Internet Marketing: Integrating Online & Offline Strategies

FOURTH EDITION

Debra Zahay, Ph.D., M.M., J.D.
Professor of Marketing and Chair of Marketing
and Entrepreneurship
St. Edward's University

Mary Lou Roberts, Ph.D.
Professor Emeritus of Management and Marketing
University of Massachusetts, Boston

Australia • Brazil • Japan • Korea • Mexico • Singapore • Spain • United Kingdom • United States

Internet Marketing: Integrating Online & Offline Strategies
Debra Zahay and
Mary Lou Roberts

Vice President, General Manager, Social Science & Qualitative Business: Erin Joyner
Product Director: Mike Schenk
Product Manager: Heather Mooney
Project Manager: Julie Dierig
Content Developer: Stacey Lutkoski and Susan McNally, MPS Limited
Marketing Manager: Katie Jergens
Content Project Manager: Darrell E Frye
Marketing Communications Manager: Audrey Jacobs
Production Service/Composition: SPi Global
Sr. Art Director: Bethany Casey
Intellectual Property Analyst: Diane Garrity
Intellectual Property Project Manager: Sarah Shainwald
Cover Image: ©iStock Photo

Copyright © 2018, 2013 Cengage Learning®

ALL RIGHTS RESERVED. No part of this work covered by the copyright herein may be reproduced or distributed in any form or by any means, except as permitted by U.S. copyright law, without the prior written permission of the copyright owner.

Unless otherwise noted, all content is © Cengage

For product information and technology assistance, contact us at
Cengage Learning Customer & Sales Support, 1-800-354-9706
For permission to use material from this text or product, submit all requests online at **www.cengage.com/permissions**
Further permissions questions can be emailed to
permissionrequest@cengage.com

Library of Congress Control Number: 2017934415

ISBN-13: 978-1-337-38561-9

Cengage Learning
20 Channel Center Street
Boston MA 02210
USA

Cengage Learning is a leading provider of customized learning solutions with employees residing in nearly 40 different countries and sales in more than 125 countries around the world. Find your local representative at **www.cengage.com**.

Cengage Learning products are represented in Canada by Nelson Education, Ltd.

To learn more about Cengage Learning Solutions, visit **www.cengage.com**

Purchase any of our products at your local college store or at our preferred online store **www.cengagebrain.com**

Printed at CLDPC, USA, 01-20

DEDICATION

The fourth edition is dedicated to students and practitioners of all forms of internet and interactive marketing around the globe who have enhanced our knowledge and understanding of these continuously evolving marketing disciplines.

MLR/DZ

Contents

Preface vii

1 INTERNET AND MOBILE MARKETING IN THE DIGITAL ECOSYSTEM 1
2 THE SUPPLY CHAIN BECOMES A VALUE ECOSYSTEM 33
3 BUSINESS MODELS AND STRATEGIES 55
4 THE DIRECT RESPONSE AND DATABASE FOUNDATIONS OF INTERNET MARKETING 89
5 SOCIAL MEDIA MARKETING AS A CORNERSTONE OF STRATEGY 123
6 EXPERIENCING THE DIGITAL CUSTOMER JOURNEY 149
7 DISPLAY AND MOBILE ADVERTISING FOR CUSTOMER ACQUISITION 170
8 CONTENT MARKETING 195
9 EMAIL MARKETING TO BUILD CONSUMER AND BUSINESS RELATIONSHIPS 225
10 SEARCH ENGINE MARKETING 254
11 PAID SEARCH AND SOCIAL ADVERTISING 280
12 MOBILE MARKETING 309
13 DEMAND GENERATION AND CONVERSION IN B2B MARKETS 335

14 CUSTOMER RELATIONSHIP DEVELOPMENT AND RETENTION MARKETING 365

15 DEVELOPING AND MAINTAINING EFFECTIVE ONLINE AND MOBILE WEBSITES 401

16 DIGITAL CUSTOMER SERVICE AND SUPPORT IN THE DIGITAL ERA 433

17 SOCIAL AND REGULATORY ISSUES: PRIVACY, SECURITY, AND INTELLECTUAL PROPERTY 455

18 MEASURING AND EVALUATING DIGITAL MARKETING PROGRAMS 492

Appendix: AdWords Online Marketing Challenge for Students 531

Glossary 544

Index 550

Preface

INTRODUCTION

Since *Internet Marketing: Integrating Online and Offline Strategies* was first published in 2003, the internet has continued to undergo rapid and often disruptive change. The internet is now a worldwide communications and transactions channel that serves billions of people. Mobile has become the driving force in the development of what is now the digital space with many, especially in developing countries having internet access only through mobile devices. Marketers' focus is on digital marketing, implying a seamless integration of internet and mobile. That focus requires a focus on seamless customer experience on the internet, in the mobile space and in traditional channels of communications and transactions. The explosive growth of digital has created a growing number of interesting and challenging jobs in the field and we have taken a variety of approaches to informing students about the nature of jobs and offering useful preparation for them. So while this book focuses on digital marketing efforts, it continues to be titled Internet Marketing as a homage to the network that binds us together for more than marketing communications channels, but also for the complex value-adding processes that support organizational prosperity and growth.

An outgrowth of digital change is the e-book format of the fourth edition and the inclusion of the book on the Mind Tap learning platform. We have tried to take full advantage of the flexibility and interactivity this platform offers and look forward to working with users to continue to improve the quality of the experience on Mind Tap. In the midst of all the change users will find familiar and useful constructs. The strategy paradigm used in the book is based on customer acquisition, lead conversion, customer retention, and growing customer value. All these subjects are given extensive treatment either in a specific chapter or integrated into discussions of tools and techniques that are most appropriate for executing the particular strategy. Other useful strategic frameworks have been retained and new ones have been added in burgeoning fields like mobile and social media marketing.

Strategy considerations are accompanied by in-depth coverage of the ever-increasing array of technologies, tools and services that support marketing program execution. The emphasis, however, is on marketing strategy and execution, not on technology for technology's sake. While keeping the focus on strategy students are introduced to and offered practical experience in using digital tools as an asset to their current or prospective jobs in digital marketing.

Search is where most consumers start the purchasing process on the web and search engine marketing that incorporates both optimization for organic search and pay-per-click is essential. Email remains a key part of the marketing programs of B2C, B2B, as well as nonprofit marketers, even as consumers continue to migrate to social media, mobile communications and text messaging. Display advertising for branding and for direct response, is undergoing a renaissance as new formats become available to better engage the viewer. Social media marketing has become an essential strategy element with paid social advertising growing in importance. And ever-present is mobile, with a growth rate that outstrips all others in every aspect of digital marketing.

The only constant in the digital space is change that often disrupts entire industries as Uber and Airbnb have done in the transportation and travel industries. Whether you call it waves of business change, stages of technology change or a Fourth Industrial Revolution, marketers must be agile and resilient to deal with on-going change.

UNIFYING THEMES

This book is uniquely positioned to take advantage of the innovation and disruptive change that is inherent in the digital ecosystem... Digital marketing is only effective if strategies and messages are integrated across media. That viewpoint is pervasive throughout this book; Digital marketing is considered in the context of overall marketing strategy executed in multiple channels. Throughout, examples show the integrated use of online, mobile and offline channels by B2C and B2B to achieve business and marketing objectives. This book also recognizes the internet as the global phenomenon it truly is. Coverage of global issues is integrated into the appropriate subject areas. Global data are presented when appropriate, and examples of programs in various countries are seamlessly woven into content coverage. Where, the stage of digital development, regulations or culture affects digital marketing activities, they are treated separately and specifically.

It is impossible to understand digital marketing without having a layperson's appreciation of the technology that makes it possible. Technology also is covered in the context of the marketing activities affected by it, not as a separate issue. Complex technological subjects are explained in a manner that can be successfully grasped by those with only introductory or user-level familiarity with computer technology. At the same time, students are encouraged to gain experience in use of technology-driven marketing tools, both to increase their knowledge and to improve their job prospects in this dynamic environment.

The overall emphasis, however, is rigorously strategic as it discusses the planning, development, execution, and evaluation of marketing campaigns across multiple channels. At every stage conceptual frameworks are presented to aid student understanding of complex topics.

NEW AND UPDATED IN THIS EDITION

The fourth edition of *Internet Marketing: Integrating Online and Offline Strategies in a Digital Environment* has been completely rewritten to incorporate the changing digital ecosystem faced by marketers. It has an entirely new chapter on content marketing. Since the influence of search has exploded, the book now has an entire chapter devoted to the search marketing process and organic search and a new chapter expands the coverage of PPC and adds paid social advertising. Most important of all, a new Appendix encourages student participation in the Google Online Marketing Challenge so students can apply what they have learned in the text with support for instructors provided in the Instructors' Manual.

The book is divided into three sections of equal length which will facilitate testing:

1. Part 1: "Foundations of Internet Digital Marketing" introduces the topic in the context of disruptive change and profiles the Internet digital audience. It has chapters on the value chain, evolving business models, and direct and database marketing. Social media marketing has been moved up to take its place as an essential element of strategy. A reconfigured chapter presents the digital customer journey in both B2C and B2B and gives early coverage of the essential topic of Customer Experience (CX).

2. Part 2: "Digital Marketing Tools and Techniques" covers various aspects of advertising as well as content marketing, email and search engine marketing.
3. Part 3: "Creating and Evaluating Digital Marketing Strategies and Programs contains completely rewritten chapters on mobile marketing, B2B demand generation, CRM, websites, customer service and social and regulatory issues. The chapter on measuring and evaluating digital marketing programs brings all metrics together instead of scattering them in various chapters.

Throughout there is emphasis on student engagement. Videos are woven through chapters with the Mind Tap platform providing easier access to them. Interactive Exercises provide learning experiences in actual tools and techniques used by digital marketers. Discussion questions and internet exercises for each chapter provide more opportunities for experiential learning. The instructor Power Point Presentations offer additional interactive opportunities in each chapter.

ACKNOWLEDGMENTS

Reviewers of both the first and second editions contributed materially to the original soundness and readability of the book. Academic users of the book and practitioners alike have made informal contributions that have been helpful throughout.

We are especially grateful to the many firms in the digital space that have provided content that is essential to a working understanding of digital marketing

This information has contributed immeasurably to keeping the book relevant and timely

There are many people involved in publishing a book

We express our appreciation to the content team at Cengage and to production contractors who have brought the book to completion. Mary Lou Roberts is particularly indebted to students and numerous guest lecturers in Internet Marketing and Social Media Marketing courses for introducing her to issues and developments she would never have otherwise recognized

Debra Zahay wishes to acknowledge the support of her husband, Edward Blatz, and her parents, Joyce and Albert Zahay, and their unswerving belief in her. She also is indebted to the insightful comments and contributions of her colleague-at St. Edward's University, Dr. Juli James and to former student Mr. Thorne Washington for his knowledge of search engine marketing, and the insights from her current students.

About the Authors

Debra Zahay is Full Professor of Marketing and Department Chair of Marketing and Entrepreneurship at St. Edward's University in Austin, Texas, where she has overseen the inclusion of digital marketing and analytics in the undergraduate curriculum. She holds her Doctorate in Marketing from the University of Illinois in Urbana-Champaign, her Master of Management from Northwestern University in Evanston, Illinois, her Juris Doctor from Loyola University in Chicago, Illinois and her undergraduate degree from Washington University in St. Louis, Missouri. Dr. Zahay researches how firms can facilitate customer relationships, particularly using customer information. She has published extensively in marketing journals in the United States and Europe. She has served as a vice president on the Executive Board of the Chicago American Marketing Association and currently serves on the Board of the Marketing EDGE organization and the editorial board of the Journal of Marketing Analytics as well as that of Industrial Marketing Management. She has been the Editor-in-Chief of the Journal of Research in Interactive Marketing since 2012, guiding the explosive growth in influence of that journal.

Mary Lou Roberts has been a tenured professor of marketing at the University of Massachusetts Boston and held a number of administrative positions there including Director of Development. She currently teaches internet marketing and social media marketing to a global cadre of students at the Harvard University Extension School. She has a Ph.D. in marketing from the University of Michigan. She is the senior author of *Direct Marketing Management*, 2e, available on her website www.marylouroberts.info. She has published extensively in marketing journals in the United States and Europe. Dr. Roberts is a frequent presenter on programs of both professional and academic marketing organizations and has consulted and provided planning services and management training programs for a wide variety of corporations and nonprofit organizations. She has been an active member of many professional organizations and has served on a number of their boards.

Chapter 1

Internet and Mobile Marketing in the Digital Ecosystem

LEARNING OBJECTIVES

By the time you complete this chapter, you will be able to:
1. Briefly describe how the internet originated and what makes it unique as a communications and transactions medium.
2. Identify waves of change from both a business perspective and a technology perspective.
3. Explain how the mobile web has affected the digital ecosystem.
4. Explain what the IoT is and some of its potential effects on consumers and businesses.
5. Discuss the implications of disruptive technologies including AR/VR, AI, and cloud computing.
6. Identify some of the sites where up-to-date digital statistics can be found.
7. Discuss the concepts of digital disruption and digital transformation.
8. Understand the generic marketing objectives that form the basis for digital marketing strategies.
9. Explain the nature of strategy for digital transformation.
10. Describe what is meant by customer experience and why it is the focus of digital transformation.

Many of you who are reading this book do not remember a world without the internet. Many of the rest of us cannot imagine what we ever did without it. That is remarkable, given the relatively short history of the network we now call the internet.

There are some wonderful accounts of the development of the internet, including one by the people directly responsible for it.[1] Those people are still active in the industry. That's true because—impossible as it seems—the internet officially celebrated its 25th birthday on August 23, 2016. That is the date on which the internet was opened to the public after years of development at the particle physics research laboratory CERN in Switzerland. Why is that such a milestone date? Tim Berners-Lee says,

> *Had the technology been proprietary, and in my total control, it would probably not have taken off. The decision to make the web an open system was necessary for it to be universal. You can't propose that something be a universal space and at the same time keep control of it.*[2]

That attitude set the standard for the World Wide Web that still rules today, although not without challenge at times. Figure 1.1 gives a capsule summary of the early days of the web. It's important to note that the internet was originally a communications network for individuals and commercial activity was not allowed. Consequently, the interest of marketers is focused on the years since 1991 when commercial traffic was first officially permitted on the internet.[3]

HOW THE INTERNET HAS EVOLVED

As you can see, major developments of the internet prior to the early 1990s were primarily technical in nature, building infrastructure and creating communications protocols. Early web browsers required extensive technical knowledge and it was not until the creation of browsers with graphical interfaces, including Netscape, that the general public became interested in the internet. Web portals Yahoo!, Lycos, and AOL gained early popularity. eBay and Amazon were among the earliest to recognize the potential of ecommerce. MySpace and Napster also achieved early popularity but most of these sites are now a mere shadow of their former selves. Starting around 2000 with iTunes, Facebook, YouTube, and others you begin to see sites that are part of your daily lives.

Why so much change in the powerhouses of the industry in such a short time? In a word—search. Google became the leading search engine in the early 2000s because it was easy to use and gave useful results. As more and more internet users turned to search as their entry point to the web, there was less need for portals, whether a "walled garden" like AOL or an open portal like Yahoo!. The portals were eclipsed and Google and its smaller competitors thrived.

On the internet disruptive change is ongoing. Author Kevin Maney describes Yahoo! as the past of technology leaders and Amazon as the future. Apple is the present, on a huge run since the introduction of the iPhone smartphone in 2007 but not having found a category-changing product like it for the future. Amazon revolutionized internet storage with Amazon Web Services, cloud-based storage, which we will discuss in detail in Chapter 2. It seems poised to disrupt another industry sector if it successfully harnesses **artificial intelligence (AI)** for use by its Echo home connectivity device. Maney describes it as "the front-end technology that will let us talk to a watch or car or loo (U.S. English translation bathroom) and make sure the device will understand who we each are, what we want, and how to get it done."[4] BMW appears first to announce that voice-activated Echo technology will be introduced for all models in 2016. It will allow a range of simple voice commands like starting the car, locking it, or following a journey route. The terminology can be a bit confusing; Echo is the home connectivity device. Alexa is the voice-activated software assistant (conversational interface[5]) that works with the Echo device or, in this case, from a smartphone app.[6] It's too soon to say that the technology is on a roll, but Hyundai has announced that voice-activated Echo technology will soon be available on its Genesis luxury line.[7]

artificial intelligence (AI) the ability of a computer to mimic human behaviors.

FIGURE 1.1
Highlights of Early Internet Development

Internet > History >

Internet History -- One Page Summary

The conceptual foundation for creation of the Internet was largely created by three individuals and a research conference, each of which changed the way we thought about technology by accurately predicting its future:

- *Vannevar Bush* wrote the first visionary description of the potential uses for information technology with his description of the "memex" automated library system.

- *Norbert Wiener* invented the field of Cybernetics, inspiring future researchers to focus on the use of technology to extend human capabilities.

- *The 1956 Dartmouth Artificial Intelligence conference* crystallized the concept that technology was improving at an exponential rate, and provided the first serious consideration of the consequences.

- *Marshall McLuhan* made the idea of a global village interconnected by an electronic nervous system part of our popular culture.

In 1957, the Soviet Union launched the first satellite, Sputnik I, triggering US President Dwight Eisenhower to create the *ARPA* agency to regain the technological lead in the arms race. ARPA appointed *J.C.R. Licklider* to head the new *IPTO* organization with a mandate to further the research of the *SAGE* program and help protect the US against a space-based nuclear attack. Licklider evangelized within the IPTO about the potential benefits of a country-wide communications network, influencing his successors to hire *Lawrence Roberts* to implement his vision.

Roberts led development of the network, based on the new idea of packet switching invented by *Paul Baran* at RAND, and a few years later by *Donald Davies* at the UK National Physical Laboratory. A special computer called an *Interface Message Processor* was developed to realize the design, and the *ARPANET* went live in early October, 1969. The first communications were between *Leonard Kleinrock*'s research center at the University of California at Los Angeles, and *Douglas Engelbart*'s center at the Stanford Research Institute.

The first networking protocol used on the ARPANET was the *Network Control Program*. In 1983, it was replaced with the *TCP/IP* protocol invented Wby *Robert Kahn*, *Vinton Cerf*, and others, which quickly became the most widely used network protocol in the world.

In 1990, the ARPANET was retired and transferred to the *NSFNET*. The NSFNET was soon connected to the *CSNET*, which linked Universities around North America, and then to the *EUnet*, which connected research facilities in Europe. Thanks in part to the NSF's enlightened management, and fueled by the popularity of the *web*, the use of the Internet exploded after 1990, causing the US Government to transfer management to *independent organizations* starting in 1995.

And here we are.

SOURCE: http://www.livinginternet.com/i/ii_summary.htm.

FIGURE 1.2

Waves of Change

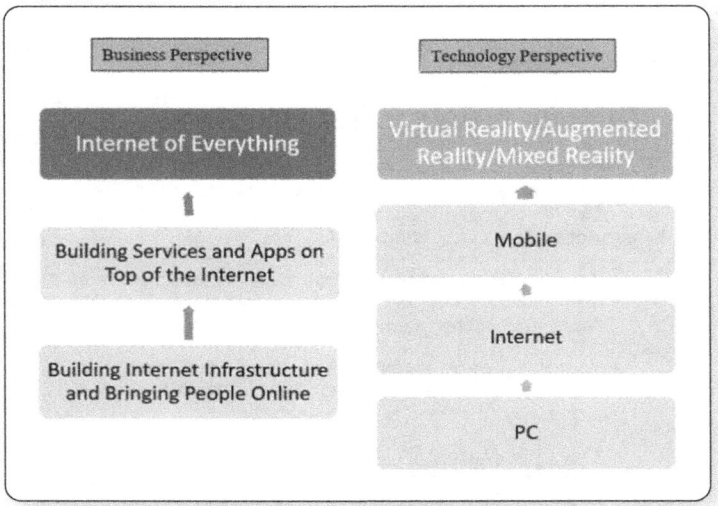

SOURCE: Adapted from http://www.forbes.com/sites/danschawbel/2016/04/06/steve-case-what-leaders-need-to-know-about-the-next-wave-of-tech/#786cb542484b http://venturebeat.com/2016/07/14/why-virtual-augment-and-mixed-reality-are-the-4th-wave-of-tech/.

Incremental change happens in technology on a daily basis. Every few years a wave of change, the introduction of the smart phone for example, occurs that disrupts the industry.

The Waves of Internet Change

Figure 1.2 shows waves of digital change from both the business and the technology perspectives. The business perspective originates with Steve Case, the founder of AOL. The technology perspective is widely recognized in the industry. As you can see they are quite different.

Steve Case lays out his business perspective in *The Third Wave*.[8] You can see the general dimensions in Figure 1.3. The first wave was the firms like AOL, other early portals, and early ecommerce firms like eBay and Amazon. That makes the discussion about Amazon Web Services, clearly part of the second wave, and Amazon Echo, a potential player in the 3rd wave of business and the fourth wave of technology all the more amazing. Also in the second wave, according to Case includes Google, Facebook, and Apple, including the mobilization of all three. Technology tends to be a winner-take-all (or at least most) scramble for market leadership. Case says the third wave will make all companies technology-based businesses that have to challenge incumbent powerhouses. Those powerhouses range from Uber to IBM and others we will discuss in Chapter 3. That means the potential for disruptive change is still present as we will discuss in the next section.[9]

Do you remember when personal computers were not connected to the internet? Again, many of you probably do not. However, many of the rest of us remember the frustrations of learning to use word processors, dumb terminals for access to a mainframe computer, and personal computers themselves. Connectivity to the internet and between our devices is now taken for granted.

The technology waves in Figure 1.2 are widely accepted and discussed in the technology industry. One writer describes it as the Fourth Industrial Revolution. He says:

> *The possibilities of billions of people connected by mobile devices, with unprecedented processing power, storage capacity, and access to knowledge, are unlimited. And these possibilities will be multiplied by*

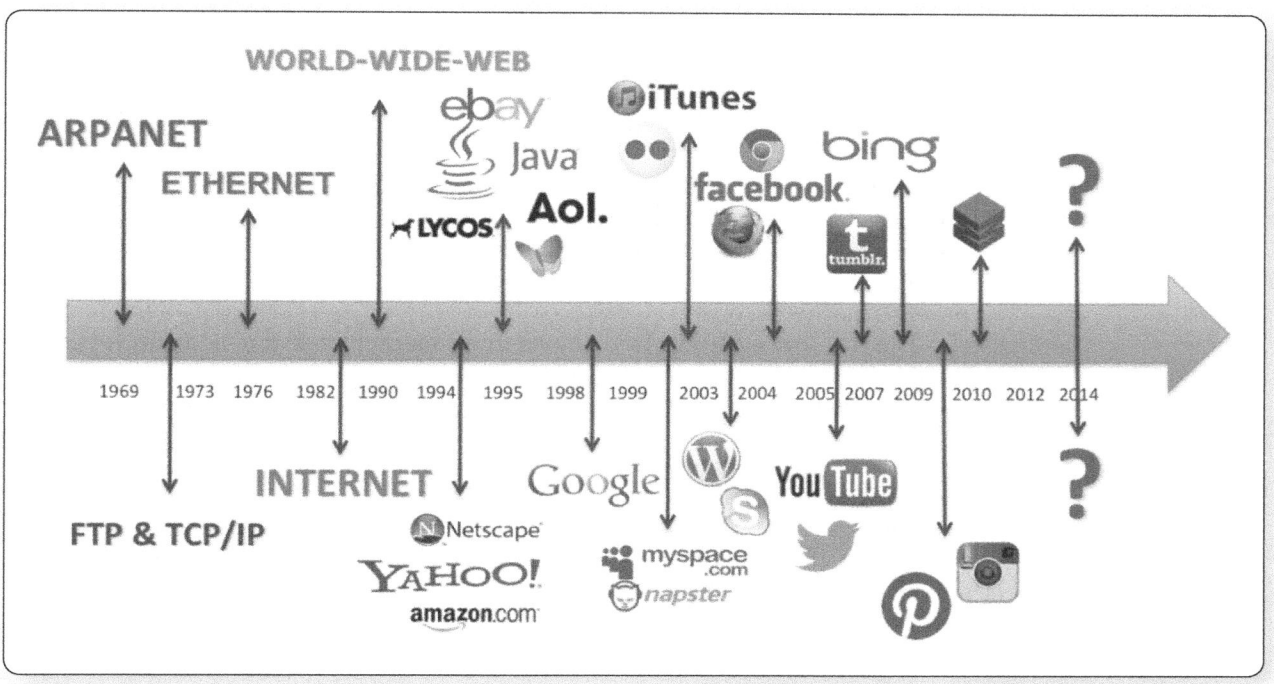

FIGURE 1.3
Highlights of Commercial Internet Development

SOURCE: https://www.tes.com/lessons/hMm6KQB3x9wzPw/web-the-history-of-the-internet.

emerging technology breakthroughs in the fields such as artificial intelligence, robotics, the Internet of Things, autonomous vehicles, 3-D printing, nanotechnology, biotechnology, materials science, energy storage, and quantum computing.[10]

Some of these issues are more in the manufacturing realm but most will over time be relevant to marketing. Artificial intelligence (AI) and **virtual reality (VR)** are of prime importance to marketers at present as you will see later in this chapter and other chapters, especially in Chapter 3. The Internet of Things (IoT) is also upon us, and the vast quantity of data it will produce intrigues marketers as we will discuss later in this chapter. The point is that the fourth wave, with all its disruptive technology, is already upon us. Marketers, and the businesses they work for, must ride the wave or the wave will wipe them out. Let's discuss the two disruptive technologies that have the most current impact on marketing before going on to the broader topic of digital disruption.

virtual reality (VR) simulation of a three-dimensional image or environment with which the user can interact by using special equipment.

Important Acronyms—IoT and AI/VR

The third wave of digital business is what Steve Case calls the Internet of Everything. The more often-heard term at the moment is the Internet of Things. What is the difference? Here are careful definitions for both:

The Internet of Everything (IoE) "is bringing together people, process, data, and things to make networked connections more relevant and valuable than ever before-turning information into actions that create new capabilities, richer experiences, and unprecedented economic opportunity for businesses, individuals, and countries. (Cisco 2013)"

The Internet of Things (IoT) is the network of physical objects accessed through the internet. These objects contain embedded technology to interact with internal states or the external environment.

The post further explains:

The Internet of Everything (IoE) with four pillars—people, process, data, and things—builds on top of The Internet of Things (IoT) with one pillar—things. In addition, IoE further advances the power of the internet to improve business and industry outcomes and ultimately make people's lives better by adding to the progress of IoT.[11]

In other words, the IoE is a broader concept with more far-reaching implications. You can see considerable similarity between this definition and the discussion of digital strategy that concludes this chapter. We will return explicitly to the concept in Chapter 3 when we discuss the transformation at GE. It is a strategy concept, not purely a marketing one.

The IoT, however, is a prime concern of marketers at the moment. It pervades many of our products and is already beginning to produce a tremendous volume of data for marketing purposes. Consequently, the IoT is our focus here.

Postscapes is a research firm that follows the evolution of the IoT. It says there are three elements—sensors, connectivity, and people and processes—that make up the IoT. They are shown in Figures 1.4 a, b, and c.

Sensors can measure changes in states like temperature, light, flow, sound seen in Figure 1.4a. In a smart home, for instance, sensors can detect water on the basement

FIGURE 1.4a

Sensors in IoT

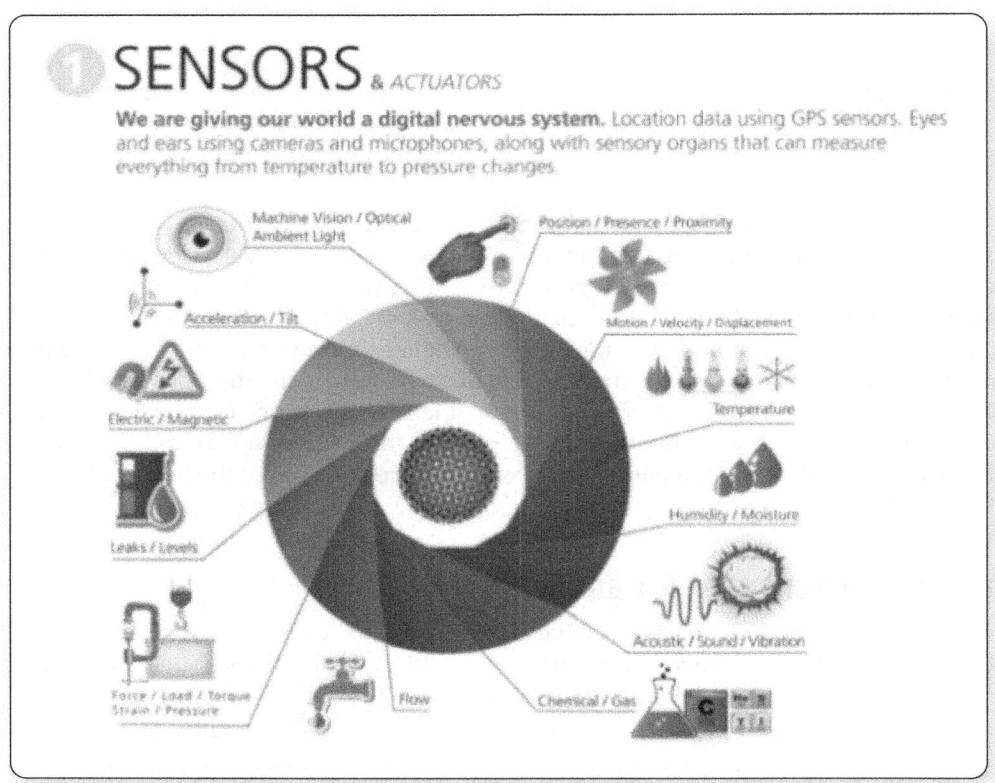

SOURCE: http://www.slideshare.net/Postscapes/what-exactly-is-the-internet-of-things-44450482.

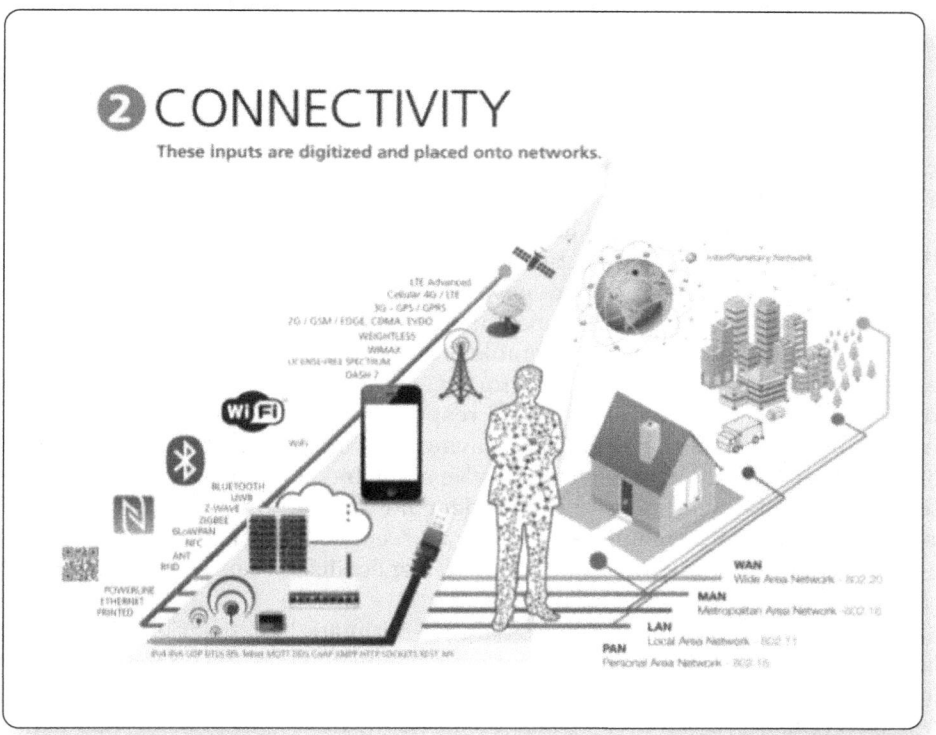

FIGURE 1.4b
Connectivity in the IoT

SOURCE: http://www.slideshare.net/Postscapes/what-exactly-is-the-internet-of-things-44450482.

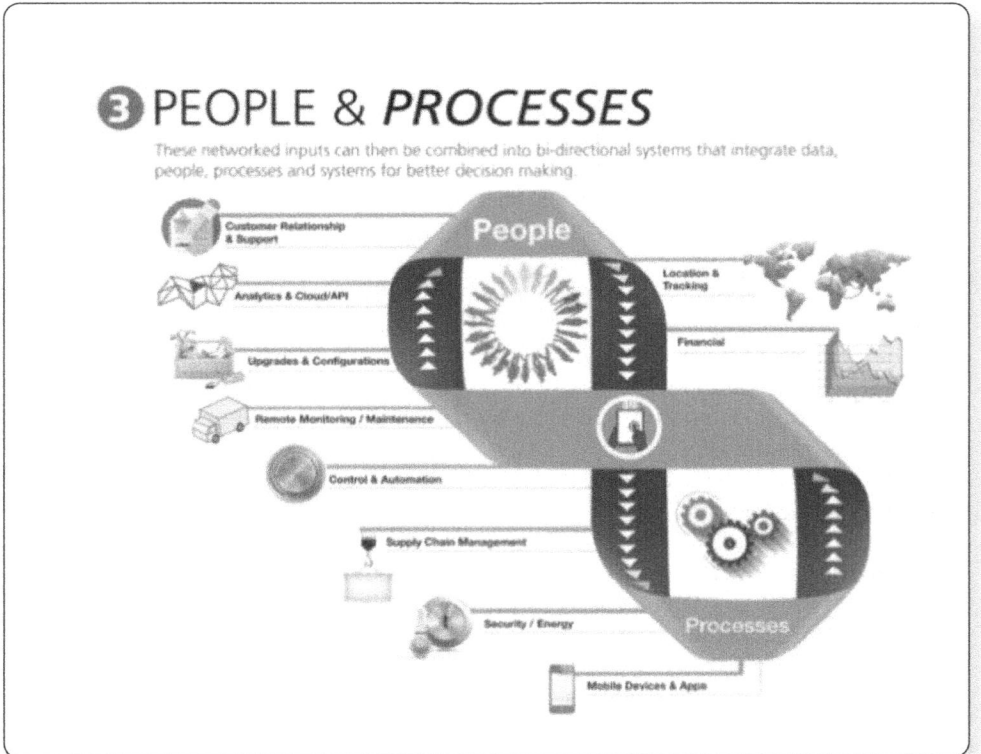

FIGURE 1.4c
What Is Connected: People and Processes

SOURCE: http://www.slideshare.net/Postscapes/what-exactly-is-the-internet-of-things-44450482.

floor and notifies the owner via smartphone app that there is a potential problem. The app allows the owner to unlock the door for a plumber who can correct the leaking pipe.

Smart cities can embed sensors in parking spaces so drivers with the appropriate app can locate vacant spaces with their smartphone or in-car connectivity.[12]

In an industrial setting sensors can monitor various aspects of the contents of large vessels in real time for process control, detect leaks of liquids or gasses from tanks or pipelines, and much more.[13]

Connectivity is the essential link in the IoT (Figure 1.4b). Sensors are embedded in houses, cars, cities, and more. Many technologies are available to connect the data from the sensors to the appropriate network. That makes connectivity essentially a technology issue, but the implications are profound.

Take healthcare as just one example. The millions of elderly or frail consumers living alone can use in-home monitoring services to report events like falls and smoke in the house to the appropriate responder. They can connect with physicians who can monitor them remotely, saving trips into the office. A smart medication dispenser can tell them whether they've taken medication or not. Hospitals can use equipment like smart beds to reduce demands on staff time. They can use smart storage (Chapter 2) to streamline inventory and reduce the risk of errors. The potential is so great that Microsoft has developed a specialized Azure Cloud to serve the healthcare industry.[14]

People and their support process are the ultimate beneficiaries of the IoT as Figure 1.4c suggests. This chart shows people connected with customer services and their financial institutions, for example. Businesses can be connected with their supply chains (Chapter 2) and with transport fleets for remote diagnostics and maintenance. Both individuals and businesses use mobile devices and apps and both can take advantage of upgrades to their devices and monitoring of their energy and security systems.

Another way of thinking about it is that people and their data-producing devices are being connected with systems and other devices that can deliver services and generally make their lives easier and more productive.[15]

The IoT is in its early days. The opportunities and potential in this market are huge. Business Insider predicts that by 2020 there will be 24 billion devices installed and investment will total 6 trillion in hardware, software, and systems. The impact will be felt on every sector of the economy.[16]

One example of the IoT is the Walt Disney Magic Band. Disney has invested $1 million in **RFID (Radio-Frequency IDentification)** technology (discussed in the context of the supply chain in Chapter 2) in colorful bands that customers at Disney World can use for everything from getting on the bus from the airport to ordering food to reserving fast passes for rides to paying for their purchases. Each band has an embedded RFID transmitter that sends data to the RFID readers placed throughout the park and resort. The bands not only make it easier to get around the park but also provide valuable information to Disney about customer habits through the data transmitted. This data will later be used by Disney to help improve the customer experience.[17]

RFID (Radio-Frequency IDentification) technology that allows the identification of tagged goods from a distance with no intervention by human operation.

The next wave of technology features AI, VR, and something called MR. These technologies are interrelated:

- Virtual reality is the embedding of graphics into actual settings. In the summer of 2016 President Obama celebrated Wilderness Week with a virtual reality tour of Yosimite National Park.[18] As this is written you can view the experience with no special equipment on National Geographic's Facebook page.[19] However, promotional content suggests that an enhanced experience will soon be available using Facebook's Oculus Rift headset.

- **Augmented reality** is the technology that takes a person's view of the real world and adds digital information or data on top of it. It is usually delivered through a wearable device with sensors such as Google Glass. In Chapter 3, we describe a Pepsi Max ad with various creatures appearing to menace London bus patrons. That ad was delivered through one window of the bus stop.[20] As many of you undoubtedly know, Pokémon Go is, in mid-2016, the poster child for how deeply engaging AR can be.

    augmented reality an enhanced version of reality created by superimposing computer-generated images on top of the user's view of the real world.

- **Mixed reality** is a combination of the two in a way that is supposed to be more flexible than either. According to *Recode*, the viewer sees the real world like AR at the same time sees believable virtual objects. This is all anchored to a point in space making it seem real to the viewer. Recode gives an example of how it works with the Microsoft Hololens:

    mixed reality combining the real and virtual worlds to produce a new environment in which objects can interact and humans can interact with them.

    To borrow an example from Microsoft's presentation at the gaming trade show E3, you might be looking at an ordinary table, but see an interactive virtual world from the video game Minecraft sitting on top of it. As you walk around, the virtual landscape holds its position, and when you lean in close, it gets closer in the way a real object would.[21]

Each of these technologies seems to have potential applications that impact marketers from games to advertising to the delivery of enhanced messages. It is a relatively new wave and like the IoT there are many opportunities and possibilities.

There are more ways that technology is disrupting the landscape of digital business and we will cover two more important ones in a later section. First, however, we should look at the nature and consequences of digital disruption and transformation itself.

DIGITAL DISRUPTION AND DIGITAL TRANSFORMATION

First, what do we mean when we talk about digital disruption and digital transformation? Are they the same? They are, in fact, both part of the same technology-driven phenomenon, but they have different implications. Straightforward definitions are as follows:

- **Digital disruption** is the change that occurs when new digital technologies and business models affect the value proposition of existing goods and services.[22]

    digital disruption change caused by digital technologies that disrupts ways of thinking and acting.

    In Chapter 3, we define a **value proposition** as the value delivered by the firm to a specific, targeted customer segment and learn how to create a compelling value proposition. Netflix, for example, has disrupted the movie offerings of the broadcast TV channels. Who would not rather have whatever movie she wants available whenever she wants it on whatever device she chooses to use at the moment? That's a big improvement over a take-it-when-we-choose-to-offer-it fixed movie schedule served up by the broadcast channels (more formally called the "linear model" in the trade). On demand mitigated the pain of the fixed schedule to some extent but Netflix offers the choice and convenience and personalization that has made it the preferred option for 81.5 million subscribers as of early 2016.[23] What the TV channels offer just can't compete with the broad range of the Netflix product and service offering.

    value proposition a description of the customer value delivered to a specific target market.

    Digital transformation is the profound and accelerating transformation of business activities, processes, competencies, and models to fully leverage the changes and opportunities of digital technologies and their impact across society in a strategic and prioritized way.[24] Put even more simply, "Digital is the application of information and technology to raise human performance."[25]

    digital transformation the rapid change in business activities and operations caused by digital disruption.

So if Netflix is disrupting the entertainment industry, their competitors from movie theatres to broadcast TV will fight back by transforming themselves, right? Companies usually are quick to sense the disruption but slow to find a good way to deal with it. The infrastructure of the movie industry, all those theatres in all those locations, makes it hard for them to change. The TV networks also have infrastructure, employees, and organizational culture that make swift and decisive action difficult, even if they were sure what would work.

CBS has made a signature effort to join the streaming ecosystem with its All Access offering. It offers on demand access to CBS series with minimal ads and ad-free access to classic series. It offers over 7,500 series episodes at a monthly price about half that of Netflix. It offers many of its televised sports events via live streaming but sometimes licensing restrictions prevent offering events like the NFL games on CBS Sports. It is available on mobile devices and computers and with Roku players, Chromecast, and Apple TV.[26] It is an interesting offer, perhaps compelling for some sports fan, but it is not streaming movies on your family TV. CBS doesn't release subscriber figures but the service appeared to have more than 100 thousand subscribers in early 2016 and CBS predicts 8 million subscribers to its All Access and Showtime streaming services by 2020.[27] None of the other streaming services like HBO and Amazon Prime releases subscriber numbers either, but it appears that none come close to Netflix's 81.5 million.[28] It's hard playing catch-up and digital transformation is, indeed, hard work.

It is probably more fun to be a disrupter and some companies in addition to Netflix have disrupted their industries more than once. See Interactive Exercise 1.2 for an interesting example of how a pizza company can characterize itself as an ecommerce company.

Engaging in Digital Transformation

MIT and European consulting firm Capgemini interviewed over 150 executives in 50 billion-dollar enterprises in 15 countries. They found all moving forward on digital transformation but at varying speeds and with varying success. None of them considered their business digitally mature but the researchers found that the more digitally mature the enterprise was, the better its operating results. The researchers identified nine building blocks of digital transformation and were able to group them into three business fundamentals—customer experience, operational process, and business models. The building blocks can be seen in Figure 1.5.

- Customer experience will be described throughout this book as the unchallenged competitive battlefield of today and the foreseeable future. Customer experience issues affect all channels, all tools, and everything the marketer does in fact. In order to create successful customer experience, marketers must have customer knowledge gained from analytics (Chapter 18) and social understanding of their lifestyles (Chapter 5 and more). Top line revenue growth requires digital selling and satisfying customer processes backed by predictive marketing. Customer experience is the focus of Chapter 6 where the emphasis is on all customer touchpoints throughout the multichannel customer journey. Predictive modeling is discussed in a number of contexts.
- The operational processes' building blocks—process automation, worker enablement, and data-driven performance management—are management topics but marketers will be affected by them in many ways. One example is the automated programmatic ad buying discussed in Chapter 7.

FIGURE 1.5
The Building Blocks of Digital Transformation

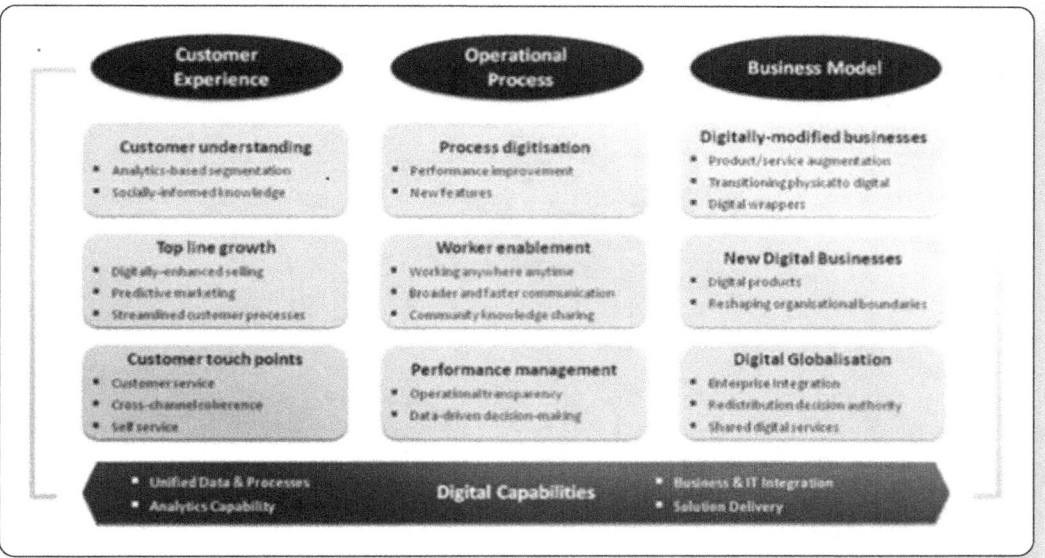

SOURCE: http://sloanreview.mit.edu/article/the-nine-elements-of-digital-transformation/.

- Changing business models and the value propositions that are one component of them are the highly visible outcomes of digital transformation. Chapter 3 explicitly covers business models old and new and gives many examples. Throughout the book we use examples taken from all over the world to stress that global marketing is an essential part of digital marketing, not a separate topic.

Achieving Digital Maturity

Accomplishing the transformation described in Figure 1.5 is clearly a major process, involving all parts of the business. Brian Solis at Altimeter has distilled the process into six stages (Figure 1.6). In the previous section we pointed out that digital disruption is ongoing and no business can afford "business as usual" in the face of change of this magnitude. The process continues through several stages of experimentation that become progressively more formalized and strategic. When there is sufficient confidence in the process, it converges into a central team that is charged with overseeing the process throughout the business. The final stage is crucial—the end result of a transformation process is a firm that is innovative and adaptive, one that is agile enough to adapt to ongoing change. As the figure says, "change is constant." There is no more business as usual. It is often said that digital transformation is a journey, not a destination. Constant adaptation to change is what that statement implies.

We will end this chapter with a discussion of digital strategy and a case example of a business that seems well launched on the road to constant innovation. In the next section, we illustrate the need for constant innovation and adaptation with a discussion of two interrelated technologies and the imminent disruption they foreshadow in marketing across all industries.

FIGURE 1.6
The Road to Digital Maturity

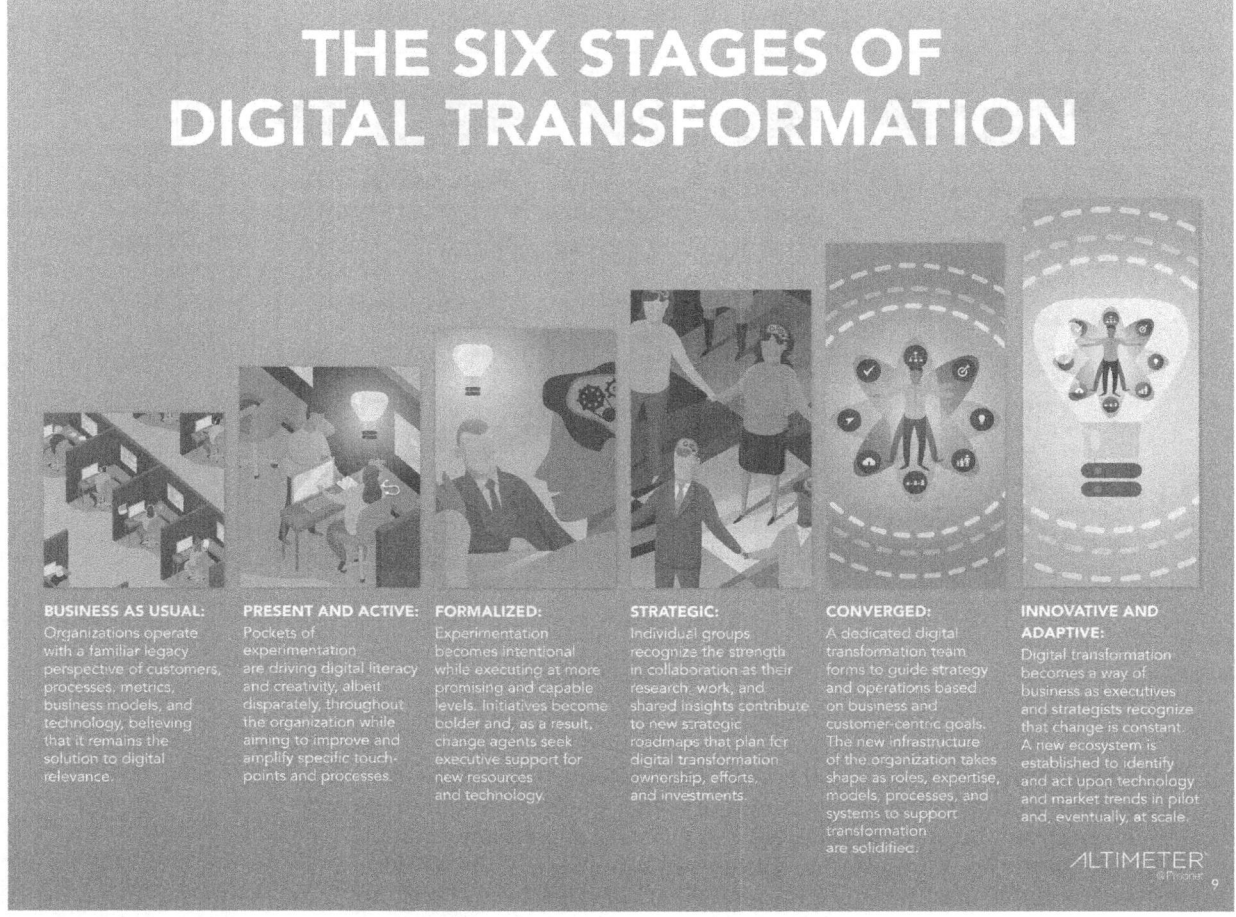

SOURCE: http://www.altimetergroup.com/pdf/reports/Six-Stages-of-Digital-Transformation-Altimeter.pdf.

ARTIFICIAL INTELLIGENCE AND CLOUD COMPUTING—SALESFORCE AND NORTH FACE

As a technology, artificial intelligence (AI) is by no means new. Throughout the ages mankind has fantasized about investing inanimate objects with intelligence or creating god-like creatures with superhuman intelligence or even creating intelligent machines. The field of computer science known as AI, however, can be traced to a conference at Dartmouth College in 1956 at which the term artificial intelligence was first used.

Six decades later there is still no commonly accepted definition of AI.[29] The Oxford Dictionary has one that is useful for general purposes:

> *Artificial intelligence is a sub-field of computer science. Its goal is to enable the development of computers that are able to do things normally done by people—in particular, things associated with people acting intelligently.*[30]

We have already highlighted one application of AI in Section 1-1—Amazon's effort to embed AI into its Echo home connectivity device. In that paragraph there was also mention of cloud-based computing, another technology that is essential to the current wave of transformation. Cloud-based computing is a simple-sounding technology with a profound impact. PC magazine explains it in nontechnical terms:

> *In the simplest terms,* **cloud computing** *means storing and accessing data and programs over the internet instead of your computer's hard drive. The cloud is just a metaphor for the internet.*[31]

cloud computing using a network of remote servers hosted on the internet, not a local server or computer hard drive, to store data and programs and to process data.

For individual users that means accessing programs and data, not on the computer hard drive or even on a network, but accessing them through the internet. As individuals most of us already use many cloud services, perhaps without knowing it. Some examples are as follows:

- Microsoft Office may be resident on the computer itself, but it now includes OneDrive, storage in the cloud. There is also Office Online in which the most popular applications are accessed over the internet.
- Google Drive offers cloud storage that can be used by various applications like Google Docs and Google Sheets. It is accessible by mobile devices like smartphones and tablets.
- Apple offers iCloud that both stores data and synchs it across devices, including Windows devices once the app is installed. Ever wonder how the Find iPhone app works? It's in the cloud!
- Amazon's Cloud Drive is mainly for things you purchase from Amazon—music and books, for example.

PC magazine points out that synchronization is an essential feature of cloud computing. It makes files and other data available, not only from all your devices, but to be shared within designated groups via apps like Dropbox and Evernote.[32] Most of this storage is what we will call "freemium" in Chapter 3. A basic amount of storage is available to the user free of charge with more storage and premium services available for a fee.

The business situation is different. As we will discuss in more detail in Chapter 3, most software is now sold as a service (**Software as a Service, SaaS**), not as a product. It means that the software is stored in the cloud and subscriber companies access it as they need it for a fee. Relationship management software firm Salesforce is sitting squarely at the intersection between the cloud and AI. Salesforce is no stranger to disruption in marketing, so the product announcement in the fall of 2016 is big news.

Software as a Service, SaaS making software available on a fee for use basis instead of on a license or purchase basis.

Salesforce first disrupted the market for CRM software with its founding in 1999. Up to that point the makers of CRM software believed, rightly, that numerous marketing and sales functions had to be integrated in order to make CRM work—customer service had to have access to marketing's customer database, for example. The result was huge integrated software systems that took months to install and were riddled with both coding and data issues. The results were budget overruns, lack of ROI and the occasional epic fail. Salesforce entered the market with a modular system. After the customer database was plugged into the software the customer service module could be added. It could be tested and debugged then could demonstrate that it was meeting objectives—performance, monetary or otherwise—before moving on to another module. This was a disruption felt throughout the specific industry sector and noted by others.

From the beginning Salesforce offered distribution of its software over the internet as an option. That required an ever growing IT infrastructure to eventually serve as many as 150,000 customers on its own cloud platform.[33] It has long been self-described as a "cloud computing company." That is itself a second disruption because cloud computing is still new to many businesses today.

Over the years Salesforce has partnered with other cloud-services firms like Microsoft and AWS. In early 2016 Salesforce announced AWS as its preferred public cloud partner while promising to continue development of its own infrastructure.[34] That can be considered a third disruption because of the shift of emphasis away from internal, owned infrastructure to cloud infrastructure. It also indicates how well established AWS has become in the field of cloud services.

The announcement expected in the fall of 2016 is expected to be genuinely disruptive. The product is called Salesforce Einstein and it will integrate AI across the Salesforce product line. Forbes described it this way:

> *Einstein will integrate AI into almost all of Salesforce's products, injecting predictive suggestion and insights into service, marketing and sales, as well as its newest efforts in collaboration and commerce. As such, [CEO Marc] Benioff tells his executives, Einstein won't just slot in as another "cloud" for them to sell. Instead, Einstein will serve as a new nerve system across the entire business. "We are going to catch our competitors by surprise."*[35]

Since there have been indications of Salesforce acquiring capabilities in AI for several years, whether it truly qualifies as a surprise is open to question. However, once again, Salesforce is opening up distance between itself and its competitors that will require tremendous effort for them to overcome.

Salesforce Einstein is a large undertaking, affecting all of its offering to customers. However, AI-enabled product may not always be so large in scope, especially in the B2C marketplace. A post on the Cloud Tech site says:

> *The future of AI isn't about one giant super-intelligence. Instead, it's about many small, dedicated agents that know you intimately and work on your behalf to improve your everyday life. That could be helping you shop, get to work or, even, find a partner. Each is focused on a discrete task, and each gets better over time and adapts to your needs as they evolve.*[36]

unstructured data data that have no predetermined models or are not organized in a predefined way. Unstructured data is often heavily text but not necessarily all text.

At roughly the same time Einstein is introduced into the B2B market retailer, North Face is going to announce an app that uses AI to help shoppers choose the best clothing to meet their needs. It is powered by IBM's Watson, which IBM describes as "a technology platform that uses natural language processing and machine learning from large amounts of **unstructured data**."[37] In this case the unstructured data includes the features of the outdoor clothing items that North Face sell.

The app has another notable feature: it is browser based. That means the user does not have to install it; the app can be used from any computer, smartphone, or tablet connected to the internet. That is possible because North Face has a responsive website,[38] a subject we will cover in Chapter 15. Experience the app for yourself in Interactive Exercise 1.3.

Both these examples not only highlight how much technology is changing but also give a sense of the myriad of ways in which technology may be employed to make our lives easier and more interesting in years to come. They also point out that not even the largest and most innovative companies can do it alone. Salesforce has chosen to use the cloud computing services of AWS in tandem with its own platform. North Face used the personal shopping assistant already developed by IBM to power its clothing app. Collaborations and partnerships between companies, even ones that may be competitors in other aspects of their businesses, are already the norm in the digital economy.

This all is happening in the context of continued growth and change in the internet and in the mobile web. We end the chapter with a brief profile of the status and change in who, how many, and for what purposes people access the internet and the mobile web.

A PROFILE OF DIGITAL USERS

It is helpful to have a broad grasp of the aspects of the digital ecosystem at the beginning. The statistics quoted here and throughout the book are mostly taken from free public sources. In some instances publishers have made paid content available to us and we are grateful for that. For you, however, it means that sources like this are available to you.

One thing you should keep in mind as you look at these data is that they are broad and, as such, of limited use to marketing practitioners. Marketers need data about specific market segments, products, geographical areas, and so forth. Much of this data is also available free of charge although it is true that the finer the detail, the more likely the data is going to behind a paid subscription wall. As you pursue your study of digital marketing, it behooves you to become acquainted with these resources and others you will find by searching on the web.

The Size and Scope of the Internet and the Mobile Web

It is generally necessary to separate statistics about the fixed internet from those that apply to the mobile web. The technology is distinctly different, but that is not the reason. Mobile has spread more quickly in Europe and in developing countries than it has in the United States and therefore the United States is not always a good indicator of status. Neither is any other single country for that matter—that is among the reasons that marketers need specific, not broad, data.

In 2016 about 40 percent of the world population had an internet connection, up from less than 1 percent in 1995. The internet reached its first billion users in 2005, its second billion in 2010, and its third billion in 2014.[39] That is fast growth by any standards, and the growth rate for technological innovations has accelerated over the past few decades.[40]

By contrast the United Nations says that by 1990 there were 11 million mobile subscribers, rising to 2.2 billion in 2005.[41] The GSMA, a trade organization of mobile operators around the world, says the number was 4.7 billion in 2015 and is expected to be 5.6 billion in 2020. That means that 71 percent of the world's population will have access to the mobile web.[42] You can see that the numbers skew heavily toward the mobile web for internet access over time. What these numbers do not tell you directly is that mobile will be the only connection for much of the world's population.

Figure 1.7 gives the picture in easy-to-grasp visuals. The 3.4 billion internet users figure is consistent with the data just quoted. The 3.8 billion unique mobile users figure is lower than previously quoted and "unique" is the reason. Many people have more than one mobile connection—multiple connections but a single user. For instance, Australian research firm Buddle quotes the number of mobile subscribers in the Philippines in 2015 as 113 million. In a country with a population of 100 million, that's a penetration rate of 114 percent![43]

Of the internet users, 31 percent are active on social media while 27 percent of mobile users are active social media users. That number can be expected to close over the next few years. In the same sense 51 percent of web page views were on a PC in 2016 contrasted with 39 percent on mobile. Notice that the growth rate for internet page views is negative while mobile web page views are up 21 percent.

The penetration rate of mobile connections overwhelms the penetration of the internet around the world. Notice also that the percentage of internet users who are on social media varies greatly throughout the world. The same is true of mobile social media use, but in some instances the penetration of mobile social media (global average 27 percent) in a given country is close to that of internet social media use (global average 31 percent) in that same country. Once again it suggests that while mobile is enjoying explosive growth, there is still ample opportunity for marketers in many aspects of mobile use.

FIGURE 1.7
The Internet, the Mobile Web, and the Social Web

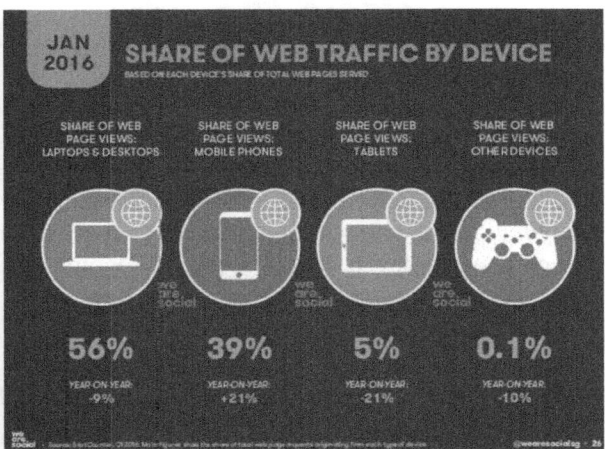
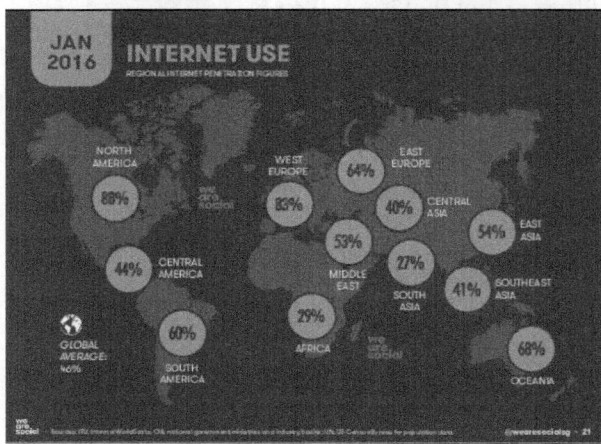
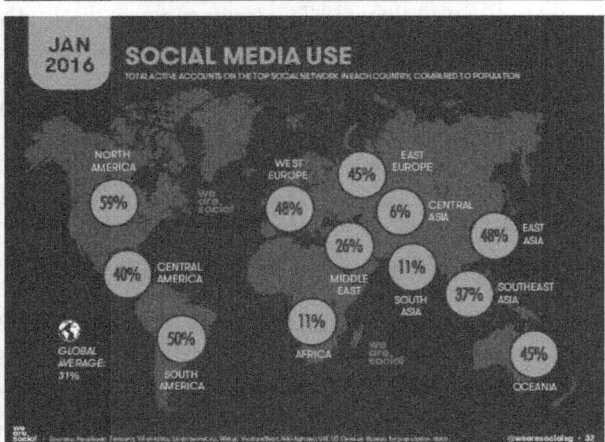
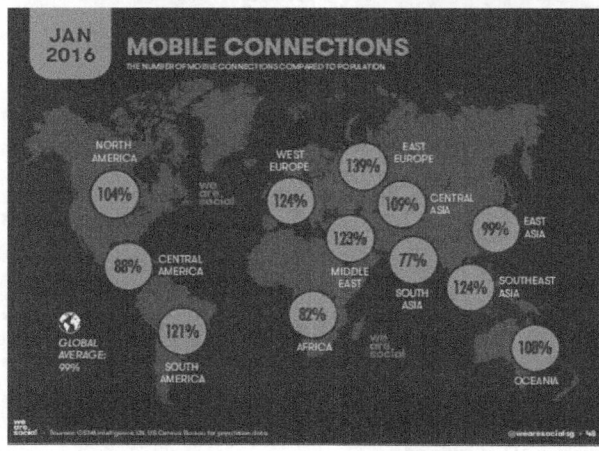
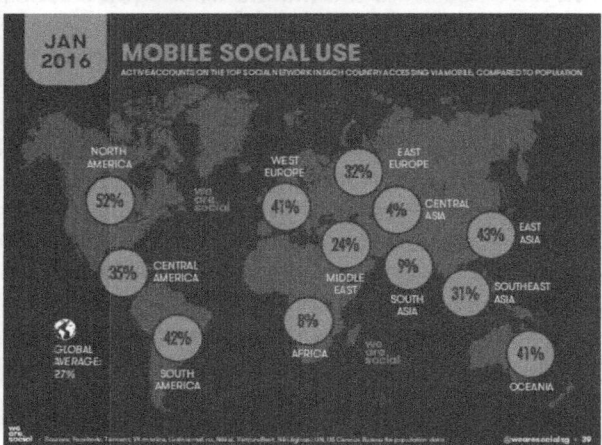

SOURCE: http://wearesocial.com/uk/special-reports/digital-in-2016.

Who Uses Digital, for What?

In January 2014, the Pew Foundation said that 87 percent of American adults were internet users. Their 2016 chart above puts the number at 89 percent for North America. It means that in terms of basic use there is little room for growth among the adult population. The adults who want to use the internet are most likely already using it. It also means that some demographic descriptors are no longer meaningful in distinguishing internet users from the general population.

The Pew data found no significant differences in internet usage between men and women or by ethnicity—White, African-American and Hispanic—or by community type—urban, suburban, or rural. It did find, however, differences between age groups, with young adults 18–29 more likely to be internet users than older age groups. In terms of educational level, adults with some college and a college degree or more were more likely to use the internet while the higher the income level, the more likely that segment was to use the internet.[43] You are probably saying that there is no real news here and you are correct. However, it does show the continuing democratization of the internet, although some differences persist.

Figure 1.8 gives a different perspective on age differences as seen in the annual internet trends report of Mary Meeker of KPCB Partners. It highlights the importance of the Millennials segment to marketers. They are young, offering a tempting acquisition target for marketers who hope to retain their business for life. Even more important, there are a lot of them. While Gen X was something of a "baby bust" generation,[44]

FIGURE 1.8

Highlights of Generational Differences

Consumer Preference / Value Evolution by Generation, USA... Millennials = More Global / Optimistic / Tolerant..., per Acosta

	Silent	Baby Boomers	Gen X	Millennials
Birth Years	1928 – 1945	1946 – 1964	1965 – 1980	1981 – 1996
Year Most of Generation 18-33 Years Old	1963	1980	1998	2014
Summary	• Grew up during Great Depression • Fought 2nd "war to end all wars" • Went to college on G.I. Bill • Raised "nuclear" families in time of great prosperity + Cold War	• Grew up during time of idealism with TV + car for every suburban home • Apollo, Civil Rights, Women's Liberation • Disillusionment set in with assassination of JFK, Vietnam War, Watergate + increase in divorce rates	• Grew up during time of change politically, socially + economically • Experienced end of the Cold War, Reaganomics, shift from manufacturing to services economy, + AIDS epidemic • Rise of cable TV + PCs	• Grew up during digital era with internet, mobile computing, social media + streaming media on iPhones • Experiencing time of rising globalization, diversity in race + lifestyle, 9/11, war on terror, mass murder in schools + the Great Recession
Core Values	• Discipline • Dedication • Family focus • Patriotism	• Anything is possible • Equal opportunity • Question authority • Personal gratification	• Independent • Pragmatic • Entrepreneurial • Self reliance	• Globally minded • Optimistic • Tolerant
Work / Life Balance	• Work hard for job security	• Climb corporate ladder • Family time not first on list	• Work / life balance important • Don't want to repeat Boomer parents' workaholic lifestyles	• Expanded view on work / life balance including time for community service + self-development
Technology	• Have assimilated in order to keep in touch and stay informed	• Use technology as needed for work + increasingly to stay in touch through social media such as Facebook	• Technology assimilated seamlessly into day-to-day life	• Technology is integral • Early adopters who move technology forward
Financial Approach	• Save, save, save	• Buy now, pay later	• Cautious, conservative	• Earn to spend

SOURCE: http://www.kpcb.com/internet-trends.

Millennials are a larger cohort than even the Baby Boomers. The U.S. Bureau of the Census says there were 83.1 Millennials in 2014 making them more than one-fourth of the total population.[45] Add to that the fact that they are technology oriented and many of them are in the household formation years, and they represent an enticing target for digital marketers of many products and services.

The generational differences highlighted in Figure 1.8 suggest that not all internet users are using it for the same activities or with the same intensity. With that in mind, let's first look at consumer use and then at business use with most of the data coming from the United States.

Consumers It is also not news that first the internet, and now mobile, have fundamentally changed the way people consume media. The big losers have been the traditional broadcast and, especially, print media. The traditional media are being forced to invent new business models, as we will discuss in Chapter 3, and the new models are digital. While Figure 1.9 shows that total time spent with digital media is increasing substantially and is expected to continue to do so through 2018, time spent on personal computers is actually decreasing. The two categories that are big winners are mobile and other connected devices like tablets and game players. eMarketer

FIGURE 1.9
Time Spent per Day with Major Media Types

Average Time Spent per Day with Major Media by US Adults, 2012–2018
hrs:mins

	2012	2013	2014	2015	2016	2017	2018
Digital	4:10	4:48	5:09	5:28	5:43	5:53	6:01
—Mobile (nonvoice)	1:28	2:15	2:37	2:53	3:06	3:15	3:23
——Radio	0:26	0:32	0:39	0:44	0:47	0:50	0:52
——Social networks	0:09	0:18	0:23	0:26	0:29	0:32	0:34
——Video	0:09	0:17	0:22	0:26	0:29	0:31	0:34
——Other	0:44	1:08	1:14	1:16	1:20	1:22	1:24
—Desktop/laptop*	2:24	2:16	2:14	2:12	2:11	2:10	2:08
——Video	0:20	0:22	0:23	0:24	0:25	0:25	0:24
——Social networks	0:22	0:17	0:16	0:15	0:14	0:13	0:13
——Radio	0:07	0:06	0:06	0:06	0:06	0:06	0:05
——Other	1:35	1:31	1:28	1:27	1:26	1:26	1:26
—Other connected devices	0:18	0:17	0:19	0:23	0:26	0:28	0:30
TV**	4:38	4:31	4:22	4:11	4:05	4:00	3:55
Radio**	1:32	1:30	1:28	1:27	1:27	1:26	1:25
Print**	0:40	0:35	0:32	0:30	0:28	0:27	0:26
—Newspapers	0:24	0:20	0:18	0:17	0:16	0:15	0:15
—Magazines	0:17	0:15	0:13	0:13	0:12	0:11	0:11
Other**	0:38	0:31	0:26	0:24	0:22	0:21	0:20
Total	11:39	11:55	11:57	12:00	12:05	12:07	12:08

*Note: ages 18+; time spent with each medium includes all time spent with that medium, regardless of multitasking; for example, 1 hour of multitasking on desktop/laptop while watching TV is counted as 1 hour for TV and 1 hour for desktop/laptop; *includes all internet activities on desktop and laptop computers; **excludes digital*
Source: eMarketer, April 2016

SOURCE: http://www.emarketer.com/Article/Growth-Time-Spent-with-Media-Slowing/1014042.

also indicates that growth in media time spent is slowing and predicts it will be only 0.1 percent by 2018. If you look at the total row in Figure 1.9, the reason seems evident; at over 12 hours each day spent attending to one medium or the other—one screen or the other—we are about out of available time!

The data by media type covers up interesting differences in what consumers do on the desktop, 35 percent of their media time, and on mobile, 65 percent of their time. According to comScore data for 2015 shown in Figure 1.10, the only three activities for which consumers are using desktop access more than half the time are portals, business news, and entertainment news. Notice that in all three categories mobile use is growing. At the other end of the spectrum are maps, photos, and online gaming, which get almost all of their traffic from mobile devices. In between are categories from health information to social networking that are showing gains in the amount of access that comes from mobile devices. Marketers ignore this change in consumer habits at their peril.

Figure 1.11a shows the number of people who shop online over the internet and Figure 1.11b shows the number who shop on mobile. These data from July of 2015 show that 66.6 percent of internet users shopped online. During the same month 41 percent of mobile users shopped using a smartphone while 48 percent shopped using a tablet. More online shopping is still done from the desktop but the mobile and tablet numbers are significant. In mid-2016 Fortune reports that a comScore survey of online shoppers found consumers buying more online than in retail stores; 51 percent of purchases were made online. The survey also found that 44 percent of smartphone users made purchase on their devices, up from 41 percent one year ago.

FIGURE 1.10

Time Spent on Various Content Types—Desktop vs. Mobile

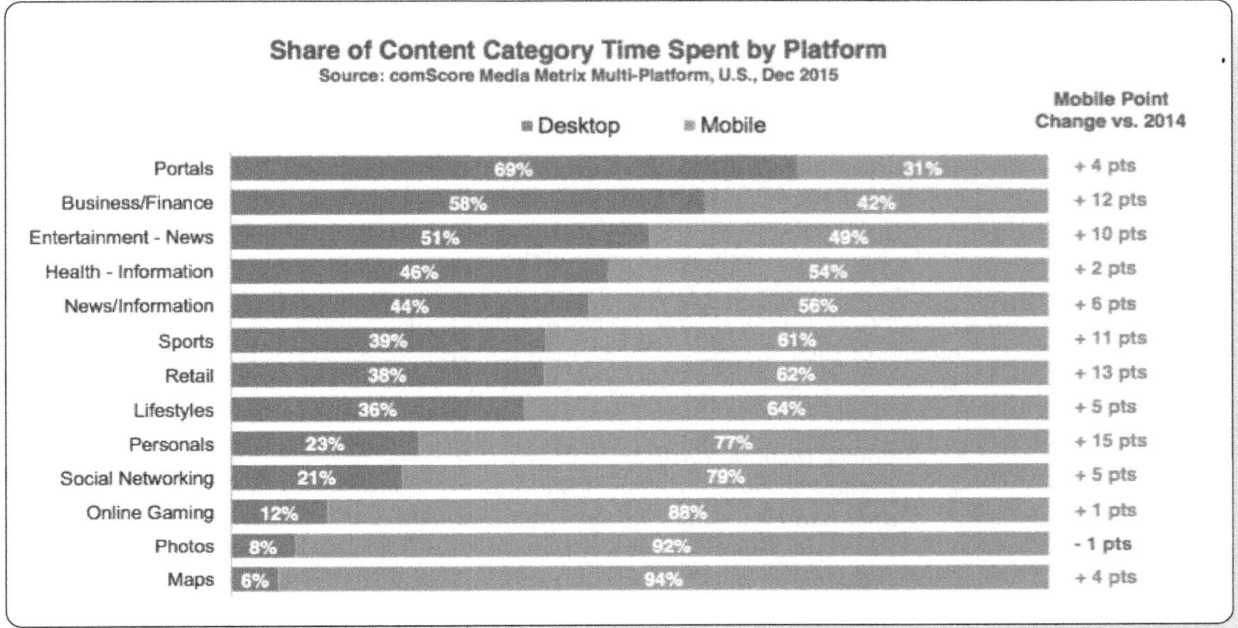

SOURCE: http://marketingland.com/digital-growth-now-coming-mobile-usage-comscore-171505.

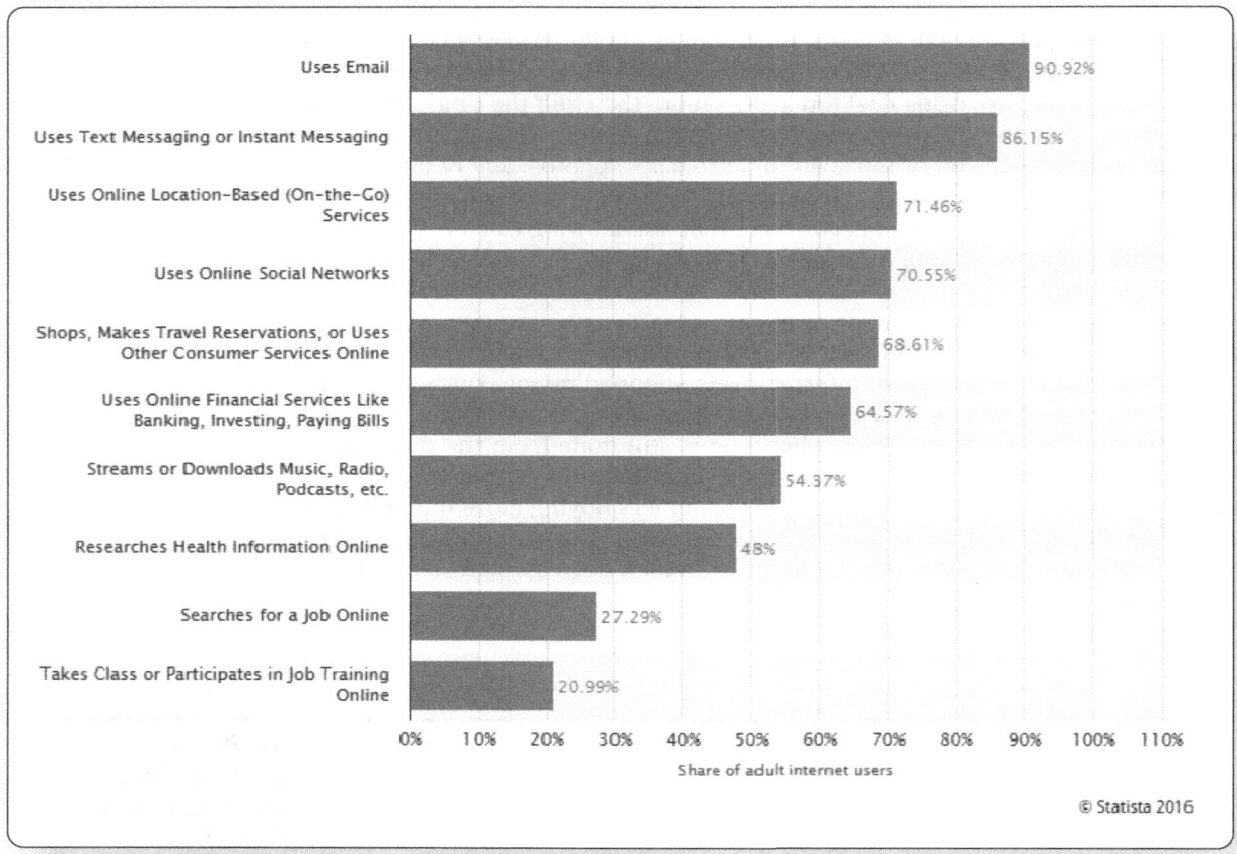

FIGURE 1.11a

Most Frequent Online Activities of Internet Users

SOURCE: http://www.statista.com/statistics/183910/internet-activities-of-us-users/.

Fortune suggests that the growth in online buying is affecting the operating results of at least the largest U.S. retailers and recommends that they act more aggressively to meet the internet and mobile challenge.

In spite of that, access to the web is not even across all market segments. In the early days of the web, we described the "digital divide" separating high- from low-income consumers in terms of access to the internet. While mobile technology has brought internet access to many low-income users, they may still be behind in the quality of their access to the web and awareness and use of collaborative services such as home and ride sharing and crowdfunding.[46]

A study from the Joan Ganz Cooney Center at Sesame Workshop found that:

> *Lower-income families in the United States have near-universal access to the internet and some kind of digital device, but they are often at a disadvantage when it comes to the quality and consistency of their connections, especially when they are limited to mobile devices such as smartphones.... "Not all connectivity is created equal, and not all devices provide the same kinds of online experiences," the report reads. "Many families face limitations in the form of service cutoffs, slow service, older technology, or difficulty using equipment because too many people are sharing devices."*[47]

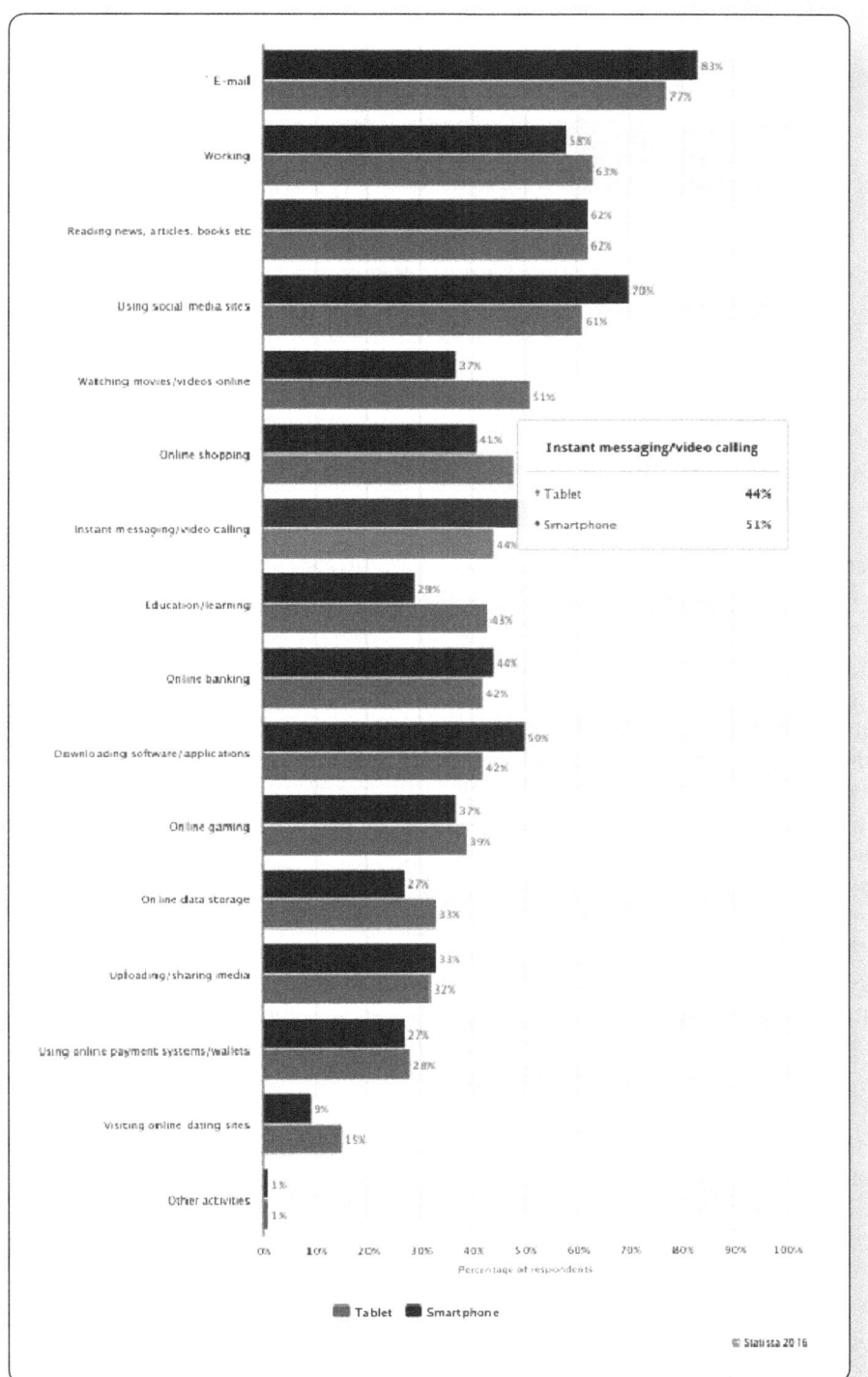

FIGURE 1.11b
Most Frequent Smartphone and Tablet Activities of Mobile Users

SOURCE: http://www.statista.com/statistics/249761/most-popular-activities-carried-out-on-mobile-internet-devices/.

FIGURE 1.12

Core Marketing Strategies

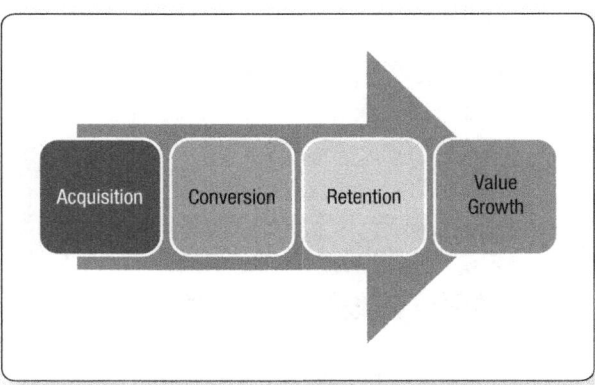

If this is true in the United States, it is also true in the areas of the world where mobile access is the norm, as shown in Figure 1.7.

Businesses In the midst of the constant change brought on by digital disruption, all the things that marketers do can be boiled down into four underlying marketing objectives as shown in Figure 1.12:

1. Customer acquisition—marketers must reach out to acquire new customers from their current market segments and to add new segments when the time is right. Customer acquisition is more costly than customer retention, but without a continuing stream of new customers it is unlikely that growth targets can be met.
2. Customer conversion (sales)—actually achieving purchases by new customers is key to marketing success. Conversion can be defined in other ways as we will discuss in Chapters 8 and 13, but sales are the ultimate goal.
3. Customer retention—it is cheaper to retain an existing customer than to acquire a new one. It makes customer retention a priority for marketers and it is the subject of Chapter 14.
4. Customer value growth—customers who remain loyal over time are likely to purchase more than other classes of customers. It is the job of marketers to facilitate the growth in customer value as we will discuss in Chapter 4.

Digital plays a key role in all four activities and the way marketers spend their money reflects that. Figure 1.13 is from the quarterly CMO/Duke University survey of marketing executives. It shows results expected from marketing activities during the 12 months beginning August 2016. It shows highest emphasis on customer acquisition followed closely by two value growth drivers, increased customer purchase volume and increased sales of related goods and services. Customer retention also plays an important role.

The report adds that over the next 12 months:

- Overall digital sales are still only 10.3 percent of total sales with highest being B2C services at 19.8 percent. Sales of B2C products are 10.6 percent.
- Marketer spending on traditional advertising is expected to decline 1.3 percent while digital grows at 9.9 percent.

In addition:

- Over the next five years marketers expect to increase spending on social media as a percent of their marketing budgets by 90 percent to 22 percent of total budget.

FIGURE 1.13

Outcomes Emphasized by Marketers in 2016

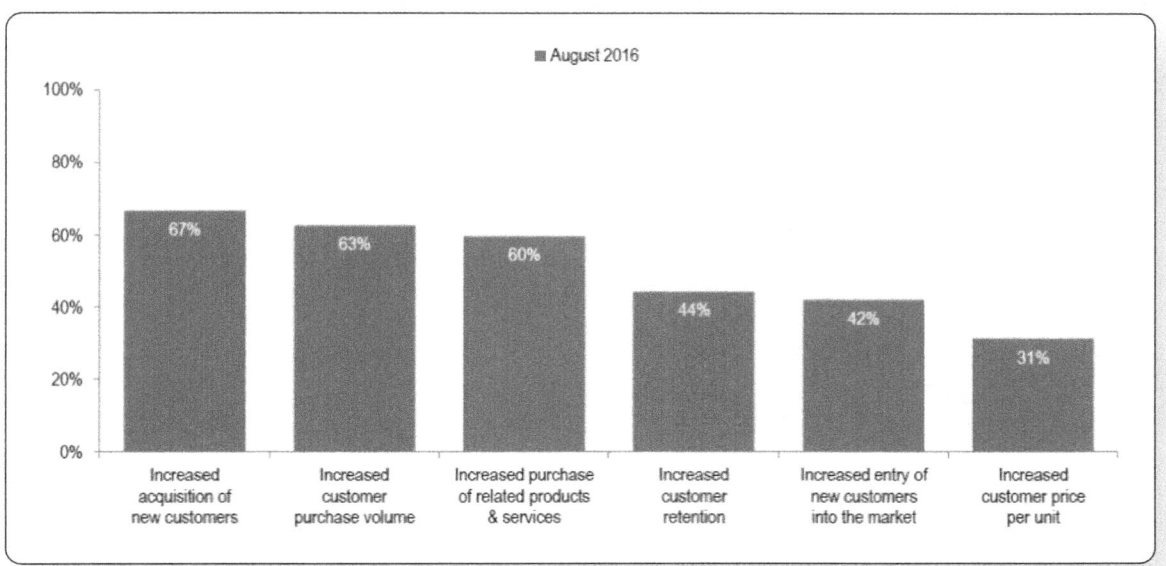

SOURCE: https://cmosurvey.org/wp-content/uploads/sites/11/2016/08/The_CMO_Survey-Highlights_and_Insights-Aug-2016.pdf.

- Over the next three years they expect to increase spending on mobile by 118 percent to 8.3 percent of their marketing budget.
- They ranked brand development and management capabilities as most important to their businesses with customer focus capabilities second and digital marketing capabilities third.
- They ranked digital marketing capabilities—which they define as digital strategy, social, and mobile activities—as the largest gap between what their organization possesses and what it needs.[48]

This survey paints a picture of strong growth in digital marketing activities with opportunities for both brands and marketers themselves. It also reflects market statistics that show all traditional media advertising except TV showing no growth or decline while digital advertising increases over 9 percent per year between 2016 and 2020. Digital advertising will actually exceed TV advertising in 2017 while mobile is expected almost half of all digital advertising by 2020.[49]

Figures 1.14a and b show how that breaks out. Paid search is still the largest digital advertising category, showing steady growth but not the explosive growth of the second largest category, mobile. Display and video advertising both show growth while classified is about steady. Mobile itself has two major categories, display advertising including video and search (PPC) ads. In the United States display is the largest category, remaining so through 2019 but search advertising is close behind. Advertising is the key channel for customer acquisition and plays a role in brand development and customer value growth. In Chapter 9 we will examine the pivotal role email plays in customer retention.

Sales are, of course, the ultimate responsibility and goal of marketers. The movement of advertising dollars away from traditional to digital media reflects the growth

FIGURE 1.14a

Global Digital Advertising Revenues, 2015–2019

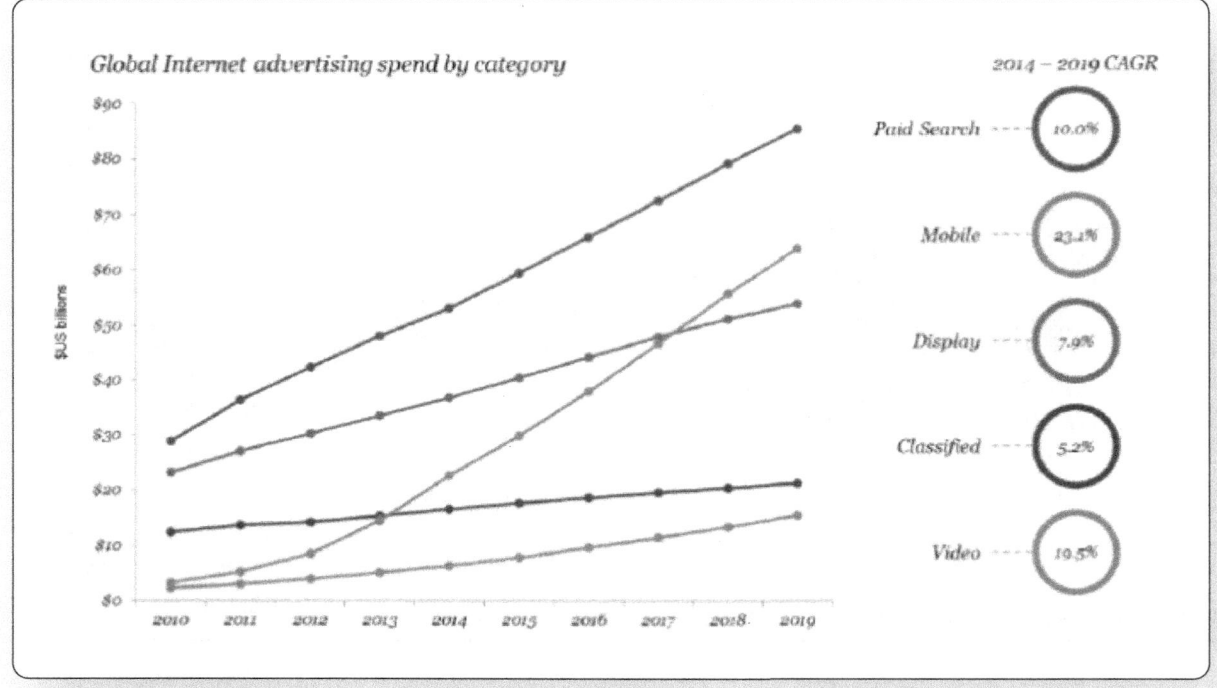

SOURCE: http://www.iab.com/wp-content/uploads/2016/04/FY2015-PwC-Matt-Hobbs-Presentation-Global-Trends.pdf.

FIGURE 1.14b

U.S. Mobile Advertising Revenues by Format 2014–2019

US Mobile Ad Spending, by Format, 2014-2019
billions

	2014	2015	2016	2017	2018	2019
Display	$9.65	$15.55	$21.58	$26.21	$29.83	$33.70
—Banners, rich media, sponsorships and other*	$8.11	$12.77	$17.50	$21.02	$23.85	$26.89
—Video	$1.54	$2.78	$4.08	$5.19	$5.98	$6.82
Search	$8.72	$13.62	$18.54	$22.18	$25.11	$28.25
SMS/MMS/P2P messaging	$0.24	$0.26	$0.27	$0.26	$0.24	$0.23
Other (classifieds, email, lead gen)	$0.55	$1.02	$1.63	$2.18	$2.77	$3.30
Total	$19.15	$30.45	$42.01	$50.84	$57.95	$65.49

Note: ad spending on tablets is included; numbers may not add up to total due to rounding; *includes ads such as Facebook's News Feed Ads and Twitter's Promoted Tweets
Source: eMarketer, Sep 2015

195307   www.eMarketer.com

SOURCE: https://www.emarketer.com/public_media/docs/eMarketer_Roundup_Mobile_Advertising_Marketing_Trends.pdf.

of ecommerce. Figure 1.15a shows the growth of global ecommerce. While it shows the rate of growth slowing between 2016 and 2019, growth is still substantial. Consequently, ecommerce is projected to be a greater percentage of total retail sales over that time. Remember that B2C online sales of services were the highest category of ecommerce sales in the CMO/Duke University survey at 19.8 percent with B2C product sales 10.6 percent of total sales.

B2B ecommerce is also a strong player in overall ecommerce growth with B2B services at 9.1 percent of total sales and B2B product at 7.3 percent.[50] In addition, there is no longer a question about whether the mobile channel can deliver sales. Figure 1.15b shows that mobile sales in the United States, which were negligible in 2013, are expected to total $284 billion in 2020, which will make mobile 20.6 percent of ecommerce sales. Remember that in developing countries more customers access the mobile web than the fixed internet, so U.S. figures understate the global reality.

As a way to reach both consumer and business customers, and then to convert them to customers, digital has demonstrated its clout. In the process, it has created some large and powerful enterprises around the world.

Some of the businesses listed in Figure 1.16, especially the top four, are the usual suspects—Apple, Google, Amazon, and Facebook. Did you expect to see a Chinese communications firm at number 5 and a Chinese marketplace ecommerce site at number 6? How about the number of huge firms—Uber and Airbnb are the Western examples—that are still privately held? The digital ecosystem is still in a state of flux and this list will change again when the sale of Yahoo! becomes final.

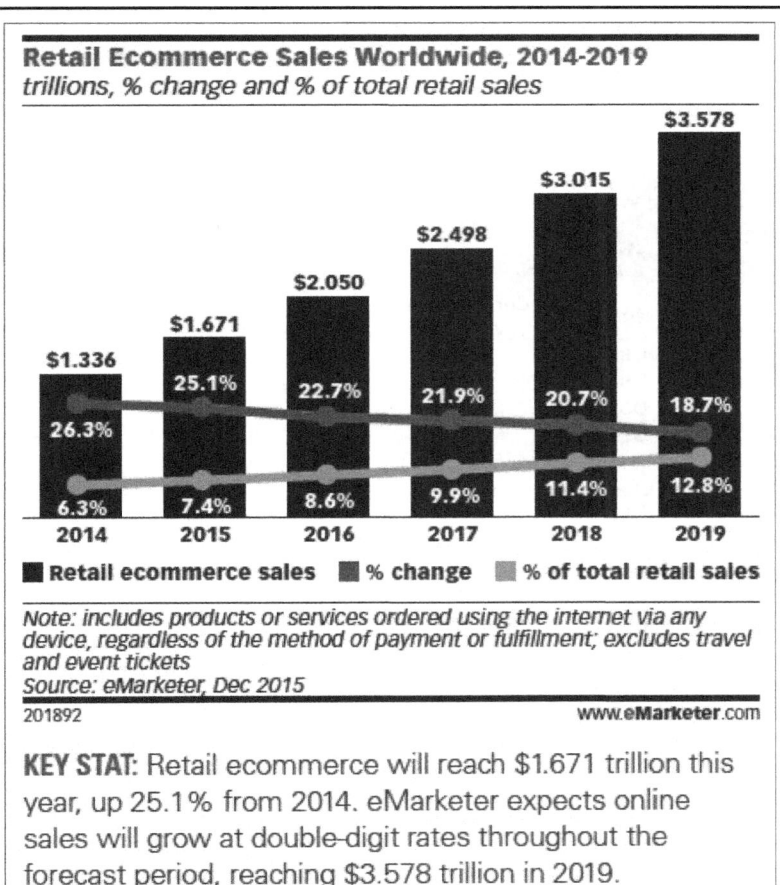

FIGURE 1.15a

Global eCommerce Sales

SOURCE: http://www.emarketer.com/public_media/docs/eMarketer_eTailWest2016_Worldwide_ECommerce_Report.pdf.

FIGURE 1.15b

eCommerce Sales—PC and Mobile

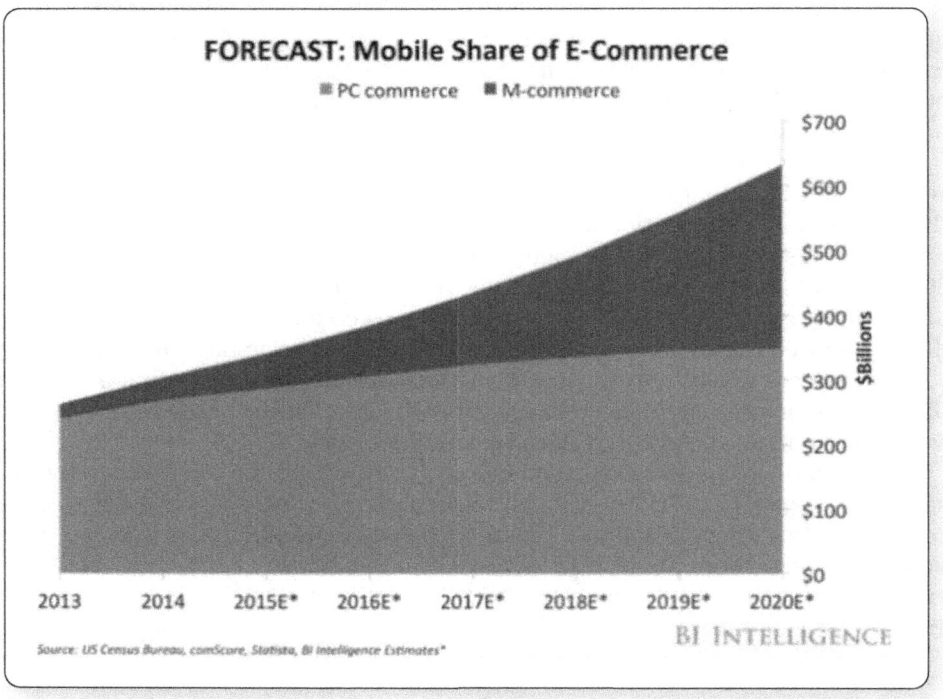

SOURCE: http://digiday.com/brands/mobile-commerce-going-2016/.

FIGURE 1.16

The Top 20 Digital Firms

Global Internet Market Leaders = Apple / Google / Amazon / Facebook / Tencent / Alibaba...Flush with Cash...Private Companies Well Represented

Rank	Company	Region	Current Market Value ($B)	Q1:16 Cash ($B)	2015 Revenue ($B)
1	Apple	USA	$547	$233	$235
2	Google / Alphabet	USA	510	79	75
3	Amazon	USA	341	16	107
4	Facebook	USA	340	21	18
5	Tencent	China	206	14	16
6	Alibaba	China	205	18	15
7	Priceline	USA	63	11	9
8	Uber	USA	63	--	--
9	Baidu	China	62	11	10
10	Ant Financial	China	60	--	--
11	Salesforce.com	USA	57	4	7
12	Xiaomi	China	46	--	--
13	Paypal	USA	46	6	9
14	Netflix	USA	44	2	7
15	Yahoo!	USA	36	10	5
16	JD.com	China	34	5	28
17	eBay	USA	28	11	9
18	Airbnb	USA	26	--	--
19	Yahoo! Japan	Japan	26	5	5
20	Didi Kuaidi	China	25	--	--
Total			$2,752	$447*	$554*

SOURCE: http://www.smartinsights.com/internet-marketing-statistics/global-internet-trends-2016-insights-kpcbs-latest-report/.

DRIVERS OF DIGITAL TRANSFORMATION

The outline of digital transformation is becoming clear even though it is in its early days. For one thing, digital transformation is more than just the adoption of digital technologies. It requires a strategy that focuses on business transformation, not just improvement at the margins. It requires leaders that understand the value of digital to the future of the organization.[51] As we discussed in Section 1.2b achieving digital maturity is a process, more a journey than a destination because the end goal is to be constantly innovating to fend off competition and take advantage of opportunities. It means taking advantage of digital technologies to improve human performance, leading to the achievement of business goals.[52]

MIT/Deloitte's 2016 digital business survey report finds that "digital congruence" is necessary to drive transformation (Figure 1.17). The strategy includes experimenting, analyzing, and implementing and requires tackling short-term projects that offer long-term benefits ("zoom out/zoom in"[53]). It further requires defining tasks, creating an innovation and risk-taking culture, and creating organizational ecosystems that include external partners as well as internal talent. The study finds that internal talent is represented more by people with soft skills including vision and the ability to collaborate than by people with detailed technological knowledge. It points to CVS Health as a company that is leading the way in digital transformation.

The company hired an experienced Chief Digital Officer in 2013 to develop an innovation lab and lead the way in strategy. The company also engaged in a number of acquisitions to bolster its retail footprint and digital capabilities. By 2015 it had demonstrated the success of the MinuteClinic concept in CVS stores and was getting ready to roll them out to many of the 1,672 newly acquired Target Pharmacy locations.[54]

FIGURE 1.17

Necessary Elements of a Digital Transformation Strategy

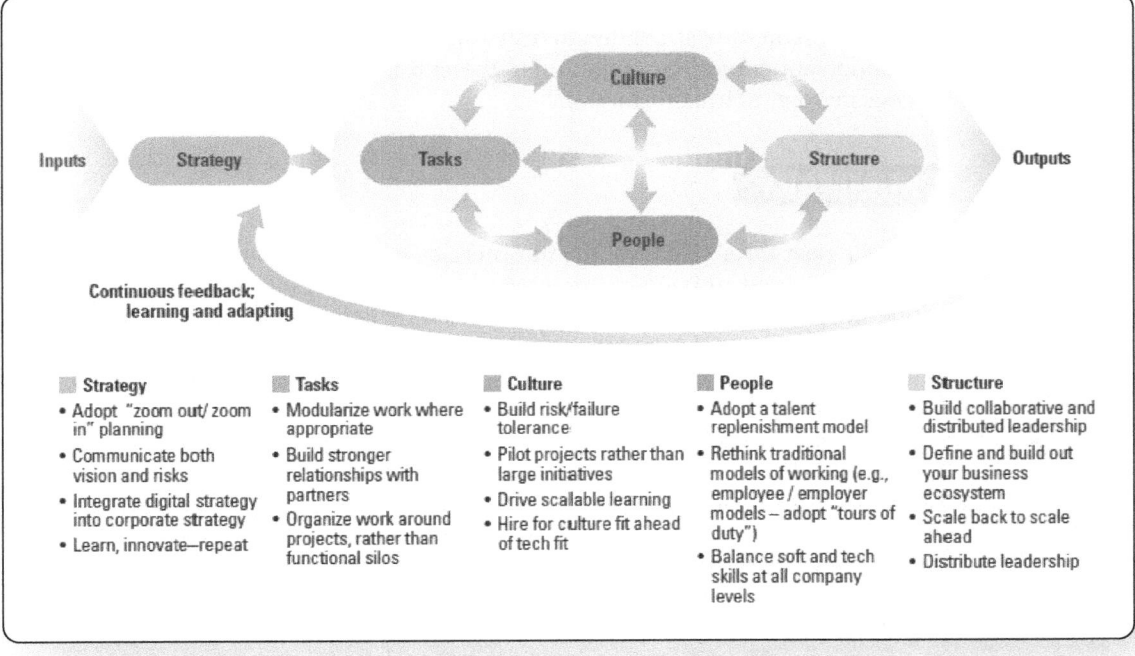

SOURCE: http://marketing.mitsmr.com/offers/DL2016/58180-MITSMR-Deloitte-Digital-Business-2016.pdf?utm_source=WhatCounts%2c+Publicaster+Edition&utm_medium=email&utm_campaign=dlrpt16&utm_content=Download+the+Report+(PDF)&cid=1.

Speaking at an industry conference in 2016 CDO Brian Tilzer listed other ways in which CVS was using technology to improve customer experience including:

- Text alerts when prescriptions are ready
- Scanning healthcare membership cards
- A pilot project for curbside pickup

None of these represents ground-breaking technology. The point is that all are chosen with excellent customer experience being the desired output.[55]

A project with potentially even broader impact was being tested in 2016. Its aim was to help customers with chronic conditions better adhere to their medication guidelines. CDO Brian Tilzer describes the CVS reach and vision:

CVS Health has an incredible scale and reach that provides us with an opportunity to use technology and innovation to improve the health outcomes of more than 5 million customers that walk through our doors every day. We have over 7,800 retail stores nationwide and 75 percent of the population in the markets we serve live within 3 miles of a CVS/ pharmacy. Since inception, our MinuteClinic walk-in clinics have seen more than 22 million patients ... we have a huge opportunity to use technology to improve the health outcomes of our customer, by extending our services to meet them anytime, anywhere. For us, the benefits of technology aren't just driving people back to our platforms: it's about uncovering the most effective ways to help all people on their path to better health. Our vision is to create a "connected" health experience that makes it radically easier for people to save time and money—and stay healthy.

The initiative is already producing tangible outcomes. Brian Tilzer continues:

10 percent more CVS/caremark members with common chronic conditions improved their medication adherence to optimal levels after enrolling online, and CVS/caremark clients could save more than $20 per registered member in unnecessary medical expenses.[56]

This is a truly transformational outcome that could improve the quality of life for people with chronic medical conditions and lower health costs in a way that could benefit an even broader population. It may be a sign of things to come as more companies begin on the path of digital transformation. Interactive Exercise 1.4 deals with the important subject of maintaining the culture of innovation that is necessary to successful digital transformation.

SUMMARY

Over the past three decades, the internet has grown from an esoteric network serving only a limited audience to an integral part of life for billions of people around the globe. It has been joined by the mobile web, which reaches even more people and is experiencing an even greater growth rate. Companies like Amazon, Google, and Salesforce are creatures of the internet itself. Old-economy companies like General Electric and IBM have integrated the internet into every aspect of their businesses in order to continue to thrive.

Digital disruption is all around us, disrupting business models and operations alike. It forces businesses—large and small, old and new—to undergo digital transformation or perish. Digital transformation is an activity that must engage the entire business in a strategic and ongoing process. Companies like Amazon, IBM, and Salesforce continue to disrupt their industries. Others like North Face and CVS are taking advantage of technology and new business approaches to better serve their customers. Few companies, however, have yet attained digital maturity.

Digital transformation must focus on providing excellent customer experience as well as on streamlining operations and reducing costs. Marketers must take the lead in creating satisfying customer experience and be an active participant in identifying needed changes in business models. They will continue to be impacted by technology that changes the way all parts of the business operate. In this chapter we have highlighted the importance of the Internet of Things, virtual and augmented reality, artificial intelligence, and cloud computing. These are among the technology drivers of change that are still in the early stages of disruption.

Marketers take advantage of the fixed internet and mobile web in various ways to perform the four basic marketing activities—customer acquisition, conversion, retention, and customer value growth. Various online and offline tools and techniques come into play at various points in the customer journey.

This chapter provides a snapshot at one point in time of the internet and mobile web and the people and companies that use them. The picture it portrays is one of rapid growth and evolution in the ways in which both people and businesses use digital. Change is universal in the digital ecosystem and any snapshot is quickly outdated. This requires the digital marketers to understand sources of information that are relevant to their specific business and/or marketing function and to track that information, usually using the web itself.

This text is premised on the need to understand how technology-driven marketing works and how it can be integrated with traditional channels and activities in order to achieve marketing success. Understanding digital marketing is, and will continue to be, something of a moving target. At the same time that we wrestle with understanding of complex, technology-driven activities, it is important to remember that good marketing puts the customer front and center and focuses on excellent customer experience at all customer touchpoints.

Businesses must maintain an innovation culture that has customer centricity at its heart and is guided by sound vision and strategy. No firm can practice business as usual. Change is a constant, making transformation a way of life, not an end goal.

DISCUSSION QUESTIONS

1. The origins of the internet are unusual in the history of commercial media. What makes it unusual and what qualities does that impart to the medium?
2. What are the waves of change in the business environment that began with the internet?
3. How do waves of change in technology parallel business change? What lies ahead in terms of technology change?
4. What are some changes in your own life and that of your family that you can reasonably expect from the Internet of Things?
5. Why is the mobile web a separate entity from the fixed internet? Why is it important that marketers track developments in mobile as well as in the internet?
6. What is the meaning of digital disruption? digital transformation?
7. How should businesses go about attaining digital maturity? What is the final outcome state that marks a digitally mature business?
8. True/False. Artificial intelligence is a new technology that promises to supplant human beings in all aspects of their daily lives.
9. Do consumers as well as businesses have an interest in the topic of cloud computing? Explain why or why not.
10. Discuss the role the internet plays in the lives of consumers and businesses. Has it changed the lives of consumers in any meaningful way? Has it changed the way businesses operate in any significant fashion? Can you give examples of the impact of the internet in B2C, B2B, or nonprofit markets?
11. Technology is at the center of all digital transformation. Why or why not?
12. What are some of the major developments that CVS can point to on its road to digital maturity?

ENDNOTES

1. Barry M. Leiner et al., "Brief History of the Internet," http://www.internetsociety.org/internet/what-internet/history-internet/brief-history-internet.
2. Anu Passary, "Happy 25th Birthday World Wide Web and Thank You Tim Berners-Lee," http://www.techtimes.com/articles/174759/20160823/happy-25th-birthday-world-wide-web-and-thank-you-tim-berners-lee.htm.
3. "Web and Commercialization of the Internet," https://www.coursehero.com/file/p4if46/23-Web-and-Commercialization-of-the-Internet-1991-NSF-lifts-restrictions-on-the/.
4. Kevin Maney, "Yahoo, Apple, Amazon: Categories Past, Present and Future," https://www.linkedin.com/pulse/yahoo-apple-amazon-categories-past-present-future-kevin-maney.
5. Tim O'Reilly, "What Would Alexa Do?" https://www.oreilly.com/ideas/what-would-alexa-do.
6. John Gregorio Zapata, "Amazon Will Open BMW Doors with Personal Assistant Alexa," http://theusbport.com/amazon-will-open-bmw-doors-with-personal-assistant-alexa/12860.
7. Anna Johansson, "Amazon's Alexa Can Now Pass Along Directions to Your Car," http://www.psfk.com/2016/08/amazons-alexa-can-now-pass-along-directions-to-your-car.html.
8. Steve Case, *The Third Wave*, Simon & Schuster (New York: April 2016).
9. Steven Levy, "Steve Case Is Bullish on Tech's "Third Wave," Even if It's Kind of a Bummer," https://backchannel.com/steve-case-is-bullish-on-tech-s-third-wave-even-if-it-s-kind-of-a-bummer-94eaadde75da#.wli7ttys4
10. Klaus Schwab, "The Fourth Industrial Revolution, What it Means, How to Respond," https://www.weforum.org/agenda/2016/01/the-fourth-industrial-revolution-what-it-means-and-how-to-respond/.
11. Ahmed Banafa, "The Internet of Everything," https://www.bbvaopenmind.com/en/the-internet-of-everything-ioe/.
12. Patrick Thibodeau, "Explained: The ABCs of the Internet of Things," http://www.computerworld.com/article/2488872/emerging-technology-explained-the-abcs-of-the-internet-of-things.html.
13. Bill Lydon, "Sensors Are Fundamental to Industrial IoT," http://www.automation.com/automation-news/article/sensors-are-fundamental-to-industrial-iot.
14. Andrew Meola, "Internet of Things in Healthcare," http://www.businessinsider.com/internet-of-things-in-healthcare-2016-8.
15. Joseph Bradley et al., "Internet of Everything in the Public Sector," http://slideplayer.com/slide/4240580/.
16. "Here's How the Internet of Things Will Explode by 2020," http://www.businessinsider.com/iot-ecosystem-internet-of-things-forecasts-and-business-opportunities-2016-2.
17. Cliff Kuang, "Disney's $1 Billion Bet on a Magical Wristband," https://www.wired.com/2015/03/disney-magicband/.
18. Adi Robertson, "Tour Yosemite in Virtual Reality with Barack Obama," http://www.theverge.com/2016/8/25/12630724/through-the-ages-obama-national-parks-vr-yosemite.
19. https://www.facebook.com/natgeo/videos/10153864841128951/.
20. Jessica Gioglio, "Pepsi Max Shocks and Delights Londoners with Augmented Reality Stunt," http://www.convinceandconvert.com/social-media-case-studies/pepsi-max-shocks-and-delights-londoners-with-augmented-reality-stunt/.
21. Eric Johnson, "What Are the Differences between Virtual, Augmented and Mixed Reality?" http://www.recode.net/2015/7/27/11615046/whats-the-difference-between-virtual-augmented-and-mixed-reality.
22. http://searchcio.techtarget.com/definition/digital-disruption.

23. "Netflix Shares How it Grew to 81 Million Monthly Subscribers," http://venturebeat.com/2016/04/21/netflix-shares-how-it-grew-to-81-million-monthly-subscribers-secrets-of-a-subscription-model-webinar/.
24. "Digital Transformation: Online Guide to Digital Business Transformation," http://www.i-scoop.eu/digital-transformation/.
25. George Westerman, Didier Bonnet and Andrew McAfee, "The Nine Elements of Digital Transformation," http://sloanreview.mit.edu/article/the-nine-elements-of-digital-transformation/.
26. "CBS All Access Review," http://www.cutcabletoday.com/cbs-all-access-review/.
27. Cynthia Littleton, "CBS Predicts 8 Million Subscribers for All Access and Showtime Streaming Services by 2020," http://variety.com/2016/tv/news/cbs-all-access-showtime-8-million-subscribers-1201730792/.
28. Tony Maglio, "HBO vs. Hulu vs. Netflix: Here's Who's Winning in Streaming Subscribers—By a Lot." http://www.thewrap.com/hbo-vs-hulu-vs-netflix-heres-whos-winning-in-streaming-subscribers-by-a-lot/.
29. Kris Hammond, "What Is Artificial Intelligence?" http://www.computerworld.com/article/2906336/emerging-technology/what-is-artificial-intelligence.html.
30. http://www.oxforddictionaries.com/us/definition/american_english/artificial-intelligence.
31. Eric Griffith, "What Is Cloud Computing?" http://www.pcmag.com/article2/0,2817,2372163,00.asp.
32. Salesforce's Data Centre Team 'Fought' AWS Cloud Outsourcing," http://www.theregister.co.uk/2016/06/03/salesforce_aws_microsoft_platform_wars/.
33. Parker Harris, "Salesforce Selects Amazon Web Services as Preferred Public Cloud Infrastructure Provider," https://www.salesforce.com/blog/2016/05/salesforce-aws-public-cloud-infrastructure.html.
34. Alex Konrad, "Nonstop Benioff: Inside the Audacious Plan to Disrupt Salesforce—and the World," http://www.forbes.com/sites/alexkonrad/2016/08/24/nonstop-benioff-inside-the-audacious-plan-to-disrupt-salesforce-and-the-world/#7d636c215747.
35. Kelly Stirman, "A Trillion Tiny Robots in the Cloud: The Future of AI in an Algorithm World," http://www.cloudcomputing-news.net/news/2015/dec/21/trillion-tiny-robots-cloud-future-ai-algorithm-world/.
36. "What Is Watson?" http://www.ibm.com/watson/what-is-watson.html.
37. Matt Marshall, "The North Face to Launch Insanely Smart Watson-Powered Mobile Shopping App Next Month," http://venturebeat.com/2016/03/04/the-north-face-to-launch-insanely-smart-watson-powered-shopping-app-next-month/.
38. http://www.internetlivestats.com/internet-users/.
39. Alexis C. Madrigal, "Most People Didn't Have an A/C Until 1973 and Other Strange Tech Timelines," http://www.theatlantic.com/technology/archive/2012/07/most-people-didnt-have-a-c-until-1973-and-other-strange-tech-timelines/260427/.
40. http://www2.unicef.org:60090/factoftheweek/index_45611.html.
41. "The Mobile Economy 2016," http://www.gsma.com/mobileeconomy/.
42. https://www.budde.com.au/Research/2015-Philippines-Telecoms-Mobile-and-Broadband.
43. http://www.pewinternet.org/data-trend/internet-use/latest-stats/.
44. Paul Taylor and George GaoGeorge, "Generation X: America's Neglected 'Middle Child,' http://www.pewresearch.org/fact-tank/2014/06/05/generation-x-americas-neglected-middle-child/.
45. "Millennials Outnumber Baby Boomers and Are Far More Diverse, Census Bureau Reports," http://www.census.gov/newsroom/press-releases/2015/cb15-113.html.
46. Chris O'Brien, "The Sharing Economy Is Creating a New Digital Divide, Says Pew Study," http://venturebeat.com/2016/05/19/pew-study-says-explosion-of-sharing-and-collaborative-services-is-creating-new-digital-divide/.

47. Benjamin Herold, "Mobile-Only Internet Access Presents Hurdles for Families, Survey Finds," http://blogs.edweek.org/edweek/DigitalEducation/2016/02/mobile_internet_access_low_income_parents_survey.html.
48. https://cmosurvey.org/wp-content/uploads/sites/11/2016/08/The_CMO_Survey-Highlights_and_Insights-Aug-2016.pdf.
49. "US Online and Traditional Media Advertising Outlook, 2016-2020," http://www.marketingcharts.com/traditional/us-online-and-traditional-media-advertising-outlook-2016-2020-68214/.
50. https://cmosurvey.org/wp-content/uploads/sites/11/2016/08/The_CMO_Survey-Highlights_and_Insights-Aug-2016.pdf.
51. Gerald C. Kane et al., "Strategy, Not Technology Drives Digital Transformation," http://sloanreview.mit.edu/projects/strategy-drives-digital-transformation/.
52. Mark McDonald, "What Is a Digital Strategy?" https://www.accenture.com/us-en/blogs/blogs-digital-what-is-digital-strategy.
53. Mark Tilberglen, "Are You Zooming In or Zooming Out? Challenging Conventional Strategic Planning," http://www.thinkadvisor.com/2015/08/03/are-you-zooming-in-or-zooming-out-challenging-conv?slreturn=1473010955.
54. "CVS Health and Target Announce Completed Acquisition of Target's Pharmacy and Clinic Business," https://cvshealth.com/newsroom/press-releases/cvs-health-and-target-announce-completed-acquisition-targets-pharmacy-and.
55. David Aponovich, "The Secret to Successful Digital Transformation? Let Your Customers Lead," https://www.acquia.com/blog/secret-successful-digital-transformation-let-your-customers-lead/23/05/2016/3295236.
56. Erica Garvin, "CVS Health Executive Talks Integration of Digital Health Tools for Pharmacy," http://hitconsultant.net/2016/02/08/cvs-health-goes-digital-to-help-its-customers-get-a-handle-on-their-health/.

Chapter 2

The Supply Chain Becomes a Value Ecosystem

LEARNING OBJECTIVES

By the time you complete this chapter, you will be able to:

1. Distinguish between the following concepts: supply chain, value chain, virtual value chain, and value ecosystem.
2. Explain the role of ecological sustainability in the supply chain.
3. List the business processes that are necessary to manage the supply chain.
4. Explain the role of information in, first, integrating the value chain and, later, making it virtual.
5. Discuss the benefits of a virtual value chain with special emphasis on its role in creating customer value.
6. Discuss the concept that all goods are services.
7. Identify technologies that allowed early process integration in supply chains.
8. Discuss the major technologies that are disrupting the supply chain at present.
9. Select one example of a business that has made significant changes in its value chain and explain why the changes were necessary and what has so far been achieved.
10. Discuss one trend that you believe will be especially important in future supply chain evolution.

Digital disruption is occurring throughout business processes. The transformation of channels of distribution has been ongoing for several decades focusing on cost reduction and speeding goods and services to market. In recent years the focus has broadened to customer-facing activities. Digital transformation that matches supply to the demands of individual customers is no longer an option; it is becoming a necessity. According to Professor William Verdini, "Businesses don't compete, supply chains compete."[1]

THE IMPACT OF DIGITAL TRANSFORMATION ON SUPPLY CHAINS

channels of distribution intermediaries through which products and information about transactions move in the course of a single exchange.

supply chain the downstream portion of the value chain, the channel from suppliers to producers.

value ecosystem connecting brands and their customers and business partners in a direct, non-linear fashion.

value chain an integrated supply chain in which transactions are conducted electronically.

value essentially the usefulness (economic utility) of the product less its price; also known as customer value or customer perceived value.

There was a time when **channels of distribution** described simple movements of goods or services through a series of intermediaries who performed a variety of business functions in the process of transporting them from manufacturer to customer. That is the linear **supply chain** portrayed in Figure 2.1a. Reaching the **value ecosystem** illustrated in Figure 2.1b is often a lengthy process.

It begins with a supply chain in which value is added at various points in the distribution process. That is the so-called **value chain**.

Michael Porter popularized the concept of the value chain in the early 1980s. His familiar graphic, which identifies the primary activities of inbound logistics, operations, outbound logistics, marketing and sales, and service and recognizes the support activities of infrastructure, human resources, technology, and procurement, provides a useful basis for understanding *how the enterprise produces* **value** *for its customers*.

Unfortunately for our ease of understanding, in the last two decades the term has been widely used in a different way. In the context of the automation of business processes and later the internet, the term "value chain" has come to mean the *seamless, end-to-end integration of activities throughout the channel of distribution*. In essence, this value chain concept incorporates two familiar business processes—the supply chain and the channel of distribution. Companies have moved, first, to integrate the supplier-facing side of their channels—the supply chain. They have been slower to integrate on the customer-facing side, the channel of distribution. When they have, they have reaped significant benefits.

Otis Elevator, a business unit of United Technologies Corp., describes itself as "The world's leading manufacturer and service provider of elevators, escalators and moving walkways."[2] Otis has been integrating with customer infrastructure for many years. In 1988 it introduced the first Remote Elevator Monitoring (REM®) system. REM® is a diagnostic system that monitors the performance of Otis elevators and other brands with which Otis has service contracts. It monitors both the usage level and individual systems within the elevator. The system schedules regular maintenance calls based on the level of usage. If it detects a problem, it reports the condition to a 24-hour communications center, which determines the severity of the problem, prioritizes service calls, and dispatches a repair person with the required tools and parts. According to Otis, the system identifies most problems before they occur, minimizing elevator downtime. By analyzing each of the hundreds of systems in an elevator, the company also maintains such that the number of service calls is minimized and the performance is optimized. Reports covering both scheduled and REM®-based service calls are available to the customer online.[3] The remote monitoring of elevators is an example of the machine-to-machine business model discussed in Chapter 3. It also illustrates how value can be added by improving product performance, and thereby improving customer service, and lowering customer costs.

Recent developments at Otis illustrate both the "greening of the supply chain" (ecological sustainability) and their continued attention to customer concerns and needs. Their GeN2 Switch product is an elevator that does not need the usual machine room full of equipment. It is described as "plug and go," just like other appliances that use available 220-volt energy, saving on installation costs. The movement of the GeN2

FIGURE 2.1

Supply Chains Evolve into Value Webs
From Linear Supply Chain to Value Ecosystem

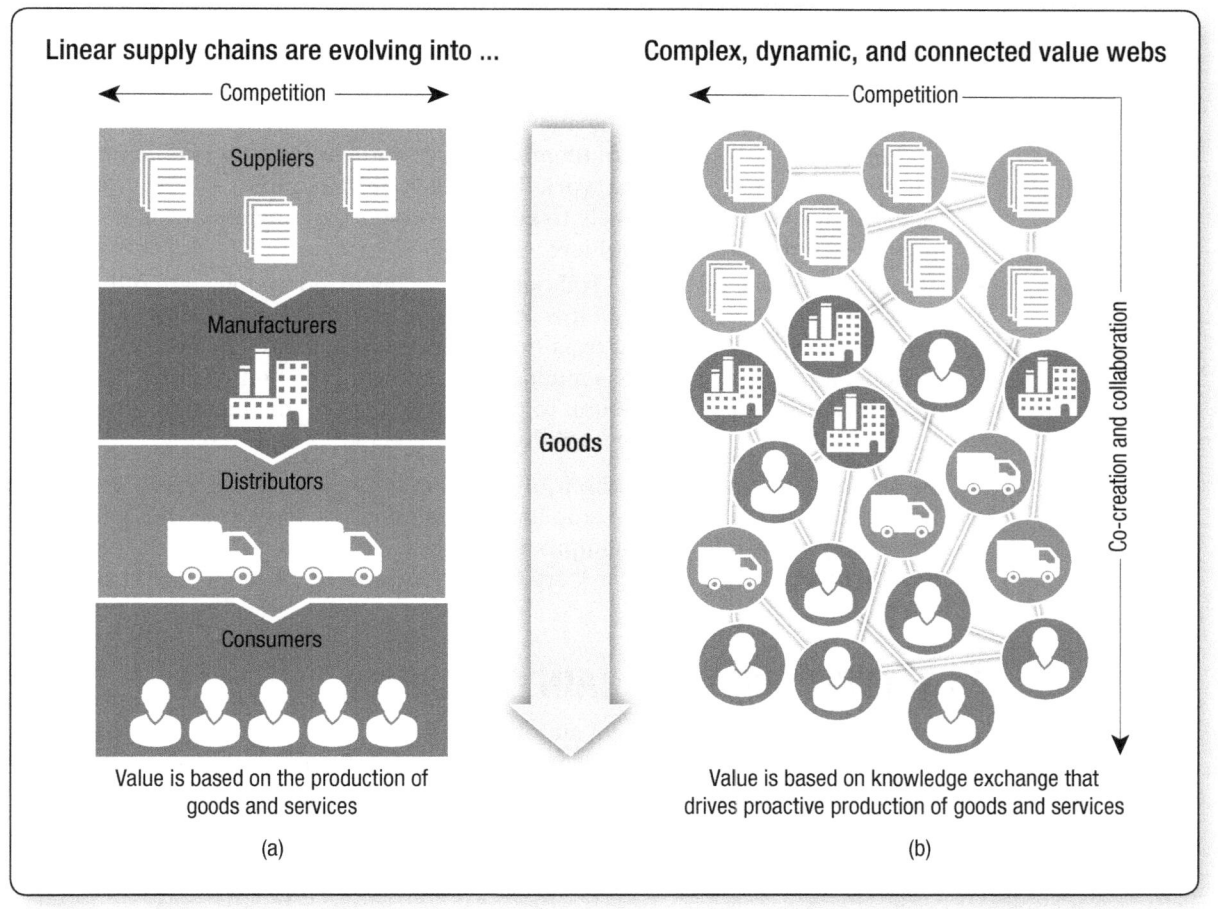

SOURCE: http://dupress.com/articles/supply-chains-to-value-webs-business-trends/

elevator generates energy, storing the excess in "accumulators." This not only saves energy costs but also allows for continued operation of the elevator in the event of power failure.[4] The elevator technology can be customized to fit customer needs in other ways. A sustainable housing development in Reze, France, will contain an elevator that derives 80 percent of its power from solar panels on the roof of the building.[5] Localization is also part of Otis's strategy. To support the "Make in India" initiative it is adding to its manufacturing capacity in Bengaluru, India. This plant will produce the GeN2 switch elevator for the Indian market, which is the second largest elevator market in the world behind China. An elevator that is not affected by power outages is seen as especially desirable by Indian builders.[6]

There is no doubt that sophisticated digital and energy technologies are key to integrated systems such as this advanced elevator. The question becomes, "how do some firms manage to use technology well to please customers and reduce costs while many still do not?" McKinsey, the global consulting firm, has found there are factors that point the way to successful digitization of business processes. Their success factors are as follows:

- Define the precise outcome to be achieved. They give as an example a bank that digitized its mortgage-application and approval process. In so doing they

cut the cost of each new mortgage by 70 percent while reducing the time for preliminary approval of the mortgage from days to just a minute.
- Create a seamless, end-to-end customer experience. This takes the cooperation of every part of the business that is part of a customer touchpoint.
- Build an in-house team that has the skills and commitment to advance the digitization process over the long term. McKinsey points out that digitization skills are in short supply in today's workforce.
- Move quickly. End-to-end processes can take years to configure and install, incurring costs but providing no payback. Like CRM systems, to be discussed in Chapter 14, projects that develop modular components that can be installed and begin to show positive outcomes in a year or less have two advantages. First, they are more likely to work than larger, more complex systems. Second, they are much more likely to generate support among management, board members, and other stakeholders.
- Do not follow the traditional roll-out process. Digitized systems are often resisted by work units in the current organization. For instance, the mortgage officers in the bank may not trust the digitized system and may continue to review mortgage applications manually, negating all the benefits of the system. It may take a new mortgage unit to prove the worth of the digital process and integrate it into the existing workflows in the bank.[7]

Providing customers with the intuitive, immediate, and seamlessly gratifying experience they expect does not stop here for many firms, however. There are many ways in which supply chains can improve business function and delight the customer. As we look at examples, it is necessary to first look at a few supply chain basics.

STRATEGIC SUPPLY CHAIN CONCEPTS

While it seems clear that the linear supply chain is a relic of the past, we need to look at the origins of today's more complex value chains and supply ecosystems to understand the basic functions and management issues.

Essentials of the Supply Chain

A supply chain maps the physical movement of goods from initial production through assembly through the distribution process to the customer in the same way but with more detail than the supply chain in Figure 2-1a. Whatever the degree of complexity, there are a set of processes that are involved in managing the supply chain (Table 2.1). As you look at the processes, which have an operations management flavor, keep in mind that a single enterprise like Nike has hundreds of suppliers whose activities must be coordinated.

Because supply chain management is such a complex task, enterprises can realize large cost savings from integrating and improving it, with best-in-class companies spending 5–6 percent less of their total revenue on supply chain costs than their median industry counterparts. They can also realize major improvements in process elements ranging from inventory (25–60 percent improvement) to overall productivity (10–16 percent improvement).[8] The classic example of a tightly integrated value chain is Dell Computer, which we will discuss later in the chapter. Zara, the European clothing chain, provides an example of combining customer information with supply chain integration to succeed in the ever-changing world of fashion.

Zara—Fast Fashion Zara, a division of Spanish conglomerate Inditex Group, had over 2,000 retail stores in more than 80 countries in early 2016 as well as growing online sales. With an estimated brand value of $9.4 billion in 2015,[9] Zara continues to capture the attention of businesses and investors as well as fashionistas around the globe.

TABLE 2.1

Supply Chain Management Processes

1. Selecting and qualifying desired suppliers
2. Establishing and managing inbound logistics
3. Designing and managing internal logistics
4. Establishing and managing outbound logistics
5. Designing work flow in product-solution assembly
6. Running batch manufacturing
7. Acquiring, installing, and maintaining process technology
8. Order processing, pricing, billing, rebates, and terms
9. Managing (multiple) channels
10. Managing customer services such as installation and maintenance to enable product use

SOURCE: Rajendra K. Srivastava, Tasadduq A. Shervani, and Liam Fahey, "Marketing, Business Processes, and Shareholder Value: An Organizationally Embedded View of Marketing Activities and the Discipline of Marketing," *Journal of Marketing*, 1999, 170.

Zara's success comes from two key drivers. First is its fashion appeal. Zara commits to only 50–60 percent of items by the beginning of the season. That leaves them with about 50 percent of the season's inventory to be produced during the season itself. Customer trends are constantly monitored. Store employees using handheld devices roam the stores, asking customers what they like, don't like, and are looking for but don't find. That information is transmitted to the design team at headquarters, which immediately begins to sketch new items. At the end of each day, store managers provide sales reports to headquarters, giving constant updates on what merchandise is and is not selling. Stores receive shipments of new merchandise twice a week, keeping stock fresh at all times.

The second driver is the ability of Zara's supply chain to produce new items and get them into stores in just two weeks. Competitive fashion chains like Swedish-based H&M and Chicos in the United States often take as much as six months to spot a trend and react to it by producing more of desired items and disposing of unpopular ones. By that time the selling season is over. As a result of its speed to market, Zara is able to sell 85 percent of its stock at full price while the fashion industry averages only 60–70 percent.

How has Zara designed a supply chain that supplies desired merchandise so quickly and so effectively? First, it owns many of its own production facilities, making about 40 percent of its own fabric in highly automated factories in Spain. It also makes about 60 percent of the garments it sells. Most are produced in small workshops throughout Spain and Portugal instead of being outsourced to lower-cost-of-labor countries. Inventory reaches stores quickly, by truck in Europe and by air in more distant locations.[10] Their marketing effort includes a website that is carefully localized for the various countries in which it operates and what appears to be a single Facebook page with over 8 million fans globally.

The importance of supply chain excellence in the fashion industry is well recognized. There are two surprising things that describe the situation in the years since Zara was founded in 1974:

1. Zara's business model has changed little since then.
2. Competing fashion chains like Gap, H&M, and Abercrombie and Fitch have not been able to emulate the fast fashion model.

That does not mean that Zara does not keep up with other developments, however. Their website is carefully localized for the many countries they serve with some exceptions. For instance, their Chinese online presence is operated on a Chinese platform. The complexity of Zara's merchandising delayed their move into online sales until 2011. By 2014, online represented only 3 percent of Zara's total sales but they were growing at a 20 percent rate and Zara continued rolling out online sales to additional countries.[11] Zara has had a global Facebook page from the early days of brand pages. The page had 23,764,176 likes in early 2016. Customers from all over the world could be seen asking for a particular pair of shoes to become available in their stores, complaining about the quality of a piece of merchandise, or even reporting a fraudulent Zara Facebook page. The operators of the Facebook page appeared to be responding within one day and providing clear and useful information.

Zara is active on other social media platforms but it seems to let its customers do a great deal of the talking—and the photographing and the sharing. According to one observer, the young consumers who are the heart of Zara's market are purchasing experiences, not just clothing. They want to parade it on Instagram and Snapchat. The fast fashion at Zara, along with the trendy but cheap fashion at Forever 21, meet young consumers' needs for a large number of images to be shared. "Their entire life, if it's not shareable, it didn't happen," Marcie Merriman, Generation Z expert and executive director of growth strategy and retail innovation at Ernst & Young, said to Business of Fashion. "Experiences define them much more than the products that they buy."[12] That kind of customer engagement may be an even more difficult standard to reach than a hyper-efficient supply chain, challenging as that is!

The Value Chain

In order to create optimal value, a company must examine the entire supply chain, from initial production to final consumption, in order to understand where costs are incurred in the process. Consultants at Bain & Company liken it to a Swahili game called Jenga. In this game, each player must remove as many blocks as possible from a tower, using them to build additional structures, all without causing the original structure to come crashing down. This seems an apt analogy.

They identify four key factors in this effort:

- Information search costs
- Transaction costs
- Fragmentation of the customer marketplace
- Standardization of products

Together information and transaction costs typically account for over 40 percent of total costs. Economists characterize these costs as "friction" in channels of distribution and they offer ripe targets for cost reduction in value chains.[13] Integrated value chains represent an important step in managing both the supply-facing and the customer-facing sides of the business. Dell's integrated value chain operates extensively in internet space, and hence it is sometimes referred to as a "virtual value chain."

Dell's Direct Model Dell Computers is one of the classic examples of creating a value chain in internet space, one that is not a series of links but a network of interconnected enterprises, both supplier and customer. Like Zara, this aspect of Dell's business model has changed little from its early days. Before Dell's direct model became a force in the industry, personal computers had important issues in all four of the categories established by Bain. Search and transaction costs were high, especially for the small business or individual customer. The fragmented market ranged from the individual customer buying a single unit to the very large corporation which might purchase several hundred computers each month. Even very large customers tended to settle for a standard product because it was cheaper to buy in a large, standardized lot until Dell. In its early years, Dell enjoyed great success as a result of its build-to-order model which featured a streamlined supply chain (Figure 2.2) and careful financial control of manufacturing and distribution operations. Touting Dell's success in 2004 *Fast Company* magazine stated that "Dell has replaced inventory with information, and that has helped turn it into one of the fastest, most hyperefficient organizations on the planet."[14]

Dell also uses information to create customer value. One primary mechanism for doing this is its Premier Pages. They were one of the first to provide each business

FIGURE 2.2a
Traditional Computer Manufacturer

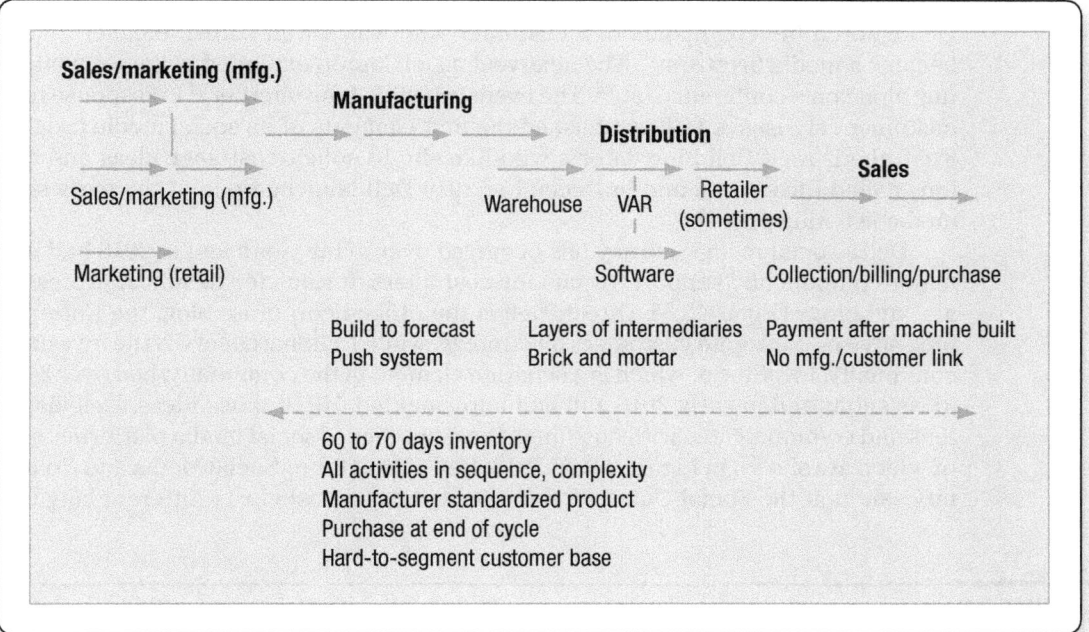

FIGURE 2.2b
Dell

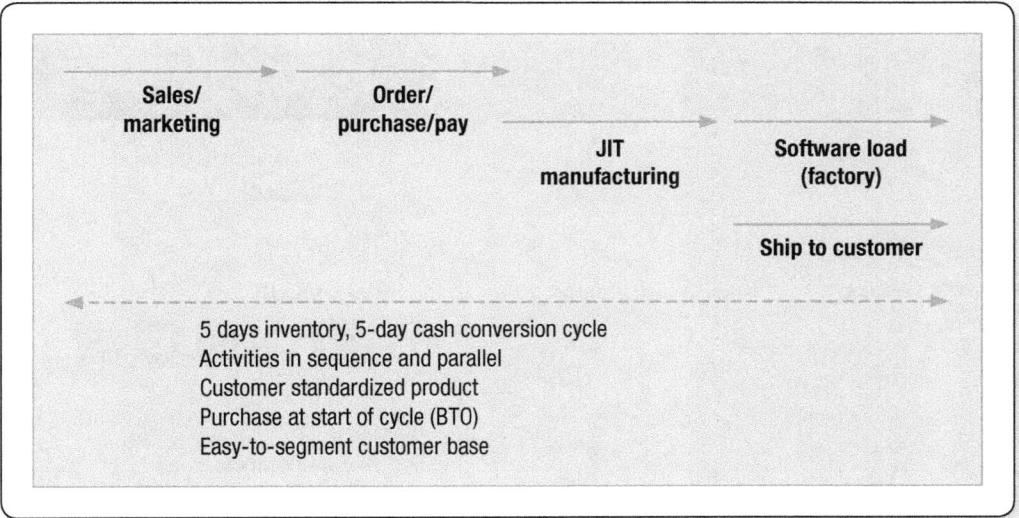

customer, from a Fortune 500 enterprise to a small local business, its own secure page on the Dell site. This includes the products that have been approved for purchase by the firm and support information for those specific products. Products not approved for purchase are not even seen, making life easier for the purchasing department. In addition, employees with purchasing authority can simply log on and make their purchase without going through purchasing, saving time for both. Dell also wins because purchases are driven to the website, where transactions are cheaper. This service is feasible for even a small business because Dell's telephone representatives have easy-to-use templates that allow them to set up a page by simply entering information provided by the customer over the phone.

Dell's success has sometimes been uneven, however. Beginning in about 2005 Dell suffered a number of issues. The company that prided itself on customer service ignored the complaints of a customer who was a well-known blogger[15] until it became a media firestorm.[16] The next year a Dell laptop exploded in flames while sitting alone on a conference table. The event transfixed the internet.[17] In response to the customer care issues Dell established the first elements of its social media program. First, the Direct2Dell blog, later a wiki-like site to solicit customer ideas and opinions called IdeaStorm, and in December 2010 Dell launched one of the early social media listening posts.[18]

Dell's social media journey has occurred over many years and in 2016 had three major components: support forums for customers, forums for technical professionals, and blogs (Figure 2.3). Direct2Dell is the official corporate blog, the Enterprise blog advises corporate customers on strategy, while DellShares serves the investment community. IdeaStorm, which is a separate element in the community, had over 24,000 ideas submitted in early 2016 and had implemented 549 of those ideas. Dell also listens and communicates with customers on a number of social media platforms, some of which are shown in Figure 2.3. In 2013, Dell's Director of Social Media and Community said that the Social Outreach team fielded 3,000 posts in 11 different languages

FIGURE 2.3
Dell's Social Media Structure

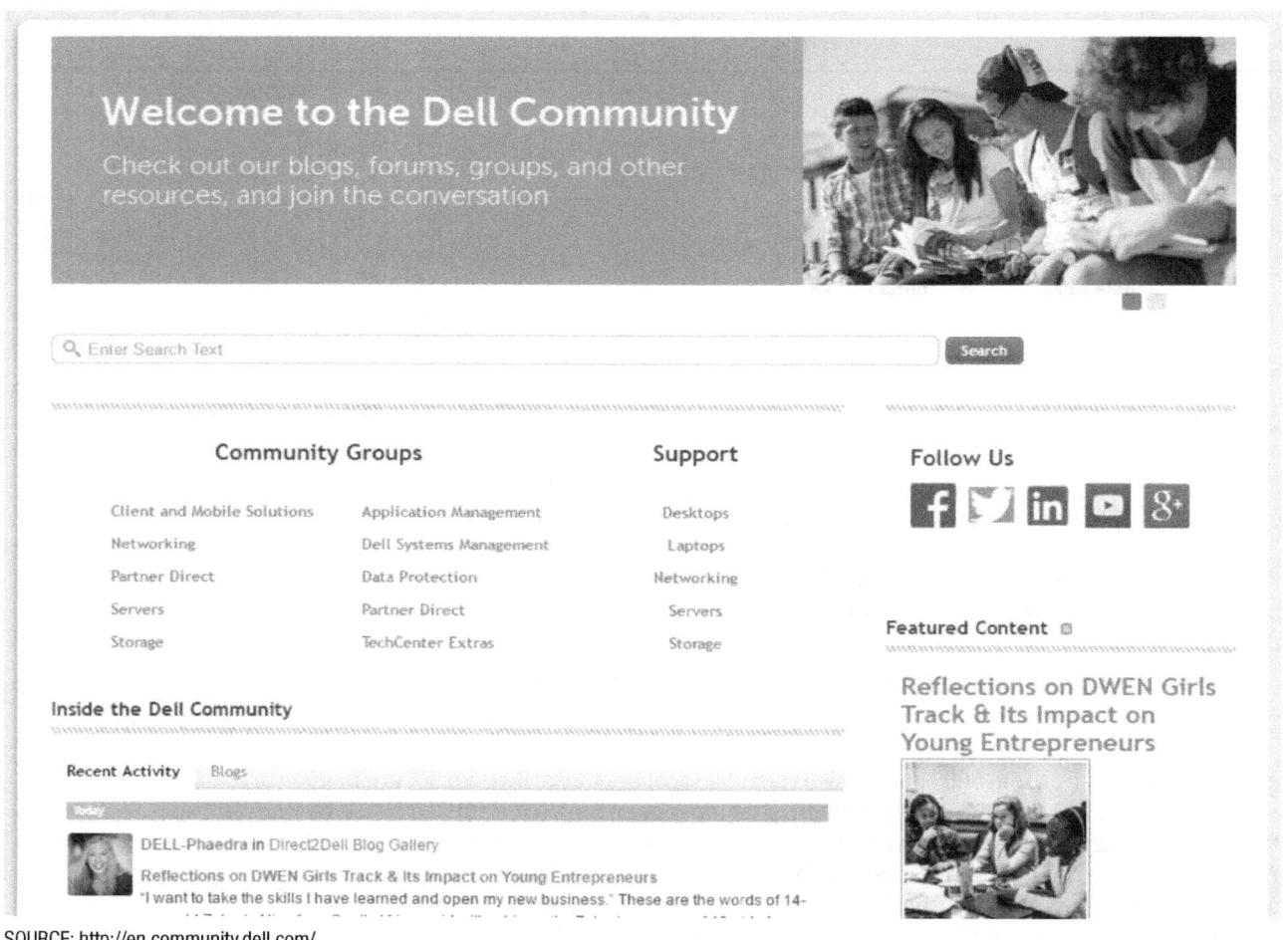

SOURCE: http://en.community.dell.com/

each week. She says that the social media program focuses on building trust through engagement and integrity, using available online and offline channels of communication, co-creation with customers and employees, and in-depth employee training.[19] These are all activities that have potential to create value for customers. They have served Dell in good stead through market disruption, economic turmoil, and the privatization of the company in 2013.[20]

One important change is a greater reliance on channels of distribution at the expense of its direct model.[21] Dell has also signaled greater emphasis on developing new markets in areas like digital services instead of relying primarily on continued streamlining of its value chain for cost effectiveness. The emphasis on new markets, one reflection of which is the merger with EMC, signals a focus on revenue generation in addition to cost reduction.[22] That requires a relentless focus on creating value for the customer.

Benefits of an Integrated Value Chain   In the internet economy customer value has taken on a special meaning. The quality of products is still unquestionably important. However, the stark truth is that many companies have mastered the art of product quality. They spent much of the last 10–15 years learning to produce products at or near the **six-sigma** level of quality (no more than 3.4 defects per million according to the American Society for Quality). That kind of quality has become expected and even standard in many applications. It is necessary, but no longer sufficient in businesses of all kinds.

It is customary to point out that customers want performance, reliability, speed, and convenience, both in products and in the distribution of those products. That is true, but Vargo and Lusch, searching for a way to integrate the subdisciplines of product marketing and services marketing, take that reasoning a step further. Their concept, which is nothing less than a new paradigm for marketing itself, has occasioned much discussion. They state that:

> the **service-centered dominant logic** represents a reoriented philosophy that is applicable to all marketing offerings, including those that involve tangible output (goods) in the process of service provision.[23]

six-sigma quality management technique that results in near-perfect products; technically, results that fall within six standard deviations from the mean of a normal distribution.

Are all goods—tangible and intangible—actually services? While that may sound like a revolutionary idea, advertisers have long known that they must sell product benefits, not product features. For the most part, people do not purchase products just to possess them; they purchase them to derive benefits of some sort, even if the benefit itself is something intangible like "status."

Vargo and Lusch have continued to update concepts and terminology associated with their logic. Their 2016 update contains several axioms that are especially relevant to value chains:

- Resources that create results, including knowledge and skills, are the fundamental basis of strategic benefit.
- Value is co-created by multiple actors of which the customer, or beneficiary, is always one.
- A service-centered view is inherently beneficiary oriented and relational.
- The beneficiary is the unique determiner of value.

In their view, "the narrative of value cocreation is developing into one of resource-integrating, reciprocal-service-providing actors cocreating value through holistic, meaning-laden experiences in nested and overlapping service ecosystems, governed and evaluated through their institutional arrangements."[24] Figure 2.4 illustrates the concept.

In this illustration of Service Dominant logic the authors use both "networks" and "ecosystem" but the word linear is not used. The actors include traditional supply chain members as well as customers, all of whom may assume different roles at various times. The actors provide resources and integrate them through collaboration with one another. The services are exchanged using the processes of facilitating institutions. All of this results in an integrated service ecosystem which has as its major purpose the co-creation of value.[25]

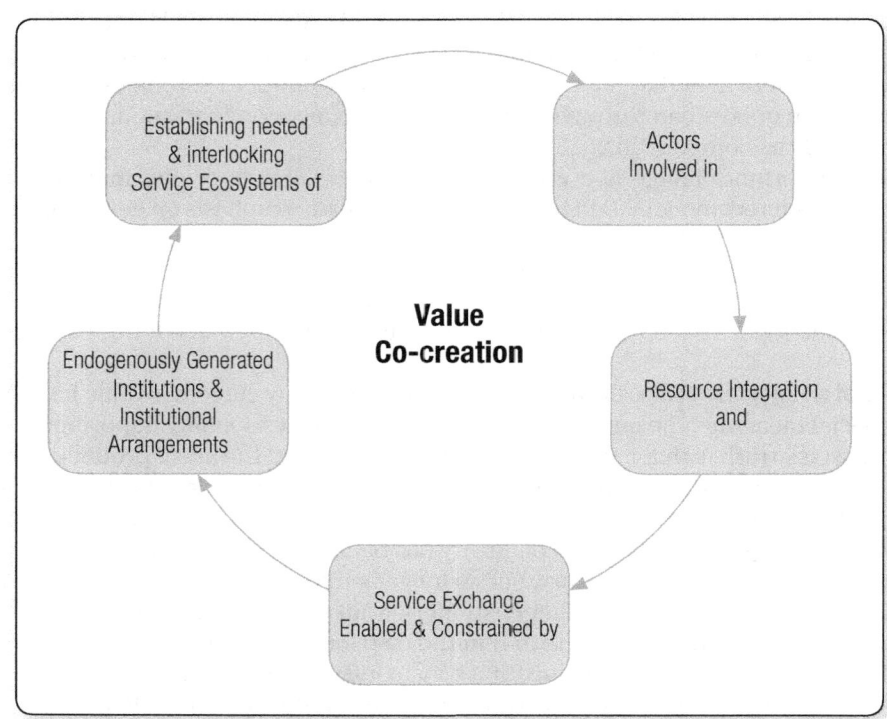

FIGURE 2.4
The Narrative and Process of S-D Logic

SOURCE: https://arizona.pure.elsevier.com/en/publications/institutions-and-axioms-an-extension-and-update-of-service-domina

Notice that customers are key to this co-creation of value; it is, after all, what they are seeking. A key task of any actor in the ecosystem is to create value. Articulating a value proposition is the first step in creating value and it is an integral part of business models. We will discuss value propositions in Chapter 3.

NEXT STEP—THE DIGITAL VALUE ECOSYSTEM

Nike's customized shoes and apparel blazed a digital trail which other brands have struggled to emulate. Recently it established a new software division, Nike Fuel, which provides an excellent illustration of the concept of collaborating to co-create value. Nike Fuel Lab was established in 2014 to build a fitness ecosystem using the Nike Fuel platform. Previously, Nike had participated alone in the fitness tracking market with its fitness tracking hardware.[26] It signaled the end of that strategy in 2014 when it announced that it was discontinuing its FuelBand tracking devices to concentrate on software.[27] The software development takes place in the Fuel Lab and includes hardware makers, fitness app developers, platform developers, scientists, and athletes as well as consumers of Nike+ products.[28]

Fast Company describes the ecosystem as revolving around the Nike Fuel fitness measurement system, which awards points to users based on their activity level. Nike+ had over 60 million users[29] of its fitness and training services. In addition to its partnership with the Apple watch, initial partners at the Fuel Lab included a running app called RunKeeper, cycling and running tracking platform Strava, and a weight loss app MyFitnessPal.[30] The Nike+ site includes a developer portal to encourage partnership activities. According to Nike, Nike Fuel is a "partnership program designed to connect Nike with industry leading companies who share our commitment to using emerging technologies to create better solutions for athletes." They add, "If you have a body, you're an athlete," and "You have a far greater chance in life winning as part of a team than as an individual."[31] Clearly this is a sweepingly inclusive activity intended to position Nike at the center of the fitness and training movement. They have also recognized that they can do this better, and faster, with partners than alone.

The customer-facing side of the Fuel Lab is portrayed in Figure 2.5. The goal is to connect the runner's environment with Nike's online environment. The graphic shows a "connected shoe" with embedded tracking devices, but there are other devices like wrist bands that can provide connectivity. Athletes are encouraged to share their accomplishments through support activities that include everything from benchmarking of athletic or fitness achievements to publication of maps of favorite running routes to weight loss updates. On the supply-facing side the developer portal provides opportunities to partner with Nike. In March 2015, they announced additional partnerships with Fitstar, Garmin, TomTom, Wahoo, and NetPulse.[32]

Nike Fuel is a good example of the platform economy. Nike has created a platform specifically for this part of the business, a platform that is open to developers who wish to either create or adapt products to participate in Nike's fitness tracking business. These developers not only bring their products or services, but also bring new members into the Nike community.

Above all, it was created as an ecosystem because Nike sees that as the road to success.

Echoing the ideas of the **Service-Dominant Logic** Accenture says that it is necessary for companies to move to an as-a-service ecosystem model even though it may cannibalize existing products or services, in this case the Nike Fuel Band. They say that ecosystems require:

- **Co-creation**. Your most valuable workforce is no longer yours. It is a me'lange of talent from different ecosystem players coming together to redefine value based on customer desires.
- Innovation. No longer an afterthought, but a process driver. Fifty-three percent of organizations indicate they are using an open innovation program with customers, suppliers, or partners.

Service-Dominant Logic the idea that service is the basis of all economic exchange making all firms service providers and all products essentially services.

Co-creation bringing business entities or businesses and their customers together to create mutually valuable outcomes.

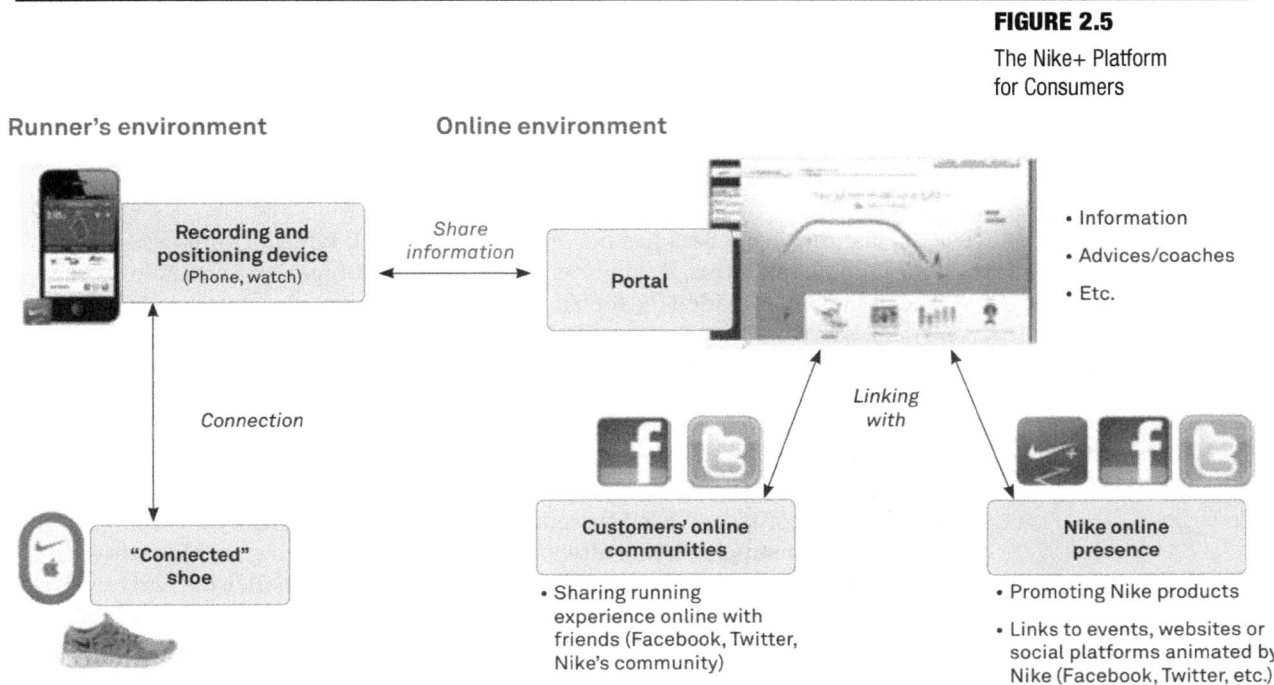

FIGURE 2.5
The Nike+ Platform for Consumers

SOURCE: https://www.capgemini-consulting.com/resource-file-access/resource/pdf/digital_transformation_at_nike_20-12_pdf.pdf

- Interdependence and dynamic roles. A good ecosystem redefines the landscape within which new solutions are developed and consumed.
- Adaptive environments. Allowing entities to respond more rapidly to disruption.
- Governance. The rules of engagement for communication, collaboration, and innovation.[33]

They assert that successful ecosystems will benefit companies in a number of ways. They will:

- Master digital relationships with customers to bring together talent—reassessing channel players and roles to foster collaboration.
- Ease adoption. Smart players will reduce risks to enable starting small and scaling fast, creating successful programs within their platform.
- Simplify the buying experience, obsessing over outcomes and solution benefits. Righting the ship means capitalizing on your indirect sales channel via an as-a-service platform you create fueled by an ecosystem of rivals and friendlies.

They conclude by asserting that, "Ecosystem as a service, done correctly, is the growth engine of the future and the battlefield on which all players now find themselves."[34] Remember that we started this chapter with the quote, "Businesses don't compete, supply chains compete." Is it now becoming clear why that is the case?

TECHNOLOGIES THAT ENABLE VALUE CHAINS AND ECOSYSTEMS

Technology and the information flows it produces have been an integral part of supply chains for decades. Exhibit 2.1 describes the most important of basic supply chain technologies. In recent years **EDI** and **ERP** have been superseded by other software technologies that are easier to use and often less costly. **RFID** technology is still in use in numerous supply chain applications.

There are a number of newer technologies that are integral to the development and functioning of integrated value chains and ecosystems. They are as follows:

- Software-as-a-Service (SaaS)
- Cloud computing
- Smart devices
- Mobile apps

Software-as-a-Service

Over the last few years **SaaS** has become ubiquitous. All kinds of software—from filing your income tax return to major enterprise applications—are available for a user fee. The definition provided by TechTarget is straightforward. "Software as a Service (SaaS) is a software distribution model in which applications are hosted by a vendor or service provider and made available to customers over a network, typically the Internet."[35] Arguably the best known application of SaaS in marketing has been SalesForce CRM, which will be discussed in Chapter 14.

The fact is that supply chain applications are moving into the cloud. That effectively makes them SaaS. The movement has been slowed by the fact that most SCM systems are part of legacy ERP systems many of which are highly customized. The overall market for supply chain software applications is growing rapidly, however, as large enterprises begin to replace their legacy systems and small firms find new SaaS applications time and cost effective. Gartner says that cloud-based supply chain software revenues grew 17 percent in 2014.[36]

Amazon Web Services is a good example of this transition. Just a few years ago if a business wanted to run on Amazon software it was necessary to download the appropriate apps. Now Amazon's description is, "Amazon Web Services (AWS) is a secure cloud services platform, offering compute power, database storage, content delivery and other functionality to help businesses scale and grow…. From data

---

EDI general term used to describe the digitizing of business information like orders and invoices so that they may be communicated electronically between suppliers and customers.

ERP implementation of processes and software that integrates all aspects of the business from manufacturing resource planning and scheduling through service functions like human resources.

RFID technology that allows the identification of tagged goods from a distance with no intervention by human operation.

SaaS making software available on a fee for use basis instead of on a license or purchase basis.

EXHIBIT 2.1 FORMATIVE TECHNOLOGIES FOR SUPPLY CHAINS

EDI (electronic data interchange)

EDI replaced the paper forms that had facilitated channels of distribution for hundreds of years. It offered speed, fewer content errors and dramatically lower processing costs. However, EDI systems were large and cumbersome and the cost was out of the reach of most small businesses.

ERP (enterprise resource planning)

ERP software allowed firms to integrate all business activities across the enterprise. All these activities, for instance accounting and human resources, had previously run separately and developing work flows to make them operate seamlessly as a single system has been a huge task. This is true in spite of the fact that ERP software is modular and can be installed one or a few activity modules at a time.

RFID (radio frequency identification) Tags

RFID technology is not new. It was used by the British in World War II to identify friendly aircraft. An RFID system begins with a **tag**, which contains a chip with a unique identifying code. As the product moves along the supply chain, its movements are recorded and sent to a tracking database.

---

warehousing to deployment tools, directories to content delivery, over 50 services are available in just a few mouse clicks with AWS."[37] On the same page is a "Get Started for Free" offer with some services being offered free for as long as a year.

A search of AWS identifies 17 supply chain management software offerings ranging from OpenERP, which it describes as a pre-configured, ready to run ERP and CRM service that connects various business processes to Sustainable Supply Chain, which enables optimal use of natural resources. One solution offered as SaaS is Retail Cloudhouse. Amazon says this business intelligence solution will allow the retail store to:

- Redesign the customer experience by analyzing customer interaction across multiple business channels.
- Reinvigorate operational excellence by streamlining Retail Store operations.
- Reimagine growth by streamlining the supply chain leading to Right-Time, Right Place merchandising inventory.[38]

It is touted as simple and easy to use. Pricing is a monthly fee per user, which is commonplace for SaaS solutions.

Cloud Computing

The AWS example shows that it is almost impossible to separate SaaS products from the cloud computing platform today. Offering access via the cloud is simply the easiest way to make the software solutions available.

One industry expert points out that the transition to cloud computing from traditional supply chain management systems is still in early stages. While it can be challenging to transition from a legacy system to a cloud-based one, he lists benefits that make it worthwhile. Cloud systems are more scalable than installed software, can be up and running quickly, they make it easy to connect new trading partners, they provide ability to connect everyone in the supply chain and more.[39]

Accenture has a nice way to cut through the technological complexities of cloud computing for the supply chain. It says that cloud computing "is the engine that makes supply chains talk to one another."[40] Pfizer has been reaping the benefits of cloud computing in its supply chain since 2012 and provides a good example of both the benefits and some of the difficulties.

Jim Cafone, VP of supply network services, calls it a virtual supply chain and says it allows Pfizer to respond quickly to both market pressures and unexpected events that might otherwise disrupt their complex supply chain. The market in which Pfizer competes is made up of two distinct segments with different issues and needs—the patented drug market and the generic drug market.

The market for drugs that are still under patent production requires responsiveness and flexibility as well as inventory to meet immediate customer needs. That means delivery strategies that can offer specialized services like temperature-controlled compartments and next-day air shipping. Speed and accuracy are the major concerns, not cost. The generic market, on the other hand, is highly cost sensitive. Logistics must focus on inventory management, efficiency, and optimized logistics that favor less costly shipping alternatives, even ocean shipping.

The complexity of Pfizer's supply chain is described by an industry publication as follows: "after more than 25 acquisitions over two decades, Pfizer has 90 plants on six continents; more than 300 external suppliers/contract manufacturers; 175 market-based logistics/distribution centers; more than 35,000 SKUs; 2,109 global logistics lanes, in 808 distinct country-lane pairs; 45,454 shipments; and 17,394 freight contract line items."[41] Before the cloud integration each of the supply chain partners had its own IT system separate from Pfizer's ERP system.

Instead of asking suppliers to implement Pfizer's existing system, Pfizer decided that a cloud-based approach that created a virtual supply chain, built in cooperation with its partners, would be more practical. All parties were required to adopt a common communications platform so they could easily send and receive information from Pfizer. Each supplier became a node on a virtual supply chain. The technology has many components but there are two key suppliers, GT Nexus and Unyson Logistics.[42] Amazon Web Services provides the cloud computing platform.[43]

Just because the cloud-based system was expected to be cheaper, faster, and much easier to install did not mean that all suppliers greeted the concept with enthusiasm. "'Not all Pfizer's partners were happy with the plan to start with, Mr Cafone says ...' There were certain providers that just didn't understand this whole world of cloud, and didn't understand this world of device agnostic and there were certain ones that didn't necessarily like it, but they decided that they wanted to build it with us and go along with us and our software partner."[44]

The project, which took about 18 months to complete, has created a number of specific benefits for Pfizer. When partners join or leave the system they can be plugged in or out easily without disrupting the entire network. The system gives Pfizer a complete view of its shipments in parts of the world where they had previously not been able to track their products. When something unexpected happens they are able to find out immediately how the product and the shipment have been affected and where the product is located.[45]

At Pfizer cloud computing now also supports other business functions. For instance, it uses cloud-based platforms in its global research and development operations. One application is a system that handles clinical trial data in partnership with research organizations Parexel and ICON as they run clinical studies. The research firms run the trials and Pfizer analyzes the data. These and other research and development activities also take place in the Amazon Web Services cloud.[46]

Pfizer uses the term **"device agmostic"** as an important descriptor of their network. That characteristic has become even more important as the Internet of Things (IoT) has entered many aspects of daily life.

The IoT Begins to Impact the Supply Chain

The IoT will eventually have a huge impact on supply chains. As digital devices are embedded in more products, an incredible amount of big data will be produced. Supply chains will be directly affected by some of these devices, smart storage, for example, and indirectly by products that include **embedded devices**, consumer wearables, for example. The data that results from the use of those products will lead to greater customer intimacy and should produce benefits for customers as well as for makers of the products.

embedded devices a device, often a microchip, that becomes part of another device, rendering various services, often doing so without human intervention.

Smart Storage Using RFID Healthcare in general and hospitals in particular are a good example of an environment in which supply chain efficiencies and careful inventory management are critical to both the cost of operations and the quality of patient care. In some cases individual items, a cardiac pace maker for instance, are quite expensive.

Enter the smart storage cabinet. Each item of inventory carries an RFID tag. The storage cabinet shown in Figure 2.6a constantly monitors inventory at the item level. When a member of the medical team removes an item the inventory is immediately adjusted. Upon reaching the operating room a bar code attached to the patient is scanned and the item is attached to the record of that patient. The cabinet monitors and reports the inventory levels and can automatically order the replacement items. If the device specified by the physician is not on hand other cabinets in the network of nearby hospitals can be searched to locate the appropriate device. The cabinets produce a great deal of data for analysis of everything from patient outcomes to inventory costs.

RFID tags are physical devices that can be attached to everything from the metal storage cabinets shown in Figure 2.6a to the cow shown in Figure 2.6b. There was a time when only a cow valued at several thousand dollars was considered eligible for an RIFD tag with its chip. Now chip technology has become so cheap that marketers can tag individual items of merchandise not just shipping pallets. Embedded chips have many other applications. Prof. Roberts's dog has an embedded microchip. Does your dog or cat have one?

Apparel with Embedded Devices A number of firms, including Nike, are producing apparel with embedded sensors used for tracking purposes. Among the well known are the Apple watch and Fitbit athletic tracking devices and shirts that collect data from daily athletic activity and display it in various ways. Many of the products are designed for athletic and physical fitness activities, but the applications to medical tracking are obvious. Some are quite sophisticated.

One of the newer applications and technologies is a pair of leggings designed by researchers at King's College in London (Figure 2.7). This application measures

FIGURE 2.6a

Smart Storage in a Hospital Environment

Source:http://www.theferrarigroup.com/supply-chain-matters/category/industry-specific-supply-chain-issues/pharmaceutical/

FIGURE 2.6b

Cow with Canadian Cattle Identification Program-compliant RFID tag

Source: http://www.canadaid.com/

muscle fatigue which previously could only be done in a lab by experienced personnel. The MIT Technology Review explains that the technology involves embroidering "an ordinary pair runners leggings with electrodes and circuitry that connect to a portable Arduino microprocessor. This then collects and analyzes the electrical stimulation data. This circuitry is double stitched in a zigzag pattern to allow for stretching. And the entire device is powered by a 7.5-volt rechargeable battery."[47] The post adds that the embroidered pattern and the stretch of the leggings automatically places the electrodes where they are needed, eliminating the need for a professional to position. This makes the product both cheaper and easier to use. It can help athletes understand how their muscles are tiring and thus avoid injury. In time it may produce data that helps design better biomechanical prosthesis.[48]

These are only two examples of hundreds of how the IoT is going to impact various elements of the supply chain.

Mobile Apps

The use of mobile devices and apps in various inventory and logistics is commonplace. It is hard to walk around a large mass merchandise outlet without seeing an employee or supplier using a device to track inventory. The principle applies to many other supply chain activities. Some of the supply chain apps are made by firms that are familiar to consumers; some are B2B supply chain specialists. Most are smartphone apps although a few require a handheld device. A few of the many apps in use today are as follows:

- Logistics by Logistics Management. This is a comprehensive app that can track drivers, vehicles, shipments, and clients.
- WEBFLEET by TomTom. This fleet management app tracks a mobile workforce.

FIGURE 2.7
Leggings with Technology Embroidered On

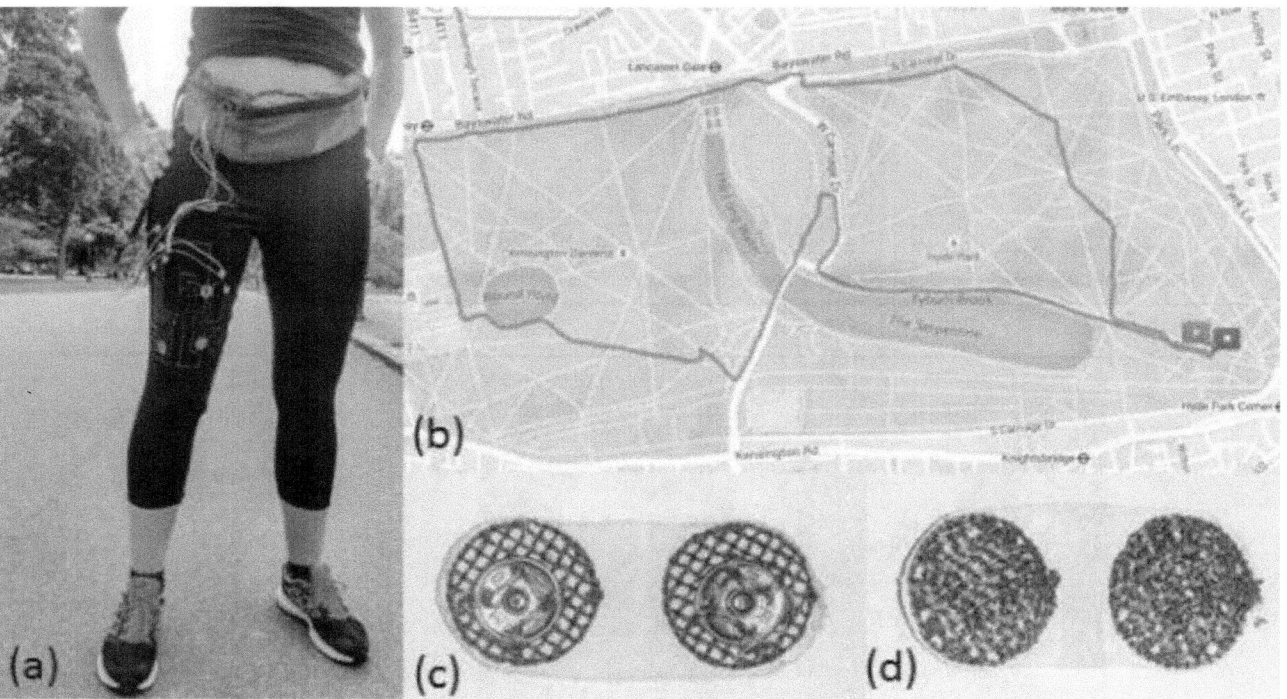

Source: https://www.technologyreview.com/s/600908/future-wearables-intelligent-leggings-measure-muscle-fatigue-in-runners/

- ServiceMax based on the SalesForce.com platform. This app offers much of the salesforce functionality including order management, call center monitoring, salesforce optimization, social media monitoring, and much more.
- GasFinder by Cheap Gas Buddy. Used by consumers and fleet operators alike, this app locates the cheapest gas in the area.[49]
- Route Plan Form by Motorola. This app for Motorola Solutions Devices develops route plans and provides details as well as storing driver and vehicle data and has the ability to capture signatures.
- Delivery Confirmation w/GPS by iPhone. This app stores relevant package data and captures delivery signature with GPS location.[50]

Mobile apps are revolutionizing SCM just as they are revolutionizing all facets of consumer life. As you can see, some of the same apps work in both B2C and B2B markets while others are specially developed to meet business needs.

WHAT COMES NEXT FOR THE SUPPLY CHAIN?

The easy answer to that question is "continuing digital disruption." A study from KPMG calls the goal a **demand-driven supply** chain that should look like the graphic in Figure 2.8. It is important to note that the graphic separates physical materials flows from information flows. Information needs to flow from consumer sources to all members of the supply chain immediately. Think of Zara and the speed with which it follows fashion trends. Materials flows are unlikely to be as swift although the importance of direct relationships with suppliers and the resulting cost and time savings have been stressed throughout this chapter. This graphic implies that information about both demand and supply should be accessible to all other members of the network. That is the all-important visibility feature of virtual supply networks.

demand-driven supply a supply chain that operates in response to demand signals from customers.

As firms work toward supply networks and ecosystems that are driven by customer demand, the technologies we have discussed in this chapter will continue to impact their design and functioning. Software provided in the cloud, embedded devices, and mobile apps will all have important places in new supply ecosystems.

Another macro trend we have not yet discussed in this chapter is **artificial intelligence** (AI). AI is a term that has been used and abused over the years. Many developers today seem to prefer some variant of "machine learning systems." IBM's Watson introduces himself: "Hello. My name is Watson. I am a cognitive system who can understand, reason and learn. I work with humans around the world."[51] IBM explains by saying: "IBM Watson is a technology platform that uses natural language processing and machine learning to reveal insights from large amounts of unstructured data."[52] You can get an idea of some of the applications and what the future might hold by doing Interactive Exercise 2.2 (accessible in the learning path).

artificial intelligence the ability of a computer to mimic human behaviors.

There are already examples of AI use in supply chains. Dell and other technology firms use control towers, a term borrowed from NASA, to collect and analyze data from across the supply chain. Many tools are used for the analytics. For instance, Dell's parts division has a control tower that uses predictive analysis, to be discussed in Chapter 4, to forecast when and how weather is going to disrupt the supply chain. That enables them to have plans ready to meet the weather emergencies when and where they occur.[53]

Another set of control towers uses **business process management (BPM)** software to support their service delivery supply chain. Dell says these control towers "provide visibility and process flows to parts, people, call center activity, and their technology resolution experts."[54] This kind of visibility allows them to meet their service level agreements. Those agreements with large enterprise customers provide for same day, 4 hour or even 2 hour guaranteed response times. The software can also do things like scan orders to see that the set of components ordered may not be the correct configuration or be technically correct in some other fashion. An analysis team does a variety of statistical tests on the data, looking at things like historical trends and deviations from expected service

business process management (BPM) a systematic attempt to make business processes more efficient.

FIGURE 2.8

Physical and Information Flows in an Integrated Supply Ecosystem

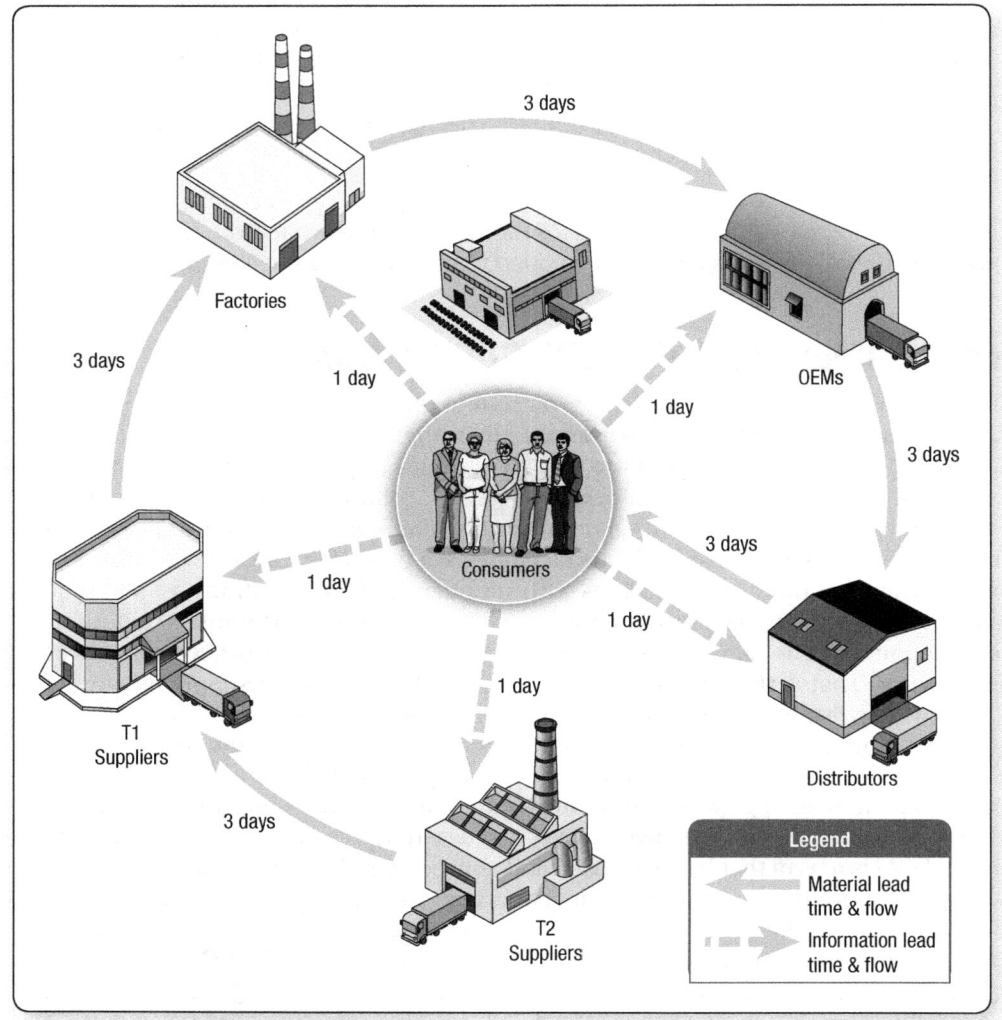

SOURCE: https://www.kpmg.com/US/en/IssuesAndInsights/ArticlesPublications/Documents/demand-driven-supply-chains.pdf

levels to detect patterns which the software can be programmed to detect and respond to in real time. No, the machine is not doing all the learning just yet, but systems that are this responsive can provide a huge competitive advantage.[55]

Some other developments you can expect to see in supply ecosystems in the coming years include the following:

- Service chains becoming more important than product chains. Service chains refer to the process by which after-sale service is delivered. This kind of service is a major customer satisfier and a potential source of strong and consistent revenue. We will discuss processes for successfully delivering after-sale service in Chapter 16.[56]
- Putting more emphasis on the "base of the pyramid." In recent years this phrase has come to mean the millions of people in underserved markets around the world. These people represent a huge market, for example, people who have no access to financial services in Brazil, but products and supply chains will have to be configured to meet their needs.

- Microsegmentation of markets becoming increasingly possible. Whether it is custom running shoes for the individual consumer at Nike or segments with only a few firms in B2B markets, information will allow supply chains to respond to the needs of individual customers.[57]
- Predictive forecasting occurring in real time. This includes abilities to predict customer demand, identify niche markets, and inform the development of products and services that fulfill marketplace demands.
- Electronic markets optimized by AI. These markets will provide transparency in terms of price, speed, and product features. They will be web based and link financial services and manufacturing to networks that provide significant competitive advantage.
- Collaborative IT infrastructures linking all parties in the network. Smarter software will lead to data-driven, agile solutions to customer demands and supply chain issues.[58]

Emerging supply chains will supply four key benefits in the future. They will provide speed in movement of both physical products and information. They will scale easily through the use of plug and play software components. They will become smarter over time. They will be inexorably connected to every node in the ecosystem of customers and suppliers.

Finally, having accomplished all of this, they will provide significant competitive advantage to firms who are diligent in creating smart, fast, demand-driven supply networks.

SUMMARY

The supply chain of the past cannot meet the requirements of the digital economy. Neither can a "one size fits all" product that is pushed through channels using conventional marketing promotional and pricing techniques. In some cases, such as configuring internal and external networks, the final product is inherently a custom proposition. In others, prospering in a competitive marketplace requires using a set of products to meet customer needs in an individualized manner. Marketers are required to achieve these outcomes in a changing business environment that has recently increased emphasis on a green supply chain.

The traditional linear supply chain has evolved into a value ecosystem made up of interconnected relationships. Each member contributes its core capability, and the final product is delivered to the customer as a single strong and recognizable brand, one that offers excellent customer experience throughout the process. This represents a revolution in business organization and management that few enterprises have yet fully achieved. As examples throughout this chapter have emphasized, it is an achievement that can be years in the making.

One way of looking at the process is through the lens of service-centered dominant logic—the marketing concept that says all products deliver services and the job of the enterprise is to create value propositions.

None of this is easy. It is likely to require reengineering of existing business processes and major projects to integrate internal systems and to communicate across organizational boundaries with both suppliers and customers. Existing technologies like EDI, ERP, and RFID will be part of this process. Newer technologies like SaaS, cloud computing, embedded smart devices, and mobile apps are part of the digital transformation. Sometimes they are disruptive as in the case of SaaS which has virtually replaced the purchase of software. Sometimes they will require new skill sets as is the case with mobile apps.

The activities required to create value chains, transform them into value ecosystems, and finally to create the demand-driven supply network of the future are many and complex. They require changes on both the supplier-facing and the customer-facing sides of the business. Some firms that are far advanced in their supply chain transformation focus relentlessly on customer experience. This increases the competitive requirements for all firms.

DISCUSSION QUESTIONS

1. Differentiate between four key concepts—supply chain, value chain, integrated value chain, and supply ecosystem.
2. The chapter lists 10 distinct business processes that are required in a supply chain. Identify those processes. Are they all required in digital supply chains? Why or why not?
3. What are the benefits of an integrated supply chain?
4. Do you agree with the concept that all goods are essentially services? Why or why not?
5. What are the business practices used by Zara that have made it responsive to customer needs and successful financially in the B2C market? What about Dell in the B2B market?
6. Which newer technologies are being used in developing integrated supply chains?
7. What are the advantages of newer technologies over the original supply chain technologies of EDI and ERP?
8. What stages is an enterprise likely to go through en route to a virtual value chain?
9. Discuss integrative elements Dell has employed on
   a. the supply side and
   b. the customer side.
10. RFID is the oldest of the technologies discussed in the context of supply chains. Why do you think it is still in use when other early technologies are being abandoned?
11. Do you think that artificial intelligence has a place in the supply chains of the future?
12. What do you expect the major characteristics of future supply chains to be?

ENDNOTES

1. Stephen DeAngelis, "Supply Chain Management: Is It Still the Next Big Thing?" March 5, 2013, http://www.enterrasolutions.com/2013/03/supply-chain-management-is-it-still-the-next-big-hting.html.
2. http://www.otisworldwide.com
3. http://www.otis.com/site/us/Pages/REMElevatorMonitoring.aspx?menuID=4
4. http://www.otis.com/site/lb/OT_DL_Documents/OT_DL_DocumentLibrary/Gen2%20Switch/Gen2%20Switch.pdf
5. Marc Howe, "The Latest Groundbreaking Vertical Transit Innovations," December 8, 2015k, https://sourceable.net/latest-groundbreaking-vertical-transit-innovations/#
6. "Otis Aims to Increase Localisation Content," February 11, 2015, http://www.deccanherald.com/content/459012/otis-aims-increase-localisation-content.html
7. Shahar Markovitch and Paul Willmott, "Accelerating the Digitization of Business Processes," May 2014, http://www.mckinsey.com/business-functions/business-technology/our-insights/accelerating-the-digitization-of-business-processes
8. Scott Stephens, "Supply Chain Council & Supply Chain Operations Reference (SCOR) Model Overviedw," Power Point Presentation, May 2000, http://www.supply-chain.org
9. "The World's Most Valuable Brands." May 2015, http://www.forbes.com/companies/zara/
10. Clara Lu "Zara's Secret to Retail Success - Its Supply Chain," December 4, 2014, https://www.tradegecko.com/blog/zara-supply-chain-its-secret-to-retail-success
11. Stephen Burgen, "Zara's Owner's Online Sales Jump 42% to L553m." November 19, 2014, www.theguardian.com/business/2014/nov/19/zara-owner-online–553m-inditex
12. Mallory Schlossberg, "Instagram and Pinterest Are Killing Gap, Abercrombie, & J. Crew," February 14, 2016, http://www.businessinsider.com/social-media-is-killing-traditional-retailers-2016-2
13. http://www.bain.com/publications/articles/the-jenga-phenomenon-how-ecommerce-is-reassembling-industry.aspx

14. "Living in Dell Time," November 2004, p. 86, www.fastcompany.com
15. http://www.buzzmachine.com/2005/08/17/dear-mr-dell/
16. http://www.buzzmachine.com/archives/cat_dell.html
17. http://gizmodo.com/#!182257/dell-laptop-explodes-in-flames
18. http://www.youtube.com/watch?v=w4ooKojHMkA
19. Liz Bullock, "How Dell Is Using Social Media to Deepen Relationships & Build Trust," April 16, 2013, http://www.slideshare.net/dellsocialmedia/how-dell-is-using-social-media-to-deepen-relationships-and-build-trust
20. http://i.dell.com/sites/doccontent/corporate/secure/en/documents/FY15-lbo-anniversary-infographic.pdf
21. Maria Deutsher, "After Privatization, Michael Dell's Vision for an End-to-End Vendor Is Finally Coming Together | #DellWorld," November 11, 2014, http://siliconangle.com/blog/2014/11/11/after-privatization-michael-dells-vision-for-an-end-to-end-vendor-is-finally-coming-together-dellworld/
22. Clark, Don, Dana Cimilluca, and Robert McMillan, "EMC Takeover Marks Return of Michael Dell," October 13, 2015, http://www.wsj.com/articles/dell-to-buy-emc-for-67-billion-1444649012
23. Vargo, Stephen L. and Robert F. Lusch. "Evolving Toward a New Dominant Logic for Marketing," *Journal of Marketing*, Vol. 68 (January 2004), pp. 1–17.; Lusch, Robert F. and Stephen L. Vargo. "Service-Dominant Logic, Reactions, Reflections and Refinements," *Journal of Marketing Theory*, Vol 6(3): 281–288. (2006), 282–288.
24. Vargo, Stephen L. and Robert F. Lusch, "Institutions and Axioms: An Extension and Update of Service-Dominant Logic," Academy of Marketing Science, 2015, https://arizona.pure.elsevier.com/en/publications/institutions-and-axioms-an-extension-and-update-of-service-domina
25. Vargo, Stephen L. and Robert F. Lusch, "Institutions and Axioms: An Extension and Update of Service-Dominant Logic," Academy of Marketing Science, 2015, https://arizona.pure.elsevier.com/en/publications/institutions-and-axioms-an-extension-and-update-of-service-domina
26. "Nike+ Moves from App to Platform with Four New Device Partners," March 6, 2015, https://gigaom.com/2015/03/06/nike-moves-from-app-to-platform-with-four-new-device-partners/
27. Nick, Slatt, "Exclusive: Nike Fires Majority of FuelBand Team, Will Stop Making Wearable Hardware," April 18, 2014, http://www.cnet.com/news/nike-fires-fuelband-engineers-will-stop-making-wearable-hardware/
28. Elizabeth Hoffman, "Nike: Creating a Digital Ecosystem (and Leaving Hardware to the Other Guys), February 5, 2015, https://openforum.hbs.org/challenge/understand-digital-transformation-of-business/why-digital/nike-creating-a-digital-ecosystem-and-leaving-hardware-to-the-other-guys/comments
29. Mark, Gurman, "Nike CEO Discusses Future of Apple Partnership, Exiting Wearables, & Apple Watch," May 8, 2015, http://9to5mac.com/2015/05/08/nike-ceo-discusses-future-of-apple-partnership-apple-watch-exiting-wearables-video/
30. Evie Nagy, "First Look at the Nike+ Fuel Lab in San Francisco," April 14, 2014, http://www.fastcompany.com/3028932/most-innovative-companies-2014/first-look-at-the-nike-fuel-lab-in-san-francisco
31. http://www.nikefuellab.com/
32. https://developer.nike.com/news/news.html
33. "Communication & Technology's New Battleground: Business Ecosystem vs. Business Ecosystem," 2016, https://www.accenture.com/us-en/insight-business-ecosystem-new-battleground?c=glb_acnemalert_10002919&n=emc_1215&emc=21091589:emc-021516
34. http://www.nikefuellab.com/
35. http://searchcloudcomputing.techtarget.com/definition/Software-as-a-Service
36. Josh, Bond, "Top 20 Supply Chain Management Software Suppliers, 2015," July 1, 2015, http://www.mmh.com/article/top_20_supply_chain_management_software_suppliers_2015
37. https://aws.amazon.com/what-is-aws/

38. https://aws.amazon.com/marketplace/pp/B0089HDOI6/ref=srh_res_product_title?ie=UTF8&sr=0-10&qid=1456859148823
39. Anthony Clervi, "Cloud Computing Is Transforming Supply Chain Management," October 12, 2015, http://www.sdcexec.com/article/12125647/cloud-computing-is-transforming-supply-chain-management
40. "Supply Chain Management in the Cloud," 2014, https://www.accenture.com/t20150523T022449__w__/us-en/_acnmedia/Accenture/Conversion-Assets/DotCom/Documents/Global/PDF/Dualpub_1/Accenture-Supply-Chain-Management-in-the-Cloud.pdf%203/2
41. "Pfizer Delivers Total Logistic, Visibility and Control," nd, http://www.supplychainbrain.com/content/research-analysis/supply-chain-innovators/single-article-page/article/pfizer-delivers-total-logistics-visibility-and-control-1/
42. Anthony Clervi, "Cloud Computing Is Transforming Supply Chain Management," October 12, 2015, http://www.sdcexec.com/article/12125647/cloud-computing-is-transforming-supply-chain-management
43. https://aws.amazon.com/solutions/case-studies/pfizer/
44. Paul Taylor, "Pfizer Moves Supply Chain to Cloud," September 22, 2012, http://www.ft.com/intl/cms/s/0/1608e5d6-fc59-11e1-ac0f-00144feabdc0.html#axzz42t7nRXXx
45. Anthony Clervi, "Cloud Computing Is Transforming Supply Chain Management," October 12, 2015, http://www.sdcexec.com/article/12125647/cloud-computing-is-transforming-supply-chain-management
46. Billy MacInnes, "How Cloud Is Finding Its Place in the Pharmaceutical Industry," February 18, 2014, http://www.cloudpro.co.uk/cloud-essentials/public-cloud/3813/how-cloud-is-finding-its-place-in-the-pharmaceutical-industry
47. "Future Wearables: Intelligent Leggings Measure Muscle Fatigue in Runners," February 26, 2016, https://www.technologyreview.com/s/600908/future-wearables-intelligent-leggings-measure-muscle-fatigue-in-runners/
48. Anthony Clervi, "Cloud Computing Is Transforming Supply Chain Management," October 12, 2015, http://www.sdcexec.com/article/12125647/cloud-computing-is-transforming-supply-chain-management
49. Dan Dowling, "8 Amazing Logistics & Supply Chain Mobile Applications," June 4, 2015, http://www.eazystock.com/blog/2015/06/04/8-amazing-logistics-supply-chain-mobile-applications/
50. "Transportation & Warehousing Mobile Apps and Forms," nd, http://www.gocanvas.com/mobile-forms-apps/48-Transportation-Warehousing/show_category
51. http://www.ibm.com/cognitive/outthink/stories/sciencefact/
52. http://www.ibm.com/smarterplanet/us/en/ibmwatson/what-is-watson.html
53. James A. Cooke, "Control Towers" Provide a Return on Risk Management Investments," http://www.supplychainquarterly.com/articles/20140826-control-towers-provide-a-return-on-risk-management-investments/
54. Steve Banker, "Dell Uses Artificial Intelligence at Global Command Centers," November 19, 2012, https://logisticsviewpoints.com/2012/11/19/dell-uses-artificial-intelligence-at-global-command-centers/
55. http://www.ibm.com/smarterplanet/us/en/ibmwatson/what-is-watson.html
56. Chuck Intrieri, "Customer Service in the Supply Chain Has Changed Drastically and the Candy Dish Is Empty," February 25, 2014, http://cerasis.com/2014/02/25/customer-service-in-the-supply-chain/
57. "10 Supply Chain Trends for the Next 10 Years," July 9, 2013, http://www.supplychain247.com/article/10_supply_chain_trends_for_the_next_10_years
58. James Canton, "The Future of Collaborative Supply Chains and Global Business," 2011, http://www.globalfuturist.com/dr-james-canton/insights-and-future-forecasts/future-of-collaborative-supply-chains.html

Chapter 3

Business Models and Strategies

LEARNING OBJECTIVES

By the time you complete this chapter, you will be able to:

1. Discuss the importance of the business model to business success.
2. Explain the concept and functions of a business model.
3. Discuss the concept of the value proposition and its importance in developing marketing strategies.
4. Explain how the Value Proposition Canvas can be used in the creation of a business model.
5. Distinguish between business models that have been transferred onto the internet, business models that prosper only with the internet, and business models that are dependent on mobile for their success.
6. Name and describe business models in each of these three categories.
7. Give examples of each of the business models.
8. Explain the nature and importance of the Business Model Canvas.

Digital disruption is present throughout the economy as we discussed in Chapter 1. Our examination of value chains made it clear that organizations that existed prior to the advent of the internet (traditional retailers and manufacturers) have been taking advantage of the opportunities the internet presents just as pure-play internet firms have. They may, however, do so in different ways. A set of **business models** has emerged to meld the best of the offline world with internet and mobile. In so doing, earlier business models have been disrupted in a way that may exceed any other aspect of digital marketing.

business models the processes by which a business creates value, provides value to its customers, and captures value in the form of profits.

In this chapter, we continue our discussion of value creation and explain how that is part of a business model. We discuss some basic business models and a few speculative but highly interesting ones.

UNDERSTANDING BUSINESS MODELS

Business models are a source of much discussion, from Shark Tank on TV to academic journals. Yet, there still seems to be no commonly accepted definition of the term "business model." An article in the *Harvard Business Review* traces the concept back to Peter Drucker, the management guru, in a 1994 article. It discussed the importance of defining what a business will and will not do and "assumptions about what a business gets paid for," but never used the term business model.[1] Later Prof. Joan Magretta defined the business model in terms of the value chain with a supply-facing side and a customer side. She says "Part one includes all the activities associated with making something: designing it, purchasing raw materials, manufacturing, and so on. Part two includes all the activities associated with selling something: finding and reaching customers, transacting a sale, distributing the product, or delivering the service."[2] Professor Alex Osterwalder, on the other hand, regards a business model as a set of assumptions about how major business activities will be carried out. He has developed a template that allows organizations to customize their own business models, which we will discuss later in the chapter.

Among marketers, Professor Michael Rappa's definition is one of the most often quoted: A "business model is the method of doing business by which a company can sustain itself—that is, generate revenue. The business model spells out how a company makes money by specifying where it is positioned in the value chain."[3]

A more detailed definition is set forth by Professors Ethriraj, Guler, and Singh. They define a "business model" as "a unique configuration of elements comprising the organization's goals, strategies, processes, technologies, and structure, conceived to create value for the customers and thus compete successfully in a particular market." The professors go on to say that a business model describes the core **value proposition**, sources and methods of revenue generation, the costs involved in generating the revenue, and the plan and trajectory of growth.[4]

value proposition a description of the customer value delivered to a specific target market.

In other words, a business model specifies how an organization *makes money*, *essentially how an entity sustains itself in the economy*. Sites of all kinds are earning revenue from *transactions*. Websites may be supporting themselves by generating advertising revenue. They may be selling products ranging from clothing to computers or services that vary from employment listings to credit cards. Sites may be selling their own products or services; they may be affiliates of large sites such as Amazon, or operate from a platform such as eBay. Sites may also be community based or ask for donations to survive, such as Wikipedia. However, they are all achieving revenue from transactions with their audience. The many ways in which they do this is the subject of the business models discussion.

FUNCTIONS OF BUSINESS MODELS

Professors Henry Chesbrough and Richard Rosenbloom explain that the functions of a business model are to:

- Articulate the value proposition, that is, the value created for users by the offering based on the technology.
- Identify a market segment, that is, the users to whom the technology is useful and for what purpose.
- Define the structure of the value chain within the firm required to create and distribute the offering.

- Estimate the cost structure and profit potential of producing the offering, given the value proposition and the value chain structure chosen.
- Describe the position of the firm with the value network linking suppliers and customers, including identification of potential partners and competitors.
- Formulate the competitive strategy by which the innovating firm will gain and hold competitive advantage over rivals.

It is important to note that *a business model and a business plan are two distinctly different entities*. A business model is a conceptual description that may have been given a name like "advertising-supported." A business plan is a detailed document that is prepared for strategic guidance and to aid in the acquisition of resources, either internal or external. There is some similarity of content between the two, but they are not synonymous. Recognizing this issue, Chesbrough and Rosenbloom go on to specify the differences between a business model and a strategy as follows:

- A business model focuses on creating value for the customer and delivering that value to the customer to a clearly defined market segment.
- It focuses on creating business value that can be translated into value for the shareholder.
- It requires that managers use technical inputs to create economic results in a context of technological and market uncertainty.[5]

Chesbrough and Rosenbloom's final point puts the business model concept firmly in the arena of business innovation including internet-based businesses. It also reinforces the focus on value creation by the firm as a key element of a business model. A bad business model or failure to execute the model effectively can often lead to failure. Examine Interactive Exercise 3.1 for the story of a digital business that had many users and raised a great deal of money but still failed. Failures often result from a myriad of business model and execution mistakes, but in the end if a business does not have a product people want at a price they are willing to pay, no business model in the world will save it.

EVOLVING BUSINESS MODELS—IBM, GE, AND AMAZON

There are many fascinating examples of businesses that have changed their models, sometimes more than once to accommodate changes in technology, the market, or both. IBM is often celebrated as a prime example of an agile business. Over the years it has morphed from a manufacturer of business machines to a maker of computers to a global technology services company. It is now in the process of transforming into a cognitive solutions and cloud platforms company. Among other things, that implies a big investment in machine learning and artificial intelligence.[6] Two case histories from researchers at Stanford University give detail on its business model changes over the years.[7,8]

> *GE is another example of transformational change. When Jeff Immelt became the CEO of GE in 2001 it was a classic 20th century conglomerate making everything from aircraft engines to refrigerators and marketing services including financial and entertainment. Now Immelt describes it as "the world's biggest infrastructure technology company."*[9]

He continues:

> *Today, everything we sell is surrounded by sensors and produces data. The data fundamentally is going to be modeled and turned into performance, outcomes. . . . So when I talk about the "Industrial*

Internet," it's about capturing data off of machines, turning it back into valuable insight for our customers and that's going to be worth trillions of dollars in the economy, and I think it's going to transform GE.[10]

Massive as the transformations have been for IBM and GE, they were both founded in the physical economy and forced to adapt to the digital economy. Amazon was founded in 1994 as a dot-com business that sold books. The vision of Jeff Bezos to be the online place "where people can come to find and discover anything they might want to buy online"[11] was dismissed as hubris by many observers. But the business held to the vision and for many years placed investment over profits. Figure 3.1 displays a timeline of major changes in the business since its founding.

FIGURE 3.1
Timeline of Major Developments at Amazon

Amazon: a timeline of major events

1995
Amazon launches in July, having been established a year earlier, as an online book retailer.

1997
Amazon floats on the Nasdaq in New York, with a market capitalisation of $438m. Acquires bookpages.co.uk and launches Amazon UK.

1998
Expands into CDs and DVDs.

1999
Expands into toys and electronics.

2000
Marketplace, Amazon's third party seller business, launches. New logo, with arrow running from the A to the Z in Amazon launches, reflecting desire to sell everything from A-Z.

2001

Photo: Alamy

Signs partnership deal to takeover running of Borders.com; Borders collapses ten year later. Amazon makes first quarterly profit at end of the year.

2002
Launches Amazon Web Services, its cloud computing platform.

2003
Expands into selling jewellery for first time.

2004
Sells shoes for the first time.

2005
Amazon Prime, its premium membership package launches in the US, followed in the UK two years later.

2006

Photo: Jonathan Alcorn / Reuters

Amazon Fresh, its online fresh food delivery business, launches in Seattle.

2007
Kindle book e-reader launches.

2008
Amazon Games launches.

2010
Amazon Studios launches to create original television content.

2011
Kindle Fire, the company's tablet, is unveiled.

2012
Acquires Kiva, a robotics company, for $775m.

2013

Photo: News Scan

Amazon Art launches. Drone delivery plans unveiled for first time under 'Prime Air' name.

2014
Echo, Amazon's voice-activated information and home gadget device, launches in the US.

2015
Celebrates 20th birthday with market capitalisation standing in excess of $245bn.

SOURCE: http://www.telegraph.co.uk/technology/amazon/11801515/Amazon-timeline-from-internet-bookshop-to-the-worlds-biggest-online-retailer.html.

Amazon's business model has many working parts. In **ecommerce** alone it has:

- Direct sales of merchandise from inventory.
- Sales from partners who list free on Amazon, maintain inventory, and pay a commission to Amazon for each sale.

It also has **subscription**-based ecommerce activities:

- Amazon Prime, which was said to reach almost half of U.S. households in 2016[12] and have as many as 80 million users worldwide.[13] Prime offers services such as free two-day delivery and free streaming TV.
- Kindle Unlimited offers an unlimited number of e-books for a monthly subscription fee.

ecommerce buying and selling goods and services online.

subscription model delivers products, services, and content for a set fee.

It also has fee-for-service activities, especially AWS (Amazon Web Services) discussed in Chapter 2.

With all these activities and various business models under one roof, how does Amazon maintain control? Students of Amazon, and there are many, have identified a number of key factors:

- It focuses on customer satisfaction.
- It focuses on innovation both to provide satisfaction and to lower costs.
- It recognizes technology as a core competency.
- It promotes a "culture of metrics" in which all activities are measured and data-driven improvements are made.
- The metrics culture also drives it to engage in experiments to improve its offerings.
- It constantly reevaluates its business model and makes changes or develops new approaches as required.[14,15,16]

THE VALUE PROPOSITION

This discussion leads us squarely to another term that is used frequently but not defined with any degree of precision. In this case, it seems to be because marketers follow the definition of "economic value," which is essentially the value of ownership and use, minus the cost of the item. The term value proposition has come to mean the value delivered by the firm to a specific, targeted customer segment. Figure 3.2 outlines what a value proposition is and is not and steps in creating and articulating one. The process shown makes it clear that customer data is one vital step on the road to developing and articulating a good value proposition. It also emphasizes that a value proposition is not an advertising slogan; it is a core element of the brand or business strategy.

From the rather simple concept, marketers can study the drivers of value in a particular market. Professors Osterwalder and Pigneur have a simple framework that is useful in that process (see Figure 3.3). It combines consideration of the needs of the target customer, which define the nature of the value desired, with an understanding of the core capabilities of the enterprise, which determines the value that can be delivered. Data can be obtained and used to understand both target customers and organizational capabilities, making developing a value proposition an information-driven marketing activity. Their Value Proposition Canvas takes a segment-by-segment approach, creating a value proposition for each customer segment. Interactive Exercise 3.2 allows you to experience the process using Osterwalder's original canvas terminology.

There are many explanations of how to use the canvas and examples of its use that do not come directly from Osterwalder. Figure 3.4a is one of those. It uses slightly different terminology, perhaps more B2C than B2B terms, but the process is the same as the one you experienced in Interactive Exercise 3.2. In this case the benefits, features, and experience are for a mobile productivity app.

The Evernote app originated from data collected by an angel investors group called Innovation Warehouse. This London-based organization maintains a large co-working space. One thing its members emphasized was the need for a space that was both quiet and productive. This was the genesis of the Evernote app, whose value proposition you can see in Figure 3.4b. The essence of the value proposition is that it is quick and easy for mobile professionals to use. Their other key segment is students.[17] As I write this, the Evernote home page showcases the student segment. Does the site know something about me or is it because I'm writing this in August? I haven't given any personal information, so my guess is that it is an appropriate seasonal emphasis.

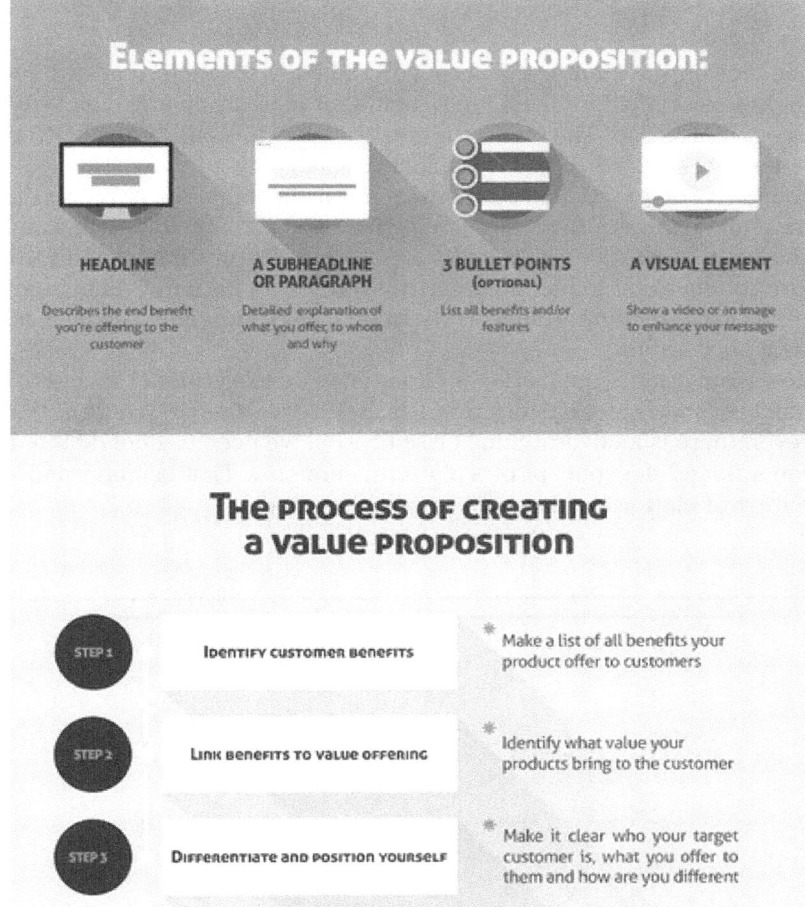

FIGURE 3.2
How to Create a Value Proposition

SOURCE: http://blog.hubspot.com/marketing/write-value-proposition#sm.0000002to08kmvcpyv7vlb6v649jq.

FIGURE 3.3
The Osterwalder and Pigneur Value Proposition Canvas

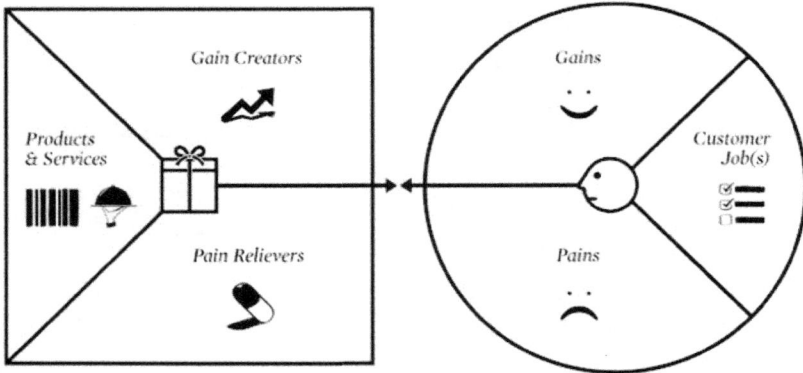

SOURCE: http://www.businessmodelgeneration.com/downloads/value_proposition_canvas.pdf.

Notice that on the main business page[18] the copy seems to come directly from the value proposition with a listing of benefits for user groups. As you scroll down, features are emphasized. The main students page has the same copy platform but it presents the information in a more graphic manner.

Although Evernote was named the *Inc.* magazine company of the year in 2011,[19] its path has not been smooth recently in the face of customer complaints and a great deal of competition. Its new CEO emphasizes listening to customers and getting back to the core product that made the company successful initially.[20] That sounds a lot like reemphasizing the importance of its value proposition and the business model that made it successful.

While a strong value proposition is essential to business model success, there are other aspects of successful business models. Before we describe some of those models, however, there is an overarching classification we need to understand. In Chapter 1 we mentioned the concept of a platform economy. That becomes more logical in the context of platform as one type of business model.

FIGURE 3.4a
A Revised Value Proposition Canvas

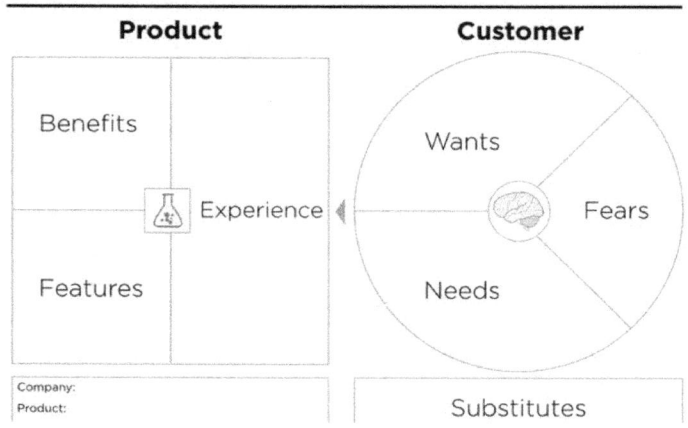

SOURCE: http://www.peterjthomson.com/2013/11/value-proposition-canvas/.

FIGURE 3.4b
The Value Proposition for Evernote

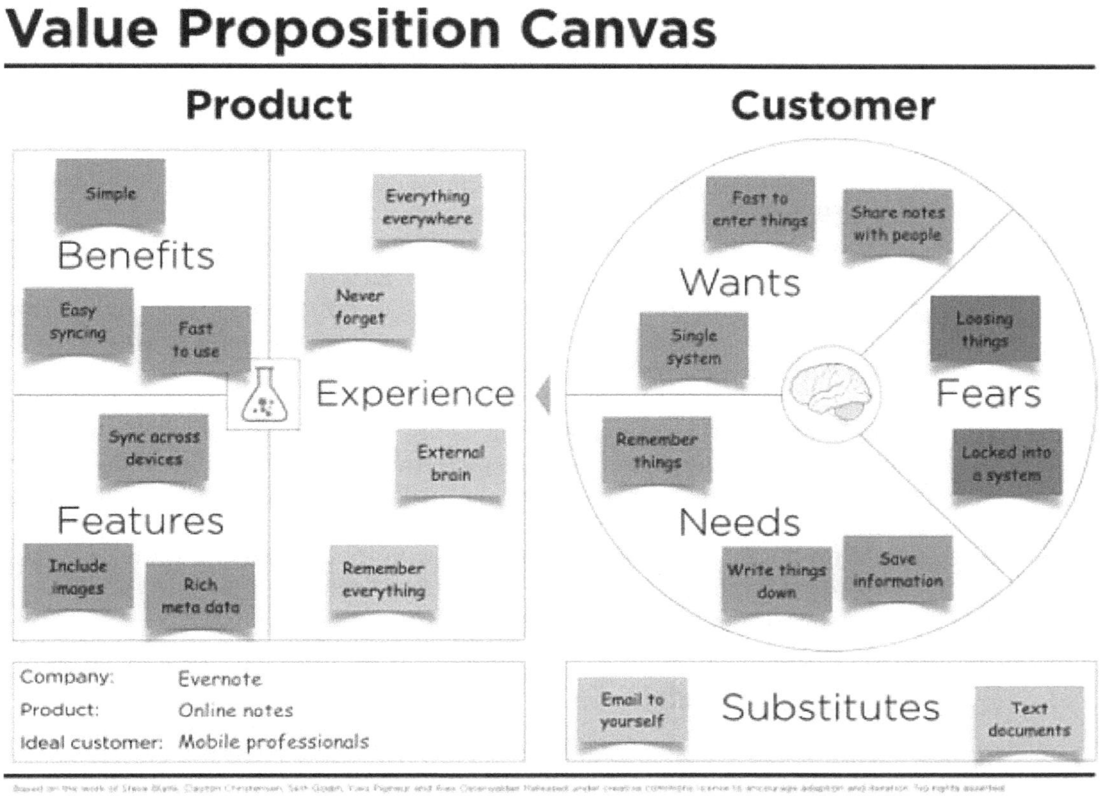

Value Proposition Canvas

Product

Benefits: Simple; Everything everywhere; Easy syncing; Fast to use; Never forget

Experience

Features: Sync across devices; External brain; Include images; Rich meta data; Remember everything

Company: Evernote
Product: Online notes
Ideal customer: Mobile professionals

Customer

Wants: Fast to enter things; Share notes with people; Single system

Fears: Loosing things; Locked into a system

Needs: Remember things; Write things down; Save information

Substitutes: Email to yourself; Text documents

Evernote's value proposition is anchored on simplicity and speed.

SOURCE: http://www.peterjthomson.com/2013/11/value-proposition-canvas/.

TYPES OF BUSINESS MODELS

In recent years a consensus has emerged in the small and somewhat rarified group of business model enthusiasts that includes the venture capitalists who fund new businesses. While the subject may seem a bit esoteric, the implications are highly practical as we learned in Interactive Exercise 3.1. The experts have divided all business models into two types—**pipes** and platforms.

pipes business models, essentially the traditional distribution models.

The Pipe Model

The pipe model describes traditional businesses of all kinds and still includes most of the major manufacturers of consumer goods. It looks like, and in fact it is, the channel of distribution model. In business model terms it looks like this:

In Section 3-3 we discussed the fact that IBM and GE are getting rid of their traditional pipes (computer hardware for IBM and all consumer appliances for GE). However, Amazon still has very profitable pipes including books and streaming video.

> Value Is Produced > Goods and Services Are Distributed > Value Is Consumed

Even more telling is the fact that there are internet-based businesses that are built on the pipes model. Zappos, now owned by Amazon, is an example of a successful e-tailer that thrives on reselling the products of many manufacturers. Zappos owes its success to fanatical customer service, not to unique merchandise. Most distributors of content are also pipes. Netflix is an example of one that has enjoyed great success. A widely distributed video shows CNBC Fast Money panelists arguing about whether Netflix is a "dumb pipe."[21] That is a term taken from discussions of data transmission on the internet—simply moving bits and bytes around without knowing what they are, much less adding value. That describes a product with no differentiation and therefore no pricing power. It is why you will not see Internet Service Providers as an identifiable business model in the table in the next section. It was not a profitable model and carriers have either diversified (Comcast), disappeared (France Telecomm's Mintel communications terminal, which was ubiquitous in France before the advent of the internet), or struggled to find a model that gets them out of the commodity trap (AOL). Trying to avoid that trap appears to be the reason Verizon acquired Yahoo!.

Figure 3.5 lists the main differences between the pipes model and platforms. Notice that in the pipes model products are prespecified, with or without detailed knowledge of customer needs. In the platforms model, users and producers not only interact with one another but often have dual roles. An interactive network connects all the roles. One company can be a user of a software tool, for example, at the same time it produces business CRM software with transactions for both SaaS products taking place on the platform. "On the platform" usually translates to "in the cloud" today as we discussed in Chapter 2.

The Platform Model

The competing type of model is the platform. There are two types of platforms—two sided and multisided. A two-sided model connects two groups—consumer credit card users and retail merchants as one example, and organizations of health care providers and patients as another. The two-sided platform differs from the pipe in that network effects occur in the platform. *HBR* describes the difference by saying that in the pipe model all cost is on the left (value creation) and all revenue is on the right (value consumption). In the two-sided platform the two sides interact with each other. For

FIGURE 3.5

Differences between Pipes and Platforms Models

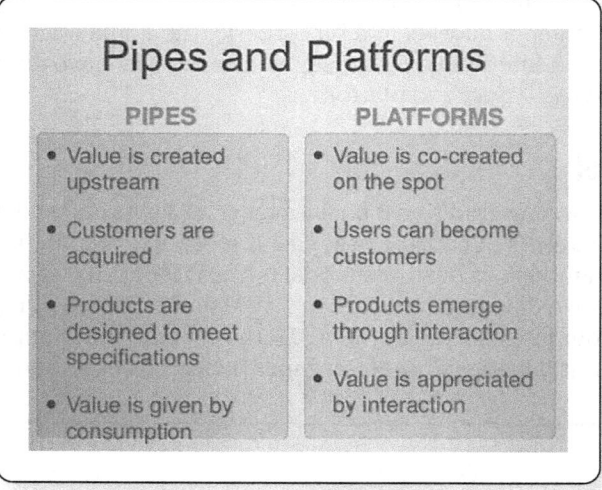

SOURCE: http://www.slideshare.net/itcocchi/pres-7jan014-short.

example, a credit card has more value to the user when more merchants accept it. The size of the network affects the value produced by it. Patients may choose a health care organization based on the number and perceived expertise of the providers.[22]

There are multisided platforms that connect more than two segments of users. In Section 2-3 we discussed the development of the Nike value ecosystem. Nike connects with both customers and retailers. Customer segments include the fitness market and professional athletes who often play a role in product development or promotion. In retailing it sells direct, through the traditional wholesaling channel and through retail partnerships like the one with Foot Locker.[23] Its Fuel Lab has added hardware manufacturers and software developers to the ecosystem. There are three clear sides—consumers, retailers, and Fuel Lab members. If you want to count segments as separate sides, there are many more.

There are other multisided platforms that genuinely have more than two sides. For instance, Google's Android platform connects smartphone makers, software developers and users, and customers who obtain Android apps from the Google Play Store, so its model is three-sided. Apple makes its own devices, so it only needs to connect with customers and developers, again using the App Store to facilitate transactions with both—a two-sided model. These models represent fundamentally different strategic decisions by businesses operating in the same market.[24]

However, if you look carefully, you will find that most platforms are two-sided today. We are newly into the platform era and that may change, but it seems to make sense that businesses will start with simpler platforms, perhaps evolving into more complex platforms as they move forward. So beware of terminology. Many authors use the term "multi-sided" to include two-sided platforms, and technically, that is correct. Just be careful to read beyond the terminology to the details of what they are discussing.

One writer gives some interesting industry examples to bolster the argument that platforms are becoming the dominant business model:

> *TV Channels work on a Pipe model but YouTube works on a Platform model. Encyclopaedia Britannica worked on a Pipe model but Wikipedia has flipped it and built value on a Platform model. Our classrooms still work on a Pipe model but Udemy and Skillshare are turning on the Platform model for education.*[25]

Disruption of business models is ongoing and it's hard to predict what the future will hold. However, it is safe to say that at present the platforms model is receiving the most attention from existing businesses and new ventures alike.

IDENTIFYING BASIC BUSINESS MODELS

Now that we understand the types of business models, it is time to look at basic internet and mobile business models. Looking at the most common models is useful to an understanding of the subject. There are three caveats as we do so:

1. There is no commonly accepted set of models. Worse, various authors have given different names to the same model. Table 3.1 gives an overview of models suggested by Professor Michael Rappa[26] and consultant Mark Johnson.[27] Both of them wrote before mobile became a major force, so mobile models were curated from a number of different sources.[28,29,30]
2. Almost no business has a pure model today. We have already discussed Amazon and some of its numerous business models. You say that's not surprising because Amazon is a large and diverse firm. While true, that is not the only reason. Attempting to monetize messaging apps is a case in point.

    Do you use WhatsApp? If so, you have a lot of company. WhatsApp, acquired by Facebook in 2014, hit the 1 billion active monthly users mark in February of 2016.[31] The app no longer charges users even the $1 annual fee, nor does it accept advertising. Announcing the acquisition by Facebook, WhatsApp CEO Jan Koum said, "Monetization is not going to be a priority for us... We're focused on the growth."[32] That assumes that with growth will come monetization opportunities and that Facebook's deep pockets will be open in the absence of profits. Not all messaging apps have the luxury of being owned by Facebook, however. Line is an example. It is the largest messaging app in Japan and neighboring countries with over 220 million monthly active users in mid-2016.[33] While provided free to users it has several revenue streams. One major source of revenue is stickers, which are souped-up emojis that users can purchase to convey a wide range of emotions. It also has major revenue sources from games and from Line Friends, animated characters that are widely used in merchandising efforts.[34] The Line Friends are so popular that there are several stores in Asia selling only Line Friends merchandise and a pop-up store operated in New York's Times Square during the Christmas season of 2015.[35] A recent addition is selling access to Line users to brands. Fast Company explains how it works this way: After Toyota airs a new commercial in its Toyotatown campaign, for instance, it can follow up by offering its 14.3 million Line followers stickers featuring AKB48, an insanely popular Japanese girl group with (at last count) 187 members. The automaker gets its message out; consumers get free stuff; Line gets paid. Everybody's happy.[36]

It's easy to assume this will not be the last revenue stream added to keep the wildly popular app free to its users.

3. The marketplace is too diverse and fluid to simply adopt a basic model, no matter how well it may have worked for another company. In the final section of this chapter we will discuss the Business Model Canvas which generates custom business models, not just for each business, but for each segment of the business's target market.

Table 3.1 is a listing of the three basic types of business models—models that thrived before the internet was established, models that owe their success to the existence of the internet, and models that are uniquely suited to the mobile environment. Adding the founding date of the company gives a bit of context. Were mobile business models, or even the internet for that matter, available when Fidelity first began operations in 1946? No, of course not. While Fidelity now has world-class internet and mobile operations, it has added those over time as the need became apparent. The dates come mostly from the Google results page for the firm, in some cases from Wikipedia.

The entries in the table are drawn from the B2C, B2B, and nonprofit domains. The list of models is not comprehensive although it does include most of the best-known models. The discussion of the models listed and the examples used are intended to stimulate thinking, not to provide a comprehensive catalog of business models.

Traditional Business Models Extended onto the Web

When traditional "old economy" firms first established websites most assumed that the business model that worked in the physical economy would work on the internet. For some that was true. For others it was highly problematic. Table 3.1 lists several models that have made the transition from the physical world to the internet and later to the mobile web.

- The advertising-supported model is the most problematic of the group. It is the traditional media model with content provided free (broadcast TV channels) or at a price that did not cover costs (newspapers). It worked in the old economy because print and broadcast media have only limited space/time for ads and can reach large audiences. The internet exploded the model because it created almost unlimited space on which advertising could be placed. Also, while it is true that some websites reach huge audiences, the internet is really better at reaching niche audiences.

  It is hard to find an internet business of any size that is purely advertising supported using the strict definition of external advertisers placing ads on its

TABLE 3.1 Basic Types of Business Models

Model	Examples	Notes
Extension of Traditional Offline Models		
Advertising-supported	YouTube (2005)	Purchased by Google in 2006
	WashingtonPost.com (1877/1996)	Purchased by Jeff Bezos in 2016
Brokerage	Fidelity (1946)	Retail locations
	TradeStation (1982)	Online only
Fund-Raising	American Cancer Society (1913)	Traditional fund-raising and online
Infomediary	InfoUSA (1972)	List broker
Manufacturer Direct	Dell (1984)	Retail distribution
	Salesforce (1999)	Software-as-a-Service
Merchant (Ecommerce)	Amazon (1994)	Extensive assortment
	Ebags (1998)	Single-product category
Subscription	Dollar Shave Club (2011)	Product
	BuzzFeed (2006)	Content
Utility	Amazon Web Services	Payment based on usage
Internet-Enabled Models		
Affiliate	Teleflora (1934)	Sales through local affiliates
	CJ Affiliate (1998 as Commission Junction)	Focuses on lead generation
	Amazon Affiliates	Focuses on sales from affiliate websites
DAO	The DAO Hub (2016)	Distributed autonomous organization with no single leader
Community/ Crowdsourcing	TripAdvisor (2000)	User-generated content is primary
	Business Model Generation	Osterwalder and Pigneur's e-book
	GoFundMe (2010)	Fund-raising
M2M	Samsung Hub and other IoT Devices	Wi-Fi home automation and security
Mobile-Dependent Models (Mobile First)		
Apps		
Ad-supported	Facebook	Targeted ads
Freemium	Spotify (2008 in Sweden)	Music
	Dropbox (2007)	File storage, synchronization and sharing
AR/VR	See Games	Mobility necessary for access, otherwise cost prohibitive in many instances
Games	Pokémon Go (2016)	AR phenomenon
	Candy Crush Saga (2012)	Mobile product extension of original Candy Crush game for browsers
Loyalty/Coupons	Starbucks (1971)	Payments, reward points
	Open Table (1998)	Real-time reservations, reviews, and loyalty points
On Demand	Uber (2009)	Taxi
	Slate (2005)	House cleaning
Payment	Apple Pay, Android Pay, Samsung Pay	Payments
	Venmo (2010)	Payments, payment sharing, and money transfer
	Cryptocurrencies	Digital financial transaction technologies

properties. YouTube may come the closest and it is not clear that YouTube is profitable on its own. It has over 1 billion accounts worldwide[37], reaches over 167 million active users each month in the United States alone[38] and actually receives 80 percent of its views from outside the United States[39] Its reach is huge.

It has one significant problem as far as advertising revenue is concerned. Approximately 82 percent of teens and 81 percent of Millennials (ages 18–35 in 2016)[40] use YouTube. The number of users in older age cohorts shrinks precipitously. Essentially, YouTube is popular for its music videos among viewers under 35 years of age. If you want further confirmation of narrow audience reach, in December 2015 the two most watched channels belonged to Justin Bieber and Adele.[41] Consumers aged 18–35 and teens are desirable target audiences for some products but not for others, and that limits the advertising attractiveness of YouTube. A partial solution may be to add subscription models for ad-free content and original content.[42] Both of those alternatives would slightly increase YouTube's costs. Would they bring in enough revenue to replace or exceed the lost advertising revenue? It's hard to say.

The *Washington Post* has suffered in the digital age like other venerable newspapers from a loss of advertising revenues and declining subscription rates. Like the others it has a content-rich website and mobile app. Unlike the others, however, it was purchased in 2013 by Jeff Bezos. He obviously brings a flair for basing strategy on technology that may or may not be the answer for the Post and other newspapers in the digital age. Innovative approaches at the Post in the Bezos age include the following:

- Journalists and technologists share space in a new office building. In the early days of news websites the online operation was generally banned to another building so it wouldn't make the traditional employees nervous. Now publisher Fred Ryan says, "We view ourselves as a technology company as well as a media company."[43] That statement has not been overlooked by others in the online news industry.
- The Post is the only major newspaper to publish all its content directly to Facebook's Instant Articles in spite of the threat this may pose to online subscription revenue.
- It is partnering with the technology industry to develop faster, more user-friendly mobile apps.
- The company is also conducting research on news bots that could provide news in the car or through Amazon's Echo voice-controlled speaker.

One Post executive sums it up by saying, "What Jeff really brought, beyond his initial investment, is more freedom to innovate and take more risk."[44]

Of course, other newspaper publishers are working to evolve their business models also. The *New York Times* has introduced 360-degree videos as an immersive experience and has a number of digital video series available on the website and through special apps.[45] GE[46] and Infiniti[47] were early triers of the VR ads. The NYT demonstrated its commitment to the technology with the purchase of a specialized agency to support its T Brand Studio as it develops the technology and helps brands integrate it into their ads.[48] On the other side of the world an Australian company has launched a platform called Subscriber First, which is being used by the *Sydney Morning Herald* and *The Age* to bring a more personalized digital news experience to their readers.[49]

The jury is still out on whether these efforts will lead to profitability, but they make clear the difficulty of adapting the advertising-supported model to the digital age. Others, fortunately, have adapted more readily.

- The brokerage model is one that has adapted relatively smoothly. **Brokers** make markets: the function of a broker is to bring buyers and sellers together and facilitate transactions. Brokers play a frequent role in B2B as well as in the two B2C examples given here. For instance, real estate brokers operate in both

brokers brings buyers and sellers together to exchange goods and services.

business and consumer markets. Usually, a broker charges a fee or commission for each transaction it enables, but not always.

Fidelity Investments is a relatively new entrant into the consumer investments field that was originally the province of old-line Wall Street firms. It is best known for its expertise in mutual funds but it offers a full range of brokerage services, including discount online brokerage and online banking which includes bill payment services. Its various product lines follow the brokerage model. The difference is primarily the availability of personal investment guidance in the original product line and limitation of personal advice in discount brokerage. Its network of about 200 retail outlets facilitates investor relationships.

Most of Fidelity's investment and other financial services are available on its mobile app. The primary benefit of the app is the ability to trade stocks and funds at any time from any location. It offers ancillary services such as the ability to get stock quotes through Amazon's Echo and to track stocks via the Apple watch.[50]

TradeStation, on the other hand, is online only and its offerings are geared to the online environment. It offers a variety of trading algorithms and educational programs to support the use of its online tools. It offers a wiki for customer-to-customer support and an online discussion community. Mobile offers the "anytime, anywhere" benefit and TradeStation says, their mobile app gives "the ability to access core features of our award-winning desktop platform, synchronized to your online account in real time."[51] That emphasizes the fact that mobile users are not looking for watered-down functionality but want a robust and complete mobile experience.

These, of course, represent traditional financial services brokerage successfully moved onto the web. There are many other examples of brokered trading on the web. The huge Chinese marketplace, Alibaba, operates much of its business on the brokerage model.[52] In addition to its B2C side, Alibaba is the largest B2B marketplace where it acts as a broker. Other large B2B marketplaces serve specialized needs—TradeIndia provides a global marketplace that fosters Indian overseas trade while TradeKey serves the electronics market globally. In all these cases the transaction mechanism is primarily brokerage.[53] Other examples abound in many different industries.

- **Fund-raising** is another model that has adapted well to the internet. Fund-raising has always been about relationships—existing relationships like a graduate to his alma mater or personal relationships developed by fund-raisers with wealthy individuals who have an affinity for their cause. Fund-raising organizations were quick to realize that internet tools like email could be useful in nurturing relationships. They also recognized the ability of websites to convey information to supporters and reach potential new donors.

fund-raising basic nonprofit business model in which money is raised from donors and grants without a traditional economic transaction.

The American Cancer Society (ACS) is a venerable fund-raiser that has adapted to the new environment. Figure 3.6 is a model of transparency in terms of where the charitable donations come from and what they are used for. It also emphasizes the extent to which ACS not only provides useful information about cancer and cancer treatment but also a great deal of information about healthy living with an emphasis on cancer prevention. This content is in line with its mission "to eliminate cancer as a major health problem."

Besides offering many cancer-survivor stories, the organization's website promotes its fund-raising events and its local chapters. It hosts numerous events but the two largest are the Relay for Life, which attracts over 4 million participants in 20 countries each year, and Making Strides against Breast Cancer, which is so widespread that it lists walks by cities in what appears to be every state in the United States. The ACS has a network of local offices that offers services as well as participating in fund-raising. That is a substantial infrastructure and is probably testimony to its early-20th century roots.[54] You will

FIGURE 3.6

Portion of American Cancer Society Infographic

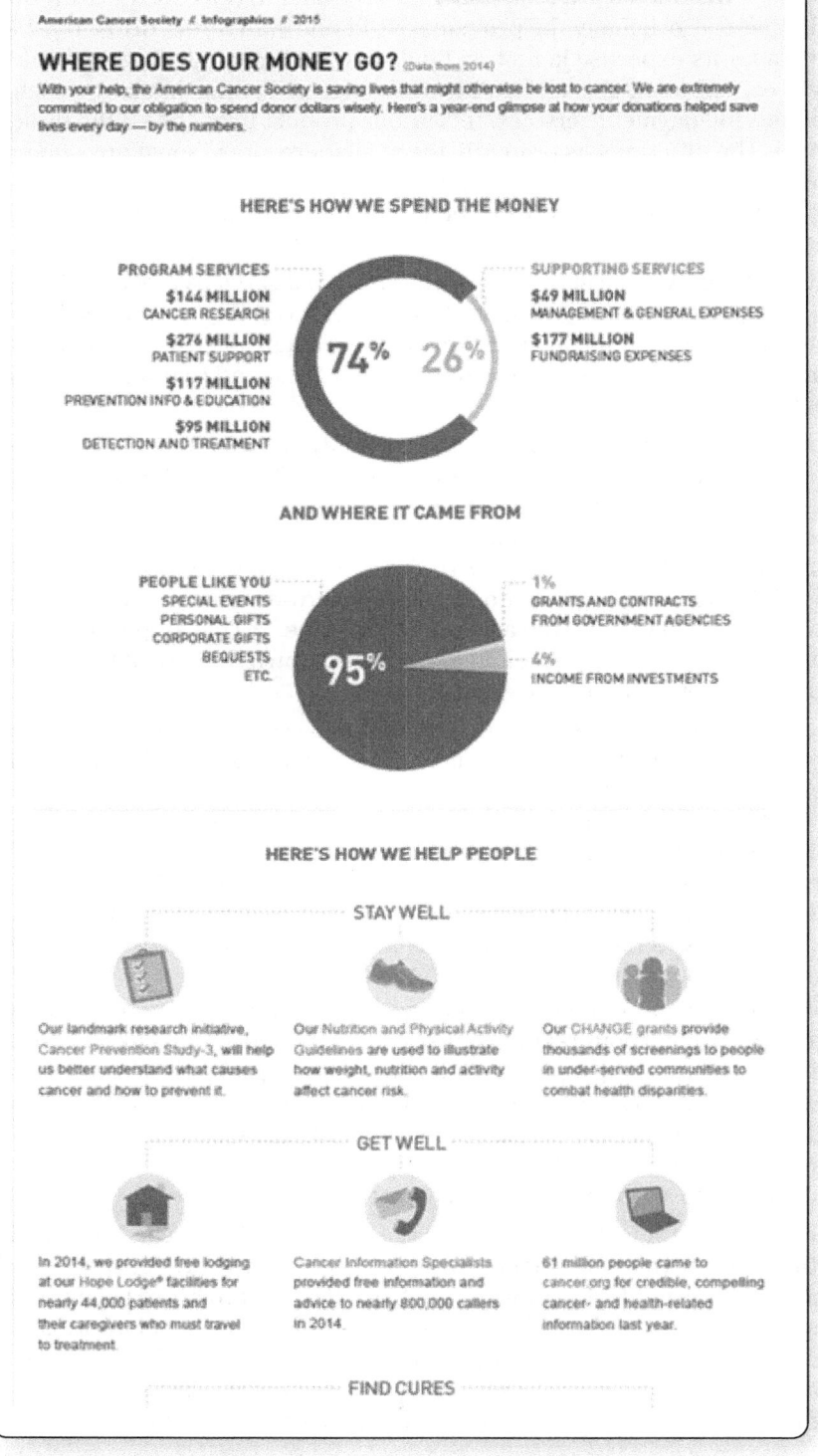

SOURCE: http://www.cancer.org/research/infographicgallery/where-does-money-go-2015

often find newer fund-raising organizations relying more on the internet. Matt Damon's The Water Project is a good example.[55]

Because fund-raising is an inherently personal activity, mobile often has a more specialized role in a fund-raising organization. In the case of the American Cancer Society it is primarily used to support its individual fund-raising activities for the Relay for Life and Making Strides against Breast Cancer events.[56] The ability for individuals to use the internet and mobile web to raise funds for causes they support is a major change from the days when fund-raising was a rather exclusive domain for the wealthy and well-connected.

- Some firms function as **infomediaries** (information intermediaries) assisting buyers and/or sellers to understand a given market. Infomediaries have always been important to direct marketers and many of those active today began as list brokers for the direct marketing industry. An infomediary on the web is a site that gathers and organizes large amounts of data and acts as an intermediary between those who want the information and those who supply the information.[57] The term is used broadly to cover virtually any third party that manages and distributes data on the internet.

    InfoUSA is one infomediary that has moved from the direct mail era smoothly into the digital era. As such, it offers a variety of both physical address mailing lists and email lists. It also offers list enhancement services that add data to the basic list address to give marketers a better picture of each list member and therefore a better ability to target their messages. They also offer the SalesGenie® lead generation tool for both B2B and B2C markets.[58] Notice that these firms are often called list brokers because they use the brokerage transactions model.

    Data about consumers and their consumption habits are valuable, especially when that information is carefully analyzed and used to target marketing campaigns. Independently collected data about producers and their products are useful to consumers when considering a purchase. The quality of medical care is one area where this kind of information is vitally important. Rating and ranking data is provided by many organizations from Consumer Reports[59] to Medicare, which provides data for health care plans[60] and nursing homes,[61] to many specialist health care rating organizations to many specialist health care rating organizations.

- The operations of the **manufacturer direct model** were discussed extensively in Chapter 2 where both Zara (Section 2-2a1) and Dell (Section 2-2b1) were used as examples.

    Many software developers sell directly to their customers. Salesforce was mentioned in Chapter 2 as an example of software-as-a-service, which some people consider a business model on its own. As we discussed in our Amazon example (Section 2-5a), SaaS involves making software available to users from the cloud, usually charging them on the usage basis. That also qualifies as the **utility** model.

    Confusing, isn't it? That was exactly the point of business models being so fluid and complex today that understanding these basic models is really only a start.

- We discussed the multiple examples of the ecommerce (**merchant**) model as part of Amazon's operations earlier in the chapter. Many firms have enjoyed success as single-line etailers, as opposed to Amazon's huge assortment.

    Zappos has already been mentioned as a limited line merchant. It has diversified into clothing from its original shoes-only offering but remains a deep assortment in shoes for the whole family and women's clothing. eBags is a model for a specialty retailer, and it does have bags—from backpacks to handbags and from durable traveling gear to high-end briefcases and laptop bags. It has suitcases of all kinds and all sorts of travel accessories including electronics for the "connected traveler." All the categories are related to the "ebags"

infomediaries intermediary in channels of distribution that specializes in the capture, analysis, application, and distribution of information.

manufacturer direct model bypassing intermediaries such as wholesalers and manufacturers' reps in the channel of distribution; direct from manufacturer to customer.

utility delivers services or content on a metered or "pay as you go" basis.

merchant see ecommerce.

- slogan "Your journey starts here," and all have a very deep assortment.⁶² That is necessary in order to be a successful specialty retailer on the web.
- The **subscription** model has been popular since long before the internet. Newspapers, of course, are a prime example as are magazines. Using the subscription model for content is popular among internet-era businesses as well. BuzzFeed is only one of many examples, but its often-irreverent approach to the news and many other subjects has made it popular. It has a dozen or so feeds to which you can subscribe. They range from News to LOL to Fail. There are more than two dozen newsletters derived from these feeds to which you can subscribe. None of these charge the subscriber. The mobile app is free. So BuzzFeed must be advertising supported—right? Not exactly. Its main revenue stream comes from **native ads**.

native ads paid media in which content follows the form and function of the site on which it is placed, not traditional advertising formats.

Native ads don't look like ads, nor are they like the thinly disguised advertising called advertorials carried by both print and online content distributors. The advertisers are called Brand Publishers and clearly identified in story listings. The day I was looking at the BuzzFeed home page Shell was sponsoring a feature called "11 Ways Energy Could Change Our World in the Future." That one uses the list format used with great success by BuzzFeed and dubbed "the listicle." An interesting feature on Johan Hills and Miles Taylor was sponsored by the War Dogs movie.⁶³

In mid-2015 Tech Times said that BuzzFeed gets about 150 million unique visitors each month, three-fourths of which come from social media platforms, and posts about 400 articles every day. It makes interesting points about this model and the future of journalism:

- *what BuzzFeed sells to brands is its ability to grow and shape what works on social. It has been producing extremely sharable content for more than eight years now and the more content it pushes out the more it discovers what does and doesn't work, thereby honing the staff's skills to create effective native advertising*
- *if this is the model that works, is all journalism doomed to be lists of date tips and LOL cat GIFs? No, it could actually mean the opposite to the point that Stratechery calls BuzzFeed the most important news organization in the world. The argument is that having created a profitable business model, BuzzFeed journalists don't have to worry about writing about what will sell, but instead have the freedom to write stories that people find important enough to share.*⁶⁴

The subscription model is not unknown on the product side of the marketplace. A number of products are sold on an automatic replenishment basis. Make-up on the home shopping channels is a good example. HP has recently started a subscription model for printer cartridges to ensure that you never run out of ink.⁶⁵ Amazon seems to want to offer subscriptions to everything through its "subscribe and save" program.⁶⁶

However, few have disrupted their industry as has the Dollar Shave Club. Dollar Shave Club's offer is simple. The customer selects his blade from three quality levels priced from $1 per month to $9 per month. The club provides a free handle. Blades are shipped each month so the user always has a supply. There are no fees, no term of commitment, the user can cancel at any time and satisfaction is guaranteed.⁶⁷ What could be simpler? Dollar Shave Club buys its blades from a Korean manufacturer and sells them directly to the customer.

The club's founder Mike Dubin did the original advertising in the form of a video that went viral. It is still posted on the home page of the site where it tells me that a favorite former student and 2.7 million others have liked it on YouTube. You should watch it if you haven't seen it as a viral share because I can't quote the slogan—or reproduce the attitude for that matter.⁶⁸ The video reportedly brought in 12,000 orders within its first 24 hours and has been seen more than 20 million times.[69]

Its success has upended the razor/razor blade industry which one writer says "has long been built on convincing people they need more and more blinged-out blades at higher and higher prices." Another adds that the success of Dollar Shave Club "shows that no company is safe from the creative destruction brought by technological change." Challenging market leader Gillette didn't require massive factories and a far-flung distribution network. It took the internet and the global economy.[70]

When Unilever bought the company for about $1 billion in 2016 Unilever CEO Paul Portman described it as an "innovative and disruptive brand with a cult-like following of diverse and highly engaged users." As a privately held company, financials were not released and it is not clear that the business is yet profitable. Still Portman described it as "inherently profitable" and pointed to its subscriber base which is heavily Millennial.[71]

Is there really big growth ahead for the subscription model? Again, you will just have to stay tuned.

- The utility model is based on metering usage, or a "pay as you go" approach. Unlike subscriber services, metered services are based on actual usage rates. Traditionally, metering has been used for essential services (e.g., electricity, water, and long-distance telephone services). The model has been picked up in the digital age by firms like Skype, which has a pay-as-you go service alongside a calling subscription plan.[72]

The utility model is most in evidence now in cloud services, as discussed in Sections 2-5a and 2-5b. Amazon Web Services has already been discussed; it clearly uses a utility payment model.[73] It is the dominant model in cloud services at the moment, popular enough that firms including IBM have developed metering and billing tools for suppliers of cloud-based software.[74]

The models we have just discussed all existed and continue to exist in offline space as well as online. Not all are entirely online, but all have flourished on the internet and mobile web. There is another category of models that are not entirely unique to internet space but that owe their ability to flourish to the internet.

Internet-Enabled Models

In this section you will see some models that are familiar and at least one that may be entirely new. That is the nature of this group of models that have prospered in the digital era.

- **Affiliate** models are an example of offline existence, online flourishing. The floral industry is a good example. Teleflora has been in existence since 1934 when telegraph was the preferred channel for quick communications. As a privately held company its growth is hard to chart but it currently has over 30,000 affiliates around the world. It offers same-day and international delivery of flower arrangements. In its early days it telegraphed, later telephoned, orders to affiliates. Support was primarily by mail, where information about new flower arrangements and promotions was shared with affiliates. The company now has a strong internet infrastructure to support its affiliates. It does have a mobile app but the app appears to be a service offered to their florist affiliates[75] and is not promoted on the Teleflora website.[76]

CJ Affiliate was originally Commission Junction. Its model is portrayed on the website as two-sided. It offers advertisers (online retailers) a variety of advertising services to both create and track the results of their listing. Payment is primarily CPA, a pay-for-performance revenue model in which payment is contingent on completion of a visitor behavior, which could be a

affiliate offers incentives to partner websites, wherein a website agrees to post a link to a transactional site in return for a commission on sales made as a direct result of the link.

sale or a request for more information or other actions specified by the retailer. Publisher affiliates can be anyone who owns a website and wants to generate more traffic from the sites of brands that partner with CJ Affiliate. Publishers are also offered a variety of ad creation and tracking services and the pay-per-call option as well as CPA.[77,78] In many ways, this is a brokerage model, but affiliate marketers operate in a specialized manner.

No mention of affiliate marketing would be complete without Amazon. The company does not release numbers but the number of what Amazon calls Associates is clearly immense. The Associates program offers links to products listed on Amazon, banner ads, and the ability to create an online store. For Associates who employ website developers, it offers advanced services.[79]

- Truly a creature of the internet is the **distributed autonomous organization (DAO)**. This model could be described as conceptual, but there is one example of an actual organization. At this moment The DAO Hub, launched in April 2016, is experiencing start-up pains. Whether it is the first, or the precursor, of an important model is open to question, but it is an excellent example of a model that could not exist without the internet. A site that follows the online payments industry has provided the following description:

distributed autonomous organization (DAO) a distributed virtual organization with no identified leader or physical presence.

> *"A distributed organization with no single leader that could theoretically exist so long as there's an Internet connection was launched last month.... "The DAO", as it's called, takes its name from the description for a new type of entity: a distributed autonomous organization. Intended to act as a vehicle for supporting Ethereum-related projects, The DAO has garnered over $50m worth of ethers (ETH) – the digital token of the Ethereum network – from investors."*
>
> *But what does The DAO do exactly? Think of it as a hub that disperses ETH to other startups and projects. Backers of The DAO receive voting rights by means of a digital token, which can be used to help determine the future direction of the organization and which projects will actually get funded following a voting period.*
>
> *Participants stand to receive possible dividends, including ether, in return for supporting the project.*[80]

blockchain a public ledger of all Bitcoin transactions. See also distributed ledger.

distributed ledger a type of data structure composed of encrypted data that is difficult to change that is digitally recorded in packages called blocks.

In order to pretend to understand this description, you must understand Ethereum and the **blockchain** concept. Figure 3.7 contrasts the traditional financial clearing house with a blockchain (**distributed ledger**). Again, we need to turn to the experts for an explanation. The *Wall Street Journal* explained the concept and its potential this way:

FIGURE 3.7
Financial Clearing House vs. a Shared Registry or Blockchain

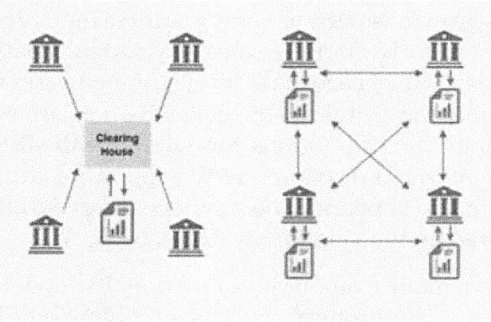

A distributed ledger is a network that records ownership through a shared registry OLIVER WYMAN

SOURCE: http://blogs.wsj.com/cio/2016/02/02/cio-explainer-what-is-blockchain/.

A blockchain is a data structure that makes it possible to create a digital ledger of transactions and share it among a distributed network of computers. It uses cryptography to allow each participant on the network to manipulate the ledger in a secure way without the need for a central authority.

Once a block of data is recorded on the blockchain ledger, it's extremely difficult to change or remove. When someone wants to add to it, participants in the network—all of which have copies of the existing blockchain—run algorithms to evaluate and verify the proposed transaction. If a majority of nodes agree that the transaction looks valid—that is, identifying information matches the blockchain's history—then the new transaction will be approved and a new block added to the chain.[81]

Finally, Ethereum. You may have heard of Bitcoin; it is also a type of payment system powered by blockchain, and it has been in existence longer. Bitcoin was the first virtual currency. It is operated by a decentralized authority unlike the central banking systems of traditional currencies. While it is not a recognized currency, it is widely recognized for payment transfers.

Ethereum is a newer platform based on blockchain technology that goes beyond just virtual currency. It allows the creation of smart contracts (computer protocols that make the contracts self-verifying and self-executing)[82] and distributed trading networks. Ether is its virtual currency which can function like a Bitcoin but also is used within the Ethereum platform to run applications and for transactions.[83]

So in some ways, investing in the DAO Hub is like investing in any business, right? Yes, in some ways it is. However, all power resides in investors who own tokens, not in any governing board or set of executives. The CTO of the open source firm that created the infrastructure for the site said, "We actually don't know who started it. Of course we can see the address on the blockchain but we don't know who owns the address. The only way to speak with the DAO is to make a proposal and vote."[84]

Is this one of many digital fads to see brief popularity followed rapidly by obscurity? Or is it the forerunner of many new virtual business models? You'll just have to stay tuned for the answer to that!

- One area where the semantics have become truly garbled is the **community model** and the **crowdsourcing model**. It is hard to find a substantive definition of the community model but it clearly encompasses a group of people with shared interests, which could be anything from obtaining recipes for nutritious meals to supporting cancer sufferers to advocating for a political or community issue to developing open-source software or content. On the other hand Wikipedia defines the crowdsourcing model as "the process of obtaining needed services, ideas, or content by soliciting contributions from a large group of people, especially an online community, rather than from employees or suppliers."[85] There is little if any difference and we have lumped them together but retained both terms for clarity.

community model connects like-minded individuals and groups for sharing.

crowdsourcing model obtains needed resources, including financing, by soliciting from a community instead of traditional funding sources.

These models rely on the internet or mobile web for their very existence. Before the internet, communication was either one-to-one (e.g., personal communications) or one-to-many (e.g., commercial advertising). The web made possible many-to-many communications, which are the backbone of the community model.

TripAdvisor was founded in 2000, four years before Yelp! democratized the restaurant review business. Founder and CEO Stephen Kauferre recalls that the concept of open user reviews was frightening to the hotel industry at that time. The original business model was to license a database of travel information to consumer-facing sites. The online travel services like Expedia and Orbitz recognized the value of the concept but never got around to licensing the product for their own use. Consequently, the founding team **pivoted** the model to a traveler-facing site, one that earned its revenue from booking referrals. At that time the button was added that allows travelers to submit their own reviews and growth exploded.[86]

pivoted a quick change from one business model to another. It is usually applied to start-ups that can make rapid model changes that may be impossible for entrenched business models of large enterprises.

In a 2016 post on the TripAdvisor blog Kaufman says the site now receives 230 pieces of new content every minute and gets over 340 million unique visitors each month. He believes in the power of its community, saying:

> *"The TripAdvisor travel community has fundamentally changed the way we travel. Our community's voice has done more to improve service standards than professional reviews ever could. And 8 out of 10 business owners agree. Our community has helped small businesses all over the globe reach a global audience; to grow and succeed based on the quality of their product and the service they offer, not the size of their budgets or the savviness of their marketing efforts."*[87]

As a very different example the Business Model Generation e-book that lays out the Business Model Canvas is described by the authors as being crowdsourced and the authors acknowledge all 470 professionals from 45 countries in the book.[88] Alex Osterwalder said in an interview,

> *"It took 9 years of research and practice 4,000-plus writing hours, 28,456 Post-it notes, 77 forum discussions, 287 Skype calls, 1360 comments, and 137,757 online views for over 470 contributors from nearly 50 countries to arrive at these nine elements of any business model and arrange them into the visual 'Business Model Canvas.'"*[89]

That represents a herculean effort on the part of authors Osterwalder and Pigneur but it paid off in a book that sets the standard for business model strategy development.

GoFundMe is one of many crowdsourcing sites for personal fund-raising. It is available to individuals or groups who wish to raise money in support of a particular individual or a cause. It is also available to charitable organizations. It has easy-to-use templates for setting up personal websites and for keeping in touch with donors by email.[90] The site is funded by a 5 percent commission on all donations received.[91]

There are many crowdfunding websites including ones that are intended for the launch of businesses or projects. They have different approaches and revenue models but overall the popularity of this model seems to be growing.

Mobile-Dependent Models

This is a category in which confusing terminology is the norm, not the exception. **Mobile first** has received huge attention since Eric Schmidt of Google first used the term in 2010.[92] The term is used in all sorts of contexts and it often seems that no two users give it the same exact meaning. You will meet the term again in Chapter 15 where it has a precise meaning in the context of designing websites.

mobile first designing the online experience for mobile before designing for the internet.

TechCrunch does a good job of cutting through the semantic thicket. In the process they create a wonderfully evocative term of their own. They say that mobile first treats mobile usage as first priority, not as an afterthought like "pave-the-goat-paths mobile" which simply tries to transfer desktop concepts to mobile screens. This is still, however, not entirely new functionality that depends on mobile for its very existence. They call this authentically mobile and contrast the three approaches in Figure 3.8. The descriptions also point out that what they describe as authentically mobile emphasizes data collection, which seems to draw it close to the IoT.

There are a number of business models that qualify as mobile dependent, some of which fit into TechCrunch's mobile first category and others that seem to be authentically mobile.

- Apps are so much a part of our mobile experience that it is hard to remember that there are desktop apps which have been around for many years. Apps will appear frequently in our discussions throughout the text and we are invariably discussing mobile apps. We list two revenue models for mobile

FIGURE 3.8

Three Approaches to Mobile

	Pave-the-goat-paths mobile	Mobile first	Authentically mobile
Target platform	Desktop	Mobile	Mobile
Target business process	Already addressed by desktop	Already addressed by desktop	Difficult to touch without mobile
Design focus	Process centric	Human centric	Human centric
Functional innovation	Functionality already exists on desktop	Functionality already exists on desktop	New-to-world functionality
Usage pattern	Periodic and typically scheduled	In-the-moment and continuous	In-the-moment and continuous
Role of data	Emphasis on presentation	Emphasis on presentation	Emphasis on collection

SOURCE: https://techcrunch.com/2015/05/17/mobile-first-but-whats-next/.

apps—advertising supported and freemium. There are many others discussed—subscription, in-app transactions, paid apps, sponsorship, and enterprise apps offered to B2B customers to name a few.[93]

Is there a new model in that list? Not really, these are existing revenue models applied to apps. Advertising supported and freemium are two of the most popular and we will illustrate them with some brief examples.

Facebook is well known for its ability to attract advertisers to its website with targeted advertising opportunities, a subject we will discuss in detail in Chapter 11. The same is true, perhaps even more so, of its mobile site. In January 2016, Fast Company reported that 80 percent of Facebook's ad revenue for the fourth quarter of 2015 had come from mobile ads—that's $4.5 billion in advertising revenue.[94] By the second quarter of 2016 Facebook's profit had tripled year-over-year with the growth being attributed to mobile ad sales and a 15 percent growth in monthly active users, making that number 1.7 billion. Facebook's emphasis on video appears to be attracting users and it plans to get more out of its advertising sales by concentrating on video advertising. It cannot host many more ads and video advertising commands a premium price.[95]

Google, of course, also sells mobile advertising that appears on its own mobile site and the sites of other publishers. In fact, eMarketer estimated that Google would have an almost 32 percent share of the mobile advertising market in 2016 compared to Facebook's approximately 19 percent.[96] Google's mobile advertising revenue, however, is dwarfed by its search revenues, just as it is on the desktop. Google's mobile advertising revenues continue to grow, primarily due to the popularity of video advertising on YouTube.[97]

The third ranking in terms of mobile ad revenue is Pandora and the fourth is the Yellow Pages app. Both of them have only a fraction of the market share of Google and Facebook. Is that the result of a business model that includes a platform for ad creation, not just selling advertising space on the app?

- The freemium model also represents a time-honored practice on the internet and in the physical world where it is often called "free trial." Freemium is in widespread use in B2B markets for both SaaS and apps. Would you adopt an app—one of many competitors—to help you manage your Facebook advertising without knowing that it worked as promised? You'd much rather try it out,

I'm sure, but that puts a premium on designing apps that are easy to use. It may also give an edge to apps from a current supplier of software that has already had at least some of the configuration done.

The same argument can also be made for apps for streaming music or video. Spotify was established in 2008 to compete with the then-largest music streaming service, Pandora. In 2015, Spotify had about 15 million paid subscribers and some 60 million active monthly users. Those numbers alone are testimony to the viability of the freemium model. On Spotify, free users do receive 15- or 30-second audio advertisements between songs. The audio quality is lower than on the Premium version and only shuffle mode is available. In addition, Premium subscribers receive additional services like on-demand access, the ability to download music for offline listening and others.[98] So the millions of free users can access the huge Spotify music catalog in a less flexible and lower-quality fashion, which seems like reasonable free trial.

The Dropbox file-sharing app is also freemium with a pricing structure that is typical for apps that serve B2B as well as B2C customers. The free version offers less storage space and fewer options for sharing with other Dropbox users. For Pro individual users, a subscription offers a considerable increase in storage space, ways to integrate content with other software and more ways to share with other users. The Business version offers a free trial and additional features for managing a multi-user platform for $12.50 per user per month. The Enterprise version provides additional management options and offers training. A "seat" (per user) price is not listed meaning that quantity discounts probably apply, depending on the size of the user base. Dropbox has grown rapidly since it was introduced in 2007 and now has 500 million users worldwide with 8 million of those being business users but it is not clear how many of those users are paid and how many are free.[99]

Notice that on the B2C side, many of the Spotify users have only free access, meaning that subscription revenues must cover costs. Considering both Spotify and Dropbox it is clear that these freemium services must have good business and revenue models to ever achieve profitability.

augmented reality (AR) an enhanced version of reality created by superimposing computer-generated images on top of the user's view of the real world.

virtual reality (VR) simulation of a three-dimensional image or environment with which the user can interact by using special equipment.

- The business model for **Augmented reality (AR)** and/or **Virtual reality (VR)** is worth mentioning both for its future potential and for its tie to mobile. In the next section we cover the explosive present of AR in the form of Pokémon Go. In terms of future potential, some technology pundits believe AR/VR is the major fourth platform after the internet, PCs, and mobile. AR puts objects into the real world for people to interact with. VR requires hardware to use, but it is expected to be a major force in the games market with VR games already in play and a number of mobile VR headsets to support the experience.[100] AR will be dependent on mobile services because using data for access to AR out of Wi-Fi range will be cost prohibitive.[101]

  Advertisers have experimented with augmented reality for a number of years. In an article entitled "Augmented Reality: the Future of Advertisement?" EuroNews describes a London ad for Pepsi Max (Figure 3.9). The ad uses a bus stop window to expose watchers to a tiger seeming to come straight at them, a tenacled monster trying to grab passers-by, and other highly unlikely but engaging stunts. The episodes were short, intended to grab awareness, not to scare people out of their wits.[102] The ad is part of Pepsi's #LiveForNowcampaign, although the purpose of this ad may be more to show that it can be done than to convey an advertising message. It created awareness, however; the YouTube video has over 3 million views.[103] That may be the prime use for now, but it may also be a peek into the future.

- Games have become franchises just like movie hits. Candy Crush Saga has been one of the leading game franchises since its introduction in 2012. In 2014 it added Candy Crush Soda Saga and in 2016 Candy Crush Jelly Saga and it

FIGURE 3.9
Pepsi Max Augmented Reality Ad

SOURCE: http://www.convinceandconvert.com/social-media-case-studies/pepsi-max-shocks-and-delights-londoners-with-augmented-reality-stunt/.

updates the games with new features and levels from time to time.[104] In 2014 Candy Crush Saga alone experienced over $1.3 billion in sales.[105] In 2015 the company reported 550 million monthly active players. Quarterly revenue for all three games declined to $604.6 million in Q1 2015 compared to $641.1 in the same quarter of 2014.[106]

How does a set of free games make that much revenue? From in-app sales of features like extra lives, extra moves, color bombs, lollipop hammers, and gold bars.[107] Why has it become so popular? *Forbes* lists reasons for the game's popularity that other brands can emulate:

- Scarcity, which in the case of Candy Crush saga means that players get only five lives then have to wait 30 minutes to play again. To a nongamer that sounds very annoying but apparently it adds to the addictive nature of the game.
- It is free to download.
- It is easy to learn to play and doesn't require extra hardware like many games do. That makes it perfect for smartphones.
- The subject matter is likeable—who doesn't love candy, soda, and jelly?
- Players get various kinds of rewards, from onscreen celebration when a new level is reached to verbal encouragement to a piece of striped candy for an especially good move. Rewards are central to the concept of gamification which brands are applying in other settings to engage customers.
- It has a community of avid players.[108]

Candy Crush was often at or near the top in app downloads until Pokémon Go came along in 2016. Its revenue quickly outstripped that of Candy Crush, earning $200 million in its first month, seven times more than Candy Crush.[109] Like

Candy Crush it is free to download and earns its revenue from in-app sales. It is also part of a game franchise which boasts over 100 games.

There are a number of important business model implications from the success of Pokémon Go. One is the importance of AR in the games market, at least for now. Another is implications of game play for businesses. When the game launched in Japan, McDonald's became its first sponsored location. That allows the location(s) to become Pokémon gyms in which players can be trained and can battle other players. (That explanation came from the Pokémon community wiki,[110] whose existence suggests just how engaged the Pokémon community is.) Being a Pokémon gym could be a big traffic builder for retailers. There are also Pokéstops where purchased Lures can attract Pokémon for about 30 minutes. That might be a traffic-building alternative to the gym. Will the success of Pokémon Go speed the adoption of AR for other business uses? It is certainly showing the viability of a well-designed application.[111]

Loyalty points or rewards are a time-honored marketing tactic that is a perfect fit for mobile. Starbucks' loyalty program predates mobile, but it was quick to see the benefits. In 2016 there were over 11 million Starbucks mobile app users in the United States. Users load value onto the app and use it to pay at Starbucks locations. In return they receive promotional offers and are able to order through the app for pick up at their designated location. The loyalty program is the heart of the mobile app, giving users free product in return for levels of purchase. Customers can also earn loyalty points for activities like filling out mobile surveys.[112] There was a huge outcry from lower-spending loyalty program members in spring 2015 when Starbucks changed its reward guidelines from number of purchases to amount spent. Customers who regularly buy a $3 cup of coffee now have to make 50 purchases to earn a reward instead of the previous 30 purchases. Conversely, higher-spending customers get rewards more often.[113] Starbucks was obviously convinced they were doing the right thing because they stuck to the program in the face of the criticism. It does suggest that loyalty programs, mobile or not, must be carefully designed because it is painful to change them.

A different business model in this space is Open Table which provides reservations and reward points for some 37,000 restaurants around the world. By giving reward points for honoring online reservations and offering restaurant reviews, it has created a platform that allows small or new restaurants to match the services of larger competitors.[114]

Both Starbucks and Open Table are successful in mobile but did not begin with a mobile model. One that did is the Indian site ShopRover. It is targeted to online mobile shoppers in India. It provides typical services such as coupons and deals for many stores so that the user does not have to deal with a multitude of store apps. At this writing it is available only for Android. It is owned by a Hong Kong performance marketing firm and does not appear to have its own website.[115] That model fits well in a country where most internet access is mobile and may be another insight into models to come.

on-demand model technology-based model in which user demand is fulfilled immediately in a location-aware manner.

- The **on-demand model** is exemplified by Uber in the minds of many. To paraphrase Uber, the site says that all the customer needs to do is to tap the app and a driver will respond to her location in any city that Uber serves any time of day or night. That is the service that Uber is famous for but it also allows customers to schedule in advance and drivers will pick up and deliver many items from a grocery order to a forgotten cell phone—an on-demand errand service if you will. Apparently Uber doesn't tell drivers that a person has to be part of the service but lets drivers decide for themselves.[116] Uber is a technology platform, not a conventional business with assets or employees or inventory. Airbnb, founded a year before Uber, could make the same claim about its real estate rentals although its services are necessarily more complex.

The basic Uber business model has been widely copied and has its own name—Uber for X. A sampling from a list of Uber for X companies:

- Shyp picks up items to ship, packages them, and ships them at the best rate.
- FoodNow picks up food ordered online and delivers it to your location.
- Wag offers on-demand dog walking, sitting, or boarding.[117]

However, Uber for X is not for all on-demand businesses. A cleaning company called Slate was started in 2005 by Miguel Zabludovsky as a courier that picked up dry cleaning, took it to a contract dry cleaners, and returned it to the owner. Two years later a dry cleaners was purchased and two years after that house cleaning services were added. Mr. Zabuldovsky did not add a technology layer until 2015. Now his daily house cleaning clients interact with the cleaning service over a mobile app, specifying the tasks each day. Mr. Zabuldovsky believes that he can provide a better quality of service by owning as much of the process as possible. Fast Company argues that many startups are emulating this model as an alternative to Uber for X.[118]

- **Mobile payments** is another natural mobile business model although the uptake has been slow, apparently because of security concerns by potential users. The Apple Pay system allows users to load their credit card details onto an iPhone or Apple Watch then pay for a purchase by simply tapping on a contactless retail terminal. As of mid-2016 there were 12 million monthly users of Apple Pay with about 5 million monthly users each for Android Pay and Samsung Pay. It's a small penetration rate; only 6 percent of Apple users with qualifying iPhones use the system compared to 4 percent for Samsung and 1 percent for Android. Samsung may have an advantage at the moment because its system can work with card readers so that the merchant does not require a contactless terminal as with Apple and Android.[119]

mobile payments payments made from a mobile device using established financial payment mechanisms.

- Venmo, owned by PayPal, is a mobile wallet founded by Millennials for Millennials. It allows users to transfer money to friends, split bills with them, and collect the rent money, among other things. It is highly social allowing users to post comments and even emojis along with their transfers. Users can post either publicly or privately and can designate "trusted" friends. For concerned users, there is a set of etiquette suggestions for using Venmo that include not using it to stalk a significant other.[120] The app has achieved considerable popularity, hosting $1billion in transfers for the first time in January 2016.[121] Venmo appears to be mobile-only with its website only providing information, not hosting transfers.[122]

- A section on mobile payments would not be complete without a mention of **cryptocurrencies** that allow users to conduct financial transactions without the assistance of a central governing body. Ethereum was discussed earlier in the section. The largest "alt currency" is Bitcoin, but it is joined in this space by as many as 500 other competitors. Beyond the bare facts there is no agreement about the future of cryptocurrencies. The *Wall Street Journal* published an article in 2015 in which one financial expert argues to let it play out and see what happens while another argues that the whole blockchain system will collapse because it doesn't follow the rules to traditional currency transfer.[123] Isn't that what disruption is all about? This is another "stay tuned" potential business model.

cryptocurrencies digital currencies in which encryption regulates the creation and use of currencies that operate outside the control of a central banking system.

Remember that this is not an exhaustive listing of business models. We have purposely discussed some of the most popular business models as well as some highly speculative ones. Does that mean that we can offer no advices except to wait and see what the future holds?

No, there is a viable alternative, the creation of a customized business model. The Business Model Canvas allows users to do just that.[124]

USING THE BUSINESS MODEL CANVAS

You have already encountered the crowdsourced e-book Business Model Generation (Section 3-6b) and the Value Proposition Canvas (Section 3-4 and Interactive Exercise 3.2). Now it is time to put it all together and to understand how this approach allows the entrepreneur or evolving business to customize a unique model, not simply to blindly pick a model from Table 3.1.

From the beginning their approach has been based on understanding the basic elements of a business model that can be applied in a traditional business setting or, even more important, in a disruptive one. The result is their Business Model Canvas (Figure 3.10) which American Express calls "the elements of an ironclad business model." They explain:

> *As Alexander Osterwalder and Yves Pigneur write in their crowdsourced book Business Model Generation: "Disruptive new business models are emblematic of our generation. Yet they remain poorly understood, even as they transform competitive landscapes across industries."*
>
> *A business model describes the rationale of how an organization creates, delivers, and captures value. And a disruptive business model is one where a non-traditional industry player enters the mix and threatens to disrupt the status quo.*[125]

The canvas has nine elements, each of which is necessary but not sufficient alone to describe a business model. The video in Interactive Exercise 3.3 examines each of the nine elements as applied to the popular coffee system Nespresso. You should complete the exercise before continuing with the remainder of the chapter.

Now that you have watched Osterwalder distill a decade of work by the Nestlé Group on its Nespresso brand, much research and at least two failed business model iterations into less than five minutes, you have a good sense of how a viable business model finally comes together. You also have a sense of the uniqueness of the Nespresso model. It works for this brand; it would not work for any other products

FIGURE 3.10
The Business Model Canvas

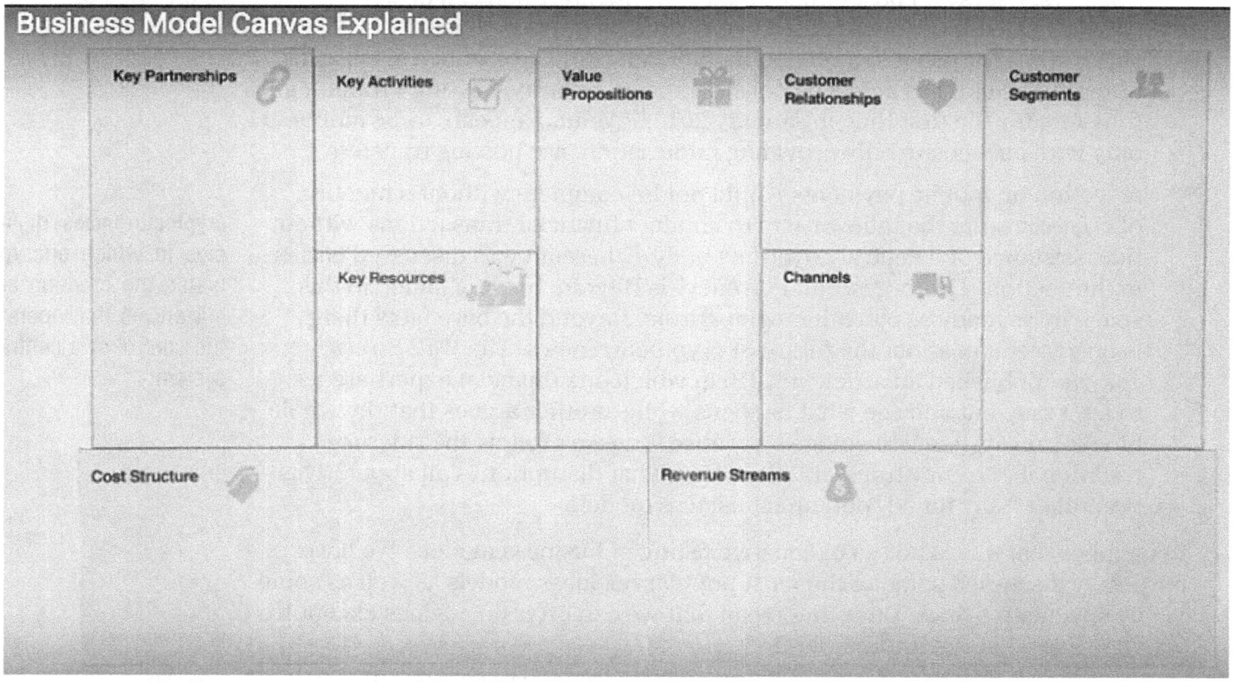

SOURCE: http://www.businessmodelgeneration.com/downloads/business_model_canvas_poster.pdf.

that did not have all nine key elements in place. Osterwalder's Strategizer website has many resources for working with business models, including the ones the company judges to be essential.[126]

You can use the Business Model Canvas to analyze existing business models, as seen in the discussion of the Evernote model. The canvas can be used to create a business model for a start-up business or to help an existing firm evolve its business model to one more in keeping with the times.

It is a powerful tool and you are encouraged to get some experience with its use.

SUMMARY

Business models are how enterprises are configured to create value for customers and to deliver that value in a profitable way in the physical world, on the internet or on the mobile web. A business model is a conceptual description of the business. Business models on the internet have been given a set of names, although there is no commonly accepted set of names or classifications of types of business models. To aid in understanding this complex space we have divided them into models that have been extended onto the internet from the physical world, models that require the internet to prosper, and models that are dependent on mobile.

The emphasis on the value proposition, however, is characteristic of all discussions of business models. The drivers of value are customer wants and needs. It is up to the business to uncover the relevant wants and needs and design products and services that meet those needs and fit with its core expertise. This is a customer-centric, not a product-centric, approach. It is captured in the Value Proposition Canvas.

There are many commonly accepted business models in all three categories and we discuss key examples of each. Most of them can be found in both B2C and B2B marketspaces and are also used by nonprofits and governmental agencies. A key point of this discussion is that many businesses now have hybrid models or multiple models. There are few examples of pure models in practice. The same is true of revenue streams that support each model. Few businesses today prosper without multiple revenue streams.

The complexity and ever-changing nature of the world we live in suggests that adopting a basic business model in its entirety may not work well for most businesses. Enter the Business Model Canvas. The canvas sections the business model into nine parts, all of which must be present and each of which can be customized to the needs of a particular business concept. An example is given and resources are presented for the use of the canvas.

The evolution of business models in the digital era continues. It is likely that different models may achieve prominence at different periods of time and possible that entirely new models may emerge as the digital space matures. It is likely that we have not seen the end of disruptive business models.

DISCUSSION QUESTIONS

1. Why is the concept of the business model important? In what ways is it useful?
2. What is the single reason that most new businesses fail?
3. Why is it sometimes necessary for existing firms to evolve their business model or for startups to pivot theirs?
4. How does the value proposition impact a firm's approach to creation of new products and new marketing strategies?
5. Can a company have more than one business model?
6. How do business models evolve?
7. What is the difference between pipe-type business models and platform-type models?

8. Would you start a business today driven by the advertising-supported model?
9. Do you agree with the statement that the community/crowdsourcing model is likely to become even more prominent in the future?
10. Why do you think the on-demand model has become so popular for so many kinds of businesses?
11. List and explain each of the nine sections of the Business Model Canvas.
12. What is the meaning of the term "disruptive business model?" Give an example of a business model that you believe is genuinely disruptive and explain why.

ENDNOTES

1. Andrea Ovans, "What Is a Business Model?" https://hbr.org/2015/01/what-is-a-business-model.
2. Andrea Ovans, "What Is a Business Model?" https://hbr.org/2015/01/what-is-a-business-model.
3. Michael Rappa, "Business Models on the Web," http://digitalenterprise.org/models/models.html.
4. Sendil Ethiraj, Isin Guler, and Harbir Singh, nd, "The Impact of Internet and Electronic Technologies on Firms and Its Implications for Competitive Advantage," Working Paper, The Wharton School, University of Pennsylvania, 18–19.
5. Henry Chesbrough and Richard S. Rosenbloom, "The Role of the Business Model in Capturing Value from Innovation: Evidence from Xerox Corporations's Technology Spin-Off Companies," *Industrial and Corporate Change*, Volume 11, Number 3, 2002, 533–534.
6. Jitender Miglani, "IBM Strategic Imperatives vs Traditional IT Business Growth," http://revenuesandprofits.com/ibm-strategic-imperatives-vs-traditional-business-growth/.
7. Michael Copeland, "What Is the Difference Between Artificial Intelligence, Machine Learning, and Deep Learning?" https://blogs.nvidia.com/blog/2016/07/29/whats-difference-artificial-intelligence-machine-learning-deep-learning-ai/.
8. Charles A. O'Reilly, Michael Tushman, and Bruce Harrell, "Organizational Ambidexterity: IBM and Emerging Business Opportunity," https://www.gsb.stanford.edu/faculty-research/working-papers/organizational-ambidexterity-ibm-emerging-business-opportunities.
9. Charles A. O'Reilly and Michael L. Tuchman, "Organizational Ambidexterity: Past, Present and Future," https://www.gsb.stanford.edu/faculty-research/working-papers/organizational-ambidexterity-past-present-future.
10. Henry Blodget, "CEO Jeff Immelt on transforming GE," http://www.businessinsider.com/interview-with-ge-ceo-jeff-immelt-on-transforming-ge-2015-12.
11. Henry Blodget, "CEO Jeff Immelt on transforming GE," http://www.businessinsider.com/interview-with-ge-ceo-jeff-immelt-on-transforming-ge-2015-12.
12. Linton Weeks, "Can Amazon's Jeff Bezos Save Planet Earth," http://www.npr.org/sections/theprotojournalist/2014/01/08/260457752/can-jeff-bezos-save-planet-earth
13. Chris Isidore, "Amazon Prime Now Reaches Nearly Half of U.S Households," http://money.cnn.com/2016/01/26/technology/amazon-prime-memberships/.
14. Tricia Duryee, "Amazon May Have Up to 80 Million High-Spending Prime Members Worldwide," http://www.geekwire.com/2015/amazon-may-have-up-to-80-million-high-spending-prime-members-worldwide/
15. "7 Surprising Things to Know About the Amazon Business Model," http://digitalsparkmarketing.com/amazon-business-model/
16. Dave Chaffey, "Amazon's Business Strategy and Revenue Model," http://www.smartinsights.com/digital-marketing-strategy/online-business-revenue-models/amazon-case-study/.
17. Karan Girotra and Serguei Netseeine, "Amazon Constantly Audits Its Business Model," https://hbr.org/2013/11/amazon-constantly-audits-its-business-model.

18. https://evernote.com/students/.
19. https://evernote.com/business/.
20. David H. Freeman, "Evernote: 2011 Company of the Year," http://www.inc.com/magazine/201112/evernote-2011-company-of-the-year.html.
21. Casey Newton, "Evernote's New CEO on the Company's Critics," http://www.theverge.com/2016/5/4/11584764/evernote-ceo-chris-oneill-interview.
22. http://video.cnbc.com/gallery/?video=3000431729.
23. Thomas R. Eisenmann, Geoffrey G. Parker, and Marshall W. Van Alstyne, "Strategies for Two-Sided Markets," https://hbr.org/2006/10/strategies-for-two-sided-markets.
24. Phalguni Soni, "NIKE's Distribution Channels," http://marketrealist.com/2014/12/nikes-distribution-channels-products-reach-customers/.
25. Ben Bajarin, "iOS, Android, and the Dividing of Business Models," https://techpinions.com/ios-android-and-the-dividing-of-business-models/32237.
26. "Why Business Models Fail: Pipes vs. Platforms," http://platformed.info/why-business-models-fail-pipes-vs-platforms/.
27. http://digitalenterprise.org/models/models.html.
28. Andrea Ovans, "What Is a Business Model?" https://hbr.org/2015/01/what-is-a-business-model.
29. Annum Munir, "App Monetization," http://info.localytics.com/blog/app-monetization-6-bankable-business-models-that-help-mobile-apps-make-money.
30. "9 Mobile Business Models that You Can Use Right Now to Generate Revenue," http://untether.tv/2010/8-mobile-business-models-that-you-can-use-right-now-to-generate-revenue/.
31. Tim Merel, "The Reality of AR/VR Business Models," https://techcrunch.com/2016/04/05/the-reality-of-arvr-business-models/.
32. http://www.statista.com/statistics/260819/number-of-monthly-active-whatsapp-users/.
33. Juro Osawa, "How Messaging Apps Make Money," http://blogs.wsj.com/digits/2014/03/03/how-messaging-apps-make-money/.
34. http://www.statista.com/statistics/327292/number-of-monthly-active-line-app-users/.
35. Leslie Hsu, "LINE-Messaging App Monetization Best Practice," https://openforum.hbs.org/challenge/understand-digital-transformation-of-business/business-model/line-the-best-practice-of-messaging-app-monetization.
36. Harry McCracken, "How Japan's Line App Became a Culture-Changing, Revenue-Generating Phenomenon," http://www.fastcompany.com/3041578/most-innovative-companies-2015/how-japans-line-app-became-a-culture-changing-revenue-generat.
37. Harry McCracken, "How Japan's Line App Became a Culture-Changing, Revenue-Generating Phenomenon," http://www.fastcompany.com/3041578/most-innovative-companies-2015/how-japans-line-app-became-a-culture-changing-revenue-generat.
38. https://www.youtube.com/yt/press/statistics.html.
39. http://www.statista.com/topics/2019/youtube/.
40. https://www.youtube.com/yt/press/statistics.html.
41. Craig Smith, "By the Numbers: 135 Amazing YouTube Statistics," http://expandedramblings.com/index.php/youtube-statistics/.
42. http://www.statista.com/topics/2019/youtube/.
43. Andrew Beattie, "How YouTube Makes Money Off Videos," http://www.investopedia.com/articles/personal-finance/053015/how-youtube-makes-money-videos.asp.
44. Christopher Payne, "Good News at the Washington Post," http://nymag.com/daily/intelligencer/2016/06/washington-post-jeff-bezos-donald-trump.html.
45. Christopher Payne, "Good News at the Washington Post," http://nymag.com/daily/intelligencer/2016/06/washington-post-jeff-bezos-donald-trump.html.
46. Erin Griffith, "Can Virtual Reality Save Journalism?" http://fortune.com/2016/05/02/virtual-reality-nyt-newfronts/.

47. P. J. Bednarski, "A simpler Way Around for 360 Degree Video Ads at "NYT."" http://www.mediapost.com/publications/article/281454/a-simpler-way-around-for-360-degree-video-ads-at.html.
48. Keith O'Brien, "360 Video Meets Display Advertising," http://www.dmnews.com/marketing-strategy/360-video-meets-display-advertising/article/513718/.
49. Marty Swant, "The New York Times Just Bought Agency Focused on Virtual and Augmented Reality," http://www.adweek.com/news/technology/new-york-times-just-bought-agency-focused-virtual-and-augmented-reality-172950
50. Miranda Ward, "Fairfax Media Launches Subscriber First Product to 'Enrich' Subscriber Experience," https://mumbrella.com.au/fairfax-media-launches-subscriber-first-product-enrich-subscriber-experience-387626.
51. https://www.fidelity.com/mobile/overview.
52. http://www.tradestation.com/trading-technology/tradestation-mobile.
53. "The Difference Between Amazon and Alibaba's Business Models," http://www.investopedia.com/articles/investing/061215/difference-between-amazon-and-alibabas-business-models.asp.
54. Gulrukh Cagatay, "Top 10 Worldwide B2B Trade Marketplaces for Exporters, Importers, Suppliers, Manufacturers," http://www.ads2020.marketing/2015/12/top-10-b2b-marketplaces-in-world.html.
55. http://www.cancer.org/.
56. https://thewaterproject.org/.
57. http://makingstrides.acsevents.org/site/PageServer?pagename=MSABC_CY15_FindAnEvent.
58. http://www.webopedia.com/TERM/I/infomediary.html.
59. https://www.infousa.com/.
60. http://www.consumerreports.org/health/doctors-hospitals/hospital-ratings.htm.
61. https://www.medicare.gov/find-a-plan/(X(1)S(wto5fwtpp133gourbudrwuq1))/results/planresults/planratings/compare-plan-ratings.aspx?PlanType=MAPD&AspxAutoDetectCookieSupport=1.
62. https://www.medicare.gov/nursinghomecompare/search.html.
63. http://www.ebags.com/.
64. https://www.buzzfeed.com/.
65. Fergal Gallagher, "How Does BuzzFeed Make Money?" http://www.techtimes.com/articles/38013/20150306/buzzfeed-make-money.htm.
66. http://www8.hp.com/us/en/instant-ink/overview.html.
67. https://www.amazon.com/gp/subscribe-and-save/details/.
68. https://www.dollarshaveclub.com/how-it-works.
69. https://try.dollarshaveclub.com/try-the-club/.
70. "Dollar Shave Club's Retail Disruption," http://theweek.com/articles/641015/dollar-shave-clubs-retail-disruption.
71. "Dollar Shave Club's Retail Disruption," http://theweek.com/articles/641015/dollar-shave-clubs-retail-disruption.
72. Laura O'Reilly, "Unilever's CEO on Why He Bought Dollar Shave Club for a Reported $1 Billion," http://www.businessinsider.com/unilever-ceo-paul-polman-on-dollar-shave-club-acquisition-2016-7.
73. https://support.skype.com/en/faq/FA1214/how-much-does-it-cost-to-call-mobiles-and-landlines-from-skype.
74. Chris Stone, "We Learned from Utilities Everything We Need to Know about Cloud Infrastructure," https://techcrunch.com/2016/05/03/everything-we-need-to-know-about-cloud-infrastructure-we-learned-from-utilities/.
75. http://www.ibm.com/developerworks/offers/lp/demos/summary/tv-saastuam.html.
76. https://www.myteleflora.com/PreLoginWireframe.aspx?pageid=5691.
77. http://www.teleflora.com/.
78. Mahesh Mohan, "The 18 Best Affiliate Programs & Networks for Anyone and Everyone," http://www.minterest.org/best-affiliate-programs-and-networks/.
79. http://www.cj.com/.

80. https://affiliate-program.amazon.icom/welcome/topic/tools.
81. Michael del Castillo, "The DAO: Or How a Leaderless Ethereum Project Raised $50 Million," http://www.coindesk.com/the-dao-just-raised-50-million-but-what-is-it/.
82. Steven Norton, CIO Explainer: What Is Blockchain?" http://blogs.wsj.com/cio/2016/02/02/cio-explainer-what-is-blockchain/.
83. http://about.smartcontract.com/#defining-a-smart-contract.
84. Prableen Bajpai, "Bitcoin Vs Ethereum: Driven by Different Purposes," http://www.investopedia.com/articles/investing/031416/bitcoin-vs-ethereum-driven-different-purposes.asp.
85. Michael del Castillo, "The DAO: Or How a Leaderless Ethereum Project Raised $50 Million," http://www.coindesk.com/the-dao-just-raised-50-million-but-what-is-it/.
86. https://en.wikipedia.org/wiki/Crowdsourcing.
87. Kyle Alspach, "TripAdvisor at 15," http://bostinno.streetwise.co/2015/01/31/tripadvisor-trip-ceo-stephen-kaufer-on-the-travel-planning-sites-first-15-years/.
88. "A Force for Good—How TripAdvisor Changed the Way We Travel"http://blog.tripadvisor.com/2016/07/13/force-good-tripadvisor-changed-way-travel/.
89. http://www.businessmodelgeneration.com/downloads/businessmodelgeneration_preview.pdf.
90. Matthew E. May, "The 9 Elements of an Ironclad Business Model," https://www.americanexpress.com/us/small-business/openforum/articles/the-9-elements-of-an-ironclad-business-model/.
91. https://www.gofundme.com/tour/.
92. https://www.gofundme.com/pricing.
93. Matt Hamblen, "Google CEO Preaches 'Mobile First' " http://www.computerworld.com/article/2520954/mobile-wireless/google-ceo-preaches--mobile-first-.html.
94. Annum Munir, "App Monetization," http://info.localytics.com/blog/app-monetization-6-bankable-business-models-that-help-mobile-apps-make-money.
95. Pavithra Mohan, "80% of Facebooks Ad Dollars Come from Mobile," http://www.fastcompany.com/3055999/fast-feed/80-of-facebooks-ad-dollars-come-from-mobile.
96. "Faebook Profit Nearly Triples on Mobile Ad Revenue and New Users," http://www.nytimes.com/2016/07/28/technology/facebook-earnings-mobile-ad-revenue.html?_r=2.
97. Jack Marshall, "Facebook to Boost Mobile-Ad Market Share as eMarketer Reverses Forecast," http://blogs.wsj.com/cmo/2015/09/08/facebook-projected-to-narrow-mobile-ad-gap-with-google-as-emarketer-reverses-forecast/.
98. "Google's Gains Slow, but Big Mobile Growth Continues," http://www.emarketer.com/Article/Googles-Gains-Slow-Big-Mobile-Growth-Continues/1013531.
99. https://support.spotify.com/us/account_payment_help/subscription_options/subscription-levels/.
100. Emil Protalinski, "Dropbox Passes 500 Million Users," http://venturebeat.com/2016/03/07/dropbox-passes-500-million-users/.
101. "6 Reaspms the Mobile VP Headset Is the Future of VR," https://i-blades.com/latest-news/future-virtual-reality-mobile-vr-headset-headsets/.
102. Tim Merel, "The Reality of AR/VR Business Models," https://techcrunch.com/2016/04/05/the-reality-of-arvr-business-models/.
103. "Augmented Reality: The Future of Advertisement?" http://www.euronews.com/2015/05/05/augmented-reality-the-future-of-advertisement.
104. Jessica Gioglio, "Pepsi Max Shocks and Delights Londoners with Augmented Reality Stunt," http://www.convinceandconvert.com/social-media-case-studies/pepsi-max-shocks-and-delights-londoners-with-augmented-reality-stunt/.
105. Pankaj, "Candy Crush Jelly Saga and Soda Saga Gets an Update with New Levels," http://www.mobipicker.com/candy-crush-jelly-saga-soda-saga-gets-update-new-levels/.
106. Joe Rossignol, "Candy Crush Saga Players Spent over $1.3 Billion on In-App Purchases," http://www.macrumors.com/2015/02/13/candy-crush-saga-revenue-2014/.

107. Jeff Grubb, "King Hits a New Record with 550 M Active Players, but Fewer Spenders Still Makes It Look Weak," http://venturebeat.com/2015/05/14/king-hits-a-new-record-for-active-players-but-one-metric-has-it-looking-weak/.
108. Joe Rossignol, "Candy Crush Saga Players Spent over $1.3 Billion on In-App Purchases," http://www.macrumors.com/2015/02/13/candy-crush-saga-revenue-2014/.
109. Roger Dooley, "Five Marketing Lessons From Candy Crush Saga," http://www.forbes.com/sites/rogerdooley/2013/11/19/candy-crush-lessons/#60291fea6e3a.
110. David Meyer, Pokémon Go Creator Is Now the Most Popular Game Publisher in the World," http://fortune.com/2016/08/12/niantic-pokemon-go-popularity/.
111. http://bulbapedia.bulbagarden.net/wiki/Gym.
112. Sarah Anderson, "Four Ways Pokemon Go Can Impact the Business World," http://newsok.com/article/5510187.
113. Colby VanVolkenburgh, "Starbucks: A Case Study in Effective Mobile App Marketing," http://www.digitalturbine.com/blog/starbucks-a-case-study-in-effective-mobile-app-marketing/.
114. "Starbucks New Loyalty Program Case Study," https://www.clutch.com/starbucks-new-loyalty-program-case-study/.
115. "Top 20 Loyalty Reward Apps for Small Businesses," http://upcity.com/blog/top-20-loyalty-reward-apps-for-small-businesses/.
116. Kishalaya Kundu, "Sponsored App Review: ShopRovers," http://www.androidheadlines.com/2016/05/sponsored-app-review-shoprovers.html.
117. Seth Porges, "How Uber Can Be Used for Far More than Just Rides," http://www.forbes.com/sites/sethporges/2014/07/27/how-uber-can-be-used-for-far-more-than-just-rides/#4295893db1f5.
118. Dylan Kissane, "The Ultimate List of Uber for X Companies," http://www.doz.com/tech/ultimate-list-uber-x-companies.
119. Sarah Kessler, "Why a New Generation of On-Demand Businesses Rejected the Uber Model," http://www.fastcompany.com/3058299/why-a-new-generation-of-on-demand-businesses-rejected-the-uber-model.
120. Michael Grothaus, "Apple Pay Leads Mobile Payments with 12 Million Monthly Users," http://www.fastcompany.com/3057353/fast-feed/apple-pay-leads-mobile-payments-with-12-million-monthly-users.
121. Christina Najjar, "3 Dos & Don'ts for Using Venmo," http://www.refinery29.com/venmo-etiquette-dos-donts#slide.
122. Megan Marrs, "4 Examples of Killer Mobile Banking Apps," http://info.localytics.com/blog/4-examples-of-killer-mobile-banking-apps
123. https://venmo.com/about/product/.
124. "Do Cryptocurrencies Such as Bitcoin Have a Future?" http://www.wsj.com/articles/do-cryptocurrencies-such-as-bitcoin-have-a-future-1425269375.
125. Matthew E. May, "The 9 Elements of an Ironclad Business Model," https://www.americanexpress.com/us/small-business/openforum/articles/the-9-elements-of-an-ironclad-business-model/.
126. Kavi Guppta, "14 Essential Links for Working with the Business Model Canvas." http://blog.strategyzer.com/posts/2016/8/8/14-essential-links-for-working-with-the-business-model-canvas?utm_source=Master+Email+List&utm_campaign=fcf9d7f2ec-Newsletter_August_11_20168_11_2016&utm_medium=email&utm_term=0_fd75a09316-fcf9d7f2ec-336682621&mc_cid=fcf9d7f2ec&mc_eid=e5d2d99da7.

Chapter 4

The Direct Response and Database Foundations of Internet Marketing

LEARNING OBJECTIVES

By the time you complete this chapter, you will be able to:

1. Explain the ways in which the internet is a direct response medium.
2. Distinguish between acquisition, conversion, retention and value growth strategies.
3. Identify the elements of a direct response marketing strategy.
4. Explain the concepts of offer, customer lifetime value, and testing.
5. Explain the role of a customer database in the development and execution of internet marketing programs.
6. Describe a data warehouse and how it is used by marketers.
7. Explain the concept of big data.
8. Define data mining and explain why it is important in making marketing decisions.
9. Discuss how strategies can become more customer focused by using information-driven marketing.

Students reading this book may never take a course in direct marketing or direct response marketing but they might have a negative opinion of direct marketing derived from late night infomercials or receiving too much direct mail perceived as "junk." However, students need to know what direct marketing is because the concepts are so widely used in internet marketing. In fact, students may not realize that they have been studying direct marketing because the method has become the dominant form of marketing and is rapidly expunging other forms marketing, like mass media advertising. In fact, as the internet has developed, it has been recognized as the ultimate direct response medium.

Whatever this approach is called, direct marketing techniques have a significant impact on the economy of the United States and other countries. In a 2011–2012 report published by the DMA, the authors estimate that in 2011 direct marketing represented a total of 52 percent of advertising expenditure and represented about 8.7 percent of U.S. GDP and was a powerful source of employment growth.[1] By 2015, when direct marketing had evolved to include all data-driven marketing efforts (DDME), it was estimated that DDME contributed at least $202 billion to the economic output of the United States and employed about 966,000 individuals.[2]

To clarify, traditional direct response channels include direct mail, fax, phone, and television, with email marketing becoming a strong direct response channel as the internet developed. According to the DMA (formerly the Direct Marketing Association but now the Data–Driven Marketing Association), direct marketing required the following:

- An organized and planned system of contacts
- Using a variety of media
- Seeking to produce a lead or an order
- Developing and maintaining a database
- Measurable in cost and results
- Expandable with confidence

Thus, any system that is based in data analysis, has a clear objective and is measurable can be considered direct marketing or direct response. In the past, it was only direct marketers who had access to data and who could truly measure results. So a direct marketer, like Land's End, would send a catalog, see if the customer responded, and then send another catalog or offer based on the data. Now, many marketing channels and many types of marketers have access to data hence the evolution to data-driven marketing versus direct marketing.

Think about Amazon and all it knows about its customers through its data collection and analysis. If someone buys a book for left-handed golfers, they are sure to be shown other products for left-handed individuals through the process known as *collaborative filtering*. Amazon's vast store of data on its customers makes it easier to target customers and get them to purchase again. This targeting is done via the internet as a direct response mechanism, without traditional forms of direct response such a mail, phone fax, or direct response television.

THE INTERNET AS A DIRECT RESPONSE MEDIUM

interactive presenting choices based on user actions and allowing for response.

Many say the internet is the ultimate direct response medium. Why? Certainly it is an **interactive** channel, allowing for a two-way dialog between marketer and prospective customer using direct response techniques or social media. It is also a sales channel, with ecommerce growing at a rapid rate from the early days of the internet to the present. The internet is also a powerful branding medium, as we discuss in various chapters. However, it is difficult to do successful internet marketing without understanding the basics of direct marketing. This chapter will focus on direct response principles and execution on the web.

The internet presents powerful opportunities to the shrewd marketer. From the consumer's perspective, it permits a seamless purchase process. From the marketer's perspective, the internet allows fine-tuning of marketing programs in ways previously unimaginable. There are four important characteristics—call them the "four Is"—that describe the ways in which marketing efforts are powerfully affected by the capabilities of the internet (see Figure 4.1).

The internet, more than any other current medium, allows *interactivity*. In direct response mode, marketers can initiate two-way communications with prospective customers by sending offers to them and tracking their responses or by initiating direct communications by way of surveys, chat rooms, or other internet-enabled techniques. Interactivity allows for marketing to become a true conversation. Marketers listen to the customer and present choices based on that feedback, changing offers and communications based on an ongoing dialog.

All marketing activities on the web also have the potential to be **information** driven. Every move a website visitor makes, every action taken—from sending an email query to purchasing a product—is a potential piece of **data** for the marketing database that drives targeted promotional activities. The internet fosters *immediacy* in a variety of ways. Marketers can reply directly to customer queries, using human agents or automated systems. The internet makes it cost-efficient to construct offers that appeal to a specific market segment or to make offers that are seasonal or that are triggered by a particular event, say the NCAA basketball finals. Internet promotions can also be *involving*. Marketers are increasingly using streaming video, games, and other types of rich media in internet advertising to attract and involve prospective customers, also known as engagement. A good direct response offer incites prospects to take action—either to request information or to make a purchase on the spot.

information data that have been processed into more useful forms using techniques that range from simple summary formats to complex statistical routines.

data raw, unprocessed facts and numbers Data mining analytic process and specialized analytic tools used to extract meaning from very large data sets.

Some marketers have learned to combine brand marketing with direct response marketing. Procter & Gamble, best known for its use of mass media and mass distribution channels, was a user of direct response long before the advent of the internet. Figure 4.2a and Figure 4.2b shows one product in its brand family, the Swiffer. Initially developed as an easy method of cleaning floors with disposable replacement cloths, the Swiffer family of products has expanded to dusters and even mopping systems to handle harder cleaning jobs. While still using mass marketing techniques, P&G has expanded its list of promotional techniques to include free samples and coupons to build a mailing list of households that needed this product. Using this list, the company can promote directly to these households by mail, a targeted and cost-effective solution.

Presently, the web is now the hub of P&G's marketing strategy. It is still necessary to use traditional techniques—in this case, often coupon offers in Sunday supplements or shared coupon mailings—in order to drive new prospects to the web page and physical store. With newspaper readership declining, the internet is replacing print as the means of delivering coupons and discount offers. P&G's Swiffer webpage includes a Call-to-Action to download coupons for the products. Although there is an opportunity to buy online, the primary objectives of the site are twofold: brand development and driving traffic to retail stores. The home page also offers opportunities for engagement by including links to a social sharing site where customers post information about the "Swiffer Effect," that is, what they are now able to do and enjoy since they were able to clean the house more efficiently.

The Swiffer line of product is featured on the P&G Everyday page, which offers coupons and samples for many brands. Customers also have to register (or sign in) to

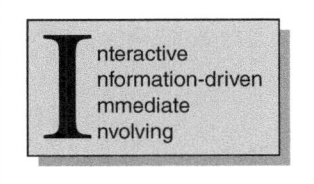

FIGURE 4.1

The Four Is of Internet Marketing

SOURCE: © Cengage Learning 2013.

92 Chapter 4 • The Direct Response and Database Foundations of Internet Marketing

FIGURE 4.2a

Swiffer Home Page

SOURCE: The Proctor & Gamble Company, http://swiffer.com/en-us

FIGURE 4.2b

Swiffer Coupon Offers on P&G Everyday

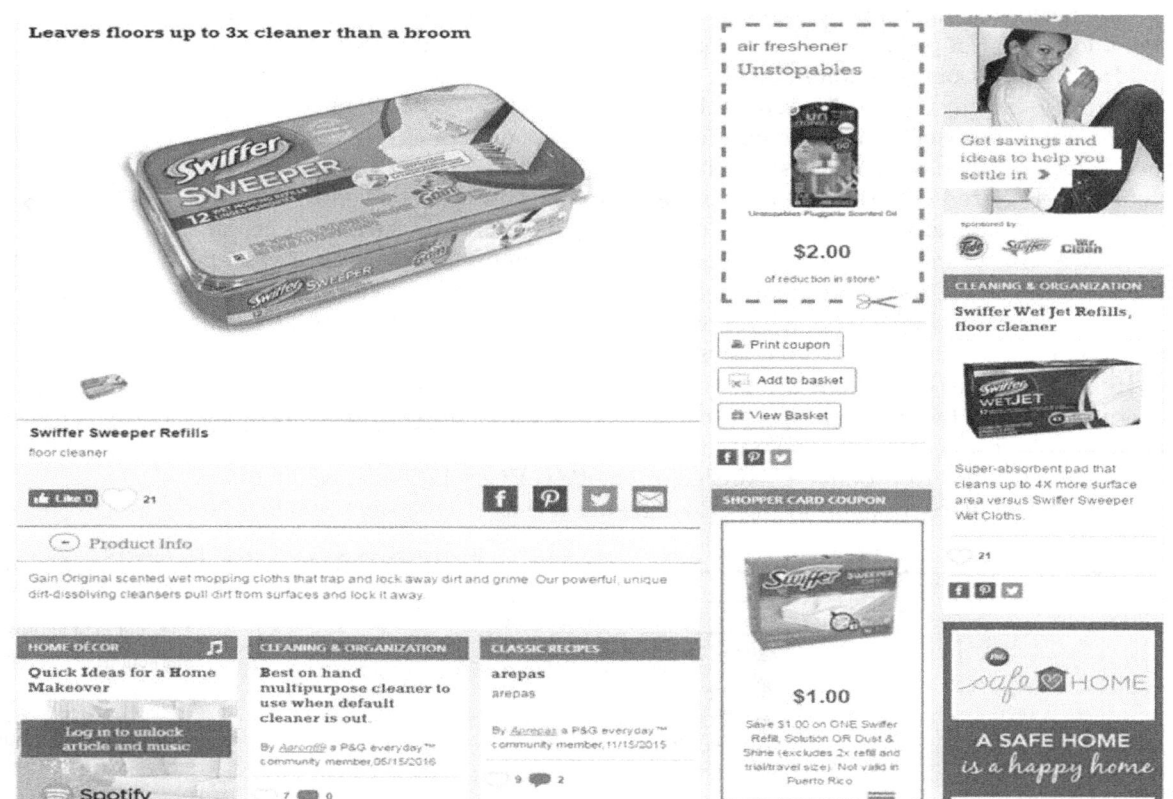

SOURCE: https://www.pgeveryday.com.

download a coupon (see Figure 4.2c). P&G offers value to the customer in return to their information, which will, of course, be used for continued promotion. Consider the fact that an email to a person who has already expressed interest in the product is a much more cost-efficient marketing approach than mailing coupons to undifferentiated audiences with the associated low redemption rate. P&G provides additional value by allowing consumers to load coupons directly to a grocery store shopping card for paperless shopping convenience. In addition to coupons, benefits of membership by registering on the page include newsletters with recipes and other tips, a community to share thoughts and the ability to tag and save favorite products and posts.

Whether the offers are for coupons, free samples, or contests, all are **sales promotions** with the objective of inducing consumers to take immediate action. One action is sign-up that provides an email address for further promotion. Each succeeding promotion invites action. Action taken—or not taken—provides additional information for the customer database, allowing the company to target more precisely its email promotions. P&G's ability to seamlessly integrate multiple channels of communications and sales to take full advantage of the cheap and effective communications abilities of the web is an important part of its ongoing global success. Recently, the company has streamlined its product portfolio to focus on key brands, an approach that, combined with knowledge of its customer, should bode well for the future.

This example illustrates that many of the time-honored tools of direct marketing can be transferred onto the web in fairly straightforward ways. It is critical for marketers to understand direct marketing methodology so they can develop and refine successful internet marketing programs.

sales promotions a marketing communication that encourages the customer to take specific action.

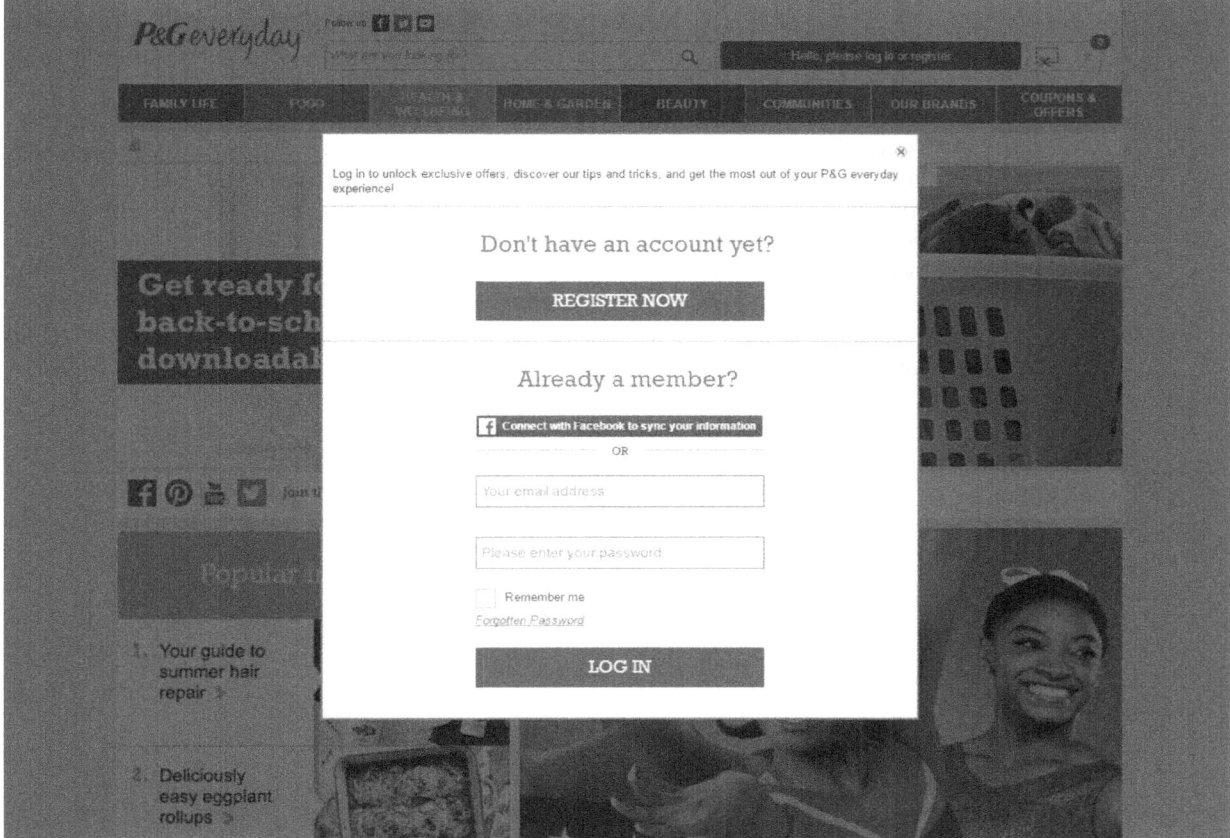

FIGURE 4.2c

The Sign Up Box

SOURCE: https://www.pgeveryday.com/?&utm_source=google&utm_medium=cpc&utm_campaign=PG+Everyday_Search_Desktop_Brand+Awareness&utm_term=p%26g%20everyday&utm_content=srHQEo6Jw_dc|pcrid|81084769400|elp%26g%20everyday&gclid=Cj0KEQjw5Ie8BRCJ9fHlr_bH24cBEiQAkoDQcRp-7klaualjbTWbFTXrk77q8w4Y6LYzwteqI8HrOa4aAjeU8P8HAQ.

In order to understand the importance of this methodology, we should look first at the basic types of direct marketing strategies. Then we will follow with specific techniques that form the basis of successful direct marketing programs.

GENERIC DIRECT MARKETING STRATEGIES[3]

Essentially, there are four types of direct marketing strategies that parallel a basic customer life cycle (see Figure 4.3). First, a customer must be attracted to the brand. This state represents trial of a product or a service. In the *acquisition* stage, the customer has made a single purchase, or perhaps engaged in free use as a result of a sample or a demonstration, but is not yet committed to the brand. The second stage is *conversion*, so called because in this step the prospect *converts* to customer. This stage may require one to three purchases, or enough to form a habitual purchasing pattern. The goal of the first two stages is *retention*, in which the customer continues to make purchases, a situation we might call behavioral loyalty. Even better, in this stage, the customer begins to exhibit loyalty in an attitudinal sense, which may result in behaviors ranging from rejecting competing offers to recommending the product to others. Finally, we continue to nurture the relationship and *grow the value* the customer represents for the brand. Marketers do this in a variety of ways, including increased engagement. Loyalty in this stage can deepen and transform into becoming a strong brand advocate.

Each of the basic strategies requires a different type of effort on the part of the marketer. *Acquisition* is roughly equivalent to the awareness stage of general advertising with an action component added. The step is focused on getting the customer to complete the desired action, whatever that might be. It requires a conscious attempt to get the attention of the prospective customer through media placement and creative execution and interest them in completing a desired action, such as a purchase, signing up for a newsletter or other specific request. Direct marketers often add an incentive to clinch product trial. We discuss customer acquisition on the internet in detail in Chapter 7.

The *conversion* step means getting the one-time purchaser to convert to being a customer. Product and service satisfaction is critical to achieving this goal. Customer contact, through media ranging from personal selling to newsletters, is often useful. Sequential incentives have also been used with good results. For example, a bank that wanted its customers to make more deposits at ATMs sent them a series of three checks, each of which could be used only with a series of ATM deposits. The first check was for $5, the second was for $3, and the third was for $1. The incentives not only were sequential, but decreased in value as the presumed habit formation was taking place. It is hard to prove habit formation, but in this case, it seems reasonable

FIGURE 4.3

The Basic Direct Response Strategies

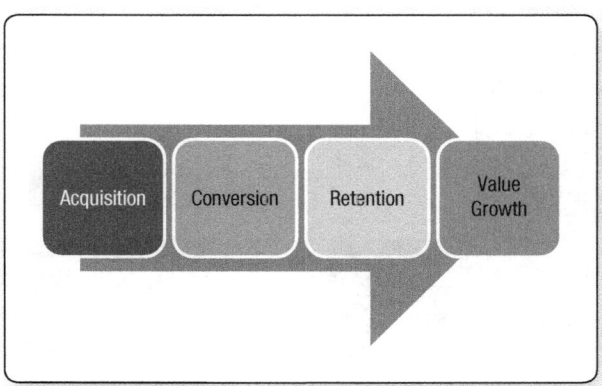

SOURCE: © Cengage Learning 2013

to assume that many customers, after three successful deposits, recognized that it is safe to make deposits through ATMs. This was a sensible, low-cost conversion program aimed at achieving a worthwhile business goal. Its only visible drawback was that the bank did not make good use of its customer database. It sent the checks to customers who regularly made ATM deposits as well as to those who never deposited through an ATM! We discuss conversion marketing in Chapter 13.

After conversion, it is important to retain customers in order to create the highest possible customer lifetime value (CLV). *Retention* is most often the result of adding value to the customer purchase and use experience and superior customer service. A planned program of customer contact, carried out at appropriate points in the purchase cycle, can also be a useful component of retention programs. We discuss retention in detail in Chapter 14.

After the customer is on board, we want them to continue to purchase but to also foster *growth* in terms of not only their overall purchases but also their commitment to our brand and product. In the *growth* stage we might involve the customer in our product line through engagement in social media, such as the sharing of brand stories in the P&G example explained previously. HubSpot says that the goal in this stage is to "delight" the customer and continue to interact with them.[4]

CRITICAL STRATEGY ELEMENTS

The marketing mix that supports direct marketing programs uses slightly different terminology from the 4Ps of traditional marketing. They are as follows:

- The offer—product, price, positioning, and any other product-related elements that make up the complete proposition presented to the prospective customer
- The list—the targeting vehicle
- The media used—with the understanding that any medium can be a direct response medium with the proper implementation
- The creative execution—which tends to play a secondary role in this action-oriented context
- The service and support—long recognized as a key element in this environment where the shopping experience and many sensory stimuli are not present

These elements are all required to implement any direct response program. It is, however, especially important to understand the role of the offer in developing internet marketing strategies.

Offers That Incite Action

The first rule of direct marketing is that the offer must include a *call to action*. Put another way, the offer must tell the viewer exactly what the marketer wants him or her to do and must make it easy for him or her to take that action. This sounds like a simple notion, but it is easy to let the call to action become buried in website pyrotechnics. It also happens all too frequently that the visitor is willing to take action but cannot find a response form, finds that the form does not work, or finds the questions on the form to be intrusive or simply too onerous. Action that is not taken when the impulse burns strong will probably never be taken.

A particular internet marketing program has one of three generic action objectives:

- *To get the visitor to remain on the site longer*, exploring more of what it has to offer. This is referred to as site "stickiness," and it has a direct bearing on the CPM (cost per thousand) rates that sites are able to charge for their advertising space. If the site does not have a transactional component, this may be a terminal objective. In the more common situation, in which sites are trying to achieve transactional as well as advertising revenue, it may be a first-stage objective with one of the other two objectives as the primary objective.

- *To cause visitors to request additional information about a product or service.* This is the conventional lead-generation objective long used in both B2C (business-to-consumer) and B2B (business-to-business) markets. When automobile manufacturers send to a carefully selected mailing list inviting consumers to come to their nearest dealership and test drive a new model, they are engaged in a multiple-step B2C lead generation and conversion program. When a software firm offers a free online demonstration of its new release, it is engaged in a B2B lead generation program. If the site requires the visitor to register and provide an email address in order to get the desired information, it is building an email list of people who have qualified themselves by indicating their interest in the product. These are clearly more qualified prospects than individuals who have the correct demographics with known or unknown buying habits that the car manufacturer or software developer obtains from a list rental firm.
- *To achieve a sale.* When the product and the purchasing situation are appropriate for a one-step sales effort, the actual sale becomes the objective.

Offers with Incentives

One of the key tools for achieving offers that compel action is the incentive. Different objectives call for different incentives. The hair care ad in Figure 4.4a offers a sample to back up its claim of increasing hair strength. Netflix, in Figure 4.4b, offers a free trial for nonmembers and access to a current film that members could access. In both these cases, the incentive is inherently related to the product itself: the mark of a good incentive. It might not be in good taste to offer an incentive with a cause-marketing appeal, but Toyota in Figure 4.4c does offer an informative video. Internet marketers have learned in recent years that free shipping is another compelling incentive. Time deadlines such as "Purchase by X to receive free shipping," often make offers more powerful.

Offers Tied to the Brand

Another tool that is a key part of the offer is the brand. In designing the offer, the marketer must consider how strong the brand is. The stronger the brand, the easier it is to get the prospect to accept a good offer. If the brand is unknown, it may be harder to compel action. A bigger incentive is one option. Another is to make use of another important tool—risk reduction. Risk is reduced when a strong guarantee is offered. Customer reviews and third-party endorsements are also useful. However, the best way to reduce potential buyers' perceived risk is to build a strong and trusted brand.

Much has been written about the issue of trust on the internet. There is no doubt that marketers need to build trust in the relationship between their company and brands and their prospective customers. In the longer term, trust is going to be achieved by the way the marketer does business—prompt and accurate fulfillment, satisfying returns and service practices, and guardianship of the customer's privacy. The immediate issue for the marketer without an established brand, however, is how to create a sense of confidence that will make the prospect feel reasonably comfortable about conducting a transaction. In the early days, Amazon recognized that, even though it was making Herculean efforts to establish its brand, many customers were still reluctant to give their credit card numbers over the web. It posted a prominent guarantee that promised to reimburse any losses customers incurred as a result of transmitting their credit card information to Amazon. This was appropriate for its time, but it has been replaced with a free shipping offer for many Amazon purchases. Today, trust is more of a concern than ever, especially with the expansion of the "Internet of Things (IoT)."[5] Products such as "Fitbit®" mean that consumers are trusting marketers with their vital statistics and there must be a level of trust that

(a)

(b)

(c)

SOURCE: Yahoo.

FIGURE 4.4
Offers with Calls to Action

this information will be kept securely and safely. This type of product requires a new, more detailed approach toward trust, privacy, and security by companies. However, there has not been a strong commitment to keeping customer data private by the "wearables" vendors in general, an issue that will no doubt receive more attention in the future.[6]

A good offer is designed to compel immediate response from the prospective customer and lays a strong foundation for future marketing efforts to a targeted, identified customer. To do this cost-effectively, the marketer must understand front-end versus back-end issues.

The Front End versus the Back End

front end all the marketing and promotional activities that occur before a sale is made.

back end activities that are required to satisfy the customer after a sale is made, including fulfillment and customer service.

Direct marketers have long used these terms although no precise definition exists. It is useful to think of the **front end** as being all the activities that are employed in making the sale. The **back end** is all the postsale activities, primarily order fulfillment and customer service. Marketers understand the front end well; that is their historical domain.

Internet marketers, however, have tended to ignore the importance of the back end. They have concentrated on what customers see—the acquisition activities on the front end—to the exclusion of what they do not see—the back-end functions. The problem with that perspective is that it is the back-end activities that create lasting customer satisfaction and lead to customer retention.

fulfillment the business processes necessary to receive, process, package, and ship orders to customers.

customer service solving customer problems.

It is also worth noting that this is an arena in which established direct marketing firms had an initial advantage over established bricks-and-mortar retailers. Established direct marketers have the infrastructure and the processes for effective order **fulfillment** and **customer service** in place. Established bricks-and-mortar businesses have infrastructure and processes that are precisely the opposite of what is needed on the web. Their back ends are designed to meet the needs of a series of stores, not to fulfill the orders of individual customers. As an internet-only retailer, Amazon understands the importance of quick and accurate fulfillment. It has dozens of fulfillment centers around the world, employing over 30,000 people.[7] This makes it possible for it to act as a contractor for firms that do not want to establish their own fulfillment operations.[8]

Many direct marketers have long concentrated on establishing superb customer service, recognizing the importance of this element in the absence of the store shopping experience. The extent to which many established retailers have slighted customer service functions is well recognized although an outstanding few like retailer Neiman-Marcus and cataloger L.L. Bean have systems that have transferred well into the web environment. Customer service must be experienced, but there is often visible evidence of commitment to providing exceptional service, as discussed in Chapter 16. (Figure 16.8 shows the customer service page of Canadian wireless carrier Koodo, which offers many types of and channels for customer self service and a strong promise that excellent service will be forthcoming.)

The line between customer service and customer experience is somewhat blurry, but it is clear that customer service is one element of overall customer experience. The luxury hotel chain Ritz-Carlton is famous for both. While home pages for its various properties emphasize the experience element, its corporate home page has a perspective on the pervasiveness of customer service culture at the Ritz. Like manufacturer P&G, they had learned their direct marketing lessons prior to the internet. The established brick-and-mortar retailer that has no experience in direct marketing will not only require a different infrastructure to be successful at internet marketing, but will also need a change of mindset in several important areas.

There are a number of other perspectives that are important in the direct marketing environment that must be adopted in order to achieve long-term success in the internet space. One is the concept of lifetime value of a customer.

THE ROLE AND IMPORTANCE OF CUSTOMER LIFETIME VALUE[9]

It has long been a truism that the role of marketing is to create a customer, not just a sale. That is true, but it has been an elusive goal for many mass media marketers. Being unable to identify their end customers, they could not interact directly with them and engage in specific attempts to retain them and to increase their long-term value. This represents another direct marketing technique that is now available to all marketers who make informed use of their internet marketing activities.

CLV (customer lifetime value) (customer lifetime value) the net present value of a future stream of net revenue from an identified customer.

The basic idea of **CLV (customer lifetime value)** is that, if the marketer understands what it costs to acquire, maintain, and service a customer, then he can make a reasoned decision about how much to spend to market to that customer. The underlying model is simple:

$$\text{Less}: \frac{\text{Net Customer Revenues Cost of goods sold}}{\text{Gross margin}}$$

$$\text{Less}: \frac{\text{Cost of servicing}}{\text{Customer Revenue}}$$

$$\text{Times}: \frac{\text{Cost of capital}}{\text{Net present value of customer revenue stream}}$$

The calculation takes into account the amount of time the customer is likely to persist with the firm. It usually takes as much as three years of data to calculate CLV with a reasonable degree of accuracy. After five years, the discount for the cost of capital becomes so high that future revenue streams have little value, so three to five years is usually satisfactory. Notice that data must be collected for as much as three years in order to begin developing CLV and marketing programs based on it.

Professors Venkatesan and Kumar use a graphic (see Figure 4.5) that helps make the issues clear.[10] Characteristics of the customer that include switching cost,

FIGURE 4.5

A Conceptual Framework for Measuring and Using CLV

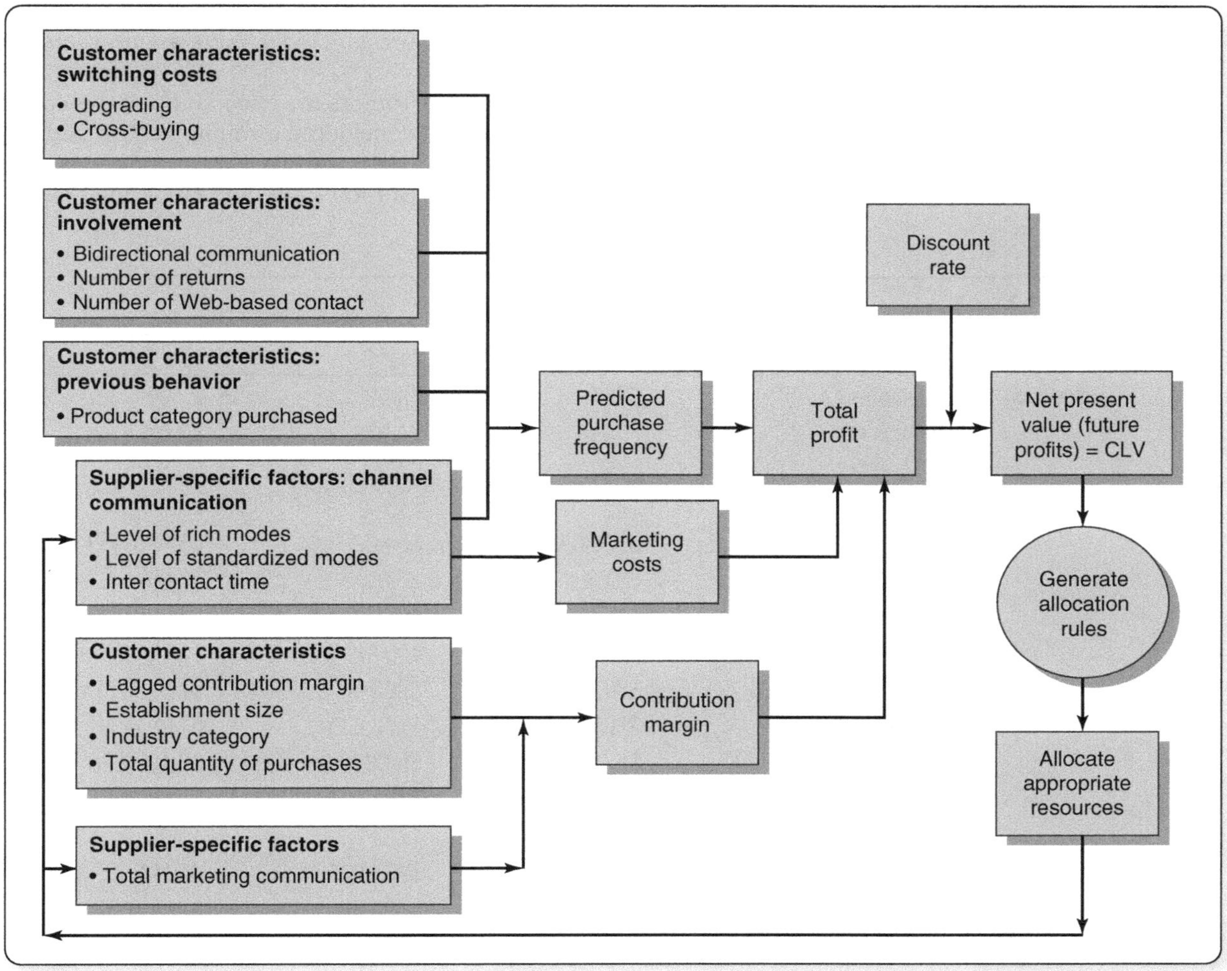

SOURCE: Adapted from Rajkumar Venkatesan and V. Kumar, "A Customer Lifetime Value Framework for Customer Selection and Resource Allocation Strategy," *Journal of Marketing*, 68, 2004, p. 110.

involvement with the product category or brand, and the customer's purchase history are used to predict his future purchasing frequency and the profit obtained from it. The cost of communicating with the customer determines marketing costs. The contribution margin from each customer is determined and the amount of communications with the customer across all channels is taken into account. The profit from the customer is based on the frequency of purchasing at a particular contribution margin (revenue times contribution percent) less the costs of marketing to the customer. The discount rate is applied and the NPV of a future stream of profits—CLV—is computed. Then the marketer determines actions that can be taken to increase CLV.

A CLV Example

The implementation is less straightforward than what the basic model may suggest. There are a number of questions even after the necessary customer-level data has been confirmed. What is the typical life span of a customer in this particular situation? What is the time period required to achieve a reasonable level of accuracy in predicting purchase frequency and contribution margin across multiple purchases in multiple time periods? Even identifying the relevant revenues and costs is not as easy as it sounds.[11] The following example will help to explain the concept and its application.

Consultant Arthur Hughes[12] gives an example that is based on the experience of the Safeway supermarket chain. Supermarkets have notoriously thin gross margins, and Safeway was concerned that it spends its scarce promotional resources in the most effective way. It turned to a CLV analysis for guidance. Table 4.1 presents the first stage of that analysis.

Assume that the firm acquires 5,000 new customers in year 1 and that the goal is to track their value over three years, generally considered a minimum for calculating customer value. These customers make 0.64 visits per week, purchasing an average of $33 each trip. Direct costs are 83 percent of total sales, and labor and benefits

TABLE 4-1 Baseline Consumer Lifetime Value Calculation

Lifetime Value Before New Programs

	Year 1	Year 2	Year 3
Customers	5,000	3,500	2,590
Retention rate	70.0%	74.0%	80.0%
Visits/week	0.64	0.69	0.78
Average basket	$33	$45	$55
Total sales	$5,280,000	$5,433,750	$5,555,550
Cost percentage	83.0%	80.0%	79.0%
Direct costs	$4,382,400	$4,347,000	$4,388,885
Labor + benefits 11%	$580,800	$597,713	$611,111
Card program $16, $8	$80,000	$28,000	$20,720
Advertising 2%	$105,600	$108,675	$111,111
Total costs	$5,148,800	$5,081,388	$5,131,826
Gross profit	$131,200	$352,363	$423,724
Discount rate	1.00	1.20	1.44
NPV profit	$131,200	$293,635	$294,253
Cumulative NPV profit	$131,200	$424,835	$719,088
Lifetime value	$26.24	$84.97	$143.82

SOURCE: Arthur Middleton Hughes, "Building Successful Retail Strategies Using Customer Lifetime Value," Database Marketing Institute, September 7, 2011 (http://www.dbmarketing.com/articles/Art181.htm).

for marketing personnel are another 11 percent. Safeway spends $16 on a shopper loyalty card program for each customer in the first year and $8 in succeeding years. Advertising is 2 percent of total sales. The calculations are as follows:

Total sales	$5,280,000
Less: Total costs	$5,148,800
Equals: Gross profit	$131,200
Times: Discount rate	1.0
NPV of first year revenue	$131,200
Lifetime value of a customer in year 1	$26.24

The item that needs particular attention—both in terms of computation and of meaning—is the discount rate. A discount rate is necessary because a future stream of revenue is worth less than revenue received in the current year. Consequently, in year 1, the discount rate is 1.0. For subsequent years, the rate is calculated using the formula

$$D+(1+i)^n$$

Where D is the discount rate, i is the current interest rate plus a risk factor, and n is the number of years that will elapse before the revenue is realized. When the gross profit for any given year is multiplied by the discount rate for that year, the result is the **net present value (NPV)** of the gross profit for that specific year.

Looking back at the baseline table, the retention rate of these customers is 70 percent in the first year. This means that, of the 5,000 customers acquired in the first year, 3,500 will persist as customers into year 2. As presumably satisfied customers, they will visit the store somewhat more frequently, buy a bit more, and cost a bit less to serve. Following through to the end of year 2, the value of an original customer in year 2 is $84.97 (the cumulative NPV of the profit stream, $424,835, divided by 5,000). Using the same reasoning, the customer value is $143.82 when a customer acquired in year 1 persists to year 3.

The first step in working with CLV is usually to identify additional marketing efforts that can be used to increase customer value. Activities that come under this heading include upselling and cross-selling. Upselling means activities designed to persuade customers to buy more, either in volume or in higher-priced items or both. Cross-selling refers to programs that attempt to sell other products to the customer; for example, a bank that markets certificates of deposit (CDs) to high-value checking account customers. This type of program is, in fact, particularly attractive in industries such as financial services where customers frequently have a number of financial products scattered among the offerings of many financial services providers. The attractiveness of persuading customers to consolidate their holdings with a single provider is obvious. This phenomenon has come to be known as "share of wallet" in the financial services industry or, more generally, "share of customer." Many marketers would argue that this is a better metric of marketing success than the more commonly used "share of market." Other types of retailers such as supermarkets are also testing programs to increase customer value.

Returning to Arthur Hughes's example, he points out that Safeway had determined that it could spend a maximum of $2 per customer per month on customer relationship management. That is not a great deal of money, and it is imperative that it be used wisely. Safeway, for example, tried giving targeted customers an ice cream cone on their birthdays and measured incremental sales that resulted from that trip to the store. Retailers have also experimented with programs including:

- Customer-specific pricing, where members get cheaper prices on certain items
- Rewards for larger total purchases
- Rewards for frequency of purchase
- Rewards for shopping on slow days
- Personal recognition and relationship programs

net present value (NPV) current value of a discounted stream of future revenues personalization.

What if the company took the major step of cutting its advertising budget in order to divert money to the customer relationship program? In Table 4.2, Hughes presents some possible results.

Assume that the company has cut advertising to 1 percent from the 2 percent in Table 4.1. That money is shown in the "Customer specific marketing" line in Table 4.2. All the rest of the cost and CLV calculations are the same. Notice, however, that the top portion of the table changes. In year 1, the retention rate goes from 70 percent to 75 percent. Visits per week increase from 0.64 to 0.68. The average basket (sale) increases from $33 to $38. As a result of the increase in number of visits per week and average sale, the CLV for year 1 goes from $26.24 to $32.96. Because the retention rate has gone up, the company starts year 2 with 3,750 customers instead of 3,500. This increases the revenue stream. Visits per week and average sales go up as compared to year 2 without the targeted programs. The same reasoning follows for year 3. At the end of year 3, the NPV of the net revenue stream is $934,183. Divided by 5,000—the original cohort of customers who have now been tracked through three years—the CLV is $186.84.

Table 4.3 shows the increase in CLV that results from the targeted programs. Since the cost of the targeted programs came out of the amount previously budgeted for advertising, there is no increase in marketing cost. The gain is therefore incremental profit.

TABLE 4-2 Increase in Customer Value Using Targeted Programs

Lifetime Value Before New Programs

	Year 1	Year 2	Year 3
Customers	5,000	3,750	2,963
Retention rate	75.0%	79.0%	85.0%
Visits/week	0.68	0.73	0.82
Average basket	$38	$50	$61
Total sales	$6,120,000	$6,843,750	$7,409,213
Cost percentage	83.0%	80.0%	79.0%
Direct costs	$5,079,600	$5,475,000	$5,853,278
Labor + benefits 11%	$673,200	$752,813	$815,013
Card program $16, $8	$80,000	$30,000	$23,700
Customer-specific marketing	$61,200	$66,438	$74,092
Advertising 1%	$61,200	$66,438	$74,092
Total costs	$5,955,200	$6,394,688	$6,840,176
Gross profit	$164,800	$449,063	$569,037
Discount rate	1.00	1.20	1.44
NPV profit	$164,800	$374,219	$395,165
Cumulative NPV profit	$164,800	$539,019	$934,183
Lifetime value	$32.96	$107.80	$186.84

SOURCE: Arthur Middleton Hughes, "Building Successful Retail Strategies Using Customer Lifetime Value," Database Marketing Institute, September 7, 2011 (http://www.dbmarketing.com/articles/Art181.htm).

TABLE 4-3 Gain in Customer Value from Using Targeted Programs

Effect of Adoption of New Programs

New lifetime value (CLV)	$32.96	$107.80	$186.84
Previous lifetime value (CLV)	$26.24	$84.97	$143.82
Gain	$6.72	$22.83	$43.02

SOURCE: Arthur Middleton Hughes, "Building Successful Retail Strategies Using Customer Lifetime Value," Database Marketing Institute, September 7, 2011 (http://www.dbmarketing.com/articles/Art181.htm).

Uses of CLV

The Safeway case study above is simple compared to the reality of customers being acquired and leaving at various times, a multiplicity of marketing programs occurring at the same time or in sequence, and the activities of competitors, all of which may have important effects on variables like retention rates. It also assumes that all customers are equally desirable prospects for targeted programs. That is usually not true. Banks, for example, sometimes find that their highest value customers are not desirable targets for additional marketing effort because they are already giving the bank as much of their business as they are likely to give. At the other end of the scale, many enterprises find that their lowest value customers are unlikely to upgrade enough to make the marketing expenditures worthwhile. An overriding issue becomes, "How much should I spend to acquire customers who fit a certain profile?"

The acquisition problem is commonly stated as, "Who are my best customers and how can I acquire more like them?" To that we should add, "And how much should I spend on the acquisition?" Identifying best customers is another time-honored direct marketing technique based on a simple RFM (recency × frequency × monetary value) model. This model does a good job of segmenting a customer database according to value in many industry sectors.[13] The issue of acquiring more customers like the best ones can be as simple, in the traditional direct marketing environment, as renting lists with similar characteristics and mailing to them. As we build databases of customer activities on the internet, the same principles will apply. To speed the process of acquiring many years of customer data, marketers have increasingly turned to predictive modeling to profile the best potential customers and to estimate a suitable acquisition cost target. We will give a brief introduction to predictive modeling in the last part of this chapter.

Many CLV-based marketing approaches are directly transferable onto the web where their value is often magnified. What if, based on available data and models, the marketer could know within seconds what the prospective value of a site visitor is and consequently could generate an offer that is both optimally cost-effective and attractive to the prospect—all done on the fly, so quickly that the viewer is unaware of the background mechanics? In fact, this is exactly what happens when a customer applies for a credit card online.

On the other hand, CLV analysis will invariably show some customers to be unprofitable. That presents two basic options. If additional analysis indicates that there are one or more sub-segments that have the potential to become profitable, marketing programs should be developed with this objective. If there are, as is often the case, other sub-segments that appear to have little probability of becoming profitable, one of two actions must be taken. The first is to cut costs—either by cutting the costs of acquiring customers in this segment or by reducing costs to serve them. For example, these customers may be offered only self-service options via telephone or web, with personal service options reserved for profitable customer segments.

Some of these applications raise the specter of overstepping the bounds of customer privacy, a subject that is covered in detail in Chapter 15. As long as we can manage issues of customer privacy, however, strategies based on knowledge and enhancement of CLV provide exciting prospects for internet marketers. This also includes the social net, where marketers are struggling to quantify the return on investment of their social media marketing investment. One aspect of that is trying to understand the value of a customer on a specific platform. Because of its dominance of the social media space, there is great interest in Facebook, which has led to a recent assessment of the value of a Facebook customer (see Figure 4.6).

The survey by Syncapse found that across the 20 consumer brands studied:

- Facebook fans spend an average of $71.84 more on the brand than nonfans.
- They are 28 percent more likely to continue using the brand than nonfans.

FIGURE 4.6
The Estimated Value of a Facebook Fan

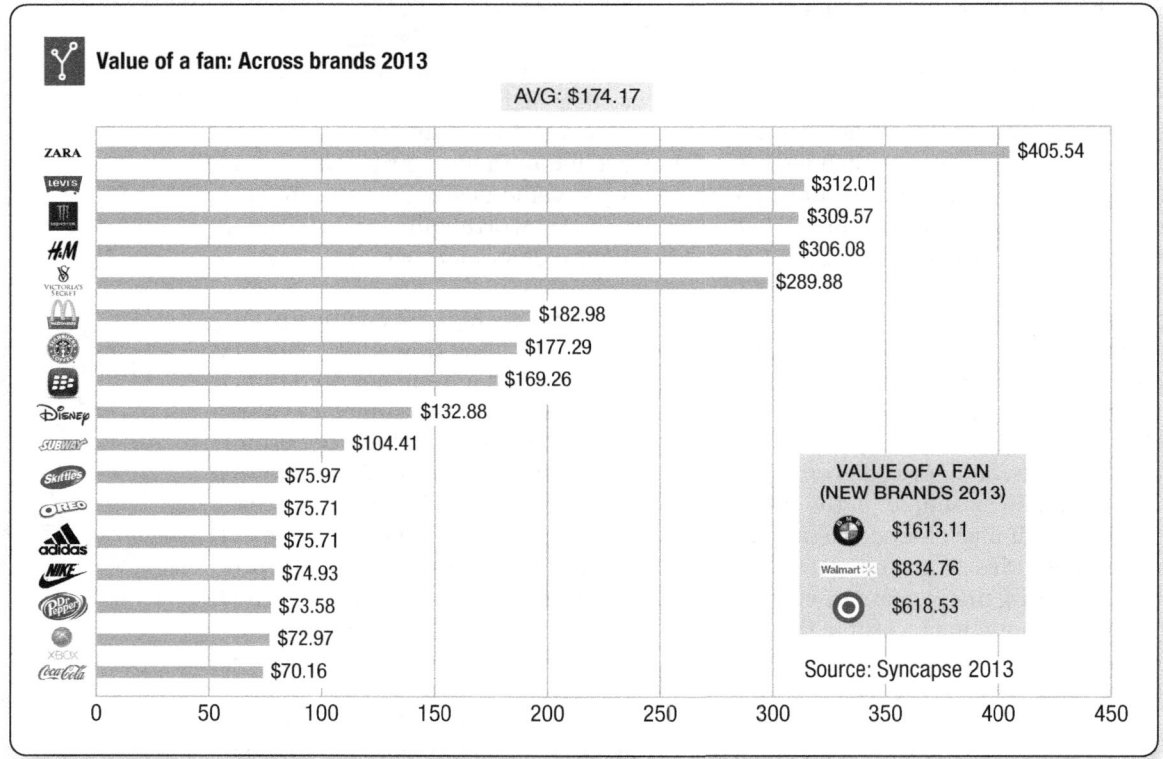

SOURCE: "The Value of a Facebook Fan: An Empirical Review," p. 14, June 2010, Syncapse Corporation (www.syncapse.com). Reprinted with permission.

- They are 41 percent more likely to recommend a fanned product than are nonfans.
- Fans were more likely to report favorable attitudes toward the brand than were nonfans.

The model also includes the value of "earned media," essentially favorable commentary by customers, a social media concept that is discussed in Chapter 9. When these five model elements were quantified, Syncapse estimated the average value of a Facebook fan to be $136.38 in 2010. Nike had the highest "best fan" value of all brands studied at $380.16. Oreo cookies had the lowest "average fan" value at $60.60.[14] That is a striking example of how the difference in product margins affects customer value. It also suggests that some people eat a lot of Oreo cookies! One can be confident that there will be many other attempts to quantify the value of customers based on their use of social networks. That is an important application of CLV concepts that is in its infancy.

The company repeated its study in 2013 and found that the average value had increased 28 percent to $174.17. The increase, the company says, is driven by the fact that fans want to be super customers. Fans spend more money, engage more, advocate more, and are more loyal than nonfans. As in 2010, there were disparities among the brands, with those brands having a higher retail prices or category purchases having a higher fan value.

The almost limitless marketing options presented by this type of information-based marketing strategy development and execution[15] call into play another important direct marketing technique, that of testing.

TESTING DIRECT RESPONSE PROGRAMS

Testing in a timely and statistically valid manner is another advantage that direct marketing has traditionally held over mass media marketing. Direct marketers are able to track each response and therefore to know whether programs are performing satisfactorily. In addition, some direct response media, mail for example, have lent themselves well to controlled testing of different offers or different creative executions. On a broader scale, offer placement in different media can also be tested. Again, this set of direct marketing tools is directly transferable to the internet space, which offers even greater potential for evaluating and refining marketing efforts on a timely basis.

Testing statistical process by which alternative marketing approaches are compared and the best is selected.

In an offline campaign, a fortunate marketer can create and launch a new campaign in eight to ten weeks. Orders begin to trickle in and maybe 80 percent of orders are in 90 days later. So a baseline is established five to six months after the idea is crystallized. To improve the baseline performance, one can try to improve the quality of the list to determine if the offer was effective. Perhaps the company can improve the order process. Companies can systematically test variables to determine critical paths, but it's hard, costly, and time consuming. In the offline world, it's basically drop the mail and hope for the best.

Now consider an email marketing campaign such as those we will discuss in more detail in Chapter 9. There's not that much left to chance. Did the message get delivered? How many opened it? Which version of the email was most effective? Did those graphics in the email help or hurt? Once those who opened the email got to your site, did they go past the home page? Where else did they go? How long were they there?

In the online world, such as email, marketers receive such answers immediately, and if the test is not meeting expectations, marketers can drop it or perform major surgery on it before doing the company any real economic damage.[16]

The simplest kind of direct marketing test is an **A/B split**. There are two key aspects of an A/B split test:

A/B split presenting one offer, creative execution, and so forth to one group of customers or prospects and another version of the same offer, creative execution, and so on to another group of customers.

1. *Change only one element.* That can be a specific element of the promotion like an offer—"15% Off" versus "Free Shipping," for example. Or it can be a promotion that is completely different in some major respect—the creative execution, for example. If only one element is changed, any differences in response can be attributed to that element and that element only.
2. *Test the big things.* Test only changes that are likely to make a substantial and profitable difference in response to the promotion.

There are also two different ways of executing the test. The classic direct marketing test pits a new (test) version against a control, which would be the promotion that has worked best in the past. It is also possible to test two versions, neither of which has been used before.

In the traditional print environment—mail or magazines, for example— testing requires different physical versions of the direct mail piece or magazine ad. Although good direct marketers tested consistently, it was slow and cumbersome compared to testing on the internet where changes to a promotion can be made with a few mouse clicks. The ease and speed of testing on the internet encouraged products that automated new test versions and placement in online media or on the website. An early entrant into this space was a firm called Offermatica; think about the name! It offered an automated approach to testing that was an important component of overall marketing optimization. Offermatica was purchased by Omniture, a metrics firm.

Omniture was subsequently purchased by Adobe, whose products are familiar to anyone who has ever read a PDF file. Adobe had been using the Omniture product line in its own testing prior to acquiring the company. It was the case of "liking the products so much we purchased the company." It was also a case of understanding that testing is essential to internet marketing success.

Figure 4.7 shows two homepage promotions for Adobe's Lightroom product—software for digital image editing. Figure 4.7 Recipe A shows the control for this test and Figure 4.7 Recipe B shows the new creative execution (the test). The fact that Recipe A is specified as the control for this test indicates that it had been successfully used in the past. However, the product managers at Adobe thought it could be improved.

Adobe wanted to test an updated page template with a shorter hero (main) image on the page and smaller Learning/Help thumbnails in order to move content higher on the page above the fold, as well as wanting to test black versus white backgrounds. Their hypothesis was that these changes would make it more likely that visitors would find what they were looking for and therefore be less likely to abandon the page. You can see (Recipe B) that the slightly smaller hero image and smaller supporting images helped condense the page, allowing visitors to consume the content on the homepage at a greater rate without scrolling down or instead, abandoning the page.

The test execution produced a revenue per visitor 15.82 percent higher and an average order value 13.3 percent higher than that achieved by the control version. Notice the metrics that were chosen to measure success. It was not a simple response measure like click-throughs. It was a measure of actual revenue by the number of visitors to the page, a comparison of success to the marketing effort required to achieve it. We will return frequently to the issue of selecting the most appropriate and powerful metric to measure internet marketing success throughout the text.

The statistical question is whether the 15.82 percent improvement is a statistically significant difference over the control. It is a notable improvement and the number of visitors to the page over the duration of the test is probably large, so the likelihood that it is statistically significant is high. In any event, the difference is enough that Adobe planned a follow-up test before making the decision to use only the winning page (Recipe B). This is also standard direct marketing procedure; do not make important decisions on the basis of a single test.

Notice that this is precisely the statistical testing process taught in basic statistics courses. As this example suggests, there are now software packages that have testing options, alternative marketer objectives, and statistical decision making built in. Another popular approach to testing is *multi-variable testing*, where multiple variables are tested simultaneously. This approach can be fraught with peril. It is often difficult to find the right combination of variables; however, when the right combination is found, the results can be rewarding.

Direct marketing testing, whether it uses a simple A/B split or a complex experimental design, is both a marketing and a statistical process. Table 4.4 summarizes the marketing approach. Paralleling the marketing activities is a set of statistical activities—establishing hypotheses, choosing the significance level, computing the sample size, and specifying the decision rule—that the student recognizes as the classical hypothesis testing process from statistics and marketing research courses. Both the marketing and the statistical activities are necessary in order to have a valid test on which to base decisions.

Some marketers test some variable on every marketing program they run. *Fast Company* magazine profiled the credit card issuer Capital One and described, "Its mission: Deliver the right product, at the right price, to the right customer, at the right time. Its method: Never stop testing, learning, or innovating."[17] Others test only when a marketing problem is evident. Whatever the corporate policy on testing, it is a powerful tool to show marketers what actually works best in a natural setting.[18]

FIGURE 4.7
A/B Split Test of Adobe Lightroom Home Page Promotion Versions

SOURCE: Courtesy of Adobe. Used with permission.

TABLE 4-4
The Testing Process
	Reasons for Conducting a Test
	• Standard practice ("We test all marketing programs.")
	• Strategy questions ("Which subset of lapsed customers can be reactivated?")
	• Tactical questions ("Which incentive works best with this offer?")
	Design the Test
	• What marketing variables to test (New offer, different creative execution, new list, or others.)
	• Type of test (Against control, A/B split, complex experimental design.)
	• Sample (Entire population or random sample; sample size.)
	Establish Test Metrics
	• Test criterion (variable on which the test is judged)
	• Decision rule (the values of the variable on which the decision will be based)
	• Cutoff date
	• Ranges for success/failure/continued testing
	• Timing and nature of reporting (online, on demand, and formal report)
	Execute and Monitor the Test
	• Ensure that test is conducted according to specifications.
	• Record results.
	• Monitor competitive/environmental activity that might affect results.
	• Record any deviations from testing plan.
	Analyze and Report Test Results
	• Which version performed best?
	• Was the difference
	   • Statistically significant?
	   • At an acceptable level of risk?
	Make Marketing Decisions
	• What changes, if any, should we make to our marketing efforts?
	• Should we repeat the test? Should we test new variables?

SOURCE: A statistical approach to marketing testing is described by Paul Berger in a chapter from *Direct Marketing Management* at http://marylouroberts.info/images/dir.mark.man.ch10.pdf.

A MORE COMPLEX ONLINE TEST

In the A/B split example, we pointed out that, in order to have a valid test, only one element of the promotion can be changed. In that case, it was the featured product offer.

Figure 4.8a shows the bare bones of another example, a test conducted by Marketing Experiments for an unidentified client. It represents another traditional direct marketing type of test. In this case, three different "treatments" are compared to a "control" in the classic experimental protocol covered in marketing research courses. In the case of marketing experimentation, the control treatment is the promotion that has been most successful in the past—implying ongoing testing. It is also a careful approach in which the historically most successful promotion (the control) is not discarded until something clearly better (i.e., a statistically significant better experimental treatment) is found.

The other difference from the simple A/B split is that the entire promotion, or major elements of the control promotion, can be revised. In this case, there were three experimental treatments. Treatment 1 was almost entirely text, as opposed to the control, which has prominent graphical elements. Treatment 2 has similar text but more graphics. Treatment 3 has the same elements, but smaller graphics.

FIGURE 4.8
Email Experiment with Control and Three Experimental Treatments

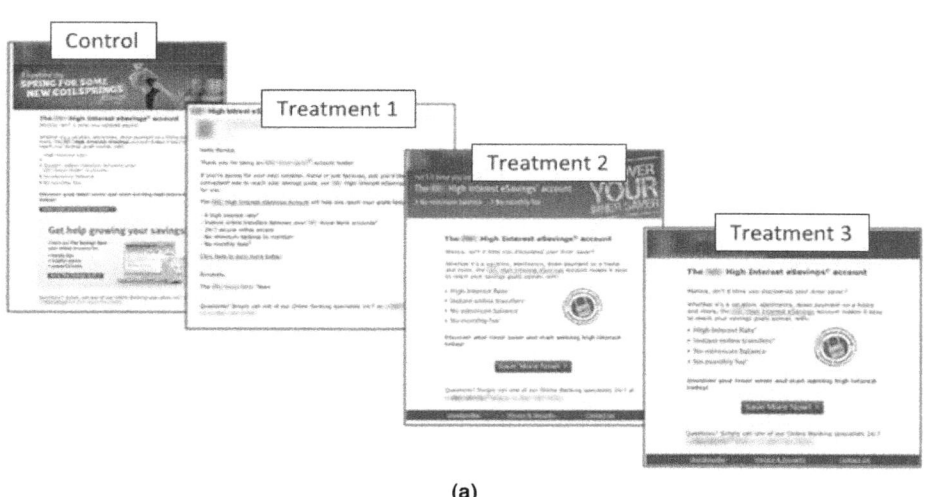

(a)

Experiment: Results

42% Increase in Clickthrough
Treatment 1 (copy rich) outperformed the control by 42.34%

Email		
Email	CTR	Rel. Diff.
C – Control email	0.51%	
T1 – Copy-rich email	**0.73%**	**42.34%**
T2 – Single CTA (w/ header)	0.63%	24.12%
T3 – Single CA (w/o header)	0.65%	26.27%

(b)

SOURCE: Marketing Experiments, http://www.marketingexperiments.com/email-marketing-strategy/the-five-best-ways-to-optimize-email-response-part-3.html.

Figure 4.8b shows that all three experimental treatments (different emails) performed better than the control. The copy is simpler and more "chunked," so that may be one explanation. However, and be honest, would you have guessed that the straightforward and not visually appealing Treatment 1 would have performed substantially better than the treatments with graphics? While many of us would not have assumed so, the hypothesis may be that there is less distraction in the text-only email, which leads to a higher click-through rate. Direct marketers would add that if you really do not believe the results, repeat the test. In the online environment, repeat testing is quick and inexpensive, and it should usually be done before the marketer adopts a "new control" on the basis of one test to replace one that has performed well over time.

Traditional direct marketers would also make a strong case for experimentation over marketing research to identify most successful promotional approaches. Testing permits the marketer to find out what people actually do when faced with an offer or another type of communication. Marketing research has to rely on what people say they will do. Online testing can be set up quickly by experienced personnel, and the conduct of the test is also quick, even compared to online marketing research.[19]

No discussion of online testing would be complete without a mention of website optimization programs. These services use the principles just described to allow marketers to develop tests of web pages to improve their performance. For example, the company Optimizely (https://www.optimizely.com/testing/) has software that allows marketers to test various images and offers across all types of platforms, including mobile devices and tablets. Google also offers this capability in Google Analytics Content Experiments. The goal of all of these tools is to increase conversion rates on whatever platform is used.

Testing various direct response options is one way in which traditional direct marketing has carried over onto the internet. Far and away, the most important transplant, however, is the use of a customer database. From the beginning, this text has pointed out that every mouse click on the internet represents a possible data point. Only marketers who capture and use this data to make better marketing decisions can tap the full power of the interactive web.

THE DATABASE IMPERATIVE

The distinctive tools and techniques of direct marketing all have a great deal to offer in the interactive marketing setting created by the internet. The foundations of virtually all the capabilities that differentiate direct response marketing from mass media marketing reside in the marketing **database**. It is the repository of all customer-related knowledge and the source of data for analytical activities. It is the knowledge resource that to some extent can compensate for the churn of human resources in many contemporary firms.

database set of files (data, video, images, etc.) organized in a way that permits a computer program to quickly select any desired piece of content.

Correctly conceptualized, however, it is not "the marketing database." When marketers refer to "the marketing database," they are generally referring to the customer database. However, there are actually numerous databases that should all be linked through some type of a central repository such as a data warehouse so information can be provided on demand to decision makers and operational personnel. Figure 4.9 provides a hypothetical mapping of a typical marketing database system indicating the nature of the data in each and its primary source.

From the marketer's viewpoint, the data warehouse, which contains multiple individual databases, can be conceptualized as having four basic components. The marketing management databases drive marketing programs, and the marketing support databases provide additional data that are important for decision-making purposes. Other functional areas of the business supply databases that are crucial to the functioning of marketing programs and customer service. These include the order-processing database and the inventory database, both of which are essential to good customer service. The sales force management and project databases also provide important marketing-related information. Finally, externally purchased or linked databases provide additional valuable data. This includes commercial scanner databases that track product movement. There are numerous database products that marketers can overlay onto the customer database to increase its predictive power. The Prizm geodemographic products of Nielsen's Claritas division are a good example of this type of external data product. There are a variety of other databases available from third parties that are important information resources to specific industry sectors. For example, the data of the large credit bureaus are used in proprietary credit scoring models by banks and other credit issuers.

Some marketers may require fewer databases for effective decision making and operations, but in reality, a large company may have dozens of databases that need to be integrated to give a full view of the customer. And the technological reality is

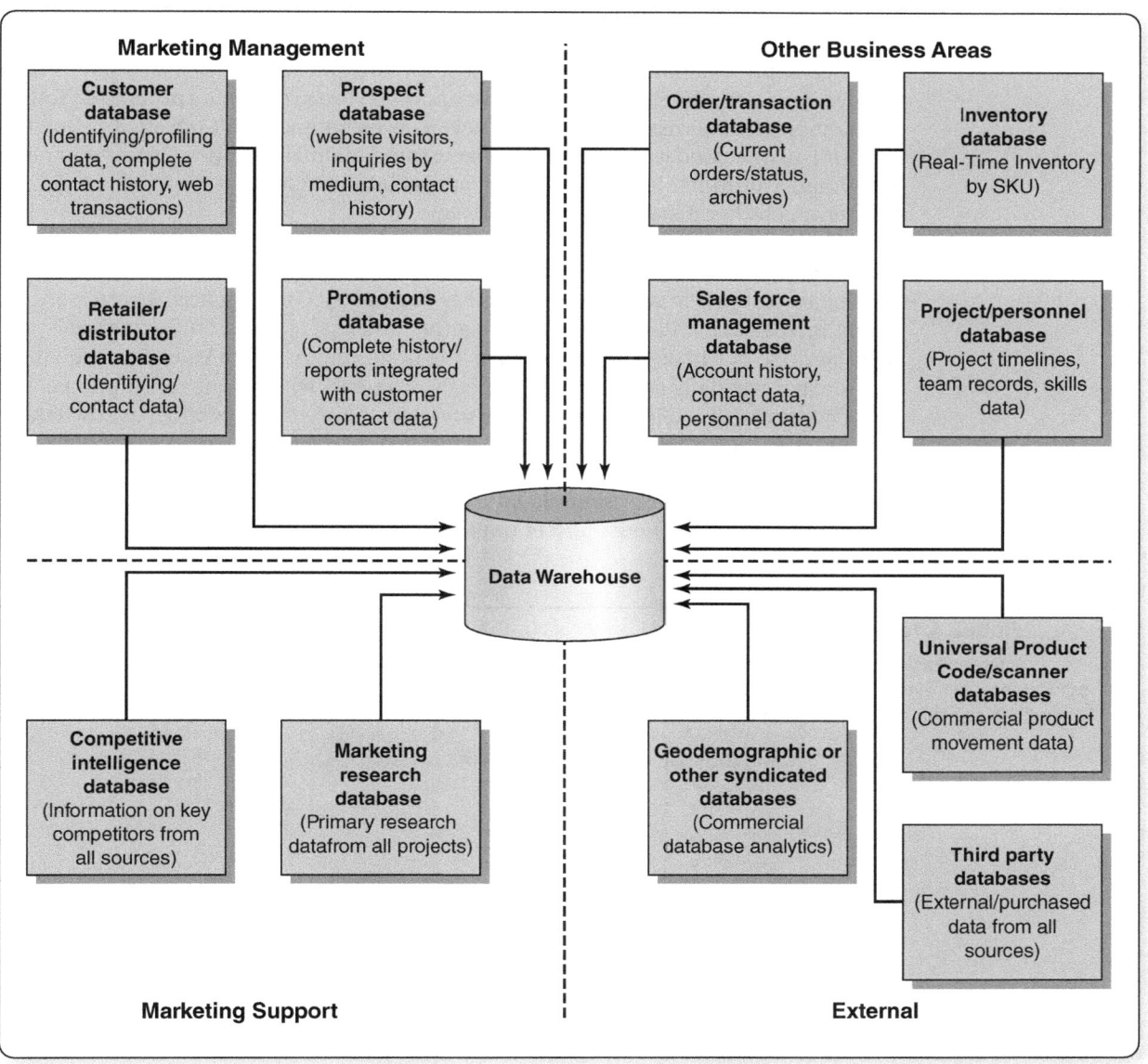

FIGURE 4.9
Marketing Database System

SOURCE: © Cengage Learning 2013.

that the individual databases are often not neatly interconnected through a data warehouse. Instead, they are sitting on various desktops, connected to one individual or unit, and essentially acting as isolated islands of information. If this is the situation, marketers will be unable to make effective use of the information resource for marketing or customer service.

The difficulty of integrating many databases that have a variety of data structures and that reside on a variety of different platforms can hardly be understated. However, integrating the databases into a data warehouse is a technical task. The job of the marketer is to determine what data need to be in the central repository and to champion its creation. In order to do this, the marketer must ask what accessible database information can accomplish for the business. In answering that question, let us focus for the moment on the database of actual and prospective customers.

BENEFITS OF USING A CUSTOMER DATABASE

The profile and customer transactions data contained in the database are captured from the clickstream created by customer activity. The challenge is to capture the data and use that data effectively for marketing decision making. Even before the internet, some companies that were not traditional direct marketers began to build and use customer databases in ways that improved their marketing programs. Today's marketers work across multiple channels to present and track offers. As shown in Figure 4.10 one good example of using a customer database across channels is American Eagle Outfitters, Inc. (AEO), a global specialty retailer that has been a solid performer in a rather dismal retailing landscape.

The company has integrated its contact strategy across all media and uses a customer database to do so. Recently, it's "Legendary Gifts" program gave customers a chance to win prizes while shopping AEO Legendary Gifts apparel. There were different prizes over a 12-day period during the holidays, starting on December 3, with a grand prize of $10,000 on the last day. The prizes increased in value but even those who did not win daily prizes received special discounts with unique redemption codes.

Those who opted in received a link to a Personalized URL (PURL) over whatever method they chose, SMS, email, etc. The PURL then opened up to reveal either a winning prize or a one-time use discount code. The campaign was integrated across all digital and traditional media in including AEOs desktop website, email, mobile web and app, SMS, social media, direct mail, and in-store Signage. The results were that

FIGURE 4.10
American Eagle Cross-Channel Campaign Captured Data Centrally

SOURCE: Experian Marketing Services "American Eagle Outfitters® Cross-Channel Marketing Holiday Case Study."

AEO was able to connect with more than $8 million email and SMS subscribers in a two-week period, building its database and allowing for unprecedented customer engagement. Engagement metrics were 50 percent to 60 percent click-through rates for daily SMS alerts, and an average of a 4.3 percent email click-through rate throughout the campaign. In-store redemption of mailings yielded a total conversion rate of 1.5. Since 50 percent of its customers shop on their phones, it is not surprising that SMS response rates were so high.[20] Most importantly, AEO was able to build a solid database for future campaigns. In fact, the company is transforming its traditional loyalty program to one that is data-based but centered around the mobile application.

The "Legendary Gifts" program in part led to AEO's nomination for the 2016 "Mobile Best-In-Class" award from eTail (and to its eventual win in that category). The company has continued its cross-channel innovation with its "Reserve, Try, Buy" functionality (https://www.ae.com/reserve-in-store) that is available on the website or the mobile app. This functionality allows customers to reserve items to try on in the store before heading out to shop. The application uses customer data as its foundation to create the best experience for the customer.

USING A CUSTOMER DATABASE FOR PROGRAM EXECUTION AND MARKETING ANALYTICS

There are two different ways to approach database use. One involves *analytics*— any statistical technique that compresses the vast amount of data into summary statistics that are useful either for managerial decision making or for program execution. The second approach involves using individual data items or summary statistics to *execute marketing programs*. Figure 4.11 presents an overview of both types of use in a hierarchical format. The programmatic activities portion is not absolute; it is rather a suggestion of the types of uses at each analytical level that are generally more appropriate.

While it is possible to develop marketing programs around a single data item—an offer to all women in the database, for example—it would be unusual for this to be an optimal use of the database. It is more likely that a **profile**, using either RFM or a special-purpose data model, will produce more precise marketing action. This action is most likely to take the form of targeting individuals who have been identified as potential best customers for a particular marketing program. It is described as "electronic targeting" because the capabilities of the web allow customers to be identified and targeted with individualized content. One type of individualized targeting is

profile summary of the distinctive features or characteristics of a person, business, or other entity.

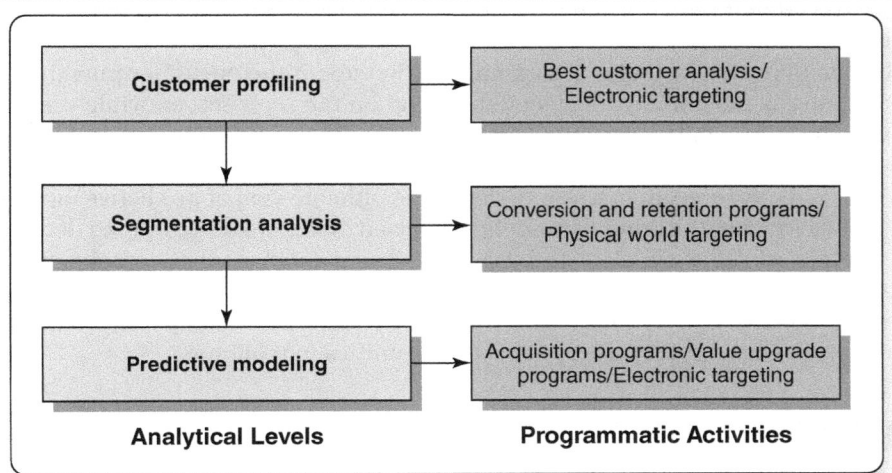

FIGURE 4.11
Analytical Database Hierarchy

SOURCE: © Cengage Learning 2013.

"event-triggered" targeting. Some event in the customer's life—anything from purchase of a new car to a birthday—triggers an automated system to communicate with that specific customer.

At the second level of complexity in analytical terms is statistical analysis, which has an important use for segmentation purposes in a database environment. When the application requires selection of a group of potential best customers out of the larger database, this will be the approach to take. Because this leads to segmentation marketing, it is an approach that is highly appropriate for the physical world in which targeting customers individually is usually cost-prohibitive. In addition, because the focus is on existing customers who reside in the database, it is particularly suitable for conversion and retention programs, which can be executed either offline or online. The most often used analysis at this level is some form of regression ranging from simple linear regression to more complex nonlinear models. Cluster analysis is also used for segmentation purposes. It is worth noting that these commonly used statistical techniques are often described as models, and they produce results that aid in understanding the relationships between variables that affect customer behavior and hence are a necessary precursor to formal model building.

predictive modeling relevant variables and associated response factors or probabilities are used to estimate the likelihood of occurrence of a specific behavior, given the existence of a given level of the specified variables.

The line between segmentation analysis and **predictive modeling** often seems blurry in actual practice, but the conceptual distinction is clear. Segmentation analysis uses statistical models to group customers on the basis of characteristics (demographic and lifestyle) and product-related behaviors. Predictive modeling uses this data to build models that predict future customer or prospect behavior. The most commonly used type of predictive modeling is response modeling in which the statistician constructs a model that predicts the likelihood of response to a given program on a customer-by-customer basis.

Capital One has used the results of its continuous testing to develop an extensive set of predictive models that are used to make an additional offer to almost anyone who calls Capital One for almost any reason. For example, if you call to activate a credit card, you are offered an associated service like balance transfer. Capital One views every call as a selling opportunity and uses models to predict which callers are most likely to buy something and what they are likely to buy. Calls are routed to call center reps who are specially trained to handle particular types of calls. According to Joey Berson, who directs cross-sell offers at Capital One:

> Every one of the three dozen non-credit-card products that Capital One offers has a statistical model behind it that outlines which kinds of customers will find it most appealing, and under what circumstances. A specific "product offer" comes to a customer-service rep in the same data burst as a caller's account information. So the decision about what to offer is made the instant someone calls.

He adds that if "you're calling because you lost your card, I'd be a fool not to sell you credit-card registration."

In practice what happens is that information about the customer plus the offer the customer is most likely to accept shows up on the rep's screen while the call is being routed through the system (a "data burst"). By the time the rep answers, she has all the information in front of her to service the customer well and to make an offer that is likely to result in a sale.[21] That is the ultimate goal of predictive modeling. Note, however, that this kind of modeling is based on extensive testing to determine which offers work for which customers as well as a database that contains the customer data, results of thousands of tests, and many predictive models, all of which can be linked together in real time. It is a complex process but nothing less would allow a company to link service calls to sales opportunities in real time.

THE POWER OF DATA MINING

The opportunities presented by the customer database are great, but you may have seen a recurring theme running through the preceding sections. The traditional approach to database marketing requires that data be captured, housed in a database, analyzed, and modeled. For databases of moderate size, this approach, using simple tools like Excel macros or multiple regression, works well. However, data warehouses like now contain many pentabytes of customer transactions and preferences data and have quickly become unwieldy, meaning more powerful tools are needed.

The solution to the problems large-scale collectors of data like Capital One is a set of statistical tools that has become known by the catch-all name of **data mining**. Kurt Thearling writing on Thearling.com gives a deceptively simple definition of data mining. He says it is *"the automated extraction of hidden predictive information from databases."*[22] He goes on to say that this includes *"automated prediction of trends and behaviors."*[23] For instance, all three of the test emails for savings accounts in Figure 4.8 performed well. Did, for example, current investment customers respond better to one email while customers with only a checking account responded better to another? Knowing this would be the next step in developing more customer-centered communications. Data mining also enables the *"automated discovery of previously unknown patterns."* Patterns that exist in data are often not intuitively obvious. Witness the often quoted finding that people who purchase diapers at the supermarket are also likely to purchase beer. The reason for patterns like this is often not known, nor may the reason even be important to the marketer. As it stands, it suggests a promotional opportunity and that is sufficient.

In other words, data mining is used to produce customer information not previously known, or perhaps even previously hypothesized, from large databases. How is it done? The simple answer is that data mining produces new knowledge because it looks for patterns in data that might not be revealed by traditional statistical analysis. Techniques like decision trees and neural networks may be used as well as techniques commonly used in marketing research like regression and cluster analysis.

One of the important aspects of data mining is that marketing managers do not have to deal directly with the complex analytics. They also do not have to request programming assistance from the IT department in order to get information from the data warehouse through the data mining routines. The software includes easy-to-use interfaces that permit managers to ask questions, often in natural language, like "What were sales yesterday in the northeastern region?" The manager can specify how the information is to be provided—a numerical report or a graphic are common options.

data mining analytic process and specialized analytic tools used to extract meaning from very large data sets.

Data Mining at Disney

Another example of data mining is the Disney Corporation. The company pioneered Disney MagicBands, stylish rubber wristbands in a variety of colors, which complement the Disney experience while providing an enormous amount of data for analysis. The bands each have an RFID chip and a radio similar to those in a cordless phone. The MagicBand can identify a customer when he or she enters a restaurant and, if he or she has pre-ordered, facilitate the delivery of the food to the table. The data from favorite rides can be crunched and result in a stress-free itinerary at the Park. "Magical Express" service for those staying at the resorts can bypass waiting for rental cars and time-consuming check-in processes. The wristband can also act as a virtual wallet and no money is needed for purchases.

All these experiences lead to turning the Magic Kingdom and the other parks at Disneyland in to a big computer. Disney can take the data about how its customers use its services to create an even better customer experience, eliminating wait times at restaurants, as noted above, and making sure that the entire experience is positive. We have just begun to see how this data can be leveraged by the company to ensure its continued success and its reputation for customer service excellence.[24]

Data Mining in the NBA

A final example illustrates data mining used in a different context. Would you believe that the NBA (National Basketball Association) has a sophisticated application based on data mining for both operations and marketing? The Orlando Magic was one of the first teams to begin using statistical software to look for patterns in the huge amount of game data. An average game has about 200 possessions and there are about 1,200 NBA games each year. The sheer volume of data was so overwhelming that initial efforts provided only the basic kind of stats that could be found in any newspaper.

Enter an IBM strategic partner by the name of Virtual Gold and a data mining application called Advanced Scout, specifically tailored for the use of NBA coaches and scouts. After two devastating losses to the Miami Heat in the 1997 finals, the coaches of the Magic turned to Advanced Scout. According to Virtual Gold press material:

> *Advanced Scout showed the Orlando Magic coaches something that none of them had previously recognized. When Brian Shaw and Darrell Armstrong were in the game, something was sparked within their teammate Penny Hardaway—the Magic's leading scorer at that time. Armstrong received more play-time and hence, Hardaway was far more effective. The Magic went on to win the next two games and nearly caused the upset of the year. Fans everywhere rallied around the team and naysayers quickly replaced their doubts with season ticket purchases for the following year.*[25]

The software application is used in tandem with video recording of games to help coaches uncover patterns they otherwise might miss. A technology note from UCLA's Anderson School of Management explains a bit more about how it works:

> *An analysis of the play-by-play sheet of the game played between the New York Knicks and the Cleveland Cavaliers on January 6, 1995, reveals that when Mark Price played the Guard position, John Williams attempted four jump shots and made each one! Advanced Scout not only finds this pattern, but explains that it is interesting because it differs considerably from the average shooting percentage of 49.30% for the Cavaliers during that game.*[26]

With that level of success, it is not surprising that NBA teams have turned to mining of their customer database as one way of dealing with the declining game attendance in the last several years. Group 1 Software consultant Jim Stafford has a case study of an NBA team that was moving into a larger arena, in the face of declining game attendance. The team needed to upgrade existing season ticket holders and identify new season ticket prospects from the ranks of single-game ticket purchasers.

After careful processing of the available ticketing data and choice of statistical models, the analysts identified patron segments that had the highest likelihood of responding to ticket offers. In addition to demographic profiles from its own data, Group 1 overlaid Prizm cluster data on its segments. Using its response model and all this data, it ranked each member of the database according to his or her probability of responding positively. That produced a list ranked from 1 (the patron who has the highest probability of responding) to the total number of database members, in this case, about 3,000 customers (the patron in this data set who has the lowest probability of responding). In this kind of predictive modeling, *each member of the database receives a score and those scores are rank ordered from highest to lowest.* Admittedly, there are some special techniques for handling large databases—perhaps a million or more members—but the principle of ranking each member holds.

The yellow bar in Figure 4.12a shows the result of the ranking—the 5 percent who had the highest probability of responding favorably to a season ticket offer. When you aggregate the top two rows, segments S1, Elite Suburbs in Prizm terminology, and U3, which Prizm calls Urban Cores, are clearly the most desirable segments; that is, they have the highest probability of responding to a season ticket offer. Analysis of demographic and behavioral data produced the profiles in Figure 4.12b. With this information, the team could devise a separate marketing approach for each of the two segments.

Even without segmentation, the analysis suggested the team could cut marketing costs substantially by just promoting to the top 50 percent of the season ticket

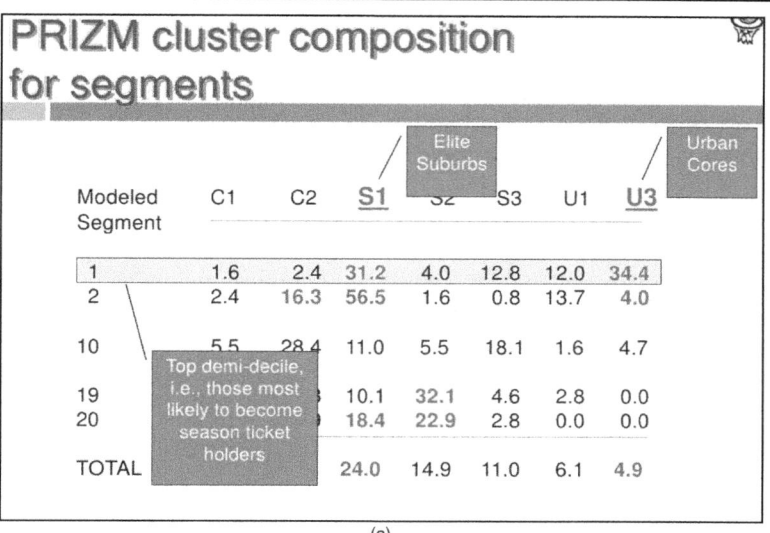
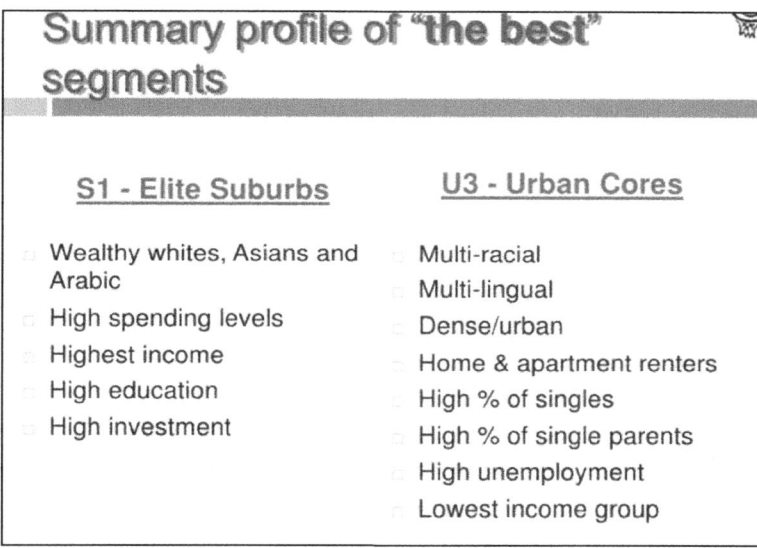

FIGURE 4.12
Data Mining in the NBA

SOURCE: SlideShare Inc., http://www.slideshare.net/jrstafford/ncdm-datamining-case-study-2010-3563095, slides 28, 33, 40.

prospects. That would produce 70 percent of the likely responses.[27] Mostly likely, other NBA teams have been successfully using data mining applications in their marketing programs for a number of years.

All the examples described in this chapter point to the detailed data collection and analysis that must take place in order to enable data-driven marketing. This is not something that happens over night. Both the Disney and the NBA examples showcase programs that have evolved over a decade or more. With that in mind, we close the chapter with a brief discussion of a hierarchy that can help to guide marketers through this process, providing a return on the investment of money and time at each step. The Orlando Magic also uses a similar segmentation approach powered by SAS statistical software that has resulted in an increase in ticket revenue by 50 percent in one year.[28] Other sports, such as baseball, have benefitted from the data mining approach also, such as the story of the Oakland A's manager Billy Beane and his successful use of statistical analysis to pick a successful team in the 2002 draft as told in the book *Moneyball*.[29]

BIG DATA

The term "big data" has been associated with database marketing in recent years. The term refers to taking data from many sources, both structured (purchase patterns) and unstructured (customer service interactions) to mine. Often "big data" requires specialized software for processing many millions of transactions and pieces of data. Because the amount of data is growing exponentially, organizations often feel overwhelmed by the data that they have. However, as the analytical software provider SAS has observed, it's not the amount of data, but what organizations do with the data they do have.[30] The examples in this chapter are some excellent ways that companies have used data intelligently for marketing insight that leads to better decisions. Many of the examples in this chapter focus on "broad data" or getting a complete view of the customer sometimes called a 360 degree view. Certainly, "smart data" or an intelligent use of existing data, is much to be desired.

THE HIERARCHY OF INTERACTIVE STRATEGIES

Marketing on the internet offers many possibilities for data analysis and strategy development that marketers have only been able to wish for in the past. At the same time, it presents many demands, both technological and strategic. Successful internet strategies appear to be moving up a hierarchy in which each stage allows more persuasive communication with the prospective customer and more compelling ways in which to create value for that customer. Each stage also places increasingly rigorous requirements on marketing strategies and operations as well as on the associated technology. The hierarchy is shown in Figure 4.13.

The underlying rationale is that as marketers learn more about their customers, they can develop more focused strategies and more targeted promotional efforts. Take as an example the new website of a hypothetical start-up business that is just beginning to develop a customer database for marketing purposes. The firm undoubtedly has some *informational* marketing material that it can make available to customers as it begins to work on a corporate site. A B2C firm might adapt advertising material, especially from print media, as site content. A B2B firm is likely to have sales support material that will provide initial content—hence the derogatory term "brochure ware." A rather static, informational site may be a viable beginning, but the business needs to have a plan to move beyond that in order to tap the power of the internet.

A reasonable next step is to add some *interactivity* to the site, both to engage the visitor's attention and to provide reasons for the visitor to return. The P&G pages shown in Figure 4.2 are good examples in a B2C context. B2B companies provide valuable information like product demonstration videos and real-time order tracking

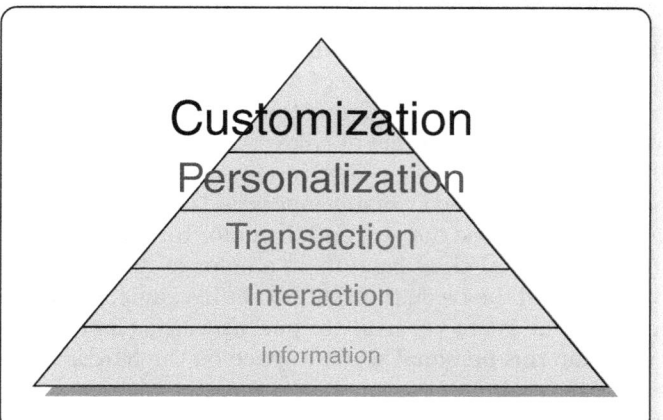

FIGURE 4.13

Hierarchy of Customer-Focused Marketing Strategies

SOURCE: © Cengage Learning 2013.

to increase their level of on-demand customer service. Egovernment sites allow citizens to handle many of the details of everyday interaction with government agencies such as renewing driver's licenses. Nonprofits allow people to join or renew memberships, to donate, or to request information or services.

At some point in the informational or interactive stages, the business needs to begin to collect the names and email addresses of visitors as it looks ahead to personalized communication. That is the beginning of the customer database.

Every organization needs to think about how it can capture the email addresses of visitors who are genuinely interested in their product and are willing to receive additional communications. This step is the beginning of the conversion and retention processes, discussed in more detail in Chapters 10 and 11. Before an organization begins to collect data, it needs to think carefully about how the data will be used to add value to the customer experience as well as to provide data for better marketing decisions. Put another way, it needs to collect useful data that visitors are willing to provide.

Moving to a *transactional* site is a big step. Transactional sites require specialized technology like shopping carts. They require the integration of back-end data—inventory databases for in-stock status, for example. The site must be sure that effective security software and procedures are in place before any transactional features are activated. These and other possible requirements are demanding in terms of both technical complexity and smoothly functioning internal business processes. This is a good point for the business to stop and recognize that any process that is not smooth, error-free, and customer-friendly in the physical should be reengineered *before* it is moved to the internet where its flaws are likely to be magnified many times over. It is also a point at which the business can turn to Web Services instead of developing all the applications on its own.

Once solid transactional functionality is in place, the site may turn to **personalization** as a reasonable next step in its attempts to attract and, especially, to retain customers. Specific personalization techniques are discussed in Chapter 11 in the context of customer relationship management. The options range from a simple greeting of a return visitor by name to the construction of individualized pages with content and functionality specified by the customer. Personalization, a technique long used by traditional direct marketers, is one way in which the internet vastly expands the opportunities for meaningful marketing actions.

Another step a site might take is to offer **customization**. At this point, the site might have so much information about individual customers that individualized products or services can be created. For example, sites like Netflix that can amass a huge set of customer preference data can customize recommendations for the next rental that are often highly satisfactory.

personalization process of preparing an individualized communication such as a newsletter or web page for a specific person based on stated or implied preferences.

customization process of producing a product, service, or communication to the exact specifications/desires of the purchaser or recipient.

A CUSTOMIZATION EXAMPLE

As discussed elsewhere, some websites can allow the customer to customize his own product in a way that takes advantage of the web's unique capabilities. NIKEiD, is a companion to the main Nike site dedicated to the task of helping customers design and purchase their own versions of Nike styles made popular by their celebrity endorsers.[31]

The customer can start with an available model and change elements or start with a plain shoe. He then can choose the size and the color for each part of the shoe. He has the option to put personal identification, in a color of his choice, on the tongue of the shoe. Having created the basketball shoe to fit his game, he can then look at it from all perspectives. If he is not yet ready to purchase, the customized shoe can be saved. In order to set up this personal storage space on the NIKEiD site, he must, of course, provide a small amount of personal information.

This is an interesting, perhaps appealing, process. Is it an indication of the type of customized products we will see more of in the next few years? Probably. Does it create real value for customers? You decide.

These stages of data-driven marketing development are reasonable and observable in current internet space. At the same time, the order is not fixed. Personalization may be interchangeable in order with the transactional stage on the website. Content-rich sites—portals, for example—may choose to personalize the visitor experience in order to retain them and build the critical mass for transactional activities. On the other hand, retail or B2B sites may transact first and then create personalized shopping experiences for consumers or accounts to encourage repeat purchases. A site like NIKEiD may even be a vehicle for new customer acquisition if the offer is sufficiently compelling.

Companies need to carefully consider, and rigorously test, the various options that are available for bringing customers to their sites and persuading them to transact or to identify themselves as sales leads for a future transaction.

SUMMARY

Good internet marketing has an existing marketing discipline—direct marketing—from which to draw tools and techniques that have been developed and honed in other media. The web permits faster, cheaper, and more precise execution of many existing direct response marketing techniques, and it often allows the development of other approaches that would not be cost effective in physical-world media. The internet marketer can profit from the knowledge of both front-end and back-end marketing requirements that successful direct marketers have accumulated over several decades. This is truly a "do not reinvent the wheel" situation in which marketers who recognize the direct response foundations of internet marketing can enjoy a very steep learning curve on the internet.

A number of tools and techniques of direct marketing find direct applicability on the internet. The offer, which is made up of product, positioning, price, and incentives, is one. A compelling offer is necessary in any marketing environment and is especially important on the web where the contact is impersonal and the time devoted to any marketer-initiated communication is usually minimal. Customer lifetime value is becoming increasingly important in both acquisition and retention programs as internet marketers make use of their ability to capture detailed customer activity and purchase data. Testing is becoming more widely used as marketers understand the opportunities offered by the internet to test alternative marketing approaches in a speedy and reliable manner. All of this is made possible by the existence of "the marketing database," actually a complex system of databases with customer, promotional, and marketing operations data, often contained in a data warehouse.

Some marketing programs will be driven by single pieces of marketing data like "registered on baseball website." Still others will be driven by profiles or the results of complex analytics, for example, segmentation by CLV, or predictive modeling. Many, if not most, of these marketing programs will be driven by the goal of increasing CLV as the most direct route to increasing the effectiveness of the marketing effort. Marketers will continue to struggle with the explosion of data and how to use "big data" in a smart way.

DISCUSSION QUESTIONS

1. Why is it important for the marketer to distinguish between customer acquisition, conversion, retention, and value growth when developing marketing strategies?
2. How does "the offer" differ from "the product" of traditional mass media marketing?
3. In addition to the offer, what are the elements of a direct marketing strategy?
4. How do direct marketers distinguish between the "front end" and the "back end" of a transaction? Why is this important?
5. Explain the "customer lifetime value" concept. Thinking about a specific firm, how could it use the concept of CLV to increase the overall profitability of its customer base?
6. How is testing different from marketing research?
7. Why and how does testing offer opportunities to internet marketers?
8. What are some types of analytics that are supported by the customer database?
9. Distinguish between the concepts of customer profiles, market segments, and predictive modeling.
10. Explain the related concepts of data warehousing and data mining.
11. What do you think the future is for customized products? Think of an example of a product that could reasonably be customized and explain why the target customer would find value in the customization.

ENDNOTES

1. IHS Global Insights, Inc., (2011–2012), The Power of Direct Marketing, ROI, Sales, Expenditures and Employment in the US, 14th ed, Direct Marketing Association, Inc., New York, NY.
2. Deighton, John and Johnson, Peter, A., (2015), The Value of Data 2015, Consequences for Insight, Innovation & Efficiency in the US Economy, DMA/DDMI, New York, NY.
3. Concepts in this chapter are based on Mary Lou Roberts and Paul D. Berger, *Direct Marketing Management*, 2nd ed., available for free download at http://www.marylouroberts.info.
4. http://www.hubspot.com/inbound-marketing.
5. Sicari, S., Rizzardi, A., Grieco, L.A., Coen-Porisini, A., Security, privacy and trust in Internet of Things: The road ahead, Computer Networks, Voume 76 15, January 2015, pages 146–164.
6. http://www.informationweek.com/mobile/fitbit-other-fitness-trackers-leak-personal-data-study/a/d-id/1324165.
7. https://www.amazon.jobs/.
8. https://services.amazon.com/fulfillment-by-amazon/benefits.htm.
9. For an extensive discussion and computational appendix, see "Profitability and Lifetime Value," in Mary Lou Roberts and Paul D. Berger, *Direct Marketing Management*, pp. 179–201, http://www.marylouroberts.info.
10. Rajkumar Venkatesan and V. Kumar, "A Customer Lifetime Value Framework for Customer Selection and Resource Allocation Strategy," *Journal of Marketing*, Vol. 68, 2004, p. 110.

11. Details can be found in other articles in journals that deal with issues of data manipulation. A classic article is Robert Dwyer, "Customer Lifetime Valuation to Support Marketing Decision Making," *Journal of Direct Marketing*, Vol. 8, no. 2 (1989), 73–81. Other publications in relevant journals include Paul D. Berger, Bruce Weinberg, and Richard Hanna, "Customer Lifetime Value Determination and Strategic Implications for a Cruise-Ship Company" *Journal of Database Marketing and Customer Strategy Management*, Vol. 11, no. 1 (2003), 40–52; and Wernar J. Reinartz and V. Kumar, "The Impact of Customer Relationship Characteristics on Profitable Lifetime Duration," *Journal of Marketing*, Vol. 67 (January 2003), 77–99.
12. This example is based on Arthur Middleton Hughes, "Building Successful Retail Strategies," Database Marketing Institute, February 5, 2002, http://www.dbmarketing.com.
13. For more detail and an example, see Arthur Middleton Hughes, "How to Succeed with RFM Analysis," nd., http://www.dbmarketing.com/articles/Art106.htm.
14. http://www.syncapse.com/value-of-a-facebook-fan-2013/#.V4FiZOsrKUk.
15. For another detailed CLV example, see http://www.kaushik.net/avinash/2010/04/analytics-tip-calculate-ltv-customer-lifetime-value.html.
16. Rick Fernandes, "Reap the Web's Testing Capabilities," *iMarketing News*, April 10, 2000, p. 28.
17. http://www.fastcompany.com/magazine/24/capone.html?page=0%2C0.
18. For a more detailed discussion, see Chapter 10; "Testing Direct Marketing Programs" in Mary Lou Roberts and Paul D. Berger, *Direct Marketing Management*, http:// www.marylouroberts.info/images/dir.mark.man.ch10.pdf.
19. http://diy-marketing.blogspot.com/2008/09/testing-to-make-im-fast-and-simple.html.
20. http://www.forbes.com/sites/jasonbloomberg/2016/03/22/mobile-first-drives-digital-strategy-at-american-eagle-outfitters/#4b2a01da4ac8.
21. http://www.fastcompany.com/magazine/24/capone.html? page=0%2C4.
22. http://www.thearling.com/index.htm.
23. http://www.thearling.com/text/dmwhite/dmwhite.htm.
24. http://www.wired.com/2015/03/disney-magicband/.
25. Bhandari, Inderpal, Colet, Edward, Parker, Jennifer, Pines, Zachary, Pratap, Rajiv, and Ramanujam, Krishnakumar, (1997) "Advanced Scout: Data Mining and Knowledge Discovery in NBA Data," *Data Mining and Knowledge Discovery*, Vol. 1(1), pp. 121–125.
26. Bill Palace, "Data Mining: What Is Data Mining?" nd., http://www.anderson.ucla.edu/faculty/jason.frand/teacher/technologies/palace/datamining.htm.
27. http://www.slideshare.net/jrstafford/ncdm-datamining-case-study-2010-3563095.
28. http://www.sas.com/en_us/customers/orlando-magic.html.
29. Lewis, Michael, (2003) *Moneyball: The Art of Winning an Unfair Game*, W. W. Norton & Company, New York, NY.
30. http://www.sas.com/en_th/insights/big-data/what-is-big-data.html.
31. http://www.nike.com/us/en_us/c/nikeid.

Chapter 5

Social Media Marketing as a Cornerstone of Strategy

LEARNING OBJECTIVES

By the time you complete this chapter, you will be able to:

1. Define social media marketing.
2. Explain why marketers find it both necessary and effective to engage in social media marketing.
3. Explain why social media marketing is not free.
4. Describe the ways in which marketer communications are different in social media from those in traditional mass media and online marketing.
5. Identify the elements of a social media marketing strategy.
6. Discuss the differences among paid, owned, and earned.
7. Give examples of engaging a social media audience.
8. Explain what it means to build a community around a brand.
9. Discuss issues involved in building a successful social media team.
10. Explain the importance of top management involvement in social media.

Social media marketing (SMM) is no longer a curiosity or even a trend. It is an established element of marketing strategy. The platforms are specific to social media and so are many of the business activities, but social media is so much a part of the daily lives of people around the globe that business underutilizes it at its peril.

THE EXPLOSION OF SOCIAL NETWORK USE

Every day people across the globe—both at home and at work—log on to social platforms on desktop or mobile devices. Figure 5.1 shows data from Smart Insights, which is taken from the GlobalWebIndex and other statistics sources.[1] Figure 5.1a shows that over 2.3 billion of the almost 7.4 billion people who use the internet are active on social media. That's almost one-third of the internet population! Although mobile users are only 27 percent of the total internet population, they are a vast majority (1.97B of 2.31B) of social media users. All these activities are growing rapidly with huge growth occurring in the Asia-Pacific where most of the new users are mobile users.[2]

Figure 5.1b shows Facebook as the largest platform globally, which is probably not a surprise. However, did you expect to see that the second largest platform is WhatsApp, a mobile messaging app that is very popular in India.? As of early 2016 WhatsApp, owned by Facebook, had over 1B users,[3] with 800 million of them in India alone.[4] The next two platforms in order of size are QQ Mobile (Chinese) and Facebook Messenger. Not only is social media growing rapidly, but it is shifting to mobile and to messaging and chat apps.

HOW MARKETERS ARE USING SOCIAL MEDIA TO ENGAGE VISITORS

There is an old advertising maxim that says marketers must "follow the eyeballs." In other words, where their customers go for information and entertainment, marketers must follow. That necessity has prompted an explosion in the use of social

FIGURE 5.1

(a) Number of Social Media Users Globally and (b) Users of the Largest Social Platforms

(a)
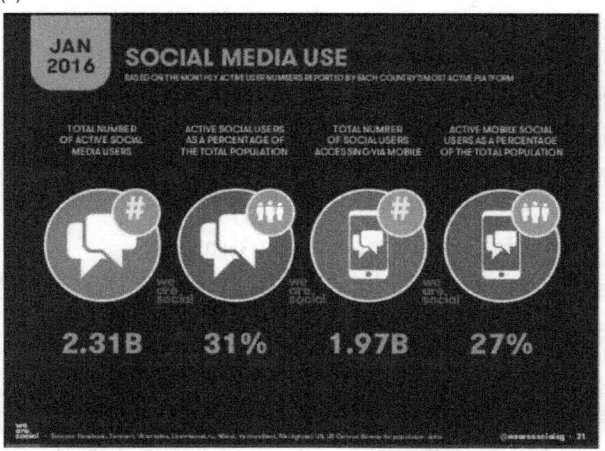

(b)
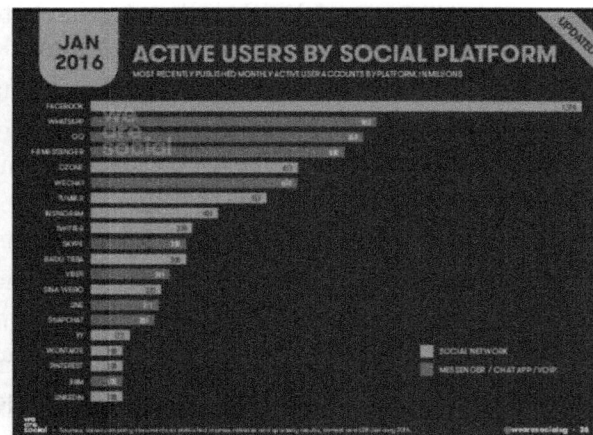

SOURCE: http://www.smartinsights.com/social-media-marketing/social-media-strategy/new-global-social-media-research/

media channels by marketers, both B2C and B2B. This new practice has presented both opportunities and challenges for marketers and for the brands and companies that employ them.

Old Spice and Android Generate Buzz in B2C Markets

The most talked-about social media campaign of summer 2010 was the Old Spice effort. It featured former *National Football League* (NFL) player Isaiah Mustafa, who debuted as brand spokesperson in a Super Bowl 2010 TV ad, "The Man Your Man Could Smell Like." The video quickly went viral on YouTube. In just two weeks following the Super Bowl, it had 1.6 million views. By fall, it was still going strong, closing in on 22 million views. In spring 2011, a new series of videos was launched and another in 2015.[5]

It has been a durable campaign, although no other single video has experienced the success of the original shown in Figure 5.2.

So far, this sounds like normal practice, right? Most national advertisers put their ads on the web. However, most of them are not compelling enough to be shared by users, making them go viral. The Old Spice video not only went viral but also spawned about two dozen more videos featuring the hunky spokesperson. Most have achieved only 2 or 3 million views, although one called "Questions" had over 16 million. This particular social media breakthrough came in July 2010 when Old Spice announced that for two days Mustafa would answer questions from the Old Spice Facebook, Twitter, and Reddit communities. Between July 14 and 16, Mustafa and the Wieden+Kennedy agency produced what has to be a record amount of content and traffic:

- Over 180 personalized videos responding to audience requests and questions. He made a voice mail message for one fan but turned down Alyssa Milano's marriage proposal.
- Over 5.9 million video views.
- 22,500 comments on the social networks.
- Number of subscribers to the Old Spice YouTube channel increased to 120,000.
- Number of Facebook fans increased to 616,000.[6]

FIGURE 5.2

The Beginning of the Video Campaign. View the first Old Spice video.

SOURCE: https://www.youtube.com/watch?v=owGykVbfgUE

On July 16, Mustafa declared victory and presumably hung up his towel, ending the questions phase of the overall campaign.

All this activity represents a tremendous creative accomplishment, but it begs the ultimate marketing question: did it increase sales? According to a Procter & Gamble representative, it did. "Since the 'Smell Like A Man, Man' campaign broke in February, Old Spice has month-over-month strengthened its market position," said (Michael) Norton in an e-mail. He added that Old Spice is now the No. 1 brand of body wash and anti-perspirant/deodorant in both sales and volume with growth in the high single/double digits. Nielsen data appeared to confirm this corporate statement, although it is hard to separate what the impact was of a two-day social media campaign out of a long-term brand campaign in multiple media.[7] However, it is clear that brand marketers, social media marketers, and technical experts worked closely together to make this campaign successful.

Making a video go viral is more luck than skill, although the most viewed viral video ad of 2015 gives some hints. Google wanted to impress on Android users that even though they had different phones, they are all part of one big user family. What made the Friends Furever ad go viral? There are probably several reasons:

1. People love animals, these animals are adorable, and the 16-second video clips show them in unusual friendly relationships.

2. It is short, lasting only 1.02 minutes. It moves quickly because of the number of short clips, so it's a very enjoyable viewing experience.

The YouTube capture in Figure 5.3 shows almost 6.4 million shares and the site showed almost 30 million views.

In addition, it was created entirely out of "found footage," video clips from the web. The agency doesn't say, but this must have made it a very cheap video to produce as opposed to shooting new footage. By November 2015, it had become the most shared ad of all time, reaching over 6 million viewers. Industry experts also noted that it was a successful ad during a year in which many powerful ads successfully engaged the emotions.[8,9] We are not told whether the campaign has lifted sales of Android phones. However, it has generated a lot of love. That may be considered sufficient for what seemed to be its relationship objective.

FIGURE 5.3 From the Android "Be Together, Not the Same" Campaign. View the Android ad.

SOURCE: https://www.youtube.com/watch?v=vnVuqfXohxc

B2B Uses Both Influencers and Content

A 2015 study by the Content Marketing Institute found that 86 percent of business marketers said their firm was using content marketing. The average B2B marketers used 6 social media channels to distribute the content. The top channels were LinkedIn, Twitter, Facebook, YouTube, Google+, and SlideShare. Many of the marketers were less confident of their content strategy or their ability to measure ROI from their investments in content distribution in social channels, but they appear to be sold on the relevance of content marketing.[10] After all, B2B buyers consume large amounts of content in order to be successful at their jobs. **Influencer marketing** is one useful strategy to develop awareness of content.

influencer marketing using people who are regarded as authorities in their field to help distribute brand content

Offering potential clients relevant content was part of the strategy when PR firm Cision partnered with Altimeter consultant Brian Solis to author an e-book called "What if PR Stood for People and Relationships?" There are many lists of marketing influencers and the listings differ wildly depending on the criteria used. Brian Solis was fifth on one list for 2015[11] with other very familiar marketing names, many of whom he writes about as part of his consulting practice at Altimeter.[12] Digital transformation and content marketing are two other areas in which he specializes. He was able not only to author a significant e-book, he was able to further promote it through his own writing and speaking.

The e-book received over 200,000 views on SlideShare by the end of the year and was shared by 11 Twitter influencers that reached a combined audience of 2 million followers. The PR firm said it generated 600 sales leads.[13]

The e-book was part of an integrated campaign called "The Future of PR." The second element was a half-day conference at Google headquarters at which Brian Solis was one of the speakers along with other marketing influencers. The third element of the campaign was a contest in partnership with design firm Canva and digital evangelist Guy Kawasaki who often leads the lists of marketing influencers. The contest allowed professionals to share their views on the future of PR by creating graphics that were shared on social networks.

This social media campaign won a Shorty Award,[14] a recognition platform for social media influencers and brands. More important, it received over 290 thousand SlideShare views (said to be 72,404% above average), was shared over 2 thousand times on social platforms and generated 60 contest entries.[15] Remember, this was for a B2B e-book about public relations. Yes, SMM does work for B2B firms!

Successful Influencer Marketing

According to eMarketer, influencer marketing is becoming pervasive among brand marketers with platforms like YouTube, Instagram, and Snapchat making it easier and more effective. Influencers are particularly helpful in activities like the content promotion for the PR e-book just described, new product launches, events and corporate communications. They are also useful in creating search visibility.[16]

In order to be successful at influencer marketing, it is necessary to:

- Know your audience. Each audience has its own set of influencers and it is important to identify the right one and be able to engage his or her services. A marketing influencer on LinkedIn will be a different person from a makeup influencer for teen-aged girls on Facebook who will be different from an influencer for local restaurants on foodie blogs. There are numerous free tools to help marketers locate the relevant influencers.
- Set clear goals. An influencer campaign is just that—a promotional campaign. Is the goal to create awareness for a new product, to encourage professionals to attend a conference, or one of many other possibilities? Without a goal the campaign will not have clear direction and it is impossible to measure its success.
- Identify success metrics. This is the subject of Chapter 18. Without defining and capturing the correct measures a marketer cannot demonstrate the success of

any SMM campaign—or any digital campaign for that matter. And a marketer who cannot demonstrate success for the current campaign will have difficulty getting budget for the next campaign.[17]

There are also useful tools that you see at work in many of these case histories. For example, the e-book campaign used the hashtag #FutureofPR. The hashtag makes it much easier to track what is going on with the campaign and therefore to measure its success. It also used not just one influencer but 40 marketing influential in various stages of the campaign. Timing of influencer activities to generate the maximum amount of buzz is important but expect buzz to be a short-lived thing.

Two other things are essential for successful influencer marketing. First, do not pay too much. Most influencers expect direct payment today. Some are setting high fees. Marketers must understand the ROI of their investment in influencer marketing—or any other type of SMM—in order to understand what they should be paying an influencer.[18] We will discuss ROI in SMM at the end of the chapter.

Second, it is essential to recognize that the Federal Trade Commission regulates the conditions for disclosure of relationships between marketers and influencers. If marketers do not follow the specific guideline for disclosure in social media[19] they risk enforcement action, including fines.[20]

Social media has also changed the face of fundraising for charities and political causes. The changes cut across all kinds of political campaigns and fundraising at all levels.

Record-Setting Fundraising in Social Media

Charitable organizations were among the first to sense the potential of the social web as a way to reach more potential donors at a lower cost. Once a donor was acquired, he could then be solicited by e-mail instead of more expensive direct mail. However, one experienced fundraising executive says that approach falls far short. She says:

> *For too long, nonprofits have been more in the getting than giving business. You secure a gift, dump the donor into a database, and you're pretty much done (until the next ask) — . betraying your donors. Fundraising, fundraising, fundraising all the time.*[21]

That standard approach ignores the relationship-building power of social media. Among the things nonprofits must do are the following:

1. Join, participate in, and guide conversations that shape the perception of your brand. Create awareness and establish you and your organization as a leader in thought and action in your field.
2. Build communities of like-minded people and tap into their influence and power. They are not just an e-mail list. They are people who care about the kinds of things your organization does.
3. Use social media to build engagement by sharing your activities and successes in the field. Donors want to know what is being done with their money. That is more successful if it is not always in the context of direct fundraising.[22]

That is also excellent advice for brand marketers!

The most successful fundraising campaign of recent years was started, not by the sponsoring organization, but by a college student who suffered from the debilitating disease ALS. Pete Franes and two of his friends came up with the idea of dumping a bucket of ice water over their heads to raise money for the ALS Association, which supports research aimed at finding a cure for the disease. They built an event around the idea and held it in downtown Boston, drawing a lot of local participation.[23] Within about a week the challenge had gone national and by the end of the month Facebook said that over 2 million ice-bucket-related videos had been posted.

Mark Zuckerberg took the challenge and simply picked up a bucket of ice water and poured over his head. He nominated Bill Gates to take the challenge. Gates designed

FIGURE 5.4
Bill Gates Takes the Ice Bucket Challenge. View Bill Gates accepting the ice bucket challenge.

SOURCE: http://mashable.com/2014/08/15/bill-gates-ice-bucket-challenge/#E8N4um5nXqq3

a contraption and released what some authors described as "the nerdiest video ever" of his soaking (see Figure 5.4). He posted the YouTube video on his blog.[24] He nominated Elon Musk, Ryan Seacrest, and Chris Anderson to take the challenge. They went on to nominate people like Johnny Depp and David Beckham who nominated people like Magic Johnson and Leonardo DiCaprio. That's influencer marketing on steroids!

But the real test is whether it worked to raise money or not; it did. The 2014 ice bucket challenge raised approximately $220 million for ALS. One year later, Business Insider reported that 67 percent of that had gone to research, 20 percent to patient and community services, 9 percent to public and professional education, and 2 percent each to fundraising and donor processing. Only 4 percent to overhead is a commendable use of donated funds by any nonprofit. The transparency of ALS in reporting detail on what was raised and how it was spent fulfills an important recommendation for positive social media engagement. In addition, researchers commented on how their research had been facilitated and at least one article was published in a highly regarded scientific publication.[25]

That kind of success, well managed, leads to further success. The ALS website now says simply #EveryAugustUntilACure.[26]

Fundraising success can also exist on a smaller, local scale that can materially improve the lives of people. Crowdsourcing fundraising sites make that possible. You may know of, or may have participated in, such a fundraising campaign. Just a few months ago one of Prof. Roberts' friends rather suddenly required a liver transplant. Using the crowdsourcing fundraising site GoFundMe[27] her co-workers set out to raise money to defray costs associated with the disease and treatments that were not covered by insurance. They began by posting the message on their own Facebook pages and pages of organizations to which she belonged. When a person donated, she went onto an e-mail list for updates. The campaign quickly raised over $5,000 and two months later it still brings in donations, mostly when the organizers update donors on the patient's good progress. The amount is not huge, but it was enough to make a difference in the life of one person, and that should be what fundraising is all about.

HOW BUSINESSES ARE USING SOCIAL MEDIA IN THE WORKPLACE

Effective use of social media in the workplace is an important issue that goes beyond marketing. Social media use can turn employees into advocates. It can also provide tools to make the workplace more collaborative and efficient.

To Engage and Motivate Employees

E-retailer of shoes and fashion apparel, Zappos has generated a great deal of buzz in recent years for its wide ranging use of social media. Its home page contains customer comments about their shoes and other fashion products. While customer reviews are a staple of digital marketing, giving them home-page prominence is unusual. The home page also features one of Zappos' Core Values, "Build Open and Honest Relationships with Communication."

CEO Tony Hsieh has been a proponent of "Delivering Happiness" through social media from its earliest days, posting personal tweets as well as content about Zappos. He has been on Twitter since 2007 and has 2.86 million followers and over 2 thousand tweets.[28] All Zappos employees are trained and encouraged to use Twitter. Zappos is also active on YouTube, Instagram, and Facebook, using the platforms to showcase its products, company culture, and engaged employees.[29] Posts range from product-related to content that includes what it's like to work @insideZappos, fun places to conduct hiring interviews, and how they welcome summer interns.[30] All this employee-centered social media activity does a wonderful job of building and humanizing the Zappos brand.

In a different business sector social media is also playing an important role. Putnam Investments has been actively training its investment advisors to use social media to build their businesses. The firm offers many web-based presentations that cater to advisors at any level of social media skill. It offers coaching to advisors one-on-one in their own offices. It offers everything from advice on using mobile and social media to proprietary apps that make the advisors more productive.[31]

Building relationships with advisors through social media has been a major focus at Putnam, says Mark McKenna, head of global marketing. "'This is really what we do hands-on with advisors,' he says. For instance, the firm recently brought about 30 advisors into its offices for a full day of training, which also included professional head shots taken in Putnam's studio, he says."[32]

Pervasive social media use is transforming firms into social businesses. Consulting firm Blue Focus Marketing lists recent statistics on benefits of being a **social business**:

social business in business terminology, a business that has adopted social communications in all aspects of internal operations and of dealing with external customers and partners

- People are three times more likely to trust everyday employees than executives.
- Employee-generated or shared content is eight times more effective than that shared by a branded account.
- Employee advocacy leads to increased visibility, inbound web traffic, brand recognition, and brand loyalty.
- Socially engaged companies are 57 percent more likely to get increased sales leads, 58 percent more likely to attract top talent, and 20 percent more likely to retain them.
- Employee networks are 10 times larger than a company's follower base.
- Salespeople who share engaging content get seven times more profile views, see their connections grow four times faster, and are 45 percent more likely to exceed their sales quota.[33]

Like other successful transformations, becoming a social business is a process that occurs over time. Blue Focus co-founder Mark Burgess says,

> *Successful social marketing is the result of a well-structured social business, and a well-structured social business requires organization-wide buy-in, employee training and an evolved infrastructure. In other words, a commitment to social marketing means a commitment to a much larger process. A brand cannot communicate externally unless it first learns to communicate internally.*[34]

One thing that is necessary to the creation of a successful social business is a social media policy that governs what employees should—and should not—do on social media. A detailed discussion is beyond the scope of this chapter, but there are good resources with many examples. They include samples from both large and small firms and from nonprofits. There are also illustrations of community guidelines.[35,36]

Using social media tools internally is an important aspect of employee engagement in the social business as well as a way to directly increase productivity.

To Increase Productivity

There are numerous software platforms that support increased business productivity. Hands-down the most popular in recent years has been Slack. It describes itself as "real-time messaging, archiving, and search for modern teams."[37] It is business collaboration software but it feels like social media. By putting many activities into a single app, employees can communicate without ever leaving the app. Good-bye office e-mail and meetings!

Slack was founded in February of 2014. Less than two years later it had 1.7 million users with 480,000 paid accounts.[38] By mid-2016 it had over 2.3 million daily users[39] and was said to be the fastest-growing piece of business software ever. Replete with emojis and other aspects of social media, it is even fun to use!

One advertising agency estimated that it was 30 percent more productive after it started using Slack to communicate with clients. The R/GA agency has 1,500 of its 1,800 employees in its 15 offices in 9 countries on the platform. Each of its offices has its own Slack channel where work is done and anyone in the company can drop in to see what's going on. It also has subject-matter channels, virtual reality for example, where employees can learn about what is going on throughout the agency. It uses private channels to communicate with clients, finding that decision-making is 30–40 percent faster when agency and client communicate on the platform.[40] Slack is only one part of the agency's technology strategy, which includes what Forbes called "The World's Most Connected Office."[41]

Slack encourages the use of bots to automate many personal activities[42] even using a Slackbot to help users fill out profiles when they sign up for the service. One of the most creative uses of a Slackbot to date is Taco Bell's TacoBot. It was built for offices that use Slack, so they could simply enter an order with the bot and drive over to pick it up, complete and correct.

The bot uses AI and natural language processing technology to carry out conversations that are strictly limited to ordering the food. "It can take down your customized order and even crack a couple of jokes. For example, if you tell TacoBot that you're drunk, it'll add a cup of water to your order. And if you ask for a food recommendation, it'll give you one in binary code that translates to Doritos Locos Taco." But it can't give you the weather or the sports score and that's intentional. It's not a chatbot, it's a TacoBot. Figure 5.5 shows how it works, complete with a little lighthearted conversation.

According to the advertising agency that helped design it, "TacoBot isn't only a means to attracting more corporate orders for Taco Bell. It's also a stake in the ground, as it shifts beyond website forms and in-app buttons to text- and voice-based conversations." "We are at a point of switching up how we use computers," said Deutsch's senior VP and creative technology director, Martin Legowiecki. "It used to be we had to talk like computers. Now computers are increasingly talking like us."[43]

Stay tuned for many other applications of bots in the coming weeks, months, and years!

The SMM campaigns are interesting and the technology can be fun. However, the effort will be wasted unless it is based on a sound SMM strategy. Preparing a plan to guide strategy execution is discussed and illustrated in *Social Media Marketing: A Strategic Approach*.[44]

FIGURE 5.5

Martin Orders Tacos for the Office from the TacoBot. You can view the human/bot interaction in this article.

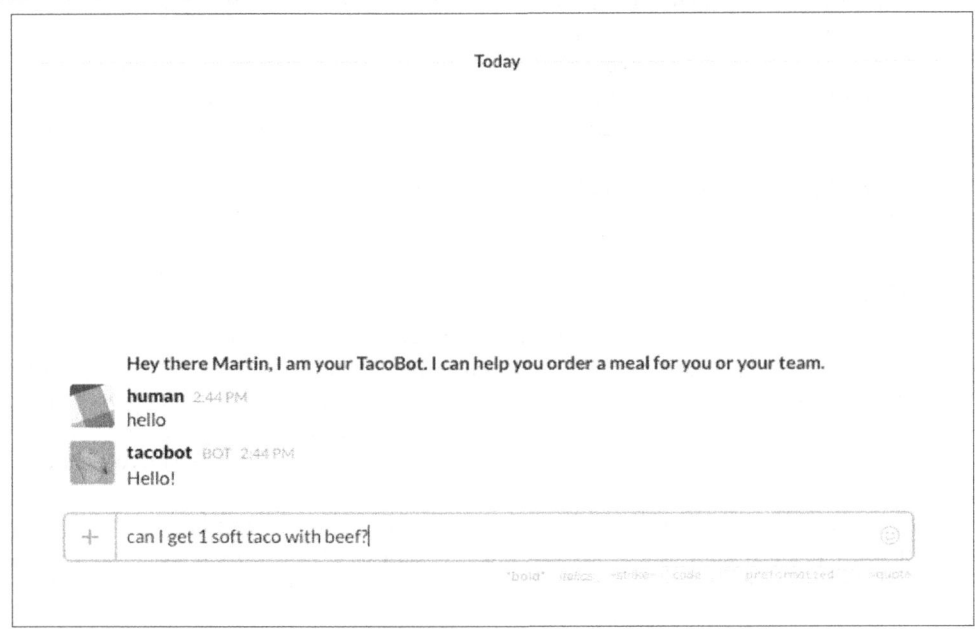

SOURCE: http://www.theverge.com/2016/4/6/11378258/taco-bell-ai-bot-slack-crunchwrap-supreme

DEVELOPING A SOCIAL MEDIA MARKETING STRATEGY

We cannot say it too often: *Good SMM results from a carefully planned strategy, not from a series of random activities.* It must also be carefully integrated into the firm's overall marketing communications strategy and activities, as case histories throughout this chapter emphasize. The first question we ask should be, "How does a business go about developing a social media marketing strategy?"

Although different authors use different terminology, there is general agreement on the steps needed to develop an SMM strategy. Following the process illustrated in Figure 5.6 leads to a deeper relationship with the customer. That kind of relationship takes time and effort—an upfront investment, if you will—but the end result is well worth the effort. Let us take a brief look at each of the steps.

Listening to the Target Audience

Whether they are your customers or people you want to attract as customers (prospects), the marketer must listen before she speaks. A good way to think of it is the way in which a socially savvy individual behaves at a party. He does not just walk up to a group of people and start talking. He listens to the content and tone of the conversation before joining in. That is exactly what savvy marketers do in the initial stages of developing an SMM strategy.

Marketers must first identify the social habitats of their defined target market. For example, young males can be found in large numbers on gaming sites, young mothers have an extensive system of "mommy blogs" that traffic in everything from coupons to parenting advice, and Millennials are watching videos on their smart phones. Both women and men are sports fans these days and can be found on league and sports commentary sites. The list could go on and on, but it is important to realize that the key issue is lifestyle and interests, not demographics *per se*.

It is also important to pay attention to what people do when they are visiting social sites. Here we are also using a broad definition of any site that allows interactivity (e.g., product reviews), not just the social networks. Forrester Research has been

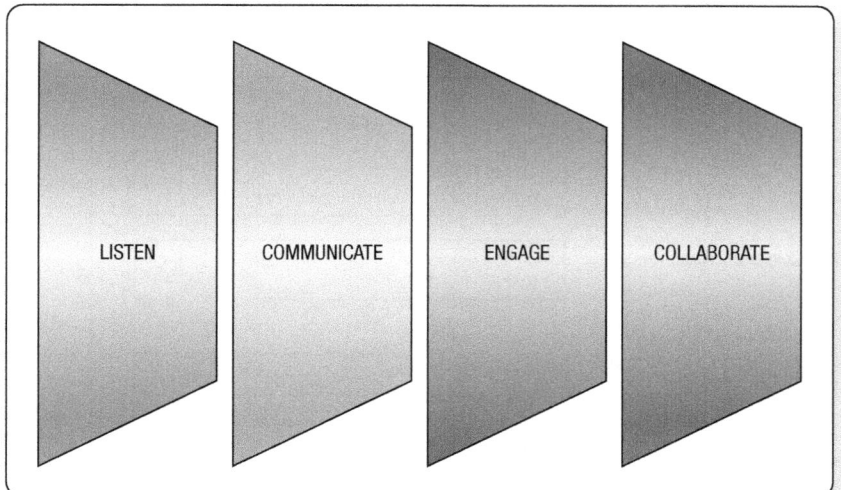

FIGURE 5.6

Steps in Developing a Social Media Marketing Strategy

SOURCE: Adapted from Jeremiah Owyang, "Social Media Marketing," Awareness, Inc. Webinars, http://www.awarenessnetworks.com/learning/webinars, December 9, 2008.

conducting research on that subject for several years; they call it the Social Technographics Ladder (see Figure 5.7).

First you should note that people can be a member of various categories over time and for various reasons, so the numbers add to much more than 100 percent. Notice, though, that there are not many people who classified themselves as totally inactive in 2010. There are, however, huge numbers of people who can be best described as consuming content or simply joining sites; but they do not contribute. There are a substantial number of people in the critics category, driven by the desire to post product and service ratings and reviews online. Likewise, there are numerous conversationalists who socialize online. There are relatively few collectors, but those are people who carefully search the web for content and aggregate it on third-party sites or on their own websites. The proportion of creators is even smaller. These are the influentials described in an earlier section, the people who create and distribute content. Forrester points out that this group has plateaued, while the proportion of joiners continues to increase.[46]

It is a big web out there; how can a business possibly keep track of what people are saying about it on the internet? The short answer is that there are many tools, some free, others paid, and still others part of comprehensive metrics platforms to be discussed in Chapter 18. The embarrassing gaff of the New England Patriots recounted in Interactive Exercise 5.2 shows that, while these tools are essential to track the huge volume of conversation on the internet, they must be used with care.

The promotional activity surrounding Super Bowl 50 had many examples of the impact of social media and marketer response. The most talked-about was the shout-out to Red Lobster from Beyoncé who was the highlight of the game half-time show (Figure 5.8a). On the Saturday before the Super Bowl, Beyoncé released the video of her new single "Formation" which contained a sexually-charged reference to the Red Lobster chain. In 15 hours it became a trending item on Twitter and quickly racked up over 300,000 tweets. No one seems to know how quickly Red Lobster became aware of the mention, but it took them 8 hours to reply.[47]

When Red Lobster did reply, it sent a rather weak tweet offering to name its cheddar biscuits "Cheddar Bey." Fans hated it and tweeted a long string of insults about the competence and sensitivity of Red Lobster. The firm tried again on Sunday but it's efforts didn't fare any better with fans. So this was a real disaster, right?[48]

FIGURE 5.7

Forrester's Social Technographics®

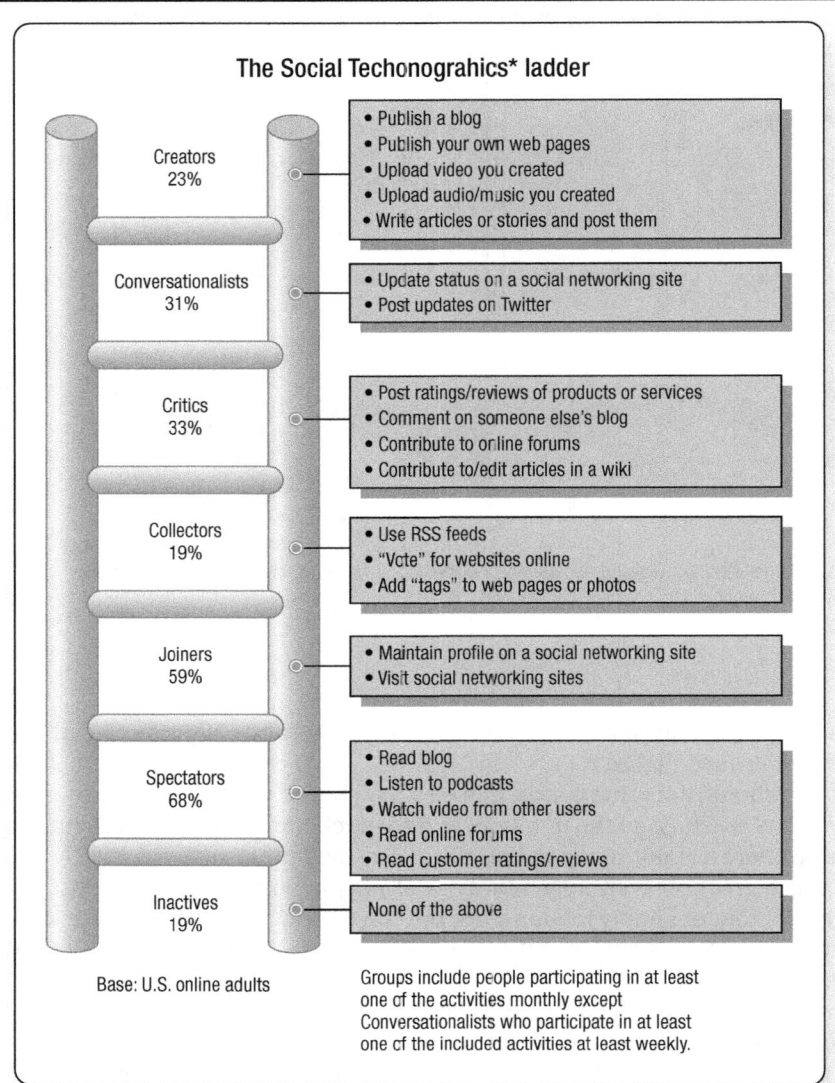

SOURCE: Forrester Research, Inc., The Latest Global Social Media Trends May Surprise You (Jackie Rousseau-Anderson), September 2010 http://blogs.forrester.com/jackie_rousseau_anderson/10-09-28-latest_global_social_media_trends_may_surprise_you.

The chain itself said its sales spiked 33 percent on Super Bowl Sunday as compared to the same day last year. Sales were still up on Monday.[49] Comparing the number of social media mentions for Red Lobster to those for Super Bowl ads costing a minimum of $5 million, one writer, "found that the one-line Beyoncé endorsement just might carry more weight than many of the highly touted 2016 Super Bowl ads."[50] That's not conclusive scientific evidence, but then the cost was "free" versus $5M.

After the game was over and the Broncos had won, quarterback Peyton Manning was recorded twice saying he was going to celebrate by "by kissing his wife and kids, celebrating with family and teammates, and that he's "gonna drink a lot of beer tonight…Budweiser. Von Miller's buying." One advertiser estimated that the amount of air time the twice-repeated comment received was worth $3.2 million at the rate of $5 million per 30 seconds charged for paid advertising.[51] By the next morning the estimated value had soared to $13.9 million because people were still talking about it on social media.[52] Budweiser repeated early and often that it did not pay Manning for this endorsement although it is no secret that he owns several Budweiser distribution franchises.[53]

FIGURE 5-8a

View Beyoncé Wowing the Audience at the Half-Time Show

SOURCE: https://www.linkedin.com/pulse/why-beyonces-word-worth-more-than-super-bowl-ad-dennis-williams-ii

FIGURE 5.8b

Peyton Manning Hoists the Super Bowl Trophy and Talks about Budweiser

SOURCE: http://www.marketwatch.com/story/peyton-manning-handed-budweiser-32-million-in-free-ads-after-the-super-bowl-2016-02-08

You could find several important takeaways in these two Super Bowl episodes but one is paramount. People are talking to one another—and to brands—on social media and brands must listen and react intelligently. That leads to the next strategy element—how should brands communicate on social media?

Communicating with Your Audience in Social Space

This one is easy, right? After all, communicating is what marketers do! The problem is that both the landscape and the rules of the road change in social media. It is no longer a one-marketer to many-audience-members type of communication. It is many-to-many. Even more difficult, marketers no longer establish the rules of communication. Audience members do.

All companies need to think of themselves as creators and communicators of content, the subject of Chapter 8. This is a tall order, especially for marketers who are used to trying to put their products in the best light, not to being responsive to what customers are saying and doing. One marketer puts it well when he says that, "No One Cares About Your Products." Sage Lewis argues that people care about what other people say, and that they care about experiences more than the products themselves. This quote captures the essence of his argument:

> *People don't care what you say about your products. They want to know what other people say about your products.*
>
> *If we don't realize this, I believe our Web sites will become obsolete.*
>
> *People simply won't go to your site if they know it's just filled with puffery, marketing-speak, and straight-up meaningless content.*[54]

Dreary product-oriented promotions also will not be shared on the web whether they originate in your website or on a branded social media platform. As the case histories in the previous section dramatically illustrate, both the cost and the effectiveness of various types of communication about brands differ greatly.

There is general agreement about requirements for effective communication in social media. Communications must be:

- Interactive, not a one-way street from marketer to customer
- Published on the platforms customers choose using the language and terms they use
- Above all, be open, transparent, and authentic in all respects.

This type of communication is aimed at building a two-way dialog between brand and customer that creates a trusting relationship.

Marketers need to develop communication strategies that leverage the various types of media shown in Figure 5.9. **Paid media** in traditional print and broadcast channels still has an important role to play. It can provide great audience **reach** and as much **frequency** as the marketer desires and can pay for. It is accessible on a national or a local level and can be implemented quickly. Marketers feel comfortable with paid media because they are in control of content as well as all the elements of execution.

Owned media refers to properties of brands on the internet and on social media. Website content and presentation is within the control of the brand. It can choose to put customer-created content on its site, like the reviews on Zappos's home page. Many other websites include customer comments and reviews. This is clearly a loss of control. Is it worth inclusion of unedited reviews to create trust? Yes, it is. Research consistently finds that consumers trust online reviews for information like quality of local stores (88 percent),[55] and influencing their product decisions (90 percent).[56]

Like all the rest of social media, owned media is not really free. It requires human effort and ingenuity to listen and respond. Still, it is within the reach of small businesses and many use it with great success to showcase their businesses to local customers.[57,58]

In earlier sections we have stressed the importance of reacting quickly when brands are mentioned on social media. Recent research suggests that consumers expect a reply on social media in less than 4 hours but it takes most companies 10 hours to respond. That harms brand loyalty and makes consumers more likely to use a competitor's product.[59] Owned properties like the brand's Facebook or Instagram page make the monitoring of comments easier. In general, branded social media pages offer many opportunities for communicating with customers in engaging ways.

Earned media is the result of doing both paid and, especially, owned media well. A great Super Bowl ad is discussed, viewed and retweeted many times. That's what the brand is counting on when it pays those exorbitant prices for an ad on game day. In fact, in recent years, a whole advertising industry has grown up around the practice

---

paid media traditional advertising on any channel, traditional or social, that requires direct payment for insertion

frequency the number of times a person is exposed to a promotional message

owned media brand pages on social platforms

earned media buzz in both social and traditional media that is generated by content distributed by the brand

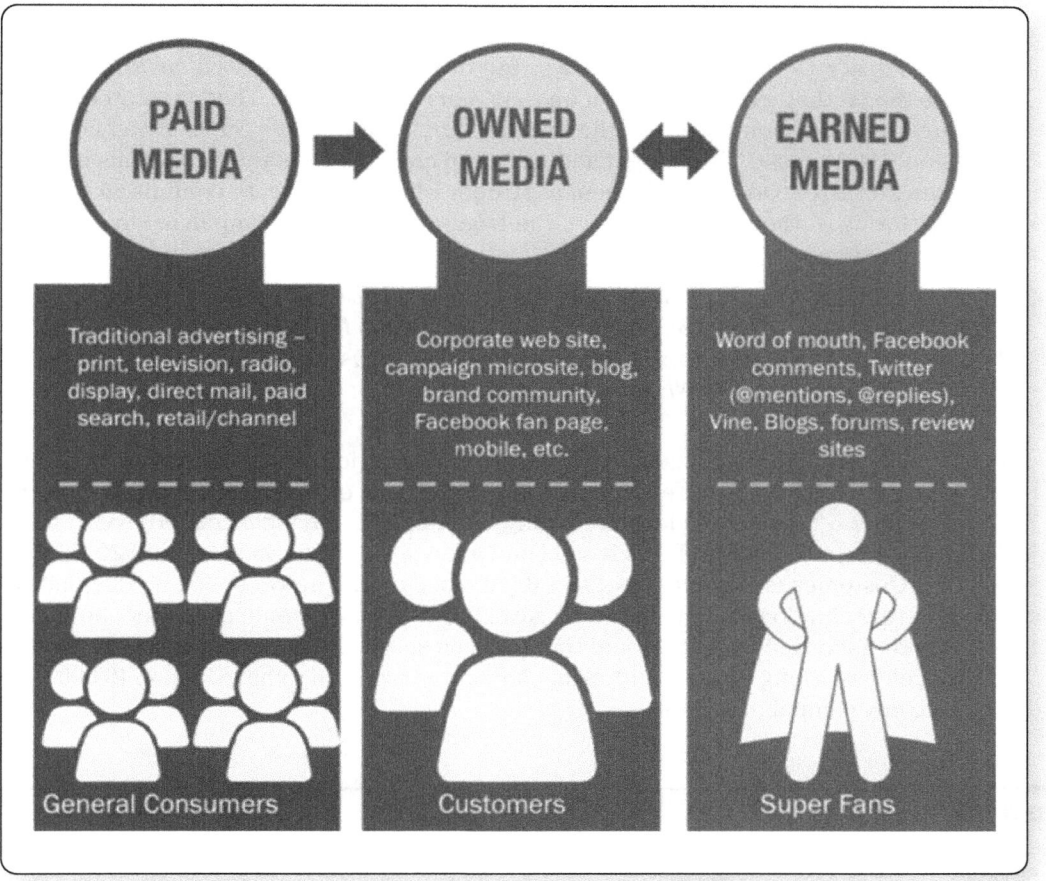

FIGURE 5.9
Types of Promotional Media

SOURCE: https://blog.hootsuite.com/converged-media-brito-part-1/

of creating buzz for Super Bowl ads—and for many other types of promotions. The whole idea of creating buzz is to get the product, ad, event, and so on, to be discussed among family and friends or on the social web. In other words, to stimulate earned media. Many marketers regard earned media as the most valuable because it carries with it the authenticity and trustworthiness of the publisher. It is also the hardest and most time consuming to generate.

Without doubt, however, the best way to generate earned media is to create engaging content—anything from furry friends, to dumping buckets of ice water, to watching Beyoncé promote her latest video.

Engaging Your Audience

First, let us admit that the line between "communicate" and "engage" is blurry. The marketer communication needs to be relevant and engaging, or it will not attract attention. However, remember the Forrester ladder. It is nice to have people who simply consume your content. It is even better to have people who post favorable reviews (while having a response strategy for those whose opinions are unfavorable) and people who actually co-create content. Users who exhibit a behavior beyond simply consuming content are usually considered engaged.

There are a number of brands who have a long history of successful customer engagement. Pepsi's Mountain Dew has often used contests to help make product line decisions. In mid-2016, it has a DEWCISION 2016 opportunity to vote whether to keep the Baja Blast or the Pitch Black flavor on store shelves. While you're on the page, there's a selection of games and sports videos.[60]

Pepsi's Doritos had a 10-year string of contests that invited customers to create the ad that would be shown on that year's Super Bowl. That generated interesting ads and much buzz, but the brand announced that the Super Bowl 50 contest would be the last. Their target audience had changed from the Millennials in 2006 to Gen Z in 2016. Doritos sees them as people who like to create content on the social platforms of their choice. Hence, the Legion of the Bold campaign. On its website Doritos says:

> *Crashing the Super Bowl was just the beginning. Together, we're going to unleash our creative talents on the world throughout the year. That means more opportunities for national exposure and more chances to win cold-hard cash or bold experiences. Sign up now, and let the boldness begin.*[61]

Red Bull has an equally long history of sports videos. The videos cover all types of sports, including extreme sports, and they focus on the athletes, not the product. The over 5 thousand videos are highly entertaining, having attracted over 5 million subscribers to the Red Bull channel and almost 1.5 billion views in mid-2016.[62]

Customer engagement is also taking place on the newer social media platforms where technology often gives an assist. The assist may come at a price, however. A senior Taco Bell executive said that the lens shown in Figure 5.10a took 6 weeks to develop working directly with Snapchat and is reported to have cost $740,000—for a one-day campaign at that!

FIGURE 5.10a

Taco Bell's Cinco de Mayo Taco Head on Snapchat

The lens also featured Taco Bell's 'Bong' sound. *Taco Bell*

FIGURE 5.10b
A Shot of Paris is Part of the #MyAmex Campaign on Instagram

On that single day the lens received 224,000 views, the most ever for a single ad. Engagement is demonstrated by statistics showing that the average user played with the ad for 24 seconds before sending the snap. Engagement and branding were heightened by the fact that the ad played the chain's distinctive "bong" sound.[63]

Users also figured prominently in a campaign from American Express. While Taco Bell has a product that lends itself to visual marketing, American Express does not. Its solution was to turn its Instagram account over to six influentials in the fields of fashion, food, and media to record their travel and dining experiences and the way in which Amex impacts their business. During the 2-week period there were 10 million views on the Instagram account, doubling its average number of daily followers. During that time there were also 40,000 "engagements."[64] Instagram defines engagement as the number of viewers who responded to a post in some way: by clicking, sharing, or commenting.[65] It is important to know how each platform defines each metric; they can be different.

These examples illustrate the fact that, while social media is not free, it has a tremendous capacity to attract and engage followers.

Creating Community

The word "community" is often used loosely to refer to like-minded people who congregate somewhere to interact on the web. A brand community is something more limited and precise. Muniz and O'Guinn have advanced a universally accepted definition:

> A **brand community** *is a specialized, nongeographically bound community, based on a structured set of social relations among admirers of a brand.*[66]

brand community like-minded people who share interests grouping around a brand on the internet to communicate with one another and the brand

In a subsequent publication, they add that:

> *These consumers are drawn together by a common interest in, and commitment to, the brand and a social desire to bond with like-minded others. New modes of computer-mediated communication facilitate and flavor communal communication.*[67]

Building a brand community is not an activity to be undertaken lightly. It takes time, resources, and experience in successful social media marketing. If the marketer is extremely lucky, there is an existing brand community that can be gently co-opted by the corporation. Such was the case with the Harley Owners Group® (HOGs) who, as early as the 1920s, banded together in the physical world to enjoy motorcycle rides together. Harley Davidson recognized its value and assigned executives to go along on the rides long before the internet. The internet gave them an opportunity to "support" the HOGs with a web page. The page facilitated many subtle marketing activities, including support of local chapters and women's activities. The brand community is also alive and well on Facebook and Twitter while many local HOG groups are active on Instagram and Pinterest.

Whenever you look, there are numerous posts from members and some from local chapters, promoting events. There are, however, few comments from page administrators (i.e., corporate social media marketers). Members are doing it all for them! That is truly a vibrant brand community. It started with an experiential product that owners were passionate about, and that is why there have been HOG groups from the brand's early days. This physical world relationship gave Harley Davidson a rich history on which to build a modern virtual community to promote the real-life experience.

The community remains strong but it has gotten older. By 2013, most of its members were over 50 and although they had disposable income it was not going to bike purchases.[68] Through 2014 and 2015 sales slumped[69] and it was clear that action had to be taken. A new global campaign "Live Your Legend" was launched on TV during the 2016 NCAA Men's Basketball tournament to encourage riders of all ages and genders to live out their dreams on their own terms. The campaign, which was planned to launch globally later in the spring, will include a series of TV spots, print and online media, enthusiast and lifestyle media outreach, social media activations, direct marketing, and retail promotions. Harley also plans on curating real-life stories from riders on its social channels and website.[70] This campaign is designed to strengthen the brand by encouraging new uses and users. A robust brand community cannot prevent all business reverses, but it does provide a strong foundation for traditional and social media promotions, whatever their objectives.

It can also provide a strong foundation from which to launch a new product. For over 13 years video game series Call of Duty has been a sensation around the globe. It has been a best-seller and in 2016 it was said that over 100 million people played it.[71] There was much interest among players in the 2016 release, Infinite Warfare.

To promote the release publisher Activision set up a 'secure channel' on which fans could chat with Lt. Reyes. That secure channel was Facebook Messenger and Lt. Reyes was a chatbot. The promotion on Twitter is shown in Figure 5.11. During the first 24 hours the chatbot exchanged 6 million chats with avid fans.

Venture Beat added that, "Activision directed players to the chatbot through Nuk-3town, a popular map in last year's Call of Duty, Black Ops III. Those who put together the right clues were able to earn a link to Infinite Warfare's trailer."[72] While this type of game promotion is not unusual except for the chatbot, the use of an existing product to promote a line extension is good marketing practice.

A strong social media strategy can provide great value to a brand or a business. In order to both develop and execute the strategy the organization must have the well-developed infrastructure necessary for a social business. We end this chapter with a discussion of two infrastructure issues, the social media team and buy-in from top management.

FIGURE 5.11
Chat with a Bot

SOURCE: http://www.thedrum.com/news/2016/05/02/call-duty-drives-fans-facebook-messenger-secure-chat-lt-reyes-chatbot

EMBEDDING SMM IN THE ORGANIZATION

There has always been one key challenge for marketers who wish to make SMM an integral part of their strategy. Top managers have been skeptical and therefore reluctant to provide necessary budgets. The reasons for the skepticism are not well documented, but there appear to be two that are especially important:

1. Marketers have found it difficult to document ROI in a way that convinces management.
2. Many top managers are not users of social media and doubt its value.

Demonstrating ROI for SMM campaigns takes some time and effort, but it can be done. Throughout this chapter you have seen examples of success measures for campaigns, some even being able to link increased sales to social media efforts. There are many useful discussions of how to compute SMM ROI that are beyond the scope of this text.[73,74] All agree on two important issues:

1. All SMM campaigns must have clearly defined objectives. Most often the objectives will be behavioral—clicks, likes, and shares, for instance—although they can include impact on sales.
2. Campaign results must be carefully tracked to measure the achievements for each objective.

We will return to these subjects in Chapter 18.

Many studies over the years have found top managers unsure of their firm's ability to track SMM results. This has been true over all the iterations of the Duke University CMO study. The February 2016 study found only 11.5 percent saying the impact could be shown quantitatively and 40.6 percent saying they had some qualitative sense of impact while 18.3 percent said social media made no contribution to the firm's performance. The study also found that the firm's ability to integrate data from social media with other channels, necessary to prove impact on sales, had actually gotten worse since the last time the question was asked. Nevertheless, the firms intend to increase SMM budgets substantially over the next 5 years.[75] This suggests that there is much work to be done.

However, there is support for the proposition that ROI on SMM can be demonstrated. When a survey of digital marketers was taken, they were able to answer an important question, Which social media platform shows the greatest return on your marketing investment? When asked to name the channels that produced the best ROI, the winners were the four usual suspects—Facebook, Twitter, Instagram, and LinkedIn, with almost 96 percent listing Facebook as a top producer (Figure 5.12).

Some firms are able to track the degree to which SMM achieves stated communications objectives. One of the requirements for this level of SMM effectiveness is a strong social media team.

Building a Successful Social Media Team

Most businesses of any size who are serious about social media will find it necessary to have a social media team whether it is solely focused on social media or whether it shares other marketing responsibilities. Finding the right people and organizing them for effectiveness is therefore of paramount importance.

There are several roles that must be filled in a social media team. They include the following:

- Social media manager
- Content creators, including search engine optimization (SEO) and platform optimization specialists
- Community management
- Campaign management and promotion. Campaign promotion often includes paid promotions as well as PR and perhaps events.
- Analytics and strategy. This may include not only analysts but people who are familiar with testing a variety of campaign elements as discussed in Chapters 4 and 18.

FIGURE 5.12
Platforms Providing Best Return on Marketing Investment

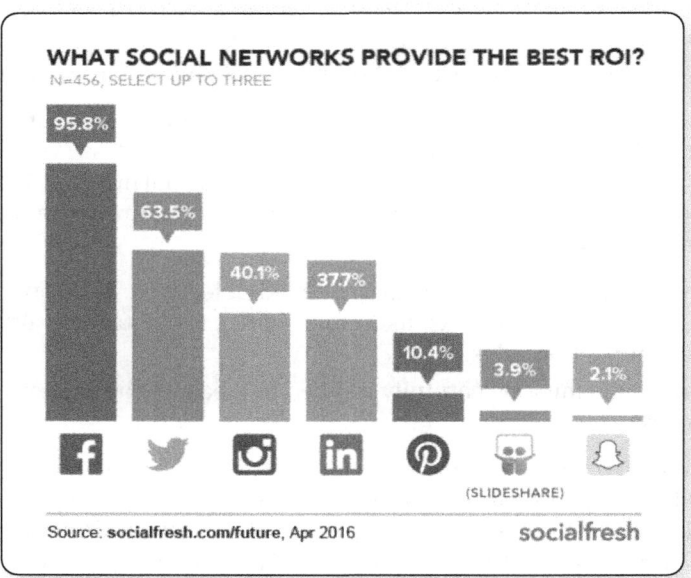

SOURCE: http://simplymeasured.com/blog/3-surprising-lessons-for-marketers-from-the-future-of-social/#sm.0000002to08kmvcpyv7vlb6v649jq

This suggest that teams will have a number of members who must work well and creatively together so choosing the right people, not just the right skills, is important.[76,77]

The video in Interactive Exercise 5.4 gives unusual insight into how one team works together. JetBlue is also well-known for social media effectiveness. It is a standout in social media customer service using a team of mostly stay-at-home moms.[78] Head of the Social Media and Customer-Commitment team Laurie Meacham says, "JetBlue's social media goal is for a truly organic experience—people talking to people." In order to make that happen JetBlue team members are trained to be their own authentic selves, being willing to engage with customers and doing so in the language of the customers. They are building a network of customer relationships that is a strong foundation for the good and the bad of everyday air travel.[79]

In spite of all the success stories in this chapter it is difficult for SMM to gain traction in a firm without the support of top management, particularly the CEO. It is even better if the CEO provides leadership in the field of social media.

Bringing Top Management into the Social Business Fold

Advocates for CEO involvement in social media often point to the 70-20-10 model. The concept is that in the digital era employee learning comes 70 percent from experience, 20 percent from social aspects like coaching and many types of collaboration, and only 10 percent from formal educational programs.[80] Seeing the CEO as a role model, mentor, and coach for social involvement can be a powerful part of that learning system as the experience of Zappos shows.

A study by BrandFog uncovered key benefits of top management involvement in social media. They are as follows:

1. Social media involvement makes better leaders. They create transparency for the brand and build connections with customers, employees, and other stakeholders.
2. Their engagement in social media builds brand trust. It helps build brand awareness and trust in the brand by communicating mission, values, and purpose.
3. Social media is modern PR for top managers. Social media engagement helps establish them as industry leaders who have credibility with the public and the media. It may help to prevent reputational crises and if an event does occur, it provides a trusted channel for communicating to transmit facts and to preserve brand reputation.[81]

There are many top executives who thrive on the open conversation of social media whether they are engaging with customers or with their own employees. A recent list of the top 100 CEOs on social media contains many familiar names. Should that surprise you? The cover photo has Richard Branson (Virgin Group), Arianna Huffington (Huffington Post), Bill Gates (Microsoft and the Gates Foundation), Jeff Weiner (LinkedIn), and Mark Benioff (Salesforce). It is an international list that contains CEOs of established firms like Unilever and GE and new entrants like Uber and Airbnb. The list makes interesting reading. You will not be surprised to see other superstars like Mark Zuckerberg and Tim Cook on it. You may be surprised to see CEOs of lesser-known firms in sectors like investments and insurance.[82]

There is widespread belief that pressure will continue to grow for top managers to have constructive social media presences. How can you lead if you do not understand important aspects of your business?

All in all, the concept of the social business—whose employees are engaged from top to bottom levels, who builds strong customer relationships through communication, and who has a trusted public presence—is a vision that will propel much corporate and personal transformation in the years to come.

SUMMARY

Well-informed marketers—large and small, B2C, B2B, and nonprofit—are finding success in social media space. In order to thrive, going forward most businesses will have to incorporate some elements of SMM into their marketing communications mix. If customers are in social space—and they are as the statistics in this chapter show—marketers must be there also. Marketers are finding that good SMM engages visitors and encourages them to participate in campaigns and to co-create content. Influencers can be a powerful force in well-designed campaigns bringing both awareness and thought leadership to the SMM effort.

Businesses of all kinds are using social media in the workplace. In some firms CEOs and other top executives are part of the social media activity. They find ways to engage and motivate employees and customers and identify tools that increase productivity. These are all steps on the way to the social business in which social media permeates all aspects of the enterprise.

All good marketing begins with customer knowledge. The acquisition of customer knowledge is facilitated in social media space where good listening is a precursor to development of SMM strategy. The steps in developing a strategy are as follows:

- Listening
- Communicating through a mix of paid, owned, and earned media
- Engaging
- Creating community

There are numerous tools that can be used to support marketer efforts in each stage.

There are also important metrics that are used to evaluate the effectiveness of each step. Some have been mentioned in this chapter, including Facebook fans or viewers or subscribers to a branded YouTube channel, for example. It is important to link social media campaigns to actual sales results and to ROI whenever possible, but that is often difficult. It is important for all SMM campaigns to have clearly defined objectives and to track and analyze the campaign results. This will produce useful insights for future campaigns.

Businesses need a strong social media team, one that has an explicit, if not a total, focus on social media. The team must have the skills needed to carry out the social media strategy and must work well together in an environment that often requires real-time response. It is helpful if top managers are part of this activity. Top management involvement enhances the brand and engages employees. This is the road to the social business.

DISCUSSION QUESTIONS

1. Why do you think social networks have grown so quickly in countries all over the world?
2. Why are messaging apps attracting numbers of users almost equivalent to the largest social platforms?
3. What are the benefits to a brand or business from the use of SMM?
4. True or False. SMM requires entirely different tools and techniques in B2C, B2B, and nonprofit markets.
5. What is influencer marketing and how is it carried out?
6. How can social media make workplaces more engaging and more productive?
7. Why do marketers consider earned media especially desirable? What other types of media are they comparing it to?
8. What are the steps in developing an SMM strategy? Why is each one important?
9. What are some examples of social media engagement beyond the ones discussed in the chapter?

10. Why do many people seem to enjoy belonging to brand communities?
11. What is necessary to build a good social media team?
12. Why do you think some managers are resistant to the idea of engaging in SMM? What could you do or say to convince your reluctant boss that SMM could be a good idea in a specific business setting?

ENDNOTES

1. http://www.smartinsights.com/marketplace-analysis/customer-analysis/digital-marketing-statistics-sources/
2. http://www.smartinsights.com/social-media-marketing/social-media-strategy/new-global-social-media-research/
3. Vidhi Choudhary, "Half of Online Indians Use Facebook and WhatsApp Daily: Report," http://www.livemint.com/Industry/vU55FbKdlz9vIfkxUb0EoL/Facebook-tops-networking-WhatsApp-in-message-apps-in-India.html
4. "WhatsApp User Base Crosses 800 Million," http://timesofindia.indiatimes.com/tech/tech-news/WhatsApp-user-base-crosses-800-million/articleshow/46985683.cms
5. http://oldspice.com/en-us/videos/videos
6. "The Old Spice Media Campaign by the Numbers," http://mashable.com/2010/07/15/old-spice-stats/#E8N4um5nXqq3
7. Noreen O'Leary and Todd Wasserman, "Old Spice Campaign Smells Like a Sales Success Too," http://www.adweek.com/news/advertising-branding/old-spice-campaign-smells-sales-success-too-107588
8. Tim Nudd, "The 20 Most Viral Ads of 2015," http://www.adweek.com/news-gallery/advertising-branding/20-most-viral-ads-2015-168213
9. http://www.digitaltrends.com/social-media/google-friends-furever/
10. Content Marketing Institute, Marketing Profs, Brightcove, "B2B Content Marketing," http://contentmarketinginstitute.com/wp-content/uploads/2014/10/2015_B2B_Research.pdf
11. Brian Solis, "StatSocial Names the Top 100 Social Media Power Influencers for 2015," http://www.briansolis.com/2015/06/statsocial-names-top-100-social-media-power-influencers-2015/
12. Brian Solis, "25 Top Marketing Influencers," http://www.briansolis.com/2015/10/25-top-marketing-influencers/
13. James Anderson, "20 B2B Content Marketing Examples and Case Studies for 2015," http://www.toprankblog.com/2015/03/20-b2b-content-marketing-examples/
14. http://shortyawards.com/about
15. http://shortyawards.com/7th/the-future-of-pr-what-if-pr-stood-for-people-and-relationships
16. "Influencer Marketing Is Rapidly Gaining Popularity Among Brand Marketers," http://www.emarketer.com/Article/Influencer-Marketing-Rapidly-Gaining-Popularity-Among-Brand-Marketers/1013563
17. https://www.tapinfluence.com/the-ultimate-influencer-marketing-guide/
18. Dom Burch, "Is it Time to Call Bullshit on Influencer Marketing?" http://www.thedrum.com/opinion/2016/05/18/it-time-call-bullshit-influencer-marketing
19. https://www.ftc.gov/tips-advice/business-center/guidance/ftcs-endorsement-guides-what-people-are-asking
20. "FTC Puts Social Media Marketers on Notice with Updated Disclosure Guidelines," http://marketingland.com/ftc-puts-social-media-marketers-on-notice-with-updated-disclosure-guidelines-132017
21. Claire Axelrad, "10 Truths About Social Media's Impact on Nonprofit Fundraising and Marketing," http://maximizesocialbusiness.com/social-media-impact-nonprofit-fundraising-marketing-8357/
22. Claire Axelrad, "10 Truths About Social Media's Impact on Nonprofit Fundraising and Marketing," http://maximizesocialbusiness.com/social-media-impact-nonprofit-fundraising-marketing-8357/

23. Freida Kahen-Kashi, "The Man Behind the ALS Ice Bucket Challenge's 'Viralstorm,'"http://abcnews.go.com/blogs/politics/2014/12/the-man-behind-the-als-ice-bucket-challenges-viral-storm/
24. https://www.youtube.com/watch?v=6TLzOW39WXw
25. Lyanne Alfaro, "Your $220 Million to the ALS Ice Bucket Challenge Made a Difference, Study Results Show," http://www.businessinsider.com/your-220-million-to-the-als-bucket-challenge-made-a-difference-2015-8
26. http://www.alsa.org/fight-als/ice-bucket-challenge.html
27. https://www.gofundme.com/
28. https://twitter.com/tonyhsieh?lang=en
29. Christopher Ratcliff, "How Zappos Uses Social Media: Twitter, Facebook, and Instagram," https://econsultancy.com/blog/65526-how-zappos-uses-social-media-twitter-facebook-and-instagram/
30. Liz Azyan, "How to Turn Employees into Social Media Advocates: Case Examples," http://www.socialmediaexaminer.com/turn-employees-into-social-media-advocates/
31. http://www.advisortechtips.com/
32. Connie Sung Moyle, "How 3 Firms Are Using Social Media Education Programs to Grown Business," http://hearsaysocial.com/2016/02/how-3-firms-are-using-social-media-education-programs-to-grow-business/
33. "Social employee advocacy pilot program made simple #marketing #business," http://bluefocusmarketing.com/2016/03/29/social-employee-advocacy-pilot-program-made-simple-marketing-business/
34. Mark Burgess, "Plotting a Course for Social Business," http://blog.ama.org/plotting-a-course-for-social-business/
35. http://socialmediagovernance.com/policies
36. http://socialmedia.biz/social-media-policies/
37. https://slack.com/
38. Jeff Bercovici, "Slack is Out Company of the Year. Here's Why Everybody's Talking About It," http://www.inc.com/magazine/201512/jeff-bercovici/slack-company-of-the-year-2015.html
39. Annalee Newitz, "What Slack Is Doing to Out Offices—and Our Minds,"http://arstechnica.com/information-technology/2016/03/what-slack-is-doing-to-our-offices-and-our-minds/
40. Lauren Johnson, "This Agency Is 30% More Productive Since It Started Using Chat Software to Connect With Clients," http://arstechnica.com/information-technology/2016/03/what-slack-is-doing-to-our-offices-and-our-minds/
41. Michelle Greenwald, "R/GA Moves Into the World's Most Connected Office," http://www.forbes.com/sites/michellegreenwald/2016/05/23/rga-moves-into-to-the-worlds-most-connected-office/#74c0bf316515
42. Nicole Nguyen, "21 Productivity Hacks Every Slack User Should Know,"https://www.buzzfeed.com/nicolenguyen/slack-attack?utm_term=.evPp4ZwRR#.wkQY9jZxx
43. Tim Peterson, "Inside the Making of Taco Bell's Artificially Intelligent, Drunk-Tolerant TacoBot," http://marketingland.com/inside-making-taco-bells-tacobot-173181
44. Melissa S. Barker, Donald I. Barker, Nicholas F. Bormann, Debra Zahay, and Mary Lou Roberts, 2nd ed. 2017, *Social Media Marketing: A Strategic Approach* (Mason, OH, Cengage Learning), Chapter 15, Appendix
45. Melissa S. Barker, Donald I. Barker, Nicholas F. Bormann, Debra Zahay, and Mary Lou Roberts, 2 nd ed. 2017, Social Media Marketing: A Strategic Approach (Mason, OH, Cengage Learning), Chapter 15, Appendix pp. 258, 259.
46. Jackie Rousseau-Anderson, "The Latest Global Social Media Trends May Surprise You," http://blogs.forrester.com/jackie_rousseau_anderson/10-09-28-latest_global_social_media_trends_may_surprise_you.
47. Dennis Williams II, "Why Beyonce's Word Is Worth More Than a Super Bowl Ad," https://www.linkedin.com/pulse/why-beyonces-word-worth-more-than-super-bowl-ad-dennis-williams-ii

48. Ian Mount, "The Twitterverse Is Hating on Red Lobster for Lame Beyonce Response," http://fortune.com/2016/02/08/red-lobster-beyonce/
49. Hadley Malcolm, "Beyonce's 'Formation Helped Boost Sales 33% at Red Lobster," http://www.usatoday.com/story/money/2016/02/09/beyonces-formation-helps-boost-sales-at-red-lobster/80055898/
50. Dennis Williams II, "Why Beyonce's Word Is Worth More Than a Super Bowl Ad," https://www.linkedin.com/pulse/why-beyonces-word-worth-more-than-super-bowl-ad-dennis-williams-ii
51. Barbara Kollmeyer, "Budweiser Inisists It Didn't Pay Peyton Manning for that $3.2 Million in Free Advertising," http://www.marketwatch.com/story/peyton-manning-handed-budweiser-32-million-in-free-ads-after-the-super-bowl-2016-02-08
52. Sean Wagner-McGough, "Peyton Manning's Budweiser Super Bowl Shoutouts Valued at $13.9M," http://www.cbssports.com/nfl/eye-on-football/25478090/peyton-mannings-budweiser-super-bowl-shoutouts-valued-at-139m
53. Sage Lewis, "No One Cares About Your Products," http://www.clickz.com/clickz/column/1707550/no-one-cares-about-your-products
54. Sage Lewis, "No One Cares About Your Products," http://www.clickz.com/clickz/column/1707550/no-one-cares-about-your-products
55. Myles Anderson, "88% of Consumers Trust Online Reviews as Much as Personal Recommendations," http://searchengineland.com/88-consumers-trust-online-reviews-much-personal-recommendations-195803
56. Amy Gesenhues, "Survey: 90% of Customers Say their Decisions Are Influenced By Online Reviews," http://marketingland.com/survey-customers-more-frustrated-by-how-long-it-takes-to-resolve-a-customer-service-issue-than-the-resolution-38756
57. Suzanne Delzio, "12 Social Media Marketing Trends for Small Business," http://www.socialmediaexaminer.com/social-media-marketing-trends-for-small-business/
58. Kristina Cisnero, "3 Small Businesses That Found Social Media Success, https://blog.hootsuite.com/small-business-social-media-success-stories/
59. Jack Loechner,"Brands Failing in Timely Response to Customers on Social Media," http://www.mediapost.com/publications/article/275848/brands-failing-in-timely-response-to-customers-on.html#reply?utm_source=newsletter&utm_medium=email&utm_content=comment&utm_campaign=92983
60. http://www.mountaindew.com/
61. https://www.doritoslegionofthebold.com/
62. http://www.statsheep.com/redbull
63. Lauren Johnson, "Taco Bell's Cinco de Mayo Snapchat Lens Was Viewed 224 Million Times," http://www.adweek.com/news/technology/taco-bells-cinco-de-mayo-snapchat-lens-was-viewed-224-million-times-171390
64. Lauren Johnson, "AmEx Generated 10 Million Impressions in 2 Weeks With Guest Photographers," http://www.adweek.com/news/technology/how-amex-used-influencers-raise-its-profile-instagram-162086
65. https://help.instagram.com/help/178043462360087
66. Albert M. Muniz, Jr. and Thomas C. O'Guinn, (2001). "Brand Community." *journal of Consumer Research* 27, p. 412.
67. Thomas C. O'Guinn and Albert Muniz, Jr., "Collective Brand Relationships," in *Handbook of Brand Relations*, eds. Joseph Priester, Deborah MacInnis, and C. W. Park (N.Y. Society for Consumer Psychology and M.E. Sharp), p. 19.
68. Jonathn Salem Baskin, "Harley-Davidson Will be a Case History in Social Branding," http://www.forbes.com/sites/jonathansalembaskin/2013/07/12/harley-davidson-will-be-a-case-history-in-social-branding/#7bc41a7b5b85
69. "Rivals Give Harley-Davidson a Case of Earnings Road Rash," http://www.fool.com/investing/general/2015/04/27/rivals-give-harley-davidson-inc-case-of-earnings-r.aspx
70. Lindsay Stein, "'Live Your Legend,' Urges Harley-Davidson in New Global Campaign, http://adage.com/article/agency-news/harley-davidson-aims-energize-brand-campaign/303141/
71. http://moviepilot.com/posts/3879408

72. Mike Minotti, "Call of Duty: Infinite Warfare's First Victory: 6M Bot Messages on Facebook," http://venturebeat.com/2016/05/03/call-of-duty-infinite-warfares-first-victory-6m-bot-messages-on-facebook/
73. Dominique Jackson, "Ultimate Guide to Measuring Social Media ROI," http://sproutsocial.com/insights/social-media-roi-guide/ https://blog.hootsuite.com/measure-social-media-roi-business/
74. Melissa S. Barker, Donald I. Barker, Nicholas F. Bormann, Debra Zahay, and Mary Lou Roberts, 2nd ed. 2017, *Social Media Marketing: A Strategic Approach* (Mason, OH, Cengage Learning), Chapter 13.
75. https://cmosurvey.org/wp-content/uploads/sites/11/2016/02/The_CMO_Survey-Highlights_and_Insights-Feb-2016.pdf
76. Sam Milbrath, "How to Build a Social Media Dream Team," https://blog.hootsuite.com/how-to-build-a-social-media-dream-team/
77. Alex York, "How to Build a Dynamic Social Media Team," http://sproutsocial.com/insights/social-media-team/
78. Jo Piazza, "The Secret of JetBlue's Social Media Success? Stay at Home Moms, Cat Memes—and a Sense of Humor," https://www.yahoo.com/style/the-secrets-of-jetblues-social-media-success-93024204957.html
79. Jason Keath, "The Secret to JetBlue's Awesome Social Engagement,"https://www.socialfresh.com/the-secret-to-jetblues-awesome-social-engagement/
80. https://www.702010forum.com/about-702010-framework
81. http://brandfog.com/CEOSocialMediaSurvey/BRANDfog_2014_CEO_Survey.pdf
82. http://www.xinfu.com/the-top-100-ceos-on-social-media/

Chapter 6

Experiencing the Digital Customer Journey

LEARNING OBJECTIVES

By the time you complete this chapter you will be able to:

1. Discuss the growth of the internet through its various stages and in different parts of the world.
2. Explain the purposes for which consumers and B2B customers use the internet.
3. Describe how media use is changing in terms of both communications channels and groups of users.
4. Discuss the concept of a resilient brand.
5. Identify key things marketers must do to be effective in the digital age.
6. Explain what the customer journey means and how the digital age has changed it.
7. Provide an in-depth explanation of what CX (customer experience) is.
8. Explain why CX is important.
9. Discuss what marketers must do to provide seamlessly excellent CX.

CX "cumulative experiences across multiple touchpoints and in multiple channels over time"

The way customers approach making a purchase has changed. This has increased the importance of **CX** at each step. We will discuss those two important and interconnected topics in this chapter. Before we do so, however, we need to look at customers themselves—who they are and how they use the internet, keeping in mind the discussions of social media usage in Chapter 5.

A PROFILE OF THE INTERNET AND ITS USERS

The original concept for the modern internet is generally attributed to MIT scientist and head of the Defense Advanced Research Projects Agency (DARPA) J. C. R. Licklider. In 1962, he envisioned a "Galactic Network" of connected computers whose primary purpose would be to share data and programs. Use would be limited to the community of scientists who were linked to research and development programs of the Department of Defense. The only flaw in his reasoning was that communications quickly became the primary use of the network among the scientist users of early days just as it is of users today.

It is also fair to say that no one foresaw the explosive growth of internet use and users that began about 1995 and continues to the present day. Figure 6.1 only covers 1991 through 2012 but it clearly shows the basic eras of the modern internet and the growth of different aspects of the network along with major technological innovations

FIGURE 6.1
Growth of the Internet

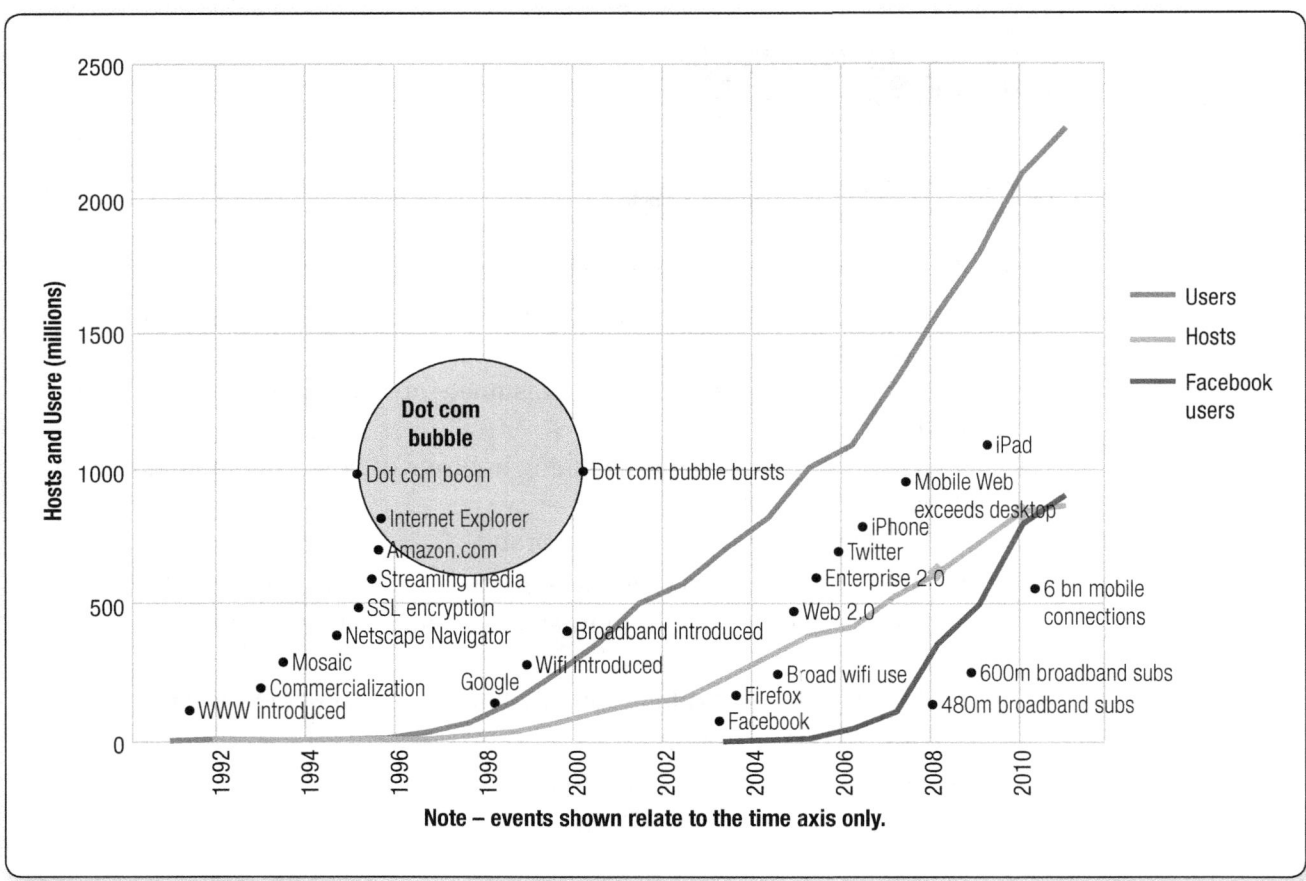

SOURCE: http://webscience.org/web-observatory/about/tracking-explosive-growth/

that spurred its growth. Just as user-friendly browsers fueled the growth of the interactive stage of the web, social platforms continue to fuel growth during the social phase. Mobile is an important aspect of growth at present, to be discussed in detail in Chapter 12.

The Size and Scope of Today's Internet

Figure 6.2 picks up the ongoing story of explosive growth in internet usage. These data from the Internet Society show 400 million users in 2000—6.8 percent of the world population. The *1 billion* user mark was reached in 2005 and the number became 2 billion in 2010. The chart shows 3.2 *billion* in 2015—46.1 of the world population.[1]

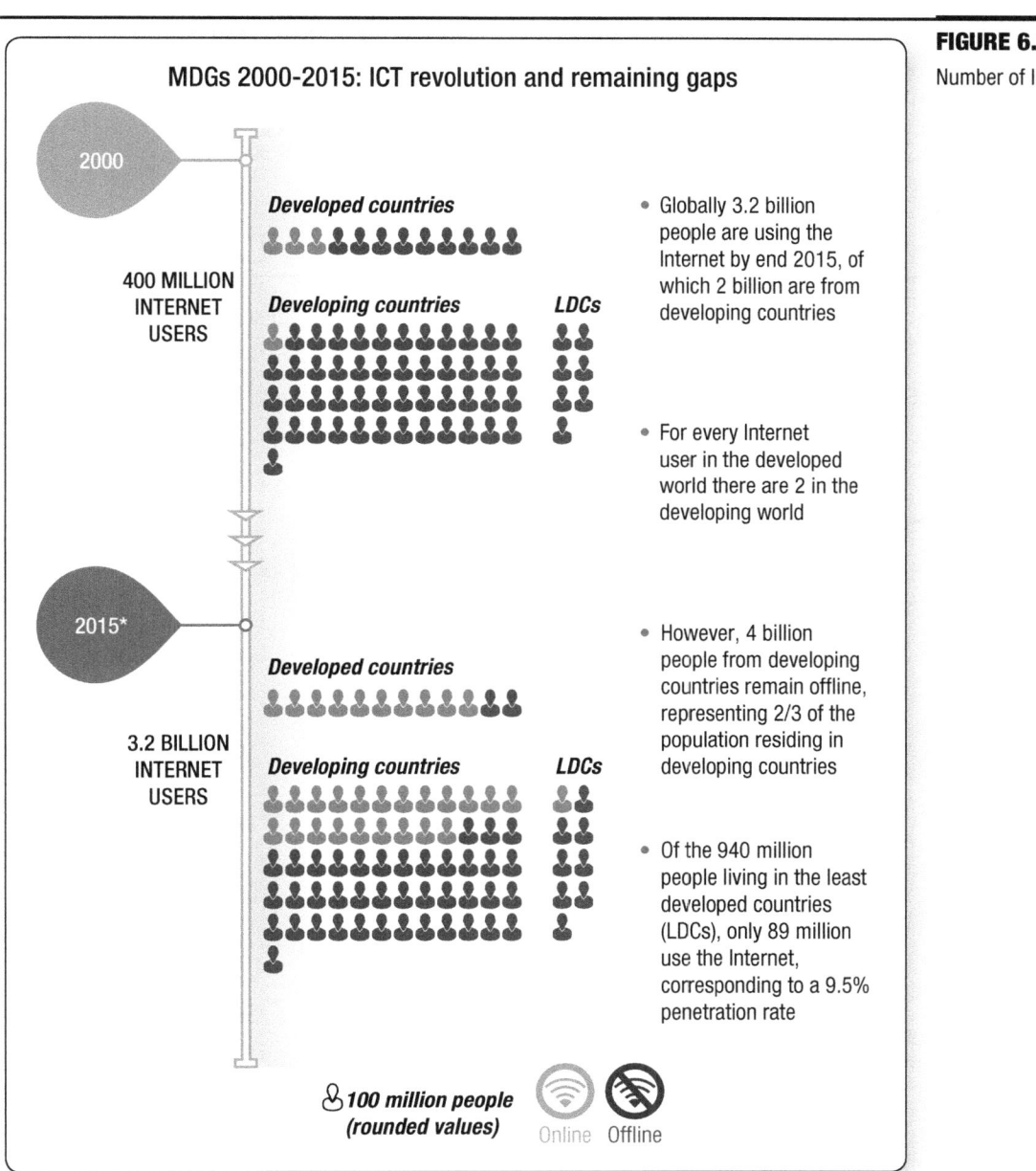

FIGURE 6.2
Number of Internet Users

SOURCE: http://www.itu.int/en/ITU-D/Statistics/Documents/facts/ICTFactsFigures2015.pdf

That is an incredible growth trajectory. But look at it the other way around. The penetration of usage in developed countries is high. Pew found it to be 84 percent in the United Stats in 2015,[2] which some would argue is about the saturation point. The chart points out that two-third of the people in developing countries lack internet access. That number rises to 90 percent in less developed countries.

That leaves a very large number of people still to gain access to the internet. Media experts estimate that 3 billion more people will be connected by the end of 2018. About one-third of them will be from India and most of them will be through mobile.[3]

Media Use in the Digital Age

Both consumers and business buyers have turned to digital channels for much of the information they consume. As can be seen in Figure 6.3, that has resulted in less time spent consuming all the traditional broadcast and print media, even though the total time spent consuming media is expected to continue to inch up through 2017. The growth is coming from digital. More precisely, it is coming entirely from mobile and other connected devices. Content consumption has truly gone mobile.

FIGURE 6.3

Daily Media Consumption

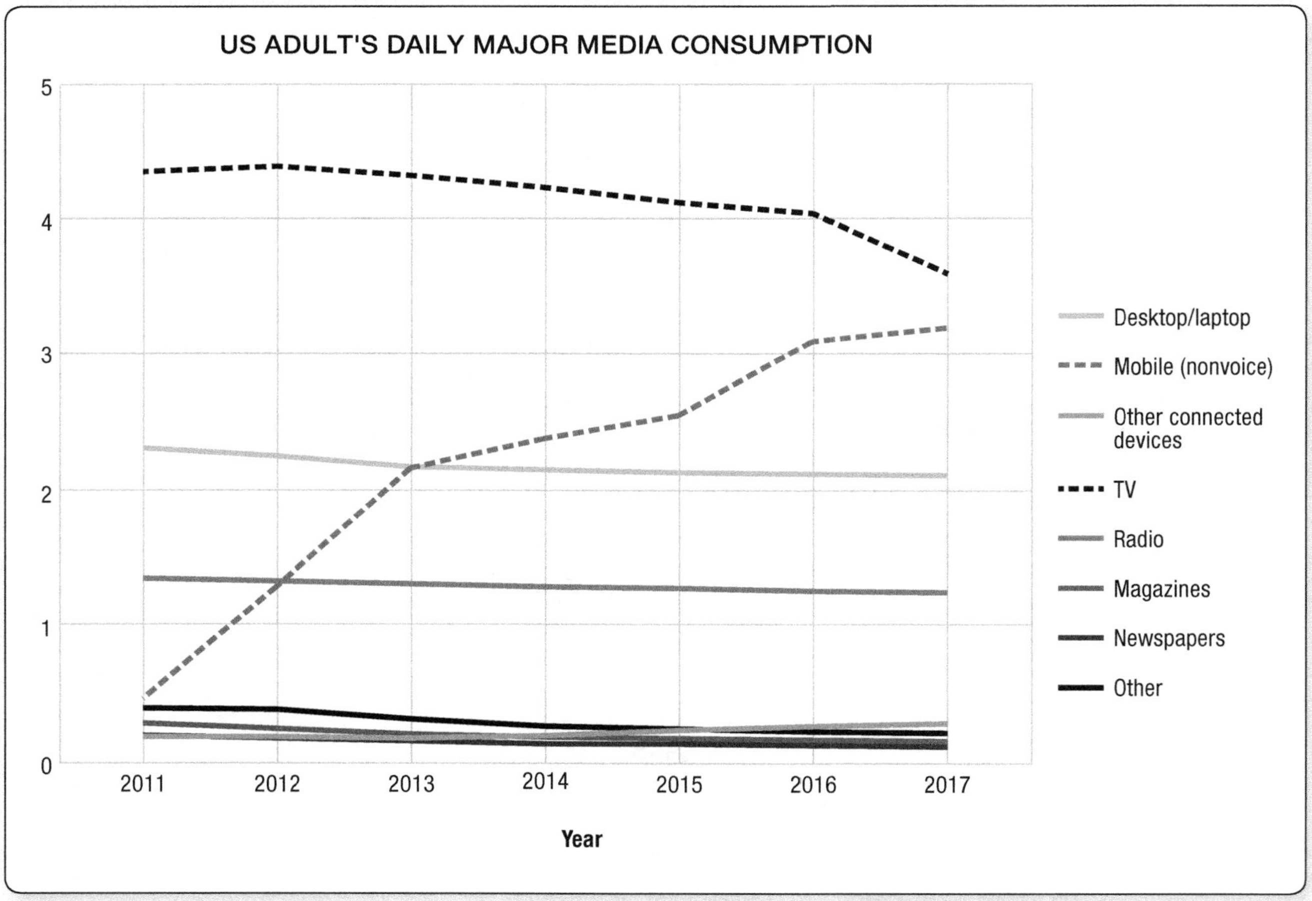

SOURCE: http://www.marketingcharts.com/traditional/us-adults-daily-major-media-consumption-estimates-2011-2017-59995/

Branding in the Digital Age

When asked if the fundamentals of brand building had changed in the midst of this disruptive change in media use, agency CEO Andrew Keller said no, they had not. However, he added that "the opportunities, touchpoints, access, and speed with which we can take action have changed dramatically. But that's really only part of the story. The digital age and social media in particular, have changed the social contract between people and brands. The expectation of the relationship has become far more intimate."[4] The resilient brand concept portrayed in Figure 6.4 captures this idea. It could also be described as an agile brand, one that is able to withstand disruption and emerge stronger and more vibrant.

The belief component of a resilient brand is best developed by interactive communications in social media. Advertising and other forms of persuasive communication play a role but, as we discussed in Chapter 5, authentic brand communications in social media are key to building trust and belief that the brand will fulfill its promise to the customer. Resilient brands also understand that customers are only a click away from peer reviews and communications about the brand. There is no place for a brand to hide in the social media ecosystem. The importance of CX, the second component, in creating brand satisfaction is a major focus of this chapter.

The approach argues for the nature and requirements of the brand as the driving force behind strategy in a way that is different from the traditional one-to-many methods of traditional advertising. Instead, it requires an always-on methodology that resonates with its connected community. According to agency Brilliant Noise that methodology "supports a narrative that builds over time, that feel fresh and in-sync with what's happening in the world. It supports dialogue with the customer. It has personality and supports personalization. The goal isn't always to push a product, but to build trust—to create a meaningful relationship with both existing customers and those who are considering the brand."[5] They add that this kind of communication is geared toward engagement and building advocates.

Engagement is a somewhat fuzzy term, as we will discuss in Chapter 18. When asked what it means in a promotional context, Chief Strategy Officer Gareth Kay of

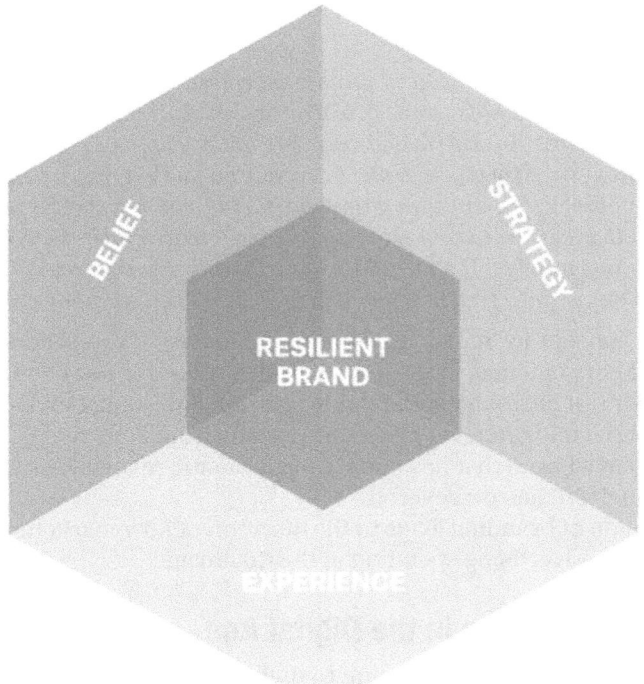

FIGURE 6.4

The Components of a Resilient Brand

SOURCE: http://www.slideshare.net/brilliantnoise/resilient-brands-49517135

Goodby Silverstein & Partners talked about the importance of engaging the emotions of customers to drive desired behaviors.[6] He pointed to studies of traditional advertising and digital advertising,[7] both of which found that creative ads that have emotional appeal were the most effective. Emotion is also an important factor in CX, as we will see later in the chapter.

Netflix has engaged in a decades-long struggle to establish and evolve a resilient brand. Its odyssey illustrates many of the issues. Netflix was established in 1997 and opened for business in 1998 as a DVD rental-by-mail firm. It struggled against retailer competition (Blockbuster) in the early years and did not have a profitable quarter until 2003. It continued to struggle with profitability, however. At times, the more subscribers a new type of rental program garnered, the more money the company lost. In spite of uneven profitability the company went public in 2002 while continuing rapid expansion in the number of distribution facilities needed to provide overnight delivery to its customers, now numbering 1 million.

By 2005, Netflix was shipping over 1 million DVDs each and every day and absorbing the high costs associated with the purchase, stocking, shipping, and restocking of physical product in its dozens of distribution centers. It was clear that content on demand was the future and in 2007 Netflix started streaming movie and video content. Netflix initially did not charge members more for the streaming content, and independent producers were often happy to furnish titles at low cost to reach Netflix's large audience. As the popularity of streaming increased so did the licensing fees, bolstered by the consumer's demand for first-run movies.

It was clear that Netflix would have to charge for streaming and in 2011 they broke the company into two parts. Netflix would continue to handle the streaming and a new company, Qwikster, would be responsible for DVD rental. The result was a significant price increase and consumer fury reverberated around the web. Netflix had to pull back from the two-company concept.[8]

What followed was a long period of rebuilding business and customer trust. Streaming continued to grow and in 2013 the company introduced its first original series. One estimate says that Netflix will have 150 million global customers for its Subscription Video on Demand services by 2020.[9] The company continues to argue that the linear model, in which programs are offered at a set time on nonportable screens, is unappetizing to modern viewers.[10]

Netflix puts it this way:

> *Sometimes it's hard to find a movie everyone can enjoy on a Friday night. For individuals and families with internet access, Netflix instantly streams an unlimited number of TV shows and movies, anytime, anywhere. Simply search, browse and watch on the easy-to-use website, mobile apps, apps on game platforms and hundreds of Internet-connected devices. With one-click anyone can watch ad-free, HD quality, TV shows and movies. It's month-to-month and you can cancel anytime. We offer a one month free trial. Netflix, it's movie enjoyment made easy.*[11]

The brand concept is "movie enjoyment made easy." The product itself and its core benefits of convenience, large selection, and value are not enough. It offers the emotional benefits of customer satisfaction and delight. Going beyond mere satisfaction, it offers a brief and often very welcome escape from daily reality. Its story is also a revealing look at a brand that has undergone dramatic reversals as well as euphoric highs and, through all, has persevered.

The discussion of branding leads to the question of how marketers are approaching marketing and advertising spending in the digital age.

Marketing Effectiveness in the Digital Age

If all customers are increasingly turning to digital channels for their content, where do you expect marketers to put their advertising dollars? Digital, of course!

Duke University's CMO survey forecasted that traditional advertising spending would go down by 2.1 percent in 2016 while digital ad spending would go up

12.2 percent.[12] Figure 6.5 gives more detailed data. It shows total ad spending declining from 2014 (which included Olympic ad spending) to 2015 by 3.9 percent. Sunday magazines were the biggest losers with Spanish language TV and newspapers also suffering big declines. The downward trend affected all types of newspapers and the free-standing inserts (FSIs) that depend on them for distribution. Digital display advertising rose sharply with paid search advertising also showing growth. The outlier was radio and the driver was spending on local radio ads. According to Kantar Media that growth came primarily from automobile dealerships, legal services, and health care providers.[13]

Marketer spending on advertising is only part of the answer to effectiveness, and not necessarily the most important part of the answer as the previous sections have demonstrated. The CMO survey identified the top three customer priorities for 2015 as superior product quality (importance trend both up and down over three years), excellent service (trend up over three years), and low price (trend down over three years).[14] Figure 6.6 offers more detail.

Good value for the money, high-quality customer service, and good prices are once again the top three issues. Customers do not articulate CX so readily; it ranks tenth on this list. But look at other issues important to them—knowing customer needs, trust, easy to do business with, high-quality sales reps, and communications that make customers feel connected. What do all those issues add up to, except excellent CX? Customers clearly know good CX when they see it.

FIGURE 6.5
How Advertisers Are Spending Their Money

US AD SPENDING TRENDS

Media platform (ordered by Q2 spend)	Q2 2015 (year-over-year change)
Total	−3.9%
TV Platforms	−4.5%
Cable TV	−5.1%
Network TV	1.0%
Spot TV	−1.8%
Spanish language TV	−22.4%
Syndication – National	−3.3%
Digital Platforms	2.4%
Paid search	7.7%
Online display (PC desktop only)	−4.7%
Magazine Platforms	−7.7%
Consumer magazines	−5.5%
B2B magazines	−6.3%
Sunday magazines	−41.9%
Local magazines	−1.2%
Spanish language magazines	−13.7%
Newspaper Platforms	−12.7%
Local newspapers	−13.9%
National newspapers	−4.2%
Spanish language newspapers	−18.9%
Radio Platforms	5.0%
Local radio	10.6%
National spot radio	1.2%
Network radio	−8.4%
Hispanic local radio	4.2%
Out of Home Platforms	4.0%
Outdoor	2.2%
Cinema	14.9%
FSIs	−15.6%

SOURCE: http://www.marketingcharts.com/online/us-ad-spending-trends-by-medium-in-q1-2015-56313/

FIGURE 6.6

Drivers of Customer Satisfaction

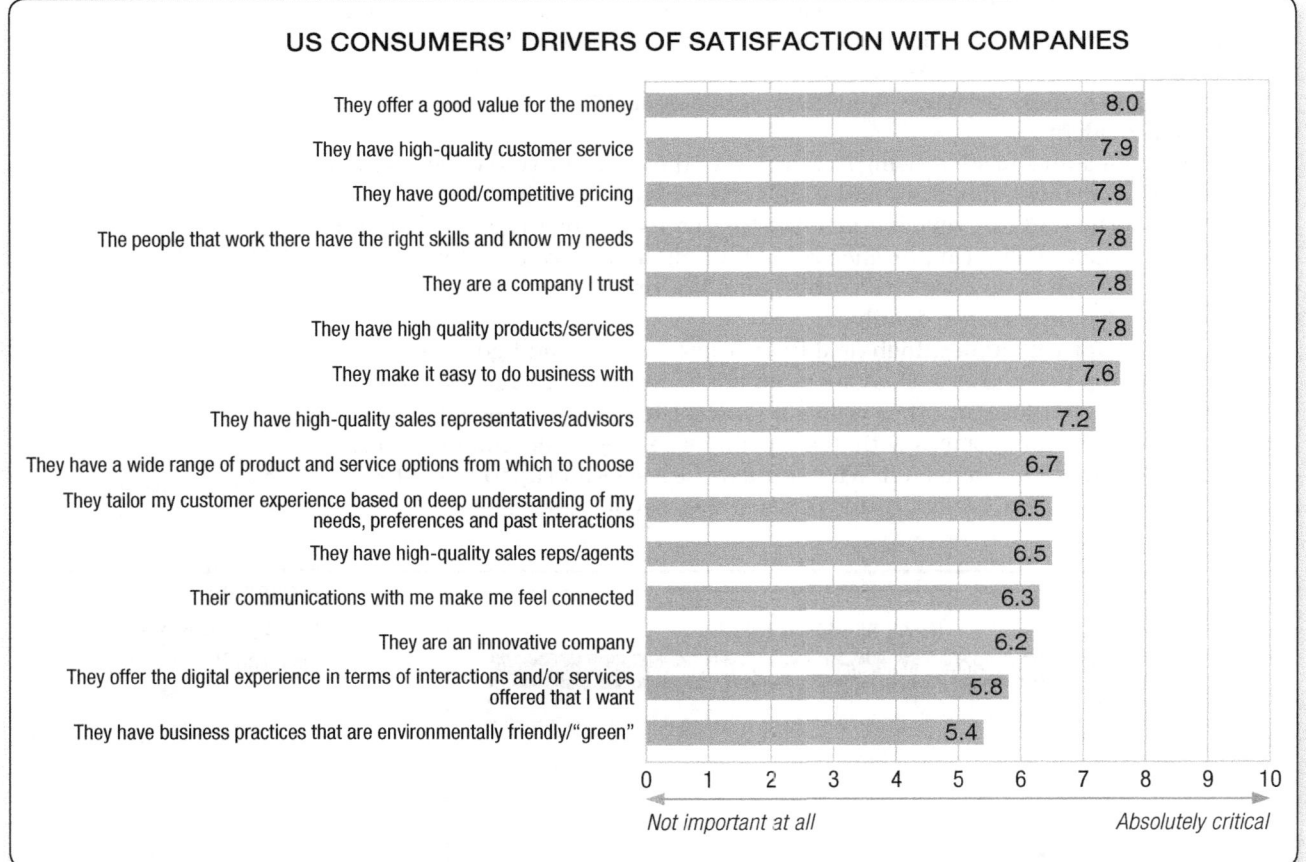

SOURCE: http://www.marketingcharts.com/traditional/what-do-us-consumers-see-as-their-core-drivers-of-satisfaction-with-companies-66657/attachment/accenture-consumer-drivers-company-satisfaction-mar2016/

Marketers are reacting to the message customers are sending. Gartner estimates that in 2016 89 percent of companies expect to compete primarily on the basis of CX—up from 36 percent in just four years.

They also predict that by 2017 50 percent of product expenditures will be directed toward CX improvement.[15] It is hard to overstate the importance of CX!

A meeting of media executives described the CX goal as "each touchpoint a customer has with your organisation must be anticipated, relevant, and effortless—every single time."[16] They stated the following imperatives for CX:

- Marketers must have a mobile-first mindset.
  "Mobile is your customer's first interaction with your brand."
- The differences between B2C and B2B marketing will disappear.
  "Whether your buyer is a business or a consumer, there's a person behind every interaction."
- Learn to know your customer intimately with analytics.
  "organisations are racing to transform the data they capture into consumable insights that foster customer engagement and retention."

- Marketing and customer service work hand-in-hand.
  "the marketing team monitoring and flagging a service-related remark on social media to the customer care team—enables brands to improve the digital CX in real-time, with personalisation, and produce responsive support and communications on the channels that customers choose."[17]

Forbes adds that "CX is the future of marketing."[18] Could there be a stronger statement?

In order to understand the all-important touchpoints, we must first look at how the customer journey has changed. Then we can examine how best to deliver excellent CX at every touchpoint.

THE CUSTOMER JOURNEY IN THE DIGITAL AGE

Over the past decade it has become clear that marketers must rethink their model of the consumer decision process. It has typically been portrayed as a linear process, often as a funnel as in Figure 6.7a. The message of the funnel is that customers begin with a set of brands in mind and over several stages of consideration narrow the set down to a single brand for purchase. The implication that this takes place in an orderly, linear set of steps does not hold true in the digital age.

Instead the term customer journey or customer decision journey has come into widespread use. Like any journey, the customer's route to a purchasing decision can experience stops and starts, wrong turns, and progress that often appears to be anything but linear. That is the result of changes in customers themselves, changes in the environment (like more brands to consider), and the disruptive changes in media we have just discussed. Actual customer journeys can be complex as we will discuss later in this section. However, Figure 6.7b is a good portrayal of the basic concept.

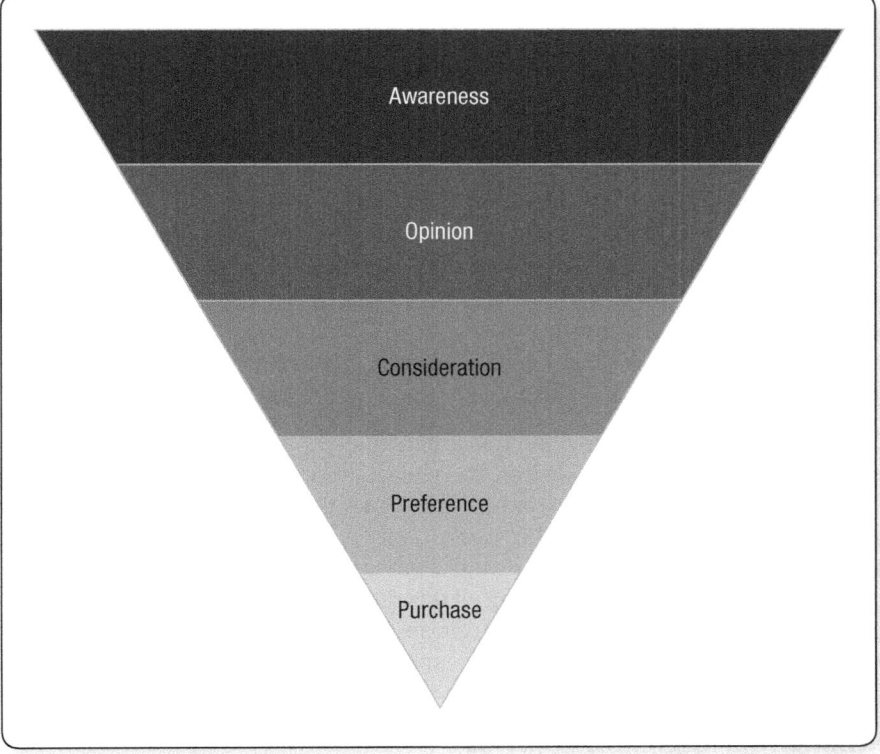

FIGURE 6.7a
The Purchase Funnel

SOURCE: http://www.forbes.com/sites/gregsatell/2015/10/12/marketers-need-to-drastically-rethink-the-customer-decision-journey/#f21bd073f285

FIGURE 6.7b

The Journey

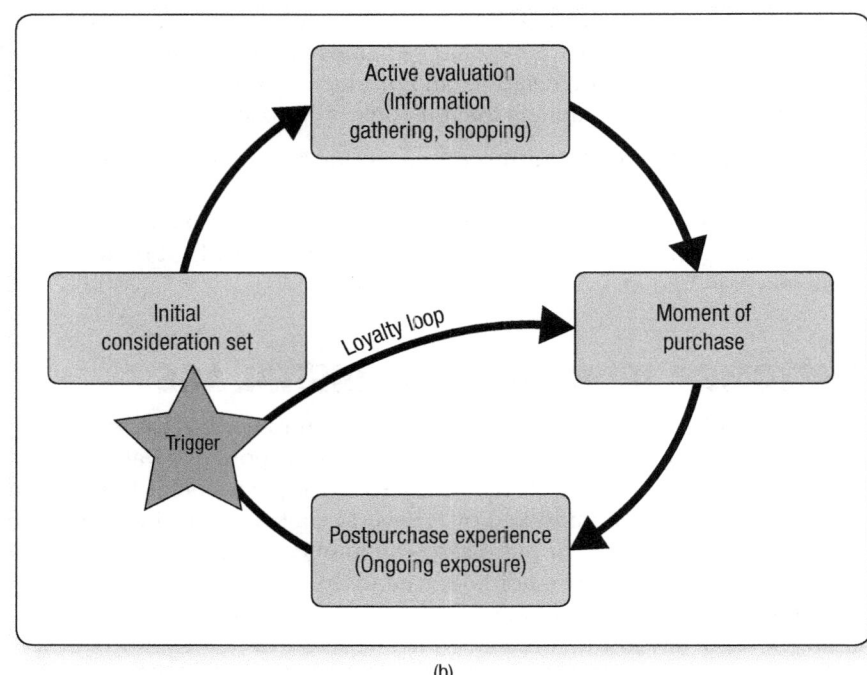

(b)

SOURCE: http://www.forbes.com/sites/gregsatell/2015/10/12/marketers-need-to-drastically-rethink-the-customer-decision-journey/#f21bd073f285

Much of the consumer decision journey as portrayed in Figure 6.7b is familiar to students of marketing. The journey begins with a trigger, perhaps the recognition of a need. Then the consumer considers an initial set of brands based on brand perceptions and recent exposure to touchpoints. A recent study found that key touchpoints to be:

- Search engine visits—consumer searches online for information about retailers, products, and brands.
- Retailer visits—consumers like to visit retail stores to actually see and experience the product and to get more information. Mobile phones are often a source of information while visiting a retailer.
- Brand visits—direct visits to brand and manufacturer sites appear to be decreasing as search uncovers brand information. Information is also available on Amazon, which many shoppers use as a price and review check either before or after visiting a retail store.
- Review site or app visits—some shoppers make additional checks through third-party reference sites, often using their mobile apps.[19]

At any point in the journey, the consumer may loop back and repeat an activity. After visiting one or more brand sites, the customer may decide to revisit the retailer (or visit another retailer) to give additional consideration to one or more brands. Alternatively, the customer may skip a step. For example, the customer may forego a retail visit if he is familiar with the product category or the brand.

Active evaluation is going on during all this time. If the decision is made to purchase, a brand is chosen at the moment of purchase. The loyalty loop begins when the consumer experiences the product and builds expectations for the next purchase situation.[20]

The Consumer Decision Journey

The description of the decision journey actually sounds quite familiar, doesn't it? It is similar to the way that we have always described the linear purchase process. It is the presence of the loyalty loop that causes marketers to look at the ongoing journey in a way that is different from a process with a beginning and an end. Research indicates that consumers are constantly reevaluating the product as a result of both their experience of using the product and the thousands of product- and brand-related messages they are exposed to during the period of using the product. The loyalty loop can be thought of as having three components as consumers experience the product and consume communications from peers as well as marketers. The loyalty stages are:

- Enjoy the use of the product
- Become an advocate for the brand
- Bond with the brand through satisfactory use and service experience and ongoing relevant and personalized content.

In other words, marketers have to develop and distribute content, not just for the purchase process but also for the loyalty process. That requires a large and detailed set of data about the individual consumer.

Figure 6.8 shows a decision journey map. In this case it is for a business trip. What additional stages might be added if it were a map for a family vacation? There would probably be a number of entertainment decisions to add if it were for a family trip.

As it is, there are a number of stages, each one of which seems to require a separate website or app. Have you booked travel through a single site that was able to meet most of your requirements? Do you think this was improved the CX over what you see in Figure 6.8?

The point is that marketers first need to understand the consumer decision journey. Then they need to look at every stage in the journey for marketing opportunities. Interactive Exercise 6.2 (which can be found in the learning path for this chapter) allows you to use one of the tools that might be helpful in this process.

FIGURE 6.8

A Customer Decision Journey

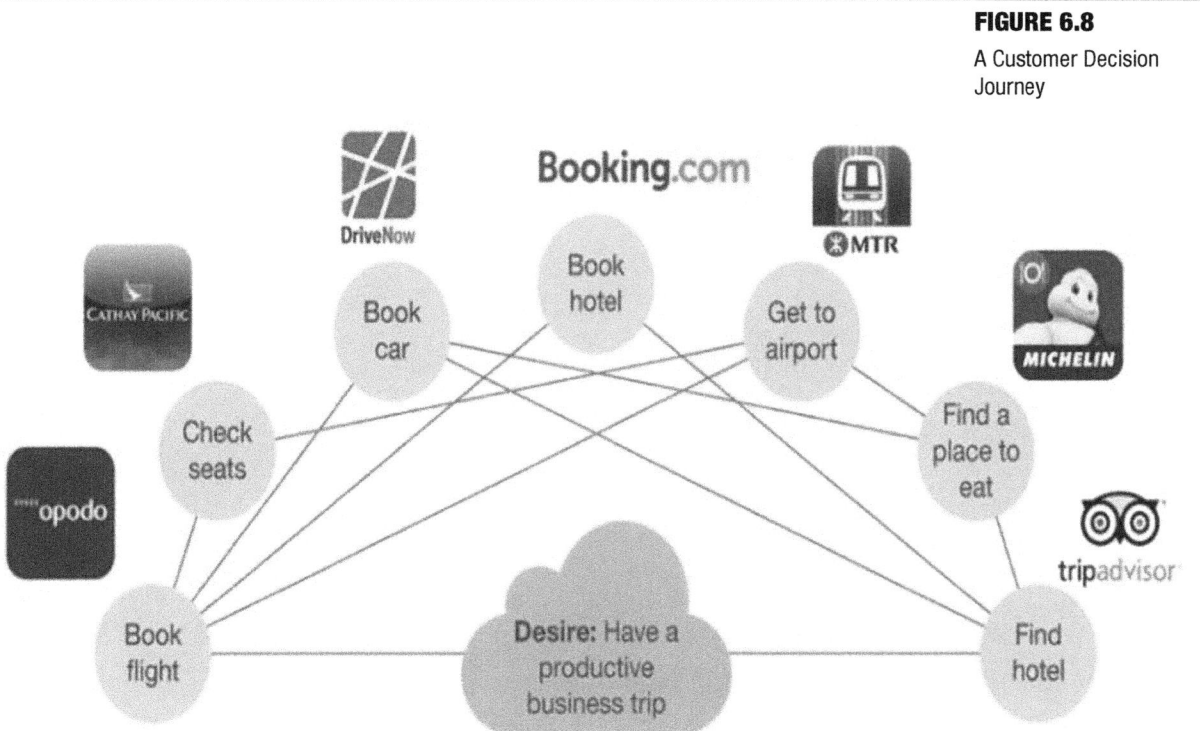

SOURCE: http://blogs.forrester.com/category/customer_experience

The B2B Decision Journey

The illustration of the journey in B2B markets in Figure 6.9 is conceptual, and it helps to understand the mapping process in either B2B or B2C markets. Notice that it is divided into just three stages—awareness, consideration, and purchase. Each stage, however, has multiple possible actions. In the awareness stage, for example, the potential buyer can search, make discoveries, and share them. Notice also that the map has many turns, forward loops, and backward loops. It looks a bit like a bowl of noodles, but it captures the multiple activities that buyers can engage in and the almost infinite number of paths they can take.

The conceptual map of the consumer journey in Figure 6.7b is much simpler. However, when you look at the discussion of consumer touchpoints and realize that there might be other touchpoints and there is likely to be much looping back and skipping forward, it is clear that the consumer journey can also be complex.

FIGURE 6.9
Conceptual Business Decision Journey Map

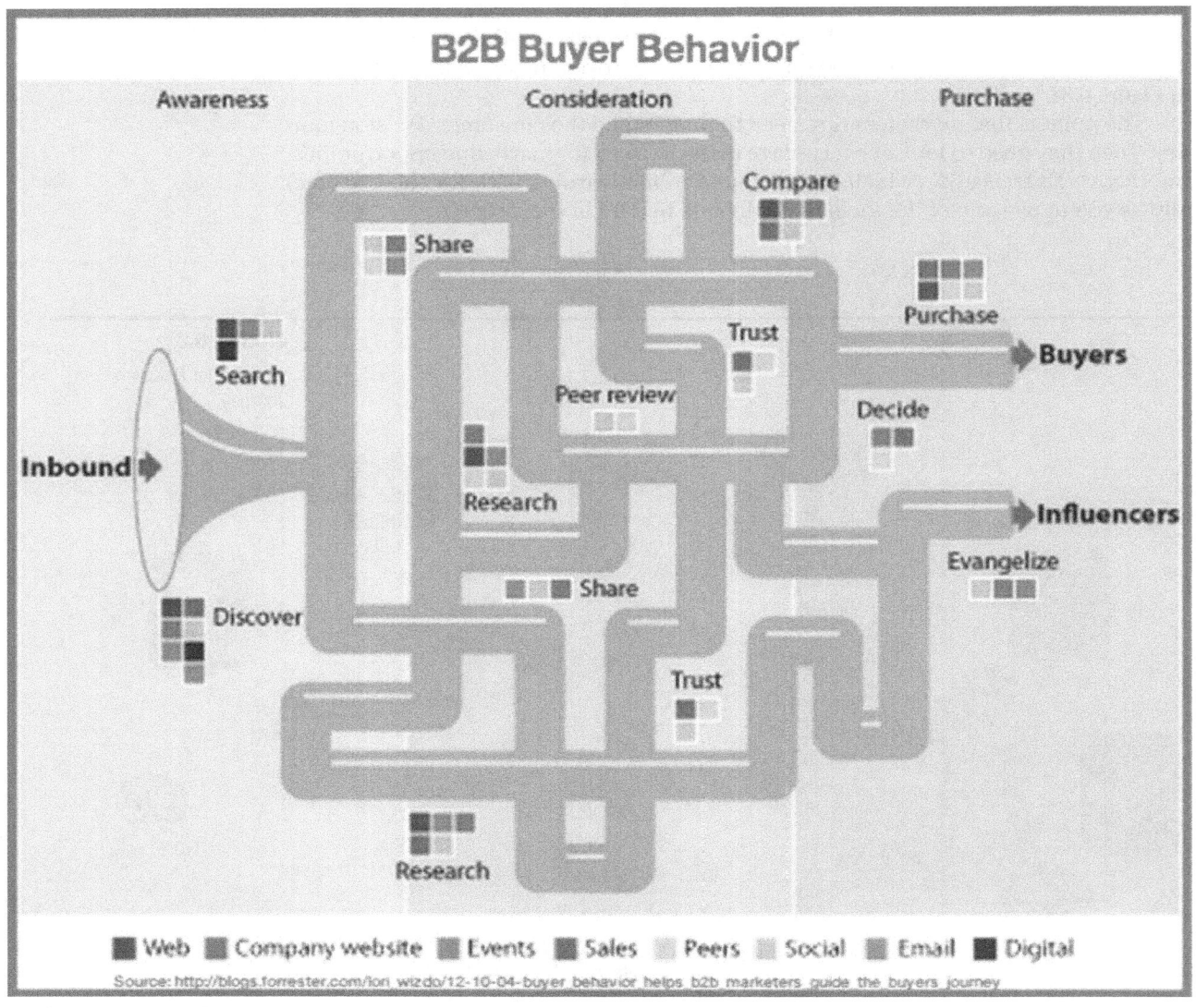

SOURCE: http://heidicohen.com/2015-b2b-purchase-decision-process/

The point of this comparison is that both concepts represent a useful starting point, but the marketer needs to create a journey map that is specific to the product (e.g., travel) and purchase situation or segment (e.g., family). As you will see in the next section, the level of specificity and detail is essential to creating a seamless CX across all journey touchpoints.

Can Marketers Track Customers Through Their Journeys?

Accepting the fact that the customer journey can be complex and that it can vary from one individual to another, it is reasonable to ask whether marketers can respond at a granular level that corresponds to the customer's journey stage and their behaviors at that time. The answer is yes. Much of the technology is not new but Facebook has made it easy to use and very popular with marketers.

It starts with Facebook's dynamic product ads. These ads essentially allow marketers to showcase multiple products in a single ad.[21] It has been likened to a catalog in which a variety of products are offered to a potential customer. The difference is the degree to which the ideal product can be identified for an individual consumer on either a laptop or a mobile device.

The second piece of technology is a Facebook **pixel**, often generically referred to as a **pixel tag**. Pixel tags have been in use since the dawn of e-commerce, but the Facebook pixel has several features. It allows a marketer to track conversions (sales) from a Facebook ad, to show the ads to people like their existing customers (optimization) and to remarket (in this chapter we will call it retargeting) to people who have looked but not purchased.[22] Setting up a pixel involves creating decision rules like "If viewer books hotel room, then offer him a rental car in the same city."

pixel a one-pixel transparent GIF that is added to the pages of a website allowing sites to track visitor activity

FIGURE 6.10

Screens from a Dynamic Product Ad

An example of a 'Dynamic Ad' on Instagram. For the first time, Facebook is bringing the popular retargeting ad format from its flagship app to its photo-and-video sharing app. (Courtesy of Facebook)

SOURCE: http://www.forbes.com/sites/kathleenchaykowski/2016/05/10/facebook-debuts-retargeted-ads-on-instagram-tests-new-travel-ads/#3062d83f480f

Instagram (owned by Facebook) has been shown to be excellent at creating awareness of a product but less successful in directly generating sales. Much of Instagram viewership is on mobile devices, which also makes it attractive to marketers. By combining marketer data (for instance, a product page visit to the website) with Facebook data, the viewer can be shown the most relevant product in the Instagram ad. Facebook says this allows the retailer to "show the right product to the right person every time."[23]

Figure 6.10 shows screens from a test run on Instagram by Canadian jewelry site Jewlr. The site had already been successful with product ads on Facebook. In this instance they "wanted to target U.S. consumers who had viewed or added a product to their cart from their website, but had not followed through with a purchase. By hitting them with Dynamic ads after the fact, Jewlr reported a nearly 300 percent increased return on ad spent, according to Facebook's internal calculations."[24]

Dynamic ads placed on either Facebook or Instagram can also take advantage of the retargeting opportunity. That allows the retailer to display ads on other sites the viewer is visiting. For instance, the jewelry retailer can show an ad on a wedding site when the viewer visits there.

Viewer tracking has opponents as will be discussed in Chapter 17. However, there seems little doubt that being able to advertise the right product to a shopper at the time he is looking for it is an improvement in CX.

CREATING SATISFYING CX IN THE DIGITAL AGE

What is this "satisfying CX" that is the focus of marketers? Harvard Business Review has a simple but powerful definition. They say CX can only be understood as the customer's *"cumulative experiences across multiple touchpoints and in multiple channels over time."*[25]

experiential marketing promotional activity that helps consumers understand a product by having direct contact with it

There are wonderful examples of great CXs from many brands. Nike has long been a master of what is called **experiential marketing**. Basketball has been one favorite focus for this kind of marketing. As part of the hoopla for the 2015 NBA final game, Nike built a responsive LED half court environment to celebrate the thirtieth anniversary of the Air Jordan franchise. Invited fans could recreate two of Michael Jordan's most iconic championship game shots, complete with crowd reaction to their individual enactment.[26] Instead of spending millions of dollars on a single Super Bowl ad in 2016, Nike staged an experiential event in nearby San Francisco. A venue called The Arena, open for the three-day Super Bowl weekend, allowed fans to try out new Nike products and interact with athletes. As part of the festivities Nike+ fans were treated to a Speed Drops event. Athletes in Nike-branded luxury cars delivered special products to lucky fans. Products included Vapor Untouchable football cleats in a golden box and limited-edition Precious Metal sneakers.[27,28]

event marketing a themed activity that promotes a product, business, or cause

Event marketing like this does a wonderful job of creating buzz around exciting CXs. And it is part—but not all—of overall CX. There is general agreement that CX is the customer's perception of the brand that results from *all interactions with the brand over all touchpoints*. It is not the result of any single event or experience, no matter how satisfying—or perhaps even unsatisfying. It is not the result of interaction with a single touchpoint. It is the result of cumulative interactions over time.

It also results from more than one type of perception. CX expert Bruce Temkin says its components are function, how well the product performs and accessibility, how easy it is to use and derive the benefits (Figure 6.11). The final component is emotion, the feelings that result from experiencing the product. If you look back at the resilient brand framework, you see these same ideas expressed with attributes as the base and something bigger than the product itself as the final achievement. Again, there is agreement that experience is a key to a sustainable brand and emotion is a key component.

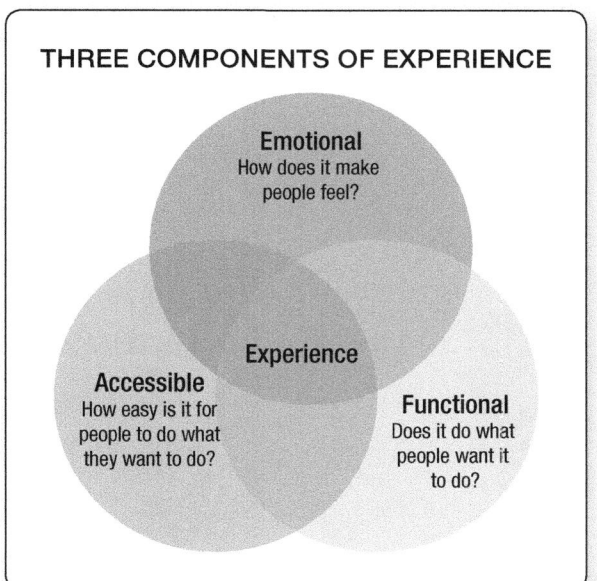

FIGURE 6.11
The Components of CX

SOURCE: https://experiencematters.wordpress.com/2011/02/28/nokia-needs-more-design-less-engineering/

Amazon has been at the top of CX award categories year after year. How do they do it? The company is obsessive in its focus on customer satisfaction and CX. It shows up in everything from its customer service to its many types of personalization that make shopping more convenient and enjoyable. It makes mobile work for its customers for both search and purchase. Jeff Bezos is often quoted as saying, "If you make customers unhappy in the physical world, they might each tell six friends. If you make customers unhappy on the internet, they can each tell 6,000." He notes that it works the other way too. According to Bezos, "word of mouth is becoming more powerful. If you offer a great service, people find out."[29]

Customers agree according to the responses to a Forrester CX survey as seen in Figure 6.12. Sparking positive emotion, making the decision process easy, and acting as a buffer against negative issues—excellent CX creates competitive strength.

In Chapter 2, we discussed Amazon Web Services as one example of how Amazon is constantly exploring new technology to enhance its business and to make the CX better. Its highly automated distribution centers are essential to swift order fulfillment that enhances experience. It has been much in the news for its experiments with drone delivery. But in the end, CX experts and successful managers alike agree that it's all about the employees.

CX—It's All About People

Wegmans is a relatively small family-run grocery chain that has been at or near the top of the grocery industry rankings for several years. What makes it so special?

"They were the first grocer to work from the customer's point of view," one food writer said[30]

Instead of simply displaying aisles of packaged products that shoppers might buy, McCauley explains, Wegmans made grocery into theater—not just with specialty food stations but also by preparing food in front of customers. Wegmans understood that, to a younger generation, "shopping" didn't mean filling your cart with canned peas, it meant hanging out, learning about food, and eating it.

FIGURE 6.12

Emotion in the Amazon CX

Emotional elements of Amazon's CX resonate with customers around the world.

It appeals to logic and emotion.

"There are multiple wish lists, a cart, and a save-for-later area, which means that Amazon recognizes that for an orgnanized shopper, one list won't do. This is why Amazon is the gold standard."

Canadian female, 35 to 44 years old

It eases the decision process.

"When I shop with Amazon, I feel nurtured, taken care of, and fulfilled. Overall, I feel like a very smart shopper. I love Amazon!"

US male, 55 to 64 years old

It controls negativity.

"Amazon is so reasonable when you actually have a problem. The company takes a common-sense approach to customer service, which is refreshing."

UK female, 25 to 29 years old

Source: Forrester's ConsumerVoices Market Research Online Community, Q4 2015 (US, UK, Canada)

SOURCE: http://blogs.forrester.com/anjali_lai/15-12-31-the_data_digest_a_happy_new_year

"Wegmans was prescient," McCauley said. "They were aware of what millennials wanted before the millennials even got there."[31]

Customers and food experts agree that the European food hall-style layout, product quality, in-store dining, selection of prepared foods, and reasonable prices all make Wegmans appealing. One points out, however, that the real secret sauce is their employees.

KMPG says about Wegmans and its CEO Danny Wegman:

> At Wegmans, there is no rule book for its employees. Staff are allowed to make their own decisions, with the only rule being that no customer is allowed to leave unhappy. CEO Wegman believes in giving employees training and experience, then trusting them to deliver the product and service experiences that are expected. It's a formula that works for both staff and customers. The company regularly ranks at the top of Fortune's '100 Best Places to Work For,' as staff feel they are trusted to have control over decisions.[32]

That results in "almost *'telepathic levels of service,'* where the staff anticipate what the customers might need before the customer is even aware."[33] That is among the many customer-pleasing characteristics of the Ritz-Carlton experience.

The Ritz-Carlton has long been famous for superb customer service, delivered in a luxury environment by employees who are not highly paid but who are empowered to do their best for customers. Even at the Ritz-Carlton, though, the saga of Joshie the giraffe is outstanding.

After a family vacation at the Ritz-Carlton in Amelia Island, Florida, the young son's beloved stuffed giraffe went missing. He was inconsolable and found it hard to sleep without his Joshie. The parents, of course, reported the toy missing and were delighted when the resort found it in the laundry, having suffered no damage. Joshie was returned, complete with pictures of his vacation—lounging by the pool, driving a golf cart, and several others that were chronicled on Huffington Post.[34]

I wish I could tell you that the little boy slept peacefully ever after with his stuffed giraffe by his side but that's not the case. Four years later the boy left the giraffe at another hotel in another city. Despite the best efforts of the hotel staff and the boy's mother, the toy was never found. Since the same model was no longer being made, the toy was replaced, if such a thing is possible, with a smaller giraffe named Tucker. Not long after this incident the family returned to the Amelia Island, Ritz-Carlton only to find that the staff remembered Joshie and were saddened over his recent disappearance. The staff presented the little boy with another giraffe, Jeffie—a long-lost cousin of Joshie's. Apparently Tucker and Jeffie now co-exist happily in their new home.[35] In addition, the Ritz-Carlton has another wonderful CX story to tell its employees in their never-ending quest for excellent customer service that creates memorable CX.

THE OVERRIDING IMPORTANCE OF CX IN THE CUSTOMER JOURNEY

Gartner estimates that 89 percent of companies will compete on CX in 2016—not on product quality, not on product benefits, but on the end-to-end CX.[36] Other reports emphasize the importance of CX in B2B markets.[37] Both B2B and B2C companies consider it a more durable competitive advantage. Considering the challenges we have discussed in this chapter, it is hard not to agree that truly satisfying CX takes time and effort to achieve. Given its basis in engaged, motivated employees, it is hard for competitors to emulate.

CX was at or near the top of marketing trends lists for 2016 as it had increasingly been for several years. IBM's SilverPop had a good summary of what it takes to provide excellent CX. Their criteria were:

- Understanding what customers want, perhaps before they even know it themselves. (That is a special skill at Wegmans.)
- Identifying the perfect moment. (That is hard enough to do in person. It is even more difficult when the contact is made through some kind of technology. We will return to the subject in Chapter 12 when we discuss Mobile Micro-Moments.)
- Adding sentiment (think Joshie the giraffe) and emotion (think the Nike+ member receiving a pair of state-of-the-art athletic shoes in a gold presentation box) to the mix.
- Using data, analytics, and predictive models to create personalized communications that impact the purchasing decision.
- Being able to bring all marketing capabilities to bear across any touchpoint in real time.[38]

Others describe this process as putting the right content into the right context. By that they mean getting it to the customer at the right time, in the right setting, and over the right communication channel.[39,40] This kind of omni-channel response is difficult, and we will further examine it in our discussion of customer service in Chapter 16.

While it is clear that most companies recognize the importance of CX, it is equally clear that the majority are not succeeding in creating excellent omni-channel CX. The numbers differ slightly from one study to another,[41,42,43] but the message of underperforming CX efforts is clear. These same studies find that companies with leading-edge CX programs outperform their competitors.

If CX is indeed the competitive battlefield of 2016 and beyond, companies need to focus their efforts on CX programs that truly result in customer satisfaction in order to achieve a truly sustainable competitive advantage.

SUMMARY

From a closed network accessible by only a few scientists, the internet has become part of the global infrastructure for both communications and transactions. Growth has not slowed in the 21st century, it has accelerated. Social media have been one growth driver; people in developing economies gaining access to the internet has been another. Access in developing economies is overwhelmingly by smart phone.

Consumers of all ages, social classes, and racial groups use the internet. One of the few demographic groups that shows less usage is rural residents who may lack good internet access. Communications have always been the primary reason for internet use but content consumption, especially video, and purchasing of goods and services are also important. Younger consumers adopted the internet more quickly, use it for more and more activities, and are often the trend setters in areas such as migration to mobile. Business customers are people too, and they use the internet for the same reasons but with a different motivation—to improve their job performance. They use information sources on the web extensively, often not bring sales representatives into the process until late in the purchase process. Use of internet media channels continues to rise at the expense of traditional print and broadcast media.

The Resilient Brand is a concept of the digital age. Resilient brands use a strategy based on interactive communications and the engagement that is engendered by open and direct communications. They focus intently on providing excellent customer experience. The communications and the experience lead to belief in the brand and create a level of trust that is vital to the brand in good times and bad. The amount spent on marketing and advertising, of course, has a bearing on brand development. However, it is all the elements that make up a seamlessly excellent customer experience that is the foundation of a strong brand.

In this digital environment, the customer journey—both B2C and B2B—has changed. It is no longer a linear progression through a few identifiable stages. It is a process with stops, starts, loops back to earlier stages, and a variety of information sources in addition to the information provided by the brand or product itself. Marketers must make the effort to track customers throughout their journeys and to communicate with them in the context of their current journey stage.

Experiential marketing using techniques like marketing events have long been part of the marketer's toolkit. While important, that falls short of the concept of customer experience which is made up of all interactions with the brand over all touchpoints over time. Customer experience is about people not technology, although technology can assist the marketer to understand and serve the customer.

Customer experience should be the focal point of marketing efforts. Providing excellent customer experience is not always easy, especially for the multichannel merchant. It is however essential because it is the competitive battlefield today and for the future.

DISCUSSION QUESTIONS

1. True/False. The internet has reached a saturation point where rapid growth is no longer possible.
2. Think about your own internet use habits. Have you changed your use of traditional media? Why or why not? How do your own habits fit the media use attitudes and patterns described in this chapter?
3. Now think about people a generation or two older than you—your parents and grandparents, perhaps. Have they changed from traditional media use patterns? In what ways?
4. True/False. There is no significant difference between the ways consumers and businesses use the internet.
5. A businessperson who is not an internet expert asks you whether the internet is useful for branding. What answer would you give and how could you support it with examples?
6. What are special tools and techniques that enterprises can use in their brand-building process on the web?
7. Do you believe that online advertising has more potential to engage viewers than mass media advertising? Why or why not?
8. Explain your understanding of the term "customer experience."
9. True/False. A linear representation of the customer journey—whether B2C of B2B—represents the situation in the digital age.
10. What is retargeting and how are marketers able to track what a prospective customer has looked at on an internet page or social media site?
11. Is experiential marketing different from customer experience? If so, explain how.
12. Discuss the three components of customer experience.
13. Do you have any personal customer experiences that parallel Joshie at the Ritz-Carlton? If you cannot think of one, think about why it is hard to think of a customer experience that truly delighted you.
14. Why is it difficult to create good customer experience in an omni-channel world?

ENDNOTES

1. http://www.internetlivestats.com/internet-users/.
2. "Americans' Internet Access: 2000–2015," http://www.pewinternet.org/2015/06/26/americans-internet-access-2000-2015/.
3. "The Next 3 Billion People on Social," https://blog.hootsuite.com/the-next-3-billion-people-on-social/?utm_source=twitter&utm_medium=owned_social&utm_campaign=social_hootsuite&Last_Associated_Campaign__c=701a0000002JXk5.
4. "Brand Building in a Digital Age with Andrew Keller," https://www.thinkwithgoogle.com/articles/brand-new-with-andrew-keller.html.
5. "Resilient Brands: A Framework for Brand Building in the Digital Age," https://brilliantnoise.com/resilient-brands/#brand-as-strategy.
6. "The Link Between Creativity and Effectiveness," https://www.thinkbox.tv/Research/Thinkbox-research/The-link-between-creativity-and-effectiveness.
7. http://www.projectrebrief.com/.
8. "Brand Building in a Digital Age with Gareth Kay," https://www.thinkwithgoogle.com/articles/brand-new-with-gareth-kay.html.
9. "Netflix, Inc. History," http://www.fundinguniverse.com/company-histories/netflix-inc-history/.

10. Joseph O'Halloran, "2015 Surge Sets Netflix on Track for 150 MN Customers by 2020." http://www.rapidtvnews.com/2016041242441/2015-surge-sets-netflix-on-track-for-150mn-customers-by-2020.html#axzz45oPlS4eL.
11. "Netflix's View: Internet Is Replacing Linear TV," http://ir.netflix.com/long-term-view.cfm
12. https://cmosurvey.org/results/survey-results-august-2015/.
13. "Kantar Media Reports Q! 2015 U.S. Advertisin Expenditures Decreased by 4.0% From Q! 2015 Olympic Spend Levels," http://www.kantarmedia.com/us/newsroom/press-releases/kantar-media-reports-q1-2015-u-s-advertising-expenditures-decreased-4-0-percent-from-q1-2014
14. http://cmosurvey.org/results/survey-results-february-2015/.
15. Jake Sorofman, "Gartner Surveys Confirm Customer Experience Is the New Battlefield," http://blogs.gartner.com/jake-sorofman/gartner-surveys-confirm-customer-experience-new-battlefield/.
16. "Marketing in 2015: Make the Customer Experience Count," http://www.theguardian.com/media-network/2015/jan/26/marketing-2015-seamless-customer-experience.
17. Marketing in 2015: Make the Customer Experience Count," http://www.theguardian.com/media-network/2015/jan/26/marketing-2015-seamless-customer-experience.
18. Daniel Newman, "Customer Experience is the Future of Marketing," http://www.forbes.com/sites/danielnewman/2015/10/13/customer-experience-is-the-future-of-marketing/#2f527a824b21.
19. Becky Wu, "5 Truths About Consumer Path of Purchase," https://luthresearch.com/whitepaper/5-truths-about-consumer-path-to-purchase/
20. David Court, Dave Elzinga, Susan Mulder, and Ole Jørgen Vetvik, "The Consumer Decision Journey," http://www.mckinsey.com/business-functions/marketing-and-sales/our-insights/the-consumer-decision-journey.
21. https://www.facebook.com/business/news/product-ads.
22. https://www.facebook.com/business/a/facebook-pixel.
23. Ingrid Lunden, "Facebook Expands Dynamic Ad Retargeting to Instagram and Travel Sector, Ramps Up Lookalikes," http://techcrunch.com/2016/05/10/facebook-expands-dynamic-ad-retargeting-to-instagram-and-travel-sector-ramps-up-lookalikes/.
24. Gavin O'Malley, "Facebook Adds Dynamic Ads to Instagram," http://www.mediapost.com/publications/article/275417/facebook-adds-dynamic-ads-to-instagram.html.
25. Alex Rawson, Ewan Duncan, and Conor Jones, "The Truth About Customer Experience," https://hbr.org/2013/09/the-truth-about-customer-experience/ar/.
26. Tim Moynihan, "Immersive Michael Jordan Simulator Is the World's Coolest Basketball Court," http://www.wired.com/2015/02/michael-jordan-simulator-the-last-shot/.
27. Tim Nudd, "Nike Athletes Dropped Some Insane Product on Fans in San Francisco Last Weekend," http://www.adweek.com/adfreak/nike-athletes-dropped-some-insane-product-fans-san-francisco-last-weekend-169635.
28. http://news.nike.com/news/super-bowl-50.
29. Zarina de Ruiter, "3 Lessons From Amazon’s Jeff Bezos to Improve Your Customer Experience Strategy," http://www.cxnetwork.com/cx-experience/articles/article-customer-experience-lessons-from-amazon-jeff-bezos/.
30. Robert Klara, "Why Do So Many People Go Crazy for Wegmans?" http://www.adweek.com/news/advertising-branding/why-do-so-many-people-go-crazy-wegmans-169396.
31. Robert Klara, "Why Do So Many People Go Crazy for Wegmans?" http://www.adweek.com/news/advertising-branding/why-do-so-many-people-go-crazy-wegmans-169396.
32. http://www.nunwood.com/?portfolio=8-wegmans-us-customer-experience-excellence-report-2015.
33. http://www.nunwood.com/?portfolio=8-wegmans-us-customer-experience-excellence-report-2015.

34. Chris Hurn, "Stuffed Giraffe Shows What Customer Service Is All About," http://www.huffingtonpost.com/chris-hurn/stuffed-giraffe-shows-wha_b_1524038.html.
35. Chris Hurn, "Great Customer Service Never Ends: Joshie the Giraffe Part 2," http://www.huffingtonpost.com/chris-hurn/great-customer-service-ne_b_8340954.html
36. Tom McCall, "Gartner Predicts a Customer Experience Battlefield," http://www.gartner.com/smarterwithgartner/test/.
37. "B2B Customer Experience Best Practices," http://www.cx-journey.com/2014/01/b2b-customer-experience-management-best.html.
38. "10 Key Marketing Trends for 2016," http://www.silverpop.com/marketing-resources/white-papers/all/2015/2016-marketing-trends/.
39. "Content × Context = Customer Experience: Driving a More Personalized Experience," thttps://www.accenture.com/us-en/insight-content-context-customer-experience-web-development-summary.aspx.
40. Lynn Hunsaker, "Customer Experience for the Future: Context is King," http://www.insidecxm.com/customer-experience-for-the-future-context-is-king/.
41. "The Customer Experience Maturity Playbook for 2015," https://www.forrester.com/The+Customer+Experience+Maturity+Playbook+For+2015/-/E-PLA690.
42. "Report: The State of the CX Management, 2015," https://experiencematters.wordpress.com/2015/05/12/report-the-state-of-the-cx-management-2015/.
43. "Lessons from The Leading Edge of Customer Experience Management," http://www.sas.com/content/dam/SAS/en_us/doc/whitepaper2/hbr-leading-edge-customer-experience-mgmt-107061.pdf.

Chapter 7

Display and Mobile Advertising for Customer Acquisition

LEARNING OBJECTIVES

By the time you complete this chapter, you will be able to:
1. List the major customer acquisition techniques, both online and offline.
2. Define display advertising.
3. Identify the major online display and mobile advertising formats.
4. Explain ad serving and how ad serving networks are used to target digital ads.
5. Identify the most common methods of targeting.
6. Explain the various types of behavioral targeting.
7. Discuss reasons for the growing importance of mobile advertising.
8. Identify issues associated with ad blocking.
9. Define publicity and affiliate marketing.
10. Explain the importance of IMC.

In Chapter 1 we defined the four basic marketing strategy objectives as customer acquisition, conversion, retention, and value growth. The concept of customer lifetime value (CLV), by which the marketer measures customer value, is discussed in Chapter 4. Conversion to a loyal customer and customer retention are very important marketing objectives discussed in Chapters 13 and 14, but, while trite, it is also true that the marketer must acquire a customer before creating loyalty and retention. It is also important to note that a steady stream of new customers is necessary to fuel growth in most organizations.

This chapter focuses on specific digital marketing tools that are most often used in customer acquisition strategy. There are other acquisition tools, most importantly search marketing, which are discussed in the later chapters. Throughout these chapters, it is important to realize that virtually any of the internet marketing tools can be used in an acquisition program, but some of them are especially well suited to acquisition efforts.

Examples also imply that there is more than one definition of *customer acquisition*. Certainly *acquisition* can be defined as "making a first purchase." However, it can also be defined as getting the customer to engage in a behavior that permits further contact—signing up for a newsletter, for example. For the social media marketer, *acquisition* may be defined as getting additional fans or followers on a social network page. We return to the issue of definitions and metrics to measure acquisition in various later chapters. For the moment, however, just try to focus on the generic concept of a "new customer."

INTERNET CUSTOMER ACQUISITION TECHNIQUES

While there are numerous ways to acquire new internet customers in B2C and B2B markets, they can best be described by the channels shown in Figure 7.1. The figure shows the channels as digital, offline, or as programs that could take place either online or offline. The channels and the tools available through each are better used in combination with one another as discussed throughout this text. There is no one "best channel" to be used independently of all others.

In order to better understand the complex issues of developing an effective media mix for acquisition, it is necessary to understand the strengths and weaknesses of each channel. In this chapter, we discuss online advertising, mobile advertising, and

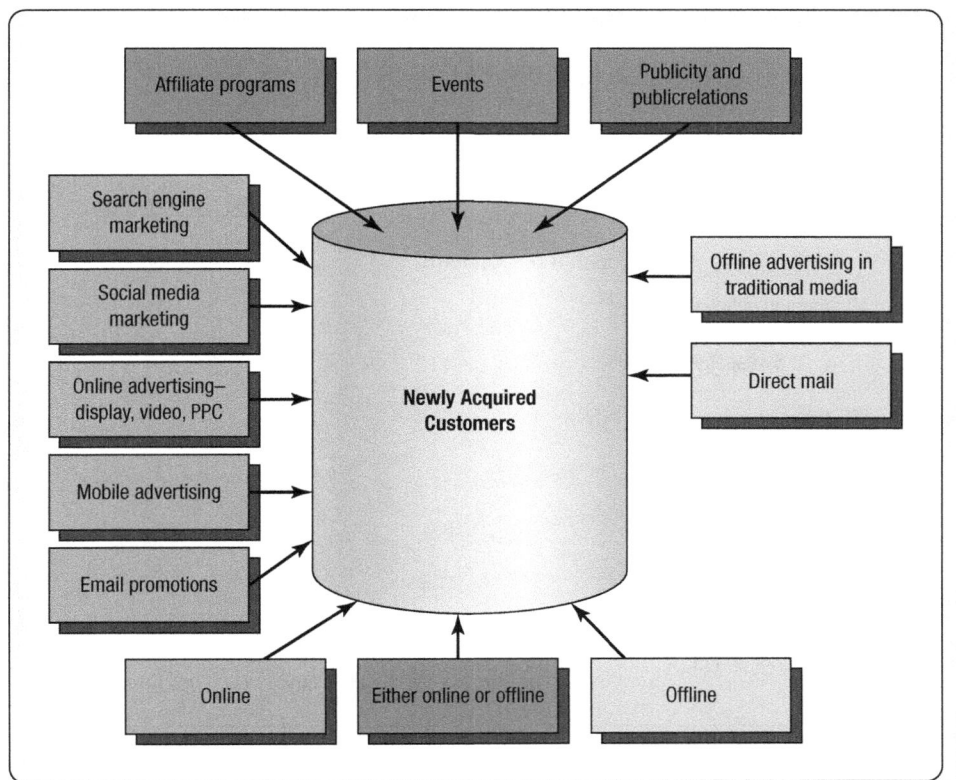

FIGURE 7.1
Channels for Acquisition of New Customers

miscellaneous acquisition techniques. In other chapters, we discuss e-mail promotions, search engine marketing (SEM), and social media marketing (SMM). In so doing, we will keep in mind the fact that any and all of these techniques can and should be used in concert with the traditional channels of offline advertising and promotion. Examples will illustrate media mixes that include various digital and offline channels and tools.

DIGITAL ADVERTISING

Take one more good look at Figure 7.1. Notice that many of the channels do not qualify as advertising by the narrow definition of paid persuasive content that is placed in commercial media. When you consider the effectiveness of channels in acquiring customers the differences become more stark. Figure 7.2 shows channels that are identified as being effective by as many as 10 percent of U.S. retailers. There are not many of them.

Search engine marketing (SEM), the subject of Chapter 10, is by far the most effective. It includes optimizing web pages for search engine visibility and paid techniques to draw search traffic to websites. Organic traffic also comes as a result of search, but not paid search. It is primarily the result of relevance to search terms used by the customer. Affiliate programs, like those offered by Amazon and eBay, drive traffic from the platform to the merchant's site where the sale is closed and fulfilled. The platforms receive a commission for the customer action.

Notice that you must get down to the fourth channel on the list before advertising is mentioned. Then the fourth and the seventh channels are specific types of online advertising—**retargeting** and **behavioral targeting**, both of which will be discussed later in the chapter.

Digital advertising is, in fact, a broad subject. It is generally described simply as paid persuasive content displayed on the web but that masks its complexity. It is necessary to begin to look at specific types of advertising to get definitions that are helpful. We will begin with display advertising.

retargeting ads for the product category are displayed based on the user's recent internet behaviors.

behavioral targeting tracking users' activities in order to display relevant ads.

FIGURE 7.2
Most Effective Customer Acquisition Channels for U.S. Retailers

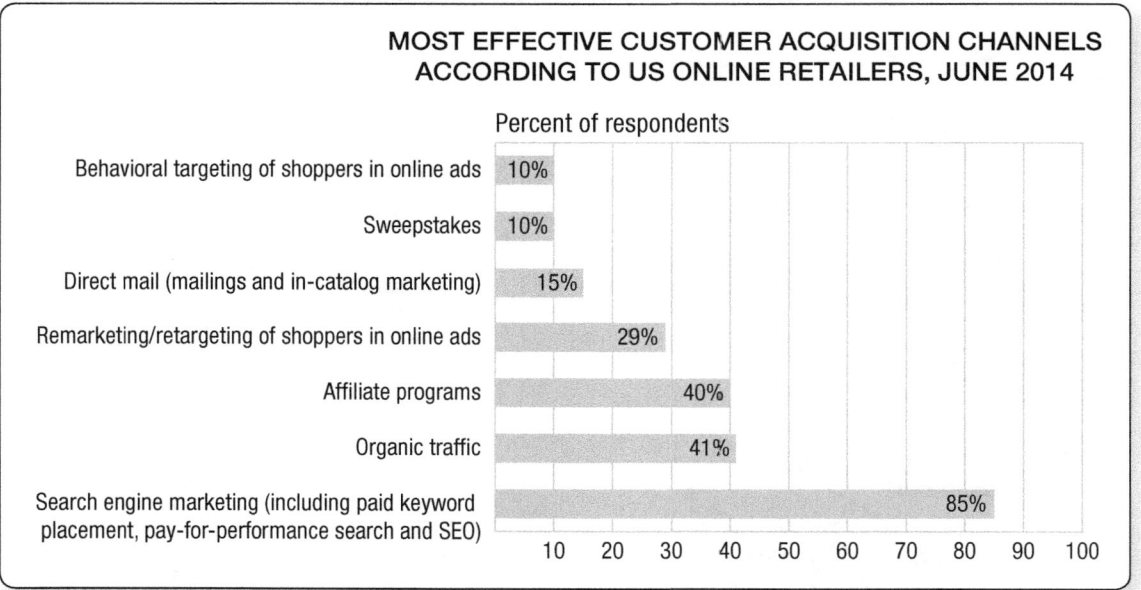

SOURCE: http://www.emarketer.com/Article/Whats-Your-Customer-Acquisition-Strategy/1011821

Display Advertising

Display advertising is a commercial message that includes not only text but also visual content and perhaps sound and motion. Display ads contain a headline, body text, and one or more visuals. Brand names and logos need to be prominently displayed in order for the ad to link the message with the brand. These statements are true whether the display add is offline, in a print magazine for example, or online, displayed on a website or a mobile site.

display advertising ads that contain headline, text copy, and visuals including the brand logo in any channel.

Digital advertising has proven that it is cost effective and it continues to grow rapidly. It is expected to maintain an annual growth rate of over 12 percent until 2019 as shown in Figure 7.3a. By that time almost 70 percent of digital advertising spending will be mobile (Figure 7.3b).

Taking the basic display ad components of headline, (copy plus visual) and adding creativity seemed enough when the advertising world was made up of traditional media. That is no longer true, and in order to begin to bring some order to our understanding of digital advertising we need to look at formats for display advertising.

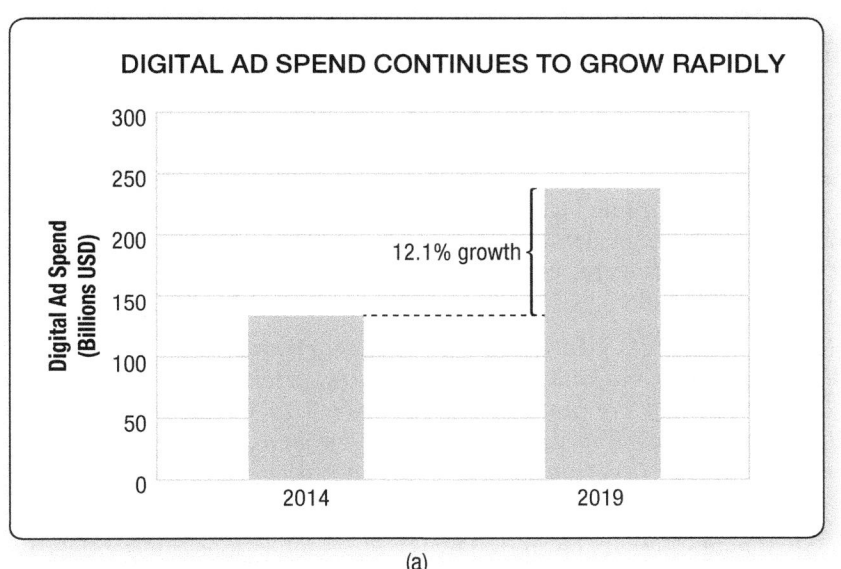

FIGURE 7.3a
Growth of Digital Advertising

(a)

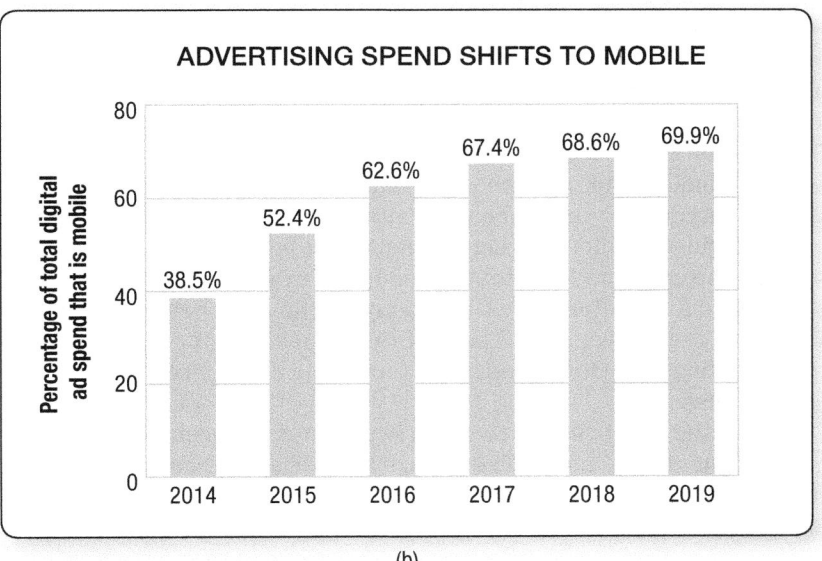

FIGURE 7.3b
Percentage of Digital Advertising that is Mobile

(b)

SOURCE: https://www.salesforce.com/blog/2016/02/key-trends-transforming-advertising-2016.html

Digital Display Advertising Formats

The number of digital display formats is limited only by the imagination of web designers and marketers, and perhaps by the size of screens. This would lead to chaos even if digital advertising space was purchased manually for each ad, but it becomes impossible when most ad placement is done with technology (that will be discussed later in this chapter). We will discuss three broad aspects:

- Digital display ads
- Rich media ads
- Video display ads.

The Internet Advertising Bureau (IAB), which is made up of 650 media and technology companies that are responsible for 86 percent of online advertising,[1] is the custodian of industry standards for digital formats. Because the number of possible display formats is so large they have developed a Universal Ad Package (UAP) that member companies have agreed to support. The formats included in the UAP are illustrated as part of Interactive Exercise 7.1 (accessible via the learning path) where you can see samples of each format.

There are other common display formats—a super leaderboard, half page, button 2, and microbar. As you can see from the standards, some of the common types of display ads allow a limited amount of video, animation, or audio.[2] However, none allow expansion—a frame that pops out a larger box when some criterion is met, for instance, a viewer spending x number of seconds on a web page. Looking at the New York Times online media kit in Interactive Exercise 7.1 you can see many variations on the basic formats.

All the IAB ad formats have been revised for the **HTML5** programming language. According to Webopedia:

> *HTML5 is a W3C [Worldwide Web Consortium] specification that defines the fifth major revision of the Hypertext Markup Language (HTML). One of the major changes in HTML5 is in respect to how HTML addresses Web applications. Other new features in HTML5 include specific functions for embedding graphics, audio, video, and interactive documents.*

Clearly the interactivity permitted by HTML5 applications is essential to ads like the deceptively simple square ad shown in Figure 7.4.

With the ability to include interactivity the options for display ads are almost limitless today. The static capture of an IBM ad in Figure 7.4 shows the sound off (upper left) and an opportunity to drive the car through some challenging streets (lower right). Notice that these features are viewer-initiated. When you watch the ad to its conclusion you find a call for action to get more information on the smart technology.[3]

rich media combination of text, images, video, and other interactive elements in a digital ad.

Rich media *formats* enable many kinds of technology and interaction in display ads. Google's DoubleClick unit is one of the largest ad servers (to be discussed later in the chapter). According to DoubleClick rich media is an "ad that includes advanced features like video, audio, or other elements that encourage viewers to interact and engage with the content. While text ads sell with words, and display ads sell with pictures, rich media ads offer more ways to involve an audience with an ad. The ad can expand, float, peel down, etc."[4] They list rich media ad options that include expanding, multi-floating, peel-down, and seven more. The number of display ad options continues to increase!

Consider the number of viewer actions that are possible in the rich media ad shown in Figures 7.5a and b. The square banner ad shows no obvious interactivity, not even a call to action, but when the viewer clicks on the square he is sent to the leaderboard where the game is accessed. In order to play, the viewer clicks on

FIGURE 7.4

An IBM Ad for its Smart Traffic Solutions. To view the animation (application) follow the link provided

SOURCE: http://digitalsynopsis.com/ibm-smart-roads/

the Expand button and is taken to another version of the leaderboard which has a QR code. When he aims a QR reader at the ad, the game itself shows on the screen. In order to play it, the viewer must verify that he is over 21 years of age and install it on his smart phone. This ad and game is part of the Heineken Legends campaign which aims to show, in TV and YouTube primarily, that every man is a legend. The campaign has won both praise for its creativity and criticism for the fact that its "legends" are paid actors.

The possibilities for online display ads are growing so rapidly that IAB has developed a *Rising Stars* category to highlight what it calls cutting edge advertising technology. The highlighted formats change from time to time but in mid-2016 they included Billboards, Filmstrips, Portraits, Pushdowns, Sidekicks, and Sliders.[5] All these units can include *Video*, which can also be considered as a separate display category.

The Samsung Galaxy "Love Every Letter" commercial was inspired by the song of the same name from Nao (see Figure 7.6). It shows people saying "I love you" in many different ways. It does not tout product features; it shows what the user can do with the phone in an emotionally-appealing way. The tag line "It's not a phone, it's a Galaxy" has several levels of meaning. In this case, the phone is being used for messaging, not calls, in the scenarios, and for relationships not business. The link is to an online media company where users can find more information about the ad and track its appearances if they desire.

Video is currently very trendy in advertising, just as it is in viewer consumption as we will discuss in Chapter 12. Video advertising, however can be very intrusive and annoying to viewers. If you examine the Rising Stars formats[6] you find requirements that allow users to control video ads to limit their intrusiveness. Going on to the description of Digital Video Display ads you find explanation of the VAST (Video Ad Serving Template) that permits streaming ads to video players. Essentially that means that ads can appear either before the video, after, or during the video. The latter, of course, interrupts the video and advertisers should ask themselves whether this is positive for their brand. There are other video servers that make up the IAB video suite, which is carefully explained—in a video of course.[7] Consider the difficulty of trying to engage viewers, or at least not annoy them, and maximizing advertising revenue for publishers. It leads to a rapidly-growing but complex digital marketing discipline that offers great opportunity to marketers who are willing to tackle the complexity.

FIGURE 7.5a

A Simple Square Banner with Rich Media Promoting a Game

(a)

SOURCE: https://www.richmediagallery.com/

FIGURE 7.5b

A Leaderboard Ad that Can be Expanded To Install and Play the Game

(b)

SOURCE: https://www.richmediagallery.com/

FIGURE 7.6

Galaxy "Love Every Letter" Ad

SOURCE: https://www.ispot.tv/ad/AYk5/samsung-galaxy-note5-love-every-letter-song-by-nao

We should end the discussion of digital display advertising with a word about two important topics. First, display ads are appearing on social platforms like Facebook[8] and Google.[9] Each platform has its own standards for display advertising but the process of creating a good ad does not differ. Which leads to the second, a good ad requires creativity. Creativity has always been a keystone of good advertising. How is advertising creatively different in digital advertising? Simply—not at all. There are just more ways to execute your creative idea. There are tools to help; tools to help design or optimize your ad for specific channels or platforms, for example. But creativity is still important as all these ads show, especially perhaps, the interactive ones. Creativity is still the product of human minds, not technology, and we can expect it to remain just that.

This section on display advertising just skims the surface of the number of online advertising formats available. There are many other specific formats in the categories we have discussed and more are being developed on an almost-daily basis. It is matched in number of available options only by the number of target market segments that can be reached in the digital environment. The technique of **ad serving** provides the methodology for reaching ever-smaller and more specific target audiences.

ONLINE AD SERVING AND TARGETING

Just as most ads are not static today, most are served onto the web page separately from the content files. **Ad serving** is an important activity of third-party marketing services firms that match an advertiser's need for targeted ad placement with a publisher's need for revenue-generating ads on its site. *PC Magazine's* encyclopedia page has a succinct definition of ad serving:

> *The hardware, software and personnel required to deliver advertisements to Web sites and ad-supported software. It also includes the monitoring of click-throughs and required reporting to the ad purchasers and Web site publishers.*[10]

Ad serving technology that places ads on websites or mobile sites.

This explanation is correct and helpful as far as it goes. But how are the destination websites chosen and by whom? These further queries require us to define ad networks and ad targeting. *PC's* definition of ad networks is:

> *Internet advertising organizations [that] act as a middleman between the advertiser and the Internet venues that display the ads. They sell the online campaign to the advertisers and then deliver the ads to the sites that display them. The site owners receive a royalty based typically on the number of times users click the ads.*[11]

In addition to charging on the basis of clicks (**Click Through Rate** or CTR) publishers can charge on the basis of exposure to the ad (**CPM**, cost per thousand viewers) just as offline print and broadcast media do.

It is true that ads can be embedded in a web page in the same sense that they are placed on a magazine or newspaper page, but that is not common except for house ads—ads for the site's own products. It is more common to serve ads separately from content. In order to meet the needs of both advertisers and publishers, complex software and systems are required. That leads to one of the hottest topics in digital advertising, **programmatic advertising**. Digiday has a definition free of jargon although they use the term buying instead of serving:

programmatic advertising automating the advertising buying process.

> *"Programmatic" ad buying typically refers to the use of software to purchase digital advertising, as opposed to the traditional process that involves RFPs, human negotiations and manual insertion orders. It's using machines to buy ads, basically.*[12]

When you stop to think about the fact that it is important to serve the best ad from *both* the website (most revenue) and the advertiser's (most **reach**, best value) point of view, the complexity begins to become obvious. When you consider that the decision must be made and the ad retrieved from inventory and sent to the appropriate site while the site content is loading—often in a matter of milliseconds if the user has a broadband connection—another layer is added to the complexity. Even though complex, this example represents the basic situation. If the advertiser wishes to use more complex targeting techniques, the question of which ad to serve to which viewer on which site becomes even more daunting, explaining why most sites of any size use ad serving technology of some kind.

Figure 7.7 provides an understanding of the various ways in which digital ads can be purchased and serviced—a technology stack for ad serving. Notice that, the more automated the process, the cheaper the ad. Automating the process also improves the ability to target specific audiences as well as lessening the labor involved. Let's look briefly at each of the types.

Direct Ad Serving refers to orders purchased directly from the publisher and represent about 50 percent of all digital ads at present.[13]

- Direct orders are placed directly with the publisher using traditional advertising insertion orders. The NYT media kit shown in Interactive Exercise 7.1 (accessible via the learning path) explains the options and the process to potential ad buyers.

- Programmatic direct is provided by third-party ad tech firms in a way that allows advertisers to purchase a preconfigured package of ad placements without direct contact with the publisher. The programmatic ad vendor supplies the ads to the publisher's ad server which, in turn, inserts them onto the user's page while it is loading.[14]

FIGURE 7.7
Methods of Buying and Placing Digital Ads

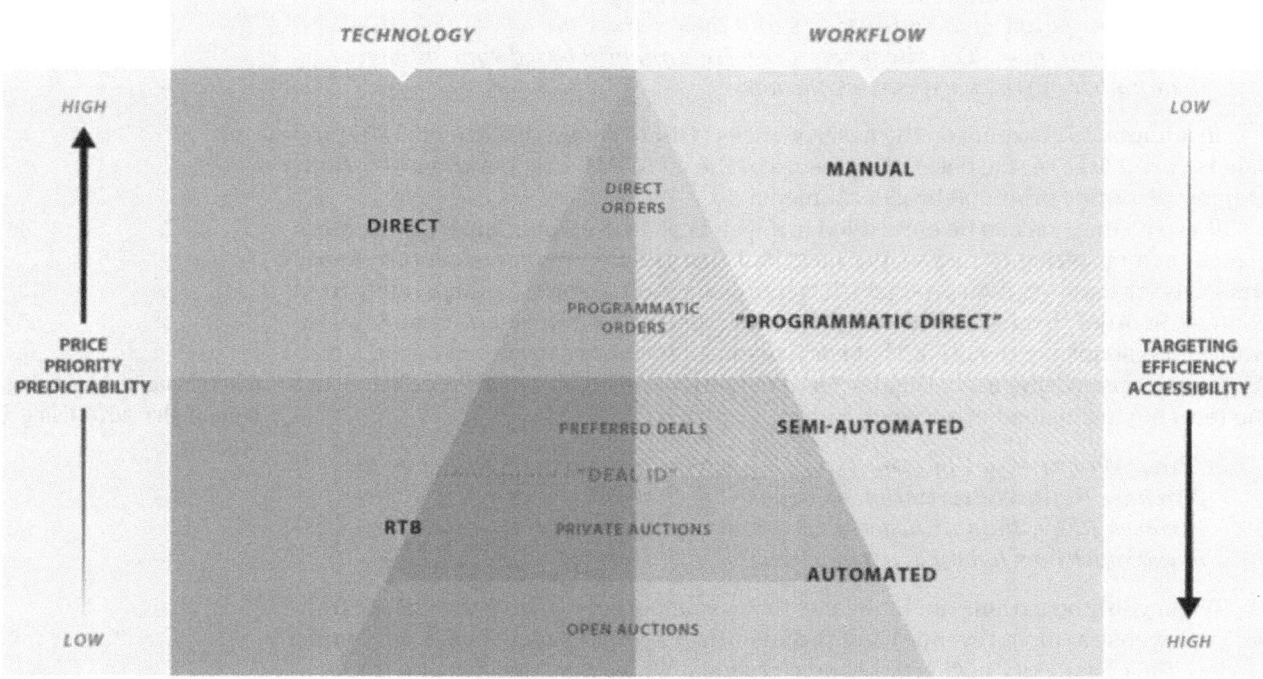

SOURCE: http://marketingland.com/navigating-modern-ad-serving-stack-part-1-direct-orders-109611

Real-Time Bidding means that ads are bought and sold by instantaneous auction, much like stocks on a stock exchange. **Ad exchanges** are the online marketplaces in which these exchanges take place.

- **Preferred deals** take place in **private marketplaces**. A private marketplace is invitation only and allows publishers of highly-desirable sites to control the brands that advertise on their site and advertisers to get the best selection of advertising inventory. A preferred deal occurs when a single buyer of ads enters into an agreement to purchase inventory with specific purchase terms. This bypasses the auction process and allows the advertiser to purchase inventory before it enters the open auction process.
- **Private auctions** take place when invited members compete (bid for) what is considered premium advertising opportunities.
- **Open auctions** are open to all advertisers unless a publisher chooses to block them. The IAB calls them the "Wild West" of auctions. Advertisers may simply "buy blind," not knowing from which publishers they are buying advertising space, only the exchanges and SSPs they have opted to participate in. In many cases the winning bidder pays only one cent more than the next highest bidder, creating a situation in which advertisers can pay what they think the advertising is worth and no more. The prices are kept low while reach to the defined target market is maximized because of the large number of sites available. Remember that this all takes place in real time, so it can become unpredictable, requiring close tracking.

The BrightRoll programmatic video platform illustrates many of these activities. BrightRoll is a third-party service provider that offers services to both the demand side (advertisers) and the supply side (publishers of digital properties who are soliciting video ads). It serves advertisers who want their video to appear on desktops, mobiles, and connected TVs. It serves publishers in a private marketplace for desktop and mobile ad inventory. It also provides inventory from other advertising exchanges and **supply side platforms** (SSPs). It offers services to advertisers including audience targeting, to be discussed in the next section, and technology necessary to interface with the exchange. It also offers creative services to improve the quality of video ads and data and measurement services to ensure that advertisers are getting value for their advertising dollar.[15] This complex ecosystem is portrayed in Figure 7.8.

real-time bidding ads are bought and sold instantaneously through electronic exchanges.

Ad exchanges digital marketplace where advertisers buy and publishers sell advertising space in an auction setting.

preferred deals offering ad inventory to buyers at a negotiated price before the inventory is made available for auction.

private marketplaces ad exchanges (marketplaces) that include both private auctions and preferred deals for the selling of publisher advertising inventory.

private auctions ad bidding in which members of the exchange are allowed to bid first.

supply side platforms software used to sell a publisher's ad inventory through programmatic advertising.

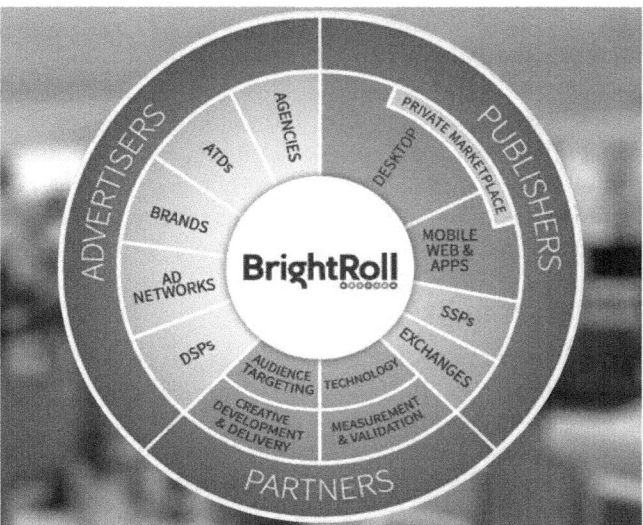

FIGURE 7.8
Marketplace for Video Advertising

SOURCE: http://news.softpedia.com/news/Yahoo-Buys-Video-Ad-Platform-BrightRoll-for-640-Million-514-Million-464764.shtml#sgal_1

This discussion of ad serving assumes B2C markets. B2B marketers do not usually want to reach business buyers on consumer websites. As a result, specialized ad exchanges have grown up to serve the B2B market. The number of B2B ad exchanges is growing and more B2B publishers try to monetize their advertising inventory.[16] The B2B exchanges operate the same way that B2C exchanges do.[17, 18]

All this begs the question of how digital ads reach their target markets. Dun & Bradstreet simplifies the issue by identifying three kinds of targeting; audience, behavioral, and retargeting.

Audience Targeting

Audience targeting involves the type of market segmentation that has always been used in offline markets. The most common types are:

- Demographics
- Geographics
- Life styles
- Behaviors.

While this is the traditional way of segmenting audiences for offline media, it is also the way that Facebook and other PPC ads are purchased. This type of targeting will be discussed in Chapter 11.

Behavioral Targeting

In the offline world, marketers have to ask customers to self-report what they do, which can have elements of unreliability. In the online world, marketers and third-party data collection services can collect data about what people actually do—what sites they visit, what pages on the site, what purchases, and much, much more. There are variations in the ways advertising networks actually carry out the process, but the three basic types of behavioral targeting are:

1. Targeting identified users (people who have registered on a website, for example)
2. Targeting unidentified users by using **cookies**
3. Targeting with predictive models

cookies a few lines of code that a website or advertising network places on a user's computer to store data about the user's activities on the site.

Targeting Identified Users

Targeting identified users is straightforward for the marketer and observable to the customer. When a customer visits Amazon, for example, she is encouraged to log in to the site. When she does, a number of Amazon services become available—the wish list, 1-Click ordering, and recommendations among them. The wish list and 1-Click ordering have been set up by the customer herself. It is obvious to even the casual observer that the recommendations are based on previous purchases. Amazon actually encourages the customer to provide additional data to improve the recommendations. Amazon is more open about what it does and how it does it than many sites,[19] but this type of targeting on the site is visible and does not arouse a lot of concern among most internet users.

Targeting Unidentified Users

Targeting anonymous users is an issue that does raise privacy concerns and we return to that aspect in Chapter 17. In this section, we discuss how it works. Figure 7.9 presents an understandable view.

This type of targeting is done by advertising networks and made it available to advertisers who use the network. The hypothetical situation set up in Figure 7.9 shows an unidentified (not signed in) user visiting a website that has information about hotels in San Francisco. The user's activity suggests intended behavior, and a cookie is set on the visitor's browser. A cookie is a piece of code that can track visitor activity but does not necessarily last beyond a single web session or link to

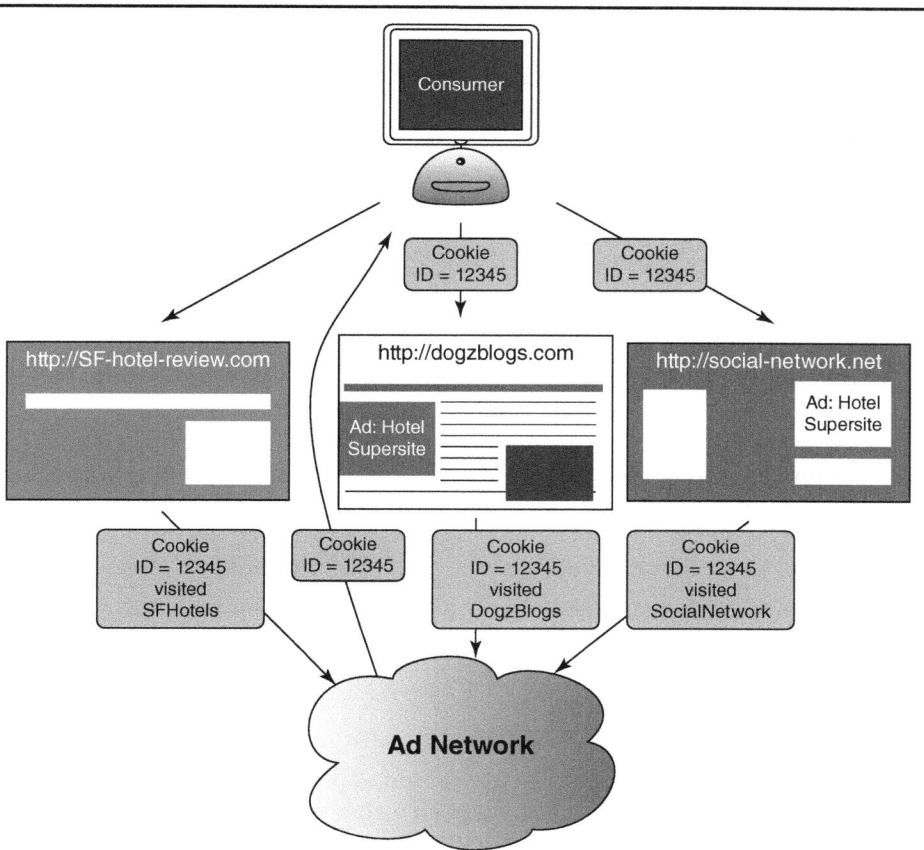

FIGURE 7.9
How Behavioral Targeting of Anonymous Users Works

SOURCE: © Cengage Learning 2013

identifiable personal information. We discuss cookies in more detail as part of the metrics process in Chapter 14. In Figure 7.9, the cookie is simply used to track the visitor to other websites and to display an ad for a hotel supersite (a client of the advertising network) on both a site about dogs and on a social page like a blog.

Cookies have been around since the dawn of the internet. Recently a new type of user tracking has come into vogue—the **hashed e-mail**. While cookies only work on the web a hashed e-mail can work on any channel. For instance, it can track the user onto Facebook on her mobile device, making it a very useful adjunct to the standard cookie. Hashing an e-mail address is a simple process. An e-mail address is run through an MD5 hash algorithm (actually a cryptographic tool) and it produces a 32-character unique identifier that cannot be reversed. This becomes a data point in the person's record in a marketing database. It allows the marketer to track the user on any device or platform where she is signed in with her e-mail address. It is a compliment to cookies, not a substitute.[20, 21, 22]

The ad networks collect huge amounts of behavioral data and mine the data to find patterns of behavior that constitute market segments. The hypothetical user in Figure 7.9 could be a "frequent traveler" or perhaps an "adventure traveler," which are fairly generic segments, although the targeting they represent is still valuable to the marketer. The network can drill down in the data to find microsegments, "architectural history traveler" or "garden traveler," for example. The ad networks actually configure the segment to be targeted for each individual advertiser, so you do not find much detail on their sites about the segments they offer. Collecting and using data like this also implies placing cookies that persist over a period of time, not cookies that are set for a single user session. Tracking a user over time also allows **retargeting** of a visitor who has left a site (one that sells shoes, for example) without making a purchase. All the shoe sites would like to reach that person. You see the results of retargeting on other sites you visit virtually every time you search for a product or service online.

retargeting ads for the product category are displayed based on the user's recent internet behaviors.

Behavioral targeting has gone far beyond simple visitor behavior—data points like websites visited, types of products examined, coupons downloaded, and so forth. There are many third-party databases that vastly expand behavioral targeting options.[23] They include:

- Values targeting, which the agency describes as being able to reach people on the basis of enduring human values.
- Cut-and-paste content sharing, which is based on items that readers cut and paste from publisher sites. This content produces search key word suggestions, as well as behavioral profile data.
- Retailer cooperative database, which identifies people who are shopping on the web for certain products. This database can be used for retargeting.
- Search retargeting, which is the ability to purchase display advertising based on search activity.
- Owner targeting, which focuses advertising based on ownership. Direct marketers have long used, for example, product registrations to confirm ownership of an article in a database. Behavioral tracking allows activities such as looking at online owner's manuals or searching for replacement parts for a product to be included in the database as evidence of product ownership.

For anything beyond simple behavioral targeting by user activities as shown in Figure 7.9 marketers turn to predictive models to construct audiences that meet their specific needs.

Targeting with Predictive Models

Behavioral targeting often makes use of the kind of predictive modeling described in Chapter 4. Predictive modeling has long been a staple of direct marketing, and Paul Berger describes it in the context of segmenting mailing lists,[24] the forerunner of online behavioral targeting.

Figure 7.10 shows the outcome of this kind of predictive modeling exercise. The client was a private online college that had been using PPC and affiliate marketing to acquire new students. The cost of leads (to be discussed in Chapter 13) was acceptable. However, not enough of those people registered and the cost per enrolled student was unacceptably high. They added SEM, SEO, and simple behavioral targeting to their acquisition media mix. That helped, but it still did not produce enough students who would enroll and persist.

The college turned to an agency that uses both traditional marketing data and big data to build predictive models.[25] The college knew who its high-value students were. Presumably these are students who took numerous courses, and perhaps completed programs of study. The college was able to provide a profile of these high-value students to the agency so it could build a model that would identify other people who have the same characteristics ("look like") as the current high-value students. These prospects will have a higher probability of becoming high-value students than will other viewers of the college's ads.

The data used for this model included 12 types of offline data that contained thousands of attributes for each individual case used to build the model. Online data for these cases was drawn from a database comprised of "220 million U.S. adults with our more than 640 million cookie profiles, 720 million hashed e-mails and 300 million mobile IDs."[26] This massive data set was fed into a scoring model with the results seen in Figure 7.10. The Key Predictive Factors are the variables that contributed most to the variance in the regression-type model. They included a number of variables that had to do with location, others that helped to identify prospects by gender-specific traits as well as occupation and political affiliation.

Looking at the pie chart you see that three broad types of variables contributed over 50 percent of the variance—financial transactions, demographics, and purchase history. It is common for only a few variables to contribute most in this type of modeling. However, the other eight types of variables give useful information, especially for identifying media channels that will reach the highest-scoring prospects.

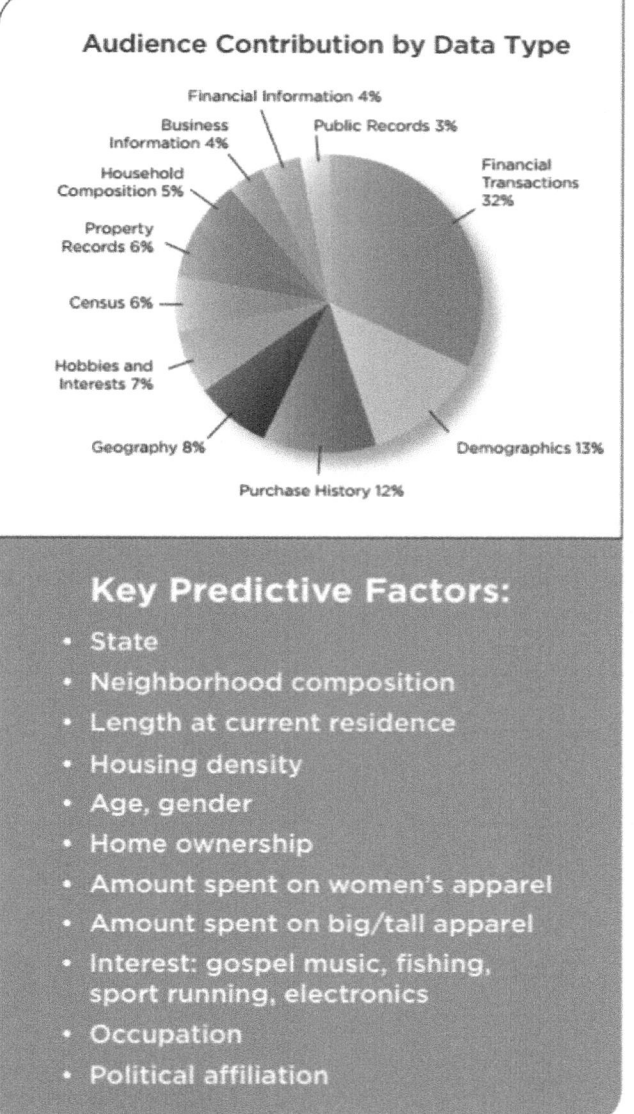

FIGURE 7.10
A Predictive Model for Private Online College Enrollment

SOURCE: http://www.tru-signal.com/wp-content/uploads/2014/11/TruSignal-Online_College.pdf

Targeted display advertising was used in a campaign to reach these prospects. Results were carefully tracked and showed a 32 percent higher enrollment rate with a cost that was 21 percent lower than the campaign target. Moreover, 84 percent of the leads from this new campaign converted within seven days of an inquiry about the college.

Predictive modeling is a demanding discipline but it is not unusual to see significant results like these. The amount of data used in this model also reminds one of the old "looking for a needle in the haystack" saying. In this case the needle is a high-value prospect and the haystack is the huge amount of data that inundates marketers today.

When you look at behavioral targeting from a marketer's point of view, the desirability of precision targeting based on actual visitor behavior data seems obvious. When you look at it from the visitor's point of view, it quickly becomes clear that a lot of internet firms know a great deal about internet users. Is that good or bad? We consider that issue in Chapter 17.

MOBILE DISPLAY ADVERTISING

Chapter 12 will provide a broad overview of mobile marketing and advertising, but no discussion of contemporary display advertising would be complete without mention of mobile display advertising. Figure 7.11 Shows that display advertising makes up a significant part of the rapidly-growing space of mobile advertising. Search advertising is the largest element, followed by display and social. Video advertising is presently the smallest element, but it is growing rapidly. In the same report Business Insider forecasts that mobile video ad revenue will grow three times faster than desktop through 2020.[27]

Experts describe several popular formats for mobile display advertising:

- Banners
- Interstitials
- Expandables
- Video
- Native.[28,29,30]

Banners and expandables were discussed in the previous section. Native advertising will be discussed in Chapter 8.

Interstitial ads are available for desktop ads as well as for mobile. In either environment they are available in different sizes but they often cover the entire screen. They are usually loaded during a pause in data transmission—as a website opens, for

FIGURE 7.11

Growth In Mobile Display Advertising Exceeds That of Other Display Advertising

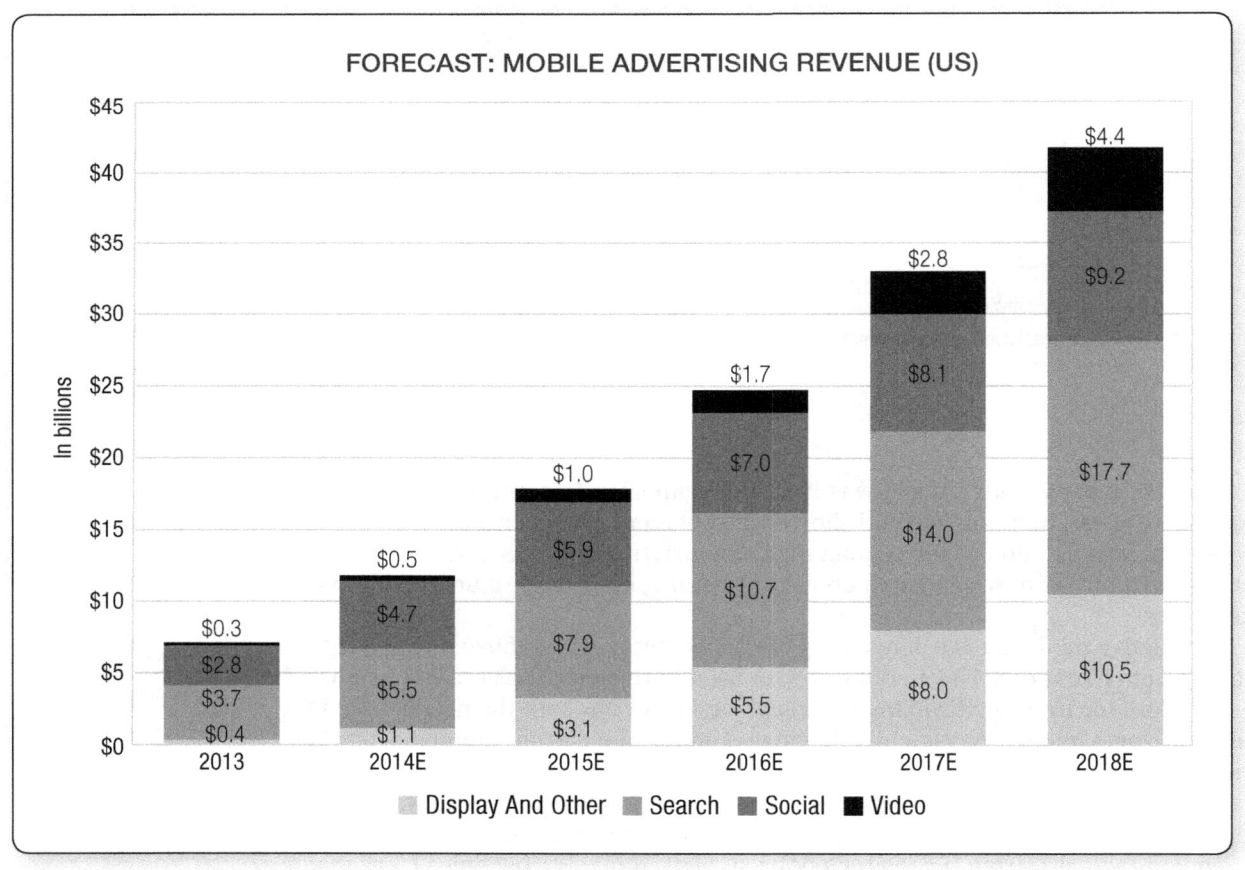

SOURCE: http://www.businessinsider.com/mobile-video-is-the-growth-area-2014-10

example, or between levels of an online game. Obviously they need to be brief enough not to seriously annoy the user.

The mobile interstitial shown in Figure 7.12 features used cars and trucks available on the lot of the local dealer. The main tab, Pre-Owned, has a "tap for more information" button with each vehicle. The video tab, shown, links to videos with additional information. The third tab features a click-co-call button and the fourth tab contains an e-mail request for more information.

If you are looking for a pre-owned car or truck, the ad is highly engaging. It offers product choice and information. This full-screen ad is also the only thing the viewer sees until it is closed. That contributes to engagement but it also adds to the annoyance factor.

Taco Bell has been an early and successful mover in both video and mobile advertising. Its target audience of Millennials devours video and can be reached on both mobile sites and with **in-app advertising**. It also has its own mobile app for ordering and payment of food items but its mobile ads appear on other platforms.

Taco Bell has been pushing its breakfast items since 2014. In early 2016, it increased its number of $1 breakfast items to 10[31] and launched a mobile push on its behalf (Figure 7.13). They wanted to get people thinking about Taco Bell for breakfast as soon as they opened their eyes in the morning. For their Millennial audience,

FIGURE 7-12

Interstitial Ad for Local Automobile Dealer. To view the animation (application) follow the link provided.

SOURCE: http://www.mobileads.com/preview/?campaignId=554a6e60b481a982a343633998dd64f5&studioId=3ee9cdc18ebe92c901a35b11af4c5d2a&adCategory=Embedded&platform=MW&dimension=300x250

FIGURE 7.13

A Screen from Taco Bell's 10 Item Morning Menu Video Ad

SOURCE: http://www.cnbc.com/2016/03/10/taco-bell-launches-1-breakfast-menu-nationwide.html

where better than their smart phones?[32] The campaign was highly targeted to early morning behavior with a variety of ad formats, heavy on the video advertising. Among the things they were able to do:

- One supplier was able to track people using data including what apps they used first in the morning, favorite news apps or what time of day they look for breakfast recipes.
- A specific app that asks viewers to choose between two photos. Taco Bell used photos of two different breakfast options.
- On the map app Waze, it used branded pins that directed the viewer to the nearest Taco Bell.

For additional reach it also ran video ads on YouTube, Facebook, and Instagram.[33]

Impressive though this is, marketers have only begun to explore the possibilities of mobile video advertising.

MISCELLANEOUS ACQUISITION TECHNIQUES

Referring back to Figure 7.1, we see that there are other acquisition techniques that can take place either on or off line. Event-driven marketing, affiliate programs and publicity and public relations are the most used. Events and experiential marketing were discussed in Chapter 6 as part of the customer experience, consequently we will end with a discussion of affiliate marketing and online press releases.

Affiliate Programs

affiliate programs offers incentives to partner websites, wherein a website agrees to post a link to a transactional site in return for a commission on sales made as a direct result of the link.

We discussed **affiliate programs** as an internet business model in Chapter 3. Since many of the prospects who enter a website as a result of an affiliate listing may be new customers, affiliate programs clearly qualify as a customer acquisition technique. Marketers like affiliate marketing because it is a relatively low-cost activity. It can largely be automated, and affiliates are paid on the basis of performance. Note that low cost, however, does not necessarily mean high revenue.

Affiliate programs follow the **80/20 rule:** about 80 percent of the affiliates are low volume, and 20 percent produce significant volume; meaning only a small number of the affiliates produce the most click-throughs and most profitable sales. Consequently, affiliate programs need to be actively managed. Networks have grown up to serve the affiliate marketing sector by finding appropriate affiliates for merchants and publishers and relevant sites for small businesses who wish to participate in affiliate marketing. There are also marketing services firms that will assume the management of an affiliate system. If you conduct a search on virtually any subject that includes the term "affiliate marketing," you will see many "make money fast and easy" sites and ads. That should be a *caveat emptor* signal to anyone trying to enter the business.

There are, however, interesting new businesses that are affiliate programs. Several of them operate in the space that is known as fintech (financial technology). Two examples are:

- Nerdwallet—an American firm that offers links to dozens of products in financial sectors including banking, credit cards, insurance, loans, and more along with advice that aims to help the user choose the best product for his circumstances. They describe the nature of their affiliate program as:

  The Nerds strive to provide consumers with transparency and in that spirit, we would like to share how we make money. Some of the financial institutions with products on our site may pay us a referral fee when customers get approved for certain products.

  When you click to apply for those products through our site, we may receive compensation from the company that issues that product. This compensation enables us to maintain our growing database of financial products, many of which we don't receive compensation for. It also helps us support our Nerds who research and stay up-to-date on the latest news and offerings for you.[34]

- BankBazaar-an Indian company that was started to take advantage of the fact that penetration of many financial services is low in India and most users patronize brick and mortar establishments. Much of the population is online through their smart phones but do not have credit cards and therefore cannot shop online. The company was founded to take advantage of the opportunities this presents.[35]

Giving customers in India and nearby countries mobile access is key to the company's business. BankBazaar offers a robust mobile app (Figure 7.14) and offers at least one third-party app on its site to assist customers with financial calculations. The app features links to information about personal finance and they have an active blog.

Like other affiliate models they make offers to customers and direct them to the financial service website. If customers enroll, they make a commission, which could be based on something like the size of the loan. At this early stage in its corporate life the company also builds and maintains websites for Indian financial services companies although it is the affiliate revenue on which it is apparently banking its future.[36]

Generating Publicity

Although **public relations** is a communications discipline separate from marketing, the two must work closely together. Staging events, arranging product placement in films and TV, and issuing press releases are all tools that the public relations professional uses to generate unpaid media attention for products, services, and causes. Of those, the issuance of press releases appears to have been most changed by the internet.

Writing press releases and distributing them to the firm's own media list or through a news wire service is the stock in trade of public relations. It has always been important to write press releases well, keeping in mind the interests of the target media, and to distribute them in a timely fashion to journalists who are likely to pick them up and use them to write an article or even write a feature article around the subject of the press release. The issue has always been that journalists are deluged with press releases. This problem has only increased with the internet, and drawing their attention to a particular one is difficult.

Making press releases visible to journalists on the internet—optimizing press releases—assumes more importance in this environment. In addition to writing the press release well, optimization requires the use of search marketing tools including:

- Selecting relevant key words.
- Using the key word or phrase in the title of the release and in the various tags that identify the content to search engines.

FIGURE 7.14

The BankBazaar Mobile App

SOURCE: https://www.bankbazaar.com/getapp.html

- Tagging images for identification by the search engines.
- Using three anchor links: one to the home page, one to the product page, and one to the most relevant blog post.[2]

The template shown in Figure 7.15. also shown RSS feeds to relevant content. Other tools of search engine marketing (SEM) are discussed in detail in Chapter 10.

The optimized press release[37] is posted with its own URL on the business' website to facilitate search. The releases are tagged with keywords and the content itself is optimized for search, both topics covered in Chapter 10. In addition, most businesses use an internet press service to distribute their releases to the largest possible set of relevant journalists, who will generally have all the information they need to write articles or posts without having to contact the marketer and wait for a reply.

- In addition to being optimized for search, press releases should also contain rich media including images and videos, providing journalists with engaging content. Figure 7.15 displays a template for an interactive press release featuring traditional elements like text and contact information plus rich media elements including links to images and videos. Other links encourage writers to post their content to book-marking sites like Delicious and news sites like Technorati. These postings add to the reach of the content and may also increase the search ranking since they represent incoming links (discussed in Chapter 8).

All these channels and techniques are important in customer acquisition. However, nothing works if the target audience does not see it. We end the chapter with two separate topics on the subject, **ad blocking** and the importance of integrated communications for reaching target audiences.

FIGURE 7.15

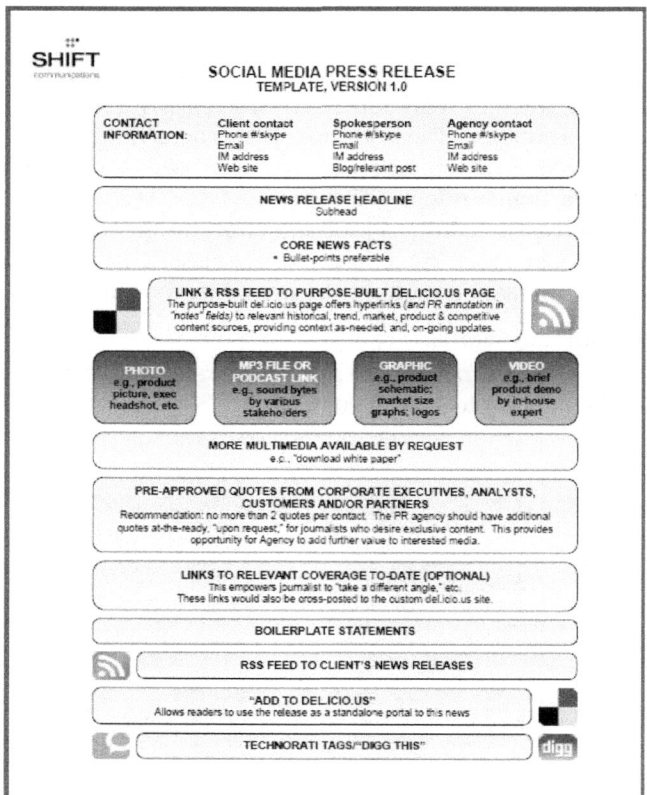

SOURCE: Shift Communications, http://www.shiftcomm.com/blog/social-media-press-release-3-0-2014-edition/

A WORD ABOUT AD BLOCKING

Ad blocking is of concern to both marketers and publishers but internet users seem to like the idea. As of late 2015, as many as 198 million of them were using ad blocking software with an estimated cost to publishers of $22 billion.[38]

The benefit of ad blockers to users who do not want to see ads is obvious. Will there be long-term harm to users if ad blocking spells the end of free content on the web? What kinds of sites are likely to suffer most from ad blocking? One study found that Millennials are willing to pay for entertainment content but unlikely to pay for news. Many older internet users do not read digital news in any event.[39] One UK study found that users were willing to sometimes turn off blockers in return for content from trusted sites.[40]

The prevalence and cost of ad blocking concerns the advertising industry. The IAB has written an ad blocking primer that suggests publishers adopt this model:

- *Detect* visitors who are using ad blockers and attempt to start a dialog
- *Explain* the value that ads offer to both readers and publishers
- *Ask* for behaviors that will help maintain the value of the exchange
- *Lift* restrictions or *limit* access, depending on user behavior.

One agency executive listed solutions that some major publishers have taken on their own sites:

- GQ and Epicurious are two sites that have asked users to disable blockers or to pay 50 cents per article. Coin Tent has been set up as a micropayments service to make it easier for users to pay for content.
- Wired asks users to whitelist the site on its blocker. In return it will serve only standard display ads to that user. Alternatively they offer an ad-free subscription for $1 per week.
- Forbes tested an "ad lite" experience in which users were asked to turn their ad blockers off for 30 days. In return, they received pages with less intrusive advertising like animation and video. They found that users in this test cell stayed on the site longer and consumed more pages than other test cells.[41] They also found that, while readers of other sections changed their viewing habits to some extent, technology readers did not.[42]

There is disagreement on the long-term danger of ad blocking to the ad industry. Some see it as a fad and others as a serious problem. All seem to agree that there needs to be better dialog with internet users about the positive and negative features of digital advertising.

INTEGRATED MARKETING COMMUNICATIONS FOR REACH AND IMPACT

The digital age has not changed another key fact. No single medium or channel of communication is enough to reach a given market segment. Examples throughout this chapter have shown that multiple channels are necessary to provide reach and do so in a way that is impactful to all members of the audience. For the foreseeable future that will require integrating both online and offline media into coherent, sequenced marketing campaigns. Coke has become an expert in integrated marketing campaigns through many years of experience in many channels, both offline and online.[43] Admittedly, most of Coke's advertising is reminder advertising, not customer acquisition. It does, however, make use of display and other components in a host of media channels.

Coke is also a master of individual campaigns under the overarching umbrella of a brand theme. Since the beginning of 2016, the brand campaign has been "Taste the Feeling" with initial TV ads (also posted on YouTube, of course) which convey the emotion of the Coke experience.[44]

The worldwide success of the "Share a Coke" campaign, which started in Australia and rolled out to other countries based on initial success, is one such example (Figure 7.16). The Australia launch featured a digital outdoor billboard with Coke users' names occupying a major square in Sydney. The campaign quickly spawned videos all over the world.[45] It was gradually rolled out to countries in all parts of the globe. In the United States it was supported by television advertising.[46] The campaign is credited with increasing sales of the soft drink by 2 percent in the United States alone.[47]

The primary goal of the campaign was to connect and engage with teens and Millennials in a personal and emotional way. Facebook and other social media are credited for much of the campaign's success.[48]

One Coke executive pointed out that:

Coca-Cola encouraged consumers to spread the word about the campaign on social media using the #shareacoke hashtag and the results were phenomenal.

- More than 500,000 photos were shared using the #shareacoke hashtag.
- Consumers created and shared more than 6 million virtual Coke bottles by September 2014.

Coca-Cola gained 25 million Facebook followers as a result of the campaign.[49]

All the evidence suggests that digital advertising in general, and mobile in particular, will continue to grow in popularity and impact. However, marketers cannot

FIGURE 7.16
The Share a Coke with Your Name Facebook Page

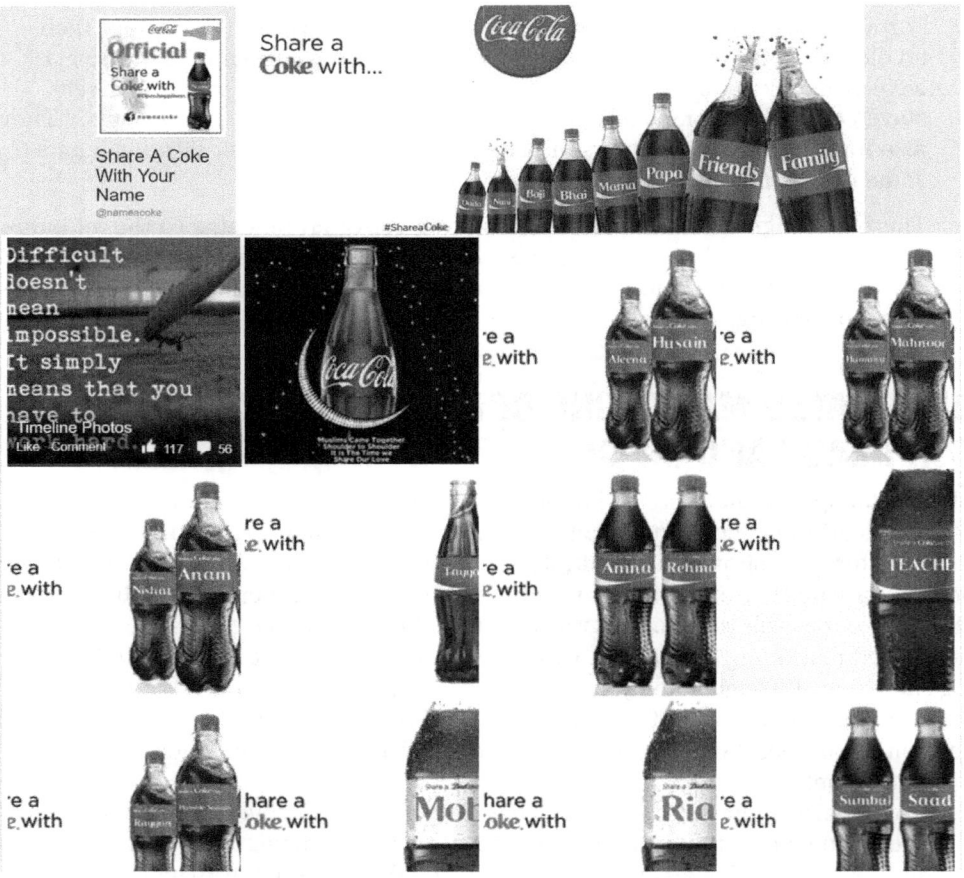

SOURCE: https://www.facebook.com/nameacoke/photos

afford to ignore other digital channels, nor should they ignore the traditional communications channels. Acquiring new customers requires broad reach. That requires an integrated marketing communications mix to expose target audiences to the acquisition marketing message.

SUMMARY

As the internet has matured and its ability to perform as a branding channel has been recognized, online advertising has become an increasingly important digital marketing tool as evidenced by its growing role in the marketing budget. This budget is still dominated by search marketing expenditures (direct response), but display advertising and, more recently, advertising on social and mobile networks continues to grow. The growth is primarily because of their reach and their effectiveness in branding, especially as new digital advertising formats are developed to more effectively engage the viewer. Each of these digital marketing tools contributes to brand development and at the same time operates as an effective customer acquisition mechanism.

There are numerous formats that can be used for online display ads. Static ads have lost popularity to rich media ads, which attract attention and deliver compelling messages. Most online ads are placed on websites by an ad serving network. The system tries to balance the requirements of the site with those of the advertiser. The site wishes to sell as many spaces as it has available on its site at the best possible rates. The advertiser wishes to reach the defined target audience with the right frequency at the lowest possible cost. Ads can be served directly to large sites or within networks of sites that have been brought into an alliance for that purpose. Programmatic advertising automates the process of identifying target markets and purchasing the ad space. Real-time bidding carries this out in nanoseconds so the visitor can be targeted with ads that match current activity like search for a specific product.

As both technology and databases improve, it becomes possible to target ads with more precision. Behavioral targeting can be based on a user activity profile, profile of either an anonymous web user or an identified user. It can also be based on more complex predictive models. Using any of these targeting approaches, the visitor is followed through the site, and ads can be served based on the visitor's segment membership without regard to the content being viewed at any given time. The visitor can be followed off the site with relevant ads being served on other websites. Advanced targeting requires the compilation and use of consumer data, often without the consumer being aware that the data are being collected.

In recent years, a new advertising opportunity has arisen as a result of the time spent on social platforms and mobile networks. The same display advertising formats and targeting options apply on both social and mobile sites. While the reach of social platforms like Facebook is huge, it is really the targeted advertising opportunities they offer that make them so attractive to the marketer. Similarly, it is the amount of time spent on mobile networks and the ability to engage visitors through video and games that makes mobile advertising the fastest-growing display segment. The growth of mobile display advertising is enhanced by the ability of apps to display advertisements.

In addition to online advertising, other customer acquisition techniques include affiliate marketing and publicity.

The ubiquity of digital display advertising has led to the practice of ad blocking by consumers. Advertisers are concerned when their ads are not being displayed to visitors. The industry is actively engaged in developing ways to make digital advertising more acceptable to visitors.

Display advertising and other customer acquisition techniques must be part of an Integrated Marketing Communications strategy that includes both digital and offline marketing efforts. In a multichannel world no single advertising technique can be effective. Marketing effectiveness requires a judicious use of techniques that are appropriate to the target user and to the nature of the campaign.

DISCUSSION QUESTIONS

1. True or False: All businesses need to create a steady flow of new customers as part of their marketing strategy. Explain your answer.
2. Identify the main customer acquisition tools.
3. What is online display advertising, and how does it relate to offline display advertising?
4. What is an online ad format? Why must marketers be familiar with the formats and understand what creating an online ad requires?
5. Why are new ad formats continually being developed? What benefits do this offer the marketer? Do any of the formats presented in this chapter have any potential downsides?
6. What is ad serving and how does it relate to targeting an ad to the correct target audience?
7. Why is ad serving an improvement over just placing an ad on a web page and just leaving it there?
8. Explain what programmatic advertising is and why it is an essential tool of both the digital publisher and the digital advertiser. What capability does real-time bidding add?
9. Behavioral advertising, is especially important on the internet. Explain why and give a hypothetical example, perhaps based on your own experience.
10. How do cookies and hashed e-mails facilitate audience targeting? Do you see any ethical problems in the use of these technologies?
11. Why do you think mobile advertising is growing at such a fast pace?
12. Discuss whether or not generating publicity is one of the few marketing communications activities that has not changed much as a result of the internet.
13. Do affiliate programs tend to attract many websites or blogs that can generate a large volume of traffic that results in sales? Why or why not?
14. What is IMC and why is it important to marketers and advertisers?

ENDNOTES

1. "Digital Ad Industry Will Gain $8.2 Billion By Eliminating Fraud and Flaws in Internet Supply Chain, IAB & EY Study Shows" http://www.iab.com/news/digital-ad-industry-will-gain-8-2-billion-by-eliminating-fraud-and-flaws-in-internet-supply-chain-iab-ey-study-shows/
2. http://www.iab.com/guidelines/other-ad-units/
3. http://digitalsynopsis.com/ibm-smart-roads/
4. https://support.google.com/richmedia/answer/2417545?hl=en
5. http://www.iab.com/guidelines/display-rising-stars-ad-units/
6. http://www.iab.com/guidelines/display-rising-stars-ad-units/
7. http://www.iab.com/guidelines/digital-video-suite/
8. https://www.facebook.com/business/ads-guide/?tab0=Mobile%20News%20Feed
9. http://www.google.com/ads/displaynetwork/why-display.html
10. http://www.pcmag.com/encyclopedia/term/37491/ad-serving
11. http://www.pcmag.com/encyclopedia/term/45193/internet-advertising
12. Jack Marshall, "WTF Is Programmatic Advertising?" http://digiday.com/platforms/what-is-programmatic-advertising/
13. Ratko Vidakovic, "Navigating The Modern Ad Serving Stack, Part 1: Direct Orders," http://marketingland.com/navigating-modern-ad-serving-stack-part-1-direct-orders-109611
14. "Programmatic and Automation—The Publishers' Perspective," http://www.iab.com/wp-content/uploads/2015/06/IAB_Digital_Simplified_Programmatic_Sept_2013.pdf

15. "Video Viewability: Measuring the Measures," http://na-ab05.marketo.com/rs/brightrollinc/images/KelloggViewabilityWhitepaper.pdf
16. "How B2B SaaS Companies Can Drive Sales With Display Advertising," https://blog.kissmetrics.com/sales-with-display-advertising/
17. Kelly Liyakasa, "B2B Advertisers Seek To Bridge The Divide Between Demand Gen and Brand Engagement" http://adexchanger.com/ad-exchange-news/b2b-advertisers-seek-to-bridge-the-divide-between-demand-gen-and-brand-engagement/
18. "The B2Bnn Primer on RTB Advertising and Its Future," http://www.b2bnn.com/2015/07/the-b2bnn-primer-on-rtb-advertising-and-its-future/
19. http://www.amazon.com/gp/help/customer/display.html?nodeId=468496
20. Dave Hendricks, "What's an Email Hash, Anyway?" https://www.clickz.com/clickz/column/2288689/whats-an-email-hash-anyway
21. https://en.wikipedia.org/wiki/MD5
22. Phil Davis, "What is a Hashed Email and Why Should Marketers Care?" https://blog.privy.com/blog/2015/8/what-is-a-hashed-email-and-why-should-marketers-care
23. Jim Nichols, "5 New (and Powerful) Targeting Methods," http://www.imediaconnection.com/articles/ported-articles/red-dot-articles/2011/jun/5-new-and-powerful-targeting-methods/
24. "List Segmentation," http://marylouroberts.info/images/dir.mark.man.ch5.pdf
25. http://www.tru-signal.com/predictive-scoring-platform/what-sets-us-apart/
26. "National Online College," http://www.tru-signal.com/wp-content/uploads/2014/11/TruSignal-Online_College.pdf
27. Mark Hoelzel, "The Digital-Video Advertising Report: Mobile and social are fueling video growth as dollars shift from display to video," http://www.businessinsider.com/mobile-boosts-digital-video-advertising-2015-4
28. "Mobile Advertising Guidelines," http://www.mmaglobal.com/files/mobileadvertising.pdf
29. Shuant," Best Mobile Ad Formats and Sizes for Display Ad Campaigns," https://www.mobileads.com/blog/best-mobile-ad-formats-sizes-display-ad-campaigns/
30. Adam Foroughi, "Which Mobile Ad Formats are Best? A Down and Dirty Guide that Spells It Out," http://venturebeat.com/2015/03/10/which-mobile-ad-formats-are-best-a-down-and-dirty-guide/
31. Jenn Harris and Noelle Carter, "Every Item on the New Taco Bell $1 Breakfast Menu, Reviewed in Emojis," http://www.latimes.com/food/dailydish/la-dd-taco-bell-breakfast-menu-review-20160313-htmlstory.html
32. Kenneth Burke, "The First Thing People Do Everyday Is Check Their Phones," https://www.textrequest.com/blog/the-first-thing-people-do-everyday-is-check-their-phones/
33. Lauren Johnson, "Taco Bell's Mobile Ads Are Highly Targeted To Make Users Crave Its Breakfast Menu," http://www.adweek.com/news/technology/taco-bells-mobile-ads-are-highly-targeted-make-users-crave-its-breakfast-menu-170155
34. https://www.nerdwallet.com/blog/how-we-make-money/
35. Catherine Shu, "India's BankBazaar Raises $60M SeriesC Led by Amazon," http://techcrunch.com/2015/07/02/bankbazaar/
36. "What is Bank Bazaar's Business Model?". https://www.quora.com/What-is-Bankbazaars-business-model-How-does-it-generate-revenue-and-is-it-profitable-If-not-then-by-when-is-the-estimated-time-to-profits
37. "Tips for Creating a Press Release that Maximizes Social Sharing," http://www.prnewswire.com/knowledge-center/how-to-optimize-your-press-release-for-social-sharing-seo.html
38. "The 2015 Ad Blocking Report," https://blog.pagefair.com/2015/ad-blocking-report/
39. Rick Edmonds, "Millennials Will Pay for Content, but News is Not High on Their List," http://www.poynter.org/2015/paying-for-news-is-not-a-popular-option-for-millennials/375848/
40. "Almost Half of those Planning to Use an Adblocker Say they Just Don't Like Ads," http://www.theguardian.com/media/2016/apr/27/adblocking-ads-kpmg-report-uk-block-ads

41. Christine Campbell, "Ad Blocking: How Worried Should You Be?" http://www.ninahale.com/blog/reactions-to-ad-blocking-marketers/
42. Lucia Moses, "Forbes: Ad Blocking Test Hasn't Cost Us Technology Readers," http://digiday.com/publishers/forbes-ad-blocking-test-hasnt-cost-us-technology-readers/
43. Gregory Stringer, "Case Study: Coca-Cola Integrated Marketing Communications,"htttps://www.linkedin.com/pulse/case-study-coca-cola-integrated-marketing-gregory-stringer
44. Will Heilpern, "Coca-Cola Just Launched a Massive New Ad Campaign to Change the Conversation Around Sugary Drinks," http://www.businessinsider.com/coca-colas-taste-the-feeling-campaign-2016-1
45. Jay Moye, "Share a Coke: How the Grandbreaking Campaign Got Its Start "Down Under,'" http://www.coca-colacompany.com/stories/share-a-coke-how-the-groundbreaking-campaign-got-its-start-down-under/
46. "Coca-Cola TV Spot, 'Share a Coke' Song by Trimountaine," https://www.ispot.tv/ad/7y_C/coca-cola-share-a-coke-song-by-trimountaine
47. "3 Marketing Lessons from the 'Share a Coke' Campaign," http://www.mayecreate.com/2015/05/3-marketing-lessons-from-the-share-a-coke-campaign/
48. Casey Neal, "Share A Coke: It's All In a Name," http://www.brittonmdg.com/the-britton-blog/share-a-coke-case-study/
49. "3 Marketing Lessons from the "Share a Coke" Campaign,"http://www.mayecreate.com/2015/05/3-marketing-lessons-from-the-share-a-coke-campaign/

Chapter 8

Content Marketing

LEARNING OBJECTIVES

By the time you complete this chapter you will be able to:

1. Identify reasons why content marketing is superseding traditional advertising.
2. Provide a definition of content marketing.
3. Explain the difference between content marketing and content strategy.
4. Discuss the kinds of content marketing used by both B2C and B2B marketers.
5. Identify and define various types of content used by marketers.
6. Explain the role of buyer personas in audience development.
7. Discuss issues involved in content distribution.
8. Identify the four types of content metrics.
9. Explain what is meant by native advertising.
10. Discuss the role of storytelling in content marketing.
11. Explain the importance of content that is valuable, engaging, and relevant.

content marketing strategic approach to creating and distributing content.

Marketing guru Seth Godin is often quoted as having said, "**Content marketing** is the only marketing left."[1] And he adds, "Marketing is no longer about the stuff that you make, it is about the stories you tell."[2]

A similar refrain is heard when advertisers and their critics alike when they say that traditional advertising as we know it is dead. An executive at a 2016 conference sponsored by the ABC network put it this way, "advertising in the current model is a dead man walking."[3] This is a disruption of huge proportions. What has caused it? The usual suspect, of course—the internet!

The web has totally upended the way marketers are expected to communicate with their target audiences: Professor Jennifer Rowley has a good comparison of the characteristics of traditional media and online media shown in Table 8.1.

TABLE 8.1 Comparison of Traditional and Online Media Channels

	Traditional media	Online
Space	Expensive commodity	Cheap, unlimited
Time	Expensive commodity for marketers	Expensive commodity for users
Image creation	Image is everything Information is secondary	Information is everything Image is secondary
Communication	Push, one-way	Pull, interactive
Call to action	Incentives	Information (incentives)
Audience	Mass	Targeted
Links to further information	Indirect	Direct/embedded
Investment in design	High	Low, allows change
Interactivity	Low	Ranges across aspectrum from low to two-way dialogue.

SOURCE: JOURNAL OF MARKETING MANAGEMENT, 2008, Vol. 24, No. 5–6, pp. 517–540. ISSN0267-257X print /ISSN1472-1376 online © Westburn Publishers Ltd.

The comparison makes it clear that information is the primary characteristic of online channels while push and image best characterize traditional media. People are tired of promotional content; they want information that helps them improve the quality of their lives. The number of communications channels has exploded and many of them give the smaller business an opportunity to be heard at an acceptable cost. The emphasis on information in digital channels and the importance of community building there means that transparency and trust are indispensable if content marketing is to achieve its goals.

In the roughly 20 years since Seth Godin made his famous statement content marketing has evolved. Instead of quantity of content, quality is more highly valued. Highly targeted distribution channels are expected. Above all, the entire content effort is driven by behavioral data from the web and marketing research that sheds light on the purchase journey. Creating an always-on content strategy that measures up to these standards and more is the subject of this chapter.

EFFECTIVE CONTENT MARKETING BY A MARKETING AGENCY

In numerous places in this book you see references to digital marketing agency HubSpot. That is neither accidental nor is it particularly intentional on the part of the authors. It happens because HubSpot has gone out of its way to create not only a thriving software business but also a place, as Figure 8.1 illustrates, "Where Marketers Go to Grow."

When Jacob McMillan examined HubSpot's content strategy, here is some of what he found:

- 7 blogs, each with several posts per day, averaging about 35 posts each day in addition:
- 5 tweets/retweets per day
- 3 Facebook posts per day
- 1 email sent out every day
- 10 Instagram posts per week
- 22 YouTube videos per month
- 2,400 total Pinterest pins

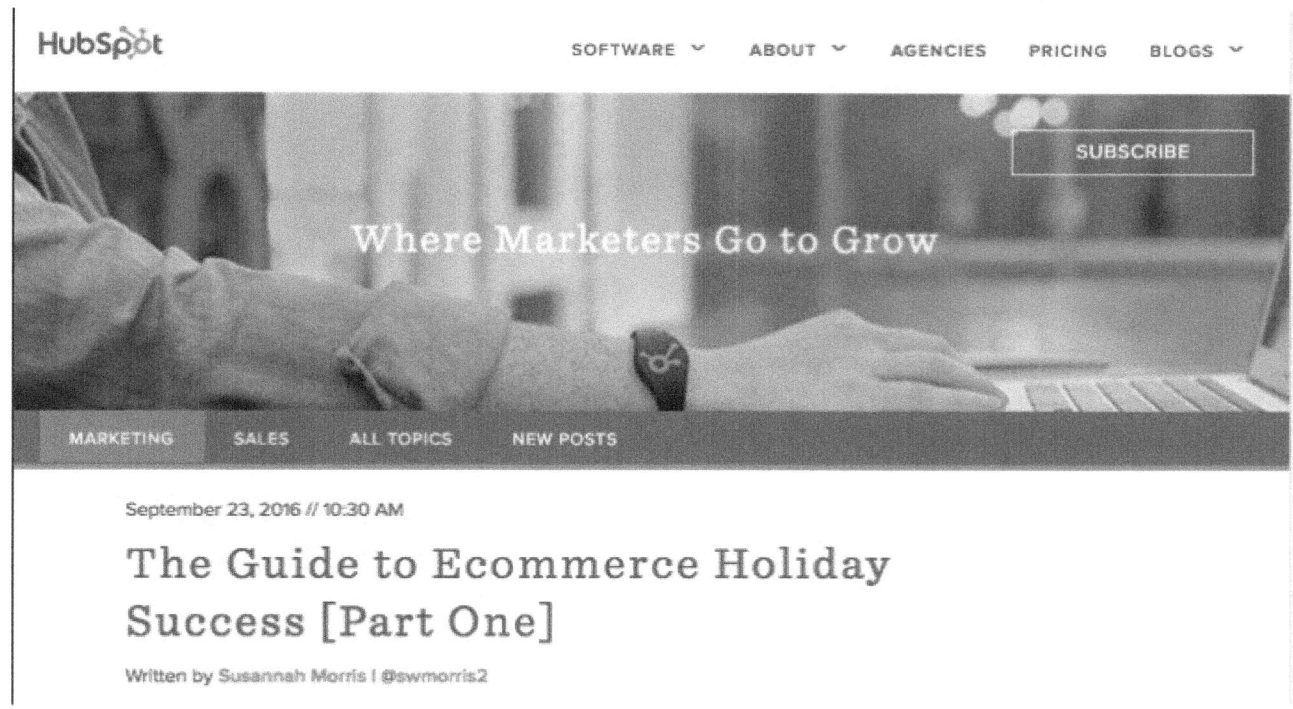

FIGURE 8.1

A Main Product Page on the HubSpot Website

SOURCE: http://blog.hubspot.com/marketing/guide-ecommerce-holiday-success-1#sm.0000002to08kmvcpyv7vlb6v649jq.

And this flood of content has resulted in a massive audience;

- 300k email subscribers (after deleting 250k inactives)
- 928k Facebook fans
- 654k Twitter followers
- 28k Pinterest followers
- 20,000 YouTube subscribers[4]

If you doubt this tsunami of content, take a look at their content library. Actually, take a look at it anyway and search for some marketing issue or event you want to know about. Chances are you'll find an informative post, ebook, video, or some other type of content on the subject you are looking for. That's how any content marketer becomes a thought leader who is frequently quoted.

And, yes, HubSpot has a thriving software business to run at the same time its employees are turning out all this content. They have created a business and a culture where that kind of productivity is possible. Figure 8.2 is from their Culture Code deck, which is famous in its own right.

If this section sounds less than totally objective, that's because it is. Prof. Roberts holds HubSpot in especially high regard because of the way it has always treated her and her students. HubSpot is located in the Greater Boston area where she taught Internet and Social Media Marketing. When asked for a guest speaker, it always supplied a top executive who came well prepared and invariably gave one of the highest-rated lectures of the semester. They practice what they preach.

FIGURE 8.2
A Slide from the HubSpot Culture Code

SOURCE: https://inbound.org/blog/ask-dharmesh-about-the-hubspot-culture-code.

Now look at content marketing from another perspective. The Lucy the Robot story is hard to classify. It is a delightful piece of content in and of itself. A search for "Lucy the Robot Buys an iPhone," returns over 500,000 items, which means it got great publicity in addition to the video going viral. Add to that, it's a very creative marketing effort that costs almost nothing. Watch the video in Interactive Exercise 8.1 and see what you think.

WHAT EXACTLY IS CONTENT MARKETING?

There seem to be as many definitions of content marketing as there are people who write about it—and most marketers seem to do so at one time or another. The definition of the Content Marketing Institute is comprehensive:

> *Content marketing is a strategic marketing approach focused on creating and distributing valuable, relevant, and consistent content to attract and retain a clearly-defined audience — and, ultimately, to drive profitable customer action.*[5]

Their definition highlights the fact that content marketing is part of overall marketing strategy. As such, content must be created with a specific, clearly-defined target audience in mind. The content must be useful to them—must resonate in their lives—and it must motivate them to take the actions the marketer calls for. That is good; isn't it enough? No, in order to accomplish the content marketing task, marketers need a content strategy. Here is a good definition that clarifies the difference:

> *Content strategy deals with the planning aspects of managing content throughout its lifecycle, and includes aligning content to business goals, analysis, and modeling, and influences the development, production, presentation, evaluation, measurement, and sunsetting of content, including governance.*[6]

In other words, content marketing is not just a bunch of people writing, filming, or otherwise creating content that they find interesting. It is an activity that is aligned with marketing and digital marketing strategy and carefully tracked and evaluated. That still leaves two interesting terms in the definition.

Sunsetting is obvious but not easy. Marketing content is not usually developed with an end date in mind. For example, if the content is the promotion of a branded marketing event, the promotion needs to have an end date—the date the event begins. However, good content marketing will transform the communications, both formal and informal, at the event into "evergreen" marketing content. Content should be so good and so relevant that is valuable for a considerable period of time—hence, "evergreen." At some point, however, specific points are no longer valid or, overall, the content is too old to be useful and, as such, reflects poorly on the brand. Who decides to take down that content? When? How? Sunsetting requires policy guidelines that specify these matters.

Governance is also a familiar term that has specific meaning when it comes to content marketing. Another definition:

> *digital governance is "a discipline that focuses on establishing clear accountability for digital strategy, policy, and standards." In other words, digital governance gives organizations a way to manage content-related decisions that does not involve the seat of anyone's pants.*[7]

Good governance, in content marketing or any other organizational activity, identifies the people or teams that make decisions. Decision makers then need to get out of the way and let people do their jobs. Governance is not micromanagement, nor does it stifle innovation or creativity. One writer has a wonderful analogy:

> *A small digital team, like a jazz ensemble, can get away with making things up as it goes along. A large team, on the other hand, needs to operate like a symphony orchestra.... Improvising doesn't scale. A large team needs to follow standards just as an orchestra needs to follow sheet music.*[8]

Content marketing represents a different way of thinking about marketing. One term that is used to describe that is "*always on.*" In the early days of content marketing it was often said that "the marketing campaign is dead." Campaigns have a beginning and an end, while content has an indefinite life span. As content marketing has matured brands have learned to treat the two separately, with content marketing as an ongoing, permanent activity—always on. Marketing campaigns are used as highlights—a new product introduction or an appeal to a new market segment for example.

Just as content marketing itself has evolved, content marketing activities within an organization mature. We will return to that issue as we discuss content marketing strategy. First, however, let's take a quick look at the growing role and importance of content marketing.

WHO USES CONTENT MARKETING—WHAT AND HOW MUCH?

The answer to that question is, "just about all marketers, many types of content in multiple channels." Here are some highlights:

- Eighty-eight percent of B2B marketers and 76 percent of B2C marketers used content marketing in 2016.
- B2B marketers spent an average of 28 percent of their marketing budgets on content marketing while B2C marketers spent 32 percent.
- Most marketers plan to increase their spending on content marketing with estimates ranging from 75 percent[9] to 51 percent of B2B and 50 percent of B2C.
- Types of content receiving increased investment include original visual assets such as infographics, original videos, original written content, and original audio.[10]

Does it surprise you to see B2B marketers spending more on most aspects of their content marketing? Business marketers have a pressing need to inform their customers and prospects and content marketing is the answer. B2C markets are increasingly realizing the need to inform their customers but they use more expensive—and entertaining—tools.

B2B and B2C content marketers have somewhat different objectives. Top objectives for B2B marketers are

- Lead generation
- Sales
- Lead nurturing
- Brand awareness.

B2C content marketers prioritize

- Sales
- Retention and loyalty
- Engagement
- Brand awareness.

The differences are less in final objective—sales—than in approach; lead generation and conversion in B2B and direct attempts at conversion in B2C. The longer sales cycle in B2B is another explanation for the slightly higher usage of content marketing in B2B. Considering the different purchase journeys, you might expect to find the content that works for B2B versus B2C marketers is also somewhat different.

Among the questions Joe Pulizzi of the Content Marketing Institute and Ann Handley of Marketing Profs ask in their annual benchmarking survey is what types of content marketers use. Are you surprised that social media is at the top of the list for B2B? Case studies and blogs rank high in usage; B2B customers are looking for detailed, product-specific information and these are two good tactics to convey it. So are e-newsletters and in-person events. Types of content not making the list include mobile apps, with only 28 percent usage, virtual conferences (25 percent) and games/gamification (12 percent). For B2B marketers the effectiveness of in-person events far exceeds other tactics with 75 percent rating it most effective (Figure 8.3b). Webinars/webcasts follow at 66 percent, case studies at 65 percent, white papers at 63 percent, and videos at 62 percent. The study found that the most effective B2B marketers allocated 42 percent of their marketing budget to content marketing while the average quoted above was only 28 percent.

The importance of content marketing in B2B is documented in recent research by Professors Geraint Holliman and Jennifer Rowley. They offer a definition of B2B content marketing that reinforces the importance of achieving business goals:

> *B2B digital content marketing involves creating, distributing and sharing relevant, compelling and timely content to engage customers at the appropriate point in their buying consideration processes, such that it encourages them to convert to a business building outcome.*[11]

They also point out that most discussions of B2B content marketing focus on unpaid content, although there are important types of paid B2B content. When they add social digital content to the framework it becomes an important way of understanding B2B content.

Content marketing is also important in B2C strategy though perhaps a bit less central. In Figure 8.4a you see that B2C marketers use an average of 12 different content tactics as opposed to 13 used by B2B marketers. Social media again leads the list with 90 percent of the B2C respondents reporting its use. Images, e-newsletters, videos, and website content are not far behind. Among the lesser-used types of content not included in the graphic are case studies (38 percent), research reports

FIGURE 8.3a
Types of Content Used in B2B

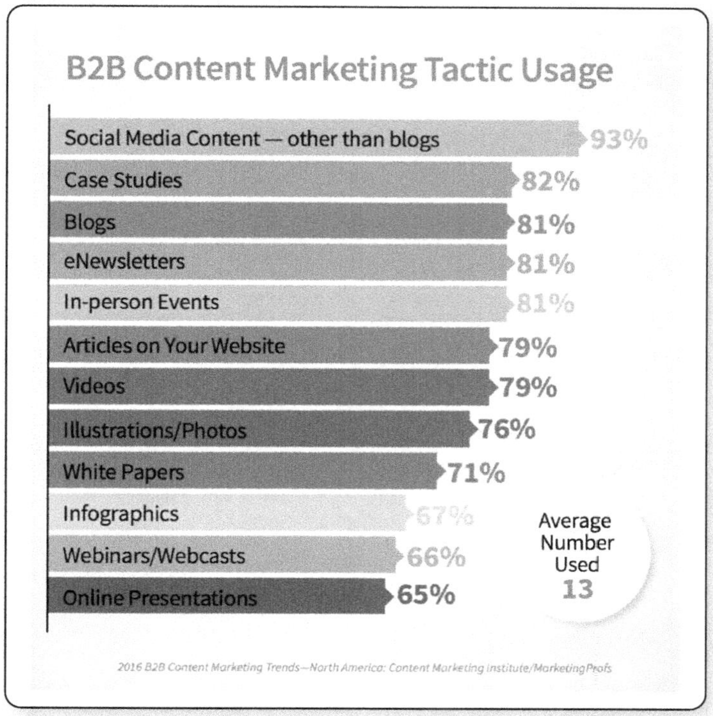

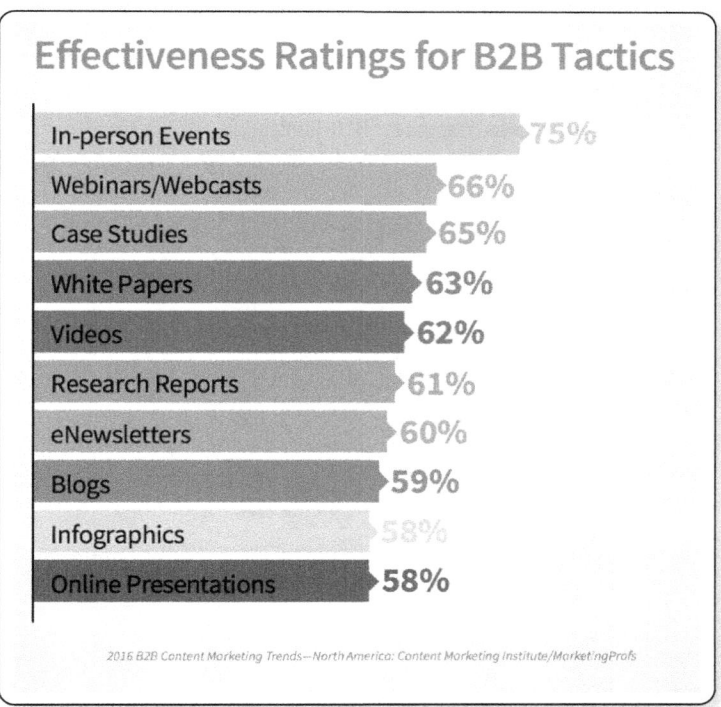

SOURCE: http://contentmarketinginstitute.com/wp-content/uploads/2015/09/2016_B2B_Report_Final.pdf.

FIGURE 8.3b
Effectiveness of Types of B2B Content

SOURCE: http://contentmarketinginstitute.com/wp-content/uploads/2015/09/2016_B2B_Report_Final.pdf.

FIGURE 8.4a

Types of Content Used in B2C

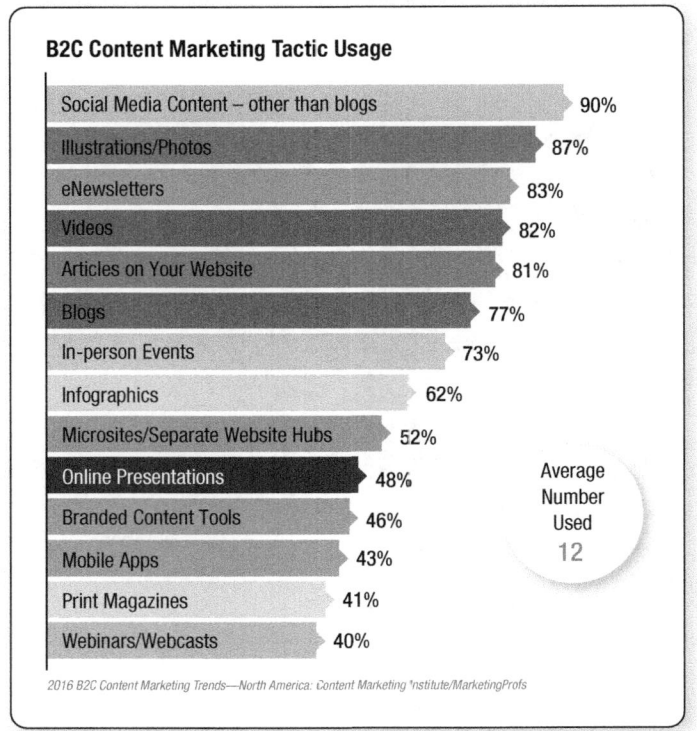

SOURCE: http://contentmarketinginstitute.com/wpcontent/uploads/2015/10/2016_B2C_Research_Final.pdf.

FIGURE 8.4b

Effectiveness of B2C Content Types

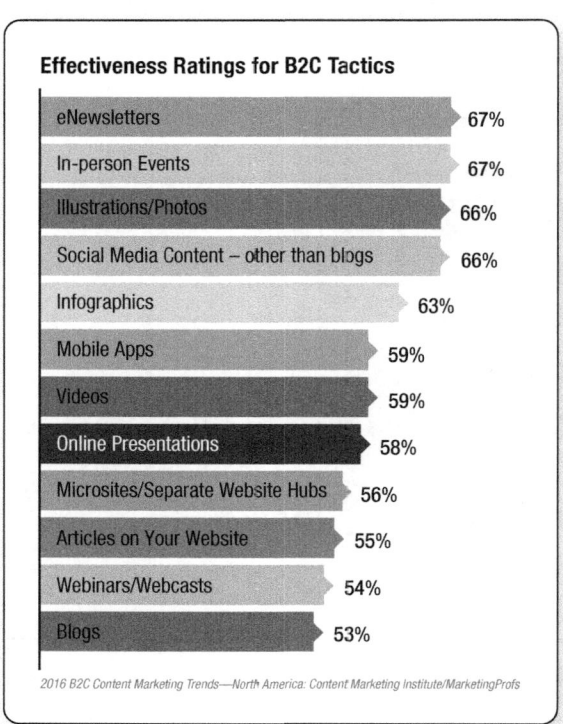

SOURCE: http://contentmarketinginstitute.com/wpcontent/uploads/2015/10/2016_B2C_Research_Final.pdf.

(36 percent), games/gamification (22 percent), and podcasts (21 percent). In terms of effectiveness, these marketers rated e-newsletters and in-person events in a tie for first place with 67 percent saying they were most effective. Notice that the usage of in-person events is much lower; they are expensive and time consuming to produce and may or may not replicate well to different venues—retail stores in different cities, for example. Images and social media content also ranked high in terms of effectiveness. The most effective B2C marketers allocated 38 percent of their budgets to content marketing as opposed to the 32 percent average quoted above.

The picture that is emerging is that of a complex, labor-intensive process. What is required to establish and perpetuate an always-on content marketing strategy?

THE CONTENT MARKETING STRATEGY PROCESS

An underlying theme of this book is that marketers need strategies and plans to guide their efforts. Otherwise, there would be no effective marketing, just marketing chaos. That is just as true for content marketing as for any other sub-discipline of marketing. However, the discussion frequently becomes confusing because people do not clearly distinguish between content marketing strategy and content strategy as we tried to do in Section 8-2. Content strategy is a broader activity and, as such, may be one foundation for content marketing strategy. Exhibit 8-1 pinpoints the origin of content strategy in web development, gives a working definition, and lists the characteristics of good content.

The distinction is important. The remainder of this chapter will concentrate on content marketing strategy which is a key job of today's marketing professionals.

Figure 8.5 describes content marketing strategy as an ongoing process, never a static document. The world in which marketers create content is constantly changing. The context in which users consume that content is constantly changing. The technology by which the content is distributed is constantly changing. In the midst of all this, marketers must create, refine, evaluate, and further refine the content that tells the brand story. That requires the guidance of a documented content strategy. Content marketing is still in early days and the CMI benchmark studies found that less than 40 percent of marketers had a documented (i.e., written) strategy while just under 50 percent had a verbal-only content marketing strategy.[12,13]

EXHIBIT 8.1 CONTENT STRATEGY

There is a distinction between content strategy and content marketing strategy but discussions often do not make that clear.

Content strategy is an integral part of website design, defining how an organization's content shapes user experience with the brand. It often is used in reference to other kinds of digital communications, but it originated with website developers.

Author Erin Kissane says that the golden rule of content is to *"Publish content that is right for the user and for the business."*

Then she goes on to explain the nature of content strategy:

There's really only one central principle of good content: it should be appropriate for your business, for your users, and for its context. Appropriate in its delivery, in its style and structure, and above all in its substance. Content strategy is the practice of determining what each of those things means for your project—and how to get there from where you are now.

Content that is right is:
- Right for the user and the user's content—what are the user's goals, what is the user doing, thinking, and feeling
- Right for the business and its objectives
- Useful in achieving the goals of both viewer and business
- Reflects how users think and talk about the subject
- Clear and easy to understand
- Consistent in presentation
- Concise
- Supported by information and data
- Updated as necessary

Adapted from http://alistapart.com/article/a-checklist-for-content-work

FIGURE 8.5

The Content Marketing Strategy Process

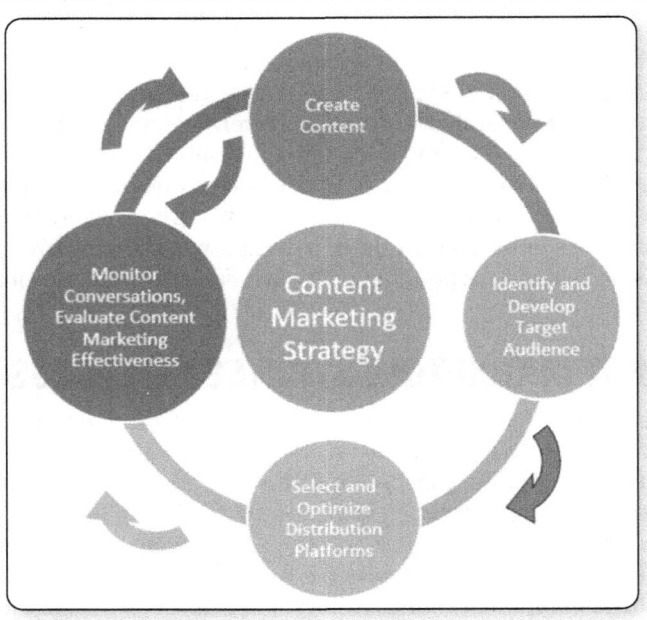

So a lot of marketers believe they have a content strategy; it just isn't written down. Is that dangerous for an essential marketing activity?

Creating Content

The first step in the strategy process is to create content. There are several ways of looking at the content marketers have available.

Sources of Content. There are three basic ways in which marketers obtain content. Marketing teams can

- Create the content themselves, which is labor intensive but hopefully produces high quality, relevant content.
- **Curate** content, which is basically locating good content from other publishers and publishing all or part of it with explanation to your audience about its relevance.
- Purchase **syndicated** content, a traditional publishing model in which content from a recognized source is republished, usually for a fee. There are a number of networks that specialize in syndicating marketing content.[14]

curate to select and prepare content from other sources for publication.

syndicated content from another source published under license.

A 2014 study by Curata showed marketers using 65 percent created content and 25 percent curated content.[15] In spite of laws governing digital content (Section 17-3) marketers need guidelines and best practices for curating content. Figure 8.6 offers a roadmap to curating a blog post.

Notice that the new title is a search issue; do not confuse the new post with the original one. The new image is more a copyright issue; images are a problem and it is better to use one whose origin and permission requirements are known. Obviously the writer is going to link to the original post but the majority of the text is commentary which links the original ideas to those of the writer's blog and puts them in context for his audience. A really good quote is essential both for the readability of the post and for search results. (The curated post will of course follow all the other requirements for effective SEM including use of keywords and tagging.) Finally there should be a call to action. Notice that the CTA in this post is the download of an ebook, which should be related to the subject of the curated post if it is to be effective.

FIGURE 8.6
Best Practices for a Curated Blog Post

SOURCE: http://www.curata.com/blog/content-curation-the-art-of-a-curated-post-infographic/.

There are two things in Figure 8.6 that good content marketers do automatically. The Curata logo is part of the image so it is captured along with the image when someone else uses it. They also have a "please cite us" statement which is a reminder to be polite along with the implication that their content is available for public use.

Hootsuite points out that effective SMM requires a substantial amount of outside content and recommends a Rule of Thirds:

- One-third of content should directly promote your business
- One-third of content should share content of thought leaders and like-minded businesses in your industry
- One-third should be brand building content.

Hootsuite makes content curation a formal part of its content marketing. Each week it does a blog post "This Week in Social" and sends an email newsletter to subscribers with the best blog posts of the week.[16]

If curated content sounds like a lot of work, it is. However, it is considerably less work than thinking of a great idea and writing from scratch. If you choose well, the curated content is likely to be effective in helping you meet business goals. It also may help you make content with influencers and thought leaders if you do the curation in a professional manner.[17] Curation is a lot of work but there are many marketing tools to assist, ranging from features of marketing platforms like Hootsuite to literally hundreds of stand-alone tools to help you find and prepare the best curated content.

Types of Content. Basic content types are shown in Figure 8.7 as a pyramid. The large foundation of the pyramid is made up of high frequency/low effort types of content while the top is made up of in depth publications that provide detailed customer

FIGURE 8.7

Types of Content by Effort and Frequency

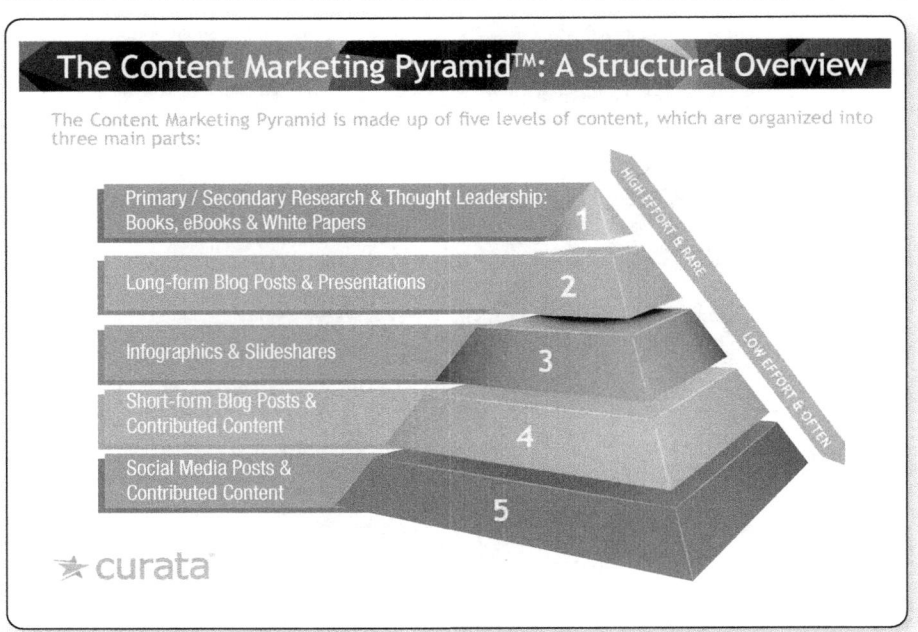

http://www.curata.com/assets/sales/Curata_Content%20Marketing%20Pyramid_v01.pdf.

assistance. You remember from Figures 8.3a and 8.4a that B2C and B2B marketers use somewhat different mixes of content types in spite of the differences in effort.

The core content at the top level of the pyramid made up of the insights and research your brand has developed. More important, it must embody the mission and values of the business: "Where Marketers Go to Grow," for example. It provides the core concepts and a great many specific ideas for content at the lower levels. For instance, research reports provide almost limitless content opportunities ranging from videos and slide shows to infographics and blog posts. Blog posts often have "tweet this" boxes with some of their better quotes. Even pdf research reports can have "tweet this" which is a powerful way to make content shareable.

The middle three rows of the pyramid, the derivative assets, are directly derived from the core content. They allow for more focused, more frequent, and perhaps more targeted pieces of content. They also lend themselves to visual images and videos that many users find more engaging than lengthy text. They improve reach as well as frequency because the basic content can be repurposed for a variety of channels—a blog with an embedded video which is then posted to YouTube or an infographic that is constructed from the data in a long set of slides. Content marketing has a voracious appetite, and successful repurposing for various channels is essential.

The high-volume promotional content at the bottom comes, in many cases, directly from the levels above but it also provides many other marketing opportunities as we learned in Chapter 5. It can be timely, appeal to emotion or humor, and is the best type of content for humanizing the brand in the eyes of its target audience. All that is very good—as long as it stays on mission as defined by the values and the message themes of the core content.

Another important way of looking at content uses stages in the customer purchase process and an emotional/rational continuum to classify content. The matrix in Figure 8.8 has stages of the purchase process across the horizontal axis and emotional/rational content on the vertical axis. It then identifies the marketing role of the content in each quadrant:

- To *entertain* is an emotional, early purchase stage activity. It aims to reach potential customers and create awareness. It includes traditional marketing activities such as brand advertising and interactive ones such as games.

FIGURE 8.8
Types of Content by Objectives and Tone

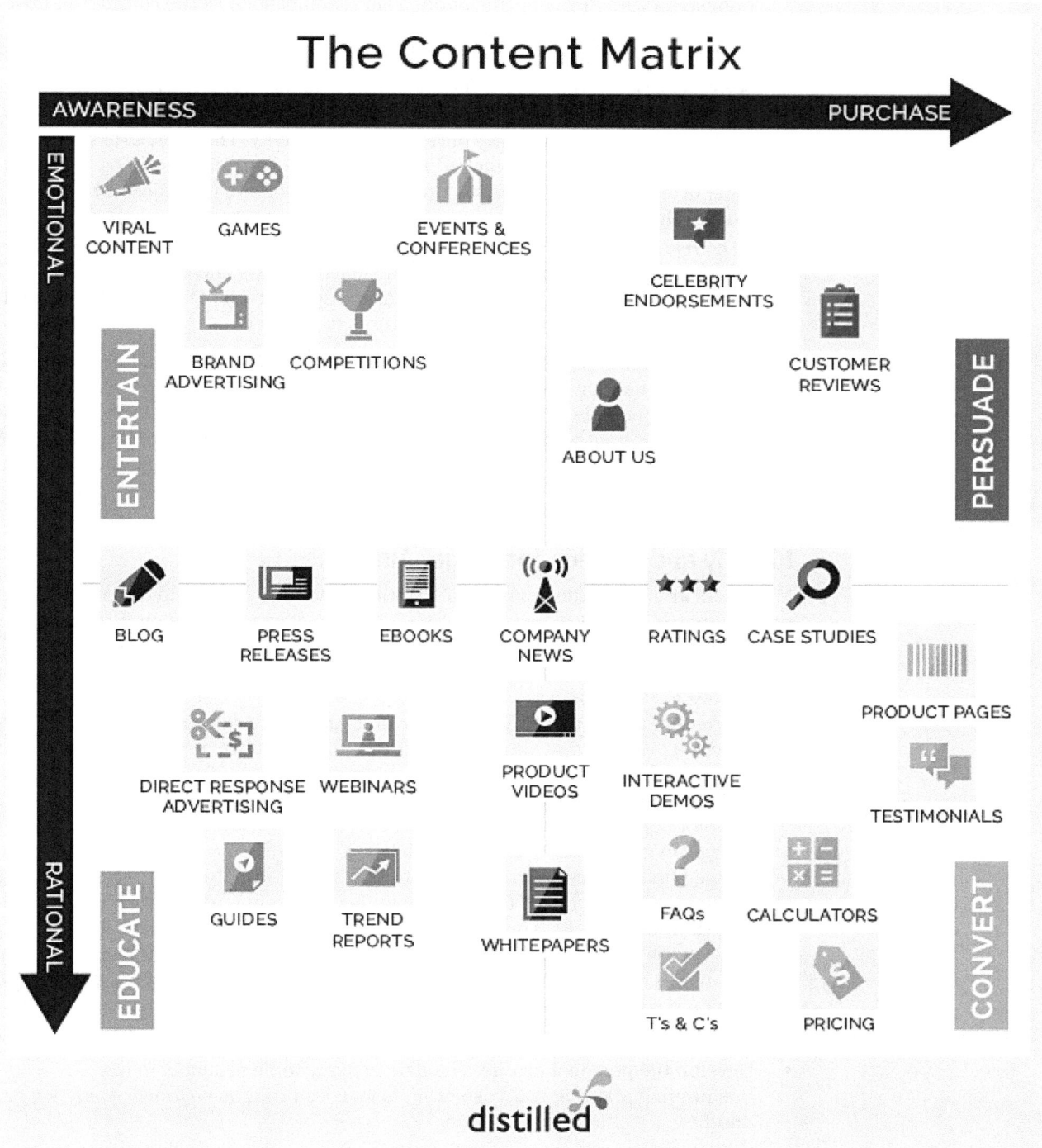

SOURCE: https://www.distilled.net/blog/the-content-matrix/?utm_content=bufferbdfa7&utm_medium=social&utm_source=twitter.com&utm_campaign=buffer.

It also lists viral content. The marketer should be aware that when a piece of content goes viral it is much more a case of luck than of skill. There are many lists of viral content and most of the content is not branded content. In one month in 2016, the most viral content came from Black History Month, the

Super Bowl, and the release of the movie "Deadpool."[18] Marketers would be wise to set their objectives in terms of shareable content, not viral. Some digital publishers have gotten very good at that. BuzzFeed is one; one analysis showed that 65 percent of its viral articles are its famous listicles.[19] There are other publishers who have become good at shareability such as the Huffington Post, which published a large-scale study of the subject.[20]

- To *persuade* is an emotional, late purchase stage activity. In that quadrant you see celebrity (or influencer) endorsements and the very powerful customer reviews.
- To *educate* is a rational, early purchase stage activity. The chart lists webinars and guides. An important addition would be informative videos. Google is reported to have found that 42 percent of consumers use video in their pre-purchase research.[21]
- To *convert* a visitor to a customer is a rational, late-stage activity. As such this quadrant contains informative content such as demos and testimonials. This quadrant might have included videos also, especially the DIY type popularized by brands from home improvement stores to makeup.

There are some popular types of content that are in the middle between emotional and rational that run from blogs to case studies.

The marketer truly has a dizzying array of content from which to choose. That is why it is so important to be guided by the core mission and values of the brand. With those firmly in mind the marketer can develop a content strategy and plan and learn from the advice about specific kinds of content that is plentiful on the web.

Identify and Develop the Target Audience

Marketers know well the types of information used to segment and target customers: demographics, lifestyles, and media use. The bare statistics—although readily available from online behavioral data and marketing research both online and offline—are cold. Consequently, marketers have turned to buyer personas to put flesh on the bare bones of the statistics.

In Figure 8.9 you meet Kyle Fisher who is in the market for a small SUV. When you read the persona, you should, indeed, feel that you have met Kyle Fisher. That is the purpose of the persona—not only to make a hypothetical person feel real but to give life to an entire target market segment.

Developing a buyer persona is not an exercise in creative writing, however. It is an exercise in gathering the right data, drawing insights from the data and creating a believable human story around it. A word of caution—much of the content you will find on personas deals with B2B personas. That is an important topic to which we will return in Chapter 13. The process described for B2B personas is similar to that for B2C but it has more steps, some of which are irrelevant to the B2C case, and that can throw you off if you are not careful. Learn from the B2B process, but be wary of the differences.

Steps in developing a B2C customer persona are as follows:

- Develop the personal profile. The data is likely to be available in the business's marketing database or in its metrics program—Google Analytics or another.
- Give the person a relevant but hypothetical name that doesn't produce any predispositions about the person.
- Include a photo.
- Financial status and preferred payment methods. There is a substantial amount of secondary data available on the finances of various cohorts of generational groups, one of which your persona should fit into.

FIGURE 8.9

A B2C Buyer Persona

- Describe "a day in the life."
- Describe the hopes and dreams of the persona.
- Also describe worries and fears.
- Explain how the persona interacts with and uses technology.
- Provide a social media profile.
- What the information the persona finds influential.
- What are the current brands used?
- Add a quote that sums up the persona.[22]

The persona in Figure 8.9 covers most of these topics but not all. It may have been done from a persona template that was designed specifically for automobile purchases. That would make it more focused that the broader template just described.

Once a persona has been developed to characterize the nature of the target market the work of **audience development** begins.

The term audience development represents another seismic shift in the post-advertising era. The advertising model is to reach people with promotions and convince them to buy. The audience development model is to create a community of people who are loyal subscribers to the brand's content. The term has long been used in nonprofit marketing, for obvious reasons, and has been popularized by content marketers. One manifestation of this approach is the creation of email lists discussed in Chapter 9 Developing an Email Campaign. Creating an email list requires that people first become aware of the brand and its content, then opt-in to joining the list and, over the long run, find the emails relevant and interesting enough to continue receiving the subscription. Email lists are a powerful marketing tool and so are audiences developed in other channels by other means.

audience development creating a loyal following for branded content.

Just as in traditional advertising, the goal of early stages of audience development is to reach as many people as possible—with content, not promotional messages. The content must be persuasive enough to get them to take action—to join an online community, to subscribe to an email list, or increasingly to permit push messaging. The content must be engaging and relevant to the early stages of the purchase journey. Is that enough? Probably not. Even well-known brands with a great story to tell like Red Bull need promotional help to build their audience.

Red Bull has a magazine which seems to be something of a hub for its audience development efforts. *The Red Bulletin* is a (mostly men's) style magazine that is available in print, online, and through a mobile app. Red Bull's 2016 media kit gives monthly circulation figures as follows:

- 2.3 million copies with 2.7 readers per copy
- 520,000 paid subscribers
- 300,000 newsletter subscribers.[23]

It gives both print and online advertising rates but not online viewership by channel, which can often be found on the site itself. Its highly regarded main YouTube channel has over 5.4 million subscribers in late 2016 and its main Twitter channel has over 800,000 subscribers, as seen in Figure 8.10. This is a capture from their media kit; their twitter account usually has a daily promotion, not necessarily the main page.

What is important is that anyone who stumbles onto this or any other Red Bull online site or account has an easy opportunity to sign up for *The Red Bulletin* magazine. The header gives a promotional message and the sign-up creates an account for the user while other pages give direct access to signing up for the magazine. It seems that Red Bull has all the bases covered when it comes to enticing viewers to join one of its many communities. That illustrates a primary principle of audience development.

In the early customer journey stages, creating interest and engagement, it is necessary to reach as widely as possible to locate people who are not yet members of the community but who are interested in becoming part of it. That requires reaching people through many media channels, online and offline, unpaid and also paid. PR and offline events can be very useful in acquiring new followers as discussed in Sections 6-5 and 7-5. It requires using all appropriate online channels in which the marketer has expertise. Increasingly, it requires paid promotions including display advertising (Chapter 7) and PPC and social media advertising (Chapter 11). Simply

FIGURE 8.10
Main Red Bull Twitter Page

SOURCE: https://www.redbullmediahouse.com/products-brands/online/social-media.html.

distributing content, even content well optimized for search, is no longer enough if it ever was. According to a 2016 Adobe study, the internet has reached the saturation point with very little organic growth to drive additional traffic. The web is now a competitive environment in which all marketers are struggling to attract the same sets of eyeballs.[24] Expect paid advertising to assume a greater role throughout digital marketing as a result.

As the customer begins to move through the purchase journey a nurturing approach is required. It includes, first, segmentation and persona development for each segment and, then, creating content for each segment with special attention to the persona's stage in the customer journey.

Select and Optimize Distribution Platforms

Figure 8.11 gives an overview of the content *distribution* process that illustrates what we have just described. It shows a basic set of platforms including the brand hub, either a website or a blog. It includes email; sponsored content on what could be thousands of websites, blogs, and other properties; and several social media platforms.

There are several important ideas in this graphic. The first is that most of the content is designed to drive people to the brand hub (pink arrows) where they can take some action such as purchase a product. Some of the content such as the sponsored Red Bull twitter account in Figure 8.10 is designed to persuade people to sign up for the email list (pink arrow). The yellow arrows signal that the brand is publishing directly to the platform regardless of whether it is a paid or free posting. In that

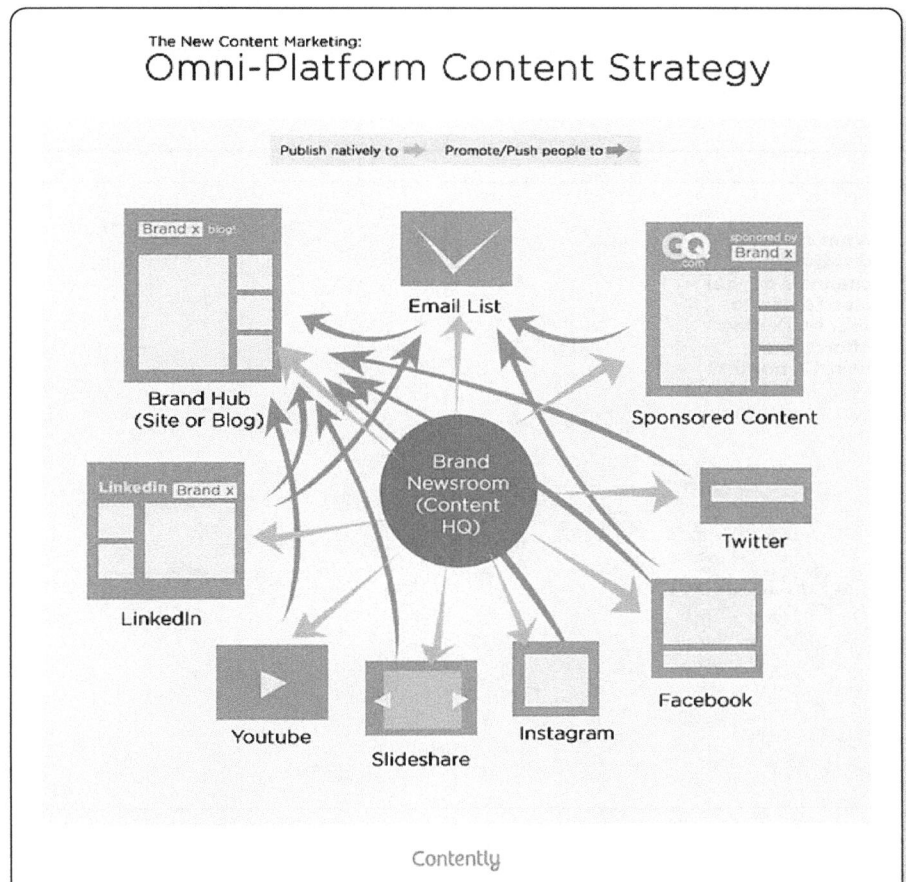

FIGURE 8.11
Native and Sponsored Content on Platforms

SOURCE: https://contently.com/strategist/2015/12/17/state-of-content-marketing-2016/.

native content content whose format is appropriate to the publication or the channel.

process there is another term used—call it **native content**. That means to publish content in a format that is appropriate for that channel; Tweeting a link to an Instagram video, for example. That is also called repurposing of content. "Native" is an important term and we will return to it later in the chapter.

Choosing platforms and sites on which to distribute content is not easy, even when guided by a strong audience definition, because there are so many options to choose from. Choosing the best set of channels with which to reach your target audience is the *optimization* step.

The advice centers around beginning with the brand's owned channels. Most brands have a website and a blog and a few social media channels including perhaps a Facebook page, Twitter account, and a YouTube channel. Red Bull lists nine video channels on its YouTube page along with a TV channel for first-run films and videos. A brand can have a great deal of owned media but it takes a great deal of effort, money and usually a lot of help from user-generated content to keep multiple channels viable. It also takes a large audience to make them worthwhile.

Then work on getting as much earned content as you can with reasonable effort and cost. That leaves paid content to fill out the picture—to be sure that the content is reaching the target audience. Paid channels provide a great deal of control and work quickly, more reasons why paid placements have become an essential part of content marketing strategy.

The need to expand content reach is illustrated in the 2016 State of Inbound report. See Figure 8.12. The chart implies that almost 80 percent of content marketers plan to add channels during their next operating year. YouTube is not a surprise but notice that the marketers specify Facebook video; the importance of video in a mobile world is clear. Instagram is working well for many marketers, but messaging apps and podcasts rounding out the top five may be less expected.

Ads on messaging apps are still unexplored territory. The two largest apps What'sApp and Facebook messenger are both Facebook properties and both currently do not allow ads. Brands can, however, communicate with an existing audience

FIGURE 8.12
Adding Channels for Content Distribution

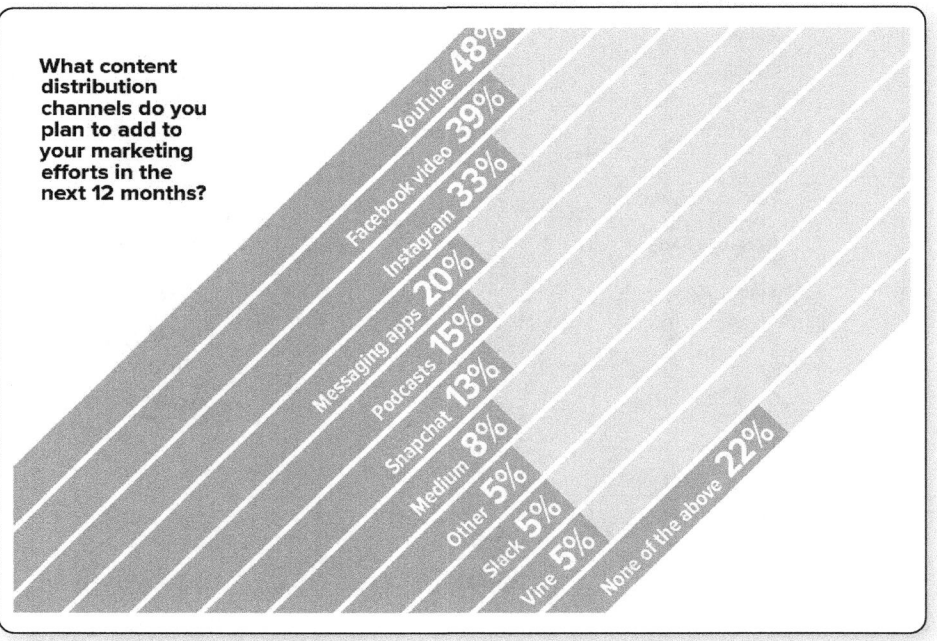

SOURCE: http://cdn2.hubspot.net/hubfs/53/HubSpot-State-of-Inbound-Report-2016.pdf?__hssc=20629287.1.1475155278674&__hstc=20629287.024c09a57966d35f8490ebcbedd7cc97.1454958488354.1474902675481.1475155278674.60&__hsfp=1097012398&hsCtaTracking=7b8dec0c-af54-4700-899c-3d4907a5cdc4%7C323c7216-def8-4f80-bb32-0ec9964b65f3.

by establishing an account. Dutch airline KLM used the platform to let their frequent flier members ask customer-service related questions. Earlier Absolut Vodka used What'sApp to invite customers to an exclusive brand launch party in Venezuela. The hook was that the customer had to convince a virtual bouncer named Sven to include them on the guest list.

Messaging apps offer potentially huge audiences, but there are important warnings. First, there are no advertising formats for messaging apps and using them effectively is likely to require creativity that is far outside the traditional advertising box. Second, messaging apps operate in what is called **dark social**, a space where traditional marketing analytics do not apply. Finally, different messaging apps are popular in different parts of the world, so marketers will have to exercise care in choosing a platform.

dark social social media exchanges that cannot be tracked or measured.

The process of selecting and optimizing platforms for distribution has a huge role in audience development and marketers need to carefully match channel to audience persona.

Having created and distributed relevant content to identified target audience segments, marketers must then measure the success of their content marketing efforts.

Monitor Conversations and Evaluate Content Marketing Effectiveness

We discussed the importance of monitoring social media conversations for content and tone in Section 5-4a. It is important to listen to the conversations that surround brand content to gain insights about what can make content more effective. Marketers also need to monitor their content for amplification—the degree to which content is shared by users. There are social media tools to measure sharing and it is a feature of many metrics platforms as we will discuss in Chapter 18. How much the content is shared tells the marketer a lot about how effective it is, but it is not the only important type of content metric.

There is a fair amount of agreement among content marketers about the four key types of content metrics. They are as follows:

- Consumption
  - How many people are consuming content?
  - Which channel?
  - How frequent and how in-depth is their content consumption?

- Sharing
  - Which items are being shared?
  - By whom and how often?
  - How and where are they sharing?

- Lead generation
  - How is content supporting lead generation and nurturing?

- Sales
  - Is content driving sales and revenue?
  - Is there appropriate content at all stages of the customer journey to support customers and move them through the journey?[25,26]

Google Analytics, which will be discussed in detail in Chapter 18, has metrics that will answer most of these questions and many content platforms and services provide their own insights. When monitoring content marketing effectiveness, it is important to remember that it is not the quantity of visitors that is critically important, it is the amount of time spent—the extent to which visitors actively engage with the content—that is important. Marketers are fond of quoting a statistic that says that 55 percent of website visitors stay no longer than 15 seconds. Whether that is true of your brand hub or not—and metrics can provide your own specific figure—the more time you can get visitors to spend with your content, the more likely it is to have impact.[27] The ability to measure content marketing effectiveness should not be taken as a given. Measuring the ROI on content marketing is difficult and many marketers admit that they do not do it well. In one study 79 percent of marketers agreed with the statement, "My team makes awesome content that our audience loves," but only 18 percent of those same marketers agreed with the statement, "We have a clear understanding of the ROI our content delivers."[28] Is that a bit of a disconnect? Another study found that while 50 percent of marketers rated their ability to measure ROI from paid search as being good, only 17 percent said that their ability to measure ROI from content marketing was good.[29]

The CMI Benchmark Study quoted earlier in the chapter asks what may be a better question, at least at this early stage of content marketing development. They asked, "In your organization, is it clear what an effective or successful content marketing program looks like?" That allows marketing teams to establish content marketing objectives and identify metrics that measure their accomplishment, not just to rely on financial ROI. Still, only 43 percent of B2C marketers and 44 percent of B2B said that they had clarity in terms of what constituted content marketing success. The study also found that marketers used a variety of metrics to measure effectiveness with 30 percent of B2C marketers saying sales was the most important measure and 31 percent of B2B marketers saying sales lead quality was most important. Other metrics considered most important included higher conversion rates, brand lift, and website traffic.[30,31]

Measuring the effectiveness of content marketing is not a one-size-fits-all process. Where it starts is clear, however. It starts with clear content marketing objectives, includes careful traffic of the metrics that measure those objectives and results in insights that improve the content marketing program.

It may be, in fact, that engagement is the most important concept in defining what is meant by content marketing success. However, before we tackle that important but rather slippery subject, we need to take a look at a concept that does not fit neatly either into content marketing or into advertising. Wherever it fits, native advertising is rapidly growing in importance.

NATIVE ADVERTISING—PROMOTION THAT LOOKS LIKE CONTENT

In our discussion of audience development we emphasized that paid promotion is necessary to get content noticed by new audience members because growth from new internet users has essentially disappeared. To put it bluntly, there are the same number of users and more content is being created, so the competition for eyeballs becomes fiercer every day. And we all know that most people don't think too highly of paid advertising of any kind on any channel.

Enter native advertising. Native content was mentioned in Section 3-6a when we discussed advertising-supported business models and in the discussion of publishing to content platforms. What exactly is native advertising? The definition of the Native Advertising Institute is:

> *Native advertising is paid advertising where the ad matches the form, feel, and function of the content of the media on which it appears.*[32]

That's clear, but the use of the term native content can muddy the waters. A definition of native content is:

> *A piece of content that has been commissioned or paid to be placed on an external website with the view that the content fits and the form and function of where it exists.*[33]

The author points out that what makes a piece of content native is:

- It fits the content style of the publisher.
- It is created or curated for that publisher's target audience.
- It is on an external website, not the brand's own.

That makes the two terms almost synonymous, just leaving the possibility that native content could be an unpaid placement. To be clear what we are discussing we will stick to the term native advertising in this section.

You see native ads on many sites today, especially the most trafficked ones. However, you may not be especially conscious of seeing them. That is exactly the point; they blend in with the other content. However, native ads must be clearly labeled as advertising whether the reader pays attention or not. The FTC released guidelines on native advertising in 2015 and it can charge advertisers with deceptive advertising if they violate them.[34]

Gentlemen's Quarterly (GQ) is a publication that has worked to create a comfortable environment for native advertising. This is how Wil Harris, digital head at the magazine's parent Conde Nast, describes it:

> *the site offers the same set of tools, the same kind of integration, and the same placement for native advertising as it does for editorial content. This means content that is created in collaboration with its commercial partners can show up in related articles, on the front page, in the story stream, and on social media in exactly the same way as its editorial content does.*

"If we are creating content with commercial partners it should be accessible in the same way that all our other content is created. This new version of the GQ website puts commercial and editorial content on complete parity" said Harris.[35]

Those are sweeping statements. Figure 8.13 shows how this works in practice. On the day in late 2016 that I looked at the site there was an article "This is How Your Hoodies Should Fit Right Now." Figure 8.13a shows only the bottom part of the article with the final, pricey sweatshirt review. Below that you see six blocks illustrating

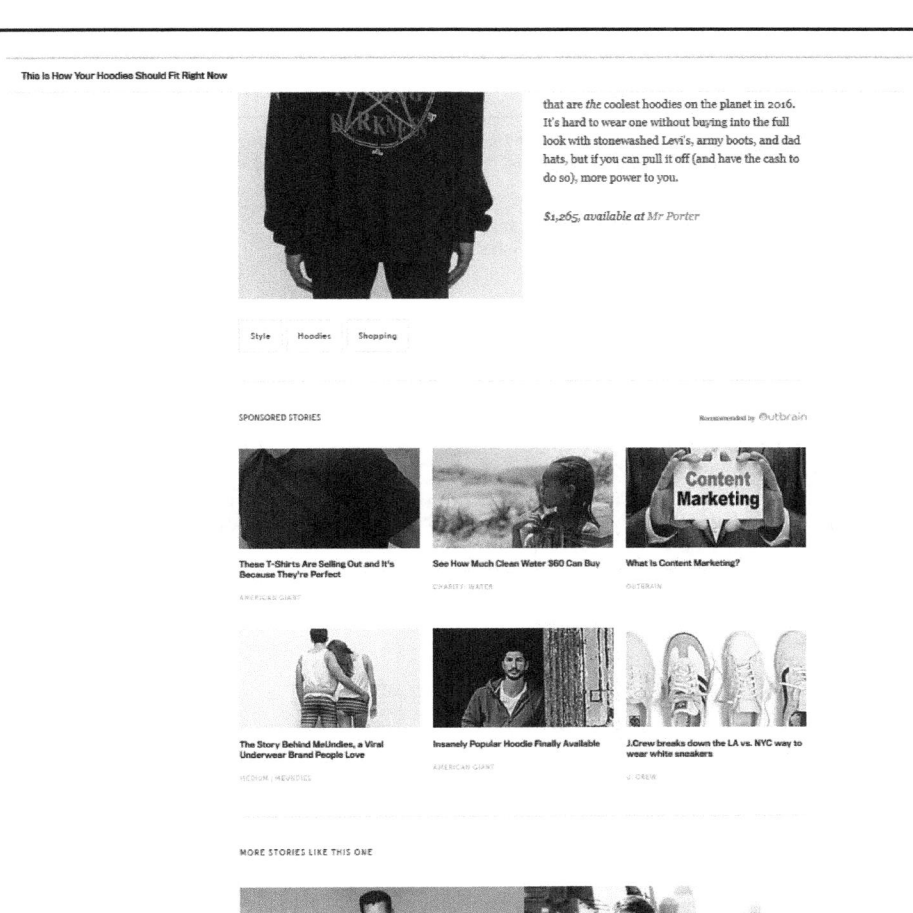

FIGURE 8.13a

The Original Article on the GQ Site

SOURCE: http://www.gq.com/story/how-hoodies-should-fit-2016

six different "Sponsored Stories," the type of labeling required by FTC rules. I clicked through on the fifth article, just because it was also about a hoodie. That led to an article on the American Giant hoodie that was essentially a press clipping of a Business Insider article (Figure 8.13b). I clicked through to read the full article on the Business Insider Retail site. Figure 8.13c shows just the bottom part of that article, which

FIGURE 8.13b

Content Clip from Business Insider

SOURCE: http://www.american-giant.com/the-insanely-popular-hoodie-2.html.

FIGURE 8.13c

Full Article from Business Insider Retail Section

SOURCE: http://www.businessinsider.com/this-hoodie-is-so-insanely-popular-you-have-to-wait-months-to-get-it-2013-12.

was substantive and which contained a three-minute video about how the sweatshirt was made. Notice the Sponsored Financial Content on the Business Insider page. The article was written in 2013, so this content is not only detailed, it really has legs! Ask yourself: would you get this much information from a display ad? Would a display ad remain interesting and eye-catching for three years?

This stream of content also deserves a small writer's whine, though. Every time I went back to check the article on GQ the six sponsored stories had changed. That, of course, is intentional and it is managed by a content discovery agency, OutBrain, that is recognized on the page.

The *New York Times* is another publisher that has placed a big bet on sponsored content, purchasing its own agency along the way. Interactive Exercise 8.3 provides insight into its approach.

USING CONTENT TO ENGAGE READERS—STORYTELLING AND MORE

The concept of engagement with content is both important and frustrating. Marketers want viewers to pay attention to their content and to react to it in some way. It is about as far as agreement goes; there is simply no agreed-upon definition of engagement. One school of thought believes that engagement means that the reader takes some action, from liking a post to purchasing a product. The other believes that engagement means building stronger emotional ties with the product or brand. You can see the divide here between sales goals and branding goals.

AOL conducted a study in eight different countries and found the motivations for engaging with content shown in Figure 8.14. They called them "content moments" and pointed out that some motives seemed more suited to certain channels. For instance, "entertain" seems tailor-made for video while "update socially" seems intended for social media content. The research also showed that motives for engagement had different prominence in different markets.

There is no single answer to the question of how to get viewers to engage with content. It is, however, clear that marketers must set their own engagement objectives in light of their overall marketing strategy and measure the achievement of those objectives. That opens another can of worms because there is endless argument over which metrics best measure engagement. Again there is a partial answer; it is usually necessary to use multiple metrics to get a clear picture of content engagement. We will discuss the measurement of engagement in Chapter 18.

In this section we will focus on the issue of creating engaging content, which is central to our discussion of content marketing strategy. That should be reasonably straightforward, but it is not. A search for "create engaging marketing content" returns over 57 million results. Many of them are interesting and give good advice. However, a remarkable number of them give the advice "have a content marketing strategy, develop audience personas, and create relevant content for the audience." That is good advice and it is what we have discussed in this chapter. However, when you bring that advice down to the granular level of a single piece of content that grabs the attention of the reader and causes some reaction, it is useless.

We shall therefore combine two approaches to present a workable method for creating engaging content. They are as follows:

1. Storytelling is at the heart of good content marketing. Many marketers agree with this statement and Neil Patel and Ritika Puri of Quick Sprout built an infographic that covers many of the issues. In it they say:

    Contrary to popular belief, brand storytelling is not about your company. It's about your customers and the value that they get when engaging with your product or service. The most powerful brand stories are the ones that prioritize customers as the stars. Think of your company as a supporting character.[36]

FIGURE 8.14
What Motivates Consumers to Engage with Online Content

Consumer Motivations for Interacting With Online Content
based on an analysis of more than 55,000 consumer interactions with online content across 8 markets
September 2016

Content "Moment"*	% Most Popular	Description	Leading Topics	Top Formats
Inspire	20%	Look for fresh ideas or trying something new	Fashion, Food	Product page, Photo gallery
Feel good	19%	Improve mood or feel relaxed	Wedding, Family	Social media post, Photo gallery
Update socially	17%	Stay updated or take a mental break	Celebrity, Sports	Social media post, Article
Entertain	15%	Look for an escape or a mental break	Comedy, Animals	Short video, Long video
Find	9%	Seek answers or advice	Health, Autos	Product page, Listicle
Be in the know	8%	Stay updated or find relevant ideas	Current events, Politics	Online information, Article, Blog
Connect	7%	Learn something new or be part of a community	Science, Comedy	Photo gallery, Short video
Comfort	6%	Seek support or insight	Relationships, Medical	Blog, Product page

* Description of the ways by which people around the world engage with content. Comprised of 4 elements before, during, and after engagement: The motivations for initiating the content experience, the emotions felt during the experience, the outcomes of the content, and the topic of the content.

MarketingCharts.com | Data Source: AOL

SOURCE: http://www.marketingcharts.com/online/what-motivates-consumers-to-engage-with-online-content-70543/.

2. Brand stories are all around the alert content marketer. Consultant Heidi Cohen has concrete suggestions for how to find those stories. She says you find stories in your company in several places:

- Your company—its heritage, "a day in the life," its community outreach and more.
- Your products—special history or product lore, famous people associated with them, unique product features, special uses and more.
- Your brand—what is special about the brand, its logo, its story over time, the causes it supports, its mascot and more.
- Your employees—who are they, what are their relationships to your products, what are their associations with causes and community activities and more.[37]

Story ideas are all around; how are they turned into compelling content storytelling? For an answer, let's turn to Shakespeare. Shakespeare, you say? What could Shakespeare have to do with marketing content?

Before we attempt to answer that question directly, do you remember the "Puppy Love" commercial from the 2014 Super Bowl in which a yellow lab puppy made friends with a Budweiser Clydesdale and played with him on the farm? All was well until people came to adopt the puppy. The puppy cried, the horses rallied to stop the car, and the friends were reunited. Nothing at all to do with beer, but a record-breaking commercial. If you don't remember it, take 1:30 to look at it on YouTube along with some commentary. There was also a sequel "Lost Dog" commercial in 2015, which is another value of storytelling done well. One good story leads to more good stories.

Writing in the Harvard Business Review, Harrison Monarth makes the connection between Shakespeare and marketing storytelling. It is Freytag's Pyramid, shown in Figure 8.15, which has actually been around for thousands of years. Shakespeare was the acknowledged master of using it to structure the acts of his plays. In the

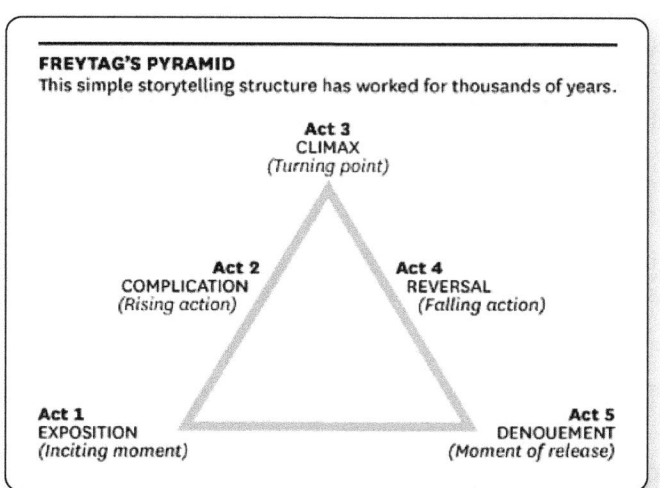

FIGURE 8.15
The Structure of a Good Story

SOURCE: https://hbr.org/2014/03/the-irresistible-power-of-storytelling-as-a-strategic-business-tool

puppy commercial, the complication occurs when the woman takes the puppy from the arms of the farmer, the climactic moment comes when the puppy turns around to his friend and cries, then the action resolves itself from there. Monarth points to research done at Johns Hopkins on commercial storytelling[38] and at Penn State's and UMass's medical schools on health issues to demonstrate that storytelling does work to change both attitudes and behaviors.

Lego is a brand that was in distress in 2003 and in 2004 suffered financial losses that threatened its existence. By 2013 it had turned the situation around and was not only realizing substantial profits but also had become one of the world's most admired brands. Customer focus, pruning a bloated product line, a return to the core product and cost control all contributed to the turnaround.[39] Along the way Lego became a master storyteller.

There are several keys to Lego's storytelling success:

- Lego created early and very successful video games beginning with *Lego Island* in 1997 and gradually creating a whole *Lego Universe* of games.
- It acquired a number of successful franchises, beginning with Star Wars and continuing through Minecraft and Harry Potter. It used the franchises as the take-off platform for Lego games and the characters and products that bring them to life in the hands of their customers.
- It created a line of toys with a storyline, *Bionicle*. According to Rick DeMott of the Animation World Network:

    Producer Bob Thompson and his team at LEGO took the concept and developed it into a multi-arc story that crossed comics, online games, TV series and movies. Unique elements of the story played out in each medium and drove fans to engage in additional story points in other mediums. Collectibles in toys drove sales and "Kanoka points" on packages allowed fans to connect toy play with online exclusives.[40]

    The *Bionicle* line was followed by the equally successful *Ningago* line. The *Lego Universe* was now populated with several groups of fascinating character/products, each with its own story to tell.

- Lego's focus on and responsiveness to its customers created a dedicated fan base. Fans' criticisms and product ideas were incorporated into Lego strategy. Many fans became part of the story.

    Former teacher Alice Finch built a Hogwarts Castle from the Harry Potter series entirely out of Legos—around 400,000 of them! It won "Best in Show" at

the 2012 BrickCon exhibition, a Seattle convention for lovers of the brand. She belongs to several Lego user groups and, along with other AFOLs (Adult Fans of Legos) was featured in the 2015 documentary, "A LEGO Brickumentary." The story goes on, and as it goes it gathers fans and participants.
- One culmination of the brand building was *The Lego Movie* in 2014 in which the toys were the stars. It got great reviews, both as a film and as a piece of branded content with one marketer calling it "the most effective 90 minute commercial for a "toy" that we've ever seen."[41]

Once again, it's easy to say that Lego has a product that lends itself to storytelling, and that is true. GE, which we described in Section 3-3 as "the world's biggest infrastructure technology company," seems a less likely candidate for engaging storytelling. Yet, GE has turned to storytelling as part of its brand transformation. Interactive Exercise 8.4 explains how.

TECHNOLOGY AND THE FUTURE OF CONTENT MARKETING

In the continuing quest for viewer engagement content marketing seems certain to add more elements of technology over the months and years to come. This is just a sampling of technology-enhanced content marketing:

- The *New York Times* has introduced a native ad format different from the ones illustrated in Section 8-5 and Interactive Exercise 8.3. The Flex Frame Everywhere is intended to replace the banner ad, which is losing popularity especially among mobile advertisers. *The Times* says "is a horizontal, large format, cross-device, responsive unit which appears in-stream alongside editorial content."[42] It can contain video, 360 images, 360 video, slideshows, static images, and other formats specified by the advertiser. Brand Studio technology along with that of advertising platform Double Click allow advertisers to configure their own ads on the NYT site.
- *Adweek* identifies VR as the "next great storytelling canvas."[43] Philanthropist Bill Gates posted a VR video of a trip to South Africa on his blog. He says:

    In this video, you will hear the stories of young women living with HIV. Sit beside me as I drive from the leafy suburbs of Johannesburg to the dusty township of Soweto. Feel what it's like to be in the center of a stomping gumboot dancing troupe. And be inspired by the power of South Africa's youth, who will drive the next generation of innovations to create a future free of AIDS.[44]

- Now anyone who has a smart phone camera with a panorama feature can take 360-degree photos and post them to Facebook.[45] Is that what NASA astronauts did in this shot of the International Space Station?
- Bots are infiltrating all aspects of our personal and professional life. That includes content marketing. One agency lists ways bots will be used in content marketing as:

    - Helping writers choose engaging topics. Some bots, for example, use trending words in search engines to help identify topics.
    - Locating content to curate. The amount of content available is huge and curators need automated systems to sift through it and locate the best possibilities.
    - Optimizing content for readability and SEO. Bots that can grade for readability level or for compliance with SEO criteria can save time and allow the writer to concentrate on content, not mechanics.
    - Optimizing content distribution. There are many publishers of content. Which platforms offer content marketers the best chances of meeting their branding or sales objectives?

- Analyzing the effectiveness of content marketing. Just as there is much content, there is much data available. Bots can automate the collection of data from platforms and the preparation of basic reports. They can even suggest insights from the data to start marketers on that all-important analytical task.

That just skims the surface of technology use in content marketing. Marketers will continue to find good ways to use the technology we now have as well as to discover new technologies to help them develop and execute their content marketing strategies.

SUMMARY

If traditional advertising is not yet dead, it has certainly been devalued in the minds of customers and marketers alike. Content marketing has taken over center stage for most B2C, B2B, and nonprofit marketers. Good content marketing focuses on being valuable and relevant to its carefully defined target audience, not on product-focused sales communications. In addition, good content is "always on." It is available to the potential customer whenever, wherever, and on whichever device she desires it.

The creation of successful content marketing is not a randomly creative act. Good content marketing is driven by a strategy that involves, first, creating or curating content, then identifying and developing loyal audiences for the content, followed by optimized distribution of content in multiple channels, and finally evaluation of the content strategy effectiveness that provides insights for future content marketing. As part of this process buyer personas are developed to give all those concerned with content marketing a deep understanding of audience segments.

Native advertising is not the same as content marketing, nor is it traditional advertising. It is a rapidly-growing type of marketer communication that places content that has no overt advertising intent into publications that can reach the target audience with content that is engaging and relevant.

There is a growing body of evidence to suggest that storytelling is not only a type of content that audiences find engaging, it is also effective in creating brand attitudes and in inciting action. Storytelling in marketing borrows structure and techniques from types of creative writing that include plays and short stories.

Storytelling and other types of marketing content are beginning to be impacted by technologies like VR and 360-degree imaging. It is likely that content marketing will take increasing advantage of technology going forward to engage and delight audiences.

DISCUSSION QUESTIONS

1. Discuss the reasons for the emergence of content marketing as a major force in marketing and give your own opinion of whether it is likely to continue to grow or, at some point, to go into decline.
2. What are some of the major differences between traditional media communications channels and digital channels?
3. Can you see a reason why B2B marketers may make even more use of content marketing than B2C marketers do?
4. Discuss the nature and importance of the four elements of content marketing strategy.
5. Discuss the three basic ways of obtaining marketing content. Which do you think is the most valuable to the brand? Which requires the most effort? The least?
6. What is the meaning of "audience development"? Why is it different from selection of a target audience in an advertising campaign?

7. Explain in your own words why buyer personas are considered essential in content marketing strategy.
8. Why are paid channels a necessary addition to owned and earned in most content marketing strategies today?
9. What are the four categories of content marketing metrics? Why is each one important?
10. Experts suggest that native advertising may make up a majority of digital advertising spending by 2020. Why do you think native advertising is growing at such a rapid rate?
11. What do you think marketers mean when they talk about engagement with their audience members?
12. Do you agree that storytelling is at the heart of good content marketing? Why or why not?
13. Do you have personal opinions about which communications channels are best for storytelling about brands and product categories with which you are involved?
14. Have you seen examples of the use of technology in either native advertising or content marketing? If so, bring a good one to class.
15. In the end, what makes a piece of content valuable to the viewer?

ENDNOTES

1. Joe Pulizzi, "Seth Godin: "Content Marketing Is the Only Marketing Left" and 10 Other Marketing Lessons," http://contentmarketinginstitute.com/2008/01/seth-godin-cont/.
2. Heidi Cohen, "Seth Godin, 7 Truths at the Heart of Marketing (and How to Use Them)," http://heidicohen.com/seth-godin-7-truths-at-the-heart-of-marketing-how-to-use-them/.
3. Helen Hoddinott, "The Advertising Model Is 'Dead Man Walking,'" http://www.campaignlive.co.uk/article/advertising-model-dead-man-walking-four-things-learnt-abc-interaction-2016/1381508#.
4. Jacob McMillen, "6 Exceptional Content Marketing Examples You Should Emulate in 2016," https://ahrefs.com/blog/content-marketing-examples/.
5. http://contentmarketinginstitute.com/what-is-content-marketing/.
6. Rahel Anne Bailie, "Rahel Bailie Provides a Content Strategy Primer," http://thecontentwrangler.com/2009/09/13/rahel-bailie-provides-a-content-strategy-primer/.
7. Marcia Riefer Johnston, "The Basics of Digital Governance: What Content Marketers Need to Know," http://contentmarketinginstitute.com/2015/11/basics-digital-governance/.
8. Marcia Riefer Johnston, "The Basics of Digital Governance: What Content Marketers Need to Know," http://contentmarketinginstitute.com/2015/11/basics-digital-governance/.
9. "2016 Content Marketing Staffing & Tactics Study," http://www.curata.com/resources/ebooks/2016-CMStaffing-Tactics-Study.
10. Michael Garard, "Content Marketing Statistics: The Ultimate List," http://www.curata.com/blog/content-marketing-statistics-the-ultimate-list/.
11. Geraint Holliman and Jennifer Rowley, "Business to Business Digital Content Marketing: Marketers' Perceptions of Best Practice," Journal of Research in Interactive Marketing, Vol. 8 Iss: 4, pp. 269–293.
12. "B2C Content Marketing: 2016 Benchmarks, Budgets and Trends—North America," http://contentmarketinginstitute.com/wp-content/uploads/2015/10/2016_B2C_Research_Final.pdf.
13. "B2B Content Marketing: 2016 Benchmarks, Budgets and Trends—North America," http://contentmarketinginstitute.com/wp-content/uploads/2015/09/2016_B2B_Report_Final.pdf.

14. Neil Patel and Aaron Agius, "The Complete Guide to Building Your Blog Audience, Chapter 8," https://www.quicksprout.com/the-complete-guide-to-building-your-blog-audience-chapter-8/.
15. Mitchell Hall, "Content Curation: The Art of a Curated Post (Infographic)," http://www.curata.com/blog/content-curation-the-art-of-a-curated-post-infographic/.
16. Kristina Cisnero, "A Beginner's Guide to Content Curation," https://blog.hootsuite.com/beginners-guide-to-content-curation/.
17. Neil Patel, "How to Do Curated Content RIGHT: A Step-by-Step Guide," https://www.quicksprout.com/2015/11/11/how-to-do-curated-content-right-a-step-by-step-guide/.
18. Perry Simpson, "The Most Viral Social Media Moments of February 2016," http://www.dmnews.com/social-media/the-most-viral-social-media-moments-of-february-2016/article/480976/.
19. Eric Brantner, "The Science Behind Buzzfeed's Viral Content," http://www.socialmediatoday.com/marketing/science-behind-buzzfeeds-viral-content.
20. Noah Kagan, "Why Content Goes Viral: What Analyzing 100 Million Articles Taught Us," http://www.huffingtonpost.com/noah-kagan/why-content-goes-viral-wh_b_5492767.html.
21. "Google: 42% of Online Shoppers Use Video During Pre-Purchase Research," https://www.clicky.co.uk/2015/10/42-of-online-shoppers-use-video-during-pre-purchase-research/.
22. Elizabeth Earin, "A Step-by-Step Guide for Creating a B2C Buyer Persona," http://iterativemarketing.net/step-step-guide-creating-b2c-buyer-persona/.
23. "The Red Bulletin Media Kit 2016 US," https://b2b.redbulletin.com/fileadmin/upload_media/redbulletin/download/ratecards/TRB-2016-Mediakit-US.pdf.
24. Giselle Abramovich, "Eat Or Be Eaten: The Internet Has Reached Saturation," http://www.cmo.com/adobe-digital-insights/articles/2016/9/13/adi-advertising-demand-report-na-2016.html#gs.EdoFsdo.
25. Pawan Deshpande, "The Comprehensive Guide to Content Marketing Analytics & Metrics," http://www.curata.com/blog/the-comprehensive-guide-to-content-marketing-analytics-metrics/.
26. Jay Baer, "The 4 Types of Content Metrics That Matter," https://www.ceros.com/blog/4-types-content-metrics-matter/.
27. Shane Snow, "Brands Are Measuring Their Content All Wrong," https://contently.com/strategist/2014/04/22/its-time-to-take-content-marketing-measurement-to-the-next-level/.
28. "Minority of Content Marketers Say They Know Their Content Production Costs," http://www.marketingcharts.com/online/minority-of-content-marketers-say-they-know-their-content-production-costs-66471/.
29. "Which Digital Channels Are Marketers Most Confident in Measuring for ROI?" http://www.marketingcharts.com/online/which-digital-channels-are-marketers-most-confident-in-measuring-for-roi-67300/.
30. "B2C Content Marketing: 2016 Benchmarks, Budgets and Trends—North America," http://contentmarketinginstitute.com/wp-content/uploads/2015/10/2016_B2C_Research_Final.pdf.
31. "B2B Content Marketing: 2016 Benchmarks, Budgets and Trends—North America," http://contentmarketinginstitute.com/wp-content/uploads/2015/09/2016_B2B_Report_Final.pdf.
32. http://nativeadvertisinginstitute.com/blog/the-definition-of-native-advertising/.
33. Ben Young, "Definition of Native Content," http://giveitanudge.com/definition-of-native-content/.
34. Will Critchlow, "A Checklist for Native Advertising: How to Comply with the FTC's New Rules," https://moz.com/blog/checklist-for-native-advertising.
35. Jessica Goodfellow, "GQ's Native Ad Offering 'Taking Inspiration' from Buzzfeed as It Puts Comercial and Editorial Content on 'Complete Parity.'" http://www.thedrum.com/news/2016/03/24/gq-s-native-ad-offering-taking-inspiration-buzzfeed-it-puts-commercial-and-editorial.

36. Neil Patel and Ritika Puri, "The Beginners Guide to Online Marketing," https://www.quicksprout.com/the-beginners-guide-to-online-marketing-chapter-3/.
37. Heidi Cohen, "How to Find Stories for Your Brand Within Your Organization," http://heidicohen.com/how-to-find-stories-for-your-brand-within-your-organization/.
38. Jill Rosen, "Super Bowl Ads: Stories Beat Sex and Humor, John Hopkins Research Finds," http://hub.jhu.edu/2014/01/31/super-bowl-ads/.
39. "The Lego Case Study 2014," http://www.thelegocasestudy.com/uploads/1/9/9/5/19956653/lego_case_study_2014.pdf.
40. Rick DeMott, "How Transmedia Made LEGO the Most Powerful Brand in the-World," http://www.awn.com/animationworld/how-transmedia-made-lego-most-powerful-brand-world.
41. "The Best Example of Brand Storytelling Ever: The lego Movie," https://www.thesaleslion.com/brand-storytelling-example-lego-movie/.
42. "The Times Works to Transform Digital Display Ad Business with Launch of Flex Frame Everywhere," http://www.nytco.com/times-works-to-transform-digital-display-ad-business-with-launch-of-flex-frame-everywhere/.
43. Gian LaVecchia, "Virtual Reality Is Becoming the Next Great Storytelling Canvas," http://www.adweek.com/news/advertising-branding/virtual-reality-becoming-next-great-storytelling-canvas-172797.
44. Bill Gates, "South Africa: Virtually There," https://www.gatesnotes.com/Health/South-Africa-Virtually-There.
45. Andy Huang, "Introducing 360 Photos on Facebook," http://newsroom.fb.com/news/2016/06/introducing-360-photos-on-facebook/.

Chapter 9

Email Marketing to Build Consumer and Business Relationships

LEARNING OBJECTIVES

By the time you complete this chapter, you will be able to:

1. Discuss reasons for the growing importance of email marketing.
2. Describe the various levels of permission.
3. List the steps involved in developing an email marketing campaign.
4. Identify the basic steps in developing an email marketing program.
5. Learn the basics of email design.
6. Recognize key provisions of CAN-SPAM laws in the United States, Canada, and Europe.
7. List the latest trends that are causing a resurgence in email marketing.

email marketing the process of developing customer relationships through offers and communications contained in email messages.

EMAIL MARKETING

Email as promotional activity has exploded in recent years, and most forecasters believe that its growth is likely to continue for the foreseeable future. A report by Marketing Charts showed that **email marketing** was the top area of business budget growth for marketers, with almost 60 percent of marketers surveyed planning to increase their spending on email marketing.[1] Why this continued growth from what has been termed the "granddaddy" or "workhorse" of internet marketing channels? After all, email started many years ago and today's focus tends to be on new media like social and mobile marketing. In the 1970s, the first email program was developed through ARPANET and was instrumental in developing the protocols to help send email messages from computer to computer. With the popularization and commercialization of the internet, email caught on quickly as a way not only to communicate but also to communicate directly with prospective customers.

Email was one of the first technologies to really take off on the internet. In spite of its early presence and the emergence of other media, the tool is not going away. In fact, email marketing continues to be one of the strongest marketing channels in terms of return on investment (ROI). According to the Direct Marketing Association (DMA), the channel yields an estimated 4,300 percent ROI. Salesforce Marketing Cloud, formerly ExactTarget, estimates that every dollar spent on email marketing offers a return of $44.[2] With numbers like these, email cannot be considered an out-of-date tool.

Many people start their day with email and 91 percent of mobile customers check their email at least once a day on the phone.[3] So it is obvious that email plays a critical role in consumers' lives. Email offers marketers a fast, flexible, and highly controllable format. Email is essentially direct mail on steroids because not only is the customer contacted directly, but also different offers and methods of engagement can be tested to find the most effective means of communication. A deep understanding of the nature of offline mail promotions is also useful to the email marketer because of the relationship between the two media channels. In both direct mail and email, the marketer needs a solid offer and time deadline, and an attention-getting device (think envelope versus subject line). In both cases, measurement is critical to gauge success.

Even better, email direct marketing offers several advantages to traditional direct mail marketing (see Figure 9.1) and was initially positioned as a cost-effective alternative to direct mail. Emails can be developed quickly, tested, revised on the fly based on almost immediate feedback, and can reach many internet users in a short period of time. Compared to other types of internet promotions, email is cheap on a per customer contact basis. Although email response rates differ widely by application and industry, email still has a favorable response rate compared to direct mail, with a strong ROI. According to the DMA, email marketing

FIGURE 9.1

Email Is Cheaper, Faster, and More Effective Than Direct Mail

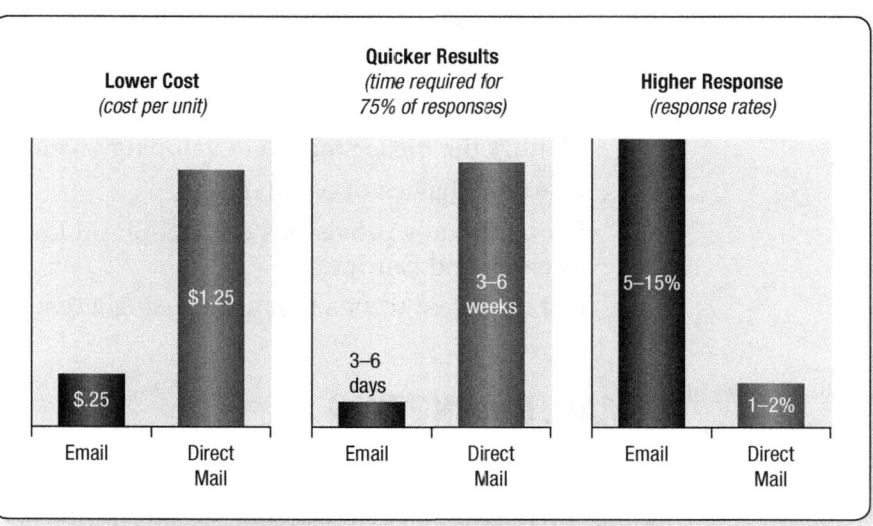

SOURCE: yesmail.com, LucWathieu, Harvard Business School, March 22, 2000, 500092-PDF-ENG.

generates about $40 for every dollar spent, outperforming both traditional direct marketing and other forms of internet marketing by several fold.[4] Forrester estimates that emails are so cost-effective that they have the ability to drive ROI two or three times higher than other forms of direct marketing, resulting in a continued increase in email spending.[5]

Additionally, email can be used by any marketer—B2C, B2B, or nonprofit—who has an acceptable way to acquire an email list of potential customers. Email, like direct mail, is also highly measurable and database driven (see Chapter 4). Email marketing systems also offer a good way to tap into data from other internal and external systems to create meaningful and relevant communications for customers.

In fact, email has proven to be a more powerful retention tool than an acquisition tool (see Chapter 14). Increasing customer engagement often tops the list of marketing goals and email is seen as the ideal retention tool. The reason email is so effective is that marketers have lists of existing customers to use, a "house" list of customers most likely to purchase again (see Figure 9.2).

Figure 9.3 illustrates how email marketing has evolved to a sophisticated tool for customer engagement from a broadcast tool highly reminiscent of spam. The trend toward a true one-to-one marketing channel is closer to becoming a reality with changes in marketing technology, including email marketing and CRM tools and customer databases. The DMA reports that about 73 percent of businesses are focused on customer retention with their email program versus 27 percent that are focused on customer acquisition.[6]

The cornerstone of a good email marketing campaign is the concept of permission, which will be discussed in detail in the next section. Targeted emails to those customers who want to hear from a company are going to get a higher response rate than a list of customers that are not familiar with a product or service. Although it is possible to conduct an email marketing campaign to unknown prospects, it is not a recommended practice. In fact, Seth Godin's book, *Permission Marketing*, outlined the concept of permission that holds true today. Customers want to interact with companies, but on their own terms and in their own time frame. Just as one would not (hopefully) propose marriage on a first date or accept such a proposal, consumers want to see that they are doing business with the right type of company for them before revealing personal information and giving companies permission to use that information. Academic research supports the use of Permission Email Marketing (PEM). A recent study indicated that PEM positively influences the experience of shopping online and thus can benefit marketers.[7]

FIGURE 9.2

Evolution of Email Marketing

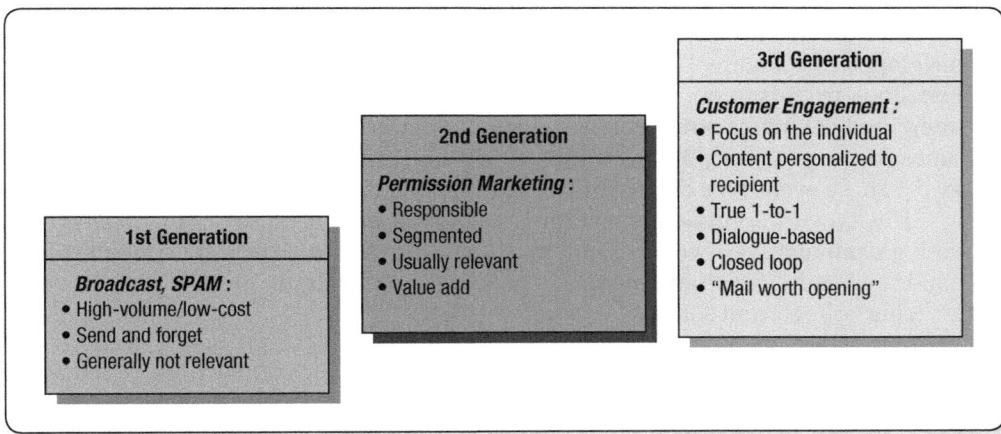

SOURCE: © Cengage Learning 2013.

FIGURE 9.3

Email Is the Most Effective Marketing Technique for Retention

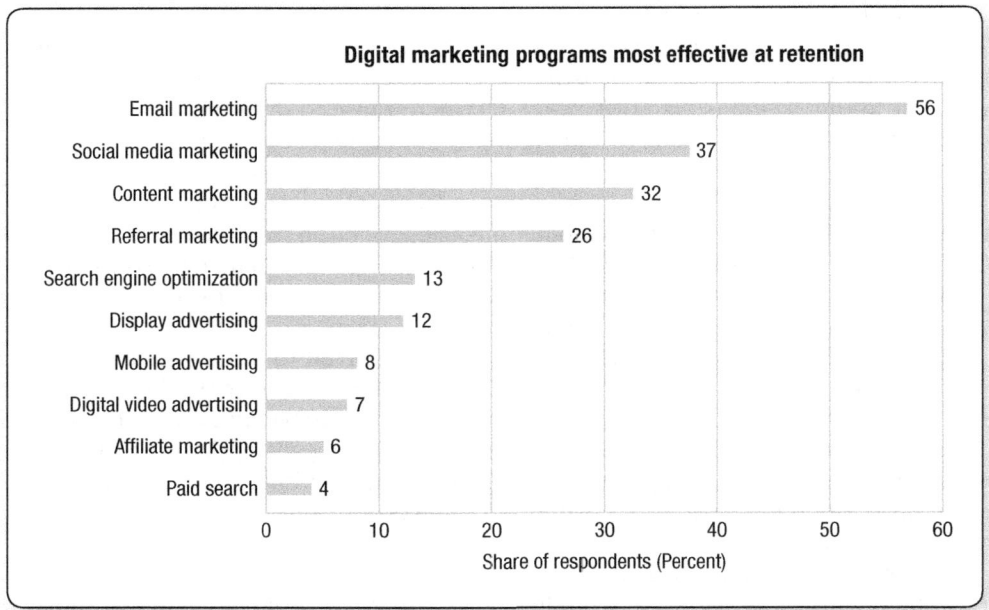

SOURCE: Gigaom Research Report: Workhorses and Dark Horses, "Digital Tactics for Customer Acquisition."

Scotts Miracle-Gro Company

Email is also ideally suited to event marketing campaigns, as discussed in Chapter 7.

The Scotts® Miracle-Gro Company, known for its lawn and garden expertise and for the Miracle-Gro product, started a lawn care update email program in the spring of 2000 and now has over a million and a half subscribers. The company uses over 355 unique geo-demographic variations of its newsletter for a variety of purposes, customizing it for the customer. The content of these updates is based on the consumer's grass type, zip code (which indicates climate zone), and possible weed and insect problems that might abound at a particular time of year. Imagine getting an email telling you it is now time to treat the lawn for grubs! A customer living in an area where grubs are a concern would be grateful.

Email marketers have integrated their campaigns with direct mail for years. As social media has become more widely used, another opportunity for engagement has developed (see Figure 9.4). In this case, Scotts® Miracle-Gro Company also invites its Facebook friends to opt-in for emails, incorporating social media and developing an integrated campaign strategy. The "events" noted in this case could be, for example, times of the year for planting seeds, fertilizing, and providing other lawn care services. These event-type emails nurture the customer relationship each step of the way.

This type of approach is just one example of how email works with event marketing campaigns. However, email marketing can just as easily be applied to other major events in a customers' life, such as high school graduation, buying a first car, entering college, and so on.

Email as a Communication Medium

Along these same lines as Scotts® Miracle-Gro Company, Johnston & Murphy, a high-end shoe company, has highly segmented its customer base and provides offers that are relevant to the consumer based on age, gender, interests, and past purchases,

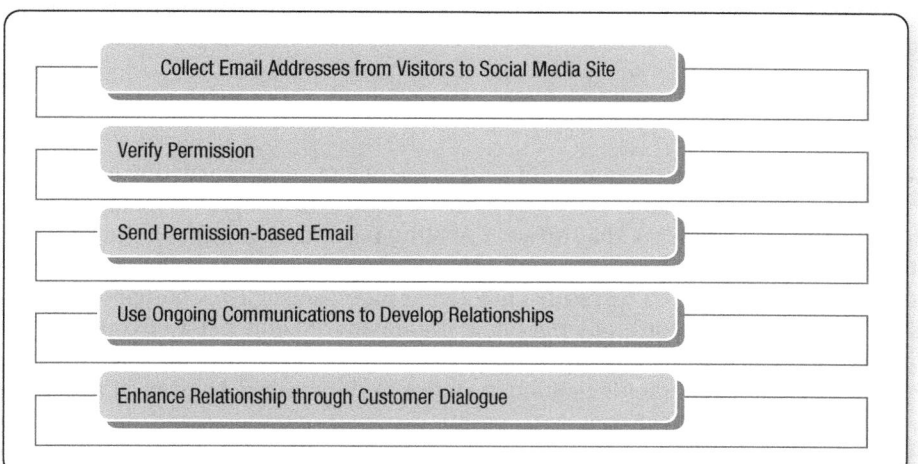

FIGURE 9.4

Integrating Email and Social Media

SOURCE: © Cengage Learning 2013.

resulting in an increase in open and response rates, as well as sales. Therefore, in spite of being one of the first communications channels to "take hold" in the marketplace, email remains a vital way for businesses to communicate with their customers.

Customers, for their part, are very active in the email space. Email is so prevalent that not only do most people check email daily but estimates are that they spend over six hours a day checking professional and personal email![8] By May of 2011, 88 percent of American internet users reported using email daily and 37 percent reported using it "constantly."[9] In fact, in 2015, the typical corporate user sent and received about 122 messages daily, a figure that is expected to grow to 126 messages sent and received per business user per day by the end of 2019. The typical consumer sent and received 93 messages per day in 2015, and about 129 messages in 2016.[10]

However, nearly three-quarters of emails received by consumers were perceived as *spam*.[11] This figure is in spite of the fact that quite often spam emails get caught in Spam filters and do not reach the recipient. **Spam** is considered unsolicited email and is in the eye of the consumer. Consumers typically report higher open rates for permission-based emails and definitely see the value in signing up for relevant commercial messages. While the latter is good news for marketers, the existence of spam provides an ongoing problem.

spam unwanted email communication.

However, in spite of the negative perception that much of email (according to Symantec about 49.7 percent)[12] is spam, consumers do value messages from commercial sources and have become more sophisticated in dealing with spam. Spam filters block many unwanted messages and consumers can manage which messages they wish to receive. Many marketers have come to rely on email marketing as a cost-effective tool, not necessarily for customer acquisition, but for customer development and retention. Salesforce Marketing Cloud (formerly ExactTarget) reports that 49 percent of research respondents have purchased as a result of an email.[13] Some purchased online immediately, others online later, and still others purchased offline at a later date. Increasingly according to eMailMonday, mobile email will account for 15–70 percent of email opens, depending on the target audience, product, and email type, which means that consumers increasingly will be able to redeem offers immediately when they are shopping.[14] These data are consistent with other research and monitoring statistics, which all testify to the power of email marketing to influence consumer behavior.

All in all, email usage is predicted to continue to grow. According to Radicati Group, Inc., the number of email accounts will increase from greater than 4.3 billion in 2015 to over 5.5 billion by 2019.[15] Not only is email usage growing, but also email marketing performance results are strong. While **click-through rates** in general have been declining and are hovering about 3.2 percent, savvy marketers realize that

click-through rates number of clicks divided by number of opens.

click-through rates can be triple that of the general rate with the use of techniques such as messages triggered by specific customer actions or events, as discussed below.[16]

Dreamfields Pasta

Dreamfields Pasta is a good example of a company using email marketing and permission to create demand for its products by building good customer relationships. Dreamfields is a specialty company that offers a healthy pasta that is suitable for everyone but targeted to diabetics and those with other health concerns. People with diabetes can enjoy Dreamfields Pasta and still control their blood sugar. The company uses SEO (search engine optimization), pay-per-click, online advertising, print advertising, and word of mouth to attract customers to its website, www.trydreamfields.com. Consumers register for the Dreamfields email newsletter and receive a $1 coupon as a thank you. Dreamfields uses these emails to create an opt-in database, with over 500,000 consumer email subscribers. The company's offers include coupons to subscribers, as well as recipes and other cooking tips via email. Integrating social media, consumers are invited to visit the company's fan page on Facebook and participate in the Dreamfields conversation. Another email campaign targets health care professionals.

The results have been astounding. In 2009, the company sold 8.3 million pounds of pasta, a 13-percent increase over the prior year. In 2010, Dreamfields sold 7.1 million pounds of pasta, a 9.6-percent increase. The company has also significantly reduced its advertising budget by more than 50 percent since converting to digital marketing. Figure 9.5 illustrates the email sign-up page, which shows the benefits of the product, as well as the incentive provided for registering. Figure 9.6 illustrates a portion of an email sent as part of a Dreamfields campaign powered by ExactTarget. These emails are attractive and offer something a consumer might want to receive, in exchange for giving part of their consumer information.

One piece of recent news is that the company made an $8 million settlement over its claims of "low carb" pasta in 2014, with half of the money going to claimants and the other half to the American Diabetes Association.[17] The company is back on track with its marketing and is making more use of various forms of social media in

FIGURE 9.5
Dreamfields Initial Permission Email Sign-Up Offer

SOURCE: Dreamfields Pasta.

FIGURE 9.6
Dreamfields' Pasta Permission Emails

SOURCE: Dreamfields Pasta, http://www.dreamfieldsfoods.com/emails/2011-June-Newsletter.html.

conjunction with email as possible; visual forms of social media, like Pinterest, are particularly well-suited to the brand and the company has an active blog with engaging contests and promotions. It is still offering a $1.00 coupon for providing an email address and offering a chance to subscribe to monthly emails.

LEVELS OF PERMISSION MARKETING

Dreamfields Pasta illustrates an important principle of email marketing—the issue of **permission**. In this text, we encourage the use of permission-based marketing, particularly in email messaging.

The first issue relating to permissions is that of spam. Unsolicited email is referred to as "spam," but it is not because the food product SPAM is unliked. Instead, the origins are from a Monty Python skit on SPAM in which it is offered on the menu of a restaurant many times (see Figure 9.7). The waitress' continued use of the word "spam" to describe the menu items made the word become annoying. (Watch the original Monty Python video online to get an idea of how really annoying spam can be.)

No responsible marketer uses or sanctions the use of spam. Ever. Period. And as stated earlier, permission-based marketing is the only responsible way to conduct email marketing campaigns.

Direct marketers have been sending unsolicited mailings for many years. Many, if not most, consumers do not like it. However, unsolicited physical mail does not appear to arouse the same level of ire in consumers that spam email does. It seems that consumers regard spam email as more intrusive than mail. Either way, it is clear that reputable marketers do not want to be identified with spam in the minds of the consuming public.

In order not to be considered a spammer, the marketer must obtain permission from the customer or prospect before sending email. There are four levels of permission:

1. **Opt-out** means that the visitor *did not* refuse to receive further communications from the marketer. This is an improvement over spam, but it does not represent a high level of commitment on the part of the visitor. Usually there is just a check box that needs to be unchecked to opt-out.

> **permission** refers to gaining the customers agreement to market to them in a certain way.

> **opt-out** taking an action to prevent the receipt of further communications, usually unchecking a box on a registration form.

FIGURE 9.7
Monty Python SPAM Skit

SOURCE: Python (Monty) Pictures.

Opt-out email addresses are often collected via online registration forms or other methods, even face-to-face. The point is to make consumers take some explicit action in order *not* to receive further communications. The theory behind opt-out seems to be that people may not bother to take the action, or be unaware that they could take it, and will therefore, almost by default, become members of the list. This is often operationalized by an already-checked box saying in effect, "Please send me email." Even if the choice is made to precheck the box, the accompanying statement must be clear about what the visitor is agreeing to. The statement should be unambiguous and it should be located in a visible place. Under the CAN-SPAM law (described in detail at the end of this chapter), all emails must have a clear option to unsubscribe.

Opt-out represents, at best, passive agreement to receiving email, but at present, it represents the minimum acceptable standard. Opt-in is the preferred method by many marketers and observers of the field.

opt-in actively choosing to receive further communications, usually by checking a box on a registration form.

2. **Opt-in** means that visitors have actively chosen to receive further communications, usually by checking a box on a registration form. It represents active acquiescence, if not enthusiasm, about receiving future communications from the marketer. Consequently, members of opt-in lists should be more receptive to messages.

double opt-in a technique by which visitors agree to receive further communications but must perform two actions, usually checking an opt-in box on a site, and then responding positively to a sent email asking for confirmation.

3. **Double opt-in** is a technique by which visitors agree to receive further communications, probably by checking an opt-in box on a site, and are then sent an email asking them to confirm their consent by replying to the email. The visitor has taken two actions, first indicating willingness to accept email, then actively confirming it by replying to the confirmation. This response should indicate an interested, potentially well-qualified prospect.

confirmed opt-in somewhere in between opt-in and double opt-in; the visitor actively acquiesces to receiving email, again probably by another email confirmation.

4. **Confirmed opt-in** is somewhere in between opt-in and double opt-in. Visitors actively acquiesce to receiving email, again probably by checking a box. They are then sent a follow-up email confirming the permission, but no reply is required.

An easy way to remember the difference between opt-in and opt-out is that in opt-in, the box is checked and in opt-out, you must uncheck the box or perform some action.

The opt-in/opt-out controversy is in part the traditional direct marketing issue of fewer, better-quality leads versus more leads of lower quality. Marketers are often wise to choose quality over quantity in lead situations. As with direct mail, the list is critical in maximizing response rate. The differences in the email context have to do with both the economics and the relationships with potential customers. The cost of incremental email is virtually zero, arguing for larger lists, even if they are less qualified. The annoyance factor is so high, however, that there is a strong argument for high quality opt-in lists of prospects who are genuinely willing to receive marketer-generated communications.

The one gray area is when the marketer has an email list that was obtained without use of specific opt-in or opt-out authorization by the consumer. These lists should be converted to either opt-in or opt-out by means of one carefully constructed email to confirm participation, perhaps including the use of incentives. There are relatively few email lists like this which were collected in the early days of the internet before the permission-based protocol became something of an accepted standard. The existence of a small number of lists in this category should not be taken as an excuse for spam by other marketers. Today when email lists are rented from a list broker, the marketer does not get the emails. Rather, the list broker who owns the permission-based list sends out the emails and the marketer only gets the addresses and other personal information if there is a response, such as an order or inquiry. Once the person or business on the list moves from a customer to a prospect and the relationship is developed, then the marketer gets information about that person or company. As in direct marketing, the "house" list is most effective, which incents the marketer to provide the best offer possible to be able to gather a new inquiry or order and, hopefully, an ongoing customer.

Both the emails in Figure 9.8 are the result of a new registration on a site. Staples replied to a new registration with a welcoming sales message that linked to promotional areas on the site. Notice that at the top of Figure 9.8a, it contains a message relating to *deliverability*, asking registrants to add the address to their address books so it will not be screened out by ISP spam filters.

FIGURE 9.8

(a) Welcome Email from Staples; (b) Weekly Featured Products Email

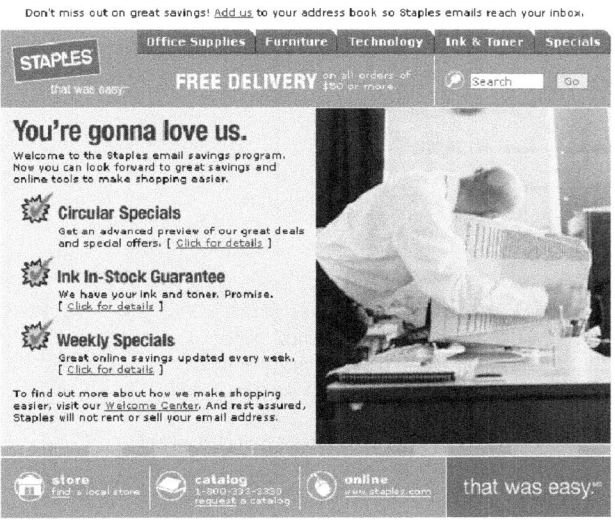

(a)

(b)

SOURCE: Copyright © Staples the Office Superstore, LLC.

DEVELOPING AN EMAIL MARKETING CAMPAIGN

The Peppers and Rogers Group, whose expertise is in relationship marketing, summarizes the email marketing process as it moves from analysis to action (see Figure 9.9). Their process involves four steps:

- *Gather customer data.* This includes contact information, physical address or email address, or both. The transactional data from the company's own files also include purchase history and a record of all customer interactions. It also includes the types of information (offers) they wish to receive, their preferences for receiving it (frequency and communications channel), and their privacy preferences.
- *Derive customer insight.* Using the different types of information that have been captured about the customer, begin to understand what the customer needs and values. The most valuable type of understanding is what should come next in the purchase cycle—an extended warranty program for a recently purchased appliance, for example.
- *Suggest proactive action.* This is the point at which the process moves from analysis to action. Email programs are developed, executed, and refined based on the results of the programs themselves, captured in the customer database.

FIGURE 9.9

The Basics of Email Marketing

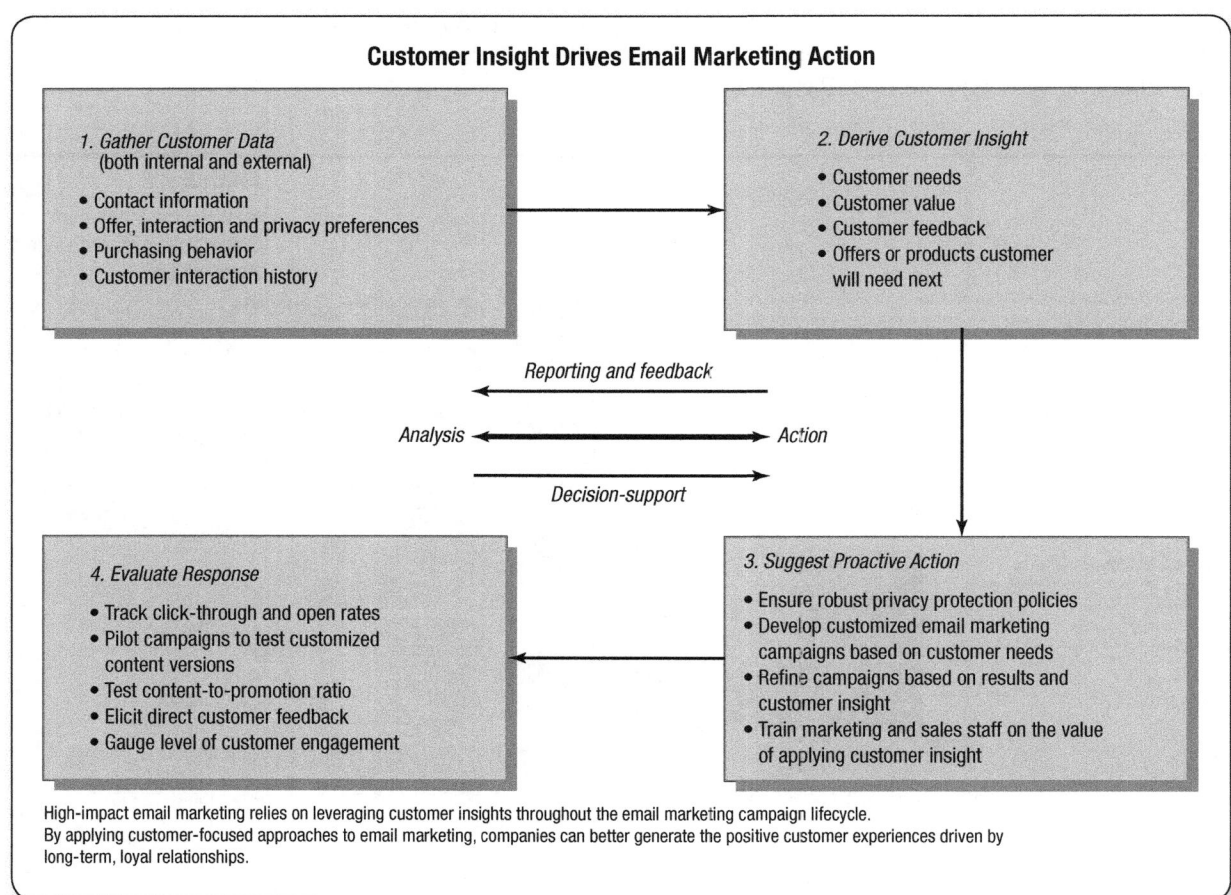

SOURCE: © Cengage Learning 2013

- *Evaluate response.* In this step, program metrics are collected and analyzed to refine existing programs and suggest new strategies. Different approaches and content should be tested to see which perform better. It is also good to encourage direct feedback from recipients in order to further understand likes, dislikes, and desires.

Peppers and Rogers present an overview of the process that applies whether email is being used for acquisition of prospects or relationship marketing to customers. Let us now turn briefly to a detailed set of steps for developing an email campaign, which also applies to either acquisition or retention settings (see Table 9.1).

- *Build or obtain an email list.* Like Rome, email lists are not built in a day, and list development needs to be an ongoing process, one begun well in advance of an actual email campaign. Marketers who wish to be welcome in the inboxes of their customers obtain permission at one of the four levels just discussed. In direct marketing terms, this becomes their own "email house list" and it is an essential foundation for permission-based email marketing.

If it is necessary to rent email lists—and there are a considerable number available—the marketer should carefully investigate the source of the list, especially any privacy promises that were made to consumers as the list was constructed. Many privacy policies make it clear that lists will "from time to time" be shared with other marketers deemed acceptable to the list owner. When this is the case, both marketers are clearly within their legal rights. However, that does not mean that the consumer will be thrilled about receiving email from a company with whom she or he may have no relationship.

Lists for acquisition programs should be rented with care, from reputable list management agencies. Although lists are available for less, good lists will run from $100 to $400 per thousand (known as CPM), with established, performing lists closer to the higher end. Extremely cheap lists have been complied by software (bots) that search the internet and snatch email addresses in public places such as chat rooms. They are the source of spam and should be avoided at all costs.

- *Profile or segment the list.* The customer/prospect database should have data, the volume of which grows over time, that allows a descriptive profile (middle-aged, high-income golfer living in an upscale suburb in the Midwest) or segmentation analysis that produces typical demographic (high-income two-worker family with school-aged children) or lifestyle segments (patron of the arts). We return to the subject of segmenting the database as an element of relationship marketing strategy in Chapter 11. It is essential in order to know what communications to address to which segments of the list in order to get the best response.

TABLE 9.1

Steps in Developing an Email Marketing Campaign

1. Build or obtain an email list
    a. Build a permission-based list
    b. Rent email lists
2. Profile and segment the list
3. Establish a communications schedule
4. Develop specific program objectives
5. Write compelling copy
6. Structure your email to be received and opened
7. Create links to further information
8. Make it easy for viewers to take action
9. Test and revise the email
10. Measure results
11. Integrate learning into next email program

SOURCE: © Cengage Learning 2013.

- *Establish a communications schedule.* The ease of sending email makes it tempting to send email whenever the firm feels like it. With the exception of important "breaking news" types of notifications, which should be rare, the organization should establish a mailing schedule and stick to it. Better yet, it should ask the subscriber for his or her preferences when he or she signs up. Then the marketer will send content that is relevant to the subscriber on the schedule she has dictated. That is the way to make email welcome in the inbox.
- *Identify the target segment and communications objectives.* Each mailing should have its own specified target segment and specific objectives. Simply sending the same message to an entire list will not often be effective. Perhaps the business marketer is announcing a new product to users of that product line. The marketer of consumer credit cards may be delivering an offer of credit card protection insurance to new cardholders. The nonprofit marketer may wish to invite large donors and prospects to a special event showcasing the successes of the organization. The objective and the target segment must be a good fit and the single campaign must fit into the overall communications and marketing strategies. Specify the action you want the recipient to take. You may, for instance, give the prospective large donor the option of calling a special phone number or visiting a special landing page to respond to the invitation.
- *Write compelling copy.* Email copy should be only as long as is necessary to convince the recipient to take the desired action. Often this action will be to click-through on a link to go to a particular page on the website, known as a landing page or micro site specific to that campaign. The target pages should be carefully examined to make sure they are consistent with the objectives and message of the email campaign. Writing short copy that persuades is not an easy task.
- *Structure your email to be received and opened.* In their effort to control spam, ISPs have set up filters in an attempt to remove the offenders. In the process they capture many messages from legitimate marketers. The "from" header and the "subject" header are both important in this respect. The source must be clear and the subject descriptive.
- *Create links to further information.* One of the beauties of email, whether text or HTML, is that links to more detailed information, usually on the website, are easy. Copy has to be written around the concept of linking. The website and/or landing page must be examined to ensure that it is ready to receive visitors from the email.
- *Make it easy for readers to take action.* Marketers need to specify what it is they want recipients to do after the recipients click-through to the site. Do they want the recipients to send for additional information? If so, create an email link, or better, a form that requests a small amount of information about the requester. Is the objective to persuade recipients to donate to a charitable cause? If so, the links to material on the site need to make the case for the contribution, with multiple opportunities to click-through to the form that accepts the donor's information.
- *Test and revise the email.* Emails can and should be tested using the techniques discussed in Chapter 4. Important things to test include the preheader, subject line, and the offer. A test can be mailed to only a selected segment of the target list or an A/B split can be used as covered in Chapter 4. Testing is a powerful tool, and it should not be overlooked.
- *Measure results.* Email service providers supply the most common metrics—delivered, opened, and clicked-through, are typical. Marketers can get more detailed results by creating special landing pages to receive click-throughs

and then tracking them through the site. Results will also include maintenance issues like bounce-backs and unsubscribes. Detailed reporting is usually available with most email service providers.

- *Integrate learning into the next email program.* Most organizations today will find themselves doing another email campaign rather quickly. An ongoing challenge is how to use the results of one campaign to make the next one better. Some companies have developed formal programs for doing so, a subject to which we will return in Chapter 11.

This list appears to be a rather formidable series of steps. However, the seasoned email marketer, with the support of a well-maintained database and suppliers of the necessary services, can develop and launch an email campaign in days, if not hours. The speed, the relatively low cost, and the ability to target and measure will only fuel marketers' interest in effective email marketing.

Email Design

There are many types of emails, such as email newsletters, new product announcements, general marketing and advertising, alerts and reminders, and market research emails—all of which need to be designed according to the objective for each. Since email marketing has its roots in direct marketing, an email for promotions and discounting—which is the majority of emails that companies send out—should follow the basic rules of direct marketing. In other words, the email should have a clearly defined offer or call to action, with a time deadline, and should also use good web design principles as discussed in Chapter 10.

In addition, there are basic elements of design that are unique to emails themselves. These design elements are summarized in Table 9.2. A good promotional email includes a preheader (a short text blurb; the part of the email that displays after the subject line and is above the text or html of the email) and can include many items. Successful preheaders restate and reinforce the offer provided, link to the online version of the email if the receiver cannot view the email, and perhaps include a short reminder of the relationship or an option to view on a mobile device.[18]

Although the preheader is important, the email subject line is often the determining factor in **open rates**. There is much debate over the email subject line and what is most compelling since what works most effectively depends on the product, the offer, and the customer. What might work for a retail environment might not work in B2B marketing. In general, the subject line should be short, less than 50 characters, which is usually the number of characters displayed on an email system and generates a higher open rate. The email subject line should also include as much as possible the reason for the email, including a brief summary of the offer.

open rates number of opens divided by number of emails delivered (sent minus bounces).

TABLE 9.2 Promotional Email Checklist

Email Element	Recommended Approach
Preheader	Link to online version of email, reminder of relationship, restates offer
Subject line	Short, include brand, call to action, urgency
Offer or call to action	Specific, clear, and meaningful
Time deadline, sense of urgency	Not only what the customer should do, but by when?
Web design principles	Above the fold, golden triangle
CAN-SPAM	Include reply-to and unsubscribe, and otherwise be compliant
Viral marketing	Include forward to a friend as well as social media links
Social media	Integrate with popular sites on social media

SOURCE: © Cengage Learning 2013.

The email itself should clearly state the offer—and only including one offer is best. Sometimes you might see emails that try to cram in a lot of information and refer to several different offers with different time frames. Studies have shown that people get fatigued by multiple messages in the same email and tend to click-through less as more, competing messages are provided. The offer should include the time deadline, that is, when the offer expires and by when the action is expected. The email should also use good web design principles, including the most important information (e.g., the offer) appearing in the "golden triangle," the upper left triangle area where the user's eye spends most of its time. Another good web design principle to apply to email design is "above the fold." Above the fold is a simple concept adapted from newspaper publishing which suggests that the reader's eye is going to concentrate above the fold of a newspaper, which, in this case, is the area above where his web browser cuts off the email. Where the fold falls depends on the physical size of the monitor used, the resolution that the screen has been set to, and the type of browser used. As Figure 9.10 illustrates, the information available can vary greatly based on these criteria. It is a good idea to test emails on multiple web browsers before sending to ensure readability and clarity. Mobile marketing campaigns also mean that emails must be designed to be read and responded to on smaller screens on various devices.

Good promotional emails are also CAN-SPAM compliant and clearly state that the message is advertising or promotional in nature; they have a valid reply-to address and street address listed; and a valid opt-out or unsubscribe feature. (We will discuss more about CAN-SPAM at the end of this chapter.)

Finally, a good promotional email takes advantage of word-of-mouth marketing and social media, including a forward to a friend feature and the ability to post on the consumers' social media accounts (which accounts depends on the consumers and where they "hang out" in social media).

Although we have focused on promotional emails, the design of other types of emails can be equally important. *Transactional emails* can be an overlooked source of marketing. *Welcome emails* typically have a higher open rate than traditional emails and can be used to up-sell and cross-sell as well as to leverage social media marketing. All these emails can benefit from the viral and social aspects of email marketing.

Figure 9.11 illustrates an email received by one of the authors that is a good example of all the elements discussed in this section. It makes good use of the preheader, provides the offer in the golden triangle space, and has pertinent information above the fold. This email also has social media integration and is CAN-SPAM compliant, although it is missing a clear time deadline in the text of the email.

Figure 9.12 clearly shows an email offer of 20 percent off if purchases are made in a certain time frame, is simple in design, and does not provide too many competing messages. Not all promotional emails illustrate the principles mentioned

FIGURE 9.10

Above the Fold Viewing Dimensions

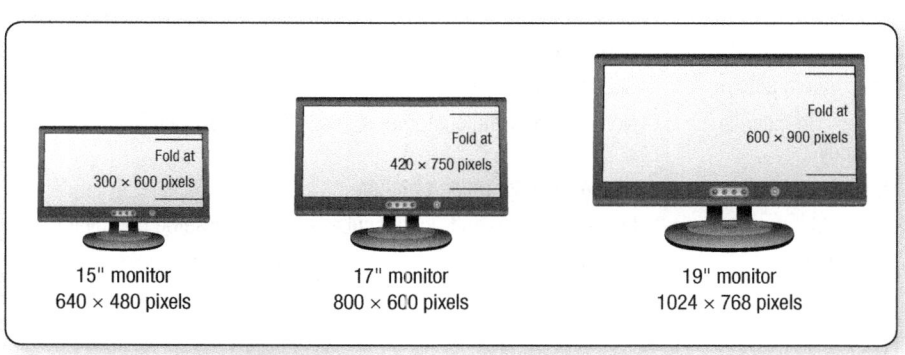

SOURCE: © Cengage Learning 2013.

FIGURE 9.11
Email Analysis

SOURCE: Hanes.

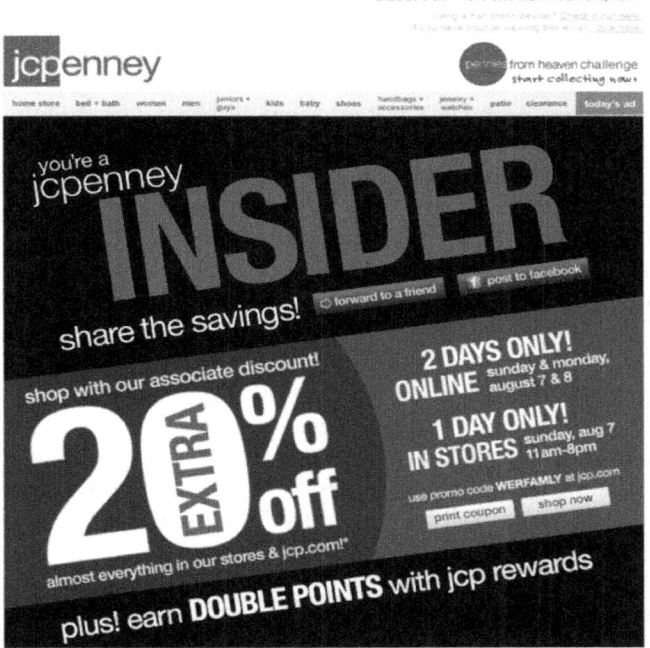

FIGURE 9.12
Email Offer with Time Deadline

SOURCE: JCP Media L.P.

here. It could be that companies not using these principles are testing different approaches or it could be that they are in need of hiring people who have taken an internet marketing course to help them with their email design. In any case, marketers will continue to test different approaches to determine what generates the best response.

Sending Emails

There are a number of different choices in sending emails, but with any type of volume, it is usually wise to use an email service provider (see list of some major providers in Table 9.4). This table includes some of the larger vendors but you will have a chance to evaluate the vendors for small- and medium-sized businesses in an Interactive Exercise. An email service provider does a number of things for its customers, including help with the design. First though, most standard email packages have limits on the number of recipients for an email in an effort to avoid spam filters, so most email service providers have the ability to help figure out what will trigger a spam filter and get emails delivered. For example, the tried and true direct marketing offering of "free," which historically has delivered the highest response to direct mail campaigns, will trigger a spam filter at some ISPs.

Other benefits of using a service company for email include help in tracking and measurement, easy integration with a company's internal database and other software programs such as salesforce.com, and other marketing campaigns.

One of the key benefits of using an ESP is usually the ability to integrate with a current database of customers and their transaction history. Integration with the database means that emails can be personalized to individuals and offers can be customized based on the data and interests of that particular customer. **Dynamic content** management is what allows Scotts® Miracle-Gro Company to send out over 300 versions of its emails or Johnston & Murphy to customize its product offerings in its promotional emails. The content and greeting change per each email, making it more personal and less like spam. When used wisely, dynamic content can increase the chances emails will be opened and responded to by the target consumer. Table 9.3 provides a summary of what an email service provider can do for a company. Some of the top email service providers that target larger customers, with the ranking of the strength of their offering on these and other dimensions, are included in Table 9.4.

dynamic content ability to change greeting and other content dynamically based on to whom the email is addressed.

Another major concern is timing—what time of day to send emails and on what date. The answer really depends on the customer base. The best way to determine when people will answer emails is to test a few different days and times, using some common sense about the habits of the customers. In general, for business customers Monday morning and Friday afternoon are bad times to send email, with Tuesday mornings or afternoons being preferred as people have gone through their inboxes the previous day. For consumer messages, weekends and evenings are preferred, but again, this timing depends on the targeted consumer and the product or service offered. The answer really is that "relativity" matters in the timing of email sends.[19] Mail Chimp analyzed the data from its customers and found that in general most days of the week are preferable to the weekend, with the "peak" time being 10:00 a.m. However, even at the peak time, marketers can only reach less than 10 percent of their subscribers, leaving the answer as to the best time to send email up to the individual subscriber and customer preferences. For example, bartenders and college students get a later start to the day and lawyers and other professionals might get an earlier start to the day. As in most things related to direct marketing, testing is the key to understanding the optimal time to send emails.

TABLE 9.3 Advantages of Email Service Providers
Help get emails delivered through ISPs
Aid in tracking, measurement
Provide database integration
Manage content dynamically
Integrate with social marketing, other campaigns

SOURCE: Adapted from the Forrester Wave™: Email Marketing Service Providers, Q4, 2009, Carlton A. Doty and Julie M. Katz for Interactive Marketing Professionals.

TABLE 9.4 Forrester List of Email Marketing Service Providers, 2014

Vendor	Product evaluated	Product version evaluated	Version released date
Acxiom	Digital Impact	9.3	Q2 2014
Epsilon	Harmony	N/A	Q2 2014
Experian Marketing Services	Cross-Channel Marketing Platform	5.7	Q2 2014
Oracle Responsys	Responsys Interact Suite	6.20	Q2 2014
Salesforce ExactTarget	Salesforce ExactTarget Marketing Cloud	N/A	Q2 2014
Silverpop	Engage	N/A	Q2 2014
StrongView	Message Studio with InteractionStore	8	Q2 2014
Yesmail Interactive	Yesmail Email Marketing Platform	7.6	Q2 2014
Zeta Interactive	Zetamail	7.0	Q2 2014

SOURCE: The Forrester Wave™: Email Marketing Vendors, Q3 2014 by Shar VanBoskirk, July 23, 2014.

SOURCE: Adapted from the Forrester Wave™: Email Marketing Service Providers, Q4, 2009, Carlton A. Doty and Julie M. Katz for Interactive Marketing Professionals.

In addition, conventional wisdom in the area indicates that email programs that delivered less than one message a month experienced a higher **bounce rate** than programs with at least a daily delivery. So more frequent email can mean better delivery prospects because lists are more likely to be updated and consumers are expecting regular communications.

bounce rate number of bounces divided by number of emails sent.

Tracking Emails

One of the biggest benefits of using an email service provider is the ability to track metrics such as click-through and open rates, and compare metrics across different offers (known as A/B testing from the direct marketing world). Email service providers make it much easier to tell which emails were effective. Here is an example of some of the email tracking available on MailChimp's Dashboard in Figure 9.13. As you can see, 919 emails were sent out but many were not delivered. This list had only a 61.6 percent delivery rate, well under the industry standard of almost 100 percent, indicating an old list that needs to be updated or one lacking permission. There were a total of 572 bounced emails. In email language, a **hard bounce** means the email address is bad or truly undeliverable, whereas a **soft bounce** means the email could not be delivered at that particular time, perhaps because of a system problem. Most of these emails in our example appear to be hard bounces, again indicated the need to update email lists frequently. There are many ways to calculate email metrics and we describe the most common method here.

hard bounce undeliverable, usually due to a bad email address.

soft bounce temporarily undeliverable, usually due to a system problem.

Of the 919 emails opened, there were 260 unique (individual) opens for a 28 percent open rate (calculation: 260/919). There were 13 click-through on 260 unique opens for a **click-to-open rate** of 5 percent (calculation: 13/260). Many other statistics are available on the dashboards of email service providers, and it is also possible to see who opened or did not open the email and where they clicked-through to find more information.

click-to-open rate number of clicks divided by the number of unique opens.

Figure 9.14 illustrates activity over time on the MailChimp platform and we can see that this email was opened primarily within three days of delivery. In fact, most activity occurred within 24 hours of delivery, down from 48 hours just a few short years ago. This figure illustrates again that fast email response rates are critical in developing effective programs. If something does not work, a marketer can try another offer, list, or design to get the desired response from the customer and provide the information the customer needs.

FIGURE 9.13

MailChimp Email Dashboard

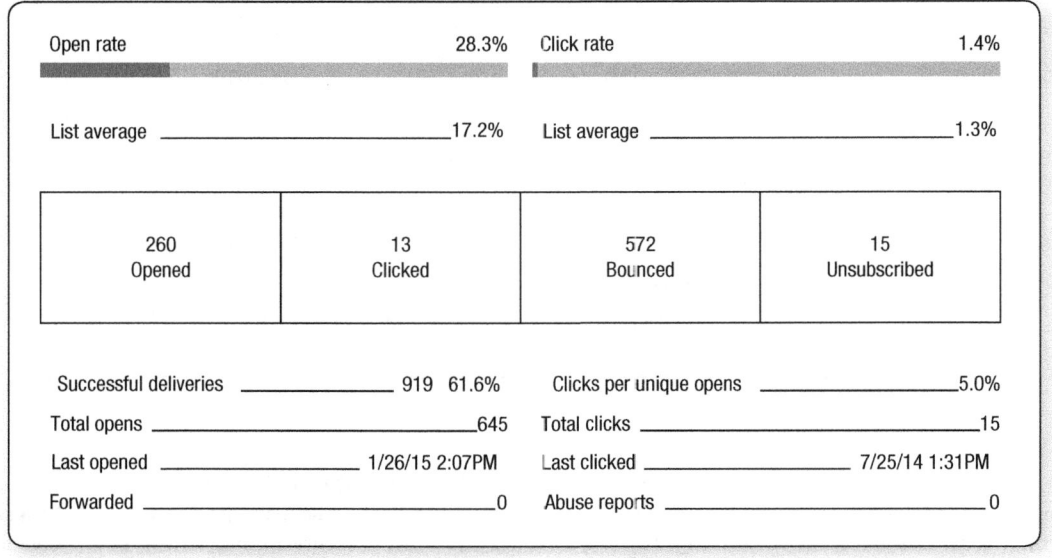

SOURCE: Mail Chimp.

FIGURE 9.14

Open Rates Decline after 24 Hours

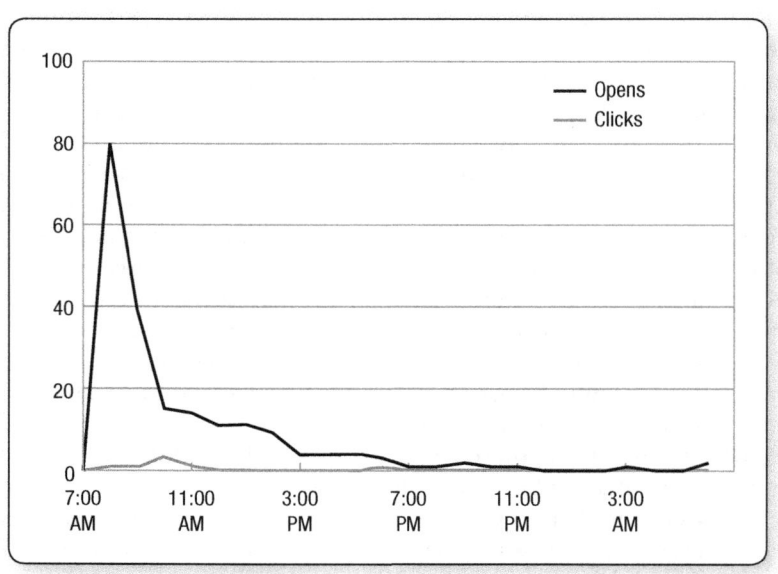

SOURCE: Mail Chimp.

THE GOLDEN RS OF EMAIL MARKETING AND TARGETING, PERSONALIZATION, AND CUSTOMIZATION

As we discuss email marketing as a whole, we enter another semantic thicket: the differentiation between targeting, personalization, and customization. These three important terms are used often, in many contexts, with many shades of meaning. When defined by various authors, they often give different definitions.[20] The distinction between "personalization" and "customization" is especially fuzzy, with some authors using them interchangeably and some attempting to give more precise meanings. For the purpose of our discussion in the remainder of this chapter, we will give the terms the following meanings, which are helpful in teasing out the specific ways in which marketers can use these techniques. These definitions were presented in previous chapters and they are still applicable:

- *Targeting* refers to directing marketing communications to individuals or businesses that have been identified as valid prospects for acquisition or retention for the good or service. Targeting can be visible, as when a marketer sends an email newsletter with personalized content to a customer who has given permission for this type of communication. It can be invisible to the receiver, as when targeted ads are served onto a website without the visitor's explicit knowledge.
- *Personalization* involves the creation of specialized content for a prospect with a known profile by choosing from an array of existing content modules. In addition to the email newsletter, just described, personalization occurs when a visitor registers on a website like Reddit and creates a list of personalized "subreddits" by choosing relevant content from extensive lists presented by the site.
- *Customization* is the creation of new content, services, or even products based on the needs and wants of an individual customer—either business or consumer. Internet marketers like NikeID are offering the ability to customize products as discussed in Chapter 2. Others like iTunes are offering customers the ability to customize their own user experience.

Note that this terminology defines customization rather tightly, calling into question the way in which the term is often used by internet marketers. Even so, there is still a gray area in which goods or services are configured to customers' orders from a standardized set of components or services. This type of customization is represented by manufacturing processes such as Dell's and NikeID's and has been called "mass customization" in discussions in both the academic and trade press.[21]

With few exceptions, internet marketers are not engaging in customization at this level, and we can therefore center our discussion on targeting and personalization. In so doing, we are not missing any important marketing issues since the processes used to identify and reach prospective customers with offers for truly customized products are the same as the ones used to identify customers in order to target them with personalized content.

In fact, email personalization does appear to be related to increased email response rates (see Figure 9.15a). Campaign monitor cites data from Experian that says; that just using the recipient's name in an email subject line can increase response rate by 26 percent. However, in this kind of claim it is important to understand that open and click-through rates are also dependent upon other factors, such as the industry involved. Open rates vary depending on the type of industry, a factor which can affect the influence of personalization (see Figure 9.15b).

Personalization research is in its infancy in academia. However, the research in general supports the use of personalization in marketing. One study in a series of randomized field experiments found that even simple personalization such as adding the name of the recipient to the subject line increased the probability of opening the email by 20 percent, translating to a 31 percent increase in sales leads and a 17 percent reduction in the number of unsubscribes.[22] Some research by White, Zahay,

FIGURE 9.15a
Personalization Increases Open Rates

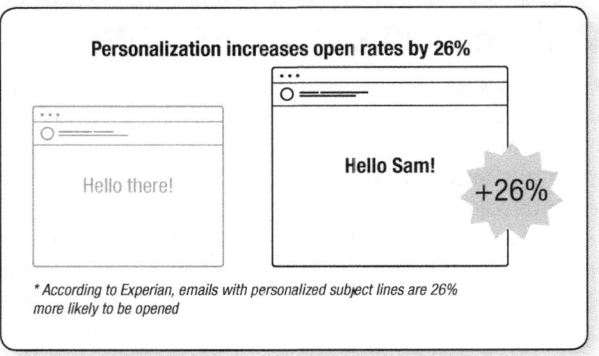

SOURCE: Campaign Monitor https://www.campaignmonitor.com/rescurces/guides/email-marketing-new-rules/.

FIGURE 9.15b
Average Opens and Click-Through Rates by Industry

	Open Rate	Click Rate
Nonprofits	30.32%	8.69%
Travel and hospitality	22.84%	3.48%
Professional & business support services	22.56%	2.40%
Hobbies	22.55%	4.51%
Marketing & advertising	20.66%	3.73%
Retail	15.43%	2.87%

SOURCE: *DMA Statistical Fact Book*, the Definitive Source for Marketing Insight, Direct Marketing Association, New York, (2016), p. 210.

Thorbjornsen, and Shavitt[23] indicates that although personalization can yield higher response rates,[24] consumers do not react well to highly personalized messages that are given too soon in the relationship. The consumer develops a response called "reactance" in response to highly personalized messages where the fit between the offer in the message and consumers' personal characteristics is not explicitly justified by firms. In other words, if Dreamfields Pasta were to make an offer based on highly personalized information, perhaps about the size of the consumer's family, too soon in the relationship, it might turn customers off and decrease response. However, starting the consumer relationship with a simple dollar off coupon as they do is not threatening and is a good idea to help develop the relationship.

Email inboxes are crammed with spam, emails of dubious value to the recipient, and a small number of communications that are welcome and that have a good chance of inciting to action. There is an approach marketers can follow to give their emails the best chance of being opened and acted upon. We call this the three "Golden Rs of Email Marketing."[25] They are as follows:

- *Relevance.* All content should be applicable to the recipient's needs and lifestyle. Content that is not relevant will not motivate the recipient to take action and it may tarnish the brand of the communicator.

- *Respect.* Relevant content cannot be generated without in-depth information about the recipient. In order to get the information and keep the trust of the recipient, the sender of emails must guard data from unwarranted or frivolous use.
- *Recipient control.* Go beyond simply obtaining permission to communicate with the recipient. Make the recipient an active partner in deciding what content he or she wants to receive and how often he or she wants to receive it. That gives the content a much better chance of being seen as valuable.

Following these three Rs will not only give the emails the best possible chance of success but it will also, over time, contribute to the creation of brand that is trusted by the members of its target market.

REQUIREMENTS OF THE U.S. CAN-SPAM ACT

Because email is open to abuse by spammers, phishers, and others who seek to dupe the unwary, legislation, the **CAN-SPAM Act**, has been passed in an attempt to curb the worst abuses. *Phishing* is the process of using emails to obtain or "fish" for a consumer's personal information, usually financial. An example of a phishing email is shown in Figure 9.16. The subject line says that it is from Amazon.com accounts management and the text asks for the recipient's personal bank account information. When receiving emails that looks suspicious, see if the emails are compliant with the CAN-SPAM Act, as discussed later. If there is a valid reply to address, a valid street address, and an unsubscribe provision, the email is less likely to be a "phishing" expedition.

CAN-SPAM Act the U.S. law regulating advertising and promotional emails.

The law, officially named "Controlling the Assault of Non-Solicited Pornography and Marketing Act," was passed in 2003 by the U.S. Congress in an attempt to curb unsolicited and, especially, offensive email. Although it does not use the terms, it distinguishes between acquisition mailings by marketers and relationship mailings. Relationship mailings, or in the terms of the Federal Trade Commission, "a transactional or relationship message," are emails that facilitate a transaction or update an existing customer. As long as the content is not false or misleading, these emails are generally exempt from the provisions of CAN-SPAM. Acquisition or promotional mailings

FIGURE 9.16
What Is Wrong?

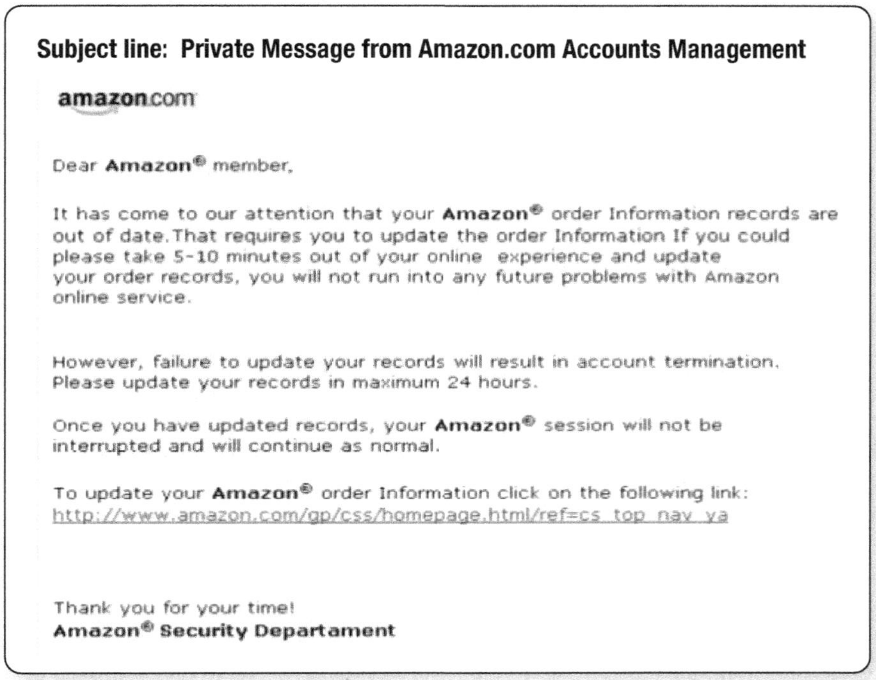
Subject line: Private Message from Amazon.com Accounts Management

amazon.com

Dear **Amazon®** member,

It has come to our attention that your **Amazon®** order Information records are out of date.That requires you to update the order Information If you could please take 5-10 minutes out of your online experience and update your order records, you will not run into any future problems with Amazon online service.

However, failure to update your records will result in account termination. Please update your records in maximum 24 hours.

Once you have updated records, your **Amazon®** session will not be interrupted and will continue as normal.

To update your **Amazon®** order Information click on the following link:
http://www.amazon.com/gp/css/homepage.html/ref=cs_top_nav_ya

Thank you for your time!
Amazon® Security Departament

SOURCE: © Cengage Learning 2013.

as we have been discussing here, however, come under the provisions of the law. It is wise to pay attention to the law since every separate email in violation of the law can be subject to a penalty of $16,000.[26]

According to the FTC website, the main provisions of the law are as follows:

- *It bans false or misleading header information.* Your email's "From," "To," and routing information—including the originating domain name and email address—must be accurate and identify the person who initiated the email.
- *It prohibits deceptive subject lines.* The subject line cannot mislead the recipient about the contents or subject matter of the message.
- *It requires that email give recipients an opt-out method.* You must provide a return email address or another internet-based response mechanism that allows a recipient to ask you not to send future email messages to that email address, and you must honor the requests. You may create a "menu" of choices to allow a recipient to opt-out of certain types of messages, but you must include the option to end any commercial messages from the sender.
  - Any opt-out mechanism you offer must be able to process opt-out requests for at least 30 days after you send your commercial email. When you receive an opt-out request, the law gives you ten business days to stop sending email to the requestor's email address. You cannot help another entity send email to that address, or have another entity send email on your behalf to that address. Finally, it is illegal for you to sell or transfer the email addresses of people who choose not to receive your email, even in the form of a mailing list, unless you transfer the addresses so another entity can comply with the law.
- *It requires that commercial email be identified as an advertisement and include the sender's valid physical postal address.* Your message must contain clear and conspicuous notice that the message is an advertisement or solicitation and that the recipient can opt-out of receiving more commercial email from you. It also must include your valid physical postal address.

Commercial email service providers as we have discussed help marketers abide by the provisions of the law. Most of them seem straightforward, but some are difficult to implement if the marketer has a large list. This is especially true of the requirements for removing "unsubscribes" from the marketer's own list as well as those of any affiliates who may have been given access. If the list is to be rented, the unsubscribes must be meticulously purged from the rental list. Software that automates this process is desirable since errors must be avoided.

There are other practices specified as unacceptable in the FTC implementation guidelines. Most are practices not used by reputable marketers in any event. These practices include harvesting of email addresses from other websites, a so-called dictionary attach in which the spammer uses computer algorithms to create email addresses, using unauthorized networks, and other practices that mislead the consumer about the results of registering with a site. The last provision means, for example, that if a marketer needs to place a special piece of software on the registrant's computer so he or she can receive emails in the desired format, the registrant must be explicitly notified of and agree to the placement of the software on his or her computer. That is an issue that can trip up even a marketer whose intentions are good.

Figure 9.17 from the DMA describes how to identify an email that is not compliant with the CAN-SPAM Act.

Advocates of permission marketing argue that the requirements of CAN-SPAM Act are simply good business practice. In fact, many of them would argue that they represent minimal acceptable levels, not best practices. Some level of opt-in is considered more effective than opt-out. Many would go a step further, arguing that segmentation and personalization of content is a requirement for effectiveness. Permission marketers speak disparagingly of "blast" emails that are sent to all members of a list, regardless of the relevance of the content.

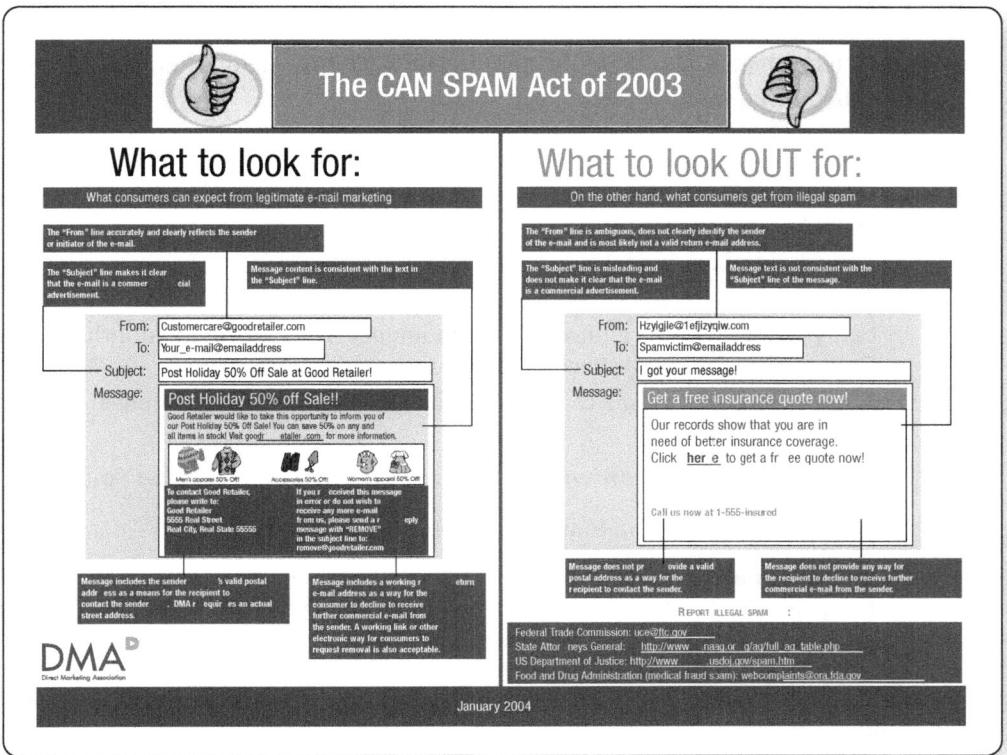

FIGURE 9.17
What to Look for in a CAN-SPAM Compliant Email

SOURCE: Direct Marketing Association, http://www.ivisionmobile.com/CanSpamPDF.pdf.

CAN-SPAM IN THE EUROPEAN UNION

The European Union's Directive on Privacy and Electronic Communications was passed in 2002 and is probably due for updates and revisions. This Directive sets out guidelines for direct marketing in all media and requires that member nations of the EU harmonize their individual laws under the umbrella of the EU Directive. Email is covered under the general policy directive and the basic requirement is that people must opt-in to receive marketer-initiated communications in all electronic media. The "technology neutral" laws resulting from the EU Directive have been criticized as being unenforceable. The very generality of laws that attempt to cover the wide spectrum of electronic media makes it hard to be specific, and therefore enforceable. The fact that the directive also covers the 27 members of the EU also creates difficulties. Finally, the fact that much spam received in Western Europe comes from outside that geographical area makes enforcement exceedingly difficult.

However, without similar antispam rules being adopted across the globe, the EU Directive is not going to stop spam sent to European email users from beyond the region."[27] That refrain sounds familiar to email users around the globe. Many spam sites are located outside the United States, for example. A summary of the EU Directive can be found online provided by the European Commission on Information, Society and Media, along with links to other information about the data privacy laws in Europe.[28]

In both the EU and the United States, CAN-SPAM laws specify legal standards that marketers must meet. They are not, however, sufficient to assure effective email marketing. Some countries, such as Canada, have taken more specific steps to reduce the occurrence of spam.

THE CANADIAN ANTI-SPAM LAW

The new Canadian Anti-Spam Law (CASL) became effective July 1, 2014 and according to Deloitte is one of the toughest laws of its kind in the world.[29] The goal is to protect Canadians from spam, particularly on an international level. The law applies to every business, including entrepreneurs, not for profits, with stiff penalties of up to 10 million Canadian dollars. The law applies equally to companies that are located in and/or doing business in Canada.

The law applies to "commercial electronic messages" or CEMs. These include emails or text messages and are considered commercial if they encourage participation in a commercial activity, such as a promotion or a sale. The law has three basic requirements:

1. *Consent* from the recipient of the email.
   a. *Implied consent* comes from an existing business relationship in the prior two-year period, like a purchase or an inquiry in the prior six months. Express consent is required outside of these timeframes.
   b. *Express consent* means the contact has given written or oral consent to receive CEMs.
2. *Identification of the organization.* Similar to the law in the United States.
3. *Unsubscribe mechanism.* Similar to the law in the United States.

What really makes the law unique is the consent requirement. Databases and ESPs can be used to track consent and make sure a company is compliant. There is a grace period for compliance also. This grace period expires July 1, 2017. If express consent was obtained before July 1, 2014, it generally does not expire. For more information on CASL watch this video. This law will make it more challenging to market via email in Canada.

THE VIBRANT FUTURE OF EMAIL MARKETING

However, email marketing continues to be a valuable tool in the marketer's arsenal because of the high ROI, the ability to target and segment customers directly, and the ability to measure results. Some current trends are making email even more relevant today:

1. *Personalization.* Personalization will continue to improve as marketers use more than name and address the next frontier on personalization will be truly one-to-one email marketing campaigns.
2. *Relevant segmentation.* Not only personalization, but targeting content to highly segmented lists, ala lawn care example above, will continue to improve the success rate and the reliability of email marketing. As Figure 9.18 illustrates, the return on segmented campaigns versus "one-size-fits-all" can be hundreds of times higher. Although many marketers are using the segmented campaigns mentioned above, there is more room to use this technique to improve response and revenue.
3. *Mobile applications.* With so many customers accessing email on their mobile devices, mobile will continue to foster the growth of email marketing. In fact, mobile open rates grew 30 percent in 2015, while desktop rates decreased (Figure 9.19). In addition, geo-targeting will improve the relevance of messages that can be delivered when and where the customer requires them. For example, novelty T-shirt vendor BustedTees went beyond mass send times to the time when the customer was most likely to open the email, based on time zone and other factors. The company experienced an 11 percent higher click-through rate and an 8 percent uplift in email revenue overnight, indicating the

FIGURE 9.18
Segmented Campaigns Drive a 760% Increase Revenue

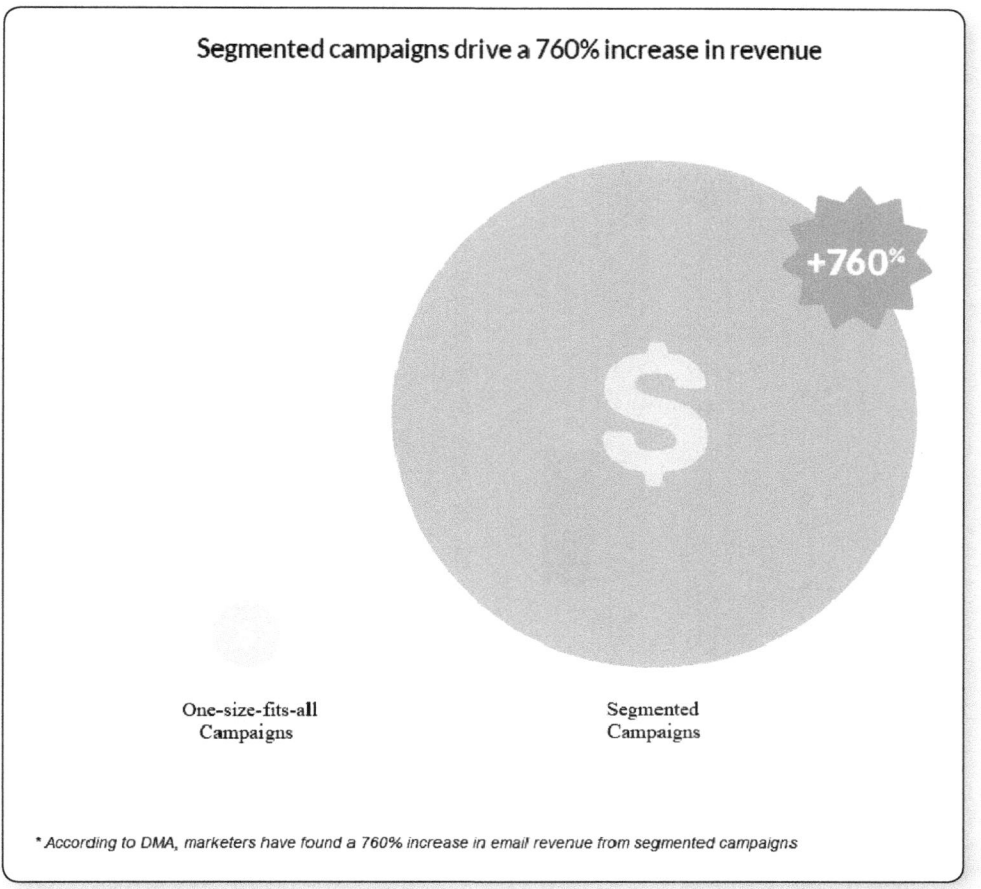

SOURCE: Campaign Monitor, https://www.campaignmonitor.com/resources/guides/email-marketing-new-rules/.

vital importance of timing for emails and the critical role of understanding customer behavior on mobile devices.[30]

4. *Triggers.* **Triggers** involve sending emails after a particular event, like a purchase, when customers are more likely to purchase again, or reminding customers to visit the website who haven't been there for a while. Triggers will continue to be an evolving trend in email marketing.[31] Trigger emails can have an open rate of 152 percent greater than a traditional email[32] and, as shown in Figure 9.20, in general have higher click, and open rates versus "business-as-usual" emails.[33] Again, these emails not only can be automated and measured effectively, but also campaigns can be "tweaked" to improve results.

triggers events or actions that prompt an email to be sent.

5. *Animation and rich content.* Animation will become more prevalent in effective email marketing, as will all rich content, such as video. The DMA estimates a 15–18 percent lift in performance metrics such as a click to open and transactions from the use of animation in emails.[34] Animated GIFs can do everything from provide humor and delight to help illustrate how to use a product.[35]

FIGURE 9.19

Email Opens on Mobile Grew 30%

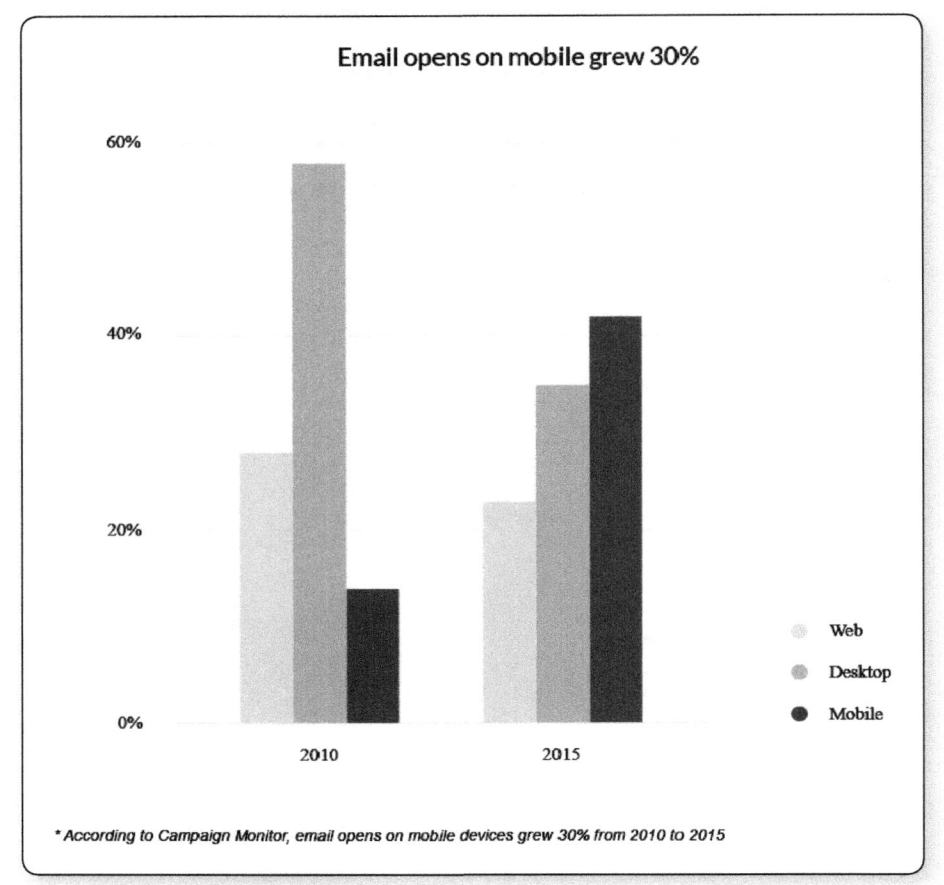

SOURCE: Campaign Monitor, https://www.campaignmonitor.com/resources/guides/email-marketing-new-rules/.

FIGURE 9.20

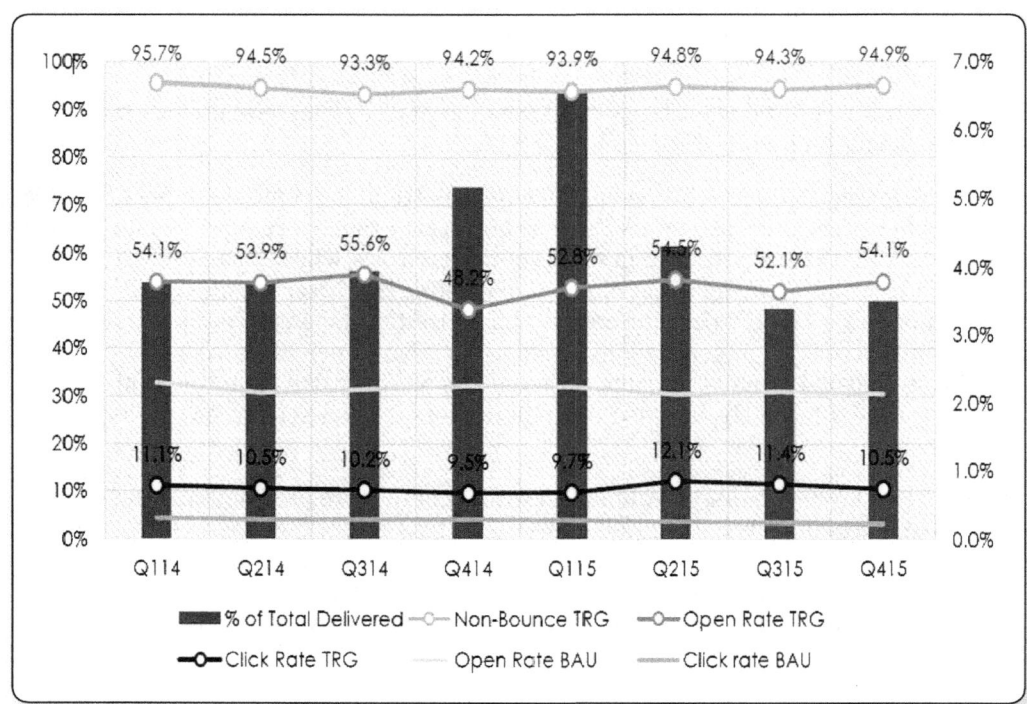

SOURCE: *DMA Statistical Fact Book*, the Definitive Source for Marketing Insight, Direct Marketing Association, New York, (2016), p. 201.

SUMMARY

The marketer's list of customer retention techniques is rich, varied, and growing. The challenge is to use the correct ones for the correct objective at the correct time and to do so in a fully integrated online and offline communications program. Emails can be used in conjunction with other communications channels such as direct mail and social media for powerful results.

Email marketing for customer retention offers a number of legitimate benefits. Not only can marketers contact consumers in a timely and more cost-effective fashion than other response mechanisms, but response is almost immediate, and offers and campaigns can be altered to increase response rate. Permission is the key to effective email marketing since email is marketing's version of a two-edged sword. Email has genuine benefits when used as part of an integrated permission marketing program. However, the volume of spam threatens to drown the efforts of legitimate marketers. Governments around the globe are attempting to stem the tide of spam.

The secret to effective email marketing, as with all direct techniques, is a good list—and in this case, permission-based lists are superior. Levels of permission range from opt-out to opt-in to double opt-in. Generally, a form of opt-in permission is considered to be most consistent with good email marketing practices. Good lists help decrease the bounce rate and increase click-through rates. Emails need to be designed with good web design principles in mind, compelling subject lines and offers, and need to take into account in their design the limitations of the computer screen on which they will be received.

Marketers need to offer the consumer the right to opt-out or unsubscribe at any time, provide a physical address on their email and a valid reply-to email address, and to otherwise comply with good email marketing practices as outlined in the CAN-SPAM provisions. Good campaign planning is critical to success and the ability to measure many aspects of response can allow the marketer to adjust the campaign accordingly in short order. Used properly, with a concern for relevance, respect, and recipient control, email can be a highly effective marketing tool. Increasing sophistication in marketing technology, including true **one-to-one** personalization and rich media content, will ensure that emails will continue to be relevant, timely, and worth opening.

DISCUSSION QUESTIONS

1. Why is email still a strong tool for internet marketers? Do you think it will be replaced by mobile applications, such as text messaging, if so why and in what time frame?
2. What is meant by permission marketing? Do you think it is an important concept to email marketers and if so why?
3. Think about email communications from marketers, perhaps some that you receive yourself. What makes them interesting and worth your time to open and read? Do you ever take any action as a result of the emails? Why or why not?
4. What are the main benefits of using an email service provider? Say you are the head of a student organization and you need to regularly contact members, would you consider using an email service provider if the cost were within your budget? Why or why not?
5. What aspects of promotional email design would you take into account if you were designing an email to invite students to a meeting of the organization mentioned in Question 4? Where would you put the most important information? What would be your call to action?
6. From your perspective, is the CAN-SPAM law working? Why or why not?
7. What emerging trends in email marketing will be the most significant in the future and why?

ENDNOTES

1. http://www.marketingcharts.com/online/2016-marketing-budget-trends-by-channel-64987/attachment/strongviewselligent-2016-marketing-budget-plans-by-program-jan2016/.
2. https://www.entrepreneur.com/article/251752 *ExactTarget* "Mobile Behavior report" (2014).
3. https://www.entrepreneur.com/article/251752.
4. *DMA Statistical Fact Book*, the Definitive Source for Direct Marketing Benchmarks, Direct Marketing Association, New York, (2009), p. 87.
5. Forrester, U.S. Email Marketing Forecast, 2009–2014.
6. *DMA Statistical Fact Book*, 30th ed., the Definitive Source for Direct Marketing Benchmarks, Direct Marketing Association, New York, (2008), p. 115.
7. Reimers, V., Chao, C.-W., and Gorman, S. (2016) "Permission email marketing and its influence on online shopping," *Asia Pacific Journal of Marketing and Logistics*, 28(2), pp. 308–322. doi: 10.1108/apjml-03-2015-0037.
8. http://www.huffingtonpost.com/entry/check-work-email-hours-survey_us_55ddd168e4b0a40aa3ace672.
9. http://www.exacttarget.com/sff, % per the May 2011 SFF survey. (This is of online consumers in the United States 15-1—weighted by age and gender.)
10. http://www.radicati.com/wp/wp-content/uploads/2015/02/Email-Statistics-Report-2015-2019-Executive-Summary.pdf.
11. https://www.symantec.com/content/en/us/enterprise/other_resources/intelligence-report-06-2015.en-us.pdf.
12. http://www.bbc.com/news/technology-33564016.
13. http://www.exacttarget.com/sff. (This is of online consumers in the United States 15-1—weighted by age and gender.) Question wording, "Have you ever made a purchase as the result of a marketing message you received through: Email (email was one of multiple yes/no questions).
14. http://www.emailmonday.com/mobile-email-usage-statistics. The Ultimate Mobile Email Stats (2016).
15. http://www.radicati.com/wp/wp-content/uploads/2015/02/Email-Statistics-Report-2015-2019-Executive-Summary.pdf.
16. Source: *DMA Statistical Fact Book*, The Definitive Source for Marketing Insight, Direct Marketing Association, New York, (2016), p. 201.
17. http://www.law360.com/articles/528234/pasta-maker-forks-over-8m-in-low-carb-labeling-deal.
18. http://www.lyris.com/Email-marketing/535-Email-Preheaders-Work-So-Make-Them-Work-For-You, retrieved July 18, 2011.
19. https://blog.mailchimp.com/insights-from-mailchimps-send-time-optimization-system/.
20. For a discussion of competing definitions see, "Is It Personalization or Customization?" Don Peppers and Martha Rogers, *Inside 1 to 1*, June 20, 2000, http://www.marketing1to1.com.
21. See, for example, James Gilmore and Joseph B. Pine, II, "The Four Faces of Mass Customization," *Harvard Business Review, 1997*.
22. Sahni, Navdeep S. and Wheeler, S. Christian and Chintagunta, Pradeep K., Personalization in Email Marketing: The Role of Non-Informative Advertising Content (January 30, 2016). Stanford University Graduate School of Business Research Paper No. 16-14. Available at SSRN: http://papers.ssrn.com/sol3/papers.cfm?abstract_id=2725251.
23. T. B. White, D. L. Zahay, H. Thorbjorsen, and S. A. Shavitt (2008). "Getting too Personal: Reactance to Highly Personalized Email Solicitations," *Marketing Letters*, 19: 39–50.
24. O. J. Postma and M. Brokke (2002). "Personalization in Practice: The Proven Effects of Personalization," *journal of Database Management*, 9: 137–42.

25. Based on a concept suggested by Bill Nussey, *The Quiet Revolution in Email Marketing* (New York: iUniverse, Inc., 2004).
26. https://www.ftc.gov/tips-advice/business-center/guidance/can-spam-act-compliance-guide-business, retrieved June 23, 2016.
27. "European Spam Laws Lack Bite," BBC News, April 28, 2004, http://news.bbc.co.uk/2/hi/technology/3666585.stm.
28. http://ec.europa.eu/information_society/doc/factsheets/024-privacy-and-spam-en.pdf.
29. http://www2.deloitte.com/ca/en/pages/risk/articles/canada-anti-spam-law-casl-faq.html.
30. http://www.marketingsherpa.com/article/case-study/personalized-send-times-email-revenue.
31. http://www.emailvendorselection.com/forrester-wave-email-marketing-vendors-2014-everything-you-need-to-know/.
32. https://blog.kissmetrics.com/6-email-personalization-techniques/.
33. *DMA Statistical Fact Book*, The Definitive Source for Marketing Insight, Direct Marketing Association New York, (2016), page 201.
34. *DMA Statistical Fact Book*, The Definitive Source for Marketing Insight, Direct Marketing Association New York, (2016), page 204.
35. https://litmus.com/blog/a-guide-to-animated-gifs-in-email.

Chapter 10

Search Engine Marketing

LEARNING OBJECTIVES

By the time you complete this chapter, you will be able to:

1. Discuss the reasons why search marketing is so important.
2. Explain the difference between a directory and a search engine.
3. Understand how search engines work and what a search algorithm is.
4. Define SEM, SEO, and PPC.
5. Understand the basic process of optimizing a website for organic search.
6. Understand how search and social work together.
7. Understand the future trends in search.

There are multiple customer acquisition techniques used by marketers in integrated programs spanning both advertising techniques and media. In this chapter, we discuss an acquisition technique that has enjoyed explosive growth on the internet and has become an integral part of how we work on the internet—search marketing. Search marketing is in a sense a true outgrowth of the direct marketing roots of the web because it allows us to be in front of the customer at the exact moment they are researching a product or service or considering purchase. Although we may not know exactly who the customer is at the point they see our organization or firm listed on the results of a search, we do know what they are interested in at the moment. If we can encourage them to learn more about us or make a purchase, we then have the opportunity to acquire them as a customer, to collect specific information about them, and to develop a long-term relationship.

THE GROWING IMPACT OF SEARCH

When the Pew Internet & American Life Project asked American consumers in 2004 about their use of search engines—websites that work to help users to find the things they wanted to find on the internet—32 percent said they "couldn't live without them."[1]

At that time, the average internet user performed 33 searches per month, a total of 3.9 billion searches on the 25 most popular search engines. To put this information in perspective, Google currently processes about 40,000 inquiries per second and growing. Check out the current statistics at: http://www.internetlivestats.com/google-search-statistics/.

The statistics above underline the fact that the trend toward search engine usage and dependence has continued at a breakneck speed. The following information puts that usage in perspective:

- 92 percent of U.S. internet users have used search engines.
- 93 percent of B2B purchase start with search.[2]
- 81 percent of retail purchases begin with an online search.[3]
- 48 percent of mobile searches start on search engines, 33 percent on branded websites, and 26 percent on branded apps.[4]
- Although 96 percent of the youngest adult internet users (ages 18–29) used search engines, 87 percent of the oldest users (65+) also still use search engines to find information online.
- There are no significant differences by gender or race/ethnicity in terms of those who say they used search "yesterday."
- Those with higher incomes and who have attended college are, however, slightly more likely to use search engines to find information online.[5]

Overall attitudes toward search are positive. A 2012 Pew study reported the following:[6]

"91% of search engine users say they always or most of the time find the information they are seeking when they use search engines

73% of search engine users say that most or all the information they find as they use search engines is accurate and trustworthy

66% of search engine users say search engines are a fair and unbiased source of information

55% of search engine users say that, in their experience, the quality of search results is getting better over time, while just 4% say it has gotten worse

52% of search engine users say search engine results have gotten more relevant and useful over time, while just 7% report that results have gotten less relevant"

Results are so positive that it appears that desktop search volumes peaked in 2013 and that about 50 percent of all searches are now performed on mobile devices.[7] However, the mobile search market only represents about a third of the revenue of desktop search, as users continue to make larger ticket purchases during the week and when they are on their desktops. Mobile users typically look to search engines for information about products but may make purchases on their desktop. We can expect those trends to reverse as mobile purchasing becomes easier and mobile ads more relevant.

Web users continue to look for information on specific topics, maps and directions, news and current events, general information, shopping, and entertainment—in other words, just about everything! Millions of searches everyday encompass a wide range of subject matter. Search has radically transformed fields such as health care and real estate, with patients walking into their doctor's office armed with information and home buyers depending on real estate search sites and virtual tours to limit their possibilities before they even set foot in a home for a real-world tour. No wonder marketers have found opportunities for marketing through search engines on the web medium and now on mobile devices.

Marketers are also using search engine marketing for just about everything. Web marketers use search for branding, online sales, lead generation for both manufacturers and dealers, driving traffic to websites, and simply to provide content. The Search Engine Marketing Professional Organization (SEMPO) in its first year of studying search engine marketing (SEM) stated that marketers in the United States and Canada spent over $4 billion on search marketing and advertising in 2004 and planned to

FIGURE 10.1
Search Marketing's Share of U.S. Digital Ad Spending Shows Continued Growth

US Digital Ad Spending, by Format, 2014-2019
billions

	2014	2015	2016	2017	2018	2019
Search	$23.44	$26.53	$29.24	$32.32	$36.41	$40.60
Display	$21.07	$26.15	$32.17	$37.20	$41.87	$46.69
—Banners and other*	$10.53	$11.57	$13.39	$14.74	$16.17	$17.68
—Video	$5.24	$7.46	$9.59	$11.43	$13.05	$14.77
—Rich media	$3.71	$5.44	$7.42	$9.17	$10.69	$12.19
—Sponsorships	$1.58	$1.68	$1.77	$1.86	$1.96	$2.06
Classifieds and directories	$2.82	$2.94	$3.07	$3.20	$3.33	$3.47
Lead generation	$1.88	$1.97	$2.06	$2.15	$2.25	$2.35
Email	$0.25	$0.27	$0.29	$0.31	$0.33	$0.35
Mobile messaging	$0.24	$0.26	$0.27	$0.26	$0.24	$0.23
Total	$49.69	$58.12	$67.09	$75.44	$84.44	$93.70

*Note: includes advertising that appears on desktop and laptop computers as well as mobile phones, tablets and other internet-connected devices on all formats mentioned; numbers may not add up to total due to rounding; *includes ads such as Facebook's News Feed Ads and Twitter's Promoted Tweets*
Source: eMarketer, Sep 2015

195251   www.eMarketer.com

SOURCE: http://www.emarketer.com/Article/US-Digital-Display-Ad-Spending-Surpass-Search-Ad-Spending-2016/1013442.

increase their search spending by an average of 39 percent in 2005.[8] SEM is now valued almost $30 billion in the United States alone and search spending, for the moment, dominates digital marketing spending.[9] (See Figure 10.1.) A study by SEMPO found that search is still the leader among digital marketing efforts, although as Figure 10.1 illustrates, display advertising is expected to outpace search in spending in the United States sometime in 2016/2017. Search is still a formidable industry, with the biggest SEO Challenges for marketers being measuring the ROI of search efforts.[10]

THE WORLD OF SEARCH

The world of search is broader than just search engines, important though they are. Search includes several types of search engines, including desktop-only search, specialty search, and another major category—directories—which are aids in finding internet websites. In fact, only 36 percent of consumers said that they would start a localized search with a general search engine.[11] Directories and classified advertising sites like Craig's list and Angie's list services still play a role in how consumers find information online.

directories aid in finding internet websites; list of sites are usually arranged by category, and the directory has a search function.

Directories create a list of sites that are usually arranged by category, and each directory has a search function. Directories emerged early in the history of the internet. For example, Yahoo! began as a directory in which Jerry Yang and Paul Filo listed their favorite websites. The essence of a directory is that it offers both free basic listings and paid enhanced listings that allow any local business to add business details, including photos and a link to their website, to their basic listing.[12]

Directories can also be compiled from other sources. The Open Directory Project by DMOZ is free and describes itself as "the largest, most comprehensive human-edited directory of the web. It is constructed and maintained by a vast, global community of volunteer editors."[13] Online directories seem to be overtaking their offline counterparts in many market sectors, ranging from finding former high school classmates to locating business services. However, directories have declined in importance in terms of SEM with the rise of search engines. In reality, the most important aspect in being able to be found on the internet is to be indexed by the major search engines, which usually requires submitting the website to these engines. Like directories, search engines have both a paid aspect and a free aspect.

SEARCH ENGINE MARKETING

The entire process of getting listed on search engines so consumers can find a company online is called **search engine marketing (SEM)**. SEMPO defines SEM as "a form of internet marketing that seeks to promote websites by increasing their visibility in search engine result pages."[14] There are two basic aspects of SEM:

- **Search engine optimization (SEO)** refers to the process of designing a site and its content whereby search engines find the site without being paid to do so. SEMPO describes SEO as "the process of editing a web site's content and code in order to improve visibility within one or more search engines." The free aspect of SEM known as SEO is also called *natural search, organic search*, and sometimes *algorithmic search*.
- **Pay-per-click (PPC)**, or paid search advertising, involves "text ads targeted to keyword search results on search engines, though programs such as Google™ AdWords sometimes referred to as Pay-per-Click (PPC) advertising and Cost-per-Click (CPC) advertising."[15] The paid aspect of SEM is also called **paid search** and is based on an advertising model where firms seeking to rank high in specific search categories will bid on certain terms or "keywords" in the hopes of a lucrative search ranking. A lucrative ranking is one that makes money for the firm and is not necessarily the number one or two spot on the page. Sometimes a number two or three spot will be just as profitable for the firm. Paid search will be covered more in depth in Chapter 11.

search engine marketing (SEM) process of getting listed on search engines.

paid search the paid aspect of SEM based on an advertising model where firms seeking to rank high in specific search categories will bid on certain terms or "keywords" in the hopes of a lucrative ad ranking; also known as PPC (pay-per-click).

Search engines used to employ paid placement or "sponsored links" to help marketers rank highly on search criteria, but they have generally abandoned this effort. Therefore, in the paid aspect, most search engines' success at bidding and creating relevant ads still determines ad placement, and in the natural search aspect, other factors are taken into account. While both paid and natural search are important, natural search brings in the majority of website visitors (anywhere from 60 to 80 percent depending on the estimates) and is the "most commonly used resource to navigate websites." Paid search advertising growth has declined but paid search is still on the upswing, driven in part by the explosion of mobile devices and the increasing ease of purchase there.[16] It is referrals and not ads that drive traffic. Referrals and social media are also playing an increasing role in helping users find websites.[17] The reason is that users want to trust the source that is recommending the site and organic search results or referrals from a friend or an often-used social media site are the most trusted ways to find information on the web.

Table 10.1 compares the advantages and disadvantages of the two types of SEM. Although SEO requires no out-of-pocket costs to pay for ad placement, there is a cost in terms of time to effectively design a site to optimize it for natural search. It is also difficult to predict search ranking with SEO and may take several months for the results of the efforts to be noted on search engines. PPC provides immediate results and allows the user to limit spending to a daily budget, but PPC campaigns also must be monitored on a daily (or hourly) basis because it is easy to lose a top search

TABLE 10.1

Comparison of SEM Techniques: SEO versus PPC

	Advantages	Disadvantages
SEO (Natural or Organic Search)	Better response since majority of clicks are organic	Results are not immediate
	More return traffic	Ranking is difficult to predict
	Lower cost	Initial time investment and time is major cost
	Long-term marketing solution	Takes time for results to be displayed
	Brand recognition and loyalty	
Paid Search (PPC, Pay-Per-Click)	Immediate results based on bidding system in which there are charges for clicks received	Easy to lose ranking or spot
		Daily budget can be expensive depending on keywords
	Daily budget can be limited	Unqualified clicks
	Gives definite search volume	
	Easy to change focus	
	Unlimited keywords	
	Ability to test (keywords, ad copy, landing pages, etc.)	

SOURCE: © Cengage Learning 2013.

ranking if another firm outbids your firm in terms of keywords. Also, the impact of SEO, while it takes longer to set up and implement, if monitored properly can have a long-term effect versus the short-term effect of PPC programs, which lasts only for the duration of the ad campaign. (Please note we are referring to search results as "search results" or "search ranking." The specific term **"page rank"** refers to a mathematical algorithm named after Google co-founder Larry Page to indicate how important a page is on the web.)

ORGANIC SEARCH

Keywords are search terms, words, or phrases, selected by the user when making a search in a search engine. The term "keywords" can refer to but is not limited to all of the following items:

1. Search terms, words, or phrases, selected by the user when making a search in a search engine
2. Terms that are bid on in a PPC system such as Google or Bing
3. A section in the hypertext markup language (HTML) code for a website where site developers put terms that they hope search engines will classify the site when users search for those terms on the web.

In other words, the same term is used in a variety of situations and contexts. If the usage seems confusing, it is. Remember that SEM is a relatively new and evolving discipline in marketing, and it is common to see the same term being used in different ways.

In the case of HTML code, keywords are designated by a "meta name" also known as a **meta tag** or meta element. An example of HTML code containing keywords used by a fictional purse website is included in Figure 10.2. The HTML code listed is within the *header* portion of the website. (You can see the header data on any website by going to View → Source in your browser.) Below the beginning of the header section is the **title tag**, a useful tag that we discuss later in this chapter. Below the title tag are two meta tags; these tags are written as meta name=. The first meta tag is the "description," which often contains a sentence or two describing the site and in this example, it describes our fictional site, Pink Handbag World. The second meta

"page rank" a mathematical algorithm named after Google co-founder Larry Page to indicate how important a page is on the web; used as a metric when evaluating websites.

keywords terms, words, or phrases that are selected by the user when making a search in a search engine; also refers to terms that are bid on in a PPC system, or a section in the HTML code for a website where site developers put terms that they hope search engines will classify the site when users search for those terms on the web.

meta tag a section in the HTML header section of a website that can be used to describe the site in more detail, including content and keywords; also known as meta name, or meta element.

title tag the title the user sees in the blue bar at the top of the web page; also known as the HTML title tag.

FIGURE 10.2
HTML Code for Title, Description, and Keywords in the Head Section of a Fictional Website for Pink Purses

```
<HEAD>
<TITLE>Pink Handbag World</TITLE>
<meta name="description" content="Pink Handbag World has a huge selection of
stylish, affordable handbags and purses for girls. Get the latest fashion trends and tips
to look your best from phw.com."/>
<meta name="keywords" content="Purses, Handbags, Purses for Girls, Pink Handbags,
Pink Purses"/>
</HEAD>
```

SOURCE: © Cengage Learning 2013.

tag is "keywords," which states the keywords for searches in which the site would like to be ranked.

In the past, search engines paid close attention to the description and keywords in the meta names. However, the major search engines, particularly Google, are now concerned with customer "intent" in search and whether the page is a good fit for the search term used. The fear with meta tags and keywords is that they may be manipulated and may not refer to anything close to the content that the site actually contains. Some search engines do look at the "description" content tag, so it is probably still useful to include that tag and, following the example here, just include a few relevant terms in the keyword tag.

SEARCH ENGINES

Search engines are the focus of attention in SEM because they are the heart of the search process. Search engines have the ability to organize and make accessible the vast amount of information available on the web.

When a user enters a query, the search engine looks for information on the web and returns a list of results known as a search engines result page (SERP). These results are in the form of suggested web pages, images, videos maps, or other types of files. Increasingly, they include results from the users' social contacts, as discussed later in the chapter. The inclusion of search results from multiple content sources such as videos, images, news, maps, books, and websites into one set of research results is called **universal search**. While the search results are rather instantaneous for the user, there are a multitude of processes that occur behind the scenes. Figure 10.3 illustrates the process of a web search.

First, the user initiates a query that goes to the search engine's web server. The web server then sends the query typically to an **index server**, which stores information on previously categorized websites as a best fit to certain keywords. In order to index all this information, search engines use **spiders** or "robots," which are programs that "crawl" the web and follow every link or piece of data that they see and bring this information back to be stored. The contents of each page— words extracted from the titles, headings, or the special fields (meta tags)—are then analyzed to varying degrees to determine how it should be indexed. (Site content, inbound and outbound links, and other information are also used, which we discuss later in this chapter.)

The relevant documents are then taken from the search engine's document server based on an appropriate *algorithm*, and then displayed for the user. The word "algorithm" in the context of search does not refer to the process of solving a mathematical problem. A **search engine algorithm** displays the search engine's "best guess" at which pages are most relevant to the user's search and in which order they should be shown.

universal search the inclusion of search results from multiple content sources such as videos, images, news, maps, books, and websites into one set of research results.

index server stores the information index, which has categorized websites as a best fit to certain keywords.

spiders programs that "crawl" the web and follow every link or piece of data that they see and bring this information back to be stored; also known as robots.

search engine algorithm displays the search engine's "best guess" at which pages are most relevant to the user's search and in which order they should be shown.

FIGURE 10.3

The Generic Search Process

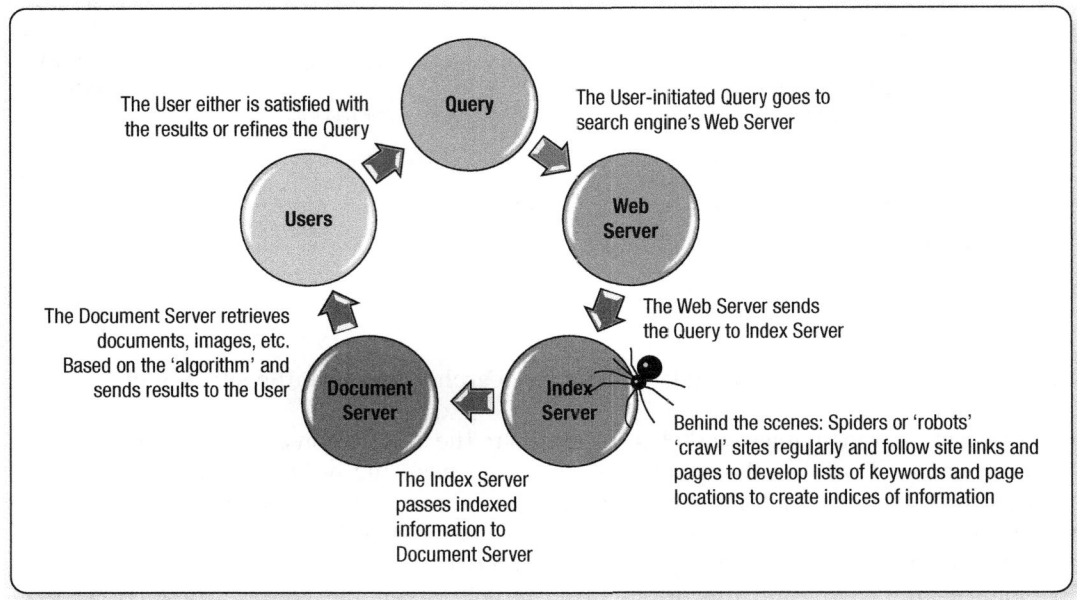

SOURCE: Adapted from "The Life Cycle of a Query" from Marketing and Advertising Using Google: Targeting Your Advertising to the Right Audience, Copyright © 2007 Google Inc., p. 12.

Figure 10.4a indicates how spiders looked at the ESPN website on a summer day in 2016. As the spiders move through a site, they are just looking to see what topics are covered and the order in which they are covered. The spiders do not make any particular judgment about the activity. In this case, the spider would pass information back to the index indicating each time the term "ESPN" had been used and on which page.

A "word cloud" of the site shown in Figure 10.4b illustrates the most frequently used terms in the site. In this case, "ESPN," "Sports," and "Olympic" are shown as larger than other terms, which indicates that they are used more often. ESPN is known for its comprehensive sports coverage so the prominence of the term Olympics is not surprising. A **keyword density** chart is also shown below the word cloud. Keyword density is the percentage of times a particular word is used in comparison to the number of words on a page. The keyword density should not be too large (less than 3 percent), which in this example (3.16 percent) indicates that the site is engaging in keyword practices that might get it in trouble with search engines. However, a density of at least 1 percent was formerly recommended in order to be properly indexed by search engines. Although 1 percent does not seem like a lot of words from one page, it is important not to overload with keywords on the page or try to trick the search engine into indexing and ranking the page a certain way.

As Jayson DeMers noted recently in *Forbes* online, while keywords and keyword density are still important, it is more important today to place keywords properly on a page and to create longer content that will get the page ranked more highly. The reason is a trend called **semantic search**, which focuses on the user's intent when searching for something. Users today might say "how do I find cheap pink purses" or "how do I find designer pink purses," depending on their intent, rather than just searching for "pink purses." The first search would yield results for clearance and discount outlets and the second search would return results for Nordstrom and other outlets that sell designer merchandise.

keyword density percentage of times a particular word is used on a website page in comparison to the number of words on that page.

semantic search focuses on the user's intent when searching for something.

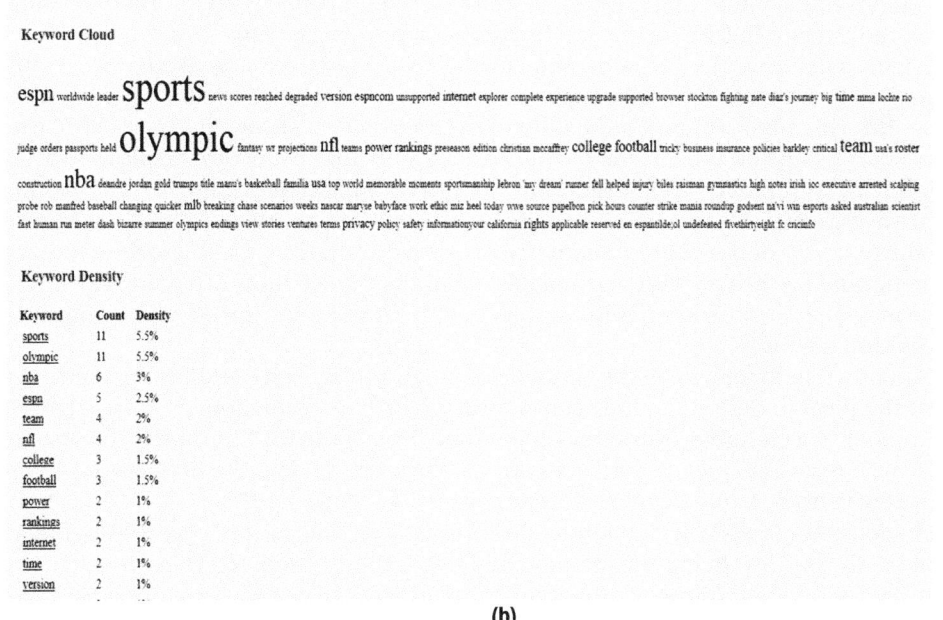

FIGURE 10.4

(a) Search Engine Spider Simulator and (b) Word Cloud and Keyword Density Chart

(a)

SOURCE: http://tools.seochat.com/tools/search-spider-simulator/.

(b)

SOURCE: http://www.webconfs.com/keyword-density-checker.php.

Semantic search has changed the game for SEO, as search engines are now programmed to return results based on intent. However, the user is still searching for something and good keyword research is still key. Put the primary keyword for the site in the header tags (H1 and H2), title tags, h1 tag, URL and the body of the text so search engines know what is important on that page.[18] Focus on creating valuable content and on the right keywords for that product or service first.

Search results can and do vary dramatically by search engine and by user. Of course search engines know our IP addresses but a search engine like Google knows a lot about us from Google+ information to Gmail, our search history, and potentially location history from an Android device.[19] The browser cache and cookies on a single device can affect search results as can previously clicked links, geographic location and type of device, whether mobile or desktop.[20] All this information is used to make search results more relevant. Those wishing to see what their SEO results look like to others should first log out of their Google accounts. Otherwise, information relating to that person will skew the search results. Figures 10.5a and b show the results before and after Dr. Zahay logs out of her Gmail account. Before she logs out of her Gmail account, her Google+ profile is prominent as well as the results from Google Scholar. After she logs out, there are more results from other web pages where she is mentioned and the results are less focused on Google sources. Students can try this activity themselves and compare the results.

Most users prefer the search engine that they believe gives them the results they want, with preferences varying depending on the searcher. And searchers are more likely now to see results that are relevant to them. So there are pluses to having more relevant search results although there are some minuses in terms of privacy concerns.

In fact, each search engine has its own algorithm for ranking entries, which is not generally published. In this chapter, we focus primarily on Google because it is the dominant platform. There are a number of search engines with significant market shares, as measured by the number of searches conducted both on desktop and mobile devices (see Figures 10.6a and b). However, Google has dominated the search market for many years, and on desktop search has a healthy 71 percent share. On mobile devices, which are the future of search, Google has almost complete dominance, with a 95 percent share worldwide. There are estimates that 90 percent of worldwide search comes from Google![21]

Yahoo! has been losing market share over time, primarily to Microsoft's Bing. Check the latest results yourself at: [https://www.netmarketshare.com/].

Figures 10.7a and b provide the results of two separate searches for "pink purses" on two separate search engines, Google and Bing. The results vary because of the differing algorithms. The results of organic search show up in the main area of the search page on the left-hand side. Exactly how the results are displayed varies from one search engine to another, but the intention is that organic search results are always ranked by relevance based on the keyword or phrase chosen and provide the majority of the content on the page. Above and below the page, the searcher will generally see boxes with text images and links. Those links are paid ads (PPC). There may also be a band of color across the top of the page that displays the highest-ranking paid ads.

As shown in Figure 10.7a the "organic" or "natural" search rankings appear to the left of the page underneath paid search terms, which also can appear to the right of the organic search terms. Marketers seek to be "above the fold" or in the top four or five search terms because most users do not scroll down past the first few rankings and rarely venture to subsequent search pages.

As stated before, search engine marketers try to "guess" or "reverse engineer" the algorithm to get their pages ranked highest in natural search. The entries to the index and the calculations of the algorithms change over time, meaning that site ranks may change just because the way of determining ranking has changed. All the search engine ranking algorithms are different, placing different weights on different characteristics. The exact ranking algorithm of any site is proprietary, although trade sources make educated guesses at the nature of the different algorithms. The meta tag "description," as we have seen, often contains a sentence or two; Google, Bing, and Yahoo! ignore it in ranking the site, and focus on the context of the search.[22] However, the meta tag and the title tag do affect how the site is displayed

FIGURE 10.5

(a) Searches Before and (b) After Logging in to a Google Account

SOURCE: Google.

on the search page and are important to searchers in deciding whether to click on a particular page. Some search engines pay attention to the description. This example is just one small indication of the difference in ranking algorithms among different search engines.

FIGURE 10.6a

Search Engine Market Share, Desktop, June 2016

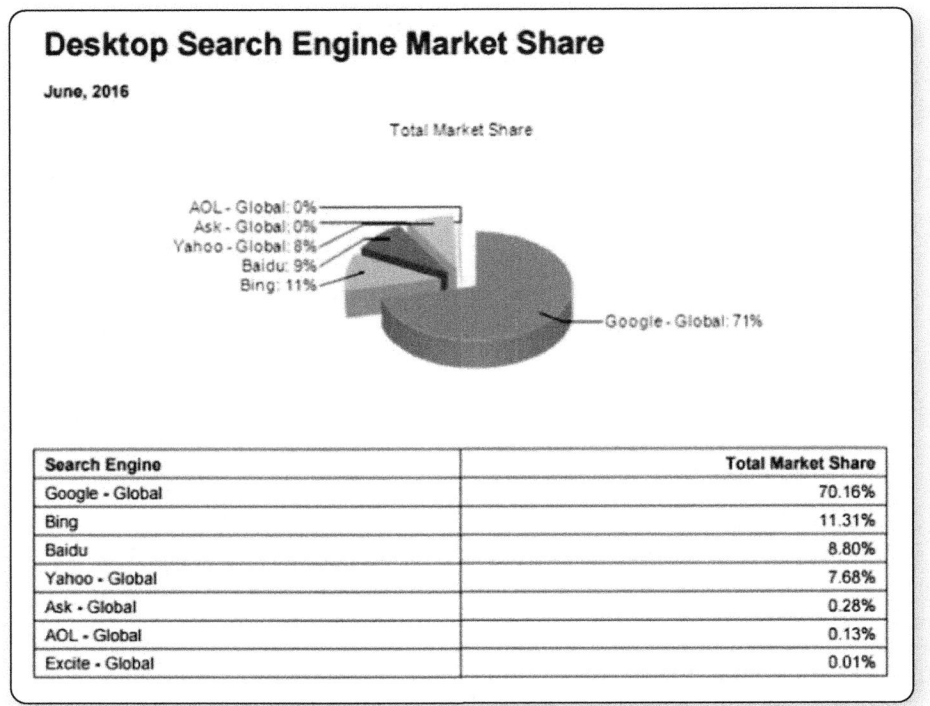

SOURCE: https://www.netmarketshare.com/.

FIGURE 10.6b

Search Engine Market Share, Mobile and Tablet, July 2016

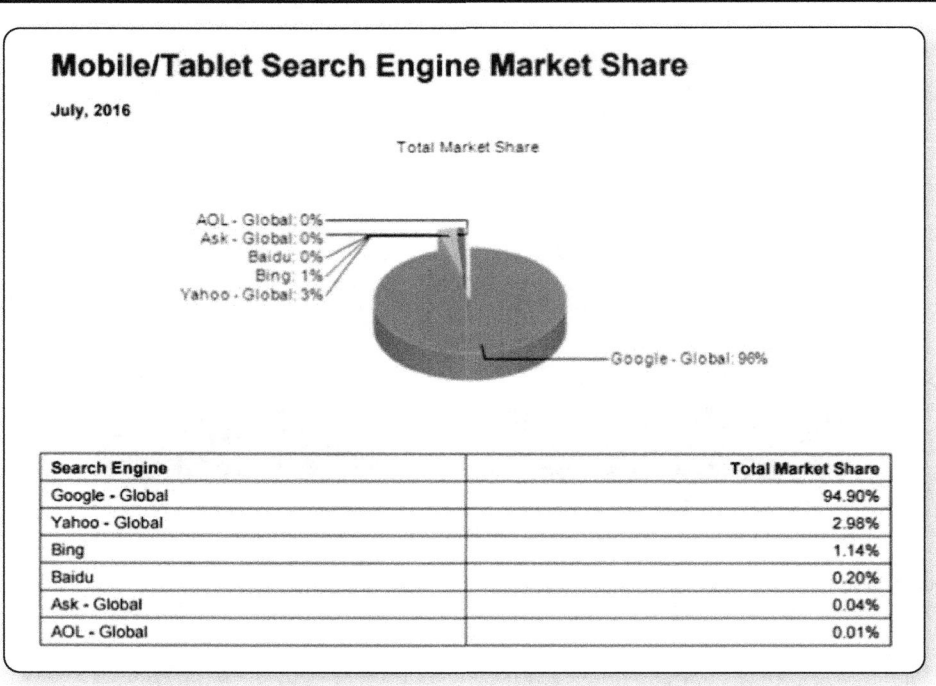

SOURCE: https://www.netmarketshare.com/.

FIGURE 10.7
Google versus Bing Search Results for Pink Purses

SOURCES: Google and Bing.

In a series of excellent articles in SearchEngineLand, Dave Davis outlines the three factors that website owners need to consider when designing their websites for search. These three factors (shown in Figure 10.8) are as follows:

- Technical
  - Indexing: Making sure the site is indexed for search
  - Single URL: Site should point back to a single source

FIGURE 10.8

Basic Approach to Search Engine Optimization

Technical	Content	Off-site SEO
• Indexing • Single URL • Sitemap • Working internal links • HTTPS • User Experience • Mobile Friendly • Page Speed • Keywords in URL • Above the fold Content	• Content with purpose • Content that attracts natural links and social signals like recency and number of social mentions • Keyword Research • Title tag and descriptions • Headings that define sections • Optimize content • Optimize images	• Google My Business listing • Name, address, phone consistency • Social media consistency • Backlinks (come from another website) • Domain name authority

SOURCE: Davis, Dave (2016) "Search Engine Land Definitive SEO Audit" Parts 1–3, https://searchEngineland.com.
1) http://searchengineland.com/definitive-seo-audit-part-1-3-technical-250541.   2) http://searchengineland.com/definitive-seo-audit-part-2-3-content-site-252492.   3) http://searchengineland.com/definitive-seo-audit-part-3-3-off-site-254344?utm_source=feedburner&utm_medium=feed&utm_campaign=feed-main.

- Sitemap: Aids in navigation
- Working internal links: Links should not be broken or redirect
- HTTPS (secure site designation)
- User experience: The number of click throughs generated by searches to that page and if the user stays on that page
- Page speed in terms of loading
- Keywords in URL that match the page
- Above the fold content that is relevant to the search

• Content

- Purposive content: Content that attracts natural links and social signal, such as recency of mention and number of social mentions (72 percent of marketers think that content is the most effective SEO technique)[23]
- Keywords: Should be consistent with the landing page and can aid search (48 percent of marketers favor this method)
- The HTML title tag (the title in the blue bar at the top of the page)
- Headings that define content
- Optimized content and images: Content relates to the subject and has meaning, and images have useful identifying tags and file names and a size that loads quickly

• Off-site SEO

- Consistency for name, address, and phone number across the web, including (for Google) a complete Google My Business listing
- Consistency across social media
- Backlinks: The number of other (legitimate) sites that link to the page
- Domain name authority

See what marketers think is important at: [http://www.marketingprofs.com/charts/2015/27941/marketers-favorite-seo-tactics-and-metrics]. An item that in the past has been considered important for inclusion in the rankings is the location and frequency (density) of keywords on the page. However, search engine optimization has become more complicated than that, particularly with the emphasis on *user intent* and the *user experience*. The user experience is how the user progresses on the site after clicking on the displayed search results. For example, if a user clicks on a result for "pink purses" and is directed to a general page for discount purchases for purses, the results from the search will not match her experience and she will quickly exit. The Google search engine in particular takes these experiences into account, particularly on mobile devices.

OPTIMIZING FOR ORGANIC SEARCH

Making organic search marketing more difficult is the fact that the search algorithms know quite a bit about users when they are searching and now deliver search results.

From the discussion in the last section, it sounds like it should be relatively easy to get a web page ranked highly on the major search engines. Simply choose the right keywords, stuff the page header and content pages with those keywords, and get ranked accordingly. There are three problems with that reasoning. First, it does not work that way. The search engine algorithms look for items, such as undue repetition of keywords, or, even worse, putting keywords on a page in an invisible way, for example, by making them the same color as the background. Second, if the search engines identify the site as an offender in terms of practices deliberately designed to trick them, they can refuse to rank it altogether. This practice is often referred to as "black hat" search.[24] Third, as stated above, the SEO process is more sophisticated now and content-driven.

As the definition of SEO suggests, practitioners try to work within the algorithms of the individual search engines to achieve the best possible ranking for the site or page on that particular search engine so their sites are listed at or near the top in the organic search listings. You may notice a problem here, however. Since the search engine algorithms are not disclosed, practitioners are working from what they believe the algorithms to be, based on their own experience and their own proprietary techniques for studying search engine rankings. This practice is not for amateurs, although nonprofessionals can certainly learn some of the main techniques and practice them.

Therefore, most practitioners of SEO follow the practices suggested here for maximizing their rankings. They start by understanding their target market and their intent in searching, developing keywords to reach that market, and defining and developing the content of their web and mobile pages around those keywords. In addition, it is important to use keywords you think are important in search engines and see if the type of company you are thinking of, yours or a competitor's, is displayed in the search results. For example, the term "dat" can be digital audio tape, the Dental Admissions Test, or the Danish Air Transport company.

The SEO Process

A good suggested process for beginning an SEO campaign is as follows:

1. Define the target market.
2. Find out what they search for and why they search.
3. Develop a search strategy: find keywords and phrases.
4. Develop a content strategy to align with the keyword strategy.
5. Redesign the site with those keywords and content in mind.
6. Register the site with search engines.
7. Implement a paid search campaign to complement or inform the organic search campaign (optional).

Starting with the customer and what they are looking for is critical and often overlooked. Sometimes search terms might be obvious and sometimes they might not. For example, there are several spray products based on Cherith Clark and Kirstin Stokes' 2008 book *Monster Spray* that produce an aroma that is supposed to convince young children that this spray eradicates or scares away monsters in their bedrooms at night. However, parents eager to allay their children's fears might not search for "monster spray" but rather search for their intention "my child is afraid of the dark," or "children afraid of the dark," or other related terms.

Even Coca-Cola[25] with its worldwide brand needed help with SEO strategies and worked with an agency to deploy a team that works internationally in 200 countries. The search tactics worked and the coca-colacompany.com set a record in 2010 of over 4 million visits, 1 million more visits than in 2009, and had good results in terms of company's return on investment (ROI). By taking its time to select and mange keywords on the site over multiple countries, Coca-Cola's organic search campaign delivers media impressions, traffic, and customer connections, particularly in one of its growing markets, China. The Coca-Cola content marketing strategy relies on "linked" and "liquid" content that can be shared and bring more users to the site.[26] We cover some tools that can help identify relevant keywords to help fuel success later in the chapter.

SEO Tools

Even when conducting an SEO campaign only, a number of tools exist to develop keywords. In addition, it is always a good idea to do market research and ask the customer how they search for your product. Looking at search trends and "hot keywords" is also a good way to select keywords. In addition, most search engines have keyword finder tools. Paid search sites also have a number of useful tools for free use that can help explore and narrow down keyword selection. One great tool available is the Keyword Tool in Google, which can be used either for free (with a credit card guarantee) or as part of the capabilities of a Google AdWords account.[27] It is also possible to access search volume information but not suggested bid strategies without a credit card. The tool shows how much competition there is for the term and the number of monthly global or local searches (local can be defined for a particular geographic area). The traffic estimator tool can then be used to give the bid estimator a better idea of how many clicks might be expected from that search term and the average CPC, or cost-per-click, to the online advertiser. This tool will be discussed in more detail in Chapter 11 and in the Appendix.

Once the proper terms have been identified, the site's title tag and content must be completely redesigned with the appropriate search terms in mind. It is a good idea to think of the top five or six terms and their variations that the company would like to be ranked on and to include those terms throughout the content of the site.

SEO Problems

In addition, many companies are unaware of these common problems in organic search that can depress search results, and it is a good idea to make note of them:

1. *Search engine spiders unable to navigate the website:* Flash is the single biggest barrier to the spiders. A Flash Player is a web browser plug-in that allows images such as videos to display on a website. The problem is that spiders cannot read these images. Opening a website entry page with video can be a problem because spiders will not know how to categorize your website. Images in general, even photos, can pose a problem for spiders and using Alt tags to describe the image can aid in SEO.
2. *No site map on website:* A detailed and accurate site map provides important assistance to the spiders. Laying out the site in an easy manner means all pages can be crawled and indexed by search engines.

3. *Nonoptimized navigation structure:* The spiders need to be able to move through the site, understand the HTML code, and determine how to best index it. Anything that makes it difficult, like the extraneous HTML code inserted by some of the website development tools, impedes their progress.
4. *Diluted link popularity of key category/product pages:* Links are important to ranking. However, they need to be relevant and represent a real relationship to the topic of the main site.

The Google Algorithm(s)

Fixing these problems can improve search rankings. However, please note that improving rankings may take several months for the changes to be made and for initial results to be seen. Michael Laps outlined these changes on the YoghurtDigital blog as follows:

> Panda (2011): Made it less easy to engage in "black hat" SEO practices and now part of Google's core algorithm. The algorithm targeted pages with poor quality and duplicate or irrelevant content.
>
> Penguin (2012): Focused on websites that were buying links such as "link farms". Such practices are employed by companies that resort to activity that, while not illegal, may be unethical and artificially raise organic search results. These companies pay to have thousands of links placed on hundreds of sites leading directly to their firm, aiming for search engines to perceive these links as valuable and raise the ranking of the site. Another example that Google perceived as a black hat practice was a firm that provided incentives for colleges and universities (typically perceived as "authority" links by search engines) to link to a particular site.
>
> Hummingbird (2013): Used Penguin and Pigeon but is essentially a new algorithm, which focused on *intent* behind the search, paying attention to each word in a query rather than keywords.
>
> Pigeon (nickname not given by Google) (2014): Upgraded accuracy and relevance of *local search* results. Especially impacts Google maps.
>
> Mobile Friendly (2015): Gave preferences to mobile-friendly pages.[28]

In spite of algorithm changes, some easy ways to rank in natural search include the following:

- *The URL or domain name:* The uniform resource locator (URL) itself should be descriptive of the firm and consistent with how a firm wants to be found. Being around for a long time and having a search history will also help.
- *Title tag, also known as the HTML title tag* (the title seen in the blue bar at the top of the page): Many companies ignore the title tag, which should include a company description and the most important search terms or keywords. A good example to follow would be to include the keyword portion first (how the firm wants to be found), followed by the branding portion (firm name or description), and to keep the title page tag short (70 or 71 characters depending on pixel width) so it can be read when it displays on search engines. An example is "University of Texas System | Fourteen Institutions. Unlimited Possibilities." Those looking for schools in the University of Texas System can see that they have many choices when deciding to enroll as the branding portion of the tag.
- *Domain name authority:* Domain name authority is the extent to which that domain name is considered to be a reputable website in a particular category. Authority comes from good behavior over time and includes the length of time links have pointed to the site and the overall authority of those sites. For example, universities, charities, and governmental agencies are in general considered to have high authority.[29]

The Top Ranking Factors on Google

However, the most recent information seems to indicate that the simpler ways of ranking highly in organic search are no longer the most influential. In fact, it appears that the most important elements of the Google algorithm are content, links, and RankBrain. Content and links are both important and neither one is given precedence, according to Google. All three elements are described below and illustrated in Figure 10.9.

- *Content:* Content includes quality and relevance to the desired search topic as well as the location and frequency (density) of keywords on the page. Certainly Google places a lot of emphasis on quality content but it is sometimes hard to determine what is meant by quality. Decide what terms are important and rewrite the page content to reflect those terms. Do not just focus on written content, although this content should contain relevant references to desired keywords. Videos and blogs are likely to improve the search ranking considerably because the search engines look upon these activities favorably, presumably because of the web traffic and links that they produce.
- *Links:* The number of other sites that link to the page, the number of pages the site links to, and their relevancy to keywords and search phrases are most important for the site. Not only the quantity but also the quality of the links is significant for search engines. It is easy to create relevant outbound links and less easy to get sites to link to you (also known as a backlink). However, backlinks are important to SEO. Authority links as previously mentioned, directory links, real-time links from blogs, and social bookmarking links all increase the chances of a high search ranking. It is estimated that 33 percent of search ranking comes from link activity, including links to blogs and social media.
- *RankBrain:* This process is related to voice usage and is a machine learning query enhancement tool. The tool can match queries to results pages taking into account relevance and the context of the search and reorder queries, looking at the context. Machine learning will no doubt play an even bigger part in search in the future as search engine firms seek to match queries to results from a relevance perspective.

FIGURE 10.9
Top Three SEO Influencers per Google

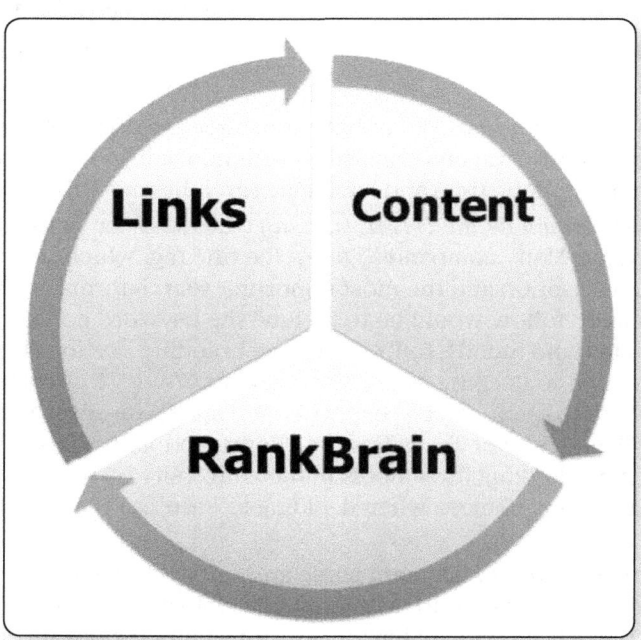

SOURCE: 1) http://searchengineland.com/now-know-googles-top-three-search-ranking-factors-245882.
2) https://youtu.be/I8VnZCcI9J4.

An Optimization Example

Ranking a site for SEO is therefore challenging and requires constant vigilance. The ebags.com site in Figure 10.10 illustrates some of the points listed above for optimizing for natural search. (To follow along with this exercise, go to the site and search for "pink purses.") Hover over the SERP tab in any browser (Explorer

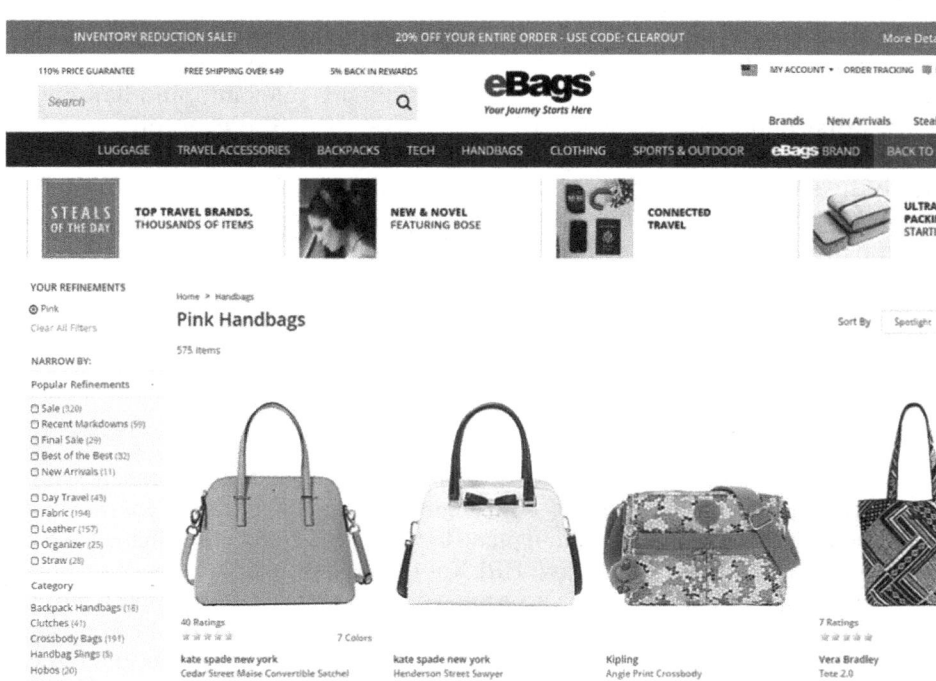

FIGURE 10.10
Optimizing the Site for SEO

(a) Search for Pink Purses on ebags.com Site Using Google **Chrome**

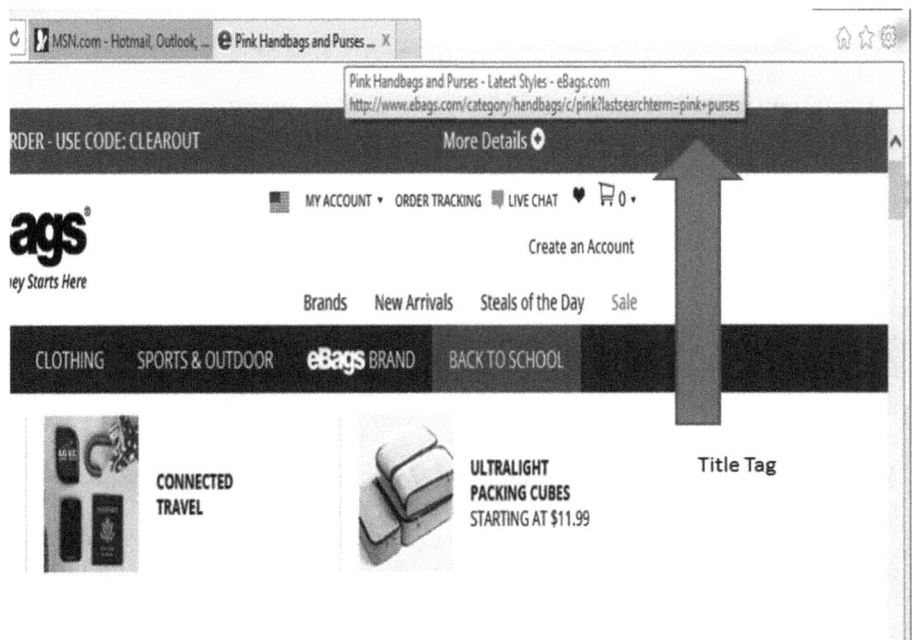

(b) How to View a Title Tag in Internet Explorer

SOURCE: http://www.ebags.com.

is shown here) to find the title tag in the HTML code displayed. The company's general URL is ebags.com. The title tag "Pink Handbags and Purses - Latest Styles - eBags.com" repeats the URL ebags.com although this landing page URL is customized for this search as http://www.ebags.com/category/handbags/c/pink based on the last search term of pink purses. This title tag also includes both a keyword piece (Pink Handbags and Purses) and a branding piece; one of the company's differentiating features, "Latest Styles." This tag line is not repeated in the site content on the first page, though it would be nice if it were to reinforce branding and optimize search. What the site does provide is a relevant landing page URL (http://www.ebags.com/category/handbags/c/pink) where the inquiry of "pink" is already listed as a filter and the search results are relevant, pink handbags. It appears that depending on what the site knows about the user, different information will be served on the page. For example, since this was the author's first visit to the site, it is possible that the big discount coupon offer of 20 percent at the top of the page was directed to her. The travel accessories links could result from the fact that she had just checked in to a flight online. This site appears optimized for search in many ways, which is why it is in the top five of the searches for "pink purses." However, since search is ever-changing, there is always room for improvement.

Other Considerations in SEO

Once the SEO changes are in place according to our suggested process, it is a good idea to register the site with major search engines, especially if the site has never been registered before. Of course the main place to register is Google because of the large volume of searches. Google's "Crawl URL Tool" says, "Google adds new sites to our index, and updates existing ones, every time we crawl the web. If you have a new URL, tell us about it here. We don't add all submitted URLs to our index, and we can't make predictions or guarantees about when or if submitted URLs will appear in our index." In other words, submitting the site might not mean being added to the index. Conversely, not submitting doesn't mean the site will not be indexed if it is perceived as important by search sites. It is most important to submit the site to the major search engines but less important to submit to the hundreds of other minor search engines. There are firms which will charge money to do so, but since organic search traffic is concentrated and some of the search sites share information anyway (like Bing and Yahoo!), submitting to hundreds of search sites is unnecessary.

Although the information above gives the tried and true information about search, there have been many changes in the recent algorithm (estimates range that there are 500 changes per day).[30] Certain other trends are affecting how websites and mobile sites can maximize their impact.

1. Voice search: As voice search, particularly on mobile devices, increases, RankBrain and semantic search will become more prominent.
2. User experience: Sometimes called user intention, this trend means that now search engines are seeing what happens beyond the click. If a person clicks on a site as a response to a query, the search engines will look to see if the person got what was needed and stayed on the site or left quickly.
3. Meaningful content length: Formerly, SEO experts would recommend short pages and blog posts. Today, the recommended for articles is 1,200 to 1,500 words, because these articles fit better in search and average word count on pages has increased to reflect that trend.[31] There are more words and images to rank on the page. As always, use subheadings, bullets, and images to make it easy to move through the pages. Tag images so spiders can index them.
4. Local intent: Local search is more complex than traditional search, with users starting with a general search and then moving along a path that might include directories, customer reviews, and coupons, sometimes taking four or five

actions and depending on mobile devices for the results.[32] Generally, less than 40 percent of local searches start with a search engine, so marketers in local businesses such as restaurants must depend on coupons, customer reviews, and local directories in their marketing tactics.
5. Video content and unique images: Search results now include videos and images to which users respond. Creating video and unique image content makes it easier to be found.
6. Mobile optimization: Search engines like Google now make sure that a mobile site is optimized for mobile devices and are more likely to serve that site up in a search if it is.
7. Social content ranking: Search engines are looking for not only your participation on social media but also how much others engage with your posts and other content.
8. Beyond keywords: In the past, SEO experts recommended repeated keyword in the body copy and the headline and even the meta description. Now, search engines are responding to more than single keywords and looking at related search. For example, people tend to search for multiple words, that is, "Mexican restaurants in Austin" and not just Mexican restaurants. Also search engines are looking for related terms. For a "Fibit," related terms might be "activity" and "tracker" and "health" and "monitor." A search for activity tracker reveals a paid ad but also blogs and magazine articles that rate the various devices. All of this again illustrates the power of content.
9. SEO as part of an inbound marketing plan: SEO needs to be seen as pulling users in to the brand and should include optimizing landing pages.

Another trend worth mentioning is vertical search, a type of specialty search. According to the *San Francisco Chronicle*, "By going vertical, search engine companies hope to reduce extraneous results for users by better guessing user intent. A query for 'great white'—the name for an '80s rock band and a shark species—can get very different results on Google compared with an engine that specializes in academic material. In other words, if you are on the academic search engine, you are going to get the listings for the shark species, not the rock band. The specialty search engine attempts to narrow the user intent. The user went to the academic search engine with a purpose—or so the search engine assumes.

Vertical search engines also can ask questions more quickly. Shopping search engines, for example, can ask up front the color, size and manufacturer of what you want to buy."[33] Some of the other types of search engines are as follows:

- Topical search: such as worldwidescience.org and WebMD
- Industry search: such as business.com and chemindustry.com
- Image search: such as Picsearch, Yahoo!, and Image Search
- News search: such as NewsNow and onlinenewspapers.com
- Blog search: such as blog-search.com
- Books and articles search: such as Google Scholar
- Social real-time search: such as Twitter Search

It is not hard to see that vertical search engines have sprung up all over the place and are of benefit to mobile users looking for something particular at a given time. There are search engines devoted to travel and others devoted to shopping, as only a few examples. The major search engines also allow for searching on images, videos, and places, among other topics. There are other types of search being introduced into the internet marketspace and as long as vertical search engines can meet the need for relevant search results, the market will continue to grow. For example, YouTube as a stand-alone company from Google is the second largest search engine in the world.

ORGANIC AND PAID SEARCH WORK TOGETHER

Before we move to the discussion of paid search in the next chapter, we would like to discuss the role of paid search in developing an organic search campaign. It is often quite useful to employ a paid search campaign before, after, or during the development of an organic search campaign to determine which keywords should be used to optimize the site for paid search. A paid search campaign can be used to finely target terms for an organic search campaign. In other words, it is useful to use paid search terms where the site is not showing up as strongly in the organic search rankings as was hoped. Equally, once the SEO campaign is successful and showing results, the terms for which the site is ranked the highest naturally can be considered as candidates for paid search. Landing page copy can also be used in paid search ads. In any case, the two campaigns should ideally work together.

iCrossing found a synergy between paid and natural search. If the keywords purchased by paid search were also ranked in natural search, clicks increased by 92 percent, time on the site increased by 39 percent, and orders increased by 45 percent.[34]

It can legitimately be said that "search is search" and that both types of campaigns should work together.[35] In the prelaunch phase, the keywords can be used to develop a consistent site message. A consistent message and the intelligent use of keywords on the site help improve the quality score during the campaign execution phase. During the reporting and analysis phase, the results of each type of search should be compared and paid keywords should be refined based on input from both the paid and organic search campaigns.

MOBILE SEARCH IS OUTPACING DESKTOP

It is clear that marketers must learn to optimize their web pages and their search capabilities for the mobile market. The year 2015 was a benchmark year in that more than half of digital ad spending (over $15 billion) in the United States was spent on mobile devices.[36] This figure highlights the shift to searching on mobile devices. For a while Google was highlighting "mobile friendly sites" as part of its AMP (Accelerated Mobile Pages) project as a way of signaling how important mobile websites were to search. The project rewards in search results those sites which are "responsive" or adaptable to different mobile devices in terms of the user experience. Although the "mobile friendly" label is going away, search engines such as Google will continue to reward mobile sites that are optimized for search.[37] The reason is that more than half of searches take place on mobile devices in countries such as the United States and Japan.[38] In addition, about half of those queries have local intent, or about 14 billion queries. Therefore, marketers may need to change their strategies in SEO to accommodate the terms that searchers would use "on the go." Also, specific vertical markets have benefitted from mobile, including restaurants, autos, consumer electronics, finance, insurance, beauty, and personal services and will continue to do so. Companies such as Groupon that provide searches and special offers related to local markets will also play a role in the expansion of local search, meaning that local and mobile search will continue to grow hand-in-hand for the foreseeable future.

However, the mobile search market will continue to experience growing pains as marketers adjust their marketing techniques to this new medium. SEO Clarity's 2014 mobile organic search study that analyzed over 2 million impressions and 2.6 million clicks, which revealed that the first position in organic search received a 19.3 percent click-through rate as compared to a 27.7 percent rate on mobile devices. However, the drop off on mobile devices for the second position is dramatic, from 27.7 percent to 9.2 percent. These data underline the importance of ranking number one in mobile searches. Mobile searchers are even less likely, in the moment while they are searching, than desktop searchers, to scroll down to the tenth search position.[39] Note that in spite of the increased traffic, conversion rate and average order value is typically still lower from searches from mobile devices than desktop devices (see Figure 10.11). Check out the latest statistics on conversion rate and order value at the IBM BenchmarkLIVE site.

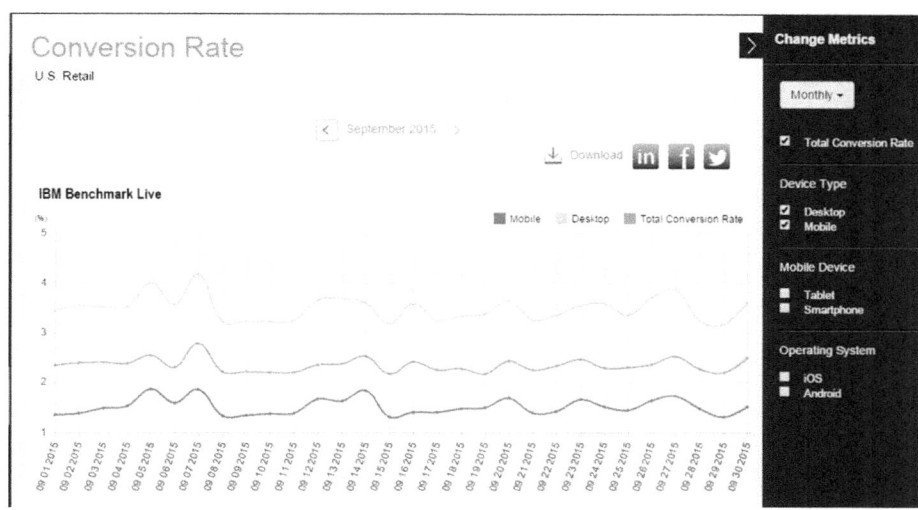

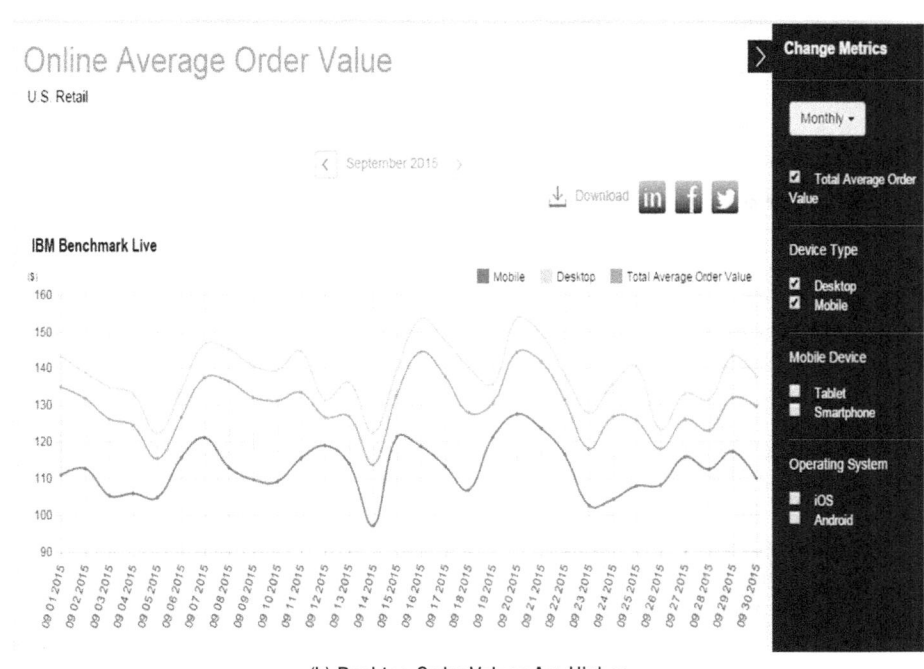

FIGURE 10.11
Desktop and Mobile Conversion Rates and Average Order Size

(a) Desktop Conversion Rates Are Higher

(b) Desktop Order Values Are Higher

THE RELATIONSHIP BETWEEN SEARCH AND SOCIAL MEDIA

This chapter would not be complete without a few more words about the integration of search and social media. Social media continues to capture the interest of digital marketers for the good reason that consumers are on social media. Figure 10.12 shows the relationship between search and social media. Search marketers are expanding their use of social media by driving inbound links from social media forums, expanding their profiles on social media accounts, and monitoring social media conversations to influence SEO. Marketers want to be where their consumers are and to participate in the conversation to engage and retain those customers. A study by business.com and BtoB Online in 2010, written by the author but no longer available online, indicated that the best-performing companies in a survey of 464

FIGURE 10.12
Use Social Media to Enhance SEO

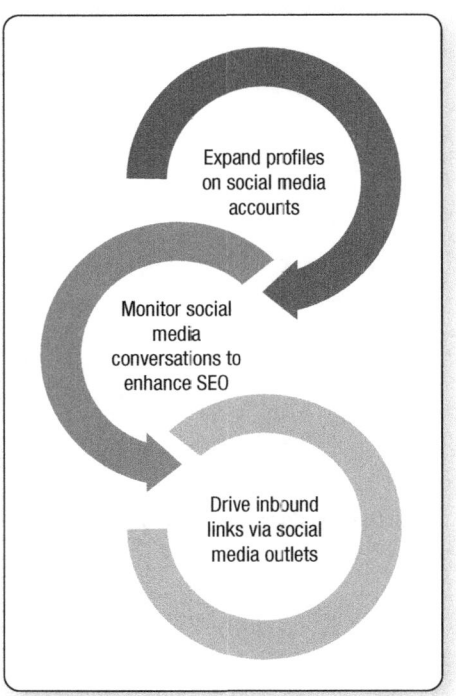

SOURCE: http://www-01.ibm.com/software/marketing-solutions/benchmark-hub.

business-to-business (B2B) online marketers were using social media to enhance their natural search efforts. Enhancement for these firms was accomplished by expanding the profiles on social media accounts, monitoring social media conversations to influence SEO, and driving inbound links via various social media outlets. Increasing the number of social media followers and encouraging them to share your content in all channels will also impact search rankings.[40] This trend will only continue in years to come.

Monitoring social media conversations is another great way to determine how to pick appropriate keywords to monitor both paid search and SEO. Using tools such as Salesforce For example, Radian6 marketers can see what and how customers and prospects are talking about it across the social web and develop search marketing campaigns based on this input. Google's social search capability means that searches conducted while signed into Google will highlight relevant content from social connections, including websites, blogs, images, and other contacts created by or shared by your social connections. Web content that has been recommended using the +1 button in Google plus will also be highlighted. Other search engines have or will have adopted a similar strategy regarding integrating social media "likes" into organic search results. Since marketers know that consumers trust recommendations of friends more than those of advertisers, the future will bring about an even greater integration between search and social media. Another related trend will be the integration of display advertising into the results of search campaigns.

SUMMARY

Search is a key focus of internet marketers at present. Other customer acquisition techniques, however, continue to evolve and remain an important part of the marketer's toolkit. Since the size of the web increases by many pages each day, the importance of search to users, B2C and B2B alike, can hardly be overstated. Because it is important to internet users, marketers and advertisers are close behind. While search has a growing impact and can be confusing for marketers to understand, the basic concept is simple.

Search engines send out spiders or crawlers that look at websites and categorize them to create indices that are used in specific search queries. The marketer needs to think about what words its customers or prospects use when trying to find a product or service. There are a number of free tools that can be used to develop these keywords. Relevant keywords can then be used in both organic and paid search. Organic search is sometimes called natural search or algorithmic search, as it depends on algorithms that are developed by commercial search engines to find the most relevant web pages to display as the result of a search query.

In organic search, content, links, and RankBrain contribute most to success, but the savvy marketer needs to pay attention to technical items such as using relevant keywords in the title bar of a website and content issues such as the website content to raise the ranking of the page as the result of a query. Other off-site SEO techniques to optimize the website include links from and to the page and the overall authority the page commands.

The search process as a whole is iterative and is "never done" as the search engines are constantly updating their algorithms and the bidding for keywords changes daily, if not hourly. The field offers a good opportunity for employment and a steady prospect for growth as new aspects of search are developed.

One can expect two levels of change to affect SEM in the years to come. At a granular level, the search engines themselves will continue to tweak their algorithms to provide more relevant results. Search engine marketers will continue to scramble to keep up with those changes. At the level of the overall search marketplace, innovations like such as vertical, local, social, mobile search, and others yet unseen will continue to proliferate and impact the ever-changing search landscape.

DISCUSSION QUESTIONS

1. Why do you think search has become such an important part of the life of internet users?
2. What options do marketers have when it comes to developing a search marketing strategy?
3. What are the three most impactful elements of a website in terms of optimizing a site for organic search and why are they important?
4. How come the major search engines do not publish their algorithms?
5. Compare the two searches in Figure 10.7. Which produces the better results in terms of quality and relevance? Why?
6. Why do paid and natural search work so well together?
7. How do search strategies differ for mobile devices?
8. Why is local search likely to be important in the future? What other trends are likely in organic search?

ENDNOTES

1. Deborah Fallows and Lee Rainie, "The Popularity and Importance of Search Engines," August 2004, http://www.pewinternet.org.
2. http://www.digitalistmag.com/customer-experience/2016/05/06/100-amazing-marketing-stats-you-need-to-know-in-2016-04163557.
3. http://www.adweek.com/socialtimes/81-shoppers-conduct-online-research-making-purchase-infographic/208527.

4. Source: http://connect.relevance.com/hubfs/2015_State_of_Search_Industry_Report.pdf
5. http://www.pewinternet.org/Reports/2011/Search-and-email/Report.aspx, retrieved September 24, 2011.
6. http://www.pewinternet.org/2012/03/09/search-engine-use-2012/.
7. http://searchengineland.com/data-show-search-query-volumes-pc-peaked-2013-245663, https://theoverspill.wordpress.com/2015/10/19/searches-average-mobile-google-problem/.
8. SEMPO, "The State of Search Engine Marketing 2004," http://www.sempo.org.
9. http://www.emarketer.com/Article/US-Digital-Display-Ad-Spending-Surpass-Search-Ad-Spending-2016/1013442.
10. http://www.sempo.org/?page=currentstateofsearch.
11. http://searchengineland.com/survey-under-40-percent-start-a-local-search-with-a-search-engine-240426.
12. http://www.ecommerceoptimization.com/local-business-listing-guide.
13. http://dmoz.org.
14. http://www.sempo.org/?page=glossary#s.
15. SEMPO, "The State of Search Engine Marketing 2004," http://www.sempo.org, 4.
16. http://searchengineland.com/adobe-paid-search-spend-growth-slowed-in-q4-mobile-continued-to-eat-into-desktop-241366.
17. Forrester titled, "How Consumers Find Websites in 2011—Trends to Consider for Your 2011 Strategy, Shar VanBoskirk, as quoted in http://www.marqui.com/blog/how-do-consumers-find-websites-in-2011.aspx.
18. http://www.forbes.com/sites/jaysondemers/2016/01/20/is-keyword-density-still-important-for-seo/2/#7e09c80e6733.
19. https://askleo.com/if-an-ip-address-doesnt-do-it-then-how-does-google-know-my-location/.
20. http://www.webpresencesolutions.net/7-reasons-google-search-results-vary-dramatically/.
21. http://www.emarketer.com/Article/How-Much-Search-Traffic-Actually-Comes-Googling/1011814.
22. https://www.woodst.com/seo-social-media-marketing/seo-do-keywords-and-meta-tags-still-matter/.
23. http://www.marketingprofs.com/charts/2015/27941/marketers-favorite-seo-tactics-and-metrics
24. http://www.beanstalk-inc.com/tactics/black-hat.htm.
25. https://www.adforum.com/agency/6655036/creative-work/34479067/drinking-global-thinking-local/coca-cola Retrived December 15, 2016
26. https://www.youtube.com/watch?v=LerdMmWjU_E.
27. https://adwords.google.com/home/tools/keyword-planner/ retrieved December 15, 2016.
28. https://www.yoghurtdigital.com.au/insights/every-google-algorithm-change-explained, https://www.rankranger.com/google-algorithm-updates.
29. http://searchenginewatch.com/article/2064461/SEO-Link-Building-The-Domain-Authority-Factor, retrieved October 29, 2011.
30. https://www.ama.org/publications/MarketingNews/Pages/seo-rules-2016.aspx, https://www.ama.org/publications/MarketingNews/Pages/seo-rules-2016.aspx.
31. http://www.searchmetrics.com/news-and-events/searchmetrics-ranking-factors-2015/, http://www.webpresencesolutions.net/150-digital-marketing-seo-statistics-2016/.
32. Source: http://searchengineland.com/survey-under-40-percent-start-a-local-search-with-a-search-engine-240426.
33. Verne Kopytoff, "New Search Engines Narrowing Their Focus," April 4, 2005, http://www.sfgate.com/cgi-bin/article.cgi?file=/c/a/2005/04/04/BUGJ9C20VU1.DTL&type=printable.

34. http://www.scribd.com/doc/2235975/icrossing-search-synergy.
35. http://searchenginewatch.com/article/2067308/Search-is-Search-Paid-and-Organic-Search-Synergies, retrieved October 29, 2011.
36. http://www.emarketer.com/Article/Mobile-Account-More-than-Half-of-Digital-Ad-Spending-2015/1012930.
37. http://venturebeat.com/2016/08/23/google-search-removes-mobile-friendly-label-will-start-negatively-ranking-mobile-interstitials-in-2017/.
38. http://screenwerk.com/2015/05/11/data-suggest-that-local-intent-queries-nearly-half-of-all-search-volume/.
39. http://www.seoclarity.net/mobile-desktop-ctr-study-11302/.
40. http://img.en25.com/Web/BusinessCom/Search%20and%20%20Social%20Integration_2921.pdf?elqIsAgent=True%2cTrue, retrieved November 21, 2011.

Chapter 11

Paid Search and Social Advertising

LEARNING OBJECTIVES

By the time you complete this chapter, you will be able to:

1. Understand the growing impact of paid search and social advertising.
2. Explain the impact of mobile technology on the search process.
3. Understand the process to implement a paid search campaign.
4. Understand the basic format of AdWords text ads and match types.
5. Understand the other forms of paid advertising on Google.
6. Understand the difference between Google search and display networks.
7. Identify basic display ad formats used on Google, Facebook, and other major social platforms.
8. Understand the process of creating a display ad on Facebook.
9. Explain the nature of a promoted post.
10. Discuss issues in choosing the best platforms on which to place paid search and social advertising.

THE GROWING IMPACT OF PAID SEARCH AND MOBILE TECHNOLOGY

Search marketing is the heart of the web because it allows advertisers to be in front of the customer at the exact moment they are researching a product or service or considering purchase. Although we may not know exactly who the customer is at the point they see our organization or firm listed on the results of a search, we do know

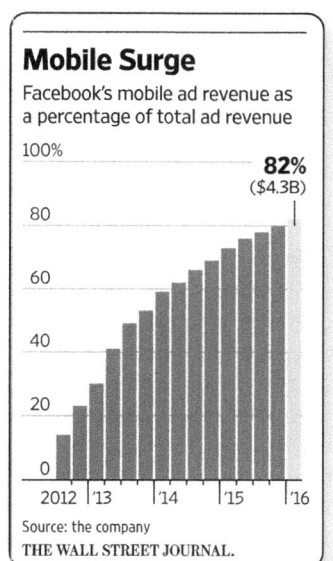

FIGURE 11.1
Facebook's Mobile Ad Revenue Soars

SOURCE: http://www.wsj.com/articles/facebook-revenue-soars-on-ad-growth-1461787856.

what they are interested in at the moment. With 94 percent of all B2B product inquires beginning with search,[1] and 81 percent of online shoppers searching online before they make a purchase, advertisers know that search is important.[2] In fact, advertisers spend much of their energy on search engine marketing, both paid and organic. The search industry is by itself a 40 billion dollar industry and growing, with job opportunities abounding.

When we consider that in 2016[3] more than half of digital advertising was spent on mobile devices, we understand that much of what is driving paid search now is mobile technology. In fact Google recently revamped its paid text ad formats in response to the market pressure and the growth of mobile advertising and is reconsidering its other ad formats as well. All of Google's new formats are more mobile friendly, displaying more copy and easier to read on a mobile device.

Google's concern stems in part from the fact that Facebook has 12 percent of the $186.8 billion global digital-advertising market, up from 10.7 percent in 2015 and 8.6 percent in 2014, according to data firm eMarketer.[4] In contrast, Google's market share was projected to decline to 31 percent in 2016 from 33 percent in 2015 and 35 percent in 2014. While that figure is still a sizeable percentage of the search market, Google is concerned. Facebook's ad revenue is soaring (see Figure 11.1) and increased 57 percent in the first quarter of 2016, growing to $5.2 billion from $3.3 billion. Even more telling is that mobile ads, which typically are more expensive and yield higher revenue, were roughly four-fifths of that revenue. Clearly, mobile searching and shopping habits have had a dramatic impact on the paid search industry.

PPC OR PAID SEARCH DEFINED

So what exactly is paid search? **PPC** involves "ads targeted to keyword search results on search engines, through programs such as Google™ AdWords are sometimes referred to as PPC advertising and Cost-per-Click (CPC) advertising."[5] In this section we will focus on AdWords as Google has the largest market share of the traditional search engines. Search advertising is growing on social networks, as more and more users spend their time on those networks. Please note that these days ads can take many formats, from the traditional text ad to video, to "call only" ads to shopping ads with high-quality images. Other formats were discussed in Chapter 7 and formats unique to paid advertising on social media platforms will be discussed in the last half of this chapter.

Whatever format is used, the paid aspect of SEM is also called **paid search** and is based on an auction model. In this model, firms seeking to rank highly in specific search categories will bid on certain terms or "keywords" in the hopes of a lucrative search ranking. Winning the auction usually means being displayed higher in search results, although search engines will take other factors such as the relevance of the ad into account.

paid search the paid aspect of SEM based on an advertising model where firms seeking to rank high in specific search categories will bid on certain terms or "keywords" in the hopes of a lucrative ad ranking; also known as PPC (pay-per-click).

In this section we will focus on creating and placing ads in Google AdWords. As with other forms of SEM, the objective of using AdWords is to attract the attention of that specific user when he or she is actively searching for information about the business's products or services, and bring him or her to its website. Google tries to find the best "match" based on the search terms used by the customer, and the keywords the advertiser associates with those search queries and the match is not just based on winning the auction.

With well-chosen keywords and appealing ad copy, advertisers can attract consumers who are searching for a specific product or service that they sell. The advertiser pays only when someone clicks on its ad, making AdWords a cost-effective means of advertising for some businesses and nonprofits. A lucrative ranking is one that makes money for the firm and is not necessarily the number one or two spot on the page. Sometimes a number two or three spot will be just as profitable for the firm. Whether or not a spot is profitable depends on the number of clicks, the CPC, and the revenue obtained from the advertisement.

Advertisers understandably want the most noticeable position in the results from a customer's search query. Certainly one of the few top spots on the page is preferred. Google decides on a company's ad position among all its advertisers based on its **Ad Rank**. The ad with the highest Ad Rank gets shown in the top position, and so on.

The Ad Rank depends on the following:

- The bid for each keyword, that is, CPC.
- The **Quality Score**—how relevant an ad and website links are to the person who will see the ad.
- The expected impact from **ad extensions** and other ad formats. Adding additional information, such as a phone number or links to specific pages is a feature called ad extensions. Adding these features to an ad may impact the attractiveness of an ad to customers.

ad extensions provide additional information with the ad such as a phone number, locations and reviews and can increase the click-through rate.

The **Quality Score** in turn depends on the following:

- Expected click-through rate
- Ad relevance
- Ad extension relevance
- Landing page experience, for example, how long the viewer dwells on the page and website, or "bounces" out quickly

The matching process starts with a query from someone using the Google search engine. When someone searches for something on the internet, Google tries to match the term the searcher uses with the most relevant terms (keywords) used by AdWords advertisers. The AdWords ads with the most relevance to that specific query get more prominent placement in the search results. Google determines if there will be an auction for the advertisers' ad placements in the search results, that is, which ad is shown in which order, on which page, and so on.

How does Google determine "relevance" in the Quality Score? That information is a closely guarded secret so that advertisers do not "game" the system, which might result in less relevant ads placed higher in search results. (Google assumes that irrelevant ads annoy users and therefore make them less likely to click on revenue-generating ads.) In general, "relevance" is determined by a combination of the past **click-through-rate (CTR)**, text-matching relevance, cookies, and the associations to the landing page, such as related business partners with strong connections to the search query. Google will downgrade the Quality Score if there are few click-throughs, quick "bounces," indicating little relevance to the searcher, and/or intentional advertiser manipulation of the search result process. As such, it is possible that no ads will appear if Google determines that none would satisfy the viewer's criteria, as evaluated by its Ad Rank, a value used to determine the ad's position. The main components of Ad Rank are bid and Quality Score. For example, even if an advertiser is the highest bidder on a its ads may not show if there is a poor match between the ad and the landing page. Conversely, another advertiser's ads with a higher Quality Score might appear even if they bid slightly less. Also included in Ad Rank is the impact of ad extensions and specific ad formats.

click-through-rate (CTR) Click-through-rate.

Advertisers identify keywords they want to bid on and how much they want to spend overall. The keywords are paired with AdWords ads the advertisers want displayed. Google then enters the keyword from the advertiser's account it deems most relevant into the auction, with the maximum bid specified, as well as the associated ad. Thus, if an advertiser wants to improve the position of its ad in the search results, it can increase the bid or improve the Quality Score of the ad, or both.[6]

THE PAID SEARCH PROCESS

The paid search process is similar in most of the major web browsers and revolves around bidding on keywords that are entered in when a user searches the web. The keywords that are bid on may or may not be the same keywords that are entered into the HTML on the advertiser's website, but there should be a relationship between the website "landing page" and the keyword term bid on in the campaign. The term "keyword" is the same as in organic search, but the purpose is quite different. In paid search, the company or individual engaged in paid search selects a number of keywords, usually at least 20 for each ad that will then be displayed in the paid search results. Figure 11.2 shows the results of a Google search

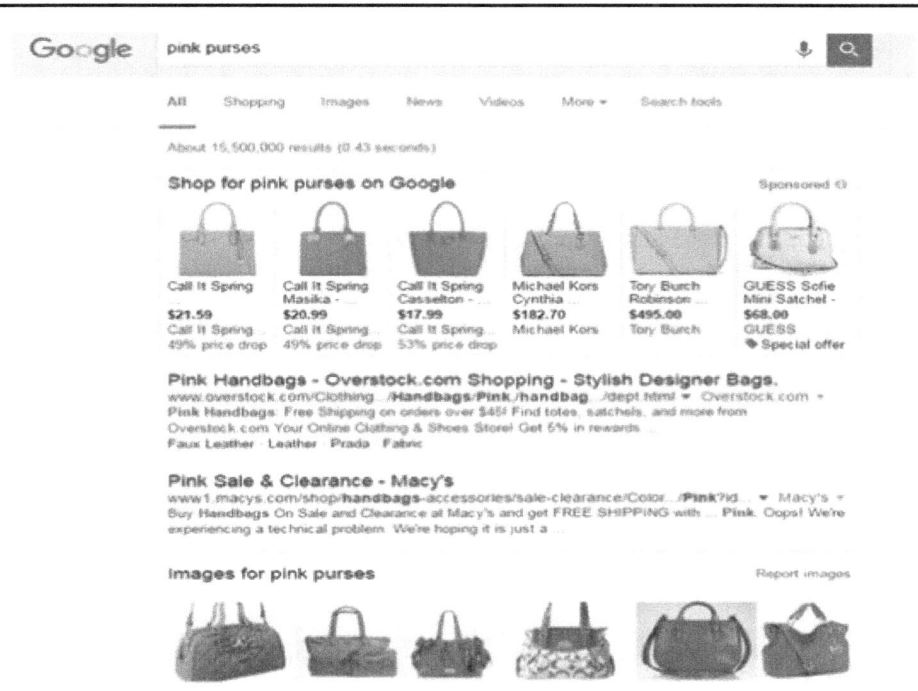

FIGURE 11.2

Google Search Results for Pink Purses Fall 2016

SOURCE: Google.

for "pink purses" in the Fall of 2016, with paid advertisements across the top of the page and organic results beneath. The hope of the paid search advertiser is that enough searchers will click on the ad to more than make up the cost of paying for the advertisement. Paid advertisements in the past used to be on the side of the page, but as our knowledge of how people browse on a web page has improved, Google has moved the ads to the places where people's "eyeballs" are most likely to scan a web page for content.

Each keyword will have a separate price that is based on its popularity. Some keywords may be priced out of the range of smaller advertisers. Some categories dominated by larger companies, such as auto insurance price quotes or mortgage loan rates, may have keywords on some days that cost over $10 per click. Other categories may, however, appear to be quite cheap and have a minimum bid of 25 cents. On some search engines, the minimum bid will actually be the lowest amount paid. Google, however, may set a higher minimum based on the popularity of the word, and often times the minimum bids suggested in AdWords is not the final minimum bid in the campaign.

In these sections, we use Google for our paid search examples because the company is the largest search firm and dominates paid search. Display advertising was discussed in Chapter 7 and social media sites and other forms of paid advertising will be covered in the rest of the chapter. Another reason to focus on Google for this paid search section is because the company has a number of programs that benefit undergraduate students hoping to make a career in digital and interactive marketing. One of the programs run by Google which may be of interest to students is a program known as the Google Online Marketing Challenge (GOMC)[7] (see Appendix A). The GOMC is an international challenge. Students work with real companies or nongovernmental organizations that have never used paid advertising from Google before and receive a $250 advertising budget. Over a three-week period, they work to optimize the PPC campaign of these organizations. The second program of interest to students is the ability to obtain certification in the AdWords tool itself. Individuals may learn about the tool in-depth and take certification exams by becoming a Google Partner. Certification should help everyone, including students, improve their chances of finding and doing well in a job in paid search. The Appendix outlines how to do well in the GOMC. Becoming a Google partner and obtaining certification is recommended before participating in the challenge to get the most out of the experience.[8]

However, there are a number of other search engines offering paid search, such as Bing and Yahoo! and sites such as Facebook also offer paid search advertisement and have separate tools to manage their campaigns. All of these tools model themselves to some extent on Google.

Google AdWords is an online platform that enables advertisers to display brief advertising copy to web users. AdWords is based on pay-per-click (PPC), or the cost-per-click (CPC) that the advertiser is willing to pay to "win" the top ad placement locations when users enter a search query into Google's search engine. This process is in contrast to SEO strategies discussed earlier in the text that rely solely on the "natural," or "organic" relationships of the search queries to the advertiser's keywords, aside from any bidding process or other forms of paid advertising.

As stated above, Google's platform for placing and managing PPC advertising programs is called Google AdWords. When embarking on a paid search campaign, remember that the steps that we listed for organic search are also steps to follow for paid search in terms of first knowing the customer and what they want from a site. These steps are

1. define the target market,
2. find out what they search for, and then
3. develop a search strategy in terms of keywords and phrases. Good keywords for paid search advertising reflect the products/services that are offered.

While the overall process for a paid search campaign is similar to an organic search strategy, the execution is different. There are more details in a paid search campaign and a more specific process is warranted to achieve good results. A more detailed suggested process for paid search campaigns as used by industry leaders is as briefly described as follows and is illustrated in Figure 11.3:

1.0 Research: Determine, using tools such as Google Trends and the Keyword Planner, what terms relating to the campaign are being used. Narrow down the terms to those most pertinent and determine cost.

2.0 Build: Develop the campaign by selecting appropriate keywords and match criteria and designing ads.

3.0 Launch: Watch results as the campaigns are running and then monitor the results and refine. Use A/B testing to test one ad against another.

4.0 Analyze and Report. Use available reporting tools to understand which ads and campaigns were the most successful and try to determine why. Make a note of any changes for the next campaign.

This process is illustrated in more detail in Figure 11.3 and described more fully in the following narrative.

Research

The first step in the research phase is to investigate broad search categories and trends. By using tools such as Google Trends and Alerts and by monitoring search traffic to one's own website using various analytical tools, advertisers get a good idea of where to start in investigating the keywords most appropriate for a paid ad campaign. Another way to research is to ask customers or other stakeholders how they search for your product and monitor their search patterns. From the information in the investigative phase, the advertiser narrows its keyword search and determines if it can afford to bid on the most appropriate keywords, adjusting its strategy if necessary.

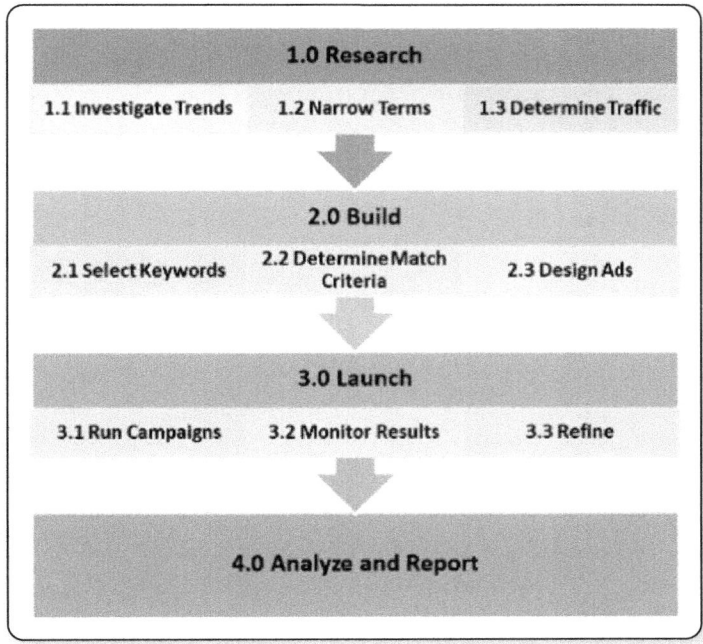

FIGURE 11.3
Paid Search Process

SOURCE: Inspired by presentation by Thorne Washington, former student and Digital Marketing Manager at Firewood Marketing.

Build

broad match search setting allowing for matching on a wide variation of a keyword or set of keywords.

phrase match search setting that includes an entire phrase.

broad match modifier allows AdWords ad to show for searches that include the broad match keyword or close variations of the broad match.

exact match paid search parameter that is set to display to those looking for a particular phase.

negative match search setting that is the opposite of what is desired; used to avoid paying for unnecessary clicks.

Next, in the Build phase of the campaign, the advertiser can make the final selection of keywords to bid on for each ad and each campaign, using tools such as the Keyword Planner (Figure 11.4). Keywords that are too expensive or don't have enough traffic will be discarded in favor of others. For matching categories, a **broad match** includes that keyword idea in any search, including synonyms and related words, whereas a **phrase match** must include that entire phrase. A **broad match modifier** will look for close variations of the keyword to show. An **exact match** will return the search volume for that particular keyword or set of keywords, and a **negative match** is a term that should not be considered (see Table 11.1). Generally, the broad match will not be most cost effective as the ad will show in response to searches that may not be relevant to the product or service.

To be more targeted, another option when developing ad campaigns is to consider the Contextual Targeting Tool, which will also provide ideas of keywords and themes of keywords, as well as ad group names that can run on the Google Display Network. Google has two networks for advertising. The first network is the broader Search Network, which displays ads in response to searches on browsers and the second is the more targeted Display Network, which displays ads on websites pertinent to the ad. Display Select will allow the advertiser to choose specific sites such as business.com and nytimes.com for ads to display for PPC campaigns.

Contextual targeting allows for advertisings on a list of websites that have partnered with a search engine to display its advertising on their site. Contextual advertising is considered a leading-edge internet advertising tactic because

FIGURE 11.4
GoogleAdWords™ Keyword Planner Tool Reports Section Showing Estimated Traffic and Suggested Bid

SOURCE: GoogleAdWords™ advertising service.

TABLE 11.1 Types of Keyword Matches

Types of Match Terms	Example
Broad match: reaches widest audience and not in same sequence	**sale purse** = **purse sale** and ad will appear
Phrase match: must be in exact sequence, enclosed in quotes	**"pink and purple purses"** in that order will trigger an ad
Exact match: most precise method, enclosed in brackets	**[pink purse]** will trigger an ad but not **pink purse store**
Negative match: uses a minus sign and prevents ads from appearing	**-handbags** and your add will not appear
Broad match modifier: allows ad to show for searches that include the broad match keyword or close variations of the broad match keyword	**+pink +purses** can match discount pink purses, best pink purses, designer pink purses, and pink bags

SOURCE: © Cengage Learning 2013/UPDATED 2016.

it allows for a more refined targeting of display ads depending on how the user is conducting the search. In Google AdWords, the Contextual Targeting Tool will serve up advertising on particular sites as deemed relevant. For our "pink purses" example, it could be a web page or it could be an email, particularly Gmail in the case of Google, or a discussion group about fashionable purses. PPC ads on Google AdWords are priced on a CPC basis, with the cost determined by the keyword as described previously.

Using the Display Network allows the advertiser to choose specific sites on which to display PPC ads. Choice of sites will be based on the product offered and the characteristics of the target market. For "pink purses," we might choose accessory or other types of shopping sites. Site placement targeting also allows the advertiser to pick specific sites or categories that match specific products and services and to select matching demographic characteristics of those who would want to see an ad. The pricing for site targeting is based on **CPM**, the **cost-per-thousand** impressions.

Of course, whether an ad does get served up to users who enter a particular match term is dependent on cost, the actual bid, and the quality of the ad. The idea is to create a "fair playing field" where it is not just the amount of money that is bid that determines whether the ad is served and discourage irrelevant advertising.[9]

The next step of the Build phase is then to design ads based on different themes known as Ad groups and then test different ads within that group to determine which ones are most effective. An Ad group might be handbags or purses, and then different types of advertisements could be created for the different types of accessories within that category, such as leather purses, pink purses, tote bags, and so on. The Quality Score will also drop when keywords are not grouped logically together.[10]

Before October 2016, Google allowed for just three lines for the copy of a text ad plus a **display URL**, which may or may not have been the same as the actual site URL. In October, Google introduced Expanded Text Ads, which will be the primary ad format after January 2017. The headline for text ads was formerly limited to 25 characters, the description line was two 35-character description lines and the display URL was entered manually. In English, in standard text ads the title can be longer, two 30-character headlines versus one with 25 characters. The ad text was formerly 70 characters, with each line limit of 35 characters each. The text of the description line of the ad has now been expanded to a single 80-character description line and the display URL can be up to 35 characters (see Figure 11.5).

- These increased character limits in text ads came about because paid search needed to evolve with the increased use of mobile technology. The examples below show how text ads can display more information in the mobile format. In

CPM the amount paid in purchasing advertising; in this case, means the cost per thousand impressions, or the cost divided by the total number of impressions.

cost-per-thousand the amount paid in purchasing advertising; in this case, means the cost per thousand impressions, or the cost divided by the total number of impressions.

display URL displays in ad but has link to another page.

FIGURE 11.5 Changes to Text Advertising

Upgraded ad components	Current	Available later this year
More prominent headlines	One 25-character headline	Two 30-character headlines
Longer description line	Two 35-character description lines	One consolidated 80-character description line
Relevant display URL	Manually entered display URL. Any mismatch between your display, final and landing page URLs will cause your ad to be disapproved.	Domain automatically extracted from your final URL to ensure accuracy. You can customize the URL path.

SOURCE: https://adwords.googleblog.com/2016/05/ads-and-analytics-innovations-for-a-mobile-first-world.html.

addition to the changes in headlines and description lines, Google added self-generating Display URLs. The display URL is automatically generated now from the ad copy to ensure accuracy, rather than leaving display URL selection up to the advertiser (see Figure 11.6). The display URL is most successful when it has content and links to the relevant page on the site. Now Google automatically generates a meaningful and descriptive display URL, perhaps in part to aid advertisers and in part to minimize potentially deceptive practices. Destination URLs can still be customized to direct to specific landing pages for campaign tracking. This customization is done using two optional "Path" fields that can be up to 15 characters each.

Part of the reason these changes were made, as noted above, is to optimize advertisements for mobile devices. Figure 11.7 shows an example of the new versus old ad format on Mobile devices. The new format provides more information and is easier to read, among other benefits.

When writing any type of ad, remember that an effective ad is persuasive, specific, and concise and distinguishes the firm or not-for-profit from the competition. A good practice is also to include an offer and a call to action, standard direct marketing best practices, to provide an incentive or benefit for clicking-through the advertisement. Of course, including the keywords that users bid on and that the user is searching for in the ad is also a best practice and a time deadline will create a sense of urgency. The ad example in Figure 11.7 for the Guitar Center suggests that there are good deals every day, a rather weak call to action implying that the viewer will get a bargain by clicking on the ad. Figure 11.8, which shows advertisements on both desktop and mobile

FIGURE 11.6 Entering in an Ad in the New Format (ETA)

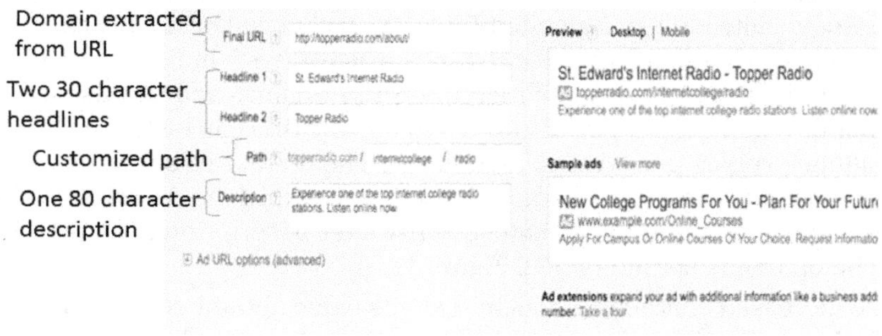

SOURCE: Google.

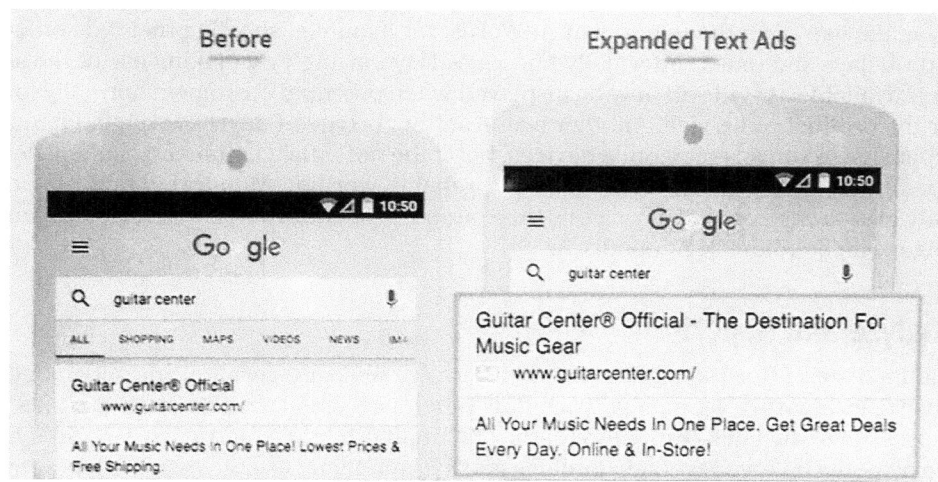

FIGURE 11.7
Results in Mobile Format Before and After ETA Format

SOURCE: http://www.wordstream.com/blog/ws/2016/05/25/google-expanded-text-ads.

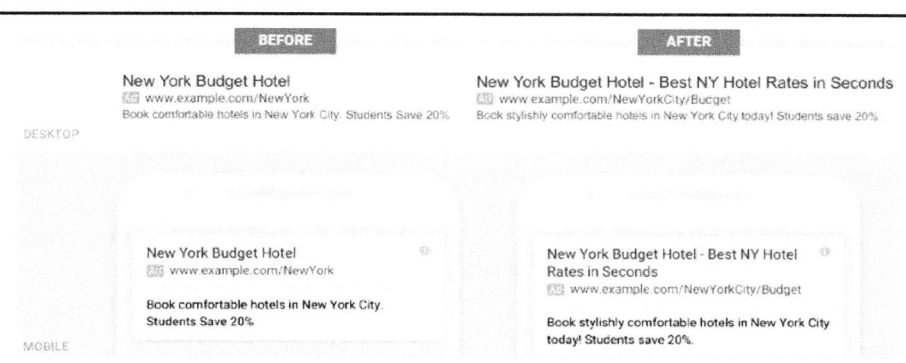

FIGURE 11.8
Desktop and Mobile Ads for Hotel Site, Old versus New ETA Formats

SOURCE: https://support.google.com/adwords/answer/1722124?hl=en.

before and after the format change, indicates that students receive a 20 percent discount, a clear offer for a particular segment.

Google recommends that to maximize the new Expanded Text Ad format the advertiser should focus on messaging and use all of the available characters to do so. Optimizing headlines and considering how they will display on mobile will also help increase CTR, as will the use of ad extensions. Ad extensions in AdWords provide additional information along with an ad, such as phone number, location information or reviews can also help increase the number of people who actually click on an ad.

Launch

During the launch phase, advertisers make sure to target their ads and monitor campaigns closely. During launch, another technique advertisers might use for increasing CTR includes using a **local search** term for ads targeted to geographic areas Google allows for targeting of ads to countries and regions within them. In the United States, regions can be as small as metropolitan areas, allowing PPC ads to be affordable and relevant to local and regional businesses. Facebook allows for more specific geographic targeting, one reason for its recent success.

local search using a local search term in a search query.

During launch, advertisers will want to monitor the campaign closely and possibly make use of all the features of AdWords, for example, showing their ads only at certain days and times (informally known as Day Parting). By making use of the settings available, the ad will only be displayed when potential customers normally look for the product or service. Another useful setting is type of device. It might be more expensive to run ads on mobile devices, but if the potential customer is making decisions when on the go, the investment is probably worth it. Monitoring budgets on a daily basis is also crucial during this time period. More information on AdWords campaigns can be found in Appendix A.

Analyze and Report

The final step after the ad campaign is run is to measure results. Not only can the advertiser measure on a daily basis how much was spent, the number of clicks or impressions, the click-through rate, the CPC, and other key metrics in AdWords but can also sign up for conversion tracking and measurement. (A conversion is any action a visitor takes on your site that is of value, such as a purchase or a request for information.) In addition, by using Google Analytics, discussed in Chapter 18, an advertiser can also determine how traffic arrived to the site, whether from search engines or other referral sites, and which keywords have been most effective. Larger and sophisticated websites rely on other reporting tools such as the Adobe®SiteCatalyst®, powered by Omniture®, to monitor site traffic, improve conversion rates, and attribute performance to the proper marketing channel.

For PPC analysis, Google AdWords and Analytics maintain a high market share among both large and small businesses. There are paid metrics suppliers that offer even more functionality and opportunities for customization and are included in the discussion in Chapter 18. Most larger and more sophisticated websites also rely on other reporting tools to monitor site traffic, improve conversion rates, and attribute performance to the proper marketing channel.

ADDITIONAL AD FORMATS

Although the chapter has focused on text ads in Google, there are many additional ad formats as shown in Figure 11.9. The formats include the following:

- Text ads, as discussed in Section 11-3, can have "extensions;" that is, they can be extended to provide more information.
- Responsive ads that change to fit the space available, for instance, from the desktop version of an ad to the mobile version.
- Image ads that can be either static or interactive.
- App promotions, which are ads specifically to drive app downloads.
- Video ads, which are more engaging to viewers.
- Shopping ads which emphasize product features to encourage purchase on a dedicated shopping page.
- Call-only ads that offer click-to-call functionality.

Ad formats should match the objective for a particular paid search ad campaign. For example, the advertisements on the top of the pink purses example in Figure 11.1 are primarily shopping ads, meant to encourage purchase. A call-only ad is quite effective in a mobile environment for a restaurant owner who knows that potential customers are searching for a restaurant on a mobile device and want to call for information or to make a reservation. All AdWords ads can be run on mobile devices as well as on desktop just by checking the Mobile box in the Device preference section when building the ad. Advertisers should carefully consider which format will be most effective in helping reach campaign objectives.

FIGURE 11.9
Other Ad Formats Available in AdWords

Ad formats available in an AdWords account

Format	Description	Main benefits
Text	Words only. *	Maintain ads quickly and easily. Reach customers when they search on Google. Use Ad extensions to provide additional details and contact information that can make your text ads more relevant to customers.
	Boston's Best Bonsais - Spring Sale Going on Now Ad www.example.com Florist And Indoor Plant Nursery. Two Locations. Spruce Up Your Desk Today!	
Responsive	Responsive ads automatically adjust their size, appearance, and format to fit available ad spaces. They can transform into text or image ads.	In a matter of minutes, create ads that fit just about any ad space available. Plus, responsive ads can show as native ads, which boost your impact by blending into publisher's websites.
Image	Static or interactive graphics. Animated ads in .gif and Flash format can be used. 	Showcase your product or service in a visual way. Reach customers on websites that partner with Google.
App promotion ads	Drive app downloads and engagement with app promotion ads.	Send your customers to download your app from an app store, or include a deep link directly into your app. Note: Ads will appear only on devices compatible with your content.
Video	Video ads that show online. Run standalone video ads or insert them in streaming video content. 	Deliver a rich and engaging experience to customers. Reach customers on websites that partner with Google.
Shopping ads	Text ads that contain product features and pricing information. Goes to a product purchase page on your website. 	Encourage your customers to learn about the products that you sell before they click to your website.
Call-only ads	Call:(555)555-555 Ad www.example.com Description Line 1 Description Line 2	Drive phone calls to your business with ads that include your phone number. People can click on these ads and then call your business directly. These ads will only appear on devices that can make phone calls, and any field in these ads can be hidden to fit on smaller screens.

* Text ads might look different on the Display Network.

SOURCE: https://support.google.com/adwords/answer/1722124?hl=en.

Remember that Google has two networks for advertising, which are the broader Search Network and the Display Network. Campaigns can be run on either the Search Network or the Display Network. If the advertiser wishes to run a campaign on both networks, Search Network with Display Select is available. Choice of network affects the formats available and the advertising features that can be selected. For example, choosing Search Network (Standard) or Search Network with Display Select (Standard) means the advertiser is restricted to text ads. Advertisers seeking to use Call-only or Mobile App ads on the Search Network are restricted to those specific ad types. On the other hand, selecting the Display Network only limits the advertiser to text, image, and video advertisements. Advertisers need to be aware of their target audiences and campaign objectives when selecting both ad formats and search networks because of these limitations.

While search advertising, especially Google AdWords, has been a staple of online marketing for many years, there is another area of paid advertising that is enjoying explosive growth—**paid social**. That type of advertising will be explored in the next section.

paid social any type of paid promotion on social media platforms.

THE EMERGENCE OF PAID SOCIAL ADVERTISING

Advertisers have been taking advantage of *free social media platforms* to listen to and engage with customers almost since their inception as we discussed in Chapter 5. More recently the growing reliance of advertisers on social media intersected with the need of the platforms to monetize their properties. At the intersection sits search advertising and newer *paid social* advertising formats that are more like the display advertising discussed in Chapter 7. Section 11-1 described the growth of paid search and the impact of mobile on that advertising sector. The growth of mobile and its impact on digital marketing will be further explored in Chapter 12. In this section we will focus on paid advertising on social platforms, both desktop and mobile. To illustrate its importance, the CMI Benchmark study for 2016 found both B2C and B2B advertisers making heavy use of the social options. They found the following:

- On the average B2C advertisers used four paid advertising types including both digital and offline.

  - Seventy-six percent used promoted posts and SEM while 74 percent used social ads.
  - The average B2C advertiser used seven social media platforms with 94 percent using Facebook, 82 percent using Twitter, 77 percent using YouTube, and 76 percent using LinkedIn. Instagram was used by only 62 percent but it was the fastest growing channel of paid social media advertising.

- On the average B2B advertisers used three of these paid advertising types.

  - Sixty-six percent used search advertising, 57 percent used offline promotion, 55 percent used traditional digital banner ads, 52 percent used promoted posts, and 51 percent used social ads.
  - The average B2B advertiser used six social media platforms with over 94 percent using LinkedIn and over 80 percent using Twitter and Facebook followed by YouTube which was used by 74 percent.[11,12]

When the subject is specifically paid social media there are two indisputable facts. First, it is growing rapidly, as shown in Figure 11.10. eMarketer adds that growth from 2014 to 2015 was 33.5 percent and by 2017 paid social is expected to reach 16 percent of total digital ad spending around the world. The second is the dominance of Facebook with a share hovering around 65 percent for the years shown. What is fueling growth of this magnitude? Consider a paid social campaign run by a niche website.

FIGURE 11.10 The Growth of Paid Social Advertising

Social Network Ad Revenues Worldwide, by Company, 2014-2017

	2014	2015	2016	2017
Social network ad revenues (billions)				
Facebook	$11.49	$16.29	$21.43	$26.98
Twitter	$1.26	$2.03	$2.95	$3.98
LinkedIn	$0.75	$0.93	$1.13	$1.33
Other	$4.36	$5.88	$7.41	$8.72
Total social network ad spending	$17.85	$25.14	$32.91	$41.00
Social network ad revenue growth (% change)				
Twitter	111.2%	61.8%	45.0%	35.0%
Facebook	64.5%	41.8%	31.5%	25.9%
LinkedIn	33.2%	25.1%	20.5%	17.8%
Other	34.4%	35.0%	26.1%	17.6%
Total social network ad spending	56.8%	40.8%	30.9%	24.6%
Social network ad revenue share (% of total)				
Facebook	64.4%	64.8%	65.1%	65.8%
Twitter	7.0%	8.1%	9.0%	9.7%
LinkedIn	4.2%	3.7%	3.4%	3.2%
Other	24.4%	23.4%	22.5%	21.3%

Note: includes paid advertising appearing within social networks, social network games and social network apps; excludes spending by marketers that goes toward developing or maintaining a social network presence; numbers may not add up to total due to rounding
Source: eMarketer, Sep 2015

196303 www.eMarketer.com

SOURCE: https://www.emarketer.com/Article/Social-Network-Ad-Revenues-Accelerate-Worldwide/1013015

This paid social campaign of early 2016 shows how the social platforms work—and work together—for advertisers. Olivia Rose is a website that offers afro hair tutorials to English- and French-speaking women. It focused on video because its videos were being monetized on Google's **AdSense** platform. AdSense is a Google platform that allows publishers of websites and blogs to display ads on their sites and receive payment when ads are seen or clicked.[13] Using AdSense allowed Olivia Rose to show its videos as ads on other websites and blogs.

AdSense a way to monetize a website or a blog on Google by showing paid ads.

The specific objectives of the campaign were to

- Increase the size of their Facebook fan base
- Increase the number of subscribers to their YouTube channel
- Increase subscribers to their blog
- Increase the number of Instagram followers

A still shot of the Facebook ad is shown in Figure 11.11. It ran for 20 seconds, including some text and a CTA, so it could be used on both Facebook and Instagram. Facebook allows videos of up to 120 minutes but Instagram's maximum length is 60 seconds, so they developed a video that would work on both. Using Facebook

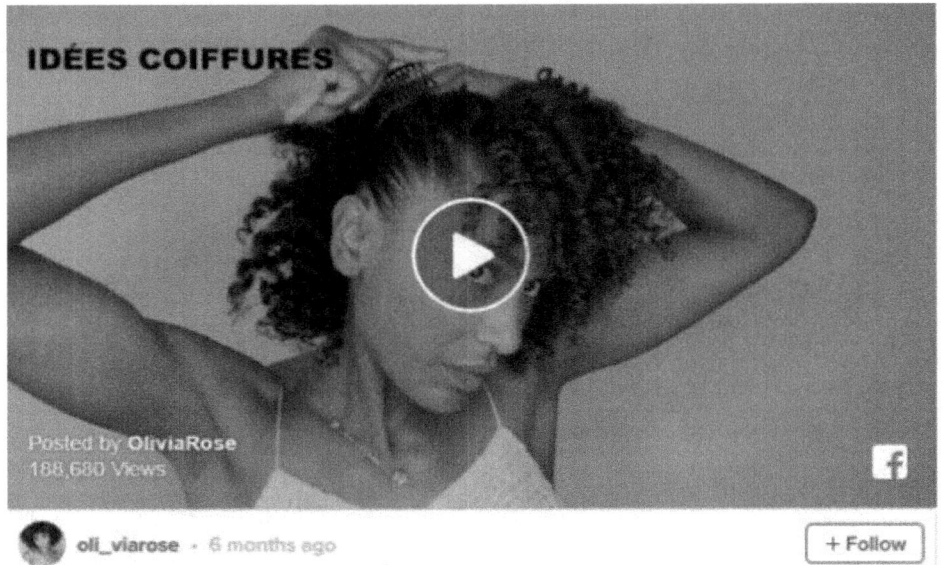

FIGURE 11.11
The Basic Facebook Video

SOURCE: http://www.marketingsherpa.com/article/case-study/olivia-rose-paid-social-media-growth.

targeting options they targeted an audience that was female only, 13–40 years old and living in French-speaking countries outside of France such as Guadeloupe and Reunion.

Olivia Rose ran a one-day Sunday trial that was so successful it broadened the campaign specifications by increasing the bid price and extending its reach to English-speaking African and Caribbean countries, the United Kingdom, the United States, and Canada. It ran the broadened campaign for four days with the following results:

- 15,647 new Facebook fans
- 1,784 new YouTube subscribers
- 1,758 new Instagram followers
- 6 new blog subscribers[14]

The company also reported an increase in engagement with its social media postings and increased inquiries about its products.

This campaign is a good example of how a well planned and executed social media campaign can produce results. It also gives an initial sense of the large number of paid social options available to advertisers.

A report from an investment house reinforces the dominance of Google and Facebook in the world of paid search and social. According to a Morgan Stanley analyst quoted in the *New York Times*, "In the first quarter of 2016, 85 cents of every new dollar spent in online advertising will go to Google or Facebook."[15] That translates into $1.48 *billion* in growth for Google, $1.0 *billion* in growth for Facebook, and $300 *million, or 10 percent of total online ad revenue growth*, for "everybody else."[16] That is a sobering statistic if you are a website or platform competing for ad dollars, but good reason for us to concentrate in this chapter on how Facebook and Google work.

promoted posts regular posts for which the marketer pays a fee to have the post prominently displayed in a feed or on the platform page.

There are two basic formats in paid social advertising—display and **promoted posts**. Table 11.2 shows the display ad formats, many of them similar to the formats discussed in Section 7-2a1. The table includes Instagram, which is owned by Facebook, and usually incorporates Facebook ad products soon after they are introduced by the parent company. Perhaps that rich assortment of options is one reason it is the fastest growing of the social media platforms in terms of ad dollars. YouTube, owned by Google, is not included in the table although ads on YouTube are discussed later in the chapter. YouTube concentrates on video advertising, although it does offer one format that it simply calls Display Ads.[17]

TABLE 11.2
Display Ad Formats Offered by Facebook and Google

Platform	Text	Links	Mobile App	Mobile App Carousel	Desktop App	Photo/Image	Video	Rich Media	Carousel	Canvas
Facebook										
Google										
Instagram										

The display formats shown in Table 11.2 fit into two categories. First, ad formats similar to the ones illustrated in the discussion of AdWords in the first part of the chapter—text and links ads. The other seven types of ad formats listed are essentially display ads, sized and otherwise constructed to meet the needs of the viewing device and the objectives of the advertiser. These nine ads make up one general category of paid social ads. Call them display ads for simplicity.

The other category is promoted posts. These are unique to the characteristics of the platform; a promoted post on Facebook is not the same thing as a promoted Tweet. And yes, Facebook does have promoted posts in addition to all the ad formats in Table 11.2. And Twitter has other ad formats unique to its platform.

In order to make this bewildering array of options as simple as possible, and to keep this chapter from turning into a book, we are going to cover the basic formats in Table 11.2. Then we are going to select some of the other social media platforms with the most advertising power and highlight nondisplay ad formats that are either unique to that platform or shared only with similar platforms. That will give a high level understanding of paid social advertising and resources to further your knowledge about advertising on platforms important to your brand or career aspirations.

DISPLAY ADS ON FACEBOOK, GOOGLE, AND INSTAGRAM

The good news is that you already know a great deal about display ads from the coverage in Chapter 7. Many of the formats for both desktop and mobile ads remain similar in appearance and the principles of serving ads to targeted audiences remain the same. In other words, the principles of display advertising on websites and social platforms are the same. Different vendors supply services such as ad creation and serving in the different markets, but the principles remain the same.

The bad news is that different terminology is used in different markets, even sometimes on different platforms. Some of those occurrences will be mentioned here, but the advertiser must exercise caution. Part of the due diligence required for running an ad campaign anywhere on the web is to read the format specifications in order to understand what can and cannot be done with a given format. The IAB establishes ad formats for the industry. For paid social ads advertisers will also need to look at the format descriptions on the platform's site because some formats are specific to that platform. Yes, it's complicated, but the information the advertiser needs is easily accessible.

Since Facebook offers more display formats than any other platform we are going to use Facebook as the primary example. The examples in this section are from the Facebook Ads Guide publication. It has detailed specifications for each ad format and shows images of each https://www.facebook.com/business/ads-guide/?tab0=Mobile%20News%20Feed. It also contains the ad formats for Instagram, owned by Facebook, as you can see in Table 11.2. On Facebook's business page you will find video tutorials on many aspects of Facebook advertising, including measuring results. On that page you will find a link to How Facebook Ads Work which has a number of tutorials including audience targeting and Facebook Ad Auction Basics. The Facebook bidding and auction processes are similar to Google's as described in Section 11-3.

FIGURE 11.12

Facebook and Instagram Display Ad Formats

Ad Placements

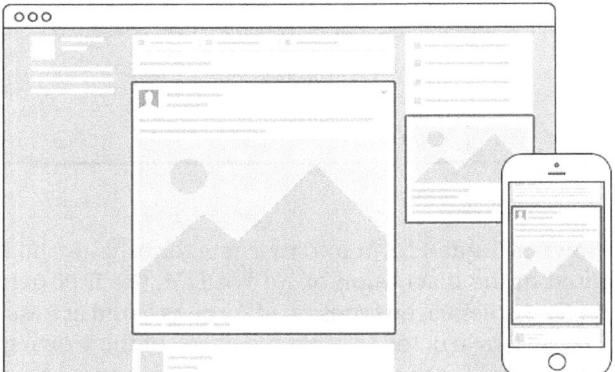

SOURCE: https://www.facebook.com/business/ads-guide?tab0=Mobile%20News%20Feed.

There are many good posts that describe Facebook ads that have worked well and the advertiser can get excellent ideas from them. However, it is essential that you consult the platform itself before trying to create your own ad. Advertising on social media sites is in a constant state of evolution and the ad format that worked yesterday might have changed today. The platform itself is the only place you can count on getting information that is up to date. Even so, the Facebook Ads Guide carries a warning that recent changes may not show up for a time. Announcements generally appear first on the Facebook blog.

Figure 11.12 shows the formats as they appear on a Facebook or Instagram page. Reading from left to right they are the Desktop News Feed, Right Column, Mobile News Feed, and Instagram Mobile ad formats.

Facebook also classifies its ads by advertiser objective. The 12 objectives are shown in Figure 11.13 with the objective for Page Post Engagement expanded to show that it offers text ads.

Text and Links Ads on Facebook and Google

Figure 11.13 shows the 12 objectives with Page Post Engagement expanded to show the four format types available. Most of the other objectives also have multiple formats that correspond to the objective. A bewildering array of options, you say?

Yes, it is a large number of options, but look at how well it is organized. The advertiser knows what he or she wants to accomplish or should take a deep breath and think about it before creating an ad. An example of a text ad (and for all of the other formats) is shown when you click on a format. Design recommendations tell how to construct the ad and give warnings such as "text longer than 500 characters will be truncated on small screens."

Figure 11.14 shows another example, the Links format for Instagram desktop and mobile. If this were a Facebook Links ad, the actual website link would be visible. In Instagram it is presented on the Learn More link.

Notice that in Figures 11.13 and 11.14 the term "Sponsored" is clearly visible in order to meet FTC guidelines as described in Section 8-5. "Advertisement" and "Promoted" are also acceptable identifiers as is #ad. On platforms that allow the user to create his or her own ads this is handled automatically.

Now for perhaps the best news of all. On each one of the Ads Guide pages there is a Create Ad button like the one in Figure 11.14. It takes you to a page that corresponds to the ad objective and format you are looking at. If the advertiser already has

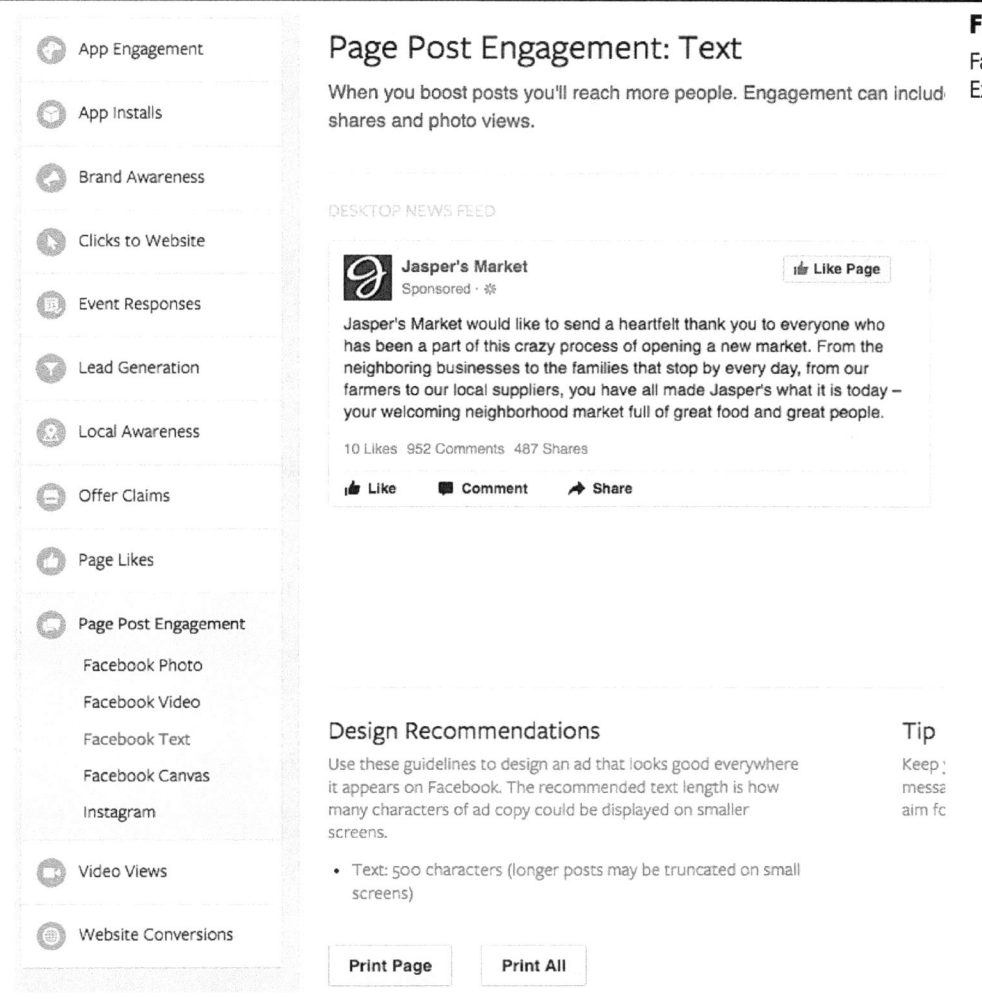

FIGURE 11.13

Facebook Ad Types and Example of a Text Ad

SOURCE: https://www.facebook.com/business/ads-guide/post-engagement/text/.

an AdWords account it shows the account settings and allows access to items like photos that have been used before. If the advertiser is satisfied with the existing Audience definition in the settings, just continue on. But first, consider once again the objectives of the specific campaign. If the objective is to reach loyal Facebook fans with a particular message, a narrowly drawn audience like fans who live in a particular geographical area or fans who have a specific set of interests may be indicated. Facebook is popular among advertisers for its ability to reach precisely defined target markets by

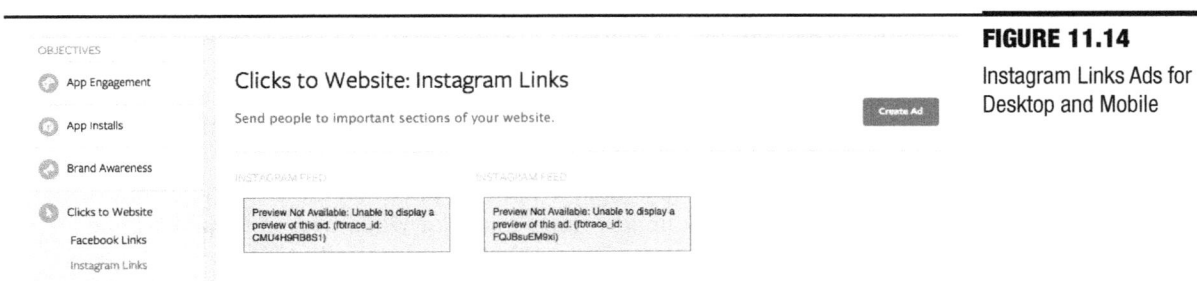

FIGURE 11.14

Instagram Links Ads for Desktop and Mobile

SOURCE: https://www.facebook.com/business/ads-guide/clicks-to-website/instagram-links/?toggle0=Photo.

location, demographics, interests, and behaviors. Facebook also has a huge reach as its user numbers indicate (Section 5-1). That makes it useful for running broadly targeted campaigns in order to build the brand's fan community on the platform.

Once the audience has been specified go on to Placements to identify the sites chosen to reach it. Many large publishers such as the New York Times, National Geographic and BuzzFeed as well as many gaming apps display Facebook ads. The advertiser may wish to use Automatic Placements until it is clear which publisher sites work well. Next set the Budget and Schedule. Then go on to create the ad by selecting the format (including images and video), choosing media and entering text. Facebook provides a lot of suggestions that is useful to the beginner. However, examine them carefully. The audience settings may not be what is needed for this campaign. At the moment on my account the Media page is connecting to an inactive Facebook page because that is the only business page on which I am identified as an administrator. Once the advertiser completes the campaign, a preview makes sure that the ad looks like what is expected.

Ads are launched on the schedule that was set and advertisers receive results on the account dashboard. Consider that this process gives more good news—it is exactly the set of steps shown in Figure 11.4—Research > Build > Launch > Analyze and Report. Remember also what the advertisers at Olivia Rose did; they performed a one-day trial, analyzed those results, and revised what became a very successful result based on the data.

Text ads on Google are the same ads used on Google Search. They are distributed on the Google Display Network as described in section 11-3.

Display Ad Formats on Facebook, Google, and Instagram

Facebook has other display ad formats in addition to text and links. All are accessed in the way described in the previous section. All can be paid for either on a per click or a per impression basis. All are reviewed before insertion is approved.[18] Bidding for Facebook ads is part of the ad creation process just as it is in Google AdWords.[19]

Here is a brief summary of Facebook ad formats:

- App Engagement. The objective is to increase activity on the brand's mobile apps. Formats offered are Facebook desktop and mobile, Instagram mobile and Instagram Carousel.
    - The Instagram Carousel format includes three to five images, each of which leads to a specific page on the brand website. Minimal text is used and the creator selects from 11 CTAs provided on the page.

- App Installs. The objective is to get viewers to download the app. The same four formats are offered.

- Brand Awareness. The title says it all; the objective is to create awareness. Formats offered are Facebook Photo (one image with opportunity to link to the website), Facebook Video (120 minutes maximum with numerous format requirements, minimal text, and opportunity to link to the website), Facebook Carousel (maximum of ten images or videos each of which can link to the site with a strict limit on the amount of text), Instagram Photo (one image with warning that amount of text may limit reach of ad), Instagram Video (a video between 3 and 60 seconds long, minimal amount of text, automatic Learn More link), Instagram Carousel (just as in App Engagement except that the CTA is an automatic Learn More link).

- Clicks to Website. Send people to specific pages on the website. Formats offered are Facebook Links (either image or video with minimal text and CTA button options), Instagram Links (photo or video with CTA options), Facebook Carousel (maximum ten images or videos, each with a link to a page on the website), Instagram Carousel (same as for App Engagement), Facebook Canvas (billed as an immersive mobile experience with text, images, videos, and numerous other options).[20]

- The Facebook Links to Website Carousel ad shown in Figure 11.15 can contain as many as ten images. The screenshot shows the opening frames of the desktop, mobile, and right side ad placements. The Instagram Carousel format includes three to five images, each of which leads to a specific page on the brand website. Minimal text is used and the creator selects from 11 CTAs provided on the page.
- Event Responses. The objective is to promote event attendance with ads on the Facebook Desktop News Feed, Mobile News Feed, or a Right Side ad.
- Lead Generation. This allows the advertiser to add a form to ads in order to collect lead information.
- Local Awareness. The objective is to attract people who live near the business with a CTA button that provides directions. This type of ad is also available on Instagram in some countries.
- Offer Targeting. The objective is to reach nearby residents with limited-time promotional offers.
- Page Likes. The objective is to connect with people who might Like your page.
- Page Post Engagement. The objective is to increase Likes, Shares, Comments, and Views of a specific post. The formats offered are Facebook Photo, Facebook Video, Facebook Text, and Instagram.

FIGURE 11.15

Facebook Carousel Ad, Desktop, Mobile, and Right Side Versions

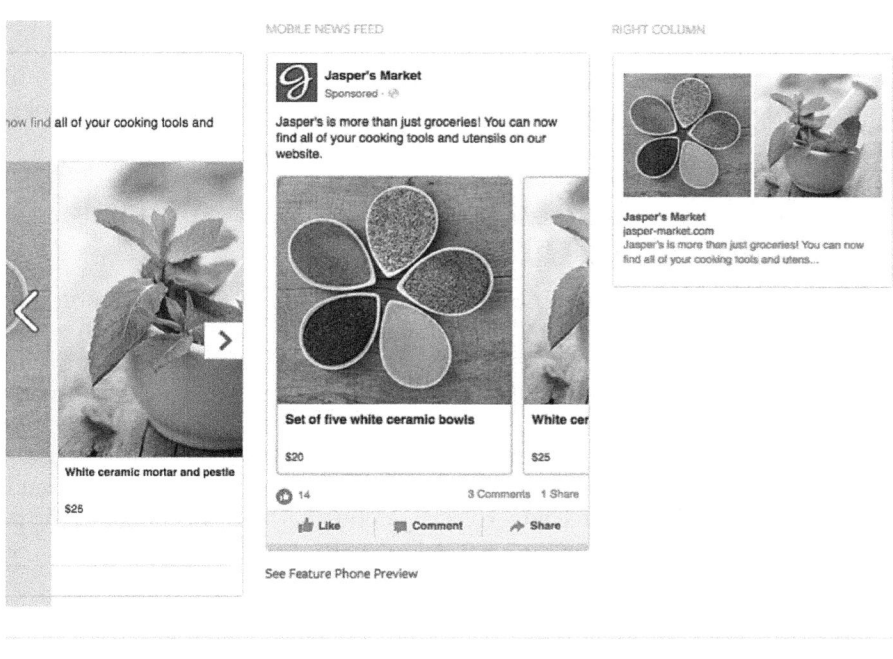

SOURCE: https://www.facebook.com/business/ads-guide/clicks-to-website/carousel/?toggle0=Photo.

- Video Views. The objective is to tell a story using a video or slide show. The video can be a maximum of 120 minutes with minimal text and an optional link to the website.
- Website Conversion. The objective is to encourage a specific behavior such as signing up for a newsletter or purchasing a product. It can include an image or a video and minimal text, and a CTA button is recommended.

Many of these ads can be shown on Facebook's Desktop News Feed, Mobile News Feed, or as a Right Side ad as shown in Figure 11.12. Facebook uses a responsive template (discussed in Chapter 15) to ensure the ad renders properly for the device or size without additional effort on the part of the advertiser.

Google classifies its display ads by format, hence Text, Image, Video and Rich Media (Table 11.2).

- Google's image ads basically follow the rules for creating text ads as explained in Section 11-3. Instead of classifying by objective as Facebook does, Google offers many options within the image format. For instance, the Lightbox format is a rich media image ad. Some of the many other options are inclusion of phone numbers and quoting of third-party reviews of the product or service. Many of the options (extensions in Google's terms) are subject to specific requirements. An example is that phone numbers must be verified before being used in an ad.
- Rich media ads are image ads that have interactive elements that can change depending on the viewer and how he or she interacts with the ad. Examples include a carousel of product images or an ad with animated layers.[21]
- Google's video ad formats are extensive because it owns YouTube and the Double Click ad serving network.
    - Any YouTube video can become an ad by promoting it on YouTube.[22]

in-stream ads video ads that appear in the video stream itself—either before (also called a pre-roll), during or after the video plays.

discovery ads YouTube video ads that are served based on the viewer's Google search activity.

Video ads can be created for either YouTube or the Google Display Network. There are two basic types; **in-stream ads** that appear before, during, or after a video on YouTube or on publisher sites on the Google Display Network and **discovery ads** that are associated with search results on Google or YouTube.[23]

Google has many options for creating ads within these basic categories. Some allow the advertiser to serve personalized content to the viewer or to set up the ad for remarketing (discussed as retargeting in Section 7-3b) and there are many others.[24]

PROMOTED POSTS AND OTHER SOCIAL MEDIA AD OPTIONS

As noted in the previous section, both Facebook and Google offer promoted posts options, Facebook on its own platform,[25] and Google on YouTube.[26] In both cases the advertiser can promote directly from the post page, specify the audience, and set a budget, which can be as low as $5 per day. Performance metrics are provided by the platform.

All the social media platforms we are discussing in this section have some type of promoted post offering and most other prominent platforms do also. Many promoted posts show in the user's main feed with a label like Sponsored or Promoted, but they blend in like other types of native advertising (Section 8-5). They can also show at the top of the feed or in the right column, depending on the format of the platform. Some examples of promoted post and other offerings include the following:

- Instagram. Accounts with a business profile get access to Insights about the performance of their posts and the ability to promote posts.[27]
    - Instagram also offers several types of display ads as shown in Table 11.2.
- Twitter. On Twitter ordinary Tweets can be promoted by any user. The tool to create them is Quick Promote.[28] Twitter also offers Promoted Accounts, which put the user's account at the top of the list to be recommended for other users to follow. Promoted Trends puts the user's ad at the top of Twitter's Trending Topics box.[29]

- Twitter also offers Twitter cards, which are essentially business cards for the user's tweets that include a link to a web page. The cards are available in a number of objectives-based formats.[30]
- LinkedIn. Sponsored Content on LinkedIn is represented by sponsored posts with targeting and tracking options.[31] LinkedIn also allows the user to upload email addresses to his or her account, which is useful in the lead nurturing and conversion process.[32]
- Pinterest. Business accounts on Pinterest can promote pins for objectives of awareness, engagement, or website traffic. Currently Pins can only be promoted directly from the Pinterest board, so content must be pinned before starting the three-step promotion process.[33]
- Snapchat. The conventional promoted post doesn't work with Snaps that disappear within 10 seconds. Instead they offer Snap Ads that appear between user stories and Snap Geofilters that are overlays on Snaps—On-demand, which are cheap and Sponsored, which can be very expensive. They also offer Sponsored Lenses such as the Taco Bell Cinco de Mayo head discussed in Section 5-4c.[34]

There is a pattern here that you can look for in other platforms. Platforms first try to monetize "native content" on their platform, whether it be a Facebook Post or a Pinterest Pin. Then, as understanding of the platform's strengths builds in both the platform itself and in its advertisers, the platform begins to offer additional advertising opportunities suited to the nature of the platform. This continuing expansion of advertising opportunities is the reason we continue warning that advertisers must stay abreast of the ad offerings on platforms that work for their target market segment. It is still early days in the world of paid social ads, however, and promoted content is still the main offering of many of the large platforms.

NATIVE ADVERTISING ON FACEBOOK AND GOOGLE

In Chapter 8 we described native advertising as advertising that matches the format, tone, and function of the publication or channel. That description fits traditional publisher sites but its meaning has become massively confused in social media. Let's try to make a bit of sense out of the confusion to help the advertiser in his or her ongoing search for what works best.

First, Facebook and Google. The Facebook Audience Network offers a native ad unit for mobile app ads. It features a series of templates that allow the app owner to design advertising options that blend with the app design and still meet the requirements of designating it as an advertisement. *Notice that this is an option for selling ads on the app, not for placing ads on behalf of the app.* The ads can contain either images or video and include a CTA. The Facebook Advertising Network then serves content provided by an advertiser into the template to create an ad on the app. The network also provides Facebook targeting options. You can see examples on the Facebook link.

Instagram does not have a native advertising option *per se*. The implication is that all ads on Instagram are native because of its unique visual platform.

Google accepts ads for its own sites and for the Google Display Network as described in Section 11-3. Its native ad format is offered through Double Click and therefore, like Facebook, *it provides an opportunity for publishers to sell ads on their sites*. Ads can appear on desktop and mobile websites and on mobile apps. Google uses two native ad templates, a content ad template and an app install template. You can see examples of both on the link. The publisher configures the template to be used. Ad Exchange then requests bids for the advertising and serves the ad content of the winning bidder. As you can see, Google's process is similar to that of Facebook's.

Remember that any YouTube video can be promoted and thereby become an ad and that video ads can also be created on the YouTube platform. These ads also seem to be, by definition, native because of the unique nature of the platform. In 2015, YouTube introduced TrueView cards. These are interactive overlays that appear on the right side of the video as seen in Figures 11.16a and b. The viewer can click on the

FIGURE 11.16a

YouTube Video Ad with Interactive Cards on Desktop

(a)

FIGURE 11.16b

YouTube Video Ad with Interactive Cards on Mobile

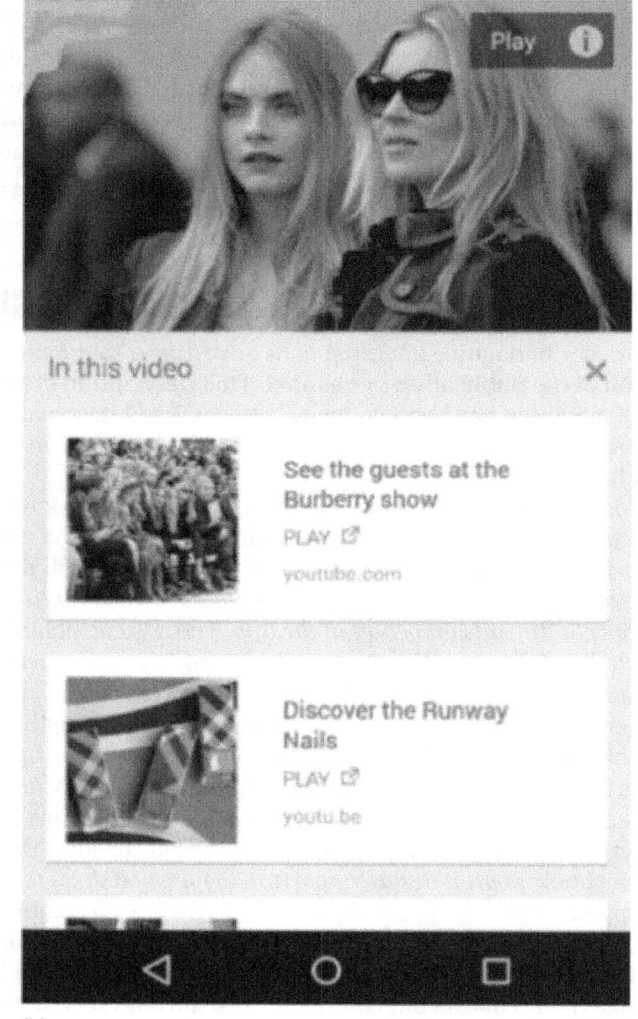

(b)

SOURCE: http://www.wordstream.com/blog/ws/2015/04/08/trueview-ads.

cards, in which case the advertiser is charged. If a viewer does not click to expand the cards, the advertiser is charged only if the viewer watches the video ad all the way through.[35] This type of video advertising moves one step closer to **social commerce**.

It is worthwhile to distinguish between sponsored content and native advertising in traditional digital media (Sections 8-3 and 8-5) and the use of native advertising on social media platforms where it is a monetization option, not a promotional one. One content marketing expert points out that native advertising is any type of advertising that mimics the format of the site on which it is placed while sponsored content is one specific type of native advertising.[36] Promoted posts on social platforms are clearly a type of sponsored content while native advertising on social platforms is a way of attracting advertising dollars to publisher sites. It is inherently confusing!

social commerce using social media platforms to assist in or to conduct ecommerce activities.

CHOOSING THE RIGHT PLATFORM(S)

How is the advertiser to make sense of all the paid search and social options? Once again, the answer is given in Figure 11.3—in a word, research! There are two basic questions: where is your target audience to be found and what is their intent? For example, if your audience is found on Google searching for products or DIY advice, then Google AdWords is an obvious choice.

It is important to identify platforms where members of the audience are spending time and engaging with content. Platforms that stimulate attention and engagement are highly desirable, sometimes even more so than platforms selected just because of their size. Then the advertiser's own objectives come into play. See Figure 11.17.

Some examples are as follows:

- Most businesses use Facebook, so ours should too. While that's not a profound reason, there is actually a grain of truth to it. With over 1.75 billion users worldwide in late 2016 and almost 40 percent of all internet users on the platform[37] Facebook's reach is tremendous. Do you need that broad reach to grow your online community or otherwise reach new customers? Then you can use Facebook Lookalike Audiences.[38] On the other hand, Facebook's precise targeting options are the reason most often given for its use. Do you

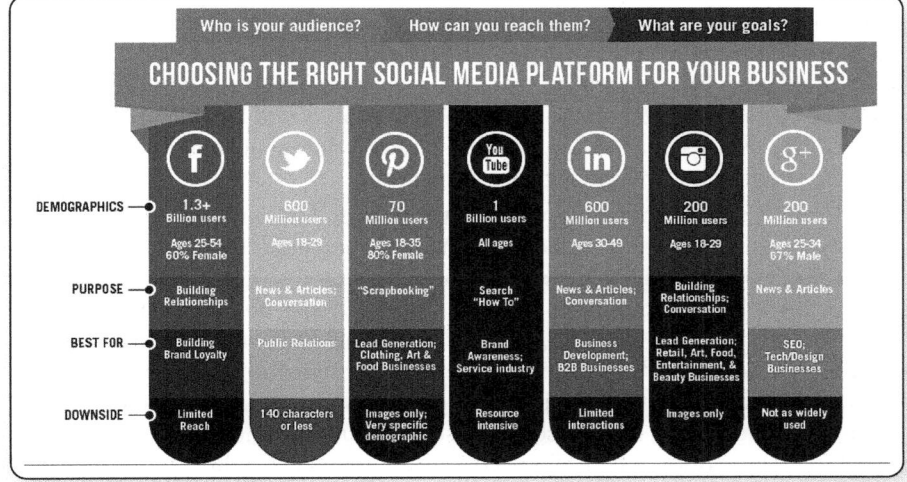

FIGURE 11.17

Features of Leading Social Media Platforms Important to Advertisers

SOURCE: http://us.accion.org/business-resources/articles-videos/choosing-right-social-media-platform-your-business.

have a precisely drawn target audience that you want to reach, knowing those people are most likely to be attracted by your product or service? Do you want to promote engagement within your existing community between purchase events? Or do you want to target your current customers with a new product ad? If so, you might want to upload an email list and create a Custom Audience.[39] While the options for using Facebook seem almost limitless they will be equally worthless unless the advertiser has clear objectives he or she wishes to accomplish.

- With over 450 million business and professional users in 200 countries LinkedIn is the leader in reach for that broad community.[40] It has good ratings on its effectiveness for content marketing and paid social from B2B advertisers,[41] adding to its leadership role. It has many targeting options and, in addition to sponsored content and display ads, it offers Sponsored InMail for direct message access to targeted users.[42]
- Is the target market the coveted Millennials segment? If so, the advertiser may wish to consider Snapchat which became the third most popular platform among Millennials (behind Facebook and Instagram) in 2016.[43] If the target audience is teenagers, Snapchat is an even more viable option since 80 percent of teens use the platform at least once a month.[44]
  - Remember, though, that numbers are not the only criterion for inclusion of a platform in a paid social campaign. Millennials have a high rate of visitation on YouTube with 93 percent visiting it at least once a month.[45] The Millennials that Comcast calls "Die Hards" are highly engaged with and very loyal to YouTube. They are digital first, they often binge watch and 62 percent of them say they take action after watching an ad.[46] Engagement and receptivity are very important in choosing platforms for advertising.
- Is the target market made up of highly educated young men who are not successfully reached by traditional media, even traditional digital media? Consider Reddit which is variously considered a major news source and a remarkably weird place on the internet. Its audience is 70 percent male with over 90 percent having at least some college.[47] Reddit is organized into conversational threads called Subreddits. There are over 850,000 Subreddits and over 11,000 active communities,[48] so it is a goldmine of interest-specific groups of users. The goldmine has proved difficult for advertisers, however, because Redditors are notoriously allergic to advertising, attacking posts that even smack of promotional intent. Reddit does offer sponsored posts. It is also offering something called Promoted User Posts in which a post that has gone viral, after receiving permission from the user who wrote the post, can be offered to the brand for sponsorship.[49] Think a Taco Bell Head as described in Section 5-4c as an example of a brand-related Reddit post that quickly went viral and thus offered an advertising opportunity.
- Is the brand looking for an audience that is heavily Millennials and teens but evenly divided between men and women? If so, consider Tumblr, the blogging platform owned by Yahoo! It has over 550 million active users and, at 28 minutes per session, a high engagement rate and its audience is heavily mobile. It has over 280 million blogs, providing a large and diverse set of topics to attract specialized audiences.[50] According to Pew, its audience is clustered at the high and low ends of the household income scale and tends to be urban and well educated.[51] In addition to sponsored posts (both image and video) it offers a Sponsored Day option which places the brand logo and tagline at the top of the Tumblr dashboard. It links to the platform's Explore page where the brand can feature its own content. Because the platform is owned by Yahoo! sponsored content can be syndicated to Yahoo! where it has the potential of reaching an even larger audience.[52] All these options are essentially native, requiring the advertiser to have a blog on Tumblr. In 2016, the platform introduced a Blogless Sponsored Post which does not require a blog on Tumblr.[53]

- Is the target market composed of women, especially women who shop? If so, the marketer should consider Pinterest. Of its 170 million registered users (100 million of whom are active each month) fully 85 percent are female.[54] They use Pinterest as a discovery engine for products to buy. They start earlier than other shoppers ahead of the holiday season, conducting 2 billion searches on Pinterest each month of which 130 million use its innovative image search tool. Pinterest is making it easy to shop, first with shopping directly from a mobile device and more recently with a shopping bag that does not expire and is available to the user on any device.[55] That represents a seductively easy shopping experience that brands with visually appealing merchandise may want to use to their advantage.

If research is the key to choosing the right platforms for a campaign—and it indisputably is—there are two more important pieces of advice. First, multiple platforms will be necessary to reach the target audience with sufficient frequency and impact. Whenever possible choose platforms for which content can easily be repurposed. Second, having chosen platforms and created content TEST, TEST, TEST (Section 4-5). Many platforms like Google have testing options built into their ad creation process. Initial testing should identify the platforms and content that works best. Testing other campaigns as they are executed allows the marketer to try other platforms that offer interesting features or focus on other types of content. Remember to test new features on the best-performing platforms. This kind of testing is the lifeblood of all good digital marketing and it is essential to bring order into the vast array of choices open to the marketer in paid search and social.

SUMMARY

Search is a key focus of internet advertisers at present and will continue to play an important role. In paid search, the advertiser bids on relevant keywords to get its advertisements displayed at the top or near the top of the paid advertisements. The bidding processes can be complicated, and there are many tools to help determine which keywords to bid on and how much to pay. Paid social also uses a bidding process for paid ads but placements are more limited, generally in the main feed or to its right. Paid social is already mobile first territory and the number of ads displayed is limited.

There are four basic steps in the search and social advertising process

Research > Build > Launch > Analyze and Report

The research step is largely about precisely defining the target audience and identifying the keyword bidding terms and the advertising appeal that will resonate with them. In the build step actual ads are created according to the specifications of the platform, bidding terms are selected, and budgets are set. The campaign is launched, either as a full-scale campaign—or better—as a test. Monitoring at least daily is essential and, depending on results, campaigns may be refined while they are ongoing. All platforms offer account dashboards that offer metrics, usually in real time, and graphics that assist in the reporting process. Analytics platforms like Google Analytics are useful in this process and there are numerous digital agencies that offer monitoring and reporting services.

Paid search offers just two basic formats, links and text, with Google having recently rolled out Expanded Text ads. Facebook is far and away the leader in paid social advertising and it offers additional display formats in addition to links and text. In addition, social platforms offer promoted posts. Facebook and Google also offer what is called native advertising, although it is a monetization option, not a promotional one. Other platforms offer advertising options unique to their own formats. The bewildering array of formats requires that advertisers retain focus on their own objectives and target audiences in order to make best platform and format choices. It also demands that advertisers continually test and refine their paid search and social advertising programs.

One can expect two levels of change that will affect paid search and social in the years to come. First, mobile advertising will continue to grow and dominate paid search as it already does paid social. Second, advertising formats will continue to adapt to user search and shopping patterns. Most assuredly, the paid search and social landscape will become more, not less, complicated over the coming years. In this chapter we have carefully pointed out that the resources advertisers need to understand paid search and social advertising—and to create and to execute their own ad campaigns if that is their choice—are readily available on the platforms with good advice available from experts all over the web.

DISCUSSION QUESTIONS

1. Compare two searches, one of desktop and one on a mobile device, using two search engines. Which produces the better results in terms of quality and relevance? Why?
2. How do the ads differ above in terms of how they are displayed? Which do you like better and why?
3. How do search strategies differ for mobile devices from the customer point of view?
4. Why is mobile search likely to be even more important in the future? What other trends are likely in the future for paid search?
5. What is the effect of the different types of ad formats on how advertisers conduct paid search campaigns?
6. Do you see paid social advertising as a useful or even a necessary element of many digital advertising campaigns? Why or why not?
7. How are display ads on social media platforms both similar to and different from display ads found on traditional digital sites?
8. What do you understand a promoted post to be? Are promoted posts the same on all platforms?
9. Explain the statement, "Any YouTube video can be an ad."
10. Do you agree or disagree with this statement? Ads on social media platforms have many of the characteristics of native advertising.
11. What are some of the elements of a paid social advertising campaign that could usefully be tested?
12. The process of developing paid search and paid social ads is quite different. Explain why you agree or disagree.

ENDNOTES

1. http://www.brafton.com/news/94-percent-b2b-buyers-research-online-purchase-decisions/.
2. http://www.adweek.com/socialtimes/81-shoppers-conduct-online-research-making-purchase-infographic/208527.
3. http://www.mobyaffiliates.com/blog/mobile-advertising-statistics-roundup-2016/
4. http://www.wsj.com/articles/facebook-revenue-soars-on-ad-growth-1461787856.
5. SEMPO, "The State of Search Engine Marketing 2004," http://www.sempo.org, 4.
6. https://www.google.com/partners/#p_content;idtf=tAQAAAAAAC0hM Search Advertising video from Google's Digital Marketing Course, "What Is Adwords?
7. https://www.google.com/onlinechallenge/.
8. https://support.google.com/partners/answer/3154326?hl=en.
9. http://adwords.google.com/support/aw/bin/answer.py?hl=en&answer=10215, retrieved October 29, 2011.

10. http://www.thewebmasterscafe.net/ppc/adwords-keyword-grouper.html, retrieved October 29, 2011.
11. "B2C Content Marketing: 2016 Benchmarks, Budgets, and Trends—North America," http://contentmarketinginstitute.com/wp-content/uploads/2015/10/2016_B2C_Research_Final.pdf.
12. "B2B Content Marketing: 2016 Benchmarks, Budgets, and Trends—North America," http://contentmarketinginstitute.com/wp-content/uploads/2015/09/2016_B2B_Report_Final.pdf.
13. https://www.google.com/adsense/start/#?modal_active=none.
14. Courtney Eckerie, "Inbound Marketing: How a Paid Social Media Campaign Drew in 1,000 New YouTube Subscribers in Just Four Days," http://www.marketingsherpa.com/article/case-study/olivia-rose-paid-social-media-growth.
15. John Herrman, "Media Websites Battle Faltering Ad Revenue and Traffic," http://www.nytimes.com/2016/04/18/business/media-websites-battle-falteringad-revenue-and-traffic.html?_r=2.
16. Jason Kint, "Google and Facebook Devour the Ad and Data Pie. Scraps for Everyone Else," https://digitalcontentnext.org/blog/2016/06/16/google-and-facebook-devour-the-ad-and-data-pie-scraps-for-everyone-else/.
17. "Ads on YouTube," https://creatoracademy.youtube.com/page/lesson/ad-types#yt-creators-strategies-2.
18. https://www.facebook.com/policies/ads/.
19. https://www.facebook.com/business/help/430291176997542.
20. https://canvas.facebook.com/.
21. https://www.google.com/ads/displaynetwork/build-your-ads/ad-formats.html#tab=text-ads.
22. https://www.youtube.com/yt/advertise/.
23. https://support.google.com/adwords/answer/6381008?hl=en&ref_topic=3119118.
24. https://support.google.com/adwords/answer/3265299?hl=en.
25. https://www.facebook.com/business/a/boost-a-post.
26. https://www.youtube.com/yt/advertise/.
27. "Coming Soon" New Instagram Business Tools," http://blog.business.instagram.com/post/145212269021/new-business-tools.
28. https://business.twitter.com/en/help/overview/what-are-promoted-tweets.html.
29. Tara, Johnson, "What Are Promoted Tweets?" http://www.cpcstrategy.com/blog/2016/01/promoted-tweets/.
30. https://business.twitter.com/en/advertising.html.
31. https://business.linkedin.com/marketing-solutions/native-advertising.
32. https://www.linkedin.com/help/linkedin/answer/4214/importing-and-inviting-your-email-contacts?lang=en.
33. https://business.pinterest.com/en/promoted-pins.
34. Roni Jacobson, "How Snapchat's Sponsored Lenses Became a Money-Printing Machine," https://backchannel.com/how-snapchats-sponsored-lenses-became-a-money-printing-machine-a1e45b0a82b#.8uknhdlob.
35. Tim Peterson, "YouTube Makes Skippable TrueView Ads More Interactive and More Lucrative," http://adage.com/article/digital/youtube-adds-interactive-cards-skippable-trueview-ads/297953/.
36. Joe Lazauskas, "Ask a Content Guy," https://contently.com/strategist/2016/04/20/ask-content-guy-whats-difference-sponsored-content-native-advertising/.
37. https://www.statista.com/topics/1164/social-networks/.
38. https://www.facebook.com/business/a/lookalike-audiences.
39. https://www.facebook.com/business/a/custom-audiences.
40. Craig Smith, "By the Numbers: 133 Amazing LinkedIn Statistics," http://expandedramblings.com/index.php/by-the-numbers-a-few-important-linkedin-stats/.
41. "B2B Content Marketing: 2016 Benchmarks, Budgets, and Trends—North America," http://contentmarketinginstitute.com/wp-content/uploads/2015/09/2016_B2B_Report_Final.pdf.

42. https://www.linkedin.com/help/linkedin/answer/722/targeting-options-and-best-practices-for-linkedin-advertisements?lang=en
43. http://mwpartners.com/snapchat-is-now-the-third-most-popular-social-network-among-millennials/.
44. Lauren Johnson, "Snapchat Beats Instagram and Facebook as the Top Social Platform for Teens," http://www.adweek.com/news/technology/snapchat-beats-instagram-and-facebook-top-social-platform-teens-174053.
45. https://plus.google.com/+GlobalWebIndexNet/posts/2wTiZmob26f.
46. Gillian Heltai, "What Millennials' YouTube Usage Tells Us about the Future of Video Viewership," https://www.comscore.com/Insights/Blog/What-Millennials-YouTube-Usage-Tells-Us-about-the-Future-of-Video-Viewership.
47. Michael Barthel et al., "1. Reddit News Users More Likely to Be Male, Young, and Digital in Their News Preferences," http://www.journalism.org/2016/02/25/reddit-news-users-more-likely-to-be-male-young-and-digital-in-their-news-preferences/.
48. Craig Smith, "By the Numbers: 60+ Amazing Reddit Statistics," http://expandedramblings.com/index.php/reddit-stats/.
49. Andrew Hutchinson, "Reddit Looking to Open Up Advertising Opportunities via Sponsored Posts," http://www.socialmediatoday.com/social-networks/reddit-looking-open-advertising-opportunities-sponsored-posts?utm_source=web&utm_medium=links&utm_content=Reddit%20Looking%20to%20Open%20Up%20Advertising%20Opportunities%20via%20Sponsored%20Posts&utm_campaign=related-items.
50. Craig Smith, "Tumblr Stats," http://expandedramblings.com/index.php/tumblr-user-stats-fact/.
51. Drew DeSilver, "5 Facts about Tumblr," http://www.pewresearch.org/fact-tank/2013/05/20/5-facts-about-tumblr/.
52. https://www.tumblr.com/business.
53. Rebecca Sentence, "Are Tumblr's Advertising Plans a Bad Idea?" https://www.clickz.com/are-tumblrs-advertising-plans-a-bad-idea/96335/.
54. Craig Smith, "Pinterest Statistics and Facts (October 2016), http://expandedramblings.com/index.php/pinterest-stats/.
55. George, "Pinterest's New Shopping Bag Is the Future of Social Commerce," http://wersm.com/pinterests-new-shopping-bag-is-the-future-of-social-commerce/.

Chapter 12

Mobile Marketing

LEARNING OBJECTIVES

By the time you complete this chapter, you will be able to:

1. Explain the concept of micro-moments and its implications for mobile marketing.
2. Discuss the current state of mobile CX.
3. Explain why mobile CX is vital and what marketers can do to improve it.
4. Identify the essential elements of a mobile marketing strategy.
5. Explain why a mobile-friendly site is necessary.
6. Identify key issues in developing mobile content.
7. Discuss the reasons for the growth of mobile advertising.
8. Explain why localized advertising is important to both brand marketers and local businesses.
9. Discuss what is necessary to create an effective mobile app.
10. Identify some important technologies that are being used by retailers.
11. Comment on the growth of wearables as an aspect of mobile technology.

From the beginning of this book the word "mobile" has reverberated. From an interesting novelty just a few years ago, mobile use has become the key driver of internet growth and mobile marketing has become a key element of digital strategy. Large enterprises and small businesses, multinational firms and local concerns—all are focusing effort on mobile marketing. Mobile CX has become a cornerstone of marketing success. Such is the disruptive change that has occurred in only a few years.

In spite of the importance of mobile and the necessity that mobile be strategic, not reactive, we must be careful to not to confuse mobile strategies with marketing strategy. Marketing strategy today is carried out in an omni-channel world as discussed in Section 6.4. Mobile is often the channel at the forefront of activity today but it cannot be successful in isolation as we will discuss throughout this chapter. Figures 12.1a and b highlight the importance of mobile in the digital channel mix.

In 2014, the time consumers spent with mobile surpassed that spent with a desktop device for the first time. Figure 12.1a shows that trend continuing. At the end of 2015, 35 percent of time was spent with desktop while 65 percent was spent on a mobile device. The trend lines show that the trend to mobile and away from desktop has continued since 2013 and looks to be continuing. Sixty-five percent of the mobile time is accounted for

FIGURE 12.1a

How People Use Digital Media Time

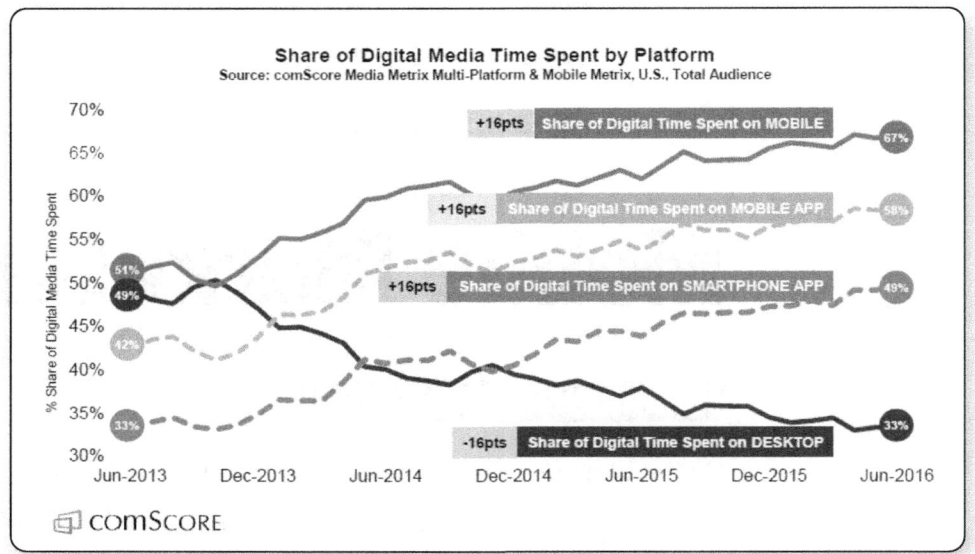

SOURCE: http://www.kpcb.com/internet-trends.

FIGURE 12.1b

How People Use Smartphones

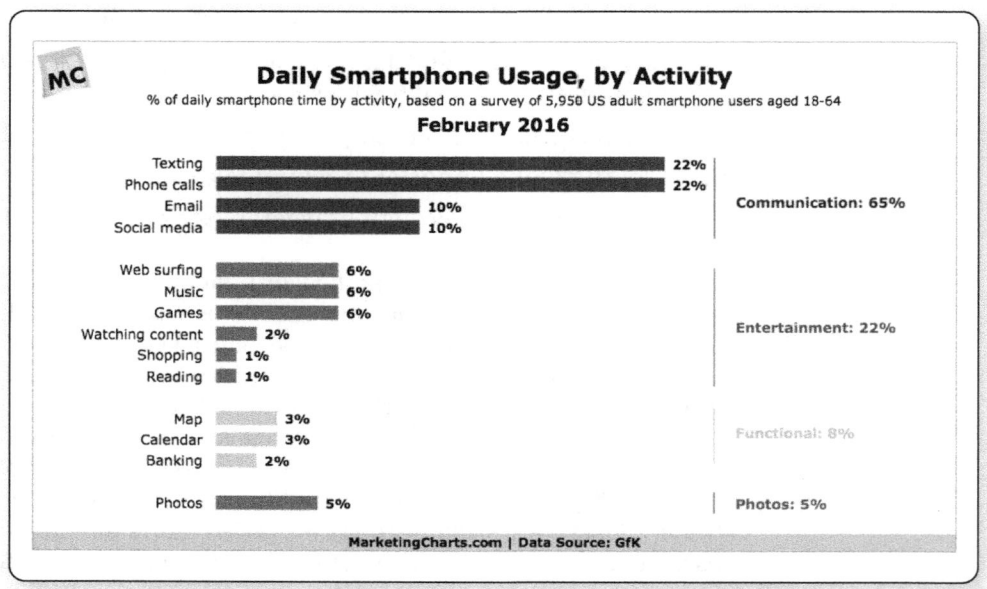

SOURCE: http://www.marketingcharts.com/online/which-activities-do-smartphone-owners-prioritize-on-their-devices-65242/attachment/gfk-daily-smartphone-use-by-activity-feb2016/.

by a mobile app of some kind with smartphone apps alone accounting for 47 percent. Figure 12.1b shows that communications, including social media, account for the lion's share of smartphone usage. The primacy of communications has been true since the beginning of the internet. In this chart, shopping is grouped into the entertainment category and represents only 1 percent of time. However that may be an understatement. What portion of the web surfing and watching content time do you guess has to do with shopping? Some of it is certainly product research, as we will see in the next section.

Mobile search (The Growing Impact of Search Section 10-1) has also grown at a rapid rate giving Google a vested interest in the success of mobile marketing. It has developed many resources and a useful way of looking at how mobile impacts the customer journey.

THE CUSTOMER JOURNEY IN MICRO-MOMENTS

The **micro-moments** perspective on the customer journey, as seen in Figure 12.2 has four stages:

micro-moments not a measure of time; a concept that describes consumer recognition of needs.

- I want to know, in which the customer does research.
- I want to go, in which the customer is considering purchasing locally and looking for a source.

FIGURE 12.2

The Micro-Moments of the Customer Journey

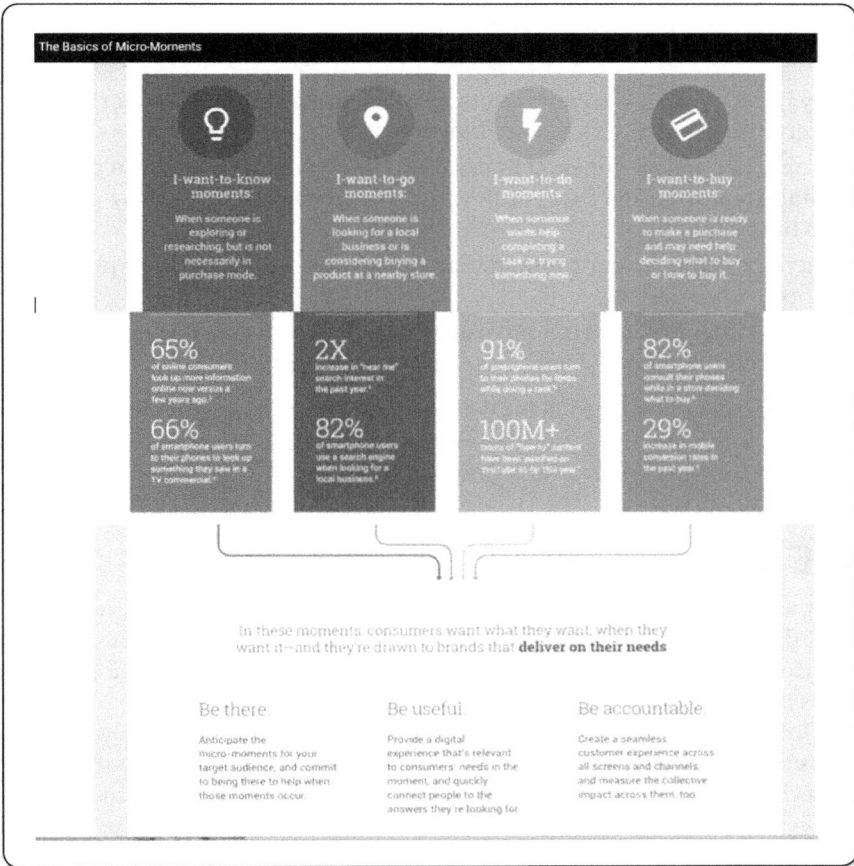

SOURCE: Adapted from https://www.thinkwithgoogle.com/infographics/micro-moments-understand-new-consumer-behavior.html.

- I want to do, in which the customer is seeking help with the purchase.
- I want to buy, in which the customer has decided to make a purchase but needs more information or help.

As you can see, these customer journey stages do not differ greatly from the underlying consumer purchase process with which we are all familiar. Notice, however, that we are being careful not to describe this as a mobile journey. It is more likely to be a multichannel journey.

The degree to which it is multichannel as well as the degree to which mobile figures in various stages is highlighted by the data that shows a 65 percent increase in online search with much of it taking place on smartphones. That is especially true when consumers are looking for a local business near themselves. A staggering 91 percent of smartphone users consult their phones while doing a task; "how do I assemble the bookcase?" for example. An almost equally large number actually consult their smartphones while in a store shopping for products. Perhaps you have noticed that many large stores are making it easy to access Wi-Fi while on the premises. Consumers want information ranging from product reviews to the how-to videos on YouTube. And last, but not least, mobile purchasing is steadily increasing as we first discussed in Section 1-4b2.

The value of this concept to the marketer lies in understanding that the consumer is looking for immediate gratification and expects the brand under consideration to meet his or her needs in real time. Micro-moments are not measured in duration of time. They are the moments in which a person turns to a device, often a smartphone, to gratify an immediate need for information or for action. The advice to marketers is to Be There when the moments occur; Be Useful by immediately providing consumers with what they are looking for; and to Be Accountable for all aspects of the CX in all channels. Only by measuring CX in all channels, at all touchpoints, can the brand know whether it is fulfilling all customer requirements.

Google makes additional points about mobile impacts along the journey:

- Ninety percent of smartphone users have used their phones to work toward a long-term goal or process like making a purchase while on the go.
- Sixty-nine percent of consumers are more likely to purchase from a company that makes information that is relevant to them easy to find. This appears to trump brand familiarity.
- Seventy-six percent of consumers who do a local search on their phones visit the store within one day.
- Fifty-one percent of smartphone users have discovered a new product or brand while searching on their phones.[1]

The micro-moment approach is customer centric and designed to help marketers create mobile marketing programs that work. In Interactive Exercise 12.1 you can see how it worked for the Best Western Hotel chain.

MOBILE CX

Since the customer interaction is taking place in micro-moments CX is the beginning and end of the encounter. What does it take to create a real-time CX that satisfies, even delights? Best Western studied the journeys of its customers. Here are some other businesses that are mastering the tools.

At *L'Oréal* the CEO recently said "It is clear that the digital changes everything. We must rethink everything differently. Today, L'Oréal no longer sells cosmetics but beauty services." One of the ways is to make women a Makeup Genius by using its app. It uses the person's digital camera to look at her face and calibrate her features. Then she can either choose from a series of premade looks or try products one by one. The app then shows a live view of the person wearing the virtual makeup. In

Figure 12.3 a customer is using the app in the retail store before she purchases. The image responds realistically, adjusting when the wearer smiles, closes her eyes, or even turns her head to see from a different angle. The *New York Times* found it easy to use and apparently found the looks appealing.[2] At this writing it had a 4+ rating on the iTunes store.

Turbo Tax managed to make it on to Saturday Night Live:

> Hands folded on the "Saturday Night Live" Weekend Update desk, mischievous grin on his face, Seth Meyers locked eyes with the camera: "Yeah, as if I don't enjoy doing my taxes enough already," he said, holding up his iPhone, "A new mobile phone app was released Friday by TurboTax, which will allow people to prepare and file their taxes from their smartphones. Finally, the stress and headache of doing your taxes comes to a much smaller screen!"[3]

How did an income tax app achieve this level of coolness? Intuit had been testing the idea of an income tax app for awhile using a typical first stage test, a paper prototype. People agreed that the idea was great, but they didn't believe their phone could take a usable image of their W2 form and use it to fill in their tax return. They had to prototype the technology for an iPhone. Then they watched users try it and see that it worked. When the users' eyes lighted up they knew they had something. It still took a lot of work to make it a mobile-only solution with which the user could capture an image of his W2, fill out a few other fields on the form and file his return—all in about 5 minutes![4] There is now a line of Intuit tax apps, but the original TaxCaster app now has over 17 thousand reviews a 4+ score on iTunes.[5]

At *Zappos* the Head of Mobile says,

"CX needs to be seamless regardless of point of entry. At Zappos, we approach mobile CX as just CX, not differentiating it, because mobile is simply who we are."[6]

Zappos has long been recognized for customer service excellence, scoring in the top ten of the United States. CX Excellence rankings for 2016 along its parent company Amazon. It earned its reputation for customer service excellence through its telephone call centers;[7] the focus carries over into its mobile CX. Customer service is emphasized on the app with free returns highlighted in the center above many mobile options ranging from shoes to gift cards to search. The aim is to keep customers

FIGURE 12.3

The L'Oréal MakeUp Genius App

SOURCE: http://www.cmo.com/interviews/articles/2016/8/18/loreal-vp-innovation-rachel-weiss.html?cid=em:MR345#gs.ipl3=U8.

engaged so they will not delete the app by creating a personalized, emotion-driven connection. Customers are encouraged to submit feedback and to review products. Special events in the lives of loyal customers are rewarded with gifts or homemade cards, making them feel like members of the Zappos family.[8]

Zappos also has a sense of humor. Cats are often a theme and at one point if you shook a phone with the Zappos app, it rained cats![9] It's all about the service and the experience. Zappos has been rated on the iTunes store over 53,000 times and has a 4+ score.[10]

At *Nespresso* the CX is truly multichannel with emphasis on both mobile and retail. They offer services that are expected at high-end coffee shops like order online and pick up in store. The mobile app encourages customers to search for more information while in the store. Store design, like the capsule wall featuring the 23 Grand Cru coffee selections, also encourages information search. Three test boutiques in Europe place mobile technology in the hands of store Coffee Specialists who can help the customer with his order and send it for immediate preparation. In the short time before the customer leaves the store with the purchase he is spending quality time with a well-informed Coffee Specialist.[11] When the customer arrives home he can brew his coffee remotely using the app—as long as the tank is full and a pod has already been inserted. It's not yet the IoT (Internet of Things) because it can't yet refill the tank or install a coffee capsule. It can, however, notify the user when the tank is low, the coffee maker needs maintenance, or when he is low on capsules.[12] With this level of services is the IoT far behind, with the ability to sense the customer's location and have coffee ready when he arrives?

These examples of excellent CX were suggested by Brian Solis in an Altimeter presentation called "The Inevitability of a Mobile-Only CX." Is he suggesting that in short order all CXs will take place on mobile? No, he is not—not yet anyway. However, he makes two important points. First, most businesses have not made a sufficient commitment to mobile, either in terms of investment or in terms of strategy. Second, a mobile-first strategy is essential for marketing leadership at present. Most experiences are partly mobile today and many are indeed mobile-only.[13] Let's look at what mobile-first means and then examine elements of a mobile strategy based on that type of approach.

ESSENTIAL ELEMENTS OF MOBILE STRATEGY

We have already encountered the term mobile-first in the context of business models in Section 3-6c but did not attempt to give it a concise definition. In the 2015 Econsultancy/Adobe study "A Quest for Mobile Excellence", executives were asked to agree or disagree with a statement that captures the essence of mobile-first: *"Mobile activities are central to our overall business and how we engage with customers."* From a strategy perspective, that is a good definition. We will give mobile-first a different definition in the context of website design in Chapter 15.

When asked to agree or disagree with the statement only 6 percent of the marketers and digital professionals who responded strongly agreed with the statement while another 23 percent agreed—29 percent in all. When specifically asked if theirs was a mobile-first organization only 7 percent strongly agreed and another 12 percent agreed for a total of 19 percent.[14] This indicates that most companies have a long way to go in terms putting mobile at the heart of their strategies. Figure 12.4 provides a set of strategy elements that are useful in that quest.

Designing a Mobile-Friendly Site

What are the characteristics of a mobile-friendly site? Google distills it down into a single piece of advice—make everything easy for your customer. Here are some specifics of what that entails:

responsive fluid site design that senses the user's device and automatically adapts to it.

- Use **responsive** technology, which we will discuss in Chapter 15, to transform your internet site into a mobile site.

FIGURE 12.4
The Elements of Mobile Marketing Strategy

SOURCE: Adapted from http://thealmostdone.com/2015/11/29/tips-on-mobile-marketing-strategy/.

- Keep the design and navigation simple.
    - Make it easy to use with just the thumbs or a forefinger.
    - Ensure that no pinching is needed to expand or contract.
- Make content, including videos short and to the point.
- Design forms for mobile use.
- Take advantage of geolocation technologies to provide maps, driving directions, store locators, and other location-specific information.
- Make it easy to find and use contact information.
- Be sure that it loads quickly, as discussed in Chapter 10 and that it operates smoothly throughout.
    - Google's mobile-friendly tool is introduced in Chapter 15 and being sure your site meets its criteria is crucial. Google recently announced that it will no longer designate sites as mobile-friendly in search results, but that does not mean it is less important. Google continues to assign severe penalties in terms of ranking to sites that do not meet its mobile-friendly criteria and to favor mobile-optimized sites in mobile search ranking.
    - Facebook has announced that it would prevent ads from showing on its platform if the websites to which the ads are linked are slow to load. Facebook's research shows that 40 percent of viewers click away if a page takes 3 seconds to load.[15]

Both sites have information for developers to help them optimize sites for mobile. Marketers need to be sure their guidance is being followed in site design and maintenance.

Designing a Site for Mobile Usability and CX

Website usability guru Jakob Nielsen famously said a few years ago that mobile usability was an oxymoron. Thankfully, he has revised that opinion in recent years, mostly as a result of responsive technology. The Nielsen Norman Group has recommendations from their research into usability techniques that contribute to good CX:

- Content is the primary focus.
    - The small screen restricts the amount of content. Plan carefully so users don't have to go back and forth from one screen to another.
    - Usability elements like buttons, menus, navigation bars, links, and others that help users find their way around are necessary. However, content should always be the priority.
- Long pages that require scrolling are a problem. Use mini tables of contents that give direct access to each section, back to the top buttons and other devices that make traveling around a long page easier.
- Layer content, with details relegated to secondary pages. Avoid linear pages such as the ever-popular listicles on some sites. They are entertaining, but can take forever to load, degrading the experience.[16]

Note the importance of content in Dr. Nielsen's recommendations. Other experts also prioritize content and have other recommendations:

- Above all, KISS. Whether the designer is keeping it simple by focusing on a single topic or with simple, easy-to-follow menus and navigation, complexity and clutter are enemies of good experience.
- Images slow down load time, so use them judiciously.
- Smartphones and tablets can make use of features that desktop applications do not have.
- Functions like such as GPS allow a store locator function; the user can then tap to call the store.
- Prepopulate forms and use autofill wherever possible.
- Put the call to action on the first page where it has a better chance of being seen.
- "Click and collect" payment is a great convenience, but customer security must always be the dominant consideration.[17,18]

Two themes run through both of these sections—the need for simplicity and the importance of page loading speed. Stuart Macmillan of U.K. online shoe store Schuh uses these two requirements to explain the essential purpose of mobile-first:

> *"Simpler is better" really would appear to be the case. Approaching it mobile first really helped us with our design. It helped us eliminate unnecessary UI elements, whereas in the past we would have included them just because we felt we had plenty of pixels to spare.*[19]

In other words, just because some element is on your internet website, it doesn't necessarily have to be on your mobile site, especially if it will slow loading time or otherwise degrade CX. It's easier to accomplish that if the mobile site is designed first, followed by the desktop site.

Mobile-friendly and good CX are not just "nice to have." Since 2015 Google has been penalizing the search rankings of websites that are not mobile-friendly. Google announced in mid-2016 that it would further emphasize good mobile **UX (user experience)** by penalizing **interstitials** and popup ads that slow user access to mobile content. This will begin in January 2017 and it creates another possibility that a site could be penalized in search ranking if it does not meet Google's criteria for acceptable use of interstitials and popups.[20]

UX (user experience) according to Jakob Nielsen, all of the user's interactions with the brand on all touchpoints, which makes it nearly synonymous with CX. Often used to describe the usability of a website or a mobile app.

interstitials ad that covers the entire screen.

Creating and Managing Mobile Content

Content is not only the focus of designing a mobile website, it is the marketer's reason for having a mobile website. The possibilities for content are enormous and creating it is labor intensive. It therefore requires a careful strategy and consistent monitoring for results.

How much of this content is consumed on mobile? Figure 12.1a puts that figure at 67 percent. In case there is any doubt whether B2B users are consuming their share of mobile media a study by Millward Brown Digital found that:

- Forty-two percent of B2B buyers used a mobile device at some time during the purchase process.
- Forty-nine percent of B2B buyers who use their mobile phone for research do so while at work.

That means that effective mobile content is essential whether the audience is B2C or B2B.[21]

What makes mobile content effective? Many of the answers are just good marketing:

- Know what the target audience is looking for. Effective content is not about what's interesting. It is about what customers want and need. It's also about their pain points—what problems do they need to resolve? Consequently, effective content starts with data that reveals customers' wants, needs, problems, and habits. Jim Yu of BrightEdge says to give each piece of content the "why this, why now" test.[22]
- Map the customer journey, identifying the moments and the type of device they are likely to turn to at a given moment.
- Develop content for each of the micro-moments, but don't underestimate the early ones. Create effective content for the I-want-to-know moments like refrigerator comparisons or even kitchen remodeling ideas. He calls the latter I-want-to-be-inspired moments.
- Tracking content performance is essential. Equally essential is to track it across the entire customer journey. Marketers need to know what content influenced customers in the early stages, not just what content they viewed immediately before they purchased.[23]

Mountain Dew has long been a digital leader and its mobile and internet sites demonstrate a number of issues about mobile design and content. The screens in Figure 12.5 were captured at the same time, within just a few minutes of one another. They are from The Latest site which is entertainment oriented. Mountain Dew has another site devoted to its products. The slogan that appeared on the site was "Do The Dew" and the theme was adventure oriented.

Obviously, the screens look different although both of them devote more space to the video than to any other piece of content. Although there are fewer items of content on the mobile screen, all of them work. The image of the Mountain Dew Pitch Black product connects to the DEWcision 2016 site which announced Pitch Black the winner of the product contest and connects to a Pitch Black VR experience. The product image connects to a video for the Kick Start energy drink that combines funny and mildly gross moments. The tabs at the bottom of the mobile screen connect the viewer with a sports site, a site with VR content, and the video for the Kick Start product. The menu button at the bottom right has those options plus the Amazon Store which offers familiar and some rather weird exclusive Mountain Dew flavors. The second page also offers a social media sharing bar and an offer to sign up for the DEWsletter—yes, really! It's necessary to click through to a third page to sign up on a minimalist form. Do you think it's a fair summary that there is a lot of content here, presented with no fuss and ease of access?

In a sense, the desktop site is even less cluttered. The tabs at the bottom are shown expanded but when the viewer accesses the site they are retracted. That leaves

FIGURE 12.5

a. Mobile Home Page and
b. Desktop Home Page

Source on both mobile and desktop: http://www.mountaindew.com/.

the screen for the auto-play video of young men "Doing The Dew" and racing their cycles and dune buggies in the desert. The video is a continuous loop; I tried to find a way to shut it down and couldn't. I don't imagine most visitors want to shut it down and just look at a static site. The tabs at the bottom include the options from the mobile site plus links to mini sites for Black Label, Dewshine, Green Label, and a trailer from the movie "We Are Blood," a movie about skateboarding. The Kitty Wop tab features the cat from the Kick Start video starring in an interactive video in which the viewer can make the cat perform all sorts of unlikely dance steps.

Is the message clear, whether it's the mobile site or the desktop site? The tone is upbeat, energetic, sports oriented, and decidedly male—all designed to appeal to a global audience of Millennial males. The President of PepsiCo's global beverage group says the Millennial males have more in common with one another than they have national differences. This makes them an ideal target for this type of global campaign. Both sites are connected to a sports mini-site but the overall emphasis is on participatory sports. That's also a good fit with the global reach.[24]

A final issue about mobile design and content is where to place content in order to maximize its impact. The newspaper concept of "above the fold" carried over into desktop website design because people don't like to scroll and often do not see the content at the bottom of the web page. Heat maps from eye-tracking studies of desktop internet pages are shown in Section 15.4d. Figure 12.6 shows a heat map of an eye-tracking study of mobile screens. The study found that viewers basically look at the center of the screen, giving 68 percent of their attention to content in the top half of the screen and 86 percent to the top two-thirds of the screen. How do you rate the placement of the "Do The Dew" theme and the "Watch the Video" CTA on the Mountain Dew mobile screen? It's right where it will get the most attention.

Mobile Advertising

As marketers "follow the eyeballs" the importance of mobile advertising increases. In Section 1-4b1, we discussed the fact that digital users spend far more of their time on mobile devices than on desktop devices and that time spent with mobile has

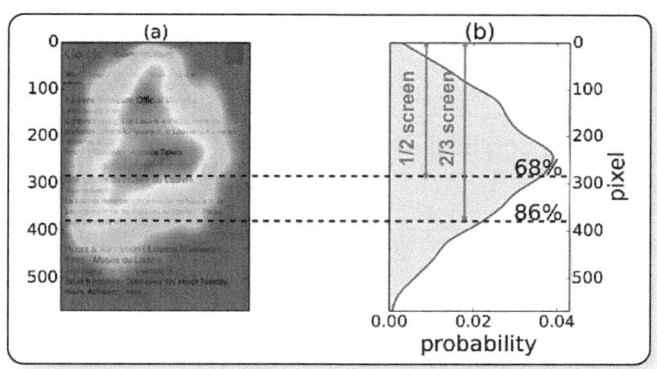

FIGURE 12.6

Heat Map for Mobile Screens

SOURCE: http://contentmarketinginstitute.com/2015/04/content-engages-mobile-readers/.

overtaken time spent with TV. In Section 1-4b2, the importance of both mobile display and search advertising was highlighted. Section 7-4 discussed the importance of mobile display advertising and various formats offered. In Chapter 11 we discussed the increasing importance of paid social advertising much, but not all, of which is viewed on mobile.

Mobile's share of advertising spending has not yet caught up, as shown in Figure 12.7. That has been true of digital advertising itself as well as other digital media channels. TV still commands top dollar because of its huge reach. Digital, and especially mobile, counter with the ability to reach highly targeted markets and to engage viewers. Mobile is also especially effective in mounting multichannel advertising campaigns.

Pepsi's "The Sound Drop" is not an advertising campaign per se, although comes from a long history of association between music and Pepsi advertising and sponsorship. It is, instead, a platform on which emerging artists will be featured. The plan is to launch ten new artists during the calendar year. An ongoing content series of this type requires promotion and that is where advertising comes in.

The program is collaborative. Pepsi's partners and their contributions include the following:

- iHeart Media which will feature ads across its broadcast radio stations, 850 station websites and iHeart Radio. iHeart says. "With over a quarter billion monthly listeners in the U.S., iHeartMedia has the largest reach of any radio or television outlet in America." It adds that through an array of iHeart and artist Facebook and Twitter pages, its social media content reaches 85 million people.[25]
- One special event will include a 24-hour takeover of the iHeart Media Snapchat Discover channel to promote the platform and the artists. The Snapchat Discover channel is a platform for entertainment publishers of all kinds that will run ads for The Sound Drop during the time frame of the channel takeover.[26]
- Shazam, the mobile music app that reaches over 12 billion people worldwide,[27] will also run ads. Those ads will direct users to personalized messages from featured artists. The ads will also run when a user tags the featured artist on the app.
- It will also use influencer marketing (Section 5-2b) to encourage influencers to remix tracks and host them on their own pages.
- YouTube is not listed as a partner, each featured artist will be the subject of a mini-documentary produced by Pepsi and hosted on its YouTube Channel. The first featured Lucas Graham with Devvon Terrell. It had garnered 384,740 views in roughly the first month since its upload in August 2016.[28]

This campaign is an example of what an experienced digital marketer like Pepsi can do with a campaign that is mostly mobile in nature.[29] It is not exclusively mobile;

FIGURE 12.7
Share of Global Ad Spending for Major Media Channels

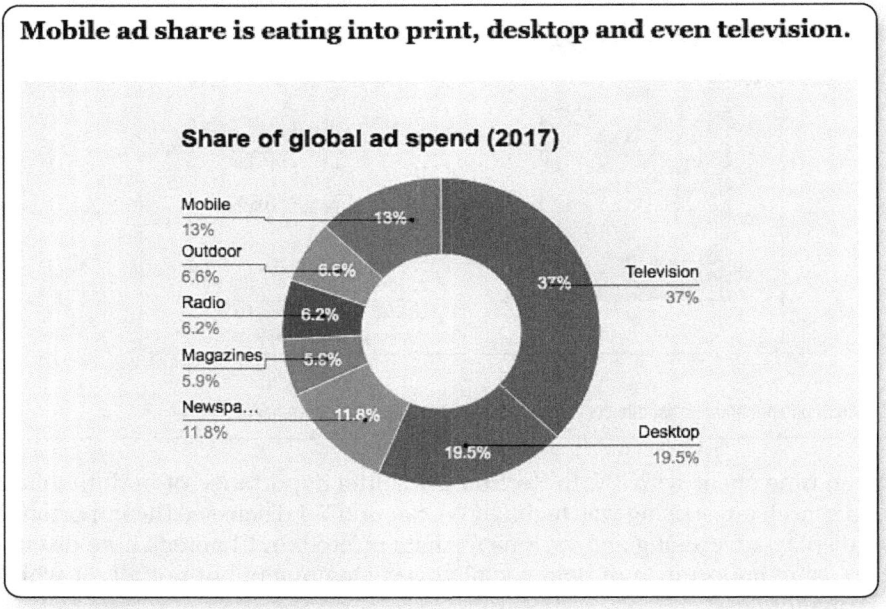

SOURCE: http://digiday.com/publishers/state-mobile-ad-spending-5-charts/.

content is available on the desktop. However, the target audience is young, so the viewership can be expected to be primarily mobile.[30]

"The Sound Drop" is an example of how one digital marketer, in collaboration with other digital marketers, can reach a potentially huge global audience. At the other extreme is the potential for mobile marketing to reach a hyperlocal audience.

Local Opportunities

Figure 12.8 shows ways in which localized targeting can work. The Rogers Centre is a multi-purpose sports and event stadium in downtown Toronto. In Figure 12.8a, a **geo-fence** or virtual perimeter has been drawn around the centre. That enables the marketer to target all cellphone users who pass through the space. If the Toronto Blue Jays are playing at the centre, that might attract a set of advertisers who wanted to reach sports fans. If Disney on Ice is playing there it would suggest advertisers of family-oriented products. That is powerful targeting.

Figure 12.8b shows how hyperlocal advertising can work in a different way. In mobile advertising contextual refers to the specific characteristic of the defined geographical area including types of locations, demographics, and other census data. In Figure 12.8b the map shows a green space near York University. The space contains a bridle path and that is the title given to the defined area. You can see how this would interest advertisers who were trying to reach the student population or advertisers of recreational products who wanted to reach a population that was enjoying an outing. Messages that reflect the context in which people receive them also represent powerful targeting.

Local businesses can, of course, develop their own local advertising campaigns and there are numerous mobile agencies that provide advertising platforms at affordable prices. Small local businesses can also place their ads on apps where localized content is already being presented like Yelp and the Weather Channel. A family-owned chain of three Mediterranean restaurants in Westborough MA used mobile network Chitka, which reached over 10,000 mobile apps in 2014. The restaurant was able to create its own ad and name its own price for the exposures. The owner chose $5 per 5,000 views and was happy to find patrons coming into the restaurant saying they had seen her ad on their phone. She was also pleased with reports that gave the number of

geo-fence software feature that lets GPS or RFID establish a geographical area that can be defined by a virtual perimeter.

FIGURE 12.8

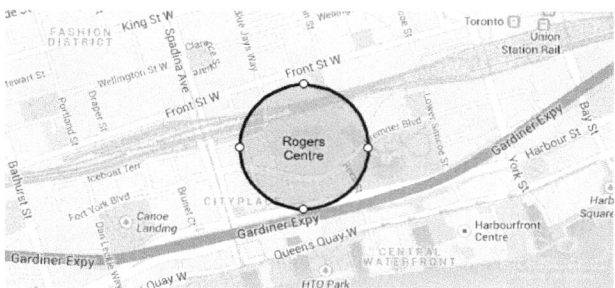

a. Geofencing

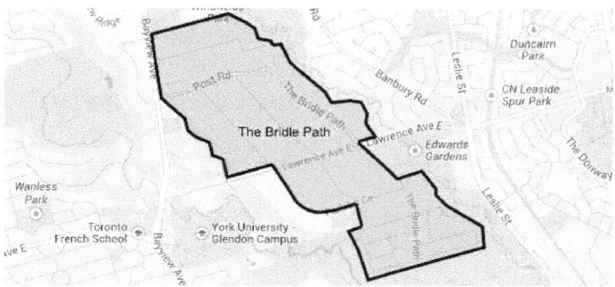

b. Contextual Local Targeting

SOURCE: http://marketingland.com/hyperlocal-mobile-advertising-changes-everything-92979.

views and where they were being seen.[31] In 2016 the network reports that it reaches 350,000 publishers and serves over 4 billion ads each month.[32] A 2016 review acknowledges complaints that some publishers do not realize substantial returns and that some of the ad placements are not relevant. Still, the reviewer found the platform easy to use and considered it an acceptable alternative to AdSense, especially for publishers like blogs.[33] This is only one of many alternatives that put mobile advertising within the reach of even the smallest local business.

Advertising on Social Media Platforms

In Chapter 11 we discussed the broader issue of paid social and made the point that only some of it is advertising, for instance display advertising, is advertising in the true sense of the term. Much of paid social is promoted content or other types of platform-specific promotions. However, advertising has its place and, like localization, social platform advertising is within the budget of small and start-up businesses. One business that has staked its growth on social media advertising from the beginning is BarkBox. It is an ecommerce subscription service that offers monthly shipments of size-appropriate dog treats and toys. Figure 12.9 shows ads from Facebook, Instagram, and YouTube.

BarkBox appears to rely solely on social media promotion. In addition to the ads, promoted posts, and videos it has a "Bark Pack" of some 400 "celebrity" dogs, each with its own Instagram account, many of which have over a million followers.[34] They also engage in partnerships and events to support rescue dog efforts. Overall, it's a robust social media effort with paid social at its core.

This section stresses that mobile strategy is a multichannel effort, whether it is the multiple social platforms and real-world efforts of BarkBox or the complex set of global partnerships and promotional activities of Pepsi's The Sound Drop campaign. One digital agency executive sums up the appeal of mobile across many communications channels: "So what does mobile lend itself to doing? Short, low-friction actions: sharing, liking, tweeting, taking pictures, looking at pictures, reading short-form content, watching videos."[35] In general, that's good advice, but remember that BarkBox succeeds with videos longer than are usually recommended.

FIGURE 12.9a
Facebook Ad for BarkBox

This Facebook ad (Figure 12.9a) is a reduced-price offer with a CTA. Facebook says that tools used include promoted posts as well as two kinds of ad targeting. Custom Audiences reach people the marketer already knows—has on an email list, for example. Look-alike Audiences use known traits like age, gender and dog ownership to create Facebook segments that look like current purchasers. Its case study says that:

- One-third of daily website traffic at BarkBox comes from Facebook.
- Fifty percent of daily conversions originate on Facebook.
- It brings in 5,000 new subscribers each month.[36]

SOURCE: http://blog.hubspot.com/marketing/social-network-advertising#sm.0000002to08kmvcpyv7vlb6v649jq.

FIGURE 12.9b
Instagram Ad for BarkBox

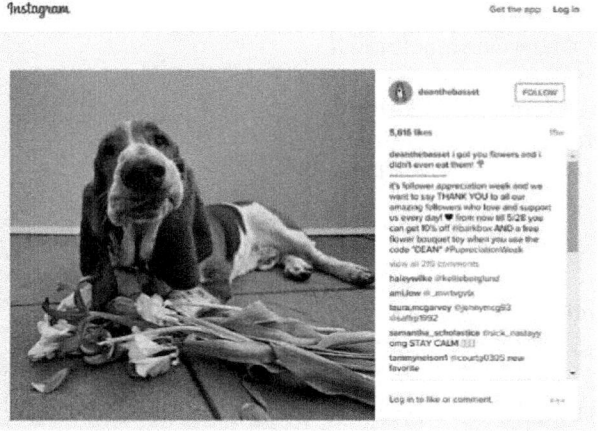

With success on Facebook and targeting experience there, it is not surprising that BarkBox also uses Instagram ads like the one in Figure 12.9b where its ads attract both Likes and Comments.[37]

In addition, BarkBox has introduced an app called BarkCam. It not only takes pictures but also offers sounds that are supposed to make your dog sit still and look at the camera. The app can post images on additional networks too.[38] The app is highly rated on iTunes and, if you are interested, there is a video app also.[39]

SOURCE: https://www.socialmediaexplorer.com/content-sections/movers-and-makers/an-interview-with-4-brands-on-the-secrets-to-their-social-media-success/.

FIGURE 12.9c
YouTube Video for BarkBox

With cute pups like Cooper, how could BarkBox not use YouTube? But it does more; its YouTube strategy is based on influencers like gamer TmarTn seen in this video helping his puppy open his first BarkBox (Figure 12.9c).[40] The gamer is an active YouTube poster and has almost 2 million followers. This video has been on YouTube since 2015 and has 799,734 views and 446 likes. Tn continues to post videos for BarkBox on his TmarTn2 channel. All the brand's YouTube videos are surprisingly long; this one is 5 minutes and 43 seconds.

SOURCE: https://www.youtube.com/watch?v=F5iJPEMmETc.

There are a number of best practices that marketers can follow to create and enhance effective mobile marketing strategies. They include the following:

- Invest in the mobile channel so all mobile experiences (say, mobile email connecting to the mobile website) are consistently pleasing.
- The first contact is very important. "You never have a second chance to make a first impression."
- Ensure that the experience remains consistently excellent, from the important first contact through repeat use which can be complicated by updates.
- Use short copy, bold colors, minimalistic visuals, and short headlines that grab attention.
- Introduce video content to engage viewers.
- Consider how location-based technologies, like such as GPS-enabled apps, can increase engagement and prompt user actions.
- Include clickable phone numbers/interactive maps and other interactive elements that make calls to action easy to take.
- Collect data and analyze it to improve mobile marketing strategy.[41]

MOBILE APPS

There are probably some marketers who would include apps as one of the essential elements of mobile strategy. However, there is a better way to look at the importance of apps. All the aspects of mobile strategy just discussed apply to apps—from design for usability and excellent CX to the importance of apps in social media. Apps are important—let there be no doubt about that!

Experts agree that users spend the majority of their mobile time using apps, not the mobile web. Figure 12.10a puts the figure at 90 percent in this 2015 study. In fact, Facebook alone accounts for 19 percent of their time with entertainment, gaming, and messaging/social close behind. However, there is a dark side. The experts also agree that the retention rate for apps is not high. Figure 12.10b shows the *three-month* retention rate in a 2016 study to be on both sides of the 20 percent often quoted. That means that about 80 percent of all apps downloaded are uninstalled within the first three months. The same study reports that 25 percent of users who download use the app only once! The study's definition of retention is that the user returns to the app

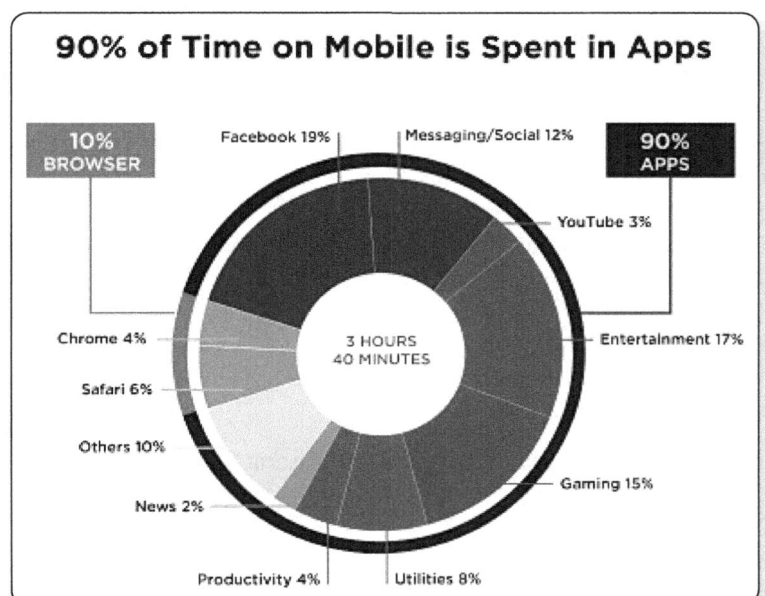

FIGURE 12.10a

How Mobile Time Is Spent

SOURCE: http://www.smartinsights.com/mobile-marketing/mobile-marketing-analytics/mobile-marketing-statistics/.

FIGURE 12.10b

App Retention Rate

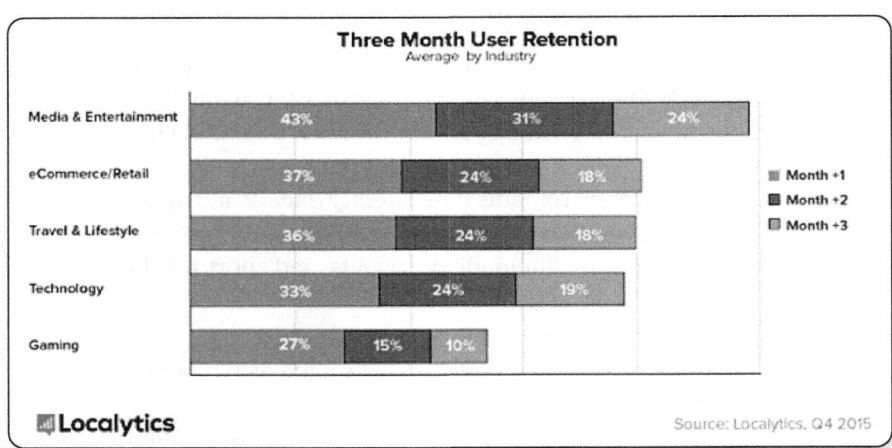

SOURCE: http://info.localytics.com/blog/mobile-apps-whats-a-good-retention-rate.

at least once within a 30-day period, which is a pretty low bar. The high for a three-month retention is 24 percent for media and entertainment apps, with 18 percent for retail apps, and a low of 10 percent for gaming apps. Does this make sense in your experience? You download an app and if it doesn't please you on the first use or two you either ignore it or delete it. This rather painful retention data puts a premium on app effectiveness.

With the data for app use and retention in mind, it makes sense that advertising dollars are concentrated on a few top apps. Figure 12.10c shows that about 70 percent of advertising dollars go to the top ten apps listed with almost 48 percent going to Google and Facebook alone.

Designing Effective Mobile Apps

Think with Google offers 25 principles of good app design and all are valuable. Notice that they have a great deal of similarity to the recommendations for designing excellent mobile CX, Sections 12.3a and 12.3b. Here are the ones that apply to all apps:

1. Address the user's task clearly and relate the app's features to the task.
2. Organize the menus in the way and using the terms that users apply to the product category.
3. Use the back button to let the user go back one step, not to the beginning.
4. Use auto-detection of user location. If users need to manually enter their location, make it easy.
5. If users need to move from the app to the mobile website, say to book a flight, make the transition easy and seamless by making the screens match. Make sure the mobile website loads quickly.
6. Display the search bar prominently.
7. Be sure the search function works well.
8. Provide easy to use filters and sort options.

Ecommerce apps have additional usability criteria and so do apps whose objective is to get the user to register for something.[42]

It is important to have a solid marketing strategy in place when an app is launched. That includes involving potential users in testing, creating buzz well in advance of launch, using influencer marketing, and more.[43] Given the sad state of app retention, careful attention must also be paid to a strong retention strategy. A good retention

FIGURE 12.10c

MostAd Dollars Spent on Top Apps

Net US Mobile Ad Revenue Share, by Company, 2013-2016
% of total and billions

	2013	2014	2015	2016
Google	37.7%	37.2%	35.2%	33.2%
Facebook	14.4%	17.6%	16.7%	14.6%
Twitter	3.0%	3.6%	3.7%	3.8%
Yahoo	-	3.2%	3.7%	4.2%
Pandora	3.5%	3.0%	2.6%	2.2%
YP	3.5%	2.7%	2.2%	1.9%
Apple (iAd)	2.44%	2.6%	2.8%	2.9%
Yelp	0.5%	0.7%	0.9%	1.0%
Amazon	0.1%	0.5%	0.6%	0.7%
Millennial Media	0.7%	0.4%	0.3%	0.3%
LinkedIn	0.1%	0.3%	0.4%	0.4%
Other	34.1%	28.4%	31.0%	34.9%
Total (billions)	**$10.7**	**$19.0**	**$28.5**	**$40.2**

Note: net ad revenues after companies pay traffic acquisition costs (TAC); includes display (banners and other, rich media and video), search and messaging-based advertising; ad spending on tablets is included; numbers may not add up to 100% due to rounding
Source: company reports; eMarketer, Dec 2014

182498 www.eMarketer.com

SOURCE: http://marketingland.com/report-mobile-users-spend-80-percent-time-just-five-apps-116858.

strategy includes the all-important ease of use but also requires segmentation-based targeting and personalization.⁴⁴

Starbucks is well known for the strength of its mobile loyalty program. The mobile app not only lets consumers order ahead and pay for their purchase with their phone, but also has a convenient visual display of loyalty points (stars) that shows how many more stars are needed to earn a free cup of coffee. Starbucks continues to enhance its loyalty program by partnering with companies like such as Lyft, Spotify, and the New York Times to let customers earn Starbucks loyalty points. One agency executive says:

> *They've built utility right into the loyalty program. There is not a lot of distinction between the mobile payment and amassing your stars and defending your gold status. They are part and parcel of the same interaction, and I think that has been a huge key to their success.*⁴⁵

Are you thinking that many of the best apps already have the excellent UX and the personalized marketing touch described here? If so, you would be correct—and you would also have pinpointed the challenge for marketers of new apps. There are a number of options for making apps great, including good old-fashioned creativity. There are also specific metrics for assessing the effectiveness of apps and app marketing that will be discussed in Chapter 18. Technology itself, however, may provide powerful options going forward.

Take the case of the app for the 2016 U.S. Tennis Open. The Tennis Open has a long history of successful apps that provide information about the current open tournament. The 2016 app, shown in Figure 12.11, was powered by IBM's Watson service,

FIGURE 12.11

Mobile App for 2016 U.S. Tennis Open

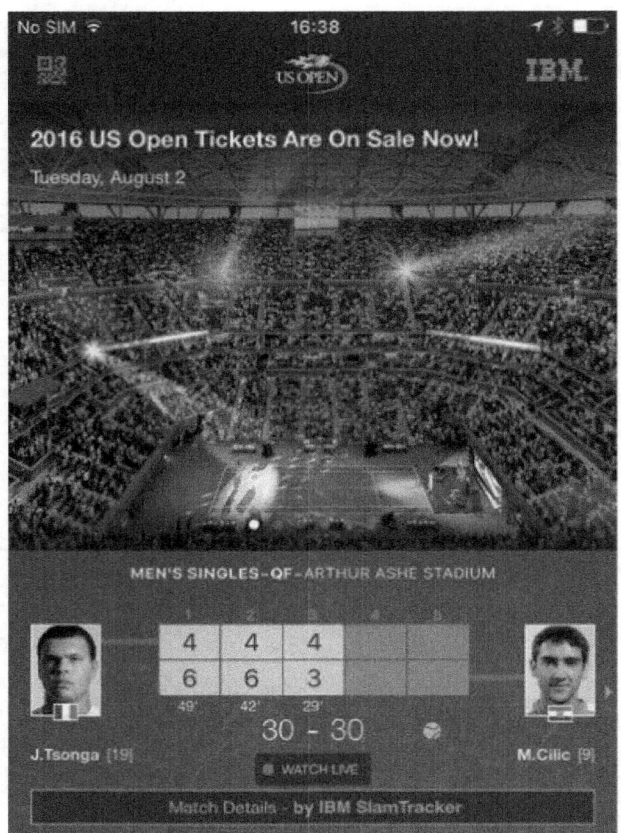

SOURCE: https://itunes.apple.com/us/app/2016-us-open-tennis-championships/id327455869?mt=8.

featured in Interactive Exercise 2.2. IBM promotes the platform as more than AI; it calls it cognitive computing. In essence, that means the system not only captures and analyzes massive amounts of data but also learns from its experiences. One IBM executive explained the experience at the U.S. Open this way:

> So far, we have had hundreds of questions come through from guests at the tournament on a daily basis, and we've seen some questions that we didn't anticipate," Kent said. "What we were noticing was that people weren't asking questions, per se - instead they'd use one word, like 'smoothie.' Now, if they type in 'smoothie,' Watson is more informed and will respond to that. That's the beauty of Watson, we don't have to re-program it, we re-educate it, we train it.[46]

natural language processing a component of AI that allows a computer to understand spoken human language.

The Watson technology includes the ability to learn as well as visual recognition technology and **natural language processing**. Natural language processing is also at the core of the chatbot, illustrated in Interactive Exercise 12.2. Watson technology is now in use in health care where it helps researchers and practitioners interpret the data they receive[47] and in fashion where cognitive capabilities are being built into garments.[48]

In retail environments apps are being paired with technology in different ways to enhance the shopping experience and drive customer loyalty.

APPS + TECHNOLOGY = RETAIL

Retail stores and shopping malls are another obvious application of localization technology (Section 12-4e). A number of large retail chains are adopting **beacon technology** that has been popularized by Apple.[49] In this context beacons are small, inexpensive Bluetooth devices that can be scattered throughout a retail location. Once the user has opted-in, mobile apps running on both Apple and Android mobile devices can receive signals from the beacons. The user can then be offered personalized deals and coupons, information, and other retail promotions, offers that should be enticing to shoppers. A study by Adobe found that convenience and the ability to achieve goals in just a few steps were the most important features of retail apps. Retail app users also wanted to be able to check prices and earn loyalty points using their apps.[50]

Target has been among the retail leaders in adopting mobile technology across the board. Their test of beacon technology began in late 2015. Figure 12.12 shows some of the key screens for the app. Notice that the user must opt in to activate the location technology and the push notifications. Target planned no more than two notifications per store visit in order not to annoy customers. Those notifications need to be chosen carefully and be based on the customer's shopping history. It is not known if that level of personalization yet exists. Target Run, which also is an opt-in feature, allows content from various social media platforms such as Pinterest.

Target's Chief Strategy and Innovation Officer comments that 98 percent of Target's customers shop digitally and three-fourths of them start on a mobile device making mobile the new front door to Target stores. Casey Carl says:

> There's no longer a delineation between how our guests live life and how they shop; they just shop whenever they have time. They want to flow seamlessly across all of our channels . . . and we've got to make that happen by having the right underlying architecture.[51]

beacon technology beacons are small pieces of hardware that use Bluetooth Low Energy technology to send signals, including messages, to nearby mobile devices.

FIGURE 12.12
Screens from the Target Retail Shopping APP

SOURCE: https://techcrunch.com/2015/08/05/target-launches-beacon-test-in-50-stores-with-expanded-rollout-later-this-year/.

That perspective seems to be paying off as Target opens its in-store communications platform to advertisers after partnering with selected brands during its development. The platform offers Target vendors targeted advertising access to Target shoppers. It points to one campaign for the Flonase allergy line in which Target was able to identify shoppers who had purchased similar products during the previous shopping year. They were reached by banner ads, content from Target's media site,[52] and manufacturer's coupons from its Cartwheel loyalty app. The campaign ran for two months and provided a 40 percent sales life for customers who received the messages over a control group who did not. For customers who had children at home the sales lift was 50 percent.[53]

Beacons determine where people are in respect to a retail location. *RFID tags* can determine where products are. Media Post reports on a prototype store in which all products had RFID tags. A reader in the ceiling was about the size of a ceiling tile and had a real-time location for each product on the store shelves. The system also knows when a shopper has put a product in a shopping cart headed for a dressing room. That would enable the store to send messages about complimentary items, assuming, of course, that the shopper has opted into the system.[54] There is legitimate concern about consumer reaction to the privacy implications of systems like this, but the convenience of being able to locate an item directly and immediately in a large store might well tip the balance in favor of the system.

Augmented and virtual reality are in their infancy in retail stores in the United States although they are better developed in European shopping environments.[55] *HBR* gives one example of the potential:

> *Your camping trip is coming up. You and a friend go shopping for a tent. Spotting one you like, you both crawl inside to check the capacity. But there's something unusual about this scenario: You're in Boston. Your buddy is in Houston. And neither of you is anywhere near a sporting goods store.*[56]

If that sounds like fun, remember the AR bus stop ad for Pepsi Max described in Section 3-6c. The technology still has implementation drawbacks as discussed in that section, but it also has great potential to create engaging shopping experiences.

MOBILE TECHNOLOGY—WILL IT BE CARRIED OR WILL IT BE WORN?

Whatever the application, whatever type of experience the marketer is creating, mobile is above all mobile! Some recent developments may change the way we interact with our mobile technology.[57]

In Section 3-6c, we discussed *mobile payments* as a business model. Mobile payments are also a matter of consumer choice and consumers, in the United States at least, have been slow to adopt mobile payments. One source says that only 6 percent of iPhone owners with compatible phones use Apple Pay and only 1 percent of Android users take advantage of Android Pay.[58]

Some recent developments that may speed the adoption of mobile payments include the following:

- With the Apple Watch version 2 Apple has introduced upgraded software for all Apple watches that makes Apple Pay easier and faster to use.[59] About 200 thousand websites are said to be planning to accept Apple Pay by holiday season 2016.[60]
- MasterCard and 17 large banks are making it possible to pay for merchandise using bank cards on their Android phones.[61] PayPal is reported to also be joining the network.[62]
- MasterCard and GM have designed a key fob that allows actions like starting your car and making mobile payments.[63]

- Facebook has allowed people to send and receive money through Facebook Messenger since 2015.[64]
- Apple added the ability to transfer funds to its iMessage app in 2016.[65]

There are rumors of payment mechanisms embedded in apparel and just about everything else for that matter; it's another manifestation of the IoT. What it will take to get consumers to use mobile payments in large numbers when they have other easy and convenient ways to make payments is another question.

Wireless headphones from several manufacturers already offer functionality beyond just music. Apple's elimination of the headphone jack in the iPhone 7 was, of course, big news and led to much speculation about additional uses. One writer has likened them to a "wearable computer." Among other features they offer easy access to Apple's Siri *virtual assistant*.[66] Amazon's Alexa assistant continues to increase its versatility with an app from Twitter that lets Alexa read the user's Twitter timeline and do other things like read aloud trending topics near where the user is at the moment.[67]

Connected clothing is also on the horizon. In Section 2-5c2, we discussed clothing with embedded sensors for fitness or medical tracking applications. Using Google's Jacquard technology, Levi's has designed a connected jacket for urban cyclists.

Mashable describes the technology:

> *The core of the technology is a fabric that's specially woven with conductive thread, which allows it to act as an interactive touchpad. Levi's Jacquard-enabled jacket contains a swath of this fabric on the edge of one sleeve (Figure 12.13).*

That touchpad itself is powered by a small dongle, or "tag," that connects to the sleeve's cuff. The tag, which charges via USB, is designed to look like the snaps and buttons on the rest of the jacket, though the current iteration is noticeably bulkier than the snaps you would typically find on a sleeve. The tag is also equipped with an LED light that changes colors based on what you're doing.

The final piece of Jacquard is a smartphone app, which allows you to configure how gestures map to the apps you use—whether you use a tap or a swipe to answer the phone, for instance.[68]

There are up to eight different signals the wearer can use to control the apps that are associated with the jacket. Besides the usual Google suspects like maps and search, other platforms like Spotify are working to integrate their services.

FIGURE 12.13

The User Interface on Levi's Connected Jacket

SOURCE: http://mashable.com/2016/05/22/google-project-jacquard/#N3E9B.MWlsqR.

Levi's plans to introduce the somewhat pricey jacket into its Commuter line in spring 2017. It is aimed at urban cyclists and can help them do things like control their music and answer phone calls in what is hopefully a safer manner. The jacket looks like a normal denim jacket and the firm says it can be treated like one—stuff it in your backpack, throw it in the washing machine, whatever!

This is just one of the early entries in the IoT connected clothing category. See Interactive Exercise 12.3 for a dress that "thinks." You may be wearing your most essential technology sooner than you think!

SUMMARY

In the early days of the internet, marketers talked about the convergence of devices into one central device that would control many aspects of our daily lives. In a sense, it has happened and the device is the smartphone. Smartphones are the constant companions of people in developed economies and are rapidly penetrating the economies of developing nations. It provides access to the mobile web to billions of people around the world and makes mobile marketing strategy a key driver of brand marketing strategies.

The central element of mobile marketing strategy must be excellent CX that is delivered through a mobile-friendly site, relevant content, advertising that is targeted and personalized, localization, and advertising on social media platforms where mobile users spend a significant amount of their time. Google and Facebook dominate the mobile advertising space as well as other aspects of mobile. Facebook has begun to penalize advertisers by not showing ads that load slowly as frequently as swifter-loading ads. Google is penalizing types of advertising that take over the mobile screen and/or slow loading time. The objective is the continual improvement of mobile CX.

Mobile users spend about 90 percent of their time on mobile apps, so creating and marketing effective mobile apps is of utmost importance. Effective mobile apps allow users to accomplish their goals in only a few steps, give them personalized content, allow them to earn loyalty points, and have overall ease of use. Most mobile users frequently use only a few of the apps installed on their devices. Even worse for the makers of apps, as many as 80 percent of apps downloaded are uninstalled within three months. That calls for a good marketing strategy and, even more, a good retention strategy that includes segment-based targeting and content personalization.

Retail apps present an equally challenging picture for marketers but they also present major opportunities when paired with other technologies. Beacons identify consumers who have opted in when they reach the store and can deliver messages, coupons, and other promotions. RFID again plays a role, this time in tags on products in the store. This permits easy location by the customer, possible in-store marketing opportunities and data for the marketer. Other technologies such as VR/AR and AI have potential in the retail setting.

At present most people are carrying their technology with them on smartphones or other devices. There is a great deal of effort being devoted to wearable technology and its future looks bright.

Mobile must be part of an all-touchpoints, all-channels strategy. It must be the welcoming doorway to excellent experiences delivered by brand marketers and retailers alike. Mobile marketing is not the only marketing challenge, but it is quickly becoming the central one.

DISCUSSION QUESTIONS

1. Explain your understanding of what mobile marketing is and what role it should play in marketing campaigns.
2. What is a micro-moment? Why is it an important concept in mobile marketing?

3. What is the nature of the customer journey in micro-moments?
4. What are the elements of a mobile marketing strategy? Give an example of how each applies in developing a mobile strategy.
5. Why has mobile advertising assumed so much importance? Do you think that is likely to continue?
6. How is advertising on social media platforms different from other types of mobile advertising?
7. How can technology enable localized advertising?
8. True/False. Mobile advertising is within the reach and capability of most small local businesses.
9. Why do mobile apps play such a large role in mobile marketing?
10. What are some of the keys to effective mobile apps?
11. What issues besides the design of their apps do app marketers need to pay attention to?
12. Explain the basics of beacon technology. How is it useful to retailers?
13. Have you seen or heard of any examples of VR or AR being used in retailing?
14. Mobile payments have been slow to catch on. Do you think that will change? Why or why not?
15. Do you have mobile technology on or with you at this moment in any other form than your smartphone?

ENDNOTES

1. "Understanding How Micro-Moments Influence Consumers," https://www.thinkwithgoogle.com/collections/how-micro-moments-influence-consumers.html.
2. Kit Eaton, "A Beauty Makeover with One Tool: Your Phone," http://www.nytimes.com/2016/08/11/technology/personaltech/a-beauty-makeover-with-one-tool-your-phone.html?_r=1.
3. Jeff Zias, "Snap and An Innovation Story Behind Intuit's TurboTax Mobile App," https://www.linkedin.com/pulse/snap-file-innovation-story-behind-intuits-turbotax-mobile-jeff-zias.
4. Jeff Zias, "Snap and An Innovation Story Behind Intuit's TurboTax Mobile App," https://www.linkedin.com/pulse/snap-file-innovation-story-behind-intuits-turbotax-mobile-jeff-zias.
5. https://itunes.apple.com/us/app/taxcaster-by-turbotax-free/id346184215.
6. Brian Solis, "A New Generation of Mobile Devices Represents the New Frontier in CX," http://www.slideshare.net/briansolis/altimeter-mobile-cx-final/14-14At_the_same_time_instore.
7. "Customer Experience Strategy: How Zappos Became a 2016 US Top Ten Customer Brand," http://www.nunwood.com/customer-experience-strategy-zappos-became-2016-us-top-ten-customer-brand/.
8. Alex Samuely, "Zappos Exec: Personalized Mobile Experiences Drive App Retention, Social Engagement." http://www.mobilemarketer.com/cms/news/database-crm/22794.html.
9. Rimma Kats, Zappos Exec: Apps Are a Loyalty Tool," http://www.mobilecommercedaily.com/zappos-exec-apps-are-a-loyalty-tool.
10. https://itunes.apple.com/us/app/zappos-mobile/id392988420?mt=8&pf_rd_r=0C74XDSYSJZG0VNHZZ1C&pf_rd_p=4c779ca8-e448-4381-b801-46aa5a6b6cd5.
11. "Nespresso Announces New Boutiques with Re-designed Shopping Experience," https://www.nestle-nespresso.com/newsandfeatures/nespresso-re-designed-shopping-experience.

12. MaurizidPesce, "But First Coffee: Now You Can Brew Your Nespresso with an App," https://www.wired.com/2016/03/nespresso-prodigio/.
13. Brian Solis, "A New Generation of Mobile Devices Represents the New Frontier in CX." http://www.slideshare.net/briansolis/altimeter-mobile-cx-final/14-14At_the_same_time_instore.
14. "Quarterly Digital Intelligence Briefing: The Quest for Mobile Excellence," http://landing.adobe.com/en/uk/products/marketing-cloud/69111-econsultancy-mobile-strategies-survey-report/GXUeEi5O.html?ev=event35&faas_unique_submission_id={A8121BDF-4F2E-DF46-D1F2-9B33C90D0BFB}&s_cid=null.
15. Garett Sloane, "Facebook Tells Advertisers to Speed Up Sites or Don't Bother Asking for Clicks," http://adage.com/article/digital/facebook-tells-advertisers-pick-pace-fast-ads/305676/?utm_source=digital_email&utm_medium=newsletter&utm_campaign=adage&ttl=1473269956.
16. Raluca Budiu, "The State of Mobile User Experience," https://www.nngroup.com/articles/mobile-usability-update/.
17. Richa Jain, "7 Best Practices for Designing a Mobile User Experience," https://www.sitepoint.com/7-best-practices-designing-mobile-user-experience/.
18. Ben Davis, "14 Features of Great Mobile Commerce Design," https://econsultancy.com/blog/64867-14-features-of-great-mobile-commerce-design/.
19. Ben Davis, "14 Features of Great Mobile Commerce Design," https://econsultancy.com/blog/64867-14-features-of-great-mobile-commerce-design/.
20. Greg Sterling, "Google Will Punish 'Intrusive Interstitials' with a Ranking Penalty in 2017," http://marketingland.com/google-will-punish-intrusive-interstitials-ranking-penalty-2017-188945.
21. Patricia Hursh, "3 Reasons B2B Marketing Must Embrace Mobile . . . Now," http://searchengineland.com/3-reasons-b2b-marketers-must-embrace-mobile-now-240820.
22. "How to Create and Measure Effective Mobile Content for Micro-Moments," https://www.thinkwithgoogle.com/articles/create-and-measure-effective-mobile-content-for-micro-moments.html.
23. "How to Create and Measure Effective Mobile Content for Micro-Moments," https://www.thinkwithgoogle.com/articles/create-and-measure-effective-mobile-content-for-micro-moments.html.
24. Nathalie Tadena, "Mountain Dew Ads Go Global with Return of "Do the Dew," http://blogs.wsj.com/cmo/2015/03/29/mountain-dew-ads-go-global-with-return-of-do-the-dew/.
25. http://www.iheartmedia.com/CCME/Pages/digital.aspx.
26. Josh Constine, "Snapchat Uncovers Discover," https://techcrunch.com/2016/06/07/snapchat-discover-previews/.
27. http://www.shazam.com/company.
28. https://www.youtube.com/watch?v=kmPabnlnotU.
29. Sahil Patel, "Inside Pepsi's New Music Program with iHeart Radio and Shazam," http://digiday.com/publishers/inside-pepsis-new-music-program-mtv-iheartradio-shazam/.
30. "Pepsi Launches The Sound Drop to Identify and Support the Next Generation of Breaking Artists in Partnership with iHeart Media, Shazam and MTV," http://www.pepsico.com/live/pressrelease/pepsi-launches-the-sound-drop-to-identify-and-support-the-next-generation-of-bre08242016.
31. Michael Barris, "Small Businesses Target Hyper-Local Mobile Ads Vis Brands' Apps," http://www.mobilemarketer.com/cms/news/advertising/19015.html
32. https://chitika.com/about
33. PriyaGopi, "Chitika Review 2016 - Contextual Advertising Network," http://blognife.com/2016/05/08/chitika-contextual-advertising-network/
34. Sarah Pike, "An Interview with 4 Brands on the Secrets to Their Social Media Success," https://www.socialmediaexplorer.com/content-sections/movers-and-makers/an-interview-with-4-brands-on-the-secrets-to-their-social-media-success/.

35. Nicolette Beard, "What You Need to Know About Mobile Content Marketing: Pros, Cons and Best Practices," http://www.toprankblog.com/2014/01/mobile-content-marketing/.
36. "Turning Dog Lovers into Subscribers," https://www.facebook.com/business/success/barkbox
37. https://www.instagram.com/p/BC3pu0boCLt/.
38. Darrell Etherington, "BarkCam, BarkBox's Instagram for Dogs, Is Now Available," https://techcrunch.com/2014/07/15/barkcam-instagram-for-dogs/.
39. https://itunes.apple.com/us/app/barkcam/id894097778?mt=8.
40. "How Dog Subscription Service, BarkBox, Is Marketing with Popular YouTubers," http://mediakix.com/2016/01/how-barkbox-is-marketing-with-popular-youtubers/#gs.fBL2eIE.
41. Nicolette Beard, "What You Need to Know About Mobile Content Marketing: Pros, Cons and Best Practices," http://www.toprankblog.com/2014/01/mobile-content-marketing/.
42. Jenny Gove, "Principles of Mobile App Design: Introduction," https://www.thinkwithgoogle.com/articles/principles-of-mobile-app-design-introduction.html.
43. "The 7 Keys to an Effective Pre-Launch Mobile App Marketing Strategy," http://savvyapps.com/blog/mobile-app-marketing-strategies-pre-launch.
44. "Mastering the Complexity of Mobile with Simplicity," https://landing.adobe.com/en/na/solutions/experience-manager/188465-mobile-consumer-study/PgevVPx8.html?ev=event35&faas_unique_submission_id={527C3F93-D9B5-7089-0ACD-BEB3B3FFAC59}&s_cid=null.
45. Rebecca Harris, "Why Starbucks Is Winning at Loyalty," http://www.marketingmag.ca/brands/why-starbucks-is-winning-at-loyalty-152974.
46. Brian Mastroianni, "IBM Watson Serves New Tech at the U.S. Open," http://www.cbsnews.com/news/us-open-tennis-ibm-watson-serves-new-cognitive-computing-tech/.
47. Brian Mastroianni, "Tech Trends that Will Make Waves in 2016," http://www.cbsnews.com/news/tech-trends-that-will-make-waves-in-2016/.
48. Brian Mastroianni, "Marchesa, IBM Watson Design 'Cognitive Dress' for Met Gala," http://www.cbsnews.com/news/marchesa-ibm-watson-to-debut-cognitive-dress-at-mondays-met-gala/.
49. https://support.apple.com/en-us/HT202880.
50. "Mastering the Complexity of Mobile with Simplicity," https://landing.adobe.com/en/na/solutions/experience-manager/188465-mobile-consumer-study/PgevVPx8.html?ev=event35&faas_unique_submission_id={527C3F93-D9B5-7089-0ACD-BEB3B3FFAC59}&s_cid=null.
51. "For Target, Mobile Is the New Front Door," https://www.thinkwithgoogle.com/interviews/for-target-mobile-is-the-new-front-door.html.
52. https://corporate.target.com/article/2015/03/welcome-to-abv.
53. Adrianne Pasquarelli, "Is Target the Next Digital Media Giant?" http://adage.com/article/cmo-strategy/advertise-a-target-shopper-luck/305753/?utm_source=daily_email&utm_medium=newsletter&utm_campaign=adage&ttl=1473912505.
54. Chuck Martin, "Store of the Future," http://www.mediapost.com/publications/article/277561/store-of-the-future-iot-to-track-products-people.html?utm_source=newsletter&utm_medium=email&utm_content=headline&utm_campaign=93587.
55. "3 Examples of Augmented Reality in Retail Industry," http://www.augment.com/blog/3-examples-augmented-reality-retail-industry/.
56. Dan McKone, Robert Haslehurst, and Maria Steingoltz, "Virtual and Augmented Reality Will Reshape Retail," https://hbr.org/2016/09/virtual-and-augmented-reality-will-reshape-retail.
57. Michael Grothaus, "Apple Pay Leads Mobile Payments with 12 Million Monthly Users," https://www.fastcompany.com/3057353/fast-feed/apple-pay-leads-mobile-payments-with-12-million-monthly-users.

58. Tom Warren, "Watch OS3 Arrives to Make Your Apple Watch a Lot Faster to Use," http://www.theverge.com/2016/9/13/12903230/apple-watchos-3-apple-watch-software-update.
59. "Apply Pay Coming to 200,000-plus Websites, Not Just In-Store or In-App," http://www.computerworld.com/article/3119735/mobile-payments/apple-pay-coming-to-200-000-plus-websites-not-just-in-store-or-in-app.html.
60. Ben Fox Rubin, "Now This May Finally Get You to Use Mobile Payments," https://www.cnet.com/news/heres-something-that-may-finally-get-regular-folks-to-use-mobile-payments/.
61. Kyle Wiggers, "PayPal Inks Agreement with MasterCard Allowing Users to Make Mobile Payments," http://www.digitaltrends.com/mobile/paypal-mastercard-agreement/.
62. Don Reisinger, "MasterCard Wants Everything to Support Mobile Payments," http://in.pcmag.com/android-pay/96962/news/mastercard-wants-everything-to-support-mobile-payments.
63. http://newsroom.fb.com/news/2015/03/send-money-to-friends-in-messenger/.
64. Laura Shin, "You Can Now Send a Payment to Anyone in the World Via iMessage," http://www.forbes.com/sites/laurashin/2016/09/13/you-can-now-send-a-payment-to-anyone-in-the-world-via-imessage/#1d224d49685d.
65. Will Oremus, "These Aren't Wireless Headphones," http://www.slate.com/articles/technology/future_tense/2016/09/apple_s_airpods_aren_t_just_wireless_earbuds_they_re_the_future_of_computing.html.
66. Tim Peterson, "Twitter Rolls Out an App for Amazon's Alexa Voice Assistant," http://marketingland.com/twitter-rolls-app-amazons-alexa-voice-assistant-190973.
67. Karissa Bell, "Project Jacquard Could Be Google's Best Shot at a Wearable Platform," http://mashable.com/2016/05/22/google-project-jacquard/#N3E9B.MWlsqR.
68. Sarah Perez, "Google and Levi's Team Up on a 'Connected' Jacket That Lets You Answer Calls, Use Maps and More," https://techcrunch.com/2016/05/20/google-and-levis-team-up-on-a-connected-jacket-that-lets-you-answer-calls-use-maps-and-more/.

Chapter 13

Demand Generation and Conversion in B2B Markets

LEARNING OBJECTIVES

By the time you complete this chapter, you will be able to:

1. Explain how the internet and search in particular has changed the B2B buying process.
2. Define the functions of a marketing automation system and its role in demand generation.
3. Define the six steps in the demand generation process.
4. Explain the difference between demand generation, lead generation, and inbound marketing, and the relationships between the three concepts.
5. Define and explain the importance of content marketing in demand generation.
6. Describe the B2B buy cycle and the Marketing Funnel.
7. Discuss the steps in the sales lead generation, nurturing, and qualification processes.
8. Identify channels that can be used to generate sales leads.
9. Discuss the issues in defining conversion.
10. Explain the meaning and use of customer personas and buying scenarios.
11. Discuss the use of landing pages and the importance of testing them.

THE GENERIC MARKETING STRATEGIES

The core marketing strategies discussed in Section 1-4b2 suggest that all marketing strategies fall into one of the four generic categories:

1. Acquisition
2. Conversion
3. Retention
4. Value growth

This book has previously discussed a number of digital marketing tools that can be used for customer acquisition. Some, like display advertising and search marketing, are primarily used for acquisition. Email marketing is primarily used for customer retention. Social media marketing falls in between, with its value for acquisition or retention depending on platform and marketer objectives.

Customer conversion is the second of the generic activities. Conversion and the processes leading up to conversion will be the focus of this chapter in terms of its end result. In its broadest sense, conversion is generally equated with making the first sale to a particular customer. This is a good place to start, but this chapter will show that conversion is a more complex process. Conversion is not a simple activity with a clear beginning and an equally clear termination. It is more like a river, with many tributaries entering it that eventually empties into the sea, which is, in this case, a customer database. This entire process of getting to conversion is today known as **demand generation**. Conversion is the ultimate goal of demand generation, the desired action by the **prospect**, or unqualified lead, but there are many steps along the way. Conversion also does not stop when the prospect becomes a customer, as continuous feedback helps refine the actions the marketer takes each step of the way. In the process of this discussion we will also distinguish between the three terms that are often loosely used, which are "demand generation," "inbound marketing," and "lead generation," and understand them in the context. However, before delving into the demand generation process, it is important to note some recent changes to the B2B (business-to-business) buy cycle and what is important in that cycle.

Demand and lead generation are the two most commonly used terms today in B2B marketing. While lead generation as an activity can stand alone, demand generation as a process includes lead generation. The demand generation process drives awareness and interest in a company's products and services, starting with attractive content and ending with a desired action, or conversion and associated metrics.

Lead generation as the second step in the demand generation process also drives interest or inquiry into products or services. The goal is the collection of qualified connections to build initial relationships with prospects so we can nurture them until they are closed as customers.[1]

demand generation entire process of developing customer demand for a product or service.

prospect an unqualified lead.

THE B2B BUY CYCLE AND THE CUSTOMER JOURNEY

Since the discipline of B2B marketing is concerned with the flow of the buying process from prospect to loyal customer, demand generation is a natural way to organize this process. Another aspect of this flow of B2B marketing is the concept of the buy cycle. Looking at Figure 13.1, it is immediately evident that the concept known as the **buy cycle** is a restatement of the consumer decision process familiar to all students of marketing. Whether using the term "B2B" or the older descriptor, industrial, it is the set of stages business buyers go through as they make a purchase. Using business marketing terminology, the process is as follows:

buy cycle process a customer goes through in deciding to make a purchase.

- *Needs awareness*, in which the potential purchaser recognizes the need for a product or service to meet the needs of a specific business activity.

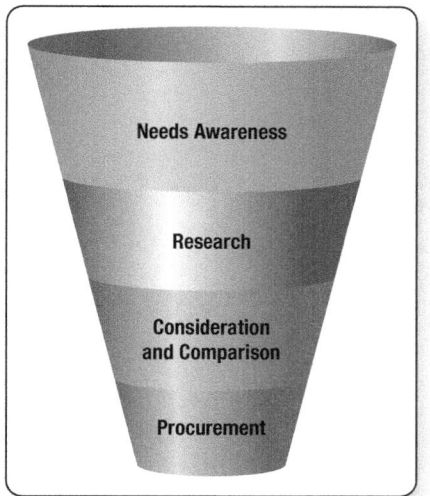

FIGURE 13.1
The B2B (Industrial) Buy Cycle

SOURCE: Marketing Maven Blog: "The Industrial Buy Cycle: Part 1," February 4, 2010, GlobalSpec. Reprinted with permission.

- *Research*, in which the potential purchaser investigates products and vendors.
- *Consideration and comparison*, in which the potential purchaser studies potential vendors and their products, arriving at a short list from which the purchase will be made.
- *Procurement*, in which the actual purchase transaction is completed.

Both the length and the number of people involved in the business purchasing process complicate the task of the marketer. These factors also enhance the importance of lead generation and management in order to understand who the information researcher (gatekeeper) for the business buying center is and to access the current stage of the buying process.

In addition to the buy cycle, today we often speak of the buying process as the **buyer's journey**[2] and seek to map the buyer's path through that journey as part of the demand generation process. Therefore, it is useful to ask the following questions in the buyer's journey:

Who is making the purchase? A majority of B2B purchase decisions are made by a group, not by a single person. That phenomenon has long been[3] called the **buying center** or the decision-making unit.

Why and what outcome is desired? What is the buyer's pain point, desired outcome, and what is his or her perception of the value from the product or service.

When is the purchase being made? The length of the purchase cycle increases as the price and the risk inherent in the purchase go up.

What content can answer the buyer's question? Is an infographic enough or will a whitepaper better answer to the question? The answer depends on the buyer and the stage in the buy cycle.

Where does the buyer seek the information? As shown in Figure 13.2, there are many sources for B2B purchase decisions, including blogs, webinars, and industry events. Where the buyer seeks information can determine marketer's actions.

From the above discussion and Figure 13.2, it is clear that the purchasing process is changing for B2B customers. Not only do those in the buying center or buy center rely now on search, social media, and other content in making their decision, but another hard fact is that quite often, much of the purchase decision has been made by the time the salesperson walks in the door. The reason for this change is that the buyer is doing much of his or her own research and is less dependent on the sales

buyer's journey the customer's path on the buying process.

buying center a group of people in an organization who make decisions for high-value and/or risky purchases.

FIGURE 13.2

The Changing Purchase Process for B2B Means Salesperson Comes Later in Process

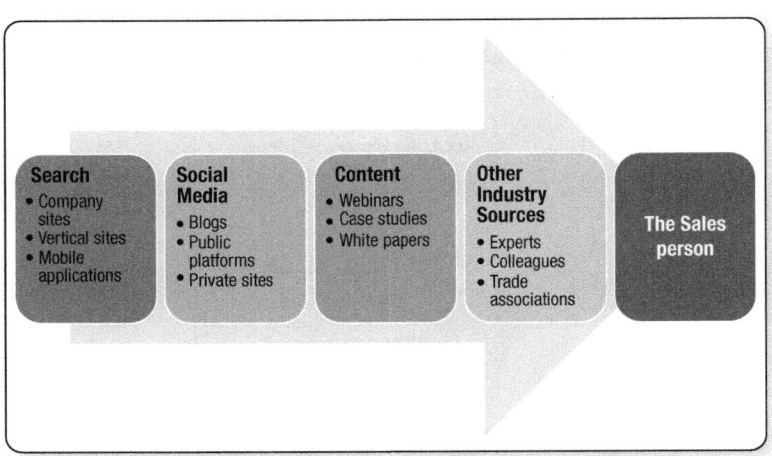

SOURCE: Zahay, Debra, Don Schultz, and Archana Kumar (2015), "Reimagining Branding for the New B2B Digital Marketplace," *Journal of Brand Strategy*, 3(4), pp. 357–372.

force as a source of information. Sources such as Marketo and Forrester Research all indicate that as soon as 2020 85 percent of the purchase decision will be made by the time the salesperson actually contacts the customer. HubSpot predicts that a full 1 million sales jobs will be lost by that year as the role of the salesperson changes to a more consultative selling orientation and there is less of a need for "order takers" in the sales force.[4]

IMPORTANCE OF SEARCH AND BRANDING IN B2B MARKETING

This changing process means that search marketing and being able to generate good quality content to attract potential buyers are more important than ever to B2B marketers. Generating high quality sales leads has traditionally been perceived as the greatest challenge by B2B marketers and we will discuss the lead generation process shortly. A large volume of leads was considered important, but much less so than *high quality* leads. While business marketers need to be concerned with high quality leads, changes in the B2B marketing process have shifted the emphasis of how leads are obtained. The change is that now most B2B buyers start their purchase process with search and rely heavily on social media and other online content for research before making a purchase decision. Therefore, buyers rely on the salesperson much later in the process and to a lesser extent (see Figure 13.2). In fact, it is predicted that by the year 2020 that 85 percent of the purchase decision will have been made before the buyer ever sees or contacts a salesperson.[5] According to the 2014 state of B2B Procurement Study, 94 percent of B2B purchasers research online.[6] Their search activity is as follows:

- 77 percent use Google Search.
- 84 percent consult business websites.
- 34 percent rely on third-party websites.
- 41 percent refer user reviews.

Therefore, B2B marketers must concentrate on being found in searches, both mobile and desktop, and having a strong presence on social media platforms. This shift in the purchase process means that branding in more critical than ever, as evidenced by the concerns of B2B marketers in a recent survey by B2B International, summarized in Figure 13.3.[7] In that survey, brand/marketing communications is seen as the top challenge by 36 percent of B2B marketers surveyed whereas concerns involving the sales function (finding top talent) were only listed as a top marketing challenge by 3 percent of those surveyed. Retaining customers and increasing brand awareness were the two items that increased significantly from 2014 to 2015, reinforcing the need for a solid demand generation process starting with content marketing as described in this chapter.

While B2B marketers will continue to have a goal the generation of high quality sales leads, priorities are shifting. Among overall business challenges, retaining customers and increasing brand awareness are seen as in the top five by half of the participants in this study, as illustrated in Figure 13.3. With branding becoming more important, so is content, as it is one way to tell the brand story. Some samples of brand reinforcing content channels such as email and social media are illustrated in Figure 13.4.

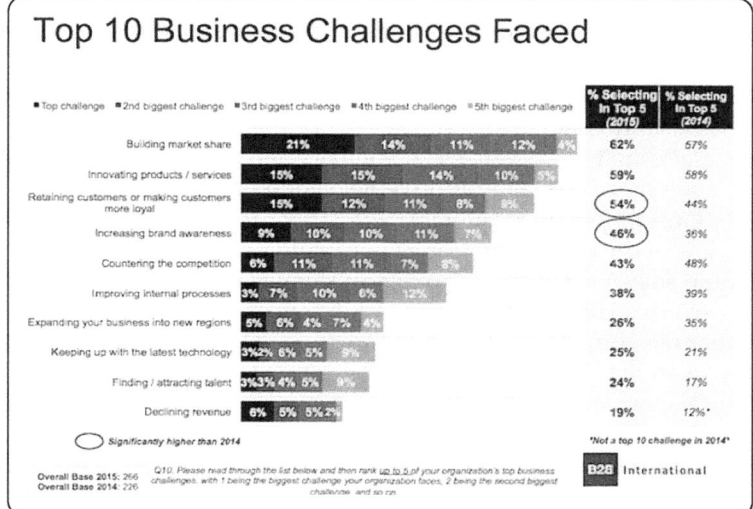

FIGURE 13.3

Top 10 Business Challenges Demonstrate Shift in Focus Away from Pure Lead Generation

FIGURE 13.4

Content Channels to Reinforce the Brand Image

SALES AND MARKETING WORK TOGETHER

Because of these changes, noted above, increasingly, the sales and marketing functions are seen as a holistic system, tied together by marketing automation systems, such as Eloqua or Marketo, which allow marketers to manage and track customer interactions and leads and measure the results. HubSpot calls this process "Smarketing," an integration of the sales and marketing process to more efficiently convert and retain customers. Marketo says that the sales funnel, which usually shows the process of leading the customer through brand awareness to conversion and then retention and **cross-selling** and **up-selling** has in the past had a gap between brand awareness and conversion by the sales team. The sales team has typically had most of the interface with the customer, with marketing providing leads that were seen as poor quality and not relevant to the sales process. The B2B Sales Funnel has changed to emphasize a more important role in marketing in nurturing leads through the process. It is marketing that decides if a prospect is more likely to move along the demand generation process to convert if they are offered a chance to view a webinar after downloading a whitepaper or receive an informational email, as seen in Figure 13.5.

From the marketing point of view, Marketo says that the corresponding gap in the marketing sales funnel between brand awareness and conversion can be filled by the processes of lead nurturing (developing relationships with customers before conversion), scoring, routing, and management, as shown in Figure 13.6. Armed with better qualified leads and prospects that are more likely to buy, the sales team can not only close the sale faster but also concentrate on postsale retention, cross- and up-sale activities. In this new perspective, marketing takes a leadership role in the sales process and is no longer seen as an ancillary and sometimes unnecessary function focused mass messages and intuitive decision-making. Hence the origin of the term "Smarketing," where sales and marketing work together. Figure 13.7 illustrates the Marketo view of the transformation of marketing that has accompanied the transformation of the sales process. Marketing's mission is now to represent the customer's view and see that the company is found in search, to use customer intelligence for the best message targeting, and also to focus on customer relationships quickly, using the best customer information possible.

cross-selling selling a different, related product to an existing customer.

up-selling upgrading an existing customer's account by selling more expensive products or packages in an attempt to increase the revenue value of that customer.

FIGURE 13.5
The B2B Industrial Sales Funnel Then and Now

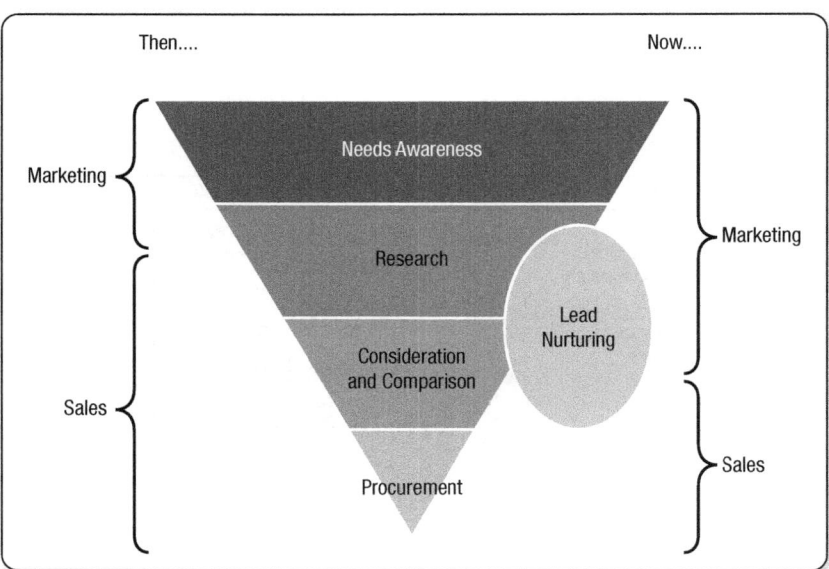

SOURCE: Zahay, Debra, Don Schultz, and Archana Kumar (2015), "Reimagining Branding for the New B2B Digital Marketplac," *Journal of Brand Strategy*, 3(4), pp. 357–372; and https://stevepatrizi.com/2012/10/23/the-new-marketing-sales-funnel/.

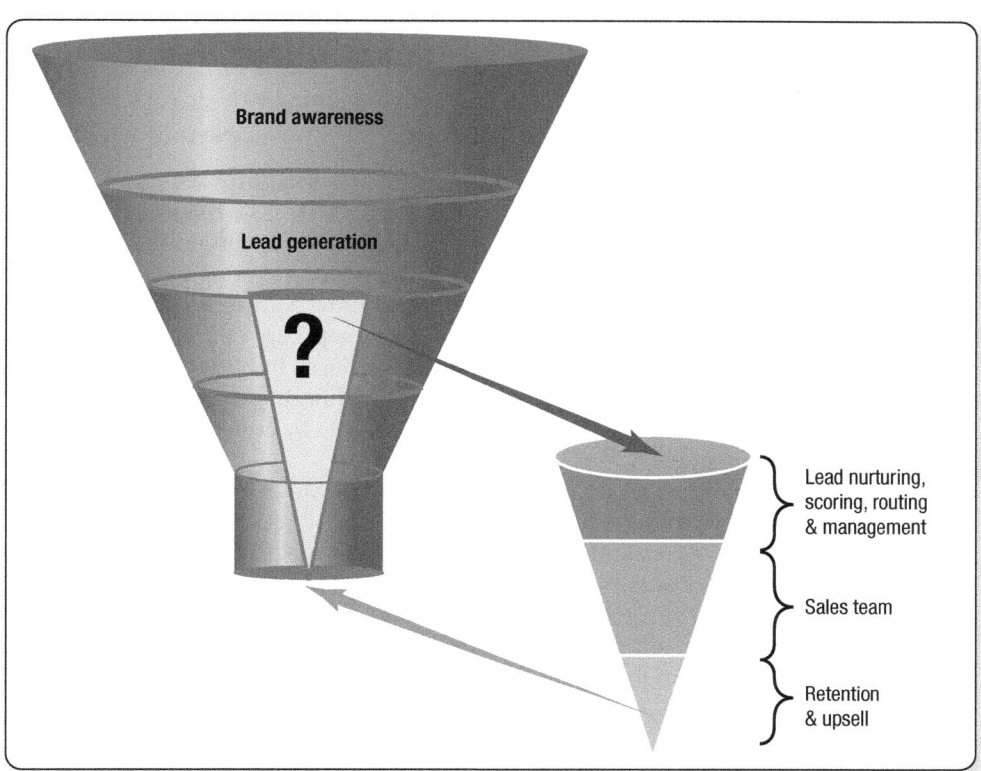

FIGURE 13.6

Filling the Gap between Lead Generation, Sales, and Customer Retention

SOURCE: Marketo

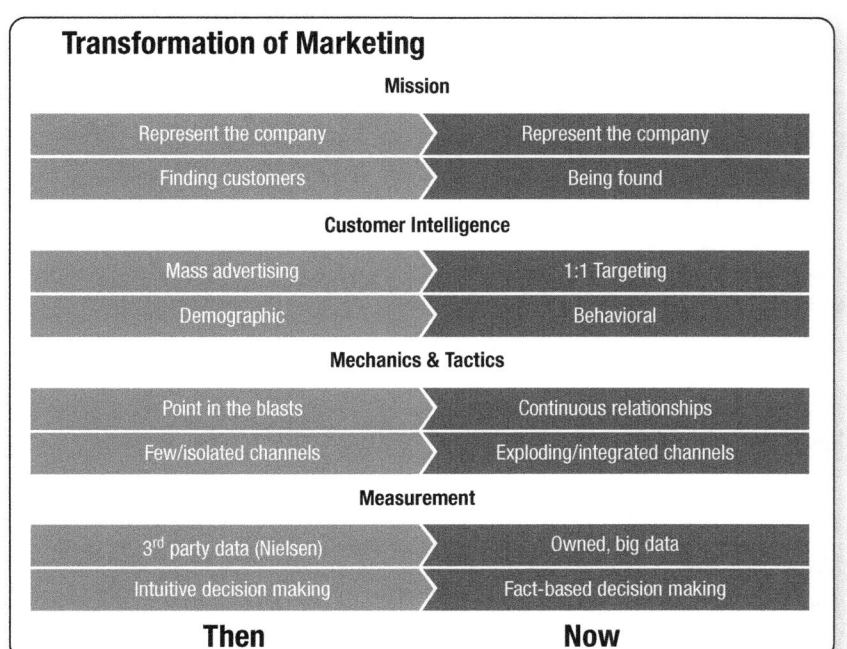

FIGURE 13.7

The Transformation of Marketing with the Rise of Demand Generation

SOURCE: https://www.marketo.com/lead-generation/.

AUTOMATION SYSTEMS FILL THE GAP

marketing automation system marketing interaction management system including a database, engagement engine, and analytics component.

This gap between marketing and sales to make both functions more effective is quite often filled by a **marketing automation system**. A marketing automation system typically includes

1. a centralized marketing database including interactions and behaviors from prospects and customers;
2. an engagement marketing "engine" that allows the marketer to manage and automate the process of interaction and conversations with customers; and
3. an analytics tool to test, measure, and optimize ROI for marketing activities.

For example, BMW has long been good at identifying potential customers and nurturing them. Its U.S. home page that is shown in Figure 13.8 offers exclusive features and the ability to "build your own" car to people who sign up for an account. These offers of information and special functions encourage people to provide their email address along with other personal information to complete account registration. Have no doubt that BMW will be in touch once a prospect has registered! This activity is a classic example of the use of the lead process in both business and consumer markets. We will focus on B2B applications in this chapter, but remember that there are also important applications in B2C (business-to-consumer) markets, and they work in the same way.

BMW might next send an email reminder to a customer who had recently been on the website looking for new car information or place an ad on a website that the consumer visits next. A marketing automation system would be able to "automate" that process and track conversion, whether the prospect actually purchased something from the site and the exact conversion path.[8] In fact, visitors to the HubSpot or Marketo sites seeking to learn about marketing topics in this chapter won't have to wait long before seeing a pop-up that tries to capture personal information and email for continued contact and communication.

FIGURE 13.8
The BMW USA Home Page

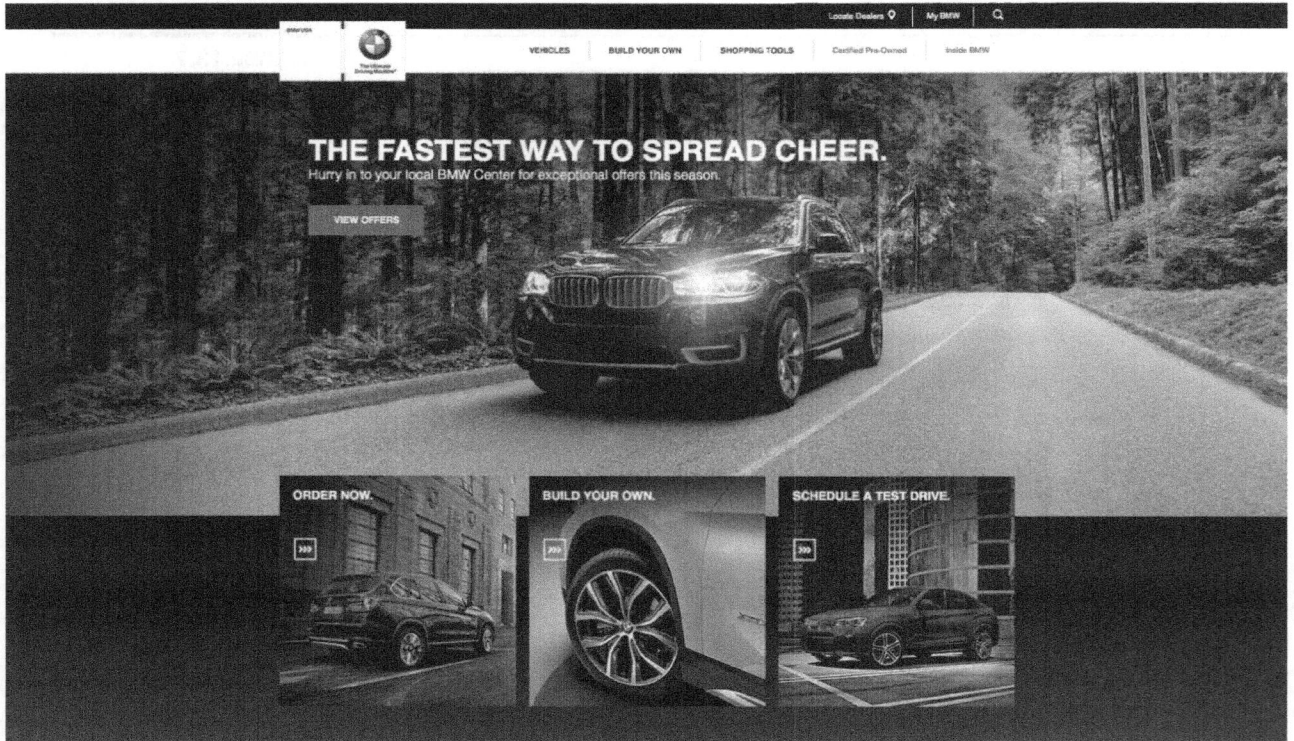

SOURCE: BMW of North America, LLC, http://www.bmwusa.com.

THE B2B PROCESS TODAY: DEMAND GENERATION

While leads will continue to be a focus of B2B marketing efforts, in recent years, as stated above, the term **demand generation** has entered the marketing lexicon as a way to organize and understand customer interaction processes. Demand generation is the process of stimulating demand and creating excitement for a product or service.[9] The idea behind demand generation is to manage, as much as possible, the process of acquisition, conversion, retention, and value growth. Demand generation begins with good content creation to attract leads. Leads are then nurtured and qualified and converted to customers, as shown in Figure 13.9. There is a "pull" aspect to this prospect and is known as Inbound Marketing and consists of attracting customers based on quality content and then converting them. The "push" aspect is known as lead generation and nurturing and in this activity marketers reach out directly to potential leads and nurture them through the sales process to conversion. After conversion, a good demand generation process involves using metrics to analyze what went well and what needed improvement through a feedback process. What this conceptualization suggests is that much of the material in this text represents demand generation activities, whether in a B2B or B2C context. However, before we go further into the lead generation and conversion processes, we will explore first the concept of content marketing in a B2B context.

demand generation entire process of developing customer demand for a product or service.

Demand Generation Step One: Content Creation and Content Marketing in B2B Markets

We discussed content marketing in detail in Chapter 8 as a strategic process to attract and retain a clearly defined target market to a brand for the purpose of profitable customer actions. B2B marketers have always done a certain amount of content marketing. Informative content in traditional B2B marketing is generally described as "collateral material." This process includes things like brochures or other "leave behinds" that salespeople use as part of the personal selling process. Collateral material has been almost an afterthought as compared to advertising and the strength of the sales force's presence in B2B markets and even less emphasized in B2C markets. However, the shift in the B2B buying process has raised the importance of collateral material and any type of relevant content about the brand and its products and services. Focusing on the concept of **content marketing** shifts the focus from traditional advertising, in offline or online media, to marketing that depends on marketer- and customer-created content that is either informative or entertaining or both.

content marketing creating and distributing content across the web that users find valuable and relevant, driving visitors to the website.

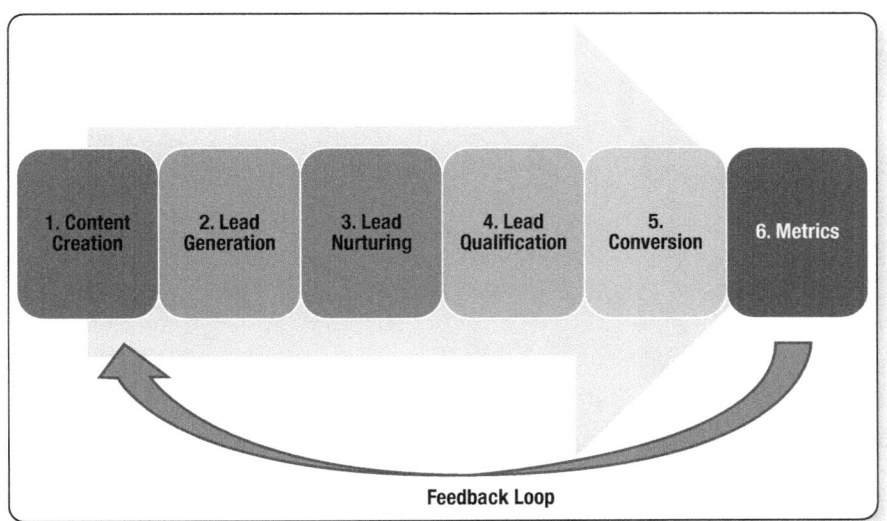

FIGURE 13.9

Demand Generation Process Begins with Good Content and Ends with Analysis

There are many types of content that are appropriate for the web. The infographic seen in Figure 13.10 characterizes the types of content, both online and offline, that can be used in lead generation. Content does not have to be completely original every time. Content can be repurposed across channels. This repurposing can mean something very simple, such as posting a video on YouTube as well as on the corporate website. Repurposing can also take more effort—using corporate material to develop a webinar, for example. Corporate content can be optimized for search in whatever channel it exists. For instance, corporations might establish YouTube channels to group their content and make it easier to locate. In addition, an individual YouTube video can be tagged to make it easier to find. Businesses can also reach out to customers in other ways on social media as discussed in Chapter 5. Social media encourages the creation of content by customers, which can be a huge asset to the content-creation effort. Any platform like a blog that encourages customer comments also creates an opportunity for customer to co-create the of content.

FIGURE 13.10

Online and Offline Lead Generation Channels

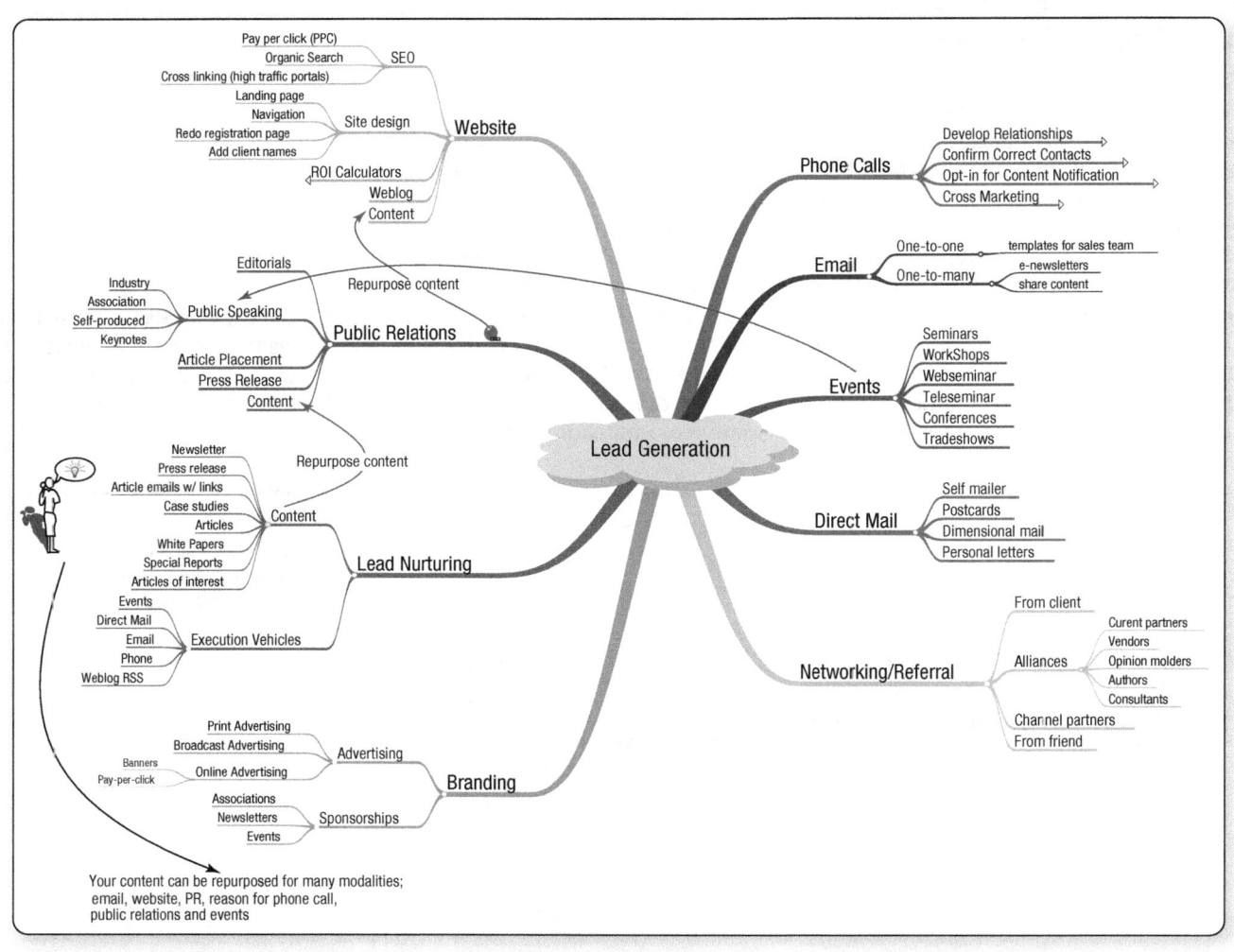

SOURCE: "Lead Generation," InTouch, http://www.b2bleadblog.com/2005/02/lead_generation-9.html.

Notice the many different types of content in this figure represented by these channels. No single firm can or should use all these techniques to repurpose content and distribute it across the web. It makes sense that companies start with only a few options that make sense for them and make it easy to repurpose important content (a feed from a Facebook page to a Twitter account, for example). The marketer should test efforts and solicit customer feedback and contributions. This testing must all be done in a context of understanding the information needs and media habits of the target audience while producing content that conveys a consistent corporate message.[10] In other words, take a strategic approach to producing and distributing content; it is the essence of being visible on the web. Being visible is the necessary forerunner to attracting people to the corporate website from which they can be identified, nurtured, and eventually converted to customers.

Therefore, content marketing means that marketing is no longer about fluffy or even persuasive advertising messages. Content marketing is a discipline that is about informational content intent on attracting prospects and converting them to customers in the brave new world of digital marketing and demand generation. The goal is to move the prospect through the demand generation process.

Demand Generation Step Two: Lead Generation; What Is Lead Generation?

After content is in place on various channels, the next step is to process the leads that result from content marketing efforts. Traditional offline direct marketers have used the process of sales **lead generation** and management since the 1950s at least. Over time, the process has taken advantage of customer databases and marketing automation software and has become a highly disciplined and cost-effective marketing technique of the business marketer.[11] The process focuses on getting individuals to self-identify as a potential decision maker in the purchase of a product or a service—a sales lead.

lead generation identifying sales prospects.

Why was this process developed by business marketers? The reason is cost. Business marketers traditionally have large field sales forces that call on customers, which is an expensive process. It is especially costly in the technology and high-ticket industrial spaces where closing a sale may require a year or more and necessitate multiple customer calls from a sales representative supported by engineers and designers. Multiple sales calls by multiple highly paid representatives can add up to an expensive process! This costly process is true even if the customer has a defined need for the product and is ready to purchase.

If the customer is early in the sales cycle—just collecting information for a possible purchase in the indefinite future, for example—personal selling is simply not cost-effective. If personal sales calls represent the only option, the company risks losing contact with a customer who may eventually make a purchase. The other option is to maintain communication in nonpersonal channels—originally by mail, now primarily in interactive channels—until that potential customer is ready to make a purchase decision. It is a simple concept that is surprisingly difficult to implement for reasons that are organizational, not technological.

It is important to understand that sales lead generation and management is a marketing tool that is used for higher-ticket sales with a longer purchase cycle. By now, you may have realized that some consumer purchases also fit that description. The purchase of a car usually fits into that category; so does the purchase of a condo or a house. In consumer behavior terms, these are situations in which the consumer goes through the entire purchase process—triggering cue, information search, selection of alternatives, purchase decision, product use, and information feedback. This type of situation is ideal for identifying someone in the initial stage of the purchase process, communicating as the process unfolds, and making an effort to close the sale when the time is appropriate. All one needs to do is look at the websites of any major automobile brand to see this process in operation. As noted above with the

BMW example, the prospect will not get far into the site before being required to give an email address in order to proceed. Shortly after registering, behaviorally targeted ads, as discussed in Section 7.3b immediately begin to appear based on prior search behavior.

The Lead Generation and Management Process The first step in the lead generation process is to get a person to self-identify as a potential sales lead. Whatever the channel, this process requires producing and distributing content that induces the reader or viewer to ask for more information. This initial stage is called a **prospect**. In other words, the marketer does not yet know whether that person—the prospect is made by a single person, whether in a B2B or a B2C market—is actually considering a purchase.

prospect an unqualified lead.

The question is not really whether a marketing department can produce leads. Anyone can produce inquiries if the marketing budget is large enough! The question is how to produce a desired quantity of leads that are worth careful qualification and potential distribution to the sales force. Putting the issues of quality and quantity together, lead generation becomes a serious marketing activity.

Now take a look at the actual content of the chart in Figure 13.10. Some of the lead generation channels are traditional in nature—telephone calls, direct mail, events (which can be virtual as well as physical), word of mouth (networking), public relations, and the various demand generation activities included under the heading of branding and those characterized as lead nurturing take place typically online. However, all channels have been profoundly affected by the internet. Much of the contact activity that was once done by mail or by phone is now done by email, and offline channels are often used to drive prospects to the corporate website for in-depth information. Events now include activities like webinars. Press releases that are an important part of public relations are now posted on the internet and optimized for search (see Chapter 6).

The connection between corporate events and public appearances by corporate personnel at industry events is a traditional one. The activity of "repurposing content" is not entirely new, but this ungrammatically titled effort has become essential in view of the endless appetite of the web for relevant new content. The corporate website and its associated corporate blog have become the hub of all this content, which needs to be widely distributed across the web in order to produce the greatest level of awareness and the largest volume of leads.

In spite of the importance of online information, marketers cannot just put content on a website and expect people to find it and respond to it in large numbers. People have to find content in places, physical and virtual, that they commonly frequent—which usually does not include corporate websites as a first step. Content distribution that aims to drive traffic to the website can also be described as "inbound marketing."

inbound marketing approach that is focused on being visible to potential customers and using the visibility to drive them to a website where they can transact.

Inbound Marketing for Lead Generation The concept of **inbound marketing** introduced a discipline on content marketing as a technique for lead generation in the sense that it outlines a clear process for managing content to reinforce a brand image and draw prospects to a web or mobile site. The term has been popularized by marketing services firm HubSpot, although concepts like "interruption marketing" and "permission marketing" were originally used by other marketers. Most notable among users of these terms is marketing guru Seth Godin, who has been preaching the doctrine of permission marketing since the early days of the internet.[12]

It has already been discussed that most potential customers turn to *search* as the first step in the purchase process, even before they consult personal sources (see Chapter 8) or corporate sources of information (see Chapters 5, 6, and 7). This association makes having all content optimized for search a top priority for internet marketers. It is also important to have content in places frequented by potential customers since they generally see corporate websites as a last stop, not a first one.

HubSpot says succinctly, "Inbound Marketing is marketing focused on getting found by customers."[13] It is not the traditional "marketer talking to customer" approaches that are also described as "interruption marketing" that might be characterized by intrusive advertising. Instead, inbound marketing involves making content available to customers when and where they want it. Inbound marketing also involves getting customers' permissions to push desired content to them through feeds or newsletters of various kinds. As noted above this marketing method has been called **permission marketing** since the early days of the internet. Students, if interested, can get certified in HubSpot's inbound methodology of Attract, Acquire, Close, and Delight which closely mirrors the Zahay and Roberts approach of Acquisition, Conversion, Retention and Customer Value Growth.

permission marketing marketing to customers who have given explicit permission to be contacted.

Cost of Lead Generation The ultimate question in B2B marketing and in deciding whether to use a sales force or inbound techniques is always, "How much does it/should it cost to generate a sales lead?" The answer, as usual, depends on the nature of the product and the competitive environment in the particular industry. Here are some generalizations. The 2010 study of lead generation by HubSpot found that companies that used mostly outbound marketing (e.g., trade shows, telemarketing, and direct mail) incurred an average cost of $332 per lead, whereas companies that used mostly inbound techniques incurred an average cost of $134. Within these figures, there are huge variations by firm and by industry. Compared to the firm's average cost per lead, 63 percent of respondents said that social media and blogs produced leads at a lower than average cost. The best performing outbound media were direct mail and telemarketing, producing leads at 37 percent and 34 percent, respectively, below the firm's average.[14] Again, industry sector and individual company variance is huge, but so are the costs to generate a sales lead, whether qualified or not. The data from HubSpot for 2016 in Figure 13.11 shows a wide variety of average costs per lead in industry, with financial services having the highest cost of $51–$100 per lead and media & publishing having the lowest cost of $11–$25 per lead.

Why the difference in the cost of leads? Think about the average price (more precisely the gross margin) of the two types of sales. In general, financial services will be more expensive and will produce a higher gross margin to cover the costs of lead generation and other marketing activities. The more competition in the field and the higher the return, the higher the cost of a lead.

FIGURE 13.11

Cost per Lead Varies by Industry

Industry	Cost Per Lead
Media & Publishing	$11 – $25
Education	$26 – $50
Healthcare & Medical	$26 – $50
Consulting	$26 – $50
Industrial & Manufacturing	$26 – $50
Travel & Tourism	$26 – $50
Consumer Products	$26 – $50
Software	$51 – $100
Information Tech & Services	$51 – $100
Marketing Agencies	$51 – $100
Financial Services	$51 – $100

SOURCE: https://research.hubspot.com/charts/cost-per-lead-benchmarks-by-industry.

When the same reasoning is applied to the cost of generating a B2B sales lead, the business marketer can accept a higher cost per lead for a higher return. The large differences in the costs and gross margins of various B2B products means there will be large variations in lead costs between industry segments in business markets. There will also be differences between inbound and outbound channels.

Purchasing Leads This discussion of generating sales leads and assessing their cost assumes that the firm, whether B2B or B2C, is generating its own sales leads, alone or with the support of a specialty marketing services firm. Typically, like the direct marketing "house list" the company's own leads will be more effective than purchased leads. However, there are thousands of firms that advertise sales leads at a low cost for virtually any business. On one end are the traditional providers of direct marketing lists, which can loosely be described as sales leads. Hoover's[15] and InfoUSA[16] are both traditional purveyors of business databases and lists to the direct marketing—and now the internet marketing—industry, for as little as a few cents per lead. The source of the leads is the business and consumer directories compiled by these firms. These are business leads that are qualified only by industry membership; the "lead" does not necessarily have a need for the marketer's product. While purchased "targeted lists" are still popular among B2B marketers, the marketer's own lists of customers and those who register over the web or click on paid advertisements are usually more likely to result in qualified leads.

There are also marketers who offer a set of "free leads" for little or nothing as an incentive for purchasing more leads. Many of these leads are of extremely poor quality and have been obtained in questionable ways like hacking. Purchasing sales leads is a "buyer beware" activity! The poorer the initial lead quality, the more it will cost to qualify them and the fewer good leads will come out the end of the lead funnel.

DEMAND GENERATION STEP THREE: NURTURING LEADS

The next step in demand generation is lead nurturing. Business marketers use lead nurturing techniques in part because they achieve results and in part because they have to get used to small numbers. Often, the total market size is rather small, perhaps a few thousand or even a hundred firms. Each sale can be quite large—in the hundreds of thousands or even millions of dollars. Consequently, each sales lead is indeed something to be nurtured.

The Buyer's Journey

Lead nurturing requires a good understanding of the buyer's purchase journey and stage in the buy cycle. Companies use campaign, industry- or persona-based nurturing "tracks" and deliver content and offer experiences relevant to that track, on average using three "touches" or interactions with each track.[17] Aberdeen's best in class companies tended to use a variety of marketing technologies to interface with and nurture leads, including both inbound and outbound telemarketing, as shown in Figure 13.12.

Kaiser Permanente Colorado (KPCO) is a healthcare organization that uses the lead nurturing process to great success. The company is Colorado's largest nonprofit health plan and is consistently rated highly by its customers. KPCO captured leads through targeted landing pages that were driven from telemarketing, email, paid search, and social advertising campaigns. Leads were also sourced from special events, industry associations, or other lead sources. Multichannel marketing programs were used to nurture leads, qualify them, and convert them into customers and messages, which were then segmented appropriately. Based on the point in the buying cycle, the customer could be closed with a quick email or might need a more detailed rate quote. Messaging and content were targeted to the buyer persona as well. The results were an increase in the "win rate" from leads of 3 percent to 33 percent and 23.4 million dollars in marketing-sourced revenue in 18 months.[18]

FIGURE 13.12
Marketing Technology for Lead Nurturing Across Company Type

	Best-in-Class	Average	Laggards
Email marketing system	88%	76%	67%
CRM/sales force automation	86%	64%	60%
Web analytics	75%	56%	64%
Marketing automation software suite	63%	40%	36%
Cookie-based website tracking	63%	46%	57%
Outbound telemarketing	63%	44%	29%
Inbound telemarketing	43%	38%	21%
Marketing analytics tools	43%	29%	7%
Marketing automation consultant/services	43%	32%	14%
Content marketing platform	38%	32%	21%
Marketing asset management	29%	13%	7%
Revenue performance management software	29%	9%	7%

SOURCE: Aberdeeen Group, May 2012

Designing and Testing Landing Pages to Nurture Leads

The Kaiser Permanente example illustrates the use of targeted landing pages in the lead nurturing process. The **landing page** refers to the page customers encounter when they click through from any channel to a business website. A landing page is constructed that is specific to the content or offer in one or more channels. This type of landing page is housed on a server but is not part of the website itself. It allows the marketer to get contact and qualifying information like that in Figure 13.13. Dr. Zahay filled out this form to receive information to help write this book. Although as an educator she is probably not a good prospect for Aberdeen, the company will use her information to make that determination in the demand generation process.

landing page a web page designed to receive visitors who are coming to the site as a result of a link from another site.

This approach is much more useful in the context of lead generation and management and it is the type of landing page we will describe in this section. There is no good reason for simply dumping click-throughs on the corporate home page. There must be a landing page, whether it already exists on the website or whether it must be constructed specifically for the ad or lead generation campaign.

There is a great deal of useful advice on the internet about best practices for creating landing pages[19] and landing page mistakes.[20] A good summary comes from Marketing Experiments, which, as the name suggests, conducts extensive testing of marketing activities throughout the sales funnel, using the techniques described in Chapter 4. It uses the term "marketing optimization," which has become popular to describe data-driven improvements at any stage of the sales funnel. From its extensive testing experience, it has settled on three criteria for landing pages that work—*simplicity, continuity*, and *relevance*.

FIGURE 13.13
A Qualification Form for Information Download

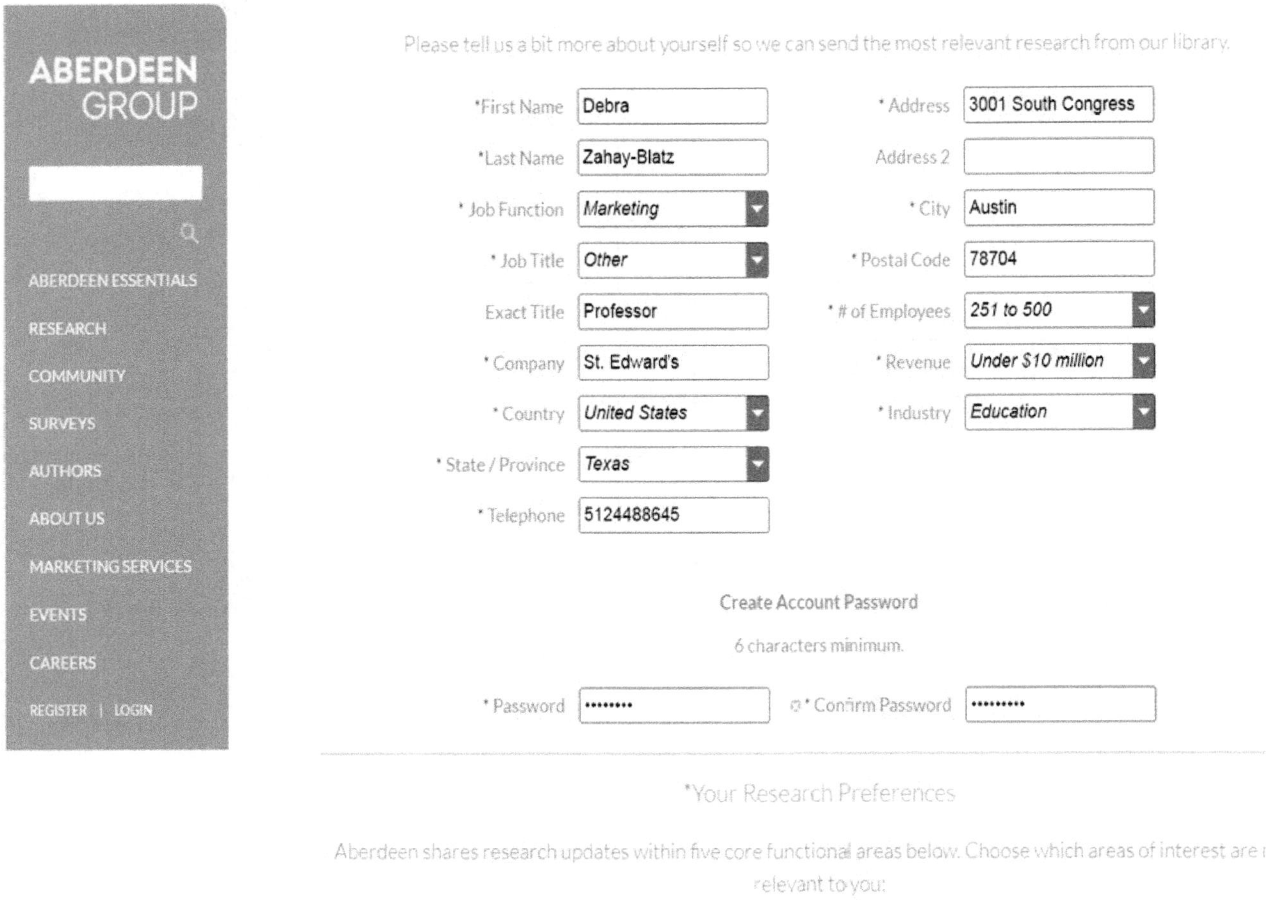

SOURCE: Aberdeen Group.

Figure 13.14 shows the second stage in an optimization process, testing and improving a landing page. The company had already tested and improved the PPC ad for this unidentified business software company, improving the click-through rate by 21 percent.

The company in the second phase made changes in the landing page to increase its simplicity, continuity, and relevance. The changes were as follows:

- To improve the layout by eliminating the left-hand navigation bar and reducing the number of call to action buttons to just one. Taking off the website navigation bar from the landing page may seem counterintuitive, but look at it this way: the marketer wants the reader to click on the call to action button, following the conversion path the marketer has designed. Clicking on anything else—any one of the links on the navigation bar—interrupts and probably destroys the conversion path. The changes created a *simpler* page.
- To "chunk" the copy into smaller bulleted units. The headline, subhead, and the award symbols directly below the subhead mirrored the "we're number 1" promise made on the PPC ad, thereby improving the *continuity* from one element of the path to another. MarketingExperiments points out that the information was already there; it just rearranged it.
- To improve the *relevance* of the landing page, it included customer testimonials. Though brief, the testimonials included numbers that demonstrated improved outcomes from use of the software.

FIGURE 13.14
Testing a Landing Page to Optimize Click-Throughs

SOURCE: MarketingExperiments. Used with Permission,

Taken together, these changes improved the click-throughs from the landing page to the forms page by 54 percent.

Marketing Experiments also optimized the forms page for this client using both design and messaging that reflected the landing page. The form looked simpler, but it actually asked for the same amount of information. And the number of forms submitted increased by 97 percent. That growth was not all the result of the improved form; more people arrived on the landing page and more people clicked through from the landing page. That meant there were many more people who arrived at the forms page where the completion rate improved by just over 7 percent from the original to the optimized form.

An improved landing page helped a great deal in this particular test. However, *it was the optimization of each page as part of a three-step process* that created the final outcome—an improvement of 272 percent in overall conversion. According to Marketing Experiments the optimized path also produced more than four times the monthly profit." This data demonstrates the value of testing in the marketing automation environment. However, it takes knowledge of everything we have discussed, including personas, the buy cycle, knowledge of the customer's journey, and learning from testing and research to create effective paths through the web or mobile site that will allow visitors to obtain the information they need to convert to customers.

DEMAND GENERATION STEP FOUR: QUALIFYING SALES LEADS TO CREATE MARKETING QUALIFIED LEADS (MQLS)

Once a prospect has been generated from an inquiry or other source, the next step is to qualify in order to determine whether the inquiry actually represents a sales lead. Marketing takes the first step in qualifying the leads best on indicated buyer interest, buyer persona fit, or other criteria. These leads that have been scored and further

Marketing Qualified Leads or MQLs leads that have been through scoring and other qualification processes and are ready to be passed on to sales for further qualification.

unqualified leads potential sales leads for which there is no qualifying data beyond membership in a relevant industry.

qualified by marketing as worthy to be passed on to sales to check their qualifications are deemed to be **Marketing Qualified Leads or MQLs**.

There are leads at the other end of the qualified/unqualified continuum. The "bingo" cards (many offers on a single response card) that you still see in some magazines tend to produce a large volume of highly unqualified prospects. So does any offer that includes a sizable free gift, especially one that is unrelated to the product itself. Any sources that produce **unqualified leads** which haven't met the MQL scoring threshold met by the organization will in turn produce major marketing expenses as the (few) good are sorted from the (many) bad.

Marketing typically uses scoring models to, as a first step, qualify leads. Lead scoring models tend to be set up and run in marketing automation systems. such as Eloqua, Pardot, and Marketo. These applications tend to make operations easier, but they do not solve the basic problem. The marketer must ensure that the scoring system genuinely expresses the lead quality, and he must revisit the items and associated scores at frequent intervals to make certain that they still accurately reflect the firm's situation and needs.

Lead scoring requires a model that requires data that includes the following:

- Online activity: Number and frequency of visits to site, multiple visitors from same firm, time spent, clicks on email newsletters, and more (negative: time spent on job openings page)
- Current or previous customer relationship
- Title; role in buying center: Purchasing agent may be a negative, depending on product in question
- Ideal customer pro Industry, size of firm, annual revenue, and more

It should be noted that most of these criteria are not simple "yes/no" questions. It may be sufficient to score them on a simple scale—1 to 3, for example. In that case, a set of categories needs to be developed for items like "number of visits to site: 1 visit in past six months, 3–5 in past six months, 6 or more in past six months." This categorization suggests that the marketer is rescoring leads every six months. It is often better to assign points for each item instead of using a scale. A point system allows the marketer to build in weights for important or negative items. For example, the VP of procurement title may be heavily weighted positively; whereas a prospect in a region where the firm does not have sales representation may be heavily weighted negatively. A scoring system can become much more complex, but it is wise to start as simply as possible and add to the complexity of the scoring only as experience clearly demonstrates the need. Figure 13.15 illustrates a real-life lead scoring form from industry. The scoring model adds points for actions such as viewing a video (10 points), completing a contact form with a request for a demo (40 points), or visiting the website multiple times in one day (5 points). The form takes away points for inactivity (-5) or unsubscribing from a newsletter (-10 points). The lead with the above-mentioned activities would have 55 positive points ($10+40+5$) minus 15 points ($-5+-10$) for a total lead "score" of 40 points. Whether this score is good or bad depends on the activity of other leads and what the threshold number of points is for a lead to be considered qualified in this round of analysis by marketing.

Deciding how much information to request from a prospect for lead scoring and qualification requires a delicate balancing act. Think of it in customer relationship terms. There really is no relationship yet, so prospects are reluctant to give up much information. The more information the marketer can get, the less it will cost to identify real leads and qualify them. The minimal amount of information is name and email address.

How does the marketer know how much information to ask in an information form used in lead scoring is too much? First, testing the response form in various versions helps determine what will optimize response. Second, continually reviewing the metrics for the form to determine how many people start to fill out the form and exit the page before completing it will improve response. It is even better if the analytics allows the marketer to see at which line in the form the visitor stops.

FIGURE 13.15
Lead Scoring Form from Industry Illustrates Complexity of Customer Interactions

Website Visits	Score
Viewed Video 75%+	10
Clicks link to Schedule Demo or Talk to Us	5
Multiple Web Visits-One day	5
Form Fill	
Complete Contact Form / Demo Request	40
Decrease Score	
Decrease Score - Inactivity, 1st time	-5
Visited Career Pages	-5
Decrease Score - Inactivity	-10
Unsubscribed from Email	-10
Banner Ad	
Converted - Response	15
Content Syndication	
Downloaded Asset - Response	20
Email Campaign	
Opened	1
Clicked Email (Social link);	2
Clicked Email;	5
Downloaded Asset - Response;	20
Unsubscribed	-10

Events (External Tradeshow)	Score
Invited;	0
Added by Sales;	0
Registered;	10
Scheduled Meeting - Response;	15
Booked Demo - Response;	15
Attended Show;	10
Visited Booth - Response;	15
Attended Seminar Session - Response;	20
Influential Meeting - Response;	40
Attended Demo - Response;	40
Executive Meeting - Response;	40
No Show;	0
Post Show Engagement - Response	25

Google AdWords	
Converted - Response	15

Events (Internal Roadshow)	Score
Invited;	0
Added by Sales;	0
Registered - Response;	10
Scheduled Meeting - Response;	15
Booked Demo - Response;	15
Attended Show - Response;	25
Influential Meeting - Response;	40
Attended Demo - Response;	40
Executive Meeting - Response;	40
No Show;	0
Post Show Engagement - Response	25

LinkedIn	
Converted - Response	15

List Purchase	
Opted-In - Response;	15

Online Advertising	
Converted - Response	15

Paid Search	
Converted - Response	15

Social Media	
Converted - Response	15

Webinar	Score
Registered;	10
Attended - Response;	25
Attended On-demand - Response;	20
Price Request - Response	25

Xing	
Converted - Response	15

SOURCE: Dr. Juli James, St. Edward's University, Marketo Champion.

The outcome of lead scoring and qualification is a set of lead categories which then can be distributed to the sales force. The essence of **lead distribution** is to categorize leads for immediate closing efforts or nurturing them with a view to future closing. There is also a delicate balance between giving salespeople only well-qualified leads that are worthy of their efforts and keeping them supplied with a target number of leads.

Scored leads are usually further qualified based on behavioral characteristics such as customer persona fit and the purchasing scenario before they are passed on to sales. Once further qualification has occurred, a minimum number of categories for lead distribution would be three:

1. Leads ready for distribution to sales force (MQLs)
2. Leads for further nurturing
3. Leads to receive no attention at present

Once MQLs are distributed to the sales force, leads that are to be nurtured might be distributed to a call center or assigned to receive periodic email communications. Some leads might percolate up the system and be candidates for future nurturing. All these nurturing activities can be managed through a marketing automation system. Leads that are to receive no attention at present might be rescored at a later date.

Using Customer Personas

As marketing seeks to further qualify leads beyond the use of lead scoring models, it looks to the concept of customer personas. Every marketing student is familiar with the concept of market segmentation and knows how important it is to select the appropriate target segment for a marketing campaign. The concept of **personas** takes the concept one step further, as discussed in the context of consumer personas in Section 8-4b. Whether B2C or B2B a persona puts flesh on the bones of a typical segment profile, which describes a customer (or perhaps a customer firm in B2B) on a series of business demographic, product use, and buying behavior items. The items are straightforward quantitative measures: "yearly revenue between $50 and 100 million," for example. A persona weaves a textual description around the set of quantitative data, making it qualitative and humanizing it.

personas a way of describing different groups of customers by giving them a unique personality.

The idea of creating personas is not new, but it has become newly popular in the context of the internet. Personas are helpful to everyone involved with customers, but they are especially helpful with the interface between marketing and IT. It is the job of marketing to select segments around which to develop marketing strategy and to profile those segments for strategy execution. It is the job of IT to design websites and landing pages that reflect the strategy and support the execution. If marketing can give IT a written depiction of a specific customer who represents a specific segment, IT will have a human image to which it can design. Such a specialized strategy should result in a better product from both the marketing and IT standpoint.

In its e-book entitled *Persuasion Architecture Future Now*, a consulting group defines personas as "archetypical fictional characters who represent your buying audience." In describing how this group creates personas for its clients, it goes on to say:

> *When we design personas for persuasive systems, we are primarily interested in understanding how they initiate relationships, how they gather information, how they approach the decision-making process, what language they use and how they prefer to obtain agreement and closure. These are the principal factors that influence how we choose and connect prospects to content that helps them buy in a manner comfortable to them.*[21]

Personas are created on the basis of detailed marketing research—both qualitative and quantitative—and website and other online metrics. Dr. Andrea Wiggins cataloged the steps used in the creation of personas, from collecting initial data to analyzing detailed website reports to the selection of and creation of living personas.[22] Use of personas in website design will be discussed in Chapter 18.

Figure 13.16 is a graphical representation of a customer persona that was developed in the specific context of lead generation and management in a B2B market. It describes a CIO (chief information officer) who is in the category of transformational

FIGURE 13.16

Persona for a CIO in the Transformational Leader Segment

	Technical Decision Maker: The Transformational Leader
	• CIO • Technical decision maker • Develops IT strategy and roadmap • Leads technology team that evaluates technology options
Key Attributes	40-55 years old; Masters in Science, Executive MBA; at least 1 leadership roles
Attitude	Leader, business savvy, frugal, skeptical of vendor claims
Reputation	Visionary, decisive, well regarded within industry, egotistical
Job Focus	Creating enterprise-wide change, shifting perception of techno
Pain Points	• Identifying most promising technology • Getting company-wide buy-in for new software initiatives • Finding ways to make measurable impact
Keywords Used to Search for Information	enterprise software ROI, strategic software investments, breaki enterprise-wide productivity
Values	• **Leadership**: Ability to see and convey the "big picture" • **Knowledge and expertise**: Broad IT knowledge but not inte • **Innovation**: Follows latest trends; seeks proof of how others • **Expectations**: High expectations of IT team and vendors/so
Fears	Making bad purchase decision, tarnishing reputation
Pet Peeves	Self-serving vendors who don't do their homework to understa implementation
Internal influences	Board of directors, CEO, CFO
Motivators	Bonus structure, ego, industry recognition
Information Sources	Peers; online search; Gartner, Forrester; Gartner CIO Leadersl magazine
Content Preferences	In-depth white papers, podcasts

SOURCE: http://www.findnewcustomers.com/buyerpersonas.

leader, one of the three types identified by *CIO* magazine.[23] It contains a great deal of detail on what this type of CIO does and how he does it. It includes data that are specific to B2B marketing like pain points. It also includes important characteristics like values and motivators and critical details like keywords used in searches and favorite information sources.

The questions a marketer needs to answer in order to develop a persona like this are laid out by Jeff Ogden, President of Find New Customers, a B2B lead generation firm. His questions include as follows:

- What pressing issues keep this person up at night?
- What motivates her to take action?
- What sources does he turn to for information and daily news?
- How does she go about making business decisions?
- What type of organizations does he belong to and what events does he attend?
- What social networks does she frequent?
- Does he seek advice from colleagues, industry peers, or unbiased third parties?
- What specific words or phrases does he use to describe the problems he is facing? (This is almost always missed!)
- What might prevent him from selecting your company or product?
- What are his content preferences throughout the buying cycle?[24]

Ogden argues that it is important to know the target buyer in as much depth and detail as possible in order to sell effectively, and that a persona is a good example of that kind of knowledge.

Developing Purchasing Scenarios

Another tool marketers used to further qualify leads is the purchasing scenario. The term scenario may be familiar to you from a strategy course. Here are two definitions from the corporate strategy literature:

1. Michael Porter defines a scenario as "an internally consistent view of what the future might turn out to be—not a forecast, but one possible future outcome."
2. Peter Schwartz describes scenario analysis as "a tool for ordering one's perception about alternative future environments in which one's decisions might be played."[25]

Marketers use scenarios to understand the customer purchasing process for uses such as developing a content strategy, to understand how the customer uses the website in making a purchase and to determine if a lead is marching down the path to purchase or just browsing.

The GrokDotCom blog defines a marketing (persuasion) scenario as follows:

A scenario consists of persuasive components that lead a visitor segment to participate in a conversion action. Some of these components will be linear; others will be nonlinear. All must be customer focused—based on how each segment approaches the decision to buy—rather than business focused.[26]

Consultant Patricia Seybold, writing about the use of scenarios by her consultancy, describes the kind of revelations marketers can find when they get the customers' perspective on the purchase process. Two of her examples are as follows:

- Monster, the job search website, is an important tool for corporate recruiters. Monster prided itself on providing a large number of qualified candidates for each job that recruiters were trying to fill. What it found was that the large number of candidates it was returning caused the recruiters to spend too much time screening. According to Seybold, "They wanted the best three candidates and they wanted them within 24 hours."

- Merck's Medco consumer prescription management service deals with a long value chain—doctors, insurers, and pharmaceutical companies to name only some. Consumers care about getting their prescriptions refilled quickly and accurately. Other members of Medco's value chain had policies and procedures in place that interfered with or slowed down refilling of prescriptions on the site. By working with the members of the value chain to align refill policies, Medco was able to eliminate 30 percent of pharmacists' and patients' telephone calls that had been coming in to its call center.[27]

In addition, the Irish consultancy iQ Content has an example of a complete scenario written for website design use. It calls it sales call back (variant 1), which reads as follows

The Sales Prospect sees an offer on the site that they'd like to avail of but they'd like more information before deciding to buy. There's a link that says you can have a member of the Vodafone customer care team call you about the offer at a time of your choosing. They click that link and because the offer is open only to existing Vodafone customers the system checks to see if they are logged in. They aren't, so they are taken to the log in screen. This also offers them the option of registering if they do not have log in details already. The Sales Prospect logs in and is taken to the call back scheduling form. The query title, relating to the specific offer the Sales Prospect expressed interest in, has already been entered on the form by the system and their personal details are already entered in the relevant form fields. The Sales Prospect schedules a call using the form controls and submits the form.[28]

Notice that this scenario works fine if the prospect is a Vodafone customer. What if she is not? One good solution would be variant 2 in which there is a different offer for noncustomers and/or a call to action to become a customer. That is a primary benefit of a scenario; it allows the marketer to see what is working or not working and what else may be needed.

To summarize, personas put life into market segment descriptors, and scenarios map out the path to conversion, which can be website-specific or more general in nature. Marketing leads will be classified by persona and marketing will also look at the purchase scenarios of prospects when qualifying leads. If a prospect is on a likely path to conversion, the lead will be deemed more worthy of qualification by the sales force.

Sales Accepted Leads (SALs) and Sales Qualified Leads (SQLs)

Sales Qualified Leads or SQLs leads that have passed through the BANT process as fully qualified potential customers.

The sales department itself usually further qualifies the leads presented by marketing based on its knowledge of the situation, such as the timing of the sale or poor product fit. These leads that pass through this process are known as **Sales Qualified Leads or SQLs**. Sales will then further qualify the leads making sure that the lead will have sufficient budget, authority, and need to purchase the product in a specific time frame. This qualification framework is known as BANT. BANT stands for the following:

B-Budget: Does the prospect have the money to purchase?

A-Authority: Is the prospect the one making the decision?

N-Need: Does the prospect have a defined need?

T-Timing: Is the prospect going to buy now or later?

Sales Accepted Leads or SALs leads that have been further qualified by sales as close to conversion.

Leads that meet the BANT qualification are known as Sales Qualified Leads.[29] A moment's reflection suggests that these issues are easily translated into specific questions that can be asked to try to qualify an MQL into an SQL. For instance, "Do you have money in this year's budget to make the purchase?" The prospect will generally know the answers to the qualifying questions and will be willing to provide them. This process saves time for both the marketer and the prospective purchaser. After further research by the sales force, SQLs that are true opportunities are then classified as **Sales Accepted Leads or SALs**.

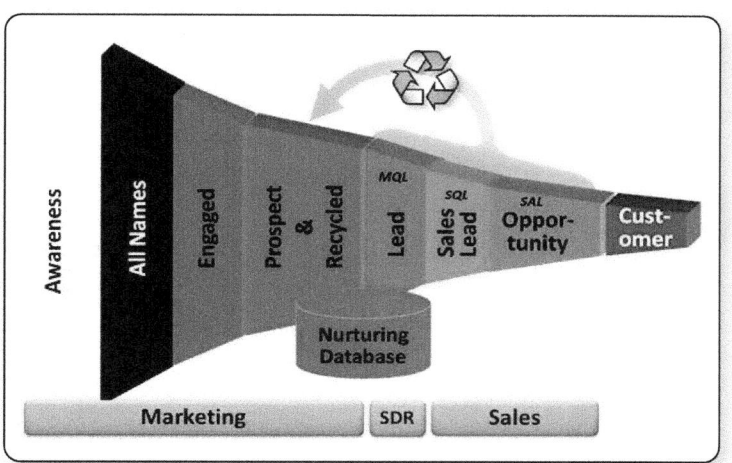

FIGURE 13.17
Marketo Marketing/Sales Funnel

SOURCE: http://global.tahono.com/images/funnel/miller_funnel.JPG.

This process is illustrated in the Marketo Marketing/Sales Funnel in Figure 13.17. Please note that a Sales Development Rep (SDR) is an outbound sales position that is relied upon heavily for lead qualification in the sales process and helps bridge the gap to turn MQLs into SQLs. The SDR might do much of the BANT qualification before the lead is delivered to the outside sales force. This process is more efficient and cost-effective for a company than having highly compensated sales representatives involved in the early stages of lead qualification. All leads are processed through a nurturing database, typically housed in the marketing automation system.

Cost of Lead Qualification

The higher the lead quality, the less it will cost to qualify it; this is the underlying rationale for getting as much information as possible in the prospect process.

David Green, director of best practices at MECLABS, has a hypothetical example of **lead qualification**, which is drawn from wide experience. The ratio of 70 valid leads per 100, as shown in Figure 13.18, is reasonable and can be affected up or down by the desirability of the offer and the amount and intrusiveness of the information requested on the prospect form.

lead qualification determining whether a prospect has the characteristics necessary to make a purchase.

Green assumes that the cost of a sales rep, including salary and fringes, is $200,000, and the rep has 1,960 productive hours available after vacation, training, and so on. If she can make 10 qualification calls per hour, that will amount to 19,600 phone calls per year. If she takes 4.2 minutes to make a qualification call, it will take a total of 40 hours to qualify all 100 leads. If only the 70 valid leads enter the qualification process, the number of hours is reduced to 34. If only sales-ready leads are called, the number of hours is less than 3, reducing the total cost from $4,082 to $286. Thus, the importance of reducing the total cost of a lead is important from a marketing management point of view. Hence the need for the more effective use of marketing automation systems.

However, decreasing qualification costs by acquiring more valid and sales-ready leads is a matter of degree, not of absolutes. It is reasonable to strive for a high proportion of valid leads, but a firm is unlikely to ever get only SALs. In fact, such a scenario would not be desirable. The lead pipeline needs to be kept stocked with leads in various stages of readiness to keep sales stable and sales costs at a minimum. Remember that these figures are hypothetical. Any good marketer tracks the success of individual lead generation programs using metrics like number of leads, cost per lead by medium, and number of qualified leads. Past performance is the best measure of success, not general or hypothetical industry metrics. Prior to the internet, qualification was almost entirely conducted by telephone. It is a process that works, but it is relatively expensive. Today, B2B marketers have other, more cost-effective, options.

FIGURE 13.18
Lowering the Cost of Lead Qualification

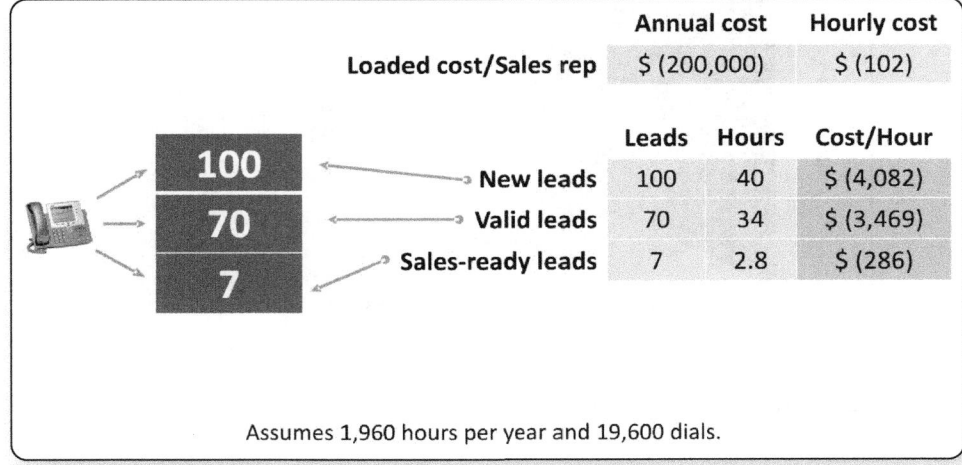

Assumes 1,960 hours per year and 19,600 dials.

SOURCE: J. David Green, "2011 Lead Generation Trends and Challenges," p. 20, November 15, 2013. Reprinted with permission of MECLABS.

Lead Generation and Qualification at EDGAR Online

Lead scoring is an area in which business marketers often seek the assistance of a marketing services firm. Silverpop, now part of the IMB Marketing Cloud, for example, was originally a supplier of email services and developed in to a firm that offered lead scoring as part of its marketing automation software.[30]

The experience of financial services firm EDGAR Online with a lead generation and qualification system represents several of the issues and solutions in this area.[31] EDGAR Online's basic problem was one shared by many marketers: EDGAR needed to increase the quality of the leads distributed to the sales force; in other words, to make sure they were indeed sales-ready leads. It began by better promoting its content with whitepapers and newsletters--and by offering free product trials as an incentive. This promotion actually increased the number of leads generated, which could have compounded its problem. Instead, the firm refined its lead scoring criteria and developed a careful, automated lead distribution process.

The EDGAR online case study recounts the following outcomes:

- Attraction of new customers and better communication with existing ones led to a 400 percent increase in sales leads, with the sales department being happier with the quality.
- The lead scoring system led to five times more qualified leads each month..
- The rate of sales closure was more than double the average for EDGAR Online's industry sector.
- The seven-day free trials for EDGAR Pro resulted in conversion rates in the 40–60% range.

This technique makes such good sense that all good B2B marketers do it, right? Sadly, that is not the case. A 2012 study by consultancy Aberdeen found only 20 percent of marketers using lead management technology were characterized as "best in class," meaning that action was taken on 85 percent of the leads passed from marketing to sales whereas 80 percent of marketers pass on 27 percent or fewer leads that are actionable by sales.[32] The low effectiveness of these systems is usually the result of an organizational disconnect between marketing and advertising, who distribute the sales leads, and sales, who are responsible for following them up and closing the sale. All too often the MQL process falls into the organizational crack between marketing/advertising and sales and is not followed up effectively. The result is that marketing spends money to generate leads. Sales complains that the leads received are of poor quality. If no one in the organization is responsible for fixing the crack, the organizational return on its marketing and sales investment suffers.

To sum up, the activities leading up to the closing step are of great importance, even though the point of the entire process is to close the sale or conversion.

DEMAND GENERATION STEP FIVE: LEAD CONVERSION

Defining Conversion

Traditional direct marketers are responsible for the term "conversion," and its original definition is making the first sale to a prospect—converting the lead to a sale. As the importance of CRM became evident in the 1980s, direct marketers were heard to speak of "converting to a loyal customer." That sounds like exactly what marketers are trying to do, but it begs the question of exact metrics. Is it the second or maybe the third sale? Is it obtaining a growing share of the customer's expenditure on the product in question? It could be either, or both! It could be another performance indicator that is more closely tied to the company's strategy.

While "lead conversion" can generically be defined as closing a sale, it too can be a deceptively simple concept. Conversion in its broadest sense is any desired action, whether it be downloading a whitepaper or registering for a webinar or subscribing to a newsletter. In terms of the demand generation process and the Marketing/Sales Funnel, conversion is getting the prospect or lead from one stage of the funnel to the next. The conversion rate is the percentage of those leads that make it from one stage of the funnel to the next.

Conversion can often be an overlooked opportunity in B2B demand generation. Omniture, now a part of the Adobe Marketing Cloud for analytics applications has said that, in general, most organizations spend more time and money promoting their websites through acquisition channels such as search or affiliate marketing than they do optimizing existing conversion rates.

Another important point to note is that there may be multiple "conversion" points in the demand generation process. For example, social media marketers often say they have "converted" a Facebook fan to a sales lead when the fan clicks on a link and provides contact information on the website in return for desired information. From the standpoint of the social media team, it seems to be a conversion, because the team has passed on the responsibility to another group. However, using conversion that way is a loose application of the term. Measurable objectives should be established for each team at each stage of the demand generation process.

Measuring Conversion

In addition to neglecting the conversion process or failing to measure the results, we tend to think of conversion too narrowly as only converting existing site visitors in the "here and now." We often overlook applying marketing fundamentals such as identifying and defining profiles that comprise our larger target audience, developing the right offer and corresponding message, and delivering it to them at the right time in their purchase cycle.

Omniture goes on to say that this is all about relevancy—the right content and offers at the right time—the customer's right time, not the marketer's! It lists seven steps in an optimized conversion process:

1. *Identify Conversion Goals and KPIs.* **Key performance indicators (KPIs)**, discussed in more detail in Chapter 18, are internal benchmarks for performance at each stage: number of advertising impressions, number of click-throughs to the site, and number of lead forms completed, for example.

2. *Define and Acquire Target Profiles—Apply 40/40/20 Rule.* There is a time-honored direct marketing rule that 40 percent of success can be attributed to

key performance indicators (KPIs) a metric that has been identified as an important measure or benchmark of business performance.

targeting and another 40 percent to the offer with 20 percent being attributable to creative execution.

3. *Organize and Optimize Site Structure.* It is important to have a site that makes it easy for visitors to find and purchase what they want.
4. *Develop a Compelling Message.* The importance of the message seems to go without saying, but in this context, it must be a message that is relevant to each specific audience segment.
5. *Place Effective Calls to Action.* Chapter 4 notes that specific and compelling calls to action are a key part of any direct-response effort. That notion applies to conversion as well.
6. *Enhance Shopping Cart and Lead Capture Processes.* A visitor with a product interest has only two action options while on the website: he purchases the product at that moment using the shopping cart function; or alternatively, he can fill out a form requesting more information or to be kept informed via newsletters. A third option, of course, is to leave without doing either. It is the job of the marketer to ensure that few qualified prospects as possible leave the site without taking positive action of some kind.
7. *Test, Measure, and Refine.* There are many steps in the conversion process that can be tested. We will discuss testing landing pages later in this chapter. Both test results and the metrics produced by the program can and should be used to improve future conversion programs.

These steps also seem to follow a commonsense approach, and they do. However, they only mention the thorny problem of defining exactly what a conversion is so appropriate goals can be set.

In most firms, there are many internal teams involved in various stages of the demand generation process, and each should have its own target to reach for that stage. The "sales funnel" is the concept that previously was commonly used to describe this process. In the sales funnel leads come in at the top and are sifted out at the bottom. Sales is considered a numbers game and if there are enough leads at the top there will be customers at the bottom. The funnel in Figure 13.17 is a marketing perspective on the sales funnel and has some useful additional strategy guidance. The Marketo Marketing/Sales Funnel is on its side and operates from left to right in an intentional manner, leading the prospect through a process that will result in conversion.

The customer is correctly portrayed as the centerpiece of the process with the funnel itself representing the stages of the B2B buying process and the categories on the middle representing the generic stages of lead qualification. All leads from whichever channel go into a central database, which identifies each lead by media source. Each lead should be tracked through to a sale or lack of one. As data throughout the chapter has indicated, leads generated from different sources tend to have different acquisition costs. To further complicate the matter, these leads also tend to have different conversion rates, making the cost per converted lead vastly different from one channel to another. This is an important input into planning future marketing strategy.

DEMAND GENERATION STEP SIX: METRICS

Calculate ROI for Demand Generation

It is obvious from the prior discussion that demand generation is a time-consuming and expensive process. Marketers need to be prepared to demonstrate that it is worth the cost. Marketers will want to calculate not only the return on investment for their efforts, but also the returns on each campaign and the maximum cost that can be spent for each lead at various stages of the funnel. Marketing will also want to attribute how much revenue came from its content marketing, lead nurturing, and qualification efforts.

Conversion Paths

For example, we know that visitors take various routes (paths) through a website. One job of the marketer is to ensure that as many of them purchase (convert) as possible. Of course, there is one further complication. Figure 13.19 shows a set of paths through an unrealistically simple video games site that explains the issue.

The complication is that different market segments take different paths through the site. Would you expect the person who comes to a video games site to purchase the latest Star Wars game to take the same path through the site as a person who came to purchase a game but did not know which specific one? Would either one of those segments take the same path as a person who just dropped by the site to see what they stocked? No; these three and other segments would take different paths, and the marketer needs to satisfy the information needs of each and provide a call to action at the appropriate time.

The figure shows that 100 visitors entered the site, and some visitors apparently came to look at games while others came to look at gaming devices. Of the 60 who came to look at games, more (40) went to the Star Wars page than to the PacMan page (20). Of those who went to the Star Wars page, half purchased while the other half was evenly split between leaving the site and going on to the product demonstration page. A majority of those who saw the demonstration purchased the game and the rest exited the site; although it is possible that they could have looped back and looked at another game. The marketer has now accounted for the 40 people who went to the Star Wars page. In order to account for all 60 who went to the games page, it is necessary to find out what happened to the 20 who went to the PacMan page. Forty went to the devices page and the chart shows that outcome. The point is that the marketer has to account for all 100 of the people who came to the site, study the actions of each segment, and locate points where the conversion outcomes might be

FIGURE 13.19

Conversion Paths through a Hypothetical Video Games Site

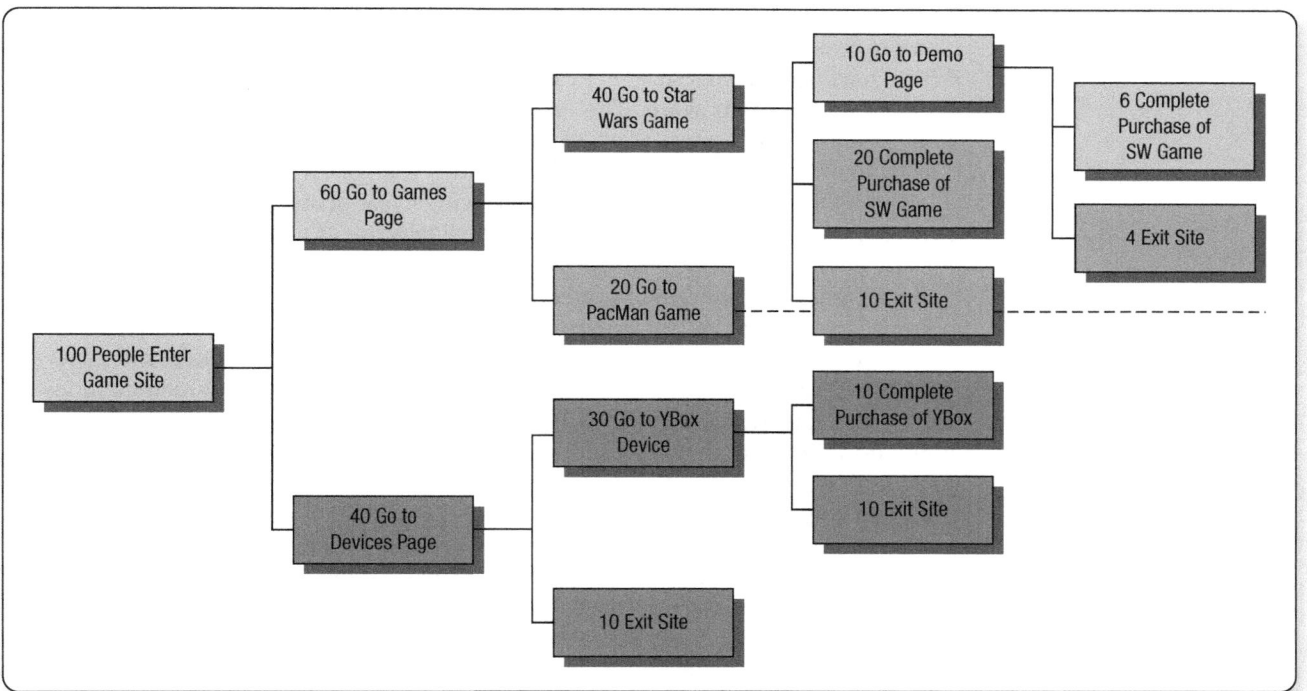

SOURCE: © Cengage Learning 2013.

improved. On a site of any size, this is a monumental task, which can be lessened by concentrating on target segments (some people got here by accident) and on the few target segments that are large enough to be worth the effort of improving outcomes. Still these measurement efforts constitute a large task. The task is also an important one because this is another instance in which it is cheaper to convert more of the target audience once they reach the site than to engage in acquisition marketing to get more people to the site in the first place. This example illustrates some of the challenges in calculating ROI for specific conversion paths.

That last point actually applies to this entire chapter. It is less expensive in the end to develop great content, generate reasonable quality leads, nurture, and qualify them well, and to convert a significant portion of them than it is to engage in endless acquisition campaigns, only to ignore or mismanage the sales leads that are produced.

THE ORGANIZATIONAL CONUNDRUM

If this complex efforts leaves students feeling lost, they are not alone! Senior marketing managers recognize the complexity and the fact that it will require an investment in process improvement and marketing automation software to resolve it. This may take some time, postponing the ROI until sometime in the future.

Even worse, all this complexity occurs in the context of organizational politics in which the leader of each internal team may be trying to maximize his team's performance, even at the expense of performance in other stages of the process—generating a large number of low quality leads, for example. The organizational context represents a serious management issue that will take time and effort to resolve. Sadly, it is often easier just to ignore the issue of an optimal lead process. Organizational issues will remain the most significant obstacle to the effective adaptation of demand generation systems and processes within B2B firms.

SUMMARY

As we have seen, the demand generation process is a key element of B2B marketing and is important in certain product categories in B2C marketing. It is a complex process full of sometimes mind-numbing detail. A large part of the challenge in B2B is because market sizes are often small and unit sales can be quite large, making each contact important. The chapter has emphasized throughout that there are many points in the process where marketing strategy or execution can be improved—improvements that can substantially raise revenue, cut marketing costs, or both.

The business buyer goes through a buying cycle process characterized by needs awareness, research, consolidation and consideration of potential vendors, and a purchasing decision. Since this process can take a year or more for a high-risk purchase, business marketers have a major challenge in keeping up with the potential customer's progress, providing the right content at the right time, and attempting to close the sale when the time is right. This leads to a formal process of demand generation (one of the most important activities of the business marketer), which includes content creation, lead generation, lead qualification by both sales and marketing, conversion, and follow-up analysis of relevant metrics. This process is a communications process that is often lengthy and begins with the concept of content marketing, providing the right content at the right time.

In the implementation of this process, many media channels, both online and offline, can be used to generate sales leads. These media include traditional outbound channels such as direct mail and email. Leads are often cheaper when generated by inbound marketing, being visible on the web in a way that draws potential customers to the website for further information. The request for information can become the beginning of the demand generation process.

Marketing lead qualification may begin with an information form filled out on the website in return for content. The purpose of the information is to determine which state of the buying cycle the prospect is in and what kind of communications are appropriate. As the process goes on, more information is obtained, and when the prospect is deemed ready, the MQL is distributed to internal and/or external sales reps for further qualification by the sales force in terms of an SQL and closing (conversion).

As we have seen, on version is not a "one size fits all" concept. Each organization is likely to have its own definition and metric for conversion. A well-managed process combines that metric with clear objectives at each stage for each team involved in the lead generation and management process. Demand generation is indeed a complex process that involves many groups within the organization. This compexity makes its implementation and execution problematic in many companies for reasons that are purely organizational, not technological.

There are marketing techniques that can improve the process. These techniques include creating customer personas, building customer journey scenarios, building and optimizing landing pages, and creating clear conversion paths through a web or mobile site. This whole process of better understanding customer market segments, developing segment-specific strategies, and testing to optimize the process can result in major improvements in ROI in the B2B marketing process.

DISCUSSION QUESTIONS

1. The chapter states that the discipline of sales lead generation and management was developed by direct marketers and later adapted to the internet. Why do you think direct marketers, and not traditional advertisers, originated the practice of sales lead generation and management?
2. What is the role of search marketing and branding in B2B marketing today?
3. Why do you think B2B marketers consider customer loyalty as one of their most important challenges?
4. Agree or Disagree: The B2B buy cycle has roughly the same steps as the consumer purchase decision process, is carried out in much the same way, and takes about the same length of time. Explain your answer.
5. What is your understanding of content marketing in the demand generation process? How does it differ from the kind of marketing or marketing communications that you are accustomed to?
6. Describe the six steps in the demand generation process.
7. Identify two or three online and two or three offline channels in which sales leads can be generated. Which channels do you think are likely to be most effective in generating leads? Which are likely to be the most expensive to use?
8. What are the Marketing Qualified Leads (MQLs) and how are they qualified?
9. What does the sales force do to further qualify leads received from marketing and what is the result?
10. What are some of the issues marketers should consider when trying to make the conversion process on their websites as effective as possible? How can personas and customer journey scenarios be helpful?
11. Why do you think it is hard to come up with a single, concise definition of conversion? Can you give at least two examples of different definitions of conversion and explain why the different definitions are needed?
12. What is the importance of the landing page in a demand generation context?

ENDNOTES

1. https://marketingtechblog.com/demand-generation-vs-lead-generation.
2. http://blogs.forrester.com/lori_wizdo/15-05-25-b2b_buyer_journey_mapping_basics.
3. http://www.globalspec.com/wp/WP_BuyCycle_Maven.

4. http://blog.hubspot.com/marketing/sales-jobs-vanishing#sm.00000iyus8ld41cqdq ta8262waubc.
5. Fox Agency, b2b marketing, "Will you take on the Challenge? "B2B Marketing Challenge, The 2016 Report, page 13.
6. http://www.brafton.com/news/94-percent-b2b-buyers-research-online-purchase-decisions/.
7. http://www.marketingprofs.com/charts/2016/29499/the-top-challenges-facing-b2b-marketers.
8. http://blog.hubspot.com/insiders/what-is-marketing-automation-a-beginners-guide.
9. http://contentmarketinginstitute.com/2014/01/content-marketing-plan-focus-lead-demand-generation/.
10. http://blog.hubspot.com/blog/tabid/6307/bid/4416/Inbound-Marketing-the-Next-Phase-of-Marketing-on-the-web.aspx#ixzzl8D7w7c4t.
11. Mary Lou Roberts and Paul D. Berger, *Direct Marketing Management*, 2nd edition. See Chapter 9, B2B Direct Marketing, available for free download at http://www.marylouroberts.info/chaptersfordownload.html.
12. http://www.startwithalead.com/article.asp?ARTICLEID=1.
13. http://www.sethgodin.com/sg.
14. http://www.slideshare.net/HubSpot/the-2012-state-of-inbound-marketing
15. http://www.hoovers.com/leads/build-a-list.
16. http://leads.infousa.com/MailingListsSalesLeads.aspx?
17. Aberdeen Research Study.
18. Marketo Marketing Success Series: "Demand Generation, How Kaiser Permanente Colorado Aligned Marketing and Sales to Drive Revenue."
19. http://www.getelastic.com/17-ways-to-minimize-friction.
20. http://blog.kissmetrics.com/5-awful-landing-pages.
21. http://www.ai-dealer.com/images/persuasionarchitecture.pdf p. -26.
22. http://www.boxesandarrows.com/view/building-a-data.
23. http://www.cio.com/article/162300/State_of_the_ CIO_2008_What_Kind_of_CIO_Does_Your_ Company_Need_.
24. https://www.youtube.com/watch?v=IcoMvaOFqtM
25. Both quoted in Frank Buytendijk, Toby Hatch, and Pietro Michell, "Scenario-Based Strategy Maps," Kelley School of Business, Indiana University, 2010, p. 337.
26. http://www.grokdotcom.com/topics/persuasionscenarios.htm.
27. http://www.psgroup.com/detail.aspx?ID=698.
28. http://iqcontent.com/publications/features/article_77.
29. http://www.pathwaysdigital.com/how-to-calculate-maximum-allowable-cost-per-lead/.
30. Adapted from http://www.yourcrmteam.com/blog/2010/11/create-a-lead-scoring-system-to-drive-more-sales.
31. http://www.demandgenreport.com/industry-events/edgar-online-quadruples-lead-gen-pipeline-results-raises-bar-on-close-rates.
32. http://aberdeen.com/research/7603/ra-marketing-lead-management/content.aspx.

Chapter 14

Customer Relationship Development and Retention Marketing

LEARNING OBJECTIVES

By the time you complete this chapter, you will be able to:

1. Explain the importance of customer retention and CLV.
2. Describe the difference between transactional and relational marketing.
3. Discuss the concept of CRM and the marketing functions on which it is based.
4. Explain the elements of CRM strategy.
5. Describe how the digital customer journey describes the next framework of marketing strategy.
6. Explain the importance of CX in CRM.
7. Discuss operational and analytical CRM and why the customer database is essential to both.
8. Describe tools for targeting customers and personalizing customer communications.

9. Explain the role of loyalty programs in CRM.
10. Discuss the growing importance of mobile loyalty programs.
11. Explain the importance of apps in CRM programs.
12. Discuss the nature and importance of social CRM.
13. Explain the benefits of CRM in the cloud.
14. Understand what is necessary to make CRM work.

CRM has become the driving force behind the strategies of leading brands around the world over the past 20 years.[1] High cost of customer acquisition is one reason. The original data supporting the relational approach posited that "It costs seven to ten times as much to acquire a new customer as it does to maintain an existing one." The customer acquisition cost argument is still compelling, although more recent studies have placed the figure anywhere from 3 to 30 times![2]

In addition to the high cost of customer acquisition, there are other issues that the adoption of a relational approach could address, alleviate, or possibly resolve:

- The loss of customers in an increasingly competitive marketplace; and the cost to reactivate them.
- Profits can increase by 25–85 percent, depending on the industry, by reducing customer defection by even 5 percent.
- Many customers who defect say they were satisfied with their former supplier.
- Customers who are extremely satisfied are six times more likely to repurchase than customers who are merely satisfied.
- A satisfied customer may tell five people, where a dissatisfied customer will tell nine.[3] In today's world of social media, the scale may be amplified when dissatisfied customers can tell thousands.
- It costs 7 to 20 times as much to sell to a new customer as to an existing customer.[4]
- Nine out of ten customers will pay more for a better CX.[5]

These data and many more have created two marketing mantras that guide customer-centric marketing programs today:

1. *"Marketing Is Dead."* This is code for the fact that the consumer decision journey has changed and traditional marketing no longer works. The new marketing is about communities and influencers, as discussed in Chapter 5, and getting both customers and influencers involved in marketing activities. Several of the case histories in this chapter make that point, chief among them, the approaches of National Geographic and Victoria's Secret.
2. *"Customer Experience Trumps Loyalty."* Brand loyalists are still desirable but the hard truth is that brands can lose even their loyal fans through poor CX. Customer loyalty and marketing loyalty programs are still important, however, as we will discuss later in this chapter.

All this argues for the importance of CRM in all marketing strategies and for its preeminence in the strategies of some brands.

THE IMPORTANCE OF CLV

customer lifetime value (CLV) the net present value of a future stream of net revenue from an identified customer.

The relationship argument relies on the concept of **customer lifetime value (CLV)**, which was discussed in Chapter 4, to demonstrate the profit impact of relationship strategies. Figure 14.1 documents the importance of relationship maintenance in the online apparel industry. After accounting for acquisition costs, the consultants identify three revenue streams associated with each customer—each one's *base* spending amount, the *growth* of spending as the customer persists with the marketer, and the revenue generated by customer *referrals*. In this example, breakeven on acquisition costs

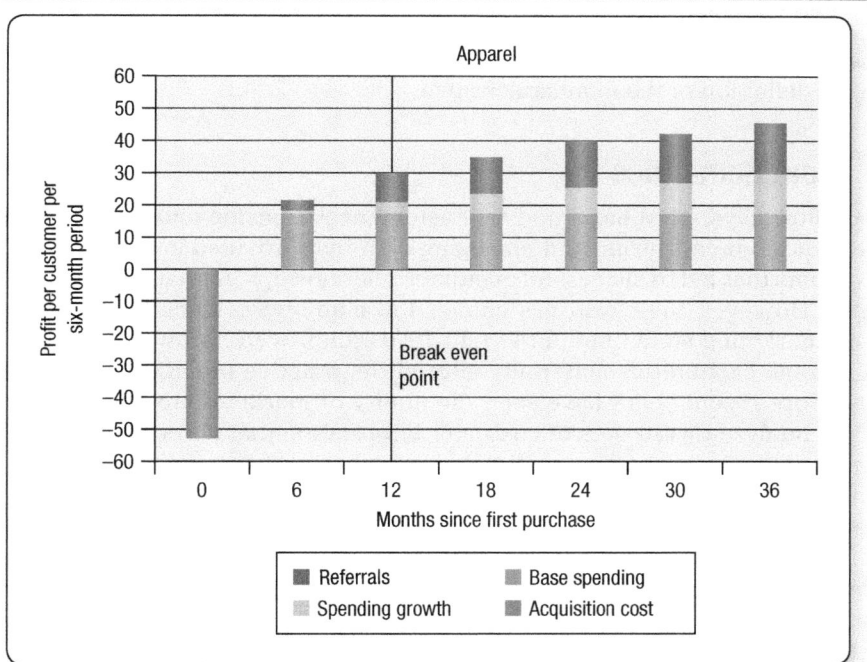

FIGURE 14.1
Components of Customer Lifetime Value for Apparel Purchases

SOURCE: Adapted from Bain & Company Mainspring Online Retailing Survey, December 1999. Copyright © 1999 by Bain & Company, Inc. All rights reserved. Reproduced with permission.

occurs after one year; in other industries it tends to be longer because of higher acquisition costs and/or longer purchase cycles. The general pattern, however, holds true across industry sectors in both consumer and business markets. It emphasizes the importance of caring for customers in a way that causes them to return, to concentrate more of their purchases with the marketer and to refer new customers.

Each of the revenue streams makes a contribution to CLV as the customer persists. In the case of the apparel industry, the data indicate that:

- The average repeat customer spent 67 percent more in months 31 through 36 of the relationship than in the initial six months.
- An average apparel shopper referred three people to the online retailer's site after the first purchase. After ten purchases, the shopper had referred a total of seven people.
- Loyal online customers would also consider buying other product lines from the online retailer outside the current merchandise offerings, indicating brand development opportunities.

Other CLV studies indicate that loyal customers are more likely to buy across a retailer's merchandise assortment, making them better targets for cross-selling and increasing share-of-wallet.[6] Further, customers who interact with the company or brand on Facebook, the major social network for brand interaction, are likely to already be customers and to buy more and to recommend more often after becoming fans.[7] CLV also supports marketers' interest in marketing to Millennials, that is, customers who potentially have a long relationship with a brand.

Although the economics of the relational concept are persuasive, implementing it requires a complete change in the way traditional marketers think about and perform their jobs. Change of this magnitude is always difficult, and such has been the case with relational strategies. In order to understand the issues, we need to contrast the older transactional model to the relationship model, and describe how the relationship model itself is evolving into a focus on the customer journey, as described in Chapter 6.

STRATEGIC CRM

Before discussing the process of developing **CRM** strategy, it is useful to understand the changing definition of the familiar acronym.

A Word about Semantics

From its earliest days, CRM has stood for customer relationship management. The discipline focused on acquiring and managing data that provided insights for marketing programs that led to successful customer relationships. In that context, CRM made sense. However, the world has changed in many ways since the advent of data-driven marketing sometime in the mid-1970s. Improved hardware, software, and data storage capabilities materially altered the practice of CRM in the 1980s and 1990s. More recent years have seen the ability of marketers to gather, build, develop, and analyze **big data** sets of customer information that allow them to track and understand customers on a more detailed level than ever before. Together, these developments allowed marketers to carry out strategies they had previously only envisioned.

> **big data** unstructured data sets that are so large and complex that traditional data processing is challenged to analyze them.

Important as these changes have been, they are dwarfed by the impact of social media SMM. The advent of SMM has allowed marketers to listen to what customers are saying and to engage in real-time dialog with them. Many marketers have adopted the terminology "customer relationship marketing," or sometimes "customer retention marketing," considering that more appropriate to the current environment. Throughout this chapter, CRM should be translated as "customer relationship marketing."

The Elements of CRM

CRM has three basic elements. The *strategic* process identifies CRM goals and objectives within the framework of overall marketing and business objectives. The strategy development process is the focus of this section. In a later section, we will discuss the *operational* or tactical program element and the *analytical* element. Each of the three elements requires different activities and expertise and needs individual attention. However, in practice, they are less distinct and may all be required at one point or another in order to carry out a CRM initiative.

The Transactional versus the Relationship Perspective

Consumer marketers in the traditional mass media environment have really had no choice except to pursue a transactional (product-centric) approach. These marketers ordinarily did not have direct contact with their customers. Consequently, they could not identify their customers as individuals nor attempt to develop an ongoing relationship with them. The mass media did not facilitate identification and tracking of individual customers and prospects. The customer relationship, if there was one, was owned by an intermediary in a channel of distribution. These two factors created a powerful barrier to the establishment of direct relationships by marketers who produced the products and services. In addition, the large up-front investment required to build a product-specific customer database could not be justified by the small gross margins provided by many frequently-purchased consumer products.

B2B marketers had different but no less serious issues. They typically dealt directly with their customers through field sales forces. Sales representatives tended to feel that they had ownership of the customer relationship and to be reluctant to provide detailed data to a centralized customer database. Even if that reluctance did not exist, contact with customers often took place in various units including field sales, the telephone call center, field service, and technical support. To make the situation even worse, if the customer purchased items from more than one division or product line within the company, multiple customer contact points existed.

This often resulted in confusion for both the company and customer, who often felt that the brand was not "speaking with one voice." Her perception was that the brand did not see her as a valued customer, but as a series of isolated problems that was the responsibility of the customer to solve.

What did not usually exist was a data repository which permitted a complete view of the customer relationship with the firm. On the positive side, however, sales reps were often able to recognize customers who were transactional in nature, usually because they were price sensitive. Relationship customers had stronger ties with the firm, perhaps since they required customized products or specialized services. Reps who recognized the difference could, on an individual basis, allocate their time and effort according to the value of the customer relationship.

As long as customer relationship knowledge was the property of individual sales reps, attempts to develop strategic CRM programs floundered. What was lacking was centralized collection and management of customer data that could be analyzed to produce customer insights and translated into strategy. The importance of data was highlighted in a study by Zahay, Peltier, Schultz, and Griffin. They studied both traditional business outcomes data, such as sales and net income, and also a type of outcome they called marketing-oriented customer performance. They operationalized the latter as retention rate plus share of wallet, CLV, and return on investment (ROI). In a broad sense, they found that relational data collected at multiple customer touchpoints were more important than transactional data in predicting both business and marketing performance outcomes.[8] It could be hypothesized that relational data are important since it is used to develop strategies that affect business outcomes.

Nonprofit organizations also need robust CRM data and strategies. They need to retain and upgrade both members and donors. Some have extensive member databases built from their direct mail and social marketing efforts. Others have little in the way of member data beyond name and address. Some still have members and donors that predate the internet who still have never been asked for addresses or other contact information. Moving to internet-based member retention programs has been difficult for many. However, as more nonprofit organizations become adept at the use of the internet, and especially as they acquire new prospects or members from web-based contacts, online CRM efforts are becoming a major part of nonprofit marketing strategies as well.

Whether in the B2C, B2B, or nonprofit marketplaces, the essentials of the two basic marketing approaches—**transactional** and **relational**—do not differ (see Figure 14.2). Traditional transactional marketing is centered on products and single economic exchanges. Marketers engage in one-way communication in the mass media, targeting market segments identified by conventional marketing research. This type of marketing is associated with traditional mass media, but online marketers can also be focused on their products at the expense of their customers.

transactional focuses on the individual sale of a product or service, in contrast to developing a long-term relationship with a customer.

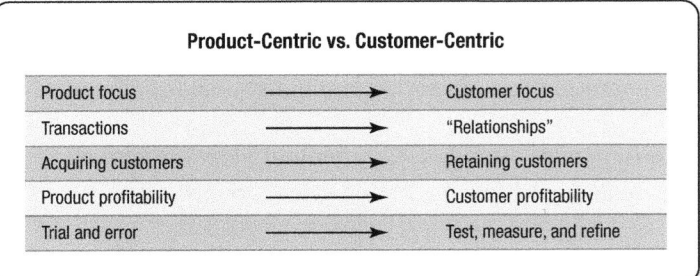

FIGURE 14.2
Product-Centric Versus Customer-Centric Marketing

SOURCE: Cengage Learning 2013.

When the marketing process moves to a relational approach, the focus shifts to customers and their relationship cycle with the organization. Customer needs and expertise in meeting them become key. Communications are targeted to individuals or carefully defined segments and contain personalized content. Goals are focused on growing customer value, not market share. CLV (Chapter 4), which incorporates both revenue and cost to serve the customer, becomes a key metric as do customer satisfaction, loyalty, and employee satisfaction. In implementing the CRM strategy, two-way communication in any channel becomes the norm with project-based marketing research taking a back seat to meaningful, ongoing dialogue with the customer. Seamlessly satisfying customer experience becomes the vision that guides all marketing activities and permeates the entire organization.

In recent years, marketers have increasingly found that relational approach could be improved to ensure lasting customer loyalty. Indeed, the phrase "Marketing is Dead" has become shorthand for a stinging indictment of traditional marketing.[9] Customers today are less influenced by traditional marketing communications, even in relational approaches by favored brands. CEOs are increasingly dissatisfied with their marketing functions' inability to deliver growth and accountability. Marketers are in the early stages of learning how to harness and use the newer levers of consumer social media influence, especially when an organization's staff doesn't come from the world inhabited by their customers. Somewhat disconcerting to many marketers, consumers' participation on social media gives them as much power to influence buying behavior as their brands or clients.

Add to that the increasing impact of mobile, and marketers face a constantly changing competitive environment that requires a fresh approach, but one that will not lose the insights gained from the past, or be unable to tap other useful resources. As discussed in Chapters 5 and 6, the marketer's objective is now to become a participant in the customer's environment, and build loyalty by communicating brand values that people want to be affiliated with. This is accomplished throughout the many dimensions of the CX process. In part, it is developed using a valuable real-time source of customer information—the digital customer journey—and delivering the content that the customer values at the appropriate time. Interactive Exercise 14-1 illustrates one approach to personalized experience. That all equates to the seamlessly satisfying CX that marketers strive to achieve—the end goal of CRM.

The B2B Foundations of CRM

While there is much inconsistency in the definition of the term CRM today, there is little disagreement on how the discipline originated. By the early 1980s, there was growing recognition among business marketers that the cost of a single sales call was spiraling out of control. Figures quoted were typically in the hundreds of dollars for one sales call. Marketers needed a way to make their field sales forces more efficient without risking their ability to grow sales. They turned to **sales force automation** in an attempt to offer more cost-effective service to customers while decreasing their overall sales costs. According to Moriarty and Schwartz, some of the sales force automation tools are:

sales force automation business processes, and the software that supports them, that permit salespeople to work more effectively both in and out of their offices by providing electronic access to important documents, customer data, and support tools like calendars.

- Sales force productivity tools such as call reporting and checking order and inventory status.
- Direct mail sales lead generation campaigns that included mail fulfillment of product information.
- Telemarketing, often to follow up the sales leads generated by direct mail.
- Sales and marketing management tools, including sales forecasting and reporting.[10]

In the intervening years, email, text messaging, social media, and other online channels have taken the place of some but not all direct mail as a means of reaching customers. This transition has not decreased the need for automating repetitive, often event-triggered, marketing activities. It has simply increased the number of activities to automate.

This is another information-driven marketing application. In the case of sales force automation, lower-cost media are used to generate (online advertising and events such as webinars, and direct mail) and qualify (telemarketing and webinars) sales leads, as discussed in Chapter 13. Field sales people are given access to a comprehensive customer/prospect database, which is also used for sales and marketing management applications. The result should be higher sales, better customer service, and lower cost to the enterprise.

Early systems focused on the sales force, with marketing developing and executing direct mail campaigns, and sophisticated call centers using the customer/prospect database to qualify leads and provide customer service. This has led to the "three-legged stool" concept of CRM portrayed in Figure 14.3. The sales force productivity "leg" has little application in the B2C marketplace, but the concept itself and the marketing and customer service components are entirely applicable. Types of software that support B2B CRM are identified and described in Table 14.1. The term CRM has been adopted to describe **relational marketing** in both the B2B and B2C spaces in spite of the differences just described. It also has the same meaning in the nonprofit space.

From the early beginnings of sales force automation to today's cloud data storage and computing and mobile apps, the whole purpose has been to make salespeople more productive. See Interactive Exercise 14.2 to learn how one software vendor makes that happen.

relational marketing a facet of customer relationship marketing (CRM) that focuses on customer loyalty and long-term customer engagement rather than short-term goals like customer acquisition and individual sales.

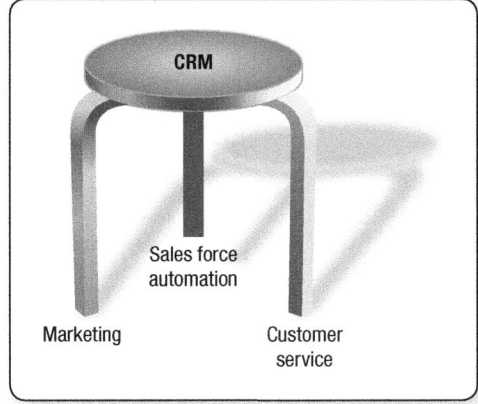

FIGURE 14.3

The B2B Foundations of Customer Relationship Management

SOURCE: © Cengage Learning 2013

Contact Management	Software with multiple modules that emulate the salesperson's address book, daily appointment log, and customer files. Key components are contact information, including name, title, address, telephone(s), email, and fax, both work and home; a daily calendar, a tickler (reminder) file, and usually an electronic notepad of some sort. Firms can have the software customized to include routine forms such as sales call and expense reports.	**TABLE 14.1** Software to Support Customer Relationships
Sales Force Automation	Takes contact management a step forward by integrating various modules and linking them to a central customer database. This lessens the bookkeeping requirements for the field sales force and permits the timely updating and transmission of customer information. For instance, sales leads can be transmitted directly from the central database to the field rep's laptop allowing immediate follow up by the rep and monitoring by sales management.	

(Continues)

	CRM	Software that is integrated on an enterprise-wide basis. The objective is to centralize all customer data and to make a **360° (complete)** picture of the customer available at each contact point within the firm. Information provision can be highly automated as when a telephone number triggers a "screen pop," making the customer record available to the call center representative by the time the call is answered. Integrated CRM software makes customer and product support data available to any authorized user anywhere in the world at any time. It also integrates all customer touchpoints into a complete view of multiple channels of communication. Integration is the precursor to marketing automation.
360° (complete) a comprehensive view of the customer, often a profile that interfaces with the firm's customer journey map.		
	SaaS or CRM in the Cloud	Cloud computing, as discussed in Chapter 1, allows many users to share a powerful computing network over the internet. In the case of CRM in the cloud that means that software, tools, and customer data are all stored on the cloud platform. This allows employees to simply log in on their browser or a mobile device to access the CRM system from their desk or from the field. Forbes predicts that by 2018, 62 percent of all CRM software will be cloud-based.[11]

DEVELOPING CRM STRATEGY

CRM consultants Don Peppers and Martha Rogers have long espoused a model that captures the essence of CRM (see Figure 14.4). Their view is an information-driven one, with every step in the process adding to the customer database that is essential to drive CRM strategy and programs. The steps are:

- *Identify* your customers by individual or household name and address.
- *Differentiate* them according to their needs and their actual or potential value.
- *Interact* with customers based on their own needs. From the organization's perspective, the interactions should become more cost effective. Each interaction should be used as an opportunity to increase the store of data about the individual or household.
- *Customize* at least some aspects of the organization's dealings with the customer. Things like tailored communications, site personalization, and specialized offers that allow the enterprise to recognize the customer as a valued supporter and that present opportunities for growing the value of the individual customer.

Customer data are the engine that drives CRM strategy forward to an ever-deepening relationship with the customer. Thoughtful use of data facilitates:

- Differentiated messages and offers that lead to effective communications channel choices.
- Customer segmentation by all the usual methods, including psychographics, and especially by customer value and the opportunity to grow value.

FIGURE 14.4

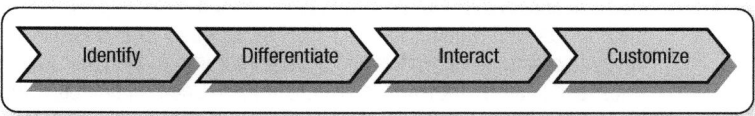

- Lifecycle communications that depend on the customer's position in the relationship cycle, from new through very active to ultimate trust in the brand.
- Active management and monitoring of performance, using KPIs throughout.[12]

McKinsey & Company suggest a plan that integrates a digital data map into the CRM/CX orientation, shown in Figure 14.5. It requires that the marketer:

- Capture customer behavioral pathways and attitudes at each stage of a purchase journey. A customer may first look for inspiration about family sports before seeking information about a vacation spot that has those activities. A website will likely show a lot of product descriptions and services before price promotions are mentioned only when visitors are closer to buying.
- Determine each customer's digital brand preference, that is, how a shopper wants to interact with a brand. Many customers use a variety of brand contact media.
- Determine the customer's "key preference indicators" for the brand, indicating the customer's affinity to spend time on the site visiting by brand, style, price point, size, etc.
- Understand their response to offers—discounts, loyalty rewards, gifts-with-purchase, etc.
- Identify life moments and context that foretell buying triggers, such as having a child, going to college, and planning a vacation.

Information about demographics, preference, and needs can be acquired beyond interactions with the company. Data aggregators such as Axiom and Nielsen's eXelate are able to append "the usual suspects" of demographics, and identify preferences

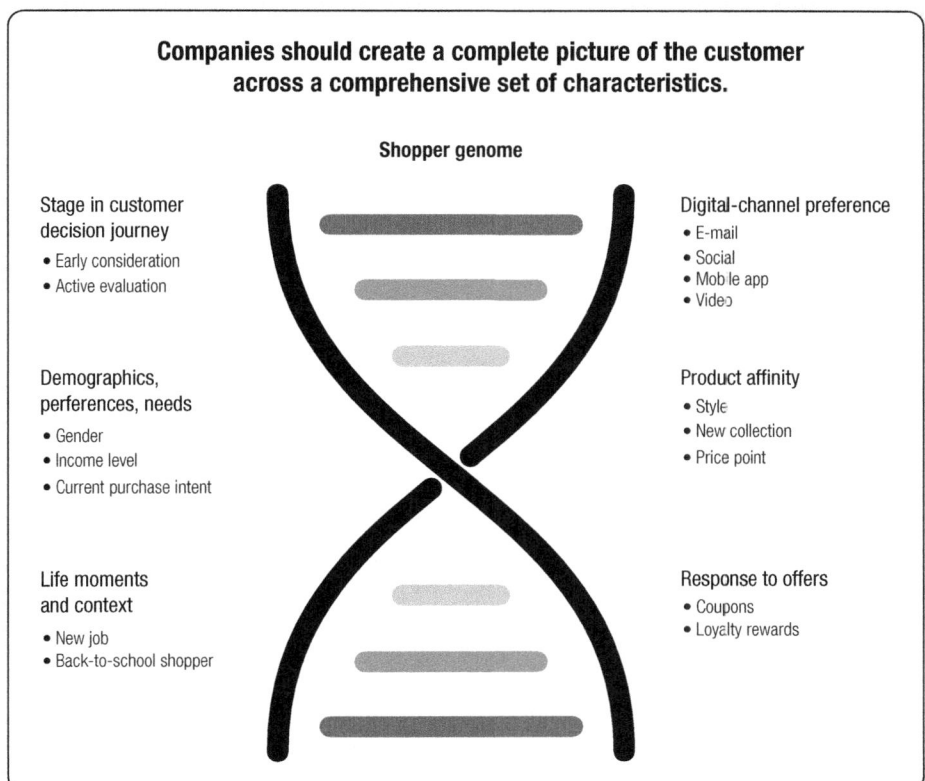

FIGURE 14.5
Characteristics of the Digital Shopper Genome

SOURCE: http://www.mckinsey.com/business-functions/marketing-and-sales/our-insights/cracking-the-digital-shopper-genome

and intent gleaned from customer browsing behavior across networks of hundreds of websites. This allows brands to understand what customers do when they are not engaging with their own brand. It is the data that allows them to provide a seamlessly excellent CX.

Proponents of moving CRM to a customer journey/CX orientation note other important changes required in marketing strategy:

- The organization's technology teams have to be involved at every stage of development, analysis, and operations. The "conversation" and tactics needed to design and understand today's CX required systems designed and built to listen, analyze, interact, and deliver the appropriate customer interaction on an increasingly real-time basis.
- Marketers must design systems that actively encourage customers to participate in the relationship, in contrast to using SMM as simply a selling tool. Bonobos, the irreverent men's clothing brand, uses social media to ask its customer base about its brand direction, including, "What PGA golfer should we sponsor?" and "Would you want our logo on a new polo shirt we are making?" Stanford Professor Jennifer Aaker calls this having the customer "message in." It's not just a way for the brand to "message out."[13]
- Brands must develop a "just-in-time" orientation to accompany individual customers throughout the CX. A study of 500 CMO's by Accenture found that 87 percent of the more successful companies have employees with specialized analytical skills to develop actionable customer insights versus their peers (36 percent). More successful companies also showed greater ability to deliver "right time" marketing and showed higher levels of integration of between their digital and traditional marketing strategies. This means delivering personalized relevant content, not just the creation of more content.[14] For example, Kohl's needed to quickly leverage the publicity it received when a customer uploaded a Facebook video of her uproarious delight with her birthday purchase from Kohl's—a talking Chewbacca mask.[15] The video attracted over 158 million Facebook views, numerous reposts on Twitter, and radio and television coverage. Kohl's also rapidly posted that the mask was sold out on its webpage. Overall good customer experience!

The importance of all these activities, especially active management and monitoring, has been heightened by the potential of SMM in CRM. SMM expands the number of communications **touchpoints** and makes it imperative to integrate communications across channels.

The International Speedway Corporation

The International Speedway Corporation (ISC) and its 13 regional racetracks already had what is arguably the world's most loyal sports followers—the NASCAR fans. They were not, however, satisfied that they were communicating with these fans and nurturing the relationship in the best possible way. They had transactional data from all the tracks, but they were not being used to develop strategic CRM insights. It was deemed important that all 13 tracks work collaboratively to focus on the customer and committing to the final program. The goal was to provide each visitor to the track an experience that was perceived as designed for him exclusively.

Building on a database that included over 3 million customers and dated back to 2002, ISC improved data collection so that all new transactions data were fed directly into the CRM software. It spent all of 2009 analyzing a mountain of data. The analysis allowed them to develop many market segments based on behavior patterns and targeted strategies that ranged from loyalty programs to up-sell programs. With better availability of transactions data, ISC was able to communicate with each ticket purchaser in accordance with the experience the individual buyer was seeking.[16]

Different tracks have approached the customer experience in different ways. Examples are:

- The Daytona International Speedway found that its patrons wanted a more in-depth look at behind-the-scenes operations. The Daytona 500 Experience is made up of an existing limited tour of the facilities and a new one-hour long tour that includes areas never before open to the public. To further engage avid driving fans, Richard Petty Driving Experiences are offered that allow fans to drive with a professional driver, try the racing skills on the actual track.[17] The Michigan International Speedway implemented new software that allows them to sell tickets directly in many channels and to retain customer data that had previously been the property of ticket agencies.[18]
- The Watkins Glenn International Speedway created personalized pages at MyTrackSchedule.com that allow the user to select relevant information, engage in discussions, and start new discussion groups.
- Kentucky Speedway operates its own campgrounds at a range of amenities and price points, but all with features that appeal to track enthusiasts.[19]
- Several of the tracks have a customer experience manager in their managerial ranks.

The volume of activity and positive reactions on the Daytona Facebook page, as one example, suggest that the enhanced customer experience is pleasing to its many fans.[20]

The Customer Lifecycle

The concept of the **customer lifecycle** (not the product) is illustrated in Figure 14.6. It starts with strategic customer acquisition—acquiring more customers like your best customers. The next step is conversion and the concept is specific in stating that conversion means a repeat customer, not a one-time purchaser. The continuing objective is to grow customer value. The other requirement of the relational approach is to identify customers who are at risk of attrition and target them for retention or for migration to a different product in the line. A classic consumer example is baby food. When the child grows too old for baby food, attrition from that product class is naturally going to occur. The wise marketer has a line of toddler foods and snacks in the wings and has the data to know when it is time to market them to a household. Capturing and using that kind of data at the individual household level is the essence of relational marketing.

customer lifecycle stages in the development of the relationship between the customer and the brand.

The attractiveness of the CRM concept quickly became apparent to marketers. After all, they had been preaching the virtues of customer orientation for many years. As a result, marketers of all kinds have taken many different paths in their search for strong and lasting relationships with their customers.

National Geographic

National Geographic is a respected global nonprofit membership organization with many facets to its mission focused on "a passionate belief in the power of science, exploration, and storytelling to change the world."[21] In addition to its research and publications, it manages an extensive travel services division of guided and individually designed tours. The target customers are segmented based on a number of factors, including interests, family life cycle, and demographics, among others. The trips take the form of various travel modes (small ship; land and sea), family travel, photo trips and workshops; private jet; active adventures; student expeditions; and small group and private "journeys." This allows customers to engage in a variety of activities complementary to the National Geographic mission (understanding science; exploring cultures of the world; related hobbies like regional foods and sports) throughout their lifetimes.

FIGURE 14.6

Mining the Customer Lifecycle

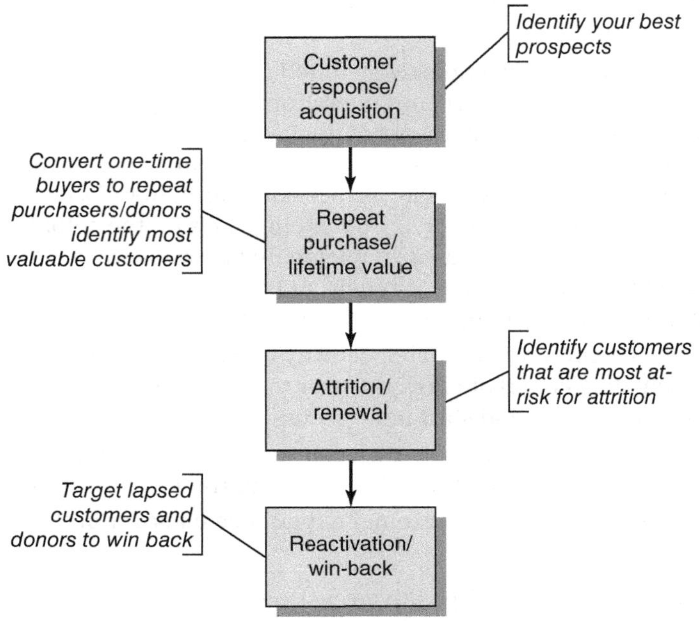

- Customer response/acquisition — Identify your best prospects
- Repeat purchase/lifetime value — Convert one-time buyers to repeat purchasers/donors identify most valuable customers
- Attrition/renewal — Identify customers that are most at-risk for attrition
- Reactivation/win-back — Target lapsed customers and donors to win back

SOURCE: © Cengage Learning 2013

For example, in the past, a person may have become curious about exploring the natural world through National Geographic publications, television shows, or films. While these venues are still important drivers of customer interest, a general interest in nature may bring today's potential customer to National Geographic's Instagram pages. With over 49 million followers, it has the largest noncelebrity brand on that platform, and is the 13th most popular overall. In addition to its already popular 15-second video clips on various channels, National Geographic plans to leverage this presence with a new digital series, including its first Instagram video series and a virtual reality platform.[22] Other digital offerings attempt to help customers develop their interests related to travel:

- Get Out: A Guide to Adventure: tips from adventure experts on navigating the outdoors;
- InTime: using hyper-lapse technology to look at travel destinations around the world;
- "Wild Life": with Bertie Gregory about wolves in the Pacific Northwest; and
- The Real (City): tips from locals in exotic cities.

The visual nature of Instagram makes it a natural for National Geographic, as shown in Figure 14.7a.

Much of this effort also supports National Geographic's web page. Here, besides exploring interests in specific topics, visitors can contribute to the website with photos; kids can play games; and learn more through blogs tied in to programs and research activities. Other initiatives encourage engagement through storytelling. For example, in the past, it has run a storytelling contest through MatadorU.com,[23] an online school and source for travel journalism. Contestant categories included blogs, magazine articles, video, and photo essays. As you can see from Figure 14.7b, at the time the website home page was captured, Nat Geo was running a "Vote Your Park" viewer poll that will direct preservation funding to the most popular parks.

In tandem with the National Parks Service, National Geographic will air a series celebrating the NPS's 100th Anniversary. As it so happens, the travel group will sponsor

FIGURE 14.7a
The National Geographic Instagram Page

SOURCE: https://www.instagram.com/natgeo/

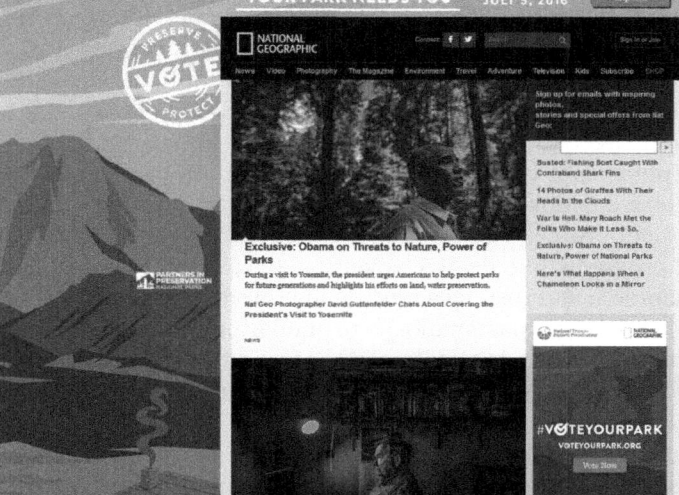

FIGURE 14.7b
The National Geographic Home Page

SOURCE: http://www.nationalgeographic.com/

a variety trips in 2016 and 2017 for a variety of customer groups: students, active adventure, photography trips, and family expeditions. In the context of her lifetime, a person could join a trip as a student, participate in a rigorous hiking adventure with friends as a young adult, and plan an assortment of family vacations in still later years, even though the relationship with natural science and National Geographic began much earlier.[24]

National Geographic continues the dialog through a variety of CX touchpoints. The National Geographic Expeditions (travel) page has the usual information about trips, destinations, and facilities, but also includes a section to "get inspired." Here, viewers can see photos from past travelers and understand more about the experts that accompany trips. Given the popularity of its various activities and social platforms, the data provided allows National Geographic to gauge interest in its travel destinations, provides insight to new program and trip opportunities, and develop communities of users to further the mission of the organization.

THE PROCESSES OF CRM—OPERATIONAL AND ANALYTICAL

The reason that CRM requires considerable discipline is twofold. First, emphasized in the preceding section, relationship marketing requires significant changes in the way marketing is done. The emphasis must move from promotional campaigns and marketing research projects to ongoing dialogue on multiple platforms, much of which can be captured and stored in a customer database. Second, it must be treated and managed as an ongoing process, not as a series of discrete events. It has often been described as "A Journey with No End." This is the antithesis of the way most marketing managers are measured, using short-term metrics, such as market share, sales growth, and expansion of customer base. The result is that, for CRM to succeed, changes in organizational thinking and action must go beyond the marketing department to the highest levels of the corporation. This degree of change is not easy and it requires a clear vision of the requirements and potential achievements of CRM.

Successful CRM cannot exist outside the context of the business unit's overall marketing strategy. The economics simply will not work unless the business identifies high value customers (initially based on marketing research if no database is available), individually or by market segment, targets those customers, and develops marketing strategies and programs that specifically meet their needs. This is a genuinely customer-centric approach; target customers are identified first and the value proposition, encompassing all aspects of the marketing mix, is then developed. It, too, is the antithesis of the traditional marketing model in which products are developed and it becomes the job of the marketing department to market and sell those products.

operational CRM designing and executing tactical CRM programs on the basis of data items or customer profiles.

analytical CRM mining the customer data and developing programs or predictive models based on the resulting insights and data discovery.

The customer database is the focal point of both **operational CRM** and **analytical CRM**. The database is developed and used to conduct segmentation analysis and to develop customer profiles that drive both outbound programs like email newsletters and inbound programs like display advertising. Analytical models include CLV, discussed in Chapter 4, and response models that predict response to future marketing programs on the basis of past response to similar programs. As programs are developed and executed, additional data are captured to enrich the database, to allow performance measurement of individual programs or customers, and to continually refine critical marketing models.

Marketers are beginning to include limited social media behavior in their databases. The data are limited because it must be usable in its raw form or quantifiable. This does not include the majority of brand-related conversations on social networks, although they have an important role in CRM. That will be discussed in the section on Social CRM.

Examples of data from social networks that can be usefully added to the database include:

- In B2B, it is possible to build apps that monitor the social conversations of a specific sales prospect on platforms such as LinkedIn, Twitter, and Facebook. This gives the sales person valuable information about what the prospect is saying and often allows him to gauge how close the prospect is to a purchase decision. Be aware of three things: First, this is social media listening data. It is ephemeral and not easily quantifiable, but it adds a useful dimension to quantitative prospect information. Second, it involves identifying individual customers in a way that probably would not be acceptable in B2C markets. Third, while this kind of data can contribute to customer qualification, it is likely to be accessed by a desktop or mobile app that lets sales reps follow customers of interest as they interact on social networks, not by entries in the customer database. Interactive Exercise 14-3 describes one approach to this kind of sales tool.

- It is difficult to link consumer social network data to identified consumers without violating privacy restrictions. On a small scale, however, there may be social data that are worth adding to consumer profiles. Marketers are always on the lookout for influentials *(opinion leaders)* who can influence others in social space. One tool is the Klout score, which measures the influence of an individual on social networks. Any individual can sign up and receive a personal Klout score.[25] Developers can create tools that filter social media messages by Klout score. In CRM, this can be used to understand how influential customers are and what topics are relevant to their sphere of influence. There is also identifiable data from sources like top blogs listings. For example, if mommy bloggers are strategically important to the brand, Babble's occasional list of top 50 mommy bloggers[26] could be entered (manually) into the blog owner's database record. If the brand needs to reach out to influential mommy bloggers, the effort could be worthwhile. There are tools for measuring influence of identified persons on various platforms. For example, there is Twitalizer for Twitter[27] and Booskaha, which aims to help small businesses identify and reward their most valuable Facebook fans.[28] Including any of these data in databases presumes the influential individual is already a customer and has a record in the database.

- Still, as the influencer sphere has become more sophisticated, the brand should investigate the influencer's audience.[29] Are they engaged? Who are they? How does the influencer engage with her audience? Does your brand make sense in their lives? It is also useful to know that some bloggers get help from brands in terms of paid promotions or assistance, which by federal law they are required to disclose. Whopaysinfluencers.com is a crowd-sourced website that reveals how much brands pay influencers and their experience in working with those brands.[30]

Integrating social media data into tactical CRM programs and potentially adding it to the consumer database is a subject of great interest to marketers. However, the privacy challenges at present are huge, and other countries are increasingly challenging information gathering about customers through digital trails.[31] For now, *the best marketing advice for including social media fans and participants in the database is to drive them to the website and persuade them to register, thereby collecting email addresses and other useful data.*[32]

Operational (tactical) CRM program execution emanates from the database of customer information. Outbound programs, which could be email promotions, Tweets, mobile posts, or marketing programs supported by physical world promotional media such as direct mail, are planned and implemented based on data from the database. One of the disciplines necessary to make CRM work is to compel programs to rely on the database. Often the pressure to get programs out the door causes marketers to want to forgo the front-end analytics and simply blast the entire list. The economics of the internet makes that a seductive argument. It is fast and inexpensive compared to any other channel. However, damage to the relationship can be caused by an onslaught of untargeted, irrelevant marketer-originated communications.

Airlines, for example, know the residential location of their frequent flyers and, if they have mined their data warehouses intelligently, they may have been able to ascertain clear flight patterns for individual customers. Why then do airlines contact their frequent fliers with promotional offers that originate in cities in which they do not live and to which they do not travel? Has your bank or credit card company recently sent you a promotion for a service or card to which you already subscribe? The cost of sending these messages may not be high, but the longer-term damage to the customer relationship and the perception of the brand may be significant. How can a customer trust a company that appears to know nothing about him, even though he has transacted with that company?

It is essential that inbound programs also depend on the customer database. Telephone call centers and web-based chat rely on the customer database for real-time data that allow representatives to provide seamless service to customers on the basis of knowledge about their dealings with the firm, both past and present. Social media data can be a useful addition to that knowledge if it can be made visible to the service rep.

Operational and analytical CRM works from the customer database. CRM strategy development should also be driven by knowledge and insights gleaned from the customer database. Strategies that revolve around customer value are the core of CRM. High value customers are targeted with value propositions developed on the basis of a deep understanding of their needs and behaviors. Care is taken to identify all customers who can be profitably upgraded, whether their current value is high or moderate. Resources are not dissipated on the attraction or even retention of low-value customers.

None of these data-driven programs or strategies is viable, however, unless we can selectively reach identified targets with content and messages custom-tailored to each. The internet provides an especially powerful medium for targeting customers with personalized content. Increasingly sophisticated technologies can take advantage of a seemingly random event if the brand can respond quickly to unpredictable opportunities or problems. As we've previously made the case, today's digital environment increasingly presents opportunities that come from outside an organization's traditional channels of communication. The importance of listening and responding to constituents on social media channel was discussed in Chapter 5.

TARGETING AND PERSONALIZATION

Direct marketing, again, provides the foundation concepts for *targeting* on the internet. Direct marketers in the physical world have long used mailing or telephone lists as their primary targeting mechanism. As we noted in Chapter 9, email lists are now available and are likely to grow in both size and number in the coming years. For the present, however, good lists (translated as opt-in lists) are expensive and short. If the right type of rental list is available, it can be useful to the internet marketer in the acquisition process, although building an opt-in list is recommended.

For retention purposes, however, the issues are different. The process that supports relationship marketing in either the physical or the online worlds is represented in Figure 14.8. The chief difference between the two is that internet marketers are able to capture more data faster and to revise their content on a more frequent, even real-time, basis.

Targeting in CRM programs is most often accomplished by developing **customer profiles** and using them to identify either customers who are appropriate to receive a particular offer (the more traditional approach) or customers who represent sufficient value, either as individuals or as a segment, to warrant the development of a unique value proposition (a CLV-based approach).

customer profiles a description of a customer or set of customers that includes demographic, geographic, and psychographic characteristics. A profile could include other relevant information, such as buying pattern, creditworthiness, and purchase history.

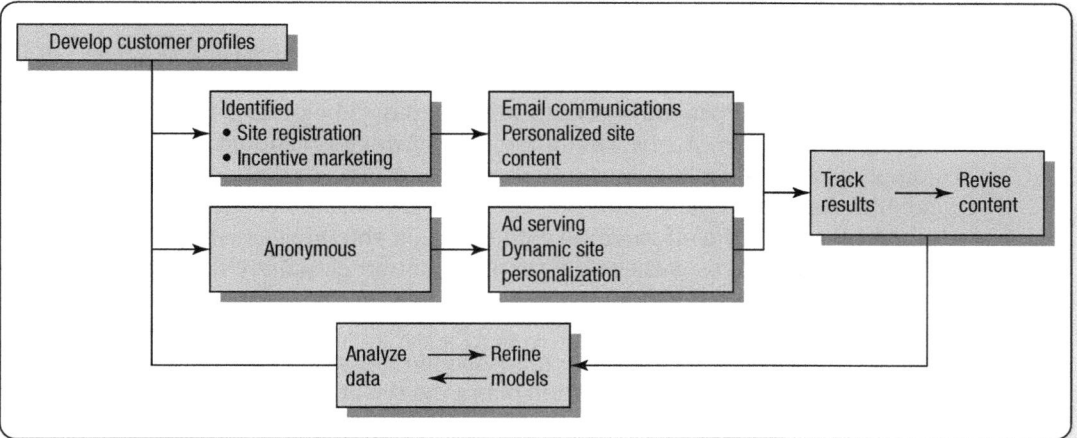

FIGURE 14.8

The Targeting and Personalization Process

SOURCE: © Cengage Learning 2013

There are two types of profiles available to marketers. *Anonymous* profiles are created without knowledge of the identity of the prospective customer. They are developed from clickstream data and perhaps enhanced with other data that belong to the marketer or are purchased from a third-party supplier. Cookies, as discussed in Chapter 7, are the most common way to develop anonymous profiles. A cookie can be used for tracking movement on the site after the click-through, for creating a user profile, or to manage the serving of ads to the user (see the discussion of behavioral advertising in Chapter 7). A cookie is also set when a user selects personalization options on a web page. However the cookie is set, when the user contacts the website again, the cookie is automatically activated. In general, a cookie can be read only by the server that sends it and can track activity only on one website, including where visitors come from and where they go as they exit. Cookie files can be located by the user and disabled, but that may prevent access to some websites. It will also erase any personalization the user has done.[33]

Identified profiles are compiled from data that are explicitly provided by a known prospect. This is often done by asking the visitor to register on a website and to provide profile information in the process. There are also infomediaries that offer incentives in return for customer information which they then sell to marketers. Companies that offer coupons from participating manufacturers over the web are an example of this type of information product.

The fastest way for a firm to build its own house list and to create its own identified profiles is *registration* on the website. This sounds simple, but it has to be done carefully. The process itself must be carefully thought out. And, of course, people must first be attracted to the site using acquisition techniques described in previous chapters.

The registration form must be carefully designed for ease and speed of completion, as discussed in Chapter 13 in the context of landing pages. A new registrant may have little, if any, existing relationship with the organization and will divulge only minimal information. Techniques that prevent error, like pull-down lists, are desirable. Even so, the form may not be completed unless there is an incentive. The incentive may be tangible, as on the many B2B sites that require visitors to register in order to get information of some type, perhaps to download a white paper. It may be intangible, as when the nonprofit offers the ability to "customize our newsletter to reflect your interests." There may be services offered to the registered visitor that are not available to the general public.

Note two things about the common strategy of providing an information incentive. First, the registrant should receive instant gratification, either by clicking on a link to download or by automatic email provision of the report. Making the person wait for something to arrive invalidates many of the special advantages of the internet. If the information comes on a scheduled basis, not on demand, automate the process to send a "thank you" email (for an email newsletter subscription, for example) immediately. Second, this is a classic direct marketing lead generation process. Consequently, enough information should be gathered to begin to categorize the desirability of the prospect. At the same time, the information should not be so detailed or complex that the visitor does not complete the form. Abandoned forms can be tracked. If there is a consistent point at which the form is being abandoned, it signals a problem with the information gathering that should be corrected immediately.

The basic rule is to gather only the information genuinely needed by the marketer to make the next communication effective. As the relationship strengthens, more information that is more detailed and more personal can be collected. Just like politeness in the physical world, do not presume too much on a brief acquaintance! There should be a relationship program plan from the beginning that specifies the data needed and the customer lifecycle stage in which it will be collected. In the absence of a plan, data collection is just a "fishing expedition" which is unlikely to be valuable to the marketer and is highly likely to be annoying to the customer. However, both the data collection and the relationship marketing strategy should be flexible and should be examined at every step for possible improvements. For example, new technological developments now allow instant shopping through social media platforms and mobile apps. These developments could make real-time purchases more relevant as target customers engage in their "native" digital environments.

The database marketing bones of CRM are clearly evident in a recent program used by Cisco to make its sales lead program more effective.

Cisco Reactivation Program

In early 2010, Cisco had a huge number of names, titles, and addresses in multiple databases all over the world. Extracting the right data to use for an operational marketing program required considerable time and effort. The effort was sometimes fruitless since the stand-alone databases sometimes did not provide a sufficient number of "marketable contacts"—businesspeople for whom Cisco had an address and who had opted-in to Cisco's digital marketing programs. "We had to be able to create an analytical environment in which we could bring together vast amounts of data and cut down on how long ad-hoc queries or segmentation would normally take," said Mike Bull, Global Database Marketing Manager at Cisco.[34] One of the first insights produced by their analysis was the fact that only about 25 percent of their addresses worldwide were classified as actively marketable. The urgent need was to find out how many of the addresses represented qualified leads and to develop an interactive relationship with them without incurring an unreasonably large cost.

In order to develop a reactivation strategy, they developed a test for their U.S. addresses. They chose about 14.5 percent of the unmarketable U.S. addresses—a number large enough to justify a strategy decision and small enough not to do substantial damage to the potential value of their database if the test failed. The latter is important because the marketer *has only one chance* to ask a consumer or business customer to opt-in for marketing purposes. After that initial offering, customer contacts would be classified as spam and Cisco does not spam.

The database marketing team segmented the test group by high- and low-level corporate titles. They decided on three test cells composed of segments and offers:

Cell 1. High-position group: Get a Starbucks card by updating your profile.

Cell 2. Low-position group 1: Get a collaboration white paper by updating your profile.

Cell 3. Low-position group 2: Update your profile to stay current.[35]

The actual messages were as similar as possible and all resembled the winning version in Figure 14.9.

The results of the campaign were:

Cell 1
- Open rate: 17.10 percent
- Click-through rate: 7.60 percent
- Conversion rate: 6.10 percent

Cell 2
- Open rate: 12.10 percent
- Click-through rate: 2 percent
- Conversion rate: 1.40 percent

Cell 3
- Open rate: 18.30 percent
- Click-through rate: 6.50 percent
- Conversion rate: 3.90 percent

Cell 3, "no offer," was the winner, which might be counterintuitive. The high-position cell 1 had a higher conversion rate, but it cost $25 for each opt-in (the definition of conversion for this program). The open rate for the low-position, no offer cell 3,

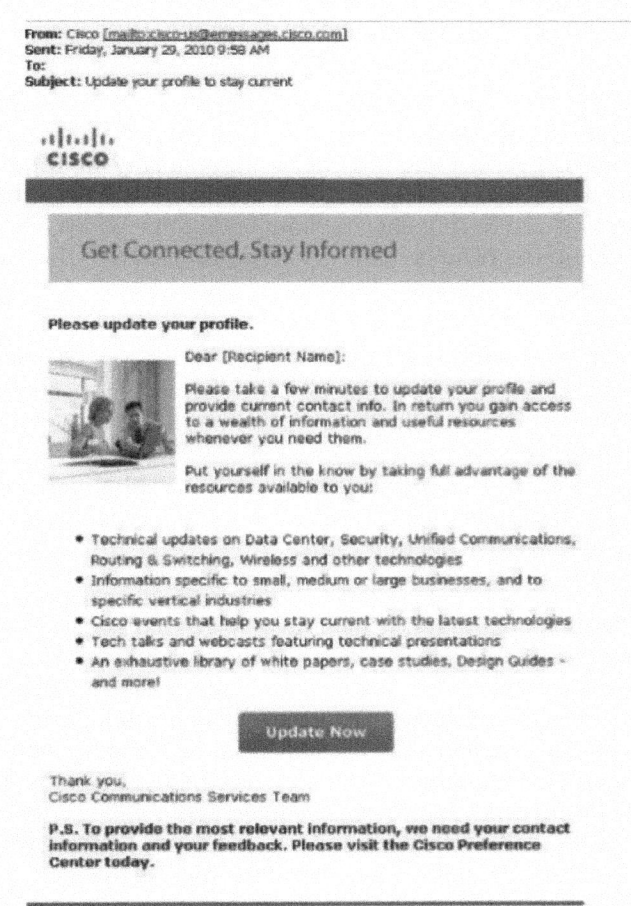

FIGURE 14.9

Cisco Reactivation to Low-Position Group 2: No Incentive

SOURCE: Marketing Sherpa, https://www.marketingsherpa.com/article.php?ident=31805

was higher, but the conversion rate was lower, and conversion was the goal. However, the lower conversion rate with no incentive for cell 3 was deemed more desirable by management because it was more cost effective. The overall conversion rate across all three versions was 2.3 percent, higher than expected.

In line with direct marketing best practices, Cisco used the success of the U.S. program to guide similar programs in other English-speaking countries, including the United Kingdom, India, Australia, New Zealand, and South Africa. They had similar results in each of the other countries, finding that contacts responded favorably to the direct approach to update their profile and to reengage with Cisco.

Overall, Bull was pleased with the program stating that they had been able reopen contacts with addresses that could not previously be reached and to do so at a reasonable cost.

At least part of the reason this program worked was that Cisco could contact these business people as individuals and indicate that they knew something about each one and valued her business. That is the goal of good personalization.

Personalized Email and Site Content

Personalized email can be a useful part of CRM as the Cisco case history illustrates. Done correctly, email personalization is an important marketing tool, as discussed in Chapter 9. Email is one tool in an outbound marketing program in which the marketer reaches out to customers.

If, however, the marketer chooses *personalized site content* part of the relationship program, that requires a different type of technology, one that can identify the customer segment in real time and make the changes needed to personalize to that segment. There are three basic types of personalized site content in use at present:

1. Rules-based personalization that chooses content on the basis of known characteristics, either from current information or from previous user information stored in cookies. Weather.com provides geographically appropriate content when the visitor enters a Zip code and remembers the Zip code for later use; both Amazon and Netflix have recommendation engines that infer additional product choices from items previously purchased. Rules-based algorithms can be quite complex and link many characteristics, but the concept is straightforward.
2. User-controlled personalization in which the user chooses the content elements to be displayed. This is the approach often used in opt-in where the subscriber is asked which newsletters she wishes to receive or the bargain hunter is asked the product categories for which he wants to receive offers.
3. Information-driven personalization uses complex profiles and models to assign content instead of simpler decision rules.[36] This uses techniques like the predictive targeting described in Section 7-3b3.

Interactive Exercise 14-3 shows personalization in action.

User-controlled personalization remains unchanged until the user decides to modify it. Rules-based personalization can also be relatively static, with rules and associated actions being established in advance and merely executed at the time of the visitor's arrival on the site. Information-driven personalization requires sophisticated quantitative models but it can be executed in real time for an inbound contact or as part of an outbound communication. The software builds a profile almost instantaneously when the visitor hits a site. It can use many types of data, depending on what is available and the level of identification of the visitor—everything from clickstream data to transactional data from the customer database. As the visitor moves around the site, the profile is updated. It also stores information, perhaps in the customer database and perhaps on a cookie on the visitor's own computer, in preparation for the next visit. Virtually any aspect of site content can be served to the visitor on the basis of the profile—the products to be displayed, incentives to be offered, and characteristics of the offer itself including price.

CRM itself and the tools of targeting and personalization all imply a continuous, closed-loop process of data capture, information-driven programs, and knowledge refinement. There is one additional technique that is widely used to increase the momentum and power of relationship marketing. That important technique is the loyalty program.

CUSTOMER LOYALTY PROGRAMS

Loyalty programs are familiar and ubiquitous. Businesses from the corner pizza parlor to the urban department store to the international hotel chain all have loyalty programs. Consumers and business travelers have wallets full of their cards. The 2015 study by Colloquy found that U.S. customers alone had over 3 billion loyalty cards, a 26 percent increase since their 2013 study. That's the good news. The bad news is that, although the average American household has 29 loyalty cards, it is active in only 12 of them![37, 38] That says that loyalty programs have their work cut out for them.

Keep in mind, though, that loyalty programs are only a part of CRM strategies. Loyalty programs alone do not represent a strategy. The key issue is that loyalty programs focus on changing behavior and their effects may not last past the reward. Strategic CRM focuses on long-term relationship and brand building and may have more long-term impact. In spite of their potential to have only short-term effectiveness, loyalty programs have become a staple of the marketing strategies of firms like Victoria's Secret, a luxury brand for the discerning female shopper. Victoria's Secret has been recognized as a leader in loyalty programs from the early days of direct mail coupons and catalogs up to the present with its email programs and mobile apps.

The end of an era was signaled in April 2016 when Victoria's Secret announced that it was shutting down its famed catalog. For a year the firm had been testing the elimination of the catalog in several markets and saw little effect on sales. In 2016, it ran the same test in two very significant markets and didn't see any difference in sales. Notably, when the number of catalogs was reduced 40 percent, online sales went up 15 percent. Eliminating the catalog would save at least $125 million each year, which could be better directed to more effective marketing actions namely its stores and its digital business.[39, 40]

In recent years Victoria's Secret has experienced considerable success with digital overall and mobile social in particular. With mobile they are able to target customers where they are, both in mind and body. A recent campaign before spring break was delivered to mobile users in a #FridayFeverContest. After viewing short Instagram videos that showed various spring break-inspired images, viewers were asked to upload a photo of their end-of-week activities because Victoria's Secret was interested to see what they were doing on Friday. Participants could win Victoria's Secret gift cards in significant amounts. While using Victoria's Secret-branded items was not required, many Instagram entrants assumed that would improve their chances of winning. Other Friday-only sales promotions were also in the mobile mix. Victoria's Secret not only got relatively cost-effective promotions among the sharing public, but also more insight into its target customers' lives.

It was also useful to promote at a time when many customers would be thinking about spring break, and perhaps beaches. Victoria's Secret later announced that it would sell off its bathing suit division in order to focus on its rapidly growing athletic wear line, and this campaign would help reduce inventory.[41]

The brand has stuck with the gold standard of digital marketing, however, the email. Both the main brand and Pink have active email lists where customers receive two or three emails each week with coupon offers, members-only shopping events, and notices of offers like sales and free shipping.[42]

Victoria's Secret has three mobile apps, two of which are shown in Figures 14.10a and b. The third is an app for coupon distribution. There are also a number of

FIGURE 14.10a
The Victoria's Secret App

SOURCE: https://itunes.apple.com/us/app/victorias-secret-for-iphone/id336860594?mt=8

FIGURE 14.10b
The Pink Nation App

SOURCE: https://itunes.apple.com/us/app/pink-nation/id463630399?mt=8

third-party apps for Victoria's Secret coupons, testifying to the brand's popularity. The fact that there have been over 12 million downloads of the Pink app shows how well their segmentation strategy is working, especially for the college-age customer targeted by Pink.

In spite of all the coupons and the incentives like free lingerie just for downloading the app, Victoria's Secret also focuses on nonprice aspects of the customer relationship. The tech people figured out how to let Victoria's Secrets mobile shoppers instantly add a valid promotion code with a click within the mobile app, rather than have to type it in.[43] A contest run on Snapchat.com asked customers snap three pictures of underwear, and after taking a screenshot of their favorite pair, to doodle on them. Snapping back the picture could win fans a recent promotional item, a do-it-yourself Valetine-themed design kit complete with panty, stickers, and rhinestones that was otherwise for sale. Victoria's Secret concluded that the promotion strengthened customer engagement through an increasingly popular mobile venue.[44]

Victoria's Secret is also nailing it in social media. A 2015 study by Spredfast ranked it number one in social media because it was the only brand to have a top score on all eight platforms studied—Facebook, Instagram, Twitter, YouTube, Pinterest, Snapchat, Tumblr, and Google+. And yes, we know what you are thinking, look at all those sexy pictures of the Angels and other models! Spredfast, though, used a number of metrics including audience size and response time, as well as volume of activity and customer engagement (comments, likes, shares, favorites). The criticism, however, was inevitable.

> *People seem to be laughing about [Victoria's Secret] having an unfair advantage, as far as content goes, but the most interesting thing to me is that they aren't actually resting on the strong brand that they have," says Chris Kerns, director of analytics and research at Spredfast. "It's not that they have a ton of people following them—that'd be one way to measure popularity, but not the best way—but they have huge engagement. They've obviously found not only a big audience, but a good core audience.*[45]

One thing it has not pulled back on is the annual Victoria's Secret Fashion Show, a big TV hit with each airing. Every year it has a full cadre of beautiful models, most recently the Angles. Over the last few years it has carefully integrated digital coverage with a dedicated website full of behind-the-scenes videos days in advance of the event.[46] All its social platforms are active in the days preceding the televised event but in 2015 Instagram appeared to lead the way. In the seven days before the show, Victoria's Secret posted 82 images and videos that generated over 216 million likes, an average of 21.7 million per post.[47] While we know that SMM is not free (Chapter 5), these figures represent a huge amount of activity on just one of several social media platforms.

This is a virtuoso IMC performance. Customer acquisition is important, especially for the Pink segment, which has a focused target market with a fairly narrow age range. But the primary emphasis is on customer retention and growing the value of the customer. All in all, Victoria's Secret seems to have done a good job moving from the traditional catalog channel, downplaying direct mail, focusing on relationship emails and finding success in mobile and social.

Victoria's Secret CRM is specifically a virtuoso performance in terms of using mobile in its loyalty program. A study by 3Cs found that 65 percent of marketers say they lack either the resources or the knowledge to launch a mobile loyalty program. On the other hand, 62 percent of consumers say that they purchase more or more often because of a mobile loyalty program. Customers want a number of things, but primarily they want to be rewarded (Figure 14.11).

The report goes on to say that brands reap a number of benefits from their mobile loyalty programs. They include larger-ticket purchases, reduced marketing costs, personalized engagement with customers, and the opportunity to differentiate themselves from competitors.

With value like that derived from mobile loyalty programs you can expect to see even more emphasis placed on newer CRM developments like apps, social media, and cloud marketing.

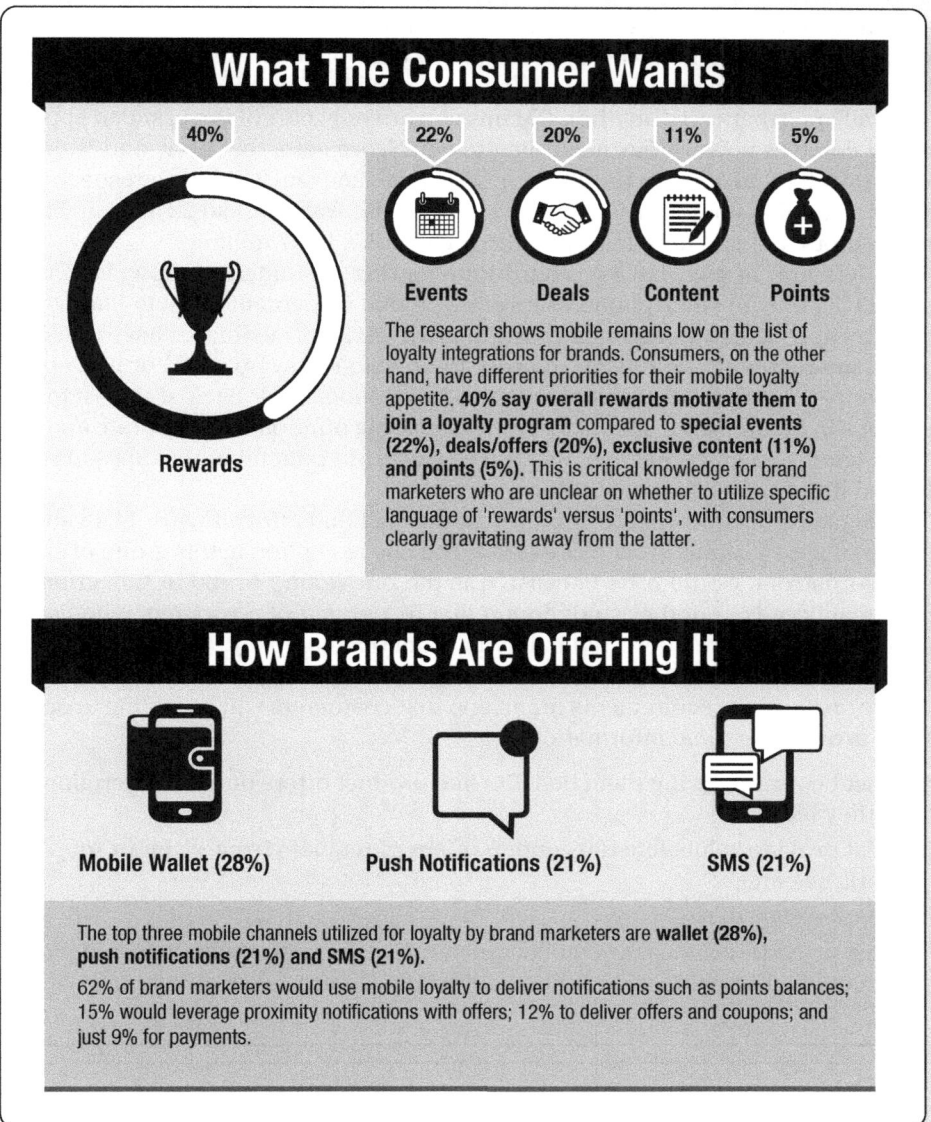

FIGURE 14.11
Consumers Want to Be Rewarded by Mobile Loyalty Programs

SOURCE: http://go.3cinteractive.com/l/13622/2016-06-15/2g6chf

THE IMPORTANCE OF APPS, SOCIAL MEDIA, AND THE CLOUD IN RELATIONSHIP MARKETING

The basic concepts of CRM have changed little over the years, but as apps and social media are changing the way they are executed. They extend reach and customer intimacy and as in the case of Victoria's Secret, they can reach customers wherever they are when they are most likely to be in a frame of mind to buy.

Mobile Apps

The changes to CRM programs that result from apps are still developing, as the previous section illustrates, but they have already had a powerful impact. Todd Wasserman of Mashable says," Branded apps these days are much more about customer retention than customer acquisition, as they go from something that surprises and delights to something that's expected."[48]

That statement is borne out by statistics about the growth of the app category. Growth in the number of apps downloaded over the next few years is expected to be great—from 65.7 billion nongame apps in 2015 to 182.1 billion in 2020. A figure for just how many of those are branded apps is hard to come by, but it is obviously substantial.[49] Retail apps that carry out the CRM mission are only part of the branded app set. So it may come as no surprise, according to comScore data, that eBay and Walmart were the only 2 retail apps on the 2015 top 25 list, in 22nd and 24th place respectively. eBay had 25 million unique visitors in June 2015 while Walmart had 22 million. That's a lot of visitors, but it is dwarfed by leader Facebook's 125.7 million.[50]

Retailers are, in fact, having a hard time getting customers to download their apps. A 2015 study of smartphone users showed that 60 percent of them had two or fewer retail apps and 21 percent had none at all. Even loyal customers have to have a reason to interact with the retailer in order to download its app. CRM or not, apparently most retailers do not provide a compelling reason. Look back at the Victoria's Secret apps in Figure 14.11. They show a free shipping offer on the corporate app and free merchandise on the Pink app. Incentives work, but remember that apps are easily deleted if they do not provide value over time.

Making apps useful appears to be worth the cost and effort. Figure 14.12 shows that users of apps visit the store more often. The one exception in this group of seven apps is Nordstrom. Could it be because it is the one luxury brand in this group of promotional brands? Another study found that 52 percent of customers who used a branded app were more interested in buying from that company.[51] So whether it is a retail app or a brand app, they do the CRM job.

There are several requirements for an app that customers will be willing to download and provide personal information:

- It must be useful, giving them benefits like product offers or even entertainment that they like.
- It must provide value, like the coupon offers of retailers from Walmart to Victoria's Secret.
- It must be easy to use.
- It must provide seamlessly excellent customer experience whether used alone or in conjunction with some other marketing message like a direct mail piece.[52]

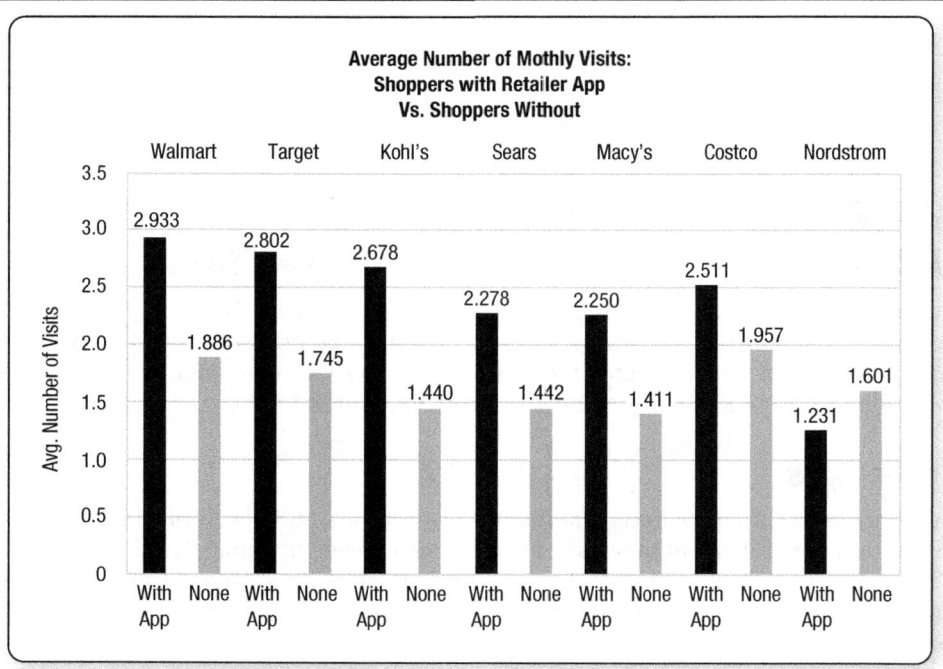

FIGURE 14.12
Branded Apps Increase Store Visits

SOURCE: http://digiday.com/brands/state-retail-mobile-apps-5-charts/

Remember that CX trumps loyalty!

Marketers should be mindful of the fact that although apps are popular and useful, it is not a case of "build it and they will come." Apps represent a marketing communications—and increasingly an ecommerce—program that needs to be targeted and executed with all the care of any other marketing program. We will discuss the issues in developing and marketing successful mobile apps in Chapter 18. It is important to remember that apps are primarily a CRM initiative. Downloading can be done on impulse, but it generally implies some level of brand familiarity and favorability.

Social CRM

Social CRM can be considered as a part of SMM, using all the brand's social media platforms, tools, and techniques to support the CRM effort. Techopedia has a good definition:

> *Social customer relationship management (social CRM) refers to the use of social media and social media techniques to engage a business's customer base.... It is seen as the next step in the evolution of social media marketing where, instead of simply focusing on sales, a company can engage the customer and get direct feedback that will improve the business. As customers see their feedback implemented by the company, they will feel more strongly about the product or service, thus becoming brand advocates for the company.*[53]

The emphasis on Social CRM offers two benefits:

1. It adds useful elements to our understanding of CRM. Traditional CRM is built around marketing and public relations, customer service and support, and transactions. Social CRM adds the role of listening to and interacting with the customer as well as meeting customer service needs in almost real time (Figure 14.13a).
2. It provides a way to transition programs to platforms like Facebook and Instagram that consumers find engaging. B2B customers can be reached through a thought leadership content strategy on LinkedIn. This extends the CRM effort to platforms that customers are using and engaging with.

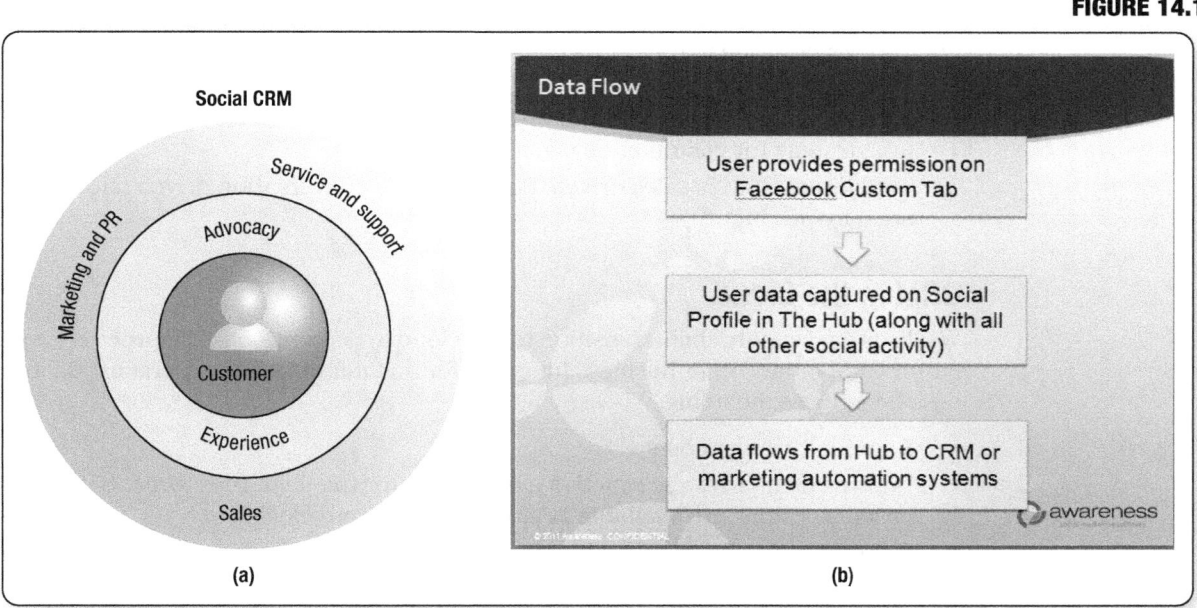

FIGURE 14.13

SM expert Jeremiah Owyang says: 'Traditional crm suppliers, such as Salesforce.com and SAP are starting to integrate data from Facebook, Twitter and other online social networks. Dell and Comcast, both leaders in social marketing and support, have already integrated Twitter data to allow brand managers and support teams to actively track what's being said in tweets'.[54]

Tools are available to enable the collection and use of data from social networks. The Facebook Campaign Manager from Awareness is such a tool (see Figure 14.13b). The Facebook Campaign Manager is part of the Awareness Social Marketing Hub, which facilitates the management and measurement of multiple social marketing channels and supports publication and customer engagement on them. The Facebook Campaign Manager is not available as a stand-alone software product, which indicates the growing importance of integrated management of channels.

The core of the campaign effort is the creation of a custom Facebook tab, which is a specialized page in the Facebook profile.[55] Tabs allow marketers to create customized, interactive pages that can take advantage of Facebook options like geotargeting and can act as landing pages for marketing campaigns. The Facebook Campaign Manager supports the creation of tabs, allowing the marketer to request data from the user and to request access to the user's social profile. When permission is given, the marketer gains access to all the data in the user's social profile which can then be incorporated into CRM solutions like Salesforce. These data allow Facebook users to be integrated into marketing activities such as lead scoring and management, email follow-up offers, and additions to email lists including event-triggered programs. Remember that the marketer must provide an incentive that makes it worthwhile for the user to provide data.

Another approach is a B2B application offered by Radian6, now part of the Salesforce Cloud. Radian6 has an analytics platform to help marketers understand how SMM is impacting their websites. It does this by importing data from the client's Google Analytics, WebTrends, or Omniture metric platform and combining it with relevant social media metrics.[56] That allows marketers to see, for example, which of their content marketing activities are generating social media activity that results in website traffic, leads, or sales conversions. That is a first step and a useful one that we can expect to develop over the next few years. However, it is a long way from putting social media *data items* from *identified customers* into a database. However, tools from companies such as Hootsuite.com increasingly allow companies to manage and track digital campaigns across a variety of social platforms simultaneously.

European social media training firm Our Social Times summarizes social CRM well when they say:

1. Today's customers are more empowered and connected than ever before. Brands need to respond.
2. Traditional CRM is about collecting and managing customer data. Social CRM is a strategy for customer engagement.
3. Traditional CRM is sales driven. Social CRM is conversation driven and sales are a by-product.[57]

CRM in the Cloud

We discussed supply chain transition to the cloud in Section 2-5b. The process is similar for CRM or any other business function, for that matter. CRM experts list the business benefits as including:

- Potentially lower costs.
- Improved employee productivity, especially for the field sales force. Cloud-based solutions are available at any location on any device.
- Better data analytics. In addition to integrating all internal data for the CRM system, cloud-based systems can pull in business intelligence data from external systems.
- Tend to be easier and more simple for employees to use.

- Easier to increase scale when more capacity is needed.
- Provide a high level of security and reliability.[58]

A small business supplier of cloud-based CRM points out that it makes daunting technology available to the small business, many of which have avoided installing CRM systems because of the cost and overall hassle.[59] The improvement in marketing results should make it worth the effort, even though the next section indicates that small businesses do not enjoy the same economies of scale with cloud CRM that larger businesses do.

THE COSTS AND FAILURE RATE OF CRM SYSTEMS PROJECTS

Consultant Arthur Middleton Hughes states the problem of understanding ROI on CRM projects well. He says,

> *If CRM success is in using customer information to create profitable customer communications, how can you measure CRM effectiveness or return on investment? To do the measurement, you have to recognize that almost all CRM's effects are incremental. If successful, CRM results in higher response rates, higher conversions, and increased sales. But the original sales are seldom due to CRM itself.*[60]

Installing a CRM system is a complex and demanding project in any business, large or small. There are cost comparisons all over the web, but they are generally comparing various software on a per seat (translate that per user) basis. Even looked at that way, costs vary dramatically. But it is the cost of licensing or purchasing the software that is the ultimate issue for management. The issue is **Total Cost of Ownership (TOC)**.

total cost of ownership (TOC) the purchase price of a product or service plus the indirect costs of operating it through its lifetime.

Consultant Vincent Lam used a hypothetical CRM project using Microsoft's CRM system to give an idea of the issues and costs involved. In order to provide an accurate TOC he used five categories of costs:

- Hardware purchase
- IT maintenance
- Consulting fees
- Server license
- User license[61]

Because there is a large difference in costs, especially of the hardware and maintenance, in systems of different sizes, he constructed scenarios for three different numbers of users—10, 40, and 100. He points out that this excludes large enterprise systems and government systems, both of which have different licensing arrangements. The bottom line is shown in Figure 14.14.

For the small firm, there is not a lot of difference between on premises (purchased) and online (cloud) systems, although online wins out slightly throughout the 5-year period. Remember the discussion of installing supply chain systems in Chapter 2, in particular how much quicker and less disruptive cloud-based systems were to install for another perspective. Then also consider the fact that small firms do not have a large IT department to manage the complexity of a CRM system. All these factors much be considered in the final decision, which will usually be made by top management.

For the 40 user system the picture is quite different. The cost for an online system and an on-premises system breaks even in year three and the on-premises system is actually a bit cheaper at the end of year five. Lam says this is because the economies of scale for hardware and licensing fees are not in favor of a business of this size.

For the 100 user system the TOC difference is more dramatic, with the online system becoming cheaper after year two and being 25 percent cheaper by the end of year five. Clearly the economics of scale work in favor of the larger installation.

FIGURE 14.14
TOC of CRM Systems for Firms of Different Sizes

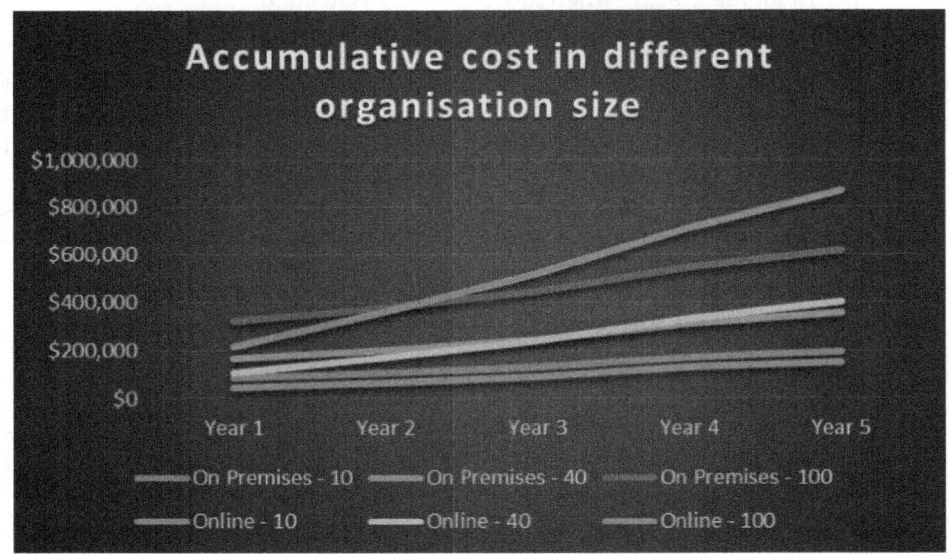

SOURCE: https://www.linkedin.com/pulse/cfos-cost-differences-between-online-premise-deployment-vincent-lam

The TOC figure itself—$200,000 for the small firm, $600,000 for the mid-sized firm, and around $900,000 for the 100-person firm—are less important than the principles involved in Lam's calculation, but they do get your attention.

The same wide variance applies to estimates of the failure rate of CRM programs. The statistic often quoted is that as many as 70 percent of CRM programs fail to provide the expected ROI. In 2009, Michael Krigsman of ZDNet reviewed studies of CRM failure rates since 2001. He was unable to document the 70 percent figure. He found estimates of catastrophic failure, failures that kept the CRM system from going live, from 18 to 31 percent. With a looser definition of failure, failure to meet ROI expectations, he found relatively recent studies that reported rates of 47 and 56 percent. On the basis of the studies he reviewed and his discussions with experts in the field, Krigsman concluded that "many organizations do achieve acceptable ROI from their CRM implementations." He further states, "Still, the data clearly states that substantial numbers of CRM customers are dissatisfied with some significant aspect of their implementations."[62]

A 2015 study by Venture Beat[63] confirms the finding that the 70 percent failure rate that is still widely quoted is a myth today—may always have been a myth, in fact. The study used big data from a number of data partners. Using only one of the data sets the author of the study, Stewart Rogers, says:

> *Of 2,119 respondents from G2 Crowd's data, only 77 (3.6 percent) stated that they had received no payback on their technology investment. A lack of payback could be for a variety of reasons. Maybe the technology isn't working for them. Maybe it isn't implemented properly. Maybe it was installed recently, and while it will gain a return, it is too soon to tell.*
>
> *Without going into all the math (I do that in the report), it means that we can state the following: With a high level of confidence, between 1.47 percent and 5.73 percent of marketing technology implementations fail to provide a return on investment over a 3.5-year life cycle. It might not sound as sexy and compelling as "70 percent fail" ... but at least it is the reality.*[64]

CRM changes the way marketers, and indeed the entire business, think about interacting with their customers. Implementing a CRM system should be seen as a process of change management with organization-wide ramifications. That is a sizeable challenge, and many businesses have fallen short. However, as the examples in this chapter have shown, there are also many paths to success and successful outcomes are rewarding.

Keeping CRM focused on the enterprise's vision of how it wishes to interact with and to be perceived by its customers is necessary to overcoming barriers and avoiding failure drivers. The generic vision for CRM can be described as "seamlessly satisfying customer experience."

THE CRM VISION—SEAMLESS CUSTOMER EXPERIENCE

The CRM vision is to provide the customer a totally satisfactory experience—through every distribution channel the enterprise employs, by means of any communications channel the customer chooses to use, 24/7/365. In an era of multichannel marketing, that is a tall order indeed!

Figure 14.15 suggests the nature of both the problems and the opportunities. Merchants can offer access to information and transactions through their retail stores, websites, telephone call centers, direct mail and catalogs, self-service kiosks like ATMs, and social networks like Facebook. Field service technicians, the person who repairs your refrigerator at home or copier at work, also represent the enterprise and can, in fact, present up-sell and cross-sell opportunities if they are properly trained and motivated. B2B marketers also have field sales forces as another important channel. No one marketer, B2B or B2C, is likely to use all these channels of distribution. However, most now offer a set—branch banks, a website, a telephone customer service center, and ATMs, supplemented with occasional direct mail promotions, would be typical for a retail bank, for example. Most nonprofits have mail, telephone, website, as well as a Facebook page, and personal contacts of various types. An industrial concern would be likely to have a field sales force, a website, printed catalogs, a telephone call center, field service technicians, a blog, and one or more brand communities for customer communication and support. Each of these channels represents a customer **touchpoint**. Each of these touchpoints provides an opportunity to serve the customer well—through information, transactions, or service. Each customer contact sends a message about the brand—positive or negative. Technology can assist on both these dimensions.

touchpoint marketing jargon for each channel available for customer interaction.

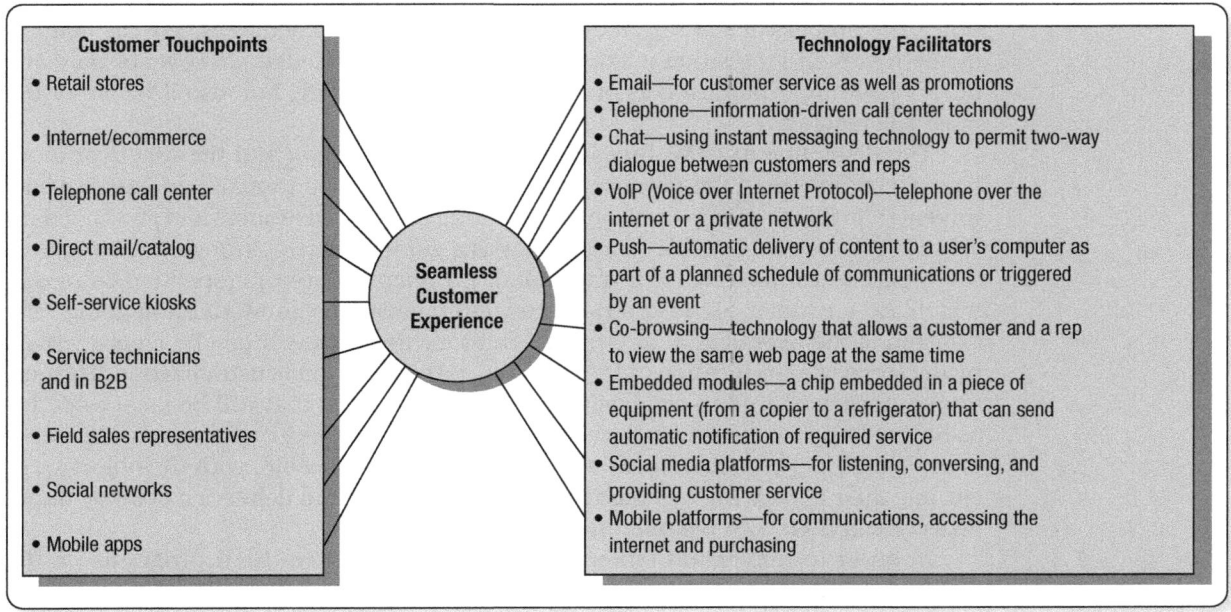

FIGURE 14.15
The CRM Vision

Figure 14.15 also lists the technologies that are in most common use in CRM applications today. The technologies have been discussed in various contexts throughout this text. They all can be applied in B2C, B2B, and nonprofit environments.

The challenge to CRM is that the customer may contact the enterprise at any time, through any of the channels, using any of the available technologies. The marketer's job is to deliver the right product, service, or information—consistently and correctly—no matter when, where, or how the customer makes contact. Further, the product, service, or information should be delivered by the agent—anyone from a call center representative to a field service technician—with whom the customer makes the initial contact. Referring the customer from one person to another in the organization in order to try to get information or settle an issue is the antithesis of "seamless customer experience." The responder on social networks may be an anonymous administrator, but quick and relevant response is essential.

In this context, it is important to recognize technology as a means to an end, not an end in itself. Jeremiah Owyang coined a phrase that has been much repeated. Superimposed on a large sledgehammer it says, "Don't Fondle the Hammer."[65] His message? Do not emphasize the technology; focus on the customer.

Writing in the *Harvard Business Review*, Bain consultants Rigby, Reichheld, and Schefter say, "Executives often mistake the easy promise of CRM software for the hard reality of creating a unique strategy for acquiring, building relationships with, and retaining customers."[66]

Their solutions, as all the perspectives presented in this chapter, are centered around acquiring and retaining high-value customers, developing the right value proposition, ensuring that all business processes are functioning properly, and motivating employees at all customer touchpoints. These are organizational and strategy issues; CRM systems can support strategies, but they cannot devise them. The enterprise must do the demanding work that goes all the way from identifying high-value customers and learning how to increase their value to reengineering processes, if necessary, to learn how to keep customers from defecting. At that point, the enterprise knows what it needs to do and it has a foundation for choosing suppliers of CRM software, systems, and integration services to assist the company in implementing its strategies.

SUMMARY

Practitioners of CRM are often heard to say that, "CRM is a journey, not a destination." The process of learning about the customer is never ending; so are the marketing activities and tools that make use of customer knowledge. CRM is not only one of the most important aspects of contemporary marketing, but also it is one of the most challenging.

The discipline of CRM focuses on customer retention and the reactivation of lapsed customers on the premise that it is less expensive to maintain existing customers than it is to acquire new ones. Acquiring the best customers and growing their value is the essence of CRM strategy. CLV is a guiding metric throughout. It requires the business to move from a traditional, product-oriented perspective to one in which the customer is the central focus and the establishment of an ongoing relationship is the overall goal of strategy. Strategy development can be characterized by the steps of identification, differentiation, interaction, and customization. The customer journey is used to establish the types of messages that will be most effective as the customer moves through relationship stages. Ongoing organizational listening to and engaging with customers will cultivate the relationship, with the objective of earning their loyalty, and encouraging their participation in delivering positive brand messages in their own communities.

In order to implement either operational or analytical CRM programs on the web, a substantial amount of customer knowledge is necessary. This knowledge is embedded in profiles of individual customers or visitors to the website as part of

operational CRM. Profiling is done either anonymously or for identified customers. While anonymous profiling has obvious relevance in the early stages of a potential customer relationship, it also has important privacy implications that should not be overlooked by the marketer. One way to avoid privacy issues is to develop value-added programs like frequent customer reward plans that deepen relationships over time and lead to willing revelation of additional information on the part of loyal customers. Identified profiles can be developed when the visitor or customer provides personal information, usually through registration on a site or making a purchase from it. This permits personalization of content that can be targeted to identified customers by email or at other touchpoints. This ability to reach identified customers with personalized content is a key reason for marketers to encourage social media followers and mobile app users to register and provide data for the database.

Moving beyond simple profiles, marketers can develop models that target customers whose value can be grown or who are likely to be responsive to a particular offer. Here, proactive marketers will supplement these models with forward-looking research regarding trends and new factors. They need to ask, "What happens if customer interest in this product line decreases?" Think about the impact of "athleisurewear," the combination of athletic clothing designed for streetwear, on how customers think about their wardrobes. Would a brand see this trend coming if it only relied on what customers were currently purchasing? Is the brand tracking trends outside of their current market offerings by engaging with their customers in Social CRM? Are they using mobile apps to reach their customers when and where they are most receptive?

Marketers have a menu of options in terms of the channels they will use and the technologies they will implement. The CRM vision is to integrate the chosen channels and technologies in such a way that customer can make contact whenever he pleases, through that channel he prefers at that particular time (the customer touchpoint) and receive the information or service he desires without delay, errors, or being transferred from one enterprise agent to another. This is the "seamless customer experience." It represents both the opportunity and the challenge facing CRM programs of all types.

DISCUSSION QUESTIONS

1. Explain, in your own words, the importance of customer-focused relationship marketing and how it differs from traditional transactional marketing.
2. What is the role of CLV in relationship marketing?
3. Customer Relationship Marketing is generally considered to have its foundations in three B2B marketing functions. Explain what the functions are and what each contributes to a CRM program.
4. Explain the steps in the Peppers and Rogers model of CRM and the importance of the customer database in the process.
5. Explain what is meant by the customer lifecycle, and how CRM strategies and messages can be crafted for its various stages.
6. Discuss how a focus on the total customer experience (CX) requires an expanded view of a marketer's relationship with its customers. What factors should be considered when developing a profile of a customer?
7. Discuss the differences between operational and analytical CRM and how they make use of the customer database.
8. Explain the difference between a customer profile and a model.
9. True or False: It is easy to include customer data from social networks in the database. Why or why not?
10. Targeting and personalization are different but related CRM concepts. Be prepared to define each, clearly explaining why they are different from one another and giving an example of each.

11. True or False: Personalization is a simple process of including the recipient's name in the subject line or body of the message. Why or why not?
12. Why have apps become an important part of CRM programs for many companies? Do you believe that apps you use are helpful in building relationships with brands? Do you think they stimulate sales?
13. Explain your understanding of Social CRM.
14. Why might businesses, large and small, transition to CRM in the cloud?
15. What are some of the major reasons that the implementation of large CRM systems may be prone to failure?
16. What do we mean by "seamless customer experience in multiple channels?"
17. Explain why CRM is a process, not a journey with a final destination.

ENDNOTES

1. Frederick F. Reichheld, *The Loyalty Effect* (Boston, MA: Harvard Business School Press), 1996.
2. Ian Kingwill, "What Is the Cost of Customer Acquisition vs Customer Retention?" https://www.linkedin.com/pulse/what-cost-customer-acquisition-vs-retention-ian-kingwill.
3. Joe Giffer, "Capturing Customers for Life," Capbridge Technology Partners, nd, www.cpt.com.
4. Ian Kingwill, "What Is the Cost of Customer Acquisition vs Customer Retention?" https://www.linkedin.com/pulse/what-cost-customer-acquisition-vs-retention-ian-kingwill.
5. Annette Franz, "A Great Customer Experience Trumps …? http://360connext.com/great-customer-experience-trumps/.
6. Sarabjit Singh Baveja, Sharad Rastogi, Chris Zook, Randall S. Hancock, and Julian Chu, *The Value of Online Customer Loyalty*, http://www.bain.com/Images/Value_online_customer_loyalty_you_capture.pdf.
7. http://www.slideshare.net/ConstantContact/10-quick-facts-you-should-know-about-consumer-behavior-on-facebook.
8. Debra Zahay, James Peltier, Don E. Schultz, and Abbie Griffin. "The Role of Transactional vs. Relational Data in IMC Programs: Bringing Customer Data Together," *Journal of Advertising Research*, March 2004, pp. 3–18.
9. Bill Lee, "Marketing Is Dead.," www.hbr.org/2012/08/marketing-is-dead.
10. Rowland T. Moriarty and Gordon S. Schwartz, "Automation to Boost Sales and Marketing," *Harvard Business Review*, January–February 1989, pp. 100–108.
11. Louis Columbus, "By 2018, 62% of CRM Will Be Cloud-Based and the Cloud Computing Market Will Reach 127.5B" http://www.forbes.com/sites/louiscolumbus/2015/06/20/by-2018-62-of-crm-will-be-cloud-based-and-the-cloud-computing-market-will-reach-127-5b/#4cd556616845.
12. http://www.1to1media.com/.
13. Douglas Quenqua, "Bonobos Takes DIY Approach to Social Media Marketing," https://www.clickz.com/clickz/news/1702634/bonobos-takes-diy-approach-social-media-marketing.
14. Elkin, Tobi, "'Just-in-Time,' vs. Mass Marketing, Delivers Higher Marketing ROI," June 7, 2016, www.mediapost.com/publications/article/277421/just-in-time-marketing-delivers-highe.html.
15. Mele, Christopher (2016) "'Happy Chewbacca' Video Is a Conquering Force on Socail Media," New York Times, May 24, 2016, www.nytimes.com/2016/05/24/us/happy-chewbacca-video.html?r=0.
16. Lisa Arthur, "International Speedway Corporation Races Ahead with Integrated Marketing Management," http://www.forbes.com/sites/lisaarthur/2011/04/13/international-speedway-corporation-races-ahead-with-integrated-marketing-management/#28a334072b3e.

17. http://www.daytonainternationalspeedway.com/Articles/2010/10/Daytona-500-Experience.aspx.
18. http://www.prweb.com/releases/2002/03/prweb35137.htm
19. http://www.kentuckyspeedway.com/camping/.
20. https://www.facebook.com/DaytonaInternationalSpeedway.
21. http://press.nationalgeographic.com/about-national-geographic/.
22. Jason Lynch, "National Geographic Readies First Instagram Video Series for Its 49 Million Followers," http://www.adweek.com/news/television/national-geographic-readies-first-instagram-video-series-its-49-million-followers-171334.
23. http://marketplace.matadoru.com/journalists/.
24. http://press.nationalgeographic.com/2016/01/04/yearlong-exploration-celebration-100th-anniversary-national-park-service/.
25. https://klout.com/home.
26. https://www.babble.com/toddler/just-arrived-the-top-mommy-blogs-of-2012/.
27. https://twitter.com/twitalyzer.
28. https://www.booshaka.com/contact2.
29. Elyse Dupre, "The Costs of Influencer Marketing," http://www.dmnews.com/marketing-strategy/the-costs-of-influencer-marketing/article/496291/.
30. http://whopaysinfluencers.com/.
31. Scott, Mark, "Europe's Privacy Watchdogs Call for Changes to U.S. Data Transfer Deal," http://www.nytimes.com/2016/04/14/technology/europe-us-data-privacy.html.
32. http://www.dmnews.com/eureka-turning-social-data-into-golden-customer-relationships/article/211407.
33. For more information on cookies, primarily from the user perspective, see http://www.cookiecentral.com/.
34. http://www.sdl.com/cxc/digital-experience/alterian.html.
35. "Email List Reactivation Incentives," https://www.marketingsherpa.com/article/case-study/gift-cards-vs-whitepaper-vs.
36. David Smith, "There Are Myriad Ways to Get Personal," Internet Week, May 15, 2000, http://www.techweb.com.
37. "U.S. Customer Loyalty Program Memberships Top 3 Billion for 2015 Colloquy Census Shows," https://www.colloquy.com/latest-news/2015-colloquy-loyalty-census/.
38. "U.S. Customer Loyalty Program Memberships Top 3 Billion for 2015 Colloquy Census Shows," https://www.colloquy.com/latest-news/2015-colloquy-loyalty-census/
39. Danila Forte, "Victoria's Secret Cuts Its Catalog—Is It an End of an Era?', www.Multi-channelmerchant.com/marketing/Victorias-secret-cuts-catalog-end-era-03062016.
40. "The Famed Victoria's Secret Catalog May Be Headed for the Recycling Bin, http://www.marketwatch.com/story/is-the-famed-victorias-secret-catalog-headed-for-the-recycling-bin-of-history-2016-04-08.
41. Alex Samuely, "Victoria's Secret Entices Mobile-Savvy Spring Breakers with Two-Pronged Sales Approach." http://www.mobilecommercedaily.com/victorias-secret-entices-mobile-savvy-spring-breakers-with-two-pronged-sales-approach.
42. "What Victoris's Secret Can Teach You About Content Marketing," http://www.mobilecommercedaily.com/victorias-secret-entices-mobile-savvy-spring-breakers-with-two-pronged-sales-approach.
43. Alex, Samuely, "Victoria's Secret Unclasps Add-On Promotional Codes for Mobile Shoppers," www.mobilemeidacommerce.com/victorias-secret-unclasps-add-on-promotional-codes-for-mobile-shoppers
44. Mike O'Brien, "Five Killer Social Media Campaigns from 2016 (so far)," https://www.clickz.com/2016/02/11/five-killer-social-campaigns-from-2016.
45. Mike O'Brien, "And the Winner of Social Media Is…Victoria's Secret [Study], https://www.clickz.com/clickz/news/2418492/and-the-winner-of-social-media-is-victorias-secret-study.
46. https://www.victoriassecret.com/fashion-show.

47. "How the Victoria's Secret Fashion Show Drove Engagement on Instagram," https://www.newswhip.com/2015/12/how-the-victorias-secret-fashion-show-drove-engagement-on-instagram/#VwdSQrC3eovPAD8W.97.
48. http://mashable.com/category/branded-apps/.
49. "5 Essential Mobile Stats Every Marketer Should Know, (Infographic)," https://www.biznessapps.com/blog/mobile-growth-statistics/.
50. "These Are the 25 Most Popular Mobile Apps in America," http://qz.com/481245/these-are-the-25-most-popular-2015-mobile-apps-in-america/.
51. "Brand' Mobile Apps Aren't Just About the Discounts" http://www.emarketer.com/Article/Brands-Mobile-Apps-Arent-Just-About-Discounts/1010100.
52. "The State of Mobile Apps for Retailers," http://www.retailmenot.com/corp/static/filer_public/78/9c/789c947a-fe7c-46ce-908a-790352326761/stateofmobileappsforretailers.pdf.
53. https://www.techopedia.com/definition/357/social-customer-relationship-management-social-crm.
54. Neil Woodcock, Andrew Green, and Michael Starkey, "Social CRM as a Business Strategy, http://link.springer.com/article/10.1057/dbm.2011.7.
55. https://www.facebook.com/note.php?note_id=%20501377617203.
56. https://www.marketingcloud.com/products/social-media-marketing/radian6.
57. "Traditional CRM vs. Social CRM," http://oursocialtimes.com/traditional-crm-vs-social-crm-infographic/.
58. "10 Benefits Associated with Cloud-Based CRM," http://nuagecg.com/10-benefits-asloud-based-crm/.
59. "The Business Benefits of Cloud CRM," http://cloudtweaks.com/2015/01/business-benefits-cloud-crm/.
60. http://www.dbmarketing.com/articles/Art204.htm.
61. Vincent Lam, "For CFOs, The Cost Differences Between Online and On Premises Deployment Microsoft Dynamics CRM," https://www.linkedin.com/pulse/cfos-cost-differences-between-online-premise-deployment-vincent-lam.
62. Michal Kingsman, CRM Failure Rates: 2001–2009," http://www.zdnet.com/article/crm-failure-rates-2001-2009/.
63. Steward Rogers, "The State of Marketing Technology Winter 2015," http://insight.venturebeat.com/report/state-marketing-technology-winter-2015-cost-ownership-and-return-investment?utm_source=vbnews&utm_medium=in-article-callout&utm_content=middle-of-article&utm_campaign=somt-2&utm_term=70-percent-of-crm-installs-fail-and-other-crap-stats-you-should-ignore.
64. Stewart Rogers, "'70 Percent of CRM Installations Fail' and Other Crappy Stats You Should Ignore," http://venturebeat.com/2015/01/23/70-percent-of-crm-installs-fail-and-other-crap-stats-you-should-ignore/.
65. http://www.slideshare.net/jeremiah_owyang/social-media-trends-for-2010?src=embed.
66. Darrel K. Rigby, Frederick F. Reichheld, and Phil Schefter, "Avoid the Four Perils of CRM," *Harvard Business Review*, February 2002, p. 9.

Chapter 15

Developing and Maintaining Effective Online and Mobile Websites

LEARNING OBJECTIVES

By the time you complete this chapter, you will be able to:

1. Understand the role websites play in the decision-making processes of both B2C and B2B customers.
2. Give your own opinion about what makes a website effective.
3. Explain each step in the website development process.
4. Identify important issues in website design.
5. Discuss the concepts of usability and its impact on customer experience.
6. Explain how a usability test might be set up.
7. Identify major cost elements involved in creating a site.
8. Explain why it is essential to have a mobile-friendly site.
9. Discuss the difference among stand-alone, adaptive, and responsive mobile sites.
10. Explain the concept of "mobile first" in the context of creating a website.
11. Identify the key elements in the development of a mobile site.

As digital and mobile marketing vie for supremacy, websites have taken on new value and faced new challenges. In the beginning of internet marketing, companies rushed to create a website just to have one. Gradually, the potential of the internet meant a movement from the idea that "everyone must have one," toward carefully crafted objectives, design for **user experience (UX)**, measurement of effectiveness, and the necessity of mobile marketing through websites or apps or both. Companies want their customers to stay on their sites as long as possible, navigate as many paths as possible, and return again and again, a concept often known as site **stickiness**. Getting the site to be "sticky" is a complex task involving the graphical design of the website, its content, the degree of personalization and interactivity, and the customer's engagement and overall experiences on the website.[1] The marketing aspects of creating and maintaining customer-effective sites will be covered in this chapter. Measurement is the subject of Chapter 18.

user experience (UX) according to Jakob Nielsen, all of the user's interactions with the brand on all touchpoints, which makes it nearly synonymous with CX. Often used to describe the usability of a website or a mobile app.

stickiness getting customers to stay on the site as long as possible, navigate as many paths as possible, and return again and again.

THE ROLE OF WEBSITES

There are two key, but not mutually exclusive, roles a website—whether online or mobile—can play in marketing strategy. A website can be a channel for providing information or a channel for generating sales or both. Information is key in both B2C and B2B markets. Both B2C and B2B marketers generate sales leads (think about retargeting of display advertising in Chapter 7) and both make sales on their websites. The order of importance for the two market sectors may be switched, though, with sales often most important in B2C and lead generation most important in B2B.

In the 30-year plus history of the commercial internet, the use of websites as an "electronic brochure" has faded, and marketers have come to understand—and generally to take advantage of—the reach and interactivity of the internet to meet a variety of marketing objectives. Some of the generic objectives that justify the existence of enterprise online and mobile websites include to:

- Increase sales revenue
- Increase the visibility of the enterprise and its products
- Advertise products and services
- Act as the focal point for a content marketing strategy
- Aid in brand development
- Interface with brand social media sites
- Provide customer service
- Generate sales leads
- Provide a platform for ecommerce
- Retain and grow customers
- Build an online community
- Provide cost savings, especially in promotion and customer service

Most firms are looking for tangible returns from their websites, either in cost savings or revenue enhancement, and are also looking for the site to reinforce their company strategy and to work in conjunction with other communications and marketing channels. Smart companies develop specific objectives for their website in terms of the stage of customer development, nurturing prospects until they become loyal customers through a series of targeted communications.

B2C consumers use websites in a wide variety of ways, both informational and transactional. A great deal of data is available about consumer use and Google has aggregated much of it into a useful tool. See how the tool can help marketers understand the web-related behaviors of various target segments in Interactive Exercise 15.1.

What B2B Marketers Expect from Websites

On the B2B side websites are also a mainstay of information acquisition and product purchase. Figure 15.1a shows the importance of the information acquisition aspect. B2B purchasers want detailed information not only about products themselves but also about service issues like in-stock availability and delivery issues.

What kind of content are they looking for if they need to verify the credibility of a brand? Outranking every other piece of content by a wide margin is contact information. This suggests that personal relationships and selling are not dead in the digital age. Establishment of a relationship is, however, likely to be based on thorough research before contact is made. Surprisingly the same study found that 51 percent of respondents found detailed contact information lacking on websites—a huge oversight! It also found, as shown in Figure 15.1b, that blogs and social media activity, and even video, do not add much to credibility. That does not mean, however, that B2B buyers do not use this type of content to get the detailed product information they want.

Think back to the B2B buyer journey, Figure 16.2. The three phases of Awareness, Consideration, and Purchase contain numerous steps, several information channels, and a lot of moving forward, then looping back. Along the way a lot of content is located and consumed, Forrester found that B2B buyers get three pieces of information from outside sources for every one piece of information marketers can deliver through their websites, email, and other channels.[2] B2B agency head Heidi Cohen adds that Google research shows that the average business buyer checks over ten pieces of content before contacting the seller. It's easy to assume that the first direct contact for many buyers will be to visit the website. Website content must recognize that potential customers may already be well into the customer journey. She suggests the following steps:

1. Know your target audience and create personas (discussed in Chapter 13).
2. Use that knowledge to create the content they want as indicated by Figure 15.1a.

FIGURE 15.1a
Information for B2B Buying Decisions

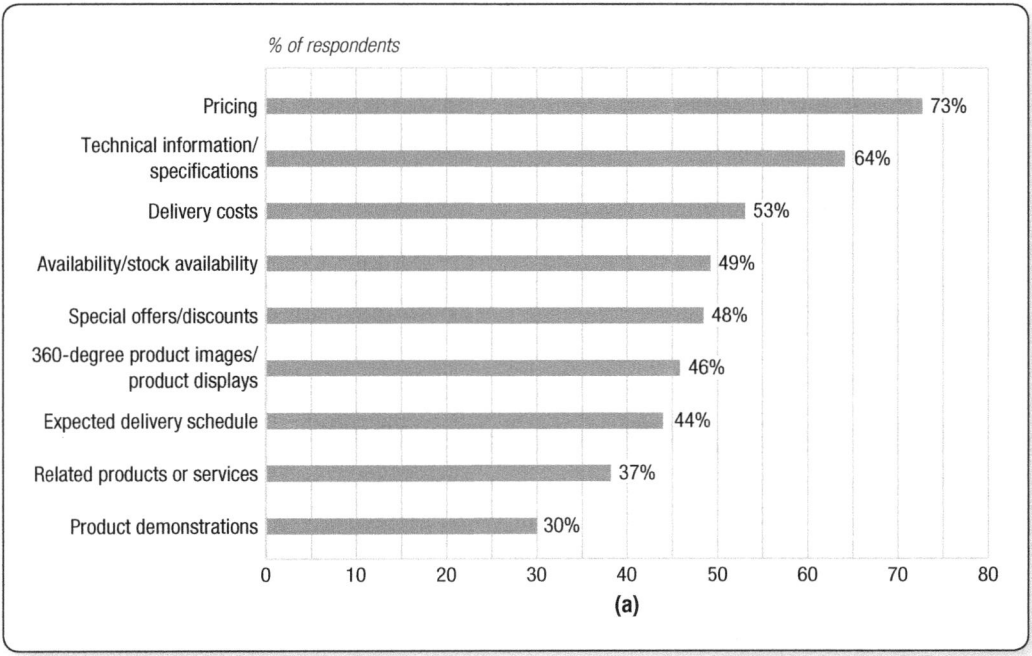

SOURCE: http://www.v3b.com/wp-content/uploads/2014/12/chart-useful-information-for-B2B-end-user-buyers.png

FIGURE 15.1b

Using Content to Establish Credibility

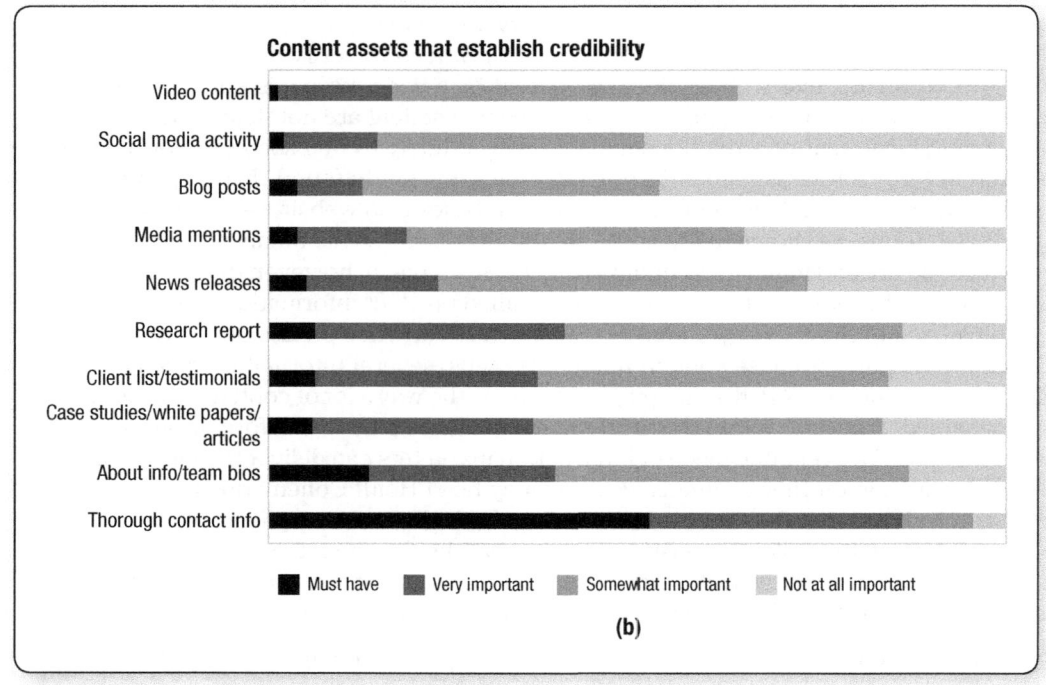

SOURCE: http://marketingland.com/less-than-20-of-b2b-buyers-say-social-media-blogs-impact-vendor-discovery-process-report-124673

3. In order to draw prospective customers to your site place your content where they are (Figure 15.2) and where they are most responsive. Not only has LinkedIn become the go-to platform for business users, they are in a business frame of mind when they are on the site.
4. Break down barriers between marketing and sales. In a multichannel, multi-platform world the two must work together, not work as independent business divisions.
5. Measure results.[3]

B2C and B2B customers prioritize different types of information on websites. Beyond that, the general principles of designing effective websites hold true in both market spaces. What makes a website effective, and how does the marketer know it is working?

WHAT MAKES A WEBSITE EFFECTIVE?

There are as many opinions of websites as there are users. There are also awards like the Webbys that can provide inspiration and some guidance. HubSpot maintains a frequently updated list of sites that appeal to marketers for their esthetic and functional qualities. Figure 15.3 shows four examples, each chosen to illustrate a web design theme.

One thing that you cannot see from the static captures is that the websites are consistent throughout. If it has clean, crisp, or even minimalist design, it maintains that theme throughout. If it relies on technology to deliver a spectacular UX, it pulls out all the technology stops. It doesn't use different styles that may confuse the message.

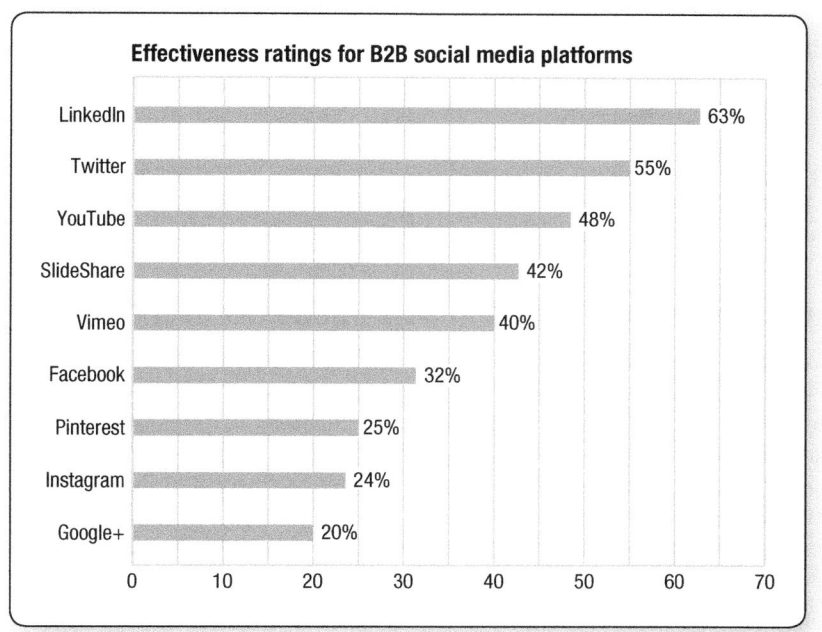

FIGURE 15.2
Which Social Media Platforms Are Effective for Reaching B2B Buyers

SOURCE: http://contentmarketinginstitute.com/wp-content/uploads/2014/10/2015_B2B_Research.pdf

FIGURE 15.3
Different Approaches to Website Design

SOURCE: http://blog.hubspot.com/marketing/best-website-designs-list#sm.0000002to08kmvcpyv7vlb6v649jq

One agency feels you can learn from a bad (intentionally) website. Canadian agency Zulu Alpha Kilo's parody site invites you to do just that. The website homepage shown in Figure 15.4 is pretty horrible, but it gets worse (and sometimes grosser) as you explore the pages. Give it a try—and think about things not to do, including all the overworked jargon.

The four highly regarded sites in Figure 15.3 and the intentionally awful one of Zulu Alpha give marketers a great deal to think about. What are your own personal criteria for effectiveness as you use websites in your daily life? Do you have any special or additional criteria when you are contemplating a purchase from a site?

Special Requirements for Ecommerce Site Effectiveness

All websites aim to inform their users in a way that helps build brand image and trust. Most also seek to inspire some kind of behavior, perhaps to sign up for an email list so they can receive further information. Ecommerce sites have the special requirement of closing the sale without assistance from any other channel. As such, they must meet the requirements for a direct response offer, as described in Chapter 4, with a clear offer and a strong call to action.

There are site design criteria that support the effectiveness of ecommerce sites in closing the sale. Ecommerce sites should have:

- Navigation that is easy to follow even though they have a large product selection. Use of filters, described later in the chapter, is desirable on sites with a large and varied product array.
- Images that present products in the most compelling way.
- Fast loading times for each page which requires compressing images among other technical requirements.

FIGURE 15-4

A Parody Website for an Advertising Agency

SOURCE: http://www.zulualphakilo.com/

- A theme and approach that is appealing to target customers. For instance, a site for a discount retailer would have a different overall look than a site for a purveyor of luxury products.
- Shopping cart, search bar, and sign-in conveniently placed, usually close to one another.
- Easy-to-find contact information. A live chat option has become very popular.
- Special offers appropriate to the target audience.
- Payment options clearly specified.
- A store finder function if the site is for a multichannel retailer.[4,5,6]

With the exception of the transaction-specific features, these are good recommendations for the effectiveness of any site.

Think about these effectiveness requirements and the sites shown in Figure 15.3 and ask yourself how marketers know that their sites are actually effective. We will discuss specific website metrics in Chapter 18, but there is a generic answer. *Marketers know that a website works if it is meeting website objectives.* That's why setting objectives is the first step in the website development process, which we now explore.

THE WEBSITE DEVELOPMENT PROCESS

Figure 15.5 summarizes the steps that are essential to the development of an effective website. It begins with the establishment of site objectives, which, in turn, should flow directly from the marketing objectives and the corporate objectives of the enterprise. It goes through six more steps—defining the target market, designing the site, conducting usability tests, deploying the site, measuring site effectiveness, and improving

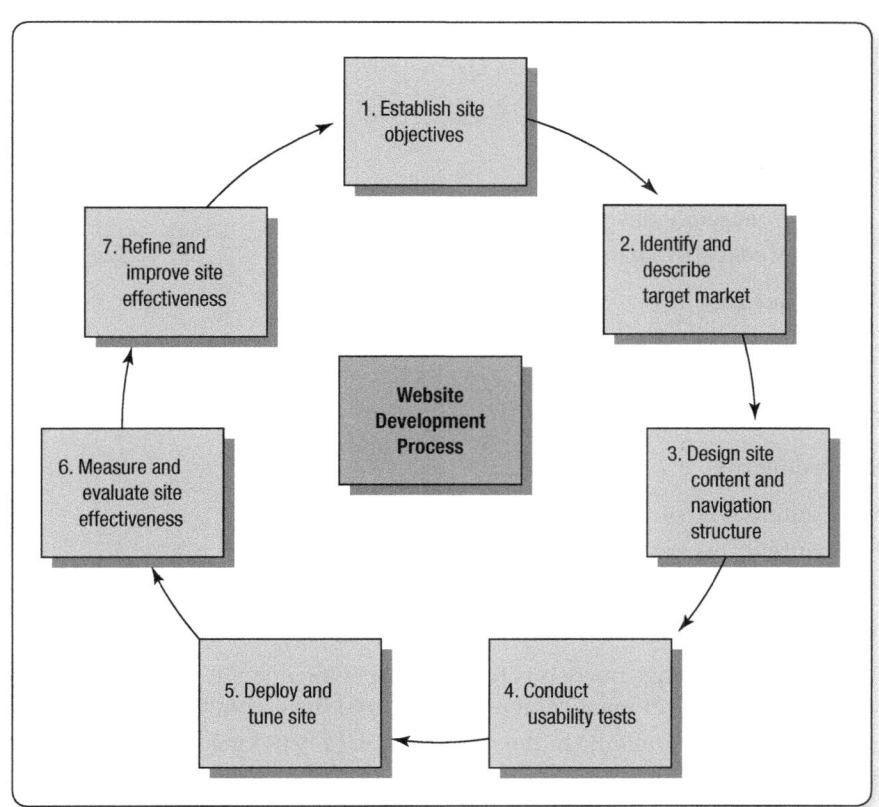

FIGURE 15.5

The Website Development Process

SOURCE: Adapted from marketing materials of Accrue Software, Inc.

the site. Some of the tasks are in marketing's domain; the target market, for instance, and others are in the domain of IT; deploying the site onto the internet, for example. Some tasks, such as designing the site structure, require substantial contributions from both departments.

The steps are the same, whether the project is the creation of an entirely new website or whether it is the modification of an existing site. A range of experience and expertise will be required in either instance. As a result, we should first consider what a website development team looks like.

Creating a Website Development Team

The size and composition of the team is, of course, going to vary by the size and complexity of the site. It will also be affected by the budget available, a subject to which we will return late in the chapter.

A website development team requires a set of skills. Within that skill set a variety of specific roles may be filled depending on the types of expertise available. Examples are as follows:

- Strategy and planning
  - The responsible executive—the internal client, in effect
  - Project leaders from marketing and IT and possibly other departments
- Project management
  - A project manager
    - Managers for one or more specific phases of the project
- Information architecture and user interface design
  - One or more persons who specialize in designing environments for shared information
  - One or more persons who specialize in designing user interfaces for optimum user experiences
- Graphic design for the web
  - Art director
    - Interactive designer
    - Media specialists—photography, videos, etc.
- Web technology
  - Applications programmers
  - Database specialists
  - Webmaster
- Site production
  - Content contributors
  - Content researchers and other support staff[7,8]

This is already a fairly complex list and it could be more detailed. Even at this low level of detail you should be aware of three important things:

1. Some of the expertise needed is for only a specific portion of the project. Other skills such as project management are required throughout.
2. If these skills are available in the organization they belong to people who already have full-time jobs.
3. External consultants or freelancers can help fill the gaps in terms of both skills and time available but will require additional management time and effort. They will, of course, also add to the cost.

Whether the project is to develop a new website or to improve an existing one, website development is a complex and demanding process. It tests both the resources and the patience of the organization. With that in mind, let's turn to the steps themselves.

Establishing Website Objectives

The objectives will depend on the nature of the product(s) and what the site is intended to accomplish.[9] There are many possible generic objectives from brand awareness to ecommerce, as discussed at the beginning of this chapter. The individual enterprise must take these generic objectives and develop them into specific, measurable objectives for the particular website. It is also important for the company to have a clear strategy so that website objectives and target markets can be well delineated.

Figure 15.6 presents the objectives cascade which gives a helpful way for marketers to look at setting their own objectives. Marketing objectives cascade down from corporate objectives, which are strategic and financial in nature.

The objectives cascade might look the examples in Figure 15.6b this for one of the several corporate long-term objectives.

Notice that one high-level strategic goal can, and usually does, generate multiple annual goals at lower levels of the organization. Notice also that Figure 15.6a also requires that objectives be SMART—specific, measurable, achievable, realistic, and time-specific.

SMART objectives are not an option. As we will discuss in Chapter 18 accurate measurement of results cannot take place without SMART objectives. Remember that *marketers can only know that a website works if it is meeting website objectives.* Then add that *marketers can only know if objectives are being met if those objectives are SMART.* Quantitative objectives such as those shown in the cascade example are a start, but they are not fully developed objectives.[11]

In the cascade example only one corporate strategic objective is shown and that is an internal operating efficiency goal. There would undoubtedly be more and most, if not all of the others, would be outward facing. For example, a corporate strategic objective might be to improve ROI by 1 percent per year for each of the next five years. That might lead marketing to adopt an objective of increasing customer retention by 5 percent in each of the next five years, with the cascade to the other departments following.

In establishing objectives, marketers must be keenly aware of their relationship with their target market and its needs and preferences. As a result, a concurrent task is identifying and describing the target market.

Identifying and Describing the Target Market

Marketing is responsible for conveying information about the target market to other participants in the process, in particular the web designers from the IT department. It is the job of the marketing department to understand how the objectives relate to a specified target market. Marketing is also the location within the firm of detailed knowledge about the needs, attitudes, and shopping behaviors of market segments targeted by the business.

It is important that marketers share this information with all who are involved in designing and building the site. Think about it. Should a site, say an entertainment-oriented one, which is targeted to teenagers look and interact like an entertainment-oriented site that is targeted to older adults? You will undoubtedly agree that it should not and that content, visual appearance, and interaction should all be designed with a specific target market in mind. It is the marketer's job to see that the site is geared to the identified target market by sharing information about the target market with web designers and developers.

The best way to transmit this information within the website development team has proven to be personas. Personas were discussed in another context in Chapter 13.

FIGURE 15.6a

How Goals and Objectives Cascade through the Organization

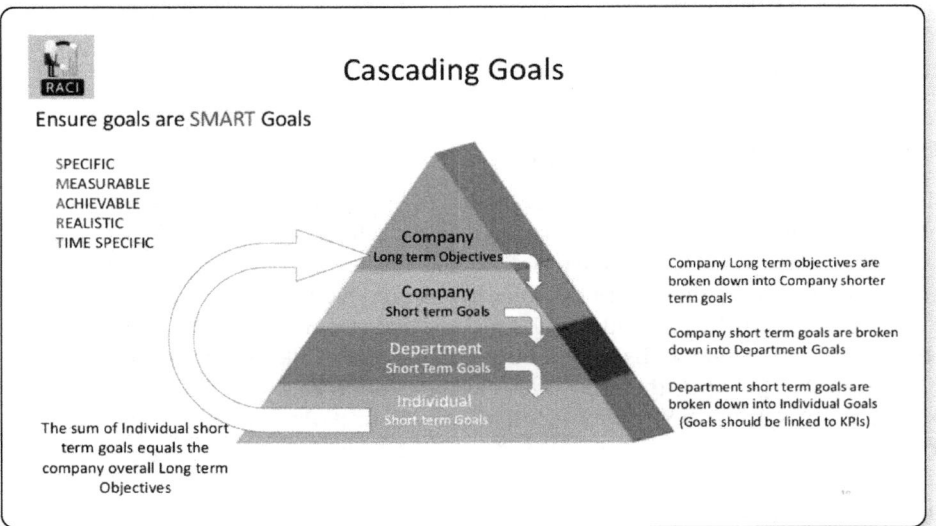

SOURCE: https://www.slideshare.net/RACI101/raci-overcoming-barriers-to-growth-session-2-51371873

FIGURE 15.6b

Examples of an Objectives Cascade

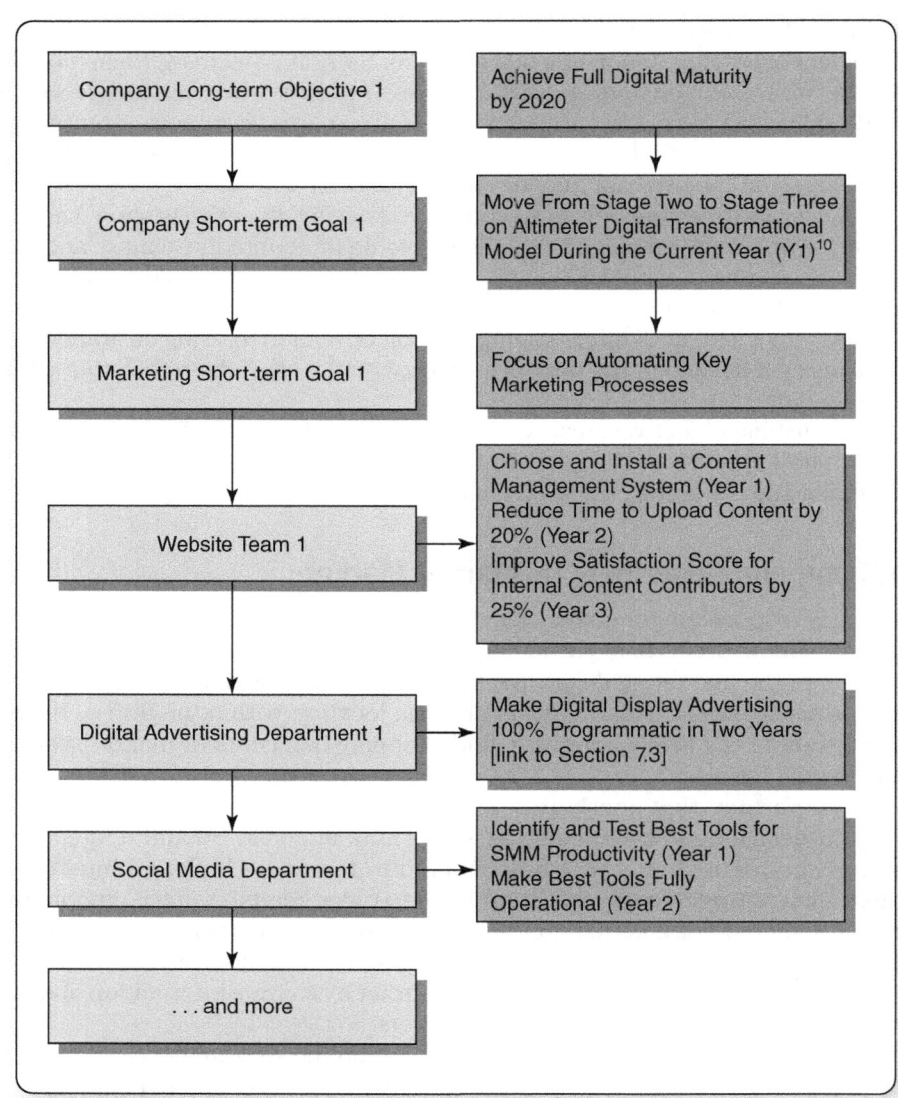

Figures 15.7a, b, c and d show one of the personas developed for a website project and how it was used. Penny is a first time buyer of this brand, a married sales assistant who lives in London. For this project a total of six personas were developed, each one representing a distinct customer segment.

Notice that the storyboard shown in Figure 15.7b is a technique taken from traditional advertising in which marketing explains to the executors of the website the kind of decision-making process this segment is likely to use and perhaps the emotional states associated with the process. With knowledge about the persona, the web designers and programmers can move from the generic home page,

FIGURE 15.7

a. First Time Buyer Penny Persona

b. Storyboard for Penny

c. Generic Home Page

shown in Figure 15.7c, to a personalized home page for the Penny persona. It caters to the decisions she needs to make when buying paint, giving her useful ideas and information.

A site may be personalized to key segments or not depending on the perceived usefulness of personalization and the time and budget available. Whether there is personalization or not the next step is to design site content and the navigational structure. This step will guarantee optimum accessibility of the content to the target market.

Designing Website Content

Identifying the necessary content and the appropriate manner of presentation are other tasks in which marketing will take the lead. The content of the site is something that, at first glance, appears quite straightforward. Marketers, after all, in every

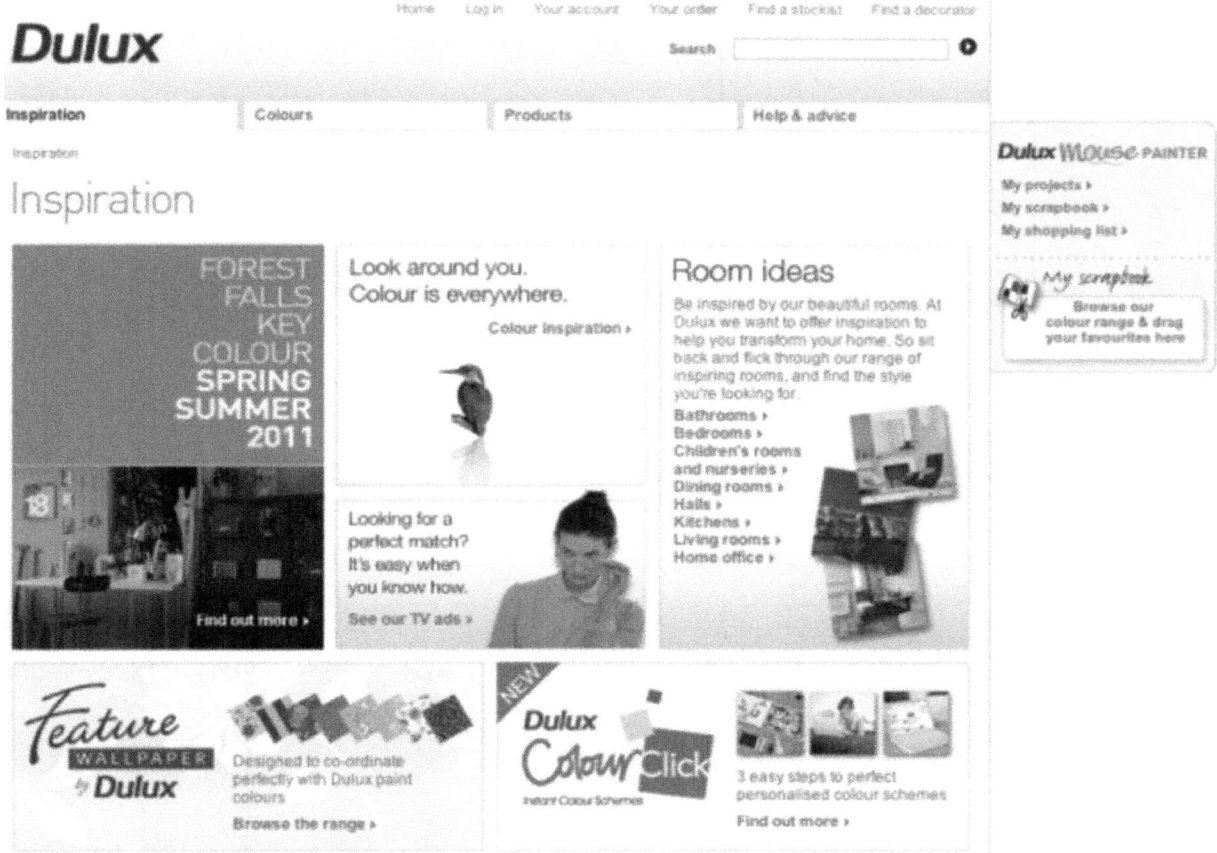

d. Home Page Design for the Penny Persona

SOURCE: http://www.smartinsights.com/marketplace-analysis/customer-analysis/web-design-personas/

business except a start-up have experience in developing communications in both traditional and digital marketplaces. As we discovered in Chapter 7, designing content for the web is both supported and complicated by technology. It is also important to take the requirements of the target market in mind. For one thing, internet marketers believe that most viewers skim instead of reading word by word. This means that copy must be laid out in short blocks, preferably in columnar fashion. When the copy is long, the marketer should assume that many visitors will not scroll down far or will not jump to a continuation page, and should place key content accordingly.

Think about the websites in Figure 15.3. All make extensive use of visuals—static, animated, and video. The ETQ site uses little copy, letting the shoes speak for themselves. Both the SwissAir and the Minimums site take a story-telling approach, with SwissAir letting visuals tell a lot of the story and Minimums using copy to tell the stories of their interesting people. For the Abbey Road site the visuals are the story. Copy, visuals, and a combination of both must engage the viewer, cause her to remain on the site, and create the brand impression, which is the goal.

Even more provocative is a series of studies that focuses on content pages conducted by the Poynter Institute, the Estlow Center at the University of Denver, and Eyetools, Inc. These studies use eye-tracking cameras in the ongoing study of how consumers read news on websites. The cameras allow the researchers to record with precision the movement of a respondent's eyes on a web page (Figure 15.8a).

FIGURE 15.8

(a) An Eye Track Map (b) The Priority Grid (c) A Heat Map

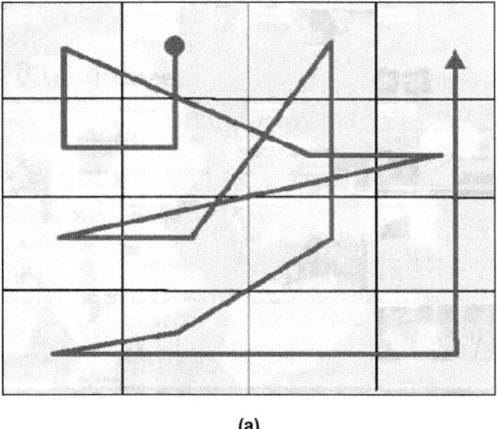

(a)

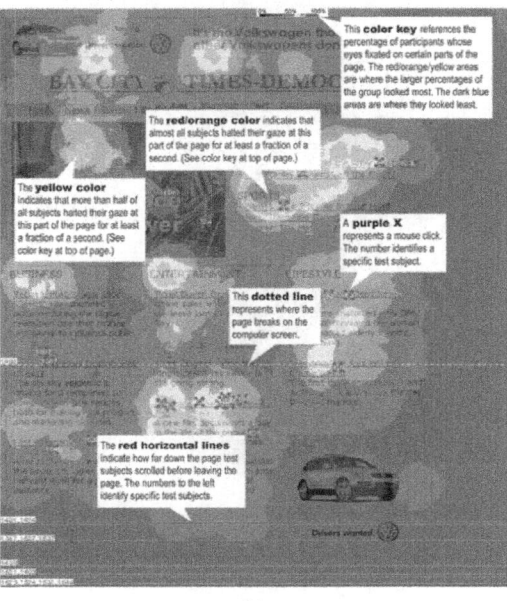

(c)

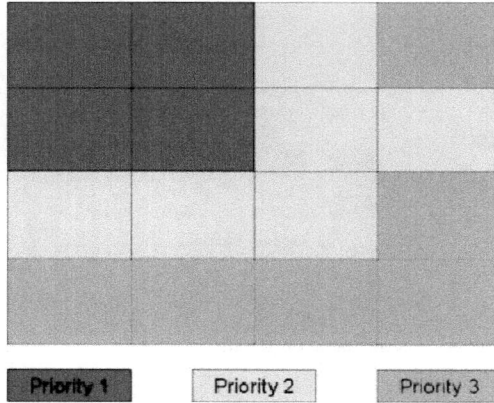

(b)

SOURCE: Copyright © The Poynter Institute, http://www.poynterextra.org/eyetrack2004/viewing.htm#1.3, and http://www.poynterextra.org/eyetrack2004/viewing.htm#1.2.

Results from a series of studies indicate that, in the absence of specific design elements:

- Eyes first land in the upper left of the page, especially if attracted by a headline.
- Users usually look at only the first few words of headlines.
- Respondents tend to look at five headlines on these news pages before clicking.

That information has led to dividing a web page into 16 quadrants, with the upper left being highest priority for content placement, roughly the middle being second priority, and roughly the right and bottom being lowest priority (see Figure 15.8b).[12]

heat maps visual representations of eye activity on a web page.

The technology has also led to the development of **heat maps**. The red to orange areas in Figure 15.8c indicate the most activity and the blue to black the least. The upper left-hand corner of the page is often called the "Golden Triangle" because it forms a triangle shape. Others refer to this area as the "F" section since the user's eyes move backward and forward in that triangle area as they examine the content. The visual also shows the page break on the viewer's browser—often referred to as "above the fold."

Recent research focusing on the reading of news on tablets shows the ongoing importance of eye tracking. Researchers from the Poynter Institute found that most readers preferred to hold their tablets vertically and to swipe horizontally even though visual content may have been set up in landscape orientation.

They also confirmed website findings that people tend to enter a site through a dominant element, often a photograph. Faces in both photos and videos attracted much viewer attention.[13]

Tools that use either eye tracking or tracking of mouse clicks are a standard part of web design. There are free-standing tools for DIY use like the one at Crazy Egg, which uses mouse clicks to produce heat maps and other website analytics.[14] Many website design and analytics platforms include these tools.

The use of heat maps and the tracking of mouse clicks argue for the importance of well-written copy on websites. The more task-oriented the viewer is and the more in a hurry he is, the more likely he is to leave as a result of poor content or poor navigation. It is also important to recognize that visitors enter the site at different times and on different pages—not necessarily the home page. Content must be relevant, make sense even if it has been archived for a long time, and repeat key points without sounding repetitive. And—of critical importance—visitors must be able to find it easily. This is the job of the content design and the navigation structure.

Designing the Navigational Structure

The first step is to design the content structure. The grammatically questionable but meaningful term "architect the information structure" is used to describe this process. The implication is that there must be a coherent structure to the content of a site, usually one that is hierarchical in nature. This enables visitors to move around the site in a manner that fits each person's individual need to merely examine summary information or to drill deeper into the site in search of detailed information about a specified topic. At the same time the site designer or information architect plans a careful and comprehensive structure, he or she should adhere to a simple premise often referred to as KISS—Keep It Simple Stupid! One way of implementing the KISS rule is to try to see that the visitor is never more than three mouse clicks away from desired information. The end goal of information architecture is to understand how the user expects to find the information presented (his or her mental model) and design the site to correspond with the way the user thinks about the content.

There are specific issues to consider when designing a site structure. The main issues and rules of thumb are as follows:

1. User intent. Visitors come to the site for a particular reason. Are they primarily searching for information or looking for a transaction, or perhaps both at different stages of the customer journey?
2. Effective communication. People scan on the web, scrolling quickly through content. Use headlines, subheads, and "chunk" information in a way that makes it quick and easy for visitors to comprehend.
3. Readable typefaces. Sans Serif fonts, those that do not have the small lines at the top and bottom of characters, are more readable on the web. A font size of 16 px (**pixels**) is good for most web applications. Use no more than three different fonts and font sizes.
4. Colors and white space. Choose colors carefully to convey the ideas and the emotions you want the visitor to experience. Use white space to give pages a modern, uncluttered look.
5. Visuals. Use images and videos to communicate the message in a way that can be more effective than the best-written copy.
6. Design for ease of use. A good navigation structure with organized layouts that facilitate eye movement is the aim.
7. Fast loading. No matter how much visual content is on your site, it must load quickly.
8. Works on different size screens and different devices.[15] We will discuss designing mobile sites later in the chapter.

9. Accessibility. Websites need to be available to people with physical challenges like low vision. Accessibility is a requirement for any organization that receives any kind of federal funds, public and research colleges, and universities, for example. It is good practice for all businesses. Your school probably has a page on its site about accessibility, and reviewing it will help you understand accessibility issues.

Figures 15.9a and b show two highly recommended steps in developing the navigational structure of a website. The first is to develop a simple graphical flow chart that shows the structure of the site. It shows the home page or parent page, second-level pages (also called "child pages") which are the entry points to major content areas of the site, and the succeeding levels that provide more detailed types of content. Notice that the persona storyboard in Figure 15.7b shows this kind of structure in an informal way. There may be more levels than shown here, but going beyond three or four levels creates a complex site that may be difficult for visitors to navigate. Even though the graphical hierarchy appears deceptively simple, it ensures that the connections are logical and it gives an overview of the navigational task that will face visitors. It is a step that must not be overlooked.

FIGURE 15.9
(a) Sample Plan of Website Hierarchy
(b) A Wireframing Tool in Action

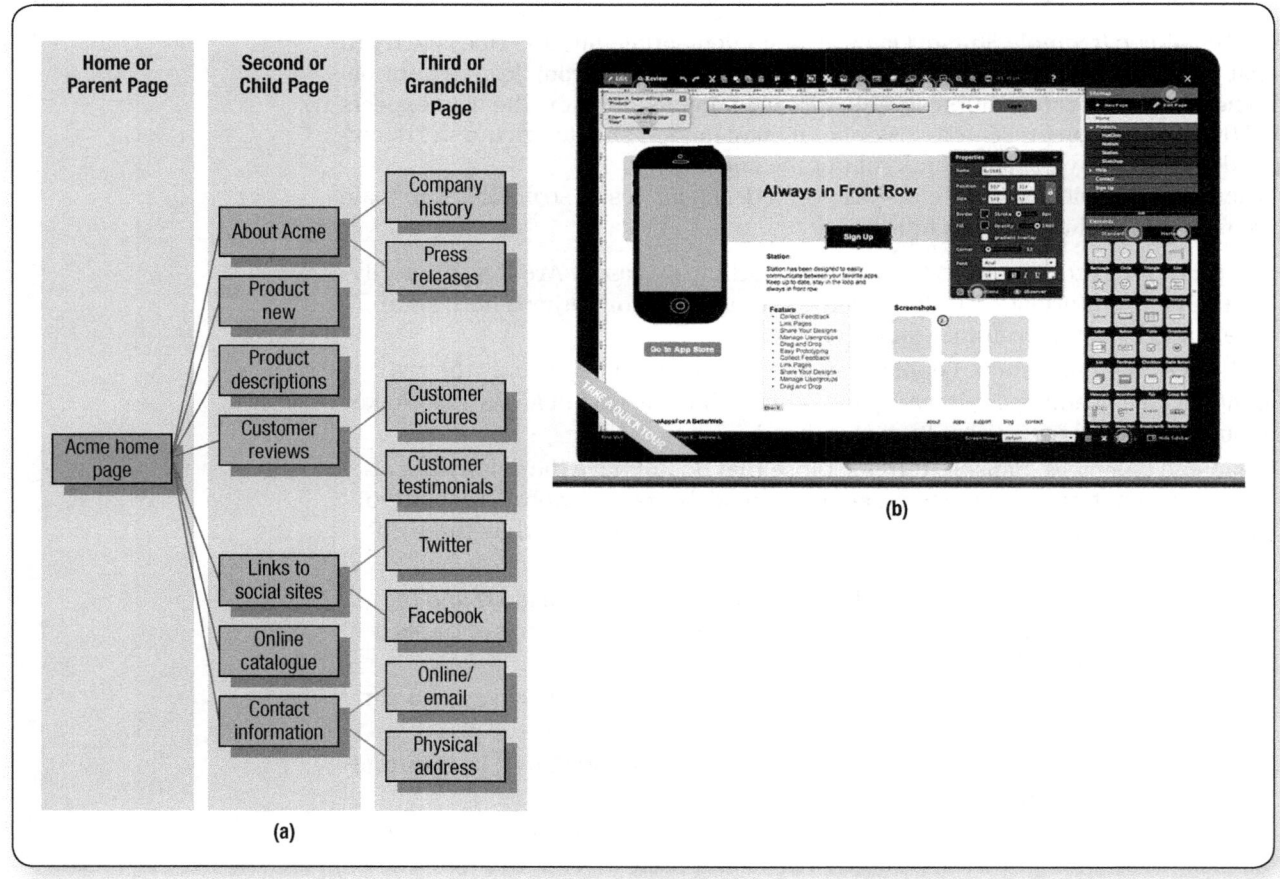

SOURCES: (a) © Cengage Learning 2013, (b) http://www.hotgloo.com/

The next step is to develop mockups of pages. A detailed mockup called a **wireframe** is shown in Figure 15.9b. A wireframe shows the type, placement, and size of each piece of content on each type of page. It also provides notes to guide the technical part of the development process. Wireframes can be developed informally, perhaps on a white board, but there are tools available to make the process faster and easier. The tool shown is from HotGloo and it works for both websites and mobile sites.

wireframe a blueprint that specifies the layout of pages on a website.

There are at least two rules that need to be followed in designing a navigation structure for any website. The first is to ensure that all key information appears on every page. Be sure that the visitor always knows where he or she is within the site. It is desirable to provide a link to the home page on every page within the site so visitors can simply start over if the path becomes a bit torturous or if they realize they are on the wrong path. This can be done by using the corporate logo as a link which fulfills two functions—branding information and the return to home page link. If that is done, the same rule holds true as it does when any icon is made into a link. Be sure that the visitor can easily identify it as a link, either by text below it or by using an **alt tag** that provides further detail about an image. The alt tag also serves an important function for visitors whose browsers are slow, cannot display graphics, or are using a screen reader for accessibility.

alt tag a tag (a type of IMG or image tag) that describes the image for people who cannot see it because of browser limitations or physical disabilities.

The second rule is that navigational structures must be simple and intuitive. That is, they should be clear and obvious to the visitor. The visitor should be able to navigate the site without instructions by following familiar web conventions (like the corporate logo as a link to the home page) or simple logic. Another way of expressing it is to say that the navigation structure should be designed with the visitor in mind, not necessarily according to the way managers and marketers are used to thinking about their corporate information. The navigational structure is commonly expressed by some combination of nav bars at the top of the page, a navigation menu in the left column of the page, mouseover menus, and text links at the bottom of the page.

Another navigational aid is **breadcrumbs**, a bar at the top of each page showing the path that the visitor has followed to reach this location in the site. Breadcrumbs look as follows:

breadcrumbs navigational aid showing path that the user has followed.

Home > About Acme Corp > Press Releases

This is a simple and useful device for letting visitors know where they are at all times.

If all else fails, the visitor should be able to do two things. The first is to refer to a site map, one of the text links that should be on the footer at the bottom of every page. The site map performs another important function, making it easier for search engines to index the site. The second thing is that there should be one or more links to the home page on every page in the site. It should be recognized, however, that having to resort to the site map or return to the home page is a failure in terms of customer-friendly websites.

Interactive Exercise 15.2 encourages you to put these steps into practice by creating a website using a commercial template. Alternatively, it offers the option of creating an infographic. The assumption is that you are going to use the site or infographic to support your career aspirations, but one could be used to further a hobby or for many other useful purposes.

Deploying and Tuning the Website

This stage is essentially a technical one. The site itself should be fine tuned, compressing images to make them load faster, checking links, and in general making sure that the site works as quickly and smoothly as possible. It is then ready to be uploaded to a host server (a computer that manages requests from browsers and returns HTML pages from the website in response to those requests) on the internet. Uploading requires working closely with the ISP or hosting service to ensure that the site meets all its technical requirements. The host will deal with technical issues like load balancing and distributing content for faster access, but the web master must continually monitor site performance.

Measuring, Evaluating, and Improving Website Effectiveness

Technical monitoring will be conducted by the IT department. Marketing is responsible for measuring and evaluating *the business effectiveness* of the site, a topic discussed in detail in Chapter 18. The evaluation metrics will provide information that points to areas in which it is possible to refine and improve site effectiveness. Possible improvements that surface as a result of site evaluation range from infrequently accessed pages to abandoned shopping carts to navigation paths that indicate difficulty in locating content. Continuous improvement should be the motto for websites. If improvements can be made without radically revising the site, they should be implemented immediately. When the burden of proof generated by the evaluation metrics and various kinds of user satisfaction measures warrants it, a full-scale redesign and relaunch of the website should be undertaken.

Looking back over this process, it should be abundantly clear that the initial steps in website development rely heavily on marketing for structure and guidance while technical design, function, and usability concerns tend to predominate in later stages. One of the worst mistakes internet marketers can make is to simply turn the process over to the technical experts and say "design us a website." The result is almost certain to be a website loaded with technical bells and whistles but without a marketing objective in sight. Yet, this is what sometimes happens in companies of all types and sizes.

The entire website development process, then, should focus on the marketing objectives of the site and the usability and user satisfaction required for the accomplishment of the objectives. The process should be seen as an iterative one, with usability tests at various stages signaling either need for more work or readiness to proceed to the next stage.

In addition to being an integral part of website development, usability testing should be done throughout the life of the site on a regular basis to uncover possible problems and to understand opportunities that are suggested by changes in customer behavior. It should also be done when there is a sign of **usability** problems—a sudden uptick in the number of people abandoning shopping carts at the payment information page, or people leaving the site because it is taking a long time to load, for example. Usability testing is an important tool of the internet marketer, and so we turn to it in the next section.

usability the ability of a site to provide a satisfactory user experience.

USABILITY TESTING

First, it is important to be clear about what usability testing is and is not. It is not conventional marketing research, although it may incorporate focus group research techniques into the testing process. It is, in fact, more similar to the testing done by direct marketers or in advertising laboratories than to the marketing research survey approach typically used by mass media marketers.[16] In addition, usability testing should not be confused with the testing of communications appeals, which should be part of the enterprise's overall marketing communications program not of the website development process itself.

Usability testing is exclusively designed to see if the site works in a user-friendly fashion according to the expectations of members of the target market. Site performance (quality assurance is another frequently used term) is a different issue that needs different metrics, which will be discussed in Chapter 18. Usability tests are essentially qualitative, and *they are performed by marketers interacting with target site users, not by technicians.*

There are many marketing services and agencies with expertise in usability testing, but the undisputed guru of web usability is Dr. Jakob Nielsen. Now a consultant, he was with the original Bell Labs and IBM before moving to Sun Microsystems where he was lead usability engineer for the establishment of the first Sun website in 1994. He has been a consultant for many years, doing research on many aspects of usability and being a tireless advocate for the importance of good UX on sites. He advocates testing early and often.

Stages of Usability Testing

Usability testing can be divided into general categories as follows:

- *Concept testing* is the earliest stage and reflects none of the actual site programming. In testing at this stage, one or more concept boards are shown to respondents who critique it from the perspective of how logical they perceive it to be and how easy they think it would be to use. Concept tests are useful at a very high level to prevent egregious design flaws and to give general guidance to the designers about what customers and prospects expect and what they think about the design concepts presented to them. This type of testing can be done relatively quickly in a focus group setting. Since it requires only the development of concept boards, it is also relatively cheap. Remember that the concept boards are testing the design of major pages on the site and the degree to which these pages communicate the desired corporate image and specific communications objectives, not the communications appeals themselves.
- *Prototype testing* is the second level. At this point in the development process, the site design is complete and at least some parts of the site are functional. Testing a prototype affords an opportunity to get reactions to the appearance of the site and to get some information about the degree to which the site structure is consistent with customer expectations. The earlier prototype testing is conducted, the more visual appearance and structure can be changed without increasing the development time and cost of the site. Early testing, however, implies that much functionality is probably not operating and that the test will be somewhat artificial. The marketer must carefully assess the trade-off between early and more complete testing.
- *Full usability testing* indicates that the site has been uploaded to a server and is fully functioning, even though it is not accessible to the general public. Dr. Nielsen has a page on his site that shows a testing setup in detail and Interactive Exercise 15.3 asks you to examine that page.

The main focus of a usability test is to ask test subjects to perform tasks that simulate what a visitor would want and expect to do on the site. In a more recent research project, Dr. Nielsen and his colleagues tested 20 ecommerce sites, and he explained the various types of tasks required in the test. First, test subjects were asked to simply explore the site for a few minutes to see what they believed the purpose of the site was. The second task was to ask them to locate a specific product on the site. For example, on one home-products site, they were asked to locate the cheapest toaster. For the third task, element test subjects were given a more open-ended task. An example was, "Pretend that you have just moved from Florida to a cold climate and that you don't own any winter clothes. Please buy what you will need to be able to go for a walk in freezing temperatures." The fourth task was for the users to answer specific questions about customer service on the site, such as whether the customer could cancel an order after placing it.

In this research project each website received attention for 35–40 minutes.[17] This is considerably less than one hour or more usually spent when a single site is being tested. Dr. Nielsen notes that after two hours, both the test subjects and the facilitators are sufficiently tired that further useful results are unlikely, no matter how many or how few sites are being tested.

Usability Testing and the Pareto Curve

Usability testing should not be considered an option or a luxury. Even the best-designed websites invariably have problems that are quickly detected by users. Even the so-called cosmetic problems will produce an inferior user experience.

The need for testing is often questioned on the grounds of both time and expense. Dr. Nielsen makes a strong case for the affordability of user testing by constructing a **Pareto curve** which shows that over 75 percent of a site's usability problems can be identified with *five user tests and that 100 percent will be found by testing 15 users*.[18] He also states that, with experience, the tests can be completed in two workdays at a cost of less than $1,000 if user recruiting has been outsourced to a commercial marketing research firm.[19] The message should be that eliminating or skimping on usability testing is a false economy. It should be a standard part of the launch of any new website, whether it is completely new or a redesign.

pareto curve a plot of number of occurrences against percent of total; the source of the 80/20 rule.

One important decision the marketer will have to make is, at which stage in the development process the usability testing should be done. The earlier it is done, the easier it will be to make fundamental changes. At the same time, the lack of prototype functionality in early-stage testing makes it somewhat artificial. On the other hand, if the functionality is nearing completion, considerable time and money have been invested in the site and it will be harder to make major changes. The issues involved in testing a prototype versus a fully functioning site suggest that several small-scale tests at various mileposts along the way will be more productive than any single larger-scale test. Once the site is launched, usability testing is one of the essential tools for monitoring its ongoing progress and for identifying areas for improvement.

Special Usability Requirements for B2B Sites

All of the requirements for good UX on B2C sites apply to B2B sites as well. However, it is important to remember that the customer journey for B2B may be longer and involves multiple parties to the buying process. That requires some additional considerations to provide good UX for B2B sites. Dr. Nielsen says, "When testing B2B sites, we often hear business customers lament the usability gap between B2B sites and the better-designed consumer sites they use after hours."[20]

Differences in the B2B customer journey and decision-making process should be accommodated by:

- Content that supports long purchase decision processes. The content should focus on solving the problems of business customers, tell why your product solves problems better than competitors' products, and provide tools to share content with buying team members. Customer success stories are helpful as are various kinds of content including white papers, blogs, and videos.
- Clear information about product integration and compatibility and about regulatory issues. Business purchasers have to know how products will fit into their existing systems and processes and process that they meet the relevant regulatory standards. Images and animations of product use are helpful.
- Content that is relevant to both "Choosers" and "Users." This is another purchasing team issue with one person (the chooser) making the final decision and many users having input into the buying. Users are focused on how products will solve their problems and make their work easier and more productive. Choosers tend to be focused on ROI details such as price, operating costs, and lifespan. They also tend to be the most concerned about regulatory issues.

- Realistic pricing scenarios. B2B pricing can be complex and it must be explained clearly. Careful design, including imagery, is an aid to understanding.
- Design that speaks to different target customer segments without confusing or alienating any of them. Dr. Nielsen explains that the typical B2B approach is to design around audience segments like Small Business and Enterprise Accounts. On the surface, this is being customer oriented.[21] He explains the problem it can present as follows:

> *audience-based navigation can cause a myriad of problems if these segments aren't clearly labeled (or if there is any overlap between them). For example, a huge enterprise customer might still have a small team with a specialized (and localized) need closely matches that of small-business customer. Whenever using visitor segments in navigation, ensure that they are clearly defined (i.e., define the number of employees for a small business versus a large business), and that they are mutually exclusive.*[22]

One way to deal with the issue of multiple target segments with different needs and purchasing behavior is the use of filters. This isn't technology, just good design as shown in Figure 15.10. American Express has credit cards specifically designed for consumers (either traditional or prepaid), small businesses, and corporations. That is clearly shown on its home page. The cards tab has a pull-down menu that gives more detail for each. The first screen of the menu shows two cards for each segment, presumably the most popular two. Then it has a "see all" link that shows a total of 11 cards in the Small Business segment, each of which is a link to detailed features of the card. That's clear, well structured, and makes it hard for the visitor to lose her way. However, when Prof. Roberts was looking at the Prepaid Cards page,[23] she found no link to get her back to the home page. Even the best sites have usability problems.

An example of a B2B site that follows many of Dr. Nielsen's principles is Zendesk (Figure 15.11). This marketing automation company was founded in Denmark and

FIGURE 15.10

The American Express Home Page with Distinctions between Card Segments

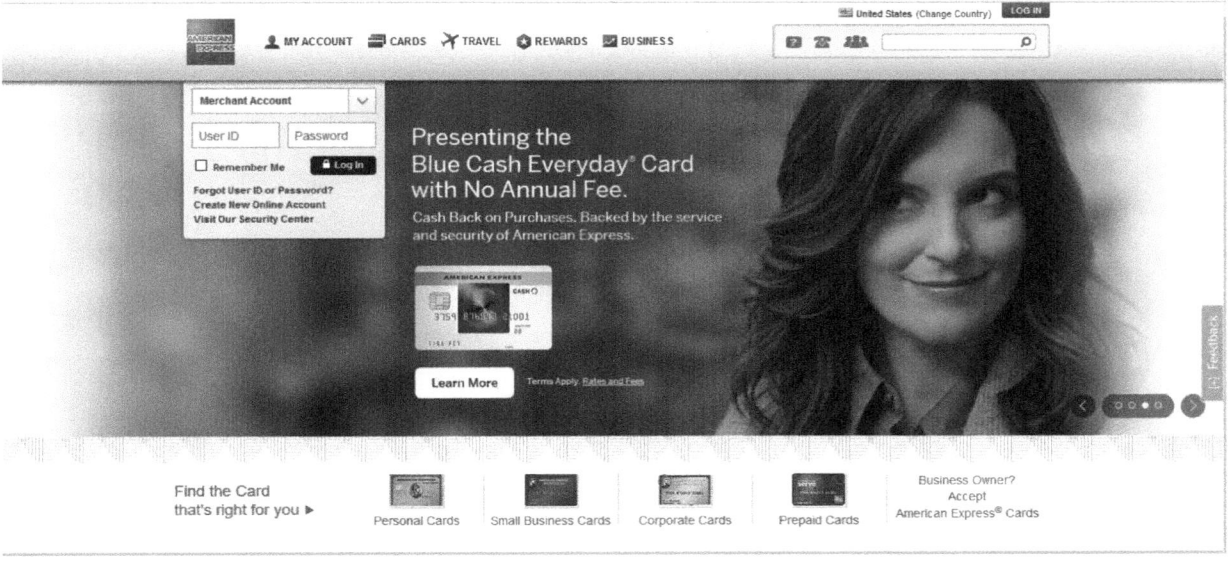

SOURCE: https://www.americanexpress.com/

FIGURE 15.11
To Come

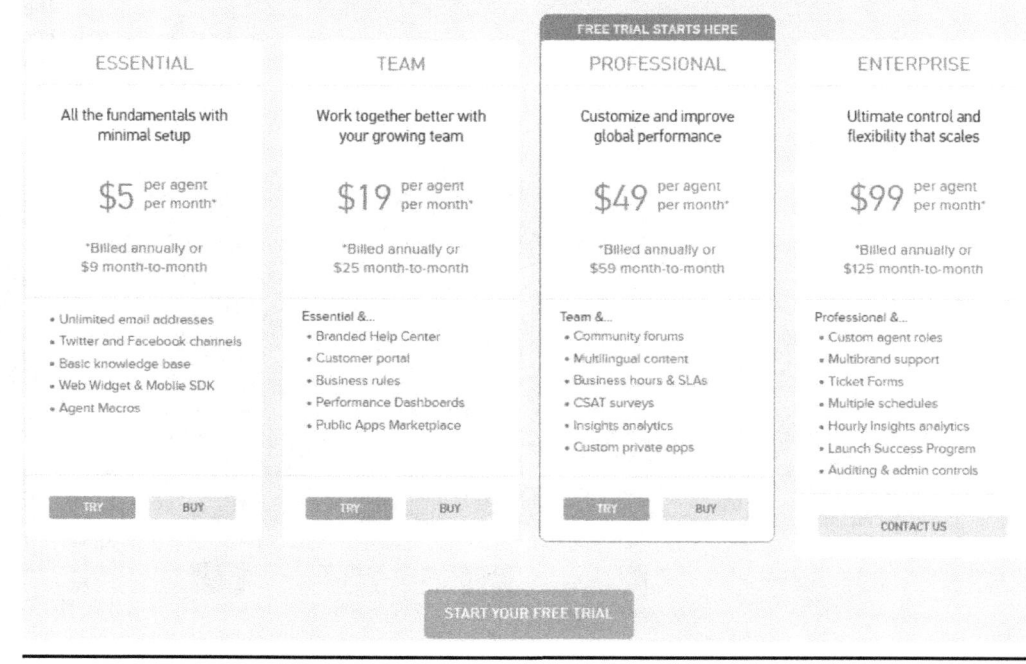

that may or may not have some bearing on the clean, crisp design and the whimsy the visitor finds on several pages. The site design and content illustrate many of Dr. Nielsen's recommendations:

- Content is well organized with the main pages shown on the top screen of the home page, which is charmingly animated. There is a lot of information about products, free trial, demos, and so forth as you scroll down to the gold screen where the two spacemen are enjoying a cup of coffee. Dr. Nielsen might object to the amount of scrolling required, but there is not much to read and it goes fast.
- The products pages use a lot of imagery and some engaging animation to lead people on through to the detail pages. There is not the clear way to share with team members that Dr. Nielsen recommends. There is, however, plenty of detail for all and the cost/ROI detail for the "Choosers" appears for each product or solution.
- There are customer success quotes on the product pages and many customer success stories in the Resources section.
- There is a brief animated demo that covers relevant issues. On the demo home screen a young office worker is typing away, looking up occasionally to smile at the viewer.

There seems little to fault in this site and the overall site design and execution is outstanding. B2B sites do not have to be dull and boring! However, all sites, both B2C and B2B must be mobile friendly.

DESIGNING SITES FOR MOBILE USE

We have probably all clicked through to a site on our smartphone or tablet only to find it unreadable—or at least not worth the effort. That is unacceptable today as more and more visitor traffic moves to mobile. Mobile-friendly sites are also important because they are essential for a high ranking in search results. Interactive Exercise 15.3 contains a Google tool for assessing whether a website is mobile friendly. Remember that not being mobile friendly is not a viable option today.

Figures 15.12 suggest that, from a business perspective, the move to mobile is ongoing but uneven. When it comes to types of user activities (Figure 15.12a) the picture is vastly different for different sectors. About half of all shopping activity occurs on a mobile device, half of all visits to finance sites are from the desktop, and well over half of all activity on media sites is either from an app or mobile browsing.

The finance share is especially interesting and one is tempted to attribute it to a concern with security of financial transactions. Not so, says a 2016 Bain study. Customers like digital transactions, partly because they are cheaper. But, beyond cost alone, digital transactions win out in customer satisfaction, measured by the Net Promoter Score (NPS) in both everyday transactions and sales transactions (Figure 15.12b). Human service providers win over digital, but only by a small margin.

So if digital transactions are cheaper for both financial services institutions and their customers and if customers seem to actually prefer them, what should the institutions do? Bain recommends that they simplify the customer journey, whether for everyday or complex transactions. For complex transactions that may mean a combination of digital and traditional delivery channels. But most of all it means removing steps to simplify the journey. In financial services that could mean anything from seeing balances without login to providing easy-to-use financial tools.

FIGURE 15.12a

Desktop versus Mobile versus Apps

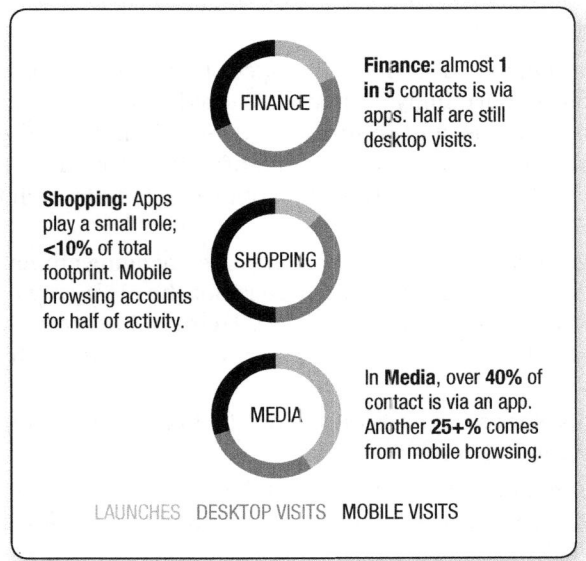

SOURCE: https://www.cmo.com/content/dam/CMO_Other/ADI/2015_Mobile_Benchmark/ADI_mobile_benchmark_report_2015.pdf

FIGURE 15.12b

Digital Satisfaction in Financial Services Transactions

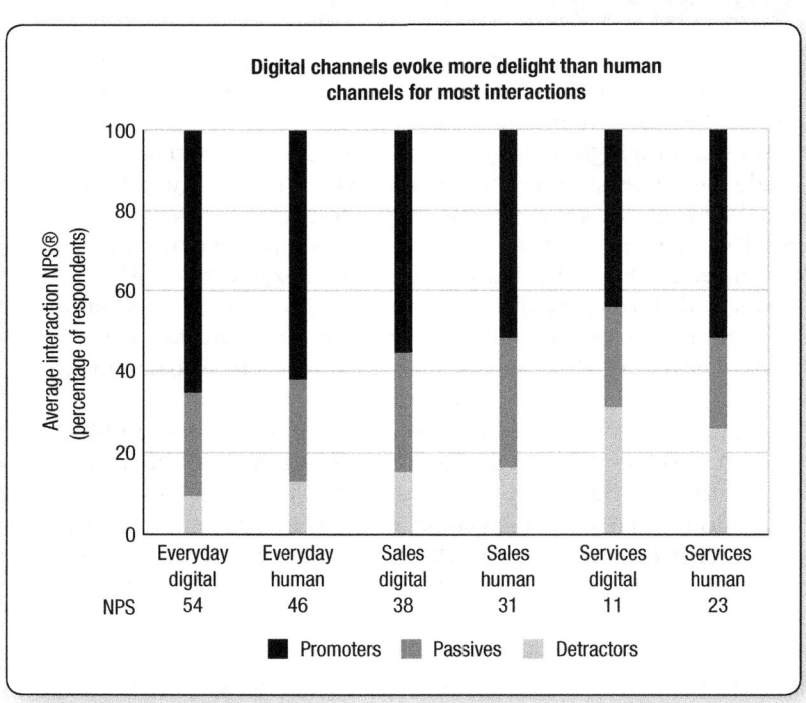

SOURCE: http://thefinancialbrand.com/59471/mobile-banking-easy-experience/

The same principles apply to any economic activity. Customers want easy-to-use digital experiences with mobile often at the forefront. The technology innovators have already transitioned; marketers must focus on making mobile technology work for technology laggards.

FIGURE 15.12c

Apps versus Mobile Sites

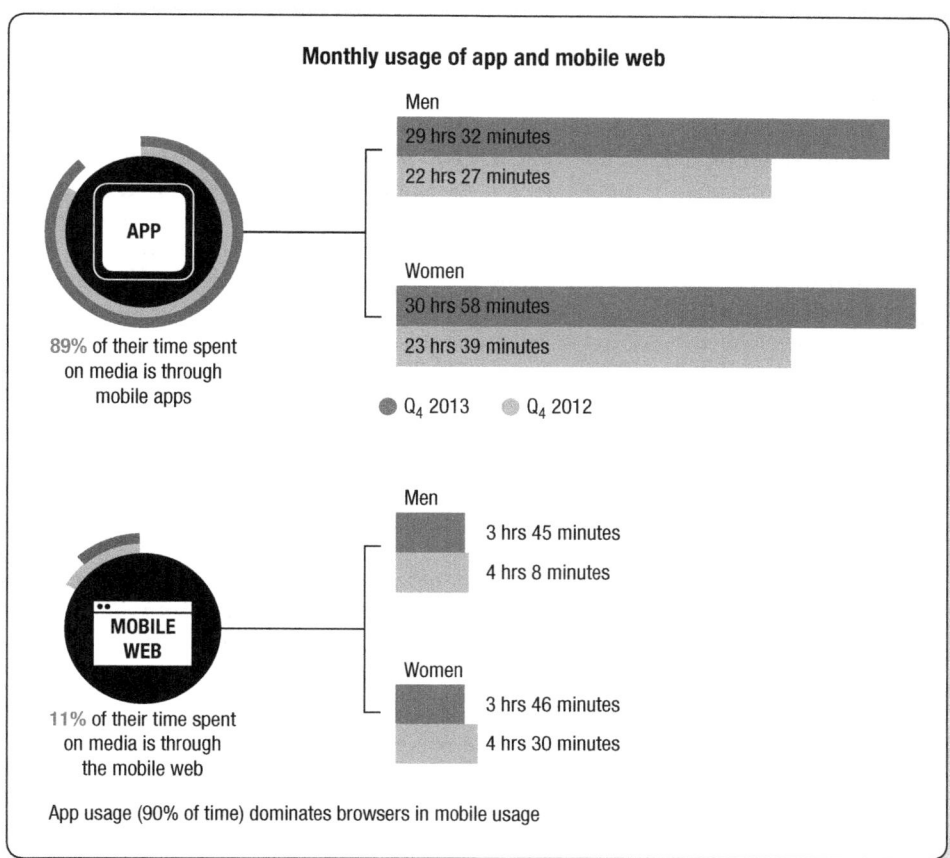

SOURCE: http://www.smartinsights.com/mobile-marketing/mobile-marketing-analytics/mobile-marketing-statistics/

Figure 15.12c emphasizes the primacy of apps over the mobile web. The data from Nielsen shows that 89 percent of mobile users' time is spent on apps leaving only 11 percent for the mobile web. Other data referenced is from Yahoo, which puts the figure at 90 percent. The point is clear; apps are the winner, hands down. However, it is important to remember that app users are spending time on social platforms and checking their email and current news. Purchasing from inside their apps is still not a major activity.

In designing sites for mobile customer satisfaction there's a piece of good news. All the basic concepts of designing good sites for the desktop apply in principle. However, that does not mean that it is easy to make a desktop site work on any mobile device—and that is the criterion—on *any* mobile device. The issue leads to two questions of process and one of strategy:

1. Should we have a mobile site that is separate from our website or should we use responsive or adaptive design?
2. Should we use the mobile-first approach to design?
3. Should we have a mobile website or an app?

There are a number of considerations when deciding on which route to follow. We have discussed apps and what makes them work in various contexts, most recently in Chapter 14. Stand-alone sites, responsive versus adaptive design and mobile-first design are issues unique to website design, however.

Stand-Alone versus Responsive versus Adaptive Site Design

a responsive site fluid site design that senses the user's device and automatically adapts to it.

adaptive site a type of site design in which a different site is created for each user device.

dynamic serving the ability to serve different site HTML without changing the URL. The term "adaptive site" is synonymous.

There are three basic ways for a business or an individual to be the proud possessor of a mobile website—a stand-alone site, **a responsive site**, or an **adaptive site** (also referred to as **dynamic serving**). A stand-alone site, identified by a separate URL such as m.yourbrand.com, is completely separate from the internet website. It was a popular early solution to the need for a mobile website. However, visitors must be redirected from the internet to the mobile site and redirects are typically time consuming and interfere with seamless CX. In addition, a stand-alone site requires extensive maintenance. For both reasons the popularity of the stand-alone site has plunged in recent years. From 2013 to 2014 the so-called mdot sites decreased from 79 to 59 percent of mobile sites used by retailers and they were expected to lose another 45–50 percent of their market share in 2015.[24] They are being replaced by either responsive or adaptive mobile sites.

Either responsive or adaptive sites sense the device on which the user is accessing the site and respond automatically, providing more seamless user experience. The technological differences in creating one or the other are complex; instead, here are two user-friendly definitions:

> ***Responsive web design*** *is comprised of a single design with a fluid layout that adjusts to screen width of the device, meaning that only one set of page templates need to be created and maintained.*
>
> ***Adaptive web design*** *uses a completely different set of designs and templates for each device being targeted. As a result, designers will create a desktop version of a website and will then design a separate mobile version (and possibly a separate tablet version also).*[25]

Think back to Interactive Exercise 15.2. In that exercise two easy-to-use website creation platforms were recommended. One was Weebly, all of whose website themes are responsive. The other was Wix, which uses a different kind of technology to make sites look good on all devices, one that IT experts do not consider to be truly responsive.[26] Whichever platform you choose for your personal website, and there are many, you need to ensure that your site does render properly on both smartphones and tablets. What if a recruiter is doing his research on a mobile device while he is in a train on the way home? Unless you are a programmer, you will probably not want to build an adaptive website. Do you want to have to build separate sites—one for the internet, one for smartphones, and one for tablets? That sounds like a lot more work. Figure 15.13 gives a technical comparison of responsive versus adaptive, providing a good list of major issues that have to be addressed by the programmer and monitored by the marketer. Surprisingly enough, from a programming standpoint adaptive is said to be easier than responsive to program,[27] although adaptive requires more ongoing maintenance.[28] For individuals using commercial templates, however, there is only one option, but the user needs to be careful to choose a responsive template.

Figure 15.13 provides a comparison between responsive and adaptive sites on several major elements of mobile-friendly site design. The technological issues are beyond our scope, but the comparison gives marketers a sense of the issues that need to be dealt with.

That still does not answer the question for a brand that has sufficient resources to make a choice. Put another way, most small businesses will use a platform with templates which will usually accommodate their relatively simple needs and perhaps their DIY requirement. For larger businesses, however, there are several pros and cons for each type of site.

Responsive sites:

- Are consistent with Google's and Bing's requirements for mobile-friendly sites.
- Take more work to program and less work to maintain.
- Are guaranteed to work on new screen sizes as they are introduced.
- Are usually slower to load.

Adaptive sites:

- Are especially desirable when dealing with making an existing site mobile friendly.
- May be desirable for new businesses because development cost is lower.
- Are more flexible.
- Are usually faster to load.
- May require substantial work to adapt to new screen sizes.
- Allow the possibility of a different user experience for each device.[29,30,31,32]

All the experts agree on one choice criterion: what works best for your users. We will discuss how to determine what types of devices are being used to access your site in Chapter 18.

If you have a blog, you want it to be mobile friendly. Platforms offer responsive blog templates and being careful to choose one is important. If you have an existing blog, the question is a bit more tricky. Your blog platform may have automatically migrated you to a responsive template or it may offer options for you to do so.

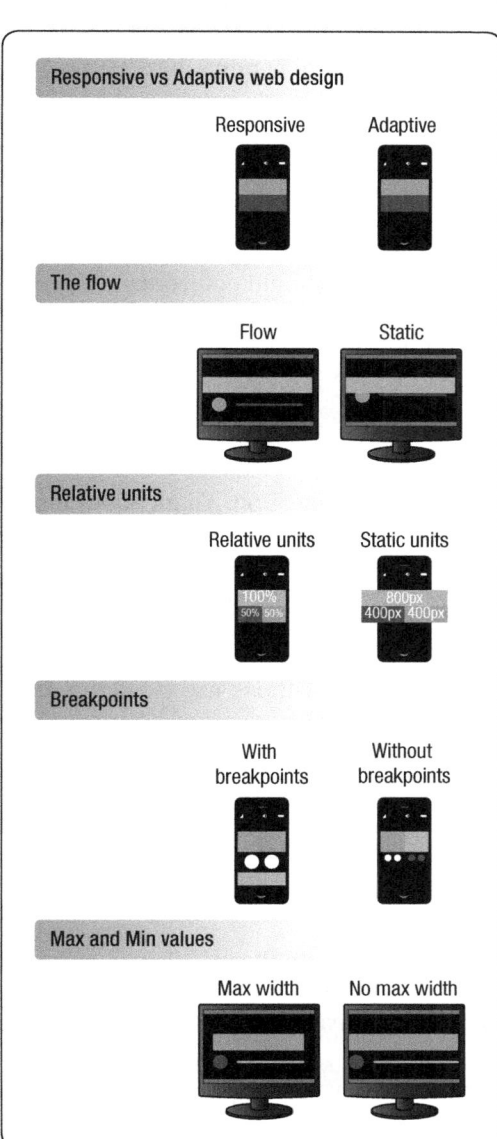
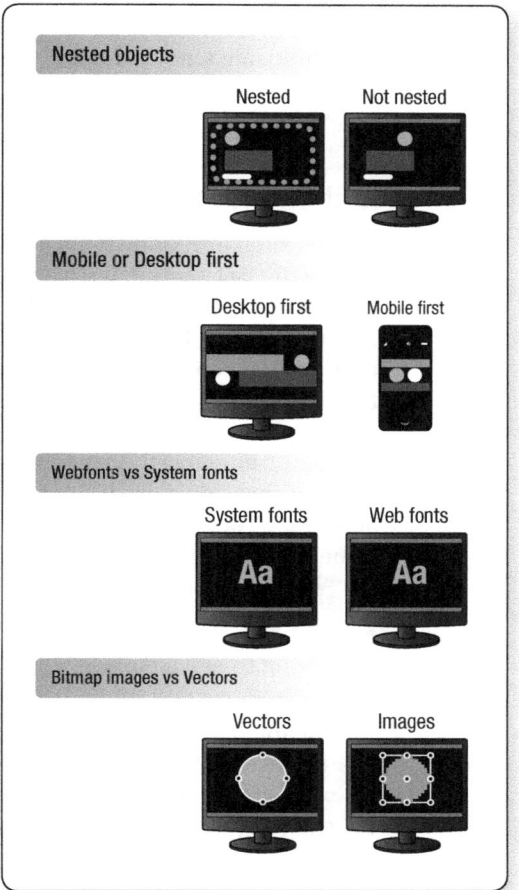

FIGURE 15.13

Comparison of Responsive versus Adaptive Mobile Website Design

SOURCE: http://blog.froont.com/9-basic-principles-of-responsive-web-design/

Both responsive and adaptive approaches assume an existing internet site and the need to retrofit it for successful mobile use. There is, however, another approach loosely called mobile first.

Designing for Mobile First

When discussing website design, there is a clearly understood meaning for the term mobile first. Designers describe it as designing from the bottom up—designing for mobile usability—while a top-down approach takes an existing internet site and recodes it for small screens. One designer explains it this way: "The top-down method of design is to create a large screen display product and then add code after code for smaller screens. In the mix of this de-evolving process, most of the time, you are overloading the smaller devices with far too information causing the smaller devices to lag at excruciatingly low speeds." The bottom-up approach starts with the lowest-tech phone expected to use the site and prioritizes content and features for that. Starting with a minimalist site, it is easier to add features than to subtract and it is more likely that mobile-specific functions like GPS and voice integration will be included.[33]

Another designer calls the approaches "graceful degradation" versus "progressive enhancement" and the terms chosen are indicative of sentiment. When the smallest site, the mobile site, is designed first, the core of the UX is revealed. Features can be added, but they are being added with the core experience in mind. If the approach is to strip features away from an existing structure, it is very easy to lose sight of what the core experience should be.[34]

Mobile first does not presume any specific outcome. What it does is to recognize that mobile is increasingly the platform of choice for access to the internet and make the experience of the mobile user primary. Could the outcome be just as successful using a responsive or an adaptive approach? Certainly it could be. Is it likely to be? That is the question marketers and their IT colleagues should confront.

Choosing among the three approaches to website design still leaves unanswered the strategic question of whether a brand should opt for a mobile app or a mobile website.

Mobile-Friendly Sites versus Apps

Mobile sites or mobile apps are really not an either-or question. Think about the fact that in the last section we were talking about how to make sites mobile friendly—not whether to have a site or not.

With apps, it is a question of whether to have an app or not. The cost of developing an app can be substantial and getting people to download them requires additional marketing effort. Remember the discussion of branded apps in section 14.10a. Few high-traffic apps are branded apps, even fewer of those are retail apps. Add to that often-quoted data that says that an app loses 77 percent of its users within the first three days after download, 90 percent within 30 days, and 95 percent within 90 days.[35] The message seems clearly to be that if you decide to build an app, it has to be a good one.

What are the requirements for a good app? They include the following:

- The brand has a clear app strategy. Is it a customer retention app or are you trying to sell a game?
- It is helpful if the task cannot be performed as well on the mobile web as on an app. For instance, if a person wants to summon a cab while standing on an urban sidewalk, doing so from an app should be easier than locating the mobile website and summoning the cab from there.
- There are skilled app developers, internal or external, available within the resources the brand is willing to commit.
- The target audience is heavily mobile and becoming more so every day.[36,37]

Here are some situations in which a mobile app seems to be a clear choice:

- When interactivity is essential, as in a game.
- When personalization is necessary, as in a financial services app.
- When complex calculations or reporting are required, as in a mortgage calculator.
- When functionality is to be built into the application, as in click to call to order a pizza.
- When the functions need to be accessible without a wireless connection being available.[38]

Even in these situations a website or a mobile site will probably be necessary. An app is really not an either-or choice. It is a matter of whether it is worth the resources to build an app that people will use consistently. Of course, if your business has sufficient resources, you may have no hesitation in deciding to have both a mobile site and a mobile app.

DESIGNING FOR THE MOBILE WEB

The final question, then, is "what are the additional considerations that apply to designing sites for the mobile web beyond the ones that provide good UX on the internet?" Keep in mind that these are also the issues you want to consider when doing your own evaluation of how well a mobile site is functioning.

Google has a detailed white paper that discusses criteria for mobile site design. The criteria are based on usability tests they performed with 119 mobile users. They uncovered 25 criteria, which were divided into five major categories:

1. Homepage and site navigation
2. Site search
3. Commerce and conversions
4. Form entry
5. Usability and ensuring that the site renders properly for the device

If you think through that list, you can probably remember instances where each factor has hindered your ability to have a good experience on a mobile site. Each one needs to be carefully considered when a mobile site is being developed or fine tuned. Google says:

> *The common thread in all sections is that mobile users tend to be very goal-oriented - they expect to be able to get what they need from a mobile site easily, immediately, and on their own terms. Ensure success by designing with their context and needs in mind without sacrificing richness of content.*[39]

HubSpot continues with factors that need to be considered when optimizing a mobile site:

- A simple, probably Sans Serif font, at least 12 pixels in size
- Touch-friendly navigation and calls to action
- Keep code as minimalist as possible to speed site loading
- All images sized to the device; none unnecessarily large
- Make sure videos load properly
- Keep forms short[40]

There are more technical issues, but just as for an internet site it is important for the marketer to establish the appropriate requirements and ask the right questions, then let the web designers do their work.

SUMMARY

This chapter sets forth a marketing perspective on building and maintaining websites without understating the effort and expertise needed for successful technical design, programming, and implementation. Marketers are primarily responsible for the initial stages of website and mobile site development in which objectives are established, the target market is identified and described to all participants, and the information architecture and navigational structure of the site are laid out. Web personas are usually developed by marketers and are a good way to understand customers and how they might interact with the site.

Marketers are also responsible for working closely with technical professionals during actual site development and closely monitoring the site for UX and consistency with business and marketing objectives. To ensure UX usability testing is essential during site development and to uncover problems on a regular basis thereafter.

In today's world, the website may play many roles and be used by marketers for everything from getting sales leads to developing online communities. In addition, customers shop across multiple channels and increasingly rely on the web for product research as well as purchasing. Mobile sites and apps are playing an increasing role in the early purchase journey stages with purchasing increasing, but more slowly.

Having a mobile-friendly site is no longer an option. The choice is between stand-alone, responsive, and adaptive sites with responsive finding most favor at present. There is also the option of following the mobile-first design process. Marketers must also decide whether to have one or more branded apps. Both the internet site and the mobile site and apps must meet the needs of multichannel shoppers. Mobile sites must display properly on all devices or they do not meet the criteria for mobile friendly.

The same overall process and the same criteria for creating user satisfaction apply to both internet and mobile sites. There are additional criteria for satisfying experience on the mobile web or with mobile apps. Customers move back and forth between devices, so it is critical that all the criteria be met to create the seamlessly satisfying experience which is the marketer's goal.

DISCUSSION QUESTIONS

1. True or False: A website development team will be made up of IT specialists and marketers. Take a position on this statement and be prepared to defend your answer.
2. True or False: It is imperative that marketers play the leading role in all stages of the website development process. Take a position on this statement and be prepared to defend your answer.
3. What are the steps involved in developing a website? What should be the marketer's role in each step?
4. True or False: SMART goals are nice but not essential. Take a position on this statement and be prepared to defend your answer.
5. Discuss the role of personas in creating a website and consider whether one persona or multiple personas are generally required.
6. Website accessibility is important to all websites and necessary for some.
7. This chapter makes references to both testing and conventional marketing research. What testing and research techniques are appropriate in the website development process and what is the role of each?
8. It is necessary to have a large, random sample in order to conduct a usability test.
9. True or False: Marketers must develop their own criteria to determine whether a site is mobile friendly or not.
10. What are key reasons why it is important to have a mobile-friendly site?

11. Why do you think stand-alone mobile sites are losing favor?
12. Responsive and adaptive mobile sites use different technical approaches to arrive at the same end result. Discuss.
13. What is your opinion on the desirability of mobile-first site design?
14. What are some of the reasons to develop a mobile app versus a responsive website?
15. True or False: All businesses must have a mobile app.

ENDNOTES

1. "5 Ways to Increase Site Stickiness with Web Design," http://www.purelybranded.com/insights/5-ways-to-increase-stickiness-with-web-design/.
2. Lori Wizdo, "Buyer Behavior Helps B2B Marketers Guide the Buyer's Journey," http://blogs.forrester.com/lori_wizdo/12-10-04-buyer_behavior_helps_b2b_marketers_guide_the_buyers_journey.
3. Heidi Cohen, "How the 2015 B2B Purchase Decision Process Has Changed," http://heidicohen.com/2015-b2b-purchase-decision-process/.
4. Nicole Kohler, "The Most Important Features of an eCommerce Sites' Design," https://woocommerce.com/2015/07/ecommerce-design-features/.
5. Ann Davlin, "10 Essential Things Your E-Commerce Site Should Have," http://www.hongkiat.com/blog/essential-things-ecommerce-site-should-have/.
6. "What Customers Want in an eCommerce Site," https://blog.kissmetrics.com/what-ecommerce-customers-want/.
7. "The Site Development Team," http://webstyleguide.com/wsg3/1-process/2-development-team.html.
8. "Building a Good Web Development Team," http://www.marketingfind.com/articles/building_a_good_web_development_team.html.
9. Andrew Kucheriavy, "Best Examples of Website Goals and Objectives," https://www.intechnic.com/blog/best-examples-of-website-goals-and-objectives/.
10. Brian Solis with Jaimy Szymanski, "Six Stages of Digital Transformation," http://www.altimetergroup.com/pdf/reports/Six-Stages-of-Digital-Transformation-Altimeter.pdf.
11. Andrew Kucheriavy, "Best Examples of Website Goals and Objectives," https://www.intechnic.com/blog/best-examples-of-website-goals-and-objectives/.
12. Steve Outing, "Eyetrack III: What News Websites Look Like Through Readers' Eyes," http://www.poynter.org/2004/eyetrack-iii-what-news-websites-look-like-through-readers-eyes/24963/.
13. Sara Dickenson Quinn, "New Poynter Research Reveals How People Read News on Tablets." http://www.poynter.org/2012/new-poynter-eyetrack-research-reveals-how-people-read-news-on-tablets/191875/.
14. https://www.crazyegg.com/.
15. Sofia Woods, "10 Top Principles of Effective Web Design," http://shortiedesigns.com/2014/03/10-top-principles-effective-web-design/.
16. See "Chapter 10, Testing Direct Marketing Programs," in Mary Lou Roberts and Paul D. Berger, *Direct Marketing Management*, 2nd ed. available for free download at www.marylouroberts.info for a detailed description of the direct marketing testing process.
17. Jakob Nielsen, Rolf Molich, Carolyn Snyder, and Susan Farrell, 2001, E-Commerce and Ussr Experience (Freemont, CA Norman Group), p. 337.
18. Jakob Nielsen, "Why You Only Need to Test with 5 Users," https://www.nngroup.com/articles/why-you-only-need-to-test-with-5-users/.
19. Jakob Nielsen, "When to Outsource the Recruiting of Test Users," https://www.nngroup.com/articles/when-to-outsource-recruiting-test-users/.
20. Page Laubheimer, "B2B us. B2C Websites: Key UX Differences," https://www.nngroup.com/articles/b2b-vs-b2c/.

21. Katie Sherwin, "Audience-Based Navigation: 5 Reasons to Avoid It," https://www.nngroup.com/articles/audience-based-navigation/.
22. Page Laubheimer, "B2B us. B2C Websites: Key UX Differences," https://www.nngroup.com/articles/b2b-vs-b2c/.
23. https://www.americanexpress.com/serve/?SOLID=4AMEX&intlink=us-amex-home-footer&inav=footer_cards_reload.
24. Caitlyn Bohannon, "Mdot Sites Expected to Lose 45-50% of Share in 2015: Report," http://www.mobilecommercedaily.com/mdot-sites-expected-to-fall-45-50pc-in-2015-report.
25. Adapted from Graham Charlton, "What is Adaptive Web Design (AWD) and When Should You Use It?" https://econsultancy.com/blog/64914-what-is-adaptive-web-design-awd-and-when-should-you-use-it/.
26. "Do Wix Websites Offer Responsive Design?" http://www.top10bestwebsitebuilders.com/how-to-create-a-website/mobile/responsive-design-on-wix-websites.
27. Matthew Harris, "Responsive or Adaptive Design – Which is Best for Mobile Viewing of Your Website?" http://mediumwell.com/responsive-adaptive-mobile/.
28. Jerry Cao, "Responsive vs. Adaptive Design: What's the Best Choice for Designers?" htt ps://studio.uxpin.com/blog/responsive-vs-adaptive-design-whats-best-choice-designers/.
29. Carrie Cousins, "Is Adaptive Better Than Responsive Design?" http://thenextweb.com/dd/2015/09/01/is-adaptive-better-than-responsive-design/#gref.
30. Matthew Harris, "Responsive or Adaptive Design—Which is Best for Mobile Viewing of Your Website?" http://mediumwell.com/responsive-adaptive-mobile/.
31. Jerry Cao, "Responsive vs. Adaptive Design: What's the Best Choice for Designers?" https://studio.uxpin.com/blog/responsive-vs-adaptive-design-whats-best-choice-designers/.
32. "Responsive Web Design vs Adaptive Web Design: What's the Difference and Should I Care?" http://www.intouchcrm.com/responsive-web-design-vs-adaptive-web-design-whats-difference-care/.
33. "Mobile First," http://zurb.com/word/mobile-first.
34. "A Hands-On Guide to Mobile-First Responsive Design," https://www.uxpin.com/studio/blog/a-hands-on-guide-to-mobile-first-design/.
35. "New Data Shows Losing 80% of Mobile Users is Normal and Why the Best Apps Do Better," http://andrewchen.co/new-data-shows-why-losing-80-of-your-mobile-users-is-normal-and-that-the-best-apps-do-much-better/.
36. Rank Fishkin, "Mobile Web vs Mobile Apps: Where Should You Invest Your Marketing?" https://moz.com/blog/mobile-web-mobile-apps-invest-marketing-whiteboard-friday.
37. Ken Lin, "The 4 Key Beliefs of Mobile-First Companies," http://www.inc.com/ken-lin/the-4-key-beliefs-of-mobile-first-companies.html.
38. Jason Summerfield, "Mobile Website vs. Mobile App: Which is Best for Your Organization?" https://www.hswsolutions.com/services/mobile-web-development/mobile-website-vs-apps/.
39. "Principles of Mobile Site Design: Delight Users and Drive Conversions," https://www.thinkwithgoogle.com/articles/principles-mobile-site-design-delight-users-drive-conversions.html.
40. "How To Make a Mobile-Friendly Website," http://offers.hubspot.com/mobile-friendly.

Chapter 16

Digital Customer Service and Support in the Digital Era

LEARNING OBJECTIVES

By the time you complete this chapter, you will be able to:

1. Explain the importance of customer service in B2C and B2B markets.
2. Identify the major goals of customer service in both B2C and B2B.
3. Describe important challenges in providing excellent customer service.
4. Discuss the channels customers want to use for service and support.
5. Explain the evolutionary stages of customer service provision.
6. Describe the various technologies and channels used to deliver customer service.
7. Explain the meaning and importance of omni-channel.
8. Understand the role of customer service in creating customer satisfaction, loyalty, and sustainable competitive advantage.

Everyone—marketers and customers alike—agree that excellent customer service is the key to customer retention, which in turn is the key to profitability (discussed in detail in Chapter 14). Unfortunately, seemingly everyone can report instances of poor customer service. Companies experience billions of dollars in lost sales each year as a result of poor customer service. This suggests that customer service is a business function that should not be overlooked.

THE IMPORTANCE OF CUSTOMER SERVICE AND SATISFACTION

There is ample evidence that customer service is important to customer satisfaction and retention. There is equally strong evidence that poor customer service hurts a business' bottom line. The research presented in Figure 16.1 indicates that businesses lose over 41 billion dollars in sales each year as a result of poor customer service. One 2015 estimate put the global value of a lost customer at $243, which pushes the cost of poor customer service to $83 billion in the United States alone.[1]

Accenture casts this as an opportunity in what they call a "switching economy." The reason is digital disruption that is causing a steady erosion of customer loyalty. This creates the "growing 'switching economy' that accounts for an estimated $6.2 trillion in revenue opportunity for providers across 17 key markets today—up 26 percent, from $4.9 trillion, in 2010."[2] For their 10th annual study of the state of

FIGURE 16.1
The Cost of Poor Customer Service

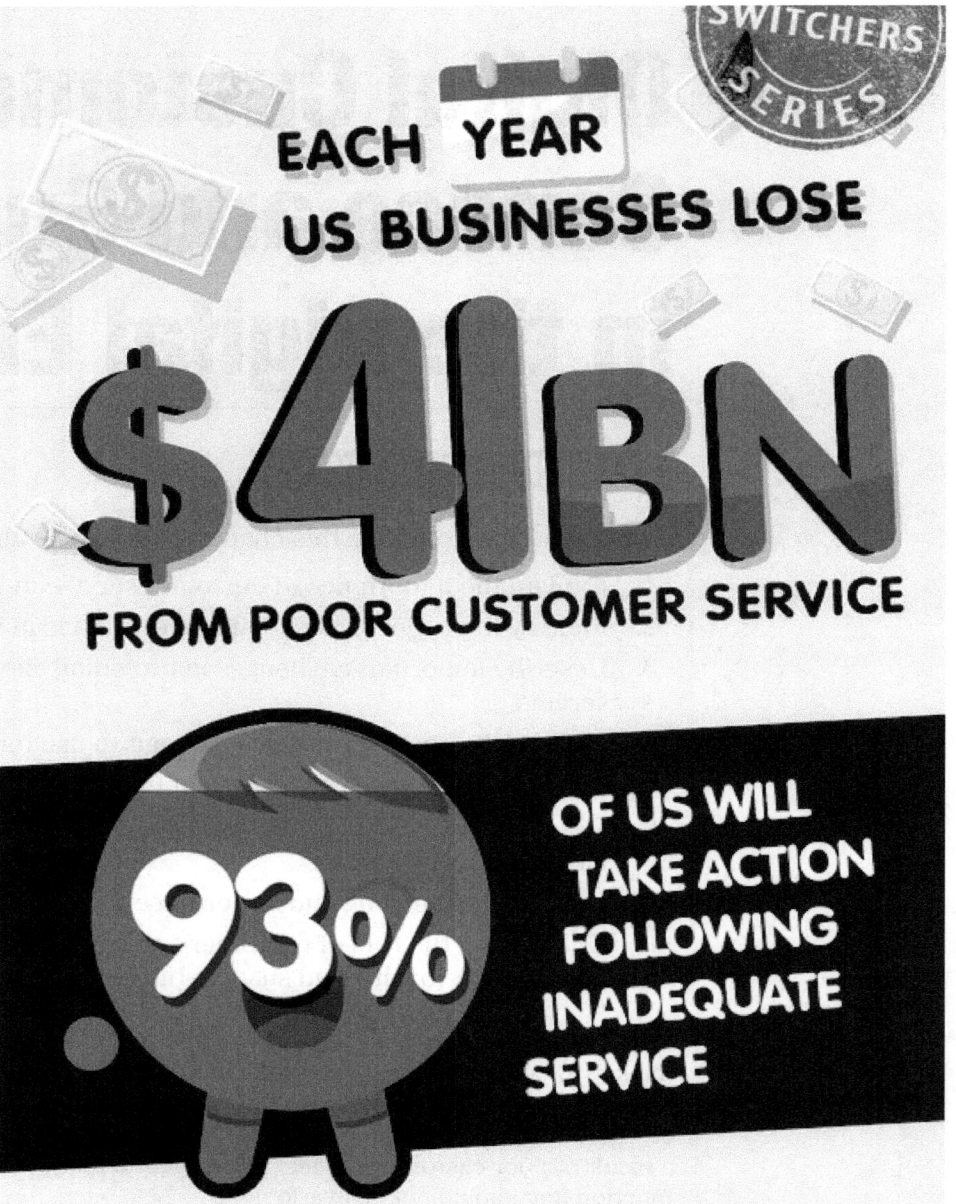

SOURCE: http://www.newvoicemedia.com/blog/the-multibillion-dollar-cost-of-poor-customer-service-infographic/.

customer service, they surveyed customer experiences in 17 different industries. Findings include the following:

- Fifty-three percent of US consumers switched providers due to poor service in at least one industry.
- However, 80 percent of poor service switching could be avoided through better resolution.
- Only 10 percent strongly agree companies effectively converge interactions across digital, social, mobile and traditional channels.
- Twenty-four percent want more digital interactions than currently offered by providers.
- Thirty-four percent would be open to offers from non-traditional players.[3]

Customers are changing with 56 percent saying they consider more brands than they did 10 years ago. Forty-six percent say that they are more likely to switch brands than they were 10 years ago. Companies are not keeping pace with their customers either in the speed of problem resolution or in the channels they offer.[4]

Burke Research used data based on industry studies to illustrate the cost of poor customer service. Its studies of the insurance industry indicate that as many as 40 percent of policyholders may experience a service problem or failure in a given year. Look at the results shown in Figure 16.2. As is typical in customer service and satisfaction studies, some of the customers (in this case, 20 percent) who experienced problems did not report them. Only 10 percent of those *unreported* will not repurchase; but keep in mind that the insurance provider has lost hundreds of opportunities to identify problems and, presumably, to correct them. Notice that if the customers were *satisfied*, they intended to

FIGURE 16.2

The Financial Impact of Customer Service Problems

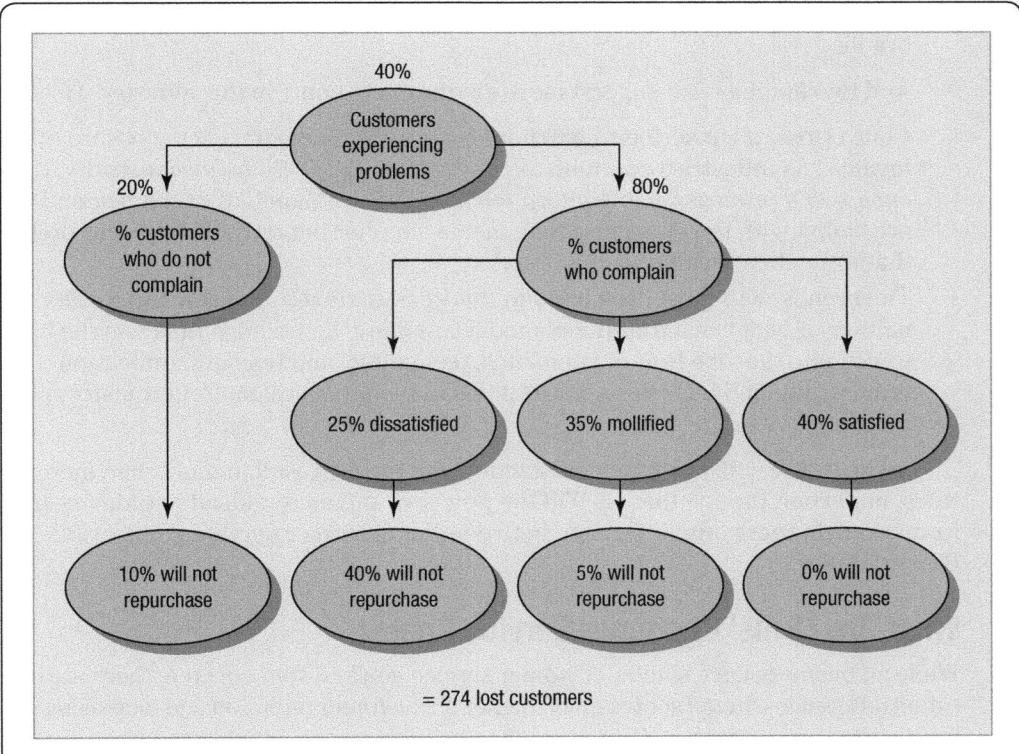

SOURCE: "Linking Measures of Customer Satisfaction, Value, and Loyalty to Financial Performance," White Paper Series, 5(3). p. 2. Copyright © 2004 Burke, Inc. Reprinted with permission.

repurchase. Of those who were *mollified* (only partially satisfied), only five percent will not repurchase, while 40 percent of those who were *dissatisfied* declared their intent not to repurchase. The result was 274 lost customers out of a total of 6,000. The study did not estimate the dollar value of the lost customers, but insurance customers represent a continuing stream of revenue, so you can imagine that their customer lifetime value (CLV) is high. This analysis also shows something else that is noteworthy about customer satisfaction: *it is not the fact that customers experience a problem that is critical to their defection; it is the fact that their problem is not satisfactorily resolved*. This places the onus for customer retention squarely on the customer service function.

THE IMPACT OF IMPROVED CUSTOMER SERVICE

Since 2010, American Express has conducted a customer service survey in global markets. The most recent in 2014 found that over two-thirds of U.S. consumers say they are willing to spend 14 percent more with brands that deliver excellent service. That number has increased every year since the study began.[5]

A 2015 survey by Xerox has interesting insights on the importance of customer service in communications, technology, and media markets. The survey covered 6,000 consumers in four generational cohorts with equal numbers of women and men in five different countries. Key consumer satisfaction findings from the media report include:

- Fifty-five percent of U.S. consumers are satisfied with their media providers.
- UK television network has the most satisfied customers at 66.7 percent followed by iTunes at 63 percent and Yahoo! at 55.9 percent.
- If customers are satisfied, the media brand is unlikely to hear from them. In this case, few interactions with the brand is a predictor of loyalty.
- Over half the respondents had recommended a media brand to friends or family.
- Only 3.1 percent of respondents were classified as influencers. They are brand advocates but would like fundamental changes in the way they interact with brands.

And two findings that suggest more disruption to come in this industry. They are:

- Churn (loss of subscribers) will not be the media industry's key measure of loyalty. "As industries continue to converge, *loyalty will be measured by a customer's propensity to sign up for more*." More than half of the respondents are happy with the concept of one media supplier but only 10.1 percent prefer that to be their current media brand.
- The brands with most credibility in this ecosystem are Amazon and Netflix, neither of which is a traditional media company. Xerox adds that, "As the battle to become the 'one brand' intensifies, technology and telecommunication brands may find business opportunities in the media realm. And transform the industry forever."[6]

In the future, will customer satisfaction and loyalty result in more than increased sales, important though that is? Will the power of satisfaction lead to industry transformation? Is there any difference between the customer service goals of B2C and B2B marketers?

What Are Firms' Customer Service Goals?

While all business have similar customer service goals to some degree, there are interesting differences. Retail scores much higher on customer retention and increasing sales from current customers. B2C companies score higher on maintaining competitive position and especially on brand differentiation. B2B scores high on increasing sales from current customers and on converting prospects into customers. Both retail and B2B, where employees have direct contact with customers, score higher on improving customer satisfaction. All these goals are important; none are easy to achieve (Figure 16.3).

FIGURE 16.3
Customer Service Goals

Customer Service Business Objectives							
Retain existing customers and reduce customer turnover	53%	55%	55%	57%	65%	48%	44%
Increase sales from existing customers	40%	33%	43%	30%	61%	43%	43%
Convert more prospects/visitors into customers	35%	47%	28%	34%	30%	28%	39%
Maintain competitive position and/or market share	31%	29%	38%	26%	30%	38%	26%
Differentiate our brand from our competitors	30%	38%	38%	29%	28%	33%	21%
Produce more with less effort and/or reduced costs	25%	22%	28%	19%	13%	18%	36%
Improve employee satisfaction	24%	17%	18%	29%	28%	20%	28%
Improve competitive position and/or market share	23%	21%	25%	30%	17%	33%	20%
Improve nouber of customer advocates or brand ambassadors	19%	10%	10%	25%	15%	20%	25%
Improve products or service offering	19%	28%	18%	17%	11%	23%	18%

KEY
- All respondents
- Communications and telecome
- Consumer goods and Manufacturing, process
- Financial services and insurance
- Retail
- Technology
- Wholesale distribution and Manufacturing, discrete

↑ RETAIL

SOURCE: http://images.forbes.com/forbesinsights/StudyPDFs/Oracle-ModernCustomerService-Report.pdf.

The knowledge needed to improve customer service is available; it is the business will that is often lacking. Take the customer service turnaround at Sprint as an example. Industry pundits have described it as "from worst to first in five years."

Improving Customer Service in B2C Markets

In 2007, a new CEO was installed to clean up the mess at Sprint. In the face of a $30 billion loss that year Dan Hess rid the company of many unprofitable customers, laid off 4,000 workers and closed 125 retail locations. The next year, the company lost over five million subscribers and suffered a severe cash flow shortage, putting its very survival in peril. Fast forward five years. By 2013, Sprint's customer service was named the most improved in the United States by the American Consumer Satisfaction Index (ACSI). Earlier that year the J. D. Powers survey had found that Sprint had the highest purchase satisfaction score in its industry for the fourth year in a row.[7] Two years later, Sprint continues to maintain a stable rating in the ASCI poll.[8]

How did the company manage a turnaround of this magnitude in customer service? Industry observers credit it to strong leadership by Dan Hess. The principles he followed were:

- To make customer experience a top priority. That required the organization to find and fix problems that were causing customer dissatisfaction and subscriber loss.
- To focus on improving the core product. In Sprint's case that required upgrading the wireless network and adding leading smart phones to the products offered.
- To recognize the role of price in an intensely competitive industry. Sprint was able to use unlimited data and lower-cost plant to make headway against larger rivals.

Sprint VP of Customer Experience said their process was data driven, supported by a long-term vision and collaboration with business partners.[9] While Sprint has never managed industry-leading ACSI scores, it continues to score competitively in its industry, which is a far cry from the original lowest-place rating.

This is one of a number of case histories we will cite in this chapter that point out that achieving customer service excellence tends to take years, even decades, to accomplish. The ongoing commitment to exceptional customer service is, therefore, difficult for competitors to emulate and it provides a sustainable competitive advantage to companies that achieve it.

Improving Customer Service in B2B Markets

An analysis by Marketing Charts in 2016 of two surveys of the state of digital marketing in B2B markets aptly summarizes the issue of improving customer service. "Despite all of the attention paid to customer experience, relatively few respondents (35 percent), by comparison, said they had improved their customer experience."[10] Recent data is hard to come by, so take a case history that aptly demonstrates the issues, Portakabin, manufacturer of modular and portable buildings in the United Kingdom. Its approach shows how important it is to cultivate an organizational culture of customer service.

"Modular Buildings on Time and on Budget" Portakabin, headquartered in Huntington, York, was established in 1961 and now does business throughout Europe. It manufactures a broad line of portable and modular buildings ranging from the Lilliput nurseries line to its Portaloo line (that is a "Porta-Potty" in the United States). It offers products either for purchase or for hire (rent).

In addition to touting the quality of its products, offering extensive visual support and linking to project case histories, the company home page makes customer service promises. They include:

- "Quality-assured customer service—with 99.7 percent of buildings delivered on time and on budget."
- "If we ever fail to meet your contract start date, we'll give you a week's free hire or, if you buy your building, we will refund 1 percent of your contract value for every week we are late."

Anyone can make promises, but there is much evidence that the company is serious. Service promises appear on product pages. Even more important, the company established a Customer Charter in 2004. It makes explicit promises in the areas of delivery time, meeting budget, customer service, quality, and safety. The case histories, organized by industry, back up the customer service claims and promises.[11]

In 2015 the U.K. Customer Satisfaction Index found that customer satisfaction in the construction industry had dropped for the fourth year in a row, citing rising customer expectations and the inability of most firms to meet them. In contrast Portakabin's customer satisfaction scores remained at 92 percent, high for any industry.

The company pointed to the fact that it is the only company in its industry to do customer service audits. It also invests heavily in the training of its employees. It describes other customer service initiative as follows:

- Two to three major research studies carried out annually to provide an in-depth understanding of customer expectations and the drivers for customer satisfaction.
- Customer satisfaction surveys—around 1,700 customers are surveyed each year.
- The development of an electronic bulletin board to test new product and service ideas that will further improve customer satisfaction.
- The publication of the Group's delivery statistics that gives customers even greater confidence of time and cost certainty and benchmarking that performance against construction industry data.

- Values Champions and an Employee Communications Forum to encourage ownership and responsibility across the business.
- Mystery shopper exercises.[12]

This is a robust customer service effort and the report provides strong evidence that it is working over a significant period of time.

Portakabin is one of many B2B firms that understand the issues in providing excellent customer service. It does not happen overnight; the company first published its customer service charter in 2004 and its customer service initiative goes back even further. It has also obviously followed the quality management literature that says that "what gets measured gets managed." The quality literature also points out the importance of "walking the walk" over "talking the talk." It is true that anyone can make promises. It takes company-wide effort and persistence to keep those promises, but that is the essence of good customer service.

WHY IS PROVIDING EXCELLENT CUSTOMER SERVICE SO DIFFICULT?

Providing an excellent customer service experience is actually becoming more difficult as time goes on. Technological change is part of the reason. The other part is changing expectations on the part of customers themselves. Specific reasons include:

- The growing dominance of mobile. In Chapter 13 we discussed the rise of mobile around the world, not only for communications, but also for information acquisition and increasingly for purchasing. That trend seems fated to continue. It means that customers can ask for support from anywhere at any time. That puts a heavy burden on marketers for responsiveness.
- Customer expectations are high. Customers expect quick resolution of their issues in a single pleasant and productive service encounter. Many marketers simply aren't set up to provide that level of service.
- Increase in self-service and crowd-based interactions. All customers have high expectations. Millennials and those younger prefer to have those expectations for immediacy and resolution satisfied by self-service. We all know that many marketers try for satisfactory self-service experiences but many fall short.[13]
- **Omni-channel** *customer service is essential.* Customers may start shopping in one channel, switch to another channel for a final purchase and request service in still another. One provider of omni-channel services says, "The number of customer service channels, including virtual agents, screen sharing, SMS, social media, and click-to-chat, has created unprecedented choice from a brand and customer perspective but creates significant challenges in terms of providing a truly integrated brand experience." Their research found that 73 percent of online shoppers think brands are making more effort in terms of omni-channel purchasing than omni-channel customer service. Even more, 78 percent say the brand's reputation for customer service is important when they are considering a purchase.[14]

omni-channel a strategy that delivers personalized and consistent customer experience across multiple channels.

In addition, the cost of providing service through various channels can differ significantly as shown in Figure 16.4.

It probably comes as no surprise that the cost of live telephone support is the highest of all channels with those served by a skilled technician, the most expensive of all. Web-enabled services are less expensive even though they require a live agent. These channels offer more opportunity to sequence and prioritize contacts and for agents to multi-task. Web self-service is significantly less expensive than the other channels.

In the face of all the challenges presented by consumer demands and differing channel costs, however, there are companies that are providing excellent customer service.

FIGURE 16.4

Cost of Customer Contact by Channel

Customer Service Channel	Approx. Cost Per Contact
Call center technical support	$12 and higher
Call center CSR	$6 and higher
Web chat or callback	$5 and higher
Email response	$2.50 to $5 and higher
Web self-service	$0.10 or less

SOURCE: https://www.salesforce.com/blog/2013/09/self-service-support.html.

WHO ARE THE CUSTOMER SERVICE CHAMPIONS?

Media firm 24/7 Wall Street has partnered with Zoby Analytics each year since 2010 to find out who those firms are. Their survey questioned over 1,500 randomly chosen respondents about customer service at 150 of the best-known firms in the United States representing 15 different industries. Table 16.1 shows the top 10 firms, based on the number of "excellent" responses received, in their customer service ranking for 2015. Table 16.2 shows the firms that had the lowest rankings based on the number of "poor" responses received.

Several things stand out in the list of the best customer service providers. First is that many of them reappear on the list year after year. Amazon has headed the list for a number of years while Marriott and UPS are consistent repeaters. Second is that firms can increase their ranking. Apple jumped from tenth to third in a single year while Sony went from number nine to number eight and Samsung appeared on the list for the first time. Mass merchandisers, fast food restaurants, and B2B firms are noticeably absent.

The list of worst customer service providers illustrates some of the same features. Of the 10 firms, only T-Mobile was on the worst providers list for the first time. Comcast has topped the list for six straight years. In fact, six of the ten worst providers are cable, satellite, or wireless companies.

Prof. Praveen Kopalle provided some insights on the results for USA Today. As we have already discussed in Chapter 5, he alluded to the importance of employee satisfaction in creating positive interactions with customers. He also pointed to the nature of various industries with tech companies having to work very hard to keep

TABLE 16.1

Customer Service Hall of Fame—2015

Rank	Company	% Excellent Scores	Survey History
1	Amazon	59.4	Sixth consecutive year at top of list
2	Chick-fil-A	47.0	Only fast food on list this year and last
3	Apple	40.0	Tenth on list in 2014
4	Marriott	39.2	Third on list in 2014
5	Kroger	38.6	Unknown
6	FedEx	37.7	Unknown
7	Trader Joe's	37.7	Number six with 36.7 percent in 2014
8	Sony	37.0	Number nine on list in 2014
9	Samsung Electronics	36.9	First time
10	UPS	36.7	On list since 2010

SOURCE: http://247wallst.com/special-report/2015/07/23/customer-service-hall-of-fame-2/.

TABLE 16.2

Customer Service Hall of Shame—2015

Rank	Company	% Poor Scores	Survey History
1	Comcast	28.3	Seventh consecutive year on list
2	DirectTV	21.5	Poor score has increased since 2014
3	Bank of America	21.4 credit card, banking	Topped list for previous four years
4	Dish Network	21.3	On list all years except 2011
5	AT&T	18.8 mobile 17.1 U-verse	Poor score higher than 2014
6	AOL	16.1	Worst or second worst 2010–2013
7	Verizon Communications	15.0	Poor score higher than 2014
8	T-Mobile	14.7	First time on list
9	Wells Fargo Credit Cards	14.0	Consistently on list
10	Wal-Mart	13.8	Consistently on list

SOURCE: http://247wallst.com/special-report/2015/07/23/customer-service-hall-of-shame/2/.

demanding customers satisfied and food chains having to use customer service to compete with mass merchandisers who have lower prices. Product is also important as in the cable and wireless industries where customers are notoriously fickle.[15]

WHAT DO CONSUMERS WANT?

While developing a customer service strategy, it is important to focus on what customers really want. Data from the 2015 Customer Rage study sponsored by the University of Arizona sheds light on key issues. They found that:

- Two-thirds of all respondents experienced customer rage.
- Thirty-five percent of complainants have yelled and 15 percent cursed when speaking to customer service about their most serious problem.
- Among complainants who reported getting something, many felt that they got very little (e.g., 75 percent of complainants wanted an apology but only 28 percent got one).
- Posting information on the web about customer problems has greatly increased since 2011, with an increase of posting to social networking sites to 30 percent from only 19 percent two years prior.
- Although posting on the web about consumer problems has increased substantially, complainants still consider the telephone their primary channel for complaining by a margin of more than six to one over the internet (72 to 11 percent).
- Word-of-mouth about product or service problems from dissatisfied complainants is more than double than the word-of-mouth communicated by those who were satisfied.[16]

Adding more detail to the description of what consumers want, The Harvard Business School found that they want resolution on the first contact (92 percent). When they received that level of customer care, their willingness to continue purchasing (86 percent), to recommend, and to spread positive WOM (88 percent) are all very high. The author asserts that it is not the number of customer service channels that is the issue, it is having channels that are perceived as convenient and that render quality service.[17]

FIGURE 16.5

Channels Most Likely to Satisfy

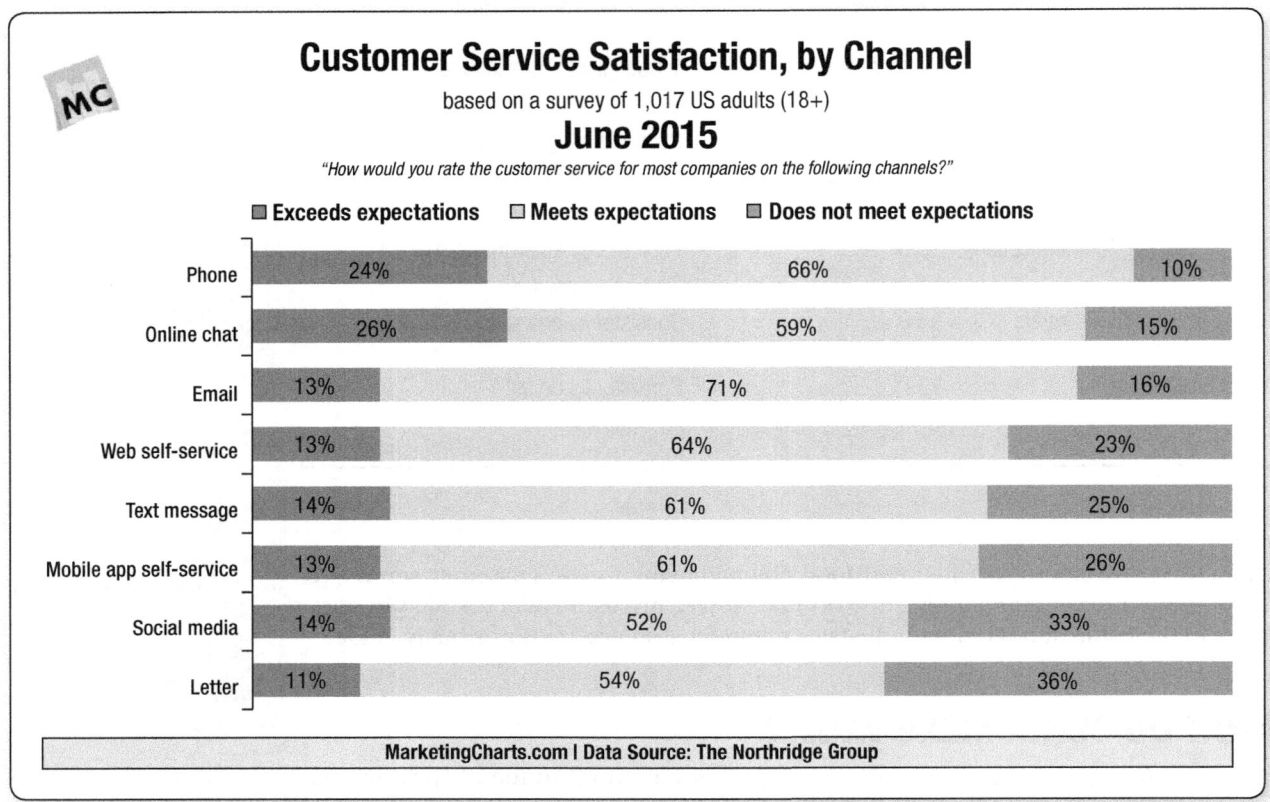

SOURCE: http://www.marketingcharts.com/traditional/customer-service-satisfaction-by-channel-55798/attachment/thenorthridgegroup-customer-service-satisfaction-by-channel-jun2015/.

The question of which channels and how many to offer continues to be a vexing one to companies. For one thing, channels differ in their ability to satisfy. Figure 16.5 shows that, as found in the Customer Rage survey, phone is found to exceed or meet expectations by most consumers. Online chat is close behind with an even higher "exceed" score. Note that both of those channels give access to a live agent. Self-service and social media do not score as high. Many consumers say they want self-service channels and only turn to other channels when self-service does not satisfy.

Remember that this is broad consumer data. If your audience is made up of tech professionals, you might place greater emphasis on self-service. If it is Millennials or younger, you might explore what it takes to use social media customer service so that it satisfies.

THE EVOLUTION OF CUSTOMER SERVICE STRATEGY

The internet is not only a key reason why the expectations of both B2C and B2B customers are rising but also can be a way in which their expectations can be met in a cost-effective manner. Figure 16.6 suggests an evolution in the way customer service is delivered that has the potential to improve service without increasing the cost of providing it. It involves, first, moving away from total reliance on *live service*, in-store service, and via telephone **call centers**, to *customer service provided on the internet*, either with or without direct human intervention. Whether live customer service is used or service over the web is the norm, notice that the first two stages are

call centers department within an organization that handles telephone sales and/or service.

FIGURE 16.6
Customer Service Evolution

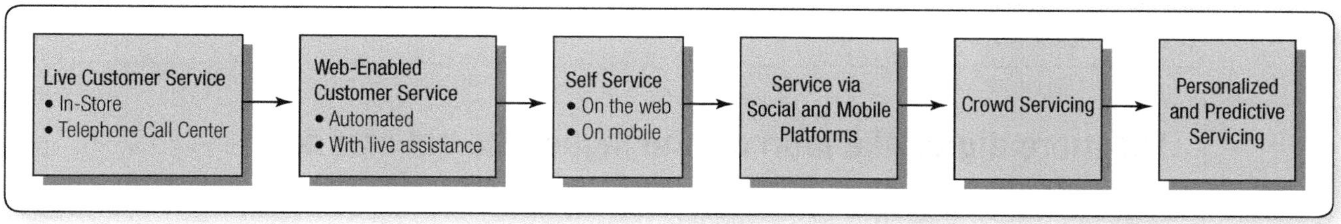

Live Customer Service (In-Store, Telephone Call Center) → Web-Enabled Customer Service (Automated, With live assistance) → Self Service (On the web, On mobile) → Service via Social and Mobile Platforms → Crowd Servicing → Personalized and Predictive Servicing

essentially reactive. The customer must ask; only then service will be forthcoming and then only if a customer service rep is available to provide the service.

Self-service is the next step and many customers are enthusiastic proponents. The reason may be that self-service is available on demand 24/7. One survey in 2012 found 75 percent of respondents preferring to use online support if it was reliable. However, only 37 percent even attempted to use it, feeling it was likely to be inaccurate or incomplete. A surprising 91 percent said they would use an online knowledge base if it was tailored to their needs.[18] Another survey in 2013 found that 59 percent of respondents were frustrated by having to reach out to a live agent instead of being able to resolve their service issue online. Seventy-one percent of these same people would prefer a virtual assistant over a static web page for their self-service.[19]

Much attention has been given in recent years to customer self-service using *mobile apps*, but there are not a great many examples of companies doing mobile customer service, in the sense of resolving problems, and doing it well. An exception is the Allianz insurance company. It had a robust call center operation supporting customers of its travel insurance with medical information at home and abroad. In 2013, it introduced a free mobile app based on its database of 2,000 hospitals in 129 countries, each accessible with one-touch dialing. The app also included a drug database with internationally recognized names for common drugs and first aid terms translated into 17 languages. There were emergency services numbers for 217 countries, which were also reached by one-touch dialing. The app also streamed travel news from USA Today.[20]

The company followed in 2014 with a more specialized Allianz MyHealth app. According to the company, features of the app include:

- First app that can photograph invoices for submission of international medical claims—with no paper claim forms to complete.
- Access to policy documents, even offline.
- Find closest hospitals and get directions to them using GPS.
- Medical term translator and Pharmacy Aid.[21]

One year later BusinessWire reported that the app had been downloaded over 60,000 times and had been used to file more than 100,000 member insurance claims. Susan Landers, Head of Market Management at Allianz Worldwide Care said that its success had exceeded all expectations. In just one year, digital claims submissions had overtaken traditional post [mail] submissions.

"With a globally mobile client base, accustomed to operating in a digital landscape, it was a natural step for Allianz Worldwide Care to enhance its service offering for members. The early response to the MyHealth app is a clear demonstration of the demand for digital services and we will continue to provide even greater value and convenience to our clients through this exciting medium."[22]

The Allianz experience supports the results of a McKinsey study (Figure 16.7) that found digital customer service channels providing 33 percent more satisfaction than traditional channels alone, with combinations of digital and traditional channels scoring next highest.

FIGURE 16.7
Digital Customer Service Channels Produce Highest Customer Satisfaction

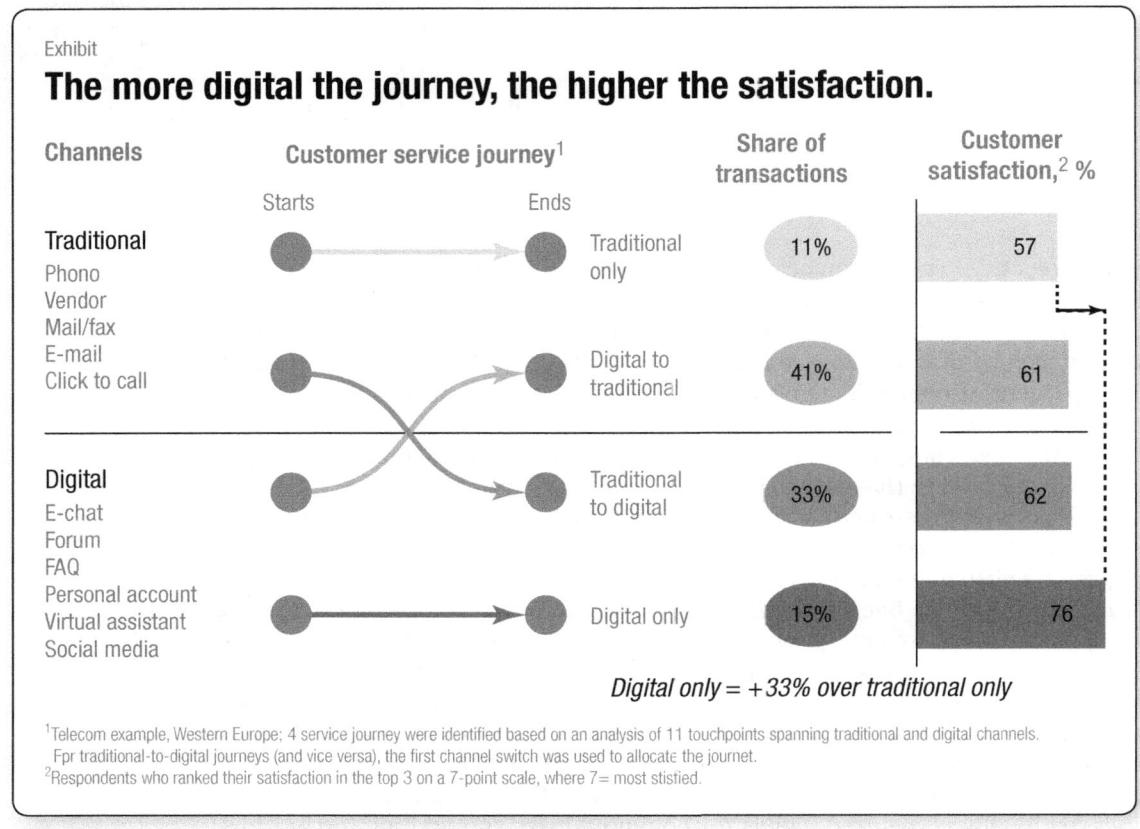

SOURCE: http://www.mckinsey.com/business-functions/marketing-and-sales/our-insights/why-companies-should-care-about-ecare.

If both what consumers do and what they say in reply to a survey supports the transition to digital customer service, what are the other options? Customer service via *social media* is another option much discussed. As we pointed out in Chapter 2, companies including Dell have long used elements of social media in dealing with customers, in some cases including customer problem resolution. Most companies, however, have been slow to jump on the bandwagon. For one thing, customer expectations of customer service on social media platforms are high. Customer expectations can be summed up in two words: *accuracy and speed*. And not in any particular order. Both are essential.

Consider a few factoids that put social media customer service into perspective:

- Companies that ignore support requests on social media have a 15 percent higher churn rate than companies who respond (Gartner, 2012).[23]
  - Another study found that 80 percent of American companies ignore service and support questions on Twitter but answer 60 percent of queries on Facebook, which has a much lower volume (Mashable, 2015).[24]
- Customers of companies that engage over social media will spend 20–40 percent more with them than other customers. They also develop more emotional commitment, giving companies an **NPS** (Net Promoter Score) that is on average 33 points higher (Bain, 2011).[25]
- Worldwide 65 percent of customers do not use social media for customer service, saying that it takes too long and is not good for complex issues (eMarketer, 2016).[26]

NPS customer satisfaction score calculated on the basis of a single question, "How likely is it that you would recommend [brand] to a friend or colleague".

If customer service on social media has so much potential—and if it is directly linked to corporate profits—why do so many companies ignore it? There are two easy answers—it is not easy and it requires a significant investment of time and money. An article in the Guardian reveals some of the good, the bad, and the ugly of Twitter customer service (Figure 16.8). The range in the response time of the fastest airline responders, from just over 4 minutes to nearly 20 minutes, is large. And remember, these are just the best!

The fastest, Volaris, is a Mexican budget airline. The company started using social media in 2009 to increase awareness and drive traffic to its website, but the turning point didn't come until 2011. In March 2011 it launched its biggest price promotion. It must have been a good one because it crashed their website and overwhelmed their telephone call center. The customer service team turned to social media to deal with disgruntled customers. Even better, it used social media after the promotion ended to follow up with customers who were unable to obtain tickets during the promotion.

Now, Volaris maintains two social media teams that are dedicated to customer service on a 24/7 basis. Team members can contact anyone in the organization to help resolve a problem. In addition, they post engaging content, including information about events they are sponsoring, on social media. They encourage customers to comment on their experiences with these events.[27]

The social media customer service odyssey of JetBlue airlines also started with a customer service disaster, the Valentine's Day snow storm of 2007. It has also taken JetBlue many years to reach the state of social media maturity that leads to its award-winning response quality and time, which we discuss in detail in the text *Social Media Marketing*.[28] Another study of airline customer service used **sentiment analysis** of tweets over the 2015 holiday season to name Spirit Airlines the least loved of 70 airlines from around the world.[29] It uses a robot to answer customer tweets.[30]

sentiment analysis the attempt to understand the emotion, positive or negative, behind a qualitative statement.

The bottom line? Social media customer service can—and does work well—but it is neither easy, quick, nor cheap. It takes commitment and patience on the part of management to make it happen.

The next stage in Figure 16.6 is called *crowd servicing*. It is a social activity, but it is considered a separate stage because it represents a separate business model—P2P instead of B2B or B2C. It is not, however, a new customer service and support activity. For almost a decade we have called it a community, and there have been many successful examples of support communities.

In the early days of the web there were a number of wildly successful branded consumer communities. Gardening and home tools firm Fiskars had a vibrant community of customers supporting one another in their crafting activities. Women's site iVilliage was founded on the idea of community but lost so much traction that it was closed down as a standalone site by purchaser, NBCU in 2014. The reason, according to one former executive, is social media. "The landscape had shifted so dramatically," a former executive said. "iVillage was a business that was built on a community. The idea of a community was completely upended as Facebook exploded, and I don't

---

Short and tweet
Airlines with the fastest response to customers' tweets
November 20th 2015 to January 9th 2016

Airline	Initial response, mins, sec
Volaris	4 min, 12 sec
JetBlue	5 min, 36 sec
Etihad Airways	9 min
Kenya Airways	19 min, 24 sec
Virgin Atlantic	19 min, 36 sec

SOURCE: Stratos Jet Charters.

FIGURE 16.8
Airlines' Twitter Response Times

SOURCE: http://www.economist.com/blogs/gulliver/2016/03/reading-you-loud-and-clear.

think people understood the impact of that."[31] B2C marketers have, however, substituted aggressive strategies to encourage consumers to review products as a way of encouraging customer input on the site.

Customer communities are now essentially the province of B2C firms. In addition to sites like Dell's Direct2Dell and Idea Storm, discussed in Chapter 2, Cisco has a long-standing and highly effective set of over 20 forums, many managed by customers, which provide technical support to their users. (Cisco's customer support activities are also discussed in detail in *Social Media Marketing*.[32]) In fact, you would be hard pressed to find a major tech firm today that did not have customer support communities of some kind.[33] Watch the video in Interactive Exercise 16.2 (found in the chapter learning path) and answer the questions to understand the reasons why.

The highest level of customer service, at least as we can see it now, is to be able to genuinely *personalize customer service and/or to be able to predict customer need* and to deliver service in anticipation of that need. This has come to be called **predictive analytics**. One industry expert describes it as follows:

predictive analytics using data, statistical algorithms, and machine learning techniques to predict the likelihood of future outcomes or behaviors.

> *Predictive analytics is data mining technology that uses your customer data to automatically build a predictive model specialized for your business. This process learns from your organization's collective experience by leveraging your existing logs of customer purchases, behavior, and demographics.*[34]

There are examples of predictive models in operation, mostly in e-commerce at this point. For instance, software makers know that I have been looking for articles on predictive analysis. Banner ads for predictive software are quickly showing up on my browser screens. A big box retailer who has set cookies on your browser has the ability to know that you have been looking at TVs online. The retailer could then e-mail you if you have given permission, send an in-store offer to your app if you have downloaded one, or simply display banner ads on your browser as you move about the web. These are both examples of using predictive cues, although not sophisticated analytical models, to offer personalized product offers.

What about customer service? There are several levels of analytics support for customer service. One is simple items of data like what page on our website is the customer currently looking at and whether we have resolved problems like this before and if so, how. It requires predictive models to be able to push relevant content to a visitor *before he asks*, anticipate when a particular customer on the website will call an agent, or predict the number of current customers who will call an agent. Each of these actions can make the corporate call center more efficient and less costly to run. The results of each interaction can be tracked to improve the model.[35]

Looking at live chat interactions another model attempts to answer the question of whether the chat session successfully resolved the problem or if the customer will be calling back again within 24 hours. This model uses AI and machine learning to predict the emotional state of the customer. The objectives are to resolve the problem with the first contact and to understand which customers are unhappy and might abandon the brand if not given additional support. A human can make these judgments by looking at the transcript of a chat session but that is labor intensive and unlikely to happen in time to intervene if the problem resolution was not satisfactory. That's an example of substituting analytics for the judgment of the best human operators.[36]

It seems obvious that with a multitude of channels and technology solutions that aim to make them more effective and more efficient, making the decisions that lead to successful omni-channel customer service is difficult.

OMNI-CHANNEL: HOW TO MAKE IT WORK

First, a definition may be in order. This one covers the issues well:

> "businesses that have a formal strategy in place to deliver personalized and consistent customer experiences across multiple channels (e.g., phone, social media, web, mobile, and e-mail) and devices (in-store, laptop, and smart phone)."[37]

While there is no doubt that this kind of omni-channel service is essential in today's marketplace, how does a company get there? There are a number of questions that need to be answered along that journey:

1. What channels do our customers want to use? A company has data on what channels their customers use for customer service, but what about the broader question of what channels they like to use in their everyday lives? What channels do they want to use for customer service? There is no real answer but to ask them, in a simple, straightforward way.
2. Which of these channels do we do well? Which of the ones we do not do well can we omit from the strategy? Customers want choice, but not all channels have to be—or perhaps should be—offered.
3. Are we using the appropriate self-service channels for our customers? Do the self- service tools provide a good experience to customers? Are the self-service tools integrated with the call center so a customer can seamlessly move from one to the other?
4. Have we given the call center agents all the tools they need to do their jobs well from the most effective call technology to access to customer records and to knowledge bases?
5. Have we made the experience a seamless whole, one in which customers are not subjected to long delays and to having to provide the same information over and over again?
6. Is some level of service available on all devices 24/7?
7. Are we getting consistently better at resolving issues on the first contact?[38]

Frank Pettinato, SVP and General Manager of Consumer Connexions of customer care company Telerx, sums it up: "We are moving to 24/7, like the news networks. Consumers are now expecting to be able to contact their brands anytime, anywhere, through any channel. The more powerful tools we can use to provide self-service will always benefit because people can get a quick answer. That's not going to mitigate and solve all problems. With self-service tools such as FAQs and interactive voice response, our hope is that we can quickly answer simple questions for customers. But as questions become more complex, we do need to engage consumers via phone, email, chat, SMS/texting, or social media to make sure that we're responding to those detailed questions."[39]

Options for channels and tools are many and can be perplexing. Two customer service successes make some of the issues clearer.

A Mobile Disruptor Offers Award-Winning Customer Service

Canadian mobile supplier Koodo launched in 2008 targeting younger mobile customers with both postpaid and prepaid plans and no fixed-term contract. Their website featured mobile-friendly responsive design that was searchable and easy to use. From the beginning it featured a customer champions program that offered "Mobile Masters" customers P2P tools that allowed them to answer questions and support other customers.[40]

Koodo launched its online community in 2011. By 2014 it was the most active of all the communities of Canadian telecommunications companies with millions of visits each year. It is self-sustaining with 99 percent of answers to customer questions coming from customers themselves. Response time averages about 4 minutes. Koodo engages with the community through gamification by allowing users to earn points and badges for answering questions and sharing ideas. The company adds that there is "a little bit of friendly competition between members to be the first to share their answer."[41] In early 2016, the community had 62,534 members.[42] The main page of the community support section (Figure 16.9) offers numerous options, most of which are self-service. It also shows that Koodo is active in social media although they only use Facebook, Twitter, and YouTube in contrast to many e-retailers who use more.

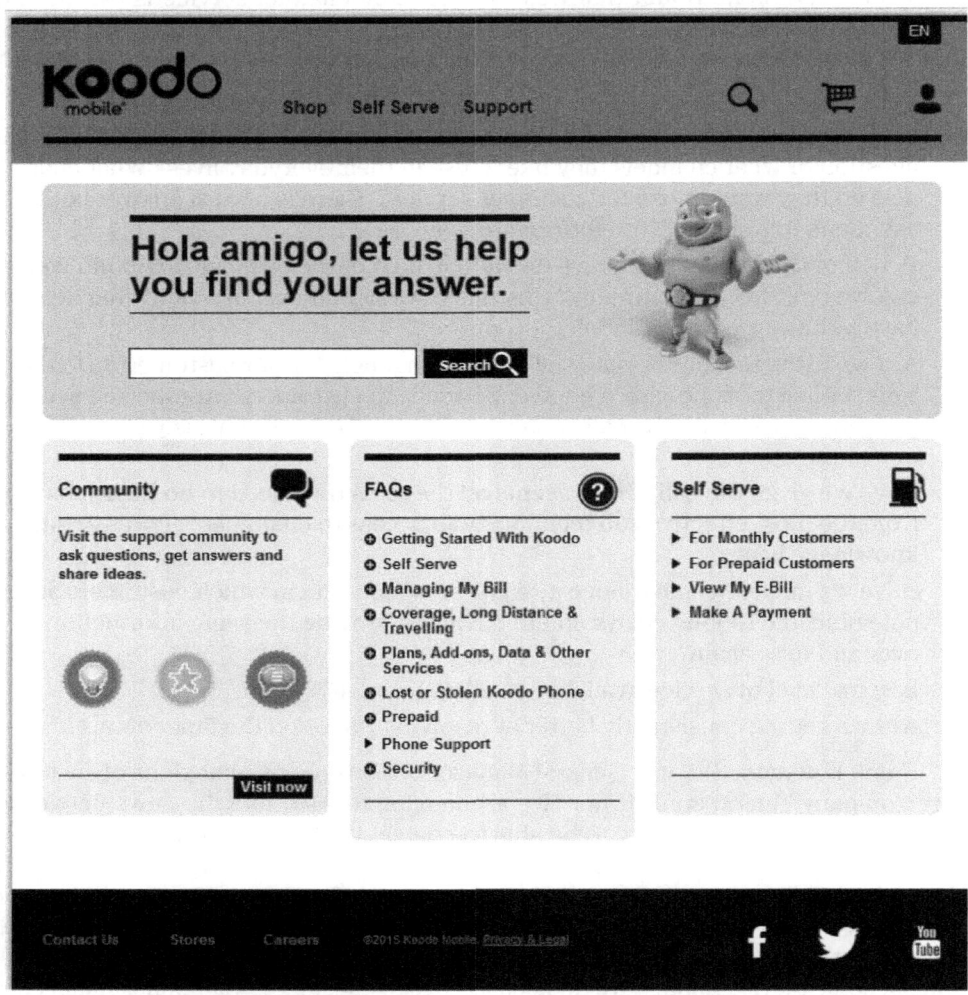

FIGURE 16.9 Main Customer Support Page

SOURCE: http://help.koodomobile.com/

In 2014 J. D. Powers ranked Koodo first among Canadian stand-alone wireless carriers and third among all carriers, behind SaskTel and its parent firm Telus.[43] Koodo maintained its industry rating in 2015.[44]

Fashion retailer Eddie Bauer presents a different picture.

The Evolution to Omni-Channel at Eddie Bauer

Eddie Bauer established his retail store in 1920 in Seattle. An avid sportsman, he called his store Eddie Bauer's Sports Shop. By 1922, he had a formal customer service creed with a delightfully old-fashioned ring and a ground-breaking guarantee policy:

Our Creed To give you such outstanding quality, value, service, and guarantee that we may be worthy of your high esteem.™

Our Guarantee Every item we sell will give you complete satisfaction or you may return it for a full refund.™[45]

This philosophy served him well when he began a mail order catalog in 1945. Successful mail order retailers have always understood that lacking an in-store experience that can have important social dimensions, top-quality customer service was essential to mail order success.

After Eddie Bauer's retirement in 1968, growth accelerated with the opening of new stores and the addition of specialty catalogs. The first international catalog was launched in Germany in 1993 followed by three stores and a catalog in Japan in 1994. There are now 370 stores worldwide. During the Christmas season of 2014, the company opened a **pop-up store** in New York City that featured a Twitter vending machine activated by @eddiebauer and #liveyouradventure. This was a centerpiece of the brand's return to its outdoor adventure heritage (Figure 16.10).

pop-up store (or popup shop) a temporary retail store.

Its 1996, website was one of the early entrants into the retail category and is now mobile-friendly. The website is easy-to-use with catalog quick order and store locator features that emphasize the multichannel nature of Eddie Bauer's business. The customer service page, which is accessible from every other page on the site, lists many

FIGURE 16.10

The First American to Summit Mt. Everest Wore Eddie Bauer

SOURCE: http://brandchannel.com/2014/11/12/eddie-bauer-scales-manhattan-with-pop-up-shop-twitter-vending-machine/

self-help options including order status and history(which allow customers to track their orders), delivery information, easy returns, size charts with instructions for measuring for a correct fit, gift certificates, watch repair, and monogramming services. It offers a number for 24-hour phone service as well as email and snail mail support.

Eddie Bauer is active on all the usual social media platforms—Facebook, YouTube, Twitter, Pinterest, and Instagram. On Pinterest it has 62 boards that feature products for specific activities. Its Instagram postings carry out the "Live Your Adventure" theme with adventure travel shots from around the globe. That is also the content strategy followed by its blog, which is accessible from its web page. The blog features adventure content and ecology-related posts that have little or no direct product reference.

The same is true of the mobile app introduced in 2014. When introduced it offered access to nine different activities at more than 10,000 locations in the United States. After answering questions about where she is, what she wants to do, what skill level she has, and how long she wants to spend the app presents a detailed guide to locations that match her requirements. It includes maps with directions, current weather conditions, and other information to make the trip safe and enjoyable. Each site features a star rating provided by outdoor experts. "With more and more people looking for an outdoor adventure to enjoy, whether it be in their own backyard or even for a few hours while traveling for work, they can now pull out their iPhone and with our app, easily find what they are looking for[46] PR Manager Molly McWhinnie said.

Continuing its progress to satisfying customer experience in early 2016, Eddie Bauer signed as a client with predictive analytics firm First Insight. Fashion is a business that has always succeeded as a result of the instinct and creativity of fashion designers and fashion buyers. Predictive analysis promises to help them offer new products that have a high probability of success, not of failure. In this case the firm collects data from online customers over a two to three day period and feeds it into its analytic models. The firm says that results are 50–100 percent more accurate than in-store testing, can analyze more products, and are delivered with greater speed.[47]

HOW CAN BUSINESSES ACHIEVE CUSTOMER SERVICE GOALS?

The Koodo and Eddie Bauer case histories reveal two very different businesses doing very different things to achieve excellent customer service. What can we learn from this?

First, never underestimate the importance of knowing your consumer. The bargain-hunting young consumers who make up Koodo's core market are oriented toward self-service and are even happy to help provide it. The perhaps older and more affluent adventure travelers that are at the heart of Eddie Bauer's strategy want a richer experience in the store, on the website, and on social media where visual marketing plays a huge role. Both companies have strategies that fit their target market segments. Both strategies produce mountains of data that can be used to further enhance strategies and delivery.

When self-service does not satisfy, the importance of good customer service representatives cannot be overstated. In order to create a good customer service team, reps must be hired with care, carefully trained and updated, motivated, and rewarded for success. Whether it is a field service force or an inside call center or some combination of both, the personnel issues are another major management task.

Technology is ever changing and customer service operations must keep abreast of current trends. The next big thing in customer service may be the IoT and the data that is being provided by connected products. In both consumer and business markets, connected devices will monitor themselves and give forewarning of failure so preemptive service can be offered. Devices will also trigger suggestions about products and activities to customers.

Data from a wide variety of sources will drive customer service strategies. If companies can understand what customers are likely to do next, they can be ready with solutions and offers that fulfill customer needs.

Above all, interactions need to be easy, resolve problems on the first contact, and provide a practically and emotionally satisfying experience that generates loyalty and additional purchases. In the end, it is the simple but monumentally challenging goal of customer service.[48]

SUMMARY

Providing superior customer service is an important part of a CRM or CX strategy. Data from various sources emphasize that service is important to both customer loyalty and profits in B2C and B2B markets. The data also point out that customer service is a multifaceted construct that includes not only service recovery but also issues like timely delivery and provision of information that makes it easier for customers to use the product. Customers have shown willingness to switch brands when customer service does not meet their expectations.

Anecdotal evidence helps us appreciate the complexity of the customer service issue and the necessity to engage in a process of continuous improvement in order to develop and maintain excellent customer service. The process includes both making sure that business systems work and implementing technology to deliver service when appropriate. The examples also stress the key role of organizational factors in creating a successful customer service system for companies like Netflix and Amazon. They rank high in the list of satisfaction with media providers even though they are not media companies. Loyalty may better be measured by willingness to sign up for additional products or services instead of by the traditional media measure of lost customers, called "churn" in the media industry.

Improving customer service is an information-driven activity. It requires segmenting and profiling customers, identifying and targeting high-CLV segments, developing differentiated service programs for different customer segments, and giving all segments seamlessly satisfying experiences appropriate to their values. Following this regimen is difficult for B2C marketers. It appears to be even more difficult for B2B marketers, few of whom rank high in customer service and satisfaction surveys.

In order to make customer service cost-effective, technology must be part of the equation. The level of customer satisfaction differs between different channels with e-mail ranking high and social media low. Perhaps that is because few companies appear to have the discipline to do social media customer service well. Customer communities are a time-honored channel for customer service, especially in the tech sector. Mobile apps are emerging as a potential customer service channel that offers convenience to both the customer and the business. Whatever channels are being used, digital channels rank high in customer satisfaction. Marketers must make careful trade-offs between what customers need and the technology solutions they offer.

Analytics will also be part of the customer service equation. Predictive analysis can enable the brand to have service available before the customer even knows he or she needs it.

Offering superb customer service and targeting customer segments with the appropriate level of service are both essential to marketing success in the global internet economy. The ability to deliver exceptional customer service as part of seamless CX has potential to produce sustainable competitive advantage that no other strategic marketing variable can match.

DISCUSSION QUESTIONS

1. Throughout the chapter, reference is made to exceptional customer service as the basis for sustainable competitive advantage. Do you agree with this perspective? Why or why not?

2. The internet has the capacity to increase customer expectations about service levels and also to be the vehicle that delivers service that meets or exceeds those expectations. Take a position on this statement and discuss it.
3. Do you believe that good customer service has a direct impact on the profitability of a business? Can you provide evidence to back up your position?
4. True or false: Customer service is less important in B2B markets than in B2C.
5. Moving all service delivery to the web where customers can access it when they need it is the most important aspect of building a successful customer service program. Do you agree or disagree? Why?
6. What channels do consumers find the most satisfactory at present?
7. Are there channels that customers would like to use but find unsatisfactory or inefficient?
8. What are the highest cost service channels? The lowest cost? What implications does that have for effective customer service strategy?
9. Can you identify industries or specific businesses for which mobile customer service apps seem especially desirable?
10. Can you find other examples of companies that are actively using social networks for customer service?
11. How does customer service on social networks differ from customer service provided by communities?
12. How could predictive analytics improve the effectiveness of customer service?
13. Why is omni-channel customer service considered a necessity by many customer service experts?
14. Think about the issue of organizational issues and the impact on the delivery of exceptional customer service. Have you encountered any customer service instances in which people in the same organization seemed to be giving you different information or advice? Why do you think this happened?

ENDNOTES

1. Rich Meyer, "The Average Value of a Lost Customer is $243," December 23, 2015, http://www.newmediaandmarketing.com/the-average-value-of-a-lost-customer-is-243/.
2. "The $6 Trillion Opportunity: How Digital Improves Customer Experience," nd, https://www.accenture.com/us-en/insight-digital-improve-customer-experience.
3. "The $6 Trillion Opportunity: How Digital Improves Customer Experience," nd, https://www.accenture.com/us-en/insight-digital-improve-customer-experience.
4. "U.S. 'Switching Economy' Up 29 Percent since 2010 as Companies Struggle to Keep Up with the Nonstop Customer, Finds Accenture," January 21, 2015, https://newsroom.accenture.com/subjects/strategy/us-switching-economy-up-29-percent-since-2010-as-companies-struggle-to-keep-up-with-the-nonstop-customer-finds-accenture.htm.
5. "Customers Reward Outstanding Service by Spending More and Spreading the Word to Friends and Family," October 28, 2014, http://about.americanexpress.com/news/pr/2014/outstanding-service-spend-more-spread-word.aspx.
6. "The State of Customer Service, Media Edition," p. 17, 2015, https://www.xerox.com/en-us/services/customer-care/insights/customer-service-2015.
7. "Sprint Most Improved Company in Customer Satisfaction Among U.S. Industries," May 21, 2013, http://newsroom.sprint.com/news-releases/sprint-most-improved-company-in-customer-satisfaction-among-all-us-industries.htm.
8. "ACSI Benchmarks by Company," nd, http://www.theacsi.org/customer-satisfaction-benchmarks/benchmarks-by-company.
9. Bob Thompson, "Worst to First: How Five Customer-Centric Habits Enabled Sprint's Dramatic Turnaround," September 1, 2013, http://customerthink.com/worst_to_first_how_five_customer_centric_habits_enabled_sprints_turnaround/.

10. "Assessing the State of B2B Digital Marketing," March 8, 2016, http://www.marketingcharts.com/online/assessing-the-state-of-b2b-digital-marketing-66007/
11. http://www.portakabin.co.uk/.
12. "Portakabin Releases Customer Services Figures Which Out-Perform National and Construction Industry Service Standards," June 2, 2015, http://www.portakabin.co.uk/portakabin-releases-customer-services-figures-which-out-perform-both-national-and-construction-indus.html.
13. Steven Van Belleghem, "The Future of Customer Support: From Personal, to Self, to Crowd Service," November 26, 2013, http://www.mycustomer.com/service/contact-centres/the-future-of-customer-support-from-personal-to-self-to-crowd-service.
14. "The Omnichannel Customer Service Gap," November 2013, https://d16-cvnquvjw7pr.cloudfront.net/resources/whitepapers/Omnichannel-Customer-Service-Gap.pdf.
15. Michael B. Sauter, Thomas C Frohlich, and Sam Stebbins, "2015's Customer Service Hall of Fame," August 2, 2015, http://www.usatoday.com/story/money/business/2015/07/24/24-7-wall-st-customer-service-hall-fame/30599943/.
16. "$202 Billion in Revenue at Risk With Poor Customer Service," December 13, 2015, http://www.customercaremc.com/wp/wp-content/uploads/2015/12/Customer-Rage-Study-2015_FINAL-PRESS-RELEASE.pdf.
17. Cynthia Grimm, "When to Offer Fewer Customer Service Channels," Mary 19, 2015, https://hbr.org/2015/05/when-to-offer-fewer-customer-service-channels.
18. "Amdocs Survey: Service Providers Have an Opportunity to Substantially Reduce Call Center Traffic with Proactive and Improved Self-Care Options," March 22, 2012, http://www.amdocs.com/news/pages/amdocs-survey-highlights-opportunity-for-service-providers.aspx.
19. "Survey Shows: Majority of Consumers Frustrated with Web Self-Service, Want a 'Human' Touch," December 16, 2013, http://www.nuance.com/company/news-room/press-releases/NinaWebSurvey.docx.
20. "Allianz Global Assistance Launches TravelSmart Mobile App," April 4, 2013, https://www.allianztravelinsurance.com/about/press/2013/aga-launches-travelsmart-mobile-app.htm.
21. "Allianz Worldwide Care Introduces the Fastest and Easiest Way to Submit International Medical Claims," August 19, 2014, http://www.businesswire.com/news/home/20140819005413/en/Allianz-Worldwide-Care-Introduces-Fastest-Easiest-Submit.
22. "One Year On, Allianz Worldwide Care's MyHealth App Hits 100,000 Member Claim Submissions," October 15, 2015, http://www.businesswire.com/news/home/20151015006185/en/Year-Allianz-Worldwide-Care%E2%80%99s-MyHealth-App-Hits.
23. "Gartner Predicts That Refusing to Communicate by Social Media Will be as Harmful to Companies as Ignoring Phone Calls or Emails is Today," August 1, 2012, http://www.gartner.com/newsroom/id/2101515.
24. Patrick Kulp, "U.S. Companies Ignore 80% of Twitter Questions from Customers, but Answer on Facebook," July 11, 2015, http://mashable.com/2015/06/13/four-out-of-five-u-s-brands-are-ignoring-your-twitter-nagging/#ia7bmuseXPq8.
25. Chris Barry et al., "Putting Social Media to Work," September 2, 2011, http://www.bain.com/publications/articles/putting-social-media-to-work.aspx.
26. "Why Consumers Don't Rely on Social Media for Customer Service," March 7, 2016, http://www.emarketer.com/Article/Why-Consumers-Dont-Rely-on-Social-Media-Customer-Service/1013670.
27. "Volaris: A Brief Biography of a Socially Devoted Company," nd, https://cdn.socialbakers.com/www/archive/storage/www/volaris-sociallydevoted-pdf.pdf.
28. Melissa S. Barker, Donald I. Barker, Nicholas F. Bormann, Debra Zahay, and Mary Lou Roberts, 2nd ed. 2017, *Social Media Marketing: A Strategic Apoproach* (Mason, OH, Cengage Learning), Chapter 2.

29. Christopher Elliott, "These 3 Airlines Get the Most Hate on Social Media," February 18, 2016, http://fortune.com/2016/02/18/airlines-hate-social-media/.
30. "Some Airlines Take Customers' Tweets More Seriously Than Others," March 18, 2016, http://www.economist.com/blogs/gulliver/2016/03/reading-you-loud-and-clear.
31. Lucia Moses, "How One-Time Dot-Com Darling iVillage Fell to Earth," October 31, 2014, http://digiday.com/publishers/ivillage/.
32. Melissa S. Barker, Donald I. Barker, Nicholas F. Bormann, Debra Zahay, and Mary Lou Roberts, 2nd ed. 2017, *Social Media Marketing: A Strategic Apoproach* (Mason, OH, Cengage Learning), Chapter 2.
33. Vanssa DiMauro, "71 Top Online Customer Communities," August 11, 2014, http://www.leadernetworks.com/2011/02/71-top-online-customer-communities-big.html.
34. R. Scott Raynovich, "The Future of Customer Service: Predictive and Personalized," March 3, 2014, http://www.predictiveanalyticsworld.com/patimes/future-customer-service-predictive-personalized/3383/.
35. Macie Dabrowski, "Four Steps – Using Data Analytics in Customer Service Solutions," April 8, 2014, http://www.altocloud.com/blog/four_steps_using_data_analytics_in_customer_service_solutions.
36. Micah Solomon, "Omnichannel Customer Experience: Expert Systems, 360 Degree Views, and AI," April 8, 2015, http://www.forbes.com/sites/micahsolomon/2015/04/08/omnichannel-customer-experience-how-a-360-degree-view-of-customer-care-can-help/#5e83df7710e1.
37. Omer Minkara, "Executive Summary: Four Steps to Smart Omni-Channel Customer Service," p. 3, March 2016, http://v1.aberdeen.com/launch/report/knowledge_brief/12038-KB-Omni-Channel.asp.
38. Omer Minkara, "Executive Summary: Four Steps to Smart Omni-Channel Customer Service," p. 3, March 2016, http://v1.aberdeen.com/launch/report/knowledge_brief/12038-KB-Omni-Channel.asp; Jacob Firuta, "6 Things You Need to Know about Multi Channel Customer Service," December 3, 2015, https://www.livechatinc.com/blog/multi-channel-customer-service/.
39. "Modern Customer Service," p. 19, 2015, http://images.forbes.com/forbesinsights/StudyPDFs/Oracle-ModernCustomerService-Report.pdf.
40. "How Koodo Created Award-Winning Self-Service," nd, https://getsatisfaction.com/corp/resource-center/case_studies/koodo.php.
41. "Industry's First Crowdsourcing Platform and Online Community Driving Forces Behind Koodo's Success," February 4, 2014, http://www.techvibes.com/blog/online-community-driving-forces-behind-koodos-success-2014-02-04.
42. https://community.koodomobile.com/koodo?INTCMP=KMNew_NavMenu_support_Community.
43. "SaskTel and Koodo Mobile Rank Highest in Wireless Customer Satisfaction for a Third Consecutive Year," May 8, 2014, http://www.jdpower.com/press-releases/2014-canadian-wireless-total-ownership-experience-study.
44. "SaskTel Ranks Highest in Wireless Customer Satisfaction with Customer Care," May 14, 2015, http://canada.jdpower.com/press-releases/2015-canadian-wireless-customer-care-study.
45. http://www.eddiebauer.com/custserv/customer-service-services.jsp.
46. Michelle Saettler, "Eddie Bauer Chooses Journeying Over Commerce in New App," July 31, 2014, http://www.mobilemarketer.com/cms/news/advertising/18357.html.
47. http://www.firstinsight.com/; Arthur Zachiewicz, "Eddie Bauer, Caleres Ink Partnership Deals with First Insight," http://wwd.com/retail-news/technology/eddie-bauer-first-insight-deal-10313140/.
48. Kate Leggett, "Trends 2016: The Future of Customer Service," January 5, 2016, http://go.genesys.com/rs/426-TDW-681/images/Trends_2016_The_Future_Of.pdf; "20 Customer Service Best Practices," 2014, https://secure.sfdcstatic.com/assets/pdf/misc/20CSBP.pdf.

Chapter 17

Social and Regulatory Issues: Privacy, Security, and Intellectual Property

LEARNING OBJECTIVES

By the time you complete this chapter, you will be able to:

1. Discuss trust as a facilitator of internet activity.
2. List some of the concerns consumers have about the privacy of their personally identifiable information.
3. Discuss the privacy issues that are especially applicable to users of social networks.
4. Identify consumer concerns about privacy and security in the mobile space.
5. Describe privacy protection efforts that affect children, financial, and health data.
6. Identify actions being taken by businesses to protect personally identifiable information.
7. Identify the Fair Information Practices Principles.
8. Discuss self-regulation and regulatory action to protect privacy in countries other than the United States.

9. Explain the significance of data breaches and other threats to the security of consumer data.
10. Discuss significant issues related to the protection of intellectual property on the internet.

From the origin of the internet as a project sponsored by the U.S. Department of Defense to its current status as a global network, the relationships among internet users, governmental agencies, and the public at large have often been strained. The internet boasts a tradition of free speech and a "caveat emptor" attitude toward information and activities that take place there. However, as the internet has evolved into a mass medium with users of all ages and degrees of technological sophistication, there has been greater concern over protection of users. Public policy makers all over the world have evidenced this concern.

There are a variety of consumer protection issues that have either arisen or become more urgent because of the internet. This chapter will examine three key issues: the privacy of **PII (personally identifiable information)**, the security of data and transactions, and the protection of intellectual property on the internet. It will consider customer attitudes and behaviors with respect to privacy and security issues. It will also consider both corporate and governmental reactions to these various issues.

The ability of business and government to assure citizens that their data are safe and being used properly affects the trust people have in those institutions. That is especially true on the internet, where consumer power and access to information has reached an all time high.[1] We should therefore begin by briefly considering the importance and role of trust as a facilitator of internet use and ecommerce activity.

PII (personally identifiable information) any piece of data that can identify a person, alone or in combination with other data items; also sometimes called personally identifying information.

THE ROLE OF TRUST IN FACILITATING INTERNET ACTIVITY

The Edelman public relations firm conducts an annual study of trust in institutions in various countries. The 2011 study was conducted among a sample of "Informed Publics," a very specific subset of the population who are college-educated, upper income, and media savvy consumers.[2] In 2015, for the first time, trust was highest in search engines versus other types of media, reflecting changes in how users access information and a growing distrust of traditional media in general (Figure 17.1a). In 2016, Edelman found a difference in trust levels between the informed publics (15 percent) and the mass populations (85 percent), the first indication of a "trust gap."[3] Trust levels have not budged with the mass populations but were slightly increased for the informed publics.

Each year Edelman has found differences, some of them substantial, among countries in the degree to which they trusted business, government, the media, and nongovernmental organizations (NGOs) to do the right thing. Looking at the trend over time in the United States, it is clear that the global financial crisis that began in 2008 damaged trust in all institutions studied. However, over time and continuing to 2015, the pattern remains the same: NGOs are most trusted, and media and government are at or near the bottom. Business retains a certain level of trust among the public, although the 2015 data shows the trust level at less than 50 percent in the United States. However, there was an increase in trust in business among the informed publics in 2016 and an agreement that business must lead the way in improving trust in society (Figure 17.1b).

The fact remains that the majority of people in the majority of countries do not trust business. Family-owned and small to medium size businesses have a trust advantage and four out of ten people do not trust CEOs. The decline in trust seems to stem from the rapid pace of change and particularly technologies that are transforming our lives, such as genetically modified organisms (GMOs) and hydraulic fracking techniques.

Consumers look to business for innovation, but now, partially due to the advent of social media, want to be involved in that innovation. In fact, according to Edelman,

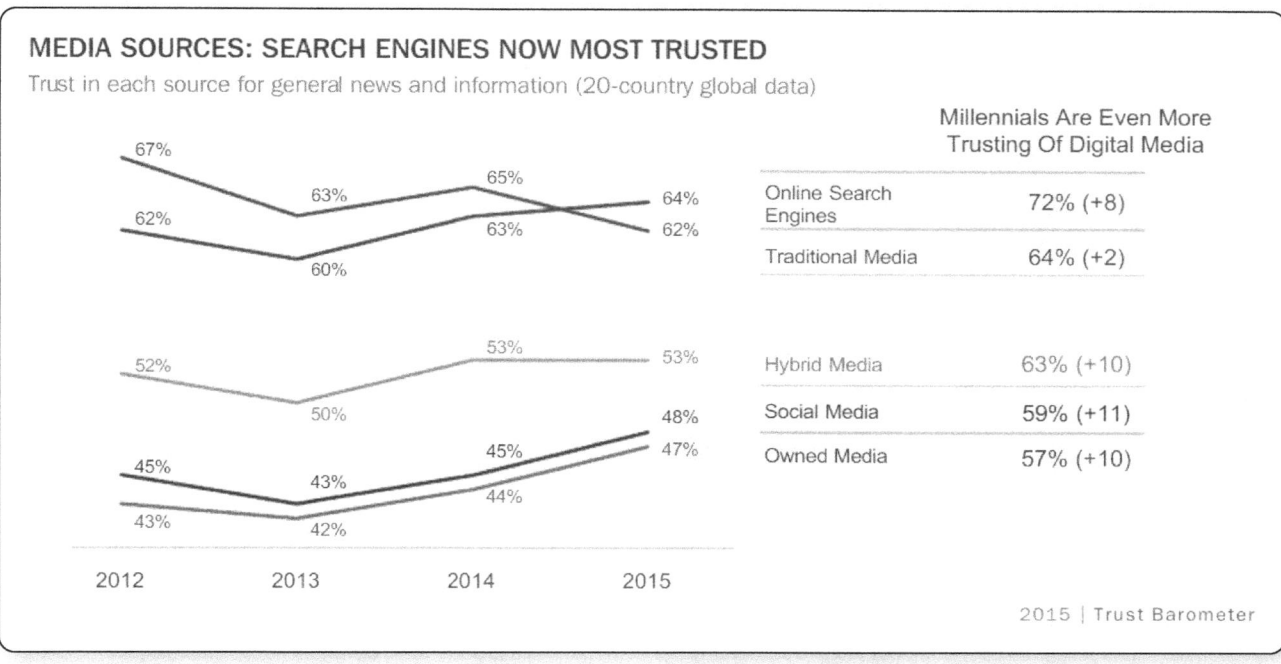

FIGURE 17.1a

A Search Engine Is Now the Most Trusted Form of Media

involvement in the innovation means that the trust level will be higher for that innovation.

Internationally, the level of trust on a national level has dropped. Figure 17.1c shows that the percent of Trusted Countries decreased from 30 percent to 22 percent in 2015 and Distrusters increased from 33 percent to 48 percent in 2015.[4] To learn more about the 2015 Edelman study, watch this video.

Businesses know that trust is important, but the question is can we get there? The 2011 Edelman report points to a high level of agreement with the statement that "corporations should create shareholder value in a way that aligns with society's interests, even if that means sacrificing shareholder value." According to the Edelman 2016 Trust Barometer, much of the trust burden falls on the executive. Today's CEOs are expected to:

- Focus on projects that are ethical and have a positive long-term impact.
- Communicate their personal values.
- Communicate with the employees and empower them to be company advocates.
- Consider all sources, including social media, to effectively engage the public.

Trust is a "protective agent," which conveys tangible benefits, while lack of trust is hard to change.[5] There is evidence that the degree of trust consumers have in the internet in general and in specific brands does influence their behavior. Milne and Culnan, in a study of who reads privacy policies, list privacy actions taken by readers after they read privacy policies:

- Eighty-seven percent refused to give information to a website because it was too personal or unnecessary.

FIGURE 17.1b

Trust Has Declined Among All Types of Institutions

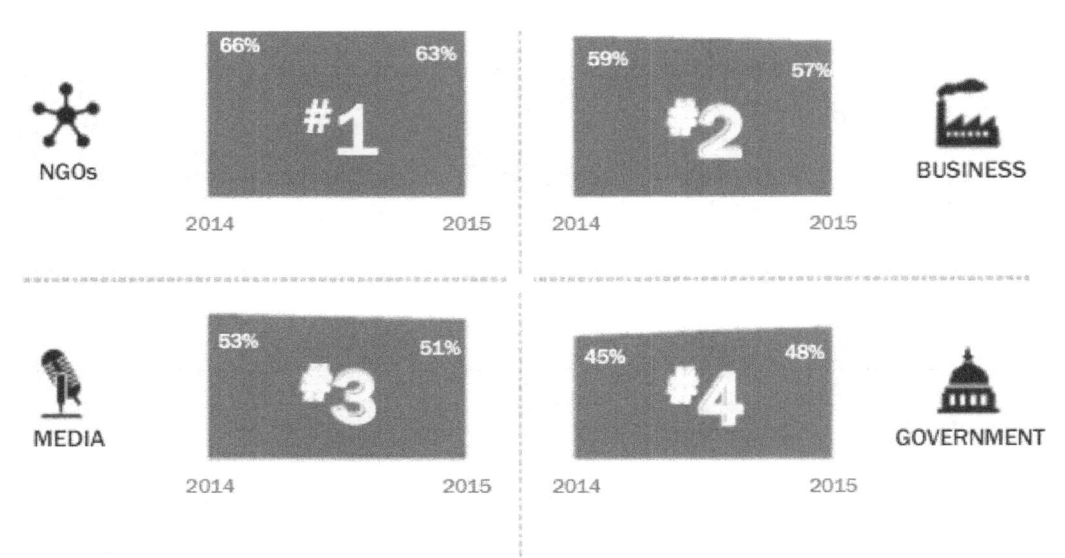

- Eighty-four percent asked to have their name and address removed from marketing lists.
- Eighty-one percent asked a website not to share name or personal information with other companies.
- Sixty-six percent decided not to use a website or to purchase because they were unsure of how personal information would be used.
- Thirty-two percent set their browser to reject cookies.
- Thirty-two percent supplied incorrect information to a website when asked to register.[6]

People are willing to take various actions to protect their PII. Those actions sometimes seem counter to the data needs of marketers.

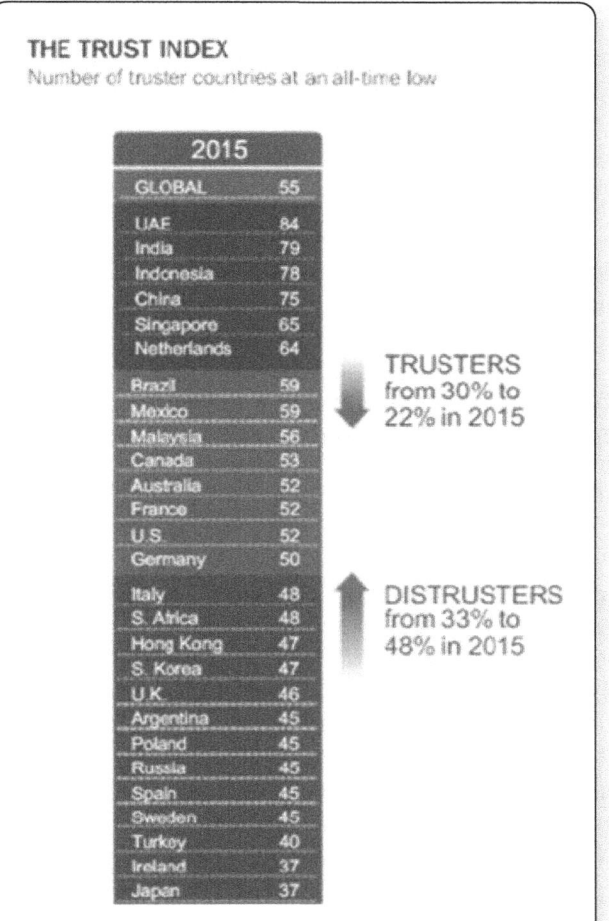

FIGURE 17.1c

The Number of Trusted Countries Has Declined Overall and Developing Countries Lead in Trust in Institutions

On the other hand, writing about "The Trust Imperative," MIT marketing professor Glen Urban points out that there are positive advantages in building trust in the customer base. He identifies those advantages as:

- *Reduced customer acquisition cost.* He argues that the advertising of trusted brands will receive greater attention. In addition, customers will be more loyal to trusted companies, reducing their need to acquire large numbers of new customers to replace defecting ones.
- *Higher profit margins.* Customers are willing to pay a premium for products or services from a trusted supplier.
- *Growth.* Trusted companies will be more successful in selling more to their existing customers and in converting visitors to customers.
- *Long-term competitive advantage.* A trusted brand and strong relationships based on understanding of customer needs will contribute to long-term success.[7]

Accenture, in its 2015 Technology Trends Report,[8] agrees, saying that the problem is not a lack of data but how to manage it responsibly to create trust. "Customers increasingly want better, faster, and cheaper all at once. In response, companies must create new ways to capture attention, deliver new services, and build trust." Accenture identifies the dimensions of trust as:

- *Security.* The protection of personal information against misuse or theft.
- *Data control.* The consumer has control over who has access to PII and when as well as what they are permitted to do with it.
- *Accountability.* Taking responsibility for and correcting incorrect information.[9]
- *Benefit.* The uses of the data provide value to the consumer as well as to the business.

Experts agree that trust can only be built, action by action, over a period of time. That emphasizes Professor Urban's contention that trust can provide long-term competitive advantage. That advantage would accrue to companies who pay immediate attention to the importance of being a trusted entity in both B2C and B2B markets. He adds that, "Trust is hard to earn—and easy to lose."[10]

The rise of social media has added another dimension to the issue of trust in businesses and their brands. Social media guru Chris Brogan has written a book called *Trust Agents* and speaks often about the importance of trust issues to businesses and their brands. He defines a trust agent as someone who is working to put a human face on a business. In an interview with HubSpot he said:

> *"The trust agent is the kind of person who, inside an organization, is translating that organization's presence on the web, how to be human at a distance. The idea is that we have all this marketing speak, PR speak, etc. What a trust agent is, is somebody that you get the feeling that you're doing business with that company through that person."*[11]

With an understanding of the importance of trust and the role of data protection and privacy in creating it, we can turn to an examination of the state of data privacy in the United States and globally.

DATA PROTECTION AND PRIVACY ON THE INTERNET

Writing in the *Journal of Interactive Marketing*, Harvard professor John Deighton pointed to the increasing vulnerability consumers feel as a result of the way business is done on the internet. According to Deighton:

> *In the physical world, they (consumers) can choose to be anonymous, trading cash for goods and moving on with no trace of their identity left behind. When they trade in cyberspace, anonymity is not an option. They have to say who they are, how to get back to them, and what their credit record is worth, or the transaction falls apart. They will give this information only if they are confident that it will not be used against them. If they are not sure of that, they know very well that there are many other ways to do business, and they will cast their vote to defer the arrival of the digital age.*

> *Deeper insight into the human need for privacy, then, is perhaps as important to the blossoming of the interactive marketing industry as any single factor. We need to understand why so often people want to be let alone, and why sometimes they do not. Marketing fundamentally, of course, is about meeting customer needs. In the matter of privacy, what are the needs that are met and not met?*[12]

In this section, we examine what is known about consumer privacy concerns in the United States and other internet economies, and what responses have been made by business and regulatory agencies in the United States and the European Union (EU).

Consumer Attitudes toward the Privacy of Their Information

There have been studies of consumer attitudes about the privacy of personal information since the beginning of the internet. In general, they have shown that consumers are concerned about the privacy of their PII, although their willingness to take action to protect it varies with issues and time. The 2010 Ponemon Institute study of trusted brands makes the following points:

- Consumers perceive loss of control of personal information. Only 41 percent feel in control and that the percentage has been dropping consistently since 2006.
- Identity theft is a major concern. Fifty-nine percent of respondents cited identity theft as a major factor in decreasing trust of brands while 50 percent said that occurrence of a data breach was important.
- Privacy protection features contributed to brand trust. Sixty percent of respondents looked for substantial security protections while 53 percent cited accurate data collection and use. They also had a positive view on limits to the collection of PII and online anonymity.[13]

These general findings are important, but it is clear that three specific issues dominated the discussion of consumer data privacy by 2011. These issues are a long-held concern about being tracked online, and newer concerns related to use of social networks and mobile technologies.[14]

Behavioral Tracking In 2008, Harris Interactive conducted a poll designed by privacy expert Dr. Alan Westin. In general, it found about 60 percent of respondents to be "uncomfortable" when major portals used information about online activities to target ads or tailor content based on a person's hobbies or interests. A quarter of the respondents were "not at all" comfortable with this practice. Only 7 percent were "very comfortable," while 34 percent were "somewhat comfortable."

The researchers then introduced four possible data safeguards based on 2007 Federal Trade Commission (FTC) recommendations. The issues covered were consumer control of their data; security and limited retention of data; express consent for changes in privacy policies; and special protection for sensitive data including data about children, sexual orientation, and health.[15] (The FTC issued revisions in 2009 that maintained these four principles but loosened the application to anonymous user data and contextual advertising.[16]) In 2012, the FTC issued a report "Protecting Consumer Privacy in an Era of Rapid Change: Recommendations for Businesses and Policymakers," which updated a 2010 finding, with more specific guidelines for protecting privacy including the following:

- **"Privacy by Design**—companies should build in consumers' privacy protections at every stage in developing their products. These include reasonable security for consumer data, limited collection and retention of such data, and reasonable procedures to promote data accuracy;
- **Simplified Choice for Businesses and Consumers**—companies should give consumers the option to decide what information is shared about them, and with whom. This should include a Do-Not-Track mechanism that would provide a simple, easy way for consumers to control the tracking of their online activities.
- **Greater Transparency**—companies should disclose details about their collection and use of consumers' information, and provide consumers access to the data collected about them."

The report included privacy practices for mobile technology and included some suggestions so as to not place an undue burden on small businesses (the report suggests that the proposed framework should not apply to companies that collect and do not transfer only nonsensitive data from fewer than 5,000 consumers a year).[17]

A recent poll by Consumer Action as reported by Marketing Charts in Figure 17.2a indicates that a majority of internet users believe there is harm to behavioral tracking and

FIGURE 17.2a
Consumer Attitudes to Online Tracking
Consumers see harm in online tracking and seek control

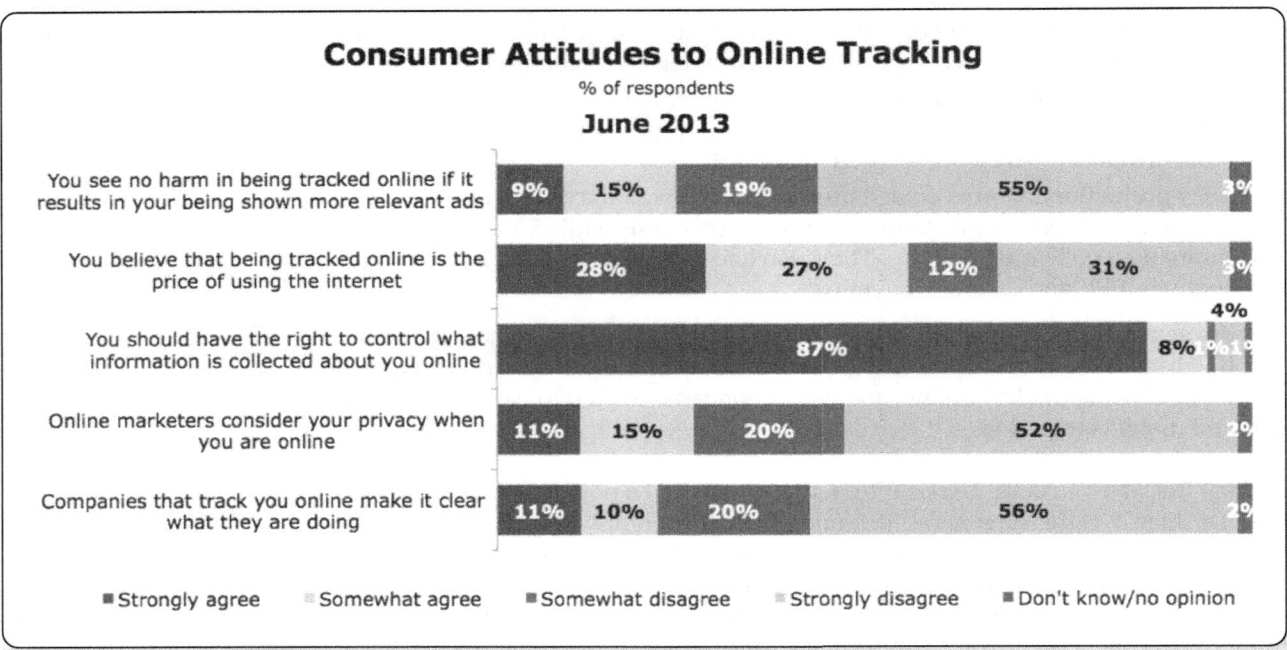

SOURCE: Consumer Action

do not believe tracking companies care about consumer privacy or consider their interests. Consumers see as an answer to this problem explicit consumer control. Figure 17.2b shows that 64 percent of consumers in a 2013 TRUSTe poll expressed concern over their privacy, up from the year before. By 2014, more than 90 percent of U.S. consumers said they worry about their personal information, with the major source of concern being business usage of data and government surveillance.[18] In addition, a recent study indicated that 33 percent of U.S. consumers were considering using ad-blocking software, a decision with serious financial consequences for advertisers.[19] Any prior reports of differences in attitudes between generations and genders appear to be narrowing, with all types of consumers increasingly concerned about privacy and data security.

One reason for this concern is the dramatic rise in incidents involving PII in the last few years, as shown in Figure 17.2c. For example, a data breach in the Target system in 2013 affected 40 million users and resulted in a $39 million dollar settlement by Target with the banking industry. This is only one of many incidents of this nature, which apparently are only going to increase in the future. Interestingly, the Target data breach was the result of hacking at its point of sale system, not at the internet interface, which indicates that consumers need to be aware of data breaches at many points.[20]

This consumer sensitivity about use of their online activity data for behavioral advertising has not escaped the notice of internet marketers. In 2009, the Interactive Advertising Bureau (IAB), in partnership with five other national advertising and marketing trade groups, set forth principles for industry self-regulation of online behavioral advertising (OBA).[21] Of several principles, the three with the most impact are:

- Education of consumers about OBA
- Transparency in the deployment of that advertising
- Consumer control over collection and transfer of data

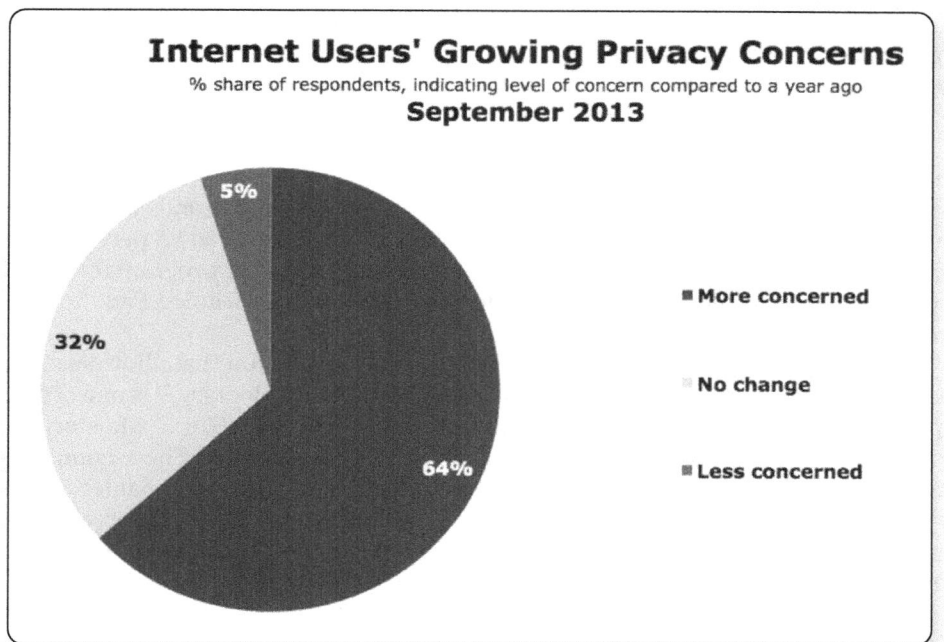

FIGURE 17.2b

Consumer Concern Is Rising

SOURCE: Marketing Charts, "Internet Users Growing Privacy Concerns," (September, 2013), http://www.marketingcharts.com/online/privacy-a-growing-concern-for-almost-2-in-3-internet-users-36781/

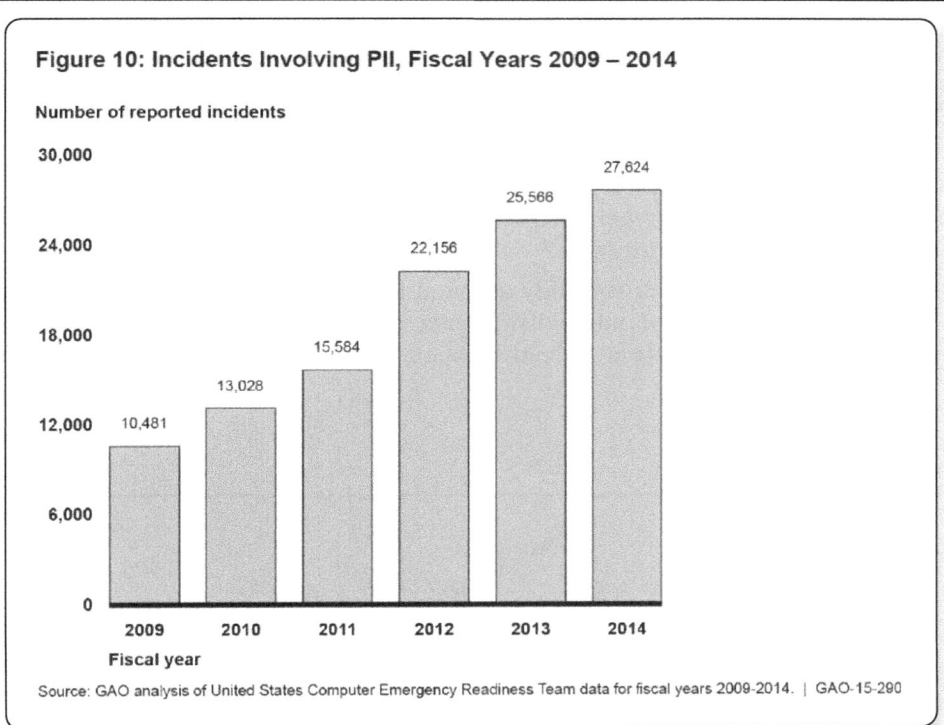

FIGURE 17.2c

Number of Incidents Involving PII Have Skyrocketed

SOURCE: Watch Blog "A Closer Look at Privacy as a High Risk Area—When Advancing Technology Meets Increasing Concerns," (May 19, 2015), https://blog.gao.gov/2015/05/19/a-closer-look-at-privacy-as-a-high-risk-area-when-advancing-technology-meets-increasing-concerns/

Practically speaking, the program offers consumers more notice that behavioral data are being collected and more choices over what data are collected and by whom. The notice is displayed near behavioral ads and on corporate websites near the point where data are being collected. Consumers can exercise choice by opting out of some or all of the business's online behavioral ads.

As of June 2016, over 400 companies participated in the DAA program,[22] entitling them to display the Advertising Option Icon shown in Figure 17.3. The participating companies include 10 of the top 20 global advertising brands and all 10 of the top 10 advertising networks, which together reach more than 85 percent of all U.S. internet households. In 2015, the DAA announced a similar program for mobile applications based on the same principles as the Consumer Choice Page for Web Browsers.[23]

Ghostery (formerly Evidon) is freeware browser extension that allows users to see which ad services are tracking them and can allow for ad blocking,[24] is one of three "approved providers" of the DAA program (the others being TRUSTe).[25] Ghostery also helps companies improve their customers' online web experiences. These companies have authorization from the DAA to distribute the DAA Icon to companies as well as provide resources for consumers, advertisers, and ad networks. Enforcement of compliance with the DAA Self-Regulatory Principles for OBA is handled by both the Council of Better Business Bureaus' National Advertising Review Council (NARC) and the Direct Marketing Association (DMA).[26] There is also concern that awareness of the meaning of the icon is low among consumers and that self-regulation therefore may not be effective.[27]

Professor Alessandro Acquisti of Carnegie Mellon University has been studying the economics of privacy for many years and has an informative resources page on the subject. On it, he points out that the subject of privacy represents an economic trade-off for both business and the consumer. As data storage has become cheap, businesses have been encouraged to collect more data about users. As the previous studies have indicated, consumers are not thrilled about the collection and use of their data. He points out the essential economic trade-off that affects both:

> *The hunger for customization and usability has led individuals to reveal more about themselves to other parties. New trade-offs have emerged in which privacy, economics, and technology are inextricably linked: individuals want to avoid the misuse of the information they pass along to others, but they also want to share enough information to achieve satisfactory interactions; organizations want to know more about the parties with which they interact, but they do not want to alienate them with policies deemed as intrusive.*[28]

A 2011 Harris Interactive study showed that most consumers still did not believe that the majority of online display ads are relevant to their needs and were reluctant to share information with advertisers. In 2015, Columbia Business School

FIGURE 17.3

Advertising Option Icon

SOURCE: Digital Advertising Alliance, http://www.aboutads.info

began a study that asked, "What is the Future of Data Sharing," which indicates that customers are still wary of sharing data, but somewhat more sophisticated than in 2011.[29] Columbia surveyed 8,000 consumers, including over 2,000 in the United States and found that they broke into four categories, that is, Defenders (43 percent), Savvy and In Control (24 percent), Resigned (23 percent), and Happy Go Lucky (10 percent). The categories rate consumers on whether they are high or low in terms of defending their data and high or low in terms of propensity to share. The Savvy and In Control, for example, rate highly on both dimensions. Figure 17.4 shows that although consumers are the most concerned about sharing PII such as name and address with brands, that this is the type of information they are most likely to share to facilitate a purchase. Types of information they are most reluctant to share include email and personal contact information. Interestingly, in the Columbia study, over 40 percent of the respondents were definitely unwilling to share their online browsing data. Since that is not an attractive solution to marketers, it is obviously important for them to try to find a way to make the internet community more comfortable with the concept of online tracking for behavioral advertising.

Even before the behavioral advertising issue has been completely settled, the new internet developments of social media and mobile have presented new privacy challenges.

Privacy, or Lack Thereof, on Social Networks   In 1999, Scott McNeely who was then CEO of Sun Microsystems famously said at an industry event, "You have zero privacy anyway. Get over it."[30] That statement received considerable attention at the time, but as the preceding section shows, many people are still concerned about lack of privacy.

FIGURE 17.4

Types of Information That Consumers Do Not Want to Share with Advertisers

FIGURE 17.4a

Consumers Consider PII to Be the Most Sensitive Data

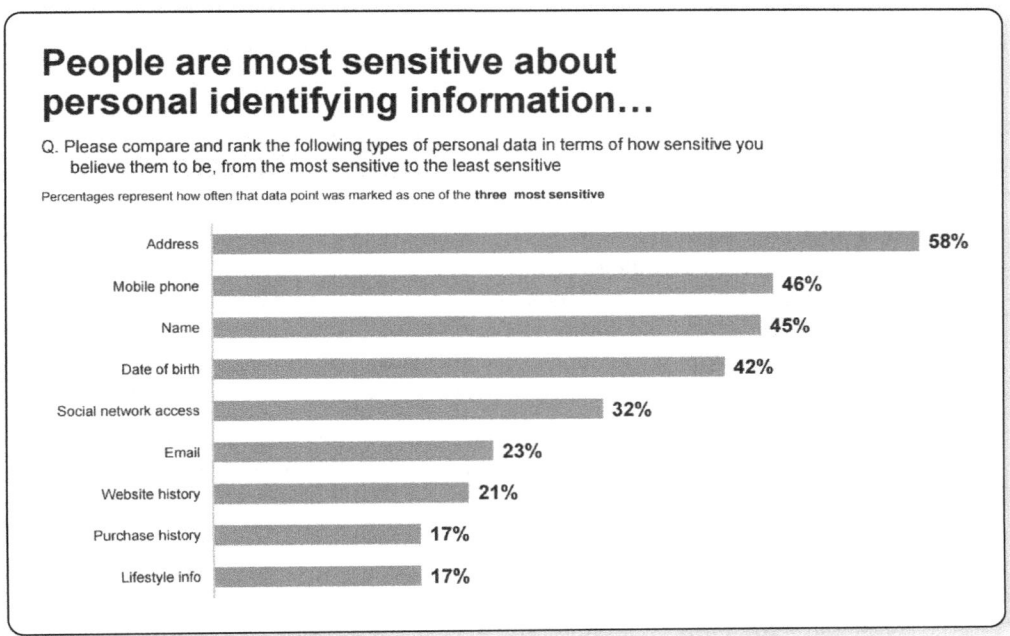

SOURCE: Columbia Business School (2015) What is the Future of Data Sharing? Consumer Mindsets and the Power or Brands, Matthew Quint and David Rogers.

FIGURE 17.4b

Consumers Are Willing to Share PII to Facilitate Purchases

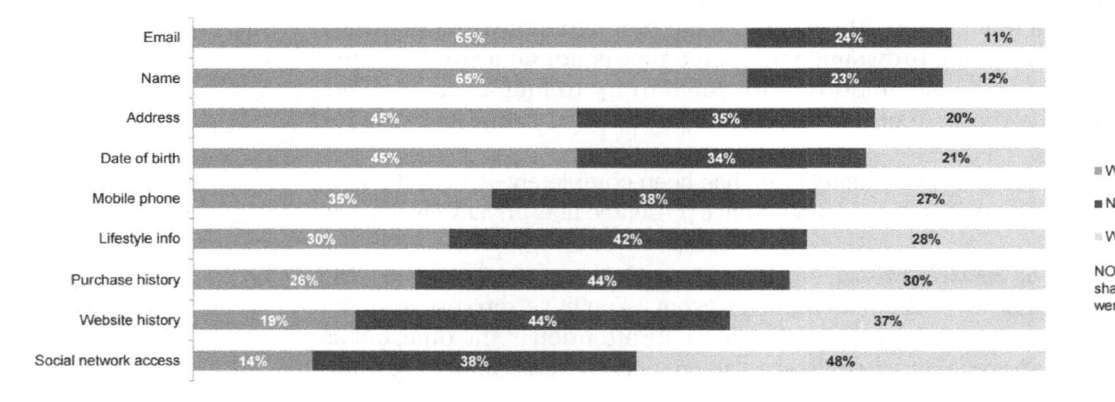

SOURCE: http://www8.gsb.columbia.edu/globalbrands/sites/globalbrands/files/images/The_Future_of_Data_Sharing_Columbia-Aimia_October_2015.pdf Types of Information That U.S. Internet Users Would Not Share with Advertisers, July 2011 (percent of respondents)

Just as famously, Facebook founder Mark Zuckerberg was quoted in 2010 as saying that people no longer have an expectation of privacy. At an industry conference he said:

> *People have really gotten comfortable not only sharing more information and different kinds, but more openly and with more people. That social norm is just something that has evolved over time.*[31]

Whether you agree with those statements or not, it is clear that the rise of social networks has added another dimension to the issue of PII privacy.

Volumes can be, and have been, written about the issue of privacy on social networks. To cut the issue down to somewhat manageable size, this section will concentrate on Facebook, which is the focus of much of the privacy controversy. However, the reader should keep in mind that to a greater or lesser extent, these issues do apply to all social networks.[32] The specifics are laid out in the privacy policy of each site, and you should consult them for more details.

Even the discussion of Facebook privacy issues can emphasize only some of the major issues confronted by the network over its lifetime. Here is a partial chronology:

- *2004: Facebook is founded as a closed network for students at Harvard.* According to the *Harvard Crimson*, Zuckerberg had already faced a privacy blowback from an earlier site, facemash.com. He told the *Crimson* that members were offered intensive privacy options:

    > You can limit who can see your information, if you only want current students to see your information, or people in your year, in your house, in your classes. You can limit a search so that only a friend or a friend of a friend can look you up. People have very good control over who can see their information.[33]

- *2006: Facebook opens registration to the general public.* Later that year, it introduced the News Feed product, which showed all the activity of friends on an individual's page. Many users were vocally opposed to the new product because it cluttered their page and others were disturbed by the information it showed. Facebook responded by pointing out that privacy options had not changed, but it was only a few days before Facebook responded to the controversy by introducing new privacy controls and admitting that they erred initially.[34]

    The author of a Facebook privacy timeline at the Electronic Frontier Foundation argues that you can see Facebook privacy protections eroding over time.[35] There is no doubt that Facebook privacy policies and options change frequently so any content you see on other sites is probably already outdated. You can see the current privacy options and find a link to Facebook's privacy policy and FAQs by clicking on the Privacy link at the bottom of your Facebook page.

- *2007: Facebook offers an advertising product called Beacon.* Essentially, it allowed subscribers to see what friends had purchased on numerous large sites who were participating in the program. As the controversy about the system built, Facebook changed the privacy option to allow users to opt out of the notifications, but it did not allow them to opt out of the system entirely, meaning that their data were still being collected.[36] A lawsuit in 2008 forced Facebook to allow members to opt out of Beacon entirely.
- In 2009, Facebook discontinued the product.
- Also in 2007, Facebook began to allow developers to create their own apps.[37] It appears that a security flaw in the Facebook platform allowed apps to access member profile data and make it available to third parties. Facebook addressed the security problem in 2011 after it was exposed by internet security firm Symantec.[38]
- *2008: Facebook Connect is introduced.* This service allows members to sign in to other websites using their Facebook username and password. Many of these other websites developed apps, some of which allowed members to post to Facebook. The privacy issue arose when privacy settings on the apps were more lenient than those on Facebook. Modifying them was initially difficult or impossible.[39]
- *April 2010: Facebook introduced the "like button" icon for websites.* The icon essentially makes a Facebook page for each product on a site that is liked by a visitor.[40] The icon also allows Facebook to collect browsing data even if the member has not liked the product.[41]
- *Late in 2010: Facebook introduced facial recognition technology that enabled automatic photo tagging.* Photos uploaded and tagged by users were matched with other photos using facial recognition software. The user was then allowed to add the tag to the other photos. Users were allowed to adjust their privacy settings to opt out of automatic tagging and were notified after they had been tagged by another user, but many users still objected to the practice.[42]

    Alessandro Acquisti and his colleagues demonstrated the power of the software by taking pictures of Carnegie Mellon students (with their permission) and matching them with Facebook profile pictures. They were able to identify 31 percent of the students by name.[43] Controversy swirled around that site feature and Germany became the first country to demand that the feature be disabled and all data about German citizens be destroyed.[44]

- *November 2011: Facebook reached what was described as "a broad settlement" with the FTC that requires the company to respect the privacy of users.*[45] In its announcement, the FTC listed a number of instances in which it alleges that Facebook did not keep privacy promises made to its users. The settlement also required that Facebook undergo regular privacy audits by independent auditors for the next 20 years.[46] In a blog post,[47] Mark Zuckerberg admitted that Facebook had made mistakes and said that many had already been corrected. The agreement is similar to one made between the FTC and Google earlier in 2011.[48]

Since that time, Facebook has tried to make it as easy as possible for users to understand how their information is being shared. Users can view the Privacy Basics information to understand how to create settings for posts, profiles, friends, and tagging.[49]

For sure, this is a story that is "to be continued." Facebook continues to add features and users continue to find additional uses for it. Remember that this is also a story that is being played out on other social networks and sites and applications that hold customer data.[50] For example, Google recently changed its privacy settings to make it easier to understand and manage information kept on Google accounts, such as G+ and Gmail. The privacy settings page can be viewed here. Mobile, however, is a bit of a different story.

Security and Privacy on Mobile Networks Previously, it appeared that security of data was the greatest concern for mobile users—both for laptop computers and for cell phones. Security of data is clearly an issue while data are being transferred back and forth over wireless networks. Other mobile security issues will be discussed in the next section.

However, recently the picture seems to have changed. TRUSTe conducted a study of smart phone users in early 2011. It found that concern over data privacy has outstripped concern over data security among its sample of smartphone users (see Figure 17.5). In addition to highlighting the importance of privacy, especially among users of mobile apps, the study confirmed that respondents distrust targeted advertising and 85 percent want to be able to opt out of targeted mobile ads. They are also distrustful of location tracking; 77 percent do not want apps to be able to track their location. Virtually all (98 percent) want more control over how apps collect and use PII. They value strong passwords and privacy trust-marks, and they pay attention to privacy policies. Are consumers more aware of both privacy and security issues in the mobile environment?

The mobile picture is also full of contradictions, with mobile users also willing to exchange PII for something of value. A 2011 study by security firm McAfee and Carnegie Mellon University deals with the blurring of the lines between personal and workplace usages of mobile devices. The report says that "mobility is changing our lives on all levels—personal, professional, and political,"[51] and that the changes offer dazzling opportunities to organizations of many kinds, but they also present security issues. Workers tend to use corporate devices, both laptops and mobile phones, for both business and personal use. They use their own equipment for business purposes. Businesses need to provide data to their workers wherever they are, whenever they need it. Lost and stolen devices are as big a worry as is hacking. All of these suggest

FIGURE 17.5

Privacy a Greater Concern than Security among Smartphone Users

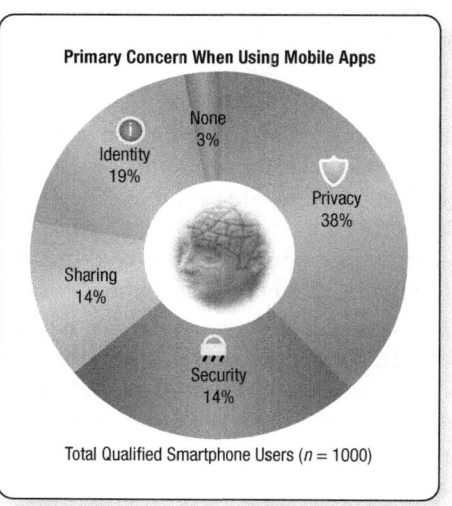

SOURCE: TRUSTe, http://www.truste.com/blog/?p=1456.

a security nightmare for corporate IT managers who need to have strong policies in place and to ensure that workers are aware and observant of them.

The conclusion is that in the current mobile environment, privacy is the chief concern of consumers while data security is the chief concern of businesses. That does suggest opportunity in both market spaces. Retailers who are seen as trustworthy, which includes providing needed security for data and transactions, have an opportunity to prosper in the mobile environment. Businesses who invest the required time and money in appropriate mobile security practices will lessen their own exposure to risk and contribute to their reputation for trustworthiness. In addition, the "Internet of Things" has produced another set of issues relating to privacy and security. The FTC recommends that privacy and security be built in to the product from the beginning. Cross-device tracking, where logins are required to identify consumers across channels and devices, will be another challenge for businesses in terms of privacy concerns.[52]

Before we leave the subject of the privacy and security of user data, we need to consider three especially sensitive subjects, data about children, financial data, and health data. In general, the United States has been unwilling to regulate internet data practices, but the sensitivity of these types of data has led to regulation in the United Sates as well as in Europe, where there has been greater willingness to regulate data practices. The first regulation in the United States was **COPPA**, the Children's Online Privacy Protection Act.

COPPA the Children's Online Privacy Protection Act regulates websites that collect information from those under 13 by, among other things, requiring prior parental consent

Regulation of Children's Privacy Issues

Whether you call them "Digital Natives"[53] or describe them as "Born Digital" (children born after 1980 who are accustomed to digital access),[54] children and teenagers are active on the web and encounter a variety of dangers there. Our concern is with the privacy of their data. The following two stories are illustrative.

1. The *Wall Street Journal* investigated the amount of data about children that is available online and found it to be substantial. It noted that the small sites that proliferate in the children's market had privacy policies that varied widely. However, Google placed the most tracking cookies of the 50 large sites analyzed. According to the journal's analysis:

    Google accurately identified a dozen pastimes of 10-year-old Jenna Maas—including pets, photography, "virtual worlds" and "online goodies" such as little animated graphics to decorate a website.

    "It is a real eye opener," said Jenna's mother, Kate Maas, a schoolteacher in Charleston, S.C., viewing that data.[55]

2. The *Washington Post* investigated the impact of smartphones on the data profiles of older teens. It focused on 13-year-old Scott Fitzsimones who had just gotten an iPhone. He immediately set up accounts with Facebook and Pandora and "went on an apps downloading spree." That involved using his parents' credit card and providing data. He told the *Post* that the first time a game asked for his location he stopped and wondered why. However, he gave it and nothing bad happened, so he has given it many times since. In fact, he "never says no."[56]

A 2012 Pew Study of teenagers and privacy (see Figure 17.6) entitled the "Pew/Internet Parent Teen Privacy Survey," teens report that they post on social media profiles the following information:

"91% post a **photo of themselves**, up from 79% in 2006.

71% post their **school name**, up from 49%.

71% post the **city or town where they live**, up from 61%. 53% post their **email address**, up from 29%.

20% post their **cell phone number**, up from 2%."[57]

FIGURE 17.6 Teen Social Media Profiles

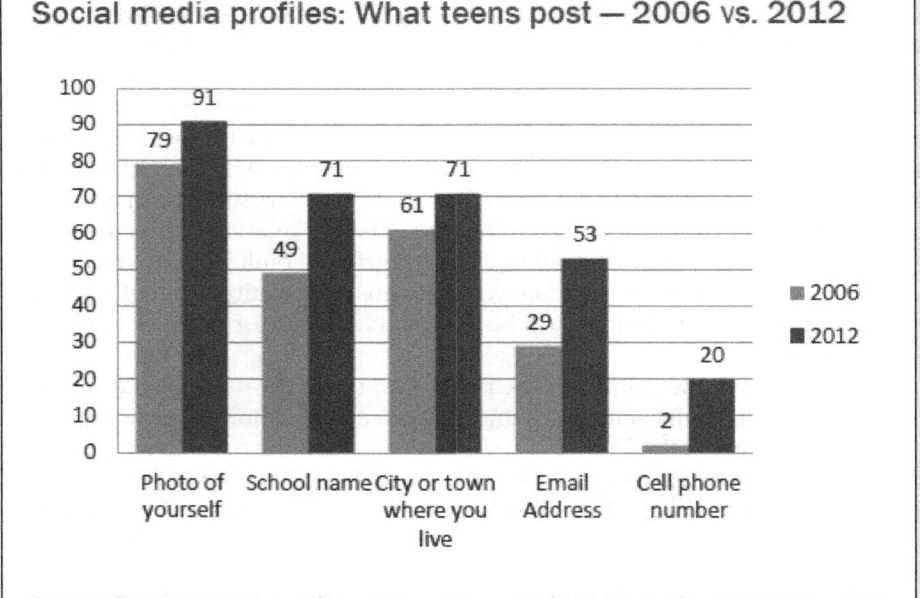

Source: Pew Internet Parent/Teen Privacy Survey, July 26-September 30, 2012. n=802 teens ages 12-17. Interviews were conducted in English and Spanish and on landline and cell phones. Margin of error for results based on teen social media users is +/- 5.1 percentage points. Comparison data for 2006 comes from the Pew Internet Parents & Teens Survey, October 23-November 19, 2006. n=487 teens with a profile online. Margin of error is +/- 5.2 percentage points.

The study of teenagers' information sharing on social networks gives insight into attitudes and practices. The Pew study focused on profile information while noting that many other kinds of data are available online. Overall, the picture is of children and teenagers who provide substantial data about themselves, both implicitly and explicitly, on the web. However, there is some evidence of self-policing, with girls being less likely to share phone numbers publicly than boys.

There is a regulatory tradition of considering children a vulnerable group in terms of marketing and advertising, and from the early days of the internet, special attention has been given to children as internet users. In 1997, the FTC brought the first-ever privacy complaint against the GeoCities website, which alleged that the site had violated its own privacy policy. Its violations were alleged to be especially serious in the case of its children's community. The issue was said to be that GeoCities collected data from children in return for free website hosting, and turned that data over to third parties who then used it in ways inconsistent with GeoCities' posted privacy statements. The complaint was settled in 1999, just after Yahoo! announced its acquisition of the site. The consent decree specified a rigorous set of privacy practices that GeoCities agreed to follow for 10 years.[58]

This move by the FTC was followed by the passage by Congress in 1998 of the COPPA. The major provisions of the act required websites that knowingly collect information from children under the age of 13 to:

- Provide parents notice of their information practices.
- Obtain prior parental consent for the collection, use, and/or disclosure of personal information.
- Provide a parent, on request, with the ability to review the personal information collected from his child.

- Provide a parent with the opportunity to prevent the further use of personal information that has already been collected, or the future collection of personal information from that child.
- Limit collection of personal information for a child's online participation in a game, prize offer, or other activity to information that is reasonably necessary for the activity.
- Establish and maintain reasonable procedures to protect the confidentiality, security, and integrity of the personal information collected.[59]

The FTC is in charge of the guidelines for implementation of COPPA. It maintains a Children's Privacy page that provides information for websites that deal with children under 13 years of age. It also has links to information for parents and teachers as they attempt to protect and educate children on issues of privacy and safety on the web.[60] In late 2011, the FTC issued its first proposed revisions to COPPA in several years. The revised guidelines stem from improved technology for parental control and technology that makes children more vulnerable, including GPS-based applications and photos and video files.[61]

Regulation of Privacy in the Financial Services Sector

Another example of regulation with broad impact is the **Gramm-Leach-Bliley Act (GLBA)**, which became law in November 1999 and took effect in July 2001. According to Robert Pitofsky, who was then chairman of the FTC:

> *The GLBA requires a financial institution to disclose to all of its customers the institution's privacy policies and practices with respect to information it shares with both affiliates and nonaffiliated third parties and limits the instances in which a financial institution may disclose nonpublic personal information about a consumer to nonaffiliated third parties. Specifically, it prohibits a financial institution from disclosing nonpublic personal information about consumers to nonaffiliated third parties unless the institution satisfies various disclosure and opt-out requirements and the consumer has not elected to opt out of the disclosure.*[62]

Gramm-Leach-Bliley Act (GLBA) the Gramm-Leach-Bliley Act requires financial institutions to disclose privacy policies and practices to customers

The law requires that each year consumers must be notified about the specific privacy policy of the institution and offered an opportunity to opt out of certain types of information collection and transmission. Anecdotal evidence in various settings suggests that few consumers read this information with care and even fewer take the opportunity to opt out of the specified data collection and transfer activities. It also requires that corporations take proactive steps to ensure the safety of consumer data.

Several years after its implementation, there is criticism of the GLBA. The Electronic Privacy Information Center (EPIC) says:

> *First, the GLBA does not protect consumers. It unfairly places the burden on the individual to protect privacy with an opt-out standard . . . Second, the GLBA notices are confusing and limit the transparency of information practices.*[63]

EPIC argues for closing loopholes in the law and improving its enforcement. Most of all, it argues for consumer opt-in to practices that involve their PII and for privacy notifications in understandable layman's language.

The Dodd-Frank law, passed in the wake of the financial crisis of 2008, appears to do little to improve the situation described by EPIC. Called the Dodd-Frank Wall Street Reform and Consumer Protection Act,[64] it sounds as if data protection might be a component. That is apparently not the case; its coverage is limited to credit data. Quoting a presentation to the American Bar Association, it does cover "analyzing, collecting, and maintaining credit report information" but not impact "data security, data disposal, and red flags."[65] The reference to **red flags** refers to corporate policies to detect and prevent identity fraud.[66] That means that GLBA is still the main law mandating the protection and privacy of consumer data.

red flags refers to the Red Flags Rule that requires certain U.S. businesses to develop and document plans to protect consumer data from identity theft

Regulation of Privacy in the Health Care Sector

Health-related information is another area of special consumer concern. In 1996, Congress added a provision on privacy of medical records to the Health Insurance Portability and Accountability Act (**HIPAA**). The provision required that, if Congress did not pass a comprehensive law on the privacy of medical data within three years, the Department of Health and Human Services (HHS) would be required to develop a set of regulations to deal with misuse and disclosure of medical records. No law was passed, and in 1999, a set of rules was issued for public comment by the HHS, with a final revision issued in December 2000. The new administration, recognizing the public concern about this issue, agreed to let the rules take effect as scheduled in April 2001. The rules give patients greater control over their health information including access to their medical records, restrict the use and release of medical records, ensure the security of personal health information, and provide penalties for the misuse of personal health information.[67] One visible result has been the posting of data policies in the offices of health care providers and the requirement that each patient sign a statement asserting that he has read and understood the service provider's data privacy policies.

The Office of Civil Rights (OCR) of the Department of Health and Human Services is responsible for enforcing the law. It maintains a web page with information for consumers and for the health care providers, insurers, and health services providers who are covered by the law. It includes compliance mechanisms and training programs for health care providers.[68]

COPPA, GLBA, and HIPAA could have important ramifications as models for regulation of other industry sectors. In addition, they have a direct effort on marketers and services firms that serve the regulated sectors. They will affect database use throughout the industry as well as list brokers, who will be asked to certify that the lists they are renting are from organizations whose practices comply with the regulations. Had the attacks of 2001 and the financial crisis of 2008 not occurred and diverted attention from general consumer privacy issues, there might have been more regulatory attempts in the recent years. However, there have been developments that point the way to the future. The law continues to be defined by the courts and penalties have been levied for breaches. In March of 2016, for example, there was a $3.9 million **Health Insurance Portability and Accountability Act (HIPPA)** settlement when data containing confidential health information was stolen from a laptop in a researcher's car who worked for the Feinstein Institute of Medical Research. The laptop included the names of research participants, dates of birth, addresses, social security numbers, diagnoses, laboratory results, medications, and medical information relating to potential participation in a research study. The OCR ruled that research institutions subject to HIPPA must follow the same standards as other institutions.[69]

Health Insurance Portability and Accountability Act (HIPPA) Health Insurance Portability and Accountability Act gives patients greater control over their medical records and provides penalties for misuse of personal health information

Privacy Issues Going Forward

Consumer concern coupled with well-publicized data breaches (discussed in the next section) cause data privacy and security to remain a concern for public policy makers around the world. Privacy expert Jay Cline suggests there are two main reasons for the recent flurry of regulatory initiatives about data privacy. They are:

1. Marketing technologies including location data, online privacy, and smart grid technology. The first two are familiar to readers of this chapter. But what does the concept of a smart grid for distributing electricity have to do with consumer data privacy? According to the Future of Privacy Forum, "the many ways in which data about consumer demand will be used for smarter electricity provision have the potential to revolutionize the electricity industry and to benefit society. However, this very same information about consumers will create major concerns if consumer-focused principles of transparency and control are not treated as essential design principles from start to end of the standards development process."[70] That is something new to worry about!

2. "Bureaucratic momentum," which he describes as regulatory agencies around the world hitting their stride. Cline points to activities of a number of U.S. regulatory agencies, including a privacy framework issued by the FTC in 2010.[71] Canada passed a new e-mail spam law which takes full effect from July 1, 2017. (See Chapter 9.) After that date, marketers may only send messages to recipients with express consent or is currently implied under the law (within 24 months of purchase or six months after an inquiry).[72] Mexico has established a well-funded data protection bureau. During the transition period, the EU continues to be aggressive in the area of data protection. The European Commission has issued notice of its intent to update the landmark 1995 Data Protection Directive.[73]

   The EU started on a new path in 2016 after, in October of 2015, the European Court of Justice declared the Safe Harbor framework invalid. The new arrangement had struck down the "Safe Harbor" provision that allowed U.S. companies to pass data back and forth and replaced it with a stronger measure. The new measure is known as "Privacy Shield" and is stronger because there will be limits and controls over the rights of public authorities in the United States to access personal data transferred there.[74] However, there is some concern that EU data regulators will go to court over the changes, which many do not view as strong enough protection for EU citizens' data.[75] The EU has also passed a far-reaching law that requires marketers to obtain consent from the user before setting almost all cookies, although that law has met with resistance in some European countries and has been difficult to implement with uniformity.[76]

3. Terror prevention versus privacy

   In 2013, US citizen Edward Snowden worked as a contractor for the US National Security Administration (NSA). He released evidence of widespread government electronic surveillance conducted by the US government by leaking classified documents without authorization. This surveillance was said to span phone, email, and web communications. In May 2015, the United States Court of Appeals for the Second Circuit held that a provision of the USA Patriot Act, known as Section 215, cannot be legitimately interpreted to allow the bulk collection of domestic calling records and ruled that this form of bulk collection of telecommunications metadata is illegal.[77] The legislation under consideration expired on June 1 of that year. On June 2, 2015, Congress passed the US Freedom Act to replace those key provisions of the USA Patriot Act that had expired. The Freedom Act now prohibits the government's bulk collection of metadata on US citizens but, according to Forrester, preserves surveillance in other forms.[78]

   While citizens recognize the need to prevent future terror attacks, there is a tension between this need and government surveillance. Increasingly, social networks such as Twitter have been placed under pressure to surrender their data and suppress activities that may lead to international terrorism.[79] Twitter has aimed for self-regulation by deleting hundreds of thousands of accounts. Terror suspects often change their accounts multiple times to evade detection, using hundreds of accounts. According to Michael S. Smith II, chief operating officer of Kronos Advisory, "No terrorist organization in history has launched as dynamic and ultimately effective global influence operation online as Islamic State."

4. The Internet of Things (IoT)

   Another potential privacy bombshell is the information contained in "smart" devices that are becoming prevalent with the IoT. Information about one's heart rate and metabolic functions are available on devices such as Fitbit™ and smart refrigerators carry information about one's daily purchases. These are all devices subject to invasion and data breaches.[80] For example, smart devices used to report energy usage in Spain have been hacked to under-report energy use. Intel calls the risk "a trillion points of vulnerability" and calls for businesses to create trust through security and data integrity and to protect the privacy of the data collected on these connected devices. In the next few years, expect to hear more about privacy and data security surrounding the IoT.

Response of U.S. Business to Privacy Concerns

Just as Twitter is trying to respond to the terror threat on its own, most businesses in the United States have argued strongly for self-regulation as the best approach to meeting consumer privacy concerns. They have been supported in their preference for self-regulation by trade associations and by the stated preference of the FTC for self-regulation. The FTC recently issued a report that includes a framework for businesses to use as they refine their approach to consumer data privacy (see Figure 17.7). Its principles are a comprehensive approach, which it calls "privacy by design," simplified consumer choice, and transparency.

As you can see from the FTC framework, U.S. businesses are expected to develop their own privacy approaches with only general guidelines. There are two types of privacy disclosures that can be enlisted in order to come up with a comprehensive privacy approach. They are:

- A *privacy policy notice* is a comprehensive description of a site's privacy practices. To be acceptable, it must be located in a single, readily identifiable place on the site. It must be easily accessible by a single link or icon. The link should be present on the home page, and it is also desirable to have it in a visible location when information is being collected, for example, on registration pages.
  - The FTC framework takes this common approach a step further by recommending a comprehensive, corporate-wide approach to privacy. The framework specifically states that privacy policies should be shorter and more understandable. Since privacy policies are written, or at least cleared, by corporate attorneys, this recommendation is difficult to implement.
- An *information practice statement* is a discrete statement that describes a specific information practice from which a potential use of the information can be inferred. Examples include: "Click here if you want to be informed about future offers of this nature" or "We will not share your information with any other organization."
  - Information practices statements are short and specific. They can be useful both to identify the choices that consumers have and to provide information about what information is being collected and how it will be used in the interest of transparency.

With the exception of financial services, health care businesses, and those that market to children under 13, the burden of designing a privacy approach and seeing that it is properly executed is left up to the business itself. There is, however, a set of privacy standards that is accepted by most of the internet-using nations called the Fair Information Practices Principles.

The Fair Information Practices Principles

The Fair Information Practices Principles have become an important international standard in the field of data privacy. They have evolved over the last quarter century as a result of analyses by governmental agencies in the United States, Canada, Australia, and Europe, and are widely accepted in regulatory frameworks around the world. The principles, as listed by the FTC,[81] are:

- *Notice/Awareness*. Customers should be given notice before information is collected in order to allow them to make informed decisions about what to divulge. Notification should include identification of the entity collecting the data, uses to which it will be put, with whom data will be shared, nature of data collection including voluntary or involuntary, methods of collection, data security measures, and consumer rights with respect to collection and use of data.
- *Choice/Consent*. Consumers should be given control over how information will be used for purposes beyond the current transaction. This includes both internal use of the information, such as putting it in a database, and external use, such as transferring it to a third party.

FIGURE 17.7
Framework for Protection of Consumer Data Privacy

Protecting Consumer Privacy in an Era of Rapid Change: A Proposed Framework for Businesses and Policymakers

Scope: The framework applies to all commercial entities that collect or use consumer data that can be reasonably linked to a specific consumer, computer, or other device.

Principles:

PRIVACY BY DESIGN
Companies should promote consumer privacy throughout their organizations and at every stage of the development of their products and services.

- Companies should incorporate substantive privacy protections into their practices, such as data security, reasonable collection limits, sound retention practices, and data accuracy.
- Companies should maintain comprehensive data management procedures throughout the life cycle of their products and services.

SIMPLIFIED CHOICE
Companies should simplify consumer choice.

- Companies do not need to provide choice before collecting and using consumers' data for commonly accepted practices, such as product fulfillment.
- For practices requiring choice, companies should offer the choice at a time and in a context in which the consumer is making a decision about his or her data.

GREATER TRANSPARENCY
Companies should increase the transparency of their data practices.

- Privacy notices should be clearer, shorter, and more standardized, to enable better comprehension and comparison of privacy practices.
- Companies should provide reasonable access to the consumer data they maintain; the extent of access should be proportionate to the sensitivity of the data and the nature of its use.
- Companies must provide prominent disclosures and obtain affirmative express consent before using consumer data in a materially different manner than claimed when the data was collected.
- All stakeholders should work to educate consumers about commercial data privacy practices.

SOURCE: Federal Trade Commission, http://www.ftc.gov/os/2010/12/101201privacyreport.pdf.

- *Access/Participation.* The consumer should be able to view data about himself or herself and to assure that the data is accurate and complete.
- *Integrity/Security.* Integrity describes the accuracy of the data; specifically that anyone who accesses the data at a given moment receives exactly the same data. Security refers to the managerial and technical measures that protect the data from unauthorized access and use.
- *Enforcement/Redress.* There should be a mechanism in place to enforce these principles of privacy protection and to provide remedies for injured parties.[82]

While these fair information principles provide a strong conceptual framework for privacy action by businesses, they do not provide sufficient guidance for the majority of firms who lack internal expertise in this area. In addition, businesses would benefit from greater understanding of privacy issues on the part of consumers while consumers would feel more confident if privacy approaches were sanctioned by a trusted third party. This has led to the establishment of various industry-supported privacy organizations.

Privacy Organizations and Seals

As part of the industry effort to achieve effective self-regulation, a number of organizations have either been formed or have added a privacy initiative to the services they offer. In general, these organizations can be characterized as nonprofit organizations that specialize in the privacy arena or trade organizations that support the privacy actions of their members. Often, as in the case of TRUSTe and the Better Business Bureau Online, compliant organizations are allowed to display their seal on the organizational web page. There is no comprehensive listing of privacy-related organizations but EPIC provides a good overview of resources available.[83]

Most industry leaders and regulators in the United States still voice strong support for self-regulation. However, many other countries have taken a regulatory approach toward internet privacy from the beginning, believing that self-regulation is insufficient to protect the public. In the next section, we will look at privacy activities in other major internet-using countries.

Privacy Regulation in Various Internet-Using Countries

Privacy is a concern in countries around the world, but it is not safe to assume that the concerns are the same from one country to another. The marketer who is conducting business globally must be aware of consumer concerns and actions as well as of the regulations in each country. While the regulations are generally based on the Fair Information Practices Principles, their degree of severity varies from one country to another.

The legislation with the most widespread impact is the EU Directive on Protection of PII.[84] It was adopted in 1995 by the Council of Ministers and took effect on October 28, 1998. Unlike the United States, the European Union has a declared preference for regulation in the area of PII privacy and has a record of action that dates back to the Council of Europe Convention in 1981. The 1995 directive was aimed at bringing the protection of PII into the internet age. Its purpose was to ensure that data could move freely between the member countries of the EU while guaranteeing a stated level of privacy protection. Its basic principles are essentially the Fair Information Practices Principles.

For its time, the regulation mandated for EU countries by the 1995 directive was strict and reasonably comprehensive. However, since then new technologies like RFID, cloud computing, and mobile have introduced new dimensions to the privacy issue. The EU responded by submitting a comprehensive. The framework, among other issues is intended to deal with new technologies and to attempt more standardization of data protection globally, as well as to give citizens more control over their data and simplify procedures for businesses.[85]

In the absence of consistency of privacy regulations around the world, it is impossible to summarize the global situation. In addition, privacy regulations change frequently. For example, India passed a strict law regulating personal data privacy in

2011.[86] The laws can also be quite complex. For example, different provinces in Canada have different privacy laws.[87] Marketers have to cope with different laws in every country, even in the countries of the EU.[88]

Privacy International is a United Kingdom-based privacy advocacy organization. In cooperation with EPIC in the United States, it conducts annual studies of privacy around the world. Its ratings focus on the trade-off between surveillance (everything from closed circuit TV cameras to maintenance of databases about citizens) and the protection of personal privacy. When that trade-off is the standard, not many countries rank well, and most are tending toward more surveillance, not more privacy of PII.[89] Forrester provides a "heat map" indicating which countries have stronger data and privacy protection. Students can interact with the map and see what countries are most strict here. As the map indicates, government surveillance may impact privacy (Figure 17.8).

FIGURE 17.8
Global Privacy and Data Protection

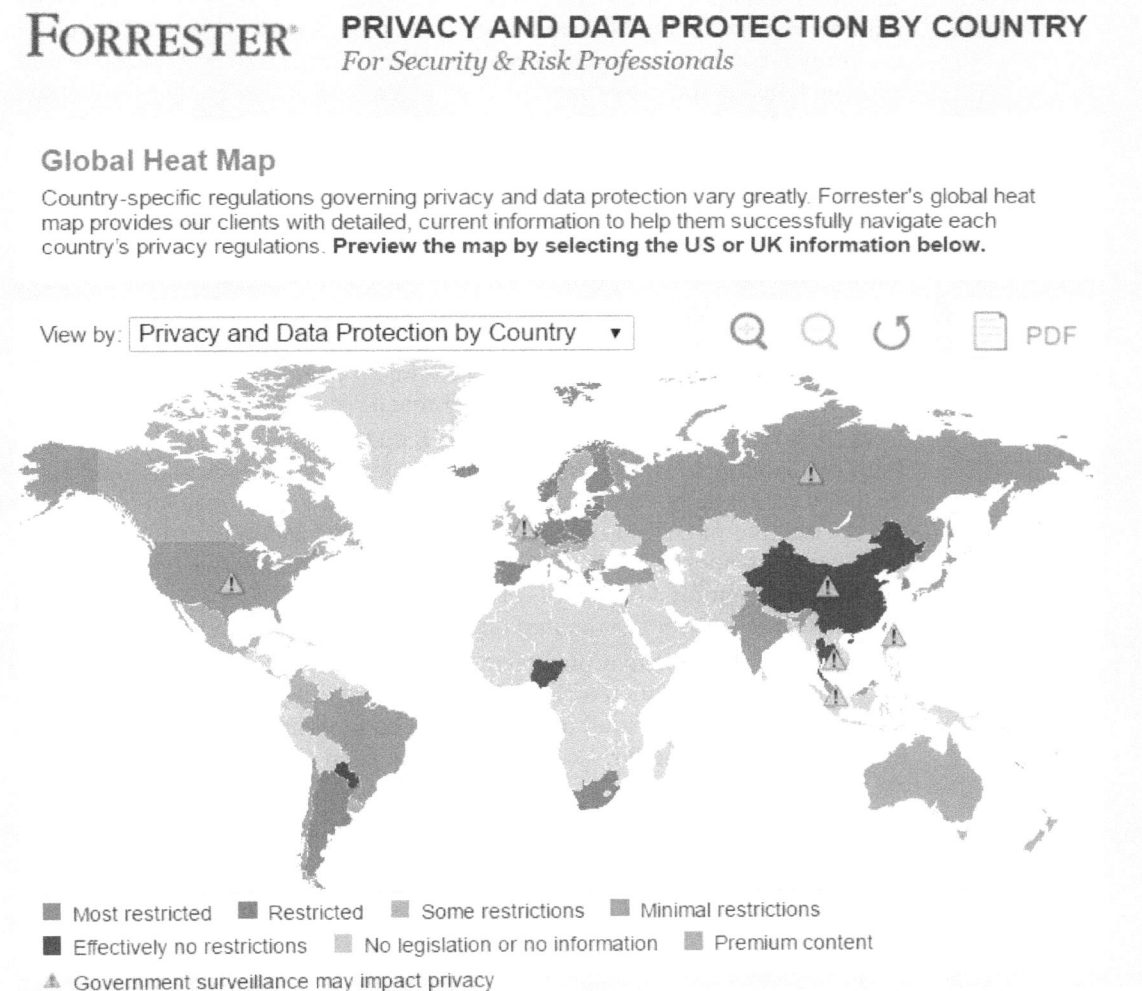

SOURCE: http://heatmap.forrestertools.com/

SOURCE: US Department of Commerce and country specific legislation

Note: This interactive map provides information on national data protection laws that have either been enacted or are currently under consideration around the world. It does not address sectoral laws, local laws, or criminal/civil code provisions that may address data protection. It is intended for information only and is not an authoritative statement or summary of the actual laws in these countries, and it may not reflect all recent changes and legislative updates.

©2013 Forrester Research. All rights reserved.

From the data presented in this section, it is clear that trust is important to the success of internet business. It is equally clear that trust in the ability of institutions to protect PII is not high around the world, and that government and corporate efforts to protect personally identifiable data vary greatly from one country to another. The other issue of special importance to the creation and maintenance of trust in internet businesses is that of the security of PII. We will now turn to a discussion of the business and marketing issues that relate to the security of data and transactions.

CONSUMER DATA SECURITY BREACHES

News about security breaches are reported on an almost daily basis. These breaches compromise the security of PII. Some are large and some impact only a few hundred consumer records. Some breaches reveal ingenious ways to obtain consumer data. For example, here is a summary of some of the largest and most widely covered data breaches:

- Began in 2005 and made public in 2007, TJX (parent company of T.J. Maxx and other retailers) suffered a massive data breach. Hackers accessed over 46 million credit card numbers and other transactions information.[90] The hack is generally attributed to weak encryption in an internal wireless database that allowed hackers to access data.[91] Urban legend has it that hackers sometimes sat in a parking lot and accessed data from their car using a laptop, a telescope antenna, and a wireless LAN adapter.[92] Estimates of the full cost to TJX vary widely, but it clearly ran into the hundreds of millions of dollars, maybe more.[93]
- In March 2011, Epsilon, a marketing services firm that maintains the email databases of over 2,500 corporate clients, announced a major data breach that allowed hackers to access email addresses. Epsilon said that about 2 percent of its clients were affected, so that could be as many as 50 large corporations, including retailers and financial services providers.[94] One expert estimates that as many as 5 million individual addresses might have been obtained, but there is no official estimate of the size of the breach.
- In April 2011, Sony announced a massive data breach in its PlayStation network. Data obtained included items like user names and passwords and could have included some credit card numbers. A second breach occurred on May 2, bringing the number of customers affected around the world to over 101 million users and 12 million unencrypted credit card numbers.[95] Sony was forced to close down the system for a period of time and to provide free usage to compensate for the downtime. Sony estimated the cost of the breach at $171 million.[96]
- In June 2011, the Privacy Commissioner of Canada announced that office supply firm Staples had failed to completely wipe out all personal information from computers that it renovated for resale. The commissioner gave Staples a year to prove it was able to wipe out all data from used computers before it sold them.[97]
- As noted above, there was a data breach in the Target system in 2013 that affected 40 million users and resulted in a $39 million dollar settlement by Target with the banking industry. The breach received a lot of publicity because it happened right before the holiday shopping season and inconvenienced a large number of users.
- In 2015, a well-publicized data breach occurred at the internet 'cheating" site Ashley Madison. It is estimated that 33 million user accounts with e-mail addresses, first and last names, and phone numbers were hacked and released to the public. The site claims that credit card numbers were not taken, but there was a lot of embarrassment as well as concern for PII.[98]

A large number of breaches originate on college campuses, which is not particularly surprising. Data in recent years show many thefts of health-related information, which is disconcerting. The Privacy Rights Clearinghouse (PRC), which has maintained a chronological list since 2005, estimated that a total of 535,363,707 data records had been compromised in 2,625 breaches reported as of August 11, 2011.[99]

The cost of data breaches to the affected organizations continues to rise. The Ponemon Institute, a research firm specializing in privacy and information management, estimated that the cost per compromised record was $204 in 2009 compared to $202 in 2008, and that the average cost per breach was $6.75 million compared to $6.65 million in 2008. The larger the breach is, the greater will be the cost.[100] An updated version of the study conducted with IBM from 2015 included 50 companies in 11 countries. The 2015 study estimated that $379 million is the average total cost of data breach, which is a 23 percent increase in total cost of data breach since 2013. The study also estimated the average cost per lost or stolen record is $154, up 12 percent per capita cost since 2013.[101] The dollar costs, of course, do not measure the loss in consumer trust that results from a data breach.

There has been considerable discussion in recent years of the importance of transparency; reporting a breach when it occurs and being accurate about the nature and possible consequences of a breach. It is important to notify customers on a timely basis and to give them all possible assistance in preventing or limiting financial damage to the consumer. Transparency may limit, although it will not prevent, damage to the consumer's trust in the organization.

Consumer Knowledge about Internet Security

Consumers appear to have a basic understanding of the importance of keeping their online activities secure. Finnish security solutions firm F-Secure conducted surveys of internet users in the United States, Canada, the United Kingdom, France, and Germany in 2008 and 2009. Findings from 2008 include the following:

- Ninety-five percent of respondents had security software on their computers.
- Only 18 percent were confident that they were completely protected from **malware**.
- Although most respondents were confident that their antivirus protection was up to date, only 10 percent were confident that they could open email attachments and 9 percent were confident that they could open email links without danger of being infected with malware. F-Secure commented that most respondents were not aware of how frequently antivirus software should be updated.
- Fifty percent of respondents in the United States, Canada, the United Kingdom, and France felt their credit cards were safe while transacting online, whereas only 15 percent of German respondents felt secure.
- Sixty-five percent of respondents in the United States, Canada, the United Kingdom, and France felt their online banking transactions were safe, whereas only 28 percent of respondents in Germany felt safe while making online banking transactions.
- Only 37 percent of respondents were confident they could identify a phishing email and 27 percent were confident they could identify a phishing site.[102]
- Twenty-eight percent of respondents used their mobile phone to access the internet, but 86 percent did not have mobile security.[103]

Their 2009 survey added respondents in Italy, India, and Hong Kong. Findings included are:

- Fifty percent felt safe when banking online but only 16 percent felt safe using a credit card to make a purchase online.
- Fifty-four percent did not agree that their children were safe online while over a third could neither agree nor disagree, indicating that they were not sure.

malware malicious software developed for the purpose of harming or taking control of certain actions on a computer or computer system

- Fifty-four percent felt confident that they would not fall for a phishing email, but 27 percent were not sure they could identify a phishing email.[104]

Once again, we see a mixed picture with internet users exhibiting a reasonable knowledge of threats but less confidence that they could deal with them successfully. With that in mind, let us look at a list of the most common types of security threats affecting both consumer and business computers.

Internet Security Threats

The ways in which cyber attacks can be carried out are myriad and seem to be growing every day. HP released a study in late 2011 that documented the costs to business and government. The head of HP's Enterprise Security division commented that, "Instances of cybercrime have continued to increase in both frequency and sophistication, with the potential impact to an organization's financial health becoming more substantial." Over the four-week period covered by the survey, responding organizations reported 72 cyber attacks in the form of malicious code, denial of service, stolen devices, and web-based attacks. That represented a 45 percent increase over the preceding year.[105] This is a huge problem for the corporate IT manager. In this section, we will concentrate on the kinds of threats and criminality that are most often directed at the individual internet user, not the corporation.

Malware Malware is literally "bad software," which is designed to cause damages. It is a generic term for much of the malicious software on the web including viruses, worms, Trojan horses, and spyware. Viruses attach themselves to otherwise legitimate software or documents and spreading across networks when their code is executed. Worms are similar, but they do not have to be attached to other software. They exploit weaknesses in the system or employ the so-called social engineering, which is simply deceiving people in order to gain access to the system. Trojan horses are manually attached to legitimate software and rely on use of the host software to spread.

spyware programs installed on consumers' computers, without their permission, that assume partial control over the operating system

adware is a free, advertiser-supported software to download and display ads when user is online

Spyware and Adware Spyware and adware are both marketer-initiated actions. Spyware works in the background as consumers move around the web, tracking their movements and recording things like keywords used in searches. Adware is free, advertiser-supported software that includes toolbars and games. It includes software for pop-up and pop-under ads. When adware is installed on a computer without the user's permission, it becomes spyware.

In many cases, spyware is simply used to create anonymous profiles. In other cases, it may be much more intrusive, for example, repeatedly changing the consumer's opening page to a specific website in spite of the consumer's efforts to specify another page or resisting all efforts to stop the advertising pop-ups. Spyware is often placed in the process of receiving a free download. The presence of spyware may, in fact, be specified in the service agreement that the consumer must sign before the download begins. Based on all we know, it seems reasonable to assume that most consumers do not read the agreements carefully and consequently are unaware of the software and the fact it may be collecting and transmitting data without their knowledge.

Phishing, Pfarming, and Spoofing Adware and spyware result from marketer-initiated efforts. A variety of other techniques are used by fraud artists to obtain the PII of consumers.

phishing emails that attempt to obtain personal information by making fraudulent claims

- **Phishing** is the practice of using fraudulent emails in an attempt to get information like consumer account numbers and passwords. These often come in the form of an e-mail that purports to be from a recognized financial services provider. They might inform customers that there is a problem with their account and they need to provide information to clear it up. From the

- **Spear phishing** is a newer and more sophisticated entry into the gallery of bad software. It is a highly targeted phishing scheme that aims to get access to an organization's entire computer system. Spear phishing is carried out by authentic-looking emails that appear to come from the organization or from an employee of the organization.[106]

  spear phishing targeted phishing attacks that use apparently legitimate communications in an attempt to breach a secure website

- **Pfarming** also attempts to obtain PII, but it does so in a different way. Perpetrators hack into the DNS (domain name system) servers that provide the IP addresses for URLs and thereby allow users to access websites on the internet. They hijack some of the pages and create a site that looks much like the original. Because they have gained unauthorized access to the DNS server, they can direct the user to the fake site and trick him into divulging personal information. Because the sites look real, this fraud is hard for consumers to detect. A similar technique has been widely used to scam charitable donations after disasters by using sites that resemble sites of legitimate charities.

  pfarming creating fake websites that are similar to legitimate business sites

- **Spoofing** is the general term that describes a situation in which a person, computer program, or website is able to masquerade successfully as another. Spoofing requires that the criminal first identify the IP address of the trusted website. Then it must waylay individual data packets and modify their identifying headers so it appears that they are coming from the trusted website. That sounds difficult to do, but there are apparently many poorly written internet protocols that make it possible for people with technical expertise to tap into the telecommunications stream that comprises the traffic of the internet.

  spoofing creating false identities in order to evade rules for conducting business and communications on the web

Whatever the method used to steal PII, the possible outcome is identity theft. Identity theft implies that a thief has obtained access to information that allows him to pose as another individual, doing things like using the other person's credit cards or bank accounts. It poses a direct threat to consumers' financial well-being and is a topic of considerable and growing concern.

Identity Theft According to the Identity Theft Resource Center, "**Identity theft** is a crime in which an impostor obtains key pieces of personal identifying information (PII) such as Social Security numbers and driver's license numbers and uses them for their own personal gain."[107] Identify theft can occur online, but many instances occur offline as a result of theft of mail, loss of personal documents, and careless disposal of documents by a person or a business. The latter often goes by the descriptive term "dumpster diving."

identity theft stealing key items of personal information with criminal intent, usually to cause financial harm

Javelin Research and Strategy conducts an annual survey that is co-sponsored by a number of financial services firms. Their 2010 report contained both good and bad news. President James Van Dyke puts the bad news first:

> *"The 2010 Identity Fraud Survey Report shows that fraud increased for the second straight year and is at the highest rate since Javelin began this report in 2003(2)… The good news is consumers are getting more aggressive in monitoring, detecting and preventing fraud with the help of technology and partnerships with financial institutions, government agencies and resolution services."*

Data from the report illustrate the magnitude of the problem:

- Eleven million Americans were affected by identity fraud in 2009. Potential losses totaled $54 billion. There is good news here also; out-of-pocket costs for resolving thefts dropped to $373 per incident.
- Time to detect and resolve fraud has dropped, primarily due to use of technology, including mobile, by financial institutions and individuals.
- Eighteen- to twenty-four-year olds take nearly twice as long to detect and report fraud and therefore remain its victims for longer. This is because they monitor their accounts less frequently.[108]

An update to that report indicated that while overall losses were decreasing, the number of victims was increasing. The 2015 Javelin report stated that in 2014 there was $16 billion stolen from 127 million identity fraud victims. Mobile devices are responsible for much of the increase and identity theft can be minimized by providing a passcode or thumbprint or other security access to the device. Credit card companies are using increased levels of security on accounts, including the newly introduced "chip" technology where the credit card is inserted and verified. Target has taken another step and requires a pin for its credit card transactions for its store credit card.[109]

There are also many ways in which corporate security can be breached and personal identity can be threatened. Individuals, corporations, government agencies, and nonprofit organizations all stand to lose financially from criminal activities that violate the security of their internet activities. Even Facebook founder Mark Zuckerberg is not immune from data breaches and potential identity theft. His Facebook account was hacked in 2013[110] and, in 2016, both his Twitter and Pinterest accounts were hacked, most probably from a password leak at LinkedIn.[111] Organizations stand to lose even more if they lose the trust of their customers, their donors, and the citizenry in general. All organizations that hold any amount of customer data have a fiduciary responsibility for the protection of that data. It is a responsibility that organizations are taking with increasing seriousness, even as cybercriminals become more ingenuous in their attempts to breach security systems.

There is one additional type of activity we need to examine before concluding this chapter. It does not usually include breaches of security, but it does involve potential theft of a possession. The subject is the thorny one of intellectual property on the internet.

PROTECTION OF INTELLECTUAL PROPERTY IN THE DIGITAL AGE

The right of persons and legal entities to protect nontangible property of importance has long been recognized. Copyright and patent laws provided reasonable protections for several centuries. Technology in the form of copiers and later computers made the protection of copyrighted material more difficult. The ease of sharing content on the internet has exacerbated the problem.

What Is Intellectual Property?

Intellectual property is a broad concept, encompassing many areas of endeavor, beyond just the copyrights of books, music, and other published material that many of us confront on a daily basis. The World Intellectual Property Organization (WIPO) defines intellectual property as:

- *Creations of the mind* [emphasis mine]: inventions, literary and artistic works, and symbols, names, and images used in commerce.

The WIPO divides intellectual property into two main categories:

- *Industrial property* includes legal constructs including patents and trademarks.
- *Copyright* applies to literary works, artistic works, and architectural designs. Literary works include not only written material from books to plays but also films and music.

The WIPO further explains the coverage of copyright laws as:

> Rights related to copyright include those of performing artists in their performances, producers of phonograms, and those of broadcasters in their radio and television programs.[112]

The Digital Millennium Copyright Act

The Committee on Intellectual Property Rights and the Emerging Information Infrastructure of the National Academy of Sciences points out that from the time of Thomas Jefferson, access to information has been a cornerstone of American democracy and the educational system. Public libraries have made printed material available to any citizen at virtually no cost. One hallmark of this system is that a published item is available to only one person at a time.

However, when that same content is published electronically, there is no theoretical limit to the number of people who can access it simultaneously. That leads to the worst nightmare of musicians and authors and their publishers—that electronic publishing will ultimately lead to the sale of only one book or recording. The rest would simply be copied.

After years of international discussion about intellectual property issues as they pertain to electronic products of all kinds, Congress passed and then President Clinton signed the Digital Millennium Copyright Act in 1998. It has many provisions that affect internet users, libraries, websites, and educational institutions. Among the provisions are to make it a crime to circumvent the antipiracy codes built into most commercial software or to make or sell code-cracking devices. Libraries and educational institutions receive certain exemptions that allow them to make copyrighted material available to authorized users. However, ISPs are required to remove material that constitutes copyright infringement from customers' websites and webcasters are required to pay licensing fees to recording companies.[113]

The issues are also difficult because the interests of various stakeholders clash with little obvious way of reconciling them. In addition, traditional practices and laws vary in different countries around the globe.[114] Links to the laws of other countries are easily found by web search. Enforcement of laws also varies around the globe, so the situation is not easy to navigate.

The WIPO is a central resource for information about the protection of intellectual property around the world. In 2011, its director general discussed three main principles for copyright protection: neutrality toward technology, comprehensiveness and coherence, and simplicity. Mr. Gurry said, "We need a global infrastructure that permits simple, global licensing, one that makes the task of licensing cultural works legally on the internet as easy as it is to obtain such works there illegally."

In the absence of a comprehensive solution in the form of copyright law, the Creative Commons offers a viable alternative.

Napster and Other Intellectual Property Controversies Napster is clearly the poster child of the intellectual property controversy on the internet. As most students know well, Napster was the home of software that makes it possible to download music over the internet. It is the prime example of the consumer **P2P (peer-to-peer)** business model, first attracting media attention when it slowed the computer systems of several universities in the United States so severely that it was banned from many campus networks.[115] Napster not only drew media attention, it also attracted the ire of the recording industry. At the end of 1999, several record companies filed suit, essentially to prevent Napster from facilitating the distribution of copyrighted music.

At its height, it is estimated that 30 million people were registered with Napster. In 2000, Bertelsmann AG, a European media conglomerate, acquired Napster with the intention of turning it into a subscription service.[116] Under that business model, Napster continued to exist but failed to thrive. It no longer exists as a separate entity but as the streaming technology for Best Buy.[117]

Perhaps the closest successor to Napster was LimeWire. It operated as a purveyor of P2P file-sharing software, but it was, in fact, widely used for the illegal sharing of music. The Recording Industry Association of America (RIAA) brought suit against LimeWire in 2006 and in 2010, it was ordered to shut down permanently and to block the unauthorized sharing of music on the software it had distributed.[118] The RIAA continues to prosecute illegal music downloading and sharing.[119] The place of

P2P (peer-to-peer) transmission of files directly from one user to another

these two sites has been taken by a host of other file-sharing products, and increasingly, music streaming sites. Music streaming sites like Spotify usually provide both a free and a fee-based alternative. The advertisements and subscription fees pay for the support of the copyright fees on the sites. These sites may be the best alternative yet to P2P file sharing.

RIAA was one of the major supporters of the Stop Online Piracy Act, introduced in October 2011. If passed, the act would have allowed the Department of Justice to force U.S. businesses, including payment systems and search engines, to stop doing business with foreign websites accused of copyright infringement.[120] Supporters include publishers and broadcasters as well as music producers. internet businesses like Google, Facebook, Amazon, and Twitter are strongly opposed to the bill, saying it would stifle internet activities. Their opposition included a threat to temporarily suspend their sites in January 2012, in protest.[121] As of this date, the legislation has not moved forward. This is the most recent, and likely not the last, salvo in the continuing battle to protect the rights of content owners while allowing unfettered access to internet content.

There tends to be considerable buzz around the issue of illegal peer-to-peer file sharing, especially because well-known artists continue to speak out against it. However, it is very hard to find credible statistics on the subject. The technology editor of the UK newspaper, *The Guardian*, affirmed the lack of statistics in 2009 but argued against the conventional wisdom that illegal downloading damages the music industry. His hypothesis is that money is being spent on DVDs and games instead of music.[122] Many others have suggested that Apple's iTunes model, because it focuses on inexpensive downloads of single tracks instead of expensive purchase of entire albums, is responsible for the presumed decrease in illegal music downloading. The thesis seems reasonable, but there is no definitive data to support it. It is also seems clear that new forms of data storage and backup, such as Apple iCloud, encourage file sharing, at least on the user's registered devices, so the controversy continues.

The Digital Millennium Copyright Act was an attempt to deal with these issues in a way that protects consumer access to information; at the same time, it protects the interests of owners of intellectual property. However, the increased use of internet technology will continue to make it difficult to enforce copyright laws internationally.

Publishing under Creative Commons

The basic meaning of copyright is best expressed by the "all rights reserved" phrase. That makes it difficult to do many things, from writing a textbook or a research paper to publishing a blog. The Creative Commons is a nonprofit organization that aims to maximize the productivity of the internet. In its own words, it "develops, supports, and stewards legal and technical infrastructure that maximizes digital creativity, sharing, and innovation."[123] It does this by offering licenses that provide more flexible choices than the "all rights reserved." The basic idea is to let the individual or organization retain the copyright to their work but choose the conditions under which people may use and distribute the content without requesting explicit permission from the owner. This extends to how people may modify the work, as long as they provide appropriate attribution. It is important to point out that the person who obtains the license must be the owner, presumably the developer, of the content. You cannot license someone else's content.

Figure 17.9 is an example of one type of license, which Creative Commons calls "ShareAlike." In this case, the content can be used and modified as long as it is attributed as the owner has specified, it is used noncommercially, and any distribution is done under a similar license. In other words, the person who modifies the content cannot choose more stringent distribution terms than the original creator. When the owner applies for a license, Creative Commons provides a badge for the content that identifies it as licensed under Creative Commons and links to the attribution criteria the owner has chosen.[124] The site has a complete list of all types of licenses available in straightforward layman's language.[125]

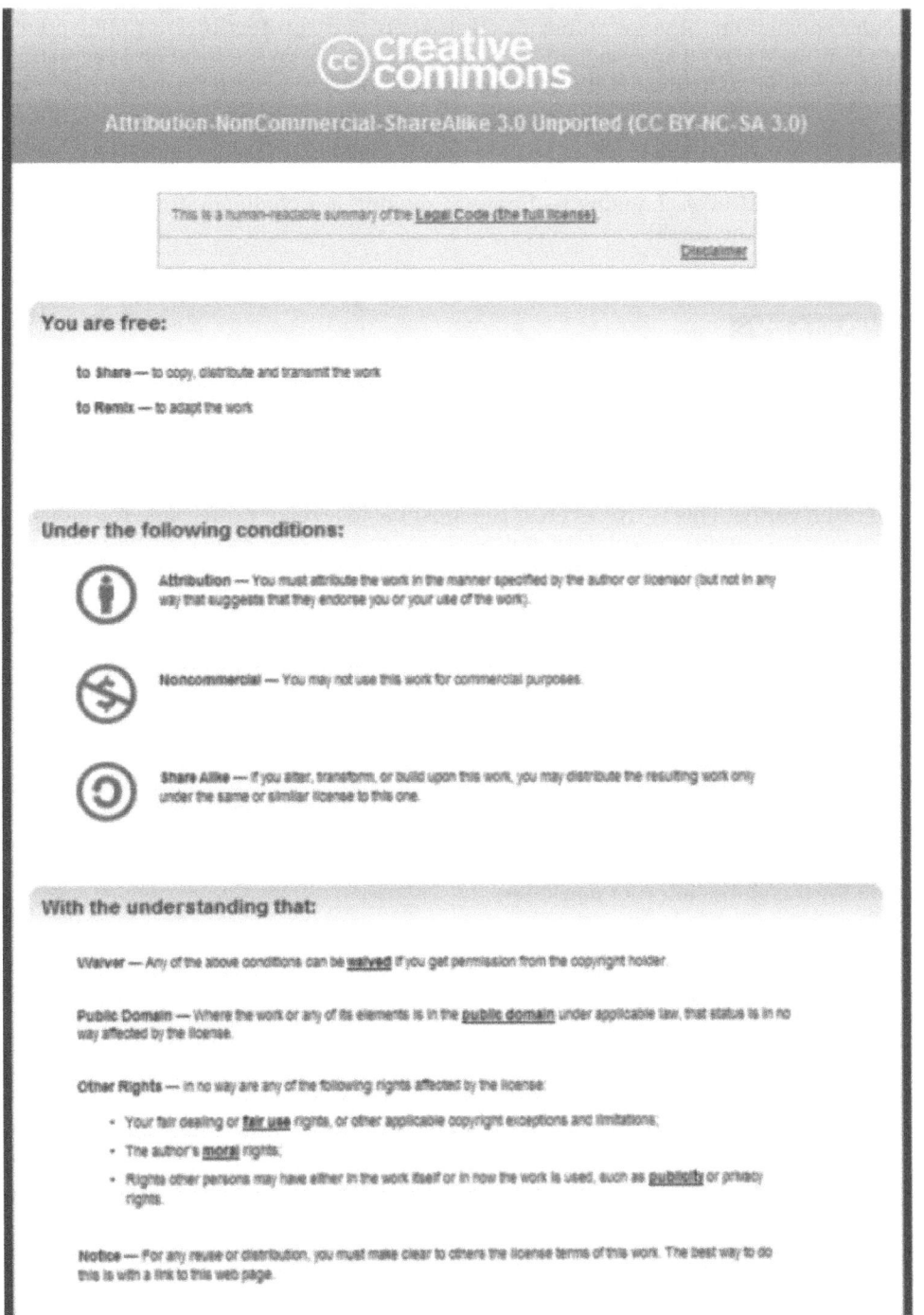

FIGURE 17.9
Example of a Creative Commons License

SOURCE: Creative Commons, http://creativecommons.Org/licenses/by-nc-sa/3.0

Creative Commons operates globally through affiliates throughout the world. It is not a panacea for all the world's intellectual property woes, but it provides an easy and workable solution for some content creators like marketers and bloggers who actually want their content to be widely shared.

There are many companies around the world working on technological fixes to the intellectual property issue, and businesses do need to employ appropriate technology. However, from the corporate point of view, it will require management skill and vigilance to protect these important assets in an ever-changing world. From a broader social point of view, online intellectual property protection is a public policy issue that needs to be approached on several fronts. There are legal and regulatory issues that need to be dealt with while providing consumers with flexibility and control in the way they access content on the internet. Finally, there is a need for better consumer understanding of the subject of intellectual property and the responsibility of consumers in helping to maintain a free and fair marketplace. All this takes place in the context of ever-changing technology, making it a challenge for public policy makers around the world.

SUMMARY

The social and regulatory issues that pertain to the internet are many and varied. In this chapter, important concerns related to the protection of PII, data security, and intellectual property were reviewed. These issues are recognized in internet-using counties around the world, although the reaction in individual countries to each issue often varies. This is true even at the most basic level of preference for industry self-regulation versus a regulatory approach.

Trust is essential to success in the information age, especially for businesses that are active on the internet.

The internet has caused intense focus on the issue of privacy of PII on the internet. Consumers in many countries are concerned about their PII security, although they do not necessarily have in-depth knowledge about the subject or examine privacy policies that are posted on the web. Studies have shown that consumers are particularly concerned about the tracking of online behavior that is widely used by behavioral advertising. Users of social networks evidence some concern for the privacy of their information there even as they actively use the networks. Mobile users are also concerned about the privacy of their personal data but even more about its security. Privacy concerns differ from one country to another, creating a difficult situation for the global internet marketer.

Businesses in the United States—with the exception of marketers of children's products, financial services marketers, and health care marketers—are essentially free to set their own privacy policies. Once they have published policies, they must then abide by them. There are third-party privacy organizations whose aid marketers can enlist in an attempt to build trust in their privacy practices. The FTC has published a privacy framework that can guide businesses as they develop a comprehensive approach to the privacy and security of consumer data.

There are many threats to data on the internet. Breaches of data stored by businesses, government, and nonprofit organizations are common and many pose the possibility of significant harm to the consumer. Other kinds of threats ranging from viruses to phishing attacks are also commonplace. The specter of identity theft is ever-present, and it presents the possibility of significant damage to consumers who experience it.

The maintenance of intellectual property rights, especially those of copyrighted literary works, is of direct concern to marketers. Illegal copying and downloading of material, including, but not limited to music, has been an internet issue almost from its beginning. The music industry, in particular, has been aggressive in pursuing legal action that has led to the shutdown of sites seen as promoting illegal downloading. Changing business models, including the ease and cost effectiveness of downloading single tracks of music, may also have affected consumer perceptions. In the absence of consistent intellectual property laws around the world, the situation is challenging. However, the presence of Creative Commons offers new options to publishers that may ease the situation for some of them.

Dealing with these concerns is an ongoing issue because new challenges continue to arise. Both business and policy makers must deal with these challenges in the face of an ever-changing technological environment.

DISCUSSION QUESTIONS

1. Explain why managers should be concerned about the trust customers have in their brand or company and what they can do to build trust.
2. Do you think consumers often take actions on the internet that reflect lack of trust in websites or marketing practices there? What might some of those actions be?
3. Discuss concerns that consumers may have about the privacy of their PII. What do you think a business can and should do to alleviate these concerns?
4. The chapter highlights online tracking for behavioral advertising as a particular concern of many internet users. Has anything you have learned in this course made you more wary of what sites you visit and what information you divulge on the internet?
5. What are some of the special privacy issues faced by users of social networks?
6. Why do you think that security seems to be a greater concern than privacy for users of mobile devices?
7. What actions would you recommend to internet users to protect the privacy of their PII?
8. What are the Fair Information Practices Principles, and why are they important?
9. Have you or anyone you know ever been informed that they had been affected by a data breach? If so, what actions were recommended for their protection? More generally, what actions should consumers take if they fear some of their data may have been compromised?
10. Have you experienced any of the other security threats discussed in the chapter? What was the result?
11. How has the internet increased both the importance and the difficulty of protecting intellectual property?
12. What do you perceive to be the attitudes of your peers to sharing of intellectual property on the web?
13. Do you think that Creative Commons licenses offer value in the protection of intellectual property on the internet?
14. Examine the complex issue of providing personal information in return for content or services and try to precisely define your own position on the issue.

ENDNOTES

1. Glen L. Urban, "The Trust Imperative," MIT Working Paper 4302–03, http://ssrn.com/abstract=400421, 1.
2. All informed publics met the following criteria: college-educated; household income in the top quartile for their age in their country; read or watch business/news media at least several times a week; follow public policy issues in the news at least several times a week.
3. https://www.youtube.com/watch?v=Kfw759dqUkY.
4. http://www.edelman.com/insights/intellectual-property/2015-edelman-trust-barometer/trust-and-innovation-edelman-trust-barometer/executive-summary/.
5. https://www.scribd.com/doc/47515988/2011-Edelman-Trust-Barometer-Executive-Summary.
6. George R. Milne and Mary J. Culnan, "Strategies for Reducing Online Privacy Risks: Why Consumers Read (Or Don't Read) Online Privacy Notices," *Journal of Interactive Marketing*, Vol. 18, No. 3, Summer 2004, p. 22.
7. Glen L. Urban, "The Trust Imperative," MIT Working Paper 4302–03, http://ssrn.com/abstract=400421.

8. http://techtrends.accenture.com/us-en/business-technology-trends-report.html.
9. https://www.accenture.com/us-en/insight-accenture-four-keys-digital-trust.
10. Glen L. Urban, "The Trust Imperative," MIT Working Paper 4302–03, http://ssrn.com/abstract=400421, 4.
11. http://blog.hubspot.com/blog/tabid/6307/bid/9242/ Becoming-a-Trust-Agent-w-ChrisBrogan-InboundNow-6.aspx.
12. John Deighton, "The Right To Be Let Alone," *Journal of Interactive Marketing*, Vol. 12, No. 2, Spring 1998, 3.
13. http://www.ponemon.org/news-2/26.
14. See a comprehensive and ongoing study of these issues in the *Wall Street Journal*, http://online.wsj.com/article/SB10001424052748703940904575395073512989404.html#articleTabs%3Darticle.
15. http://www.ftc.gov/os/2007/12/P859900stmt.pdf.
16. https://www.ftc.gov/news-events/press-releases/2009/02/ftc-staff-revises-online-behavioral-advertising-principles.
17. https://www.ftc.gov/news-events/press-releases/2012/03/ftc-issues-final-commission-report-protecting-consumer-privacy.
18. https://www.truste.com/resources/privacy-research/us-consumer-confidence-index-2014/.
19. http://www.mediapost.com/publications/article/265041/one-in-three-americans-consider-using-ad-blockers.html.
20. http://money.cnn.com/2015/12/02/news/companies/target-data-breach-settlement/p://money.cnn.com/2015/12/02/news/companies/target-data-breach-settlement/.
21. http://www.iab.net/behavioral-advertisingprinciples.
22. http://www.aboutads.info/participating.
23. http://www.aboutads.info/digital-advertising-alliance-announces-mobile-privacy-enforcement-begin-september-1.
24. On a recent visit to the Target.com site, for example, Ghostery found 19 "trackers" including 24]7 Bing Ads, DoubleClick, Facebook Connect, MediaMath and Google AdSense.
25. http://www.aboutads.info/participants/icon/.
26. http://www.iab.net/media/file/OBA_OneSheet_Final.pdf.
27. http://adage.com/article/privacy-and-regulation/study-consumers-adchoices-privacy-icon/291374/.
28. http://www.heinz.cmu.edu/~acquisti/economics-privacy.htm.
29. Columbia Business School (2015) What is the future of Data Sharing? Consumer Mindsets and the Power or Brands, Matthew Quint and David Rogers.
30. http://www.wired.com/politics/law/news/1999/01/17538.
31. http://www.guardian.co.uk/technology/2010/jan/ll/facebook-privacy.
32. http://www.mediapost.com/publications/?fa=Articles.showArticle&art_aid=139417.
33. http://www.thecrimson.com/article/2004/2/9/hundreds-register-for-new-facebook-website.
34. http://www.guardian.co.uk/technology/2006/sep/08/news.newmedia1.
35. http://www.eff.org/deeplinks/2010/04/facebook-timeline.
36. http://www.ft.eom/cms/s/0/f66elf9e-9eec-lIdc-b4e4-0000779fd2ac.html#axzzlURwCj7zf.
37. http://www.facebook.com/press/releases.php?p=3102.
38. http://online.wsj.com/article/SB10001424052748703730804576315682856383872.html?KEYWORDS=symantec+facebook+security+flaw.
39. http://news.cnet.com/8301-13577_3-10419950-36.html.
40. http://diy-marketing.blogspot.com/2011/09/discovering-facebook-like-button.html.
41. http://online.wsj.com/article/SB10001424052748704281504576329441432995616.html.
42. http://nakedsecurity.sophos.com/2010/12/17/facebook-friendships-get-creepier.

43. http://latimesblogs.latimes.com/technology/2011/08/facebook-photos-facial-recognition-puts-names-to-faces-at-black-hat-conference.html.
44. http://www.pcmag.com/article2/0,2817,2390440,00.asp.
45. http://www.nytimes.com/2011/ll/30/technology/facebook-agrees-to-ftc-settlement-on-privacy.html?_r=1.
46. http://www.ftc.gov/opa/2011/11/privacysettlement.shtm.
47. http://blog.facebook.com/blog.php?post=10150378701937131.
48. http://online.wsj.com/article/APfc8ffb68f4374e238cda0636a7faec90.html.
49. http://www.wired.com/2015/08/how-to-use-facebook-privacy-settings-step-by-step/
50. The case of British football star Ryan Giggs is instructive. His marital woes were aired on Twitter leading to a court injunction forbidding people to talk about it and heated discussion in the British Parliament, http://www.guardian.co.uk/politics/2011/may/23/ryan-giggs-named-footballer-injunction-row.
51. http://www.mcafee.com/us/resources/reports/rp-cylab-mobile-security.pdf, 3.
52. http://www.dataprivacymonitor.com/mobile-privacy/2016-mobile-data-privacy-and-security-update-and-2015-review/.
53. http://www.cnn.com/2012/12/04/business/digital-native-prensky/.
54. http://www.borndigitalbook.com.
55. http://online.wsj.com/article/SB10001424052748703904304575497903523187146.html.
56. http://www.washingtonpost.com/business/technology/parting-with-privacy-with-a-quick-click-for-adolescents/2011/04/28/AF2gSjTG_story.html.
57. http://www.pewinternet.org/2013/05/21/teens-social-media-and-privacy/.
58. Mary L. Roberts, "Geo-Cities (A) and (B)," *Journal of Interactive Marketing*, Winter 2000, 60–72.
59. "Children's Online Privacy Protection Rule: Notice of Proposed Rulemaking," *Federal Register Notice*, nd, http://www.ftc.gov.
60. https://www.consumer.ftc.gov/articles/0031-protecting-your-childs-privacy-online.
61. https://www.ftc.gov/news-events/blogs/business-blog/2012/12/ftcs-revised-coppa-rule-five-need-know-changes-your-business.
62. Prepared Statement of the Federal Trade Commission on "Recent Developments in Privacy Protections for Consumers, October 11, 2000, http://www.ftc.gov.
63. http://epic.org/privacy/glba.
64. See an explanation that is in laymen's terms but biased toward the positive from the Senate Banking Committee at http://banking.senate.gov/public/_files/070110_Dodd_Frank_Wall_Street_Reform_comprehensive_summary_Final.pdf; and a careful, ongoing study of the implications of the law by consulting firm PWC at http://www.pwc.com/us/en/financial-services/regulatory-services/publications/closer-look-series.jhtml?WT.mc_id=cpc_Google_financial+services+regulatory+services+publications&WT.srch=1.
65. http://apps.americanbar.org/buslaw/committees/CL230000pub/materials/2011/winter/2011_confin_winter_privacy_and_data_sec_after_doddfrank.pdf.
66. http://www.ftc.gov/bcp/edu/microsites/redflagsrule/index.shtml.
67. "Protecting the Privacy of Patients' Health Information," Department of Health and Human Services, May 9, 2001, http://www.hhs.gov.
68. http://www.hhs.gov/ocr/privacy/index.html.
69. http://www.hhs.gov/about/news/2016/03/17/improper-disclosure-research-participants-protected-health-information-results-in-hipaa-settlement.html#.
70. http://www.futureofprivacy.org/leading-practices/smart-grid-privacy.
71. http://www.ftc.gov/os/2010/12/101201privacyreport.pdf.
72. http://kb.mailchimp.com/accounts/compliance-tips/about-the-canada-anti-spam-law-casl.
73. http://europa.eu/rapid/pressReleasesAction.do?reference=IP/10/1462&format=HTML&aged=08danguage=EN&guiLanguage=fr.
74. http://techcrunch.com/2016/02/02/europe-and-us-seal-privacy-shield-data-transfer-deal-to-replace-safe-harbor/.

75. http://arstechnica.com/tech-policy/2016/04/eu-us-privacy-shield-problems-article-29-german-leak/.
76. http://www.pcworld.com/businesscenter/article/235985/eu_orders_member_states_to_implement_cookie_law_or_else.html.
77. http://www.nytimes.com/2015/05/08/us/nsa-phone-records-collection-ruled-illegal-by-appeals-court.html.
78. https://www.forrester.com/report/Quick+Take+The+Patriot+Act+Is+Dead+Long+Live+The+Patriot+Act/-/E-RES123081.
79. http://www.wsj.com/articles/twitter-and-islamic-state-deadlock-on-social-media-battlefield-1460557045.
80. http://www.securingtomorrow.com/blog/knowledge/3-key-security-challenges-internet-things/
81. http://inflection.com/privacy/frameworks-were-watching/ftc-fair-information-practice-principles, https://www.ftc.gov/reports/privacy-online-fair-information-practices-electronic-marketplace-federal-trade-commission.
82. Federal Trade Commission, "Privacy Online: A Report to Congress, Part III," June 1998, http://www.ftc.gov.
83. https://epic.org/privacy/privacy_resources_faq.html.
84. http://eur-lex.europa.eu/LexUriServ/LexUriServ.do?uri=CELEX:31995L0046:EN:HTML.
85. http://www.statewatch.org/news/2010/oct/eu-com-draft-communication-data-protection.pdf.
86. http://www.informationweek.com/news/government/policy/229402835.
87. http://www.pillsburylaw.com/siteFiles/Events/F1F60C7E25AC560FFD-55F268A477DD84.pdf.
88. http://www.informationshield.com/intprivacylaws.html.
89. https://www.privacyinternational.org/article/leading-surveillance-societies-eu-and-world-2007#summary.
90. http://www.computerworld.com/s/article/9014782/TJX_data_breach_At_45.6M_card_numbers_it_s_the_biggest_ever.
91. http://www.msnbc.msn.com/id/20979359/ns/technology_and_science-security/t/encryption-faulted-tjx-hacking.
92. http://www.informationweek.com/news/201400171.
93. http://www.informationweek.com/news/199203277.
94. http://www.databreaches.net/?p=17374.
95. http://www.reuters.com/article/2011/04/26/us-sony-stoldendata-idUSTRE73P6WB20110426.
96. http://www.zdnet.com/blog/btl/sonys-data-breach-costs-likely-to-scream-higher/49161.
97. http://news.cnet.com/8301-17938_105-20073515-1/canadian-staples-in-customer-privacy-hot-water.
98. http://www.bankrate.com/finance/banking/us-data-breaches-3.aspx.
99. http://www.privacyrights.org/data-breach.
100. http://www.ponemon.org/news-2/23.
101. http://www-03.ibm.com/security/data-breach/.
102. http://www.f-secure.com/en_EMEA-Corp/pressroom/news/2008/fs_news_20080228_01_eng.html.
103. http://articles.yuikee.com.hk/newsletter/2008/03/f.html.
104. http://www.f-secure.com/en_EMEA-Corp/pressroom/news/2009/fs_news_20090305_01_eng.html.
105. http://www.thenewnewinternet.com/2011/08/02/hp-study-cyber-criminals-are-reaching-into-your-companys-pocket.
106. http://www.microsoft.com/canada/athome/security/email/spear_phishing.mspx.
107. http://www.idtheftcenter.org.
108. http://www.prnewswire.com/news-releases/javelin-study-finds-identity-fraud-reached-new-high-in-2009-but-consumers-are-fighting-back-83987287.html.

109. https://www.javelinstrategy.com/press-release/16-billion-stolen-127-million-identity-fraud-victims-2014-according-javelin-strategy.
110. http://pix11.com/2013/08/19/zuckerbergs-facebook-page-hacked-to-prove-security-glitch-how-safe-is-your-fb-page/.
111. http://venturebeat.com/2016/06/05/mark-zuckerbergs-twitter-and-pinterests-accounts-hacked-linkedin-password-dump-likely-to-blame/.
112. http://www.wipo.int/about-ip/en.
113. The UCLA Online Institute for Cyberspace Law and Policy, "The Digital Millennium Copyright Act," http://www.gseis.ucla.edu.
114. For a detailed examination of the issues from a global perspective see the *Primer on Electronic Commerce and Intellectual Property Issues*, World Intellectual Property Organization, n.d., http://ecommerce.wipo.int/primer/primer.html.
115. http://www.sfgate.com/cgi-bin/article.cgi?file=/chronicle/archive/2000/03/03/MN97266.DTL&type=tech_article.
116. "Napster Audience Surges Ahead of Appeal," *Reuters*, October 2, 2000, http://www.techweb.com.
117. http://top40.about.com/od/top40andpoponline/tp/Top-5-Music-Streaming-Services.htm.
118. http://online.wsj.com/article/SB10001424052702303341904575577192244735152.html.
119. http://www.riaa.com/faq.php.
120. http://www.pcworld.com/businesscenter/article/244011/the_us_stop_online_piracy_act_a_primer.html.
121. https://www.washingtonpost.com/politics/2012/01/17/gIQA4WYl6P_story.html.
122. http://www.guardian.co.uk/news/datablog/2009/jun/09/games-dvd-music-downloads-piracy.
123. http://creativecommons.org.
124. http://search.creativecommons.org/?q=licensechooser.
125. http://creativecommons.org/licenses.

Chapter 18

Measuring and Evaluating Digital Marketing Programs

LEARNING OBJECTIVES

By the time you complete this chapter, you will be able to:

1. Identify reasons that good marketing metrics are both essential and often difficult for marketers to obtain.
2. Discuss the various types of marketing metrics that are available for websites, mobile sites, social media, and video campaigns.
3. Explain how usability testing, discussed in detail in Chapter 15, fits into the overall picture of internet metrics.
4. Identify the reasons why traffic, audience, and campaign measurement are central issues in digital marketing.
5. Understand the process of collecting data using cookies and tagged web pages.
6. Define key traffic, audience, and campaign metrics and the purpose of each.
7. Identify quantitative and qualitative metrics that can be used to analyze each stage in the customer journey.
8. Discuss the role of objectives and KPIs (Key Performance Indicators) in the identification and use of metrics.

9. Discuss the importance of segmentation in understanding visitor activity.
10. Identify the differences between internet metrics and metrics for mobile apps, social media, and video and give examples of metrics and KPIs.
11. Identify issues involved in obtaining a complete picture of the customer buying process, both on and off the web.

Like everything else in digital space, the role of data and metrics has been rapidly evolving. Chapter 4 discussed customer data and the importance it plays in guiding strategy and digital marketing programs. Throughout the book we have emphasized the importance of the insights data can produce in making marketing effective. However, the process is not automatic; the correct metrics must be selected, analyzed, and practical insights derived from them. Digital marketers subscribe to the Quality Management maxim that "What gets measured gets managed."

Producing insights from customer data has always been a difficult process. Four trends have upped the bar even further.

1. The amount of data is increasing rapidly. In numbers that are too big to comprehend, EMC provides figures that say there were 4.4 zettabytes (a zettabyte is computed as 2^{70} bytes, or 1 sextillion) of data produced each year; by 2020 it will be 44 **ZB**. Much easier to understand—the amount of data is growing by 40 percent each year, doubling every two years.[1] That is a torrent of data!

    ZB another iteration of byte; this is multiplication by the 7th power of 1,000 or 10^{21}.

2. A phenomenon called "democratization of data" has occurred. Infor describes this as "the process of expanding business information and the tools to analyze it out to a much broader audience than traditionally has had access. In most companies, the IT department has long been the gatekeeper of BI and analytical tools, not because of a desire to control information but out of necessity."[2]

    That means data and the necessary analytic tools are available to small businesses as well as to all corporate employees who need to use it. In the process, data *per se* has become less of a competitive advantage—every business has it and tools to use it are available.[3]

3. By all accounts there are too few data scientists to deal with the massive amounts of data produced by businesses.
4. The analytical skills of managers are improving, but they cannot keep up with the increasing volume and sophistication of data analytics. That implies that they are often making business decisions on the basis of information they do not completely understand.[4]

    The *Harvard Business Review* adds:
    a. Data comes from a variety of sources (e.g., website and social media) in a variety of formats and it is difficult to integrate into a single database that can be analyzed.
    b. Unstructured data can have limits to its use. It is best to first use new data for old purposes to understand how it can and cannot be useful.
    c. A well-known marketing professor once said that everything is correlated with everything else at least at the 20-percent level. Run field experiments to understand causality. It is often a mistake to try to infer it from correlations.
    d. Managers tend to underestimate the amount of skilled human judgment that is needed to make data useful. Someone has to understand what customers really want in order to produce insights that work.[5]

Marketing is responsible for the use of a large swath of business data. This data is essential to proving that marketing expenditures are worthwhile. Demonstrating the effectiveness of marketing expenditures turns out to be another difficult task.

DEMONSTRATING MARKETING EFFECTIVENESS

From the beginning of this book, we have discussed the important role that customer information plays in all aspects of digital marketing. Not all digital marketing functions are created equal, however, when it comes to being able to demonstrate ROI and the importance of ROI data in securing marketing budgets.

Figure 18.1a shows marketers' evaluations of their ability to measure ROI from various channels with PPC and email marketing leading the way. At the bottom are a variety of functions including social, mobile, personalization, and video. Notice that each time customer acquisition is broken out from customer retention, acquisition is easier to measure. It's easier to count the noses of new customers than to determine whether a customer doesn't repurchase or leaves. Marketers and their IT counterparts are adamant about what they most need to know in order to get the budgets they request (Figure 18.1b). They rate Return on Marketing Investment (ROMI) far ahead of any other effectiveness measure.

We will break this task down into several distinct types of evaluation—website effectiveness, traffic and audience data, and campaign effectiveness on the internet and the mobile web. These metrics will be organized according to the stages of the customer journey.

Then we will look more briefly at evaluating the effectiveness of social media and video efforts. Those metrics are organized according to a model of social media effectiveness. Throughout all of this runs the basic theme of setting measurable objectives, choosing the right metrics, and analyzing them to gain insights that will improve future programs.

FIGURE 18.1a

How Well Can Marketers Measure ROI from Digital Channels?

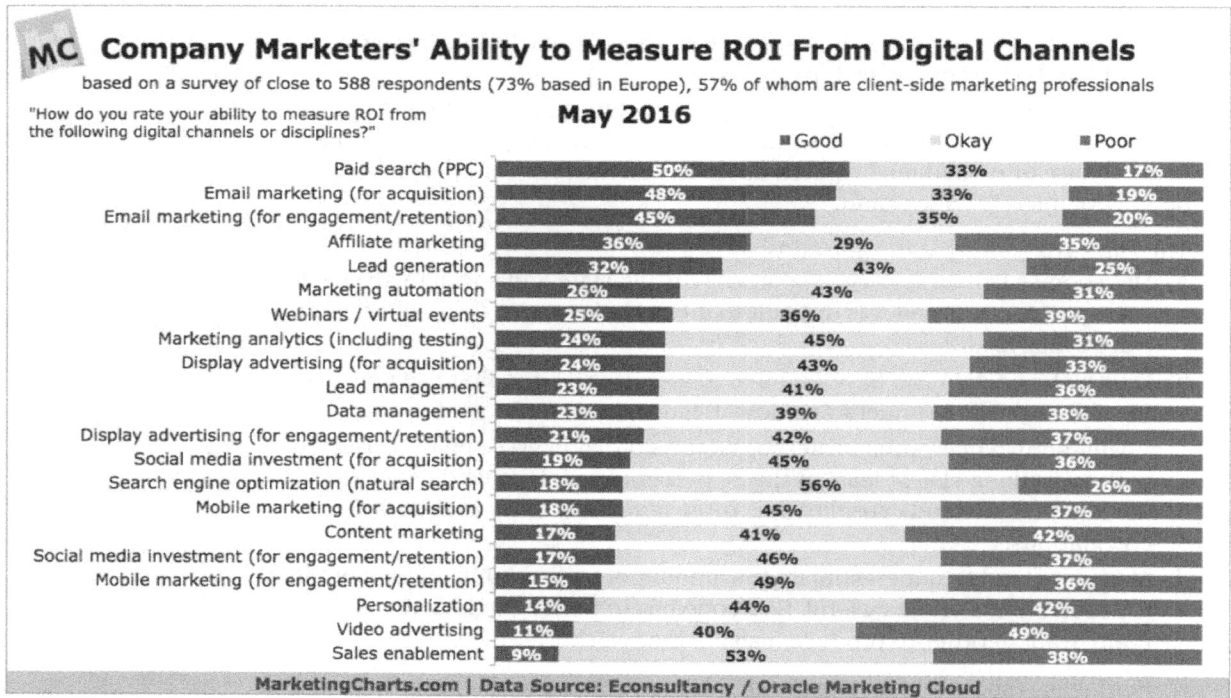

SOURCE: http://www.marketingcharts.com/online/which-digital-channels-are-marketers-most-confident-in-measuring-for-roi-67300/

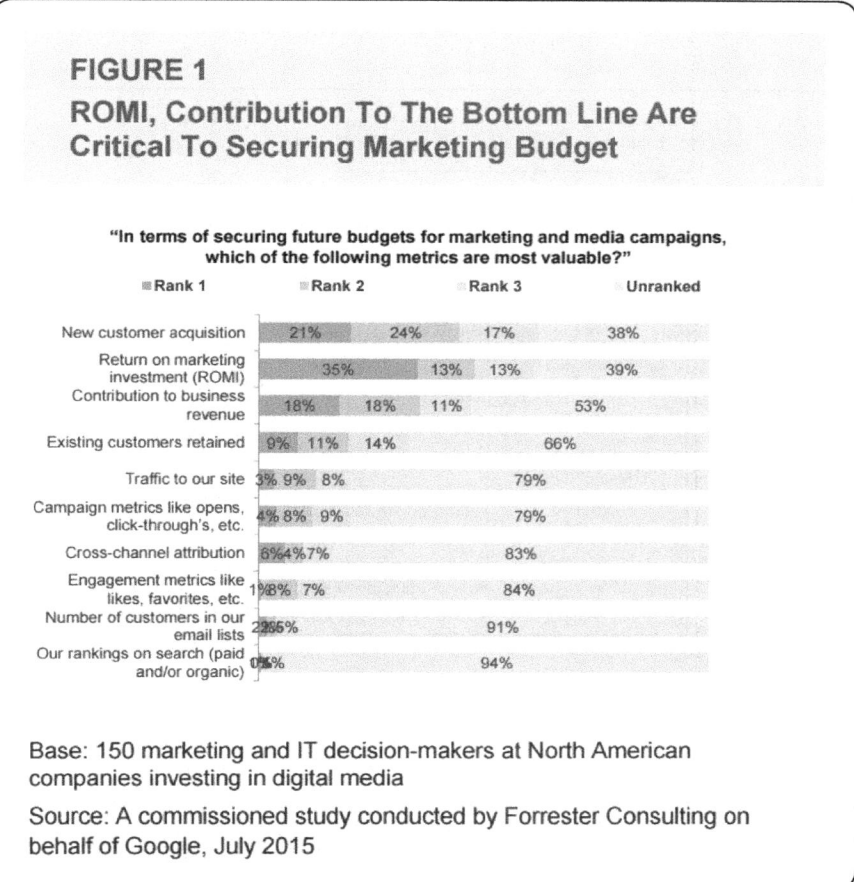

FIGURE 18.1b
How Important Is ROI to Securing Marketing Budgets?

SOURCE: https://services.google.com/fh/files/misc/discover-how-marketing-analytics-increases-business-performance.pdf.

WAYS TO EVALUATE WEBSITE EFFECTIVENESS

In Chapters 6 and 15 we have discussed the concepts of usability and customer experience, both of which lead to website effectiveness in a business context. It is important to take a high-level view of that term, because it can have different but equally important meanings. Figure 18.2 lays out the issue.

Unfortunately, the term "website effectiveness" is strategically appropriate when used in three different but related ways as shown in Figure 18.2. The one is *site usability*, which is essential to good customer experience and resultant business success. This usability is the way *the visitor* looks at the site, the way he gauges its ease of use and its value to him. If the visitor finds the usage experience satisfactory, the site has a greater chance of being successful in the long run. That is why usability testing is so important.

The second perspective is "traffic," "audience," and "campaign measurement"—the terms used to describe metrics that provide effectiveness data vital to marketing programs. We will discuss those measurement techniques in detail in this chapter because they are measures of business performance. The third perspective is that of *site performance*. This is the data that is needed by site technicians to gauge and improve site performance. Even though it is the responsibility of the technical side of the web team, marketers should be familiar with the basic approaches, which we will cover along with other metrics.

FIGURE 18.2

Perspectives on Website Effectiveness

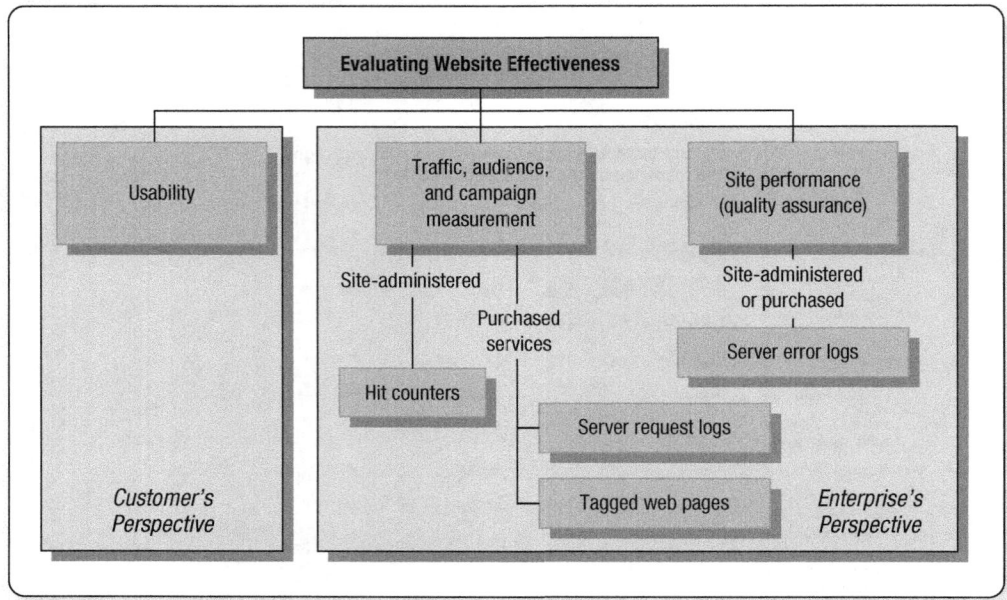

SOURCE: © Cengage Learning 2013

ENTERPRISE METRICS FOR EVALUATING WEBSITES

Site metrics fall into two basic categories—measures of business performance and measures of site performance. These business effectiveness measures provide data by which marketers can judge the success of marketing programs both on and off the website. They are key to managing internet marketing activities and demonstrating ROI (return on investment) on those activities.

FreshDirect has succeeded in the fresh-food delivery business where other, earlier entrants failed. It made its first deliveries in 2002, and by 2010 it had acquired 600,000 customers in the New York City metropolitan area and processed over 25,000 orders per week.[6] Since then it has expanded to other large cities on the East Coast and will double its warehouse distribution capacity in 2016.[7] In order to compete with supermarkets, FreshDirect had to offer quality, on-time deliveries and the brands that discriminating New York shoppers demanded. In addition, it had to maintain a content-rich website, Figure 18.3a, to convince people of the desirability of shopping for food on the web. It had an early transactional mobile app and now has both iPhone and Android apps so busy customers can "order groceries on the go!" (Figure 18.3b)

Early in its development FreshDirect recognized the need for an in-depth understanding of the best product categories for its clientele, which elements of its website were most popular, and how well its marketing campaigns and product promotions were working. Its website provides a great deal of information and has various promotional offers as you can see in Figure 18.3a.

Analysis of metrics yielded the following insights:

- Like other retail sites, FreshDirect used a recommendation engine. For example, when a shopper orders a steak, a dialog box on the confirmation page recommends complementary items such as potatoes, herbs, and steak sauce.

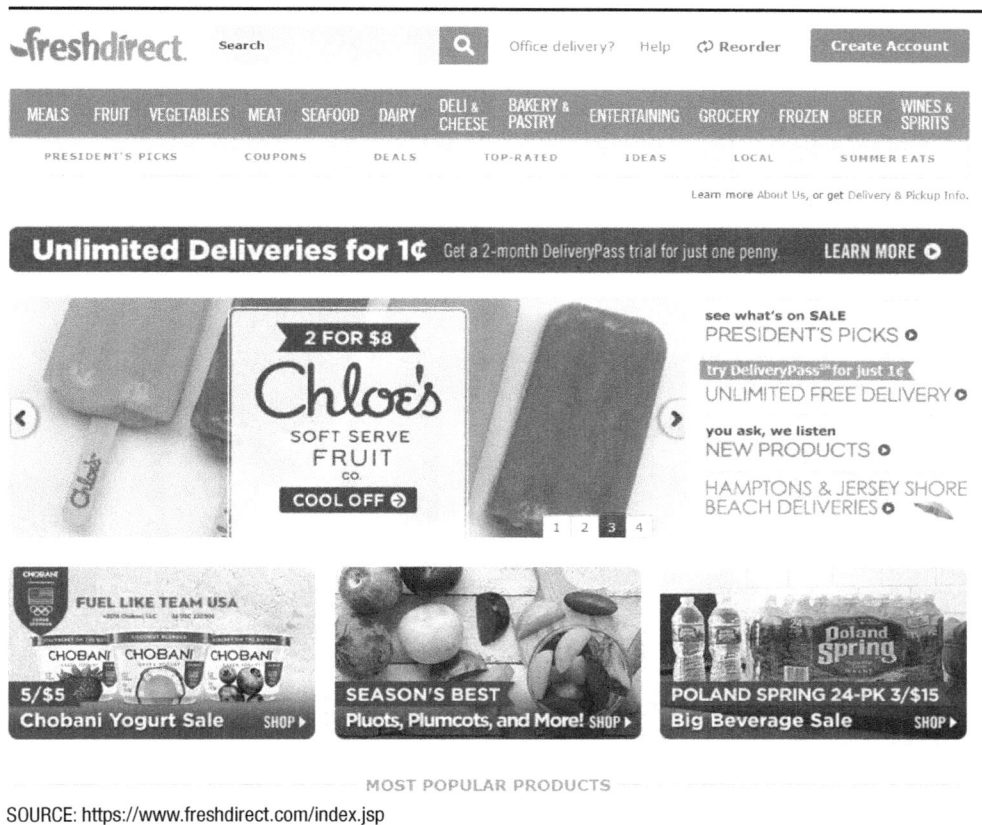

FIGURE 18.3a
The FreshDirect Home Page

SOURCE: https://www.freshdirect.com/index.jsp

Metrics showed that customers frequently purchased the recommended items, so the complementary items were given greater prominence on the site.

- FreshDirect was able to segment its database by variables that include purchase history, order size, and geography. That segmentation enabled it to target a promotion for a new prime meat product line to customers who had previously purchased meat. For one Valentine's Day, the company sent all customers an email offering meal suggestions and related specials. Metrics were able to relate purchases back to the email campaign and revealed that 50 percent of the recipients opened the email and 15 percent of them clicked-through to the site. Sales of the promoted products increased substantially, and the success of this seasonal email has influenced the company's email campaign planning.
- FreshDirect used metrics on local keyword searches to add frequently searched products—organic produce or specific brands, for example—to guide the addition of products to its selection.
- It monitored a wide variety of metrics related to checkout including most frequent shopping time, most frequent checkout time, duration of shopping visits, time required to make a purchase, and how frequently and at what point shoppers drop out of the checkout process. The site has undergone many usability tests, so the rate of shopping cart abandonment is satisfactorily low.
- Using marketing research, FreshDirect found that 50 percent of its customers used iPhones, so in 2010 it introduced its first app. It allowed users to purchase virtually all the items offered on the regular website and has features like lists and frequently purchased items (Figure 18.3b).

FIGURE 18.3b
FreshDirect Mobile Apps

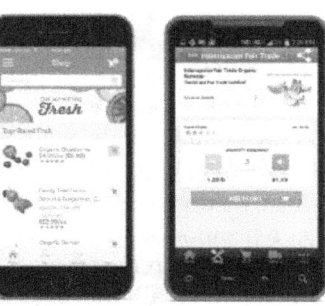

SOURCE: https://www.freshdirect.com/browse.jsp?id=mobile

Interactive Exercise 18-1 picks up the story with the next wave of data development and use at FreshDirect, the effort to personalize its interaction with customers at the individual level, not just at the segment level.

The data-driven saga continues with a 2016 partnership with third-party data supplier Hook-Logic. *Ad Age* explains that, "HookLogic sells the equivalent of search and digital end-cap advertising within ecommerce sites Walmart.com, Target.com, Costco.com, Peapod, and more. Rather than work out deals individually with these retailers, brands bid across HookLogic network sites to improve their display position or insert product listings in ads that appear next to search results. Then Hook-Logic tracks the online sales impact across the network." The CEO of HookLogic explains that this is the digital equivalent of in-store retail promotions, and Hook-Logic provides the platform that lets retailers compete for the same type of visibility in digital space.[8]

There are many other metrics available to and used by FreshDirect. These examples highlight just some of the metrics and the direct impact they have on business decisions. It also suggests the importance of integrated metrics solutions that can provide views of not only the website but also internet and mobile advertising and email campaigns and related online activities like keyword searches.

Business effectiveness measures like those used by FreshDirect are vital to marketing managers. We will devote the majority of the chapter to discussing the source, nature, and use of detailed business effectiveness measures, discussing first websites on the internet and mobile web, mobile app, social media, and video metrics. If the firm has a separate mobile site as discussed in Section 18.2b, the metrics will be much the same as those for an internet site. App metrics, however, are different and will be discussed later in the chapter.

First, however, let us take a brief look at measures of website performance. Measures of site performance give directions to the technicians who maintain the site. In the words of the website development process, this means tuning the site to maintain and improve the manner in which it functions. While the performance measures are not the job of marketing, smooth site performance is essential to CX and marketing managers should be attentive to them.

Website Performance

Figure 18.4 shows a report of the performance of a single web page—the page itself—and each file on it. Timing starts from the time the URL (www.alertsite.com in this example) is translated into the **IP (Internet Protocol)** address which in turn triggers the **DNS (Domain Name System)**. Lookup on the legend at the bottom of the chart. The more detailed printed report (not shown) indicated that it required 0.0024 seconds to look up the IP address on the network. Then the page starts loading, file by file. Each file loaded is measured as a **hit**. For each file, the webmaster can see how many seconds it took to connect with the file, how long it took for the first byte of information to load, and how long it took for content to load. Notice that many of the files are graphics—.gifs or .jpegs—and do not have significant text content. It took 1.3902 seconds for the page to load completely, which would be acceptable to most users. Reports like this are available in real time, that is, the webmaster can call up a status report for any page or many other elements of web functionality at any time.

IP (Internet Protocol) address a number assigned to each device that uses the internet.

DNS (Domain Name System) the process for converting the name of a website into its IP address.

hit any file, including a graphic, that is requested from a server.

AlertSite[9] is one of numerous businesses that specialize in website monitoring as part of software firm SmartBear. It offers monitoring and reporting services for mobile sites and apps as well as conventional websites. It also offers tools like on-demand load balancing test to ensure that pages load properly under different usage scenarios. Other tools allow webmasters to create scripts that mimic user activity. The scripts are sets of instructions that allow technicians to test many aspects of site performance in a controlled laboratory-like setting often referred to as **synthetic performance testing**.[10]

synthetic performance testing website performance testing conducted in a laboratory setting as opposed to measuring performance using actual visitor data.

Website performance data is clearly essential to the web technicians whose job it is to make sure the site functions at an optimal level. Marketers should also be concerned about the smooth functioning of the site, because it has direct impact on their customers. Walmart, for example, studied the impact of site performance on sales. It found that:

1. Conversions (sales) decreased as page loading time increased from 1 to 4 seconds.
2. Visitors who converted experienced load times that were twice as fast as visitors who did not convert.
3. There was a significantly higher bounce rate for slower-loading pages. Pages that experienced a high bounce rate were as much as 9 seconds slower than pages with a low bounce rate.[11]

Website performance is akin to daily housekeeping for digital marketers. It is necessary but not particularly exciting. The real excitement occurs when there are digital, social media, and mobile promotional campaigns to monitor.

FIGURE 18.4

Sample Web Page Performance Report

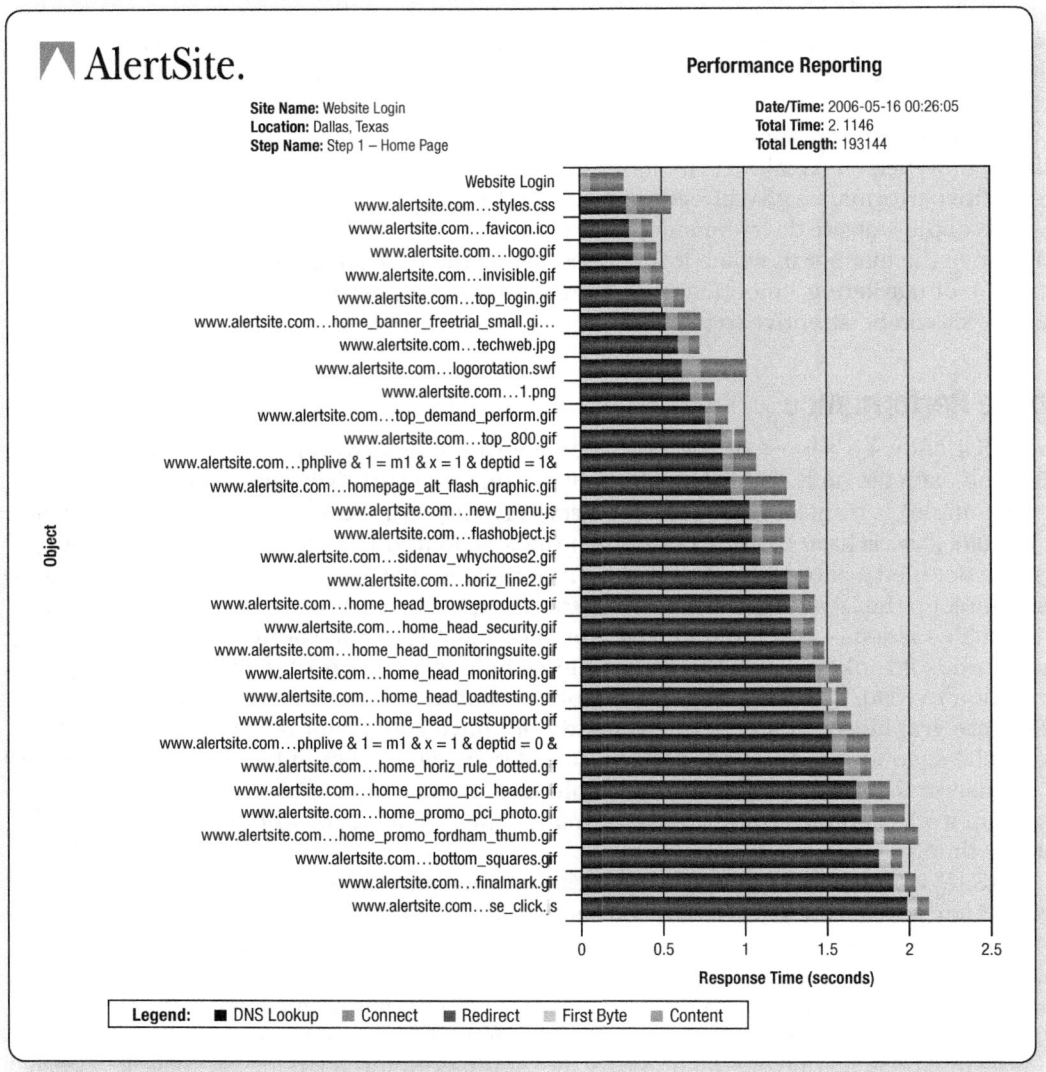

SOURCE: http://www.alertsite.com.

Collecting Website Traffic, Audience, and Campaign Data

Before we address the actual metrics there are two important issues to consider. First is the issue of quantitative versus qualitative data. Second is the discussion of tagging and cookies since these aspects of technology are crucial to campaign tracking.

The Issue of Quantitative versus Qualitative Data Data is basic to all marketing research as well as to metrics. Numerical data has benefits, especially in terms of model development like the predictive targeting models discussed in Section 7-3b3. Qualitative, or nonnumeric, data has the potential benefit of producing an understanding of buyer motives and perceptions. Table 18.1 shows basic types of both quantitative and qualitative data. Topics like why people buy (buyer motivations-qualitative) and customer product use (quantitative) are familiar from marketing research. Traffic reporting is a class of metrics specific to the internet. The principle of counting quantitatively versus

TABLE 18.1 Basic Types of Data

Quantitative	Qualitative
Traffic reporting	Why people buy
Customer product use	Perception of brand value proposition
Customer activities in various stages of the purchase journey	How customers talk about the product

Based on: https://blog.kissmetrics.com/qualitative-quantitative-analytics/

probing for understanding still applies. The web is awash with quantitative data as we will discuss in this chapter. Qualitative data can be collected online as well as offline using tools such as virtual focus groups and panel reporting.

While the distinction between the two types of data is clear, it is not now, nor has it ever really been, a choice between one type of data and the other. Anmol Rajpurohit from data science firm KDnuggets says that as Customer Experience Management becomes the paramount concern of CMOs, "there is an increasing need for holistic understanding of customer experience across the complete sale cycle. This can be achieved only through deploying qualitative analytics and integrating it with quantitative analytics to provide 360-degree data analysis."[12] This should not be taken as a recommendation for which comes first—qualitative or quantitative. There are good arguments for doing qualitative first to understand the questions for quantitative research. There are equally good arguments, especially among digital marketers who already have a trove of quantitative data, for following quantitative data with qualitative in order to unlock deeper meanings.

Although the argument for using both kinds of data for a thorough understanding of the customer is hard to refute, the data collected on the web itself is primarily qualitative and it will be the main focus of this chapter. Social media and specialized data collection tools, however, do bring qualitative data into play and will be discussed later in the chapter. For the moment, however, we stay with quantitative data and a discussion of tags and how they are employed to collect user data.

Tagged Web Pages Tagged Web Pages

Tags have been mentioned in a number of chapters, among them the discussion of following customers through their purchase journey, Section 6.4c. The terms tags, pixel tags, and beacons are synonymous and do not represent a new technology; they have been in use since the beginning of the commercial internet. Tags and tagged web pages seem to be the most used terms today.

A tag, then, is a few lines of code that are placed on each page in the site that is to be tracked. Tagged web pages allow the marketer to track a visitor as he or she moves from one page of the site to another. It also allows tracking events that occur on the page, like changing a piece of data in a form or selecting an item from a dropdown menu.[13]

Table 18.2 gives an example of the visitor data that can be captured using tagged pages, and the resulting metrics that are made available to the marketer. The metrics aggregate the data from many visitors into information that marketers need.

In order to capture the data, a cookie must be set on the user's computer. The two technologies—tags and cookies—work together to collect detailed information about visitor activity. Cookies themselves have become controversial as discussed in Chapter 17.

Tagged Web Pages a technique in which a small image is placed on a web page; used in conjunction with a cookie on the user's computer, the image returns data about user activity on the web page.

Cookies Cookies are small data files that are stored on the user's computer that transmit data back to a web server. There are several types of cookies:

- *Session cookies* are effective for only one visit. They are placed when the visitor enters and expire when he or she leaves.
- *Persistent cookies* remain for a specified period of time, a year perhaps, and then they expire.

TABLE 18.2 Examples of Data Made Available by Tagged Web Pages

Information About the Visitor (often called "Dimensions" in the metrics literature)	Metrics Produced for the Marketer
• Page	• Number of visitors
• Entry page	• Number of views
• Exit page	• Number of visits
• Referrer	• Number of new visitors
• Browser	• Number of repeat visitors
• Platform	• Total time online
• Geographic data (Country, City, Time zone, Organization, etc.)	• Average viewing time
	• Average visit duration
• Date	• Views per visit
• Time	
• Day of the week	

SOURCE: Adapted from http://ems.eos.nasa.gov/NI82/UnicaNetInsight821PageTagGuide.pdf.

FIGURE 18.5 Interaction between Cookie, Tagged Web Page, and Metrics Platform

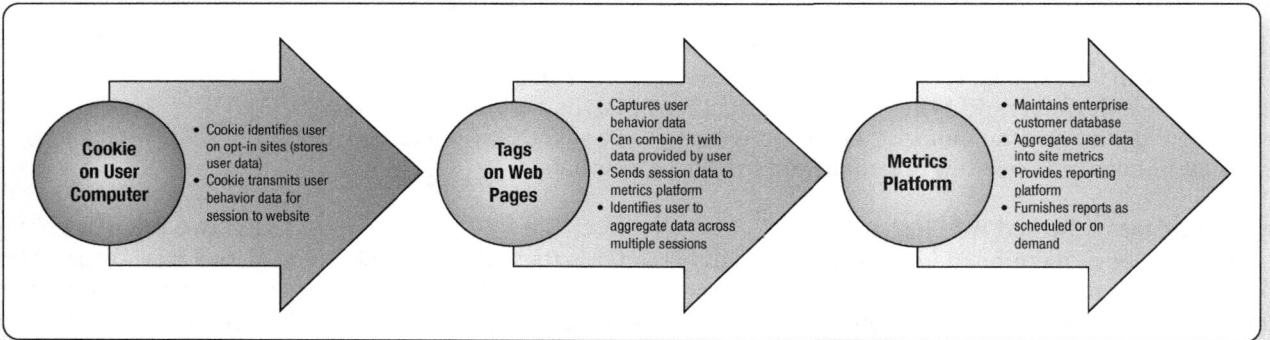

SOURCE: © Cengage Learning 2013

- *Third-party cookies* are set by an outside services provider like an ad serving firm or a metrics service.
- *First-party cookies* are set by the website itself.

Cookies can also be set to retrieve personal information or not, which should be controlled by the privacy options the user has selected.

Minus all the technical issues—and there are many—the concept is a simple one. The concept is portrayed in Figure 18.5. The cookie—set on each visit or on first visit if a persistent cookie—stores data that makes the user experience easier like remembering user names and passwords for sites where the user has registered. The tags on web pages allow the capture of user behavior and its attribution to the individual—identified or anonymous. Data are transmitted to the metrics platform, which stores enterprise customer data and maintains it for the sole use of that client and perhaps for purposes of model construction by the vendor. There is no movement of data between clients of a metrics service; that would be an egregious violation of client trust. Site metrics are aggregated from individual-level data and reported to the client according to the client's instructions.

The marketer needs to have a basic understanding of tagging and other methods used to collect traffic and audience data, but her primary job is to select the metrics that can accurately evaluate the effectiveness of the website and marketing campaigns. Let us turn now to a discussion of the metrics that are available.

Measuring Website Traffic, Audiences, and Campaigns Many of these terms show their origins in traditional advertising while others are unique to the web. The definitions that follow are generally accepted within the industry.

Traffic measures simply document site activity. Some of the key traffic metrics are as follows:

- Hits: the number of files requested. The hits metric is of little use to the marketer, although it is important to the webmaster as explained in the website performance section.
- Impressions: the number of times an ad banner is requested by a browser.
- **Page views** or deliveries: the number of times a web page is requested. Although you often see page views reported, they must be viewed with caution. Many sites use the Ajax technology to load multiple items on a page before the user requests them. Think of a retail ecommerce page with thumbnails that can be clicked on to get a larger image and text description. The entire page is loaded when the user requests it, although the user may choose to view none, all, or some of the full-size product images. What matters is which of the products are viewed, not the page view itself.[14] The various metrics platforms can handle this issue, but it requires special attention by the webmaster.
- **Sessions**: the amount of activity on a site during a specified period of time.
- Click-throughs: the number of times any link is clicked.

page views a page actually seen by a visitor; generally measured as a page being delivered to the visitor, which is not exactly the same thing.

sessions a time-dependent measure of site use; the amount of time a unique user spends on the site.

Audience measures provide data about the people who visit the site. Key audience metrics include:

- Visitors: the number of people who visit a site.
  - Total (includes multiple visits by the same user) or unique (different people) during a specified time frame
  - Unidentified (anonymous) or identified (registered or customer)
  - Unique (each visitor is counted only once during a specified time period)

- Behavior on the site
  - Number of page views
  - Session time
  - Path through the site
  - Shopping cart abandonment
  - Entry page (many visitors do not enter through the home page)

And there are many others. You should be aware that there is no clear dividing line between traffic and audience measures, but traffic always implies general information about site activity while audience always implies information about the demographics and behaviors of visitors to the site.

In addition, there are measures of marketing campaign effectiveness:

Campaign measures provide data about the effectiveness of marketing efforts.

- By communications channel: email, mail, mobile apps, online banners, and so on
- By offer: free shipping versus 25 percent off, for example
- Search effectiveness by keyword

And, again, many others.

Campaign measures have the ability to integrate measures about social media and offline activity (e.g., direct mail), or activity off the website (e.g., search keywords). Results are shown in terms of metrics like page views, number of visitors, number of unique visitors, and sales revenue. For multichannel marketers, the ability to see reports that cover all types of marketing activities across all their channels is essential.

In order to be meaningful, all these measures must be taken during a specified period of time. That leads to an almost endless set of metrics that can be produced, depending on the needs of the marketer. Some common metrics are as follows:

- Average number of visits per day
- Number of page views per month
- Average visitor session length last month
- Number of hits for each hour of the day
- Paid search results for the most recent seven-day period

And so it goes—almost infinitely.

Choosing the Right Metrics Choosing the right metrics is essential, but it is not easy. Digital executive and author Ben Yoskovitz puts it well when he says:

> *remember: analytics is about measuring progress towards goals. It's not about endless reports. It's not about numbers that go constantly 'up and to the right' to impress the press, investors or anyone else. Good analytics is about speeding up and making better decisions, and developing key insights that become cornerstones of your company, large or small.*[15]

To answer the question of "how to choose" let's first think about the customer journey and how metrics are needed to follow customers through each stage of their journey. Figure 18.6 shows basic steps in the customer journey and metrics that might accompany each. Remember that, as we discussed in Chapter 6, the customer journey is often more complex than this. Remember also that it is important to map the actual customer journey for specific products instead of simply relying on a hypothetical purchase process. With those *caveats* in mind we can use this simple journey model to tackle the question of how to choose metrics.

FIGURE 18.6

Sample Metrics for the Stages of Customer Journey

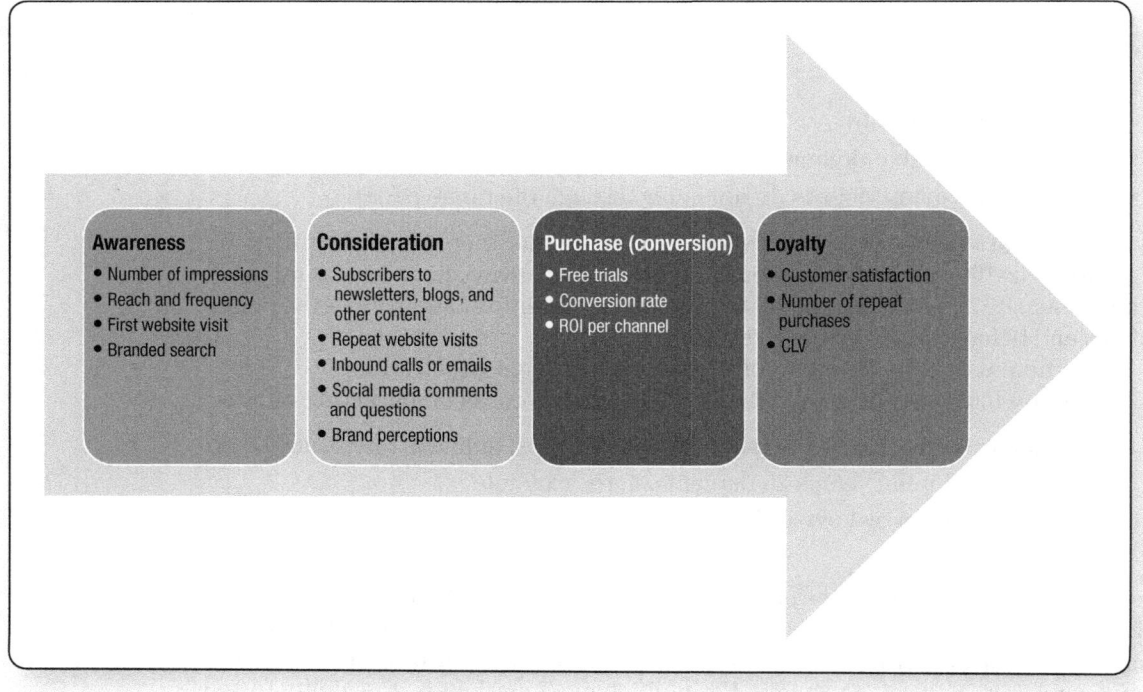

Notice that the first two samples of awareness metrics shown come directly from traditional advertising. First website visit and branded search, searches that use your brand name, are web specific. For the consideration stage inbound contacts and brand perceptions (measured by some type of marketing research) are traditional while subscriptions, repeat site visits, and social media comments are web specific. All of the sample metrics listed for purchase (the term "conversion" is often used, especially in B2B) and for loyalty are traditional marketing measures of accomplishment.

These examples help set the stage but they don't answer the "how to choose" question. There is only one answer: matching marketing objectives to marketing metrics. Figure 18.7 shows three typical marketing campaign objectives and some of the metrics that might be used to measure them. The objectives are SMART—that is, they are specific, measurable, achievable, realistic, and they have a time frame. We discussed SMART objectives in the context of website development in Section 15.4b. Later in the chapter, we will present an example using KPIs, which is another approach to establishing metrics that measure business success.

Take, for example, the first objective listed; to increase the number of registrants for an email newsletter in the first quarter of the fiscal year. How many people come to the site and how many continue on to the registration page are clearly important. Where they come from (the referral source) is likely to reveal important data for planning future programs. Would you hypothesize that the longer a visitor remains on the site, the more likely he or she is to register for the newsletter before leaving? Probably so. Take a careful look at the drill down to specifics about activity on the registration page. It is important to know how many registered as a percentage of

FIGURE 18.7

Matching Marketing Campaign Objectives to Program Metrics

Sample Campaign Objective	Corresponding Metrics
Increase Number of Email Captures by 5% in Q1	Number of unique visitors Referral source Length of visit Number of unique visitors to registration page • Number of completed registrations • Number of incomplete registrations • Last form box completed
Reactivate 10,000 Lapsed Customers in Q4	Number of emails sent • Reactivation message A/B Number of click-throughs A/B Bounces from reactivation landing page Number of incentive offers accepted A/B
Convert 2,000 Newsletter Recipients to New Customers in Last Six Months of FY	Number of emails sent Monday/Friday • Product offer A/B/C Number of click-throughs for each newsletter link Number of sales • By newsletter edition • By product Value of average sale by product Bounces from offer page A/B/C Heat map of offer page A/B/C

SOURCE: © Cengage Learning 2013

total site visitors; that is essentially a conversion measure. It is equally important to know how many people started to register—they apparently were interested—but did not complete. Why did they abandon the registration page before completing it? The last box completed may suggest the reason. Did the following box ask for information that the potential registrant did not want to reveal? That is often the case. If many people terminated registration at that point, a redesign of the registration page is in order.

For both the reactivation objective and the conversion objective, it is obvious that alternatives are being tested—a simple A/B split for the reactivation objective, different incentives perhaps, and a three different product offers being tested in the conversion appeal.

There is a logic to each set of metrics beyond just arriving at a measure of campaign success. In each case, the metrics begin with a baseline of activity and drill down to the specifics that measure campaign success. In each case, the objectives guide the choice of metrics. *Mapping metrics to objectives, in a clear and explicit manner, is the only way to bring order to the mind-numbing array of metrics choices.*

USING GOOGLE ANALYTICS

There are many good metrics platforms; many of them offer at least part of their functionality for free. Why single out Google Analytics? Exact numbers are hard to come by but in 2015 it was estimated that between 30 and 50 million sites had installed Google Analytics.[16] Is the heavy usage because Google Analytics is free? While that certainly does not hurt, Google Analytics provides robust analytics that many users need. Google gives good explanations of how to use it, and a small industry of marketing services firms and consultants offers assistance. Exercise 18-2 gives an overview of how the system works and the surrounding YouTube listings show many of the other tutorials available.

A good piece of advice for most new users is to start small, with a free platform, and determine what is really needed in terms of metrics, reporting, and access by various individuals within the firm. It will be obvious when the business outgrows the free platform and needs a paid metrics provider.

Posing and Answering a Question in Google Analytics

The platform provides the website owner with a dashboard and many options for accessing more detailed metrics. While blogs provide some metrics, they are not very flexible or detailed. It is easy for a blog owner to connect to Google Analytics to get more detailed metrics.

Figure 18.8 shows the dashboard in our example—one of Prof. Roberts's blogs—for a specific month. (The time frame is a variable and the user can request comparisons; the current week to the same week last year, for example.) The overview on the dashboard shows some of the basic metrics we have just discussed (e.g., the number of visits and page views). Most visitors appear to come for information on a particular subject because only a small number of them visit a second page. The pie chart says that most of them come from a search engine, the result of tagging and content designed for search (the good news). The bad news is that the bounce rate is high. In this example, by clicking-through on the bounce rate metric, I get a detailed chart that shows the bounces for this particular month by day, by week, or by month, as I choose.

Google defines "bounce rate" as the number of people who leave from the page on which they entered, further confirmation of the fact that few readers go on to a second page. Other metrics services define bounce rate by the amount of time readers remain on the page; for example, 5 seconds or less might constitute a "bounce." This

FIGURE 18.8
Dashboard for A Google Analytics Account

SOURCE: Google, Inc., http://www.google.com/analytics.

discrepancy is a warning that definitions vary between platforms, and the user must be certain of the interpretation of the metric. It makes this a good time to review key Google metrics definitions shown in the video in Interactive Exercise 18-3.

Continuing on through the dashboard, I see that the number of visitors do not vary much by day of the week. Most come from the United States and Canada, although I have former students in Europe and Asia, especially India, who are loyal followers, as shown by the heat map in Figure 18.9. Another aspect of a metrics report is that just about any term or image is linked to more detailed data; the user simply clicks on the item to access it in greater detail.

The most skewed data on my dashboard summary is that more than 34 percent of the page views go to one post that is over a year old ("Do Facebook Ads Work?" from October 2010) and should not be getting that kind of traffic. I want to drill down in an attempt to find out why. First, I look at some other elements on the dashboard by simply clicking on the link or the image. When I click on the country map, I see that the Indian traffic comes from large cities, which makes sense because my former students there are working professionals.

At this point, I have looked at only overview (dashboard) data. Remember that I am focusing on a single question: why is there so much traffic on a single, older post? I have to visit pages with more detail (drill down) in order to try to understand the answer to that question. But unless I have a clear focus—an important marketing question—I will get lost in all the detailed data.

The process itself is like a detective story. The analyst follows clues, hoping to find an answer. Some of the clues lead to useful data; others are dead ends. The dead ends have been eliminated from this story, leaving only the data that aid in understanding the single marketing question. Still, it takes four more Google Analytics pages to understand the nature of this traffic.

FIGURE 18.9

Blow-Up of Map Area on Analytics Dashboard

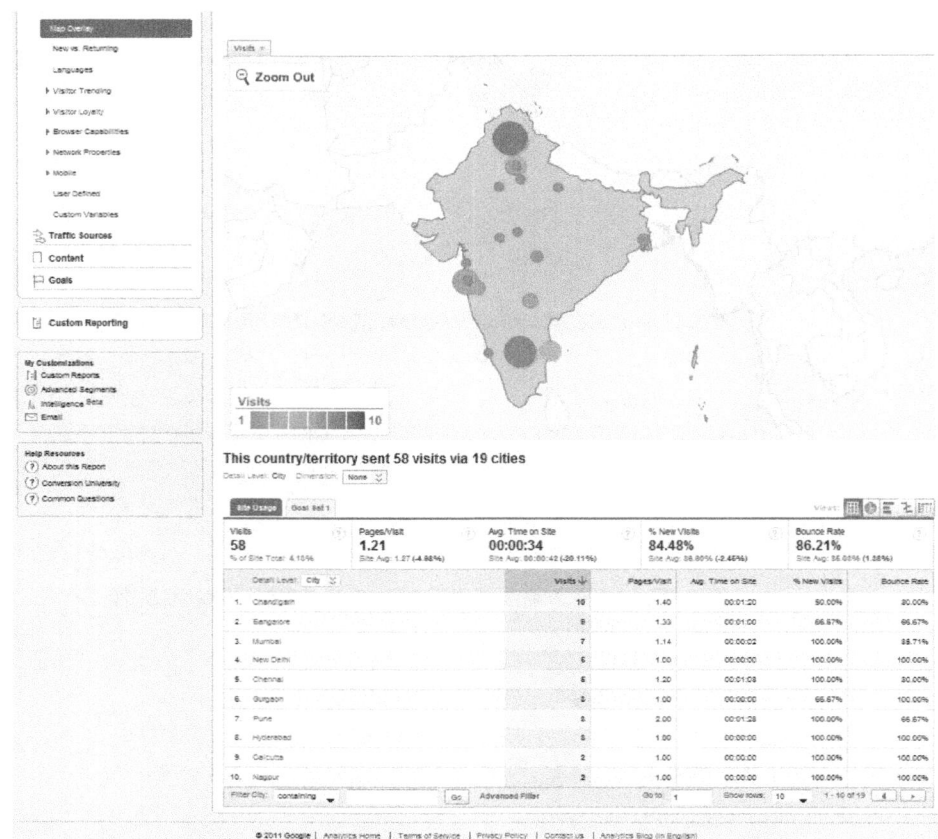

SOURCE: Google, Inc., http://www.google.com/analytics.

Each page has text beside it so you can match interpretation to data. While this creates a long figure, it is still important to review closely, and to do so with the understanding gained from Interactive Exercise 18-3. We start with one of the pages on the left navigation bar of the Dashboard, the Content page. From there we go to Traffic Sources and look at Search Engine referrals (Figure 18.10b), and from there to Keywords (Figure 18.10c). Finally, I look at an overlay called In-Page Analytics (Figure 18.10d) that shows click-throughs on the blog post I am researching. Each of these pages can be expanded into a number of subpages, as shown in Figure 18.10a, where the Content bar on the navigation pane is expanded to see a variety of content-related metrics options.

There is a little more to this story than simply writing a blog post for search visibility, although the keyword report (see Figure 18.10c) shows a number of different referrals. Note that these are not just "keywords." They are "search strings," the detailed phrases that searchers find more effective than single words. The search engines screen (see Figure 18.10d) shows that Ask.com referred three visitors to the page during that month. That is not much, but I do not see Ask.com on the referral pages for any of the other posts. A quick search on Ask.com reveals that this post has been linked to that site and usually shows up on the first screen when the question "Do Facebook Ads Work?" is entered on Ask.com. There are times when the marketer has to do some sleuthing above and beyond the metrics reports to understand what is occurring, and it is important to really understand the content, not just to look at a few numbers.

FIGURE 18.10

Google Analytics Walk-through I

Next, I click on Content > Top Content (left sidebar) in an effort to understand why the Facebook ads post is getting an inordinate amount of traffic. This page gives me a list of data, and while it is interesting that viewers spend over 3 minutes on this page as compared to only 42 seconds on the average for the site, the data do not indicate *how* they found the post.

(a)

Next, I click to Traffic Sources > Search Engines, since the majority of the traffic is referred by search engines. Seven search engines sent traffic to the blog during that month, with Google far out in front.

(b)

Clicking on the Google link on that page leads to another page with the search terms (keywords) that led users to this post. The keywords have a lot of variations on the post title, "Do Facebook Ads Work?"

(c)

Finally, I check the In-Page Analytics screen that overlays data on the page itself. While it does not help me understand the traffic to that page, it does answer another question. There are two more posts on the effectiveness of Facebook ads that were added to this post later to try to take advantage of the traffic it gets. Those links are at the bottom of the post. The overlay data shows that 15 percent of the readers clicked-through to the later post on whether Facebook ads work while only 10 percent clicked-through on the targeting post. While the ratio makes sense, it is disappointing that so few of the readers were interested in the more recent data.

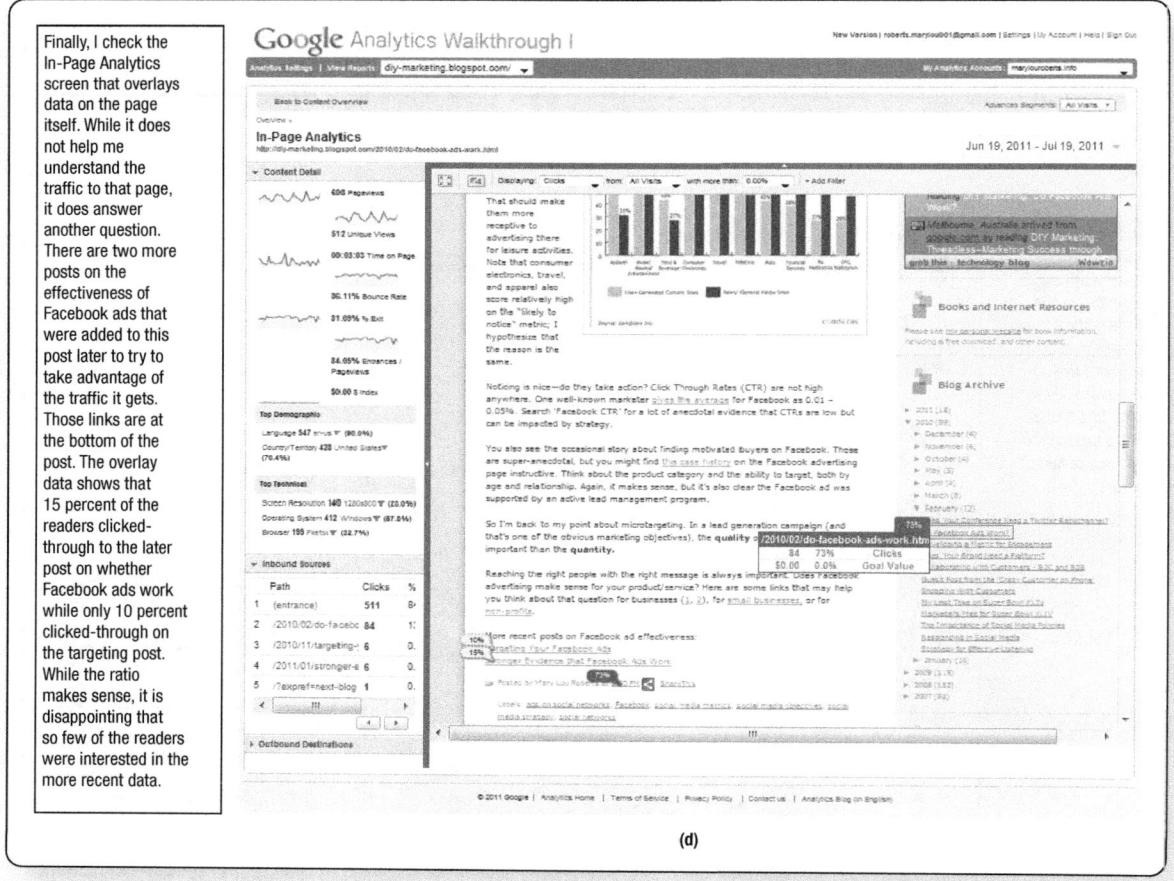

(d)

SOURCE: Google, Inc., http://www.google.com/analytics.

Adding Social and Mobile to the Picture

Fast forward just a few years to another blog. This blog was created for a specific event, a garden tour sponsored by the local Chamber of Commerce, one of many tours held over a 10-day time period. It was built on Google's Blogger, where all the Designer templates are responsive (Section 15-8a). In addition to content on the Chamber of Commerce website, event promotion included traditional print brochures and posters with the URL of the blog prominently featured. The membership of the gardening group definitely skews older, but some are active on social media, primarily Facebook. Those who are active usually join gardening groups, so an email campaign urged members to post about the tour on social media.

Figures 18.11a, b, c show key results taken from Google Analytics. The results are just for the eight days leading up to the event and one day following. The blog had been up for several months, but, not surprisingly, the greatest volume of traffic occurred within the time period leading up to the event.

Figure 18.11a shows that, in spite of the fact that the audience also skewed older, just like the garden owners, a significant minority of the sessions came from either cell phones or tablets. Developers care that most of these were Apple devices (not shown); marketers usually do not.

Perhaps equally surprising for an older audience is that over 20 percent of the traffic came from social media, almost entirely Facebook. The majority of the referrals did come from the large and highly visible Chamber of Commerce site while a reasonable number came to the site directly. The direct traffic was from people typing in the URLs from print promotion. The small amount of organic search traffic came almost entirely from people searching for their friends, presumably because they knew their gardens were on the tour.

Does this storyline make sense? It does if you know the members of the organization and the promotion that was used on behalf of the tour. It may not be what you would have predicted if you have stereotypes about older people's use of mobile and social media, but when you hear the story, it makes sense. That is an important metrics lesson. If it is not what you predicted but it makes sense when you stop and think about it, fine. If it does not make sense, keep digging because there is something going on. Unfortunately, the "something" will often be spam like the floating-share buttons or downright fraud, including interference by a competitor. None of the platforms likes spam or fraud, but if you need action taken you must bring proof to the platform.

Finally, take a look at Figure 18.11c. How does Google collect lifestyle and behavioral data like that shown from the click-stream of blog traffic? The simple answer is that it doesn't. Because Google owns the DoubleClick advertising platform it is able to collect lifestyle-related data from advertising results. Think back to the discussion of tagged web pages in Section 18-3b2. Can you sketch out how Google does this? Tags on pages and individual pieces of content. Cookies everywhere!

If that creeps you out a bit, remember that it is all kept scrupulously anonymous. That is not much comfort to some consumers, but for younger consumers it seems to be accepted and for marketers it is a treasure house of data.

There is only one major difference between traditional internet metrics and mobile metrics that marketers need to keep in mind. It is the difference between a *pageview* on the internet and a *session* on the mobile web or an app. A pageview is recorded each time a page is viewed whether as a new entry, a refresh, use of the back button, or in other ways, all of which can occur during a single visit.[17] A mobile session, on the other hand, is of limited duration. On Google Analytics the duration is 30 minutes unless the marketer sets it for a longer time period.[18] A video platform, for example, could define a session as 60 minutes if most of its videos run about 40 minutes.

FIGURE 18.11

(a) Devices Used to Access Blog
(b) Channels Used to Access Blog

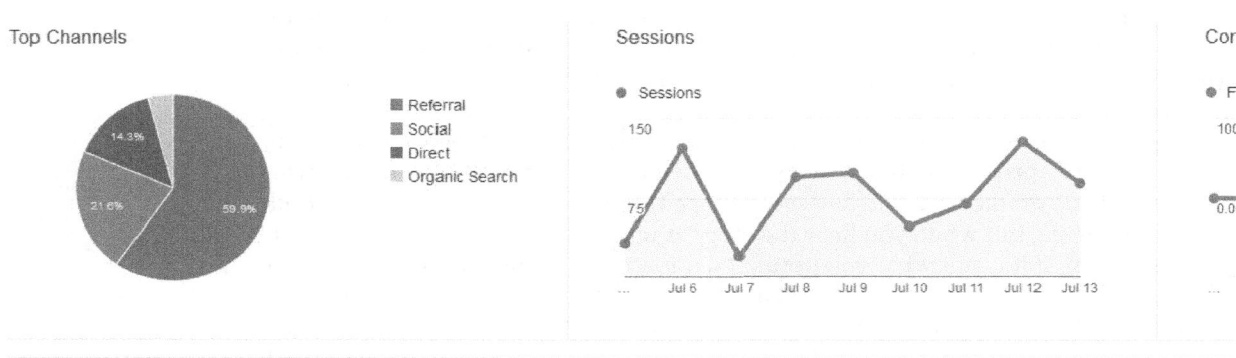

(a)

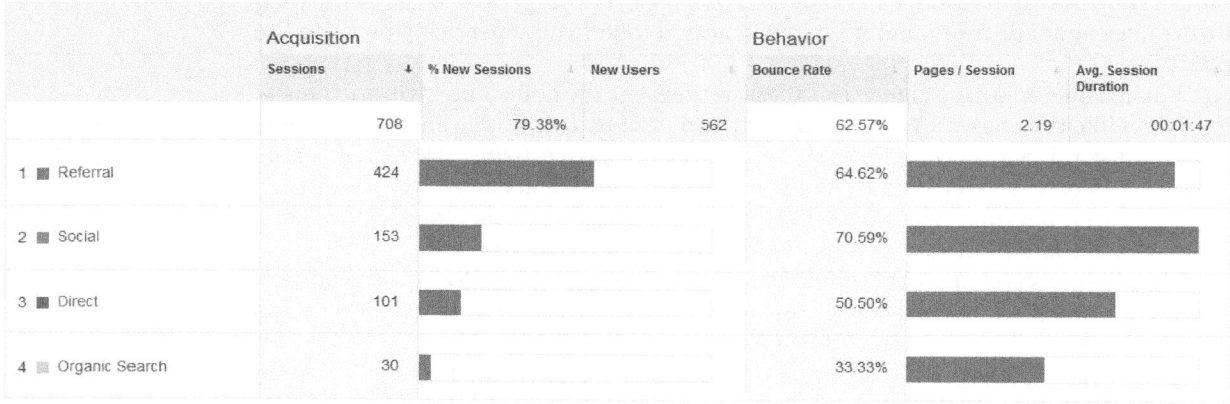

(b)

SOURCE: Google, Inc., http://www.google.com/analytics.

Segmentation and Conversion Metrics

Virtually all metrics platforms, including Google Analytics, provide the opportunity to segment data to uncover most and least profitable market segments and to provide data about what marketing approaches work best with the most profitable segments. The primary difference between segmentation of digital data and traditional market segmentation is that behavioral data is available to the internet marketer. Conventional internet marketing wisdom is that behavioral segmentation is more likely to reveal segment

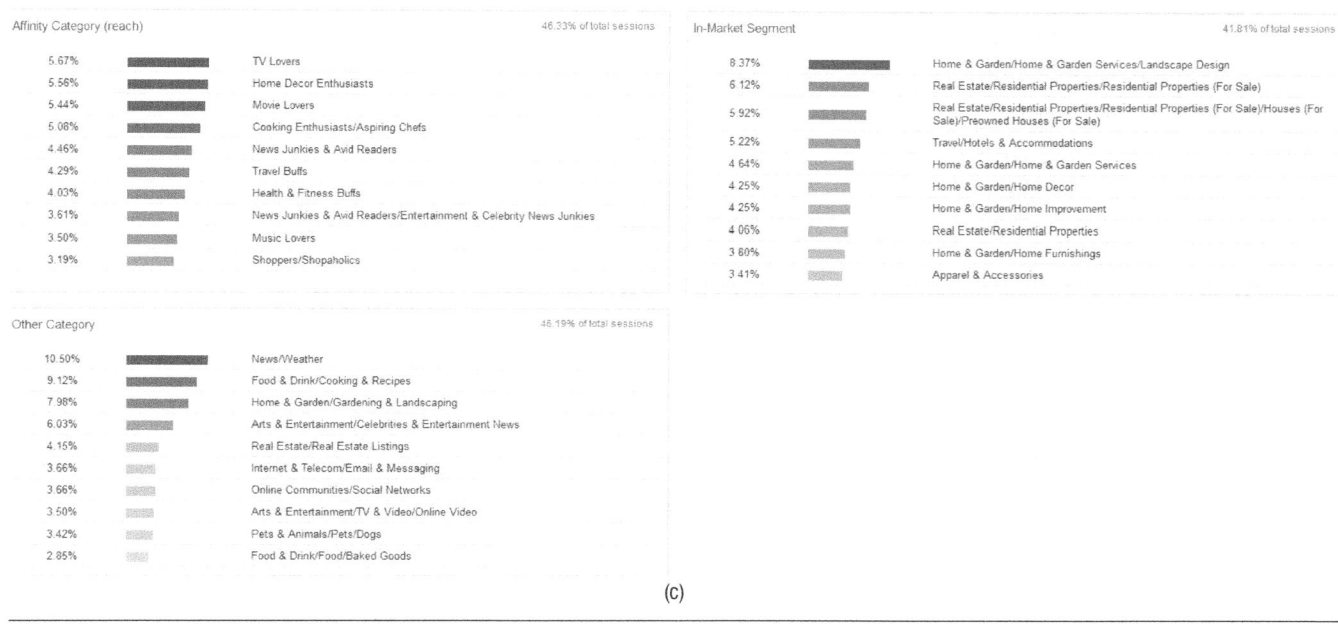

(c)

profitability, although conventional segmentation criteria like gender or geography may be necessary to understand how to reach segments.

With that in mind, let us look at a few of the types of segmentation and conversion analytics that are available from WebTrends, a metrics platform designed primarily for the enterprise user.

WebTrends offers what it calls "predefined segments" like new versus returning visitors and new versus repeat buyers. They are predefined because the coding and report formats have already been set up and are therefore quick and easy to use. The example that begins with Figure 18.12a focuses on new versus returning visitors. While you look at it, you should keep in mind that customers of sophisticated metrics platforms can develop customized segmentation approaches, using variables of their own choice, to meet virtually any marketing need.

Figure 18.12a shows the report for an email campaign carried out by hypothetical electronics supplier Zedesco. For returning visitors, it shows that average revenue per order—an important retailing metric—was highest for returning visitors who were referred by an affiliate network. While that is an important piece of information, the marketer must couple it with the fact that the affiliate network referred fewer visitors than any other referring source. The marketer can also see that the free shipping offer was more productive in terms of number of orders and average revenue per order than either of the other email campaigns. For the new visitor segment, the free shipping offer was also the most productive. It produced a higher average order size than affiliate referrals for the new visitors, which is different from the data for returning visitors. These data, and more that could be accessed by expanding the various lines on the report, provide the marketer with important information for planning future marketing programs of various types.

Figure 18.12b shows an overlay on the home page of Motorcycle Superstore for a one-month period. Beside the link to each of the site's product pages, the report shows the average revenue per order for each order placed after a click-through on that link. In terms of data, it shows a higher average order size for returning buyers than for new buyers. While this might be expected, it provides guidance for the marketer. In terms of metrics presented, New Buyer, Repeat Buyer, and month of September are all choices of the metrics user; there are other segmentations and time periods available. The tabs indicate that there are other data sets available for this site, so once again consider the huge number of metrics that can be chosen when evaluating the most profitable elements of a website.

FIGURE 18.12a

New Versus Returning Visitors Segmentation for Zedesco Email Campaign—Report Format

New vs. Returning Visitors Campaign Drilldown	Visits	Page Views	Clickthroughs	Orders	Revenue	Average Revenue per Order
1 ▼ Returning Visitors	37,273	489,783	38,129	2,761	$692,171.86	$250.70
▼ Email Campaign	30,502	300,543	26,481	1,482	$364,707.08	$246.09
▼ Zedesco	30,502	300,543	26,481	1,482	$364,707.08	$246.09
▼ Free Shipping on Everything	18,815	183,543	16,408	935	$240,540.43	$257.26
▷ Direct Email	18,815	183,543	16,408	935	$240,540.43	$257.26
▷ Zedesco Anniversary Sale	8,454	83,686	7,085	400	$89,667.52	$224.17
▷ Zedesco Take a Picture Week	3,322	33,314	2,988	147	$34,499.13	$234.69
▷ Portal	11,566	129,037	7,900	877	$225,336.99	$257.62
▷ Advertising Partner	4,627	52,301	3,325	354	$96,759.16	$245.09
▷ Affiliate Network	579	7,902	423	48	$14,768.63	$307.68
2 ▼ New Visitors	24,922	272,515	25,784	534	$77,292.93	$144.74
▷ Portal	14,277	158,465	14,390	285	$40,080.32	$140.63
▷ Advertising Partner	6,070	66,441	6,124	120	$17,640.43	$147.00
▼ Email Campaign	3,793	40,500	4,442	113	$17,660.76	$156.29
▼ Zedesco	3,793	40,500	4,442	113	$17,660.76	$156.29
▼ Free Shipping on Everything	1,700	18,142	2,374	60	$10,545.85	$175.76
▷ Direct Email	1,700	18,142	2,374	60	$10,545.85	$175.76
▷ Zedesco Anniversary Sale	1,280	13,611	1,255	33	$4,667.00	$141.42
▷ Zedesco Take a Picture Week	813	8,747	813	20	$2,447.93	$122.40
▷ Affiliate Network	821	9,110	828	16	$1,911.40	$119.46
Total		762,299	63,913	3,295	$769,464.79	$233.52

(a)

SOURCE: Webtrends, http://product.webtrends.com/WRC/8.7/ResourceCenter/rc/library/pdf/hdig/How_Do_I_Use_WebTrends_for_Audience_Segmentation.pdf.

As a final perspective on the analytics commonly available from metrics suppliers, consider the conversion funnel in Figure 18.13. This is a graphic representation, complete with data, of the traditional conversion funnel. The steps in the funnel are user defined, that is, the user specifies which behaviors to show including, for example, viewing a product page and adding an item to the shopping cart.

The left pane shows the point at which visitors entered the process. Most came from sources like search or from various other pages in the site. The right pane shows when they left the process: many moved on to other pages in the site, a considerable number ended their visit instead of adding an item to their cart, and some started the checkout process but did not complete it. About 3 percent did complete a transaction (clicking checkout complete at the bottom of the figure), but what goes on in between is even more informative to the marketer.

Take just one path as an example:

- 38,232 visitors viewed the product page
  - 10,966 added something to their shopping carts
  - 28,264 visitors went somewhere else—many of them went to another Zedesco page; over 18,000 went to other sites
- Of those who added something to their shopping carts, 4,106 started the checkout process
  - 6,529 did not start checkout and went somewhere else—most went to another Zedesco page; 1,539 ended their visit by exiting the Zedesco site

Why did they leave without making a purchase? What can the marketer do to keep them on the site and persuade them to complete a purchase? These are the kind of questions marketers should be asking. If visitors went to another Zedesco page and purchased something there, then it appears they found what they were looking for and metrics provided the answer. If visitors added something to their shopping carts but

(b)

SOURCE: Webtrends, http://product.webtrends.com/WRC/8.7/ResourceCenter/rc/library/pdf/hdig/How_Do_I_Use_Web-Trends_for_Audience_Segmentation.pdf.

FIGURE 18.12b
New Versus Returning Visitors Segmentation for Web Pages—Overlay (WebTrends SmartView) Format

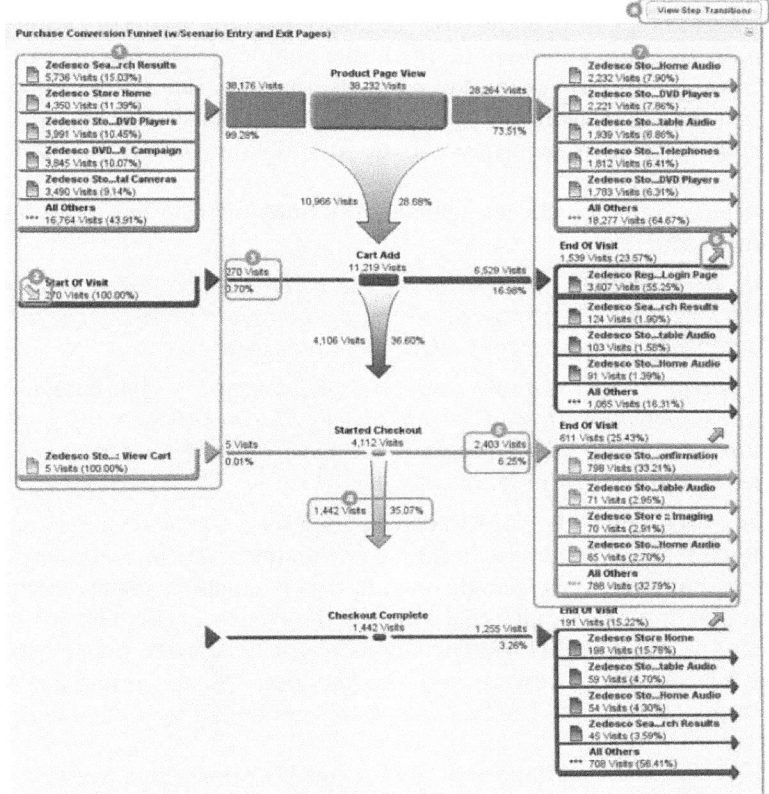

FIGURE 18.13
A Conversion Funnel Showing Paths Through the Website

SOURCE: Webtrends, http://product.webtrends.com/WRC/8.7/ResourceCenter/rc/library/pdf/aug/Tracking_Conversion_and_Abandonment_through_Scenario_Analysis.pdf.

exited after seeing the shipping charges (more detail than is on this chart, but available from metrics), then shipping charges seem to be a problem. What can the marketer do about that? If people simply looked at the product page and then left the site, where did they go (also available from another metrics report)? If they left and went to a competitor site, then they apparently did not like what they saw on the Zedesco site—which could suggest a product or maybe a pricing problem that should concern the marketer. If they left and went back to search, they did not find the product they were looking for and that may be of less concern to the marketer.

This path analysis and many other views can be very helpful to the marketer trying to understand what is happening on the website. The metrics do not answer all the questions. Sometimes that will require looking at other metrics, as just suggested. Sometimes, it may suggest that marketing research is needed, for example, to find if the product is not viewed as satisfactory by many potential customers. Whatever the situation, *metrics point the way*.

To gain some experience looking at metrics, carry out Interactive Exercise 18-4 and explore free website metrics available from two different services.

FROM METRICS TO KPIS

Throughout the chapter, we have emphasized the almost infinite number of metrics available to the digital marketer and both the difficulty and the importance of choosing the right ones. One of the undisputed authorities on web metrics is Avinash Kaushik, who is Google's Digital Marketing Evangelist and founder of a firm that offers certification in web analytics. In April, 2010, he wrote a blog post called "Metrics 101" that is worth reading in its entirety because the concepts it explains so well have not changed.[19] In it, he distinguishes between a metric, which is simply a number, and a **KPI (key performance indicator)**, which is "a metric that helps you understand how you are doing against your objectives." There are more complex definitions of both concepts, but none that are more helpful to marketers who are attempting to make sense of the metrics issue.

KPI (key performance indicator) a metric that has been identified as an important measure or benchmark of business performance.

The table in Figure 18.14 is the work of one of the metrics certification students. He focused on a presumably hypothetical bike company. The framework included high-level business objectives, marketing goals, the KPIs that will be reported, and the numerical target for each KPI. The implication is that the KPIs are the result of a conscious decision by management about what data are essential to the management of the business.

Kaushik's comment on the student's work points out another advantage of this type of framework:

> *I really liked Matt's presentation for his motor bike company analysis. In less than half a page one could see the complete picture of what the business was solving for and what the expectations were.*
>
> *Particularly clever I thought was his inclusion of the segmentation in his framework presentation. At a glance for the most important goal for the quarter (build a robust customer database for future marketing) you can see how their campaign strategy worked.*[20]

In other words, the choice of KPIs sets a long-term framework for management in controlling the effectiveness of, in this case, the marketing operation. All the KPIs are important, but strategy can single one out for emphasis in one fiscal time period. In this example, Kaushik implies that building the customer database by increasing the number of new registrants was the key focus for the chosen time period. Consequently, the analyst drilled down into the segmentation figure to find out where the most registrants came from. The fact that paid search lead by a huge margin points the way to future strategy.

Kaushik makes another important point in his blog post, "In aggregate almost all data is useless (like # of Visits)."[21] The actionable data is found by drilling down—to

FIGURE 18.14
Web Analytics Template

Bike Company X Web Analytics Framework

1 Business Objective	2 Goal	3 KPI	4 KPI Target
Sell Bike Parts	More sales	Monthly revenue	$15,000/mo
	Increase unique visits	Monthly unique visitors	13,000
	Make a profit	Profit margin/sale	40%
Effective Marketing	CRM–build a customer DB	# of new registrations/mo	300/mo
Build Goodwill	Draw qualified customers	Conversion rate	3%
	Serve as resource to riding community	# of page views of resource pages	1500/mo

5 Segmented KPI: (example) # of new registrations/mo

Total Reg Goal = 300	Result = 332 (110% of Goal)	Percent
Paid Search	223	67%
Organic Search	67	20%
Referrals	17	5%
Direct	25	8%

SOURCE: Figure: Bike Company X Web Analytics Framework by Matt Smedley, appearing on Occam's Razor by Avinash Kaushik. Reprinted with permission.

where the visits came from or to the source of the new registrants, for example. *Metrics—numbers—alone do not meet marketing and management needs. Only when the metrics are carefully chosen and reported in sufficient detail to guide strategic choices are business needs met.*

This is a high-level overview of how businesses use metrics to understand their current operations and to plan for the future. Would you be pleased if we could just stop here and say we have covered the subject? Unfortunately, we have not. There are more issues to consider, but there is good news as well in this picture.

The good news is that social and mobile metrics are being collected by the metrics platforms and are available without extra effort on the part of the marketer as shown in Section 18-4b. That does not answer questions, however, about social media campaigns like, for example, the ALS campaign described in Section 5-2d. The integration of social media data into standard Google Analytics reports was shown in Section 18-4b. We have not yet shown the integration of video metrics, but that will be covered in a later section.

The good news is very good indeed because some of the metrics the marketer needs are readily available. However, in order to understand the accomplishments of mobile app, social media, and video campaigns different sets of metrics are required.

APP, SOCIAL, AND VIDEO METRICS

Mobile apps, social media, and video all represent unique kinds of communication channels that have different issues from the traditional internet. As such, they present unique measurement issues. The three sections that follow will give a brief overview of basic measurement strategies in both spaces.

Mobile App Metrics

As we have discussed in other chapters, especially in the discussion of apps for CRM in Section 14-10a, the app marketing issue is, first, to get customers to *install* them, and second, to get them to *use* them. According to Kissmetrics:

> *Mobile app analytics is about converting ad budgets to installs, and installs to repeated app usage and in-app purchases. Ultimately, the objective of a mobile app developer is to evaluate user lifetime value, retention, and the frequency of usage.*[22]

Beyond installation and usage there is no general agreement on the stages of mobile app adoption and retention. This is a set of mobile app metrics that suggests elements of a customer journey and recognizes that different kinds of apps may require different metrics. Depending on how the marketer defines business objectives for the app, revenue and interest/intent may also be app KPIs.

Installation

- Number of installs
- Source: app store, website, other
- User characteristics

Engagement

- Number of times accessed in first 24 hours
- In-app session time
- Session intervals
- Consumer data access permissions granted
- Number of screens accessed per session

User Experience

- Screen flow (customer journey through the app)
- App performance (loading time, errors, crashes, and others)

Revenue for Transactional Apps

- Number of paid subscriptions
- In-app purchases

Interest and Intent for Media Apps

- Number of articles read
- Number of pages visited
- Social shared

KPIs for All Types of Apps

- Retention rate
- CLV[23,24,25]

Persuading customers to install a given app from among the thousands available is no easy task. However, the difficulty of generating installation and trial pales in comparison to generating engagement that leads to repeat use. Statistics suggest that only 20 percent of apps are used more than once and 95 percent are deleted within the first 90 days after installation.[26] Clearly the app must offer real value to the customer to get her to use it even a second time. Beyond the app value proposition the statistics suggest that there should be major emphasis on UX. Google has published a detailed set of instructions for testing both Android and iOS apps[27] and offers a cloud-based testing laboratory for Android apps.[28] There are other tools and other services that also provide testing capabilities. Marketers should have objectives that include successful app use, retention beyond the three-month time frame, and a satisfactory

CLV and test their apps before introduction to have the greatest probability of meeting their objectives.

As mobile marketing matures, app marketing may acquire a more strategic framework. Perhaps it will be similar to the one developed over several years of effort for SMM.

SMM Metrics

In Chapter 5 we described the process of developing a social media strategy (Section 5-4) as

$$\text{Listen} \rightarrow \text{Communicate} \rightarrow \text{Engage} \rightarrow \text{Collaborate}.$$

That is significantly different from strategy development for the traditional consumer purchase model. Because social media is so different from offline media or traditional digital media, it requires different measurement.

The issues of measurement in social media are made more complicated by the fact that social media are essentially qualitative in nature. Yes, there are things that can be measured quantitatively like number of visits to a brand's Facebook page. However, many of the issues that matter most to marketers in social media are essentially qualitative—engagement with the brand, for example.

Marketers wrestled with these issues for a number of years before settling on the Valid Metrics Framework shown in Figure 18.15. While the model is grounded in traditional advertising measurement theory, it captures the activities of SMM and produces metrics that marketers can use to make decisions.

FIGURE 18.15

Valid Metrics Framework with Metrics Categories, Definitions, and Sample Metrics

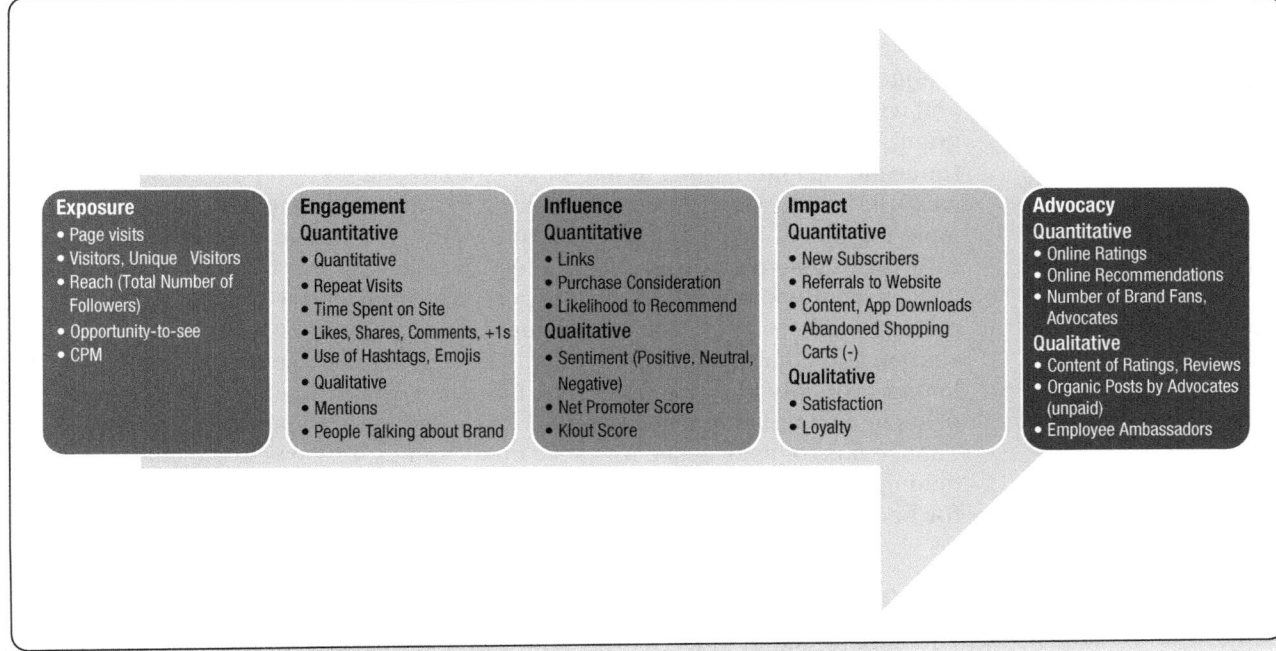

SOURCE: Barker, Barker, Bormann, Zahay and Roberts, *Social Media Marketing: A Strategic Approach*, p. 230.

First, some definitions:

- **Exposure** is taken directly from advertising metrics. It represents the opportunity to see or hear any type of content in any communications channel.
- **Engagement** is a term most used by social media marketers and it has not yet achieved a consistent definition among them. The most popular is the amount of time spent—on the platform, with the brand post, and so forth. However, definitions vary, so it is important for the marketer to understand how the term is being used in any given context.
- **Influence** is the ability to affect attitudes and behavior, whether the actor is a piece of content or a social media influencer as described in Sections 5-2b and 5-2c.
- **Impact** is the effect of SMM activities on business results.
- **Advocacy** is the likelihood that one person will recommend the brand to another.

Figure 18.15 uses these stages to categorize some of the most important SMM metrics. There are two things to keep in mind as you look at this figure. First, there are numerous qualitative as well as quantitative metrics. In each stage of SMM there can be numerous qualitative and some quantitative metrics as indicated in Table 18.1.

Second, the Valid Metrics Framework ends with advocacy, not purchase. That's a significant difference from the familiar purchase behavior model. While there are impact metrics that attempt to capture the role of SMM in a customer purchase, they are not universally accepted. More important, the nature of the model indicates that purchase is not always the expected outcome of a SMM campaign. Marketers must therefore set objectives with care in order to select metrics that genuinely measure what they set out to do.

Consider the SMM campaign of the Beggin' pet food brand. You may have seen their TV ads, but this campaign took place entirely on social media and featured the hashtag #BecauseBacon. Taking a look at Figure 18.16a, provided by social media analytics platform Zuum's Subject Analyzer tool, it's easy to just ask how anyone could resist those cute faces! It certainly makes sense to show images, or in this case videos, of adorable dogs instead of a piece of dry bacon jerky. If you are judging engagement by number of likes (and there is more to it than that as you will see in a moment) Facebook is a big winner with over 9 thousand to Instagram's 1 thousand. That can be explained by the fact that Beggin' had just over 53 thousand Instagram fans in mid-2016[29] and over a million Facebook fans as early as 2013,[30] with over 1 million fans liking a single post in mid-2016.[31] That's not the most important metric, though. Figure 18.16b shows that the overall engagement rate with these posts was 2.08 percent. For Instagram the engagement rate was 2.88 percent while it was only 0.04 percent for Facebook. That's even more compelling when you see that engagement on Facebook is a combination of likes, shares, and comments while it is only comments on Instagram. The Beggin' marketers probably already knew this, but it is certain that they concentrated their posts on Instagram for the remainder of the time period measured (Figure 18.16c). That seems to make sense for these cute canines. It worked; the engagement rate held up over that period of time with 3.09 percent for Instagram and 0.02 percent for Facebook.

Video Marketing Metrics

The importance of videos, especially video advertising, was emphasized in Chapter 12 on mobile marketing. This section looks exclusively at video content marketing. It excludes the many issues specific to measuring video advertising. The IAB is

FIGURE 18.16a
Most Engaging Posts

The campaign aligns with a mass media event, the Grammy Awards, with event-related content. The campaign content includes videos, photos and music tracks.

SOURCE: http://zuumsocial.com/blog/top-social-media-campaigns-for-pet-foods-q1-2015/

FIGURE 18.16b
Post Engagement Across Platforms

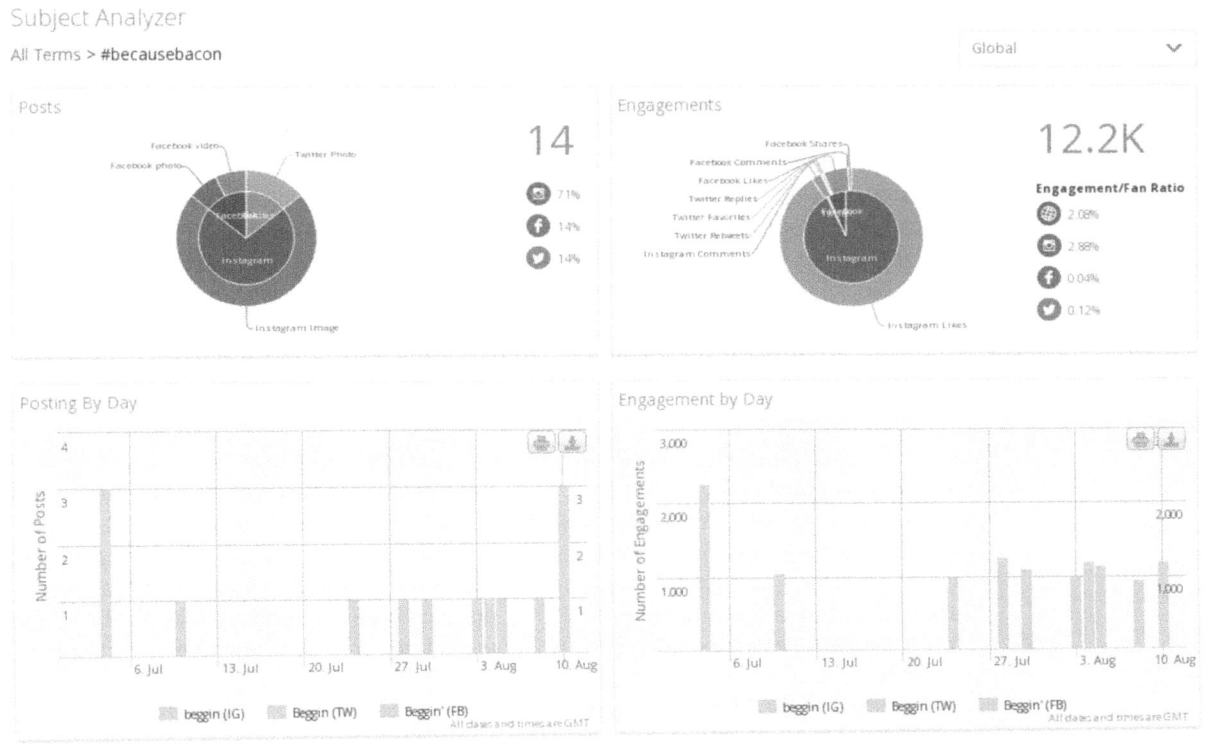

FIGURE 18.16c

Post Engagement on Instagram

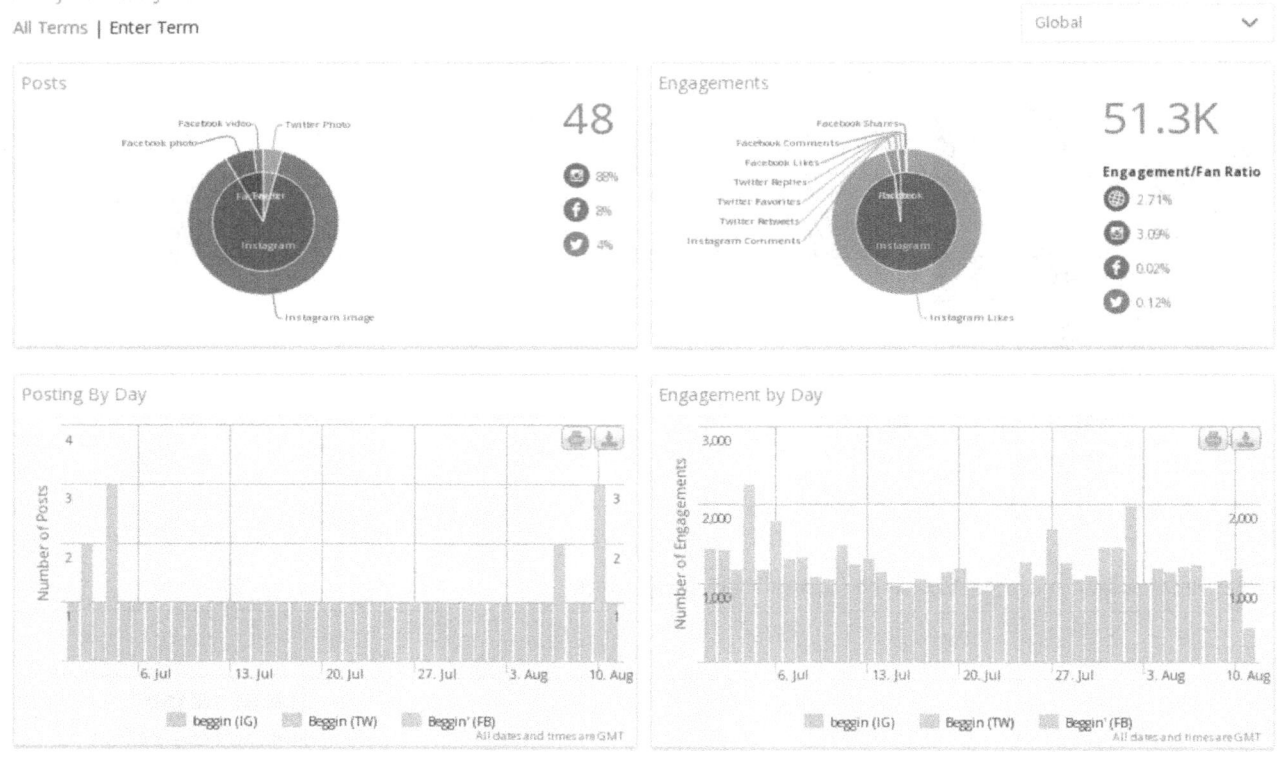

http://zuumsocial.com/blog/pet-food-social-media-campaign-becausebacon-analyzed/.

the primary source for video advertising metrics.[32] Mark Waugh, Global Managing Director, of Newcast puts the situation into context:

> *Consumers all around the world are rapidly embracing online video, because it offers them a near limitless array of engrossing content. Some of the keenest users are the young, affluent viewers who are hardest to reach on television. Brands are finding online video a particularly effective way to reach these valuable audiences, not just with advertising, but also with branded content; content that can inform or entertain consumers in a deeper and richer way than is possible with short, interruptive ads.*[33]

Like mobile metrics, video metrics are also based on time. For videos to have the greatest marketing impact they must be watched through to the end. Otherwise important content, and probably the call to action, will be missed. Beyond that simple concept there are a seemingly endless number of lists of video metrics, all of which categorize them in different ways, mostly using the same metrics. Table 18.3 shows commonly used video metrics categorized in a way that fits with content strategy issues. The use of these metrics is demonstrated in Interactive Exercise 18.5.

Notice that the final column is user experience, a recurring theme throughout the text. From a metrics perspective it is important that the user experience metrics are

TABLE 18.3
Frequently Used Video Metrics

Reach	Engagement	Relevance	User Experience
Number of views	Percent of video viewed	Play rate	Bounce rate
Click-through rates	Comments		Time spent on page
Audience characteristics	Social shares		Subscriptions/Signups
			Conversions

https://wistia.com/library/guide-to-video-metrics
https://hbr.org/2015/04/video-metrics-every-marketer-should-be-watching

not produced by the video itself. They are website metrics that we have already discussed. Each of these website metrics should be improved when videos are part of the content or the videos are not doing their job. Bounce rate should be lower and time spent on page should be higher. Subscriptions or signups to website content should increase as should the conversion rate, either in terms of purchases or of some other specified conversion objective.

In order for people to have an opportunity to view the video they must first be exposed to it. The video can be embedded on a web page, linked to the page, promoted in an email, or posted to a social media site. Reach, then is measured by the appropriate metric—number of page views for the site or number of Facebook fans for a Facebook posting, for example. Once a user has been exposed, he or she makes the decision to click the play button or not. Once again, audience characteristics are not collected directly from the video interaction. On Facebook, the marketer knows the composition of his or her fan base, although not the exact composition of the audience that viewed the video. Videos viewed as a result of emails can be linked to the email recipient. If that person has registered with the site and provided personal information, that data can be linked directly to video viewership as a result of the email.

Most marketers would agree that engagement is the primary contribution of videos. They are inherently engaging. Even branded videos can be highly engaging as evidenced by the Old Spice Guy and the furry friends videos shown in Section 5-2a. Engagement is most often measured by the percent of the video viewed—total video length to time from hitting the play button to time clicking away from the video. Be careful of a simple measure of engagement; the definitions of what portion of the video must be viewed to constitute engagement differs from platform to platform. Comments and social shares play the same role as in social media metrics—important indicators of how and how much viewer interact with the content. Play rate is a less rigorous metric than percent viewed. It is merely the number of people who clicked the play button and started watching—presumably a sign that the content held some relevance for the viewer.

Some of these metrics are illustrated in the Facebook insights capture in Figure 18.17. This 18-second video received over 16 thousand views using a definition of watching for 3 seconds to constitute a Unique view. Notice that both Total and Unique views show how many are delivered by paid advertising. The chart also shows how many of the Total and Unique viewers viewed as much as 95 percent of the video. At the top of the chart the average duration is shown as 12 seconds. Both these items of data support something that advertisers have known for years. Be sure your brand (or in this case, movie) name is mentioned early because viewers may never get to your call for action, especially if it is the last piece of content.

The video in Figure 18.18 is a good example of taking an intrinsically boring subject like getting dirty clothes clean and making an engaging branded video of it. It may

FIGURE 18.17
Some of the Metrics Produced by a Video Posted on Facebook

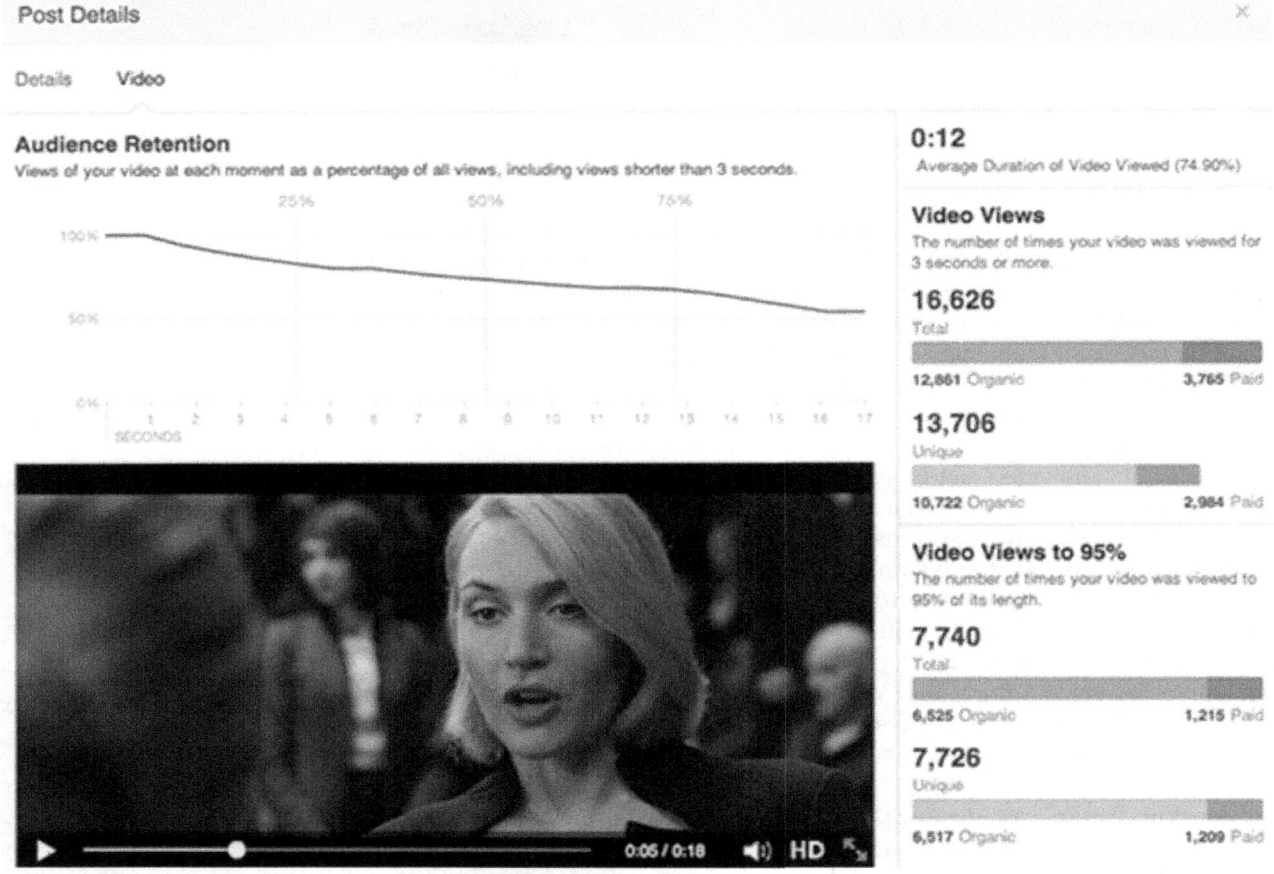

SOURCE: https://www.facebook.com/business/news/Coming-Soon-Video-Metrics

not be the best video you've ever seen, but considering the subject you may agree that it's pretty good. According to Google:

- The main objective of the YouTube video was brand consideration.
- P&G chose view-through rate as their primary KPI for the video.
- Metrics were obtained from YouTube Analytics and they showed Tide's highest-ever VTR and a high Brand Lift score. Brand Lift is a Google score that is obtained from online surveys and search results in the days immediately following the airing of a video.[34]

In the second iteration of the video campaign P&G retargeted to members of its YouTube channel and to the subscribers to the channels of the creators of the video. The retargeting netted P&G a Cost Per View (CPV) of 50 percent less than its previous campaigns.[35]

Carrying out a video campaign, or any type of digital campaign for that matter, and being rewarded with metrics that show a successful outcome is the goal of any marketer. Unfortunately, there is always one more question: Can the metrics be believed?

FIGURE 18.18
Identifying KPIs for the Tide Pod Challenge

Tools for Measuring KPIs	Awareness KPIs	Consideration KPIs	Action KPIs
YOUTUBE ANALYTICS GOOGLE ANALYTICS ADWORDS	Views Impressions Unique users	View-through rate Watch time	Clicks Calls Signups Sales
BRAND LIFT	Awareness lift Ad recall lift	Favorability lift Consideration lift Brand interest lift	Purchase intent lift
GOOGLE CONSUMER SURVEYS		Answers to custom questions	

SOURCE: https://www.thinkwithgoogle.com/articles/how-identify-right-kpis-online-video.html.

FRAUDULENT METRICS

The marketer must remain vigilant about the quality of metrics data. There is a great deal written about click fraud, which is a big issue in PPC advertising. That is costing advertisers money, hence the high level of interest and prevention attempts. When the problem is with owned content on any platform it is generally referred to as spam.

This kind of fraud is an ongoing issue for all platforms and the marketers who use them. You saw a mention of floating-share-button spam recorded as blog visits in the discussion of Figure 18.11b. This spam is generated by a site called Floating-share-buttons.com which is used to promote low-quality, spammy websites and to create backlinks for them in an effort to raise their Google search ranking.[36] I pointed out that half the referrals during one period of time came from those spam visits. The spamming also destroys the value of other metrics. For example, the bounce rate of the spam visits is 100 percent because the bot lights on a page then leaves, but this is very difficult to separate from the valid bounce metrics.

The most common kind of website spam is **comment spam**, examples of which are shown in Figure 18.19. The spammers either post a link with their meaningless, often irrelevant, comment or the blog template may create a link automatically. Either way, the blog is linked to a disreputable site. If you have a low-volume blog you can remove the comments by hand. Blog platforms have filters available and there are other filters available. Google has a discussion of the harm done by comment spam and ways to prevent it.[37]

Fake reviews are the big headache for websites. While there is not a lot of data on the subject, a 2011 study at the University of Chicago found that as many as 30 percent of the online reviews for some categories of products are fake. A 2013 Business

comment spam abusive practice in which comments are placed on a blog or website, perhaps robotically, for the sole purpose of generating a backlink in an attempt to improve search results.

FIGURE 18.19

Examples of Comment Spam

Submitted on 2015/09/04 at 2:23 pm

The official trailers of the interlude are quite tempting because they reveal a lot about upcoming events. Download Bucky Larson: Born to Be a Star Movie. An undistinguished low-budget Western, Buffalo Gun (1961) which he had made for the obscure
Globe in 1958 and which was released in 1961, was his last picture.

Submitted on 2015/09/04 at 11:28 am

best for soundcloud marketing and social media like facebook and instagram also youtube is blackhaty they also give's you free trial of 1000 soundcloud plays or likes followers reposts must give it a try 1+ delivery speed and service quality http://blackhaty.com

Submitted on 2015/09/05 at 9:44 am

Hey very cool website!! Man .. Excellent .. Amazing .. I will bookmark your web site and take the feeds additionally...I am happy to search out so many helpful info right here in the publish, we need work out extra techniques in this regard, thanks for sharing......

SOURCE: https://smartblogger.com/comment-spam/.

Insider post said that 30 percent of Yelp reviews are fake.[38] Not surprisingly Amazon is a huge target for the bots that distribute fake reviews. Amazon itself has taken legal action against the spammers[39] and there are a number of online tools the consumer can use to detect fake product reviews on Amazon. For smaller websites, the rule is *caveat emptor*.[40]

Marketers need the help of their corporate IT departments to filter out the type of spam that affects their blogs or websites and there are many tools available to do so. However, marketers must not rely on someone else making sure their metrics are clean. They should be constantly vigilant and research any strange metric that appears.

SUMMARY

The ability to track and measure visitor activities is one of the unique capabilities of the web. If marketers are not using appropriate traffic, audience, and campaign metrics, they are missing out on a major benefit conferred by digital marketing. However, the number of metrics is enormous and choosing the right ones and applying them to marketing decision making are huge challenges.

There are two different perspectives on the effectiveness of websites and internet and mobile web marketing programs. The user perspective is concerned with the usability of the website itself, which in turn leads to a satisfying user experience, discussed in Chapter 6.

From the business perspective there are a number of important types of metrics. Site performance metrics are important to the technicians whose job is to keep the site working smoothly but have little direct relevance for marketers. They do, however, impact the performance of marketing programs. Marketers focus on traffic, audience, and campaign metrics in order to provide information about site visitors and to measure marketing campaign effectiveness. Today these metrics are usually obtained from a combination tagged web pages and cookies placed on user computers that return data to the database. Internet enterprises, large and small, usually outsource the collection and reporting of these metrics to marketing services firms that have the specialized platforms and consulting expertise required for this demanding endeavor.

The use of traffic, audience, and campaign metrics to gauge effectiveness presupposes that marketers have clear marketing objectives. These objectives may range from provision of information to customer service to sale of products. When the objectives are transactional in nature, behavioral measures in the form of traffic and audience metrics are needed. When there are branding objectives, marketing research may be required to measure the attitudinal variables that are used to assess the effectiveness of branding efforts, both online and offline.

Whether the marketer relies on SMART marketing objectives or the business has identified key performance indicators, mapping metrics to objectives is a key task. Then the marketing analyst must uncover the detailed metrics that point the way to marketing planning and strategy decisions.

Mobile web metrics differ from internet metrics primarily in that they are time dependent, not number of visits. The time dependency also applies to mobile apps but apps have a download and use cycle that needs metrics that measure the importance of engagement with and retention of the app. SMM has a Valid Metrics Framework that identifies relevant metrics at each stage of the social media campaign. Video metrics are also time dependent and many are unique to the video medium.

Measurement on all these platforms must be accomplished in a multichannel environment in which customers interact with various marketing touchpoints over a buying cycle that can last for days or weeks or even longer. Only if all channels, all touchpoints are monitored can the marketer obtain the desired 360-degree view of the customer that informs decisions that improve business results. That defines the challenge for both the analyst and the user of digital marketing metrics.

DISCUSSION QUESTIONS

1. The term "metrics" is commonly used by digital marketers. Explain your understanding of the meaning of the term.
2. True or False: Internet marketers need to decide whether they will conduct measurement from a visitor usability perspective or from a traffic and audience measurement perspective. Defend your answer.
3. True or False: The webmaster and the marketer use the same metrics when assessing website effectiveness.
4. What are the uses of tagged web pages and cookies in the collection of website effectiveness data? In what other contexts have you seen tags discussed in this text?
5. What are some of the specific metrics that measure traffic, audiences, and campaigns? Which ones do you think are most important?
6. Why do you think Google Analytics is so popular? Can you think of any other indicators of popularity besides the number of sites and blogs that use it?
7. How should the marketer go about choosing the right metrics to measure website or campaign effectiveness?
8. What role do SMART objectives play in establishing and using metrics?
9. What is the meaning and importance of the term "KPI"?
10. What is the critical difference between website metrics and mobile metrics?
11. Why is it necessary for mobile apps to have a separate set of metrics?
12. Why is it necessary to measure video marketing separately from the website, blog, or social platform on which the video is embedded?
13. What are the chief metrics used to measure video marketing success?
14. True or False. The small website or blog does not have to worry much about fraudulent metrics.
15. Do you believe that most commercial websites are using metrics to improve customer experience and enhance marketing effectiveness? Do you have any personal experiences that support your view?

ENDNOTES

1. http://www.emc.com/leadership/digital-universe/2014iview/executive-summary.htm.
2. "The Democratization of Data," http://www.infor.com/content/whitepapers/democratization-of-data.pdf/?&isGated=no.
3. David Kiron, Pamela Kirk Prentice, and Renee Boucher Ferguson, "The Analytics Mandate," http://sloanreview.mit.edu/projects/analytics-mandate/?source=0514&utm_medium=synd&utm_campaign=mr.
4. Sam Ransbotham, David Kiron, and Pamela Kirk Prentice, "Minding the Analytics Gap," http://ilp.mit.edu/media/news_articles/smr/2015/56320Wx.pdf.
5. Anja Lambrecht and Catherine Tucker, "The 4 Mistakes Most Managers Make with Analytics," https://hbr.org/2016/07/the-4-mistakes-most-managers-make-with-analytics.
6. Micah Steiger, "Fresh Direct's Success," https://novoed.com/venture1-2014-1/reports/197804.
7. Paula Vasan, "Tech Giants Serving Up Competition for Fresh Direct," http://www.cnbc.com/2015/06/12/tech-giants-serving-up-real-competition-for-freshdirect.html.
8. Jack Neff, "HookLogic Expands Network That Lets Brands Bid for Online Clout," http://adage.com/article/clients-at-cannes/hooklogic-expands-network-effort-extend-brand-clout/304062/.

9. https://smartbear.com/product/alertsite/overview/.
10. Tammy Everts, "Performance Monitoring 101," https://www.soasta.com/blog/synthetic-real-user-measurement-monitoring-rum/.
11. Tammy Everts, "Performance Monitoring 101," https://www.soasta.com/blog/synthetic-real-user-measurement-monitoring-rum/.
12. Anmol Rajpurohit. "Qualitative Analytics: Why Numbers Alone Do Not Tell the Complete Story," http://www.kdnuggets.com/2014/02/qualitative-analysis-why-numbers-dont-tell-complete-story.html.
13. "Tag Management 101," http://www.signal.co/resources/tag-management-101/.
14. "Ajax Counting Nightmares," https://www.clickz.com/ajax-counting-nightmares/61765/.
15. Ben Yoskovitz, "Measuring What Matters: How to Pick a Good Metric," http://onstartups.com/tabid/3339/bid/96738/Measuring-What-Matters-How-To-Pick-A-Good-Metric.aspx.
16. Matt McGee, "As Google Analytics Turns 10 We Ask: How Many Websites Use It?" http://marketingland.com/as-google-analytics-turns-10-we-ask-how-many-websites-use-it-151892.
17. "Google Analytics Definitions," http://www.analyticsmarket.com/blog/google-analytics-definitions.
18. "How a Session Is Defined in Analytics," https://support.google.com/analytics/answer/2731565?hl=en.
19. Avinash Kaushik, "Web Analytics 101: Definitions: Goals, Metrics, KPIs, Dimensions, Targets," http://www.kaushik.net/avinash/web-analytics-101-definitions-goals-metrics-kpis-dimensions-targets.
20. http://www.kaushik.net/avinash/web-analytics-101-definitions-goals-metrics-kpis-dimensions-targets/.
21. "The Must-Have Mobile App Metrics Your Business Cannot Do Without," https://blog.kissmetrics.com/must-have-mobile-metrics/.
22. "Top 12 Key Performance Indicators for Maximizing Mobile App Revenue," http://www.adweek.com/socialtimes/top-12-key-performance-indicators-for-maximizing-mobile-app-revenue/621659.
23. Bryn Adler, "The 8 Mobile App Metrics That Matter," http://info.localytics.com/blog/the-8-mobile-app-metrics-that-matter.
24. Codrin Arsene, "Measure the Success of Your Mobile Application Using These 17 Detailed Mobile App Analytics Strategies," http://www.ymedialabs.com/mobile-app-analytics/.
25. Codrin Arsene, "Measure the Success of Your Mobile Application Using These 17 Detailed Mobile App Analytics Strategies," http://www.ymedialabs.com/mobile-app-analytics/.
26. Eduardo Bravo Ortiz, "How the Google+ Team Tests Mobile Apps," http://google-testing.blogspot.com/2013/08/how-google-team-tests-mobile-apps.html.
27. "Firebase Test Lab for Android," https://firebase.google.com/docs/test-lab/.
28. https://www.instagram.com/beggin/.
29. "Beggin'® Celebrates One Million Bacon-Loving Fans with Week-Long Sweepstakes," http://newscenter.purina.com/2013-09-30-Beggin-Celebrates-One-Million-Bacon-Loving-Facebook-Fans-With-Week-Long-Sweepstakes.
30. https://www.facebook.com/beggin/.
31. "Digital Video Metrics Modernized," https://www.iab.com/wp-content/uploads/2015/06/VideoMetricDefinitions.pdf.
32. Jonathan Barnard, "Mobile to Drive 19.8% Increase in Online Video Consumption in 2016," http://www.zenithoptimedia.com/mobile-drive-19-8-increase-online-video-consumption-2016/.
33. "Brand Lift," https://www.thinkwithgoogle.com/products/brand-lift.html.
34. Kim Larson and Rachel Salberg, "How to Identify the Right KPIs for Online: Video: Lessons from the Google Brand Lab," https://www.thinkwithgoogle.com/articles/how-identify-right-kpis-online-video.html.

35. "2 Simple Ways to Block "Floating-Share Referral Traffic," http://botcrawl.com/block-floating-share-buttons-referral-traffic/.
36. "Ways to Prevent Comment Spam," https://support.google.com/webmasters/answer/81749?hl=en.
37. Whitney C. Gibson and Jordan S. Cohen, "Online Reviews: Ten Things You Should Know," http://www.defamationremovalattorneysblog.com/2015/11/online-reviews-ten-things-you-should-know/.
38. Chris Morran, "Is Amazon Doing Anything to Fight Latest Wave of Fake, Paid-For Reviews?" https://consumerist.com/2016/02/08/is-amazon-doing-anything-to-fight-latest-wave-of-fake-compensated-reviews/.
39. "How to Spot Fake Online Product Reviews," http://www.realsimple.com/work-life/life-strategies/fake-online-reviews.
40. Ben Popken, "30 Ways You Can Spot Fake Online Reviews," https://consumerist.com/2010/04/14/how-you-spot-fake-online-reviews/.

Appendix

AdWords Online Marketing Challenge for Students

THE GOOGLE ONLINE MARKETING CHALLENGE

This Appendix provides guidance to student teams that are seeking to enter the Google Online Marketing Challenge (hereafter GOMC). This worldwide paid search marketing competition gives students the opportunity to create online marketing campaigns using Google AdWords. The Challenge tests a team's ability to write advertisements that will be displayed on Google's search network. There are often other award opportunities such as the Social Impact Awards for working with nonprofit organizations. In 2017, there will be a special award for teams undergoing Google AdWords: Certification as a Google Partners. Under the supervision of a cooperating instructor, each student team of three to six members receives an AdWords advertising budget of $250 to run a campaign on behalf of a business or nonprofit organization for three weeks over a period of up to 31 days. Exhaustive information on the Challenge is available online and is also referenced in this document. The objective of this Appendix is to provide some helpful tips and resources for the Challenge and to point students in the right direction for online resources.

To set the stage, in the Challenge, each team submits a preliminary report that details the client background and campaign plan. If the GOMC team at Google approves the plan, the team gets an AdWords budget and permission to run the campaign. After running the campaign, the team again submits a report about running the campaign and the results. A panel of global academic scholars judges the entries and awards prizes based on the quality of the AdWords strategy, the success and reporting of the campaigns, and the quality of the competition reports.

FIGURE A.1
Considerations before Entering the Challenge

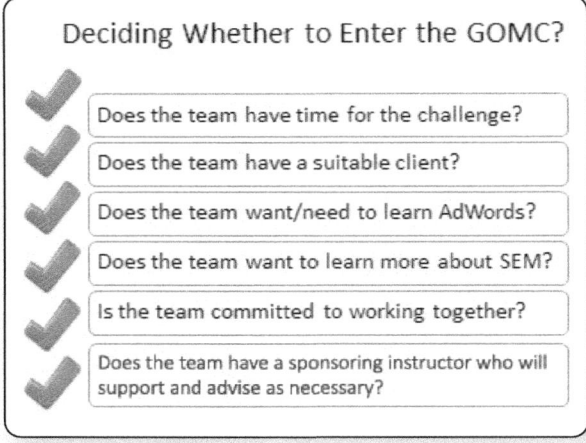

Before entering the Challenge, students should consider if they have time for the effort. The project involves pre and post work and the three-week campaign. The campaign must be monitored every day and someone has to do it. Students will also need to learn AdWords and have a suitable client and an effective team. Students might want to allow time to become AdWords certified before beginning the campaign, using resources from the Digital Marketing Course. If students want to learn more about Search Engine Marketing and pay-per-click (PPC) in particular, the GOMC is a great opportunity. Figure A.1 indicates key considerations for entering the Challenge.

PRELIMINARY STEPS FOR THE CHALLENGE

While deciding whether to enter the competition, students should carefully read through the general orientation and most current information about the competition process on the GOMC website at https://www.google.com/onlinechallenge/. This process will start the student team thinking early about the structure and rules of the competition. This page also has links to some valuable tools for designing the AdWords campaign. In addition, the GOMC has a community of users on its own Google+ site that often provides helpful insights and answers to issues as they arise: https://plus.google.com/+GoogleOnlineMarketingChallenge/posts. It is a good idea for at least one member of the team to follow this page.

Students can register for the Challenge as soon as their professor is registered. It is advisable to start the initial registration process as soon as possible after finding a client, and then get started on the pre-campaign report. The idea is that the campaign should be ready-to-go when students receive permission to launch the campaign from AdWords.

Before the Challenge three-week period begins, each team member should understand the "mechanics" of using AdWords and building campaigns. "Slackers" and "Free Riders" will not help the team optimize their search efforts so students should set clear roles and expectations within their groups. Since the campaign must be active for three weeks over a period of up to 31 days, all students in the team should take their turns monitoring the campaigns and ads and making changes to optimize their campaigns.

Google has a series of key video tutorials about the structure of AdWords under a "Search Advertising" tab in the Digital Marketing Course, which can be found on the GOMC website: https://www.google.com/onlinechallenge/dmc/. Each team member should at least complete the tutorials in the introductory sections ("What Is AdWords?" and "Search Advertising and Google AdWords") and in sections Search 101–302. This module provides some of the best, up-to-date information about the many settings and options in running a campaign. Since major changes to AdWords text ads were implemented for the Fall of 2016, Google's site itself is the best source of the latest formats and settings. In addition, a reference for all AdWords terms can be found at https://support.google.com/adwords/topic/24937?hl=en&ref_topic=3121777.

HOW TO CHOOSE AN ADWORDS CLIENT

A critical step in the success of the Challenge is to find a client appropriate for this competition and one that could successfully benefit from using AdWords. To participate in the GOMC, a student team's client must have a web page in place. The team should not rely on promises from the client that "it will be ready by the time the students start the competition in two weeks." Teams have failed based on promises not kept by clients in the competition. The web page must also have keywords and content that can be associated with the ad campaign. For example, if a client wants to advertise a new product line but product line information is not online, the ad campaign will not be successful. Google has a brief online section that describes how to pick keywords that relate to a website for a paid search campaign at https://support.google.com/adwords/answer/2453981?hl=en.

Google also asks the students to select a client that has not used AdWords in the last six months. This requirement often means a business or nonprofit that is new to AdWords. There are also restrictions about the types of sites that are acceptable, such as no websites promoting alcohol (depending on country) counterfeit designer goods, information harvesting, illegal activity, and others. Avoid industries with expensive keywords such as insurance or involving medical claims (i.e., mesothelioma). Avoid any product or category with significant national competition as well (i.e., mortgage loans), particularly if there is no unique, differentiating feature. A small, local business or nonprofit often works well in the Challenge.

Generally, tangible products or unique destinations and services seem to work best in AdWords campaigns. Some suggestions for businesses or nonprofits that can do well are as follows:

- Specialized products or services with limited competition in a geographic area.
- Industrial products that are fairly unique, especially when customers are looking for clear purchase specifications.
- Unique products in small categories that result in less advertising competition, such as some auto accessories.
- Products in categories where there is not a lot of brand recognition, especially when a well-crafted ad with a call-to-action can differentiate a company.
- Categories of services that do not have high name recognition or frequent purchase behavior but have geographic limitations. Infrequent purchase behavior often results in less word of mouth, which encourages online search, such as for the local market in tuxedo rentals.
- Products and services targeting clearly defined organizational or lifestyle groups, such as "Christian Retreats" or "Children's Birthday Parties" that can be limited in AdWords by geographic reach.
- "Event-driven" occasions such as holidays are opportunities for special items (i.e., Hanukkah Menorah) and timely messages.
- When the advertiser uses frequent promotions, for example, "Cheesehead Hats—50% Off" is likely to get a high CTR for Wisconsin fans in the market for Cheesehead Hats.

Figures A.2 and A.3 summarize some guidelines for choosing a client.

Teams should also choose a client that will communicate with them about business objectives, customer segments and behavior, and other business-related issues that might not be evident to the casual observer. The client should also be open to suggestions about changes in the landing page or pages from the results of specific AdWords ads in order to improve performance. In addition, the client should keep the student team informed about any changes to the website or the business as the

FIGURE A.2

Choosing a GOMC Client

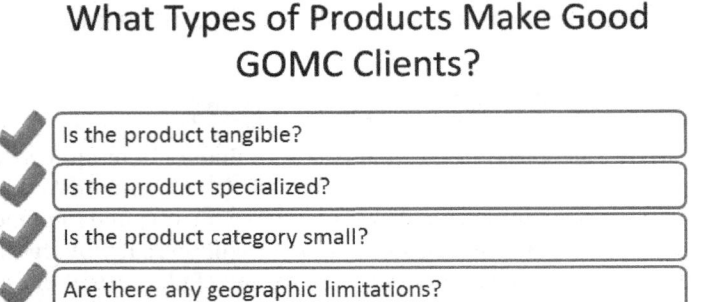

FIGURE A.3

Avoid Certain Types of Clients

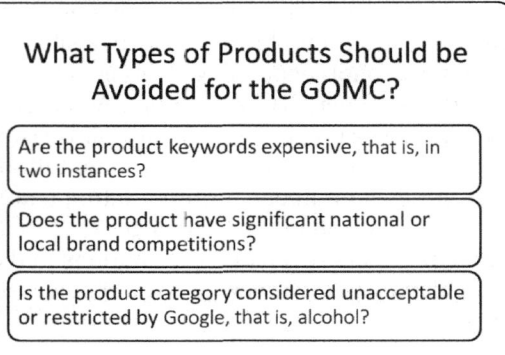

Challenge progresses so the team can keep campaigns updated. For example, an AdWords ad showing a promotional discount should only be "live" while that promotion is running on the website. It is also useful if the client enables Google Analytics and gives students access to the data for deeper analyses.

Before making a client selection, students can search for a few terms or keywords relevant to the client's business to determine the level of competition in that category. Test searches can also reveal how easy it might be to "find" that business using what students think of as obvious terms (which might not be so obvious). A review of the winners of past Challenges may also provide some good ideas for clients: https://www.google.com/onlinechallenge/past/index.html. For example, the 2015 winners show a good range of businesses and nonprofits. Finally, it seems that most of the winners involve a client with a tangible product or a unique situation of "place marketing," such as a special-interest museum.

Be sure to review the latest instructions on the GOMC website about the specific details of selecting a client for the competition as these can be changed or refined over time: https://www.google.com/onlinechallenge/discover/select-business.html.

THE GOMC COMPETITION REQUIREMENTS

In fact, the best way to start the process is by carefully reviewing the link about the Competition Process and running a campaign: https://www.google.com/onlinechallenge/discover/.

Google expects the student team to submit a Pre-Campaign Report through the student Dashboard Account. The Dashboard Account is separate from the AdWords account used for the Challenge. When reviewing the Competition Process page, students should pay special attention to the details about the required formats and campaign information it needs in future research and in discussions with the client. Pay attention to the required formats and campaign information. The team will need this information for reporting requirements for the Challenge and for discussions with the client. Before beginning work on the campaign, the team should ensure that each member has completed the Digital Marketing Course described in Section A-2. The video tutorials in the Digital Marketing Course are marked with a tab on the GOMC website. The Challenge is described in the Pre-course Preparation Video: https://www.google.com/onlinechallenge/dmc/prep.html. The following sections are particularly useful for running the basic AdWords campaign:

- Introduction to Digital Marketing
- AdWords Fundamentals (There is also a review course on AdWords Fundamentals that takes about 2 hours. Look for the link in the AdWords Fundamentals module).
- Search Advertising

Some additional helpful resources include the following:

- AdWords Help Center—detail about designing and managing AdWords ads, campaigns, and accounts at https://support.google.com/adwords#topic=3119071
- AdWords Glossary—common features and concepts defined at https://support.google.com/adwords/topic/3121777?hl=en&ref_topic=3119071
- Google AdWords Keyword Planner—useful when students have access to a Google AdWords account
- AdWords Fundamentals Review Exam—available for https://www.google.com/partners/#p_certificationexam;cert=0;exam=0;

These and other online materials can help students understand the technical aspects of running a campaign. Students should review the Display Advertising, Mobile Advertising, Video Advertising, and Shopping Advertising Modules on the Digital Marketing Course, as appropriate, if the team plans on running those types of campaigns.

DEVELOPING THE CAMPAIGN REPORTS

The written information required by Google is critical to the team's success because Google strictly enforces competition guidelines. Reports are required before and after the campaign (called Pre- and Post-Campaign Reports) and must be in a certain format. Google also asks teams to deliver a letter to the business or nonprofit selected informing the business of the team's interest and requesting its permission and a meeting with the team. Teams should first review the information requirements for writing the campaign reports at https://www.google.com/onlinechallenge/discover/campaign-reports.html. Next, students should examine the Pre- and Post-Campaign Reports of the recent winners of GOMC competitions at the above link. These reports indicate the preparation, strategy, and quality that have impressed the judges. Note that both reports are rather brief yet contain a fair amount of qualitative and quantitative information, so there is a benefit to using concise, professional writing supported by insightful discussion and analytics. Often using a chart or table better conveys pertinent information than lengthy paragraphs. This combination of quantitative metrics and verbatim insight seems to characterize winning entries, as well as sound marketing strategy. Students should not ignore writing quality, that is, logical flow and good organization, and should make sure that the document has no typos or grammar mistakes. Figure A.4 provides some guidelines for successful writing for the Challenge.

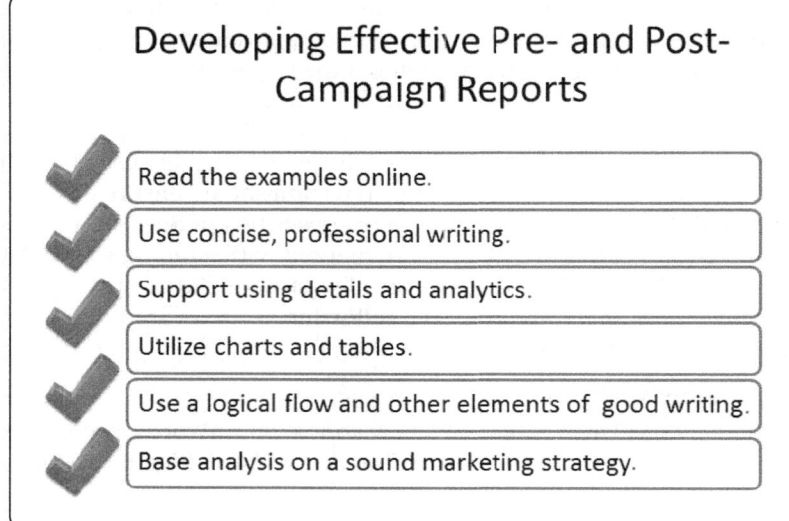

FIGURE A.4 Pre- and Post-Campaign Report Guidelines

Finally, while there have been many excellent winners in the GOMC over the years, the information and presentation in the Pre-and Post-Campaign Reports for 2015's Global Business Award, for the Devgad Alphonso Mango cooperative are particularly good models https://www.google.com/onlinechallenge/past/winners-2015.html.

DESIGNING A WINNING ADWORDS STRATEGY

Strategy is the foundation of good marketing and paid search is no exception. The team should first decide on the objectives of the AdWords strategy, based on conversations with the client and a SWOT analysis. A good idea is to map the "customer journey," that is, typical search paths and purchase behavior. Any information about the company such as sales data and best-selling products will be helpful on how successful a nonprofit has been at fund-raising. The client may not want to disclose sensitive information, but it might be possible to get ballpark estimates. From this research, students develop objectives for the campaign. Google has a list of suggested objectives at the following link: https://support.google.com/adwords/answer/6238033#define-students-marketing-goals.

Remember, the best objectives are SMART:

- Specific
- Measurable
- Achievable
- Realistic and relevant
- Time-based

For example, a basic objective in an AdWords campaign might be to achieve a certain click-through-rate (CTR) from the advertising campaign over the 21-day period or to achieve an average ad position of 2.5. It is useful to have additional performance metrics and sources such as from Google Analytics, indicating sources of web traffic and conversions. For example, an objective can be to increase visits to the campaign landing page by 10 percent during the run of the campaign, as evidenced by traffic from Google Analytics reports. Finally, good overall objectives can be written by speaking directly to the client, such as increased sales on the website for a product advertised in an AdWords ad. Often paid and organic search work together and there might be increased sales during the time of the campaign in addition to those generated by the paid advertisements.

The judging process consists of three elements:

1. Campaign Statistics (assessed by Google)
2. Campaign Structure and Implementation of Best Practices (assessed by Google)
3. AdWords Pre-Campaign and Post-Campaign Reports (assessed by an independent Global Academic Panel)

While the algorithm to assess campaign statistics, campaign structure, and implementation is constantly changing, in the past Google has outlined its expectations for a well-run AdWords campaign to include the following:

- Account structure is well defined, as illustrated in Figure A.5 and Table A.1.
- Campaign is continually monitored.
- Accounts are adjusted appropriately during the three-week Challenge.
- AdWords budget is used effectively to get desired results.
- Ads are "Relevant," of ads to the landing page, which will affect their position in search results.

A key criterion in "relevance" is the CTR. Remember that the AdWords Auction rewards bids that have both effective and relevance ads. Relevance is part of the overall Quality Score, which can lead to a better AdRank (the position of the ad). The Quality Score also includes expected CTR and the landing page experience for users. Participants in the Challenge should use the Quality Score as a means of adjusting their ad copy and making sure that the ads are relevant to the landing page to which they point.

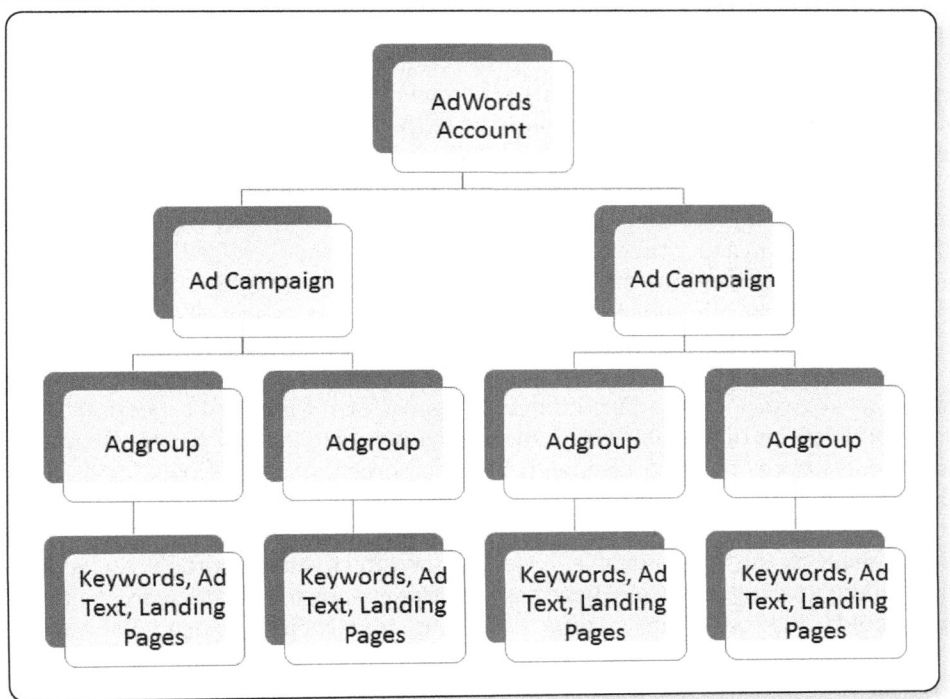

FIGURE A.5

Outline for an Account Structure

TABLE A.1

Proposed Account Structure: Ad Campaigns, Ad Groups, and Relevant Details for World Burger Bistro

Campaign Names	#1 The Meeting Place	#2 World Burger Awareness	#3 Ready for the Best Burger
Objective in the Customer Journey	Request for information or estimate for group events	Brand awareness	Purchase, Interest
Sample Ad Groups (Title of Ad Group)	Estimate Request Full-Service Event Space	Neighborhood Spot Convention Center	Best Gourmet Burger Promotional Specials
Keywords/Matching Options (all phrase match)	Party Room Event Space Event Venue Meeting Room Group Meeting	Downtown Centerville Restaurants Restaurants near Centerville convention Burger Pub Brewpub Craft Beer	Best Burger Centerville Burger Gourmet Burger OpenTable Burger Burger OpenTable Burger Brewpub
Geo-Targeting	Regional area	Centerville city zips	Centerville and Gotham metro areas
Success Indicators	No. of requests	CTR; hits on website	Increased website traffic; increased dining traffic
Device	Desktop, Tablet	Desktop, Mobile	Desktop, Mobile

Google has also prepared an extensive AdWords help center that can provide details about AdWords Set-up and Basics, Managing Ads, Measuring Results, Billing, and more. Find it at https://support.google.com/adwords#topic=3119071.

Figure A.5 shows the big picture of how an account structure can support strategy. A solid structure can ensure the organization implementation of the campaign strategy. Within the AdWords Account, Adgroups are associated with those specific campaigns and also have specific keywords and ads associated with them. Targeting landing pages helps with both relevance and Quality Score. Google has advice about setting up ad groups at https://support.google.com/adwords/topic/3121942?hl=en&ref_topic=3119116.

When running the campaign, it can also be useful to build a table like the one shown in Table 1. This example is an account structure of a Gourmet Burger restaurant and Brewpub in a city called Centerville, which is a small city with business professionals and a convention center, that is, business-related tourists. This table lays out the campaign visually and manages ads during the process as well as helping meet the strategic objectives of the campaign.

Google will also expect specific ad copy for two ads in the same ad group and samples of keywords in the Pre-Campaign Report (see Chapter 11, Section 11.3). Some modifications of the table above for that report could include creating to a table of sample keywords for each campaign, and the percent of budget paid for the keywords. (Students will not have access to specific cost-per-click (CPC) rates until the team is fully registered and the campaign is live.) GOMC assumes that students will make changes as the weeks evolve, based on the effectiveness of the selected keywords, timing of campaigns, and perhaps a rotation of ads for the keywords and students should briefly but clearly outline the strategy for any changes that will be made.

Before beginning the campaign and submitting the report, think about spending the budget. The budget is a key element of the strategy behind any AdWords campaign. Typically for the GOMC Google gives each team $250 to cover campaigns of up to 21 days in duration over a 31-day period. With budget limitations, use the money wisely. If students limit the campaign budget in the first active 7-day period to 25 percent or less, then the team can test the effectiveness of the strategy and the ads and keywords after their Challenge launch. Since the 21-day campaign must be concluded in 31 days and may be paused during that time, plan the start date accordingly, especially if the team wants to target any specific dates to include in an event-driven campaign. The campaign cannot receive clicks for more than 21 days in the 31-day period, but campaigns can be paused for up to ten days during that time. If there is more than one campaign, a chart displaying budget allocation and dividing the budget for each week can be helpful. In AdWords, advertisers can limit their total budget per day, per keyword, set when the ad might be displayed, and also use other parameters to keep within their budget.

GOMC teams should also analyze the competitor ads that appear in the top search results. This activity allows students to study their toughest competition (if the search terms were at all relevant) and make changes to strategy. Team members should think about what the team's client delivers that none of the competitors can and what is valuable to that client's customer, and plan the campaign accordingly.

Finally, each campaign might first test a few ads related to a campaign to see which works best, and to keep copy fresh for the viewer. For example, an online shoe retailer might highlight specific styles, selected brands, special promotions, or event-driven purchasing.

For 2017 Google expanded the types of ads to include not only text ads on the Search Network but also image ads, video ads, shopping ads, call-only ads, dynamic ads, lightbox ads, Gmail ads, and app install/engagement ads. Ads can run on the Search Network, Display Network, Gmail, or YouTube. The following campaign types are now factored into the algorithm to evaluate AdWords performance by teams:

- Search Network Only Campaigns
- Display Network Only Campaigns
- Video Campaigns
- Shopping Campaigns
- Mobile App Promotion/Universal App Campaigns

Students can run any of the above campaigns but need not run all of them. Campaign types should be appropriate for the client's business and should take into account the budgetary considerations. Further information on campaign types and new features such as the AdWords Certification Award is included in the PDF for updates for the 2017 campaign.

https://static.googleusercontent.com/media/www.google.com/en//onlinechallenge/pdfs/2017/updates-for-returning-participants.pdf.

KEYWORD BIDDING

During the campaign, keyword bidding is critical. The Keyword Planning Tool [https://support.google.com/adwords/topic/3175091?hl=en&ref_topic=3119130] will allow students to estimate anticipated search volume and data trends, and click and cost performance forecasts.

Students can set up their own account (requires a credit card) to get access to the details of the Keyword Planning Tool before the competition begins. Without a credit card, students can get access to rough estimates of volume for keywords but not details to flesh out a bidding strategy. Typically students cannot use the Keyword Planning Tool on the client account before the Challenge begins because they don't get the client account until the Pre-Campaign Report is approved. If they desire, students can also use a free tool such as keywordtool.iohttps://www.keyword.io/ to get an idea of possible keywords (but not volume or cost).

Besides the GOMC video tutorials, Google's guidance on Budgets and Bids is found at https://support.google.com/adwords/topic/3119127?hl=en&ref_topic=3119122,3181080,3126923. The sections that are particularly valuable to the GOMC are "Choose How You Bid" and "Choose Your Bid Amount."

Teams bidding on specific keywords should always consider the result for both cost paid in CPC and total spend. This requirement may be difficult to achieve if the objective is to "create awareness," that is, bringing viewers to a website. However, comparing click-through-rates for different keyword terms or ad copy will indicate which are the most expensive and which are more cost-effective in building awareness, and potential sales in the future.

Be aware that just because there is low competition for a keyword does not mean that it will be inexpensive. The price paid per click is also a function of the quality of ads. The team will pay at least the minimum amount bid for the position if the team wins the bid. However, students may have to bid higher if the quality score is low, and the ad may hardly show at all, even by raising the bid.

Consider varying bids for the same ad based on different days, or times of day, or different devices. The client can probably tell students things such as the website activity increases on certain days, or if customers are likely to search for their product or service during their lunch hours on Thursdays.

There are some special considerations for mobile ads. Consider bidding more for mobile-based searches, since a customer may be ready right at that moment to make a purchase. In contrast, recognize when a customer may just be browsing, as for expensive goods such as a new car purchase. Also, for mobile search, consider bidding on shorter keywords. Using a smartphone is different from using a desktop since mobile users tend to use shorter words and abbreviations.

RUNNING THE CAMPAIGN

Once students have been given permission to set up the AdWords account and have received the AdWords budget credit, the next steps are to build campaigns, enter ads, and bid on specific keywords to start running the campaign through the GOMC Competition Account.

In addition to the GOMC video tutorials, there are other excellent resources in the AdWords support group. The "Set Up and Basics" page is found at https://support.google.com/adwords/topic/3119071?hl=en&ref_topic=3181080,3126923. This page includes detailed guidance and interactive features about "Setting Up Ads and Campaigns" and "Choose Where and When Ads Appear."

Review the information about the various tools to monitor the account and progress of campaigns. The following site https://support.google.com/adwords/topic/3121769?hl=en&ref_topic=3119115 describes the various tabs in the account (home, campaigns, tools, billing, etc.) The Campaigns tab is particularly useful because it presents an overview of the structure of the accounts, and provides access to finer-grained information about the performance of ads, ad groups, keywords, and so on. In addition, Google will allow basic search marketing campaigns to specify the following features:

- Basic location targeting: This feature may be useful to service-type businesses or if the client only sells in a certain geographic region.
- Language targeting: This feature may be useful if a target customer is more comfortable in a language other than English, the default.
- Day parting: This feature may be used to stop a campaign during days and times when customers do not normally search for the product and it is started again when they do.

Figure A.6 shows the typical AdWords campaign dashboard, which has many diagnostic tools.

To choose optional settings for a campaign, review the details of campaign settings at https://support.google.com/adwords/answer/1704395?hl=en&ref_topic=3121941.

This web page provides brief guidance about the information needed in each section, such as choosing a campaign name, designating locations and languages, and other information.

FIGURE A.6
Campaign Dashboards Can Help Diagnose Problems

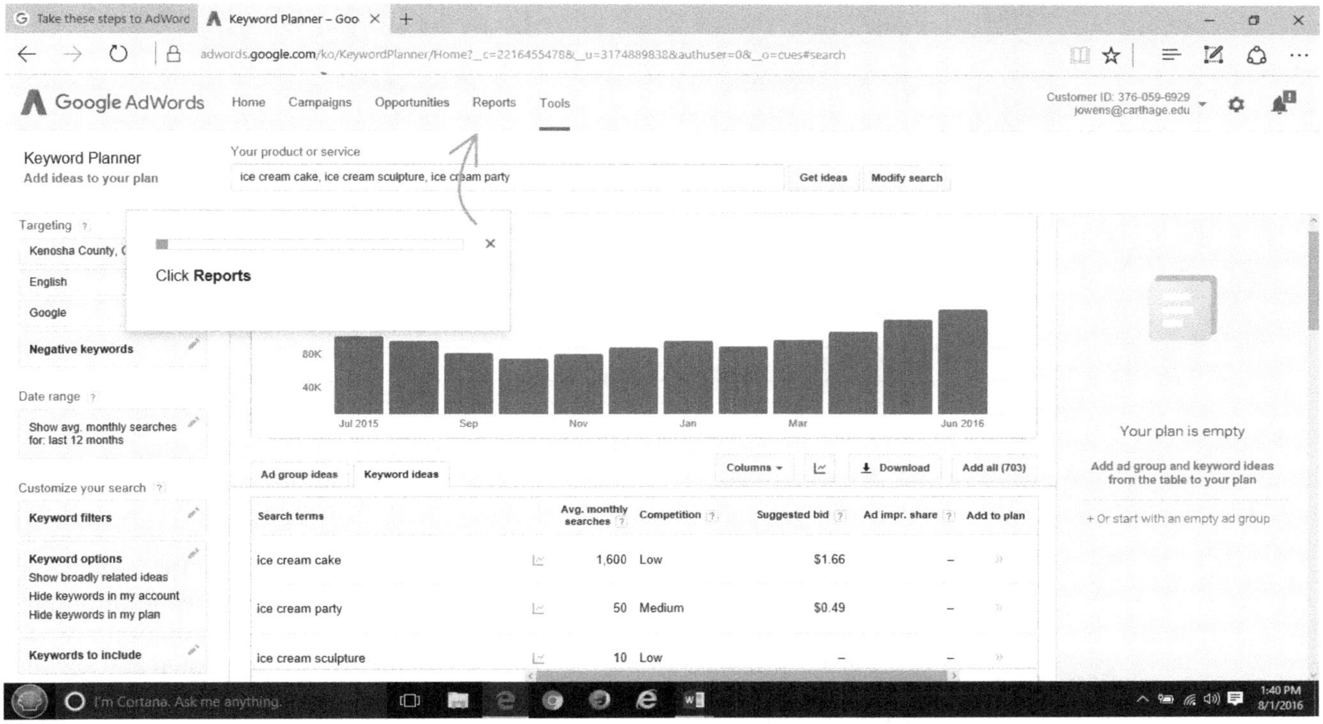

MONITORING AND EVALUATING

During the campaign, teams should regularly check how each campaign is performing. The GOMC Digital Marketing Course modules related to the Search Advertising exam provide a good overview of the different types of reports that allow students to track the performance of campaigns, specific keywords, ad groups, geographic areas, and others. The module also provides guidance about optimizing the various components of campaigns. Since the GOMC competition puts a strong emphasis on how well students use the budget, it is useful to pay attention to the sections on optimizing CTR. There is also guidance online on how to choose keywords and match types and some troubleshooting.

The following site provides text-based reviews of how to understand the status of various performance indicators (CTR, CPC, total budget spend on a keyword and total campaign, etc.): https://support.google.com/adwords/topic/3122861?hl=en&ref_topic=3119078. The site also provides guidance about changing campaign settings and temporarily pausing or removing a campaign.

Figure A.7 shows some common problems with AdWords campaigns and possible solutions. For example, if impressions are high but there are no clicks, ad copy is the most likely culprit. A low ad position can indicate that bidding just a bit more might help display the ad in a higher position. Ads that are not showing might need help in terms of relevance, overall quality, and bidding strategy. A sudden spike in CPC may be due to faulty account settings. It is important to monitor the account every day to forestall problems that might mean under or overspending the budget.

Also, if possible, check the analytics on the client website landing page. Some good questions to ask are as follows:

1. How long does the viewer stay ("bounce rate")?
2. Does the person entering from an ad or keyword click to other web pages?
3. Does one ad or keyword result in more customer "dwell time" than others?

   All these metrics can provide clues to optimize the campaign.

FIGURE A.7
Some Common AdWords Problems and Possible Solutions

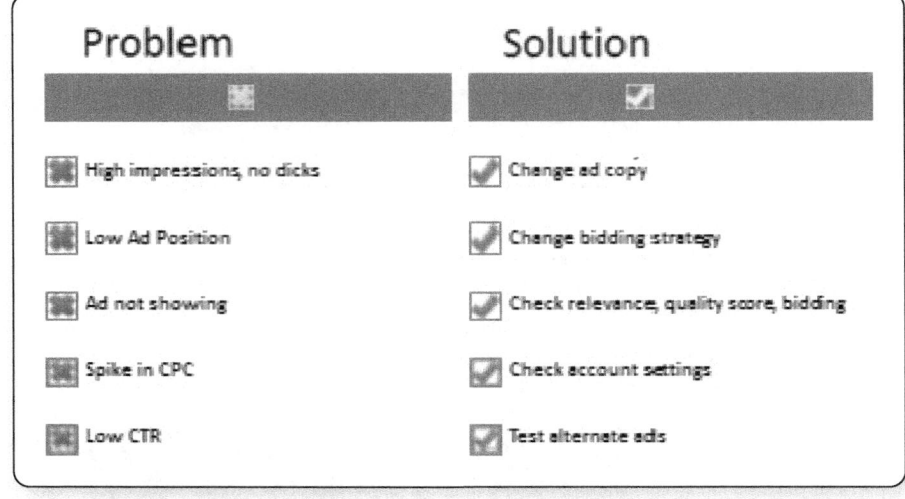

For mobile ads, consider increasing bids on mobile sites if CTR is low. Mobile searchers often look at only the top 1–3 listings, compared with desktop or tablet users who scroll through more of the first page. Also, make sure that the client's mobile ads are leading to the mobile web page, not the web page meant for desktop or tablet users.

Google also provides a valuable Tools tab to improve the campaign and account results called "Opportunities," a tab found in the account page. This tab displays the areas where Google sees ways to improve the AdWords campaign. Some of these suggestions include the following:

- Ads and ad groups: changing headlines
- Ad extensions and creating more ads
- Keywords, targeting, and reach: adding keywords, adding negative keywords, phrase matching, and showing ads on mobile devices
- Bids and budgets: raising/lowering bids, raiding budgets, and using estimated top or first page bid suggestions

Since Google does not always offer suggestions in every area in the "Opportunities" tool, other useful tools include the following:

- The Bid Simulator: "What if" scenarios about the search results (CTR; page placement) expected from raising or lowering a bid.
- **Enhanced CPC**: A bidding feature that looks for ad auctions that are more likely to raise sales results, and raises the CPC bid by 30 percent to compete harder for those clicks. When the auctions do not look promising, it lowers the bid as much as 100 percent, saving money. This option is for websites that offer purchasing capabilities online.

enhanced CPC Google AdWords tool that adjusts Cost per Click to improve conversions.

Remember, the Google GOMC team will evaluate student performance in terms of how students have selected keywords, monitored CTR, and how they have made cost-per-click adjustments to keywords. Students can find this information on the Campaigns tab, as shown in Figure A.8.

Besides the GOMC video tutorials, Google's guidance on improving the results of bids is found at https://support.google.com/adwords/answer/2472712?hl=en&ref_topic=3122864.

FIGURE A.8
AdWords Campaigns Tab

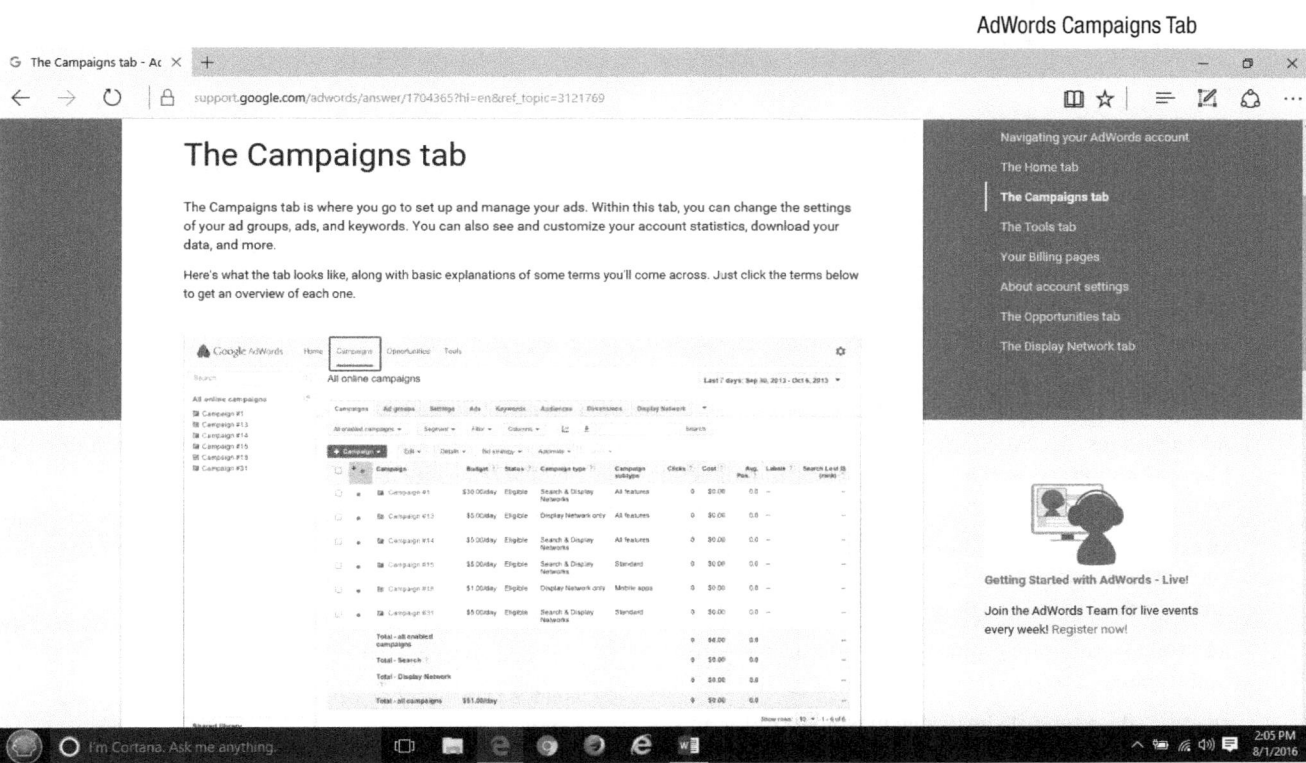

FINAL NOTE: Remember to TURN OFF the campaign within the three-week period students choose. Google disqualifies campaigns that serve impressions for less than seven days, or run longer than the three-week period, or run over budget. Good luck!

Glossary

360° (complete) a comprehensive view of the customer, often a profile that interfaces with the firm's customer journey map.

a responsive site fluid site design that senses the user's device and automatically adapts to it.

A/B split presenting one offer, creative execution, and so forth to one group of customers or prospects and another version of the same offer, creative execution, and so on to another group of customers.

Ad exchanges digital marketplace where advertisers buy and publishers sell advertising space in an auction setting.

ad extensions provide additional information with the ad such as a phone number, locations and reviews and can increase the click-through rate.

ad serving technology that places ads on websites or mobile sites.

adaptive site a type of site design in which a different site is created for each user device.

AdSense a way to monetize a website or a blog on Google by showing paid ads.

adware is a free, advertiser-supported software to download and display ads when user is online.

affiliate offers incentives to partner websites, wherein a website agrees to post a link to a transactional site in return for a commission on sales made as a direct result of the link.

affiliate programs offers incentives to partner websites, wherein a website agrees to post a link to a transactional site in return for a commission on sales made as a direct result of the link.

alt tag a tag (a type of IMG or image tag) that describes the image for people who cannot see it because of browser limitations or physical disabilities.

analytical CRM mining the customer data and developing programs or predictive models based on the resulting insights and data discovery.

artificial intelligence (AI) the ability of a computer to mimic human behaviors.

audience development creating a loyal following for branded content.

augmented reality (AR) an enhanced version of reality created by superimposing computer-generated images on top of the user's view of the real world.

augmented reality an enhanced version of reality created by superimposing computer-generated images on top of the user's view of the real world.

back end activities that are required to satisfy the customer after a sale is made, including fulfillment and customer service.

beacon technology beacons are small pieces of hardware that use Bluetooth Low Energy technology to send signals, including messages, to nearby mobile devices.

behavioral targeting tracking users' activities in order to display relevant ads.

big data unstructured data sets that are so large and complex that traditional data processing is challenged to analyze them.

blockchain a public ledger of all Bitcoin transactions. See also distributed ledger.

bounce rate number of bounces divided by number of emails sent.

brand community like-minded people who share interests grouping around a brand on the internet to communicate with one another and the brand.

breadcrumbs navigational aid showing path that the user has followed.

broad match modifier allows AdWords ad to show for searches that include the broad match keyword or close variations of the broad match.

broad match search setting allowing for matching on a wide variation of a keyword or set of keywords.

brokers brings buyers and sellers together to exchange goods and services.

business models the processes by which a business creates value, provides value to its customers, and captures value in the form of profits.

business process management (BPM) a systematic attempt to make business processes more efficient

buy cycle process a customer goes through in deciding to make a purchase.

buyer's journey the customer's path on the buying process.

buying center a group of people in an organization who make decisions for high-value and/or risky purchases.

call centers department within an organization that handles telephone sales and/or service.

CAN-SPAM Act the U.S. law regulating advertising and promotional emails.

channels of distribution intermediaries through which products and information about transactions move in the course of a single exchange.

click-through rates number of clicks divided by number of opens.

click-through-rate (CTR) Click-through-rate.

click-to-open rate number of clicks divided by the number of unique opens.

cloud computing using a network of remote servers hosted on the internet, not a local server or computer hard drive, to store data and programs and to process data.

CLV (customer lifetime value) (customer lifetime value) the net present value of a future stream of net revenue from an identified customer.

Co-creation bringing business entities or businesses and their customers together to create mutually valuable outcomes.

comment spam abusive practice in which comments are placed on a blog or website, perhaps robotically, for the sole purpose of generating a backlink in an attempt to improve search results.

community model connects like-minded individuals and groups for sharing.

confirmed opt-in somewhere in between opt-in and double opt-in; the visitor actively acquiesces to receiving email, again probably by another email confirmation.

content marketing creating and distributing content across the web that users find valuable and relevant, driving visitors to the website.

content marketing strategic approach to creating and distributing content.

cookies a few lines of code that a website or advertising network places on a user's computer to store data about the user's activities on the site.

COPPA the Children's Online Privacy Protection Act regulates websites that collect information from those under 13 by, among other things, requiring prior parental consent.

cost-per-thousand the amount paid in purchasing advertising; in this case, means the cost per thousand impressions, or the cost divided by the total number of impressions.

CPM the amount paid in purchasing advertising; in this case, means the cost per thousand impressions, or the cost divided by the total number of impressions.

cross-selling selling a different, related product to an existing customer.

crowdsourcing model obtains needed resources, including financing, by soliciting from a community instead of traditional funding sources.

cryptocurrencies digital currencies in which encryption regulates the creation and use of currencies that operate outside the control of a central banking system.

curate to select and prepare content from other sources for publication.

customer lifecycle stages in the development of the relationship between the customer and the brand.

customer lifetime value (CLV) the net present value of a future stream of net revenue from an identified customer.

customer profiles a description of a customer or set of customers that includes demographic, geographic, and psychographic characteristics. A profile could include other relevant information, such as buying pattern, creditworthiness, and purchase history.

customer service solving customer problems.

customization process of producing a product, service, or communication to the exact specifications/desires of the purchaser or recipient.

CX "cumulative experiences across multiple touchpoints and in multiple channels over time".

dark social social media exchanges that cannot be tracked or measured.

data mining analytic process and specialized analytic tools used to extract meaning from very large data sets.

data raw, unprocessed facts and numbers Data mining analytic process and specialized analytic tools used to extract meaning from very large data sets.

database set of files (data, video, images, etc.) organized in a way that permits a computer program to quickly select any desired piece of content.

demand generation entire process of developing customer demand for a product or service.

demand-driven supply a supply chain that operates in response to demand signals from customers.

digital disruption change caused by digital technologies that disrupts ways of thinking and acting.

digital transformation the rapid change in business activities and operations caused by digital disruption.

directories aid in finding internet websites; list of sites are usually arranged by category, and the directory has a search function.

discovery ads YouTube video ads that are served based on the viewer's Google search activity.

display advertising ads that contain headline, text copy, and visuals including the brand logo in any channel.

display URL displays in ad but has link to another page.

distributed autonomous organization (DAO) a distributed virtual organization with no identified leader or physical presence.

distributed ledger a type of data structure composed of encrypted data that is difficult to change that is digitally recorded in packages called blocks.

DNS (Domain Name System) the process for converting the name of a website into its IP address.

double opt-in a technique by which visitors agree to receive further communications but must perform two actions, usually checking an opt-in box on a site, and then responding positively to a sent email asking for confirmation.

dynamic content ability to change greeting and other content dynamically based on to whom the email is addressed.

dynamic serving the ability to serve different site HTML without changing the URL. The term "adaptive site" is synonymous.

earned media buzz in both social and traditional media that is generated by content distributed by the brand.

ecommerce buying and selling goods and services online.

EDI general term used to describe the digitizing of business information like orders and invoices so that they may be communicated electronically between suppliers and customers.

email marketing the process of developing customer relationships through offers and communications contained in email messages.

embedded devices a device, often a microchip, that becomes part of another device, rendering various services, often doing so without human intervention.

ERP implementation of processes and software that integrates all aspects of the business from manufacturing resource planning and scheduling through service functions like human resources.

event marketing a themed activity that promotes a product, business, or cause.

exact match paid search parameter that is set to display to those looking for a particular phase.

experiential marketing promotional activity that helps consumers understand a product by having direct contact with it.

frequency the number of times a person is exposed to a promotional message.

front end all the marketing and promotional activities that occur before a sale is made.

fulfillment the business processes necessary to receive, process, package, and ship orders to customers.

fund-raising basic nonprofit business model in which money is raised from donors and grants without a traditional economic transaction.

geo-fence software feature that lets GPS or RFID establish a geographical area that can be defined by a virtual perimeter.

Gramm-Leach-Bliley Act (GLBA) the Gramm-Leach-Bliley Act requires financial institutions to disclose privacy policies and practices to customers.

hard bounce undeliverable, usually due to a bad email address.

Health Insurance Portability and Accountability Act (HIPPA) Health Insurance Portability and Accountability Act gives patients greater control over their medical records and provides penalties for misuse of personal health information.

heat maps visual representations of eye activity on a web page.

hit any file, including a graphic, that is requested from a server.

identity theft stealing key items of personal information with criminal intent, usually to cause financial harm.

in-stream ads video ads that appear in the video stream itself—either before (also called a pre-roll), during or after the video plays.

inbound marketing approach that is focused on being visible to potential customers and using the visibility to drive them to a website where they can transact.

index server stores the information index, which has categorized websites as a best fit to certain keywords.

influencer marketing using people who are regarded as authorities in their field to help distribute brand content.

infomediaries intermediary in channels of distribution that specializes in the capture, analysis, application, and distribution of information.

information data that have been processed into more useful forms using techniques that range from simple summary formats to complex statistical routines.

interactive presenting choices based on user actions and allowing for response.

interstitials ad that covers the entire screen.

IP (Internet Protocol) address a number assigned to each device that uses the internet.

key performance indicators (KPIs) a metric that has been identified as an important measure or benchmark of business performance.

keyword density percentage of times a particular word is used on a website page in comparison to the number of words on that page.

keywords terms, words, or phrases that are selected by the user when making a search in a search engine; also refers to terms that are bid on in a PPC system, or a section in the HTML code for a website where site developers put terms that they hope search engines will classify the site when users search for those terms on the web.

KPI (key performance indicator) a metric that has been identified as an important measure or benchmark of business performance.

landing page a web page designed to receive visitors who are coming to the site as a result of a link from another site.

lead generation identifying sales prospects.

lead qualification determining whether a prospect has the characteristics necessary to make a purchase.

local search using a local search term in a search query.

malware malicious software developed for the purpose of harming or taking control of certain actions on a computer or computer system.

manufacturer direct model bypassing intermediaries such as wholesalers and manufacturers' reps in the channel of distribution; direct from manufacturer to customer.

marketing automation system marketing interaction management system including a database, engagement engine, and analytics component.

Marketing Qualified Leads or MQLs leads that have been through scoring and other qualification processes and are ready to be passed on to sales for further qualification.

merchant see ecommerce.

meta tag a section in the HTML header section of a website that can be used to describe the site in more detail, including content and keywords; also known as meta name, or meta element.

micro-moments not a measure of time; a concept that describes consumer recognition of needs.

mixed reality combining the real and virtual worlds to produce a new environment in which objects can interact and humans can interact with them.

mobile first designing the online experience for mobile before designing for the internet.

mobile payments payments made from a mobile device using established financial payment mechanisms.

native ads paid media in which content follows the form and function of the site on which it is placed, not traditional advertising formats.

native content content whose format is appropriate to the publication or the channel.

natural language processing a component of AI that allows a computer to understand spoken human language.

negative match search setting that is the opposite of what is desired; used to avoid paying for unnecessary clicks.

net present value (NPV) current value of a discounted stream of future revenues personalization.

NPS customer satisfaction score calculated on the basis of a single question, "How likely is it that you would recommend [brand] to a friend or colleague".

omni-channel a strategy that delivers personalized and consistent customer experience across multiple channels.

on-demand model technology-based model in which user demand is fulfilled immediately in a location-aware manner.

open rates number of opens divided by number of emails delivered (sent minus bounces).

operational CRM designing and executing tactical CRM programs on the basis of data items or customer profiles.

opt-in actively choosing to receive further communications, usually by checking a box on a registration form.

opt-out taking an action to prevent the receipt of further communications, usually unchecking a box on a registration form.

owned media brand pages on social platforms.

P2P (peer-to-peer) transmission of files directly from one user to another.

"page rank" a mathematical algorithm named after Google co-founder Larry Page to indicate how important a page is on the web; used as a metric when evaluating websites.

page views a page actually seen by a visitor; generally measured as a page being delivered to the visitor, which is not exactly the same thing.

paid media traditional advertising on any channel, traditional or social, that requires direct payment for insertion.

paid search the paid aspect of SEM based on an advertising model where firms seeking to rank high in specific search categories will bid on certain terms or "keywords" in the hopes of a lucrative ad ranking; also known as PPC (pay-per-click).

paid social any type of paid promotion on social media platforms.

pareto curve a plot of number of occurrences against percent of total; the source of the 80/20 rule.

permission marketing marketing to customers who have given explicit permission to be contacted.

permission refers to gaining the customers agreement to market to them in a certain way.

personalization process of preparing an individualized communication such as a newsletter or web page for a specific person based on stated or implied preferences.

personas a way of describing different groups of customers by giving them a unique personality.

pfarming creating fake websites that are similar to legitimate business sites.

phishing emails that attempt to obtain personal information by making fraudulent claims.

phrase match search setting that includes an entire phrase.

PII (personally identifiable information) any piece of data that can identify a person, alone or in combination with other data items; also sometimes called personally identifying information.

pipes business models, essentially the traditional distribution models.

pivoted a quick change from one business model to another. It is usually applied to startups that can make rapid model changes that may be impossible for entrenched business models of large enterprises.

pixel a one-pixel transparent GIF that is added to the pages of a website allowing sites to track visitor activity.

pop-up store (or popup shop) a temporary retail store.

predictive analytics using data, statistical algorithms, and machine learning techniques to predict the likelihood of future outcomes or behaviors.

predictive modeling relevant variables and associated response factors or probabilities are used to estimate the likelihood of occurrence of a specific behavior, given the existence of a given level of the specified variables.

preferred deals offering ad inventory to buyers at a negotiated price before the inventory is made available for auction.

private auctions ad bidding in which members of the exchange are allowed to bid first.

private marketplaces ad exchanges (marketplaces) that include both private auctions and preferred deals for the selling of publisher advertising inventory.

profile summary of the distinctive features or characteristics of a person, business, or other entity.

programmatic advertising automating the advertising buying process.

promoted posts regular posts for which the marketer pays a fee to have the post prominently displayed in a feed or on the platform page.

prospect an unqualified lead.

real-time bidding ads are bought and sold instantaneously through electronic exchanges.

red flags refers to the Red Flags Rule that requires certain U.S. businesses to develop and document plans to protect consumer data from identity theft.

relational marketing a facet of customer relationship marketing (CRM) that focuses on customer loyalty and long-term customer engagement rather than short-term goals like customer acquisition and individual sales.

responsive fluid site design that senses the user's device and automatically adapts to it.

retargeting ads for the product category are displayed based on the user's recent internet behaviors.

RFID (Radio-Frequency IDentification) technology that allows the identification of tagged goods from a distance with no intervention by human operation.

rich media combination of text, images, video, and other interactive elements in a digital ad.

SaaS making software available on a fee for use basis instead of on a license or purchase basis.

Sales Accepted Leads or SALs leads that have been further qualified by sales as close to conversion.

sales force automation business processes, and the software that supports them, that permit salespeople to work more effectively both in and out of their offices by providing electronic access to important documents, customer data, and support tools like calendars.

sales promotions a marketing communication that encourages the customer to take specific action.

Sales Qualified Leads or SQLs leads that have passed through the BANT process as fully qualified potential customers.

search engine algorithm displays the search engine's "best guess" at which pages are most relevant to the user's search and in which order they should be shown.

search engine marketing (SEM) process of getting listed on search engines.

semantic search focuses on the user's intent when searching for something.

sentiment analysis the attempt to understand the emotion, positive or negative, behind a qualitative statement.

Service-Dominant Logic the idea that service is the basis of all economic exchange making all firms service providers and all products essentially services.

sessions a time-dependent measure of site use; the amount of time a unique user spends on the site.

six-sigma quality management technique that results in near-perfect products; technically, results that fall within six standard deviations from the mean of a normal distribution.

social business in business terminology, a business that has adopted social communications in all aspects of internal operations and of dealing with external customers and partners.

social commerce using social media platforms to assist in or to conduct ecommerce activities.

soft bounce temporarily undeliverable, usually due to a system problem.

Software as a Service, SaaS making software available on a fee for use basis instead of on a license or purchase basis.

spam unwanted email communication.

spear phishing targeted phishing attacks that use apparently legitimate communications in an attempt to breach a secure website.

spiders programs that "crawl" the web and follow every link or piece of data that they see and bring this information back to be stored; also known as robots.

spoofing creating false identities in order to evade rules for conducting business and communications on the web.

spyware programs installed on consumers' computers, without their permission, that assume partial control over the operating system.

stickiness getting customers to stay on the site as long as possible, navigate as many paths as possible, and return again and again.

subscription model delivers products, services, and content for a set fee.

supply chain the downstream portion of the value chain, the channel from suppliers to producers.

supply side platforms software used to sell a publisher's ad inventory through programmatic advertising.

syndicated content from another source published under license.

synthetic performance testing website performance testing conducted in a laboratory setting as opposed to measuring performance using actual visitor data.

Tagged Web Pages a technique in which a small image is placed on a web page; used in conjunction with a cookie on the user's computer, the image returns data about user activity on the web page.

Testing statistical process by which alternative marketing approaches are compared and the best is selected.

title tag the title the user sees in the blue bar at the top of the web page; also known as the HTML title tag.

total cost of ownership (TOC) the purchase price of a product or service plus the indirect costs of operating it through its lifetime.

touchpoint marketing jargon for each channel available for customer interaction.

transactional focuses on the individual sale of a product or service, in contrast to developing a long-term relationship with a customer.

triggers events or actions that prompt an email to be sent.

universal search the inclusion of search results from multiple content sources such as videos, images, news, maps, books, and websites into one set of research results.

unqualified leads potential sales leads for which there is no qualifying data beyond membership in a relevant industry.

unstructured data data that have no predetermined models or are not organized in a predefined way. Unstructured data is often heavily text but not necessarily all text.

up-selling upgrading an existing customer's account by selling more expensive products or packages in an attempt to increase the revenue value of that customer.

usability the ability of a site to provide a satisfactory user experience.

user experience (UX) according to Jakob Nielsen, all of the user's interactions with the brand on all touchpoints, which makes it nearly synonymous with CX. Often used to describe the usability of a website or a mobile app.

utility delivers services or content on a metered or "pay as you go" basis.

UX (user experience) according to Jakob Nielsen, all of the user's interactions with the brand on all touchpoints, which makes it nearly synonymous with CX. Often used to describe the usability of a website or a mobile app.

value chain an integrated supply chain in which transactions are conducted electronically.

value ecosystem connecting brands and their customers and business partners in a direct, non-linear fashion.

value essentially the usefulness (economic utility) of the product less its price; also known as customer value or customer perceived value.

value proposition a description of the customer value delivered to a specific target market.

virtual reality (VR) simulation of a three-dimensional image or environment with which the user can interact by using special equipment.

wireframe a blueprint that specifies the layout of pages on a website.

ZB another iteration of byte; this is multiplication by the 7th power of 1,000 or 10^{21}.

Index

A

Abbey Road, 412
above the fold (email marketing), 238
Absolut Vodka, 213
A/B split, 105–107
accelerated mobile pages (AMP), 274
Accenture, 43, 45, 460
   switching economy, 434
acquisition. *See* customer acquisition
Acquisti, Alessandro, 464, 467
Ad Age, 498
adaptive site, 426–429
adaptive web design, 426–428
ad blocking, 189
ad exchanges, 179, 180
ad extensions, 282
ad formats
   additional, 290–292
   digital display, 174–177
   expanded text ad (ETA), 289
   Facebook display, 298–300
   Google display, 295–300
   Instagram display, 295–300
   mobile display, 184
   paid search advertising, 290–292
ad networks, 177, 181
Adobe Lightroom, 106, 107
ad rank, 282, 283
AdSense, 293
ad serving, 177–180
Advanced Scout, 116
advertising. *See also* digital advertising; display advertising
   option icon, 464
   spending, 154–155
advertising-supported model, 66, 68, 77
advertorials, 72
adware, 480
affiliate models, 73–74
affiliate programs, 172, 186–187
The Age, 68
Airbnb, 80
AlertSite, 499
algorithmic search, 257, 259
Alibaba, 69
Allianz MyHealth, 443
ALS Association, 128
alt tag, 417
Amazon
   affiliate marketing, 74
   Alexa, 2, 329
   Associates program, 74
   brand, 96
   business model, 58–59
   Cloud Drive, 13
   cumulative experience, 163, 164
   Echo technology, 4, 68, 69
   fraudulent metrics, 527
   fulfillment, 98
   Kindle Unlimited, 59
   Prime, 59
   "subscribe and save" program, 72
   targeting identified users, 180
   Zappos, 64
Amazon Web Services (AWS), 2, 14, 44–46, 60, 73
American Cancer Society (ACS), 69–70
   Making Strides against Breast Cancer, 69
   Relay for Life, 69
American Consumer Satisfaction Index (ACSI), 437, 438
American Eagle Outfitters, Inc. (AEO)
   Legendary Gifts program, 112–113
American Express, 139, 421, 436
analytical CRM, 378–380
Android, 126
   apps, 518
   Google's, 65
   mobile devices, 262, 327
   Pay, 81, 328
animation, in email marketing, 249
anonymous users, targeting, 180–182
AOL, 2, 64
   content moments, 217
   internet change, 4
apparel with embedded devices, 47–48
Apple
   App Store, 65
   customer service, 440
   iCloud, 13, 484
   iPhone smartphone, 2
   Pay, 81
apps
   Android, 518
   CRM, importance of, 389–393
   in-app advertising, 185–186
   metrics, 518
   mobile (*See* mobile apps)
   promotions, 290
   review site/app visits, 158
articles search, 273
artificial intelligence (AI)
   definition of, 2, 5, 12–14
   use in supply chains, 49
as-a-service ecosystem model, 43
Ashley Madison, 478
Ask.com, 508
audience
   content marketing, 208–211
   development, 209–210
   measurement, 495, 503
   targeting, 180
audience, social media
   communicating with, 135–137
   engaging with, 137–139
   listening to, 132–135
   reach, 136
augmented reality (AR), 9, 78–80
Azure Cloud, 8

B

back end, in direct marketing, 98
backlink, 270
BankBazaar, 187
Beacon, 467
beacon technology, 327
Beggin' SMM campaign, 520
behavioral loyalty, 94
behavioral targeting
   defintions of, 172, 180
   of identified users, 180
   with predictive models, 182–183
   of unidentified users, 180–182
behavioral tracking, 461–465
Bertelsmann AG, 483
Better Business Bureau Online, 476
Beyoncé, 133–135, 137
Bezos, Jeff, 68, 163
big data, 118, 368
Bing
   Microsoft, 262
   search results, Google *vs*, 265

bitcoin, 75, 81. *See also* cryptocurrencies
blockchain, 74–75
blog post, 206, 272
blog search, 273
BMW
   USA Home Page, 342
   voice-activated Echo technology, 2
bokers, 68–69
books search, 273
bots and content marketing, 220–221
bounce rate, 241, 506–507
branding
   cumulative experiences, 153
   customer engagement, 153–154
brands
   community, 139–140
   and direct marketing, 96–97
   lift, 524
   resilient, 153, 154
   stories, 217–218
   visits, 158
breadcrumbs, 417
BrightRoll, 179
broad match
   definition of, 286
   modifier, 286
brochure ware, 118
Brogan, Chris, 460
brokerage model, 68–69
brokers
   defintion of, 68
   list brokers, 71
Budweiser, 134
build-to-order model, 38
bureaucratic momentum, 473
Burgess, Mark, 130
Burke Research, 435
business decision journey, 160–161
business, digital users in, 22–26
Business Insider, 216–217
Business Model Canvas, 76, 82–83
business models
   basic, identifying, 65–81
   definition of, 55, 56
   evolving, 57–60
   functions of, 56–57
   internet-enabled models, 73–76
   mobile-dependent models, 76–81
   pipe model, 63–64
   platform model, 64–65
   traditional, 66–73
   types of, 63–65
   understanding, 56
   value proposition, 60–63
business plan, 57
business process management (BPM), 49
business-to-business (B2B)
   ad exchanges, 180
   collateral material, 343
   content marketing, 199–201
   customer service in, improving, 438–439
   decision journey, 160–161
   ecommerce, 25
   industrial sales funnel, 340
   lead generation program, 96
   marketers expectations from websites, 403–404
   online marketers, 276
   sites, special usability requirements for, 420–423
   use of influencers and content, 127
business-to-consumer (B2C)
   content marketing, 199–200, 202, 203
   customer personas, 208–209
   markets customer service in, improving, 437–438
BusinessWire, 443
BustedTees, 248–249
buy cycle process, 336
buyer's journey, 337, 348
buying center, 337
BuzzFeed, 72

C

Cafone, Jim, 45
call centers, 442
Call of Duty (video game), 140
call-only ads, 290
call to action (CTA)
   in content marketing, 204
   in direct marketing, 95–97
campaign measurement, 495, 503–504
Canadian Anti-Spam Law (CASL), 248
Candy Crush Saga, 78–79
Capital One, 106, 114, 115
Case, Steve, 4, 5
caveat emptor, 456, 527
CBS All Access, 10
Chamber of Commerce, 511
channels of distribution, 34
Children's Online Privacy Protection Act (COPPA), 469–472
children's privacy issues, regulation of, 469–471
Cisco reactivation program, 382–384
Cision, 127
CJ Affiliate, 73–74
Clark, Cherith, 268
click and collect payment, 316
click-through-rate (CTR), 177, 229–230, 283
click-to-open rate, 241
Cline, Jay, 472
Clinton, Bill, 483
cloud computing
   -based supply chain, 44–46
   customer relationship marketing (CRM), 372
   definition of, 12–14
   software as a service (SaaS), 13
cluster analysis, 114
Coca-Cola, 189–190
   SEO strategies, 268
   social media campaign, 190
co-creation, 43
Cohen, Heidi, 218
Coin Tent, 189
collaborative filtering, 90
Columbia Business School, 464–465
comment spam, 526
commercial electronic messages (CEMs), 248
Committee on Intellectual Property Rights and the Emerging Information Infrastructure, 483
communications objectives, email, 236
communications schedule, email, 236
community model, 75
community, social media, 139–141
concept testing, 419
confirmed opt-in (email permission), 232
connectivity, IoTs, 6–8
consumer(s)
   attitude toward privacy of information, 461–469
   behavioral tracking, 461–465
   data security breaches, 478–482
   as digital users, 18–22
   expectations, 441–442
   knowledge about internet security, 479–480
content marketing
   B2B, 199–201
   B2C, 199–200, 202, 203
   conversations, monitoring, 213–214

content marketing (*Continued*)
   creating content, 204–208
   curation, 204, 205
   customer engagement, 217–220
   definition of, 195, 198–199, 343
   demand generation, B2B markets, 343–345
   distribution platforms, 211–213
   effective, 196–198
   effectiveness, evaluation of, 213–214
   identifying and developing target audience, 208–211
   moments, 217, 218
   native advertising, 214–217
   sources of, 204–205
   strategy, 198, 203–214
   and technology, 220–221
   types of, 205–208
   users of, 199–203
Content Marketing Institute, 127, 198
Controlling the Assault of Non-Solicited Pornography and Marketing Act. *See* U.S. CAN-SPAM Act
control towers, 49
conversion metrics, 512–516
cookies, 180–181, 501–502
cost per-click (CPC), 257, 268, 281
cost per thousand (CPM), 95, 177, 287
Council of Better Business Bureaus' National Advertising Review Council, 464
Council of Ministers, 476
coupons, 91–93
CPA, 73–74
Crazy Egg, 415
Creative Commons
   copyright law, 483
   license, 484, 485
   publishing under, 484–486
creativity
   in diaplsys ads, 176–177
   publishing under creative commons, 484–486
cross-selling, 101, 340
crowd servicing, 445
crowdsourcing
   fundraising sites, 129
   model, 75, 76
cryptocurrencies, 81
Culnan, Mary J., 457–458
cumulative experiences (CX)
   branding, 153
   components of, 163
   defintion of, 150, 155–157

designing site, 316
   importance in customer journay, 165–166
   mobile marketing, 312–314
   satisfying, creating, 162–165
curation of content, 204, 205
customer acquisition
   ad blocking, 189
   affiliate programs, 186–187
   channels, 171
   definition of, 22, 171
   digital advertising, 172–177
   effective channels for US retailers, 172
   integrated marketing communications, 189–191
   internet techniques, 171–172
   mobile display advertising, 184–186
   online ad serving and targeting, 177–183
   public relations, 187–188
customer branding, 153–154
Customer Charter, 438
customer conversion, 22, 94–95
customer database
   benefits of, 112–113
   for program execution, 113–114
   for program execution and marketing analytics, 113–114
customer emotions, 154, 162, 164
customer engagement
   and branding, 153–154
   in content marketing, 217–220
   social media, 137–139
customer experience, 98
   CRM, 395–396
   end-to-end, 36
   marketing strategy, 375
customer journey, digital
   B2B decision journey, 160–161
   decision journey, 158–159
   importance of cumulative experiences in, 165–166
   purchase funnel, 157
   tracking customers through, 161–162
customer lifecycle
   definition of, 375
   mining, 376
customer lifetime value (CLV)
   calculation, 100
   components of, 367
   definition of, 95, 98–100, 366, 436
   example of, 100–102
   importance of, 366–367

uses of, 103–105
using targeted programs to increase, 102
customer loyalty programs
   CRM, 385–389
   Pink Nation app, 387
   Victoria's Secret app, 386
customer personas, 208–209, 353
customer privacy, 103
customer profiles, 380
Customer Rage Study (2015), 441, 442
customer relationship marketing (CRM)
   analytical, 378–380
   apps, importance of, 389–393
   B2B foundations of, 370–372
   big data, 368
   Cisco Reactivation Program, 382–384
   cloud computing, 372
   cloud in relationship marketing, 389–393
   contact management, 371
   costs of, 393–395
   customer knowledge, 396
   customer loyalty programs, 385–389
   definition of, 368
   developing strategy, 372–378
   digital shopper genome, characteristics of, 373
   elements of, 368
   failure rate of, 393–395
   key preference indicators, 373
   mobile loyalty programs, 389
   operational, 378–380
   personalization, 380–385
   personalized email, 384–385
   processes of, 378–380
   product-centric *vs.* customer-centric marketing, 369
   relational marketing, 371
   sales force automation, 370, 371
   seamless customer experience, 395–396
   social media, importance of, 389–393
   targeting, 380–385
   360° (complete), 372
   threelegged stool, 371
   total cost of ownership (TOC), 393
   touchpoint marketing, 395
   transactional *vs.* the relationship perspective, 368–370
   vision, 395–396

customer retention
   in business, 22
   definition of, 94, 95, 368
   and email marketing, 226, 227
customer satisfaction, 434–436
   drivers of, 156
customer service
   in B2B markets, improving, 438–439
   in B2C markets, improving, 437–438
   champions, 440–441
   definition of, 98
   difficulties in, 439–440
   goals of, 436–437, 450–451
   importance of, 434–436
   omni-channel, 439, 446–450
   problems, financial impact of, 435
   strategy, evaluation of, 442–446
customer value growth, 22, 94, 95
customization, 119, 120
   email marketing, 243–246
   mass, 243
cut-and-paste content sharing, 182
CVS Health, 27–28

D

dark social, 213
data
   burst, 114
   definition of, 91
   democratization of, 493
   protection, 460–478
   qualitative vs. quantative, 500–501
   types of, 501
database
   customer, 112–114
   definition of, 110
   marketing, 110, 111
data-driven marketing efforts (DDME), 90
data mining
   at Disney, 115
   in NBA, 115–118
   power of, 114–118
data privacy
   children's privacy issues, regulation of, 469–471
   consumers attitude toward, 460–469
   in financial services sector, regulation of, 471
   framework for protection of, 475
   in health care sector, regulation of, 472
   internet, 460–478
   on mobile networks, 468–469
   organizations and seals, 476
   regulation in internet-using countries, 476–478
   on social networks, lack of, 465–468
   U.S. business response to, 474
Data Protection Directive (1995), 473
data warehouse, 110, 111, 115
day parting, 290
decision journey
   B2B, 160–161
   consumer, 158–159
Deighton, John, 460
Dell
   control tower, 49
   DellShares, 40
   Direct2Dell, 446
   direct model, 38–41
   IdeaStorm, 40, 446
   mass customization, 243
   social media structure, 40
demand-driven supply, 49
demand generation, B2B markets
   automation system, 342
   branding, importance of, 338–339
   buy cycle, 336–338
   calculate ROI, 360
   changing purchase process, 338
   content creation, 343–345
   content marketing, 343–345
   conversion paths, 361–362
   customer personas, 353–355
   definition of, 336, 343
   developing purchasing scenarios, 355–356
   generic marketing strategies, 336
   lead conversion, 359–360
   lead generation, 345–348
   lead qualification, cost of, 357
   marketing transformation, 341
   metrics, 360–362
   nurturing leads, 348–351
   process, 343–362
   qualifying sales leads to create MQLs, 351–359
   sales and marketing work together, 340–341
   SALs, 356–357
   search, importance of, 338–339
   SQLs, 356–357
DeMers, Jayson, 260
democratization of data, 493
DeMott, Rick, 219
Department of Health and Human Services (HHS), 472
desktop, time spent on, 19
device agnostic, 46
digital advertising
   ad formats, 174–177
   customer acquisition through, 172–177
   definition of, 23
   display advertising, 173–177
   global revenues in, 24
   growth of, 173
   methods of buying and placing ads, 178
   mobile, 173
   spending in, 154–155
Digital Advertising Alliance (DAA), 464
digital age
   branding in, 153–154
   marketing effectiveness in, 154–157
   media use in, 152
digital congruence, 27
digital disruption
   definition of, 9
   and supply chain, 49
digital firms, 25, 26
digital governance, 199
digital marketing
   audience measurement, 503
   campaign measurement, 503–504
   cookies, 501–502
   fraudulent metrics, 526–527
   key performance indicators, 516
   marketing effectiveness, demonstrating, 494–495
   metrics, 504–506, 516–519
   programs, measuring and evaluating, 492–527
   quantitative vs. qualitative data, 500–501
   SMM metrics, 519–520
   tagged web pages, 501, 502
   traffic measurement, 503
   using Google Analytics, 506–516
   video marketing metrics, 520–525
   website effectiveness, 495–496
   website performance, 499–500
   websites evaluation, enterprise metrics for, 496–506
digital maturity, 11–12, 27
Digital Millennium Copyright Act, 483–484
Digital Natives, 469

digital transformation
  building blocks of, 11
  definition of, 9
  drivers of, 27–28
  engaging in, 10–11
  impact on supply chain, 34–36
digital users, 15–26
digital value ecosystem, 42–44
digitization of business processes, 35–36
direct ad serving, 178
Direct2Dell blog, 40
direct marketing
  back end in, 98
  brands, 96–97
  call to action (CTA), 95–97
  critical strategy elements, 95–98
  definition of, 90, 254
  front end in, 98
  incentives, 96
  strategies, 94–95
  testing, 108–110
Direct Marketing Association (DMA), 464
direct orders, 178
directories, 256–257
direct response medium, internet as, 90–94
direct response programs, testing, 105–110
discount rate, 101
discovery ads, 300
Disney Corporation, 115
Disney MagicBands, 115
display advertising
  definition of, 173
  formats, digital, 174–177
  mobile, 184–186
  PPC, 23
display URL, 287
distributed autonomous organization (DAO) hub, 74, 75
distributed ledger, 74
distribution platforms, content, 211–213
DMOZ Open Directory Project, 257
DNS (domain name system), 499
Dodd-Frank Wall Street Reform and Consumer Protection Act, 471
Dollar Shave Club, 72–73
domain name. *See* uniform resource locator (URL)
domain name authority, 269–270
double opt-in (email permission), 232

Dreamfields Pasta, 230–231
Dropbox, 78
Drucker, Peter, 56
Dubin, Mike, 73
dumb pipe, 64
dumpster diving, 481
Dyke, James Van, 481
dynamic content, 240
dynamic products ads, 161–162
dynamic serving. *See* adaptive site

E

earned media, 104, 136–137
eBags, 71–72
Echo technology, 2, 4
ecommerce
  Amazon, 59
  business-to-business (B2B), 25
  global sales in, 25
  marketplace, 25
  PC and mobile sales, 26
economic value, 60
Eddie Bauer, 448, 450
EDI (electronic data interchange), 44, 45
80/20 rule, 186
Electronic Frontier Foundation, 467
electronic markets, 51
Electronic Privacy Information Center (EPIC), 471, 476, 477
electronic targeting, 113
email(s)
  address, hashing, 181
  analysis, 239
  checklist, 237
  as communication medium, 228–230
  design, 237–240
  lists, 209, 233, 235
  offer with time deadline, 239
  opt-in (email permission), 232, 233
  opt-out (email permission), 231–233, 246
  profiling/segmenting, 235
  sending, 240–241
  service providers, 240–241, 246, 248
  structuring, 236
  testing and revising, 236
  tracking, 241–242
  welcome, 238
email marketing
  advantages of, 226
  basics of, 234
  campaign, developing, 234–242

Canadian Anti-Spam Law, 248
CAN-SPAM in European Union, 247
and customer retention, 226, 227
customization, 243
definition of, 225
Dreamfields Pasta, 230–231
evolution of, 227
future of, 248–250
golden Rs of, 244–245
golden triangle, 238
levels of permission marketing, 231–233
requirements of U.S. CAN-SPAM Act, 245–247
respect, 244
Scotts Miracle-Gro Company, 228
targeting, personlization, and customization, 243–244
embedded devices
  apparel with, 47–48
  definition of, 46
emotions of, customers, 154, 162, 164
employee
  learning, 143
  motivation, and social media, 130–131
end-to-end customer experience, 36
engagement, 91
Epicurious, 189
Epsilon, 478
ERP (enterprise resource planning), 44, 45
e-tailers, 64
Ethereum, 74, 75
ETQ, 413
European Commission, 473
European Commission on Information, Society and Media, 247
European Union (EU), 473, 477
  CAN-SPAM in, 247
  Directive on Privacy and Electronic Communications, 247
  Directive on Protection of PII, 476
event marketing, 162
event-triggered targeting, 114
Evernote (app), 60, 61, 63
Evidon. *See* Ghostery
execute marketing programs, 113
expanded text ad (ETA) format, 289
experiential marketing, 162, 166
Eyetools, Inc., 413

F

Facebook
- Ads Guide, 296
- Ads types, 297
- Audience Network, 301
- BarkBox, Ad for, 322
- Campaign Manager, 392
- display ads formats, 295–300
- dynamic product ads, 161–162
- Facebook Connect, 467
- fan, value of, 103–104
- links ads on, 296–298
- Lookalike Audiences, 303
- Messenger, 140
- mobile ad revenue soars, 281
- mobile advertising, 77
- native advertising, 301–303
- privacy issues, 466–468
- text ads on, 296–298

Fair Information Practices Principles, 474, 476
Federal Trade Commission (FTC), 245–246, 467, 469–471, 473, 474, 486
- "Protecting Consumer Privacy in an Era of Rapid Change: Recommendations for Businesses and Policymakers," 461

Feinstein Institute of Medical Research, 472
Fidelity Investments, 69
financial clearing house, vs. blockchain, 74
financial services
- regulation of privacy in, 471
- transactions, digital satisfaction in, 424

Finch, Alice, 219
first-party cookies, 502
Fiskars, 445
Fitbit®, 96
Forbes, 189, 260
Forrester, 403, 477
Fourth Industrial Revolution, 4
fraudulent metrics, 526–527
Freedom Act, 473
freemium, 13, 77–78
free trial, 77
frequency (promotional media), 136
FreshDirect, 496–499
Freytag's Pyramid, 218, 219
front end, in direct marketing, 98
F-Secure, 479
fulfillment, order, 98
full usability testing, 419

fund-raising
- definition of, 69–71
- mobile role in, 71
- in social media, 128–129

Future of Privacy Forum, 472

G

Galactic Network, 150
games, mobile, 78–80
Gates, Bill, 128–129, 220
GE
- business model, 57–58
- pipe model, 63–64

generic search process, 260
Gentlemen's Quarterly (GQ), 189, 215–217
geo-fence software, 320
geo-targeting, 248
Ghostery, 464
Giggs, Ryan, 489
global ad spending, 320
Godin, Seth, 195, 196, 227
GoFundMe, 76, 129
golden triangle (email marketing), 238
Google
- account, logging in, 263
- AdSense, 293
- AdWords, 257, 282, 286
- algorithms, 269
- Android platform, 65
- vs Bing search results, 265
- children's privacy issues, regulation of, 469
- content, 270
- display ads formats, 295–300
- Display Network, 287, 300
- DoubleClick, 174
- Drive, 13
- expanded text ads, 305
- Friends Furever ad, 126
- Gmail, 262, 468
- Google+, 262, 468
- Jacquard technology, 329
- Keyword Planner, 268, 285
- links ads on, 296–298
- mobile advertising, 77
- mobile app metrics, 518
- mobile friendly sites, 274
- native advertising, 301–303
- PPC, 284
- privacy settings, 468
- RankBrain, 270
- search engine, 282
- search links, 270
- search results, 283
- by showing paid ads, 293
- text ads on, 296–298
- top ranking factors, 270
- Trends, 285
- video marketing metrics, 524

Google Analytics, 213, 506–516
- question, posing and answering, 506–510
- segmentation, 512–516
- social and mobile to picture, adding, 511–512

Google Online Marketing Challenge (GOMC), 284
governance, and content marketing, 199
Gramm–Leach–Bliley Act (GLBA), 471, 472
Griffin, Abbie, 369
Guardian, The, 484

H

Handley, Ann, 200
hard bounce, 241
Harley Davidson Live Your Legend campaign, 140
Harley Owners Groupr (HOGs), 140
Harris interactive, 461, 464
Harris, Wil, 215
Harvard Business Review, 493
Harvard Business School, 441
hashed e-mail, 181
healthcare
- Azure Cloud, 8
- regulation of privacy in, 472
- supply chain, 46–47

Health Insurance Portability and Accountability Act (HIPAA), 472
heat maps, 414
Heineken Legends campaign, 175, 176
Hess, Dan, 437
hit, 499
Holliman, Geraint, 200
home shopping, 72
HookLogic, 498
HP Enterprise Security, 480
Hsieh, Tony, 130
HTML5, 174
HubSpot, 196–197, 404, 429, 460
- Culture Code, 198

Hughes, Arthur Middleton, 100, 101, 393
hypertext markup language (HTML) code, 258, 259, 269
Hyundai, voice-activated Echo technology, 2

I

IBM
- ad for smart traffic solutions, 174, 175
- business model, 57
- pipe model, 63–64
- SilverPop, 165
- Watson, 14, 49

Ice Bucket Challenge, 128–129
identified users, targeting, 180
Identity Fraud Survey Report (2010), 481
identity theft, 481–482
Identity Theft Resource Center, 481
image ads, 290
image search, 273
immediacy, 91
in-app advertising, 185–186
inbound marketing, 346, 347
incentives, and direct marketing, 94–96
index server, 259
industry search, 273
influencer marketing, 127–128
infomediaries, 71
information
- attitude toward privacy of, 461–469
- definition of, 91
- intermediaries, 71
- personally identifiable information (PII), 456, 458, 461–463, 465, 466, 468, 471, 478, 480, 481, 486

informational marketing material, 118
information practice statement, 474
InfoUSA, 71
in-home monitoring services, 8
innovation warehouse, 60
Instagram
- BarkBox, ad for, 322
- desktop and mobile, links ads for, 297
- display ads formats, 295–300
- dynamic products ads, 161, 162
- #MyAmex campaign, 139
- page, National Geographic, 376, 377

in-stream ads, 300
integrated marketing communications, 189–191
integrated supply ecosystem, 50
integrated value chain, 41–42
Intel, 473

intellectual property
- definition of, 482
- in digital age, protection of, 482–486

Interactive Advertising Bureau (IAB), 462
interactive channel, 90
interactive strategies, hierarchy of, 118–119
interactivity, 91, 118–119
internet
- access, 20
- development, 3
- evolution of, 2–9
- generational differences in using, 17–18
- growth of, 150–151
- profile of, 150–157
- size and scope of, 15–16, 151–152
- users, frequent online activities of, 20
- users, number of, 151
- waves of change, 4–5

Internet Advertising Bureau (IAB), 174, 179, 189, 520, 522
Rising Stars category, 175
internet-enabled models, 73–76
internet of everything (IoE), 5, 6
internet of things (IoTs), 5, 314, 450, 469, 473
- connectivity in, 6–8
- impact on supply chain, 46–48
- sensors in, 6, 8

internet security
- consumers knowledge about, 479–480
- threats, 480–482

interruption marketing, 346
interstitial ads, 184–185, 316
involvement, 91
IP (Internet Protocol), 499

J

Jacquard technology, 329
Javelin Research and Strategy, 481, 482
J. D. Powers, 448
Jenga, 38
JetBlue Airlines, 143, 445
Johnston & Murphy, 228–229, 240

K

Kauferre, Stephen, 75
Kaushik, Avinash, 516
Kawasaki, Guy, 127
Kay, Gareth, 153

Keller, Andrew, 153
Kerns, Chris, 388
key performance indicators (KPIs), 359, 505, 516, 518, 525
keyword bidding, 305
keyword density, 260
keyword matches, types of, 287
keywords, 258, 259, 273
Kissane, Erin, 203
Kissmetrics, 518
KISS (keep it simple, stupid) rule, 415
KLM, 213
Koodo, 447–448, 450
Kopalle, Praveen, 440–441
Koum, Jan, 65
Krigsman, Michael, 394
Kumar, V., 99

L

Lam, Vincent, 393, 394
Landers, Susan, 443
landing page, 236
landing pages, 236
- continuity, 349, 350
- definition of, 283, 349
- designing, nurturing leads, 349–351
- relevance, 349, 350
- simplicity, 349, 350
- testing, nurturing leads, 349–351

Laps, Michael, 269
lead conversion
- definition of, 359
- measuring conversion, 359–360

leaderboard ad, 174–176
lead generation
- business challenges, 339
- cost of, 347–348, 357
- customer retention, 341
- definition of, 345
- inbound marketing for, 346–347
- management process, 346
- offline channels, 344
- online channels, 344
- purchasing leads, 348
- qualification at EDGAR online, 358–359

lead qualification, 357
Lego, 219–220
Legowiecki, Martin, 131
Lewis, Sage, 136
Licklider, J. C. R., 150
LimeWire, 483–484
Line (messaging app), 66

links
  in emails, 236
  site, 270
list brokers, 71
local search, 272, 289
Lost Dog commercial, 218
loyalty loop, 158–159
Lucy the Robot story, 198

M

machine learning systems, 49
machine-to-machine business model, 34
magazines, 72
MailChimp, 241–242
malware, 479, 480
Manning, Peyton, 134, 135
manufacturer direct model, 71
marketing analytics
  technology for, 349
    using customer database for, 113–114
marketing automation system, 342
marketing database, 110, 111
marketing effectiveness, demonstrating, 494–495
Marketing Experiments, 108
marketing optimization, 349
marketing-oriented customer performance, 369
marketing outcomes, expected by marketers, 23
marketing qualified leads (MQLs), 352
marketing strategy
  core, 22
  customer experience approach, 375
  customer lifecycle, 375
  data from social networks, 379
  International Speedway Corporation (ISC), 374–375
  just-in-time, 374
  key preference indicators, 373
  National Geographic, 375–378
  right time marketing, 374
  touchpoints, 374
marketing technology
  CRM tools, 227
  for lead nurturing across company type, 349
marketplace
  B2B, 69
  B2C, 14
  ecommerce, 25
  for video advertising, 179

Marriott, 440
mass customization, 243
McAfee, 468
McDonald's, 80
McKenna, Mark, 130
McMillan, Jacob, 196
McNeely, Scott, 465
Meacham, Laurie, 143
media. *See also* social media
  comsumption, daily, 152
  frequency (promotional media), 136
  owned, 136
  paid, 136
  promotional media, types of, 136, 137
  rich, 174–176
  time spent with, 18–19
  types of, 136, 137
merchant. *See* ecommerce
messaging apps
  in content marketing, 212–213
  Facebook, 66
meta name. *See* meta tag
meta tag, 258
metered services, 73
"Metrics 101," 516. *See also* blog post
micro-moments, 311
microsegmentation of markets, 51
Microsoft Hololens, 9
Microsoft OneDrive, 13
millennials, 17–18
Milne, George R., 457–458
minimums site, 413
mixed reality, 9
mobile
  approaches to, 76
  email, 229, 238, 248–250
  role in brokerage model, 69
  role in fund-raising organization, 71
  sales, 25, 26
  time spent on, 19
  users, smartphone and tablet activities of, 19, 21
mobile advertising
  digital, 173
  display, 184–186
  revenues, U.S., 24
  strategy, 318–320
mobile apps
  branded apps increase store visits, 390
  cloud CRM, 392–393
  designing effective, 324–326

metrics, 518–519
  social CRM, 391–392
  use in supply chain, 48–49
  for 2016 U.S. Tennis Open, 326
  Victoria's Secret, 389–391
mobile cumulative experience, 312–314
mobile-dependent models, 76–81
mobile digital advertising, 173
mobile display advertising, 184–186
  formats, 184
  growth in, 184
mobile disruptor, 447–448
mobile first
  definition of, 76
  designing, 428
mobile-friendly sites, 428–429
mobile loyalty programs, 389
mobile marketing
  apps + technology, 327–328
  beacon technology, 327
  digital media time, 310
  micro-moments, 311–312
  mobile apps, 323–326
  mobile cumulative experiences, 312–314
  mobile strategy, essential elements of, 314–323
  mobile technology, 328–330
  natural language processing, 326
  smartphones, 310
mobile networks, 468–469
mobile optimization, 273
mobile payments, 81, 328
mobile search
  is outpacing desktop, 274
mobile strategy
  creating, 317–318
  designing site
    CX, 316
    mobile-friendly, 314–315
    mobile usability, 316
  local opportunities, 320–321
  managing mobile content, 317–318
  mobile advertising, 318–320
  social media advertising platforms, 321–323
mobile technology
  mobile marketing, 328–330
  paid search, 280–281
mobile use, site designing for, 423–429
mobile web
  designing, 429
  size and scope of, 15–16

Monarth, Harrison, 218, 219
Monster Spray (Clark and Stokes), 268
Monty Python, 231, 232
Motorcycle Superstore, 513, 515
multichannel marketing, 348
multisided platforms, 65
multi-variable testing, 106
Muniz, Albert M., Jr., 139
Mustafa, Isaiah, 126
MyFitnessPal (app), 42

N

Napster, 483
National Academy of Sciences Committee on Intellectual Property Rights and the Emerging Information Infrastructure, 483
National Advertising Review Council (NARC), 464
National Security Administration (NSA), 473
native advertising, 72, 214–217, 301–303, 305
Native Advertising Institute, 214
native content, 211, 212, 214
natural language processing, 326
natural search, 257
navigational structure, designing, 415–417
NBA (National Basketball Association), 115–118
NBCU, 445
negative match, 286
Nerdwallet, 186–187
Nespresso, 82
Netflix, 9, 10, 64, 96, 119, 154, 436
net present value (NPV), 101
newspapers, 72
news search, 273
New York Times, 68, 217, 220, 313
 online media kit, 174
Nielsen Claritas division, 410
Nielsen, Jakob, 316, 419–423
Nike, 162
 Nike+, 42, 43
 Nike Fuel, 42–43
 NIKEiD, 120, 243
 value ecosystem, 65
North Face, 14
NPS (net promoter score), 423, 444
nurturing leads
 buyer's journey, 348
 designing landing pages, 349–351
 testing landing pages, 349–351

O

Offermatica, 105–106
offers, and direct marketing, 95–97
Office of Civil Rights (OCR), 472
Office Online, 13
O'Guinn, Thomas C., 147
Old Spice
 'Smell Like A Man, Man' campaign, 125–126, 523
 video, 125
omni-channel customer service, 439, 446–450
Omniture, 105–106
on-demand model, 80–81
online behavioral advertising (OBA), 462, 464
online media
 New York Times, 174
 vs. traditional media, 196
online shopping, 19–20
open auctions, 179
OpenERP, 45
open rates, 237
Open Table, 80
operational CRM, 378–380
optimization, of content distribution, 212
Optimizely, 110
opt-in (email permission), 232, 233
opt-out (email permission), 231–233, 246
organic search
 optimizing for, 267–273
 SEM, 257–259
 work together, 274
organic traffic, 172
Orlando Magic, 115–116, 118
Osterwalder, Alex, 76
Otis Elevator GeN2 Switch, 34–35
owned media, 136
owner targeting, 182

P

Page, Larry, 258
page rank, 258
page views, 503, 511
paid media, 136
paid search advertising
 ad formats, 290–292
 analyze and report, 290
 build phase, 286–289
 definition of, 23, 257, 281–283
 discovery ads, 300
 in-stream ads, 300
 launch phase, 289–290
 native advertising, 301–303
 platforms, 303–305
 research phase, 285
 SEM, 274
 social media ad options, 300–301
paid search process, 283–285
paid social advertising
 growth of, 293
 promoted posts, 294
Pandora, 77
Pareto curve, and usability testing, 420
Patel, Neil, 217
"pay as you go" approach, 73
pay-for-performance revenue model, 73
pay-per-click (PPC)
 definition, 257, 281–283
 Google AdWords, 284
 growing impact of, 280–281
Peltier, James, 369
Pepsi
 Doritos, 138
 Legion of the Bold campaign, 138
 Max augmented reality ad, 9, 78, 79
permission email marketing (PEM), 227, 230–233
permission marketing, 346, 347
persistent cookies, 501
personalization
 definition of, 119
 email marketing, 243, 244, 248
personalized email, 384–385
personalized site content, 384–385
personalized URL (PURL), 112
personally identifiable information (PII), 456, 458, 461–463, 465, 466, 468, 471, 478, 480, 481, 486
personas, customer, 208–209, 353
Pettinato, Frank, 447
Pew Internet & American Life Project, 254
"Pew/Internet Parent Teen Privacy Survey," 469–470
pfarming, 481
Pfizer, 45–46
P&G, 524
phishing, 245, 480–481
phrase match, 286
Pigneur, Yves, 76
Pinterest, 482
pipe model, 63–64
Pitofsky, Robert, 471
pixel tages, in Facebook, 161
platform economy, 43
platform model, 64–65
Pokémon Go, 79–80

Ponemon Institute, 461, 479
Portakabin, 438, 439
Porter, Michael, 34
Portman, Paul, 73
Postscapes, 6
Poynter Institute, 413, 414
P2P (peer-to-peer), 483, 484
predictive analytics, 446, 450
predictive forecasting, 51
predictive modeling, 114, 116, 182–183
preferred deals, 179
preheaders (email), 237
press releases, 187–188
privacy
    children's privacy issues, regulation of, 469–471
    customer, 103
    data, 460–478 (*See also* data privacy)
    by design, 461, 474
    disclosures, 474
    mobile networks, 468–469
    organizations and seals, 476
    policies, of email lists, 235
    policy notice, 474
    regulation in various internet-using countries, 477–478
    vs. terror prevention, 473
    U.S. business response to privacy issues, 474
Privacy Commissioner of Canada, 478
Privacy International, 477
privacy policies, of email lists, 235
Privacy Rights Clearinghouse (PRC), 479
Privacy Shield, 473
private auctions, 179
private marketplaces, 179
Procter & Gamble, 91–93
productivity, and social media, 131–132
profiles
    customer, 380
    definition of, 113
    of internet, 150–157
program execution, customer database for, 113–114
programmatic advertising, 177
programmatic direct, 178
promoted posts, 294, 304
promotional media, types of, 136, 137
prospect, 336, 346
prototype testing, 419
public relations, 187–188

publishing, under Creative Commons, 484–486
Pulizzi, Joe, 200
Puppy Love commercial, 218, 219
purchase funnel, 157, 157f
Puri, Ritika, 217
Putnam Investments, 130

Q
QQ Mobile, 14
qualitative data, 500–501
quality score, 282–283
quantitative data, 500–501
Qwikster, 154

R
Rajpurohit, Anmol, 501
RankBrain, 270
reach, audience, 136
reactance (email marketing), 244
real-time bidding, 179
recipient control (email marketing), 244
Recode, 9
Recording Industry Association of America (RIAA), 483–484
Red Bull, 138, 210, 212
The Red Bulletin, 210
red flags, 471
Red Lobster, 133–135
regression analysis, 114
relational marketing, 369, 371
relationship mailings, 245
relationship marketing
    cloud in, 389–393
    email marketing process, 234
relevance (email marketing), 244
Remote Elevator Monitoring (REM®) system, 34
repurposing of content, 212
resilient brands, 153, 154, 166
respect (email marketing), 244
response modeling, 114
responsive ads, 290
responsive technology, 314
responsive web design, 426–428
Retail Cloudhouse, 45
retailer cooperative database, 182
retailer visits, 158
retargeting ads, 172, 181, 182
return on investment (ROI)
    on content marketing, 214
    digital channels, 494
    on email marketing, 226, 227
    on social media marketing, 142
return on marketing investment (ROMI), 494

review site/app visits, 158
reward programs, 80
RFID (Radio-Frequency IDentification) tags, 8, 44–47, 328
RFM (recency × frequency × monetary value) model, 103
R/GA agency, 131
rich media
    definition of, 174
    in emails, 249
    formats, 174–176
    in press releases, 188
risk reduction, 96
Ritz-Carlton, 98, 165
Rogers, Stewart, 394
Rowley, Jennifer, 195, 200
Rule of Thirds, 205
RunKeeper (app), 42

S
"Safe Harbor" provision, 473
Safeway, 100–101
sales, 96. *See also* customer conversion
sales accepted leads (SALs), 356
Salesforce, 13–14, 71
    Einstein, 14
sales force automation, 370, 371
SalesGenie®, 71
sales promotions, 93
sales qualified leads (SQLs), 356
Samsung
    customer service, 440–441
    Galaxy "Love Every Letter" commercial, 175, 176
    Pay, 81
SaskTel, 448
Schultz, Don E., 369
scoring model, 182
Scotts Miracle-Gro Company, 228, 240
search advertising, 23, 184
search engine algorithm, 259
search engine marketing (SEM)
    definition of, 172, 257
    SEO *vs.* PPC, 258
Search Engine Marketing Professional Organization (SEMPO), 255, 256
search engine optimization (SEO)
    basic approach to, 266
    Coca-Cola strategies, 268
    definition, 257
    keywords, 273
    marketing plan, 273
    meaningful content length, 272

search engine optimization (SEO) (*Continued*)
- mobile optimization, 273
- optimization example, 271–272
- *vs.* PPC, 258
- problems, 268–269
- process, 267–268
- search, 275–276
- social content ranking, 273
- social media, 275–276
- tools, 268
- unique images, 273
- user experience, 267, 272
- user intent, 267
- use social media to enhance, 276
- video content, 273
- voice search, 272

search engines
- algorithm, 259
- definition of, 259–267
- Google, 282
- growing impact of, 254–256
- market share, 264
- spider simulator, 261
- types of, 273
- visits, 158

search engines result page (SERP), 259

search marketing, 254
- growing impact of, 254–256
- U.S. digital Ad spending growth, 256

search ranking, 258
search results
- definition of, 258
- Google *vs* Bing, 265

search retargeting, 182
security, mobile networks, 468–469
segmentation
- analysis, 114, 118
- campaigns, email, 248, 249
- digital marketing, 512–516

self-service, 443
semantic search, 260
sensors, 6–8
sentiment analysis, 445
service-centered dominant logic, 41–43
service chains, 50
sessions, 503, 511
- cookies, 501

70-20-10 model, 143
Share a Coke campaign, 190
share of customer, 101
share of market, 101
share of wallet, 101
Shavitt, S. A., 244

shopping ads, 290
shopping, online, 19–20
ShopRover, 80
Shorty Award, 127
site performance, 495
site stickiness, 95
site usability, 495
six-sigma, 41
Slack, 131
Slate, 81
Small Business and Enterprise Accounts, 421
smarketing, 340
SmartBear, 499
smart beds, 8
smart cities, 8
smart home, 6, 8
smart medication dispenser, 8
SMART objectives, 409, 410, 505, 527
smartphone, users activities, 19, 21
smart storage, RFID tags, 46–47
Smith II, Michael S., 473
Snowden, Edward, 473
social and mobile to picture, adding, 511–512
social business, 130–131, 143
social commerce, 303
social CRM, 391–392
social media
- advertising platforms, 321–323
- chief executive officers involvement in, 143
- conversations, monitoring, 213–214
- customer service, 444
- and email, integration of, 228, 229
- marketing, ROI, 142
- and productivity, 131–132
- users, 15, 124

social media marketing (SMM)
- communicating with audience in social space, 135–137
- content marketing, 127
- creating community, 139–141
- definition of, 123–124
- embedding in organization, 141–143
- engaging and motivating employees, 130–131
- engaging with audience, 137–139
- influencer marketing, 127–128
- listening to target audience, 132–135
- metrics, 519–520, 527
- Old Spice and Android, 125–126

- productivity, increasing, 131–132
- record-setting fundraising, 128–129
- return on investment on, 142
- social media team, building, 142–143
- strategy, developing, 132–141
- top management, involvement of, 143
- use in workplace, 129–132
- visitors, engaging, 124–129

social networks, use of, 124
social platforms
- display ads in, 176
- owned media, 136

social real-time search, 273
Social Technographics Ladder (Forrester Research), 132–134
soft bounce, 241
software as a service (SaaS), 13, 44–45, 71
Solis, Brian, 11, 127
Sony, 440, 478
spam, 229, 231
spear phishing, 481
spiders, 259
spoofing, 481
Spotify, 78
spyware, 480
Stafford, Jim, 116
stand-alone site design, 426–428
Staples, 233
Starbucks' loyalty programs, 80
statistical analysis, 114
stickiness, 402
Stokes, Kirstin, 268
Stop Online Piracy Act, 484
storytelling, 217–220
Strava, 42
streaming services, 10
subject line (email), 237
Subreddits, 304
Subscriber First, 68
subscription-based ecommerce, 59
subscription model, 72–73
sunsetting, 199
Super Bowl, 133–138
supply chain
- cloud computing, 45–46
- definition of, 34
- and digital disruption, 49
- digital transformation, impact of, 34–36
- essentials of, 36–38
- formative technologies of, 45
- integrated supply ecosystem, 50

IoTs, impact of, 46–48
management process, 37
mobile apps use in, 48–49
Software as a Service (SaaS), 44–45
strategic concepts, 36–42
value chain, 38–42
supply side platforms (SSPs), 179
Swiffer, 91–93
SwissAir, 413
Sydney Morning Herald, 68
synchronization, in cloud computing, 13
syndicated content, 204
synthetic performance testing, 499

T
tablet
activities of users, 19, 21
SEM share, 264
Taco Bell, 138–139, 185
TacoBot, 131–132
tagged web pages, 501, 502
targeted display advertising, 183
targeting
audience, 180
behavioral, 180–183
customer relationship marketing (CRM), 380–385
email marketing, 243
predictive models, 182–183
target market
definition of, 179
websites, 409–412
target segment, email, 236
Target system, 462, 478
team, social media, 142–143
TechCrunch, 76
Teleflora, 73
Telus, 448
Temkin, Bruce, 162
terror prevention *vs.* privacy, 473
testing, of direct response programs, 105–110
text advertising
changes to, 288
definition, 290
Thearling, Kurt, 115
third-party cookies, 502
Thorbjorsen, H., 244
Tide, 524, 525
Tilzer, Brian, 28
timing of sending emails, 240
title tag, 258, 269
TJX, 478
T-Mobile, 440
topical search, 273

top management, involvement in social media, 143
total cost of ownership (TOC), 393
touchpoint marketing, 374, 395
Toyota, 66, 96
tracking emails, 241–242
TradeIndia, 69
TradeStation, 69
traditional advertising. *See also* native advertising
paid media, 136
spending in, 154, 155
traditional business models, 66–73
traditional media
consumers, 18
earned media, 136
vs. online media, 196
traffic measurement, 495
transactional emails, 238
transactional marketing approaches, 369
transactional sites, 119
trigger emails, 249, 250
TripAdvisor, 75–76
trust
advantages, 459
and branding, 153
dimensions of, 460
internet, 96–97
as protective agent, 457
role in facilitating internet activity, 456–460
Trust Agents, 460
Trust Barometer, 457
TRUSTe, 462, 464, 468, 476
Twitter, 210, 212, 445, 473, 474, 482, 484
two-sided platform model, 64–65

U
Uber, 80–81
U.K. Customer Satisfaction Index, 438
unidentified users, targeting, 180–182
uniform resource locator (URL), 269
Unilever, 73
Universal Ad Package (UAP), 174
universal search, 259
University of Denver Estlow Center, 413
unqualified leads, 352. *See also* prospect
unstructured data, 14
UPS, 440
upselling, 101
up-selling, 340

Urban, Glen L., 459
usability
definition of, 418
Pareto curve and, 420
special requirements, for B2B sites, 420–423
stages of, 419–420
testing, 418–420
USA Patriot Act, 473
U.S. CAN-SPAM Act, 245–247
U.S. Department of Defense, 456
user experience (UX)
definition of, 316, 402
SEO, 267, 272
user intent, SEO, 267, 269
utility model, 71, 73

V
Valid Metrics Framework, 519, 527
value, 34
value chains
definition of, 34
Dell's direct model, 38–42
integrated, 41–42
technologies enable, 44–49
value ecosystem, 34, 35, 44–49
value proposition, 9, 56, 60–63
Value Proposition Canvas, 60, 62
values targeting, 182
VAST (video ad serving template), 175
Venkatesan, Rajkumar, 99
Venmo, 81
video advertising, 23, 175, 179, 184, 290
video marketing metrics, 520–525
virtual reality (VR), 5, 8, 78, 220
voice search
Hyundai, voice-activated Echo technology, 2
SEO, 272
Volaris, 445

W
Wall Street Journal, 74, 81, 469
Walt Disney Magic Band, 8
Washington Post, 68, 469
Wasserman, Todd, 389
Waugh, Mark, 522
Webbys, 404
websites
audience measurement, 503
content designing, 412–415
cookies, 501–502
deploying and tuning, 417–418
describing, 409–412
designing, 405

websites (*Continued*)
   development process, 407–418
   development team, creating, 408–409
   effectiveness of, 404–407, 418, 495–496
   evaluation, enterprise metrics for, 496–506
   identifying, 409–412
   measurement, 503–504
   metrics selection, 504–506
   navigational structure, designing, 415–417
   objectives, establishing, 409
   performance, 499–500
   qualitative *vs.* quantitative data, 500–501
   role of, 402–404
   tagged web pages, 501, 502
   target market, 409–412
   traffic measurement, 503
WebTrends, 513
Wegman, Danny, 164
Wegmans, 163–164
welcome emails, 238
Westin, Alan, 461
WhatsApp, 65, 124, 212
White, T. B., 243
Wired, 189
wireframe, 417
workplace, using social media in, 129–132
World Intellectual Property Organization (WIPO), 482, 483

X
Xerox, 436

Y
Yahoo!, 2
   directories, 256
Yellow Pages, 77
Yoghurt Digital, 269
Yoskovitz, Ben, 504
YouTube, 68, 212
   BarkBox, Video for, 322
   TrueView cards, 301
   video ad with interactive cards, 302

Z
Zabludovsky, Miguel, 81
Zahay, Debra, 243, 369
Zappos, 64, 71, 130, 136
Zara–Fast Fashion, 36–38
Zedesco, 513, 514, 516
zettabyte, 493
Zoby Analytics, 440
Zuckerberg, Mark, 128, 466, 467, 482
Zulu Alpha Kilo, 406
Zuum, 520